MOOD MUSIC
POPULAR DANCE
BILL HALEY
Belafonte
HERE'S
RICHARD
a tribute to James Dean
a million strings
helmut zacharias
werner müller

1 I WANT TO HOLD YOUR HAND The Beatles
2 GLAD ALL OVER The Dave Clark Five
3 SHE LOVES YOU The Beatles
4 YOU WERE MADE FOR ME Freddie & The Dreamers
5 I ONLY WANT TO BE WITH YOU Dusty Springfield
6 24 HOURS FROM TULSA Gene Pitney
DOMINIQUE The Singing Nun
8 SECRET LOVE Kathy Kirby
9 SWINGIN' ON A STAR Big Dee Irwin
10 HIPPY HIPPY SHAKE Swinging Blue Jeans
11 MARIA ELENA Los Indios Tabajaras
12 DON'T TALK TO HIM Cliff Richard
13 I WANNA BE YOUR MAN The Rolling Stones
14 THE BEATLES (L.P.) The Beatles
The Shadows
(E.P.) The Beatl
Elvis Presley
ALK ALONE Ge
Chris Sandf
(E.P.) The

THE STORIES BEHIND EVERY NUMBER ONE SINGLE SINCE 1952

1000 UK NUMBER ONE HITS

OMNIBUS PRESS
www.omnibuspress.com

COMPILED AND WRITTEN BY JON KUTNER & SPENCER LEIGH

ACKNOWLEDGEMENTS

Cover & book designed by Chloë Alexander
Picture research by Dave Brolan

ISBN: 1-84449-283-4
Order No: OP50039

The Authors hereby asserts their right to be identified as the authors of this work in accordance with Sections 77 to 78 of the Copyright, Designs and Patents Act 1988.

Exclusive Distributors:
Music Sales Limited,
8/9 Frith Street,
London W1D 3JB, UK.

Music Sales Corporation,
257 Park Avenue South,
New York, NY 10010, USA.

Macmillan Distribution Services,
53 Park West Drive,
Derrimut, Vic 3030, Australia.

To the Music Trade only:
Music Sales Limited,
8/9 Frith Street,
London W1D 3JB, UK.

Photographs courtesy of:
Harry Borden. George Chin, Corbis, Ian Dickson, Getty Images, Harry Goodwin, LFI, Pictorial Press, Spiros Politis, Popperfoto, Redferns, Rex, Mick Rock, Star File, Topfoto, Tracks.
Elvis image on page 588 used by permission,
Elvis Presley Enterprises, Inc.

Every effort has been made to trace the copyright holders of the photographs in this book but one or two were unreachable. We would be grateful if the photographers concerned would contact us.

Printed and bound in Great Britain by CPI Bath

A catalogue record for this book is available from the British Library.

Visit Omnibus Press on the web at www.omnibuspress.com

The authors would like to thank:
Dave Ball, Trevor Cajiao, Chris Charlesworth, Ossie Dales, Geoffrey Davis, Karen Freedman, Tim Fuller, Han Olof Gottfridsson, Carena Kutner, Anne Leigh, Howard Marks, Bernd Matheja, Del Mitchell, Mick O'Toole, Carl Magnus Palm, Keith Parkinson and Paul Rhodes and all the people who agreed to be interviewed for this book.

Opening page: Elvis Presley checks the selection in a Memphis record store, 1957
Page 2: Jimmy Savile opens Top Of The Pops, Manchester, January 8, 1964
This page: Spinning the platters in 1963
Page 12: Paul Anka on stage. His debut single 'Diana' made number one in the UK and US in 1957

Introduction

THROUGHOUT THE AGES MUSIC HAS BEEN A CRUCIAL PART OF the fabric of our lives. Anyone born after the Second World War recognises the potency of the best-selling record charts. The finest records transcend the generations, but every one of the titles in this book also acts as a photo album, prompting both happy and sad memories. At a rough guess, the first thing that most readers will do is check out what was number one on the day they were born.

Records in one form or another have been around for almost 100 years, and the UK charts have been with us for about half that time. They began in November 1952 – some 12 years behind America – and now, more than 50 years later, we have our 1,000th number one. This book tells 1,000 stories.

The list of hit songs and performers is a social, cultural and musical history, and although much has changed, the core is that each week we like a song more than any other and choose to buy it on record. These 1,000 number one singles are based entirely on record sales; unlike some charts, radio play is not taken into account, although radio plays may have prompted their purchases in the first place.

In the future the charts may change dramatically with the advent of downloads, itunes and ipods but the principle is still the same: in 1952 a customer went into a store and bought a black 10-inch double-sided shellac single, and now in 2005 the customer buys a silver CD with the hit song and bonus tracks, still called B-sides. Along the way, the much loved seven-inch vinyl single has come and gone.

Many of the records that have made number one are classics – Bill Haley & His Comets' '(We're Gonna) Rock Around The Clock' introduced modern rock music as we know it, and, among so many others, who could dispute the merits of Elvis Presley's 'Jailhouse Rock', The Righteous Brothers' 'You've Lost That Lovin' Feelin'', Abba's 'Dancing Queen' and Sinead O'Connor's 'Nothing Compares 2 U'? And for some people, nothing compares to U2. For a host of non-musical reasons, Band Aid's 'Do They Know It's Christmas?' may be the most significant record in the book, while the biggest seller – and our longest entry – is Elton John's 'Candle In The Wind 1997', his tribute to Princess Diana.

These unchained melodies cover all forms of music – easy listening ballads, rock'n'roll, blues, rock, heavy metal, folk, reggae, country, rap and all forms of dance and disco. In 1952 the songs were written by professional songsmiths and competently performed, but the excitement, well, that would have to wait until 1956 when teenagers at long, long last had some spending money. Nowadays teenagers have more cash and are more disposed to buying albums but, nevertheless, more interest still lies in the singles chart than the corresponding one for albums.

For many years, Elvis Presley and The Beatles were in a perfect equilibrium with 17 number ones apiece, but, thanks to JXL and the 70th birthday celebrations, Elvis has gone into the lead. Elvis has also spent more weeks at number one (79 weeks) than anyone else, and John Lennon (30 titles) and Paul McCartney (29) are the top writers. That's probably what you would expect, but whoever would have guessed that the UK's fifth most successful songwriter in this book is Mel C from the Spice Girls with her name on 11 number ones?

Of course some great songs and artists missed out on the top spot (Nat 'King' Cole, Billy Fury, The Who, Bob Marley, Elvis Costello, Depeche Mode, The Stranglers and R.E.M.) and some really naff records went all the way, but that is part of its fun and unpredictability. Chuck Berry created rock'n'roll's templates in the Fifties, but he had little success in the UK charts. Then, all of a sudden, he went to number one in 1972 with 'My Ding-A-Ling', which owes more to George Formby than rock'n'roll.

Buying records is always a luxury, and there have always been competing attractions. In the Fifties, it was magazines, the cinema and football; today it's computer games, PlayStation and football. Maybe that's why the charts move much faster these days and new number ones come straight in from nowhere week after week. The measure of a real hit nowadays is how slowly it goes down the chart.

Many commentators have predicted the end of the hit single, but it stubbornly refuses to die. We may become more and more inclined towards an albums culture, but the three-minute song will continue. Sometime in the future, we are sure that someone will publish a book on the 2,000 number ones.

In October 2004 there was major press coverage about the UK singles market being at its lowest ever and, indeed, much fuss was made of the fact that Eric Prydz had sold only 23,500 copies to reach number one. What wasn't mentioned was the number of sales he accumulated as a downloaded track, which, as yet, is not included into the singles chart; nor the fact that it was on several big selling compilations.

On the other side of the coin, the album market is booming. When Robbie Williams topped the singles chart in October 2004 with 'Radio', he did so by selling almost 42,000. A fortnight later, his *Greatest Hits* album entered the chart at number one after selling over 320,000 copies.

The contents of this book are remarkable. Try to read it all and not just the entries that interest you. Each of the stories is fascinating and represents, in its own way, a groovy kind of love. And the race for the next number one is never ending.

Jon Kutner & Spencer Leigh
January 2005

INDEX OF TITLES

1952-1959

BUDDY HOLLY is getting into the Presley-Donegan-Boone disc class

says KEITH GOODWIN

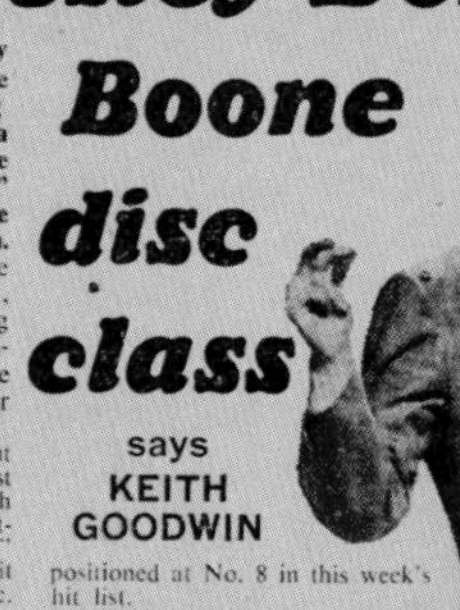

FOR sheer, solid consistency young Buddy Holly — the tall, bespectacled, guitar-playing Texan—is rapidly building up a reputation that puts him in line with such hit parade "regulars" as Elvis Presley, Pat Boone and our own Lonnie Donegan.

Apart from leading the dynamite-packed Crickets, Buddy is also a solo recording star in his own right, and his distinctive, electrifying vocal style has been linked with six major best-selling records to date.

It was Buddy who pounded out the lyrics on the record that first catapulted The Crickets to British and American fame—the pulsating "That'll Be The Day," which subsequently topped the hit lists on both sides of the Atlantic.

Hat-trick

A quick follow-up came with the release of "Oh! Boy," which made a rapid rise into Britain's top five best sellers, and more recently, The Crickets have completed their hat-trick with the high-flying "Maybe, Baby." Both records placed a heavy emphasis on Buddy's singing.

As a "single," Buddy has notched three hits in a row, starting with the Afro-tinged "Peggy Sue."

When "Maybe, Baby" started moving up the hit parade ladder, Buddy told record buyers to "Listen To Me," his recording of which was placed in the lower regions of the charts.

Right now, the gangling rocker who delighted British audiences during a tour earlier this year is making swift headway with his latest Coral release, "Rave On," positioned at No. 8 in this week's hit list.

Buddy's popularity, however, isn't confined merely to "singles." He and The Crickets did exceptional business at record counters all over Britain via their Coral album, "The Chirping Crickets," and this month's new releases by that company include Buddy's first solo album—an LP that is assured of widespread attention.

It's easy to see why Buddy is such a success with teenage audiences. He's a relaxed, easy-going sort of guy, charming and amiable and thoroughly convincing in his stage manner.

Quiet sort

He looks the quiet sort—until he begins to sing, that is! He generates excitement, and believes in having a good time—the sort of good time that others can enjoy, too. And on more than one of his concerts here, he proved himself to be a slick, amusing *ad lib.* comedian.

One of the main reasons behind Buddy's remarkable consistency as a recording artist is that the standard of his work never fluctuates. The excitement that he creates during "in person" appearances is always accurately reflected within the grooves of a record, and the aspect of his performance which pleased British fans most was that he sounded the same "in the flesh" as on wax.

This is a difficult thing to achieve, and in this respect, Buddy has a head start over many of his contemporaries, some of whose personal appearances have come as an anti-climax after their records.

To be associated with six consecutive hit records — all within the space of nine months —is no mean feat. And it all adds up to proof positive that Buddy Holly is going to be around for a long time to come!

EDITED BY ISIDORE GREEN

The Record Mirror

Editorial and Advertising Offices:
116 SHAFTESBURY AVENUE, LONDON, W.1.
Telephones: GERrard 7460; 3785; 5960

THE PAPER FOR ALL MUSIC AND SHOW BUSINESS FANS

...HALEY, SINATRA, STEELE, VAUGHAN A... THE TOP FOUR OF THE LAST FOUR YEA...

... AS A RULE, HE STILL LEAVES ROOM FOR THAT WHICH IS FORSEEABLE, FOR SEQUENCES OF EVENTS WHICH FOLLOW ONE ANOTHER MORE OR LESS LOGICALLY.

But in show business, he rations the latter type of happening to a minimum. In reasonable probability, a boxer knows he'll become a champ if he knocks all his opponents cold; a publican to succeed ...

... get nowhere; others, thought utter rubbish, and published with private embarrassment, become the rage of the nation! Plays and films run the same indeterministic gamut: the modest, tentative promotion boosts bank balances: the "dead cert" becomes dead in a different meaning of the term.

So with the four years of events covered by the 200 editions of the RECORD MIRORR. No one, in 1954, could have plotted their course with the faintest hope of even the most general accurcy. Take a line from the verse of "Love Is Here To Stay" viz. *"The more I read the papers the less I comprehend the world and all its capers."*

Apply that to the world of show business in general and ... those four ...

... But when, some weeks later, it was put before the less inhibited audiences of the provinces, and the London suburbs, its effect was a sort of psychological H-bomb.

IT DETONATED SCENES OF MENTAL HYSTERIA AND PHYSICAL STAMPEDING AMONG MASSED TEENAGERS, WHO DEMONSTRATED THAT, HOWEVER MIXED-UP THEY MIGHT BE ABOUT THE WORLD IN GENERAL, THEY CERTAINLY WEREN'T IN TWO MINDS ABOUT THEIR ADDICTION TO MR. HALEY.

Yet when, at last, in February of 1957, the ... Rock visited ...

Had the first visitor from Outer Space arrived at the time, he'd have been lucky to make a front-page!

When Ha... don's West E... there was a... hearing him... on tickets, ... was about a... Dartmo... e in, yo...

The rot had set in the rock. The Comets left Britain amid anti-climax. Haley stated they'd be back in the autumn. *They* ...

JERRY LEE LEWIS, SHIRLEY BASSEY AND THE SILLY SENSATIONALISM OF THE FLEET STREET SCRIBES

A paradise for bird-brains; a holiday for half-wits; a fantastic fiesta for feckless, fixated fools.

That's what show business, judged in terms of mass press publicity, is fast becoming. Jerry Lee Lewis may now be back in the States, cooking up fresh outbursts of his subtle artistry for tolerant fellow-countrymen. Miss Shirley Bassey may have completed her week at Chiswick Empire with no guerilla warfare other than the odd egg or two heaved her way at the first performance. Yet there remains the need for a word or two about the press repercussions ...

Readers Also Complain

I am particularly annoye... at the trouble-making nation... newspapers, as I wanted to ... Jerry Lee Lewis perform.

It was not the teenager... Britain who ruined his ... and I'm sure he still ... thousands of fans over ...

This is not the first ti... press have tried to ru... chances of artistes w... agers like.—E. J. LEW... 4 Warwick-road, Eali...

★

I am not a teena... am I a fan of Jerry ... So I've no axe to ...

Free For All

MOST CONTROVERSIAL LETTER PAGE IN SHOW BUSINESS

Here's another instalment of the battle of words between pro-Steele and pro-Presley fans—to say nothing of the infuriated letters from other readers who wonder whether all this shindy about Messrs. S. and P. is really necessary.

Drawings by Valerie Green.

ON AND ON goes Tommy v. Elvis. More and more insistent are the voices of protest. "Can anyone tell me," asks Mrs. C. M. Searson (160 Longmoor Road, Long Eaton, Notts.) "what is gained by all this petty name-calling? When they have finished pulling Tommy and Elvis apart, can I have the pieces?"

"The 'R.M.' must be the only music publication with a Laugh Parade," reckons Thomas Gomez (1 Abbey Street, Edinburgh). "You've no idea the laugh I get every week reading the silly insinuations of Steele and Presley fans. I'd like to see Presley thrown into a jailhouse, and Steele stranded on an island with no food, water,

Sir,—

PERRY COMO, PAT BOONE, MARTIN, DONEGAN FOR 20?

Bill Haley Serves R & R Piping Hot

WAXING IS FAST AND FURIOUS on that sensational hit "Volare", but to take the lead over other renditions already reviewed comes a Dean Martin disc.

A great recording with Dean capturing the Italian atmosphere perfectly — and at no loss to commercial presentation. There are two instrumentals of this melody by Cyril Stapleton and Nelson Riddle.

Both excellent, but don't rule out the Domenico Modugno original.

A star week this, for jumping back into the lists come Perry Como, Lonnie Donegan and Pat Boone, all with new discs worthy of Top Twenty honours.

Bernard Bresslaw, Private Popplewell of "The Army Game" fame, does platter duty alone with two novel and contrasting titles, "Mad Passionate Love" and "You Need Feet"!

Successful American vocal group "The Beavers" have a first British release.

SPINNING POPS

tender for TOP TWENTY veller" begins on the honours.

Steele: New York This Week?

ALL IS SET for Tommy Steele to fly to New York at the end of this week. He is to meet Oscar Hammerstein, co-writer of the "Cinderella" panto in which Tommy is to star at the London Coliseum this Christmas.

John Kennedy, one of Steele's managers, told the RECORD MIRROR on Tuesday this week: "Seats are booked on the plane for Tommy, Ian Bevan, of the Harold Fielding Agency, and myself.

"Tommy is recording a new 78 on Wednesday this week. On Thursday and Friday he is cutting tracks for his next LP. So he should be clear to travel on Saturday."

● *New Steele one-night dates: September 21, Civic Hall, Wolverhampton; (22), St. George's Hall, Bradford; (23), City Hall, Hull; (24), Victoria Hall, Hanley.*

WEEK ENDING JUNE 14

Last Week	This Week	Title	Artist
1	1	WHO'S SORRY NOW	Connie Francis (M.G.M.)
5	2	ALL I HAVE TO DO IS DREAM/ CLAUDETTE	Everly Bros. (London)
2	3	TOM HARK	Elias and his Zig Zag Jive Flutes (Columbia)
9	4	ON THE STREET WHERE YOU LIVE	Vic Damone (Philips)
3	5	WONDERFUL TIME UP THERE/ IT'S TOO SOON TO KNOW	Pat Boone (London)
4	6	WITCH DOCTOR	Don Lang (H.M.V.)
10	7	TULIPS FROM AMSTERDAM/ HANDS	Max Bygraves (Decca)
6	8	STAIRWAY OF LOVE	Michael Holliday (Columbia)
12	9	THE ARMY GAME	T.V. Cast (H.M.V.)
14	10	TWILIGHT TIME	Platters (Mercury)

1 Al Martino
Here In My Heart

Label & Cat No.: **Capitol CL 13779**

Producer: **Voyle Gilmore**

Writers: **Pat Genaro / Lou Levinson / Bill Borelli**

Date reached No.1: **15 November 1952**

Weeks at No.1: **9**

Many top American singers were of Italian extraction including Frank Sinatra, Dean Martin, Perry Como, Tony Bennett and Mario Lanza. Al Martino was another, being born Alfred Cini in South Philadelphia on October 7, 1927. He worked as a bricklayer, but he sang in local clubs. In 1950, his friend, Mario Lanza, suggested a move to New York, where he signed with the little-known BBS Records. His recording debut was with 'Here In My Heart', which had been intended for Lanza, and the thrilling top E at the start is comparable to anything from Lanza.

'Here In My Heart' was a transatlantic number one and led to a succession of hit records – 'Take My Heart', 'Now Before Another Day Goes By', 'Rachel', 'Wanted' and the western theme, 'The Man From Laramie', James Stewart being that man from Laramie. But these hits only made somebody else rich. "My manager was forced to sell my contract to some underworld figures in New York City," he later confessed, "and I had no idea where my money was going. There was some physical harm and I decided to flee to Great Britain. That cloud lived over my head for seven years."

After the hits stopped, Al became popular in cabaret and, in 1972, accepted the small but significant role of Johnny Fontane in *The Godfather*. Martino thought that Mario Puzo's creation paralleled his own life but Sinatra thought he was the model for the Fontane character. Al was the first to record the film's theme, 'Speak Softly Love' and the following year Al returned to the Top 10 with 'Spanish Eyes', which he had actually recorded in 1965.

In 1999 Al Martino performed at Billy Joel's fiftieth birthday party and in 2004, he returned to the UK playing large concert halls. Although Al knew 'Here In My Heart' was a UK number one, he remarked, "I had no idea that I had the first number one in the UK until someone said that I had made *The Guinness Book Of Records*."

2 Jo Stafford with Paul Weston & His Orchestra
You Belong To Me

Label & Cat No.: **Columbia DB 3152**

Producer: **Paul Weston**

Writers: **Pee Wee King / Redd Stewart / Chilton Price**

Date reached No.1: **16 January 1953**

Weeks at No.1: **1**

The lyrics of 'You Belong To Me' make little sense today – why is this man globe-trotting and leaving his girlfriend at home, and where does his money come from? The answer is that he was one of the millions doing compulsory national service, and several songs reflected the separation of servicemen from their loved ones – 'Auf Wiederseh'n Sweetheart' (Vera Lynn, 1952), 'Arrivederci Darling' (Anne Shelton, 1955) and 'Sailor' (Petula Clark, 1961).

Although 'You Belong To Me' was initially a country song from the writers of 'Tennessee Waltz', it crossed over to pop and Jo Stafford's version topped the US charts for five weeks. Other versions came from Joni James, Patti Page and Dean Martin, although the song made less sense when sung by a man. There were further cover versions in the UK, notably from Alma Cogan, Dickie Valentine and Jimmy Young, but surprisingly, the Sweetheart of the Forces, Vera Lynn didn't record it.

Jo Stafford, who was born in California, joined The Pied Pipers vocal group with Tommy Dorsey's Orchestra in 1941 and had several hits with a young Frank Sinatra. She left Dorsey in 1944 and most of her subsequent career was with her husband, the orchestra leader, Paul Weston. She had a strong, clear voice with marvellous phrasing and excelled with standards. Like an antecedent to *Phoenix Nights*, she and Paul made humorous records as America's worst club act, Darlene and Jonathan Edwards.

'You Belong To Me' was number two on the first UK chart but it took 10 weeks for her to dislodge 'Here In My Heart'. By the time Jo Stafford finally made the top, her follow-up, a pop version of Hank Williams' 'Jambalaya' had already come and gone.

3 Kay Starr
Comes-A-Long A-Love

Label & Cat No.: **Capitol CL 13876**

Producer: **Mitch Miller**

Writer: **Al Sherman**

Date Reached No.1: **24 January 1953**

Weeks at No.1: **1**

The daughter of an Irish mother and a full-blooded Iroquois Indian father, Kay Starr was born Katherine LaVerne Starks in the tiny village of Dougherty, Oklahoma, on July 21, 1922. When she was three, the family moved to a farm in Dallas, Texas where the young Kay would look after and regularly sing to the chickens, presumably to encourage egg laying. Her aunt appreciated her talent and, in 1937, she encouraged Kay's mother to enter her for a talent contest on local radio station WWR – Dallas. The road manager of the jazz violinist Joe Venuti heard her performance and told Joe that she could be the female singer he wanted for the band.

Joe visited Kay's house to talk to her parents about hiring Kay as a vocalist. Her parents agreed but her mother had to accompany her. In 1939, she joined Glenn Miller's Orchestra to replace his resident singer Marion Hutton who had fallen ill. After recording two songs with Miller, 'Baby Me' and 'Love With A Capital U', she joined Charlie Barnet's band as

Al Martino, whose recording of 'Here In My Heart' became the first ever UK Number One

a replacement for Lena Horne.

Al Sherman was a Russian-born lyricist and composer who, in the Thirties, composed songs that became standards for Al Jolson, Louis Armstong and Maurice Chevalier. Al's two sons, Robert and Richard, followed in their father's footsteps. In 1960 they signed a contract with Walt Disney productions and became their exclusive staff songwriters throughout the decade.

In early 1952 Kay recorded a new song for Capitol called 'Wheel Of Fortune' which was rush released to gain the advantage over competing cover versions. The wheel of fortune proved a winner for her as she topped the US chart. Although the producer Mitch Miller recognised the talent of his artists, he preferred the easy option and saddled them with light-hearted novelty songs such as 'Comes A-Long A-Love'. In the Sixties, Kay Starr sought to regain her composure by recording albums of standards.

4 Eddie Fisher with Hugo Winterhalter's Orchestra & Chorus Outside Of Heaven

Label & Cat No.: **HMV B10362**

Producer: **Hugo Winterhalter**

Writers: **Sammy Gallop / Chester Conn**

Date reached No.1: **30 March 1953**

Weeks at No.1: **1**

THE BALLADEER EDDIE FISHER WAS born in Philadelphia in 1928 and was a protégé of Eddie Cantor. He had a record contract when he was 21 and some of his most successful records were in the pre-chart days – 'Turn Back The Hands Of Time', 'Tell Me Why' and 'I'm Yours'. In 1951 he was drafted and spent part of his army service entertaining in Korea. He was in Korea when 'Outside Of Heaven' was number one and he was discharged in April 1953. His pay went up instantly from $94 a week to $7,500.

'Outside Of Heaven' was typical of Eddie Fisher's style – he was far more comfortable belting out ballads than doing rhythmic songs. His single climbed to number eight in the US, while another version by Margaret Whiting made number 22. The single was practically a double-sided hit in the UK as the British song, 'Lady Of Spain', was also popular. In June 1953 he was the headline act for two weeks at the London Palladium and he was delighted to be here at the time of the Coronation.

When he was asked to perform at a charity ball for royalty, Princess Margaret asked him to sing 'Outside Of Heaven'. In his autobiography, *Been There, Done That*, Eddie says that he introduced the song as being for 'someone special', adding, "Maybe she blushed – or maybe that was her complexion. When I sang the song, I gave her my most seductive Philadelphia stare." He wishes that he had got to know her better and then England might have had its 'first Jewish princess'. Instead, Eddie married Debbie Reynolds in 1955 and their daughter is the actress, Carrie Fisher. You may come across the daughters of his marriage to another actress and singer, Connie Stevens, Tricia Leigh Fisher and Joely Fisher, in TV movies. Tricia Leigh also made the US charts with 'Let's Make The Time' in 1990. Eddie was also married to Elizabeth Taylor who left him for Richard Burton.

Eddie Fisher

5 Perry Como with The Ramblers Don't Let The Stars Get In Your Eyes

Label & Cat No.: **HMV B 10400**

Producer: **Eli Oberstein**

Writer: **Slim Willet**

Date Reached No.1: **7 February 1953**

Weeks at No.1: **5**

BING CROSBY ONCE SAID THAT PERRY Como was "the man who invented casual", although Bing himself was hardly dynamic. He was born Pierino Como on May 18, 1912 in Canonsbury, Pennsylvania. Perry's father was a barber in Canonsburg and, as soon as his son was tall enough to cut hair, he worked in the shop but had ambitions to set up on his own. He started his own business on Third Street when he was 17 and he would entertain his customers by singing Crosby's songs. Years later, Third Street was renamed Perry Como Avenue, but he never called an album, *Short, Back And B-sides* or *Something For The Weekend*. His hair, however, was always as trim and smooth as his voice.

Many of Perry's customers urged him to sing professionally, so perhaps he wasn't so good as a barber after all. In 1935 he began a seven-year residency as singer with Ted Weems' Orchestra. In 1942 he briefly returned to hairdressing but preferred singing and just a few months later, he signed what was to be a 50-year contract with RCA Victor. His first recording was 'Goodbye Sue' in 1943.

'Don't Let The Stars Get In Your Eyes' was first recorded by the writer, Slim Willet, who had taken the song to number one on the US country chart. Perry's version gave him his ninth US, but first UK number one.

Perry's deep melodic baritone voice made it easy to emulate his idol, Bing Crosby. Like Bing, he enjoyed singing ballads like 'Melancholy Baby', but Perry liked to include light-hearted novelty songs such as 'Hot Diggity (Dog Ziggity

Boom)'. "I prefer the romantic ballads," said Perry, "but the novelty songs are frequently requested." Show tunes were also a favourite.

In the mid-Forties, Como was lured to Hollywood and made three films: *Something For The Boys* (1944), *Doll Face* (1945) and *If I'm Lucky* (1946). Before long he grew tired with the film industry and moved into the new up and coming medium, television. He was one of the first artists to pioneer a variety show. *The Perry Como Show* not only gave him a chance to sing and communicate with his audience via song, but also the opportunity to interview guests.

Perry Como said, "I've heard it said that you never get anywhere by copying someone. Well, I copied Bing and got somewhere".

6 Guy Mitchell with Mitch Miller & His Orchestra & Chorus
She Wears Red Feathers

Label & Cat No.: **Columbia DB 3238**

Producer: **Mitch Miller**

Writer: **Bob Merrill**

Date Reached No.1: **13 March 1953**

Weeks at No.1: **4**

"I'VE ALWAYS LIKED SONGS THAT HAVE a story to them and most of all, I like something that people can sing along to," said the man who made a string of catchy records during the Fifties.

Guy was born Al Cernik in Detroit, to Yugoslav parents on February 22, 1927. In 1938 the family moved to Los Angeles. As they travelled across the country by train, Guy entertained the other passengers. One of them worked for Warner Brothers pictures and saw his potential as a child star. Once the family arrived, Guy received tuition, but the family soon moved again, this time to San Francisco.

In 1947 after a year in the US Navy, Guy auditioned for Carmen Cavallaro's Orchestra and, still using his given name, he recorded for Decca. Guy recalled, "I remember being nervous on the first few occasions, because I knew I was being watched by people like Bing Crosby and The Andrew Sisters." After three singles, Guy was forced to leave the orchestra due to a throat infection.

In the late Forties, Guy recorded for the King record label under the name Al Grant. He was also a winner on the popular Arthur Godfrey Talent Show. The show was probably the US equivalent of *Opportunity Knocks* and assisted, among others, Pat Boone, Tony Bennett, Eddie Fisher, Connie Francis, George Hamilton IV and Patsy Cline with their careers.

In 1950 top producer Mitch Miller wanted Frank Sinatra to record 'My Heart Cries For You' in New York. When Frank heard it, he refused to sing it and left saying, "I would never record such rubbish." Mitch was livid. He had an orchestra in the studio and no one to sing the song. He liked Al Cernik's voice and asked him to come to the studio straightaway. Guy said, "Frank was supposed to sing that song on his next session for Columbia but he quit the label just before that, and that's how I got it."

It was Mitch who suggested a name change. When Al was on stage, the fans used to chant, `Hey guy, hey guy' so that seemed a natural first name. Guy chose the surname as a tribute to his producer. He was teamed with songwriter Bob Merrill and between them had hits with 'Sparrow In The Tree Top', 'My Truly, Truly Fair', 'Pittsburgh, Pennsylvania' and the song that appeared on the first UK chart, 'Feet Up'.

'She Wears Red Feathers' was Guy's first UK number one, but one of his least successful hits Stateside. The American people loved all things English, so it was surprising that a song about an English banker and his love for a native hula-hula girl failed to make an impact.

7 The Stargazers
Broken Wings

Label & Cat No.: **Decca F 10047**

Producer: **Dick Rowe**

Writers: **John Jerome / Bernard Grun**

Date reached No.1: **10 April 1953**

Weeks at No.1: **1**

CLIFF ADAMS WAS A PIANIST, WHO WROTE arrangements for Ted Heath and Cyril Stapleton and their orchestras. In 1950 the singer Dick James suggested that he and Cliff should form a singing group and write vocal arrangements for them. The group became The Stargazers, but James was only with them for a short time, eventually becoming a successful music publisher. Generally, there were five singers in The Stargazers and during their 10 year existence, their personnel, besides Adams, included Ronnie Milne, Fred Datchler, Bob Brown, Dave Carey, Marie Benson and Eula Parker. Their first single was 'Me And My Imagination' (1950) and they did well with 'A-Round The Corner' and 'Sugarbush'. In 1951 they recorded 'On Top Of Old Smokey' with the US folk singer, Josh White.

The battle for the chart supremacy on the ballad of lost love, 'Broken Wings' was a tough one. The original American version was by the New Jersey husband and wife team, Art & Dotty Todd, who were modelled on Les Paul & Mary Ford. Their version peaked at number six and Dickie Valentine reached number 12, but The Stargazers went all the way, thus becoming the first British act to top the UK chart. The Dickie Valentine version was also on Decca but record labels didn't mind two of their artists being in competition. As it turns out, Valentine was very friendly with The Stargazers and the group can be heard supporting him on two other number ones, 'The Finger Of Suspicion' and 'Christmas Alphabet'. They also made records with Dennis Lotis, Ray Ellington and Jimmy Young, not to mention many of their own. In 1958 Art & Dotty Todd recorded the original version of 'Chanson D'Amour'.

8 Lita Roza (How Much Is) That Doggie In The Window

Label & Cat No.: **Decca F 10070**

Producer: **Dick Rowe**

Writer: **Bob Merrill**

Date reached No.1: **17 April 1953**

Weeks at No.1: **1**

"I HAVE A LOT TO THANK THE CITY FOR," laughed Lita Roza, when she unveiled Liverpool's Wall of Fame in 2001. "I think my voice can be attributed to a good pair of lungs and the Liverpool air." Lita, who was born there in 1926 as Lilian Roza, created her own stage name, sang with Ted Heath & his Orchestra and, in pre-chart days, she sold well with 'Allentown Jail' and 'Blacksmith Blues'. She says, "I didn't want to do these songs. I saw myself as a torch singer and I wanted to sing nice, sentimental songs."

Worse was to follow. Decca producer Dick Rowe saw the potential of '(How Much Is) That Doggie In The Window', a US hit for Patti Page. The American singer, Mindy Carson, had rejected the song before Patti, and Lita was of the same opinion: "Dick Rowe asked me to sing 'Doggie In The Window' and I said, 'I'm not recording that, it's rubbish.' He said, 'It'll be a big hit, please do it, Lita.' I said that I would sing it once and once only, and I would never sing it again, and I haven't. The only time you'll hear it is on that record."

Even when the record was number one, nobody could persuade Lita to perform the children's novelty. She retained her integrity and it seemed to work as she won polls in both the *Melody Maker* and *NME* as the UK's Favourite Female Vocalist.

In 1955 Lita had hits with two songs she liked – 'Hey There' and 'Jimmy Unknown' – and then contributed 'A Tear Fell' to the All Star Hit Parade, a charity single for The Lord's Taverners Association, which made number two. In May 1956 Lita married a trumpet player from Heath's band, Ronnie Hughes and although their marriage did not last, their friendship has endured.

Lita sang with the reformed Ted Heath band for many years, but has now retired: "I spent 30 years on the road, sleeping in strange beds and now I have a nice home and I want to live in it. I keep reading about people making comebacks, but I have never wanted to do that. I like my life the way it is."

9 Frankie Laine with Paul Weston & His Orchestra I Believe

Label & Cat No.: **Philips PB 117**

Producer: **Mitch Miller**

Writers: **Erwin Drake / Irvin Graham / Jimmy Shirl / Al Stillman**

Date reached No.1: **24 April 1953**

Weeks at No.1: **18 (3 runs)**

BOB HOPE CALLED FRANKIE LAINE A 'foghorn with lips', an accurate description as Frankie Laine is best-known for his powerful, full-blooded treatment of romantic ballads. Frankie Laine won a gold disc with his first record, 'That's My Desire' (1947). Laine recalled, "That record started selling in Harlem first of all because everyone assumed I must be black."

Laine had further successes with 'S-H-I-N-E', 'On The Sunny Side Of The Street' and 'We'll Be Together Again', which featured his own lyric. Laine's bellowing style was heard to good effect on 'Mule Train' (1949), which he sang to a whip-cracking accompaniment. He made his film début in *When You're Smiling* (1950) and sang the title song. Laine made several romantic comedies but he never appeared on film with Nan Grey, a leading lady from the Thirties, whom he married in 1950.

Also in 1950, Laine followed the producer Mitch Miller to Columbia Records and Miller found him one hit song after another. 'I Believe' was co-written by Erwin Drake, who wrote the standards 'Good Morning Heartache' (Billie Holiday) and 'It Was A Very Good Year' (Frank Sinatra). The song contained powerful imagery, and Frankie Laine has said, "It accomplished an awful lot in its day because it said all the things that need to be said in a prayer and yet it didn't use any of the holy words – Lord, God, Him, His, Thine, Thou. It said it all and it changed the whole spectrum of faith songs." No record has been at the top longer than Frankie Laine's 'I Believe', managing 18 weeks in three different runs during 1953. The song reached number two for the Irish trio, The Bachelors, in 1964 and then it was reinstated at number one by Robson & Jerome in 1995.

10 Eddie Fisher featuring Sally Sweetland, with Hugo Winterhalter & His Orchestra I'm Walking Behind You

Label & Cat No.: **HMV B10489**

Producer: **Hugo Winterhalter**

Writer: **Billy Reid**

Date reached No.1: **26 June 1953**

Weeks at No.1: **1**

'I'M WALKING BEHIND YOU' WAS A BRITISH song written by Dorothy Squires' husband, Billy Reid. Eddie Fisher discovered the song and rushed to record it before he came to the UK to appear at the London Palladium. He shared the credit with the soprano Sally Sweetland, but she is not even mentioned in his 1999 autobiography, *Been There, Done That*. She sang with the Sauter-Finegan Orchestra, which was noted for 'Midnight Sleigh Ride' and featured such unlikely instruments as comb and tissue paper. Like Eddie Fisher, the Orchestra was also on RCA Records in America and when a female vocalist was needed for the song, it was natural to

Lita Roza, who only ever sang her number one hit once because she hated it so much

pick someone on the same label, and she also did the wordless singing behind Perry Como on his version of 'Summertime'. Sally Sweetland is best known for being unknown as she was the voice for several American actresses in film musicals of the Forties, notably for Joan Leslie in *Rhapsody In Blue* (1945).

Maybe it's just as well that Sally Sweetland isn't mentioned in *Been There, Done That* as this is the kiss-and-tell memoir to beat them all. Eddie Fisher was married to Debbie Reynolds (1955-59), Elizabeth Taylor (1959-64) and Connie Stevens (1968-69) but he also had affairs with Joan Collins, Angie Dickinson, Marlene Dietrich, Mia Farrow, Judy Garland, Abbe Lane, Sue Lyon, Jane Morgan, Ann-Margret and Kim Novak. Along the way he turned down Lucille Ball, Zsa Zsa Gabor, Hedy Lamarr, Jayne Mansfield, Marilyn Monroe and Edith Piaf. And they're just the entertainers! How he found the time to make any records at all defeats us and, indeed, he hardly mentions them in his extraordinary book.

Being a wedding song, 'I'm Walking Behind You' was the 'We've Only Just Begun' of its day. The B-side was a revival of the 1933 song, 'Hold Me', and we all know what P.J. Proby was to do with that.

11 Mantovani & His Orchestra
The Song From Moulin Rouge (Where Is Your Heart)

Label & Cat No.:	**Decca F 10094**
Producer:	**Frank Lee**
Writer:	**Georges Auric**
Date reached No.1:	**14 August 1953**
Weeks at No.1:	**1**

UNLIKE BAZ LUHRMANN'S EXTRAVAGANZA in 2001, the first *Moulin Rouge* film was more or less a straightforward account of artist Toulouse-Lautrec's time in Montmartre, starring José Ferrer, who was married to Rosemary Clooney. Its wide-ranging cast included Christopher Lee, Peter Cushing and Zsa Zsa Gabor. The award-winning film was directed by John Huston and had a fine score from Georges Auric.

Most record labels wanted the theme from the night club, Moulin Rouge, in their catalogues: some of the treatments were instrumental, while others used the lyric, 'Where Is Your Heart?'. Nine versions were released, and the public chose the instrumental arrangement by Mantovani & His Orchestra.

Mantovani was Annunzio Paolo, born in Venice in 1905 and whose father became the principal violinist under Toscanini at La Scala, Milan. The family moved to England in 1912 and he used his mother's maiden name, Mantovani, when he became a professional musician, playing violin and piano. He felt that "the lighter side of music had never received its proper dignity" and so he formed a string orchestra (40 pieces with 28 of them string players) and said, "I wanted an overlapping of sound as though we were playing in a cathedral."

If the charts had started at the beginning of 1952, Mantovani may have had the first number one with 'Charmaine', which became his signature tune. However, the credit for the cascading strings associated with Mantovani also belongs to the splendidly-named arranger, Ronald Binge, and the studio engineer, Arthur Lilley. The result was a Wall of Sound long before Phil Spector's, but made from more delicate materials.

Mantovani was a proud man who believed that his records were the best on the market. He died in 1980 and would be horrified to know that his albums are now dismissed as schmaltz and on sale for pennies at car boot sales. Still, he did achieve the UK's first instrumental number one and he was also the first chart-topping artist to write a number one, namely 'Cara Mia' for David Whitfield.

12 Guy Mitchell
Look At That Girl

Label & Cat No.:	**Phillips PB 162**
Producer:	**Mitch Miller**
Writer:	**Bob Merrill**
Date Reached No.1:	**12 September 1953**
Weeks at No.1:	**6**

SURPRISINGLY, 'LOOK AT THAT GIRL' never made the US chart, but the day it hit the top spot in Britain, the American people turned their attention to another girl on her wedding day. That girl was Miss Jacqueline Bouvier, who was to become Mrs. Jacqueline Kennedy.

In 1952 Guy could have sung the same song to his new wife, Jackie Loughery, a former Miss USA, but that only lasted two years. Three years later he wed another beauty queen, Miss Denmark, Else Soronsen, but that didn't last long either. He finally found the right woman in his third wife, Betty Stanzak, whom he married in 1973 and would spend the rest of his life with.

Guy appeared at the 1954 *Royal Variety Performance,* he also appeared at the first *Sunday Night At The London Palladium* a year later. Guy had many ambitions, one was to buy his parents a new and comfortable home, so in order to make some extra money, he made regular appearances on the radio shows *Housewives' Choice* and *Family Favourites*. He appeared in his first film starring opposite Gene Barry and Teresa Brewer in *Those Redheads From Seattle*. The hit single from the movie was 'Chicka Boom'.

Bob Merrill was a brilliant novelty songwriter. '(How Much Is) That Doggie In The Window', (Patti Page / Lita Roza), 'Nairobi' (Tommy Steele), 'Mambo Italiano' (Rosemary Clooney / Dean Martin) and 'Where Will The Dimple Be?' (Rosemary Clooney) were all hits. But he could also write serious songs. Barbra Streisand's definitive version of 'People' is a fine example. 'Look At That Girl' was intended as a serious song, but was still bouncy enough to fit in with Guy's image.

13 Frankie Laine with Paul Weston & His Orchestra Hey Joe

Label & Cat No.: **Philips PB 172**

Producer: **Mitch Miller**

Writer: **Boudleaux Bryant**

Date reached No.1: **23 October 1953**

Weeks at No.1: **2**

WHEN THE FIRST UK RECORD SALES chart was published in November 1952, the Chicago-born Frankie Laine was at number seven with the theme song from the Gary Cooper film *High Noon* and at number eight with 'Sugarbush', a romantic duet with Doris Day. Speaking of *High Noon*, he commented, "I didn't sing that song in the film, although I'd have been glad to have done so. Tex Ritter did the soundtrack, but I had the hit."

Frankie Laine's 'I Believe' was still at number two when 'Hey Joe' entered at number three on October 17, 1953. A fortnight later, Frankie was number one with 'Hey Joe', number three with 'Answer Me', number five with 'Where The Wind Blows' and at number six with 'I Believe'. In 1964 The Beatles had the top five records in the US but they never achieved Laine's level of short-term penetration in the UK.

The cajun-influenced, 'Hey Joe', was originally recorded by Carl Smith, the father of Carlene Carter, and it topped the US country charts in 1953. A cover version by Kitty Wells also did well. Frankie Laine covered 'Hey Joe' for the US pop market, although retaining a steel guitar solo, and his version also beat off a UK response from Frankie Vaughan. The songwriter, Boudleaux Bryant, wrote 'Love Hurts' and many hit records for The Everly Brothers, often with his wife Felice. Despite its playfulness, 'Hey Joe' is about infidelity, and the consequences of which can be seen, quite coincidentally, in Jimi Hendrix's entirely different record of the same name.

14 David Whitfield with Stanley Black & His Orchestra Answer Me

Label & Cat No.: **Decca F 10192**

Producer: **Bunny Lewis**

Writers: **Gerhard Winkler / Fred Rauch / Carl Sigman**

Date reached No.1: **6 November 1953**

Weeks at No.1: **2 (2 runs)**

MÜTTERLEIN, AN OLD-FASHIONED German term of endearment for a mother, was used as a title by the Berlin songwriter, Gerhard Winkler to celebrate his mother's 75th birthday in 1952. Leila Negra was the first to record it, and versions in Danish, Swedish, Finnish and Norwegian followed. In America, Carl Sigman wrote a controversial English lyric, 'Answer Me', completely changing the song's intention of a thank you from a son to a mother.

So, after 'I Believe', Frankie Laine was again in trouble. 'Answer Me' opened with an organ and Frankie singing as reverently as he could, "Answer me, Lord above, Just what sin have I been guilty of, Tell me how I came to lose your love, Please answer me, oh Lord". That was dynamite in 1953. The record was banned throughout the States, although it still sold well, if not spectacularly.

Enter the light operatic singer from Hull, David Whitfield, who had had his first hit early in October 1953 with 'Bridge Of Sighs'. His manager and record producer, Bunny Lewis, asked Carl Sigman to amend his words, and with a few deft changes, it became 'Answer Me, My Love'. David Whitfield recorded the 'safe' lyric and he beat Frankie Laine's original, which was hampered by a BBC ban, to the top.

In December 1953 Nat 'King' Cole recorded 'Answer Me, My Love' very successfully for the American market, securing him a gold disc, and although his single was released in the UK in February 1954, it was far too late.

Meanwhile, back in Germany, the lyricist Fred Rauch had put new German words to 'Mütterlein', following Sigman's lead and calling it 'Glaube Mir' ('Believe Me'). It sold half a million copies for Wolfgang Sauer, a blind singer and pianist.

15 Frankie Laine with Paul Weston & His Orchestra Answer Me

Label & Cat No.: **Philips PB 196**

Producer: **Mitch Miller**

Writers: **Gerhard Winkler / Fred Rauch / Carl Sigman**

Date reached No.1: **13 November 1953**

Weeks at No.1: **8**

FRANKIE LAINE'S EARLY FIFTIES HITS, 'Jezebel' and 'Satan Wears A Satin Dress', were regarded as controversial for their religious references. "I didn't pay much attention to the fuss being made over them," Laine said in 1978. "I was being given great songs and I'd have been a fool to turn them down." The controversy surrounding Frankie Laine increased with 'I Believe' and then 'Answer Me' with the singer asking God why his relationship has failed. The record was banned by the BBC. However, many listeners heard David Whitfield's amended lyric, 'Answer Me, My Love', and then bought Frankie Laine's original. Both versions made number one.

Frankie Laine's 'Answer Me' remained on the charts for four months, taking him well into 1954 where one stentorian performance followed another – 'Blowing Wild' (2), 'Granada' (9), 'The Kid's Last Fight' (3), 'My Friend' (3), 'There Must Be A Reason' (9) and 'Rain Rain Rain' with The Four Lads (8). There wasn't a number one but that's an impressive performance.

In 1955 Frankie went to number two with 'Cool Water', one of the many western songs with which he is associated, but, contrary to what many people think, he did not sing the theme on the soundtrack of the TV series, *Champion The Wonder Horse*. Frankie was busy at the time and so Norman Luboff, whose choir was often on his records, impersonated him instead. Frankie recorded his own version for a single in November 1955, and he was back at the top a year later with 'A Woman In Love'.

16 Eddie Calvert
Oh Mein Papa

Label & Cat No.: **Columbia DB 3337**

Producer: **Norrie Paramor**

Writers: **Paul Burkhard / John Turner (Jimmy Phillips) / Geoffrey Parsons**

Date reached No.1: **8 January 1954**

Weeks at No.1: **9**

EDDIE CALVERT WAS BORN IN THE HEART of brass band country, Preston, in 1922 and encouraged by his father, he was guesting with The Preston Town Silver Band from the age of six and became their principal cornet player when he was 11. He also played with several dance bands and after being invalided out of the army after an accident as a dispatch rider, he formed his own band and then joined The BBC Dance Orchestra in 1943.

In the Forties, 'Oh Mein Papa' had been written by Paul Burkhard for a stage musical, *Der Schwarze Hecht (The Black Pike),* in Switzerland. In 1949 it became a European hit for Lys Assia, who was to win the first Eurovision Song Contest with 'Refrain' in 1956.

In 1953 the EMI record producer, Norrie Paramor asked Eddie Calvert to make a solo record. The A-side was 'Mystery Street', and the B-side, 'Oh Mein Papa'. Eddie's B-side caught on in the UK and became the first number one to be recorded at EMI's Abbey Road studios. Surprisingly for a British record of the period, it made the US Top 10 but Musicians' Union restrictions prevented him from touring America. The best-known vocal version of 'Oh Mein Papa' is by Eddie Fisher, which topped the US charts and also made the UK Top 10.

Taking its cue from Nelson Algren's novel *The Man With The Golden Arm*, Calvert became known as the Man with the Golden Trumpet but he came to hate his number one. In the Seventies he said, 'Hearing 'Oh Mein Papa' is like having a six-inch nail jammed through my head."

17 The Stargazers with Syd Dean & His Orchestra
I See The Moon

Label & Cat No.: **Decca F 10213**

Producer: **Dick Rowe**

Writer: **Meredith Willson**

Date reached No.1: **12 March 1954**

Weeks at No.1: **6 (two runs)**

A CHILDREN'S PRAYER IN AMERICA went "I see the moon, The moon sees me, God bless the moon, And God bless me." It was turned into a popular song by Meredith Willson, who wrote the 1957 musical *The Music Man* and it was recorded with barbershop harmonies by The Mariners and produced by Mitch Miller. The Decca producer, Dick Rowe, asked The Stargazers to cover it for the UK and they agreed, provided they could add some humour.

The Stargazers excelled at jingles like "I see the moon, The moon sees me". They introduced themselves on radio with "The Stargazers are on the air", and their leader, Cliff Adams was gifted at writing advertising hooks. His work includes 'All because the lady loves Milk Tray', 'Fry's Turkish Delight' and 'For mash, get Smash'. In 1960 The Cliff Adams Orchestra (in reality, a group of session musicians) had a hit record with 'The Lonely Man Theme', based upon his cigarette commercial, 'You're never alone with a Strand', which featured the actor, Terence Brooks.

The Stargazers appeared on three Royal Variety Performances and they were regularly featured on The Light Programme's *Top Score* with Stanley Black & His Orchestra and *Show Band* with Cyril Stapleton. They provided vocal accompaniments on *Sunday Night At The London Palladium*, but they were reprimanded for breaching advertising regulations when they included Cliff Adams' jingle, 'Murray Mints, Murray Mints, the too good to hurry mints', as part of their performance.

The BBC has had many long-running radio programmes, but *Sing Something Simple* featuring the Cliff Adams Singers was exceptional. It was broadcast every week on either the Light Programme or Radio 2 from 1959 until Adams' death in 2001. Its format of 30 minutes of warm ballads and cheerful novelties never changed and, as the songs generally ranged from 1900 to 1970, *Sing Something Simple* provided the perfect singalong for senior citizens.

Today, if you were at an alehouse singsong, somebody may chirp "I see the moon, The moon sees me". Everybody would join in but hardly anyone would know where it came from or know more than the title line, which, thanks to The Stargazers, can be expressed in so many ways.

18 Doris Day with orchestra conducted by Ray Heindorf
Secret Love

Label & Cat No.: **Philips PB 230**

Producer: **Ray Heindorf**

Writers: **Paul Francis Webster / Sammy Fain**

Date reached No.1: **16 April 1954**

Weeks at No.1: **9 (two runs)**

BETTY GRABLE HAD IMMENSE SUCCESS in *Annie Get Your Gun* with Howard Keel, so Hollywood decided to film a raucous musical about another western tomboy, Calamity Jane. Calamity yearned after Wild Bill Hickok but, being skilled in ropin', ridin', shootin' and fightin', did not know how to attract him, pouring out her heart in 'Secret Love'. The film musical starred Doris Day as Calamity and, as if to emphasise the link to *Annie Get Your Gun*, Howard Keel as Bill.

The key songs from the film, 'Secret Love' and 'The Deadwood Stage', were put on the same Doris Day single and it went to the top of the US charts, repeating its success here. Doris had her own secret at the time as she had discovered a breast lump and was afraid to mention it to anyone. Eventually she collapsed from exhaustion and she made a complete recovery, the lump proving to be benign.

Because of her problems, Doris Day could not appear at the Oscar ceremony and the song was performed by Ann Blyth who, much to public's amusement, sang "My secret love's no secret anymore" while heavily pregnant. The song won an Oscar, one of the also-rans being Dean Martin's 'That's Amore'.

Slim Whitman took 'Secret Love' onto the US country charts and, in 1963, Kathy Kirby revived the song for her first Top 10 entry. The song again became a US country hit when Freddy Fender sang it in both English and Spanish in 1975. The film musical was converted to a stage show in the Nineties and it toured with great success and was taken into the West End in 2003 with Toyah very energetically reprising Doris Day's creation.

19 Johnnie Ray
Such A Night

Label & Cat No.: **Philips PB 244**
Producer: **Mitch Miller**
Writer: **Lincoln Chase**
Date reached No.1: **30 April 1954**
Weeks at No.1: **1**

ALTHOUGH JOHNNIE RAY WORE evening dress and is usually bracketed with lounge singers like Tony Bennett and Vic Damone, he had a distinctive approach and, like Elvis Presley and later The Beatles, he sought out powerful rhythm and blues songs, which hadn't crossed to the white market. His style and influences are therefore different from other artists recorded by Mitch Miller, and in 1953 he brilliantly covered The Drifters' suggestive 'Such A Night'. The song was written by Lincoln Chase, who also wrote 'Jim Dandy' for LaVern Baker. In the Sixties, he became the songwriter, manager and producer for Shirley Ellis ('The Name Game', 'The Clapping Song'). The Drifters' original of 'Such A Night' featured a frantic but passionate lead vocal from Clyde McPhatter, but Johnnie Ray added an animal sexuality, albeit with a middle-of-the-road arrangement.

And maybe this is why. Johnnie Ray was gay and, in 1952, he married an eager fan, Marilyn Morrison, probably to allay probing into his sexuality. Marilyn was soon drinking hard and early in 1954, she filed for divorce in Mexico. Johnnie Ray told reporters, "Someday I plan to marry again. Every man wants a home and children," but what else could he say? His real feelings were made clear in 'Such A Night', where he yowls and yelps as he responds to sexual excitement. It was the frankest exposition of gay sex put on record, and yet nobody knew it. 'Such A Night' was banned by the BBC and so fans could not hear it on the radio. Nevertheless, Johnnie Ray was a major star and so they still bought it. Seeing him in concert was something else again as Ray would whip himself into a frenzy, drop to the floor and wrap himself around a piano leg.'

Although his producer Mitch Miller loathed rock'n'roll, Johnnie Ray paved the way for Elvis Presley, and Elvis can be heard impersonating him on 'White Christmas'. Both of them made records that were bathed in echo and Johnnie has been wittily described by the writer Nik Cohn as John the Baptist to Elvis' Jesus. Both, too, were parodied on comedy records by Stan Freberg – 'Try' and 'Heartbreak Hotel' respectively – although Ray hated Freberg's pastiche. Elvis recorded 'Such A Night' in 1960 and it was released as a single in 1964, making the Top 20, but even Elvis did not want to sound as orgasmic as Johnnie Ray. Whoever thought 'Je T'aime...Moi Non Plus' was something new?

20 David Whitfield with Mantovani & His Orchestra and Chorus
Cara Mia

Label & Cat No.: **Decca F 10327**
Producer: **Bunny Lewis**
Writers: **Lee Lange / Tulio Trapani**
Date reached No.1: **2 July 1954**
Weeks at No.1: **10**

DAVID WHITFIELD WAS AN OPERATIC tenor who came from Hull and could be regarded as the Mouth of the Humber. He was discovered by Hughie Green and signed to a management contract by Bunny Lewis who wrote 'Cara Mia' with the orchestra leader, Mantovani, although their names are not in the credits. He says, "My name appears on very few of the songs that I wrote because I was working for Decca, and rival companies might not record them: also, it wouldn't make me very popular with Decca. I wrote 'Cara Mia' under the name of Lee Lange, which were my wife's father's Christian names, and Monty used Tulio Trapani. I had wanted to use the famous Mantovani falling string sound with voices on the song and Frank Lee, who was the head of A&R at Decca, said, 'The only way you'll get Mantovani to cooperate is by cutting him in.' I showed Mantovani the song and he rewrote a bit of the music. I gave him half the song and it's now a standard, which brings me quite a bit of money every year."

The combination of David Whitfield with Mantovani's cascading strings worked perfectly and gave both artists their second number ones. Their record even made the US Top 10. Whitfield had several more hits including 'My September Love' and 'Adoration Waltz', but his career had lost its momentum by the Sixties where he was playing summer seasons and pantomimes. He died in Sydney in 1980 after entertaining passengers on a cruise ship and only a few weeks after Mantovani's own death.

Whitfield was noted for the throb in his voice, and Bunny Lewis reveals, "If I wanted what we called 'the throb', I would go down into the studio and goose him. He'd produce it and it was as simple as that."

21 Kitty Kallen with orchestra directed by Jack Pleis Little Things Mean A Lot

Label & Cat No.: **Brunswick 05287**

Producer: **Milt Gabler**

Writers: **Carl Stutz / Edith Lindeman**

Date reached No.1: **10 September 1954**

Weeks at No.1: **1**

KITTY KALLEN, WHO WAS BORN IN Philadelphia in 1922, began her career singing with popular bands, Artie Shaw's in 1938 and Jack Teagarden's in 1940. She married Teagarden's clarinettist, Clint Garvin, and when Teagarden fired him in 1942, she left as well. She then replaced Helen O'Connell in Jimmy Dorsey's orchestra. Working through the big bands, she joined Harry James & His Orchestra and sang on their hit recording of Duke Ellington's 'I'm Beginning To See The Light' in 1945. She became a solo artist in 1949 and her only UK hit was with 'Little Things Mean A Lot' five years later. The record topped the US charts for nine weeks and was the year's biggest seller.

'Little Things Mean A Lot' was written by a DJ, Carl Stutz, and a newspaper journalist, Edith Lindeman (later Edith Calisch), both from Richmond, Virginia, and it is a 'list' song. You get an idea such as 'You're The Top', 'Anything Goes' or 'Little Things Mean A Lot' and then list one item after another. As with most successful list songs, the song was parodied with such lyrics as "Throw me a brick from across the room." Carl and Edith never repeated their success but they did write one of the staples of Willie Nelson's act, 'The Red Headed Stranger' as well as Perry Como's 1959 hit, 'I Know'.

Kitty Kallen had further US hits with 'Go On With The Wedding' (1956), 'If I Give My Heart To You' (1959) and 'My Colouring Book' (1963), but she became the first number one never to return to the UK charts. The only others from the Fifties are The Dreamweavers, The Kalin Twins (also arranged by Jack Pleis) and Jerry Keller.

22 Frank Sinatra with orchestra conducted by Nelson Riddle Three Coins In The Fountain

Label & Cat No.: **Capitol CL 14120**

Producer: **Voyle Gilmore**

Writers: **Sammy Cahn / Jule Styne**

Date reached No.1: **17 September 1954**

Weeks at No.1: **3**

IN 1954 SAMMY CAHN AND JULE STYNE were writing a film musical for Marilyn Monroe and Frank Sinatra, *Pink Tights*. The project was scrapped when Marilyn absconded to Japan with the baseball star, Joe DiMaggio ("Where have you gone, Joe DiMaggio?"). The 20th Century Fox producer, Sol Siegel, immediately asked them to write the title song for another picture, saying "We just made a movie in Italy, *We Believe In Love*. I hate the title but if we can get 'em a song called 'Three Coins In The Fountain', we can dissuade them." As the film was not available for showing, the composers asked for the script. "Script?" snorted Siegel, "There's no time to read a script. Three girls go to Rome, throw coins in a fountain and wish for love. Now, write the song!"

Sammy Cahn immediately hit upon the lyric and Jule Styne gave the melody a Latin flavour. When Sammy ran dry, Jule said, "You haven't mentioned Rome yet", hence the line, 'Somewhere in the heart of Rome'. Later that day, they gave the song to Siegel who knew Sinatra was walking around with a quarter of a million for not making a film with Marilyn Monroe. He recorded the song within a few days, but it had all been done so fast that nobody had made a deal for the song. Fox realised their mistake too late and the songwriters ended up with more royalties than normal. "I sang 'Make it mine, make it mine, make it mine' and that is what happened," said Sammy Cahn.

23 Don Cornell with orchestra directed by Jerry Carr Hold My Hand

Label & Cat No.: **Vogue Q 2013**

Producer: **Bob Thiele**

Writers: **Jack Lawrence / Richard Myers**

Date reached No.1: **8 October 1954**

Weeks at No.1: **4**

ONE OF THE MANY ITALIAN-AMERICAN singers to come from New York, Don Cornell (born Luigi Varlaro) worked as a guitarist in Red Nichols' Five Pennies, but he was soon concentrating on singing. He was spotted by the bandleader, Sammy Kaye, but Kaye thought his name was cumbersome and introduced him one night as "Don Cornell" without telling him first. He based the name on his former trumpet player, Dale Cornell. Cornell sang on a succession of Kaye's hit records – 'That's My Desire' (a US number three that was on the charts for five months in 1947), 'The World Is Waiting For The Sunrise', 'Careless Hands' (a UK hit for Des O'Connor in 1967), 'It Isn't Fair' and 'Room Full Of Roses'.

Following the lead of so many dance band singers, Don Cornell went solo in 1950. He had reasonable success during two years with RCA including 'Ask Me No Questions' (with Mindy Carson) and 'I Need You So'. He moved to Coral

Frank Sinatra with arranger Nelson Riddle, in the studio in 1954

in 1952 but they did not have a UK outlet for their releases. As a result, Eddie Fisher had a UK hit with Cornell's American success, 'I'm Yours'. Eventually, in 1954, his 18th Coral release secured a UK release and it was followed by his most successful record, 'Hold My Hand'.

Jack Lawrence and Richard Meyers wrote 'Hold My Hand' for a light-hearted film, *Susan Slept Here*, about a Hollywood scriptwriter (Dick Powell) and a delinquent girl (Debbie Reynolds). Cornell's record is played by Reynolds as she makes breakfast in Powell's apartment. The powerful ballad received an Oscar nomination, but lost to 'Three Coins In The Fountain'. 'Hold My Hand' went to number two in the US but topped the UK charts despite competition from Lorrae Desmond, Ronnie Harris and Gary Miller and a campaign against it.

The BBC objected to the line, "This is the kingdom of heaven", although now it is hard to fathom why they thought it profane. An amended line, "This is the wonder of heaven", was agreed and, by overdubbing, Cornell recorded a revised version for airplay. The purchased record still contained the original words, but the sheet music gave the lyric as "This is the wonder of heaven".

When Cornell came to the UK, he learnt that the Archbishop of Canterbury had been criticising his record. "It was all over the newspapers," said Cornell, "and I was so annoyed that I broke some furniture in front of the press. The headline was 'Archbishop Of Canterbury Angers US Singing Star'. The audiences were wonderful: they would shout out, 'Sing your banned song, Donny boy!'"

Although Don Cornell had further US hits in 1955 ('Most Of All' / 'The Door Is Still Open To My Heart', 'The Bible Tells Me So' / 'Love Is A Many-Splendored Thing' and 'Young Abe Lincoln'), they made no impression in the UK. He returned to the UK Top 20 in 1956 with another 'hold my hand' song, 'Stranger In Paradise'. "This was now the rock'n'roll era," said Cornell, "and Coral had the bright idea that I should be recording for teenagers. I did some horrible songs – 'Sittin' In The Balcony', for instance – and it was humanly impossible for me to do these well."

When the hits stopped, Cornell toured the States in *The Pajama Game, A Streetcar Named Desire* and other well-known productions. In 1963 he was among the first stars on the Hollywood Walk of Fame and, in 1993, he was inducted into the Big Band Hall of Fame. Throughout the Sixties and Seventies, he was performing in nightclubs and making occasional guest appearances including the TV series, *Miami Vice*.

In 1979 Cornell moved to Florida and played golf with his old friend, Perry Como. His second wife and biggest fan, Iris, encouraged him back to singing and he combined business with pleasure by performing on cruise liners and recording new albums. He died in February 2004 a few weeks short of his 85th birthday.

24 Vera Lynn with Frank Weir, His Saxophone, His Orchestra & Chorus
My Son, My Son

Label & Cat No.: **Decca F 10372**

Producer: **Frank Lee**

Writers: **Bob Howard / Melville Farley / Eddie Calvert**

Date reached No.1: **5 November 1954**

Weeks at No.1: **2**

Vera Lynn was known as the Forces' Sweetheart during World War II and established herself with such stirring songs as 'The White Cliffs Of Dover' and 'We'll Meet Again'. She continued her success after the war and, most unusually for a UK act, she topped the US charts in 1952 with 'Auf Wiederseh'n Sweetheart', which sold 12 million copies worldwide. Had the charts been started a few weeks earlier, Vera would have had the first UK number one.

Eddie Calvert recorded an instrumental version of his tune, 'My Son, My Son', but it was Vera Lynn's vocal version which became the hit. She adapted to the new medium of television with ease, having successful series throughout the Fifties and Sixties. "She was the easiest artist I ever worked with," says the arranger Tony Osborne, "She always came to the studio note perfect. The standard practice was to record four numbers in three hours but we could be out in 90 minutes with Vera. We would have two perfect takes of each song and there was no point in asking her to do them again as they would sound exactly the same."

In 1968 Vera Lynn was awarded the OBE and in 1975 she became a Dame, the first popular entertainer to receive such an honour. She no longer performs but still takes an active interest in charitable work for the Forces.

25 Rosemary Clooney with Buddy Cole & His Orchestra
This Ole House

Label & Cat No.: **Philips PB 336**

Producer: **Mitch Miller**

Writer: **Stuart Hamblen**

Date reached No.1: **26 November 1954**

Weeks at No.1: **1**

In 1928 Rosemary Clooney was born into an Irish Catholic family in Maysville, Kentucky. She sang with her sister, Betty, as The Clooney Sisters and her voice was praised by Billie Holiday, who said, "You sing from the heart. I like that." In 1949 she was signed to US Columbia Records by Mitch Miller and like many of Miller's artists, she was persuaded to sing novelty songs – 'Me And My Teddy Bear' and 'Little Johnny Chickadee' among them. Easily the most intriguing of her novelties is her playful 'Too Old To Cut The Mustard' with Marlene Dietrich, whose voice was even huskier than Clooney's.

The country music songwriter, Stuart Hamblen, who wrote 'It Is No Secret (What God Can

Do)', stumbled across the body of a prospector in a rundown hut miles from anywhere. The incident inspired 'This Ole House', which was a transatlantic chart-topper for Clooney in 1954 and then Shakin' Stevens in 1981. Also in 1954, Clooney topped the US charts with the ballad 'Hey There' from *The Pyjama Game* and made a novelty single, 'Man', with her philandering husband, José Ferrer, performing 'Woman' on the other side. They separated in 1961, divorcing in 1967, but Clooney was not the totally innocent party as she had a long-standing affair with the orchestra leader, Nelson Riddle. Again in 1954, she starred with Guy Mitchell in the film musical, *Red Garters*, and Bing Crosby and Danny Kaye in *White Christmas*.

"Rosemary Clooney has that great talent which exudes warmth and feeling in every song she sings," said Frank Sinatra, "She's a symbol of modern American music." Despite Sinatra's accolade, Clooney is remembered for novelty songs, but her Eighties homage albums to the great songwriters deserve to be considered alongside Ella Fitzgerald's She died in 2002 and although he has acknowledged her influence, it seemed mean-spirited that her nephew, George, didn't select one of her records in *Desert Island Discs*.

26 Winifred Atwell & Her 'Other' Piano
Let's Have Another Party

Label & Cat No.:	**Philips PB 268**
Producer:	**Johnny Franz**
Writers:	**See below**
Date reached No.1:	**3 December 1954**
Weeks at No.1:	**5**

IN THE FIFTIES THERE WERE MANY SOLO instrumentalists who did well on the UK charts – Winifred Atwell, Russ Conway and Joe Henderson (piano), Eddie Calvert (trumpet) and Bert Weedon (guitar) amongst them. Between 1952 and 1960, Winifred Atwell had 11 Top 10 hits and in 1954 she became the first black artist to make number one. Her hands were insured by Lloyd's for £40,000 (though her insurers can't have been happy when she played in the lions' den at a circus for charity) and her fan club had 50,000 members. She even had a house in Hampstead built in the shape of a grand piano.

Although Atwell was a trained concert pianist, she also featured a tinny, honky tonk piano in her act. This so-called 'Other Piano' was played on her number one medley, 'Let's Have Another Party', which contained snatches of 10 songs on its two sides. What is most interesting is the age of these songs – they are not contemporary hits, but their choruses would be known in any pub singalong, possibly even today. The songs are:

1898 'Lily Of Laguna' (Leslie Stuart) – Southport's top composer, he also wrote 'Soldiers Of The Queen'. Just as well that Stuart hadn't visited Laguna as, despite its magical name, it was known for its mosquito-ridden swamp.

1901 'The Honeysuckle And The Bee' (Albert Fizz / William Penn)

1905 'Nellie Dean' (Harry Armstrong) – performed by Cilla Black & Ringo Starr with Peter Brough & Archie Andrews on BBC-TV in 1968

1916 'Another Little Drink Wouldn't Do Us Any Harm' (Nat D. Ayer / Clifford Grey)

1916 'Broken Doll' (James W. Tate) – a minor hit for Tommy Bruce in 1960

1918 'Somebody Stole My Gal' (Leo Wood) – a Top 10 hit for Johnnie Ray in 1953

1921 'The Sheik Of Araby' (Ted Snyder) – performed on stage by The Beatles

1926 'Bye Bye Blackbird' (Ray Henderson / Mort Dixon)

1926 'I Wonder Where My Baby Is Tonight' (Gus Kahn / Walter Donaldson)

1926 'When The Red Red Robin (Comes Bob Bob Bobbin' Along)' (Harry Woods) – the inspiration for Phil Spector's 'To know, know, know him is to love, love, love him'.

Winnie especially loved the ragtime era and her version of 'Black And White Rag' (1952), which was written by George Botsford in 1908, was the signature tune for the BBC-TV snooker series, *Pot Black* (1969-1984).

27 Dickie Valentine with The Stargazers and Johnny Douglas & His Orchestra
The Finger Of Suspicion

Label & Cat No.:	**Decca F 10394**
Producer:	**Dick Rowe**
Writers:	**Al Lewis / Paul Mann**
Date reached No.1:	**7 January 1955**
Weeks at No.1:	**3 (2 runs)**

DICKIE VALENTINE, REAL NAME Richard Bryce, was born in London in 1929. He wanted to work in show business and his first job was as a call-boy at the Palace Theatre in Manchester. He moved to the London Palladium but left after an argument with the chief messenger. "I'll be back," he snarled, "and I'll be top of the bill." The Canadian singer, Bill O'Connor, realised he had talent and arranged some music lessons. Ted Heath invited him to be a vocalist with his dance band and sensing the young lad with dark, curly hair could be a heart-throb renamed him Dickie Valentine. His first performance with the band was singing 'It's Magic' at the London Palladium in February 1949.

In 1953 he had hits with 'Broken Wings', 'All The Time And Ev'rywhere' and a song for the Coronation, 'In A Golden Coach (There's A Heart Of Gold)'. He was voted Britain's Top

Male Singer in the *NME* poll for 1953, a position he retained until 1959.

Dickie left Ted Heath in 1954, but continued his success with his first number one 'The Finger Of Suspicion' in January 1955. The American song had been recorded by Jane Froman and Bonnie Lou. Dickie toured on the strength of the single and when his hotel was besieged in Belfast, the fans would only leave if he would sing 'The Finger Of Suspicion' from the balcony. The Finger of Suspicion was pointing to the Scottish ice-skater, Elizabeth Flynn, and 4,000 fans turned up at Caxton Hall for their wedding. In April 1955 Dickie was starring at the London Palladium and no doubt giving the chief messenger hell.

28 Rosemary Clooney & the Mellomen Mambo Italiano

Label & Cat No.:	**Philips PB 382**
Producer:	**Mitch Miller**
Writer:	**Bob Merrill**
Date reached No.1:	**14 January 1955**
Weeks at No.1:	**3 (2 runs)**

IN 1951 ROSEMARY CLOONEY THOUGHT 'Come-On-A My House' (1951) was trite and did not want to sing in a mock-Italian accent, but she dutifully did as Mitch Miller instructed and the song topped the US charts for six weeks. She kept the accent for the follow-up hit, 'Botch-A-Me', and returned to it for 'Mambo Italiano'. The song was written by Bob Merrill, who wrote many of Guy Mitchell's novelty hits as well as Barbra Streisand's remarkable 'People'. 'Mambo Italiano' might have appeared too dated for a revival, but in 2000, Clooney found herself back in the charts when her vocal was recreated by Claire Vaughan and used by the production team, Shaft, for a Top 20 single. The song was also given a stunning arrangement by Lesley Garrett, who made it sound like a song from *West Side Story*.

Despite her happy-go-lucky records, Clooney had a troubled life, suffering from depression and addiction to tranquillisers and alcohol. She cursed audiences and sobbed uncontrollably when she announced her retirement. She wrote candidly about her problems in her autobiography, *This For Remembrance* (1977), which was made into a TV movie, *Escape From Madness* (1982), with Sondra Locke miming to Clooney's vocals. By then her career was undergoing a renaissance as she had overcome her problems and she would receive an Emmy nomination for an appearance with her nephew, George Clooney, in the medical drama, *ER*.

29 Ruby Murray with Ray Martin & His Orchestra Softly, Softly

Label & Cat No.:	**Columbia DB 3558**
Producer:	**Norrie Paramor**
Writers:	**Mark Paul / Paddy Roberts / Pierre Dudan**
Date reached No.1:	**18 February 1955**
Weeks at No.1:	**3**

IN 1954 A SHY BELFAST GIRL, RUBY Murray, replaced Joan Regan as the resident singer on the BBC-TV programme, *Quite Contrary*, and won the affection of the British public. A French song, 'La Tamise Et Mon Jardin', was given an English lyric, 'Softly, Softly', by the cabaret entertainer, Paddy Roberts and the BBC executive Robin Scott (writing as Mark Paul), which was perfect for her personality.

'Softly, Softly' topped the charts for three weeks in February 1955 and during that time, Ruby was also at number four with 'Heartbeat', number six with 'Happy Days And Lonely Nights' and number 14 with 'Let Me Go, Lover' – and then, on 19 March 1955, she had five titles in the Top 20 at one and the same time. This feat has never been equalled and the entries were 'Softly, Softly' (2), Let Me Go, Lover' (5), 'Happy Days And Lonely Nights' (14), 'Heartbeat' (15) and 'If Anyone Finds This, I Love You' (a duet with Anne Warren, 17).

Ruby – whose name lingers on as Cockney rhyming slang for curry – commented, "All my success didn't really sink in. I was working at the London Palladium twice nightly with three shows on Saturday, and I had my own TV series which I had to rehearse each morning. I was working so hard that I didn't have time to enjoy anything. I look back and wonder how I coped."

30 Tennessee Ernie Ford with orchestra conducted by Billy May Give Me Your Word

Label & Cat No.:	**Capitol CL 14005**
Producer:	**Lee Gillette**
Writers:	**George Wyle / Irving Taylor**
Date reached No.1:	**11 March 1955**
Weeks at No.1:	**7**

BORN IN BRISTOL, TENNESSEE IN 1919, Ernie Ford had a Christian upbringing, which led to him recording numerous albums of hymns and gospel tunes. In 1947 he created the hillbilly character of Tennessee Ernie Ford for a radio show, but when Lee Gillette at Capitol Records heard him, he realised that his rich baritone would be ideally suited to romantic ballads. These three strains (inspirational songs, comic songs and big ballads) can be found throughout his 28 year recording career with Capitol Records. His early successes include 'Mule Train', 'I'll Never Be Free' (with Kay Starr) and a candidate for the first rock'n'roll record, 'Shotgun Boogie' (1953).

Ford became an American star with his US TV variety show, which was not screened here, despite a guest list which included Greer Garson, Gary Cooper and John Wayne. In 1955 he broke through in the UK with 'Give Me Your Word. "It was so surprising when somebody sent me the paper that said 'Give Me Your Word' was number one on your charts," recalled Ernie in 1989, "I said, 'When did I record that?' because it wasn't that big in America and I had forgotten about it. It was a beautiful song, though, and I started singing it again."

Ernie Ford could have been a much bigger star than he was but he chose to concentrate on gospel music in later years and shunned world tours. He closed all his interviews with the words, "Bless your pea-pickin' heart", and he died in 1991.

31 Pérez Prado & His Orchestra
Cherry Pink And Apple Blossom White

Label & Cat No.: **HMV B 10833**

Producer: **Herman Diaz**

Writers: **Jacques Larue / Louiguy**

Date reached No.1: **29 April 1955**

Weeks at No.1: **2**

'Cerisier Rose Et Pommer Blanc' was a French pop song by Jacques Larue & Louiguy (the pseudonym of Louis Guiglieml), given an English lyric by Hal David's brother, Mack, in 1951. (Hope you can keep up with this – we're going to test you later.) It was recorded at the time by the Havana ensemble, Pérez Prado & His Orchestra, who emphasised its dance rhythms and turned it into a mambo, a rhythm he had pioneered in the late Forties.

The producers of the 1955 film, *Underwater*, liked what Prado had done and asked him to play it on the soundtrack, and this version, with a trumpet solo by Billy Regis, was issued as a single. It topped the US charts for 10 weeks and was easily the best-known Latin record of the Fifties. The film did well as it displayed Jane Russell's heavenly body to its best advantage. Pérez Prado's Orchestra also topped the US charts with 'Patricia' in 1958 and it was used as the theme music for Fellini's film, *La Dolce Vita* (1960). Pérez Prado was called King Of The Mambo. His brother, who was born Panteleón Pérez Prado, set up a rival orchestra and Pérez had to sue his brother to preserve his reputation. Pérez was particularly annoyed when he was in Paris and someone tried to expose him as the fake.

The détente between America and Cuba did not particularly effect Pérez as he had already left Cuba. In the Seventies and Eighties, he retained his popularity in Latin-American countries. The revival of Cuban music in the Nineties came too late for Pérez Prado as he died in Meixco City in 1989 but his 'Guaglione' was used in a Guinness commercial and was a UK number two in 1995. Then his 'Mambo No. 5' found a new home with Lou Bega.

32 Tony Bennett with Percy Faith & His Orchestra and Chorus
Stranger In Paradise

Label & Cat No.: **Philips PB 420**

Producer: **Mitch Miller**

Writers: **Robert Wright / George Forrest**

Date reached No.1: **13 May 1955**

Weeks at No.1: **2**

Frank Sinatra called Tony Bennett his favourite singer and it's easy to see why. Bennett is a supreme interpreter of the popular song, and his versions of 'If I Ruled The World', 'The Good Life', 'Who Can I Turn To' and '(I Left My Heart) In San Francisco' are definitive. As great as these records may be, Tony Bennett has only topped the UK charts once and that was with 'Stranger In Paradise'.

The song came from the musical, *Kismet*, whose music was based on themes by the Russian composer, Aleksandr Borodin. Tony Bennett recalls, "It was released three weeks before the show opened on Broadway, right in the middle of a newspaper strike. On the opening night when the audience heard the song they had heard me sing on the radio, they cheered. That helped *Kismet* become a huge hit without any reviews, just word of mouth. There have been hundreds of versions of that song but I guess mine beat the competition."

As well as Tony Bennett at number one, the charts also included versions of the same song by the Four Aces (6), Tony Martin (6), Eddie Calvert (14), Bing Crosby (17) and Don Cornell (19). Vic Damone sings 'Stranger In Paradise' in the film of *Kismet*, and Tony is still performing it in his concert appearances.

33 Eddie Calvert
Cherry Pink And Apple Blossom White

Label & Cat No.: **Columbia DB 3581**

Producer: **Norrie Paramor**

Writers: **Jacques Larue / Louiguy**

Date reached No.1: **27 May 1955**

Weeks at No.1: **4**

Eddie Calvert, who secured his second number one with a cover version of 'Cherry Pink And Apple Blossom White', had his golden lips insured for £25,000 and was a top concert attraction before the advent of rock-'n'roll. Nevertheless, he continued to have hits with 'Stranger In Paradise' (a number one for Tony Bennett), 'John And Julie', 'Zambesi', 'Mandy (The Pansy)' and 'Little Serenade'. His musicians had to get used to playing in the dark as he loved to play in a spotlight!

By the Sixties his star had waned in the UK and in 1968, he emigrated to South Africa. He became immersed in African culture and was the official liaison officer for the Government with the Bantu tribe. He died in 1978 at the age of 56 following a heart attack in Johannesburg.

BBC

In the early Eighties, Modern Romance picked up on the vibrant rhythms of Latin-American music and the song was reprised with John du Prez on trumpet. As the versions by Alan Dale and Georgia Gibbs had not been hits, this was the first vocal version to make the charts, albeit with some new lyrics from the group.

34 Jimmy Young with Bob Sharples & His Music
Unchained Melody

Label & Cat No.: **Decca F 10502**

Producer: **Dick Rowe**

Writers: **Alex North / Hy Zaret**

Date reached No.1: **24 June 1955**

Weeks at No.1: **3**

YOU MAY HAVE WONDERED WHY 'Unchained Melody' is so called as the phrase does not appear in its lyric. The answer is that the song was written for a long-forgotten prison drama, *Unchained*, starring Elroy Hirsch and Barbara Hale. Todd Duncan sang it in the film but the US hit versions came from the blind balladeer, Al Hibbler, and, instrumentally, from Les Baxter. It was a UK number one for Jimmy Young, who suffered from stomach pains whilst recording the song and had to be rushed to hospital – after he'd finished the recording, y'understand.

His version started to sell well but a 'go slow' at the pressing plant meant that his record could not always be despatched and it looked as though Al Hibbler might have the number one instead. After a few anxious weeks, the stocks were available and Young's version topped the UK charts, while Al Hibbler was a respectable number two. Four versions made the Top 20 with Les Baxter reaching number 10 and the flamboyant pianist Liberace sliding in at number 20. However, the publishers did not permit an hilarious pastiche by Peter Sellers and Spike Milligan to be released.

There is a whispered rock'n'roll treatment from Gene Vincent (1957) and a frantic doo-wop version by Vito & The Salutations (1963). It was recorded by The Righteous Brothers in 1965, and this version was revived for the pottery-in-motion scene in *Ghost* in 1990. Maybe it should be retitled 'Ghost Melody' now. In 1995 it became a number one for the third time when it was revived by the TV soldiers, Robson & Jerome, and then again, in 2002, for Gareth Gates. Elvis Presley loved Roy Hamilton's recording of the song and, in 1977, he took to playing it himself on stage with his own piano accompaniment.

35 Alma Cogan with Vocal Group & Orchestra by Frank Cordell
Dreamboat

Label & Cat No.: **HMV B 10872**

Producer: **Wally Ridley**

Writer: **Jack Hoffman**

Date reached No.1: **15 July 1955**

Weeks at No.1: **2**

ALMA COGAN WAS KNOWN AS 'THE GIRL With The Giggle In Her Voice', but her record producer, Wally Ridley, recalls that it had not come naturally: "It took two and a half years to find that. Her father brought her to me and although she didn't have a natural, God-given talent like Streisand, she had enormous character. I saw her for about two minutes and I thought, "This girl is going to be a star." She sounded the same as many other singers and I had to find something different. When we were clowning round with 'Bell Bottom Blues', she giggled, and I said, "Hey, that's great" – and it was."

Her first success came with a stroke of luck. She covered Teresa Brewer's US hit, 'Bell Bottom Blues' in 1954, but Teresa's version was not released here. The following year Alma secured her only number one with 'Dreamboat', a cover of an American song recorded by the De Marco Sisters and the Paulette Sisters. Alma released an astonishing 11 singles in 1955, which included 'The Banjo's Back In Town' and the double-sided novelty, 'Twenty Tiny Fingers' and 'Never Do A Tango With An Eskimo'. Part of Alma's popularity can be attributed to her many television appearances, often with Benny Hill, where she was always glamorous and dressed in luxurious frocks.

She had hits throughout the Fifties and then became a star in Japan, topping their charts with 'Just Couldn't Resist Her With Her Pocket Transistor'. As the Sixties evolved she kept abreast of fashion by recording songs by The Beatles, with whom she was on friendly terms, and making records with Chris Curtis of The Searchers and Andrew Loog Oldham. It was too late as she contracted cancer and died, only 34 years old, in 1966. Ian Dury described her as "the greatest popular singer Britain has ever had."

36 Slim Whitman
Rose Marie

Label & Cat No.: **London HL 8061**

Producer: **Lew Chudd**

Writers: **Rudolf Friml, Otto Harbach, Oscar Hammerstein II**

Date reached No.1: **29 July 1955**

Weeks at No.1: **11**

THE TWENTIES OPERATTA, *ROSE MARIE*, which tells how a Canadian mountie always gets his woman, was staged on Broadway in 1924 and two songs became standards, the title song and 'Indian Love Call'. It was filmed with Joan Crawford (1928 – a silent musical!), Nelson Eddy & Jeanette MacDonald (1935) and Howard Keel (1954).

The country singer, Slim Whitman, at his wife's suggestion, had success with both songs, and he recalls, "I was a postman when 'Love Song Of The Waterfall' was selling half a million copies. I was a Top 10 artist and I was delivering mail.

Alma Cogan, described by Ian Dury as "the greatest popular singer Britain has ever had"

When I had 'Indian Love Call' in the charts, I decided it was time to go. I was told that if I ever wanted my job back, I could have it."

No need. After 'Indian Love Call', 'Rose Marie' topped the charts for 11 consecutive weeks and Slim commented, "Everyone thinks I'm singing falsetto, but that's my normal singing voice." A young Paul McCartney saw Slim Whitman at the Liverpool Empire and realised you could play the guitar left-handed. Slim couldn't play it any other way because he had lost part of a finger.

In the Seventies, Slim toured the UK regularly and made a succession of best-selling albums, topping the albums chart with *The Very Best Of Slim Whitman* (1976) and *Red River Valley* (1977). Slim's achievement with 'Rose-Marie' was not topped until Bryan Adams' '(Everything I Do) I Do It For You' in 1991, and Bryan invited a rather stout Whitman to perform 'Rose Marie' at a Wembley concert.

37 Jimmy Young with Bob Sharples & His Music The Man From Laramie

Label & Cat No.: **Decca F 10597**

Producer: **Dick Rowe**

Writers: **Lester Lee / Ned Washington**

Date reached No.1: **14 October 1955**

Weeks at No.1: **4**

JIMMY YOUNG HAD TWO SEPARATE SHOW business careers: one as a chart-topping vocalist in the early Fifties and the other as a consummately professional presenter of a highly-rated weekday show on BBC Radio 2 which combined current affairs, consumer news and popular music in a seemingly effortless mix.

In 1951 Young started recording for the small Polygon label, some of his first records being with Petula Clark. When he heard a new song, 'Too Young', which had been recorded by Nat 'King' Cole, he liked both the tune and the link with his own name. "I always enjoyed working with Jimmy Young," said the arranger Ron Goodwin, "because he was always so enthusiastic. He thought everything we did was going to be a hit."

In 1953 Young moved to Decca Records and again found himself in opposition with Nat 'King' Cole, this time with 'Faith Can Move Mountains', and Young appeared one place below Cole, at number 11, on the newly established record charts. He made the Top 10 with a vocal version of Charles Chaplin's theme for the film, *Limelight*, 'Eternally'.

Young became the first British artist to have consecutive number one records, the first being 'Unchained Melody' and the second a jaunty cover of Al Martino's western theme, 'The Man From Laramie'. The man from Laramie was played by James Stewart. Young ended 1955 by performing in a pantomime of *Robinson Crusoe* with Hylda Baker in Wolverhampton: 'The Man From Laramie' (which had no relevance to a desert island) was sung by Young and children with cap guns. Young made many concert appearances but he found performing 'hell on earth' and later said that he was not 'put on this earth to strut my stuff in front of hysterical, screaming women.' Instead, he was to give them Raymondo's daily recipe and write *The Jimmy Young Cook Book*.

By not keeping to pre-arranged questions when interviewing royalty, Young broke with protocol when he became a DJ on Radio 2, although the Duke of Edinburgh commended him on his approach. "His technique is courtesy with a cutting edge," said Lord Hattersley. "He rarely interrupts, is never rude and hardly ever raises his voice. He simply asks questions which are all the more difficult to answer because the listeners know that they are being posed by an eminently reasonable man." Young commented, "You catch more flies with honey than vinegar." Jimmy Young was awarded the OBE in 1979 and when he was knighted in 2002, he dedicated the honour to his listeners. Shortly afterwards, he was dropped by Radio 2 but then wrote his autobiography and did theatre tours.

38 The Johnston Brothers with Johnny Douglas & His Orchestra Hernando's Hideaway

Label & Cat No.: **Decca F 10608**

Producer: **Hugh Mendl**

Writers: **Richard Adler / Jerry Ross**

Date reached No.1: **11 November 1955**

Weeks at No.1: **2**

THE *PAJAMA GAME*, WITH CHOREOgraphy by a young Bob Fosse, opened on Broadway in 1954. The musical with its unlikely theme of union problems in a garment factory became an instant success, largely because of its score which included 'Hey There' (sung by John Raitt, Bonnie Raitt's father) and 'Hernando's Hideaway' (sung by Carol Haney). The show opened in the West End in 1955 with Max Wall, Joy Nichols and Edmund Hockridge. Hockridge became associated with 'Hey There', but by the time he recorded it, the UK was awash with alternative versions, four of them making the Top 20 – Rosemary Clooney (4), Johnnie Ray (5), Lita Roza (17) and Sammy Davis Jr (19). The Johnston Brothers topped the charts with 'Hernando's Hideaway', but Johnnie Ray's version, which was a double A-side with 'Hey There', reached number 11. Alma Cogan's version, surprisingly perhaps, remained in the record shops. Perhaps Elsa Brunelleschi's prominent castanets gave The Johnston Brothers the edge: who knows? The week the Johnston Brothers were number one, one of the writers, Jerry Ross, died from leukaemia.

The Johnston Brothers were not a family group. Their leader was Johnny Johnston, whose first vocal group, The Keynotes, was featured on numerous BBC radio programmes in the Forties and Fifties. He then formed The Johnston Singers and an offshoot, The Johnston Brothers. The other 'brothers' were Miff King, Eddie Lester and Frank Holmes. Their other hits included 'Oh Happy Day' (4, 1953) and 'Join In

And Sing Again' (9, 1955). They backed Suzi Miller (Happy Days And Lonely Nights'), Joan Regan ('Wait For Me, Darling') and Dickie Valentine ('Raindrops') on hit singles, and the Soldiers & Airmen of Her Majesty's Forces who accompanied Vera Lynn on 'Auf Wiederseh'n Sweetheart' was simply Johnny Johnston and his mates. With the advent of ITV, Johnston moved into commercials and became known as a Jingle King.

39 Bill Haley & His Comets (We're Gonna) Rock Around The Clock

Label & Cat No.: **Brunswick 05317**

Producer: **Milt Gabler**

Writers: **Jimmy DeKnight (pseudonym for Jim Myers) / Max C. Freedman**

Date reached No.1: **25 November 1955**

Weeks at No.1: **5 (2 runs)**

'We're Gonna Rock Around The Clock' may not have been first rock'n'roll record or even the best, but its arrival in the charts in 1955 announced that the future of popular music lay in rock'n'roll: music that placed less emphasis on the melody than the beat of a bass and drum rhythm section. The world wasn't the same after 'Rock Around The Clock' and for this reason many would consider it to be the most important record of the 20th century.

Bill Haley, whose mother came from Ulverston in Lancashire, ran a country band, The Saddle Men and then The Comets, but he started covering black music ('Rocket 88') in 1951 and then performing teenage dance tunes – 'Rock The Joint' and 'Crazy, Man, Crazy'. On 12 April 1954 they cut 'Rock Around The Clock', which had previously been recorded by Sonny Dae & His Knights, at the Pythian Temple studios in New York, although most of the three hour session was spent on the other side, 'Thirteen Women'. The lead guitarist was Denny Cedrone, and their tenor sax player, Joey D'Ambrosia recalls, "Danny Cedrone had a group with his brother, The Esquire Boys, around Philadelphia. He was a great guitarist and a good friend of ours. About three weeks after we recorded it, Danny fell down some steps and died. He never knew that the record was a hit."

Jim Myers, the publisher and co-writer of 'Rock Around The Clock', placed the song in a film about juvenile delinquency, *The Blackboard Jungle*, starring Glenn Ford, and so a tense drama became the springboard for the record's success. Haley was not featured in the film, and his record is only heard over the credits. However, youngsters were so starved of the new music that they lapped it up: the DJ and promoter, Alan Freed, branded it 'rock'n'roll' but the label of the original Bill Haley single describes it as 'a foxtrot'. It led to the exploitation film, *Rock Around The Clock*.

Bill Haley's double-bass player, Marshall Lytle, recalls, "We didn't know the song was a success until it hit the theatres and the kids started dancing in the aisles. Then it took the world by storm. 'Rock Around The Clock' was the lead song and it took off. It has become the all-time best-selling rock'n'roll record. It has sold over 50 million copies, been in 35 movies and been performed in 36 different languages. It is the international anthem of rock'n'roll." And of teenage rebellion as cinema seats were ripped as a matter of course when the film was screened.

Bill Haley died in 1981, and, in 2002, The Comets embarked on a UK tour. The group featured five original Comets, the eldest being 81 years old, but The Comets never had youth on their side. Bill Haley was 30 when the record topped the UK charts, while one of the writers, Max C. Freedman, was 66 years old. And they called it teenage music.

40 Dickie Valentine with Johnny Douglas & His Orchestra Christmas Alphabet

Label & Cat No.: **Decca F 10628**

Producer: **Dick Rowe**

Writers: **Buddy Kaye / Jules Loman**

Date reached No.1: **16 December 1955**

Weeks at No.1: **3**

In 1949 Buddy Kaye wrote a very successful song for Perry Como, 'A – You're Adorable' in which Perry praises his girl by finding romantic words for each letter of the alphabet. (Well, not quite, there are a couple of dodgy lines!) Realising this was a winning idea, Kaye reprised it as 'Christmas Alphabet' for The McGuire Sisters in 1954. The following year it was covered by Dickie Valentine for the UK market, and how ironic that the record which deposed the iconoclastic 'Rock Around The Clock' should be some seasonal fluff. Before Cliff Richard, Dickie was the king of Christmas hits. 'Christmas Alphabet' was followed by 'Christmas Island' (1956) and 'Snowbound For Christmas' (1957).

His move from Decca to Pye started well with 'Venus' (1959) but a 30-year-old man shouldn't be asking "Why must I be a teenager in love?". One single was called 'How Unlucky Can You Be'. Indeed. He concentrated on live performances and an album for Philips shows how 'How Do You Do It?' might have been recorded by Nat 'King' Cole, Captain Bird's Eye and his rival, David Whitfield. Performing at the Campbelltown Catholic Club in Sydney, he added Sir Winston Churchill to the list of impersonations and was thrown out by the manager who said, "Yours in the dirtiest act I have ever seen", which suggested that not many acts had come to Campbelltown. Whilst returning from a club engagement in Wales in 1971, Dickie Valentine was involved in a car crash and died.

41 Tennessee Ernie Ford with orchestra conducted by Jack Fascinato
Sixteen Tons

Label & Cat No.: **Capitol CL 14500**

Producer: **Lee Gillette**

Writer: **Merle Travis**

Date reached No.1: **20 January 1956**

Weeks at No.1: **4**

TENNESSEE ERNIE FORD WAS SO BUSY with a daytime television show five days a week that he fell behind with his recording commitments for Capitol. He recalled, "Capitol told me that I would be in breach of contract if I didn't record soon, but I was always thumbing through songbooks looking for music. I liked Merle Travis' Songbook. He wrote workingmen's songs like 'Dark As A Dungeon' and 'John Henry'. He'd lived in the coalmining community, and my grandfather and my uncle had mined coal. I showed 'Sixteen Tons' to my conductor as I liked it very much. Capitol kept telling me to get over there so we went with 'Sixteen Tons' and 'You Don't Have To Be A Baby To Cry' and we recorded them with a six-piece band. Lee Gillette said from the control, "What tempo do you want it in?" and I snapped my fingers to show him. He said, "Leave that in", and that snapping on 'Sixteen Tons' is me."

In a humorous way, the song revealed the unfair practices before the coalminers' unions started. The mineowners also owned the stores and as the miners were paid in tokens, they were cheated at every turn. 'Sixteen Tons' went gold in America within a month and then topped the UK charts. "Every recording artist dreams of something like this," said Ernie. "It was almost equal to Bing Crosby's 'White Christmas'. People say to me, 'Why don't you record another "Sixteen Tons"?', and I say, 'There is no other "Sixteen Tons".'"

Ernie proudly stated, "I was the first person to take country music to the Soviet Union. They didn't know a lot about me but everybody knew that song."

42 Dean Martin
Memories Are Made Of This

Label & Cat No.: **Capitol CL 14523**

Producer: **Lee Gillette**

Writers: **Terry Gilkyson / Richard Dehr / Frank Miller**

Date reached No.1: **17 February 1956**

Weeks at No.1: **4**

THE SONGWRITER, TERRY GILKYSON, IS one of the great, unheralded writers. His daughter, the folk singer and songwriter, Eliza Gilkyson, says, "He hated people looking for hidden meanings in his songs and he did it as a job. He went to the office every day and often wrote about us. 'Memories Are Made Of This' is about our family: it's about him meeting my mother and having three kids. He left us a wonderful legacy."

On the other hand, Dean Martin was going through hell in 1956. His marriage was on the rocks and his hugely successful comedy partnership with Jerry Lewis was all but over. He told Gilkyson that memories were made of shit as far as he was concerned ("All I want is a bottle of Scotch and a blow-job"), but he recognised it as a hit song. He recorded it with The Easy Riders, the name given to Gilkyson's group with his fellow songwriters, Richard Dehr and Frank Miller.

Dean's single topped the US charts for six weeks, with a cover version by Gale Storm reaching number five. In the UK, Dean faced competition from the TV comedian, Dave King, whose version also stopped at number five. The song again made the Top 20 when it was revived by Val Doonican in 1967.

'Memories Are Made Of This' is Dean Martin's only UK number one, but with luck, he might have had five. 'That's Amore' (1954), 'Return To Me' (1958), 'Volare' (1958) and 'Gentle On My Mind' (1969) all faltered at number two. His other US number one, 'Everybody Loves Somebody' (1964) only made number 11 here and 'Little Ole Wine Drinker Me' wasn't a hit at all. He couldn't have cared less: all he wanted was that Scotch and a blow-job.

43 The Dream Weavers
It's Almost Tomorrow

Label & Cat No.: **Brunswick 05515**

Producers: **Wade Buff / Gene Adkinson / Milt Gabler**

Writers: **Wade Buff / Gene Adkinson**

Date reached No.1: **16 March 1956**

Weeks at No.1: **3**

A VOCAL GROUP OF TWO GUYS AND A girl, The Dream Weavers, sang around Miami in the mid-Fifties, and recorded a demo that had been written by two of them, 'It's Almost Tomorrow'. Wade Buff wrote the words and Gene Adkinson the music. This was a wedding song with a difference as the singer is losing his girl to another man.

They impressed Milt Gabler at US Decca, the man who had signed Bill Haley, and he was equally quick to spot the potential of 'It's Almost Tomorrow'. The song went to number seven on the US charts and won The Dream Weavers a gold record. Their only other US hit was with 'A Little Love Can Go A Long, Long Way' from a TV play, *Joey*, the following year, and their other singles were 'Into The Night' and 'Give Us This Day' but they soon disbanded. There can never be a Dream Weavers CD as they only recorded eight tracks.

The Dream Weavers competed for UK chart success with five other versions including Eve Boswell's and Jo Stafford's. They went to number one and the song was also featured by David Whitfield on the Top 10 charity single, 'All Star Hit Parade', in June 1956. The song was revived by Mark Wynter with a new arrangement from Tony Hatch in 1963, and Mark reflects, "The

Dream Weavers did it in 3/4 waltz time and we changed it to 4/4 with a country feel."

44 Kay Starr with Hugo Winterhalter's Orchestra And Chorus
Rock And Roll Waltz

Label & Cat No.: **HMV POP 168**

Producer: **Joe Carlton**

Writers: **Dick Ware / Shorty Allen**

Date Reached No.1: **31 March 1956**

Weeks at No.1: **1**

THERE IS ONLY ONE UK CHART-TOPPER with 'rock'n'roll' in its title and only one with 'rockabilly' (see entry 58) and both are simple, cosy middle-of-the-road pop songs.

Kay Starr won her first gold disc with 'Wheel Of Fortune' and her second with 'Rock And Roll Waltz'. In 1955 she switched from Capitol to RCA Records in America but she wasn't comfortable with the recording studio. "It was a huge studio," she remembered, "completely foreign to any kind of recording I had done before and I had never sung with strings either. I was also used to singing gutbucket songs that were loud and boisterous and when they handed me 'Rock And Roll Waltz', I thought they were playing a joke on me. It was so simple, it was almost like they were insulting my intelligence".

Despite 'Rock And Roll Waltz' selling over a million copies, her audience never requested her to sing it. "That always puzzled me" she said, "They preferred my early novelty songs like 'Side By Side', but I didn't." On her tours during the Sixties, she preferred doing the standards.

In the Eighties, she toured as '4 Girls 4' with Helen O'Connell, Rosemary Clooney and Margaret Whiting, singing swing songs in various combinations. In 1982 when Martha Raye replaced Margaret Whiting, they were renamed The New Four Girls.

In 1993 Kay toured with Pat Boone on his *April Love* tour and in 2000 sang 'Blue And Sentimental' with Tony Bennett on his Grammy award winning album *Playin' With My Friends: Bennett Sings The Blues*.

45 Winifred Atwell & Her 'Other' Piano
The Poor People Of Paris

Label & Cat No.: **Decca F 10681**

Producer: **Hugh Mendl**

Writer: **Marguerite Mannot**

Date reached No.1: **13 April 1956**

Weeks at No.1: **3 (two runs)**

WINIFRED ATWELL, WHO WAS BORN near Port of Spain, Trinidad, in 1915, was a trained classical musician and she came to the UK in 1946 determined to become a concert pianist. She married the variety agent, Lew Lewisohn, in 1947 and she was soon sidetracked, playing classical pieces to be sure but becoming known for her knees-up singalongs played on her 'other' piano. She wrote the highly successful 'Britannia Rag' for her appearance on a Royal Variety Performance in 1952, and in 1953 she was back in the charts with 'Coronation Rag' to join the celebrations for our new queen.

The singalong medleys on that 'other piano' provided the karaoke of the day but, considering her ability, Winnie was dumbing down. 'Let's Have A Party' was followed by 'Let's Have Another Party' and then 'Let's Have A Ding Dong' and 'Make It A Party'. Realising there were new kids on the block, the original honky tonk woman came up with 'Let's Rock'n'Roll' and mixed standards with skiffle songs on 'Let's Have A Ball'. All these records made the Top 10 and were used for community singing throughout the land. Winnie was supplanted in the UK charts by Russ Conway, but she emigrated to Australia and remained popular there until her death in Sydney in 1983.

Before Winnie left, she discovered a young balladeer called Terry Parsons. He was so grateful that he called himself Matt Monro: the name came from Matt White, the first journalist to write about him, and Monroe Atwell, Winnie's father.

In 1954 Edith Piaf had recorded 'La Goualante Du Pauvre Jean', effectively 'The Street Ballad Of Poor John'. It was passed to Capitol Records in America, who misheard the title, writing down 'gens (people)' for 'Jean'. As Piaf always sang about Paris, the song was given an English lyric as 'The Poor People Of Paris'. It was a US hit for the orchestras of Les Baxter (number one for six weeks), Lawrence Welk and Russ Morgan, but only Winnie's version made the UK charts.

Some years later, Ralph McTell wrote a song about the homeless people he saw in the French capital but when he realised there was a 'Poor People Of Paris', he changed the title to 'Streets Of London'.

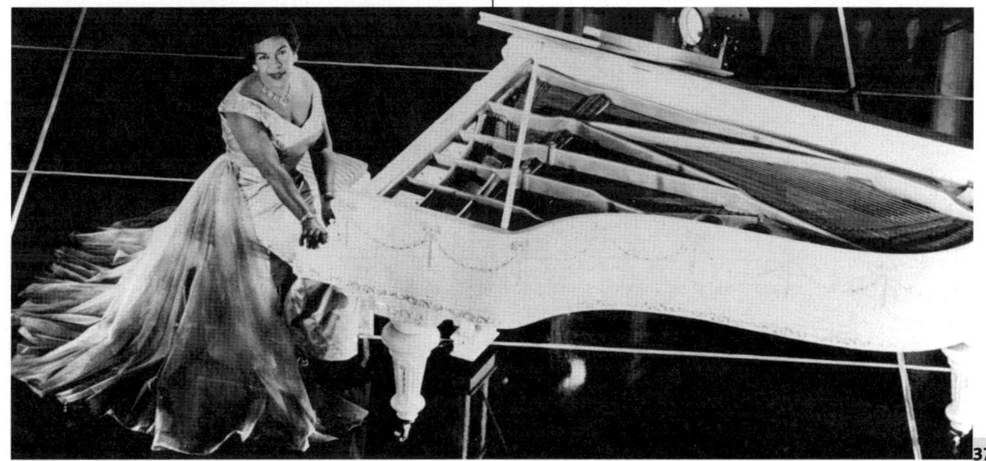

Winifred Atwell and Piano

46 Ronnie Hilton with choir and orchestra conducted by Frank Cordell No Other Love

Label & Cat No.: **HMV POP 198**
Producer: **Wally Ridley**
Writers: **Richard Rodgers / Oscar Hammerstein II**
Date reached No.1: **4 May 1956**
Weeks at No.1: **6**

In May 1956 Elvis Presley was becoming an international sensation with his first RCA single, 'Heartbreak Hotel'. The record topped the US charts but it couldn't dislodge Ronnie Hilton, who held onto the top spot for six weeks.

Ronnie Hilton, who was born Adrian Hill in Hull in 1926, had a fine, semi-operatic voice, although he spoke in a broad Yorkshire accent. Encouraged by his first wife Joan, he recorded for HMV and had hits with 'I Still Believe' (1954), 'Veni Vidi Vici' (1954) and 'A Blossom Fell' (1955) amongst others, before going to the top with 'No Other Love'.

Ronnie recalled, "Perry Como was my favourite singer and he had recorded 'No Other Love' and got a gold disc in America. Wally Ridley told me that they weren't going to release his record until he came over, so could I do it and get on TV and radio? I knew it was a good song – the music was taken from a melody that Richard Rodgers had written for a television series, *Victory At Sea*, which had a commentary by Sir Winston Churchill. The melody was called 'Under The Southern Cross' and was based on the tango. Oscar Hammerstein put words to it for their musical, *Me And Juliet*, which never came to England. We made a good record but we never let anything be released until we were satisfied with it ourselves."

Wally Ridley adds, "Frank Cordell did a superb arrangement and I remember Ronnie saying, 'If I can't sing with that, I can't sing with anything.' He was one of the few singers who listened to what the orchestra was doing."

In later years, Ronnie became a popular Radio 2 presenter with his series, *Sounds Of The Fifties*. He continued to perform and his arrangements were marked 'SHE'. "That stands for Standard Hilton Ending," said Ronnie, who died aged 75 in 2001. "I'm a glutton for punishment and I love songs like 'No Other Love' that I can belt out. There's nothing like a good stand-up-and-fight big ballad to finish the act, but I sing about eight of them in one performance."

47 Pat Boone I'll Be Home

Label & Cat No.: **London HLD 8253**
Producer: **Randy Wood**
Writers: **Ferdinand Washington / Stan Lewis**
Date reached No.1: **15 June 1956**
Weeks at No.1: **5**

Considering Pat Boone's long run for hit records (1955 – 1962) and the fondness with which many of them are remembered, it is surprising that he had only one UK number one. He had six in the US ('Ain't That A Shame', 'I Almost Lost My Mind', 'Don't Forbid Me', 'Love Letters In The Sand', 'April Love' and 'Moody River'), but 'I'll Be Home', a cover of an R&B hit by The Flamingos, only made number four. For a time he was Elvis Presley's closest rival and he topped the UK chart first. "We were both Tennessee boys and we got to know each other well," says Pat today, "I had to follow him on stage once and I didn't like walking out there with my narrow tie, button-down shirt and white buck shoes, but I'd had a couple of hits so I was all right."

With conscription still in force, many ballads of the day were for servicemen abroad, the most successful being 'You Belong To Me' (Jo Stafford) and 'I'll Be Home' (Pat Boone). Boone himself was the typical American clean-cut kid, a University graduate bringing up a young family with his wife, Shirley, the daughter of country singer, Red Foley. Some think that Boone was exploiting black music like The Flamingos for his own success, but Bobby Vee is quick to defend him: "Pat Boone is not responsible for the way our country was, he was just a guy looking for material. He introduced the white population to black R&B and black rock'n'roll. They might not have heard it otherwise until much later."

He was very religious – refusing for some time to even kiss a girl in his films – and many people were baptised in the pool at his Hollywood home. He came to the UK in 1963 but his record label wouldn't let him record a potential hit he had heard – 'From Me To You' by the Beatles. Pat and Shirley's children followed them into the business and Debby had a US number one with 'You Light Up My Life', the biggest selling record in America in the Seventies.

48 The Teenagers featuring Frankie Lymon Why Do Fools Fall In Love?

Label & Cat No.: **Columbia DB 3772**
Producer: **Richard Barrett**
Writers: (in dispute) **Frankie Lymon / George Goldner**
Date reached No.1: **20 July 1956**
Weeks at No.1: **3**

A group of New York teenagers, The Premiers, auditioned for the producer, Richard Barrett. He renamed them The Teenagers and he liked a song based on a poem from a friend of the group, Richard White. He played the song, 'Why Do Fools Falls In Love?', to the notorious record label owner, George Goldner. Whilst Goldner liked Herman Santiago's lead vocal, he realised that 13-year-old Frankie Lymon was sensational. The record starts with some wonderfully loony doowop harmonies and is then followed by Lymon's soaring voice, which had not yet broken. The record reached number six in the US, despite strong opposition from Gale Storm, and they topped the UK charts, with a cheerful cover version from Alma Cogan also making the Top 30.

Their follow-up hits included 'I'm Not A Juvenile Delinquent', but that is precisely what Lymon was. He was involved all manner of wheeling and dealing and taking drugs. Nevertheless, Lymon was the first black rock'n'roll star and the group can be seen in the film, *Rock! Rock! Rock!* : although the movie wasn't so hot, it didn't have much of a plot. His young brother, Lewis Lymon, formed The Teenchords and appeared in another rock'n'roll film, *Disc Jockey Jamboree.*

The Teenagers split with Frankie Lymon in 1957 and neither had much success on their own. In the mid-Sixties, Frankie Lymon joined the US army and during leave in February 1968, he had a recording session scheduled. He took heroin to celebrate his return to the studio and died from an overdose, one of rock'n'roll's first drug casualties. In 2002 The Teenagers performed in the UK with Lewis Lymon singing his brother's parts.

Ronnie Spector, Diana Ross and Smokey Robinson are three stars who have acknowledged Lymon's talent. If he had exercised self-control, he would have been much bigger.

49 Doris Day Whatever Will Be, Will Be

Label & Cat No.: **Philips PB 586**

Producer: **Mitch Miller**

Writers: **Ray Evans / Jay Livingston**

Date reached No.1: **10 August 1956**

Weeks at No.1: **6**

IN 1956 ALFRED HITCHCOCK WAS MAKING a thriller, *The Man Who Knew Too Much*, with Doris Day and James Stewart, and the producers insisted that Doris must have a song. Hitchcock fought this but met the songwriters, Ray Evans and Jay Livingston, and said that a song might be appropriate when she puts her young son to bed. The songwriters had been watching *The Barefoot Contessa* with Rossano Brazzi and they based a song around his motto, 'Que Sera Sera'. When Hitchcock heard it, he said, "Gentleman, I told you I didn't know what kind of song I wanted, but that is the kind of song I want." The Hitchcock blonde sang it in the film but she was reluctant to release it as a single as she felt it was a children's song. Que sera sera, her record was a transatlantic number one.

The song was retitled 'Whatever Will Be, Will Be' because a title in a foreign language would not be eligible for an Oscar. (Talk about xenophobia!) The song won the Oscar, much to Cole Porter's annoyance as he had expected to win with 'True Love' from *High Society.*

The song became the theme tune for the TV series, *The Doris Day Show*, and she said that it reflected her philosophy of life, "I strongly believe in the inevitability of everyone's life pattern. Our destinies are born with us."

Mary Hopkin had planned to revive ''Whatever Will Be, Will Be' as a single to follow 'Those Were The Days'; but the publishers objected to some rewriting from Paul McCartney and another song was chosen. A few months later Hopkin's version was cleared and included on an album.

50 Anne Shelton with Wally Stott & His Orchestra Lay Down Your Arms

Label & Cat No.: **Philips PB 616**

Producer: **Johnny Franz**

Writers: **Leon Land / Åke Gerhard / Paddy Roberts**

Date reached No.1: **21 September 1956**

Weeks at No.1: **4**

LIKE VERA LYNN, ANNE SHELTON – real name, Pat Sibley – was a Forces' Sweetheart during World War II and her big songs were 'Lili Marlene' and 'I'll Be Seeing You'. Towards the end of the war, she met David Reid, who became her manager and husband.

She continued her success after the war with 'Galway Bay', 'Arrivederci Darling' and 'Seven Days'. When Johnny Franz came across a new song with servicemen connections, he thought it would be ideal for Anne, but she was not so sure. She recalled, "When Johnny Franz played it for me, I said I didn't like it. It had a Swedish lyric at the time, but Johnny said I'd change my mind when Paddy Roberts came up with the English one. I loved it then."

The original song was 'Ann-Caroline' and it was a number one hit in Sweden for the female singer, Thory Bernhards. It was about a soldier returning from the war to find his girl had found another man. It was written by Åke Gerhard (lyrics) and Leon Land (music). They wrote many Swedish hits together and then, in the Sixties, Land became the manager of an amusement park. Gerhard wrote several Swedish entries for the Eurovision Song Contest. He managed The Hep Stars, which featured a young Benny Andersson, later of Abba, on keyboards. The English lyric for 'Ann-Caroline' was by Paddy Roberts, best known as a satirical songwriter, a prototype for Jake Thackray if you like, having hit albums with *Strictly For Grown-Ups* (1959) and *Paddy Roberts Tries Again* (1960).

Anne Shelton's recording session, which was engineered by Joe Meek, had its problems: "I had the most beautiful Christian Dior suit on, a beautiful black one. I stood by the microphone and there was a lovely man close by who had a box with stones in to give the effect of marching feet by shaking it backwards and forwards. My whole suit was covered in grey dust and I could never get it out."

Not to worry, the record was a number one Anne Shelton never lost her links with the services, often working with charities. She sang 'I'll Be Seeing You' in the film, *Yanks*, and performed 'You'll Never Know' as a special request for the Queen Mother's 80th birthday celebrations. She was, however, reluctant to tour and, by the time of her death in 1994, she was unknown to anyone under 50.

51 Frankie Laine with Percy Faith & His Orchestra A Woman In Love

Label & Cat No.: **Philips PB 617**

Producer: **Mitch Miller**

Writer: **Frank Loesser**

Date reached No.1: **19 October 1956**

Weeks at No.1: **4**

DAMON RUNYON'S GANGSTER YARNS were the basis for the 1950 Broadway musical, *Guys And Dolls*, with a superb score by the bad-tempered Frank Loesser. He was so grumpy that when he attended show-business functions with his wife, he was called "the evil of two Loessers".

The show became a Hollywood musical in 1955 and Frank Sinatra was brilliant as Nathan Detroit. Marlon Brando was less convincing as Sky Masterson and one song, 'My Time Of Day', was dropped because he couldn't manage the notes. In its place, Loesser wrote a new ballad with a limited range, 'A Woman In Love', which annoyed Sinatra because he liked the song and wanted to sing it himself. Sinatra should have swallowed his pride and recorded it as a single as he left the door open for Frankie Laine (1), the Four Aces (19) and Ronnie Hilton (30).

Frankie Laine lost much of his chart potential during the rock'n'roll years, but he had success with the theme from the TV western, *Rawhide!* (1959), which was revived with hilarious consequences by Jake & Elwood, The Blues Brothers. Laine's style influenced Tom Jones. He returned to the US charts in 1969 with 'You Gave Me A Mountain' and, in 1974, he recorded the theme for *Blazing Saddles*, which parodied his own style.

Laine continued to tour, but he was plagued with health problems and had quadruple bypass heart surgery in 1985. It didn't affect his performance as he still favoured songs with big endings and he celebrated his 91st birthday in 2004.

52 Johnnie Ray Just Walkin' In The Rain

Label & Cat No.: **Philips PB 624**

Producer: **Mitch Miller**

Writers: **Johnny Bragg / Robert S. Riley**

Date reached No.1: **16 November 1956**

Weeks at No.1: **7**

THE WRITER OF 'JUST WALKIN' IN THE Rain', Johnny Bragg, was born in the poorest part of Nashville in 1926. He was born blind but his sight came to him when he was six. He grew up wild but, when he was 16, in what appears to be a stitch-up by the police, he was accused of six rapes and sentenced to serve concurrent terms of 99 years for each. The Tennessee State Prison was a vicious institution and he was sometimes beaten unconscious but in 1953 a new warden brought about reforms and encouraged Bragg to develop a band of inmates, The Prisonaires. They could be booked for local functions and although it might be assumed that audiences would stay away, they turned up to watch a band of three murderers, one rapist and one car thief, who were watched by armed guards.

In the winter of 1953 Bragg was walking across the courtyard to his duties in the laundry with a burglar, Robert Riley. The rain was beating down and Bragg said, "Here we are just walking in the rain and wondering what the girls are doing." Riley said, "That's a song." Within a few minutes Bragg had written two verses and was convinced it was a hit. As he was illiterate, he asked Riley to write it down in exchange for a writing credit. It became their first single for Sun Records in Memphis and despite the fact that they could hardly tour, it made the R&B charts.

In 1956 the producer for US Columbia, Mitch Miller, thought that the song could be a pop hit for Johnnie Ray. It was given a full orchestral accompaniment and his emotional treatment was equally expansive. Starting with 'Cry' and 'The Little White Cloud That Cried' in 1951, Johnnie Ray was associated with songs where he could break down in tears. In their 1999 duet, 'Sometimes We Cry', Tom Jones and Van Morrison accuse Ray of artifice: "I ain't gonna fake it like Johnnie Ray", but this is unfair. Ray's UK agent, Kenneth Pitt, recalls, "When Johnnie Ray came over, I watched him very closely and I am certain that his crying was genuine, and that he could do it to order, twice nightly. I put it down to the fact that he was a very emotional boy. He was very lonely and he often went back to his hotel room and cried."

Bragg was released on parole in January 1959. He was 32 years old and had spent 15 years in prison. Unusually for a black performer, he sang on the *Grand Ole Opry* and he also opened for Sammy Davis Jr in Las Vegas. He met Johnnie Ray and gave him a follow-up, "Laughin' In The Rain", but Ray was not interested. Bragg was in and out of prison for the next 20 years but then he had a straight run until his death in 2004 and he did much for those in need.

53 Guy Mitchell with Ray Conniff & His Orchestra Singing The Blues

Label & Cat No.: **Phillips PB 162**

Producer: **Mitch Miller**

Writer: **Melvin Endsley**

Date Reached No.1: **5 January 1957**

Weeks at No.1: **3 (3 runs)**

IN 1954, AT THE AGE OF 20, THE ARKANSAS-born songwriter Melvin Endsley wrote 'Singing The Blues'. A victim of polio from the age of three, he spent his life in a wheelchair. It caused his hands to become cramped and had to use a special steel bar so that he could change chords on the guitar.

He moved to Nashville but found only one artist who would listen to his material, country singer Marty Robbins. Marty cut the first version of 'Singing The Blues', which spent 13 weeks at number one on the US country chart in 1956.

Guy heard Marty's version and asked his producer, Mitch Miller, if he could also record it. Guy recalled, "I didn't want to record it unless Marty agreed. I asked him and he said 'Okay, maybe it'll give my own record a push'. My version sold eight million copies and it also established Marty, as his version sold a million."

Ray Conniff provided the whistling on Guy's version, although Brook Benton once claimed to English producer, Stuart Colman, that he did it. 'Singing The Blues' spent nine weeks at number one in America, but only three in the UK, tying with Tommy Steele's version during the final week.

Endsley stuck to his winning formula with the follow-up, 'Knee Deep In The Blues'. Again, Marty recorded it first and both Guy Mitchell and Tommy Steele covered it. Guy won the chart battle when his version peaked at number three, 12 places higher than Tommy's.

The song was to become a favourite for chart revival acts. Dave Edmunds took it back into the chart in 1980 and 10 years later Status Quo included it in their 'Anniversary Waltz (Part Two medley)'. In 1994 it went full circle when country singer Daniel O'Donnell took it back to number 23.

54 Tommy Steele & The Steelmen
Singing The Blues

Label & Cat No.: **Decca F 10819**

Producer: **Hugh Mendl**

Writer: **Melvin Endsley**

Date reached No.1: **11 January 1957**

Weeks at No.1: **1**

BRITAIN'S FIRST ANSWER TO THE SULLEN Elvis Presley was Tommy Steele with his million-watt smile but his heart was never in rock'n'roll and he describes his first hit, 'Rock With The Cavemen', as being like 'a Monty Python satire'. However, he does display a feel for the music in his cover of 'Singing The Blues'. Just listen to that mumbled opening line – pure Elvis.

The session singer Mike Sammes recalled, "I was asked to do the whistling on 'Singing The Blues'. Tommy was very keen to have a whistle through the teeth, which I couldn't do but it was on the American record by Guy Mitchell. You need a gap in your front teeth to do that. I added a few 'boom-boom-booms' too and some clapping on the offbeat. At the end of the first chorus, there's a three-headed Mike Sammes as I'm doing it all at the same time."

Steele also covered Guy Mitchell's 'Knee Deep In The Blues' (Mitchell number three, Steele number 15), but many of his hits ('Butterfingers', 'A Handful Of Songs') were written by Lionel Bart. Encouraged by his manager Larry Parnes, he was intent on becoming a family entertainer, moving into pantomime and then light-hearted comedy films like *Tommy The Toreador,* which contained a children's favourite, 'Little White Bull'. He revived 'What A Mouth', simply to show his East End father that he was as good as the music hall act, Two Bills From Bermondsey, who performed the original.

Tommy Steele became a Hollywood star, often working for Disney, and he has returned to the UK for stage musicals such as *Hans Christian Andersen* and *Singin' In The Rain.* He is a fine sculptor (his 'Eleanor Rigby' can be seen in Liverpool) and of late, he has been starring in the Christmas musical, *Scrooge*, written by Leslie Bricusse.

Tommy Steele

55 Frankie Vaughan
The Garden Of Eden

Label & Cat No.: **Philips PB 660**

Producer: **Johnny Franz**

Writer: **Dennis Norwood**

Date reached No.1: **25 January 1957**

Weeks at No.1: **4**

FRANKIE VAUGHAN WAS BORN FRANK Abelson into a family of Russian émigrés in Liverpool in 1928: "I decided the day after I signed my contact that Frankie Abelson didn't sound very showbiz and so I rang my mother to see what she thought. My grandma, God rest her soul, said in the background, "Whatever he picks, he'll always be my number Vorn." I was her number one grandchild and so Vaughan it was."

Frankie was the most popular Liverpool entertainer before The Beatles and he had success with 'My Sweetie Went Away', 'Give Me The Moonlight' (which became his signature tune), 'My Boy Flat Top', 'Green Door' (number two), and then his first number one in 1957 with an American song, 'The Garden Of Eden'. "There were about 16 cover versions of 'The Garden Of Eden'," recalled Frankie, 'and I was very lucky to be the one to make it. The original was by an American who had been put in prison and so the song was up for grabs. There were jokes flying around the country. Kids would ask their religious teacher, 'Who came out of the Garden of Eden?' and the answer was 'Frankie Vaughan'."

The song was also a Top 30 hit for Gary Miller (14), Dick James (18) and Joe Valino (23), whose version was the American original. Perhaps it is just as well that Dick James didn't make the best-selling version. He moved into music publishing and signed Lennon & McCartney and Elton John.

56 Tab Hunter with Billy Vaughn's Orchestra and Chorus Young Love

Label & Cat No.: **London HLD 8380**

Producer: **Billy Vaughn**

Writers: **Carole Joyner / Ric Cartey**

Date reached No.1: **22 February 1957**

Weeks at No.1: **7**

In this book, you will find many artists with number one records that follow an appearance in a film or a TV series. The first is Tab Hunter, born Arthur Kelm in New York in 1931. He made his film debut in *The Lawless* (1948), and although he came from the Timberland school of acting, his all-American blond looks made him a teenage idol. In early 1957 he was promoting the film, *The Spirit Of St. Louis*, which starred James Stewart as flying pioneer Charles Lindbergh.

The first recorded version of 'Young Love' was by one of the writers, Ric Cartey. The rockabilly singer, Sonny James, picked it up and when his version appeared in the charts, Randy Wood, the owner of Dot Records, asked Tab Hunter to record it. They raced up the US charts with Sonny James reaching the top first to be replaced by Tab Hunter for a further six weeks. In the UK, Sonny James only reached number 11, but he did have a long run of hits on the US country chart.

Hunter hadn't much of a singing voice but he could get by with this easy-paced song and its follow-up, 'Ninety-Nine Ways' (US number 11, UK, number five). He continued to record sporadically and, despite appearances in the musical *Damn Yankees* (1958), *The Life And Times Of Judge Roy Bean* (1972) and *Grease 2* (1992), his films were mostly down-market. He appeared with the ultra-camp Divine in *Polyester* (1981) and *Lust In The Dust* (1985). He is currently narrating the TV series, *Hollywood On Horses*, and his autobiography was published in 2004.

57 Lonnie Donegan & His Skiffle Group Cumberland Gap

Label & Cat No.: **Pye Nixa B 15087**

Producer: **Alan A. Freeman**

Writer: **Traditional, arranged by Lonnie Donegan**

Date reached No.1: **12 April 1957**

Weeks at No.1: **5**

Lonnie Donegan, who played banjo in Chris Barber's Jazz Band, had a surprise hit in 1956 when he revived Leadbelly's blues song, 'Rock Island Line'. This song launched the so-called skiffle craze in the UK, wherein thousands of adolescents played cheap guitars, home-made tea-chest basses and washing boards (with thimble-clad fingers). Lonnie left Chris Barber and was acknowledged as the King of Skiffle. The only other skifflers to have hit records were The Vipers, Johnny Duncan and The Chas McDevitt Skiffle Group featuring Nancy Whiskey, and they all rose to fame in 1957.

Cumberland Gap is a pass through the Appalachian Mountains. The first recorded version of 'Cumberland Gap' was by Riley Puckett & Gid Tanner in 1924, but Lonnie took it at a more frenetic pace, making it possibly the most exciting UK pop record until the advent of The Beatles. Lonnie was touring the US in 1957 and while in Louisville, Kentucky, he received a telegram to say that the single was number one. When he looked out of the window, he could see the Cumberland Gap itself. "Most of the people who bought the record thought it was in the Lake District," said Lonnie.

Although Lonnie maintained an energetic act until his death in November 2002, he stopped doing 'Cumberland Gap'. When someone shouted for it, he would shout back, "I'm 70 years old, are you a sadist?"

58 Guy Mitchell with Jimmy Carroll Rock-A-Billy

Label & Cat No.: **Phillips PB 685**

Producer: **Mitch Miller**

Writers: **Woody Harris / Eddie Deane**

Date Reached No.1: **18 May 1957**

Weeks at No.1: **1**

Much of the material recorded on Sam Phillips' Sun record label in the mid-Fifties was rockabilly. It was the term coined for a style of music, which combined rock music with hillbilly. Although the lyrics of Guy's last UK number one attempt to describe what rockabilly is, the rhythm bore little resemblance to the fast, uptempo jiving sounds that came from Tennessee.

Woody Harris was a songwriter best known for songs that he wrote for Bobby Darin. 'Early In The Morning', 'Queen Of The Hop' and 'Clementine' were all hits, but it was his song 'Was There A Call For Me?', which appeared on the B-side of 'Mack The Knife' that must have made him a rich man, as royalty rates are the same for both sides of a record.

Rock'n'roll had firmly established itself by 1957 and this was Guy's attempt to jump on the bandwagon with a repetitive, yet catchy number.

In 1958 Guy was offered his own 30-minute *Guy Mitchell Show* on NBC television. It featured the Guy Mitchell Singers, Van Alexander and his Orchestra as well as the Ted Cappy dancers. The show only ran for a year, but Guy carried on recording with Ray Conniff and Jimmy Carroll, although without success.

Guy's chart career faded when the decade ended. For his last UK hit, he teamed up with Joe Sherman's orchestra for a country song originally recorded by Ray Price, 'Heartaches By The Number'. The sad tale gave Guy his final American number one. So popular was the song, that during the Sixties, Guy recorded a couple of albums of country songs.

With the Sixties beat boom on the way, Guy's

songs were not in favour. When his contract with Columbia Records expired in 1962 it wasn't renewed. In 1968 he contracted cancer, but made a full recovery. He began drinking and by the early Seventies he was in semi-retirement.

In the early Eighties he appeared on a three-hour television special tribute to Mitch Miller. Guy was given a 15-minute spot and by the end of it, the standing ovation proved he had not been forgotten. He recorded versions of 'Always On My Mind' and 'The Wind Beneath My Wings', which turned out to be crowd favourites when performed.

In 1990 he appeared as Jim Bob O'May in the BBC television series *Your Cheatin' Heart*. A year later, during a successful tour of Australia, Guy was seriously injured in a horse riding accident but after a short period in intensive care, he was back on the road. Guy toured throughout the Nineties until a few weeks before his death on July 2, 1999.

59 Andy Williams with orchestra conducted by Archie Bleyer Butterfly

Label & Cat No.: **London HLA 8399**

Producer: **Archie Bleyer**

Writer: **Anthony September**

Date reached No.1: **24 May 1957**

Weeks at No.1: **2**

When Bernie Lowe started Cameo Records in 1956, he persuaded his partner, Kal Mann, that rock'n'roll songs would be simple to write. "All we have to do," said Lowe, "is rewrite somebody else's hit record." 'Singing The Blues' was turned into 'Butterfly', and 'Don't Be Cruel' into 'Fabulous'.

Bernie and Kal wrote a song about Elvis Presley's passion for stuffed toys, 'Teddy Bear' – it was untrue of course, Elvis preferred real dolls, but the concept appealed to younger fans. They disliked the deal they had with Presley's organisation and they didn't want them to know of their next song, 'Butterfly'. They used the pseudonym of Anthony September, the first names of Tony Mammarella, the producer of Dick Clark's TV show, *American Bandstand*, who would receive a one-third cut-in. Clark himself received 25% of the publishing and, lo and behold, Charlie Gracie's version was heavily promoted on *American Bandstand*.

Archie Bleyer, the owner of Cadence Records, thought it was a hit song and had it covered by Andy Williams, who had already scored with 'Canadian Sunset' and 'Baby Doll'. Both versions topped the US charts, and Gracie reached number 12 in the UK. Andy followed his hit with a playful duet with an uncredited Peggy Powers, 'I Like Your Kind Of Love'. Andy remained with Cadence until 1961, when he switched to US Columbia and became the Emperor of Easy.

In the Seventies Andy Williams dismissed his Cadence records, even securing the masters so that they could not be reissued. He is more relaxed about them today as several compilations have been permitted. When you consider 'Can't Get Used To Losing You', 'Can't Take My Eyes Off You', 'Can't Help Falling In Love', '(Where Do I Begin) Love Story' and 'Solitaire', it is surprising that Andy Williams has only ever topped the UK and US charts with 'Butterfly'.

Andy Williams

60 Johnnie Ray Yes Tonight Josephine

Label & Cat No.: **Philips PB 686**

Producer: **Mitch Miller**

Writers: **Winfield Scott / Dorothy Goodman**

Date reached No.1: **7 June 1957**

Weeks at No.1: **3**

Which number one starts with the words, "Poor old Johnnie Ray"? The answer is Dexy's Midnight Runners' 'Come On Eileen' from 1982. Ray, despite all his success, was a sad case. He had difficulty with his relationships and he had impaired hearing as a result of a childhood accident. As his hearing got worse, he became increasingly reluctant to learn new material and so he never recaptured his glory days from the early Fifties. In 1966 he was signed to Frank Sinatra's label, Reprise, but he didn't know that Frank wanted to humiliate him by turning down his work as he suspected the bisexual Ray of having an affair with his former wife, Ava Gardner. When Ray found out, he destroyed all his Sinatra albums in a tantrum.

By 1957 he seemed an anachronism in his smart dinner-suit, although he was only 30 and a great live performer and the first major artist to work with a long microphone lead. Ray did make some inroads into rock'n'roll – his version of Smokey Robinson's 'Shop Around' is superb but was not released until a Bear Family boxed-set in the Nineties – and 'Yes Tonight Josephine' is a crossover between the MOR cabaret songs and rock'n'roll. One of the writers, Winfield Scott, also wrote 'Tweedle Dee' (LaVern Baker), 'Burn That Candle' (Bill Haley), 'Many Tears Ago' (Connie Francis) and 'Return To Sender' (Elvis Presley).

'Yes Tonight Josephine', a reversal of Napoleon's alleged rebuff to his empress, only made number 18 on the US chart, so its runaway success in the UK was unexpected. The song was a Top 30 hit for The Jets when it was revived in 1981, but, by and large, it has been forgotten.

61 Lonnie Donegan
Gamblin' Man / Puttin' On The Style

Label & Cat No.: **Pye Nixa N 15093**

Producers: **Alan A. Freeman / Michael Barclay**

Writers **Woody Guthrie / Lonnie Donegan; Traditional, arranged by Norman Cazden**

Date reached No.1: **28 June 1957**

Weeks at No.1: **2**

'GAMBLIN' MAN' IS A TRADITIONAL SONG with many, many verses – "I wouldn't marry a railroad man", "I wouldn't marry a farmer" and so on. Vernon Dalhart was so delighted with the song that he recorded it for six different labels in 1925. American folk singer Woody Guthrie knew several variants and recorded his version in 1944. Lonnie Donegan upped the tempo, but he took both lyrics and melody from Guthrie's record.

'Puttin' On The Style' was again recorded by Vernon Dalhart, this time in 1924, but the lyrics had been updated by a Harvard graduate, Norman Cazden. Dalhart refers to riding horses, but the trendy young man in Donegan's version drives a hot-rod car. Lonnie's flippant verse about a minister nearly caused the record to be banned by the BBC. It was sung with just banjo, bass and tambourine accompaniment and, ironically, Lonnie was mocking his fans as he is acknowledging that he is no longer young. The implication is, I've seen it all before and it's boring.

Both songs were recorded at the London Palladium where Lonnie was second billed to The Platters. There was a cover version by Dickie Valentine, and the song soon returned to the charts, performed by the band leader Billy Cotton, as part of the charity single, 'All Star Hit Parade, Volume 2'. Donegan parodied his own song in his Top 30 entry, 'Lonnie's Skiffle Party', an ill-advised attempt to regenerate some life into skiffle.

62 Elvis Presley with The Jordanaires
All Shook Up

Label & Cat No.: **HMV POP 359**

Producer: **Steve Sholes**

Writers: **Otis Blackwell / Elvis Presley**

Date reached No.1: **12 July 1957**

Weeks at No.1: **7**

4.35AM, JANUARY 8, 1935, EAST TUPELO, Mississippi – Elvis lives.

The 19-year-old truck driver, Elvis Presley, started recording for Sun Records in Memphis (pronounced "Memphus") in the summer of 1954 and his first few records (including 'That's All Right (Mama)', 'Good Rockin' Tonight', 'Baby Let's Play House' and 'Mystery Train') with Scotty Moore's guitar and Bill Black's bass could be the most significant recordings in the whole history of popular music. At the time, they enjoyed only regional success in America and weren't even released in the UK. In 1956 Elvis left Sun for RCA and the hits flowed at an astonishing rate – 'Heartbreak Hotel' (1 US: 2 UK), 'Blue Suede Shoes' (20 US, 9 UK), 'I Want You, I Need You, I Love You' (1 US, 14 UK), 'Hound Dog' (1 US, 2 UK), 'Blue Moon' (5 US, 9 UK), 'Love Me Tender' (1 US, 11 UK), 'Love Me' (2 US only) and 'Too Much' (1 US, 6 UK). The UK chart entries and positions were impressive, but Elvis had been kept off the top, despite five US number ones with a 28 week residency. He finally cracked it with 'All Shook Up' which spent seven weeks at the top of the UK charts as well as nine in the US.

A key reason for Elvis's success was the extraordinary songs by the new breed of Brill Building composers. Otis Blackwell, a black writer who had written 'Fever', wasn't streetwise enough to avoid being conned on 'Don't Be Cruel', the equally strong B-side of 'Hound Dog'. He sold the publishing for $25 and gave away half of his writer's royalties to Elvis. Undeterred (Colonel Parker must have been brilliantly persuasive!), he passed over 'All Shook Up' and again Elvis is shown as a co-writer, even though the song had previously been recorded by both David Hill and Vicki Young.

These shenanigans aside, 'All Shook Up' is a marvellous, mid-tempo rock'n'roll single with a shuffle rhythm and an R&B feel, described at the time by *Billboard*, the principal US music industry trade paper, as a "hoarsely belted swinging rockabilly job". He recorded it on the same day as 'I Believe' (how's that for versatility, and who said rock'n'roll was the Devil's music?). Apart from allegedly corrupting the young, the 'squares' accused Elvis of poor diction. Elvis does mumble on 'All Shook Up', but it's hard to believe that anyone couldn't make out the lyrics. Still, what on earth does "itching like a man on a fuzzy tree" mean?

'All Shook Up' returned to the Top 30 when Billy Joel revived it for the *Honeymoon In Vegas* soundtrack in 1992. The film starred Nicolas Cage, who in real life (though it sounds more like fiction) had a short-lived marriage with Presley's daughter, Lisa Marie.

63 Paul Anka
Diana

Label & Cat No.: **Columbia DB 3980**

Producer: **Don Costa**

Writer: **Paul Anka**

Date reached No.1: **30 August 1957**

Weeks at No.1: **9**

A 15-YEAR-OLD CANADIAN, PAUL ANKA, had a crush on the family's 18-year-old babysitter, Diana Ayoub, who would watch over his younger brother and sister. She wanted nothing to do with him, so he wrote her the poem which became the lyric for 'Diana'. When he won a trip to New York in a competition sponsored by Campbell's Soup, he sought out Don Costa, a producer at ABC-Paramount Records, and played him his song. Costa immediately signed the boy and at age of 16, Paul Anka was an international star.

Lonnie Donegan, the King of Skiffle, considered by many to be the founding father of British rock'n'roll

The clumsily-written 'Diana' is hardly Paul Anka's best song but its innocence was refreshing and it led to a succession of hit records – 'I Love You Baby', '(All Of A Sudden) My Heart Sings', 'Lonely Boy', 'Put Your Head On My Shoulder' and 'Puppy Love'. In 1963 he recorded the sequel, 'Remember Diana', but nobody did. Donny Osmond revived 'Puppy Love' in 1972 and Anka himself returned to the charts with '(You're) Having My Baby', which had the feminist movement up in arms. However, Anka's most enduring copyright is his English lyric for Claude Francois' 'Comme D'Habitude', now better known as 'My Way'.

In 1997 only minutes before the accident which killed Princess Diana, Bob Harris on BBC Radio 2 played a listener's request for 'Diana'. Then came Queen's 'Heaven For Everyone'. Psychic or what?

64 The Crickets
That'll Be The Day

Label & Cat No.: **Vogue Coral Q 72279**

Producer: **Norman Petty**

Writers: **Buddy Holly / Jerry Allison / Norman Petty**

Date reached No.1: **1 November 1957**

Weeks at No.1: **3**

In 1956 John Wayne starred in the John Ford western, *The Searchers*. Buddy Holly went to see it in Lubbock with his drummer, Jerry (J.I) Allison. J.I recalls, "John Wayne said, 'That'll be the day', about five or six times in that film. We were repeating it for a couple of days afterwards and then we wrote the song." Their guitarist, Sonny Curtis, says, "When they wrote that song, I remember thinking, 'Boy, that's a good idea', but I didn't imagine any of us making hit records. Everything was just fun and games. We played our music and we didn't worry about tomorrow."

Buddy, J.I, Sonny and a double-bass player and friend, Don Guess recorded the song at Bradley's Barn in Nashville for US Decca. According to J.I, "The producer said, 'That's the worst song I've ever heard.' It hurt my feelings because it was first song I'd written." Perhaps it was best that its potential was not appreciated. It was still country music with Buddy's voice being recorded too high and the beat too rigid. A few months later they would see things more clearly.

When Buddy became associated with an independent producer, Norman Petty, in Clovis, New Mexico, he wanted to re-record 'That'll Be The Day', but Petty, knowing of the earlier version, said that Holly was not contractually free to record a second one. Having a brainwave, Petty realised that they could cut it under a group name. "What about The Beetles?" said Buddy. "No," said J.I, "that's just a bug you step on." They chose another insect name, The Crickets, because of their happy, chirping sound.

The Crickets, without Sonny Curtis who had joined Slim Whitman but with Larry Welborn on double-bass, recorded the new version of 'That'll Be The Day'. Norman Petty persuaded them that his name should be added to the writers, and Holly and J.I were good ol' Christian boys who also tithed songwriting royalties to the Baptist church. Over in Liverpool, a group of lads saw *The Searchers* and thought about a name for themselves.

65 Harry Belafonte
Mary's Boy Child

Label & Cat No.: **RCA 1022**

Producer: **Rene Farron**

Writer: **Jester Hairston**

Date reached No.1: **22 November 1957**

Weeks at No.1: **7**

Just as we associate Lonnie Donegan with skiffle, Harry Belafonte's name will be forever linked with calypso. Born in New York in 1927, he began his career as an actor, studying with Marlon Brando and Tony Curtis. Opening a restaurant in Greenwich Village to gain a steady income, he became captivated by the folk songs he heard around him. He was soon researching material for himself at the Library of Congress. His first success came with 'Hold 'Em Joe', which he had sung in a Broadway show, *John Murray Anderson's Almanac*, in 1954. When Rolf Harris heard this song, he converted it to 'Tie Me Kangaroo Down Sport'.

Belafonte became a film star when he appeared opposite Dorothy Dandridge in *Carmen Jones*. His third album, *Calypso*, celebrated the happy, partying music he had heard in the West Indies. Both 'The Banana Boat Song' and 'Jamaica Farewell' were international hits. For a Christmas single in 1957, he recorded a West Indian carol written by Jester Hairston, 'Mary's Boy Child'. The song returned to the UK charts on the next two Christmases, while there was also a hit version by Nina & Frederick, not to mention the disco-styled revival by Boney M.

One of his most delightful records is 'There's A Hole In The Bucket' with Odetta and his films include *Odds Against Tomorrow* (1959), *Buck And The Preacher* (1972) and *Uptown Saturday Night* (1974), the last two with his partner in Civil Rights campaigns, Sidney Poitier. He and Petula Clark encountered much criticism in the late Sixties after holding hands on a US TV show.

Harry Belafonte has also increased awareness of poverty in Third World countries. Although he still acts and performs, most of his time in spent in humanitarian work. He was an instigator of USA For Africa's 'We Are The World' and he can be regarded as the first World Music star.

66 Jerry Lee Lewis
Great Balls Of Fire

Label & Cat No.: **London HLD 8529**

Producer: **Sam Phillips**

Writers: **Otis Blackwell / Jack Hammer**

Date reached No.1: **10 January 1958**

Weeks at No.1: **2**

Dennis Quaid portrayed Jerry Lee Lewis as the cartoon wild man of rock'n'roll in the 1989 bio-pic, *Great Balls Of Fire!*, and although it was very entertaining, the truth is far more complex. Jerry Lee Lewis was a deeply religious Southern boy who was unsure about performing at all. The recording engineer Jack Clement switched on the tape recorder when Jerry Lee was having one particularly explosive argument with the owner of Sun Records in Memphis, Sam Phillips. Sam tells him that his music can help people, can save souls, and Jerry Lee responds, "How can I save souls when I have the Devil in me?" To try to end the discussion and record 'Whole Lotta Shakin' Goin' On', Clement says, "Okay, Jerry, we'll split your royalties with the Holy Ghost," but nobody laughs.

The Brill Building songwriter, Otis Blackwell, saw Jerry Lee perform the lascivious 'Whole Lotta Shakin' Goin' On' on *The Steve Allen Show* and set about writing a song for him. The song was 'Great Balls Of Fire' and Jerry was again in two minds as the song had obvious sexual connotations (later emphasised in a bizarre cover by Mae West). Jerry performed his new record in the rock'n'roll film, *Disc-Jockey Jamboree*, and it went to number two in the US and a step higher here. The B-side was a stunning version of 'Mean Woman Blues' which outclassed Elvis's original from the film, *Loving You*.

A few months later, Jerry Lee's career took a nosedive when he visited the UK with his bride and third wife, his 13-year-old second cousin, Myra. It took him some years to recover from the scandal, although such marriages were permitted in Louisiana. In Jerry Lee's case, however, he hadn't yet divorced his previous wife. In the mid-Sixties, Jerry Lee returned as a country music star. He has been dogged by controversy ever since as, indeed, has his cousin, the famed preacher, Jimmy Swaggart. To a degree, Jerry and Jimmy have wanted to be each other and this is what makes their relationship so fascinating.

When Jerry Lee toured the UK in 2004, he told audiences, "John Lennon told me that 'Great Balls Of Fire' was the greatest record ever made, and I agree with him."

67 Elvis Presley
Jailhouse Rock

Label & Cat No.: **RCA 1028**

Producer: **Steve Sholes**

Writers: **Jerry Leiber / Mike Stoller**

Date reached No.1: **24 January 1958**

Weeks at No.1: **3**

NOWADAYS IT IS FASHIONABLE TO SNEER at Elvis Presley's movies. True, he made some dreadful ones, often with appalling scores, but, in his early years, they were fine. There's not much wrong with *King Creole* or *Flaming Star*, but best of all is *Jailhouse Rock*, a rock'n'roll film directed by Richard Thorpe, who had made *The Student Prince* with Mario Lanza.

The score by Jerry Leiber & Mike Stoller, who had written 'Hound Dog and 'Loving You', was perfect, if a little short. They wrote the whole thing in a day, surely the most productive day in the history of film music. There's the sensuousness of 'Treat Me Nice', the tenderness of 'Young And Beautiful', the anguish of 'I Want To Be Free' and the chirpiness of 'Baby I Don't Care'. Elvis must have liked 'Don't Leave Me Now' as he sings it three times in the film. Nothing, however, competes with the excitement of the title song, which was inspired by Memphis Slim's 'Comeback'. 'Jailhouse Rock' was performed in a dance routine involving cells and convicts. It is the only example of full-blooded Hollywood choreography in any of his films and offered an early, non-sexual example of pole-dancing.

The 'Jailhouse Rock' single was a smash hit in the US, topping the pop, country and R&B charts. In the UK, it was the first single to debut at number one, a common occurrence in these marketing-driven times, but, in 1957, regarded as a near impossible feat – and the *Jailhouse Rock* EP was also in the Top 20. Elvis is forced to sing at the top of his range and because it is difficult to perform well, relatively few artists have covered it. Besides, who could better Elvis's record, which also features Scotty Moore's power chords and D.J. Fontana's drumming? The lyrics, delivered at a tongue-twisting pace, are both charming and witty. 'Jailhouse Rock' is sometimes considered a gay anthem. Number 47 flirts with Number Three and, as since prisons weren't sexually integrated, both must be male.

In April 2004 Mario Kombou recreated Elvis' role of Vince Everett for the West End production of *Jailhouse Rock – The Musical*. Ironically the song does not feature in the show as the publishing is controlled by Elvis Presley Enterprises, the official Elvis company, who are not involved in this production.

68 Michael Holliday
The Story Of My Life

Label & Cat No.: **Columbia DB 4058**

Producer: **Norrie Paramor**

Writers: **Burt Bacharach / Hal David**

Date reached No.1: **14 February 1958**

Weeks at No.1: **2**

MICHAEL HOLLIDAY, BORN NORMAN Milne in Liverpool in 1925, was able to sing just like Bing and he recorded several tributes to his idol. Indeed, Ken Crossland's biography of the star is called *The Man Who Would Be Bing*.

After three years as the featured vocalist with Eric Winstone's band, Mike attracted attention with his first solo record, 'The Yellow Rose Of Texas', in 1955. A number of hits followed – 'Nothin' To Do', 'Gal With The Yaller Shoes' / 'Hot Diggity', 'Ten Thousand Miles' – and he went to the top with a Burt Bacharach & Hal David song, 'The Story Of My Life', which had been originally recorded by the country artist, Marty Robbins. Holliday beat off competition from Gary Miller (14), Dave King (20) and Alma Cogan (25).

Mike had a busy day at Abbey Road on 10 December 1957. He recorded the title song for the John Gregson film, *Rooney*, in the afternoon, and in the evening it was the turn of 'The Story Of My Life', which had been arranged by Ken Jones. The session sheets reveal that the day's expenses were £138 including the cost of The Mike Sammes Singers with Mike Sammes providing the deep-voiced 'bom-boms'.

The engineer, Stuart Eltham, developed an echo effect with a second tape head and created a fuller sound for Mike's voice. Mike was not too happy with his vocal as he drops the first 'h' on the issued take on 'And how my heart can't forget'. He told *Hit Parade* magazine in 1958, "Just what's so different between 'The Story Of My Life' and my other records, I will never know. I am seldom happy with my recording and this one pleased me least of all. Just shows how wrong you can be." In truth, Mike was keener on the B-side, a very pleasant ballad he had written himself, 'Keep Your Heart' and he was flattered when it was covered by Pat Boone.

His TV series, *Relax With Michael Holliday*, can be seen as the prototype for the very successful *Val Doonican Show*, but Mike's casual image was deceptive. He was plagued with nerves and would ensure that the words of even his best-known songs were to hand – and even written on his hand – for TV shows and concert dates.

The story of Michael Holliday's life is short as he died from an overdose of sleeping tablets in 1963 at the age of 38. What prompted his death is unknown, but he had twice taken overdoses on the days he had received tax demands and he had recently settled an expensive dispute out of court with a former manager. He also bitterly regretted his foolishness as his wife, Margie, had left him following a string of affairs. However, the press reports of a gangland killing linking his death to that of the boxer and London club owner, Freddie Mills, appear to be totally unfounded.

'The Story Of My Life' had originally been recorded by Marty Robbins in 1957 and so, trivia buffs, Bacharach & David's first-ever number one record was on the US country charts. The lyric is not typical of Hal David's work as relatively few of his protagonists remember the good things that have happened to them!

In 2004 this hit record had a new lease of life as the theme music of Rob Brydon's ITV comedy series, *The Director's Commentary*.

69 Perry Como with Mitchell Ayres' Orchestra and The Ray Charles Singers Magic Moments

Label & Cat No.: **RCA 1036**

Producer: **Joe Reisman**

Writers: **Burt Bacharach / Hal David**

Date Reached No.1: **1 March 1958**

Weeks at No.1: **8**

In 1958 Eddie Fisher's US TV show was beaten in the ratings by *The Perry Como Show*. He didn't mind: he said, "When I try to romance a woman, I play Perry Como records. What finer tribute could I pay him?" Unlike most American variety shows, Perry's was screened in the UK, thus enabling viewers to witness legendary acts for the first time and to appreciate how casual Mr C was. His relaxed and easy-going style was to be copied by Val Doonican.

At the time, Burt Bacharach's regular job was conducting for Marlene Dietrich and although he showed considerable originality in his arrangements, he and his lyricists were writing typical Tin Pan Alley songs, albeit often of a high quality. Hal David was becoming his favoured lyricist and, in one of the cubicles at Famous Music, they wrote 'Magic Moments' for Perry Como. It was ideal for the relaxed crooner, but surely Bacharach himself would have written a more imaginative arrangement. The song replaced another Bacharach and David song at the top, 'The Story Of My Life', and both records featured whistling – the old grey whistle test was the mark of a hit song in the Fifties. Despite being so relaxed, Perry Como won a Grammy for the Best Solo Male Vocal Performance, but the committee viewed rock'n'roll with suspicion, thus eliminating several major acts from the judging.

The B-side, another Tin Pan Alley song, 'Catch A Falling Star', showed more originality. The single was listed at number nine in the UK and also topped the US chart. A parody version, "Catch a Perry Como, wash him in some Omo," was popular in schools.

'Magic Moments' was revived for the Quality Street advertising campaign in the Eighties. Perry Como was still performing and recording from time to time and he died in May 2001, a week short of his 89th birthday.

70 Marvin Rainwater Whole Lotta Woman

Label & Cat No.: **MGM 974**

Producer: **Jim Vinneau**

Writer: **Marvin Rainwater**

Weeks at No.1: **3**

"It would have been a very nice thing if I had been a full-blooded Indian," says Marvin Rainwater, "but I got blue eyes and Indians have got brown eyes, and they get uptight if they think you're putting them on." Nevertheless, Marvin Rainwater's Cherokee ancestry was a publicity gimmick to sell his records.

Marvin Rainwater's first record was a tribute to Hank Williams, 'Heart's Hall Of Fame', in 1953 and Hank's record label, MGM, took him under their wing. He had success with 'Gonna Find Me A Bluebird' and a duet with Connie Francis, 'The Majesty Of Love', but his major breakthrough came with 'Whole Lotta Woman': "We got Grady Martin, Floyd Cramer and Hank Garland on that record, and I loved that infectious beat that Grady Martin was playing on guitar. MGM held it back because I was flat on the line, 'I know I've been had'. They told me to overdub my voice on top of it in unison and they managed to cover it."

'Whole Lotta Woman' proved to be controversial: "Many of the networks banned it as they thought it was dirty and shouldn't be played on air. That song was how I felt about women. I was singing about a beautiful, wonderful, marvellous woman."

When Marvin came to the UK for TV and concert dates, the airline lost his arrangements: "It was the best thing that could have happened because I ain't suited to 40-piece orchestras," says Marvin today, "They gave me Johnny Duncan & his Blue Grass Boys instead and we did them country.

Marvin's follow-up, 'I Dig You Baby', was recorded in London, and although he did not have lasting chart success, Marvin often performs at rockabilly and country clubs in the UK.

71 Connie Francis
Who's Sorry Now?

Label & Cat No.: **MGM 975**

Producer: **Harry Myerson**

Writers: **Ted Snyder / Bert Kalmar / Herman Ruby**

Date reached No.1: **16 May 1958**

Weeks at No.1: **6**

THE NEW YORK SINGER, CONNIE Francis, had made 10 singles for MGM, but the one that had sold was 'The Majesty Of Love' with Marvin Rainwater. Curiously, this is listed as a gold record, although the US chart placing (number 93) hardly bears this out. More to the point, the record company's management only gave her one more chance to have a hit record.

Her father, George Franconero, suggested that she could strengthen her chance of success by recording a well-tested standard – his suggestion was 'Who's Sorry Now', which had been introduced by Isham Jones and his Orchestra in 1923. The song was revived by Harry James in 1946 and was then sung by Gloria De Haven in *Three Little Words*, the 1950 bio-pic about the songwriters Bert Kalmar (Fred Astaire) and Harry Ruby (Red Skelton). Then it was a Top 20 hit for Johnnie Ray in 1956. Connie thought another revival was a terrible idea, saying "The kids on *American Bandstand* will laugh me off the air." "No," her dad insisted. "The adults will like it and if you put a rock'n'roll beat behind it, the kids will dance to it too."

Legend has it that Connie Francis recorded two new songs with Joe Lippman's orchestra but in the 20 minutes at the end of the three hour session, she added 'Who's Sorry Now?' to humour her father. Good story, but the session sheets tell a different story. On October 2, 1957, Connie Francis recorded 'Who's Sorry Now?' first and then 'The Promise Of Love' (which remains unissued) and 'You Were Only Fooling', the B-side of her single.

Nobody played 'Who's Sorry Now?' until Dick Clark featured it on *American Bandstand* on New Year's Day, 1958 and called her "a new girl singer who's headed straight for the number one slot." "And he continued playing it until it sold a million," said Francis, "Without Dick Clark, I wouldn't have stayed in show business. I was ready to go back to school to study medicine."

72 Vic Damone
On The Street Where You Live

Label & Cat No.: **Philips PB 819**

Producer: **Mitch Miller**

Writers: **Alan Jay Lerner / Frederick Loewe**

Date reached No.1: **27 June 1958**

Weeks at No.1: **2**

IN 1956 THE LYRICIST ALAN JAY LERNER and the composer Frederick (Fritz) Loewe converted George Bernard Shaw's satire, *Pygmalion*, into a musical, *My Fair Lady*. It opened on Broadway in 1956 with Rex Harrison as the language teacher, Professor Higgins and Julie Andrews as his unlikely pupil, Eliza. The ballad, 'On The Street Where You Live', had almost been dropped after a preview in New Haven where it was received badly because the audiences were unsure who was meant to be singing it. Alan Jay Lerner rewrote the song to introduce Freddie Eynsford-Hill as a possible threat to Professor Higgins. Lerner was very proud of the double and triple rhymes in the lyric, but he wished he could have improved on the false rhyme of 'bother me' and 'rather be'.

The *My Fair Lady* score included 'With A Little Bit Of Luck', 'I Could Have Danced All Night' and 'I've Grown Accustomed To Her Face', but 'On The Street Where You Live' was the hit song.

Vic Damone was one of the great vocalists of the 20th century. Like Mario Lanza, Frank Sinatra and Al Martino, Damone came from an Italian family in New York. He had his first successes in 1947 and his biggest sellers were 'Again' (1949), 'You're Breaking My Heart' (1949), 'An Affair To Remember (Our Love Affair)' (1957) and 'You Were Only Fooling' (1965). He appeared in several films including the 1955 musical, *Kismet*, in which he sang 'Stranger In Paradise'. In 1987 the actress and singer Diahann Carroll became his third wife.

73 The Everly Brothers with orchestra conducted by Archie Bleyer
All I Have To Do Is Dream / Claudette

Label & Cat No.: **London HLA 8618**

Producer: **Archie Bleyer**

Writers: **Boudleaux Bryant; Roy Orbison**

Date reached No.1: **4 July 1958**

Weeks at No.1: **7**

ROCK'N'ROLL IS SEEN AS THE MUSIC OF teenage rebellion, but, in truth, all the major acts were supported and encouraged by their parents. None more so than The Everly Brothers. Don, who was born in Brownie, Kentucky, in 1937, and Phil, who followed in Chicago in 1939, were appearing on their parents' radio shows from a young age. They developed their harmonies from listening to country acts like The Blue Sky Boys and The Delmore Brothers and their 1958 album, *Songs Our Daddy Taught Us*, was a beautiful tribute to their upbringing.

In 1954 Don Everly was making headway as a writer in Nashville with songs recorded by Kitty Wells and Justin Tubb. Their first recording session was not a success, but then they met the husband and wife songwriters, Felice & Boudleaux Bryant, and their publisher, Wesley Rose, at Acuff-Rose Music. Archie Bleyer signed them to his label, Cadence, and the first single was the Bryants' 'Bye Bye Love' which had been rejected by several country acts. The song was an international hit, encouraging the Bryants to write for teenagers. 'Wake Up Little Susie' was equally successful.

Boudleaux Bryant wrote 'All I Have To Do Is Dream' in 15 minutes. The 38 year old had perfectly captured the angst of teenage love, especially with the phrase, "Only trouble is, gee whiz". "I can't explain why I put that in there," recalled Boudleaux, "It was just a lucky rhyme fall. When Richard Chamberlain recorded the song, his producer wanted to change it and I said, 'No way!'"

Phil Everly remembers, "I first heard 'All I Have To Do Is Dream' on an acetate and it was just Boudleaux and his guitar. I said, 'You could put that out and it would be a hit.'" The Everlys retained that simplicity, opening with a unique tremolo chord from Chet Atkins. Boudleaux Bryant was so confident with the result that he bought himself a new Thunderbird.

On the other side was Roy Orbison's tribute to his wife, 'Claudette'. The Everlys recorded an excellent version of this fast-moving song. "The idea was always to put the best up-tempo song and the best ballad back to back," says Phil, "When we were in Chicago, we asked Roy if he'd got a song for us. He gave us 'Claudette'."

Tim Rice recalls, "When I was a teenager, going to buy a record was a great event and there were many factors to consider, not only the artist and whether you liked the song, but also who wrote it, the label it was on and, most important of all, the B-side. If you were spending six and threepence, you wanted to make sure that you liked the B-side. Many artists made great B-sides and sometimes they were better than the A-sides. I couldn't believe my good fortune with 'All I Have To Do Is Dream' as 'Claudette' was almost as great."

74 The Kalin Twins
When

Label & Cat No.: **Brunswick 05751**

Producer: **Jack Pleis**

Writers: **Jack Reardon / Paul Evans**

Date reached No.1: **22 August 1958**

Weeks at No.1: **5**

Harold & Herbie Kalin were identical twins from Port Jervis, New York, born in 1934, although the publicity at the time stated 1939. They formed a duo to sing hits from the pre-rock'n'roll era, but when they added some Everly Brothers numbers, the crowds went wild. Their manager, Clint Ballard Jr, who was to write 'You're No Good', wrote their first single, 'Jumpin' Jack'.

The Brill Building songwriter, Paul Evans, recalls, "We sent 'When' to the Kalin Twins' record producer and he didn't like it much. He put it in a pile of rejects, but when the Kalins got to his office, he wasn't there and they started playing those records by mistake. They pulled it out and loved it and their producer was too embarrassed to tell them that he had rejected it. He let them cut it and it had a thrilling arrangement, which really helped the record."

Because of problems over the publishing, Paul Evans never got to submit another song to the Kalins and he himself had UK hits – 'Seven Little Girls Sitting In The Back Seat' (1959) and 'Hello This Is Joannie' (The Telephone Answering Machine Song)' (1978). Although the Kalins didn't have a second UK hit, they toured with a young Cliff Richard. Rather like The Beatles touring with Tommy Roe and Chris Montez in 1963, Cliff stole the show every night.

The Kalin Twins continued to record, one of their US singles being a cover of Joe Brown's 'A Picture Of You'. In 1977 'When' was revived by Showaddywaddy and went to number three, but the original was not reissued. Then, in 1989, Cliff Richard invited them to join him on stage for an *Oh Boy!* sequence for *The Event* concerts at Wembley Stadium.

75 Connie Francis
Carolina Moon / Stupid Cupid

Label & Cat No.: **MGM 985**

Producer: **Connie Francis / Leroy Holmes**

Writers: **Benny Davis / Joe Burke; Neil Sedaka / Howard Greenfield**

Date reached No.1: **26 September 1958**

Weeks at No.1: **6**

After Connie Francis' father had proved correct in suggesting 'Who's Sorry Now?' she was looking for standards and her second number one came when he recommended 'Carolina Moon', originally recorded by one of the first crooners, Gene Austin, and America's favourite song at the time of the Wall Street crash in 1929. One of its songwriters, Benny Davis, befriended Connie and proved capable of writing contemporary material, notably her 1962 US number one, 'Don't Break The Heart That Loves You'.

Not being a songwriter herself, Connie was also looking for new songs, but she was choosy. She turned down some new songs by Burt Bacharach & Hal David, and Burt was so annoyed that he mentions it in concert to this day. When she invited the new kids on the Brill Building block, Neil Sedaka and his lyricist partner Howard Greenfield, to her apartment in New Jersey to play some songs for her, they assumed she was looking for emotional ballads. When she showed no interest in what they were offering, Neil jumped into a rock'n'roll song, 'Stupid Cupid', which they had written for The Shepherd Sisters. The result was a double-sided hit, and Neil and Howie wrote several other songs for Connie including 'Fallin'' (1958), 'Frankie' (1959) and 'Where The Boys Are' (1961), the title song from a beach movie starring Connie and George Hamilton.

Connie Francis, whose repertoire was a study in contrasts, shifting from tearful ballads to lively up-tempo numbers

76 Tommy Edwards It's All In The Game

Label & Cat No.: **MGM 989**	
Producer: **Harry Myerson**	
Writers: **Charles Gates Dawes / Carl Sigman**	
Date reached No.1: **7 November 1958**	
Weeks at No.1: **3**	

CHARLES DAWES WAS A BANKER AND A politician, who helped stabilise America's finances after the First World War and was awarded the Nobel Peace Prize in 1925. He became the Vice-President to Calvin Coolidge from 1925 to 1929 and was then appointed the US Ambassador to Great Britain. He played the flute and, in 1912, he wrote a tune which he called 'Melody In A Major'. It wasn't until 1951 that the tune was given a lyric, namely 'It's All In The Game', by the noted songwriter, Carl Sigman.

'It's All In The Game' was covered by several artists in 1951, but the US hit record was by Tommy Edwards, which reached number 18. The song had the makings of a standard with Louis Armstrong (1952) and Nat 'King' Cole (1957) also recording it. In 1958, Tommy Edwards suggested that he re-cut 'It's All In The Game' using this new-fangled technique called 'stereo' and giving it a more contemporary arrangement. It worked as the new version was a transatlantic number one. The follow-up, 'My Melancholy Baby' edged into the Top 30 in 1959, while Donny and Marie Osmond revived Tommy's first-ever success, 'Morning Side Of The Mountain' in 1974. With his fine voice, Tommy Edwards deserved more hit records, but it's all in the game and he died, largely forgotten, in 1970.

'It's All In The Game' endures as it has been a hit for Cliff Richard (1963) and the Four Tops (1970), but many think that the best-ever version is by Van Morrison (1982).

77 Lord Rockingham's XI Hoots Mon

Label & Cat No.: **Decca F 11059**	
Producer: **Harry Robinson**	
Writer: **Harry Robinson**	
Date reached No.1: **28 November 1958**	
Weeks at No.1: **3**	

EVERY SATURDAY EVENING ITV'S *OH Boy!* was a must-see programme for Britain's teenagers. The show made stars of Marty Wilde and Cliff Richard and featured a repertory company of rock'n'roll performers who zipped through 20 numbers in 26 minutes. Its producer, Jack Good, relied on Rita Gillespie for the choreography and Harry Robinson for the arrangements. Jack Good remembers, "The original Rockingham was a British Prime Minister. I thought Rocking 'Em, you know, it's a silly name but it might work. I called it Lord Rockingham's XI to make it sound like a cricket team but there were 13 of them."

The musicians were organist Cherry Wainer, drummer Don Storer, Reg Weller (percussion), Red Price and Rex Morris (tenor saxes), Benny Green and Cyril Reubens (baritone saxes), Ronnie Black (bass), Bernie Taylor, Kenny Packwood and Eric Ford (guitars) and Ian Frazer (piano). That's a line-up of session musicians supreme, but the jazz-oriented Benny Green became a Radio 2 presenter and an avid opponent of rock'n'roll. Cherry Wainer, whose singles included 'Itchy Twitchy Feeling' and 'The Happy Organ', was Cliff Richard's confidante, if not his girlfriend.

Harry Robinson had combined his Scottish roots with rock'n'roll for a single with Jackie Dennis, 'Linton Addie'. Amused with the outcome, he turned to '100 Pipers' and converted it into a lively instrumental they called 'Hoots Mon!'. "You couldn't have a rock'n'roll instrumental without somebody saying something in it," he said, "We wanted a voice to recite a couple of silly couplets. I did it because I'm Scottish, but I overdid the accent which resulted in people in Scotland thinking it must be a Sassenach. When we heard the playback, we fell about laughing and we couldn't play anything for 15 minutes. The engineer couldn't get the bass right when the sound was transferred to disc, and he wanted us to re-do it. A lot of record-buyers complained because if you used a lightweight needle, it jumped off the disc because of the tremendous bass parts. It was banned in certain factories because of its pounding sound: it made the workers want to smash the tools up."

Despite all this nonsense, 'Hoots Mon!' turned serious when it was number one and there was litigation to determine whether Jack Good or Harry Robinson was Lord Rockingham. Jack Good says, "In the end, they decided that I had the rights to Rockingham on records and television, but Harry could use it on the road. The whole incident was a pain in the neck because Harry and I were the greatest of friends. The argument was between lawyers and agents and we ourselves didn't give a damn."

78 Conway Twitty It's Only Make Believe

Label & Cat No.: **MGM 992**	
Producer: **Jim Vinneau**	
Writers: **Conway Twitty / Jack Nance**	
Date reached No.1: **19 December 1958**	
Weeks at No.1: **5**	

IN 1956 HAROLD LLOYD JENKINS MADE his first recordings for Sam Phillips' Sun Records in Memphis, but Phillips didn't even bother to issue them. Jenkins moved to Mercury and changed his name to Conway Twitty, taking the pseudonym from a signpost giving pointers to the towns, Conway and Twitty. Well, it was better than being named after a slapstick comedian. His records still didn't sell and tiring of playing small Southern clubs, he moved to Canada and found some success in Ontario.

In 1958 Conway Twitty and his drummer Jack Nance wrote 'It's Only Make Believe' in 20 minutes, but it's possible that it came to them so easily because of its similarity to a French chanson, 'En Ecoutant Mon Coeur Chanter', which is known in the UK as '(All Of A Sudden) My Heart Sings'. The matter was settled out of court and rather mischievously, Paul Anka revived the song in 1959. When Peter Sellers recorded a rock'n'roll parody, he called his singer, Twit Conway.

Conway Twitty, with his distinctive croaking style, had further hits with 'Mona Lisa' and 'C'Est Si Bon', but his big US success of 'Danny Boy' (1959) could not be issued in the UK as the words were still in copyright and permission was refused. In the late-Sixties Conway Twitty turned to country music and scored an unheralded 40 US Country number one hits, specialising in such cheating songs as 'I See The Want To In Your Eyes', 'You've Never Been This Far Before' and 'There's A Honky Tonk Angel (Who'll Take Me Back In)'. He recorded many duets with Loretta Lynn and one title features in lists of the worst song titles of all-time, 'You're The Reason Our Kids Are Ugly'.

In Nashville, you could visit Twitty City, but his Twittyburgers came to a greasy end. Conway's beautiful coiffure became as much a country music joke as Hank Snow's, neither of them being around when it was styled. Nevertheless, he made some fine records including a stunning duet of 'Rainy Night In Georgia' with Sam Moore of Sam & Dave, recorded shortly before his final croak in 1993.

Conway Twitty

79 Jane Morgan
The Day The Rains Came

Label & Cat No.: **London HLR 8751**
Producer: **Vic Schoen**
Writers: **Gilbert Becaud / Carl Sigman**
Date reached No.1: **23 January 1959**
Weeks at No.1: **1**

THE FRENCH SINGER-SONGWRITER Gilbert Becaud only had one UK hit, ('A Little Love And Understanding', 1975), but he wrote some classic songs. 'Et Maintenant' became 'What Now My Love', 'Je T'Appartiens' is 'Let It Be Me' and 'Le Jour Où La Pluie Viendra', 'The Day The Rains Came'. Becaud had many hits in France and 'Le Jour Où La Pluie Viendra' reached number three in September 1958. Carl Sigman, whose lyrics include 'Answer Me' and 'You're My World', captured the unusual nature of the song and it was recorded by Jane Morgan.

Jane Morgan, born Jane Currier, came from Boston, Massachusetts and was a trained soprano at the Juilliard School of Music in New York. She had a US Top 10 hit with 'Fascination' in 1953 and she accepted a lengthy contract for a club in Paris. Whilst there she heard 'Le Jour Où La Pluie Viendra' and said she would like to record an English version. Her single featured both her English and French interpretations of the song.

Although Jane Morgan never recaptured the success of this recording, she had minor hits with 'If I Could Only Live My Life Again' (1959, UK), 'With Open Arms' (1959, US, and an excellent, but little-known Bacharach & David song) and 'Romantica' (1960, US). She married the impresario Jerry Weintraub and died in 1974 at the age of 54.

80 Elvis Presley
One Night / I Got Stung

Label & Cat No.: **RCA 1100**
Producer: **Steve Sholes**
Writers: **Dave Bartholomew / Pearl King; Aaron Schroeder / David Hill**
Date reached No.1: **30 January 1959**
Weeks at No.1: **3**

THE FILM *JAILHOUSE ROCK* WAS A SMASH hit in America, but Elvis' joy was short-lived when he received his call-up papers for the US army. He was enjoying himself too much to succumb to army discipline, but his manager Colonel Parker told him it was his duty. He would have to enlist, once he'd finished *King Creole* and stockpiled some singles, of course.

Elvis often covered R&B music, but Parker must have blanched at the thought of him performing Smiley Lewis's 'One Night Of Sin', a suggestive song about a liaison with a prostitute. Elvis did record the song with its original lyric – maybe he did it for fun and had no intention of releasing it – but someone had the good sense to ask him to repeat it with an amended lyric. Ironically, the second version is far more sensuous than the first and there is no question as to what is in Elvis's mind. Keith Strachan, the composer of Cliff's 'Mistletoe And Wine', has written that "'One Night' is a wonderful, animal-like performance and Elvis hits a powerful high G sharp at the end." It's a tough song to cover and Mud's revival in 1975 ended a long run of Top 10 singles.

'I Got Stung' was a fast and furious rocker, co-written by the noted music publisher Aaron Schroeder, and David Hill, who was studying at the Juilliard School of Music. Hill recorded the original version of 'All Shook Up' and he was to record the demo for 'It's Now Or Never'. Again, 'I Got Stung' is a difficult song to perform, but one of the few cover versions was by Paul McCartney in 1999.

81 Shirley Bassey with Wally Stott & His Orchestra As I Love You

Label & Cat No.: **Philips PB 845**

Producer: **Johnny Franz**

Writers: **Jay Livingston / Ray Evans**

Date reached No.1: **20 February 1959**

Weeks at No.1: **4**

SHIRLEY BASSEY WAS BORN IN 1937 in the Tiger Bay area of Cardiff, the daughter of a West Indian merchant seaman. Her first job was wrapping parcels in a factory, but she could sing well and was soon able to break loose. She made an impression as part of Al Read's revue, *Such Is Life*, at the Adelphi Theatre in London in 1955. Her first hit was with a cover version of 'The Banana Boat Song' in 1957.

'As I Love You' was an American song written by Jay Livingston and Ray Evans, who had written 'Whatever Will Be, Will Be' for Doris Day. They wrote 'As I Love You' for the jazz singer Carmen McRae but her version went unnoticed when it was released in the UK in March 1958. Shirley Bassey's cover version was released in August and that, too, did not make the charts. In December Ronnie Hilton thought he would try his luck and Philips Records decided to promote the Shirley Bassey recording again. Her version went to the top and Ronnie's made no impact at all.

The irony is that Shirley Bassey's next single had already been released. This was a cover of Gogi Grant's 'Kiss Me, Honey, Honey, Kiss Me'. This sultry, sizzling, sexy record might have been number one, but as it happens, Shirley spent eight weeks with both records in the Top 10 with 'Kiss Me, Honey, Honey, Kiss Me' peaking at number three. This rush of hit singles came too late for Philips as Bassey had signed a contract with EMI's Columbia label and in the summer of 1960, she went to number two with 'As Long As He Needs Me' from Lionel Bart's *Oliver!*

82 The Platters Smoke Gets In Your Eyes

Label & Cat No.: **Mercury AMT 1016**

Producer: **Buck Ram**

Writers: **Jerome Kern / Otto Harbach**

Date reached No.1: **20 March 1959**

Weeks at No.1: **1**

"TONY WILLIAMS HAD THE BEST, THE clearest, the truest voice I have ever heard in pop music," says Gene Pitney and certainly Williams's soaring lead vocals for The Platters were extraordinary. The Platters bridged the gaps between pop ballads, rock'n'roll and doowop. The five vocalists appeared in rock'n'roll films and sang their ballads, 'Only You (And You Alone)', 'The Great Pretender' and '(You've Got) The Magic Touch'. The group also featured Zola Taylor, David Lynch, Paul Robi and the bass voice of Herb Reed. "Not a group out there could touch us when we walked out on stage," said Zola Taylor, "We were a God-blessed winning team."

The Platters were managed by Buck Ram, a songwriter who had been a member of The Three Suns in the Forties. In 1958 they revived The Three Suns' 'Twilight Time'. Reaching number three, it was the first rock'n'roll hit with a string arrangement. Pleased by the success, they turned to Jerome Kern & Otto Harbach's torch ballad from 1933, 'Smoke Gets In Your Eyes', from their Broadway musical, *Roberta*, which has echoes of a melody written by Chopin. The biggest-selling recording had been by Paul Whiteman & his Orchestra.

'Smoke Gets In Your Eyes' has also been a hit for Bryan Ferry (1974) and John Alford (1996) and despite anti-smoking lobbies, the song will always be an evergreen. Tim Rice has described it as the greatest lyric of all-time. The original Platters left the group one by one but they found it tough going as Buck Ram owned the name and they had difficulty trading on their past association with the group. Even though Ram died in 1991, the Buck Ram Platters still tour the world, a fine group but with no original members.

83 Russ Conway Side Saddle

Label & Cat No.: **Columbia DB 4256**

Producer: **Norman Newell**

Writer: **Trevor Stanford (Russ Conway)**

Date reached No.1: **27 March 1959**

Weeks at No.1: **4**

TREVOR STANFORD WAS AWARDED THE DSM for his achievements in the Royal Navy but he also lost the tip of a finger in a kitchen accident, a mishap which he thought gave his piano playing a distinctive sound. He was signed to EMI's Columbia label by Norman Newell who renamed him Russ Conway as a tribute to the late singer Steve Conway. Russ recorded party medleys similar to those by Winifred Atwell ('Party Pops', 'More Party Pops', 'More And More Party Pops', 'Even More Party Pops') and played serious pieces ('The World Outside', 'My Concerto For You'), but he was best known for his own jaunty compositions which he introduced on *The Billy Cotton Band Show* with a smile to the camera.

Russ and Norman Newell were commissioned to write a TV musical of *Beauty And The Beast* with David Hughes, Inia Te Wiata and Ivor Emmanuel. Russ wrote a gavotte, which was played on flutes, for the ballroom scene. A few months later, he was playing rather majestically for a television executive who told him to "honky tonk it up". He added another tune he had written, 'Anything Can Happen', and 'Side Saddle' was born.

Then Russ had an extreme piece of good fortune. He recalled, "Bill Cotton Jr had a problem with *The Perry Como Show*. One of the guests didn't want his performance to be seen in Britain and so they were going to fade down the show, come to me in the studio, and go back to Perry Como. To all intents and purposes, it would be like I was Perry Como's guest. I played 'Side Saddle' and the next morning there was a mad rush in Tin Pan Alley to find out who had published it. I gave it to Mills Music as they published Leroy Anderson's instrumentals and it

The Platters, featuring the extraordinary voice of Tony Williams (centre)

went wallop! and stayed at number one for four weeks. When they launched 'Side Saddle' in America, they dressed someone up as Lady Godiva in a body stocking on a white horse with a van following her along Broadway playing 'Side Saddle'. No wonder it wasn't a hit there."

84 Buddy Holly
It Doesn't Matter Anymore

Label & Cat No.: **Coral Q 72360**

Producer: **Norman Petty**

Writer: **Paul Anka**

Date reached No.1: **24 April 1959**

Weeks at No.1: **3**

When Buddy Holly got married he felt he had been cheated out of his royalties and to pay the bills, he agreed to headline a rock'n'roll tour, the *Winter Dance Party*. The audiences were very appreciative but the weather was appalling and the tour bus had no heating and kept breaking down. On February 2, 1959, Buddy Holly had had enough – he hired a plane to take him, the Big Bopper and Ritchie Valens to the next venue after they had played the Surf Ballroom at Clear Lake, Iowa. The pilot, Roger Peterson, was not licensed to fly in such conditions and the plane crashed, killing all the occupants. In his song 'American Pie' Don McLean describes it as "the day the music died".

Shortly before the tour, Buddy Holly had done his first session with strings, recording Paul Anka's 'It Doesn't Matter Anymore' and Boudleaux Bryant's 'Raining In My Heart', which were combined for a powerful single. 'It Doesn't Matter Anymore', a title almost as ironic as "That'll Be The Day (When I Die)," climbed the charts after Holly's death, making number 13 in the US and number one here.

Although it is only 18 months from 'That'll Be The Day' to 'It Doesn't Matter Anymore', Buddy Holly left us one of the great legacies in popular music. His simple, plaintive style has been copied and developed by numerous performers, notably The Beatles. He was also the first guitarist to popularise the Fender Stratocaster which at the time looked like something from outer space. His drummer, Jerry Allison, says, "Buddy was always full of ideas. He wanted to do a gospel album with Ray Charles. He would have loved The Beatles and The Rolling Stones and the whole British invasion. He would have kept coming out with stuff himself because he was always coming up with something new."

85 Elvis Presley with The Jordanaires
A Fool Such As I / I Need Your Love Tonight

Label & Cat No.: **RCA 1113**

Producer: **Steve Sholes**

Writers: **Bill Trader; Sid Wayne / Bix Reichner**

Date reached No.1: **15 May 1959**

Weeks at No.1: **5**

The country star, Hank Snow, was in partnership with Colonel Parker, but they fell out over Elvis Presley because Parker wanted everything for himself. Snow had no ill feelings against Presley himself and his son, Jimmie Rodgers Snow, was one of Elvis's close friends. Elvis sometimes dipped into the Hank Snow songbook and '(Now And Then, There's) A Fool Such As I' had been a US Top 10 country hit in 1953. "I don't mean to brag but Elvis was a big fan of mine," bragged Hank Snow, "and he was always sitting around singing my songs, which tickled me to death."

Elvis's version featured the bass voice of The Jordanaires' new boy, Ray Walker: "It was my first session with Elvis," he says. "I was singing solo and I didn't have anything before that to break me in."

Considering the quality of his song, it's surprising that the South Carolina songwriter, Bill Trader wrote no other hits, but his compositions include the Cold War saga, 'Mr. Stalin You're

Buddy Holly

Eating Too High On The Hog', recorded by Arthur 'Guitar Boogie' Smith and 'I Found Love Again', which he wrote with Hoagy Carmichael. In the Sixties he recorded an album, *Bill Trader Sings His Own*, for the obscure Jim Dandy label, which included his own version of 'A Fool Such As I'. He died at age of 81 in October 2003.

The single was promoted as a double A-side and 'I Need Your Love Tonight' was a frenzied rocker, specifically written for him. Sid Wayne went on to write 30 more songs for the King, but such songs as 'He's Your Uncle, Not Your Dad' and 'A Dog's Life' indicate that he played a significant part in his decline.

Both songs were recorded while Elvis was on a furlough from the army and the crack band featured Hank Garland and Chet Atkins on guitars, Bob Moore on bass, Floyd Cramer on piano, Buddy Harman and D.J. Fontana on percussion, Nashville legends one and all.

86 Russ Conway
Roulette

Label & Cat No.: **Columbia DB 4296**

Producer: **Norman Newell**

Writer: **Trevor Stanford (Russ Conway)**

Date reached No.1: **19 June 1959**

Weeks at No.1: **2**

"I CAN'T PRETEND I HAD ANY DIFFICULTY in following up 'Side Saddle'," said Russ Conway, "I can't really explain it but it was as though the songs were dormant within me, just waiting to be brought out. I had five records in the Top 10 in 1959, which is no big deal for a singer but it was very unusual for an instrumentalist." Russ even named an instrumental after his achievement, 'Lucky Five'.

After number one records with 'Side Saddle' and 'Roulette', Russ missed the hat trick when 'China Tea' stalled at number five. "I never tire of playing 'Side Saddle' and 'China Tea' but I do get fed up with 'Roulette', so maybe that was really the weakest record of the three," said Russ, but then 'Roulette' had been written in ten minutes. The other hits that year were 'Snow Coach' and 'More And More Party Pops'.

In 1960 Russ wrote 'Royal Event' for the opening of the Theatre Royal in Lowestoft. "I was annoyed when Pete Murray said on *Juke Box Jury* that I was cashing in on the birth of Prince Andrew," he said. "I would never do a thing like that." Russ teamed up with The John Barry Seven for the theme from *Pepe* (1961) and played for Dorothy Squires on 'Say It With Flowers' (also 1961). He wrote Danny Williams' ballad success, 'Jeannie' and his own narration, 'Always You And Me' is one of his best records.

In 1965 Russ Conway suffered a stroke while recording a BBC special for Christmas. He returned to work too early and collapsed again in 1968. He planned to marry his fan club secretary, Carol Wayne in 1974 but she died of lung cancer. Russ himself contracted stomach cancer in 1989 and on his recovery, he set up a charity fund for a Bristol hospital. Many of his concert appearances from until his death on 15 November 2000 were to help others, and he was also responsible for encouraging Joan Regan to perform again after a bad fall.

87 Bobby Darin
Dream Lover

Label & Cat No.: **London HLE 8867**

Producer: **Ahmet Ertegun**

Writer: **Bobby Darin**

Date reached No.1: **3 July 1959**

Weeks at No.1: **4**

"IF I'M GREAT NOW," BOASTED BOBBY Darin, "What will I be like when I'm Frank Sinatra's age?" Darin's lack of tact lost him admirers, but he had confidence in his own talent: "I'm glad I'm not a poor introverted slob," he once remarked. He also had a heart damaged from rheumatic fever and he knew it would be unlikely that he would reach 50.

Walden Robert Cassotto was born in New York in 1936. He hung around the Brill Building, recording demos for songwriters and writing the occasional song, notably Gene Vincent's 'Wear My Ring'. When he passed the Mandarin restaurant with its unlit letters MAN, he decided to rename himself Bobby Darin. He

Russ Conway

wrote his first hit, 'Splish Splash' in 15 minutes and then he wrote one of the catchiest songs from the rock'n'roll era, 'Dream Lover'. Neil Sedaka, who played piano, was let loose on the B-side, a frantic rocker called 'Bullmoose'.

But Darin was restless. While 'Dream Lover' was in the charts, he recorded an album of standards, *That's All*, which included his second number one, 'Mack The Knife'. After that, Darin went country ('You're The Reason I'm Living') and sang folk-rock ('If I Were A Carpenter'). He wanted to enter politics but to avoid a scandal coming to light, his 'sister', Nina, told him that she was his mother. Jack Nicholson and Eric Clapton have had to wrestle with the same problem.

Darin was effectively a man in love with himself and his talent, and his show-business marriage to Sandra Dee did not last. He died in 1973 and left his body to medical research.

88 Cliff Richard & The Drifters Living Doll

Label & Cat No.:	**Columbia DB 4306**
Producer:	**Norrie Paramor**
Writer:	**Lionel Bart**
Date reached No.1:	**31 July 1959**
Weeks at No.1:	**6**

AGAINST ALL THE ODDS, A 17 YEAR OLD living in a London suburb, Cliff Richard, recorded a song, 'Move It!', written by his friend, Ian Samwell, and created a record which could rival the Americans. This was not a number one as it couldn't dislodge 'Stupid Cupid', but it is the finest of all the UK rock'n'roll records.

Cliff played Curly, a delinquent's young brother, in the film, *Serious Charge*, and Lionel Bart wrote the music. "I don't think he cared for the songs," said Lionel Bart, "but one of them was 'Living Doll'. I had taken it from one of those ads in the Sunday papers for a doll that did everything and I wrote it in 10 minutes flat."

Both Cliff & The Drifters thought that a song about a blow-up doll was naff, but Bruce Welch realised that if the tempo were slowed down, it would work better. He was right: 'Living Doll' became Cliff's first chart-topper, but the American Drifters took exception to the name of Cliff's group and they stepped into the Shadows.

Jack Good, who produced the teenage music show, *Oh Boy!*, generated headlines like "Is Cliff too sexy for TV?," says, "He threw it all away with (sings) 'Got myself a laughing, crying, living, dying, blah blah blah!' I thought, 'My God, I spent all these hours making Cliff mean and magnificent, and he throws it all away with one bloody song.' I love Cliff but he should have stayed moody."

Tim Rice would disagree: "There were some wonderful writers in Britain before The Beatles, and one of the best was Lionel Bart. Tommy Steele's 'A Handful Of Songs' was a lovely composition, a show song disguised as a pop song and it showed the way both of them were heading. I don't think 'Living Doll' is naff at all. It's a great song with some very good internal rhyming. I love the bit that goes, 'Gonna lock her up in a trunk, so no big hunk can steal her away from me'. If the Beatles had written 'Living Doll', I'm sure they'd have been very proud of it."

89 Craig Douglas Only Sixteen

Label & Cat No.:	**Top Rank JAR 159**
Producer:	**Bunny Lewis**
Writers:	**Barbara Campbell (Lou Adler / Herb Alpert / Sam Cooke)**
Date reached No.1:	**11 September 1959**
Weeks at No.1:	**4**

TERRY PERKINS WAS BORN IN NEWport, Isle of Wight in 1941, one of three sets of twins in a family of nine children, possibly a record in itself. He became a milkman, but his mother encouraged him to be a singer. He was spotted by Bunny Lewis, who became his manager, and in 1958 he appeared on *Six-Five Special*. The following year he had a chart race with Marty Wilde and Dion & The Belmonts on 'A Teenager In Love' and had his first Top 20 hit.

'Only Sixteen' was written under a pseudonym by Sam Cooke, Lou Adler and Herb Alpert and, surprisingly, Cooke's original version only scraped into the US Top 20. Indeed, 'Only Sixteen' wasn't a Top 10 hit in America until Dr. Hook's revival in 1976. It was a different story in the UK. Craig Douglas topped the charts for four weeks, outselling the opposition, Sam Cooke (23) and Al Saxon (24). He says, "I was very pleased when 'Only Sixteen' made the Top 10, but I didn't think I'd get to the top. Cliff was there with 'Living Doll' and he looked set for a long stay. When I did get there, Cliff sent me a note saying that he was glad to be knocked off by a British singer, not an American."

Craig continued to have hits, often with cover versions such as 'Pretty Blue Eyes' (Steve Lawrence), 'A Hundred Pounds Of Clay' (Gene McDaniels), 'When My Little Girl Is Smiling' (Drifters) and 'Oh Lonesome Me' (Don Gibson). When the hits faded, Craig settled down for a life of entertaining on cruise ships. "Cruise audiences are there, they have no where else to go," he says. "It's very easy once you know how to work them. You tend to know everybody after a fortnight and it becomes very informal and very nice. If I'm performing for Americans, I can do my hit records because they know the originals."

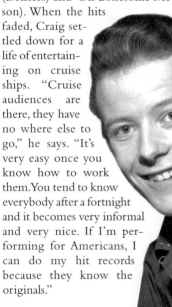

Craig Douglas

90 Jerry Keller
Here Comes Summer

Label & Cat No.: **London HLR 8890**

Producer: **Richard Wolf**

Writer: **Jerry Keller**

Date reached No.1: **9 October 1959**

Weeks at No.1: **1**

JERRY KELLER IS A GOOD EXAMPLE OF Andy Warhol's dictum about 15 minutes of fame. He was born in Fort Smith, Arkansas in 1937 and he sang in a gospel choir as a child. He formed his first group, The Lads Of Note, in Tulsa. In 1956 he moved to New York, thinking he had a better chance of hitting the big-time. He worked for an oil company and in his spare moments, cut demos and wrote songs.

His break came when he went to church one Sunday and met Pat Boone, who recognised his talent and recommended him to Dave Kapp, who owned Kapp Records. His first single was a cheerful song he had written himself, 'Here Comes Summer', which contained the memorable line, "And when we kiss, she makes my flat-top curl." The single was a Top 20 hit in the US and although it made the UK charts in August, it didn't make number one until October. In other words, 'Here Comes Summer' wasn't a summer hit.

Eddie Cochran died in a car crash on the last night of a UK tour in April 1960 and he had been scheduled to return for further dates with Gene Vincent. Vincent, although injured himself in the accident, was forced to continue with his contract, and Jerry Keller was added to the bill. Keller had no further hits as a performer but 'Here Comes Summer' is an evergreen, in particular being revived by The Dave Clark Five in 1970. Jerry Keller is not to be confused with the Brill Building writer, Jack Keller, and Jerry's song hits include 'Almost There' for Andy Williams and the lyrics for Francis Lai's much-recorded theme for *A Man And A Woman*.

91 Bobby Darin
Mack The Knife

Label & Cat No.: **London HLE 8939**

Producer: **Ahmet Ertegun**

Writers: **Bertolt Brecht / Kurt Weill**

Date reached No.1: **16 October 1959**

Weeks at No.1: **2**

BERTOLT BRECHT, SURELY THE INventor of designer stubble, was a serious writer who put his Communist philosophies into his writing, which included musicals for the Berliner Ensemble with the composer Kurt Weill. In 1928 they wrote *The Threepenny Opera* (*Die Dreigroschenoper*), which starred Lotte Lenya, Weill's wife. The score included 'Moritat', better known as 'Mack The Knife'. The lyric about Macheath, a gangster in the Berlin underworld, makes little sense outside the musical, but the melody was truly catchy and made it a hit song regardless. In 1956 five versions appeared on the US Top 40 – the Dick Hyman Trio (8), Richard Hayman & Jan August (11), Lawrence Welk & his Orchestra (17), Louis Armstrong (20) and Billy Vaughn & his Orchestra (37).

In 1959 when Bobby Darin was considering an album of standards, *That's All*, his friend, Buddy Greco, told him that he was going to revive 'Mack The Knife'. Darin took the idea for himself: he describes Macheath's talent with a jackknife and his ability for disposing of the bodies, but he omits the verses about rapes and bomb explosions. He made a passing reference to Lotte Lenya, his 'uh uh' after the words 'sidewalk' and 'tugboat' became his trademark, and his closing 'Look out, ol' Mackie is back' was a mastertouch. The record was a transatlantic number one and won him a Grammy for Best Male Vocal Performance. Ella Fitzgerald makes reference to Darin in her own hit-making version, while Frank Sinatra gave 'Ol' MacDonald' the Darin treatment. In 1960 Buddy Greco eased into the charts with 'The Lady Is A Tramp' and he made a resolution never again to tell another singer what he was working on.

Bobby Darin

92 Cliff Richard & The Shadows
Travellin' Light

Label & Cat No.: **Columbia DB 4351**

Producer: **Norrie Paramor**

Writers: **Sid Tepper / Roy C. Bennett**

Date reached No.1: **30 October 1959**

Weeks at No.1: **5**

SID TEPPER AND ROY BENNETT WERE Brill Building songwriters who had written for Elvis Presley's films, *Loving You* ('Lonesome Cowboy') and *King Creole* ('New Orleans'). One of the songs they intended for *King Creole* was 'Travellin' Light', which contained some neat imagery. The travelling light would guide the singer's way and as he was carrying very little, he was also travelling light. Like 'Danny' which was recorded by Marty Wilde and Conway Twitty, the song was rejected for *King Creole*, so the publishers passed it to Cliff Richard's management. Cliff loved the song and it was given a similar sparse arrangement to 'Living Doll', although Hank Marvin is given a guitar solo. Cliff recorded it just a few days before 'Living Doll' hit the top.

Cliff was well aware that the die-hard rockers were accusing him of selling out, so the B-side was one of his most frantic performances, Ian Samwell's 'Dynamite'. It made number 16 in its own right and is almost as good as 'Move It!'.

93 Adam Faith
What Do You Want?

Label & Cat No.: **Parlophone R 4591**

Producer: **John Burgess**

Writer: **Les Vandyke (Johnny Worth)**

Date reached No.1: **4 December 1959**

Weeks at No.1: **3**

Les Reed, the pianist with the John Barry Seven heard Johnny Worth's song, 'What Do You Want?', in its early stages. "Johnny Worth had written it in a 4/4 rock version and he asked me to go and see Johnny Kidd with him as he felt he would be right for the song. We went to a pub in Wandsworth and thumped it out on the piano and Johnny Kidd hated it. We went back to Johnny Worth's house and I said, 'It should be more in a Buddy Holly style' and I played that little figure you now hear on the record. Johnny agreed and it changed the whole character of the song."

Johnny Worth, a member of The Raindrops vocal group, remembers: "Adam had a face that could launch a million records, an amazing face, a most endearing face, and something within me said, 'This kid is going to be a star. It doesn't matter that he doesn't sing very well'." Stewart Morris liked to present him with a stern, rocker, motorbike image on *Drumbeat!* and I told Adam to smile at the camera, gently, and the world would light up when he did. In those days you couldn't edit a television show and Stewart Morris was furious when he was stuck with a smiling Adam Faith singing 'Love Is Strange'. He tore him off a colossal strip and told him not to do it again, but I knew he was wrong. When Adam did 'What Do You Want?' on *Cool For Cats*, he sat on a stool, smiled that wistful smile and went zonk! into the hearts of millions."

'What Do You Want?' was released by EMI's Parlophone label in November 1959. Pop encyclopedias liken the record to Buddy Holly's 'It Doesn't Matter Anymore' but Faith disagreed. "I didn't think I was influenced by Buddy Holly. My biggest influence was the British singer, Roy Young. Roy and I were going to Oxford before I recorded 'What Do You Want?'. I sang 'What Do You Want?' to him and he didn't like the way I sang it. He coached me all the way to Oxford and by the time we got there, 'baby' had turned into 'bay-beh'. John Barry decided that there should be strings on the record and at the time the only pop record with strings on it was 'It Doesn't Matter Anymore', but Buddy Holly's pizzicato strings were more aggressive. Johnny Worth, John Barry and myself were such a team that when I got my silver disc for 'What Do You Want?" I seriously thought about splitting it in three."

'What Do You Want? (if you don't want money)', a perfect title for Faith's own philosophy of life, was selling 50,000 copies a day and topped the UK charts for three weeks. Fans would also copy Faith's brushed-forward hairstyle, and Tony Hancock concurred: "There's Adam Faith earning ten times as much as the Prime Minister. I ask you, is that right? I suppose it depends on whether you like Adam Faith or what your politics are."

94 Emile Ford & The Checkmates
What Do You Want To Make Those Eyes At Me For?

Label & Cat No.: **Pye Nixa N 15225**

Producer: **Michael Barclay**

Writers: **Joseph McCarthy / Howard Johnson / Jimmy Monaco**

Date reached No.1: **18 December 1959**

Weeks at No.1: **6**

Emile Ford was born in St. Lucia in 1937 and he came to the UK to study engineering. He perfected a sound system which he demonstrated in dance-halls and coffee-bars. He and his band, The Checkmates (which included his brother, George) won a Pye recording contract in a talent competition run by *Disc* newspaper. Pye selected 'Don't Tell Me Your Troubles' for the A-side and left half an hour for the B-side. Emile says, "I'd heard a version of the oldie, 'What Do You Want To Make Those Eyes At Me For?', by Marie Adams with The Johnny Otis Show, but they had ruined its simple charm with screaming. I added a beat, almost as though I'm saying, 'You've asked for trouble and here it is.'"

Pye's selection panel preferred the intended B-side and, even though Emile was unknown, the single went into the charts at number 12. He said, "I was shocked to be at number one because I wasn't a singer and all I wanted was to demonstrate my sound system. Pye asked me to sign a five-year contract but I would only do two as I wanted to go back to engineering."

Emile insisted on using his sound system on tour with him which caused many ructions with theatre managers. He has been proved right as his systems have now been used throughout the world.

1960-1969

5 YEARS AGO

TOP TEN 1964 Week ending Oct 1

1	1	**I'M INTO SOMETHING GOOD** Herman's Hermits (Columbia)
5	2	**OH, PRETTY WOMAN** Roy Orbison (London)
2	3	**WHERE DID OUR LOVE GO** Supremes (Stateside)
3	4	**RAG DOLL** Four Seasons (Philips)
4	5	**I WOULDN'T TRADE YOU FOR THE WORLD** Bachelors (Decca)
10	6	**THE WEDDING** Julie Rogers (Mercury)
7	7	**I WON'T FORGET YOU** Jim Reeves (RCA)
12	8	**TOGETHER** P. J. Proby (Decca)
6	8	**YOU REALLY GOT ME** Kinks (Pye)
15	10	**I'M CRYING** Animals (Columbia)

new MUSICAL EXPRESS

WORLD'S LARGEST CIRCULATION OF ANY MUSIC PAPER

EVERY FRIDAY PRICE 6d. MAR. 4, 1966 Registered at the G.P.O. as a Newspaper

PROBY-PITNEY CLA

ELVIS • HOLLIES

Petula Clark at home in Paris

FORTUNES • CONWAY JAMES BROWN

Top Pop News

No. 25 LITTLE BY LIT DUSTY SPRINGFIEL

I GOT YO JAMES BROWN

PYE 7N 17064

'Dedicated Follower of Fashion' THE KINKS

18 RECORD MAIL December 196

LATEST 'SINGLE' RELEASES

VERVE

THE MOTHERS OF INVENTION
It can't happen here/How could I be such a fool — VS545
RIGHTEOUS BROTHERS
Island in the sun/What now my love — VS547

TAMLA MOTOWN

BRENDA HOLLOWAY
Hurt a little every day/Where were you — TMG581
MARTHA AND THE VANDELLAS
I'm ready for love/He doesn't love her anymore — TMG582
THE ELGINS
Heaven must have sent you/Stay in my lonely arms — TMG583
THE MIRACLES
(Come 'round here) I'm the one you need/Save me — TMG584
THE SUPREMES
You keep me hangin' on/Remove this doubt — TMG585

CAPITOL

DAVID McCALLUM
In the garden (under the tree)/The house in Breckenridge Lane — CL15474
MATT MONRO
Wednesday's child/When you become a man — CL15477
THE STACCATOS
Let's run away/Face to face (with love) — CL15478
AL MARTINO
The wheel of hurt/Somewhere in this world — CL15479
THE OUTSIDERS
Help me girl/You gotta look — CL15480
VERDELLE SMITH
I don't need anything/If you can't say anything nice — CL15481
JODY MILLER
If you were a carpenter/Let me walk with you — CL15482
LIZA MINNELLI
Middle of the street/I who have nothing — CL…
PATRICE HOLLOWAY
Love and desire/Ecstasy

M-G-M

CONNIE FRANCIS
Spanish nights and you/Games that lovers play — MGM1327

LIBERTY

JOHNNY SAYLES
Deep down in my heart/Anything for you — LIB12042
JAN AND DEAN
Tennessee/Horace the swingin' school-bus driver — LIB12052

WAVERLEY

KEN AND ALAN HAYNES
The house with the spire/The waters of Kylesku — SLP540

STATESIDE

DALE BROOKS
I wanna be your girl/Like other girls do — SS553
KENNY PRICE
Walking on new grass/Wasting my time — SS554
GLORIA JONES
Finders keepers/Run one flight of stairs — SS555
SLIM HARPO
I'm a king bee/I got love if you want it — SS557
GENE PITNEY
Just one smile/The boss's daughter — SS558
THE CHIFFONS
Stop, lo… listen/March — SS559
ERN… …SCA
…rd street/Am I better off — SS560
…AU — SS561
…EN AND HIS ORCHESTRA

COLUMBIA

THE ATTRACTION
Party line/She'…
VINCE HILL
Invisible tears…
TONI DALY
Like the big m…
GERRY AND…
Girl on a swing…
GUY CARAW…
Ain't you got a…
TOMMY TAT…
Big blue diamo…
JOHNNY ASI…
Big country/The…
THE CHEATI…
Zip-tease/The b…
THE SHEPHE…
Morning town r…
HAYDOCK'S…
Cupid/She thinks…
THE RICHARD…
You can't put m…
JACKIE LEE
The town I live… heartaches)
JIMMY YOUN…
Half a world awa…
WALTER JACK…
A corner in the s…
NINA AND FR…
Baby, it's cold ou…
FENELLA FIELD…
Big bad mouse/La…
THE COACHM…
Gabrielle/Seasons…
LITTLE RICHAR…
I need love/The co…
SOUNDS OF JO…
Goal/Themes from…
THE SEEKERS
Morning town rid… to fall
TOMMY VANCE
Off the hook/Summ…
DAVID AND MA…
Ave Maria no mor…
THE C-JAM BLU…
Candy/Stay at home…
THE TWILIGHTS
Needle in a haystac… wind will blow me…

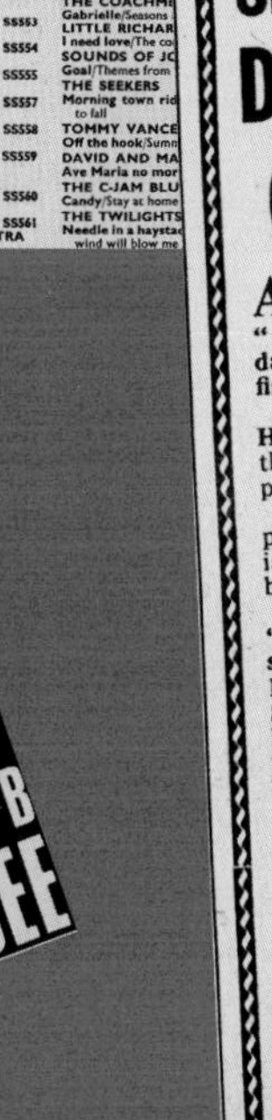

New Year are NEIL SEDAKA…

NEW RELEASES

Left to right: JOE COCKER, SANDIE SHAW, CLIFF RICHARD and JOE SOUTH.

Singles coming from— DUSTY, KINKS, TOPS, GAP, COCKER, CLIFF & SANDIE

A NEW British-recorded single by DUSTY SPRINGFIELD is being issued by Philips next Friday (5) — it is a vocal version of "Soulful Strut," and is titled "Am I The Same Girl." Out the same day is "A Delta Lady" (Regal Zonophone) by JOE COCKER — his first single since his No. 1 hit "With A Little Help From My Friends."

September 5 is also the release date for the CLIFF RICHARD-HANK MARVIN duet "Throw Down A Line" (Columbia) — and for the new Capitol single by JOE SOUTH and the Believers, his self-penned "Don't It Make You Want To Go Home."

"Shangri La" (Pye) by the KINKS is a track from the group's pop opera "The Rise And Fall Of The British Empire" — it is issued on September 12, although the LP of the entire work will not be out until November.

The first single from LOVE SCULPTURE since "Sabre Dance" is "Seagulls" (Parlophone), released on September 12. Coming out the same day are "Do What You Gotta Do" (Tamla Motown) by the FOUR TOPS; "Heaven Knows I'm Missing Him Now" (Pye) by SANDIE SHAW; "Me And Bobby McGee" (Philips) by ROGER MILLER; "Everything I Do Gonh Be Funky" (Bell) by LEE DORSEY; "Star Review" (Atco) by ARTHUR CONLEY; and "Reaching For The Moon" (Atlantic) by BILLY VERA and JUDY CLAY.

The latest from GARY PUCKETT and the UNION GAP is "This Girl Is A Woman Now," and is issued by CBS on September 19.

The waxing by Beatle GEORGE HARRISON of the Indian chant "Hare Krishna Mantra" is being rush-released by Apple today (Friday). Harrison is mentioned on the label only as producer, and the performance is credited to the Radha Krishna Temple (London).

A collection of titles recorded by LULU for Columbia, before her departure from the label, is out today in an LP called "Lulu's Album." Among September 12 releases on Pye's cut-price Marble Arch label are "The World Of DONOVAN," "The SANDIE SHAW Supplement" and "Uptight" by GENO WASHINGTON. A double-album by PINK FLOYD titled "Umma Gumma," including extracts from live performances in Manchester and Birmingham, is issued by Harvest on September 19.

SCOTT: OWN SERIES ON TV IN SPRING

SCOTT WALKER has just fulfilled a life long ambition—to have his own series on television.

Following the tremendous success of his single half-hour show in August, the BBC have signed him up to do a six week series. He will start the series probably in March. He is planning on sophisticated shows, starring talented musicians, especially his own favourites.

His publicist David Sandison told FAB: "There will be an accent on good jazz and blues rather than pop music. I think Scott is trying to get his very special favourite singer Jacques Brel on the show." (Jacques, a Belgian, wrote *If You Go Away* and *Jackie*.)

Scott, who has always seen a TV series as a sure sign of "being accepted", was given his TV break some months back when the BBC asked him to do a 'pilot' show. It received such a great audience reception that the BBC immediately planned a series. He has also done a second 'pilot' show which is likely to be shown in early December. It was scheduled to be shown earlier but had to be put off because of the BBC's wide coverage of the Mexico Olympic Games.

The 30 minute shows will be screened during the peak viewing period. Following the series, Scott is expected to start a British concert tour before going to Japan in mid-July.

STIFF UPPER | BEATLE COMMERCIAL

NEW MUSICAL EXPRESS * On sale Friday, week ending December 3, 1966

NME POLL SENSATION

BEACH BOYS BEAT BEATLES

WEST END FINAL

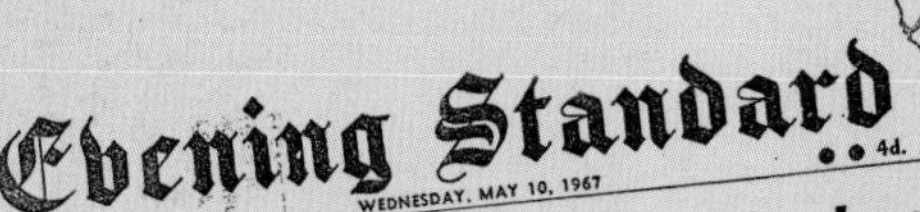

TIO PEPE THE SHERRY OF SPAIN

Evening Standard 4d.

WEDNESDAY, MAY 10, 1967

Mick Jagger hears court story of incense

AT A STONES' PARTY—'HEMP AND HEROIN'

Police tell of night raid at Redlands

Evening Standard Reporter: Chichester, Wednesday

Hemp, heroin and incense-sticks were found by police at the home of one of the Rolling Stones when they interrupted a seaside house party. This was stated by the prosecution at Chichester today.

It was suggested that the incense might have been used to mask the smoking of hemp in the house.

Detectives who searched the house and party guests at West Wittering, Sussex, were said to have found hemp in a briar pipe without a stem in a drawing room, and in ash in a pudding basin left on a bedside table.

Summonses accusing them of drug offences were heard against Michael Philip (Mick) Jagger and Keith Richard, both 29, of the Rolling Stones pop group, and Robert Hugh Fraser, 29, who runs a West End art gallery.

Lead guitarist Richard was accused of permitting his home at Redlands Lane, West Wittering, to be used for the purpose of smoking cannabis resin on February 12, this year.

Lead singer Jagger faced a summons of being in

POP 30 MAKER

WHITER SHADE OF PALE .... Procol Harum, Deram
HERE GOES MY EVERYTHING Engelbert Humperdinck, Decca
TERNATE TITLE .... Monkees, RCA
RRIE ANNE .... Hollies, Parlophone
D RATHER BE WITH ME .... Turtles, London
Y! ...... Dave Dee, Dozy, Beaky, Mick and Tich, Fontana
R SUN .... Traffic, Island
COME THE NICE .... Small Faces, Immediate
VIN' .... Young Rascals, Atlantic
T BE HIM .... Vikki Carr, Liberty
SLEEP IN THE SUBWAY .... Petula Clark, Pye
PPENING .... Supremes, Tamla Motown
E A RICH MAN .... Topol, CBS
OOMS OF GLOOM .... Four Tops, Tamla M...
BREW
S GOLDEN
SUNSET

There's nothing ICKYBOO about the

Small FACES

says DOUG PERRY who reports on them for FAB

which gets him around rather quickly. Plonk told me that he ... to get a similar car soon.

ON their occasional days off the boys enjoy going to the ... but their filmic tastes vary. ... likes Peter O'Toole, Kenny ... Anita Ekberg, while Jimmy ... Marlon Brando.

16th DECEMBER, 1967

Fabulous 208 1/-

GROOVIN'

SUPER DOUBLE PAGE COLOUR PICTURE OF TRAFFIC

KING SIZE COLOUR PIN-UPS OF PROCOL HARUM ● PAUL & BARRY RYAN ● JULIA FOSTER

PAUL & JANE ● WITH SPECIAL COLOUR PIX OF MIKE NESMITH & MICKY DOLENZ

●●● ALSO YOUR RADIO LUXEMBOURG PROGRAMMES FROM 12th DECEMBER TO 18th DECEMBER ●●●

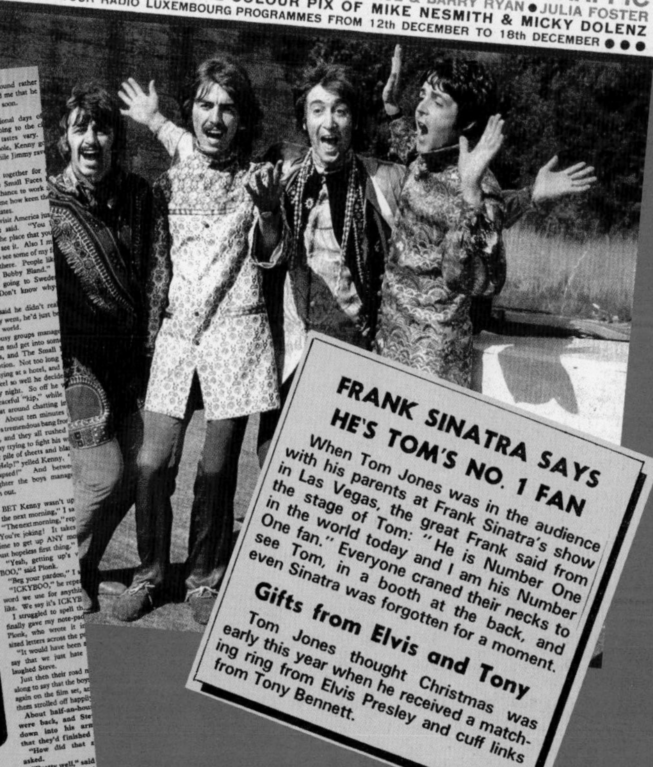

FRANK SINATRA SAYS HE'S TOM'S NO. 1 FAN

When Tom Jones was in the audience with his parents at Frank Sinatra's show in Las Vegas, the great Frank said from the stage of Tom: "He is Number One in the world today and I am his Number One fan." Everyone craned their necks to see Tom, in a booth at the back, and even Sinatra was forgotten for a moment.

Gifts from Elvis and Tony

Tom Jones thought Christmas was early this year when he received a matching ring from Elvis Presley and cuff links from Tony Bennett.

95 Michael Holliday
Starry Eyed

Label & Cat No.: **Columbia DB 4378**

Producer: **Norrie Paramor**

Writers: **Earl Shuman / Mort Garson**

Date reached No.1: **29 January 1960**

Weeks at No.1: **1**

MICHAEL HOLLIDAY WAS AN EXCELLENT middle-of-the-road ballad singer, but the Denmark Street writers rarely wrote anything good enough for him. As a result, he and his record producer, Norrie Paramor, relied on cover versions of US hits. Following successes with 'The Story Of My Life' and 'Stairway Of Love', they knew they had found another winner with 'Starry Eyed', which had been recorded by the Denver singer, Gary Stites.

Mike's suggestions for a low-key arrangement for this simple song were ignored as Eric Jupp wrote an elaborate arrangement for six violins and an eight-strong vocal group. Although Mike dutifully recorded 'Starry Eyed', he rang Norrie the next day and told him of his misgivings about the arrangements. Norrie was nursing similar doubts, feeling that they had failed to bring out the song's commercial potential. He told Mike that he could record the song again a week later with just guitar, bass and drums.

The effort paid off as 'Starry Eyed' Mark 2 was the first new number one of the Sixties. Mike followed it with two minor hits, 'Skylark' and 'Little Boy Lost', but in both cases, perhaps the wrong sides were being promoted as 'Dream Talk' (also written by Earl Shuman) and 'One Finger Symphony' were stronger. The team of Earl Shuman and Mort Garson also wrote a 1961 hit for Cliff Richard, 'Theme For A Dream'.

But is 'Starry Eyed' Michael Holliday's major contribution to 1960? Maybe not, as he also provided Tex Tucker's voice for the puppet western, *Four Feather Falls,* on Granada TV. The series was made by Gerry Anderson, who then created *Stingray* and *Thunderbirds*. Mike also recorded the TV adverts, 'You can be sure of Shell' and 'Make the day with Cadbury's Milk Tray'.

96 Anthony Newley
Why

Label & Cat No.: **Decca F 11194**

Producer: **Ray Horricks**

Writers: **Bob Marcucci / Peter De Angelis**

Date reached No.1: **5 February 1960**

Weeks at No.1: **4**

A CHILD ACTOR IN *OLIVER TWIST* (1948), Anthony Newley starred in a spoof about Elvis Presley being conscripted, *Idle On Parade* (1959), but one of the songs, 'I've Waited So Long', made him a star. The songwriter, Jerry Lordan, said, "Anthony Newley had a most unusual delivery and I loved his accent. Later on, you got David Bowie and Chas & Dave, but Anthony Newley was one of the first."

Its success prompted a serious attempt at making pop hits, and Newley went to number one with a cover version of Frankie Avalon's 'Why'. He reflected, "I thought 'Why' was charming. We worked very hard to get me sounding as innocuous as the original American performance. Frankie Avalon was one of those watered-down American teenagers who sang as if he'd only had lessons in potty training. The trick was to get Newley as simple as that and I think, to my credit, we did succeed." And back to the "potty training" – 14 year old Donny Osmond revived 'Why' and went to number three in 1972.

The 1980 film, *The Idolmaker,* employed the songwriter and manager, Bob Marcucci as a consultant and is loosely based on the stars he created – Frankie Avalon and Fabian. He and Peter De Angelis wrote many songs for them. Peter De Angelis was a fine musician who wrote, arranged and conducted many sessions for Al Martino including 'Painted, Tainted Rose', 'Just Yesterday' and 'Always Together'.

Although he was to live in America, Anthony Newley didn't derive much pleasure from covering American songs: "I wanted to retain my Englishness and 'Strawberry Fair' was one of several English folk songs that I adapted to a more modern setting. It's one of my favourites as it sounds like me as a young man. I tried hard to retain the English flavour which I thought was so important to someone like myself. I didn't want to sound too American is what I'm saying."

97 Adam Faith
Poor Me

Label & Cat No.: **Parlophone R 4623**

Producer: **John Burgess**

Writers: **Les Vandyke (Johnny Worth)**

Date reached No.1: **10 March 1960**

Weeks at No.1: **2**

TERENCE NELHAMS' LIFE WAS EXTRAordinary from the very start as he was born under a kitchen table in an air raid over London on June 23, 1940. After a succession of part-time jobs, he became a messenger boy for the Rank Organisation and wanted to work in films. He sang at the Two I's coffee-bar and changed his name. "The TV producer Jack Good and myself were sitting in his flat and he had a book of kids' names," recalled Nelhams. "He thought I ought to change mine because Terry Nelhams didn't sound right and there already was Terry Dene. I flicked through it and came to 'Faith' in the girls' names and 'Adam' at the start of the boys." Jack's wife came in and he said, 'He's just chosen Adam Faith' and she fell about laughing."

The team of Adam Faith, songwriter Johnny Worth and arranger John Barry repeated the success of 'What Do You Want' with 'Poor Me', and Faith used the title for his first autobiography. Adam almost had a hat-trick of number ones but 'Someone Else's Baby' couldn't shift 'Cathy's Clown'. Faith's records were erratic, the nadir being 'Lonely Pup (In A Christmas Shop)'. He said, "At the time I thought, 'Why not? It's going to be a hit.' I didn't appreciate the damage a hit can do for you if it is not the right sort of hit."

In December 1960 and against the advice of his management, Adam appeared on the BBC's interrogative television programme, *Face To Face.* It was anticipated that the host, John Freeman,

Anthony Newley, whose typically 'English' vocal delivery was an unlikely influence on David Bowie

would expose his shallowness, but Faith skilfully held his own and, in an astonishing revelation for its time, not only admitted to pre-marital sex but also said that he enjoyed it.

Films like *Never Let Go* and *Mix Me A Person* showed his acting potential and he was to star in the TV series, *Budgie*. He wrote about finance in the tabloids, but lost his job after saying he could make anyone a millionaire in six months. In 1991 he starred alongside Zoë Wanamaker in the BBC romantic drama, *Love Hurts*, which ran for three series.

Short of stature, Adam Faith nevertheless enjoyed a reputation as a ladies' man and his marriage to dancer Jackie Irving suffered as a result. In 1999 he started a digital station, The Money Channel, but it attracted few viewers. The station closed with debts of £32m and Faith was declared bankrupt. At the time of his death in 2003, he was in a touring production of *Love And Marriage*. His final words were, "Channel 5 is shit, isn't it?"

98 Johnny Preston
Running Bear

Label & Cat No.: **Mercury AMT 1079**

Producer: **Bill Hall**

Writer: **J.P. Richardson**

Date reached No.1: **17 March 1960**

Weeks at No.1: **2**

J.P. RICHARDSON HAD WRITTEN A novelty hit for his DJ persona, The Big Bopper, called 'Chantilly Lace'. He thought that 'Running Bear' was too serious a song for the Bopper – it was a 'Romeo And Juliet' for the native Americans – and so he passed it to his friend, Johnny Preston. Preston, who played cajun music, was unsure about the material, but he was persuaded, and the session at the Gold Star Studios in Houston was great fun as the Bopper and the country singer, George Jones, did the 'ook-a-chunka' back-up vocals.

Because of legal constraints following the Big Bopper's death in February 1959, the release of 'Running Bear' was delayed. When it did come out, it went to number one in both the US and the UK. A song with nursery rhyme lyrics, 'Cradle Of Love', got to number two in the UK and 'Feel So Fine' made the Top 20, but his best single outside of 'Running Bear', a revival of Little Willie John's 'Leave My Kitten Alone', made no impression at all.

Johnny toured the UK in 1960 on an all-star rock'n'roll package show with Freddy Cannon, Conway Twitty and Wee Willie Harris, but after a succession of misses, "I slowly slipped by the wayside". Not to worry because he bought a ranch with the proceeds from 'Running Bear' and now he tours on oldie packages for fun. In 1997 Johnny Preston added the chant for the Big Bopper Jr's version of 'Running Bear'.

99 Lonnie Donegan
My Old Man's A Dustman (Ballad Of A Refuse Disposal Officer)

Label & Cat No.: **Pye Nixa N 15256**

Producers: **Alan A. Freeman / Michael Barclay**

Writers: **Traditional, new lyrics by Lonnie Donegan, Peter Buchanan and Beverly Thorn**

Date reached No.1: **31 March 1960**

Weeks at No.1: **4**

LONNIE DONEGAN SAID, "'MY OLD Man's A Fireman (on the Elder Dempster Line)' became a student's union song in Birmingham, and then it was picked up by the troops in the First World War as 'My old man's a dustman, he fought in the Battle of Mons. He killed ten thousand Germans with only a hundred bombs.' We used it as a joke on stage, and then the A&R department at Pye told me to 'Write it', and so we took it away and wrote it, guv'nor. We performed new verses every night until we had ones that would work well on record. You need a lot of verses for a song like that, anyway. It's a joke song and people aren't going to keep laughing at the same jokes."

Most of the new verses were written by Lonnie's road manager, Pete Buchanan, who said, "Lon had great timing – he was bloody good at delivering jokes." The dustman's union didn't, however, think so – they complained about its irreverence and typecasting.

'My Old Man's A Dustman' was recorded at the Gaumont Cinema in Doncaster in February 1960. Lonnie performed the song on *Sunday Night At The London Palladium*, and as a result, it became the first UK single to enter the UK chart at number one.

The song was as much a millstone as a milestone for Lonnie Donegan and it can be viewed in the same light as Chuck Berry's 'My Ding-A-Ling'. Drummer Pete Merrett says, "I remember him saying in the Seventies, 'You may be fed up with 'Dustman', I am fed up with 'Dustman', but it is paying the mortgage. We are booked 'act as known' and we have to do it.'"

100 Anthony Newley
Do You Mind

Label & Cat No.: **Decca F 11220**

Producer: **Ray Horricks**

Writer: **Lionel Bart**

Date reached No.1: **28 April 1960**

Weeks at No.1: **1**

"I WAS VERY FOND OF LIONEL BART," recalled Anthony Newley. "He was very persuasive but I was usually a pushover for a suggestion anyway. I remember being wooed by Lionel, who really wanted me to sing 'Do You Mind', and I didn't mind because it was a very good song."

Lionel Bart continued the story, "Newley was very meticulous. We had a big orchestra and an enormous arrangement and it went into three sessions, which meant nine hours. During that time, we kept losing musicians as they had to go elsewhere and also we wanted a simpler sound. It wound up with just the rhythm section and me snapping my fingers."

Both Bart and Newley were to write ground-breaking musicals – Bart with the lavish *Oliver!* and Newley with the witty and avant-garde *Stop The World – I Want To Get Off*. Newley and Leslie Bricusse's score included the standards, 'What Kind Of Fool Am I' and 'Gonna Build A Mountain'. Newley was constantly experimenting – he wrote a parody on the Profumo affair, *Fool Britannia* (1963), and the film, *Can Heironymus Merkin Ever Forget Mercy Humppe And Find True Happiness?* (1969), was a remarkably off-beat way to end his marriage to Joan Collins. Newley had the glitz to become a Las Vegas star and he returned to the UK in the Nineties for a very successful starring role in the Leslie Bricusse stage musical, *Scrooge*. He also had an occasional role in *EastEnders*. When he died in 1999, his mother, Grace, was still alive at the age of 96.

101 The Everly Brothers
Cathy's Clown

Label & Cat No.:	**Warner Brothers WB 1**
Producer:	**Wesley Rose**
Writers:	**Don Everly / Phil Everly**
Date reached No.1:	**5 May 1960**
Weeks at No.1:	**7**

After a string of hits for Cadence Records, The Everly Brothers' contract came up for renewal in 1960. Archie Bleyer couldn't compete with the film giants, Warner Brothers, who wanted to move into records and offered the Everlys what is reputed to be the first million dollar contract to sign with them for 10 years.

For their first single, they recorded 'Cathy's Clown', which was attributed to Don Everly at the time and indeed written about his high school sweetheart. However, a subsequent court case revealed that Phil was a co-writer: the melody and the chorus were Don's but the verses were Phil's. (There's nothing like brotherly love.) The Everlys were backed by the best session musicians in Nashville and the stunning drumming is by Buddy Harman. "I remember him playing different patterns on the drums," says Phil, "then he hit upon that 'Cathy's Clown' riff and I thought, 'Bam, we're home.'" Don's slurred vocals on the verses contrasted with the precision of their harmonies on the chorus.

'Cathy's Clown' got the Warners label off to a remarkable start as it topped the charts in both the UK and the US. The B-side, 'Always It's You, was a delicate ballad written by Boudleaux & Felice Bryant, and both sides were included on their album, *A Date With The Everly Brothers*. That album included the first recorded version of the Boudleaux's 'Love Hurts'. How could the Everlys have missed that as a single and possible number one? "I don't know," says Phil, "but we should have put it out."

Graham Gouldman of 10cc remembers "I loved the Everly Brothers and still do. They would sound like three people singing and they recorded brilliant songs, looked great and played beautiful guitars. 'Cathy's Clown' was the first record I bought and I can still hear its influence in my writing. I loved the fact that one note was being held with another melody descending underneath it. I used that idea in 'For Your Love' for the Yardbirds."

102 Eddie Cochran
Three Steps To Heaven

Label & Cat No.:	**London HLG 9115**
Producers:	**Eddie Cochran / Jerry Capeheart**
Writers:	**Eddie Cochran / Bob Cochran**
Date reached No.1:	**23 June 1960**
Weeks at No.1:	**2**

On January 8, 1960, the night before he came to the UK for a lengthy tour with Gene Vincent, Eddie Cochran recorded three new songs with Sonny Curtis and Jerry Allison from The Crickets. They were 'Three Steps To Heaven', 'Cut Across Shorty' and 'Cherished Memories'.

Gene and Eddie's UK tour was dynamic and it inspired numerous UK musicians, both in the audience and on stage. Eddie was generous with his directions, showing Joe Brown a whole new style for playing guitar and telling Brian Bennett how he could make the drums sound more exciting. Still, there were indications that Eddie wanted to change his sound, telling Brian Matthew on *Saturday Club* that he wanted to develop. On April 17, 1960 and after the final date at Bristol Hippodrome, Eddie Cochran, his girlfriend the songwriter, Sharon Sheeley, and Gene Vincent were involved in a car crash, which resulted in Eddie's death.

Although Eddie was only 21, he had made scores of recordings, either for himself or backing others. His rock'n'roll standards include 'Summertime Blues', 'C'mon Everybody' and 'Somethin' Else' and his ballad, 'Three Steps To Heaven', was released shortly after his death. The song went to number one and also made number two for Showaddywaddy in 1975. The equally strong B-side, 'Cut Across Shorty', was an updated version of Aesop's fable about the tortoise and the hare.

It's nonsense to say that famous artists had premonitions of their deaths but the final recordings of famous stars include 'I'll Never Get Out Of This

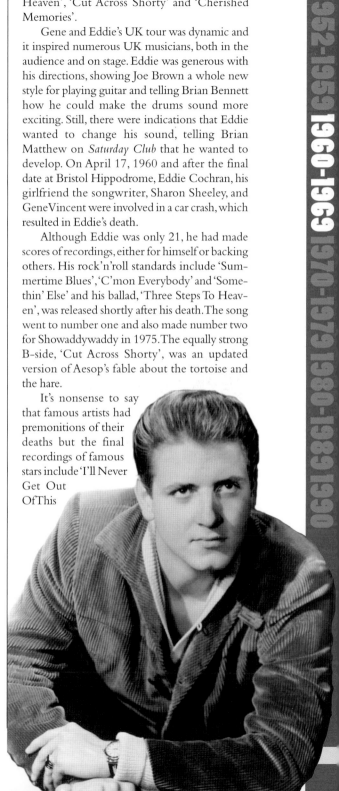

Eddie Cochran

World Alive' (Hank Williams), 'I Fall To Pieces' (Patsy Cline), 'Way Down' (Elvis Presley) and 'It Doesn't Matter Anymore' (Buddy Holly).

103 Jimmy Jones Good Timin'

Label & Cat No.: **MGM 1078**

Producer: **Otis Blackwell**

Writers: **Fred Tobias / Clint Ballard Jr**

Date reached No.1: **7 July 1960**

Weeks at No.1: **3**

JIMMY JONES, BORN IN BIRMINGHAM, Alabama in 1937, recorded demo records for songwriters in the Brill Building in New York. He played his song, 'Handy Man', to Otis Blackwell, who had written 'All Shook Up' and 'Great Balls Of Fire'. Blackwell made a few changes and decided to produce the record himself. Blackwell had thought of having a flute on the record, but when the musician failed to turn up, he whistled instead and that, with Jimmy Jones' high-pitched vocals, is what made the record so distinctive. The record climbed to number two in the US and number three in the UK.

'Good Timin'' followed the same path, but this time the song was written by Fred Tobias (part of a remarkable songwriting dynasty – eight members of the family wrote hit songs) and Clint Ballard Jr (the manager of The Kalin Twins and the writer of 'You're No Good'). The record made number three in the US and topped the charts here, enabling him to tour the UK. Sadly though, he could not match the quality of those two singles and his chart career was soon over. One of the tracks on his first album was the original version of 'Wondrous Place', which should have been tried as a single.

Jimmy Jones has continued to sing and record, sometimes revisiting his hits with titles like 'Mr Fix-It' and 'Handyman's Back In Town'. His publishers accused Boy George of basing 'Karma Chameleon' on 'Handy Man'. "I might have heard it once," said Boy George, "but it was certainly not something I sat down and copied. We gave them ten pence and an apple."

104 Cliff Richard & The Shadows Please Don't Tease

Label & Cat No.: **Columbia DB 4479**

Producer: **Norrie Paramor**

Writers: **Pete Chester / Bruce Welch**

Date reached No.1: **28 July 1960**

Weeks at No.1: **3**

HANK MARVIN AND BRUCE WELCH began their professional career with The Five Chesternuts, a group fronted by drummer Pete Chester, the son of the comedian, Charlie Chester. Hank and Bruce moved on but they retained their friendship with Pete Chester. An easy-paced rock-a-ballad that Bruce wrote with Pete, 'Please Don't Tease', was recorded by Cliff, but it wasn't the obvious choice for a single. For some reason (probably publicity!), Cliff invited a handful of fans to hear his latest recordings and they chose his next single, the majority of them going for 'Please Don't Tease'.

Cliff had time for such stunts as he and The Shadows were featured in *Stars In Your Eyes* at the London Palladium from June to December, alongside Russ Conway, Joan Regan and Edmund Hockridge. "I remember 'Please Don't Tease' of course," says Bruce Welch, "but I don't remember writing it. Personally, I think Cliff's next record, 'Nine Times Out Of Ten', deserved to go all the way as it was one of his best."

Cliff returned to 'Please Don't Tease' in 1978, recording a new, slower version on the back of his single, 'Please Remember Me'. As 'Please Remember Me' failed to chart, it should have been the A-side.

105 Johnny Kidd & The Pirates Shakin' All Over

Label & Cat No.: **HMV POP 753**

Producer: **Wally Ridley**

Writers: **Fred Heath / Gus Robinson**

Date reached No.1: **4 August 1960**

Weeks at No.1: **1**

VERY FEW BRITISH ROCK'N'ROLL records could match their American counterparts, the main candidates being Cliff Richard's 'Move It!', Billy Fury's 'Wondrous Place' and Johnny Kidd's 'Shakin' All Over'. Kidd's record came about by chance as his bass player, Brian Gregg, recalls, "Wally Ridley's assistant, Peter Sullivan, said, 'We're going to do the old trad tune, "Yes Sir That's My Baby", and you can have the B-side.' The day before the session we were in the Freight Train coffee-bar in Berwick Street and we said, 'Let's write any old rubbish.' There was Johnny, the guitarist Alan Caddy and myself. We didn't have any instruments and we sang the parts to 'Shakin' All Over'. We got up early in the morning, had a run-through in my front room – not plugged in, and we went to the studio and recorded it. We thought it would be a B-side but Jack Good loved it and pushed it on his new programme, *Wham!*, and it went straight up the charts."

'Shakin' All Over' was also the first record that Clem Cattini played on, while a few months down the line, Kidd, whose real name was Fred Heath, was joined by another young guitarist, Mick Green. Kidd never repeated the success of 'Shakin' All Over', although some of his singles ('Linda Lu' and 'A Shot Of Rhythm And Blues') can be seen as forerunners of the British beat boom. His Top 10 single, 'I'll Never Get Over You' (1963), was pure Merseybeat, and Mick Green was to join The Dakotas before becoming an acclaimed session guitarist. Kidd and his stripe-shirted Pirates had a lively stage act in which Kidd brandished a cutlass. Kidd died in a car accident in 1966, but the Pirates reformed

Johnny Kidd & The Pirates, whose line-up of singer/guitarist/bass/drums was the first of its kind in the UK; left to right: Johnny Spence, Frank Farley, Kidd and Mick Green

during the punk era and became a raucous, cult band.

106 The Shadows
Apache

Label & Cat No.:	**Columbia DB 4484**
Producer:	**Norrie Paramor**
Writer:	**Jerry Lordan**
Date reached No.1:	**25 August 1960**
Weeks at No.1:	**5**

INSTRUMENTAL RECORDS MEAN LITTLE now, but the early Sixties was a golden age with The Shadows, Duane Eddy, The Ventures and Johnny & The Hurricanes as well as the middle-of-the-road acts like Russ Conway and Bert Weedon. Indeed, the songwriter Jerry Lordan had intended Bert Weedon to record his composition, 'Apache', first. When Top Rank procrastinated over its release, Jerry passed it to The Shadows.

The Shadows had to persuade Norrie Paramor that it should be the A-side over the naval tune, 'Quatermasster's Stores'. Norrie played them to his daughters, who agreed with The Shadows. It was a very atmospheric record which established the echo-laden sound of Hank Marvin's lead guitar. Bert Weedon's version was released at the same time but only reached number 24.

For once, it looked as though a British record would have a real chance in America, but another company pushed a rival version by Jorgen Ingmann, which went to number two. Cliff Richard says, "Jorgen Ingmann put in a few tricky bits, but essentially it was a cover job. If the Shads had made the charts there with 'Apache', things might have been very different for us."

The Shadows are often compared with The Ventures, but Jet Harris says, "I think we were better than The Ventures, who were very clean-cut and precise. Hank was more raunchy and I certainly tried to give the bass some guts and so did Tony Meehan on the drums. We were at the London Palladium when 'Apache' was number one. We were sent 'Walk – Don't Run' and were told that The Ventures were releasing it in three weeks. We loved the tune, but we didn't want to do it because 'Apache' was still selling so well."

107 Ricky Valance
Tell Laura I Love Her

Label & Cat No.:	**Columbia DB 4493**
Producer:	**Norrie Paramor**
Writers:	**Jeff Barry / Ben Raleigh**
Date reached No.1:	**29 September 1960**
Weeks at No.1:	**3**

ALTHOUGH THE WORKS OF HOMER, Shakespeare and Dickens are strewn with corpses, the BBC steadfastly refused to play records connected with death and so one way to court controversy was to make a so-called 'death disc'. They included 'Ebony Eyes' (Everly Brothers), 'Teen Angel' (Mark Dinning), 'Leader Of The Pack' (Shangri-Las) and 'Terry' (Twinkle). Perhaps the best-known is 'Tell Laura I Love Her', the story of a dying stock-car racer's love for his girlfriend.

'Tell Laura I Love Her' was written by the Brill Building writer, Jeff Barry, before he teamed up with Ellie Greenwich and it was given to Ray Peterson. Peterson's first hit had been 'The Wonder Of You', which ten years later would become a monster hit for Elvis Presley. 'Tell Laura I Love Her' went into the US Top 10 but RCA were reluctant to release it here as they would be accused of bad taste by the BBC.

EMI's Columbia label saw their chance and quickly recorded a cover version by the Welsh singer, Ricky Valance. RCA changed their minds and released Peterson's version but Ricky Valance had the edge. He recalls, "I had a lot of faith in that song because it stirred something in me. I wasn't surprised when it was a hit because the melody was so beautiful, it's a song in a lifetime, one of those songs you never can match. I hated being regarded as a one-hit wonder, though. I sold 40,000 copies of some of my other records."

Those records are 'Jimmy's Girl' and 'Movin' Away', but his return to death discs with 'Bobby' (a girl in hospital) and 'Six Boys' (all of them pall-bearers at a girlfriend's funeral) didn't work. Ricky Valance has sung both country and gospel music and, most appropriately, has toured in the musical, *Leave Him To Heaven*.

108 Roy Orbison
Only The Lonely (Know How I Feel)

Label & Cat No.:	**London HLU 9149**
Producer:	**Fred Foster**
Writers:	**Roy Orbison / Joe Melson**
Date reached No.1:	**20 October 1960**
Weeks at No.1:	**2**

ROY ORBISON FORMED HIS FIRST BAND in 1949 when he was 13 and he was in a number of groups that were popular around Odessa, Texas in the early Fifties. Inspired by the success of Elvis Presley on Sun Records in Memphis, Roy and his other Wink Westerners auditioned for Sam Phillips. Roy Orbison made some commendable rockabilly records for Sun – 'Ooby Dooby' and 'Rockhouse' – but Phillips didn't appreciate the uniqueness of his voice. Roy's confidence as a songwriter increased in 1958 when he wrote a number one hit for The Everly Brothers, 'Claudette', in actuality a song about his wife.

In 1959 on the recommendation of the music publisher Wesley Rose, Roy Orbison signed with Fred Foster's new Monument label. Rose suggested that he got together with Joe Melson, another Acuff-Rose writer who also came from West Texas. Their first songs, which include 'Uptown', were good but then they hit upon 'Only The Lonely (Know How I Feel)'. Part of the title was put in brackets to avoid confusion with 'Only The Lonely', which Sammy Cahn and Jimmy Van Heusen had written for

Frank Sinatra in 1958.

Roy, still lacking some confidence, took it to The Everly Brothers, but they told him that he should cut it himself. Roy Orbison's single with its 'dum dum dum dummy doo-wah' arrangement peaked at number 2 in July 1960, but a few months later, it hit the top in the UK. Roy Orbison, commenting on his stage persona in the Eighties, said, "The sadness idea has a lot to do with my image over the years – the black clothes and the shades. Also, it has to do with the fact that 'Only The Lonely' was my first hit and that was an incredibly sad song. People obviously assume that my life is like that song, which is not really true at all. For the most part, it's been a glorious life."

109 Elvis Presley
It's Now Or Never (O Sole Mio)

Label & Cat No.: **RCA 1207**

Producer: **Steve Sholes**

Writers: **Eduardo di Capua / Aaron Schroeder / Wally Gold**

Date reached No.1: **3 November 1960**

Weeks at No.1: **8**

THE ITALIAN ARIA, 'O SOLE MIO', WHICH means 'My Sunshine' was written in 1901 and was famously recorded by Enrico Caruso in 1916. In 1949 Tony Martin recorded an English version with the title, 'There's No Tomorrow'. Elvis Presley was very fond of 'O Sole Mio', but when his publishers, Hill & Range, couldn't reach a deal over 'There's No Tomorrow', they asked four Brill Building writing teams for new lyrics. The best was by Aaron Schroeder & Wally Gold and Elvis, now out of the army, brought Mario Lanza's version of 'O Sole Mio' to the session so he knew what he had to match. (For the record, Presley hits a G sharp at the end as opposed to Lanza's high B.)

'It's Now Or Never (O Sole Mio)' became a US number one, but a difference in the copyright laws between the US and UK meant that its release was postponed. The US B-side, the wonderful 'A Mess Of Blues' became a UK A-side, reaching number two and then it was followed by 'It's Now Or Never (O Sole Mio)', which became Elvis' biggest-selling single in the UK. It marked Elvis' change from a rock'n'roll singer to an adult entertainer. Heck, the new arrangement is almost a cha-cha.

Elvis did not often perform 'It's Now Or Never (O Sole Mio)' in concert, but sometimes he combined it with the Italian words of 'O Sole Mio'. The melody is also known with a more recent lyric, the Walls' ice-cream ad 'Just One Cornetto'.

110 Cliff Richard & The Shadows
I Love You

Label & Cat No.: **Columbia DB 4547**

Producer: **Norrie Paramor**

Writer: **Bruce Welch**

Date reached No.1: **29 December 1960**

Weeks at No.1: **2**

CHRISTMAS 1960 WAS PROBABLY THE worst time in Cliff Richard's life. His father, Rodger [sic], a heavy smoker, collapsed and was rushed into hospital. He was released but after a relapse, he died, only 56 years old, on May 15, 1961. On a lighter note, Cliff's dad had always teased him by saying he should sing like Marty Wilde, and he encouraged his career, negotiating and arguing with his managers, and telling Cliff that 'I Love You' was his best single to date.

'I Love You' was written by Bruce Welch of The Shadows, who recalled in 2003, "I used to be writing all the time, any spare time I had, either twanging away on the coach or in the flat when I wasn't working. I haven't written a song in 14 years now, so it's very strange to look back on those years." The B-side, 'D In Love' was written by Sid Tepper and Roy Bennett about an American high school but the British fans loved it.

Cliff started 1961 in fine style but the year would see him and The Shadows go from strength to strength. Between them they had nine Top 10 singles, and Cliff was so popular that Columbia even released an album to celebrate his coming of age, *21 Today*.

111 Johnny Tillotson
Poetry In Motion

Label & Cat No.: **London HLA 9231**

Producer: **Archie Bleyer**

Writers: **Paul Kaufman / Mike Anthony**

Date reached No.1: **12 January 1961**

Weeks at No.1: **2**

JOHNNY TILLOTSON WAS A LOCAL SINGER in Florida who was discovered by Mae Boren Axton, the writer of 'Heartbreak Hotel' and the mother of Hoyt. He had his first US hit in 1958 with 'Dreamy Eyes' and he broke through internationally with 'Poetry In Motion'. Like Bobby Vee, Frankie Avalon, Fabian and Bobby Rydell, Johnny Tillotson was one of the good-looking, coolly-dressed teenage idols who came along while Elvis was in the US army.

Johnny Tillotson recalls, "Archie Bleyer, who owned Cadence Records, brought me a song called 'Poetry In Motion' and I couldn't get it out of my mind. It was such a perfect picture of the beauties of ladies on every level. I kinda felt we had a hit there. It was written by Mike Anthony & Paul Kaufman and a couple of years ago, just before he passed away, Mike had a number one country record for John Michael Montgomery, 'I Miss You A Little'. He was the sweetest man and he never gave up. The whole Nashville A-team was playing on 'Poetry In Motion': Boots Randolph on sax, Floyd Cramer on piano, Hank Garland on guitar and Buddy Harman on drums. The B-side, 'Princess Princess' was one I wrote and it was how I felt about the girls in the audience."

Johnny Tillotson had further UK hits with 'It Keeps Right On A-Hurtin'' and 'Send Me The

Pillow That You Dream On'. 'Poetry In Motion' returned to the charts in 1979, this time presented as a double A-side with 'Princess Princess'. In 2000 he came to the UK for a lengthy and very successful tour with Bobby Vee and Freddy Cannon. He says, "I never walk through a show. I feel a deep sense of responsibility to each person in that audience. They come to be entertained and that's what I attempt to do."

112 Elvis Presley with The Jordanaires
Are You Lonesome Tonight?

Label & Cat No.: **RCA 1216**

Producers: **Steve Sholes / Chet Atkins**

Writers: **Roy Turk / Lou Handman**

Date reached No.1: **26 January 1961**

Weeks at No.1: **4**

'Are You Lonesome Tonight?' was written in 1926 by two Tin Pan Alley songwriters, who included a narration based on Jacques' speech from Shakespeare's *As You Like It*. Several artists have recorded it, notably Vaughn Deleath (a female despite the name) first in 1927 and Henry Burr shortly after. In 1950 the song was revived by the bandleader Blue Barron with his vocalist Bobby Beers, but a disc jockey, John McCormick, was asked to do the narration. Al Jolson didn't cut it until 1953.

Outside of publishing deals, 'Are You Lonesome Tonight?' is the only song which Colonel Parker asked Elvis Presley to record, a request emanating from Parker's wife. Elvis copied Jolson's arrangement note for note and almost word for word. He recorded it late at night during a marathon session with eight other songs and he put the lights out for 'Are You Lonesome Tonight?' in order to increase his emotional feelings. Chet Atkins found Elvis' working hours interfered with his day job at RCA and so he stopped producing him after this.

Despite being a translatlantic number one in 1961, 'Are You Lonesome Tonight?' was one of Elvis's most controversial recordings as rock-'n'roll fans felt he was selling out. This was nonsense as the B-side of 'All Shook Up', for example, was another lost love song with a narration, 'That's When Your Heartaches Begin', which was associated with The Ink Spots.

Elvis's laughing version, caught in concert in 1969, is taken by some as evidence that he was perpetually high and by others that he had a wonderful sense of humour. Elvis had simply forgotten the words, but the song title summarised Elvis's later life and became the title of a West End play by Alan Bleasdale featuring Martin Shaw as the broken King.

Dodie Stevens recorded an answer version, 'Yes, I'm Lonesome Tonight', but the best adjustments to the lyric came from Elvis himself who sang such variations as "Do you gaze at your bald head and wish you had hair?" in concert.

113 Petula Clark
Sailor

Label & Cat No.: **Pye 7N 15324**

Producer: **Alan A. Freeman**

Writers: **Fini Busch / Werner Scharfenburger / David West (Norman Newell)**

Date reached No.1: **23 February 1961**

Weeks at No.1: **1**

In 1960 Lolita had her eighth Top 20 hit in Germany with 'Seemann (Deine Heimat Ist Dar Meer)', which climbed to number two. The record then became a Top 10 hit in the US in its original form. 'Seemann' was a very catchy song and the EMI producer, Norman Newell was asked for an English lyric for a Petula Clark session. He recalls, "The publisher phoned me one Friday and said he would like me to do it over the weekend. I agreed and he said that a messenger would pick it up on Monday morning. I don't know why, but I completely forgot about it. I was astonished when I saw the messenger boy on Monday, so I took him to the canteen and wrote the lyrics in about ten minutes. I wondered if it was good enough, but it became a tremendous hit, thank heavens."

Petula Clark had been a child performer during the war and she became nationally known on both radio and film as Jack Warner's daughter in the Huggett family. She made the transition to adult entertainment with 'Suddenly There's A Valley' (7, 1955), 'With All My Heart' (4, 1957) and 'Alone' (8, 1957), but then had a dry spell. 'Sailor' was a chart race for Petula Clark on Pye and Anne Shelton on Philips with both records making the Top 10, and Petula, now 29, having her first UK number one. She followed it with 'Romeo' (3) and 'My Friend The Sea' (7), both records with a similar feel. She married a Frenchman, Claude Wolff, and this led to her recording many Continental songs. She made the UK Top 20 in 1962 with a single in French, 'Ya Ya Twist'.

114 The Everly Brothers
Walk Right Back / Ebony Eyes

Label & Cat No.: **Warner Brothers WB 33**

Producer: **Wesley Rose**

Writers: **Sonny Curtis; John D. Loudermilk**

Date reached No.1: **2 March 1961**

Weeks at No.1: **3**

After Buddy Holly's death, the Crickets worked on stage backing The Everly Brothers. Sonny Curtis, who had rejoined The Crickets, recalls, "I got the idea for 'Walk Right Back' when I was in England picking for the Everlys, but during that tour I was drafted into the US Army. When I got to basic training in California, I played a beat-up guitar that somebody had and completed the first verse. I got a three-day pass and went to Hollywood to see The Everlys. They were studying acting for Warners, but nothing came of it. We had a few laughs and I sang 'Walk Right Back'. They said they'd record it if I wrote another verse. Well, the army keeps you pretty busy and it took me two weeks to come up with something. I put it in the

Brothers Don (right) and Phil Everly, the first great duo in rock'n'roll

mail, but the next day I got a letter from JI (Jerry Allison) to say that The Everlys had cut it. I knew that they hadn't had time to get my verse and it turned out that they sang the first verse twice." If you catch Sonny Curtis in concert, you will hear the complete lyric. Not to worry, it's the best half-song ever to make number one.

The double A-side was completed by a death disc, 'Ebony Eyes', written by John D. Loudermilk, the quirkiest of all Nashville's songwriters. The song featured a narration from Don Everly about the plight of Flight 1203. "I used a bit of my acting thing in the recitation," says Don, "and also we got to sing with The Anita Kerr Singers, which was a step up for us." The Everlys refused to perform the song in concert as they had to fly to bookings. However, in the Nineties, they included it in their act, albeit without the narration.

115 Elvis Presley
Wooden Heart

Label & Cat No.:	**RCA 1226**
Producer:	**Steve Sholes**
Writers:	**Bert Kaempfert / Kay Twomey / Fred Wise / Ben Weisman**
Date reached No.1:	**23 March 1961**
Weeks at No.1:	**6**

THE GERMAN BANDLEADER BERT Kaempfert is the only musician to have worked with the three greats of popular music – he produced the first records by The Beatles, he adapted a German folk song for Elvis Presley and wrote 'Strangers In The Night' for Frank Sinatra. 'Wooden Heart' is based on 'Muss I Denn Zum Staedtele Hinaus? (Do I Really Have To Miss This Little Town?)' and after Kaempfert considered it right for *G.I. Blues*, it was given an English lyric by three American writers.

Elvis performs the children's song delightfully at a puppet show with tuba and accordion accompaniment. The score also includes 'Frankfurt Special', 'Didja Ever' and the much overlooked ballad, 'Doin' The Best I Can'. Juliet Prowse played the romantic lead: she was Frank Sinatra's girlfriend at the time, but that didn't stop Elvis.

Although 'Wooden Heart' was a UK number one and on the West German charts for five months, it wasn't issued as a single in the US as they were promoting the theme from another Elvis film, *Flaming Star* instead. As a result, a cover version by Joe Dowell with Ray Stevens on organ became a hit.

G.I. Blues was a light-hearted, fictitious account of Elvis's army life in Germany. It makes out that Elvis, or Tulsa McLean as he is called, did little army work and spent most of his time partying. The truth is somewhat different. Elvis spent all of his time partying and was lucky to have escaped Germany without several court martials, paternity suits and criminal charges. Had the journalists then been as intrusive as today's, his career would have been ruined. Now there's a film for you.

116 The Marcels
Blue Moon

Label & Cat No.:	**Pye International 7N 25073**
Producer:	**Stu Phillips**
Writers:	**Richard Rodgers / Lorenz Hart**
Date reached No.1:	**4 May 1961**
Weeks at No.1:	**2**

IN 1933 RICHARD RODGERS AND LORENZ Hart were asked to write a film song for Jean Harlow. The song, called 'Prayer', wasn't used in the film, *Hollywood Party*, and nor, for that matter, was Jean Harlow. Undeterred, Hart wrote a new lyric and submitted it as the title song for *Manhattan Melodrama*. It wasn't used, but a third lyric, 'The Bad In Every Man' was sung by Shirley Ross in the film. It was an apt title as the bank robber John Dillinger was watching *Manhattan Melodrama* before being gunned down outside a cinema in Chicago.

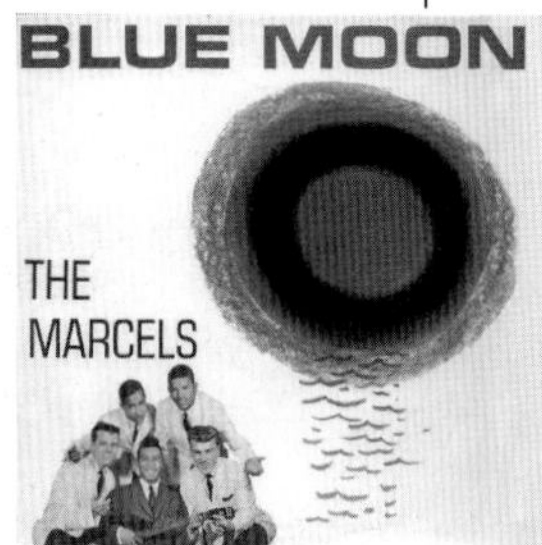

Jack Robbins, the head of MGM's music publishing division and the founder of Robbins Music, said he would promote the song if Hart wrote something more commercial and, keen to oblige, Hart wrote 'Blue Moon'. It was recorded by Glen Gray and the Casa Loma Orchestra in 1935 and it is the only well-known Rodgers & Hart song not introduced via a stage show or a film. Having said that, Robbins licensed it for one film after another and it has been included in the Rodgers & Hart bio-pic, *Words And Music* (1948), Fellini's pioneering *8½* (1963) and in two versions, one by Bobby Vinton and one by The Marcels, in *An American Werewolf in London* (1981). The many familiar interpretations include Glenn Miller and his Orchestra, Billy Eckstine, Mel Tormé, Vaughn Monroe, Frank Sinatra, Tony Bennett and Julie London. Elvis Presley recorded a slow, sensual version while at Sun Records, which became a UK Top 10 single in 1956.

Also in 1956 the doowop group, The Cadillacs, recorded 'Zoom' and its busy and intricate vocal arrangement was the inspiration for a wild, up-tempo reworking of 'Blue Moon', this time by a Pittsburgh group named after a hairstyling, The Marcels. Lorenz Hart's magnificent lyrics were upstaged by 'bomp ba ba bomps', 'dang da dang dangs' and 'dit da dit dits', not to mention 'ding a dong dings' – and it worked. Not admittedly with Richard Rodgers, who called the record 'an abomination', although it's unlikely he complained when the royalty cheques arrived.

Murray The K loved the record so much that he played it 26 times in one show on WINS and it soared to number one in the US. Unusually for the period, The Marcels were a racially integrated group – Richard Knauss and Gene Bricker were white, and Cornelius Harp (the lead singer), Fred Johnson and Ron Mundy were black, but Knauss and Bricker soon left. The Marcels had further success with 'Summertime' and 'Heartaches' and sang 'Merry Twistmas' in the film, *Twist Around The Clock*. 'Blue Moon' was back in the charts for Showaddywaddy in 1980 and John Alford in 1996.

117 Floyd Cramer
On The Rebound

Label & Cat No.: **RCA 1231**
Producer: **Chet Atkins**
Writer: **Floyd Cramer**
Date reached No.1: **18 May 1961**
Weeks at No.1: **1**

FLOYD CRAMER, WHO WAS BORN IN Shreveport, Louisiana, in 1933, was a pianist who became an integral part of the Nashville session scene in the Sixties. He played on thousands of records including most of Elvis Presley's hits from 1956 to 1968 – those piano fills on 'Heartbreak Hotel' are his – and he also can be heard on Jim Reeves' hits. Cramer became known for his 'slip note' style, which he described as 'a lonesome cowboy sound' and said it was a 'near miss' – you hit the note below the one you want and slide up into it. This technique was developed with the songwriter, Don Robertson, and first heard in the Hank Locklin hit, 'Please Help Me I'm Falling' and Cramer's own 'Last Date', which went to number two in the US. Ironically, Cramer was kept off the top by Elvis Presley's 'Are You Lonesome Tonight?' on which he played piano.

'Last Date' was not a UK hit but Cramer followed it with the lively 'On The Rebound', which went to number one. However, Cramer was reluctant to leave his lucrative session work by touring. Instead, he released numerous easy listening albums including *America's Biggest Selling Pianist* (1961), *Floyd Cramer Gets Organ-ised* (1961), *Country Piano, City Strings* (1964) and *Floyd Cramer Meets The Monkees* (1967) as well as albums with Chet Atkins, Boots Randolph and Danny Davis. In 1980 he had some popularity with the theme from *Dallas* but by then he was being overtaken by younger musicians. At the time of his death in 1997, he was recording albums for sale on CMT (Country Music Television).

118 The Temperance Seven with vocal refrain by Mr. Paul McDowell
You're Driving Me Crazy

Label & Cat No.: **Parlophone R 4757**
Producer: **George Martin**
Writer: **Walter Donaldson**
Date reached No.1: **25 May 1961**
Weeks at No.1: **1**

THE BRILL BUILDING SONGWRITER, Walter Donaldson spent as much time at the racetrack as he did writing songs and he was forced to be prolific simply to cover his debts. He wrote 'Yes Sir That's My Baby', 'My Baby Just Cares For Me' and 'My Blue Heaven'. In 1930, Guy Lombardo and his Royal Canadians introduced one of his biggest successes, 'You're Driving Me Crazy'.

Traditional jazz ('Trad') regained its popularity in the UK in the early Sixties with the 3B's – Ball, Barber and Bilk – but The Temperance Seven were different. They played their wistful, melodic jazz sitting down with virtually no movement and their lead vocalist, Whispering Paul McDowell, sang through a megaphone. They played an eclectic collection of instruments and were also influenced by the screwball comedy of The Alberts and The Goons. Watch *It's Trad, Dad!,* which is packed with jazz and pop acts, and it is the immobile Temperance Seven you will remember. The Temperance Seven worked with both film director Richard Lester and record producer George Martin before The Beatles; indeed, 'You're Driving Me Crazy' was George Martin's first number one.

The Temperance Seven – there were actually nine of them – had further hits with 'Pasadena' (4), 'Hard Hearted Hannah' / 'Chili Bom Bom' (28) and 'The Charleston' (22), but they could not find a way to develop their sound. The Bonzo Dog Doo Dah Band and The New Vaudeville Band would later find greater success with similar style music, though the Bonzos added an element on zany humour into the mix. The group's trombonist, John R.T. Davies did impressive work restoring old recordings from the Twenties and Thirties, and a version of The Temperance Seven tours to this day.

119 Elvis Presley with The Jordanaires
Surrender (Torna A Sorrento)

Label & Cat No.: **RCA 1227**
Producer: **Steve Sholes**
Writers: **Ernesto de Curtis / Claude Aveling / Doc Pomus / Mort Shuman**
Date reached No.1: **1 June 1961**
Weeks at No.1: **4**

THE ITALIAN BALLAD, 'TORNA A Sorrento', written in 1911, has been sung by famous tenors from Enrico Caruso to Luciano Pavarotti. In 1947 it was given an English lyric, 'Come Back To Sorrento', which has been recorded by many artists including Gracie Fields, Josef Locke and Dean Martin.

Elvis was so pleased with his performance on 'O Sole Mio' ('It's Now Or Never') that he asked his publisher, Freddy Bienstock, to commission a new lyric for 'Torna A Sorrento'. Mort Shuman was not impressed and, contradicting the credits, told his songwriting partner, Doc Pomus, "Why should I want to write for some redneck idiot who has so far forgotten his roots that he thinks it's a good career move to sound like Mario Lanza? You write it, Doc, you've already got the music." And the title too, as Doc immediately saw that 'Sorrento' could become 'Surrender'.

Although Elvis's record is only 90 seconds long, he does hit a high B flat, far higher than anything he'd done before. The record also soared up the charts, rising from number 27 to number one – at the time it was the biggest leap in chart history, but it has since been beaten by Captain Sensible and DJ Otzi. Yorkshire's TV diva, Lesley Garrett, put Doc's words into an operatic setting in 2001 and they sound fine.

Mort's right: Elvis Presley is the man who wanted to be Mario Lanza. They were both on RCA, they both ate too much, they both recorded operatic arias, and they both took drugs excessively and died at an early age. They were The Super Mario Brothers.

120 Del Shannon
Runaway

Label & Cat No.: **London HLX 9317**

Producers: **Harry Balk / Irving Micahnik**

Writers: **Del Shannon / Max Crook**

Date reached No.1: **29 June 1961**

Weeks at No.1: **3**

BATTLE CREEK, MICHIGAN IS affectionately known as the Cereal City USA as Kellogg's has its headquarters there. In 1959 the workers would unwind at the Hi-Lo club and listen to 25-year-old Charles Westover fronting the resident band. "There was a guy in the club who wanted to be a wrestler called Mark Shannon," he recalled, "and I thought Shannon was a great name and borrowed it. Mark Shannon wasn't right though as it sounded like a detective. I was selling carpets by day and the guy who owned the store had a Cadillac DeVille, which was beautiful and so I became Del Shannon."

Max Crook auditioned for Del's band with his electronic keyboard, the Musitron. It was a prototype synthesiser and could copy violins and other instruments. As soon as he heard it, Del said, "Man, you're hired." A music publisher, Ollie McLaughlin, was impressed with the group and asked Del and Max for original songs. Max wrote the instrumental, 'Mr. Lonely', the B-side of Johnny & The Hurricanes' 1961 hit, 'Ja-Da'.

Del Shannon recalled, "We were on stage and Max hit an A minor and a G and I said, 'Max, play that again, it's a great change.'" The drummer, Dick Parker, followed them and after 15 minutes, the manager of the club shouted, "Knock it off, play something else." The next day, in-between serving customers in the carpet store, Del Shannon wrote some lyrics. "That night I went back to the club", said Del, "And I told Max to play an instrumental on his Musitron for the middle part, and when he played that solo, we had 'Runaway'."

A modest man, Del never claimed he was doing anything original with his vocal, saying that it borrowed from The Ink Spots' 'We Three', Jimmy Jones' 'Handy Man', Bobby Darin's 'Dream Lover' and Dion & The Belmonts' 'I Wonder Why'.

In January 1961 Del and Max and their wives, Shirley and Joann, went to New York and the two men recorded with session musicians. The record company, Big Top, was to speed up 'Runaway' causing Del to remark, 'That doesn't sound like me.' 'But nobody knows what you sound like, Del' said the record executive. While they were recording, Shirley and Joann joined the audience of a TV show and Joann ended up as a winning contestant on *Beat The Clock*. Almost nine months to the day, Shirley gave birth to their daughter, whom they named Jody, after the B-side of 'Runaway' and itself named after a girl who went to the Hi-Lo.

The UK release supposedly featured the same titles, but by mistake an instrumental by Maximillian (that is, Max Crook) called 'The Snake' was put on the B-side. The record was amended and Maximillian was given a separate release, but the faulty singles are collectors' items.

Del Shannon's 'Runaway' was a great recording debut and led to a succession of excellent records – 'Hats Off To Larry', 'The Swiss Maid' and 'Little Town Flirt'. Max's Musitron can be heard at its note-bending best on 'Don't Gild The Lily, Lily', the B-side of 'Hats Off To Larry'. With his cover of 'From Me To You', Del was the first person to take a Lennon and McCartney song into the US Hot 100. However, he denied that his 1965 hit, 'Keep Searchin' (We'll Follow The Sun)', owed something to Merseybeat. "No, that song is the same as 'Runaway'. I strum hard, double." Bonnie Raitt revived 'Runaway' in 1977 and, in 1986, Del Shannon remade it for the soundtrack of the TV series, *Crime Story*.

Anyone who has toured with Del Shannon knows he was full of obsessions – one day he was attacking sugar and the next day scooping down ice-cream – and he went from one fad to another. His songs reflect his paranoia. He took his own life in 1990.

121 The Everly Brothers
Temptation

Label & Cat No.: **Warner Brothers WB 42**

Producer: **Wesley Rose**

Writers: **Nacio Herb Brown / Arthur Freed**

Date reached No.1: **20 July 1961**

Weeks at No.1: **2**

NACIO HERB BROWN ISN'T A NAME ON everyone's lips but he wrote numerous standards for Hollywood musicals, often produced by one of his songwriting partners, Arthur Freed. His many hit songs include 'Singin' In The Rain', 'You Were Meant For Me' and 'Make 'Em Laugh'. In 1933 he and Freed wrote 'Temptation' for Bing Crosby to sing in *Going Hollywood*. Perry Como revived the song with immense success in 1945 and Jo Stafford recalled a million-selling parody, 'Tim-tay-shun', as Cinderella G. Stump two years later.

Don Everly loved the song and saw a way to give it a beat treatment. He took it to their producer, Wesley Rose, who hated the concept, in truth because the song was not published by Acuff-Rose. The Everly Brothers felt that he had sabotaged their arrangement and so they insisted on doing it again without him. This new version was released as a single, much against Wesley Rose's wishes. The single caused a split with Rose, and the Everlys were prevented from recording new songs by their regular writers, Boudleaux & Felice Bryant.

Don's drug addiction did not help the situation but the Everlys staggered through the Sixties, making many fine albums, notably *Roots* (1968), and recording some classic singles – 'Crying In The Rain' (1962), 'The Ferris Wheel' (1964), 'The Price Of Love' (1965) and 'Love Is Strange' (1965). The friction between the two

Del Shannon: the solo in his hit 'Runaway', played on a prototype called the Musitron, was years ahead of its time, and continues to amaze four decades later

brothers led to a humiliating, public break-up in 1973, but, after varying success as solo performers, they returned as a duo at the Royal Albert Hall 10 years later. In 2003 they toured American arenas as the special guests of Simon & Garfunkel, a duo they had strongly influenced.

122 Eden Kane
Well I Ask You

Label & Cat No.: **Decca F 11353**

Producer: **Bunny Lewis**

Writer: **Les Vandyke (Johnny Worth)**

Date reached No.1: **3 August 1961**

Weeks at No.1: **1**

RICHARD SARSTEDT WAS BORN IN Delhi in 1942 and came to the UK after the death of his father when he was 12. In 1960 he won a talent contest at a cinema in Chelsea and found himself promoting a Cadbury's drink with his single, 'Hot Chocolate Crazy'. He was named as both a nod to Adam Faith and the film, *Citizen Kane*, and he was groomed for pop stardom with a song from Faith's songwriter, Johnny Worth, 'Well I Ask You'.

Johnny Worth was impressed: "Eden Kane was one of the legion of Elvis Presley imitators but he had more appeal than most of them. He was a striking-looking chap and he looked like The White Tide Man. He'd wear a white suit and he would fling his arms about in dramatic gestures. The growl was developed in the same way as Adam Faith's 'bay-beh' and that became his trademark."

Eden Kane recalls, "Johnny Worth played 'Well I Ask You' to my managers and myself. I wasn't crazy about it at the time but my managers recognised its potential and I took their advice. When we got to the studio, the whole thing took on a very different feel and I'm very glad we did it. 'Get Lost' was the inevitable follow-up. We had a winning formula and we stuck with it. That growl was part-accident and part-deliberate. It was a mixture of laryngitis and bronchitis."

Adding to the gimmicks, Kane was known as the man with the hully gully beat. He changed his style for his romantic revival of 'I Don't Know Why', and its narration was the highlight of his stage act.

In 1964 Kane was astute enough to team himself with a Liverpool band, the TTs, and he returned to the Top 10 with 'Boys Cry'. In 1969 his brother, Peter, hit the top with 'Where Do You Go To, My Lovely?' and in 1976, brother Clive, now known as Robin, had a Top 10 hit with 'My Resistance Is Low'. All three brothers made the album *Worlds Apart Together* (1973) and in recent years, they have worked together on stage in different combinations.

123 Helen Shapiro
You Don't Know

Label & Cat No.: **Columbia DB 4670**

Producer: **Norrie Paramor**

Writers: **John Schroeder / Mike Hawker**

Date reached No.1: **10 August 1961**

Weeks at No.1: **3**

NORRIE PARAMOR'S ASSISTANT, JOHN Schroeder, went to audition the pupils at Maurice Berman's singing academy in London and was impressed by 14-year-old Helen Shapiro. When Schroeder played him a tape, Paramor was astonished by her deep voice and was sure he was listening to a male singer. Her first hit single was 'Don't Treat Me Like A Child', and John Schroeder remembers, "I thought the most important thing about a song is its title. Fourteen-year-olds didn't like being treated as children and that gave me 'Don't Treat Me Like A Child'. It was the first song I'd written and it was very successful. Writing the follow-up was harder as I wanted something that was different and luckily, I came up with 'You Don't Know', which was my first number one."

Like Norrie Paramor, the media was fascinated by Helen's deep voice, but she says, "That never bothered me. Ever since I was a kid, I was called 'Foghorn'. I was used to it. The main thing is whether you've got talent and actually, it's handy to have something distinctive. Whether they like it or not, people recognise my voice."

Being more interested in jazz, Helen has stopped singing her golden oldies but she reflects, "'You Don't Know' is a song that could stand reviving. It has a very strong melody line. A lot of the other stuff I did was just good pop music of its day."

124 John Leyton
Johnny Remember Me

Label & Cat No.: **Top Rank JAR 577**

Producer: **Joe Meek**

Writer: **Geoff Goddard**

Date reached No.1: **31 August 1961**

Weeks at No.1: **3 (two runs)**

JOHN LEYTON, WHO WAS BORN IN Frinton-on-Sea in 1939, went to drama school and achieved recognition when he played Ginger in the Granada TV series, *Biggles*. In 1961 when he was offered the role of Johnny St. Cyr, a pop singer opening a record department, in the ATV series, *Harper's West One*, his record producer, Joe Meek, asked Geoff Goddard for a song. Goddard, who had been trained at the Royal Academy, recalled, "It came to me off the top of my head in ten minutes. 'Johnny Remember Me' created an image for John Leyton, that of a young man who'd lost his true love and was going down the road of life on his own, looking for another girl to fall in love with." It was originally intended as a death disc but Goddard amended the lyric from "The girl I loved who died a year ago" to "The girl I loved and lost a year ago."

It was a wonderfully atmospheric recording, made above a leather goods shop on the Holloway Road in North London. Producer Joe Meek, who brought in session singer Lissa Gray to sing the high ghostly voice, somehow achieved a sound quite unlike most other British records of the time. John Leyton remembers the session, "Anything at EMI would be squeaky-clean, even the engineers wore white coats. Joe Meek was the first independent producer and when I recorded 'Johnny Remember Me', the string section was up the stairs, the backing vocalists were in the bathroom, I was in the sitting room and Joe was in the kitchen. It was a great song, very well-written and Geoff Goddard deserves as much credit as Joe Meek. 'Johnny Remember Me' was voted a Miss on *Juke Box Jury* and I was a surprise guest. David Jacobs, to his credit, said the panel was wrong."

125 Shirley Bassey with Geoff Love & His Orchestra
Reach For The Stars / Climb Ev'ry Mountain

Label & Cat No.: **Columbia DB 4685**
Producer: **Norman Newell**
Writers: **Udo Jürgens / David West (Norman Newell); Richard Rodgers / Oscar Hammerstein II**
Date reached No.1: **21 September 1961**
Weeks at No.1: **1**

SHIRLEY BASSEY'S RECORD PRODUCER, Norman Newell, was always looking out for European hits that he could adapt for the UK market. He heard a song written by the Austrian singer and songwriter, Udo Jürgens, 'Woher Ich Auch Komm, Wohin Ich Auch Geh (Wherever I Come From, Wherever I Go)', and a few months later, it became 'Reach For The Stars' and was recorded by Shirley Bassey. Strangely, Jurgens never recorded the German lyric himself but he did sing 'Reach For The Stars' as late as 1966. Another song of Jürgens, 'Warum Nur Warum' became, with Don Black's lyric, 'Walk Away' for Matt Monro.

For this double A-side, Shirley had the good sense to cover Mother Abbess' ballad from *The Sound Of Music*, 'Climb Ev'ry Mountain', the equivalent of 'You'll Never Walk Alone' from *Carousel*. The song showcases Shirley Bassey's considerable range as this is almost an operatic aria. Richard Rodgers wrote in his autobiography, *Musical Stages*, "Given my lack of familiarity with liturgical music as well as the fact that I was of a different faith, I had to make sure that what I wrote would sound as authentic as possible. For the first time in my life, I did a little research."

In view of her success with this inspirational double-sider, Shirley Bassey recorded 'Ave Maria' as a single in 1962. Dame Shirley has made several hit records since -'What Now My Love?', 'I (Who Have Nothing)', 'Something' and 'For All We Know' among them – but some of her best-known records were not big hits – 'Goldfinger' (21), 'Big Spender' (21) and 'Diamonds Are Forever' (38). Her version of 'I Am What I Am', the gay anthem from *La Cage Aux Folles*, was not even in the charts and yet it is a staple of her stage act. See Shirley in concert and, despite being a grandmother, she still strips to 'Big Spender'.

In 2003 when the BBC's high profile poll of the 100 Greatest Britons did not include a single black person, a black history website conducted its own poll. The results, announced in February 2004, included Dame Shirley Bassey in the Top 10.

126 The Shadows
Kon-Tiki

Label & Cat No.: **Columbia DB 4698**
Producer: **Norrie Paramor**
Writer: **Michael Carr**
Date reached No.1: **5 October 1961**
Weeks at No.1: **1**

THE NORWEGIAN SCIENTIST AND explorer, Thor Heyerdahl, wanted to establish that ancient civilisations could have crossed the oceans. In 1947 he sailed with five companions on a large raft from South America to Polynesia. He called the raft, Kon-Tiki, after one of the gods of the Incas. They travelled 5,000 miles and reached their destination, thereby demonstrating that the Polynesians may have originated in South America. (But would the South Americans have set out not knowing what was out there?) Heyerdahl's book, *Kon-Tiki*, was a best seller and it appealed to the veteran UK songwriter, Michael Carr, who had been a film stuntman, seaman and general adventurer. He celebrated Heyerdahl's achievement with an instrumental which captured his pioneering spirit.

Carr had already penned the follow-up to the Shadows' 'Apache', 'Man Of Mystery', which was also the theme music for the short films made around Edgar Wallace's crime stories. 'Kon-Tiki' was the last of the Shadows' records to feature Tony Meehan. His poor timekeeping was annoying them and when he turned up an hour later for a gig in Leeds, they kicked him out by saying, "Heck, if Thor Heyerdahl can get to Tahiti on time, you can make it to Leeds." His replacement was Brian Bennett from Marty Wilde's Wildcats. Because Hank, Bruce and Jet didn't know how long he was going to be around, he was a Shadow in name only, being paid a weekly salary.

The Kon-Tiki raft survived the voyage and has been preserved in a museum in Oslo.

127 The Highwaymen
Michael

Label & Cat No.: **HMV POP 910**
Producer: **Dave Fisher**
Writer: **Traditional arranged by Dave Fisher**
Date reached No.1: **12 October 1961**
Weeks at No.1: **1**

PROMPTED BY THE SUCCESS OF THE Kingston Trio, clean-cut college kids in

Cliff Sings
SPIN WITH THE
RCA
Capitol
BLUES BY BASSEY
Music For Every Mood
RCA

America formed vocal groups with acoustic instruments and started performing on campuses. The Highwaymen, five students from the Wesleyan University at Middletown, Connecticut, did just that and proved so popular that they were encouraged to seek a recording contract in New York.

In the 19th century, some slaves living off the coast of Georgia had to cross the river to reach the plantation and they would sing "Michael row the boat ashore" every morning. The Highwaymen's lead tenor and banjo player, Dave Fisher, gave the spiritual a sweet and gentle setting. Bob Burnett, the second tenor and percussionist, was the university's pole vault champion. Steve Trott, president of the student's union, was a third tenor. Steve Butts, who commented on sports on the campus radio station, played guitar and sang bass. Their baritone singer, Chan Daniels, played a charango, made from the shell of an armadillo.

The UK songwriter, Tony Hiller, formed a vocal group to cover 'Michael', and recorded it for Pye, but the record was never released as Lonnie Donegan had decided to record it himself. He upped the tempo, changed the arrangement and called it 'Michael Row The Boat' – that's so he could place it with his own publishing company. Lonnie was acting as a highwayman, stealing their song, but the real Highwaymen overtook him and went to the top.

The Highwaymen had a second US hit with another slave song from the previous century, 'Cottonfields'. Although they had a versatile stage act, being able to sing in French, Spanish and Hebrew, they disbanded upon graduation. Bob Burnett and Steve Trott, the first to go, were replaced for a short time by Gil Robbins, whose son, Tim, became a Hollywood star.

The Highwaymen did have a brief reunion in the late Seventies and they threatened to sue the country stars, Johnny Cash, Kris Kristofferson, Waylon Jennings and Willie Nelson, when they also used the name The Highwaymen. Willie Nelson resolved the matter by offering the original Highwaymen an opening spot on one of his concerts. The 2004 film, *A Mighty Wind*, affectionately parodies campus groups like The Highwaymen.

128 Helen Shapiro
Walkin' Back To Happiness

Label & Cat No.: **Columbia DB 4715**

Producer: **Norrie Paramor**

Writers: **John Schroeder / Mike Hawker**

Date reached No.1: **19 October 1961**

Weeks at No.1: **3**

THE POP PAPER, *DISC*, DESCRIBED 'Walkin' Back To Happiness' as a "cute bouncy ballad with thumpy backing of rhythm and girl group directed by Norrie Paramor. This one should please her fans all right." But not Helen Shapiro herself: "I was brought up on blues and jazz and I thought 'Walkin' Back To Happiness' was corny – all that 'woop-bah-oh-yea-yeah'. I still don't like the song but everyone goes mad for it so I've been proved wrong. That kind of rhythm was not my scene and I didn't really want to do it. I preferred the B-side, 'Kiss And Run', which was written by Norrie and was more gutsy."

The single was promoted by a 15-minute *Look At Life* cinema feature which showed Helen making the record, but although it went to number one, Helen's records never took off in America: "I blame Capitol for that. They released 'You Don't Know' and then they immediately released 'Walkin' Back To Happiness'. By the time The Beatles had opened the way for British artists, I'd stopped having hits."

Helen Shapiro was rarely comfortable as a pop singer and she recorded a hit EP, *A Teenager Sings The Blues*, in 1962. Following an appearance at a Duke Ellington tribute concert in 1984, she started making concert appearances and records with Humphrey Lyttelton and his Band. Humph comments, "I always thought her voice was marvellous. It is a unique voice, especially when it was coming out of a 14-year-old. We didn't care much for the songs, but we all knew the voice was tremendous."

129 Elvis Presley
(Marie's The Name) His Latest Flame / Little Sister

Label & Cat No.: **RCA 1258**

Producer: **Steve Sholes**

Writers (both sides): **Doc Pomus /Mort Shuman**

Date reached No.1: **9 November 1961**

Weeks at No.1: **4**

THE RECORD PRODUCER SNUFF Garrett invited Doc Pomus & Mort Shuman to Los Angeles to write for an album Bobby Vee was making with The Crickets and also for some other Liberty acts. They proffered 'Little Sister' and '(Marie's The Name) Her Latest Flame', but they were a little late and so they passed the songs to Elvis. As a result, Doc & Mort wrote both sides of the grittiest single Elvis had made since leaving the army.

Mort's voice and guitar demo for 'Little Sister' shows the song to be a furious rocker, but Presley wisely slowed down the tempo. Elvis may not have appreciated its worth as he only performed the song in concert as part of a medley with The Beatles' 'Get Back'. LaVern Baker's 'Hey, Memphis' is a very sassy female version of the song, which was produced by Phil Spector.

The *Rolling Stone* writer, Dave Marsh, has commented that 'Little Sister' with its Scotty Moore lead guitar sounds like a forerunner to The Who. It could easily have been a Who record. Robert Plant performed 'Little Sister' on *The Concert For Kampuchea* at Hammersmith Odeon, while Ry Cooder's 1979 reworking with an insidious rhythm and upfront backing vocals is on par with the original.

Lots of songs have been written around the 'shave and a haircut, two bits' rhythm – 'Not Fade Away', 'Willie And The Hand Jive', '(Marie's The Name) His Latest Flame' and half of Bo Diddley's repertoire. When Doc and Mort wrote '(Marie's The Name) His Latest Flame', they also gave the song to Del Shannon, but he jettisoned this potential single in favour of his own song, 'Hats Off To Larry'.

Helen Shapiro: happiness in 1961 was a pile of 45s, an auto-change record player and the house to yourself

Mort Shuman's demo had an unusual organ effect in the middle and Elvis rang Doc to ask about it. Doc gave him the answer but it wasn't until later that he realised he had been talking to Elvis himself, the only time he spoke to him. As Mort remarked, "It's said that Elvis was very generous and gave Cadillacs to his friends, but I wrote several of his hits and he never sent me a Christmas card."

130 Frankie Vaughan
Tower Of Strength

Label & Cat No.: **Philips PB 1195**

Producer: **Johnny Franz**

Writers: **Burt Bacharach / Bob Hilliard**

Date reached No.1: **7 December 1961**

Weeks at No.1: **3**

"I WAS NEVER JUST LOOKING FOR SONGS TO record," said Frankie Vaughan, "I wanted songs that I could do in my act, songs that I could give a performance to, and 'Tower Of Strength' was right up my street. It's a great arrangement by Wally Stott and the percussion was played by the jazz drummer, Phil Seaman, and you can't get better than that."

The song, originally recorded by Gene McDaniels, became the third UK number one for the composer Burt Bacharach, although he had yet to develop his trademark sound. Although the record made the US Top 10, Bacharach felt that the arrangement was too hurried and, in his anger, he wrote a bluesy reply, '(You Don't Have To Be A) Tower Of Strength', which was recorded by Gloria Lynne. On the other hand, 'Tower Of Strength', taken at its explosive full throttle was perfect for Frankie Vaughan with his stylised kicks. He promoted fitness and his illustrated feature for the 1962 Radio Luxembourg book of stars is called *How To Be A Tower Of Strength And Stay Fit.*

Frankie did much for charity, both for the National Association Of Boys' Clubs – remember those charity singles with harmonies from The Kaye Sisters? – and then the show business organisation, The Grand Order Of Water Rats. He was King Rat in both 1967 and 1998, and, in 1993, he was appointed the Deputy Lord Lieutenant of Buckinghamshire. Frankie was awarded a CBE for his public-spiritedness and he is one of the few showbiz stars untainted by scandal: in 1960, he even declined the opportunity of an affair with Marilyn Monroe while making *Let's Make Love*! He married Stella Shock in 1951 and they remained together until his death in 1999. He said, "She accepted my proposal, so how lucky can you get? I also believe that you must put something into life. If you've got health and strength, you must do something to help others."

131 Danny Williams
Moon River

Label & Cat No.: **HMV POP 932**

Producer: **Norman Newell**

Writers: **Henry Mancini / Johnny Mercer**

Date reached No.1: **28 December 1961**

Weeks at No.1: **2**

ONE OF THE KEY FILMS OF 1961 WAS *Breakfast At Tiffany's*, which was about an eccentric girl from the American south who is looking for a wealthy husband in New York. Henry Mancini was asked to write a song for Holly Golightly (Audrey Hepburn) in a balcony scene, knowing that her vocal range was limited. He gave the melody to the veteran lyricist, Johnny Mercer, and fortunately, they ditched his first effort, 'I'm Holly'.

Johnny Mercer tried again and this time wrote 'Blue River', but when he found a songwriting colleague had already used that title, he wanted to change it. He suggested 'June River' but Henry Mancini said it was too summery for the melancholy tune. With Georgia on his mind, Johnny Mercer remembered Moon River, reasonably close to his hometown of Savannah. The new lyric was as much about Johnny Mercer wanting to leave Savannah for New York as Holly Golightly's plight. When his cousin, Walter Rivers, heard the song, he told Johnny that the 'huckleberry friend' line made him recall playing along the river bank. Johnny Mercer said, "It should do because you're the huckleberry friend."

Enter Danny Williams, a South African who had modelled himself on Nat 'King' Cole. He recalls, "My first singles were rubbishy-type things, but they were stepping-stones to the actual event. My name was getting known and then the song, 'Moon River', arrived. The songwriters came over for the première and the British publishers of 'Moon River' told them that I would be perfect for the song. At first, I turned it down because I couldn't understand the phrase, 'My huckleberry friend'. It didn't mean a thing to me. Then I saw the film and realised that the theme was running through the film."

Danny Williams' version of 'Moon River' was the UK Christmas number one, but the Oscar-winning song was a US hit single for Henry Mancini himself and the soul singer Jerry Butler. However, 'Moon River' is most often associated with Andy Williams, who used it as the theme music for his TV variety show. Andy owns his own Moon River Theater in Branson, Missouri.

Danny Williams, unexpectedly, made the US Top 10 in 1964 with 'White On White'. He tours on oldies packages and also presents a tribute show to Nat 'King' Cole.

In 1962 Johnny Mercer, who by then was an alcoholic, poured his feelings into the title song for *Days Of Wine And Roses*, another Oscar-winning song for him and Henry Mancini.

Frankie Vaughan

132 Cliff Richard & The Shadows
The Young Ones

Label & Cat No.: **Columbia DB 4761**	
Producer: **Norrie Paramor**	
Writers: **Sid Tepper / Roy C. Bennett**	
Date reached No.1: **11 January 1962**	
Weeks at No.1: **6**	

BRITISH POP FILMS BEFORE *A HARD Day's Night* tend to be dismissed, but *The Young Ones* compares favourably to its American rivals. It has the standard plot (a property tycoon wants to tear down a youth club and he ends up rock'n'rolling), but it is performed with panache, largely because the director, Sidney Furie, had the good sense to surround Cliff with excellent character actors, notably Robert Morley but also Melvyn Hayes, Richard O'Sullivan and Grazina Frame, who, incidentally, married the songwriter Mitch Murray.

The film had an excellent score, conducted by Stanley Black. The first single from the film was the ballad, 'When The Girl In Your Arms Is The Girl In Your Heart' (3), backed with 'Got A Funny Feeling'. Then The Shadows released 'The Savage' (10) and 'Peace Pipe'. Cliff took the title song to the top, backed by the film's closing rocker, 'We Say Yeah'. The pop duo, The Allisons, realised that Cliff wasn't doing anything with 'Lessons In Love' and that became a Top 30 single for them. The soundtrack topped the UK album charts for six weeks.

With its variety of styles (including a lengthy let's-put-on-a-show sequence), it is evident that Sidney Furie was wanting to make an MGM-styled Hollywood musical. However, *The Young Ones* was not deemed a commercial title for the US and the film was given a new title and a new song, *It's Wonderful To Be Young*, written by Burt Bacharach and Hal David. They need not have bothered as the film did little business there.

The song, 'The Young Ones' is a plea for tolerance as Cliff realises that they may not be the young ones very long. Cliff performs it to this day and his most famous performance was during a rain-sodden Wimbledon in 1996, released, some months later, on the B-side of his single, 'Be With Me Always'.

133 Elvis Presley with The Jordanaires
Rock-A-Hula Baby (Twist Special) / Can't Help Falling In Love

Label & Cat No.: **RCA 1270**	
Producer: **Steve Sholes**	
Writers (Rock-A-Hula Baby): **Fred Wise / Ben Weisman / Dolores Fuller**	
Writers (Can't Help Falling In Love): **George David Weiss / Hugo Peretti / Luigi Creatore**	
Date reached No.1: **22 February 1962**	
Weeks at No.1: **4**	

BLUE HAWAII MARKS THE END OF ELVIS' golden period and the start of his decline. It contained both the magical 'Can't Help Falling In Love' and the dire 'Rock-A-Hula Baby (Twist Special)', and its huge success led to a succession of cheapo-cheapo beach party movies with identical plots. Well, when we say 'cheapo-cheapo', Elvis didn't come cheap but everything else did. As Patrick Humphries has written, "You only ever got one crack at growing up, but you knew that the soundtrack to your adolescence deserved to be better than *Blue Hawaii*."

Elvis sounds bored on 'Rock-A-Hula Baby' which was designed to show Elvis could twist during a party scene. Forget it – Elvis did, he never sang it again.

After giving an old lady a music box for her birthday, Elvis sings 'Can't Help Falling In Love'. Its melody was taken from the French tune, 'Plasir D'Amour', which was written around 1800. It has been recorded in its original form by Mary Hopkin and Joan Baez, but is now better known as 'Can't Help Falling In Love'. Andy Williams upped the tempo in 1970 and took the song to number three, followed by a soul treatment from The Stylistics, produced by its writers Hugo and Luigi, at number four in 1976. Elvis loved the song but followed Andy Williams's arrangement. He closed every concert with 'Can't Help Falling In Love' and didn't do encores. Instead, somebody intoned that Elvis had left the building, which meant he could move pretty fast when he wanted to.

134 The Shadows
Wonderful Land

Label & Cat No.: **Columbia DB 4790**	
Producer: **Norrie Paramor**	
Writer: **Jerry Lordan**	
Date reached No.1: **22 March 1962**	
Weeks at No.1: **8**	

LIKE 'APACHE', THE SHADOWS' 'WONderful Land' was written by Jerry Lordan. He recalled, "I got the first phrase and it took me six months to get to the middle. I knew it had to have a second part and I couldn't think of anything. The Shadows did it marvellously and Norrie Paramor added strings very sympathetically. I thought it was fantastic but it didn't get a unanimous vote on *Juke Box Jury*."

Bruce Welch adds, "Norrie Paramor was a great help to us, a father-figure if you like, an older man but a trained musician. Jerry Lordan had given us 'Wonderful Land' and we recorded it knowing that there was something missing. What we'd done wasn't enough. We had it in the can for nine months and while we were on tour, Norrie added French horns, strings and a little vocal bit. Then it was a classic record and we were so excited about it. It was the first time that a rock group had used an orchestra and it was number one for weeks." What's more, the only instrumental to be on top for a longer spell was Eddie Calvert's 'Oh Mein Papa', which had also been produced by Norrie Paramor.

Jerry Lordan revealed that the title was not his: "I'm pretty feeble with titles and I could not think of a title for that instrumental. Hank called it 'Wonderful Land' and I don't like it. I wish I could have come up with something better." 'Wonderful Land' was a reference to America.

Should you want to hear 'Wonderful Land' without embellishments, a 'naked' version was issued on CD, *The Shadows At Abbey Road*, in 1997. Even without the strings, it sounds like a number one. In 2004 the reformed Shadows recorded an instrumental tribute to Jerry Lordan, 'Life Story'.

135 B. Bumble & The Stingers Nut Rocker

Label & Cat No.: **Top Rank JAR 611**

Producer: **Rod Pierce**

Writers: **Pyotr Ilyich Tchaikovsky / Kim Fowley**

Date reached No.1: **17 May 1962**

Weeks at No.1: **1**

In 1891 St. Petersburg Opera asked Tchaikovksy to write the music to a German story, *The Nutcracker*, that they wanted to perform as a ballet. At first he was unhappy with the setting of a Christmas party for children, but the choreographer persuaded him by giving exact specifications of the rhythms and tempos needed for each dance. *The Nutcracker* opened in December 1892 and was very popular, although Tchaikovsky died within a year from drinking contaminated water. *The Nutcracker* was not performed outside Russia until 1934, when it was staged in London.

Early in 1961 a pianist, James Wisner, became Kokomo and took his rock'n'roll version of a section of Grieg's *Piano Concerto*, now called 'Asia Minor', into the US Top 10 and UK Top 40. Thinking this a good idea, the Los Angeles label, Rendezvous, asked four session musicians to rock up Rimsky-Korsakov's *The Flight Of The Bumble Bee* and, called *Bumble Boogie*, it was the first US hit for B. Bumble & The Stingers. Also in LA, one of rock's mavericks, Kim Fowley, had the idea of updating the main theme from *The Nutcracker*. Five-hundred copies of his production by Jack B. Nimble & The Quicks on Del Rio were pressed, but the label's owner in a tantrum smashed most of them. Fowley took his concept to Rendezvous, who duplicated the arrangement and released it by B. Bumble & The Stingers. Fowley persuaded them that changing the title to 'Rickshaw Run' was not a good idea.

B. Bumble's piano was played by Al Hazan, who became a psychologist in Beverly Hills, but he was not interested in touring. A group assembled around the roly poly pianist, R.C. Gamble, stung the public on a UK tour, with Gamble claiming that his name was William Bumble. They were the first rock act to appear at Croydon's Fairfield Hall and the vocals were taken by Jimmy King, who himself was the rockabilly singer, Lou Josie. The Stingers never admitted that they had nothing to do with the record and music journalists in the Sixties were more believing.

B. Bumble & The Stingers' other singles included 'Dawn Cracker', 'Apple Knocker' and 'Baby Mash'. In 1972 Emerson, Lake & Palmer performed 'Nut Rocker' as a party piece on tour: they issued it as a single in the US, but it was B. Bumble & The Stingers who returned to the Top 20.

136 Elvis Presley with The Jordanaires Good Luck Charm

Label & Cat No.: **RCA 1280**

Producer: **Steve Sholes**

Writers: **Aaron Schroeder / Wally Gold**

Date reached No.1: **24 May 1962**

Weeks at No.1: **5**

Nothing really wrong with 'Good Luck Charm' except that Elvis was treading ground with the song in the same familiar territory as 'All Shook Up' and 'Stuck On You'. It was a Brill Building composition by a top writer (Wally Gold) and a publisher (Aaron Schroeder), the musicians (including Scotty Moore, Floyd Cramer and Boots Randolph) were first class and Elvis' performance, assisted by a strong harmony vocal from Gordon Stoker of The Jordanaires, was spot on. Somehow though, the excitement was missing. Perhaps that's why Merseybeat was only just around the corner. Time has shown that the B-side, an exquisite Don Robertson ballad, 'Anything That's Part Of You', was the stronger side.

'Good Luck Charm' was not taken from a film and something was wrong as a single wasn't released from Elvis's current film, *Follow That Dream*. An EP called *Follow That Dream* did make the Top 40 and did top the EP charts for 20 weeks, not that there was much competition, but, once again, the songs were just not strong enough. One of them, 'I'm Not The Marrying Kind', fuelled the rumour that Elvis Presley was gay. How wrong could the public be...

137 Mike Sarne featuring Wendy Richard
Come Outside

Label & Cat No.: **Parlophone R 4902**
Producer: **Charles Blackwell**
Writer: **Charles Blackwell**
Date reached No.1: **28 June 1962**
Weeks at No.1: **2**

MIKE SARNE, WHOSE FATHER HAD revealed that The Piltdown Man was a fraud, was a bit part actor (*The Guns Of Navarone*), who could sing a bit. He suggested a wry song about teenage romance to Charles Blackwood and 'Come Outside' was written. The song, written by Joe Meek's arranger Charles Blackwell, included some repartee ('You don't 'arf need a shave', 'Lay off!') with Wendy Richard. "She was a model in those days," says Mike Sarne, "absolutely beautiful with a great figure, and a really typical cockney." Wendy Richard was later to find fame in *Are You Being Served?* and *EastEnders*.

Sarne followed it with the carbon copy, 'Will I What?' this time with Billie Davis, who had a Top 10 hit with 'Tell Him' in 1963. His third single, 'Just For Kicks', was banned by the BBC for encouraging reckless driving. "I don't think people understood that these records were satire, but there you go. I rather resented being a gimmicky singer with a cockney accent and I tried to change it, but with no success."

The advent of The Beatles and The Rolling Stones made life difficult for the existing stars. Mike Sarne: "We used to dress in shiny suits and we wore stage makeup like actors. I was on tour with The Rolling Stones and Brian Jones thought you should wear what you wore in the street. He thought we were ponces and what we were doing was against his rhythm and blues ethic. I felt like a real phony – and The Rolling Stones had 4,000 screaming girls in the audience to make their point."

Don't feel sorry for Mike Sarne: he had a short, torrid affair with Brigitte Bardot when they made the film, *A Coeur Joie (Two Weeks In September)* in 1966. He has had an erratic career as a film director, making one of the cinema's greatest turkeys, *Myra Breckinridge* (1970) with Mae West and Raquel Welch. "Actually," says Mike, "there was a really good review in *The Times*. I suppose the critic lost his job."

In 1986 Mike Berry and Wendy Richard, both from the cast of *Are You Being Served?*, updated 'Come Outside' with references to medallion men. Mike Sarne has acted in *The Bill* and in recent years has been performing his hits again.

138 Ray Charles
I Can't Stop Loving You

Label & Cat No.: **HMV POP 1034**
Producer: **Sid Feller**
Writer: **Don Gibson**
Date reached No.1: **12 July 1962**
Weeks at No.1: **2**

RAY CHARLES BEGAN HIS CAREER AS A blues singer in 1949 and, on joining Atlantic Records in New York, in 1952, he fashioned a unique blend of rhythm and blues by merging the blues with the call and response of gospel music. He wrote and recorded 'What'd I Say' and 'I Got A Woman' and he toured with his band and The Raelets, so called because they let Ray have his way with them.

In his final months at Atlantic in 1959, he was experimenting with country music and he recorded Hank Snow's 'I'm Movin' On', while Solomon Burke thought along the same lines with 'Just Out Of Reach' (1961). Moving to ABC-Paramount and by now using the phrase, 'The Genius', in album titles, Ray recorded the comic 'Hit The Road, Jack' and an aching, poignant 'Georgia On My Mind'. Ray Charles wrote in his autobiography, *Brother Ray*, "Calling someone a genius is some heavy shit, and I'd never have used that word in regard to myself. I think I'm pretty good at what I do, but I've never considered myself a genius."

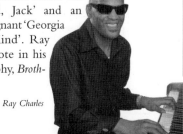

Ray Charles

In 1962 he made his best-selling album, *Modern Sounds In Country And Western Music*, in which he reworked many country favourites. He gave Don Gibson's 1958 US country hit, 'I Can't Stop Loving You', a soulful vocal and added a middle of the road choir and strings, but note the ingenious way he allows the chorus to lead the lyric.

Ray was annoyed when Tab Hunter released a note for note copy of 'I Can't Stop Loving You' as a single, even duplicating the cracks in his voice, and he insisted that his own version be issued immediately. Its worldwide success prompted further country songs, 'You Don't Know Me', 'Take These Chains From My Heart' and 'Cryin' Time' as well as a second volume of *Modern Sounds In Country And Western Music*.

Ray Charles' innovations were stifled by drug addiction, and the public had lost interest in his work by the mid-Sixties. He overcame his problems and continued as a world concert performer until his death in June 2004. He was part of the USA For Africa hit single.

139 Frank Ifield
I Remember You

Label & Cat No.: **Columbia DB 4856**
Producer: **Norrie Paramor**
Writers: **Johnny Mercer / Victor Schertzinger**
Date reached No.1: **26 July 1962**
Weeks at No.1: **7**

FRANK IFIELD, WHO WAS BORN OF Australian parents in Coventry, had been a child performer in Australia and toured with the wrestler, Big Chief Little Wolf, who told him, "If you're not prepared to make a fool of yourself, you should not be in this business." Frank, who did rope tricks and sang cowboy songs, eventually moved to pop and had several Australian hits, besides opening for Buddy Holly in 1958. He came to the UK when he was 21 in 1959 with a view to international success. He had minor hits with 'Lucky Devil' and 'Gotta Get A Date', but 'Alone Too Long' failed to secure the UK entry in the 1962 *Eurovision Song Contest*.

"My three year contract with EMI was just about up," says Frank, "and Norrie Paramor said that he would do the arrangement on the next record to see if we could get something. I came up with the idea of the Johnny Mercer song, 'I Remember You', which came out of a film, *The Fleet's In*, from 1942. He knew the song very well but he said, 'You've changed it beyond recognition. The chords are all different and you've added falsetto.' Rather reluctantly, he took my guitar and vocal down on a tape-recorder and did the arrangement. I recorded it a bit tongue-in-cheek, the harmonica is playing the first few bars of 'Waltzing Matilda'."

Frank says that the harmonica on 'I Remember You' was inspired by working with Bruce Channel and hearing Delbert McClinton's playing on his hit record, 'Hey! Baby'. If, in August 1962, you were lucky enough to see The Beatles in the Cavern, Paul McCartney would have been singing 'I Remember You' with John Lennon on harmonica. Frank's record, along with Bruce Channel's 'Hey! Baby', inspired their arrangement of 'Love Me Do'.

'I Remember You' was originally a hit for Jimmy Dorsey & His Orchestra and we would add that 1942 was a very good year for Johnny Mercer: not only was he writing hit songs, he also established Capitol Records, which became one of the world's leading labels.

The B-side, 'I Listen To My Heart', was Frank's own song and it became a Top 40 hit for the Swedish group, The Spotnicks as 'Just Listen To My Heart' in 1963.

The lyricist Johnny Mercer was having an affair with Judy Garland and when they decided to break it off, he for the sake of his family and she to avoid scandal, he wrote 'I Remember You': that is, "You're the one you made my dreams come true, A few kisses ago." Judy Garland recorded the song, although the hit versions were by Harry James and Jimmy Dorsey and their orchestras. Johnny Mercer's wife, Ginger, was furious, knowing she was being humiliated in front of those in the know. Judy Garland's name could not be mentioned in her presence.

When Johnny Mercer died in 1976, Ginger flew into a rage when the words, 'I remember you', were suggested for his tombstone. In 1982 she edited a collection of his lyrics, *Our Huckleberry Friend*, and refused to allow the inclusion of 'I Remember You'. The song, however, was to have the last word and when her life was through, someone, perhaps innocently, put 'I Remember You' on the cover of the programme for her memorial service. When the angels ask Johnny Mercer to recall the thrill of it all, we wonder who gets his vote.

140 Elvis Presley with The Jordanaires

She's Not You

Label & Cat No.: **RCA 1303**

Producer: **Steve Sholes**

Writers: **Doc Pomus / Jerry Leiber / Mike Stoller**

Date reached No.1: **13 September 1962**

Weeks at No.1: **3**

WITH DOC POMUS' PERMISSION, THE songwriters and producers, Jerry Leiber & Mike Stoller, altered one of his songs, 'Young Blood', and turned it into a 1957 US hit for The Coasters. In 1962 Doc's regular songwriting partner, Mort Shuman, wasn't around and he asked them to help out with a song for Elvis, 'She's Not You'. At the time, Jerry & Mike had been given the cold shoulder by Colonel Parker as they had recommended a film musical to Elvis, and Colonel Parker regarded it as interference.

Doc had a Fats Domino sound in mind for 'She's Not You', but Leiber & Stoller convinced him that it would work better as a beat-ballad with a shuffle rhythm. Not wanting to waste the opportunity, Leiber & Stoller also submitted an older song of theirs, 'Just Tell Her Jim Said Hello', which Elvis recorded as an easy-paced ballad for the B-side.

Curiously, 'Suspicion' was recorded at the same session and put on the *Pot Luck* LP. How come that nobody realised that this was the best of the bunch? Terry Stafford had a US Top 10 single with it in 1964 at a time when Elvis wasn't selling well. Still, if Elvis had released 'Suspicion', would he have accepted the similarly-titled and themed 'Suspicious Minds' in 1969? Perhaps it was for the best.

141 The Tornados

Telstar

Label & Cat No.: **Decca F 11494**

Producer: **Joe Meek**

Writer: **Joe Meek**

Date Reached No.1: **6 October 1962**

Weeks at No.1: **5**

BRITAIN'S FIRST TRULY INDEPENDENT record producer, Joe Meek began his career as an engineer and worked on a number of big hits, including 'Cumberland Gap' (Lonnie Donegan), 'The Green Door' (Frankie Vaughan) and 'What Do You Want To Make Those Eyes At Me For?' (Emile Ford). His first hit as a producer came with Humphrey Lyttelton's 'Bad Penny Blues' in 1956. He began to write songs and was delighted when Tommy Steele recorded his song, 'Put A Ring On Her Finger', as the B-side to 'Come On Let's Go'. Les Paul & Mary Ford had a minor US hit with it in 1958 as 'Put A Ring On My Finger'. Joe secured a job at jazz producer Denis Preston's Lansdowne Studios in West London working with various jazz bands. Within 18 months he moved to, and worked from, a homemade studio above a leather goods shop at 304 Holloway Road in North London. He named it RGM Music, taken from the initials of his real name, Robert George Meek.

At the beginning of 1961 he formed The Outlaws as his resident session musicians and used them to back Mike Berry. However, by the end of 1961 The Outlaws went on tour, which displeased Joe. So he decided to form a new house band, The Tornados, to back artists such as Billy Fury, Don Charles and John Leyton. They comprised Alan Caddy (lead guitar), George Bellamy (rhythm guitar), Heinz Burt (bass), Roger LaVern (organ) and Clem Cattini (drums). Their debut single, 'Love And Fury', which failed to chart, was a nod to Billy Fury.

For their next release, Joe took a tape of 'Try Once More,' which he had written with songwriter Geoff Goddard, to Alan and Clem. Joe sang wordless vocals over Geoff's backing track. As Clem Cattini recalled, "He played us this tape of him singing and the music didn't really sound right. It had all wrong time and key signatures. So we listened to the tape to get the idea and basically re-wrote the music." The track features Geoff deputising for Roger on clavioline, a portable, monophonic, battery powered keyboard. Geoff also gave his services free of charge because his composition, 'Jungle Fever', appeared on the B-side.

Opening with a rumble intended to sound like a spaceship taking off, 'Telstar' was named after the American communications satellite, launched on July 10, 1962. The record topped the American chart, giving The Tornados the distinction of becoming the first British group to have a US number one. In fact, they were the *only* British group to achieve that feat until The Beatles came along.

The Tornados received little money from the song. Joe had leased the record to Decca and, having negotiated a 5% royalty of the record's sales, he banked £29,000, very little of which was passed to The Tornados. Maybe Joe was not being generous because his songwriting royalties had been frozen. A French composer, Jean Ledrut, was suing him for plagiarism. His earnings of £150,000 were frozen and although it is not known why Joe committed suicide in 1967, this could have been a factor. The matter was settled a year later with Ledrut receiving £8,500 from Joe's estate.

On Clem Cattini's living room wall, there is one silver and one gold disc for 'Telstar'. The gold one was presented to him by Billy Fury on *Thank Your Lucky Stars*, but the silver one was bought from a friend who found it in a car boot sale.

Over the next 12 months, they had three further hits, 'Globetrotter' (5), 'Robot' (17) and 'The Ice Cream Man' (18). Heinz left to pursue a solo career and achieved five hits, the biggest being his tribute to Eddie Cochran, 'Just Like Eddie'. The remaining Tornados had one further chart success, 'Dragonfly' (41), but it was time to move on and Clem dismantled the group. With the exception of Alan Caddy, they reformed in 1975 to re-record 'Telstar' but, as Clem said, "We could never emulate that original sound."

The echo-laden track, which became the UK's biggest selling instrumental, was named by Margaret Thatcher as her favourite song of all time.

142 Frank Ifield
Lovesick Blues

Label & Cat No.: **Columbia DB 4913**

Producer: **Norrie Paramor**

Writers: **Irving Mills / Cliff Friend**

Date reached No.1: **8 November 1962**

Weeks at No.1: **5**

CLIFF FRIEND, A TEST PILOT AND vaudeville pianist from Cincinnati, wrote the melody for 'Lovesick Blues' and the words were added by Irving Mills. It was for a long forgotten musical about lonesome pilots, *O-oo Ernest*. Mills, who became Duke Ellington's publisher, realised the song's potential and bought out Friend's interest. The song was first recorded by Elsie Clark in 1922, but The Minstrel Man From Georgia, Emmett Miller, added the yodel in 1925. Then, in 1939, Rex Griffin recorded the song and became known for that and 'The Last Letter'.

Rex Griffin and Hank Williams, both drunks, were drinking companions. Hank Williams could only record songs published by Acuff-Rose and so Hank told Fred Rose that he had purchased the rights to 'Lovesick Blues' from Rex Griffin, which, in any event, were not his to sell. In 1949, Hank Williams' record was a smash hit – he got seven encores when he sang it on the *Grand Ole Opry* – and Acuff-Rose had to contend with an irate Irving Mills.

After 'I Remember You' established Frank Ifield in 1962, he discussed the next move with his record producer, Norrie Paramor. Frank's friend, Ronnie Carroll, had suggested 'Lovesick Blues'. Frank recalls, "Norrie said, quite correctly, 'Let's not go the American way of a carbon copy follow-up, let's go for something different.' Hank Williams had been a tremendous influence on me in my youth and I liked the idea of doing 'Lovesick Blues' but with a twist beat as the twist was the current rage. The combination of the two made it a million seller for me."

The B-side, 'She Taught Me To Yodel', attracted sales in its own right and featured some full-blooded yodelling from Frank. In 1991 a house version, now called 'The Yodelling Song', restored Frank to the Top 40.

143 Elvis Presley with The Jordanaires
Return To Sender

Label & Cat No.: **RCA 1320**

Producer: **Steve Sholes**

Writers: **Otis Blackwell / Winfield Scott**

Date reached No.1: **13 December 1962**

Weeks at No.1: **3**

SEEKING TO RECAPTURE THE SUCCESS of *Blue Hawaii*, Elvis Presley returned for a second helping with *Girls! Girls! Girls!*, although, despite the title, there were only two girls vying for Elvis' attention – *Playboy*'s Stella Stevens (real name, Estelle Eggleston) and newcomer Laurel Goodwin (later in the pilot for *Star Trek*). Just before filming, the title had been changed to *Girls! Girls! Girls!* from *Gumbo Ya-Ya*, a Creole expression for 'Everybody talks at once'.

The score was fair to middling – 'Because Of Love' became a ballad hit for Billy Fury while 'Song Of The Shrimp' and 'We're Coming In

Loaded' (about tuna fish!) were ridiculous. Stella Stevens had the best song as she revived the standard, 'The Nearness Of You', but Elvis does perform one excellent song, another rocker from Otis Blackwell, 'Return To Sender'. The Jordanaires are high in the mix and the musicians include Boots Randolph on sax and Scotty Moore and the renowned jazz musician Barney Kessel playing guitars.

Postal deliveries have always been a regular topic for songwriters – 'Death Letter Blues' (Son House), 'Sealed With A Kiss' (Brian Hyland), 'Letter Full Of Tears' (Billy Fury), 'Love Letters' (Ketty Lester), 'Please Mr. Postman' (Marvelettes) and not forgetting The Singing Postman or Slim Whitman, another singing postman. In 1993 when the US Mail issued its Elvis stamp, there was a tenfold increase in the number of letters it was obliged to return, duly marked "Return to sender – address unknown".

144 Cliff Richard & The Shadows
The Next Time / Bachelor Boy

Label & Cat No.: **Columbia DB 4950**
Producer: **Norrie Paramor**
Writers: **Sid Tepper / Roy C. Bennett; Bruce Welch / Cliff Richard**
Date reached No.1: **3 January 1963**
Weeks at No.1: **3**

Like Elvis Presley, Cliff Richard was a fine ballad singer. Encouraged by his producer Norrie Paramor, he enjoyed singing standards ('I'm Looking Out The Window', which was associated with Peggy Lee, 'It's All In The Game', 'The Twelfth Of Never') and new songs which could become standards ('The Next Time', 'When The Girl In Your Arms Is The Girl In Your Heart'). 'The Next Time', a ballad which could have been written 30 years earlier was a new song from Sid Tepper & Roy Bennett, who wrote many songs for Elvis, was included on the soundtrack of Cliff's film, *Summer Holiday*. Their record producer, Norrie Paramor, joined them on keyboards.

The B-side, 'Bachelor Boy', written by Cliff and Bruce Welch, turned out to be prophetic as, after 1962, Cliff was rarely linked romantically with anyone. "Cliff was becoming a family entertainer," recalls Bruce Welch, "and I thought 'Bachelor Boy' would be a great title for him. I wrote most of it and when I got stuck on one of the verses, I got Cliff to help me out. The producers decided to add it to the film and so we did it in a mock-up of a roadside in Greece, which was done in the Elstree studios. That awful little dance is almost as embarrassing to me as hearing 'a wife and a child' because we had the stress on the wrong syllable. I can't complain though as it was a million-seller."

145 The Shadows
Dance On!

Label & Cat No.: **Columbia DB 4948**
Producer: **Norrie Paramor**
Writers: **Valerie Murtagh / Elaine Murtagh / Ray Adams**
Date reached No.1: **24 January 1963**
Weeks at No.1: **1**

The Avons was a UK family group comprising Ray Adams and his wife Elaine, and Val who was married to Elaine's brother. They had chart hits with covers of 'Seven Little Girls Sitting In The Back Seat', 'Four Little Heels' and 'Rubber Ball', but they developed into a reliable songwriting team. Elaine Adams, the Avon lady, remembers "We spent so much time together and when Ray would pick up his guitar, we would start humming along. We had written an instrumental, 'The Hired Gun', and given it to our publisher, Dick James, who passed it to Norrie Paramor. Norrie kept it on his desk for a year and we had forgotten about it. Then one day when we were on tour, we were told to watch *Sunday Night At The London Palladium*. There weren't many TVs about then, so we went into a pub where some guys were watching football. When the time came for the *Palladium*, Val switches over the programme, saying, 'Sorry, lads, we've got to watch this.' The Shadows came on and did our tune which was now called 'Dance On!' and we were absolutely thrilled."

'Dance On!' demonstrated that The Shadows could dance on with a change in personnel – now it was Hank Marvin, Bruce Welch, Licorice Locking and Brian Bennett. The veteran Denmark Street composer, Marcel Stellman, loved the tune and asked the Avons if he could add some words. Kathy Kirby recorded that and it was her first Top 20 hit in August 1963. At the same time, Billy Fury was in the charts with another Avons' song, 'In Summer'. Val also wrote Olivia Newton-John's 1974 Eurovision entry, 'Long Live Love'.

146 Jet Harris & Tony Meehan
Diamonds

Label & Cat No.: **Decca F 11563**
Producer: **Dick Rowe**
Writer: **Jerry Lordan**
Date reached No.1: **31 January 1963**
Weeks at No.1: **3**

Although Jet Harris was an excellent bass player and the most charismatic personality in The Shadows, he was dismissed for his wayward behaviour – and part of that was caused by his wife, Carol, having an affair with Jet's boss, Cliff Richard. Jet was signed to Decca as a solo artist and he developed a deep and resonant bass sound for his first solo hit, 'Besame Mucho'

Another former Shadow, Tony Meehan was working as a producer at Decca, but he was looking for a new challenge. He suggested that he and Jet should team up and he asked Jerry Lordan, the writer of 'Apache' and 'Wonderful Land', for an

Cliff & The Shadows, two hit acts in one, left to right: Brian Bennett (drums), Cliff, Hank B. Marvin (lead guitar) and Bruce Welch (rhythm guitar)

instrumental which would feature bass guitar with space for a drum solo. Jerry Lordan gave them 'Diamonds', but Jet Harris had other ideas: "I took an ordinary Fender guitar and detuned every string a whole tone which enabled me to hit notes which were much lower than an ordinary guitar. A lot of people wondered how I'd done that. It was murder to work with on stage because once you slacked off those strings, they go out of tune so easily. 'Besame Mucho' was on a six-string bass but 'Diamonds' was using a detuned six-string ordinary Fender guitar."

Jet and Tony had further instrumental hits with 'Scarlett O'Hara' and 'Applejack', but when Jet was involved in a car accident, he was so annoyed that his manager still wanted them to appear on *Ready, Steady, Go!* that he hid in Brighton for three months. Tony mimed to his drumming without Jet by his side, and the partnership was over.

147 Frank Ifield
The Wayward Wind

Label & Cat No.: **Columbia DB 4960**

Producer: **Norrie Paramor**

Writers: **Stan Labowsky / Herb Newman**

Date reached No.1: **21 February 1963**

Weeks at No.1: **3**

THE SONGWRITERS, STAN LABOWSKY and Herb Newman, were playing Gogi Grant some of their material. They played her western song, 'The Wayward Wind', purely for her opinion as they were looking for a big-lunged male singer to record it. She insisted that she could do it justice and, in 1956, she took 'The Wayward Wind' to number one in the US, but in the UK, the sales were split between Gogi (9), Tex Ritter (8) and Jimmy Young (27).

Frank Ifield had had two consecutive number ones and he says, "No British artist had had three number ones. We had quite a few tracks in the can and the one that appealed to me was 'The Wayward Wind'. Although I like Tex Ritter's a lot, it was the Gogi Grant version that I'd heard. It was a bit of a battle to get that number one because The Beatles had come out of nowhere with 'Please Please Me', but I did make it."

It is often said that no British country performer has ever made it big, but Lonnie Donegan insisted he was the best country singer that Britain had ever produced and Frank Ifield's own hits were ascloseasthis to country. 'I Remember You' had a country arrangement and both 'Lovesick Blues' and 'The Wayward Wind' were country songs. Frank's next single, again a country arrangement of an oldie, 'Nobody's Darlin' But Mine', made number four and then he returned to the top with 'Confessin' (That I Love You)'.

148 Cliff Richard & The Shadows
Summer Holiday

Label & Cat No.: **Columbia DB 4977**

Producer: **Norrie Paramor**

Writers: **Bruce Welch / Brian Bennett**

Date reached No.1: **14 March 1963**

Weeks at No.1: **3**

THE STRAPLINE FOR THE FILM, *Summer Holiday*, was "The 'Young Ones' have gone abroad". Cliff plays a mechanic who drives a London bus across Europe, and he and his friends encounter The Shadows in Yugoslavia, Greece and everywhere else they go. Cliff found the film, which was shot in June 1962 in gruelling heat, exhausting, but it was a family affair as he had rented a beach villa in Athens for his mother and two sisters.

Bruce Welch and Brian Bennett wrote the title song in 20 minutes, but it was a perfect 20 minutes as the song has been used on endless holiday programmes ever since. The single was backed by the popular dance routine, 'Dancing Shoes', and Cliff's previous number one, 'The Next Time' / 'Bachelor Boy' had also come from the film.

It seems curious that *Summer Holiday* should have been released during the winter, but the producers had, unknowingly, made the best decision. The film was an enormous success and the soundtrack topped the album charts for 14 weeks. And why was it the best decision? The Beatles were just around the corner, about to hit the charts in a big way, and their first film, the monochrome *A Hard Day's Night*, was to make the vivid colours of *Summer Holiday* look pallid.

In 1984 The Young Ones sang 'Summer Holiday' on a bus in the last episode of their TV series, while Kevin the Gerbil, a close friend of Roland Rat, returned the song to the charts. Darren Day starred in a stage version *of Summer Holiday* with his medley of its hit songs making the Top 20 in 1996. That same year Cliff Richard included 'Summer Holiday' in his own medley when he was singing in the rain at Wimbledon.

149 The Shadows
Foot Tapper

Label & Cat No.: **Columbia DB 4984**

Producer: **Norrie Paramor**

Writers: **Hank Marvin / Bruce Welch**

Date reached No.1: **29 March 1963**

Weeks at No.1: **1**

IN ANY DISCUSSION OF THE FUNNIEST film of all-time, Jacques Tati's brilliant *Monsieur Hulot's Holiday* (1953) is bound to figure. The Shadows loved the film and they were very surprised when Tati himself turned up to see them at the Olympia in Paris in 1961. He asked them to write something catchy for his next film and, as soon as he had left, Hank Marvin and Bruce Welch wrote a tune for him. That tune became 'Foot Tapper'.

There's no doubt that 'Foot Tapper' would have lent itself to Tati's masterful clowning, but he ran into funding difficulties and the film was not made. Indeed, Tati's next film, *Playtime*, did not appear until 1967.

The Shadows only have a subsidiary role in *Summer Holiday*, but they responded as soon as they heard the director, Peter Yates, say that he needed something for the radio in the bus scene. Hank and Bruce passed over 'Foot Tapper' and although it was wasted in the film, it was issued as a single and went to the top. Why didn't the producers invite Jacques Tati for a guest appearance and get him to do a comic mime to 'Foot Tapper'?

The song has had a long life as it is the theme music for BBC Radio 2's *Sounds Of The Sixties* with Brian Matthew.

150 Gerry & The Pacemakers
How Do You Do It?

Label & Cat No.: **Columbia DB 4987**

Producer: **George Martin**

Writer: **Mitch Murray**

Date reached No.1: **11 April 1963**

Weeks at No.1: **3**

MITCH MURRAY WAS A YOUNG, enthusiastic Denmark Street songwriter, who had written B-sides for Mark Wynter and Shirley Bassey, but Adam Faith rejected the very catchy 'How Do You Do It?'. Mitch recalls, "A singer called Johnny Angel was going to record 'How Do You Do It?', but he changed his mind and recorded another song, 'Better Luck Next Time', so better luck next time, Johnny Angel."

Undeterred, Mitch's publisher, Dick James, passed the song to the label manager of Parlophone Records, George Martin. He considered it suitable for his new signings, The Beatles, and although they did record it under sufferance, they really only wanted to release their own material. "It makes me cringe," says Mitch, "to think that George Martin asked them to come up with a song as good as mine. It also makes me cringe to hear their version as I felt that they had screwed up the song, perhaps deliberately."

The Beatles' manager, Brian Epstein, passed 'How Do You Do It?' to another Merseyside group, Gerry & The Pacemakers, which featured Les Chadwick on guitar, Les Maguire on piano and Gerry's brother, Fred, on drums. "We were very surprised when we recorded it," said Gerry, "because we had only heard our voices on crummy tape recorders before. We couldn't believe we sounded so good."

Unlike The Beatles, Gerry & The Pacemakers went to number one with their first single, so Gerry had shown The Beatles how to do it. Gerry's album, *How Do You Like It?*, made number two on the album charts, but couldn't dislodge The Beatles' LP, *Please Please Me*.

151 The Beatles
From Me To You

Label & Cat No.: **Parlophone R 5015**

Producer: **George Martin**

Writers: **John Lennon / Paul McCartney**

Date reached No.1: **2 May 1963**

Weeks at No.1: **7**

WHEN THE BEATLES RECORDED 'Please Please Me', George Martin told them, "Congratulations, you have just made your first number one", but although it was a far bigger hit than their debut single 'Love Me Do', which reached number 17 the previous year, it failed to dislodge Frank Ifield and his 'Wayward Wind'. So it was that their third single, 'From Me To You', became the first of the Fabs' 17 number ones. In many ways, it is an archetypal Merseybeat recording, upbeat and strong in the harmony and melody department, and performed by a white male group with lead, rhythm and bass guitars and drums. It marks the debut of The Beatles' landmark 'Woooooo' which was borrowed from The Isley Brothers' 'Twist And Shout'.

'From Me To You' was a joint composition from John Lennon and Paul McCartney, and although their names would appear together on over 200 Beatles compositions, very few are genuine examples of them writing together. Paul said, "We wrote 'From Me To You' on the bus. It was great, that middle eight was a very big departure for us. Going to a G minor and a C takes you to a whole new world." John commented. "It was far bluesier than that when we wrote it. You could rearrange it pretty funky."

The titles of John and Paul's early songs were based around personal pronouns, and this one was doubly useful as it became 'From Us To You' for their BBC radio series. This revealed the song's inspiration – the *New Musical Express'* letter page, *From You To Us*.

152 Gerry & The Pacemakers
I Like It

Label & Cat No.: **Columbia DB 7041**

Producer: **George Martin**

Writer: **Mitch Murray**

Date reached No.1: **20 June 1963**

Weeks at No.1: **4**

LIKE A CHAMPIONSHIP FIGHT, GERRY & The Pacemakers were replaced at the top by The Beatles, but seven weeks later, they knocked them off with 'I Like It', again written by Mitch Murray. It had the same cheekiness as 'How Do You Do It?' but contained more innuendo. It was Merseybeat with a touch of George Formby. Gerry said, "Although I liked it, I wasn't sure about it because it had the same chords and the same feel as our first hit. However, everybody felt that it had a lively spirit that would do the trick. It went to number one and I was happy to be proved wrong and I'm still singing it today."

But Gerry's second single could easily have been a Lennon & McCartney song. Mitch Murray comments, "I wrote 'I Like It' for Gerry's follow-up, but John Lennon had given him 'Hello Little Girl'. John threatened to thump me if I got the follow-up, and I thought it was worth a

thump. 'I Like It' went to number one and I didn't get a thump." Gerry's version of 'Hello Little Girl' remained unissued until 1992 but the song became a Top 10 hit for another Liverpool group, The Fourmost, later in 1963.

153 Frank Ifield
Confessin' (That I Love You)

Label & Cat No.: **Columbia DB 7062**

Producer: **Norrie Paramor**

Writers: **Al J. Neiburg / Doc Daugherty / Ellis Reynolds**

Date reached No.1: **18 July 1963**

Weeks at No.1: **2**

FRANK IFIELD RETURNED TO THE FEEL OF 'I Remember You' with another oldie, 'Confessin' (That I Love You)', which had been written in 1930. The first hit recording was by Guy Lombardo and the Royal Canadians and although Guy was known as the 'King of Corn', this was a compliment in 1930. Among the many other versions are ones by Louis Armstrong, Ella Fitzgerald, Thelonius Monk and the duo of Les Paul and Mary Ford.

'Confessin'' gave Frank his fourth number one within a year, although the charts would soon be dominated by the Liverpool groups. Indeed, one of the world's most valuable records is *Jolly What! – Frank Ifield Meets The Beatles*, on the US Vee-Jay label. Frank says, "The album implied that it was us live on stage which was a load of hooey. It was just a compilation of singles although it said on the back, 'We hope you like this copulation.'"

As always, Frank's single was helped by a strong B-side: in this case, an up-tempo arrangement on the best known of Australian songs, 'Waltzing Matilda': "I love that song, I can smell the gum leaves every time I hear it," says Frank, "They used to march to the song but you couldn't march to my version."

As well as singles hits, Frank had two hit albums in 1963, *I'll Remember You* and *Born Free*. He starred on variety bills around the UK and he was a major success in pantomime at the London Palladium, *Babes In The Wood*, which involved both fencing and archery. When the hits stopped, he switched completely to country music, working with Barbary Coast and often appearing at the annual Wembley festival.

However, unlike many performers, Frank has been unable to work on the oldies circuit. In 1988 he had an operation which damaged his vocal cords and although he can work as a TV presenter in Australia, he can no longer sing effectively. "I haven't quite given up," he says. "I can do the high notes and I can do narrations."

154 Elvis Presley with The Jordanaires
(You're The) Devil In Disguise

Label & Cat No.: **RCA 1355**

Producer: **Steve Sholes**

Writers: **Bill Giant / Bernie Baum / Florence Kaye**

Date reached No.1: **1 August 1963**

Weeks at No.1: **1**

FEBRUARY 1963 SAW THE RISE OF Beatlemania and popular music would never be the same again. Elvis, hitherto invicible, should have been all right as nine of his last ten singles had made number one. He needed a strong single to compete with The Beatles, but he released 'One Broken Heart For Sale', a lackadaisical song from *It Happened At The World's Fair* and, surprisingly, omitted one of the verses so was only 90 seconds long. As a result, Elvis's single didn't reach the Top 10 in either Britain or America. So what happened next?

Bill Giant, Bernie Baum and Florence Kaye were staff writers for Hill & Range Publishing in the Brill Building. Hill & Range selected the songs for Elvis Presley and as the Sixties rolled by, Elvis became more and more likely to sing whatever was put in front of him. To quote his most notorious biographer, Albert Goldman, "Elvis would be appalled by what he was given and then he would go out and do it. There you have the essential Elvis Presley – he was a mule pulling a plough."

Although this partnership wrote 40 songs for Elvis, only one of them, '(You're The) Devil In Disguise' had any significant success – number one in the UK, number three in the US. A mediocre song was helped by a fine performance from Elvis with a neat stop-start arrangement. To give Bill Giant his due, he did write a wonderful rock'n'roll song that was never a big hit – Billy Fury's 'Wondrous Place' – if only Elvis had recorded that.

The musicians included Scotty Moore and Grady Martin on guitars, Harold Bradley on bass, Floyd Cramer on piano, Boots Randolph on sax, D.J. Fontana on drums and The Jordanaires, and you couldn't get a better Nashville A-team than that. Although Steve Sholes was producing, this was largely a titular role as, by this time, Elvis knew what he wanted to sound like even if the songs weren't great.

155 The Searchers
Sweets For My Sweet

Label & Cat No.: **Pye 7N 15533**

Producer: **Tony Hatch**

Writers: **Doc Pomus / Mort Shuman**

Date reached No.1: **8 August 1963**

Weeks at No.1: **2**

WHO KNOWS WHY THE DRIFTERS' 1961 single, 'Sweets For My Sweet', was not a UK hit? No matter, the Liverpool group, The Searchers, realised the potential of this classic pop song and performed it on Merseyside and in Hamburg.

The Searchers, who had taken their name from the John Ford western, originally had Johnny Sandon as their lead singer, but 'Sweets For My Sweets' shows it was no handicap when he left. Tony Jackson, who was inspired by Lonnie Donegan's nasal singing, took the lead vocals,

The Searchers' original 1963 line-up featured, left to right: Chris Curtis, Tony Jackson, John McNally and Mike Pender

while Mike Pender, John McNally and Chris Curtis added the ooh's.

They made an audition tape for Pye Records at Liverpool's Iron Door club and it is surprising to hear how close their arrangement of 'Sweets For My Sweet' is to the released version. Their record went to the top following an appearance on the Merseybeat edition of *Thank Your Lucky Stars*.

The songwriter, Mort Shuman, commented, "Well, they got the words wrong – it's 'your tasty kiss' not 'your fair sweet kiss' – but I thought it was fine. They had a different sound to The Drifters, but it wasn't necessarily inferior. It was so infectious and that was all you wanted from those singles."

The Searchers' follow-up, 'Sugar And Spice', written by Tony Hatch under the pseudonym of Fred Nightingale, was effectively a rewrite of 'Sweets For My Sweet', but it still made number two. They did, however, consider Mitch Murray's 'You Were Made For Me' was too lightweight and Murray passed the song to Freddie & The Dreamers.

As an agreement could not be reached, The Searchers' version of 'Sweets For My Sweet' could not be put on the soundtrack of the Robin Williams film, *Good Morning, Vietnam*, in 1987 and 'Sugar And Spice' was used instead. The song has been covered on several occasions, notably by Tina Charles and C.J. Lewis, and The Searchers themselves still perform it night after night.

156 Billy J. Kramer with The Dakotas
Bad To Me

Label & Cat No.: **Parlophone R 5049**

Producer: **George Martin**

Writers: **John Lennon / Paul McCartney**

Date reached No.1: **22 August 1963**

Weeks at No.1: **3**

The Bootle-born singer, William Howard Ashton, changed his name to Billy Kramer, and John Lennon added the 'J' to make him sound even more American. His group, The Coasters, did not want to go professional, so his manager, Brian Epstein, teamed him with the Manchester band, The Dakotas.

Their first single, a cover of 'Do You Want To Know A Secret?' from the Beatles' first LP, *Please Please Me*, made number two and, by way of appreciation, John Lennon passed him an original song, 'Bad To Me', which he wrote while on holiday with Brian Epstein in Spain. With its reference to the birds being lonely and the leaves getting messages from the breeze, it sounds more like a pop song of the Forties than a Merseybeat rocker, especially one written by John Lennon. John and Paul also gave Billy 'I'll Keep You Satisfied' and 'From A Window'. 'I'll Keep You Satisfied' deserved to be another number one but its chances were wrecked by a disastrous live performance when Billy was overcome with nerves on *Sunday Night At The London Palladium*.

The Dakotas had an instrumental hit with 'The Cruel Sea' and to resolve a much-repeated trivia question, it was their drummer, Tony Mansfield (aka Tony Bookbinder) who was Elkie Brooks' brother and not Billy J.

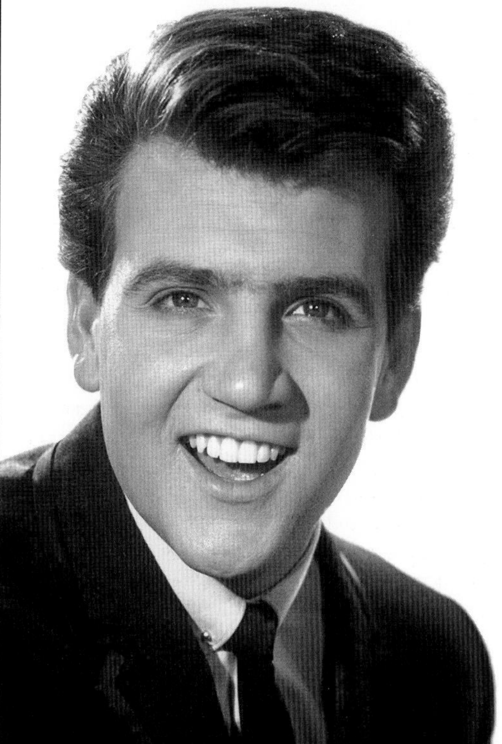

Billy J Kramer

157 The Beatles
She Loves You

Label & Cat No.: **Parlophone R 5055**

Producer: **George Martin**

Writers: **John Lennon / Paul McCartney**

Date reached No.1: **12 September 1963**

Weeks at No.1: **6 (two runs)**

'She Loves You' was the anthem of Beatlemania, the late summer hit that rang out of transistor radios throughout the land, joyously proclaiming The Beatles as the best thing ever to happen to British pop. The nation was entranced: there wasn't a teenager in the land who didn't feel great to be alive.

Johnny Dean, the editor of the monthly *Beatles Book*, says, "I got to the number two studio in Abbey Road, and Brian Epstein, George Martin and Dick James were waiting for The Beatles to turn up. I learned that the boys would write a song on the way to the studio. They walked in and they sang a song with acoustic guitars and with everyone cocking an ear to hear what it was like. It was 'She Loves You' and it didn't sound very impressive. The song when I first heard it and the song when they'd finished with it were totally different. What they did in-between was The Beatles' magic."

John Lennon commented, "It was Paul's idea and instead of singing 'I love you' again, we brought in a third party. That kind of detail is in his solo work while I'm more inclined to write about myself." Maybe, though, there is something of John's toughness in there. The song is saying, "She loves you and if you can't see that, I'm going to go after her."

Their producer, George Martin, was delighted: "The 'yeah, yeah, yeah' was a curious singing chord. It was a major sixth with George Harrison doing the sixth and the other two, the third and fifth. It was just the way Glenn Miller wrote for the saxophone." Paul McCartney later commented, "We did some great stuff, but exact analysis was never our bag."

On the other hand, the singer Kenny Lynch was more surprised by something else in the song. He heard the song whilst on tour with them and Helen Shapiro. He recalls, "I remember travelling on a coach from Warrington and they were singing 'Woooo, woooo'. I said, 'You can't do that, you sound like a bunch of fairies.' They said, 'The kids'll like it' and they were right."

Indeed. 'She Loves You' was the first single ever to sell a million copies in the UK alone.

158 Brian Poole & The Tremeloes
Do You Love Me?

Label & Cat No.: **Decca F 11739**
Producer: **Mike Smith**
Writer: **Berry Gordy Jr**
Date reached No.1: **10 October 1963**
Weeks at No.1: **3**

On New Year's Day, 1962, two groups auditioned for Decca Records – The Beatles and Brian Poole & The Tremeloes. The label chose Brian Poole & The Tremeloes, which on any other day of the week would have been a good choice. Their first hit was with 'Twist And Shout', an R&B screamer that had been recorded by The Top Notes, then The Isley Brothers and then The Beatles.

They followed it with a cover version of one of the first Tamla-Motown US hits, The Contours' 'Do You Love Me?', written by label owner, Berry Gordy Jr. Brian Poole recalls, "We bought The Contours' record and it was a great dance record. I suppose we were the original punk band, we played everything fast and furious and so we put our own interpretation on it. Faron's Flamingos from Liverpool did a very good R&B version of it, but Dave Clark's version was rubbish."

The group had further hits with 'Candy Man', 'Someone Someone' and 'The Three Bells', but something went wrong when Poole split from the Tremeloes. The Trems became a major cabaret act, and Poole's singles failed to chart. For some years, Poole went from beat to meat as he worked in the family business of a chain of butcher's shops and factories around Barking, but in the Eighties he was back performing, first with Black Cat and then with Electrix. "I am always thinking, 'Another couple of years and then I'll call it a day' but then I find I'm enjoying it and don't want to stop," says Brian.

And there is another family business. Brian's daughters, Karen and Shellie, have had hits as Alisha's Attic.

159 Gerry & The Pacemakers
You'll Never Walk Alone

Label & Cat No.: **Columbia DB 7126**
Producer: **George Martin**
Writers: **Richard Rodgers / Oscar Hammerstein II**
Date reached No.1: **31 October 1963**
Weeks at No.1: **4**

The score of the Rodgers & Hammerstein musical, *Carousel*, includes 'June Is Bustin' Out All Over' and 'If I Loved You', but even those songs are outclassed by the extraordinary ballad, 'You'll Never Walk Alone', in which the dead Billy says he will always be offering support. The musical was written in 1945 and the song captured the optimism that followed the conclusion of World War II. The original lyric says "Hold your chin up high", but today everyone sings "Hold your head up high".

Several American rock'n'rollers alighted on the song – Roy Hamilton, Conway Twitty, Gene Vincent and Johnny Preston – and the UK rock'n'roller, Tony Sheridan, added it to his repertoire for the beat clubs in Hamburg. "No one ever gives that man enough credit," says Chris Curtis, the drummer with The Searchers, "We heard him sing it and I'm sure Gerry did."

Gerry & The Pacemakers included the song in their stage act and George Martin enhanced their performance by adding strings. The song soared to number one and was at the top when Oswald shot Kennedy. Gerry & The Pacemakers thus became the first act to reach number one with their first three singles. "We could have made it four if they'd released 'Pretend' as a single," says their drummer, Freddie Marsden.

Gerry had to strain for the final notes but this only added to its charm. Partly for its sentiment and partly for those final notes, it is beloved by football choirs around the world, even becoming the Germans' official anthem for Euro 2004. It has been used in different formats by Belgium, French and Italian teams.

'You'll Never Walk Alone' is especially associated with the Kop choir. They would play Gerry's version over the tannoy at Anfield and fade it out so that the Kop could take over. Gerry, who supported Everton FC, became a staunch Liverpool supporter.

160 The Beatles
I Want To Hold Your Hand

Label & Cat No.: **Parlophone R 5084**
Producer: **George Martin**
Writers: **John Lennon / Paul McCartney**
Date reached No.1: **12 December 1963**
Weeks at No.1: **5**

Oh yeah, we'll tell you something: 1963 is the greatest year in Liverpool's musical history. For a 40-week period from April 1963 to January 1964, eight of the 11 number one records were by Liverpool artists, who occupied the top spot for an unprecedented 34 weeks. Seven of those records were produced by George Martin who spent most of the year in a recording studio.

The year ended with the definitive, and most important, single from The Beatles' early years, 'I Want To Hold Your Hand', which was to break them in America early in 1964 when they went over for *The Ed Sullivan Show* and appearances at the Washington Coliseum and Carnegie Hall in New York.

John Lennon told *Playboy*, "We wrote a lot of stuff together, one on one, eyeball to eyeball, like in 'I Want To Hold Your Hand'. I remember when we got the chord that made the song." Paul added, "'Eyeball to eyeball' is a very good description. 'I Want To Hold Your Hand' was very co-written."

Bob Dylan praised Lennon & McCartney for introducing a drug phrase into a hit record – he thought that they were singing "I get high" rather than "I can't hide" – but sly little jokes and innuendos appear in The Beatles' records from this point on. Actually though, isn't the lyric a euphemism? Surely The Beatles had something more than holding hands in mind.

161 The Dave Clark Five
Glad All Over

Label & Cat No.: **Columbia DB 7154**

Producer: **Dave Clark**

Writers: **Dave Clark / Mike Smith**

Date reached No.1: **16 January 1964**

Weeks at No.1: **2**

PERHAPS IT SHOULD HAVE BEEN THE Mike Smith Five as Mike Smith sang lead vocals and played keyboards, but when it came to business, the leader was their drummer, Dave Clark. The group was completed by Lenny Davidson (guitar), Rick Huxley (bass) and Denis Payton (saxophone). They had released five singles before 'Glad All Over', and Mike Smith recalls, "We had lost out on 'Do You Love Me?' to Brian Poole and so Dave thought we should do an original. He asked me to come up with something and I looked through my record collection for a suitable title." Mike alighted on Carl Perkins's 'Glad All Over', and wrote a new song with the same title.

Dave Clark says, "I knew that we needed a song with the thumps in. We had been playing dance halls and we were getting a great audience response to the stomping things we were doing."

The engineer, Adrian Kerridge, worked out a thunderous drum sound and the relentless 'thump, thump' was to be called the Tottenham sound. It was so powerful that The Dave Clark Five managed to depose The Beatles' 'I Want To Hold Your Hand' from the top. "We were still doing our daytime jobs when 'Glad All Over' was number one," says Dave Clark, "We released 'Bits And Pieces' in February and by then we were pros." Some dance hall managers were, however, wary of the records being played as they were worried about the state of their floorboards.

The Dave Clark Five had international success, particularly in America where they had several hit records that were not hits here – for example, their US number one 'Over And Over' barely made the UK Top 50. Dave Clark became a businessman, buying up the tapes of the *Ready Steady Go!* TV shows and producing, as well as co-writing, the hit musical, *Time*, starring Cliff Richard and then David Cassidy. "You can't go back," he says, "so I would never reform The Dave Clark Five, but I am very proud of what we did. Mike had a great voice, he was the Sixties' Rod Stewart."

162 The Searchers
Needles And Pins

Label & Cat No.: **Pye 7N 15594**

Producer: **Tony Hatch**

Writers: **Jack Nitzsche / Sonny Bono**

Date reached No.1: **30 January 1964**

Weeks at No.1: **3**

EARLY IN 1963 JACKIE DE SHANNON recorded the original version of 'Needles And Pins', which had been written by her arranger, Jack Nitzsche and session musician, Sonny Bono. Cliff Bennett & The Rebel Rousers, who, incidentally, included future Searcher, Frank Allen, learnt the song and performed it at the Star-Club in Hamburg. The Searchers heard them and recorded the song before Cliff.

The Searchers' drummer, Chris Curtis, says, "If you haven't got the listeners in the first few seconds, you haven't got them, and we had them with that. That opening A chord on 'Needles And Pins' will never be topped. It must have been a good riff as The Byrds have used it countless times – upside down, this way, that way."

'Needles And Pins' was The Searchers' third single and it attracted controversy. Mike Pender, who sang the lead vocal, recalls, "The producer of *Crackerjack* said the song was too heavy for his programme. It was a very intimate song and many people relate to it." 'Needles And Pins' prevented Gerry & The Pacemakers having their fourth chart-topper with 'I'm The One'. "I used to ring John McNally up and say, "John, will you get off the top?" says Gerry, "I'll never forgive them, the buggers."

The group returned to the Jackie De Shannon songbook for 'When You Walk In The Room' (3, 1964) and it seems unfair that this wonderful artist never had had a UK chart entry.

163 The Bachelors
Diane

Label & Cat No.: **Decca F 11799**

Producer: **Shel Talmy / Mike Stone**

Writers: **Erno Rapée / Lew Pollack**

Date reached No.1: **20 February 1964**

Weeks at No.1: **1**

THE NOVELTY ACT, THE HARMONIchords, featured the brothers, Con and Dec Cluskey, and their friend, John Stokes, but,

The Bachelors

despite success, the Dubliners knew it would be better to concentrate on straight singing and playing. Although they were all married, they called themselves The Bachelors and secured a recording contract with Decca. Dick Rowe told them, "Do something like Frank Ifield but with a Karl Denver feel." The result was 'Charmaine' and that full-blooded singing of sentimental songs became their trademark – three of their hits, 'Charmaine', 'Diane' and 'Ramona' were written in the late Twenties.

Janet Gaynor played Diane in the 1927 film, *Seventh Heaven*, and the song was a declaration of love by her boyfriend, Charles Furrell. The lyrics were by Lew Pollack, who also wrote the tear-jerking favourite, 'My Yiddishe Momme', and the music was by Erno Rapée, who also scored the gangster movie, *Little Caesar* (1930), which starred Edward G. Robinson. The song, sometimes known by its full title of Diane (I'm In Heaven When I See You Smile)', was covered for the UK market by Cavan O'Connor with Harry Bidgood & His Broadcasters and by Jack Hylton & His Orchestra. In 1937 Joe Loss & His Orchestra recorded a Film Memories medley which combined 'Charmaine', 'Diane' and 'Ramona'.

Dick Rowe was convinced that 'Diane' would be a major hit, but the first attempt with an American arranger didn't work. Johnny Keating was asked for a new one and he stripped the rhythm section to a minimum and added strings. The Bachelors preferred 'I Believe' and Decca told them that if 'Diane' wasn't a hit within five weeks, they would release that. At first the single didn't take off, but when they sang it to a girl on *Ready, Steady, Go!*, it leaped into the charts. 'I Believe' was still scheduled for release and so both records were in the chart together. 'I Believe' faltered at number two in the UK as it couldn't dislodge 'Can't Buy Me Love', but 'Diane' established The Bachelors in the US. Maybe, with a little change in their marketing, they could have become a major country act.

The Bachelors had the most public of break-ups in 1983 when the brothers sacked John Stokes. The matter went to court with the brothers claiming that he sang 'like a drowning rat' and that his voice had been overdubbed on recordings without his knowledge. Stokes retaliated that his voice was 'perfect'. When the dispute was settled, John Stokes said that he would rather listen to drowning rats than see the new Bachelors on stage.

164 Cilla Black
Anyone Who Had A Heart

Label & Cat No.: **Parlophone R 5101**

Producer: **George Martin**

Writers: **Burt Bacharach / Hal David**

Date reached No.1: **27 February 1964**

Weeks at No.1: **3**

PRISCILLA WHITE HELPED OUT AT THE Cavern's cloakroom and sang with the groups whenever she could. She changed her name after a tired Bill Harry accidentally renamed her in the *Mersey Beat* newspaper. Bill and The Beatles recommended her to Brian Epstein and she became the only girl in the NEMS stable.

Paul McCartney wrote her first single, 'Love Of The Loved', which made the Top 50, and when Brian Epstein returned from America, he gave George Martin the new Dionne Warwick record, 'Anyone Who Had A Heart'. "What a lovely song," said George, "This will be ideal for Shirley Bassey." Brian said, "I wasn't thinking of her, I was thinking of Cilla."

Somewhat reluctantly, George Martin asked Johnny Pearson for an orchestration, and his arrangement, which went from poignant start to shrieking finish, was perfect for Cilla's voice. The arrangement is similar but the saxophone solo is replaced by a bassoon. Cilla went to number one and Dionne, who was definitely not a good loser, only made number 42. If anyone had a broken heart, it was Dionne Warwick: "If I'd coughed on the record, Cilla Black would have done the same," she said, adding that her voice was 'dreadful'. She has since praised her rival, while Burt Bacharach & Hal David were so impressed that they wrote 'Alfie' for her. 'Alfie' is Cilla's crowning moment and yet it barely made the Top 10.

165 Billy J. Kramer with The Dakotas
Little Children

Label & Cat No.: **Parlophone R 5105**

Producer: **George Martin**

Writers: **Mort Shuman / John Leslie McFarland**

Date reached No.1: **19 March 1964**

Weeks at No.1: **2**

'LITTLE CHILDREN' IS AN AMERICAN song, but Billy J. Kramer recorded the original version, although he nearly lost out to Marty Wilde. Mort Shuman played it to Marty a few days after Billy bagged it and, although he wanted it, Mort said no. Not that it was certain that Billy would cut it. "I had to fight a lot of people to get 'Little Children' on the market," Billy recalls, "Brian Epstein wanted me to do another Lennon & McCartney song. I got a big kick when 'Little Children' came out and sold 78,000 in one day. The previous record for the number of singles sold in one day was The Beatles with 76,000."

Brian Epstein was concerned that the song was wrong for Billy's image. Until that point he had only sung straightforward love songs and here he was bribing a couple of young kids so he could have it away in private with their big sister. Although it sounds mild today, it did engender controversy at the time. As well as being Billy's second UK number one, it was his biggest US hit, but being a star is not all that glamorous – he spent four months of 1964 in variety with Tommy Trinder at the North Pier in Blackpool.

Mention should be made of Mort's little known co-writer, John Leslie McFarland, who had escaped from prison, gone to an airfield and stolen a plane without ever having flown one before. Another time he got an advance from a publisher by turning up in bandages and claiming that he had been beaten up. One of the great characters of the Brill Building, he also wrote Elvis Presley's 1960 hit 'Stuck On You'.

166 The Beatles
Can't Buy Me Love

Label & Cat No.: **Parlophone R 5114**
Producer: **George Martin**
Writers: **John Lennon / Paul McCartney**
Date reached No.1: **2 April 1964**
Weeks at No.1: **3**

THE MOST FAMOUS CHART OF ALL-TIME has to be *Billboard's* for April 4, 1964 where the top five singles were all by The Beatles: 'I Saw Her Standing There' (5), 'I Want To Hold Your Hand' (4), 'She Loves You' (3), 'Twist And Shout' (2) with their new release, 'Can't Buy Me Love' soaring to the top. The Beatles were on the verge of untold riches and how appropriate that Paul McCartney should write a song about the importance, or otherwise, of wealth, 'Can't Buy Me Love'. Was a Beatle learning about life and finding that money didn't buy him love?

The R&B flavoured song is very much Paul's, featuring his double-tracked vocal instead of harmonies from John Lennon, but it does contain a memorable guitar solo from George Harrison and Ringo plays tom-toms as well as drums. McCartney's chord changes were sophisticated and this new maturity was recognised by other performers, notably Ella Fitzgerald who wowed audiences with her swinging interpretation. After Ella, it became OK for middle-of-the-road and jazz singers to do Beatle songs, although some of them were merely jumping on the bandwagon.

'Can't Buy Me Love' was in the soundtrack of *A Hard Day's Night*, but it was released before the film. It might have stayed on top for longer, but it was replaced by another McCartney song, this time 'A World Without Love' for Peter & Gordon.

167 Peter & Gordon
A World Without Love

Label & Cat No.: **Columbia DB 7225**
Producer: **Norman Newell**
Writers: **John Lennon / Paul McCartney**
Date reached No.1: **23 April 1964**
Weeks at No.1: **2**

PETER ASHER AND GORDON WALLER started singing together at Westminster School and enjoyed performing songs associated with The Everly Brothers. They continued after they left and were spotted by the EMI producer, Norman Newell, at The Pickwick Club: "I introduced myself and told them that I was very impressed. I knew that they had an individual sound and I didn't know when I signed them that Paul McCartney was dating Peter's sister."

Peter's sister was the aspiring actress Jane Asher, with whom Paul would enjoy a five-year relationship during the mid-Sixties. A guest at the Ashers' residence in central London, he gave the duo 'A World Without Love', which he had written in 1962 but had no intention of recording. John Lennon was amused by the opening line, "Please lock me away", and would tease him about it. On the other hand, the noted songwriter, Doc Pomus, was to describe 'A World Without Love' as his favourite Lennon & McCartney composition: possibly it is the one that is closest to a classic Brill Building song of the early Sixties.

Peter & Gordon's version of 'A World Without Love' went to number one and it was followed by a new Lennon & McCartney song, 'Nobody I Know'. They also had hits with 'True Love Ways', 'To Know You Is To Love You' and 'Lady Godiva'.

After they split up in 1968, Gordon Waller recorded solo singles and found success in stage musicals, while Peter Asher worked for Apple and produced a fine album by James Taylor. In the Seventies, he became a noted producer, working with Taylor and Linda Ronstadt. When asked if Peter Asher had learnt some production techniques from Norman Newell, Newell replied, "Oh, I don't think Peter learnt anything from me. This was the nearest to a beat group recording that I had done so it was a new world for me. I think I was learning from him."

168 The Searchers
Don't Throw Your Love Away

Label & Cat No.: **Pye 7N 15630**
Producer: **Tony Hatch**
Writers: **Jimmy Wisner / Billy Jackson**
Date reached No.1: **7 May 1964**
Weeks at No.1: **2**

"PAT PRETTY, THE PUBLICIST IN PYE Records, had come across a song on the B-side of an American hit by The Orlons and I thought it was a great title," says Chris Curtis, the original drummer with The Searchers. The US chart band, known for their dance song 'The Wah Watusi', had made a mistake as 'Don't Throw Your Love Away' was far superior to their A-side, 'Bon Doo Wah'.

The Searchers arranged 'Don't Throw Your Love Away' in their sweeter and more melodic style and it became their third number one. Chris says, "The guitar riff came out similar to 'Needles And Pins', so again it was following a hit with a semi-copy of a hit. Mike Pender's voice was brilliant on that, just like a little boy wandering through the streets, and I joined in with that very high harmony, and it really worked. It was one of the nicest tunes that the Searchers ever did. The B-side, 'I Pretend I'm With You' was good too, one of my little gems."

This was the last record to feature the group's original line-up of Tony Jackson, Mike Pender, John McNally and Chris Curtis. Tony left in 1964, Chris in 1966 and now there are two bands playing The Searchers' hits – the original Searchers with John McNally and Tony's replacement, Frank Allen, and Mike Pender's Searchers.

169 The Four Pennies
Juliet

Label & Cat No.: **Philips BF 1322**

Producer: **Johnny Franz**

Writers: **Mike Wilsh / Fritz Fryer / Lionel Morton**

Date reached No.1: **21 May 1964**

Weeks at No.1: **1**

THE FOUR PENNIES WERE A BEAT group from Blackburn, Lancashire and individually they were Lionel Morton, a former cathedral choirboy on lead vocals and guitar, Fritz Fryer on lead guitar, Mike Wilsh on bass, and Alan Buck on drums. In 1963 they won a talent contest which secured them a recording contract with Philips. Their first single, 'Do You Want Me To?', made the Top 50 and they followed it with 'Tell Me Girl'. The B-side was 'Juliet'.

Mike Wilsh had written a plaintive tune that was reminiscent of 'Donna' and he and Lionel Morton went to Fritz Fryer's house to sort out the lyric. Fritz's two-year-old niece was there and they realised that her name was perfect for the song. Although it went on the B-side, the disc-jockeys started playing it and it soon was climbing the charts.

The Four Pennies had further hits with 'I Found Out The Hard Way', 'Black Girl' (based on a Leadbelly blues), Buffy Sainte-Marie's 'Until It's Time For You To Go' and 'Trouble Is My Middle Name'. They made two fine albums, *2 Sides Of 4 Pennies* and *Mixed Bag*, which, as the titles indicate, display their versatility.

When the hits stopped, Lionel Morton became a children's TV presenter on *Play School* and he played the title role in *Jesus Christ Superstar* in London's West End. Fritz Fryer became a record producer, working at Rockfield in Wales, Alan Buck went into music publishing, and Mike Wilsh has continued with The Four Pennies in various combinations.

170 Cilla Black
You're My World

Label & Cat No.: **Parlophone R 5133**

Producer: **George Martin**

Writers: **Umberto Bindi / Gino Paoli / Carl Sigman**

Date reached No.1: **28 May 1964**

Weeks at No.1: **4**

THE ITALIAN SONG, 'IL MIO MONDO', was given an English lyric, 'You're My World', by Carl Sigman, who died in October 2000 at the age of 91. His portfolio includes 'Pennsylvania 6-5000', 'It's All In The Game', 'Buona Sera', 'Robin Hood' and 'Theme From Love Story'. The ballad, 'You're My World', was given a beautiful arrangement by Johnny Pearson and was Cilla Black's third single. Despite its passionate ending, you may recall Cilla performing the song on the *Royal Variety Show*, arms held stiffly by her side and with a typical early Sixties hairstyle. She became more animated as the years went by, becoming the flamboyant TV host of *Surprise, Surprise!* and *Blind Date*.

Despite an appearance on *The Ed Sullivan Show* the same week as The Beatles, 'You're My World' was Cilla Black's only US hit. Following 'You're My World', she often recorded English versions of European songs and had hits with 'Don't Answer Me', 'A Fool Am I' and 'I Only Live To Love You', which were all Italian, and 'Love's Just A Broken Heart', which was French.

Like many of Cilla's records, the B-side, 'Suffer Now I Must', was written by her manager and husband, Bobby Willis. Cilla never trusted him with an A-side but they were good, well-constructed songs.

Cilla Black

171 Roy Orbison
It's Over

Label & Cat No.: **London HLU 9882**

Producer: **Wesley Rose**

Writers: **Roy Orbison / Bill Dees**

Date reached No.1: **25 June 1964**

Weeks at No.1: **2**

LIKE ROY ORBISON, BILL DEES WAS IN A rock'n'roll group playing all over the Texas panhandle. In 1964 Orbison, by now a star, returned to Odessa for a show and asked Bill if he had any songs. Bill sang him 'Borne On The Wind', which Roy reshaped and it became a UK Top 20 single. And this was how their songwriting partnership worked: Bill would present Roy with songs or fragments of songs and Roy would take and mould the sections he wanted. Bill Dees' song, 'It's Over At Last' was combined with two others to make 'It's Over', which became a vocal *tour de force* for Roy Orbison.

'It's Over' broke a straight run of 16 number one singles by UK acts. Despite the British beat boom, Roy Orbison retained his popularity and even held his own on a tour with The Beatles. He had left his spectacles with clear lenses on the plane and so the image of the man in black with his prescription sunglasses emerged. He was immobile on stage but he could even silence audiences wanting The Beatles with his presence. One night John and Paul held him in the wings as he was about to go on stage and said, "Yankee, go home"!

Roy was back in the UK when 'It's Over' was number one and in a state of euphoria, he bought a 1939 Mercedes in London. It was shipped to New York and Roy's drummer, Paul Garrison, was asked to collect it and drive it to Nashville. Easier said than done as it broke down in New Jersey and Paul had to stay in a motel while he waited for the new part to come from Germany.

In 1966 Jimmie Rodgers made the US Top 40 with a different song called 'It's Over' and the following year, Gene Pitney combined them in a medley.

172 The Animals
The House Of The Rising Sun

Label & Cat No.: **Columbia DB 7301**

Producer: **Mickie Most**

Writer: **Traditional, arranged by Alan Price**

Date reached No.1: **9 July 1964**

Weeks at No.1: **1**

EARLY IN 1964 MICKIE MOST, BY touring the provinces in a rock'n'roll package show, was looking for acts to produce. He spotted The Animals at a club in Newcastle and his first record with them, 'Baby, Let Me Take You Home', was a Top 30 hit. Their drummer, John Steel, recalls the next single: "We played Liverpool on May 17, 1964 and then drove to London, where Mickie had booked a studio for a recording for ITV's *Ready, Steady, Go!* Because of the reaction we were getting to 'Rising Sun', we asked to record it and he said, 'Okay, we'll do it at the same session.' We set up for balance, played a few bars for the engineer – it was mono with no overdubs – and we only did one take. We listened to it and Mickie said, 'That's it, it's a single'. The engineer said it was too long, but instead of chopping out a bit, Mickie had the courage to say, 'We're in a microgroove world now, we will release it.' We got a few hours sleep and went off to the Southampton Gaumont. A few weeks later, it was number one all over the world. When we knocked The Beatles off the top in America, they sent us a telegram which read, 'Congratulations from The Beatles (a group).'"

Mickie Most had similar memories: "Everything was in the right place, the planets were in the right place, the stars were in the right place and the wind was blowing in the right direction. It only took 15 minutes to make so I can't take much credit for the production. It was just a case of capturing the atmosphere in the studio."

Although it was written to be sung by a girl, the plight of the prostitute in New Orleans is related with fiery conviction by Eric Burdon. The song was 100 years old at the time and had been revived by Josh White in the Forties. Bob Dylan recorded the song acoustically in 1962. The Animals heard his version but whether they all contributed to the electricified and electrifying arrangement, or whether it was just Alan Price's work, is a matter for debate. Whatever, the fact that the songwriting royalties went into Alan's bank account was a source of discontent that would eventually split the band.

173 The Rolling Stones
It's All Over Now

Label & Cat No.: **Decca F 11934**

Producer: **Andrew Loog Oldham**

Writers: **Bobby Womack / Shirley Womack**

Date reached No.1: **16 July 1964**

Weeks at No.1: **1**

MICK JAGGER, CLUTCHING SOME R&B records, met Keith Richards, holding a guitar, on a London bound commuter train, and a friendship was established. Blues guitarist Brian Jones placed an ad in *Jazz News* for musicians to join a band and Jagger joined with his new mate, Keith. At first, the line-up was fluid but it settled on Jones, Jagger, Richards (who curiously dropped his 's' to copy Cliff), bassist Bill Wyman and drummer Charlie Watts. The Famous Five were augmented by Ian Stewart on piano, who was never officially part of the Stones as he did not project the right image. Andrew Loog Oldham, who had worked with Brian Epstein on publicising The Beatles' first single, became their manager and they were signed to Decca by Dick Rowe. The man who turned down one legendary group didn't do it twice.

Although lacking experience, Oldham produced their singles – the first, Chuck Berry's 'Come On', made the Top 30, the second John & Paul's 'I Wanna Be Your Man' the Top 20, and the third, Buddy Holly's 'Not Fade Away' the Top 10. They were well received on a UK nationwide tour with The Everly Brothers, Little Richard and Bo Diddley and their long hair (that is, 'long' by the standards of 1963) led to them being the bad boys of pop and headlines like "Would you allow your sister to marry a Rolling Stone?" kept appearing. Andrew Loog Oldham, a master of spin and publicity, encouraged these stories. *The Rolling Stones* was the first LP that did not name the act on its cover – the photo was sufficient.

On their first US tour, the DJ Murray The K played them a new R&B record by The Valentino's, 'It's All Over Now'. The Rolling Stones covered the song during sessions at Chess Studios in Chicago. The Stones added an abrasiveness and the interplay between Keith's echoing lead guitar and Brian Jones' blues rhythms is tremendous. In 1986 The Rolling Stones worked with The Valentinos' lead singer, Bobby Womack, on their *Dirty Work* album.

174 The Beatles
A Hard Day's Night

Label & Cat No.: **Parlophone R 5160**

Producer: **George Martin**

Writers: **John Lennon / Paul McCartney**

Date reached No.1: **23 July 1964**

Weeks at No.1: **3**

PRIOR TO *A HARD DAY'S NIGHT*, POP music films tended to be publicity vehicles for their stars with little substance or plot, but director Richard Lester was determined to create something with more style and quality from Alun Owen's script, which captured what it was like to be a Beatle effectively living in a goldfish bowl. They did not have anything more than a working title (actually, *Beatles Number One*) until Ringo made an off-the-cuff remark about a recording session being 'a hard day's night' and Lester knew he had the right title. John liked the title too and wrote the song overnight. Quite possibly, Ringo was quoting the title of Eartha Kitt's recent single, 'I Had A Hard Day Last Night'.

Play the opening chord of 'A Hard Day's Night' and nearly everyone will identify the record, and the rest of the song is equally distinctive. The score led to a remarkable album, the

The Beatles arrive at the London Pavilion in Piccadilly Circus for the UK premiere of A Hard Day's Night, *July 6, 1964*

TELL
andy
e world

DRESSING
COIFFEUR
G GUM
ch Ales

BAR
WARDS
GUINNESS
ON DRAUGHT

THE BEATLES
IN THEIR FIRST FULL LENGTH,
HILARIOUS, ACTION-PACKED FILM!
A HARD
DAY'S NIGHT
12 SMASH SONG-HITS!

THE BEATLES

12 SMASH SONG-HITS
CONFECTIONERY
CIGARETTES

JOHN
GEORGE
RINGO

only one where every song was written by Lennon & McCartney. As well as 'A Hard Day's Night' and 'Can't Buy Me Love', there's 'If I Fell', 'And I Love Her' and 'Things We Said Today'. The film itself was such an instant success that it recouped its production costs over the first weekend.

Like many Beatle songs, 'A Hard Day's Night' has been recorded in numerous ways, most notably by Peter Sellers impersonating Laurence Olivier, a Top 20 hit in 1965.

175 Manfred Mann
Do Wah Diddy Diddy

Label & Cat No.: **HMV POP 1320**

Producer: **John Burgess**

Writers: **Jeff Barry / Ellie Greenwich**

Date reached No.1: **13 August 1964**

Weeks at No.1: **2**

Like The Rolling Stones, Manfred Mann was formed by musicians from London's jazz and R&B clubs. The band, named after its leader, Manfred Mann, who had come from South Africa and played keyboards, consisted of Paul Jones (lead vocals, harmonica), Mike Vickers (guitar and saxophone), Tom McGuinness (bass) and Mike Hugg (drums). They sang about themselves in 'The One In The Middle', the title track of a hit EP in 1965.

The Manfred Mann group wrote their first hit, '5-4-3-2-1', the theme of ITV's *Ready, Steady, Go!,* but most of their hits were cover versions of American songs. Manfred says, "We weren't great songwriters and we knew we had to have great songs. The Beatles, The Rolling Stones and The Kinks all had wonderful, original songs, but we succeeded through a sense of judgement. The Hollies were in the same position as us."

In 1963 the Brill Building songwriters, Jeff Barry and Ellie Greenwich, had written 'Da Doo Ron Ron' for The Crystals. Ellie Greenwich: "We thought we would write another song like that and came up with 'Do Wah Diddy Diddy'. The Exciters recorded it but it never made it. Jeff and I were about to record it ourselves as The Raindrops when we heard that Manfred Mann had released it in England."

Paul Jones: "We were working our way through my record collection. I had 'Do Wah Diddy Diddy' by The Exciters, 'Sha La La' by The Shirelles, 'Oh No Not My Baby' by Maxine Brown and 'Come Tomorrow' by Marie Knight. I always had something that we ought to do. I loved The Exciters' version of 'Do Wah Diddy Diddy' – what a great song and what a great euphemism for sexual dalliance."

'Do Wah Diddy Diddy' is now performed by The Manfreds in a ten-minute audience workout. "That's great," says Ellie Greenwich, "I look at 'Da Doo Ron Ron' and 'Do Wah Diddy Diddy' as nursery rhyme songs. Everybody of every age can sing them because they are so easy to remember." Also, if you catch Paul and Tom in their other incarnation as The Blues Band, you may hear them perform a blues song by Blind Blake from 1929, 'Diddy Wah Diddy'.

176 The Honeycombs
Have I The Right?

Label & Cat No.: **Pye 7N 15664**

Producer: **Joe Meek**

Writers: **Ken Howard / Alan Blaikley**

Date reached No.1: **27 August 1964**

Weeks at No.1: **2**

Martin Murray, a part-time guitarist, owned a hairdressing salon in north London where Anne Lantree worked. She played drums and had a brother, John, who played bass and so The Honeycombs were formed with Dennis D'ell on lead vocals and Alan Ward on rhythm guitar. Two BBC employees, Ken Howard and Alan Blaikley, heard them at a pub in Ball's Pond Road and they wrote 'Have I The Right?' for them which was recorded by the independent record producer, Joe Meek. EMI said it had 'no commercial value' but it was released by Pye. As Anne's nickname was Honey and both Anne and Martin were hairdressers (that is, combers), the group was called The Honeycombs.

The single was plugged on Radio Caroline, particularly by Tony Blackburn, and the publicity surrounding a group with a girl drummer was enormous. Her drumming, accompanied by stomping feet, was likened to Dave Clark's on 'Bits And Pieces'. Joe Meek retaliated that he had been into heavy marching feet since he worked on Anne Shelton's 'Lay Down Your Arms'.

'Have I The Right?' was a UK number one and also went into the US Top 10. It was enormously successful round the world, particularly in Italy, Sweden and Japan. Murray injured himself by falling off a stage (too much stomping?) and was replaced by Peter Pye.

The Honeycombs had further UK chart entries with 'Is It Because?' (38), 'Something Better Beginning' (39) and 'That's The Way' (12), but there was a much-publicised court dispute over the authorship of 'Have I The Right?', which established Howard & Blaikley as the writers. A sad consequence is that it destroyed the confidence of the songwriter, Geoff Goddard, who had claimed the song was his composition.

To make matters worse, Joe Meek committed suicide in February 1967 and his estate was in such a mess that their unissued tracks could not be released. The Honeycombs split up but they have reformed on occasion. Howard & Blaikley managed and wrote for The Herd and Dave Dee, Dozy, Beaky, Mick & Tich.

The Honeycombs

177 The Kinks
You Really Got Me

Label & Cat No.: **Pye 7N 15673**
Producer: **Shel Talmy**
Writer: **Ray Davies**
Date reached No.1: **10 September 1964**
Weeks at No.1: **2**

POPULAR MUSIC IS FULL OF SIBLING rivalries – Tommy and Jimmy Dorsey, The Louvin Brothers, The Everly Brothers, The Kinks and Oasis, among them. Their quarrels have been very public and it could be argued that the tension has, in some way, strengthened the partnership. That is certainly true of the fiercely competitive Ray and Dave Davies from The Kinks. In his autobiography, *Kink* (1996), Dave Davies admires the insight and compassion in Ray's songs, but describes him as 'venomous, spiteful and completely self-involved'. Often though it was the other members of The Kinks who had the worst time as they were caught in the crossfire. The angry and passionate 'You Really Got Me' reflects the fire of that relationship.

The Kinks, taking their name, rather controversially, from a newly-minted word 'kinky', consisted of Ray and Dave with Pete Quaife on bass and Mick Avory on drums. Their first singles, 'Long Tall Sally' and 'You Still Want Me', did little business but the third was Ray's song, 'You Really Got Me'. Shel Talmy, their record producer, recalls, "I thought it was a wonderful riff and I knew right away that we could make a number one record. A lot of articles have said that Jimmy Page was playing lead guitar on that record, but it's not true. It was Dave Davies."

In his autobiography, *X-Ray* (1994), Ray Davies reveals that, with his long hair, he might be mistaken for being gay and so he changed a line from 'You really got me, yeah' to 'You really got me, girl' to emphasise his sexuality. Shel Talmy was right: this is one of the great riffs of rock'n'roll on a par with 'La Bamba', 'Bo Diddley', 'Louie Louie' and the opening notes of 'Johnny B. Goode' and 'What'd I Say'.

178 Herman's Hermits
I'm Into Something Good

Label & Cat No.: **Columbia DB 7338**
Producer: **Mickie Most**
Writers: **Gerry Goffin / Carole King**
Date reached No.1: **24 September 1964**
Weeks at No.1: **2**

AFTER DISCOVERING THE ANIMALS and The Nashville Teens, Mickie Most was bombarded with potential clients. One possibility was Herman's Hermits – a Manchester band featuring vocalist Peter Noone (a young actor who had played Len Fairclough's son in *Coronation Street*), Derek Leckenby (lead guitar), Keith Hopwood (rhythm guitar), Karl Green (bass) and Barry Whitwam (drums). Herman's name was derived from the group mishearing the names of the cartoon characters, Sherman & Bullwinkle, and Herman & The Hermits became Herman's Hermits after seeing a Liverpool band, Faron's Flamingos.

It was not the music which drew Mickie Most to Herman's Hermits, but the look of their lead singer, 16 year-old Peter Noone. He recalled, "Their manager sent me a photograph of Herman's Hermits at Piccadilly Station in Manchester, and Peter Noone looked like a young Kennedy. I thought this face is saleable, especially in the United States. All I need to do is find cute songs to go with it."

Most's prime ability was in finding ideal material for his artists. He asked Herman's Hermits to cover a new song by Gerry Goffin & Carole King, 'I'm Into Something Good', and the sultriness of Earl-Jean's original was replaced by Peter's boyish enthusiasm. Like Little Eva, Earl-Jean McCrea was a member of The Cookies and they recorded 'Chains', which was covered by The Beatles.

Herman's Hermits version of 'I'm Into Something Good' topped the UK charts and also broke the band in the States. Strangely, the band never had another UK number one. They topped the US charts with 'Mrs. Brown, You've Got A Lovely Daughter' and 'I'm Henry VIII, I Am', but Most decided against novelties for UK singles.

Peter Noone comments, "Mickie Most was the perfect record producer. He was more a record director actually, if I can use a film analogy. He made me believe in what I was doing and he helped me to imagine that every situation I was singing about was real."

To this day, Peter Noone opens his stage act with 'I'm Into Something Good'. Herman's Hermits may be regarded as naff today but hearing Peter in concert, you realise the strength of many of their hits – 'No Milk Today', 'There's A Kind Of Hush' and 'I Can Take Or Leave Your Loving'. They compare favourably to anything by another Manchester group, The Hollies.

179 Roy Orbison
Oh Pretty Woman

Label & Cat No.: **London HLU 9919**
Producer: **Wesley Rose**
Writers: **Roy Orbison / Bill Dees**
Date reached No.1: **8 October 1964**
Weeks at No.1: **2**

ROY ORBISON WAS WRITING WITH Bill Dees at his house when his wife, Claudette, came in and said flirtatiously, "Give me some money, honey. I'm going to the store." Bill Dees offered, "A pretty woman don't need no money" and Roy started singing, "Pretty woman walking down the street." "He sang it while I was banging my hand down on the table," recalls Bill, "and by the time she returned, we had the song." Fred Foster at Monument Records said it needed an ending so that they added a coda in which Roy gets the girl.

Bill Dees says, "I love the song. From the moment that the rhythm started, I could hear the heels clicking on the pavement, click, click, the pretty woman walking down the street, in a yellow skirt and red shoes. Perhaps it's a sailor singing the song. She goes by and flashes him a half-smile as if to say, 'I am above this.' He looks at his watch and when he looks back, she's looking at him. We wrote 'Oh Pretty Woman' on a Friday, the next Friday we recorded it, and the next Friday it was out. It was the fastest thing I ever saw. Actually, the 'yeah, yeah, yeah' in 'Oh Pretty Woman' probably came from The Beatles."

Roy's growl and cry of 'Mercy' also make the record distinctive. "I can't do that growl like Roy," says Bill Dees, who performs 'Oh Pretty Woman' in his own act, "but the 'Mercy' is mine. I used to say that all the time when I saw a pretty woman or had some good food. Still do." Dees said 'Mercy' when he found that the song was being used in the Julia Roberts' film, *Pretty Woman* (1990).

180 Sandie Shaw
(There's) Always Something There To Remind Me

Label & Cat No.: **Pye 7N 15704**

Producer: **Tony Hatch**

Writers: **Burt Bacharach / Hal David**

Date reached No.1: **22 October 1964**

Weeks at No.1: **3**

SANDRA GOODRICH WAS BORN IN Dagenham, Essex in 1947, home of UK-built Ford cars, girl pipers and Dudley Moore. She worked as a machine operator for IBM but wanted to be a singer. When Adam Faith & The Roulettes were appearing on a charity concert in Hammersmith, Sandie went to see them and sang in the dressing-room. Both Adam and his manager, Eve Taylor, were impressed and in no time, she had a new name, Sandie Shaw, and a Pye recording contract. The first single, 'As Long As You're Happy', drew comparisons with Cilla Black, but the song was not strong enough to break through.

Lou Johnson, a much underrated singer in the Ben E. King vein, recorded the original version of the Burt Bacharach & Hal David song, '(There's) Always Something There To Remind Me'. Eve Taylor thought that the song would be perfect for Sandie and the arrangement was by a classical musician, Les Williams, making his pop debut. Considering that Sandie was an inexperienced 17 year old, she did extremely well in attempting the same vocal nuances as Dionne Warwick and the single entered the charts a fortnight after release.

Sandie Shaw was a publicist's dream – tall and skinny with a model's looks, but also short-sighted and performing barefoot. Sandie's autobiography, published in 1991, was called *The World At My Feet,* but that's not wholly accurate. At first, she was barred from performing in America because she was "not of sufficiently distinguished ability to get a work permit". The authorities relented and after appearing on *The Ed Sullivan Show*, her follow-up to '(There's) Always Something There To Remind Me', 'Girl Don't Come' was a minor US hit.

Although Sandie has never performed on the oldies circuit, she did record '(There's) Always Something There To Remind Me' with a new arrangement for the 1986 film, *Letter To Brezhnev*.

181 The Supremes
Baby Love

Label & Cat No.: **Stateside SS 350**

Producers: **Brian Holland / Lamont Dozier / Eddie Holland**

Writers: **Brian Holland / Lamont Dozier / Eddie Holland**

Date Reached No.1: **21 November 1964**

Weeks at No.1: **2**

THE HISTORY OF MANUFACTURED singing groups stretches back to over 40 years and continues to this day. Among the most successful group mentors was Milton Jenkins who created two hugely successful acts of the Sixties, The Temptations and The Supremes.

Jenkins discovered Eddie Kendricks, Cal Osbourne and Paul Williams singing together in Alabama and brought them to Detroit. Naming them The Primes, he signed them to Tamla Motown in the late Fifties. He then decided to assemble an all-female group to complement The Primes, and in1959 persuaded his friend Florence Ballard to give up training as a nurse to become a singer. She brought in her school friend Mary Wilson and, between them, decided on the third member, Betty Travis. However, Betty's mother felt that her daughter's studies were suffering and pulled her out of the group, so she was briefly replaced by Barbara Martin. Most girl groups of the day were made up of four members, so they went in search of a final member. Paul Williams, from The Primes, discovered Diane Ross and brought her to Milton's attention. The line-up was now complete and given the name, The Primettes. At the end of 1960, Barbara left and the group reverted to a trio. The Primes became The Temptations and The Primettes were renamed The Supremes.

The Supremes wanted to be signed to Motown and Diane (who changed her name to Diana) asked her friend and neighbour, Smokey Robinson, to introduce them to Berry Gordy Jr. They auditioned for him by singing The Drifters' 'There Goes My Baby' but were unsuccessful and signed with Lu-Pine records instead. Still keen to be signed to Motown, they spent time at the studio and were eventually invited to provide hand-claps and backing vocals for Marvin Gaye. Gordy, who had become attracted to Diana, eventually signed them to Motown.

'Where Did Our Love Go', which was written for, but rejected by, The Marvellettes, became their first of 12 US chart toppers. When 'Baby Love' became their only British number one, The Supremes achieved the distinction of being the first all-girl group to top the chart.

The Supremes complained to the writers about being given 'baby-type songs', preferring faster and beefier numbers like Martha & The Vandellas' 'Heatwave'. As they became more established, they soon had first refusal of Holland, Dozier & Holland material, which Martha Reeves later complained about. 'Where Did Our Love Go' and 'Baby Love' were simple songs with repetitive verses and Diana's breathy "Oo ooh's" gave both songs their sexy feel.

Once Gordy and Diana became a couple, he began to promote her more than the band, even changing the group's name to 'Diana Ross & The Supremes', much to her fellow band members' chagrin.

'Where Did Our Love Go' was such an instant US smash, that there was no time to demo the follow-ups, 'Baby Love' and 'Come See About Me'. All three songs were written in one session and recorded within two weeks. Lamont Dozier recalled, "I'd usually come up with an idea, Brian and I would finish it off and then straight off to the studio and cut it with the band". Not bad for a day's work.

Although 'Baby Love' was their only UK number one, they charted with 18 UK hit singles before Diana broke free to launch a successful solo career. The remaining Supremes, with various personnel changes over the years, managed five Top 10 hits before going their separate ways.

182 The Rolling Stones
Little Red Rooster

Label & Cat No.: **Decca F 12014**

Producer: **Andrew Loog Oldham**

Writer: **Willie Dixon**

Date reached No.1: **3 December 1964**

Weeks at No.1: **1**

"MORE POWER TO THE ROLLING Stones," says Manfred Mann's lead singer, Paul Jones, "I think it was a fantastic achievement to take a down-home blues to number one. That can never be taken away from them. It's a great song, a very funny one."

'Little Red Rooster' was a coyly erotic blues song written by the Chess bass player, Willie Dixon, who also wrote 'Hoochie Coochie Man', 'Pretty Thing' (a UK hit for Bo Diddley in 1963), 'I Just Want To Make Love To You' (a UK hit for Etta James in 1996) and 'Back Door Man'. The cantankerous Howlin' Wolf recorded a bellowing, highly-charged 'Little Red Rooster' for Chess in 1961. Sam Cooke with Billy Preston on organ gave the song a more laid-back, sophisticated styling in 1963 and it reached number 11 on the US pop charts, again a very respectable position for a blues song.

The Rolling Stones recorded their version in November 1964 in the Chess studio with Willie Dixon looking on. Jagger's vocal is full of witty innuendo and Brian Jones played some beautiful slide guitar. The single was certainly controversial and many wondered why the BBC hadn't banned it for its sexual content. Doubtless no-one at the Beeb realised why the rooster's absence led to mayhem in the farmyard.

The B-side, 'Off The Hook' showed that Jagger & Richards could write fine R&B songs of their own and from then on, they would be writing their own A-sides.

183 The Beatles
I Feel Fine

Label & Cat No.: **Parlophone R 5200**

Producer: **George Martin**

Writers: **John Lennon / Paul McCartney**

Date reached No.1: **10 December 1964**

Weeks at No.1: **5**

THE BEATLES WERE CONSIDERING A track from *Beatles For Sale* as a Christmas single, but then John Lennon came up with 'I Feel Fine'. Or did he? Would John have written that tricky little riff if he hadn't heard Bobby Parker's R&B single from 1961, 'Watch Your Step'?

It was a great rock'n'roll single, although when interviewed John seemed more proud of the introductory noise than the song itself. The sound isn't Ringo's new electric shaver, but the feedback from John's Rickenbacker which wasn't as spontaneous as he would have you believe. John claimed, "It's the record with the first feedback anywhere." Probably recorded in the first flush of the group's encounter with marijuana, he wanted to claim that The Beatles were doing it before The Who.

'I Feel Fine' was The Beatles' sixth consecutive number one and not even Elvis had achieved such a run. A track from *Beatles For Sale* would have worked just as well as 'Eight Days A Week' became a US number one.

'I Feel Fine', also a US number one, was first played in America by a radio station in Los Angeles. Because of audience demand, the station, KRLA, played it every hour. To celebrate The Beatles' achievements, Baskin-Robbins created a new flavour of ice-cream – Beatle Nut.

184 Georgie Fame & The Blue Flames
Yeh Yeh

Label & Cat No.: **Columbia DB 7428**

Producer: **Tony Palmer**

Writers: **Rodgers Grant / Pat Patrick / Jon Hendricks**

Date reached No.1: **14 January 1965**

Weeks at No.1: **2**

CLIVE POWELL WAS BORN IN LEIGH, Lancashire in 1943 and he says, "I had piano lessons when I was seven but I was thoroughly bored and gave it up. Then I heard Fats Domino and Little Richard and Jerry Lee Lewis and that was the great inspiration." When Clive was only 16, he was hired as a pianist by the impresario, Larry Parnes. Parnes was planning to call him Lance Fortune, but another singer had nicked the name, and so he went to the next one on his list, Georgie Fame: "I loathed the name, Georgie Fame, at first. Larry said, 'You remind me of Wee Georgie Wood and you're going to be famous.' He also said that if I didn't accept the name, he wouldn't give me the job, and I needed the job."

The newly-named Georgie Fame found himself on that fateful tour with Eddie Cochran and Gene Vincent in 1960, but shortly afterwards Parnes sacked him for playing jazz on a concert with The Shadows at the Olympia in Paris. To the end of his life, Larry Parnes was disappointed with Fame, "I don't know why he was so keen on jazz. I could have made him into another

Tommy Steele and got him pantomimes and West End shows."

Georgie established his own group, The Blue Flames, and they became known around London clubs like The Flamingo and The Marquee: "I loved Mose Allison and I remember an American GI giving me a single of 'Green Onions' by Booker T. & The MG's. I was so impressed that I bought a Hammond organ the next day." Their 1963 album, *Rhythm And Blues At The Flamingo*, soon acquired a cult status, but their first singles, '(Do) The Dog' and 'Do Re Mi', didn't sell.

The group made number one with 'Yeh Yeh', on some copies 'Yeah Yeah', which was a most unlikely choice for a commercial single. "No, I disagree," says Georgie, "It was commercial in a way. It was recorded originally by Mongo Santamaria. Jon Hendricks put lyrics to it and recorded it live at The Newport Jazz Festival. I played it up and down the country for months before we recorded it. We were wondering what to do as a single and somebody said, 'Why don't you do 'Yeh Yeh'?' and it went down well."

185 The Moody Blues
Go Now

Label & Cat No.: **Decca F 12022**
Producer: **Denny Cordell**
Writers: **Larry Banks / Milton Bennett**
Date reached No.1: **28 January 1965**
Weeks at No.1: **1**

THE PREDICTION, "LIVERPOOL TODAY, Birmingham tomorrow", did not materialise, but some excellent performers did emerge from Brum beat – The Moody Blues, The Move, Idle Race, ELO, Raymond Froggatt and Steve Gibbons.

El Riot & The Rebels was a skiffle group which turned to beat and became Birmingham's most popular group around 1962, but they broke up after failing an EMI audition. Ray Thomas and Mike Pinder formed a new group, The Krew Cats, and went to Hamburg. When they returned some months later, they found 200 groups in Birmingham, many of them copying The Beatles. Realising that the only way to make an impact was to form a local supergroup, they teamed up with Denny Laine, Graeme Edge and Clint Warwick. They called themselves The M&B 5 as they were playing Mitchells & Butlers pubs. When the brewery refused to sponsor them, they became The Moody Blues.

The Moody Blues signed with the London manager, Tony Secunda, and he secured a recording contract with Decca. Their first single, a Mike Pinder original, 'Lose Your Money', lost money, but the next was 'Go Now' with an impassioned lead vocal from Denny Laine. The gospel-styled love song, written by Larry Banks, had been recorded by his wife, Bessie, for Blue Cat Records in 1964. Her record was produced by Jerry Leiber and Mike Stoller and is an emotional *tour de force* though not as commercial as the Moodys' treatment.

Alan Freeman was one of the first to play The Moody Blues' 'Go Now' and Paul McCartney was so impressed that he rang the BBC to praise the record and hopefully hear it again. The switchboard, doubting his call was genuine, refused to put him through to Fluff.

The Moody Blues had minor chart entries with 'I Don't Want To Go On Without You' (33), 'From The Bottom Of My Heart' (22) and 'Everyday' (44), but even a change of management to Brian Epstein didn't restore their success. In 1967 they reconstituted themselves with Pinder, Thomas and Edge remaining and John Lodge and Justin Hayward coming in. The new look Moody Blues made a fortune with their orchestral-styled rock but they never got back to number one.

The Moody Blues

And as for Denny Laine? Well, turn to 'Mull Of Kintyre'.

186 The Righteous Brothers
You've Lost That Lovin' Feelin'

Label & Cat No.: **London HLU 9943**
Producer: **Phil Spector**
Writers: **Barry Mann / Cynthia Weil / Phil Spector**
Date reached No.1: **4 February 1965**
Weeks at No.1: **2**

THE NEW YORKERS, BARRY MANN and Cynthia Weil often wrote songs for Phil Spector's acts and he invited them to Hollywood to see his latest signing, The Righteous Brothers. The duo, Bill Medley and Bobby Hatfield, were becoming known for R&B shouters such as 'Little Latin Lupe Lu' and 'My Babe', but Phil wanted a strong ballad for his Wall of Sound treatment.

Cynthia Weil remembers, "We started to write 'You've Lost That Lovin' Feelin'' and we called Phil and played it to him, and I said, 'You've Lost That Lovin' Feelin'' is not the right title, we'll get something better,' and he said, 'No, that's the title' and we finished it with him. That whole middle section was Phil's idea. We played it for Bill Medley and Bobby Hatfield, and Bobby was not happy because Bill had the whole first verse. He said, 'What am I supposed to do while the big guy's singing?' and Phil said, 'You can go to the bank!' That record had Phil Spector's touch; he created a whole new sound. We knew that this was somebody who had vision."

Barry Mann: "We knew we had written a great song. The production was so great that I felt nothing could stop this record, but when Phil first played it for me over the phone, I thought it was at the wrong speed."

The Righteous Brothers topped the US chart but in the UK they had to compete with a cover version from Cilla Black. At first, Cilla climbed the chart faster, but Stones manager Andrew Loog Oldham took out an ad in *Melody Maker* praising the Righteous Brothers' record and they came to the UK for a week's promotion which swung it round. Says their publicist, Tony Hall, "Thank God the British public came to their senses and bought the magnificent record by The Righteous Brothers in vast quantities. Cilla Black's version soon disappeared." Nevertheless, Cilla did reach number two.

Curtis Stigers commented, "The way that record unfolds is one of the greatest moments of popular music. 'You're All That Matters To Me' was my homage to Phil Spector and to The Righteous Brothers. How can you not love his records?"

187 The Kinks
Tired Of Waiting For You

Label & Cat No.: **Pye 7N 15759**

Producer: **Shel Talmy**

Writer: **Ray Davies**

Date reached No.1: **18 February 1965**

Weeks at No.1: **1**

After two wild singles, 'You Really Got Me' (1) and 'All Day And All Of The Night' (2), Ray Davies wrote a much gentler song, 'Tired Of Waiting For You' which suggested a talent which could rival that of Lennon & McCartney. By the end of the year, we knew that was true.

When Ray and brother Dave were practising in their Muswell Hill home, Ray had written an instrumental inspired by Chet Atkins' guitar style. Late in 1964 he realised that he could rework this 'plink-plonk country song' and it became 'Tired Of Waiting For You'. Dave Davies recalled, "The recording went well but there was something missing and it was my raunchy guitar sound. Ray and I were worried that putting that heavy-sounding guitar on top of a ponderous song might ruin it. Luckily, it enhanced the recording, giving it a more cutting, emotional edge. In my opinion, 'Tired Of Waiting' was the 'perfect pop record'."

The Kinks had further hits in 1965 with Ray Davies' songs, 'Everybody's Gonna Be Happy' (a tribute to Tamla-Motown), 'Set Me Free' (a public message to his management), 'See My Friend' (a touching, Indian-influenced song about the loss of friendship) and 'Till The End Of The Day' (a return to the prototype heavy metal of 'You Really Got Me'). The sarcasm and cynicism which is such a feature of his later work can be heard in 'A Well Respected Man', the lead track on their number one EP, *Kwyet Kinks*. The development of his songwriting skills can also be heard in the hit albums, *Kinda Kinks* and *The Kink Kontroversy*.

188 The Seekers
I'll Never Find Another You

Label & Cat No.: **Columbia DB 7431**

Producer: **Tom Springfield**

Writer: **Tom Springfield**

Date reached No.1: **25 February 1965**

Weeks at No.1: **2**

Despite a lifelong struggle with bronchiectasis, Judith Durham, who was born in Melbourne in 1943, sang classical music as a child and traditional jazz in her teens. She met Athol Guy who was singing with Keith Potger and Bruce Woodley and he told her that they were looking for a girl singer and wanted to form an Australian equivalent to The Weavers. "I started listening to Ronnie Gilbert of The Weavers, of course," says Judith, "but I do think there's a bit of Joan Baez, Bessie Smith, Vera Lynn and Maria Callas in me as well."

The Seekers had success around Melbourne and made a few records. Athol worked for an advertising agency that had a shipping company amongst its clients and he arranged for The Seekers to entertain the passengers sailing to England. He sent tapes of the group to various promoters and when they landed in the UK, they found work was waiting for them. "We were on a big variety bill in Blackpool with Dusty Springfield," recalls Judith. "She had left The Springfields, but she said that her brother, Tom, might write us a song. Tom listened to our records and wrote 'I'll Never Find Another You' for us. Tom took us into a studio and it was recorded on a very low budget. Actually, I slept through the alarm and had to get a taxi to the session which was a big deal for me. They'd done everything else by the time I'd got there, so once I'd put my vocal on, it was complete."

'I'll Never Find Another You' would have suited The Springfields, so does Judith think that Dusty might have wished 'I'll Never Find Another You' for herself? "No, but she very much admired Tom's work and he wrote that wonderful hit, 'Losing You', for her. She left The Springfields because she wanted to sing with more soul. The Springfields, on the other hand, were very much in our image, very middle of the road, if you like."

189 Tom Jones
It's Not Unusual

Label & Cat No.: **Decca F 12062**

Producer: **Peter Sullivan**

Writers: **Gordon Mills / Les Reed**

Date Reached No.1: **13 March 1965**

Weeks at No.1: **1**

A little fibbing in the beginning didn't do Tom Jones' career any harm at all. The original press release for 'It's Not Unusual' stated that 'He's Tom Jones, he's 22, single and a miner'. Actually, he was Thomas Woodward, 25, married (with a son) and had never been down a mine in his life.

88.3
RADIO SYD

Tom was born in Pontypridd, South Wales in 1940. He formed a group called The Senators and, adopting the stage name Tommy Scott, went out on the road. Before coming to the attention of The Viscounts' singer Gordon Mills, Tom & The Senators had set up a recording session in London with Joe Meek. Although they signed a contract, Tom and Joe were ill-matched and so they parted company.

"Gordon came to see us at the Top Hat Club in Cwmtillery" explained Tom, "He said, 'My God, you should be in London'. I said, 'I understand that, but who do I talk to when I get there?'" Gordon promptly left The Viscounts and signed a management deal with Tom and, to cash in on the success of the film of the same name, Gordon renamed him Tom Jones.

His first release was a cover of Ronnie Love's 'Chills And Fever', but when that made no impact, Gordon dropped The Senators to concentrate on Tom's solo career.

"Gordon and Les Reed wrote 'It's Not Unusual' with Sandie Shaw in mind," said Tom, "and I was asked to record the demo." Gordon took it to Sandie's manager, Eve Taylor, who hated it and sent them on their way. The song was then offered, unsuccessfully, to Frankie Vaughan. Tom continued, "I then decided that I wanted to release it myself and was adamant about it. I said to Gordon, 'If you don't let me record this, then you're not my manager any more.'"

"We did two very different versions of the song," recalled Tom. "The first one was milder with just one trombone doing the brass riff, then Les Reed came up with the idea of the brass following the bass drum and it made it a much hotter record. There was nothing like it at the time, maybe the closest thing was Motown, who also used brass in a pop song, but it sounded very unique in 1965."

'It's Not Unusual' broke Tom in the US and it was with Les' Las Vegas-styled, punchy arrangement that Tom was able to show off his powerful voice. Tom flirted with the women in the audience by swaying his hips around in a sexual way. His stage presence and raw sex appeal caused women to remove their underwear and throw it at him.

Tom, like Cliff Richard, has stood the test of time, having hits over five decades. In 1997 he was awarded an OBE and a year later, Welsh band Space, together with Cerys Matthews from Catatonia, paid tribute to him with the Top five hit 'The Ballad Of Tom Jones'.

190 The Rolling Stones
The Last Time

Label & Cat No.: **Decca F 12104**

Producer: **Andrew Loog Oldham**

Writers: **Mick Jagger / Keith Richards**

Date reached No.1: **18 March 1965**

Weeks at No.1: **3**

Mick Jagger & Keith Richards were becoming increasingly proficient as songwriters, writing album tracks and B-sides as well as a hit for Marianne Faithfull ('As Tears Go By'). Their first A-side was 'The Last Time' and they also wrote the slow and insidious 'Play With Fire' on the flip. As in the best blues tradition, the song borrowed from existing records – James Brown's 'Maybe The Last Time' and The Staple Singers' 'This May Be The Last Time'.

In January 1965 The Stones recorded 'The Last Time' at the RCA Studios in Hollywood with both Phil Spector and his arranger, Jack Nitzsche in attendance and making suggestions to Andrew Loog Oldham. Indeed, Spector plays an acoustic guitar and Nitzsche harpsichord on 'Play With Fire'.

Even with this amount of production talent available, Mick Jagger was unhappy with his vocal and he returned to re-record it a month later. It was worth the effort as Jagger's vocal is superb, while Keith Richards' guitar riff propels the song along.

Andrew Loog Oldham recorded an orchestral version of 'The Last Time' for the 1966 LP, *The Rolling Stones Songbook*. This was sampled, without permission, on The Verve's 1997 number one, 'Bitter Sweet Symphony', which led to Richard Ashcroft having to share his songwriting royalties with Jagger & Richards.

191 Unit Four Plus Two
Concrete And Clay

Label & Cat No.: **Decca F 12071**

Producer: **John L. Barker**

Writers: **Brian Parker / Tommy Moeller**

Date reached No.1: **8 April 1965**

Weeks at No.1: **1**

The key BBC radio programme for hearing the current hits was *Pick Of The Pops*, which the presenter Alan Freeman had divided into units. Hence, the group name – Unit Four Plus Two – for a six man band from St. Albans, also the home of The Zombies. They made the Top 50 in 1964 with 'The Green Fields', a cheerful Seekers-styled song.

Their founder, Brian Parker, formerly a guitarist with The Hunters, had had the melody for 'Concrete And Clay' for some months, and Tommy Moeller, in a burst of inspiration added the lyric in 10 minutes. "I was working in the Stock Exchange," he says, "and I remember taking bets that it would get to number one. I liked our version and I also liked the revival by Randy Edelman when he added violins." Unit Four Plus Two's sound was enhanced on the single by guitarist Russ Ballard and drummer Bob Henrit, who left Adam Faith's Roulettes to join the band for six months.

The B-side was a very pleasant, close harmony version of 'When I Fall In Love': "That shows The Letterman as being one of our influences. It also shows how naïve we were. Why didn't we put one of our own songs on the B-side?" says Tommy Moeller today.

The follow-up, 'You've Never Been In Love Like This Before', reached number 14. "It's rather a clumsy title," admits Tommy, "but I wasn't a good enough singer for that song, Buster Miekle should have done it."

Billy Moeller, Tommy's brother, was the group's roadie but he had his own moment of pop fame when the record producer Noel Walker, masquerading as Whistling Jack Smith, had a Top 10 hit with 'I Was Kaiser Bill's Batman' in 1967. Noel didn't want to appear on *Top Of The*

A threat to the nation! The Rolling Stones in 1965, left to right: Bill Wyman, Brian Jones, Mick Jagger and Keith Richards with Charlie Watts on drums at the back

Pops, so Billy Moeller took his place.

Tommy Moeller returned to his Australian homeland after his hits. He supported himself by writing advertising jingles. He wrote songs for the films *Cathy's Child* and *Mango Tree*, and he returned to the UK in 1993 when he wrote a West End musical, *Leonardo*, with another brother, Greg. The musical took a hammering, but as Tommy says, "Critics are always going to be critical when you write about a genius." *Leonardo* had been financed by an independent republic, Nauru, which made its money from fertiliser taken from guano, the excrement of sea birds. No prizes for guessing what the critics said.

192 Cliff Richard
The Minute You're Gone

Label & Cat No.: **Columbia DB 7496**

Producer: **Norrie Paramor**

Writer: **Jimmy Gately**

Date reached No.1: **15 April 1965**

Weeks at No.1: **1**

SONNY JAMES ONLY MADE THE UK charts with 'The Cat Came Back' (30, 1956, but a great children's favourite) and 'Young Love' (11, 1957), but he had a succession of American country hits. In 1963 he made number nine on the US country charts with the ballad, 'The Minute You're Gone', which also scraped into the US Hot 100. The writer, Jimmy Gately, played fiddle for Bill Anderson's Po' Boys and wrote his 1965 country hit, 'Bright Lights And Country Music'.

In the early Sixties it was fashionable for leading British stars to record in Nashville, and both Lonnie Donegan ('Fisherman's Luck') and Helen Shapiro (LP, *Helen In Nashville*) did good work there. In August 1964 Cliff Richard went to Nashville to record with the young producer, Billy Sherrill and he was backed by top flight session musicians as well as The Jordanaires. The three sessions yielded eight songs including the hit singles, 'The Minute You're Gone', 'On My Word' (10) and 'Wind Me Up (Let Me Go)' (2). Unfortunately, Cliff didn't record enough for an album. The producer, Billy Sherrill, went on to produce Charlie Rich and Tammy Wynette as well as Elvis Costello's Nashville album, *Almost Blue*.

Cliff then headed to New York where he recorded 'Angel'. A few weeks later he was in Lisbon, recording an album called *When In Rome*. He was moving so fast, he probably didn't know where he was.

193 The Beatles
Ticket To Ride

Label & Cat No.: **Parlophone R 5265**

Producer: **George Martin**

Writers: **John Lennon / Paul McCartney**

Date reached No.1: **22 April 1965**

Weeks at No.1: **3**

IN 1960 THE TEENAGE JOHN LENNON AND Paul McCartney hitch-hiked to Ryde in the Isle of Wight to visit a couple of Paul's relatives who ran a pub. Five years later, that holiday inspired the punning title, 'Ticket To Ride', one of those puns being an allusion to drugs. The song was mostly written by John who described it as 'one of the earliest heavy metal records' and, inspired by The Who, it had their fullest and toughest sound to date. The track is an early example of the band starting to experiment, and Dave Ballinger, drummer with The Barron Knights, says, "Just listen to that record for the drums. The part Ringo plays is fantastic. He shows that you don't have to be a technical, Buddy Rich-type drummer to be inventive."

'Ticket To Ride' was on the soundtrack of their second film, *Help!*, which also included 'You're Going To Lose That Girl' and 'You've Got To Hide Your Love Away'. A highlight of the album was what became The Beatles' most covered song, 'Yesterday', although their version was not issued as a single in the UK at the time.

'Ticket To Ride' was number one when Liverpool FC reached the FA Cup Final and won the trophy for the first time. Fans who obtained tickets would tell their friends that they had a ticket to ride to Wembley.

194 Roger Miller
King Of The Road

Label & Cat No.: **Philips PB 1397**

Producer: **Jerry Kennedy**

Writer: **Roger Miller**

Date reached No.1: **13 May 1965**

Weeks at No.1: **1**

EVEN BY COUNTRY MUSIC STANDARDS, Roger Miller wrote some of the quirkiest songs in the business. They include 'You Can't Roller Skate In A Buffalo Herd', 'My Uncle Used To Love Me But She Died' and best of all, 'Pardon This Coffin (My Brother Just Died)'. His 1964 US hits, 'Dang Me' and 'Chug-A-Lug', failed to connect with the British public, but he broke through the following year with 'King Of The Road'.

Roger Miller was on tour and coming into Chicago, he saw a sign, "Trailers For Sale Or Rent". He wrote the first verse of 'King Of The Road', but got no further. In Boise, Idaho, he saw a statuette of a hobo in the airport and he bought it and stared at it until he had completed the song. He included 'King Of The Road' in a live concert that he recorded in Printers Alley in Nashville, but he left it off the album as it deserved a studio recording.

Listeners are divided as to whether his 1966 hit, 'England Swings', is a parody or a tribute, but Miller loved the UK and just thought it would be fun to include the sights that American tourists seek out. Roger could sing sentimental songs and he was the first to record Bobby Russell's 'Little Green Apples' and Kris Kristofferson's 'Me And Bobbie McGee'. His King Of The Road Motel in Nashville proved to be a solid investment.

In 1985 he wrote a Broadway musical, *Big River*, but he had to stop singing when he contracted throat cancer. Still bursting with humour, he went on stage at the *Grand Ole Opry* and croaked to Bill Anderson, who was known for his intimate narrations, 'Hey, Anderson, I'm stealing your act.' In 1992 it was Roger and out.

195 Jackie Trent
Where Are You Now (My Love)

Label & Cat No.: **Pye 7N 15776**

Producer: **Tony Hatch**

Writers: **Tony Hatch / Jackie Trent**

Date Reached No.1: **22 May 1965**

Weeks at No.1: **1**

JACKIE WAS BORN YVONNE BURGESS IN 1940 in Newcastle-Under-Lyme. As a young girl she showed all the signs of being a star. At eight, she appeared in *Babes In The Wood*, and at the tender age of 12, she decided on a name change, after the town close to where she grew up – Stoke-On-Trent. By 18 she was making a name for herself on the cabaret circuit and landed some television appearances on the *Saturday Night Specials* with Morecambe & Wise and *The Mike & Bernie Winters Show*.

Tony Hatch was born on June 30, 1939. He briefly joined Top Rank Records in 1960 and had his first hit as a producer with Bert Weedon's 'Twelfth Street Rag', later the same year he joined Pye Records. Under the pseudonym, Mark Anthony, he wrote songs for Julie Grant and Benny Hill. He met Jackie in 1965. She had already been writing material for her own stage act and they found songwriting together came easy. Tony explained, "I would always write the tune and I would always suggest the title for it as I find that helps with the formation of the tune. I would often do the chorus and one or two lines of the verse. I do a quick cassette for her and say, fill in the holes, and then I would review the whole thing with her and probably make some more alterations, but it worked out quite well."

They married in August 1967 and their songs have been covered by an array of artists including Scott Walker ('Joanna'), Frank Sinatra ('Call Me') and Sammy Davis Jr ('I Know A Place'). Jackie said, "It was like a sausage factory, we were churning out hit after hit after hit. Petula Clark recorded 13 of our songs." Jackie also wrote Val Doonican's number two hit, 'What Would I Be?'.

In the Seventies an Australian friend of Jackie and Tony's, Reg Watson, was working for Associated Television on a new soap opera. He asked them to write a signature tune. The show became *Crossroads*.

Jackie and Tony spent a lot of time on the road. They regularly toured Australia, so much so that they made it their home in the Eighties. Meanwhile, Reg Watson had left the UK and after moving back to his native country, began working for the Reg Grundy organisation. He wanted to introduce a new series that was set in Australia, but would be marketable, at least in Britain. The series became *Neighbours* and again, Jackie and Tony were asked to compose the theme.

Jackie and Tony left Australia in 1995 and moved to Spain but split a year later. Both still live in Spain. Tony married his third wife Maggie. Jackie worked with British songwriter, Roger Cook, in Nashville in the late Nineties.

196 Sandie Shaw
Long Live Love

Label & Cat No.: **Pye 7N 15841**

Producer: **Chris Andrews**

Writer: **Chris Andrews**

Date reached No.1: **27 May 1965**

Weeks at No.1: **3**

ALTHOUGH BURT BACHARACH & HAL David wrote '(There's) Always Something There To Remind Me', the follow-up, in the same dramatic vein, was 'I'd Be Far Better Off Without You' written by Chris Andrews. Chris Andrews was a singer and songwriter, also managed by Eve Taylor, and he was soon tailoring material especially for Sandie. "I looked upon Chris like a big brother," says Sandie now, "I would tell him what was happening in my life, and many of his songs are about a teenage girl's angst, my angst, if you like. 'Stop Feeling Sorry For Yourself' is a good example of that, although it was a song that Adam Faith released. It's a great song and I wish I'd had it as a single myself."

'I'd Be Far Better Off Without You' did not send fans rushing to the shops, but the DJ's picked up on the B-side, also written by Andrews, 'Girl Don't Come'. That made number three and then another Andrews's song, 'I'll Stop At Nothing', was number four. By now, Sandie Shaw was a fashion icon and admirers wanted to copy her dresses and her hairstyle. Even though she was famous for being barefoot, there was Sandie Shaw footwear.

Sandie's fourth hit, again written by Chris Andrews, was a cheerful song with a reggae flavour, 'Long Live Love', which Chris also used in his own act. It had all the ingredients of a Eurovision song (although it wasn't) and the title was used for a different song, which was Olivia Newton-John's entry in 1974. Sandie's song was revived by Nick Berry in 1992.

197 Elvis Presley with The Jordanaires
Crying In The Chapel

Label & Cat No.: **RCA 1455**

Producers: **Steve Sholes / Chet Atkins**

Writer: **Artie Glenn**

Date reached No.1: **17 June 1965**

Weeks at No.1: **2 (two runs)**

AS A TEENAGER, ELVIS PRESLEY WOULD watch gospel groups in Memphis and wanted to join The Blackwood Brothers. He recorded gospel songs whenever he could and his first album devoted to the music, *His Hand In Mine* (1960), won him a gold disc. In 1965 came the bizarre news that an outtake from the *His Hand In Mine* sessions, 'Crying In The Chapel' was to be released as a single. After a succession of feeble singles, it was hard to understand what RCA was doing.

The truth was somewhat different. Elvis had recorded 'Crying In The Chapel' at the *His Hand In Mine* sessions, but its release had been withheld because Colonel Parker wanted the publishing rights. Hard to see why he expected to succeed as it was an established song, being written by Artie Glenn in 1953 and making the US charts for Artie's son, Darrell, the singing cowboy Rex Allen and the doowop group, The Orioles. Intuitively, Elvis brought his sexuality to the song, which widened its appeal. Neal Matthews of The Jordanaires recalled, "Elvis was feeling really good that day. He fooled around with it and then he cut it in five minutes."

Elvis won his first Grammy for *How Great Thou Art*, the Best Sacred Performance of 1967. In that same year, Elvis released the single, 'Indescribably Blue', which was written by Darrell Glenn and made the UK Top 30.

198 The Hollies
I'm Alive

Label & Cat No.: **Parlophone DB 5287**
Producer: **Ron Richards**
Writer: **Clint Ballard Jr**
Date Reached No.1: **26 June 1965**
Weeks at No.1: **3 (2 runs)**

THE BEATLES WERE FANS OF BUDDY Holly and picked their name as a variation on The Crickets, Buddy's backing group. The Hollies were also influenced by Buddy Holly and chose their name as a tribute to him.

Graham Nash and Allan Clarke met at school and soon struck up a friendship and an interest in music, particularly the influential Lonnie Donegan. They formed a duo, originally called The Two Teens, then The Four Tones and finally Ricky & Dane. They had a guest spot with The Flintstones, whose bass player was Eric Haydock. They decided to expand and recruited Eric along with guitarist Tony Hicks and drummer Don Rathbone. After a couple of brief spells as The Dominators Of Rhythm and The Deltas, they settled on The Hollies. After two singles, Rathbone was replaced by Bobby Elliott.

The Hollies, who had been billed, to their irritation, as Manchester's answer to The Beatles at the Cavern, followed the Fabs by having several US hits, but a number one US hit eluded them.

Clint Ballard Jr had already written songs for Frankie Avalon ('Gingerbread'), Jimmy Jones ('Good Timin'), Swinging Blue Jeans ('You're No Good') and Wayne Fontana & The Mindbenders ('The Game Of Love'). He wrote 'I'm Alive' for The Hollies, but when they passed on it, it was offered to another Manchester band, The Toggery Five. The Toggery Five's version, having been recorded at Abbey Road studios, was never released because The Hollies decided to record it after all.

'I'm Alive', which spent three weeks at the top in two separate stints, was later used in two different commercials; firstly in 1996 for *Boots* Winter medicine and again in 2001 for *Holland & Barrett* stores.

199 The Byrds
Mr Tambourine Man

Label & Cat No.: **CBS 201765**
Producer: **Terry Melcher**
Writer: **Bob Dylan**
Date Reached No.1: **24 July 1965**
Weeks at No.1: **2**

ALTHOUGH THE ANIMALS, WHO HAD topped the UK singles chart a year earlier, combined both folk and rock music in the form of 'The House Of The Rising Sun', it is really The Byrds who are credited for pioneering folk-rock music.

The Byrds' lead singer, Jim McGuinn, who had toured with the Chad Mitchell Trio and played guitar for Bobby Darin, was inspired to buy his first 12-string Rickenbacker after seeing George Harrison play one in *A Hard Day's Night*. Realising he wanted to form his own group, he recruited Gene Clark and David Crosby along with session bassist Larry Knechtel and drummer Hal Blaine and they called themselves The Jet Set. Shortly after, Crosby suggested that Michael Clarke be brought in as resident drummer and Chris Hillman on bass. On Thanksgiving Day 1964, with a nod to The Beatles by mis-spelling their name, they became The Byrds.

Doris Day's son, Terry Melcher, was Columbia records' youngest producer and had been assigned to work with The Byrds. A&R man Jim Dickson had a demo with Bob Dylan on vocals and Ramblin' Jack Elliott singing the high harmony, it was in 2/4 time and had a country feel. He gave the tape to Terry and urged him to record it with The Byrds. Jim explained, "It was Terry's idea to use the 'A-team'. They were a group of musicians who were doing most of the stuff in L.A. at the time. Glen Campbell was supposed to be on the session but was unable to make it. Terry also wanted to put a kind of Beach Boys feel to it. I think he was trying to emulate 'Don't Worry Baby'." In turn, Jim created a unique vocal resembling the diversity of John Lennon and Bob Dylan. The line-up was Jim on guitar and lead vocals, Gene and David on backing vocals, Jerry Cole (rhythm guitar), Larry Knetchel (bass), Leon Russell (electric piano) and Hal Blaine (drums).

Bob Dylan had the idea for 'Mr Tambourine Man' after seeing folk guitarist Bruce Langhorne playing a gigantic tambourine. As Bob said, "It was as big as a wagon wheel and that image stuck in my mind."

In 1967 Jim briefly converted to the Subud religion. He changed his christian name to Roger after an Indonesian spiritual guru asked him to list 10 names beginning with letter R. Jim, a Sci-Fi fan, replied with names like 'Rocket' and 'Ramjet'. But the only real name he included was Roger, which he liked because it stands for OK in the radio telecommunications language and that was the one the leader chose.

'Mr Tambourine Man' originally had four verses but eventually was cut down to just one. Jim now includes any number of those verses in his solo performances.

Many critics have suggested that the tam-

The Byrds, America's answer to The Beatles and the architects of folk rock, left to right: David Crosby, Chris Hillman, Gene Clark, Michael Clarke and Roger McGuinn

bourine man is a drug dealer, but Bob Dylan maintains a silence about his compositions. Nevertheless, it is hard to see how a bona fide tambourine player could take you on board a magic swirling ship…

200 The Beatles
Help!

Label & Cat No.: **Parlophone R 5305**
Producer: **George Martin**
Writers: **John Lennon / Paul McCartney**
Date reached No.1: **5 August 1965**
Weeks at No.1: **3**

THE SECOND BEATLES' FILM, *HELP!*, was more conventional than the first and although it had its moments, it lacked the originality of *A Hard Day's Night*. It was saved by an extraordinary score, although, like its predecessor, none of the songs were nominated for Oscars. The Academy Awards Committee preferred to ignore the existence of rock'n'roll.

As with *A Hard Day's Night, Help!* was directed by Dick Lester and this time The Beatles were supported by a great team of character actors including Patrick Cargill, Eleanor Bron, Victor Spinetti, Warren Mitchell, and Leo McKern. Patrick Cargill recalled, "Dick Lester made himself into a fifth Beatle so that he could get onto their wavelength. He made it appear as though they had invented what to do, where he was still directing it. He got them to be totally at ease and I thought it was a very clever thing to do. I remember them coming in and saying that they had written a tune the previous night. They played 'Help!' and I thought it was terrific. I said, 'That'll go straight to the top of the charts' and it did."

'Help!' rescued the film from its naff original title, *Eight Arms To Hold You*, but it is more than the title song for a pretty daft film: it was John Lennon in the psychiatrist's chair. "When 'Help!' came out, I was actually crying for help," he reflected, "I didn't realise it at the time. I just wrote the song because I was commissioned to write it for the movie." But was John right? Tony Barrow, The Beatles' press officer, believes that John was talking with hindsight and it is just coincidence that the song turned out that way.

John was proud of the song's vocabulary: how many pop songs included such multi-syllabled words as 'independence'? He explained, "Maureen Cleave asked me, 'Why don't you ever write songs with more than one syllable?' In 'Help!' there are three syllable words and I very proudly showed them to her, and she still didn't like it."

Roger Cook, who co-wrote the 1965 number two by The Fortunes, 'You've Got Your Troubles', says, "There isn't a musician in England who didn't learn something from The Beatles, but I like to think that they picked up a trick or two from us. Roger Greenaway and I wrote a counter-melody on 'You've Got Your Troubles' and there hadn't been one in a hit song for years. A few weeks later, The Beatles came out with 'Help!' and there is a counter-melody in that."

201 Sonny & Cher
I Got You Babe

Label & Cat No.: **Atlantic AT 4035**
Producer: **Sonny Bono**
Writers: **Sonny Bono**
Date reached No.1: **26 August 1965**
Weeks at No.1: **2**

SONNY BONO WAS A JOBBING SONGwriter (he wrote 'You Bug Me Baby', the B-side of Larry Williams's 1958 hit, 'Bony Moronie') and he worked as a studio lackey for Phil Spector. Whilst there, he met the backing vocalist Cher (Cherilyn Sarkisian) and they recorded as Caesar & Cleo in 1963, the year they got married. Falling in line with hippie trends, they wore outlandish clothes and sang their declaration of love, 'I Got You Babe'. Sonny, then aged 30 but not admitting it, looked the oldest teenager in the business.

'I Got You Babe' topped the US charts and Larry Page was in charge of their UK promotional tour. He asked them to dress in their hippiest of clothes and then register at The Dorchester Hotel. Naturally, they were asked to leave and Page arranged for a photo-shoot of them pitching their wigwam in Hyde Park. Outstanding publicity, and the single soared to number one. The duo was also helped by a bizarre mime on *Ready, Steady, Go!* in which Brian Jones and Cathy McGowan became Sonny & Cher.

Almost immediately, the market was saturated with Sonny & Cher records ('Baby Don't Go', 'But You're Mine') as well as solo ones by Sonny ('Laugh At Me', 'The Revolution Kind') and Cher ('All I Really Want To Do', 'Bang Bang (My Baby Shot Me Down)'). They had a popular TV variety show in the US for many years, but by 1974, they had split, both professionally and privately. Sonny became the Mayor of Palm Springs and was elected to Congress in 1994, dying in a skiing accident in 1998. His headstone bears the title of Sonny & Cher's 1967 hit, 'The Beat Goes On'. Cher became a superstar with further entries in this book.

202 The Rolling Stones
(I Can't Get No) Satisfaction

Label & Cat No.: **Decca F 12220**
Producer: **Andrew Loog Oldham**
Writers: **Mick Jagger / Keith Richards**
Date reached No.1: **9 September 1965**
Weeks at No.1: **2**

'(I CAN'T GET NO) SATISFACTION' WOULD be a great record even if it ended before Mick Jagger sang. Keith Richards wrote an explosive rock'n'roll riff which belongs alongside 'Bo Diddley', 'Sweet Little Sixteen', 'La Bamba', 'Louie Louie' and 'Summertime Blues'. Like those classics, the riff hypnotically continues throughout the record. You become hooked to the rhythm which is why 'Satisfaction' is such a perfect party record as well as one which summed a whole

Sixties attitude.

The Rolling Stones were on a schedule of non-stop touring and, early in 1965, they were in America. Keith normally partied until dawn but one night in Clearwater, Florida, he was tired. A riff was going through his head, so he switched on his recorder. He fell asleep and he recalls, "The next morning I listened to the tape. It was about two minutes of this acoustic guitar playing a very rough riff of 'Satisfaction' and then me snoring for 40 minutes." Keith thought his riff was inspired by Martha & The Vandellas' 'Dancing In The Street', although that was a song of happiness and 'Satisfaction' is one of frustration.

Mick came up with the title, '(I Can't Get No) Satisfaction', and he could speak for his fans by writing some anti-establishment lyrics. It was the first of the Stones' compositions with a social bite as Mick complains of being bored, the low quality of television, fraudulent advertising and his problems with girls. In one sense, Mick is being as world-weary as his blues heroes: in another, he is a frustrated, suburban youth, and the song could be seen a precursor for The Clash and The Jam in the late Seventies.

The Stones recorded four album tracks and a first take of 'Satisfaction' at a marathon session at Chess Records in Chicago on May 1965. Then they went to RCA in Hollywood and completed their hit song. Keith was not convinced: "I wanted to cut it again but I don't think we could have done it right. You need horns to knock that riff out."

The US radio stations thought the record was controversial and the reference to "trying to make some girl" was bleeped when they appeared on *The Ed Sullivan Show*. The record became a US number one but because Andrew Loog Oldham did not like the Stones in opposition to The Beatles, its release was delayed in the UK until 'Help!', another song of frustration, had run its course. The pirate stations took to playing it long before release and as it was so familiar, it did not stay on top as long as expected. The B-side, 'The Spider And The Fly', was a hilarious slow blues about an ageing groupie. 'Satisfaction' was number one in 38 different countries and Keith was delighted with Otis Redding's cover version – at last the horns were playing his riff.

When a reporter asked Keith if he still had the tape on which he had composed 'Satisfaction', he replied, "No, tapes rot after 100 years, you know."

203 The Walker Brothers
Make It Easy On Yourself

Label & Cat No.:	**Philips PB 1428**
Producer:	**Johnny Franz**
Writers:	**Burt Bacharach / Hal David**
Date reached No.1:	**23 September 1965**
Weeks at No.1:	**1**

SCOTT ENGEL, JOHN MAUS AND GARY Leeds have a background of working with different American musicians – the drummer Gary Leeds, for example, had come to the UK with P.J. Proby in 1964. Calling themselves The Walker Brothers, they impressed the TV producer, Jack Good, who put them on the *Shindig* TV show and encouraged them to go to the UK.

The Walker Brothers' first hit, 'Love Her', had been made in America with Phil Spector's arranger, Jack Nitzsche, and produced by Nick Venet. It sounded like a lush Phil Spector production for The Righteous Brothers and it became the template for the Walker Brothers' hits. The UK producer, Johnny Franz, was impressed but he felt Scott could do better and sent him to a vocal coach, Freddie Winrose, who expanded his range. It was a brilliant move and Franz found them some wonderful songs – 'Make It Easy On Yourself' (Jerry Butler), 'The Sun Ain't Gonna Shine Anymore' (Frankie Valli) and 'My Ship Is Coming In' (Jimmy Radcliffe). Their records were very slow, very echoey, very powerful, very orchestrated, very confident and very Spector. What's more, their cover version of "Walking In The Rain" is superior to Spector's original with The Ronettes.

Praise too for Ivor Raymonde's arrangements. "I used to play piano on the sessions," says songwriter Phil Coulter, "and I would pilfer the arrangements. I would take them home and study exactly what Ivor Raymonde was doing. He was the best in the country and I learnt a lot from him."

'Make It Easy On Yourself' was originally recorded by The Isley Brothers under the title, 'Are You Lonely?', but their version was not to be released for almost 40 years. The song was apparently promised to Dionne Warwick for her first single and she was furious when Bacharach & David reneged on their word and gave it to Jerry Butler. It must be said that Dionne claims the rights to almost every Bacharach & David song from the Sixties and woe betide anyone who recorded them first! Jerry Butler's version was a US Top 20 hit in 1962 but it had no UK success. "It happens sometimes," says John Walker. "A record gets lost when it shouldn't have been. Scott was an excellent singer but very demanding and I had to match him note for note to make it work. Scott preferred to be in the studio, but I liked working live even though I couldn't hear him on stage once Walkermania started." And just what did Gary do? "Oh, Gary was Gary," says John, "He was always happy and he had a great fan following."

It is surprising that no one has had a hit record with this song since 1965, although it has been covered by Johnny Mathis, The Three Degrees and The Divine Comedy. In 2001 its majestic opening was sampled by Ash on their Top 20 single, 'Candy'.

204 Ken Dodd
Tears

Label & Cat No.:	**Columbia DB 7659**
Producer:	**Norman Newell**
Writers:	**Billy Uhr / Frank Capano**
Date reached No.1:	**30 September 1965**
Weeks at No.1:	**5**

WHAT WAS THE TOP-SELLING RECORD of 1965? It came from Liverpool, but surprisingly, it wasn't anything by The Beatles or a

Merseybeat group, it was by the comedian Ken Dodd.

Variety hall comics like to end their act with a song and some of them (Charlie Drake, Benny Hill, Tommy Cooper) have had hit records. Ken Dodd was better placed than most as he had a trained voice and had sung in his church choir. "Well, I did 'til they found where the noise was coming from," he jokes. "My father had a musical ear – it was shaped like a French horn."

Starting with 'Love Is Like A Violin' in 1960, Dodd had a succession of hits, the zenith being 'Tears', which had been recorded by the original megaphone man, Rudy Vallée, in 1929. "It had been a waltz and we thought we'd have a hit if we did it four beats to the bar," says Ken, "I love singing songs about love and romance, it's the Mills & Boon in me."

"The disc-jockeys hated it," he adds. "They couldn't find words that were bad enough to say about it, but it didn't matter. The public was ready for a tuneful, singalong song and you can't keep a good song down. You can be the squarest of squares, but if you make a good record, you can still get there."

Ken Dodd still performs 'Tears' in his three-hour stage shows, but his signature tune, 'Happiness' (1964) remained outside the Top 30.

205 The Rolling Stones
Get Off Of My Cloud

Label & Cat No.: **Decca F 12263**
Producer: **Andrew Loog Oldham**
Writers: **Mick Jagger / Keith Richards**
Date reached No.1: **4 November 1965**
Weeks at No.1: **3**

FOLLOWING 'SATISFACTION', THE Rolling Stones were moving into the same league as The Beatles, and so Andrew Loog Oldham asked the New York accountant, Allen Klein, to negotiate better royalty rates for them with Decca Records. This he did and the first single under the new deal was 'Get Off Of My Cloud'.

As with 'Satisfaction', adolescent *angst* was the subject of The Rolling Stones' 'Get Off Of My Cloud'. Mick lives in a high-rise flat and he wants to be left alone, but he has trouble with nuisance callers, noisy neighbours and parking tickets. The reference to his car misled some into thinking that the song was about a Rolls-Royce Silver Cloud, but more likely, Jagger was advocating flying away on a marijuana-induced trip.

David Jacobs' complained on *Juke Box Jury* that he couldn't hear the lyrics, prompting Keith Richards to remark, "Maybe he's a bit deaf. He should stick to records like 'Tears'." However, Oldham liked to use Mick's voice as an instrument in the mix and the vocals were deliberately submerged by the driving rhythm with Charlie effectively playing lead drums. Although there are very few covers of this song, it has become an anthem with crowds at Stones' concerts picking up on the 'Hey, you' chant.

The Stones now had five consecutive number ones, but the run was broken when the next single, '19th Nervous Breakdown', made number two.

206 The Seekers
The Carnival Is Over

Label & Cat No.: **Columbia DB 7711**
Producer: **Tom Springfield**
Writer: **Tom Springfield**
Date reached No.1: **25 November 1965**
Weeks at No.1: **3**

MIKE HURST OF THE SPRINGFIELDS assesses Tom Springfield's songwriting, "This is going to sound like I am putting him down but it's quite the opposite. Tom was immensely good at finding old folk tunes and doing something new with them. 'Say I Won't Be There' is 'Au Clair De La Lune' and 'Island Of Dreams' is a mixture of 'Carry Me Back To Old Virginny' and 'The Rose Of Tralee'. 'The Carnival Is Over' is the cleverest of all as he revamped a Russian folk tune and wrote an English lyric."

The Seekers had followed 'I'll Never Find Another You' with 'A World Of Our Own', which reached number three, but they returned to the top with 'The Carnival Is Over'. Judith Durham reflects, "That was a great song that still lives on today. It is a perennial favourite and it is sung at weddings. We were very, very blessed to have met Tom Springfield as he never compromised the integrity of the group and he never got us to do things that we didn't want to do. We were, after all, completely different from everything else that was happening at the time."

Although The Seekers followed 'The Carnival Is Over' with a new Paul Simon song, 'Someday One Day', it only made number 11. The children's favourite, 'Morningtown Ride', made number two and became the theme music for the BBC request programme, *Junior Choice*. The title song of the film, *Georgy Girl*, written by Tom Springfield and Jim Dale was a number three. "I was struggling with my weight and I identified with that frumpy, overweight kindergarten teacher played by Lynn Redgrave. We became friends and she wrote a foreword for my autobiography," says Judith, now slim and svelte and much admired by audiences on the UK tour to celebrate her 60th birthday in 2003.

207 The Beatles
We Can Work It Out / Day Tripper

Label & Cat No.: **Parlophone R 5389**
Producer: **George Martin**
Writers (both songs): **John Lennon / Paul McCartney**
Date reached No.1: **16 December 1965**
Weeks at No.1: **5**

THE BEATLES, WHO HAD BEEN IRRITATED by poor B-sides on some of their favourite records, always determined to give value for money. They couldn't decide which side was the stronger – 'We Can Work It Out' or 'Day Tripper'

– and so it was issued as a double A-side with both sides being listed on the charts.

More than any other song, 'We Can Work It Out' demonstrates the differences between Lennon and McCartney's personalities and writing skills. McCartney writes the upbeat, optimistic verses and then Lennon crashes in with the bitter-sweet middle eight which gives the song its bite. 'We Can Work It Out' also illustrates McCartney's tendency to be always in the right – "Try to see it my way", that is, no room for debate here.

'Day Tripper' started as a private joke – "She's a prick teaser" – but quickly became a commercial song – "She's a big teaser", indeed. "We liked putting in references that we knew our friends would get, but the mums and dads wouldn't," admitted Paul McCartney, who also acknowledged the references to drugs. The song and its arrangement is a homage to Stax Records and Otis Redding repaid the compliment with a trenchant cover. Curiously though, Otis didn't regard his versions of 'Satisfaction' and 'Day Tripper' as covers: he told his friends that he had written both songs.

208 The Spencer Davis Group
Keep On Running

Label & Cat No.:	**Fontana TF 632**
Producer:	**Chris Blackwell**
Writer:	**Jackie Edwards**
Date reached No.1:	**20 January 1966**
Weeks at No.1:	**1**

THE BROTHERS, MERVYN, KNOWN AS Muff (born 1943), and Steve (born 1948), Winwood were playing in their father's dance band in Birmingham from an early age. In his short trousers, Steve would play a rock'n'roll medley on the piano. They met a blues singer and guitarist, Spencer Davis, who had a degree in modern languages and taught German. With Spencer's friend, Pete York, on drums, they formed The RBQ (Rhythm And Blues Quartet) for a residency at The Golden Eagle in Birmingham. "He was still a pupil at Great Barr Comprehensive," says Spencer, "while I was a schoolteacher in Wittington Oval. It was an unusual set-up but it worked. The first love was the music, not how old we were, and we sounded great."

Chris Blackwell heard the group when he came to Birmingham with his artist, Millie of 'My Boy Lollipop' fame. They were renamed The Spencer Davis Group as he made the decisions and they liked his distinctive name. Blackwell became their manager and secured a leasing deal with Millie's label, Fontana, for their work with his fledgling Island Records. He and his friend, Guy Stevens, who ran Island's Sue label, looked for obscure but distinctive R&B songs that the group could cover. Their first single, John Lee Hooker's 'Dimples', was issued in April 1964 and they had their first chart entries with The Soul Sisters' 'I Can't Stand It' (47, 1964), Brenda Holloway's 'Every Little Bit Hurts' (41, 1965) and The Malibus' 'Strong Love' (44, 1965).

The breakthrough came when Blackwell asked one of his Jamaican artists, Jackie Edwards, if he had anything suitable. He played them a ska song he had written, 'Keep On Running', which Steve reworked on the piano. Following Keith Richards' lead in 'Satisfaction', Muff Winwood used a fuzzbox and the resulting record was upbeat and catchy with a riff to die for.

The Spencer Davis Group was praised by The Beatles and many were fascinated by Steve's voice as he sounded much older than he was. Spencer says, "No one had seen a picture of the group in America and in 1966, the radio was split into black and white stations. 'Keep On Running' was played on black stations in the States and when they saw a picture of these four shining little white boys, the record was dropped from the playlists, so the momentum was lost. We got through to America in the end with 'Gimme Some Lovin'."

209 The Overlanders
Michelle

Label & Cat No.:	**Pye 7N 17034**
Producer:	**Tony Hatch**
Writers:	**John Lennon / Paul McCartney**
Date reached No.1:	**27 January 1966**
Weeks at No.1:	**3**

WHEN PAUL MCCARTNEY WAS DATING Jane Asher, he liked to amuse their friends with a song in cod French. He played it to John Lennon who thought it had potential and John added a middle section – "I love you, I love you, I love you" – which he took from Nina Simone's 'I Put A Spell On You'. Paul wrote a lyric that was partly English, partly French and he later recalled, "I got the French off Jan, who is the wife of Ivan Vaughan, and years later I sent her a cheque. I thought I better had as she is virtually a co-writer on that, From that I pieced together the verses."

The Beatles put 'Michelle' on their 1965 album, *Rubber Soul*, and it was briefly considered for a UK single. However, The Beatles' favoured up-tempo 45s, not even releasing 'Yesterday' as a single. Knowing that The Beatles wrote potential hits, one British act after another raided *Rubber Soul;* The Hollies recorded 'If I Needed Someone' (to George's distress), Three Good Reasons and The Settlers 'Nowhere Man' and St. Louis Union and The Truth 'Girl'.

The Overlanders were a folk-based group very much in the mould of The Springfields, The Seekers and The Settlers. The nucleus of the group had been Laurie Mason (the blond lead singer), Paul Arnold and Peter Bartholomew, and they added Terry Widlake and David Walsh when they wanted a fuller sound. They had been recording for Pye since July 1963, but none of their nine singles, including The Shadows' song, 'Don't It Make You Feel Good', had made the charts.

'Michelle' was also covered by David & Jonathan, actually the songwriters Roger Greenaway and Roger Cook, and their record was produced by George Martin. Both versions made

the charts but David & Jonathan's stopped at number 11. "Our version was the hit in America and we did get to tour there on account of that," says Roger Cook. "There was a rumour that we were John and Paul incognito and hundreds of girls would be waiting and screaming when we got to a radio station. I hope they weren't too disappointed."

Somewhat foolishly, The Overlanders rush-released a cheapskate album, *Michelle*, that simply gathered their old singles together. Their follow-up, 'My Life', a catchy but predictable song written by Tony Hatch, failed to connect.

Roger Greenaway says, "The Overlanders had a more original treatment than us as we merely copied what The Beatles had done, and thank goodness they had the number one and not us. Lots of acts had hits with The Beatles' songs and were never heard of again."

210 Nancy Sinatra
These Boots Are Made For Walkin'

Label & Cat No.: **Reprise RS 20432**

Producer: **Lee Hazlewood**

Writer: **Lee Hazlewood**

Date reached No.1: **17 February 1966**

Weeks at No.1: **4**

IN 1965 THE SONGWRITER AND producer, Lee Hazlewood, was living off the royalties from Duane Eddy's hits. His friend, Jimmy Bowen, worked for Frank Sinatra's label, Reprise, and offered him exceptional terms to make stars of the boy band, Dino, Desi & Billy. This he did with 'I'm A Fool' and ' Not The Lovin' Kind' and he also secured a US hit for Dino's dad, Dean Martin, with 'Houston'.

Next up was Frank's daughter, Nancy, who had cut several singles without success. She had been recording drippy teen songs and Lee wanted something with more bite. As he said to her, "You're not a virgin, you're a grown woman, we have to reflect that." The first attempt was 'So Long Babe' and the second, 'These Boots Are Made For Walkin'', which Lee had written about her crumbling marriage to the rock'n'roll singer, Tommy Sands. Nancy regretted the tough, trampling 'Boots': "The image created by 'Boots' isn't the real me," she said in 1971, "'Boots' was hard and I'm as soft as they come."

But then Lee had written the song for himself. "It was a party song I had written two or three years before that. It was a joke to begin with and we were doing the follow-up to 'So Long Babe', which made the charts just a little bit. I had written a beautiful song for her, 'The City Never Sleeps At Night', and she said, 'Do you think this will sell?' I said, 'Three times more than 'So Long Babe' and that did 60,000. We're building up your career.' I changed my mind and put it on the back of 'Boots' and that sold six million."

Nowadays record companies have their contracts on computer but in 1966 everything was by hand, and something could be missed. Lee Hazlewood reveals what happened: "When 'Boots' was number one in half the countries in the world, Nancy came over to my house and she was crying. She said, 'They didn't pick up on my option at Reprise and they said that I owed them $12,000.' I said, 'You're kidding, we've got the biggest record in the world.' I rang my lawyer in New York and I rang Nancy the next day and said, 'How would you like $1m? I've got three labels that are offering that for you right now, and I can get something pretty good for myself as well.' She talked to Daddy who said she could write her own contract with Reprise – after all, she was selling more records than him at the time. I said, 'Okay, what we'll say is – you never pay any musicians, you never pay studio time and after three years, you get your masters.' She said, 'That sounds good.' I said, 'Just don't tell them it was me as I've got to work with the other artists here.'"

'These Boots Are Made For Walkin'' was a transatlantic number one and sparked off a succession of hits including 'Sugar Town', 'Somethin' Stupid' (with her dad), the James Bond theme 'You Only Live Twice' and some oddball duets with the deep-voiced Hazlewood, 'Jackson', 'Ladybird', 'Sand' and 'Some Velvet Morning'. She was the female lead in the 1968 Elvis Presley film, *Speedway*, and she returned to the charts in 1971 when a playful duet with Lee Hazlewood, 'Did You Ever', reached number two. In 1981 she recorded an album of duets with the country star, Mel Tillis, but, by and large, she stopped performing.

In 1995 Nancy wrote a lavish biography of her father, *Frank Sinatra – An American Legend*, which offered no criticisms of his behaviour. She is back on stage now and has made a stance for the older woman by posing nude for *Playboy*.

211 The Walker Brothers
The Sun Ain't Gonna Shine Anymore

Label & Cat No.: **Philips BF 1473**

Producer: **Johnny Franz**

Writers: **Bob Crewe / Bob Gaudio**

Date reached No.1: **17 March 1966**

Weeks at No.1: **4**

BOB GAUDIO, A MEMBER OF THE Four Seasons, co-wrote 'The Sun Ain't Gonna Shine Anymore' with The Seasons' producer, Bob Crewe: "It was written for The Righteous Brothers. Bob Crewe and I were working on it one day when Frankie passed Bob's office and said, 'That's mine. I want that song and I'm going to record it.' We never did send it to The Righteous Brothers and I'm sorry that Frankie's version didn't become a major success. It was Top five in a number of local markets, Boston, Hartford, Philadelphia, but we suspected that the record company didn't want it to become a success because they were afraid that Frankie might leave the group. Lo and behold, eight months later and on the same label, Smash Records in the US, The Walker Brothers released it with a similar arrangement but a faster tempo, and that was number one in England. I thought it was fabulous but I preferred it at our tempo. Of course, that might have been the difference between success and failure."

The Walker Brothers, John Maus, Gary Leeds and Noel Engel, who relocated from the US to the UK in 1965 to find success

The record achieved notoriety. When Ronnie Kray burst into an East End pub, The Blind Beggar, to shoot George Cornell, 'The Sun Ain't Gonna Shine Anymore' was playing on the jukebox. One of the bullets hit the jukebox and the record kept repeating, 'The sun ain't gonna shine anymore, anymore, anymore' as Cornell lay dying.

The Walker Brothers' record restored them to number one but none of their subsequent records including 'Another Tear Falls' and 'Stay With Me Baby' made the Top 10. Scott Walker had some solo success – 'Joanna', 'Lights Of Cincinnati' and some highly original Jacques Brel songs including the controversial adventures of a gigolo, 'Jackie'.

The trio reformed in 1976, securing another Top 10 hit with 'No Regrets', but the reunion was short-lived. Scott Walker has organised a Meltdown Festival on London's South Bank and made some experimental CDs, but he has never returned to performing his hits. In 2004 John Walker performed a Walker Brothers set to great acclaim on a UK tour with Peter Noone, Brian Hyland and Wayne Fontana.

212 The Spencer Davis Group
Somebody Help Me

Label & Cat No.: **Fontana TF 679**
Producer: **Chris Blackwell**
Writer: **Jackie Edwards**
Date reached No.1: **14 April 1966**
Weeks at No.1: **2**

JACKIE EDWARDS' SONG, 'KEEP ON Running', did so well for The Spencer Davis Group that he was asked for another. There's nothing wrong with 'Somebody Help Me', except that 'Keep On Running' was first. It repeated the strengths of 'Keep On Running', but when Edwards and The Spencer Davis Group tried it a third time with 'When I Come Home', written by Jackie with Steve Winwood, the record only reached number 12.

By now The Spencer Davis Group were starting to write their own material – 'Gimme Some Loving' was a Top 10 single in November 1966 and is now also associated with The Blues Brothers. It was followed by 'I'm A Man', which was revived with great success by Chicago in 1970. They decided to promote 'I'm A Man' and then split up in April 1967.

The Spencer Davis Group released three fine albums – *Their First LP, The Second Album* and *Autumn '66* – as well as performing on the soundtrack of the Swinging Sixties film, *Here We Go Round The Mulberry Bush*. Steve's new group, Traffic, is also featured on that soundtrack. He is now a major solo artist, working as Steve Winwood and having a US number one with 'Higher Love' (1986). Muff Winwood became an A&R man and was appointed head of A&R at CBS Records in London, and many of the acts in this book owe their break to him. The Spencer Davis Group remains a working band, playing club dates and festivals around the world.

213 Dusty Springfield
You Don't Have To Say You Love Me

Label & Cat No.: **Philips PB 1482**
Producer: **Johnny Franz**
Writers: **Pino Donaggio / Vito Pallavicini / Vicki Wickham / Simon Napier-Bell**
Date reached No.1: **28 April 1966**
Weeks at No.1: **1**

DUSTY SPRINGFIELD BEGAN HER HIT-making career as part of the folk group, The Springfields, but she developed a more soulful voice with her solo career, becoming the best British female singer of the Sixties. Her successes included the bouncy 'I Only Want To Be With You', the Bacharach & David ballad, 'I Just Don't Know What To Do With Myself' and two poignant Carole King & Gerry Goffin songs, 'Some Of Your Lovin'' and 'Goin' Back'. The highpoint of her career is the 1968 album, *Dusty In Memphis*, which is as good as anything by Aretha Franklin and includes another hit single, 'Son-Of-A Preacher Man'.

In 1966 Dusty heard an Italian song she liked at The San Remo Festival, 'Io Che No Vivo Senza Ta', performed by its composer Pino Donnagio, and she brought it back to the UK. She asked her friend, Vicki Wickham, who produced *Ready, Steady, Go!* if she could write an English lyric. "Vicki and I used to eat together," says Simon Napier-Bell, the manager of The Yardbirds, "And she told me that Dusty wanted a lyric for this song. We went back to her flat and started working on it. We wanted to go to a trendy disco so we had about an hour to write it. We wrote the chorus and then we wrote the verse in a taxi to wherever we were going. It was the first pop lyric I'd written, although I've always been interested in poetry and good literature."

And is it a translation of the Italian song? "Oh, no, we'd no idea what the Italian lyric said. That seemed to be irrelevant and besides, it is much easier to write a new lyric completely." Though they didn't know it, the title translates to 'I Don't Want To Live Without You', so there wasn't much difference. The song has been recorded hundreds of times with further hit versions from Elvis Presley (1971), Guys And Dolls (1976) and Denise Welch (1995): "Yes, but most of them are a bit limp. Only Elvis and Dusty gave it that real kick."

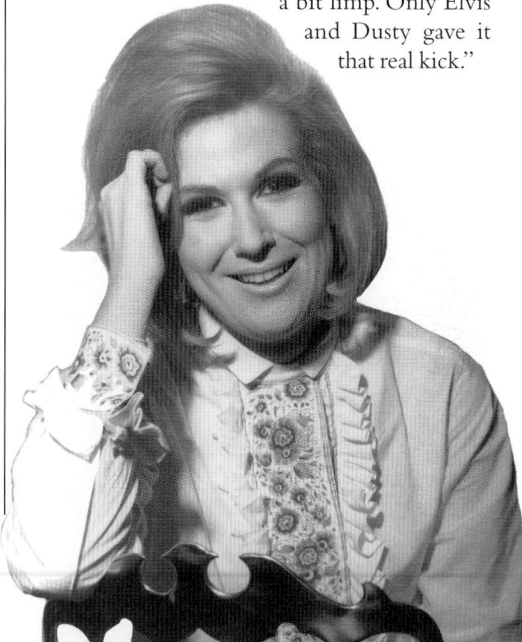

Dusty Springfield

214 Manfred Mann
Pretty Flamingo

Label & Cat No.: **HMV POP 1523**

Producer: **John Burgess**

Writer: **Mark Barkan**

Date reached No.1: **5 May 1966**

Weeks at No.1: **3**

"MANFRED MANN WAS A COOPERATIVE," says Manfred, their keyboard player from South Africa. "We shared the money equally but I was seen as the big mouth, the spokesman. I can see now that it was because I was an immigrant. If the band didn't work out, the rest could simply go home, but I couldn't. I wanted to stay in England so the band had to be successful."

As a result of Manfred's skill in picking and arranging songs, the group had a succession of hits -'Do Wah Diddy Diddy' first and then there was 'Sha La La', 'Come Tomorrow', 'Oh No Not My Baby' and 'If You Gotta Go, Go Now'. "My favourite of all our records is 'If You Gotta Go, Go Now'," says Tom McGuinness, "The lyric still makes me smile and the record has an atmosphere about it."

Manfred Mann's record producer, John Burgess, brought the group a new song, 'Pretty Flamingo', written by Mark Barkan from a psychedelic group from Philadelphia, The Deep. Manfred Mann's lead singer Paul Jones, recalls, "'Pretty Flamingo' was the first song that was brought to the band from someone other than ourselves. I didn't like it much as it didn't have a black flavour, but I see now that it could have been done by The Drifters. Ben E. King could have done a great job on it."

Although the Manfreds were immensely successful, Paul Jones had already handed in his notice – he would give them time to recruit a new singer. He reflects, "I was after more fame and glory than they were able to provide – oh, and more money. I was a bit sick of people saying 'Wotcha, Manfred' to me. A lot of people in the business were telling me that if I did go solo, they could arrange this or that, and I said, 'All right then'. I don't regret it. I did earn a lot more on my own."

"I wasn't sure what would happen when Paul left," says Tom McGuinness, "I thought 'Pretty Flamingo' might be our swan song."

Bruce Springsteen and his E Street Band often performed a knockout version of 'Pretty Flamingo' in his pre-'Born To Run' days, always prefaced by a hilarious Bruce 'rap' about a girl the band idealised, but they never recorded it officially.

Manfred Mann

215 The Rolling Stones
Paint It, Black

Label & Cat No.: **Decca F 12395**

Producer: **Andrew Loog Oldham**

Writers: **Mick Jagger / Keith Richards**

Date reached No.1: **26 May 1966**

Weeks at No.1: **1**

BILL WYMAN SAYS, "I DIDN'T THINK MY bass was punchy enough on 'Paint It, Black' and I asked if I could overdub something. I laid on the floor and I played the organ pedals with my fists, and I got a double beat going with the bass and the bass pedals of the organ. It worked as it gave the record a completely different feel." The record also sounded distinctive because of Brian Jones' sitar playing: the Indian instrument had hardly been used in rock before 'Norwegian Wood' (1965) and Jones handled it far more rhythmically than George.

'Paint It, Black' was released at the same time as The Rolling Stones' album, *Aftermath*. Mick Jagger and Keith Richards had written all the songs on *Aftermath* as well as both sides of the single, 'Paint It, Black' (No one knows why Decca put a comma in the title as Mick doesn't sing it that way) and 'Long Long While'. 'Paint It, Black' was included on the US copies of *Aftermath* as the authorities objected to the saga of drug-taking amongst suburban housewives in 'Mother's Little Helper' and the song was removed to prevent the album from being banned by record stores.

In May 1966 *NME* asked Mick about 'Paint It, Black' and he responded, "It means paint it black. 'I can't get no satisfaction' means I can't get no satisfaction. The rest of the song is expanding on that."

216 Frank Sinatra
Strangers In The Night

Label & Cat No.: **Reprise RS 23052**

Producer: **Jimmy Bowen**

Writers: **Bert Kaempfert / Charles Singleton / Eddie Snyder**

Date reached No.1: **2 June 1966**

Weeks at No.1: **3**

THE GERMAN BANDLEADER AND composer, Bert Kaempfert, had written the score for the spy spoof, *A Man Could Get Killed*, starring James Garner, Melina Mercouri and Sandra Dee. When Frank Sinatra's producer, Jimmy Bowen, heard one of the melodies, he told the publisher, Hal Fine, to come up with some English lyrics and Sinatra would record it. Two lyrics were written and rejected before Bowen approved of 'Strangers In The Night' for Sinatra. However, by then the publisher had become somewhat disillusioned and had passed the song to both Jack Jones and Bobby Darin.

When Jack Jones released 'Strangers In The Night' as a single, Sinatra wanted to hire stranglers in the night to teach the publisher a lesson. Bowen coaxed him into the studio to record a

cover version and within three days, Sinatra had nailed 'Strangers In The Night' with a fine arrangement from Ernie Freeman with Glen Campbell on lead guitar.

The UK impresario Jeff Kruger recalls, "I represented Frank Sinatra's publishing for countless years and when they were doing 'Strangers In The Night', Glen Campbell didn't know the song and had been brought in at the last minute. Sinatra liked to do his recordings in one take and then go home or play golf. Glen hadn't heard the song and he was busking on the first take but listening to the melody. When they told Sinatra, he would have to do it again, he yelled out to Glen, 'Is that guy with us or is he sleeping?' He was learning the song and he came up with that famous guitar phrase which helped to make it a hit."

The wordless vocalising at the end (the "dooby dooby doo") was added spontaneously, and it became one of Sinatra's trademarks. Despite Jimmy Bowen's approval, Sinatra never cared for the song thinking it was "about two fags in a bar". In Jerusalem in 1975, he told his audience, "Here's a song I cannot stand, but what the hell..."

The single was rush-released in the States and Frank Sinatra had the satisfaction of having a number one on his own record label. Surprisingly, Sinatra's best-known Reprise single, 'My Way' (1969) only made number 27 in the US and number five here.

217 The Beatles
Paperback Writer / Rain

Label & Cat No.: **Parlophone R 5452**

Producer: **George Martin**

Writers (both songs): **John Lennon / Paul McCartney**

Date reached No.1: **23 June 1966**

Weeks at No.1: **2**

IN A SENSE, 'PAPERBACK WRITER' WAS A throwback to The Beatles' early work as it is based upon their love of Chuck Berry. On the other hand, the storytelling aspect of the song is very much in the style that Paul McCartney was developing. It is an unusual composition as it is written entirely in the form of a letter to an anonymous publisher: "Dear Sir or Madam".

John dismissed the song, describing it as 'son of 'Day Tripper''. Paul was playing a new Rickenbacker bass guitar and The Beatles' engineer, Geoff Emerick, recorded it as powerfully as he could. John and George are clearly having a lot of fun – have you noticed that they sing 'Frère Jacques' for their harmonies in the third verse?

Although 'Paperback Writer' is fictional, Paul had in mind Royston Ellis, the beat poet who had shown them how to get high on Vick inhalers when he came to Liverpool in 1960 and who wrote the first history of rock'n'roll music, *The Big Beat Scene*, in 1961. Possibly, too, Paul was having a little joke at John's expense as he had had success with his books of poetry and stories, *In His Own Write* and *A Spaniard In The Works*.

The day before The Beatles were to perform 'Paperback Writer' on *Top Of The Pops*, Paul had a minor accident on his moped while he was visiting his dad in the Wirral. Rather than have make-up patch it up or even see a dentist, he chose to appear on *Top Of The Pops* and make the promotional films for 'Paperback Writer' and 'Rain' with half of his front tooth missing. In 1958 in similar circumstances, Buddy Holly plugged his gap with chewing-gum before taking the stage for *Sunday Night At The London Palladium*.

Paul was very much a part of the Swinging Sixties scene in London (hence, the moped!) and he crafted the song while he was helping John Dunbar and Miles establish their counterculture Indica bookshop in Southampton Row. The record became the theme tune for the BBC series, *Read All About It*.

The John Lennon song on the B-side, 'Rain', had a strong following in its own right and marked the start of their psychedelic recordings. George Martin slowed down their vocals and reversed the music at the end. Ringo always regarded it as his best ever performance on drums. 'Rain' was one of John's first 'acid' songs, a pointer to the startling 'She Said She Said' and 'Tomorrow Never Knows' on The Beatles' forthcoming *Revolver* album.

218 The Kinks
Sunny Afternoon

Label & Cat No.: **Pye 7N 17125**

Producer: **Shel Talmy**

Writers: **Ray Davies**

Date reached No.1: **7 July 1966**

Weeks at No.1: **1**

WITH SONGS LIKE 'A WELL RESPECTED Man' and 'Dedicated Follower Of Fashion', Ray Davies was able to mock the people he saw in London. He turned his attention to the idle rich in 'Sunny Afternoon', although the opening line, "The taxman's taken all my dough", was also a comment on the tax rates imposed on high earners. George Harrison expressed the same view in 'Taxman', the opening cut of The Beatles' *Revolver*.

Ray wanted to write about his own situation and he said, "The only way I could interpret how I felt was through a dusty, fallen aristocrat who had come from old money as opposed to the wealth I had created for myself." As he thought that listeners might sympathise with this sad, decadent Conservative, "I turned him into a scoundrel who fought with his girlfriend after a night of drunkenness and cruelty."

In May 1966 'Sunny Afternoon' was recorded by the four Kinks with Nicky Hopkins guesting on keyboards. The Kinks thanked Hopkins by writing an affectionate song about him, 'Session Man': "He's not paid to think, just play."

Ray had hay fever and could only manage one vocal take on 'Sunny Afternoon'. He had been listening to Frank Sinatra and Glenn Miller, which accounts for the song's jazzy feel and it showed that Ray was becoming a rock Noël Coward. "I prayed for a very hot summer," says Ray, "because the longer the sun stayed out, the more records we would sell." The record spent two months in the Top 10.

The Kinks continued this theme of social commentary with 'Dead End Street' (the bleakness of being unemployed), 'Waterloo Sunset' (originally called 'Liverpool Sunset'), 'Autumn Almanac' ("I go to Blackpool for my holidays")

Ray Davies, the principal composer in The Kinks, remains of one of the UK's most respected songwriters

and 'Lola' ('L-O-L-A, Lola'). As well as these singles there is *The Village Green Preservation Society*, a much neglected album from 1968.

219 Georgie Fame & The Blue Flames
Get Away

Label & Cat No.: **Columbia DB 7946**
Producer: **Tony Palmer**
Writer: **Clive Powell (Georgie Fame)**
Date reached No.1: **21 July 1966**
Weeks at No.1: **1**

After a number one with 'Yeh Yeh', Georgie Fame & The Blue Flames had minor hits with 'In The Meantime', 'Like We Used To Be' and 'Something'. "Everybody seems to think that we had trouble following up 'Yeh Yeh'," says Georgie, "but we didn't care. We just wanted to record things that sounded good. 'Like We Used To Be' was my first attempt at songwriting and so that was pretty important for me."

Because he was writing songs, Georgie was invited to write a commercial: "I was asked to write a happy piece of music which would encourage young kids with their first cars to buy National Benzol petrol. They would give away our record to people who bought four gallons of petrol. It was a big promotion campaign and because we didn't mention the name of the company in the song, we were able to release it as a single." With its theme, 'Get Away' was the perfect summer record.

The Blue Flames, which included Pete Coe on sax and Speedy Acquaye on congas, had a distinctive sound, but in September 1966, Fame disbanded the group and worked instead with the Harry South Big Band. His final album with The Blue Flames, *Sweet Things*, included another hit single, his cover version of Billy Stewart's 'Sitting In The Park'.

220 Chris Farlowe
Out Of Time

Label & Cat No.: **Immediate IM 035**
Producer: **Mick Jagger**
Writers: **Mick Jagger / Keith Richards**
Date Reached No.1: **30 July 1966**
Weeks at No.1: **1**

Chris Farlowe's first professional engagement was as leader of The John Henry Skiffle Group in 1957. In 1962 Chris, who was born John Henry Deighton in Essex in 1940, recruited Albert Lee (guitar), Pete Sheridan (bass) and Ian Hague (drums) as his backing group and named them The Thunderbirds. Three years later they signed to Immediate Records, which was run by Andrew Loog Oldham, manager of The Rolling Stones.

His first hit was 'Think', a cover of a Jagger & Richards track from The Rolling Stones' 1965 album, *Aftermath,* which peaked at number 37. His next choice was another song from the same album, 'Out Of Time'.

Ten years on from *Aftermath*, Decca Records issued The Rolling Stones' version of 'Out Of Time' as a single, to coincide with the release of *Metamorphosis*, an album of Sixties tracks Jagger & Richards had demoed for other artists. It differed from the original album cut with the backing track being identical to Chris Farlowe's and that's explained by the fact that Mick had laid down a new backing with session musicians Jimmy Page, Joe Moretti, Reg Guest, Eric Ford, Andy White and both Mick and Chris recorded their versions at the same session.

Chris has an interest in Nazi memorabilia and between 1969 and 2001 he owned a shop in North London selling such artefacts. He also owned a costumiers shop, which supplied the uniforms for the TV show *Allo! Allo!*

221 The Troggs
With A Girl Like You

Label & Cat No.: **Fontana TF 717**
Producer: **Larry Page**
Writer: **Reg Presley**
Date reached No.1: **4 August 1966**
Weeks at No.1: **2**

With their 'oo-ahs', the Andover group, The Troggs, were the British beat equivalent of The Wurzels, but their records had more credibility. They approached the manager, Larry Page, and said that they were better than his group, The Kinks. Page was impressed and found them an American song by Chip Taylor, 'Wild Thing'.

In a defiant gesture which would be copied by a certain Declan Patrick MacManus, the lead singer Reg Ball became Reg Presley and the rest of the band was Chris Britton (lead guitar), Pete Staples (bass) and Ronnie Bond (drums). They called themselves The Troglodytes and then shortened it to The Troggs. They converted Chip Taylor's pop song into a declaration of lust, but it was kept from the top by 'Paint It, Black'.

Surprisingly perhaps, The Troggs' only number one was with the semi-novelty 'With A Girl Like You'. "I wrote that while I was still a bricklayer," says Reg Presley. "We recorded it at the same time as 'Wild Thing' and either of them could have been released first. I liked the way The Beach Boys were going 'Ba-ba-ba-Barbara Ann' and it was lovely to

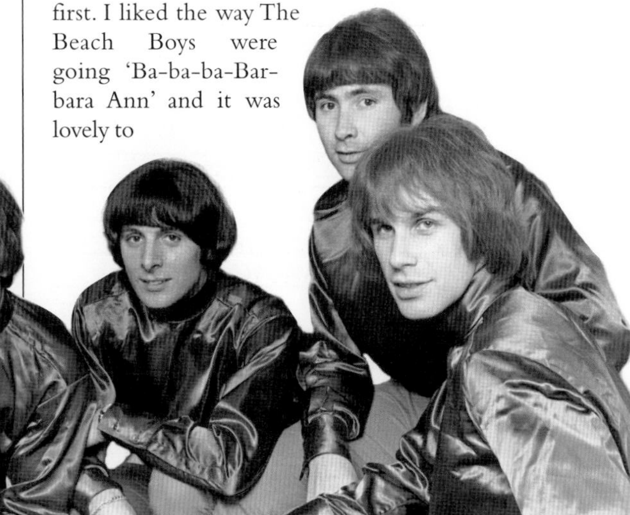

do something like that in 'With A Girl Like You'. We nearly had a trumpet playing it, but it sounded it better when we sang it."

The Troggs courted controversy with their mock orgasm in 'I Can't Control Myself' and Reg wrote a romantic ballad in 'Love Is All Around', later revived by Wet Wet Wet.

Larry Page says, "You had to record The Troggs quickly. More than three takes and they would fall to pieces. I also had to be in charge. The so-called *Troggs' Tapes* show what happened when nobody knew what was going on." In that instance, the tapes were kept running while The Troggs were arguing over a song called, of all things, 'Tranquillity'. "I was livid when I first heard those tapes were around," says Reg, "but I laugh about it now. If a young band is nervous, an engineer might say, 'Listen to this' and it makes everyone relax."

222 The Beatles
Eleanor Rigby / Yellow Submarine

Label & Cat No.: **Parlophone R 5493**
Producer: **George Martin**
Writers (both songs): **John Lennon / Paul McCartney**
Date reached No.1: **18 August 1966**
Weeks at No.1: **4**

ONE HALF OF A DOUBLE A-SIDE, 'Eleanor Rigby' may have been inspired by the gravestone for Eleanor Rigby in St. Peter's churchyard in Woolton where John and Paul first met in 1957, or it may have been coincidence. Paul himself says that he liked the name of the actress, Eleanor Bron, who had been in *Help!*, and he had seen a shop called Rigby's in Liverpool. The songwriter, Lionel Bart, says that the song had been written as 'Eleanor Bygraves' and he was the one who suggested 'Eleanor Rigby'.

Whatever, the name is perfect and the song is imbued with the spirit of Liverpool even though the city is not named. Another scouser, George Melly, says it reminds him of "The very respectable Liverpool women, living in two-up, two-down streets with the doorsteps meticulously holystoned, and the church the one solid thing in their lives. It was a complete portrait, a thumbnail sketch as solid as a Rembrandt drawing."

The priest in the song was originally Father McCartney but their close friend and original Quarry Man, Pete Shotton, said, "That's a bit hard on your poor old dad," and they went through the phone book and changed it to McKenzie. As luck would have it, there was a Father McKenzie in Woolton, which was another coincidence.

From the sublime to the cor blimey, the other side was the best song that Lennon & McCartney wrote for Ringo Starr, 'Yellow Submarine'. Or rather Paul McCartney and Donovan. Paul said, "I thought it up in bed. When you're drifting and you've got that 5 or 10 minutes before you go, there's that nice little netherworld. Somehow I got this idea of submarines; there were going to be blue ones and green ones, but in the end it all came down to this yellow one. I thought it'd be nice as a children's song." Paul showed his work to Donovan, and he came up with the line, "Sky of blue and sea of green". "Not a very difficult thing to write," says Donovan today.

The Beatles' chauffeur, Alf Bicknell, was roped into the chorus for 'Yellow Submarine': "The sound of the anchor going down is me standing by a microphone with an old tin bath and a piece of chain. I can honestly say that I've had a number one hit."

'Yellow Submarine' became the starting-point for a cartoon feature film. At the time it was popular but not highly praised. The critical response to the reissued version in 1999 showed just how innovative this film had been and what remarkable vision Heinz Edelmann had shown as the master illustrator.

In 2003 during the protests in London against the war in Iraq, the demonstrators were singing "We all live in a terrorist regime." This would have pleased John immensely. His great anthem 'Give Peace A Chance', which reached number two in July 1969, has become a rallying cry for peace campaigners the world over, and is still chanted by those protest against wars.

223 Small Faces
All Or Nothing

Label & Cat No.: **Decca F 12470**
Producer: **Don Arden**
Writers: **Steve Marriott / Ronnie Lane**
Date Reached No.1: **17 September 1966**
Weeks at No.1: **1**

IN 1964 RONNIE LANE WALKED INTO an East London music shop and bought a bass guitar that sales assistant Steve Marriott sold to him at a heavy discount. He was so bowled over by the gesture that they formed an instant friendship.

Steve had been a child actor and appeared on the London stage as the Artful Dodger in *Oliver!* Ronnie Lane had his own band called The Pioneers, which featured Kenny Jones on drums. Ronnie invited Steve to a gig where he was briefly introduced to the rest of the band before getting on stage to play the piano. Kenny and Ronnie were so impressed that they decided to split The Pioneers and form a new band, but only on the proviso that Steve learned to play guitar. The band's line-up was completed in November 1965 when organist Ian McLagan was recruited.

The Who were the innovators of the Mod music scene. A Mod was a product of the working class British youth of the mid-Sixties and essentially from the London area. They wore suits and a narrow tie and typically rode around on Lambretta motor scooters. The Small Faces took their name because of their lack of height (they were all under five feet six inches) and 'Faces', which was a Mod slang term for cool guys.

The Who's manager Kit Lambert failed in his attempt to sign them. Instead, Don Arden, a manager whose tactics were often likened to Al Capone, phoned Steve Marriott's mum and persuaded her that her son and his band would benefit by signing with him and recording for Decca. He offered them £20 a week and an account in every clothes shop in Carnaby Street. Arden is father to Sharon and father-in-law to Ozzy Osbourne.

Kenny Jones said of 'All Or Nothing', "It was

us getting to where we wanted to be musically. It wasn't as poppy as our previous hits, but still commercial enough and better than anything we'd done before."

Steve Marriott said in 1984, "I think 'All Or Nothing' takes a lot of beating. To me, if there's a song that typifies that era, then that might be it."

In mid-1967, they left Decca and signed with Andrew Loog Oldham's Immediate label. After five Top 20 hits, Marriott left to form Humble Pie with ex-Herd singer Peter Frampton. The band drafted in Ron Wood for one single 'Afterglow Of Your Love' which only just scraped into the Top 40. They briefly reformed in 1976 but by 1978, they had split again. When Who drummer, Keith Moon, died in 1978, Kenny Jones was his replacement.

In 1990 Steve Marriott returned to touring with his new band, Steve Marriott & The Packet Of Three. He had begun working on some new material with Peter Frampton, until April 1991, when he perished in a fire at his Essex home.

224 Jim Reeves
Distant Drums

Label & Cat No.: **RCA 1537**

Producer: **Chet Atkins**

Writer: **Cindy Walker**

Date reached No.1: **22 September 1966**

Weeks at No.1: **5**

Cindy Walker was one of Nashville's top songwriters, writing 'You Don't Know Me' (Eddy Arnold, Ray Charles) and 'Dream Baby' (Roy Orbison). Jim Reeves recorded several of her songs and she wrote 'Distant Drums' especially for him, even including a reference to his wife, Mary, in the lyric. Jim liked the song very much but it was considered unsuitable by his producer, Chet Atkins.

By way of a thank you, Jim Reeves recorded a demo at Starday Studios with the group, The Blue Boys, and he gave it to Cindy, saying, "You shouldn't have any trouble getting someone to record this now." Roy Orbison picked up on the song and it was the B-side of his 1963 hit, 'Falling', which, incidentally, was a much weaker song.

Jim Reeves was killed in a plane crash at the height of his fame in July 1964. 'I Love You Because' and 'I Won't Forget You' were two of the biggest hits of 1964, and RCA perpetuated his memory with such ironic titles as 'This World Is Not My Home' and 'Is It Really Over?' They came across Jim's demo of 'Distant Drums' and, after overdubbing a fuller accompaniment with Bill McElhiney on trumpet and Floyd Cramer on vibes, released it. 'Distant Drums' topped the US country charts and part of its US popularity was the lyric's relevance to the Vietnam war and American casualties.

At the time The Who were at number two in the UK with 'I'm A Boy' and Roger Daltrey remarked, "There should be two charts – one with Jim Reeves and the other for the likes of us. Then we'd be number one."

225 The Four Tops
Reach Out I'll Be There

Label & Cat No.: **Tamla Motown TMG 579**

Producers: **Brian Holland / Lamont Dozier**

Writers: **Brian Holland / Lamont Dozier / Eddie Holland**

Date reached No.1: **27 October 1966**

Weeks at No.1: **3**

The Four Tops with their stentorian lead vocalist Levi Stubbs made the most forceful of all the Tamla Motown records. Their sound bulldozed you into submission, but it was a cover version of 'Baby I Need Your Loving' by the Liverpool group, The Fourmost, that made the UK charts in 1964. Their first UK hit was with 'I Can't Help Myself' in 1965, but they followed it with 'It's The Same Old Song', which, displaying their cynicism, was precisely that.

In 1966 the writing and production team of Holland, Dozier and Holland combined both rock and R&B influences for 'Reach Out I'll Be There', which became a transatlantic number one. The sound was as dense as anything from Phil Spector, and Levi Stubbs' vocal, as much shouting as singing, over the thunderous, galloping beat was extraordinary, especially with such asides as "I know what you're thinking". And whoever thought of putting flutes in there? An uncanny, exotic touch that works perfectly.

As with 'I Can't Help Myself', the follow-ups, 'Standing In The Shadows Of Love' (US 6, UK 6) and 'Bernadette' (US 4, UK 8) were similar to 'Reach Out I'll Be There'. They had many other hits including 'Walk Away Renee', 'If I Were A Carpenter', 'Simple Game' and 'Loco In Acapulco'.

The contribution of the other Tops – Duke Fakir, Lawrence Payton, Renaldo Benson – is often overlooked, but the group was based on friendship and they remained together until Payton's death in 1997. *Standing In The Shadows Of Motown*, a 2003 film documentary, gives credit to Tamla Motown's session musicians, The Funk Brothers, but they over-egg the pudding when the drummer Steve Jordan says, "Anybody could have sung them, you could have had Deputy Dawg singing on some of this stuff." One listen to 'Reach Out I'll Be There' and you'll know he's talking rubbish.

226 The Beach Boys
Good Vibrations

Label & Cat No.: **Capitol CL 15475**

Producer: **Brian Wilson**

Writers: **Brian Wilson / Mike Love**

Date Reached No.1: **19 November 1966**

Weeks at No.1: **2**

In 1966 there was some creative rivalry between The Beach Boys and The Beatles. "When I first heard *Rubber Soul* and *Revolver*", said Brian, "I flipped. I wanted to make an album like that." He was also influenced by Phil Spector's production sound, so before long,

Brian sat down and began working on his own masterpiece, *Pet Sounds*.

Once *Pet Sounds* was completed, Brian set to work on 'Good Vibrations'. It was an extravagant and elaborate masterpiece created by a perfectionist. It took six months to complete, used 100 hours of recording tape, was recorded over 17 sessions in four different studios and cost around $16,000 to produce, which made it the most expensive number one at the time.

In an interview with *Rolling Stone*, Brian explained how 'Good Vibrations' came about. "My mother used to tell me about vibrations. I didn't really understand too much of what she meant when I was a boy. It scared me, the word 'vibrations' – to think that invisible feelings existed. She also told me about dogs that would bark at some people, but wouldn't bark at others, and so it came to pass that we talked about good vibrations."

Around 30 different takes were recorded until Brian Wilson was satisfied. One of the early takes had been in an R&B vein and although the studio personnel loved it, Brian wasn't happy. He explained, "I wanted to experiment by combining different studio sounds. Every studio has its own marked sound. I used cellos, wind chimes, flutes, organ, a jew's harp, sleigh bells and a theremin." The device, an electronic instrument invented by Russia scientist Lev Sergeivitch Theremin in 1921, makes a wavering sound that had been used to startling effect in the Alfred Hitchcock film, *Spellbound*. At every studio recording different musicians were used but after about four months everyone was growing impatient, including Capitol Records. Brian was not concerned about the time factor. He knew exactly how he wanted it to sound and wasn't giving in until he was satisfied. It was take 28 that became the finished master.

Although none of The Beach Boys played on the track, they all sang backing vocals. Mike Love, who sang the main chorus whilst Carl Wilson sang lead, admitted "'Good Vibrations' was a radical departure for us musically." It was a far cry from the archetype surf sound they had created but Love certainly wanted them to remain a surf band. Twenty musicians contributed to the session and not one of them could make head nor tail of the song. Glen Campbell, who at the time was a session guitarist and had stood in for Brian briefly on tour, enquired, "What were you smokin' when you wrote that?" Brian admitted that LSD was an influence and a contributory factor. "I completed the lyrics on the way down the Hollywood Freeway about 10 minutes before the session," remembered Mike Love. "It was a unique experience as I was dictating the words as we were driving down the freeway." The new sound was welcomed everywhere. Even *The Sunday Express* carried the headline, 'They've found a new sound at last!'

The three and a half minute track was Grammy nominated for Best Contemporary Rock-'n'roll Recording, but lost out to the song it knocked off the top of the US chart, The New Vaudeville Band's 'Winchester Cathedral'.

227 Tom Jones
Green Green Grass Of Home

Label & Cat No.: **Decca F 22511**

Producer: **Peter Sullivan**

Writer: **Curly Putman**

Date Reached No.1: **3 December 1966**

Weeks at No.1: **7**

When Tom arrived on the scene in 1965, he did so in spectacular style. Not only was his debut hit, 'It's Not Unusual', a million seller, he also became the first solo British artist to win a Grammy award for Best New Artist.

Tom had always claimed that his biggest regret was not getting into movies. Although he hated the film *What's New Pussycat?*, in 1965, he delivered the title song, which was very timely as it gave Tom's chart career a much needed boost. It also gave him his biggest US hit of the Sixties. Following its success, a year later, Tom recorded the title song to the latest James Bond movie *Thunderball*. Although the film was a success and Tom often opened his shows with the song, it failed to make the Top 20 on both sides of the Atlantic.

Marilyn Monroe made her screen debut in the 1950 film *The Asphalt Jungle*. It was a crime scene during the film that inspired Nashville songwriter Curly Putnam to write 'The Green Green Grass Of Home'. It is the tale of a prisoner who dreams of going back home, but when he awakes, he remembers where he is about to face the electric chair. Like any archetypal country song, it makes references to the old hometowna girl called Mary, a preacher, a death and a funeral.

Country singer Johnny Darrell first recorded the song in 1964. A year later, Jerry Lee Lewis, who was moving towards country music, recorded a version on his album *Country Songs For City Folks*. It was Jerry Lee's version that Tom heard and he recalled, "I said to my recording manager, Peter Sullivan, I'd like to record this. He said, 'a country song?' I said 'yeah', because I hadn't done a country song up to that point. Les Reed did the arrangement and played piano on the track and made it more of a pop song than a country song, because when Jerry Lee Lewis did it, it was strict country. When I came back to England I recorded the song on TV and we did it like in a jail. But you don't know it is a jail, until the camera pulls back and you see the bars, and there I am in this jail, singing 'The Green Green Grass of Home'."

Les Reed, with his writing partner, Barry Mason, began to write more songs for Tom Jones. "He always loved good lyrics but he liked melodies with a little blues touch now and again and he's home. Everything we wrote for him after that was completely tailored for Tom Jones. Like 'I'm Coming Home'. When I recorded it in the studio, he insisted on singing amongst the strings, which is very hard for the engineer but he gave such a performance on that first take that all the musicians had tears in their eyes," revealed Les.

During Christmas 1966 Elvis was driving from California back to his home in Memphis when 'Green Green Grass Of Home' came on the radio. He couldn't stop raving about the song and got a friend of his in Arkansas to call the radio station and have them play it repeatedly.

Red West, one of the members of 'The Memphis Mafia' – a group of men who were with Elvis every day between 1965 and the day

he died – heard Elvis was delirious about the song and called to remind him he had already heard Jerry Lee Lewis' version.

228 The Monkees
I'm A Believer

Label & Cat No.: **RCA 1560**
Producer: **Jeff Barry**
Writer: **Neil Diamond**
Date reached No.1: **19 January 1967**
Weeks at No.1: **4**

THE ADVERT INSERTED IN THE Hollywood *Daily Variety* in August 1965 told of auditions for a new TV series with "running parts for 4 insane boys, aged 17-21". As a result, 437 hopefuls were auditioned by the producers, Bob Rafelson and Bert Schneider. Stephen Stills was rejected, but he found fame elsewhere. The successful applicants were Davy Jones (a Mancunian who had played Ena Sharples' grandson in *Coronation Street* and The Artful Dodger in *Oliver!* on Broadway), Mickey Dolenz (the child star of the TV series, *Circus Boy*, and a competent drummer and singer), Michael Nesmith (a singer and songwriter working in folk music) and Peter Tork (a singer and guitarist who opened for José Feliciano).

The Beatles were outgrowing their young fans and The Monkees were intended to fill the gap, their half-hour TV series including the same zaniness as *A Hard Day's Night*. The songs were all commissioned by Screen Gems, but that was no hardship as their writers included Carole King, Neil Sedaka, Tommy Boyce and Bobby Hart. The music would be recorded by top session men including Glen Campbell, Leon Russell and Hal Blaine, and The Monkees themselves would simply add their voices.

Their first single, 'Last Train To Clarksville', was a close cousin to 'Paperback Writer' and then came 'I'm A Believer', written by the up and coming singer/songwriter, Neil Diamond. He had intended the song to be recorded by the country artist, Eddy Arnold, and was surprised when Don Kirshner at Screen Gems passed it instead to The Monkees. Michael Nesmith, probably being awkward, would have nothing to do with it – "I'm a songwriter," he told the producer, Jeff Barry (of Greenwich & Barry fame), "and that's no hit." Barry wouldn't stand for this insolence and banned him from the studio while Mickey Dolenz put on his lead vocal. The song was a transatlantic number one and Neil Diamond also wrote their follow-up, 'A Little Bit Me, A Little Bit You', but it was a weaker song.

The Monkees were hurt by press comments that they did not play their instruments, and encouraged by Mike Nesmith, they insisted on making their own records. Surprisingly, The Monkees only had five more records in the Top 20 – 'Alternate Title', 'Pleasant Valley Sunday', 'Daydream Believer', 'Valleri' and 'D.W. Washburn'. After they split, Mike Nesmith had by far the most interesting musical career – 'Joanne', 'Silver Moon', 'Rio' – but looking after his inheritance (his mother invented Tippex), meant that he has only recorded sporadically.

229 Petula Clark
This Is My Song

Label & Cat No.: **Pye 7N 17258**
Producer: **Ernie Freeman**
Writer: **Charles Chaplin**
Date reached No.1: **16 February 1967**
Weeks at No.1: **2**

MOST PEOPLE WOULD REGARD 'Downtown' as Petula Clark's biggest record but although it was a US number one, it was kept off the top of the UK charts by The Beatles' 'I Feel Fine'. That song was written by her record producer, Tony Hatch, who also wrote her hits, 'I Know A Place' (17, 1965), 'My Love' (4, 1966) and 'I Couldn't Live Without Your Love' (6, 1966).

In 1967 the 77-year-old Charlie Chaplin was making *A Countess From Hong Kong*, a romantic comedy on board an ocean liner with Marlon Brando and Sophia Loren. The theme was also written by Chaplin, who had written the standards, 'Smile' and 'The Theme From Limelight'. Petula Clark met Chaplin and says, "We got on very well and he told me that he wanted me to record it, but I was second choice to Al Jolson. He would not believe that Jolson was dead, and the producers had to show him a photograph of Jolson's tomb."

Petula Clark was in Reno, Nevada and an orchestration was sent from France: "It was the most dreadful, wishy-washy backing track and so we asked Ernie Freeman, who had done some arrangements for Frank Sinatra, to do something new. The poor man hated flying and he got himself completely drunk so that he could come and see me. I thought the record was going to be awful, but we flew to Los Angeles a week later and there was an extremely commercial arrangement waiting for me. There was so much confusion about that song as Harry Secombe recorded it before me and he didn't know I was doing it."

After Pet's stint at number one, Harry Secombe went to number two. "I didn't think my version would get anywhere at all," he recalled, "and I went to Singapore. I got a telegram from Russ Conway, who had written my B-side, saying, 'YOU BIG FAT TWIT. YOU ARE IN THE TOP TEN. COME HOME QUICK."

230 Engelbert Humperdinck
Release Me

Label & Cat No.: **Decca F 12541**
Producer: **Charles Blackwell**
Writer: **Eddie Miller / Robert Yount / Dub Williams**
Date Reached No.1: **4 March 1967**
Weeks at No.1: **6**

IN 1946 COUNTRY MUSIC SONGWRITER Eddie Miller wrote 'Release Me', but after four years trying to find someone to record it, he gave

The Monkees, the world's first 'boy band', left to right: Mike Nesmith, Davy Jones, Peter Tork and Mickey Dolenz

up and recorded it himself.

The writing credit on Engelbert's single is Eddie Miller, Robert Yount, Dub Williams and Robert Harris. All other versions of the song fail to credit Robert Harris. It later transpired that Dub Williams and Robert Harris were two pseudonyms for James Pebworth. This brazen attempt ensured a double pay packet for the impudent songwriter.

The idea for the song came to Eddie in a bar in San Francisco. He overheard a husband and wife talking about their marital troubles. The wife said, "If you'd release me, we wouldn't have any problems and everything would be all right".

Eddie had a tendency to write songs backwards. He said, "I know what the end is going to be before I start. I don't follow a trend, I go to the opposite. I think a writer should set a trend and not follow one". Eddie recorded and released half a dozen versions of 'Release Me', and at one point, held three separate positions on the US country chart, with the same song.

Engelbert Humperdinck was born Arnold George Dorsey in India in 1936. His family moved to England when he was seven and settled in Leicester. By the age of 11, he had aspirations to be a musician and took up the saxophone. In 1955, having completed two years of National Service in Germany, he began singing in public for the first time under the name Gerry Dorsey. Three years later a friend talked him into entering a talent show where he was spotted by an agent who was impressed with his voice, despite his lack of training, as well as his comic impressions, which included Jerry Lewis. He toured the UK with Marty Wilde and made his television debut on *Oh Boy!* This in turn led to a record contract with Decca and in 1959 he cut his first single 'Crazy Bells'.

His career came to a temporary halt in 1961 when he contracted tuberculosis, which kept him out of action for six months.

In 1965 having struggled for a few years, he contacted an old roommate, Gordon Mills. Gordon, who was already Tom Jones' manager, took George under his wing. He suggested a name change to Engelbert Humperdinck! after the German composer of *Hänsel And Gretel*. Engelbert recorded 'Stay' and 'Dommage Dommage' for Decca, but both flopped.

His luck changed in 1967 when he was invited to appear on the variety show *Sunday Night At The London Palladium*, to replace the scheduled star Dickie Valentine who had become ill. He performed 'Release Me' and the response was phenomenal. Not only did the song top the UK chart, it went on to spend 56 consecutive weeks on the chart, a record he still holds today.

The Beatles had established a new record of 10 straight number one hits. That run was halted when 'Release Me' kept the double A-sided 'Strawberry Fields Forever' / 'Penny Lane' at number two. In 2002 that fact upset one contestant who lost out on £25,000 on Chris Tarrant's breakfast show on London's Capital Radio. Chris asked the multiple-choice question: "What kept The Beatles' 'Strawberry Fields Forever' / 'Penny Lane' off the number one spot? Was it A) 'This Is My Song' – Petula Clark, B) 'Release Me' – Engelbert Humperdinck or C) 'I'm A Believer' – The Monkees". The lady answered B, only to be told she was wrong. The next contestant went for Petula Clark and won 25 grand...

231 Nancy Sinatra & Frank Sinatra Somethin' Stupid

Label & Cat No.: **Reprise RS 23166**

Producers: **Jimmy Bowen / Lee Hazlewood**

Writer: **C. Carson Parks**

Date reached No.1: **13 April 1967**

Weeks at No.1: **2**

In the mid-fifties, Frank Sinatra said that he hated rock'n'roll and that it was made by 'cretinous goons'. When he formed his own record label, Reprise, he soon realised that he needed some rock acts to balance the books and what's more, his daughter, Nancy, and Dean Martin's son, Dino, wanted to rock. Frank himself was swept along with the tide and 'Everybody's Twisting', a 1962 hit, found him following the new dance sensation. The best, or worst, example of somethin' stupid comes with 'Mrs. Robinson' in 1969 where, for reasons best known to himself, he sings the praises of his favourite restaurant, Jilly's. Talk about product placement.

Lee Hazlewood has a detached amusement about how things worked at Reprise: "Nancy and I were having hits and Nancy said that her dad wanted something for them. A few days later, he said, 'Well, have you got anything for the kid and I?' but I didn't have any good ideas at the time. I lived in a beach house at the cheap end of Malibu – not a $3m. house but a nice house – and he called me to his office and told me that he had found the song but Nancy wouldn't work with any producer but me. He played me the demo of 'Somethin' Stupid' and said, 'Do you like it?' I said, 'I love it, and if you don't do it with Nancy, I will.' He said, 'We're gonna do it, book a studio.'"

Actually, the demo of 'Somethin' Stupid' had been released by its writer, C. Carson Parks, but it hadn't got anywhere. When Frank and Nancy recorded the song, there was some doubts within the record company as to whether a father and daughter should be singing a love song. Frank Sinatra told them not to worry and the single, with Nancy getting top billing, topped the charts in both the UK and the US. The Sinatra expert, Will Friedwald, has written that "It may be the most un-Frankish performance Sinatra ever recorded, with the two Sinatras chanting away in bland folkish harmony." The co-producer Jimmy Bowen said, "I do know that Frank was pleased with the results of 'Somethin' Stupid'." Of course. It might win him teenage fans.

Even more untypical, however, was another collaboration, also in 1967. Frank recorded a stunning Brazilian album with Antonio Carlos Jobim, joking "I haven't sung so softly since I had laryngitis." Nancy performed the James Bond-styled title song for the Frank Sinatra thriller, *Tony Rome*. Frank was also heading a national campaign to discourage identification of gangsters in ethnic terms. Er, yes. Little did he know that *The Godfather* was just around the corner.

Frank & Nancy never made an album together, although the famous picture of them touching noses would have made a brilliant cover shot. Their only other duets are on light-hearted novelties and Christmas songs.

In 1995 Ali Campbell revived 'Somethin'

Stupid', with his daughter, Kibibi, but despite considerable airplay, the Christmas single only reached number 30. Following her success in the film musical *Moulin Rouge*, Nicole Kidman sang 'Somethin' Stupid' with Robbie Williams in 2001 and the song returned to the top.

232 Sandie Shaw
Puppet On A String

Label & Cat No.: **Pye 7N 17272**

Producer: **Ken Woodman**

Writers: **Bill Martin / Phil Coulter**

Date reached No.1: **27 April 1967**

Weeks at No.1: **3**

THE EUROVISION SONG CONTEST WAS launched in 1956 but up to 1967, the United Kingdom had not won. It had been second with 'Sing Little Birdie' (Pearl Carr & Teddy Johnson, 1959), 'Are You Sure?' (Allisons, 1961), I Love The Little Things' (Matt Monro, 1964) and 'I Belong (Kathy Kirby, 1965), but 1966 proved disastrous as the light operatic singer, Kenneth McKellar, unwisely wearing a kilt, found himself in ninth place. Still, compared to 2003, that was good.

Over the years there have been many different processes for choosing the UK entry for The Eurovision Song Contest, but in the mid-Sixties, a popular performer would sing six songs on a top variety show and the public would vote accordingly. Drastic action was needed in 1967 and a major chart name was recruited to give the UK a boost. Sandie Shaw was chosen and she says, "I hated 'Puppet On A String' from the start and I wish 'Tell The Boys' had won, but the songs were chosen by old people who watched *The Rolf Harris Show* and not my normal fans."

Phil Coulter says, "A lot of writers made the mistake of writing for Sandie Shaw, while we wrote a song for Europe. The song was geared to Europe, even down to using a bassoon on the intro. Right away you are in a fairground and we don't waste any time. You have three minutes for a Eurovision song and the meter's running. That long note at the beginning from Sandie is a rip-off from 'Volare'."

Sandie took off to Luxembourg like a puppet on a string. "I took part in the contest with no confidence in the song, but I had confidence in myself. As a singer, I felt that I had to sing the truth and that song conveyed no truths to me." 'Puppet On A String' was an easy winner, scoring more than twice as many points as the number two. It was a strong year as the Luxembourg entry, 'L'Amour Est Bleu', became an international hit as 'Love Is Blue' by Paul Mauriat and his Orchestra.

Sandie reflects, "'Puppet On A String' may have been a big hit but I took a long time to recover from it. I lost work because of it, I'd lost my credibility." Bill Martin, who wrote the song with Phil Coulter, has a different view: "I love the song and it has a circus atmosphere which suits it very well. Sandie made nearly a million pounds that year, but she said she hated the song. Well, the song is going to outlive her, I've no doubt about that." Since her second retirement she has used her experience in the music business to help artists combat problems of stress, drug dependency and eating disorders.

233 The Tremeloes
Silence Is Golden

Label & Cat No.: **CBS 2723**

Producer: **Mike Smith**

Writers: **Bob Gaudio / Bob Crewe**

Date reached No.1: **18 May 1967**

Weeks at No.1: **3**

AFTER SPLITTING FROM BRIAN POOLE, The Tremeloes moved to CBS but continued working with their Decca producer, Mike Smith. They had a Top 10 hit with a Cat Stevens' song, 'Here Comes My Baby', which set the template for many happy-go-lucky, partying hits such as 'Even The Bad Times Are Good', 'Suddenly You Love Me' and 'Helule Helule'.

The Trems had recruited Chip Hawkes as a singer and guitarist and the other members were Rick West (guitar), Alan Blakely (guitar) and Dave Munden (drums). They specialised in close harmony work, and they included the B-side of The Four Seasons' 1964 hit, 'Rag Doll', 'Silence Is Golden', in their stage show to feature Rick's falsetto. Chip Hawkes recalls, "We were on tour with The Hollies and we were getting standing ovations for 'Silence Is Golden'. We recorded it immediately and by the end of the tour, it was in the charts. Tony Hicks of The Hollies said to me, 'It's a good thing you did that as we were going to record it'."

'Silence Is Golden' was recorded on a four-track machine and, as a result, The Tremeloes had a much fuller sound than before. Unusually perhaps, their cover version was also better than the American original, as Bob Gaudio from The Four Seasons admits, "We were so excited about 'Rag Doll' that 'Silence Is Golden' was pushed to the side. It only seemed like a B-side compared to 'Rag Doll' but The Tremeloes saw something in it and made a wonderful record."

234 Procol Harum
A Whiter Shade Of Pale

Label & Cat No.: **Deram DM 126**

Producer: **Denny Cordell**

Writers: **Keith Reid / Gary Brooker**

Date reached No.1: **8 June 1967**

Weeks at No.1: **6**

THREE GREAT, HIGHLY APPROPRIATE records were number one during the Summer of Love in 1967 – 'A Whiter Shade Of Pale', 'All You Need Is Love' and 'San Francisco (Be Sure To Wear Some Flowers In Your Hair)'. What could be more suitable for someone tripping than the image-laden, allegorical words of 'A Whiter Shade Of Pale'? And, if you want to argue that rock lyrics are poetry, what better place to start?

The words were by the non-playing lyricist

of Procol Harum, Keith Reid, and the music was by vocalist and pianist, Gary Brooker. The melody itself is original but 'Suite Number 3 in D Major (Air On A G String)', 'Sleepers Awake' (both by Bach) and Percy Sledge's 'When A Man Loves A Woman' were inspirations. Shane MacGowan puts it best: "People say they nicked it from Bach but it doesn't matter. What they did with it was much better than what Bach did with it."

The classical element was enhanced by featuring an organ, played by Matthew Fisher. A few weeks earlier Matthew had been with Screaming Lord Sutch & The Savages and he was unsure about joining Procol Harum because Sutch gave him regular employment. Gary and Keith assured him that Procol Harum was going to be bigger than The Beatles. He brought theatrics to the group, notably via a masked appearance in a cloak on *Top Of The Pops.*

The DJ at the trendy Scene club in London and the UK manager of the American R&B label, Sue, Guy Stevens had taken Keith to his flat in Gloucester Avenue for some late night drugging. At half-past four, he offered to take him home and looking at his tired wife, Diane, he said, "You're just turned a whiter shade of pale." Guy also came up with the name, Procol Harum, a Latin phrase which happened to be the pedigree name of a friend's cat. Pretentious, moi?

So much is known. Keith Reid prefers to let the lyrics retain their mystery. The truth is not plain to see, but most likely the song is about a drunk at a party trying to make it with a girl. The drunk's mind wanders and different images come into his head. There is a reference to Chaucer's *The Miller's Tale*, but it could just be to rhyme with 'pale'. If the words are too much for you, check out the instrumental version from the saxophonist King Curtis, which plays majestically behind the opening credits of the 1988 film *Withnail & I.*

Procol Harum followed 'A Whiter Shade Of Pale' with 'Homburg', which contains the riveting opening line, "Your multilingual business friend". And to think they had their origins in an R&B band, The Paramounts. After 'Homburg', Procol Harum became an albums act and although they occasionally made the charts, it was albums like *A Salty Dog* and *Broken Barricades* that enhanced their reputation.

Procol Harum split up in 1977 but they reformed in the Nineties, adding an extra, equally impenetrable verse to 'A Whiter Shade Of Pale'. A missing fourth verse has appeared in print, but nothing helps to explain this song, a favourite for university theses.

235 The Beatles
All You Need Is Love

Label & Cat No.: **Parlophone R 5620**
Producer: **George Martin**
Writers: **John Lennon / Paul McCartney**
Date reached No.1: **19 July 1967**
Weeks at No.1: **3**

'PENNY LANE' / 'STRAWBERRY FIELDS Forever' couldn't dislodge Engelbert Humperdinck's 'Release Me' from number one, so were The Beatles slipping? Evidently not as *Sgt. Pepper's Lonely Hearts Club Band* became the most highly-fêted album of all-time and 'All You Need Is Love' restored them to number one.

The Beatles stopped performing in public after the end of their 1966 US tour as they felt they couldn't do justice to the music they now made but, perversely, they agreed to perform live on *Our World*, a unique, satellite TV programme to be beamed to 24 countries. With a potential audience of 500 million, they didn't take the easy option of performing something well-known, and 'All You Need Is Love' marks John Lennon's first attempt to write a message song that everybody could sing. The Beatles and their audience (including Mick Jagger, Jane Asher, Eric Clapton and Marianne Faithfull) were dressed in designer hippie gear and the song was perfect for the Summer Of Love. It is now an anthem for all occasions, and who could argue with its sentiments?

Lennon's lyrics have been dismissed as simplistic but this is to overlook its purpose. Millions of viewers could not speak English or only had a very rudimentary knowledge. John was showing good sense by writing simply, both in words and melody. George Harrison said, "John has an amazing thing with his timing. On 'All You Need Is Love', it just sort of skips a beat here and there and changes time. But you question him as to what's he actually doing and he doesn't know. He just does what comes naturally."

The introduction borrows from the French national anthem and the fadeout incorporates snatches from 'She Loves You', 'In The Mood'. 'Greensleeves' and some Bach.

236 Scott McKenzie
San Francisco (Be Sure To Wear Some Flowers In Your Hair)

Label & Cat No.: **CBS 2816**
Producer: **Lou Adler / John Phillips**
Writer: **John Phillips**
Date reached No.1: **9 August 1967**
Weeks at No.1: **4**

HIPPIES TODAY CALL THEMSELVES New Age Travellers, but hippies then were young hedonists who believed in sexual freedom, getting high, psychedelic rock music and an end to the Vietnam war. The hippie anthem, written by John Phillips of The Mamas & The Papas was perfect, "If you're going to San Francisco, be sure to wear some flowers in your hair."

Scott McKenzie and John Phillips had performed together, singing standards in The Smoothies and folk in The Journeymen. Phillips then formed a hippie vocal group, The Mamas & The Papas, and had hits with 'California Dreamin'' and 'Monday Monday'. He organised the first great pop festival, which took place at Monterey, a sleepy fishing village on the coast of California. They'd had jazz festivals at Monterey, but the residents were very worried about tens of thousands of hippies descending on the town. The song was partly written to comfort the

residents, to tell them that they had nothing to fear.

John Phillips remembered, "I wanted a song that would express the feelings of the people coming to the festival, something that would put them in the right state of mind and tell them to relax. The Olympics appealed to me because they had laurel wreaths in their hair. I wrote it in an afternoon, did a rough dub that evening, hired the players the next morning, and finished it the next night. 36 hours and it was done. I'd known Scott since we were teenagers and his voice was perfect for the song."

McKenzie agrees, "My heart was in that song and I didn't have to change my image. I already had a pretty loose life. I was wearing flower shirts, weird flowing robes and kaftans, and we picked flowers the day I recorded the song. One girl gave me a garland of flowers and my friends were sitting in the lotus position, meditating, while I was recording it."

The record features the noted session musicians, Larry Knechtel (piano), Joe Osborne (bass) and Hal Blaine (drums). Blaine's drumming is so steady that some have thought itwas a prototype drum machine. Handclapping is courtesy of The Mamas & The Papas. For all the spirit of love, the Mamas and the other Papa wished that John Phillips had kept the song for themselves.

The Monterey International Pop Festival was a spectacular success. Appearing after Jimi Hendrix, Otis Redding and The Who, Scott McKenzie closed the festival with 'San Francisco'. McKenzie had difficulty following 'San Francisco', although another John Phillips song, 'Like An Old-Time Movie', deserved to do much better than number 50. Scott was to replace Denny Doherty in The Mamas & The Papas.

237 Engelbert Humperdinck The Last Waltz

Label & Cat No.: **Decca F 12655**

Producer: **Peter Sullivan**

Writer: **Les Reed / Barry Mason**

Date Reached No.1: **9 September 1967**

Weeks at No.1: **5**

FOLLOWING HIS APPEARANCE ON *Sunday Night At The London Palladium* in early 1967, Engelbert immediately attracted a legion of female fans.

Gordon Mills had promoted Engelbert as a middle-of-the-road singer, but many critics dismissed him as a crooner. Engelbert once said, "If you're not a crooner it's something you don't want to be called. No crooner has the range I have. I can hit notes that a bank couldn't cash. What I am is a contemporary singer, a stylised performer".

Les explained how he came to write 'The Last Waltz'. "When I was a little kid, my father was in the army and my mother and her sisters used to go to a dance every Friday evening at the local YWCA. We could hear the band just across the allotment and I used to wait for the last waltz which was 'I'm Taking You Home Tonight', and as all the men were in the army, the women were dancing together and I knew that when the last waltz came, I would be getting my supper within 10 minutes. Mum would just walk across the allotment and get our supper. This would be about half past nine or 10 and it was during the war. I relayed this story to Barry Mason and he said, 'Why don't we write a last waltz'. I was very influenced by Burt Bacharach, so I gave Barry a tape of a melody with a Bacharach type feel to it. When he came back, it was nothing like the story that I had related to him, but in retrospect he was right to do something more universal. Simplicity came through. It has now taken the place of the last waltz that I used to listen to, in whatever country."

When Les and Barry played the demo of 'The Last Waltz' to friends, they laughed at the title as it was considered too square. But sometimes things can be so old-fashioned they can be considered cool. No one laughed when Andy Williams returned to the Top 10 with 'Music To Watch Girls By' in 1999.

'The Last Waltz' seemed like the right song for the French market, with their passion for romance. With lyrics translated by Hubert Ithier, it was re-titled 'La Derniere Valse' and recorded by French teenager Mireille Mathieu. Her version also made the UK chart in December 1967 where it reached number 26.

After years of performing in Las Vegas and noticing the success Tom Jones was now having with younger audiences, Engelbert sought to reinvent himself. In 1996 he recorded 'Lesbian Seagull' for the *Beavis And Butt-Head Do America* soundtrack and it was released as the B-side of the Red Hot Chili Peppers' Top 10 single 'Love Rollercoaster'. Three years later he ventured into the dance-pop world and was back in the singles chart with the Latin-tinged 'Quando Quando Quando'.

Scott McKenzie (second from right) with The Mamas & The Papas

238 The Bee Gees
Massachusetts (The Lights Went Out In)

Label & Cat No.: **Polydor 56 192**
Producer: **Robert Stigwood / The Bee Gees**
Writers: **Barry Gibb / Robin Gibb / Maurice Gibb**
Date reached No.1: **11 October 1967**
Weeks at No.1: **4**

In 1999 The Isle Of Man honoured The Bee Gees by representing their work on a series of postage stamps. Douglas, the capital of the small island in the Irish Sea is where all three Gibb brothers were born, Barry Alan Crompton Gibb in 1946 and twins, Robin Hugh and Maurice Ernest, in 1949. Their father, Hugh, was a dance band leader and drummer and he found work hard to come by in the winter months. The family, wracked by poverty, moved to Manchester in 1955 and took an assisted passage to Australia in 1958.

Encouraged by listening to The Everly Brothers, the three boys were soon harmonising and they had various band names – The Rattlesnakes, The Brothers Gibb and The B.G.s before concluding, in 1963, with The Bee Gees. They had some regional success with their records around their home town of Sydney and then an Australian number one with 'Spicks And Specks'.

The Bee Gees wanted to establish themselves outside Australia and they begged their parents to return to the UK. In 1967 they came back and signed with the Australian manager, Robert Stigwood, a director in Brian Epstein's NEMS organisation. The group expanded from three brothers and two guitars by their friends from Australia, guitarist Vince Melouney and drummer Colin Petersen. Their first record, the quirky 'New York Mining Disaster 1941' (there was no such event), was a hit in both Britain and America. It was followed by their first great soul ballad, 'To Love Somebody', which became a mainstay of Nina Simone's repertoire.

'Massachusetts' was a response to Scott McKenzie's 'San Francisco' – the lights were going out because all the hippies were going to San Francisco. They weren't sure that it was a Bee Gees song at first and offered it to The Seekers, but then changed their minds. Says Robin Gibb, "We had never been there but we loved the word, and there is always something magical about American place names. It only works with British names if you do it as a folk song. Roger Whittaker did that with 'Durham Town' (laughs). Maybe I'll write 'I'm going to Norwich City'."

239 The Foundations
Baby Now That I've Found You

Label & Cat No.: **Pye 7N 17366**
Producer: **Tony Macaulay**
Writers: **Tony Macaulay / John McLeod**
Date reached No.1: **8 November 1967**
Weeks at No.1: **2**

The Foundations were as much pop as they were soul, and they were a bunch of musicians from around the world who had formed a group in London. There was Mike Elliott (tenor sax, born 1929), Eric Allandale (trombone, 1936), Pat Burke (flute, 1937), Clem Curtis (lead vocals, 1940), Alan Warner (lead guitar, 1941), Peter MacBeth (bass, 1943), Tim Harris (drums, 1948) and Tony Gomez (organ, 1948). The soul singer Edwin Starr heard the band and invited them to join him on tour. That got them playing tight and when they returned to London, they auditioned for Pye producer Tony Macaulay.

Tony Macaulay remembers, "I woke up that morning with a stinking hangover and when I got to the studio and heard The Foundations, I thought they were pretty terrible. I decided that it was my hangover that was to blame and so I gave them the benefit of the doubt and the only song I could think of was something John McLeod and I had had some time, 'Baby Now That I've Found You'. I didn't have a lot of faith in the song but they recorded it with a lot of energy and I learnt a lot from making that record."

'Baby Now That I've Found You' was an international hit. Clem Curtis says, "That was brilliant for us. We got to play 32 States on a tour with Fifth Dimension, Big Brother & The Holding Company, The Crazy World Of Arthur Brown, The Byrds, Tim Buckley, Solomon Burke and Maxine Brown, and it was only $3 to get in."

The follow-up to 'Baby Now That I've Found You' was the similar sounding 'Back On My Feet Again': "Well, what's wrong with that?" says Clem, "All Hot Chocolate's records sounded the same for the first few years." 'Back On My Feet Again' made number 18 and they had further hits with 'Build Me Up Buttercup' (written by Macaulay with Mike D'Abo) and 'In The Bad Bad Old Days'. A very catchy film theme, 'Take A Girl Like You', failed to chart in 1970 and the group disbanded. They have never reformed.

A sharply-dressed Clem Curtis toured the UK in 2004 on a soul package with Jimmy James & The Vagabonds. When Jimmy James invited him back on stage at the end of the show in Liverpool, Jimmy said, "I don't like him and he don't like me, but that's all right. Here's Clem Curtis." They then sang a duet of 'Love Train'.

240 Long John Baldry
Let The Heartaches Begin

Label & Cat No.: **Pye 7N 17385**
Producer: **John MacLeod**
Writers: **Tony Macaulay / John McLeod**
Date reached No.1: **22 November 1967**
Weeks at No.1: **2**

In 1949 when John Baldry was only eight, he heard the blues harmonica player, Sonny Terry, and became fascinated by the blues. He made his first public appearance in 1956, played in several blues bands and he took over Cyril Davies' band following his death in 1964, changing the name to the Hoochie Coochie Men. Hearing Rod Stewart playing a harmonica riff from 'Smokestack Lightnin'' on Twickenham Railway Station, he invited him to join the band. A short while later, he formed Steampacket with Rod, Julie Driscoll and Brian Auger.

Another of Baldry's backing bands was Bluesology, which featured a young Elton John on keyboards. "Apparently, I gave Elton some very good advice when he was in a pickle," says John, "and he wrote a song about it, 'Someone Saved My Life Tonight', but I still can't figure out what the song is all about."

Although Long John Baldry had made blues and R&B records, the Pye producers, Tony Macaulay and John McLeod, wanted him to record with studio musicians. The general consensus is that John hated recording 'Let The Heartaches Begin': "That's not true at all. I liked doing anything in the studio and I was very happy that Pye was employing me. I was hugely flattered to be backed by a large orchestra and it's not a bad song – it's a much more worthy tune than a lot of hits I can mention. Until 2002 I hadn't done it for 30 years because I'd been living in North America and they didn't know it there. I feel that if it had been treated in a different manner, it could have become an R&B standard."

And possibly recorded by The Foundations. Clem Curtis recalls, "Tony Macaulay gave us two songs. One was 'Let The Heartaches Begin' and the other was 'Baby Now That I've Found You', and we chose 'Baby Now That I've Found You'. Long John Baldry recorded the other one and that knocked us off the top."

Tony Macaulay adds, "It was very like The Drifters and John McLeod's arrangement is excellent. He makes a fairly ordinary song sound great and also Long John Baldry sings it extraordinarily well, thanks to three-quarters of a bottle of Courvoisier."

Long John Baldry has lived in Canada for 30 years and released a host of blues albums including *It Still Ain't Easy* (1991), *Right To Sing The Blues* (1996) and *Remembering Leadbelly* (2001). And just how tall is Long John Baldry? "Sadly, I'm shrinking as I have osteoporosis of the spine and I'm getting a buffalo hump. I have to be very careful about getting out of the bath as if I broke my hip it might take forever to repair. I'm Shrinking John Baldry now, but I was six foot seven."

241 The Beatles
Hello Goodbye

Label & Cat No.: **Parlophone R 5655**
Producer: **George Martin**
Writers: **John Lennon / Paul McCartney**
Date reached No.1: **6 December 1967**
Weeks at No.1: **7**

THE BEATLES HAD THE CHRISTMAS number one and two in 1967 as their single 'Hello Goodbye' topped the charts, while their double-EP the six-song *Magical Mystery Tour* was number two. Much to John's annoyance, his highly experimental 'I Am The Walrus' was relegated to the B-side of the single, but as his song was on the EP set as well, it was effectively at numbers one and two.

The *Magical Mystery Tour* TV film was heavily panned when it was screened over Christmas, but this was partly due to nonsensical programming by the BBC. The first screening was in black and white with the colour print following a few days later. The concept for a touring party travelling on a yellow and blue bus was Paul McCartney's and although nothing much happens, the guests included the whimsical Scottish poet Ivor Cutler and the rubber man, Nat Jackley. The one standard to emerge from the film is Paul's ballad, 'The Fool On The Hill'.

'Hello Goodbye' sounded great, but John was not happy with it. "That's another McCartney," he said in 1980, "Smells a mile away, doesn't it?" "It's a song of duality, with me advocating the positive," said Paul, and despite John's comments, the song is not far from the sentiments of 'All You Need Is Love'. Paul had written the song after playing word associations on the harmonium with their 'Mr. Fixit', Alistair Taylor.

As well as singing and playing bass, Paul adds piano and percussion to the recording. With overdubbing, John played rhythm guitar and organ, George lead guitar and tambourine, and Ringo drums and maracas. They were supplemented by two viola players. The Beatles referred to the false ending as their Maori finale and on the promotional film shot at the Savile Theatre in London, they featured dancers with grass skirts.

Paul McCartney revived the song as his opening number on his 2003 world tour, which played to over two million fans.

242 Georgie Fame
The Ballad Of Bonnie And Clyde

Label & Cat No.: **CBS 3124**
Producer: **Mike Smith**
Writers: **Mitch Murray / Peter Callander**
Date reached No.1: **24 January 1968**
Weeks at No.1: **1**

THE SONGWRITERS, MITCH MURRAY and Peter Callander, went to see the film, *Bonnie And Clyde*, about the two Thirties gangsters starring Warren Beatty and Faye Dunaway. "We both decided that they had blown the music," says Mitch. "They should have had a hit song and so we thought we would write one. At first we considered giving it to Joe Brown or Lonnie Donegan, but they didn't seem quite right for the song. Then the managing director of CBS told Peter that they had signed Georgie Fame and were looking for a big hit. We added a special jazzy bit for Georgie – 'Bonnie and Clyde got to be Public Enemy Number One' – as we thought that would sell it to him, but he wasn't very keen on the song. We did a demo with machine guns and skidding cars and we were asked to go to the session with our sound effects."

Georgie Fame: "I was working up north and I had to fly down to London, do the track, and go back up north for that night's show. I was working pretty hard at the time and I hadn't even seen the film when I recorded the song."

The producer, Mike Smith, had his problems: "The sound effects were wonderful, but we discovered an electrical fault and we had clicks all through the rhythm track. I had to go back into the studio and using George's vocal track and the front line from the brass, the musicians had to put down a new rhythm track, which is not easy.

To this day, Georgie doesn't quite believe that they did it, but we ended up with an outstanding record."

Mitch Murray remembers this well: "We didn't feel that we could get Georgie to do it again because he hadn't wanted to sing it in the first place! Clem Cattini came in and put the drums back on the track and that is not easy as he was doing it the wrong way round. He did a brilliant job."

With their husky voices, Georgie Fame and Alan Price are often confused and they increased the confusion by making an album, *Fame And Price Together*, which included their hit single, 'Rosetta'. "We both play the piano and sing," says Georgie, "but I don't see a lot of similarity. Still, people genuinely come up to me and ask for 'Simon Smith And His Amazing Dancing Bear' and Alan gets requests for 'The Ballad Of Bonnie And Clyde'."

243 The Love Affair Everlasting Love

Label & Cat No.: **CBS 3125**

Producer: **Mike Smith**

Writer: **Buzz Cason / Mac Gayden**

Date Reached No.1: **3 February 1968**

Weeks at No.1: **2**

The Rolling Stones were often classed as the 'bad boys' of rock, but just before Christmas 1967, the newly formed Love Affair did a publicity photo shoot in London's Piccadilly Circus where they were arrested for insulting behaviour and causing an obstruction. Whilst in court, they received the news that 'Everlasting Love', had entered the Top 20. Their arrests turned out to be a publicity stunt.

Steve Ellis and two friends answered an ad placed in *NME* by actor/comedian Max Bacon. The idea was that his 14-year-old nephew, Maurice Bacon, could fulfil his dream of playing drums with a band.

Steve recalled, "I remember Decca Records came to a rehearsal and said they loved the band. They said we were just what they were looking for to follow on in a Small Faces vein. They told us they'd sign us up if we got rid of our drummer. Maurice was not that bad, so we all rallied round and said 'No'. They signed us anyway. We called ourselves The Soul Survivors and were mostly doing Stax and Motown covers. But then the management wanted us to change our name to the The Love Affair, which I thought was a crap name but was out-voted."

Their debut release, in 1967, was a Jagger and Richards composition 'She Smiled Sweetly'. The song bombed. Decca Records had acquired a reputation of being hard to work with, so The Love Affair once again followed The Small Faces and left the label.

Having left Decca, The Love Affair then moved to CBS who suggested they record a cover of 'Everlasting Love'. It had already been a US hit for Robert Knight, who was discovered by the song's co-writer, Buzz Cason, performing in a trio with Daniel Boone and James Tait called The Fairlaines.

Steve Ellis wanted to get a version out before Robert Knight's was released in the UK. The first recording session, with Spencer Davis Group bass player Muff Winwood producing, was deemed a failure. So the track was re-recorded with CBS producer Mike Smith and arranger Keith Mansfield, who often employed session musicians to provide a more commercial and orchestrated feel. Steve recalled, "I didn't think the first version with the band was all that bad, but they insisted on me doing it with an orchestra and then giving it a Phil Spector-type production".

As the song climbed the chart, Love Affair appeared on a Jonathan King hosted show called *Good Evening*. When they had finished their set, Jonathan asked the bass player if they had played on their records, and he admitted they didn't. The next day the tabloids attacked them for admitting they didn't play on their records and were banned from appearing on some television stations.

The Love Affair followed up 'Everlasting Love' with 'Rainbow Valley', another Buzz Cason and Mac Gayden composition and again originally recorded by Robert Knight. "We recorded an album, *The Everlasting Love Affair*", said Steve, "But there was no big campaign to promote it. When we were labelled teenybop idols and not being taken seriously, I got very disheartened and left the band".

In 1981 Steve retired to become a docker but was involved in a horrific accident, which took him the best part of 10 years to recover. During the Eighties and Nineties there was a touring 'Love Affair' that didn't include any of the original members, so in 1994, he went back on the road as Steve Ellis' Love Affair.

244 Manfred Mann The Mighty Quinn

Label & Cat No.: **Fontana TF 697**

Producer: **Mike Hurst**

Writer: **Bob Dylan**

Date reached No.1: **14 February 1968**

Weeks at No.1: **2**

Paul Jones' replacement in Manfred Mann was Mike D'Abo from A Band Of Angels. The group's recording contract was up for renewal and EMI decided that a Manfred Mann without Paul Jones was not a viable proposition. Despite this set-back, Manfred Mann found a home with Philips and the group continued their hits with 'Just Like A Woman', 'Semi-Detached Suburban Mr. James' and 'Ha, Ha, Said The Clown'. Having had hits with two Bob Dylan songs ('If You Gotta Go, Go Now, 'Just Like A Woman'), they had a number one with 'The Mighty Quinn'. Bob Dylan is reputed to have said that Manfred Mann did his songs better than anyone. Tom McGuinness says, "Yes, Dylan did say that, but he probably said it about The Byrds as well. He also said that Smokey Robinson was the world's greatest living poet."

Mike D'Abo recalls, "We met in a publishers's office as Bob Dylan was making some new material available to other artists. We heard about 10 songs and I thought 'This Wheel's On Fire' would be the one to do, but Manfred liked 'The

Mighty Quinn', which was called 'Quinn The Eskimo' then. It was sung in a rambling montone but Manfred had recognised its potential. If nothing else, Manfred was a brilliant arranger and very good at extracting the meat from a song. He sold me on the idea of doing this song, but I had to make up some of the words as I couldn't make out everything he was saying. It was like learning a song phoentically in a foreign language. I have never had the first idea what the song is about, except that it seems to be 'Hey, gang, gather round, something exciting is going to happen 'cause the big man's coming.' As to who the big man is and why he is an Eskimo, I don't know."

Bob Dylan, true to form, has never commented on his composition, but Anthony Quinn did play an eskimo in *The Savage Innocents* (1960).

245 Esther & Abi Ofarim Cinderella Rockefella

Label & Cat No.: **Philips BF 1640**

Producers: **Abi Ofarim / Ady Semel**

Writers: **Mason Williams / Nancy Ames**

Date reached No.1: **28 January 1968**

Weeks at No.1: **3**

Abi (actually, Abraham Reichstadt) was born in Zafed in 1937, while Esther Zaled was born in Nazareth four years later. Esther was in the Israeli army but was able to leave when she married Abi. They became a popular act in Israel, having a successful album, *HaOfarim (The Ofarims)*, in 1961. Esther had a minor role in the film, *Exodus*, and also opened for Frank Sinatra. She also represented Switzerland in the 1963 Eurovision Song Contest, coming second with 'T'en Vas Pas'. As a duo, they recorded several more albums, usually with Esther singing lead and Abi playing guitar.

In 1967 they recorded an album, *2 In 3*, which consisted of 13 songs in eight languages and was made in three cities – London, Paris and Munich. The album included a Twenties style song, 'Cinderella Rockefella', which had been given to them by a writer on *The Smothers Brothers Show*, Mason Williams. He had written the song with the singer Nancy Ames as "a song to have fun with, just a diversion."

Esther & Abi Ofarim sang 'Cinderella Rockefella' on *The Eamonn Andrews Show* on ITV and the demand was such that it was immediately released as a single. As well as topping the UK charts, it also went to number one in Holland and Sweden. Although Esther and Abi followed their UK hit with another novelty, 'One More Dance', which reached number 13, they had more success in other countries, notably Germany where 'Sing Hallelujah' and 'Morning Of My Life' (written by The Bee Gees and with their backing vocals) were hits.

'Cinderella Rockefella' was written by Mason Williams, who had his own UK hit with the instrumental, 'Classical Gas', also in 1968. He issued the albums, *The Mason Williams Phonograph Record* (1968) and *The Mason Williams Ear Show* (1969), the second of which included his version of 'Cinderella Rockefella' on which he was joined by Jennifer Warren, one of the supporting cast on *The Smothers Brothes Show*.

Esther and Abi divorced in 1970: Esther appeared on the Scott Walker LP, *Til The Band Comes In* (1970) and made a noted LP, *Israeli Song* (1983). She makes regular appearances in Europe including songs by Kurt Weill, Ewan MacColl and Noël Coward in her concerts, but not 'Cinderella Rockefella'. Abi Ofarim has worked with two partners, Sima and Sharon, and is currently involved in music publishing and managing his son, Gil.

Right, altogether now, "You're the lady, you're the lady that I love."

Esther & Abi Ofarim

246 Dave Dee, Dozy, Beaky, Mick & Tich The Legend Of Xanadu

Label & Cat No.: **Fontana TF 903**

Producer: **Steve Rowland**

Writers: **Ken Howard / Alan Blaikley**

Date reached No.1: **20 March 1968**

Weeks at No.1: **1**

Dave Harman (Dave Dee) was born in Salisbury in 1943. He became a police cadet and was called to the car accident which killed Eddie Cochran in Chippenham in April 1960. Dave and his friends formed a beat group: "We were The Boppers first and then The Beatniks. We had jackets with 'B' on so we had to stick with that letter. We became The Bostons and then I became 'D' for David, and Tich said we should be like Cliff Richard & The Shadows and call ourselves Dave Dee & The Bostons."

In 1962 Dave Dee & The Bostons, who played American R&B songs, secured a residency at The Top Ten club in Hamburg, moving on to The Star-Club. When they returned to the UK, they became Dave Dee, Dozy (Trevor Davies), Beaky (John Dymond), Mick (Michael Wilson) and Tich (Ian Amey). "The nicknames were already there," says Dave, "We wanted something that sounded original and we were almost The Slugs. We thought that no one would remember it, but they would know us as the band with the long hair and the long name. Once people got used to the name, they wanted to know which was which and we all had our own following. People used to say, 'Where's Sleepy? Where's Grumpy?' A lot of people didn't know that Dave Dee was one person, so it was thought that there were six of us."

In 1964 the band worked a summer season at Butlins in Clacton and on a night off, they played a ballroom in Swindon. Topping the bill were The Honeycombs, and Dave Dee & Co impressed their managers, Ken Howard and Alan Blaikley. They were signed to Fontana Records by Jack Baverstock and assigned to the producer, Steve Rowland.

The group made the Top 30 with 'You Make It Move', in 1965, but their breakthrough came in March 1966 with 'Hold Tight'. Only Jim Reeves with 'Distant Drums' kept their innuendo-laden 'Bend It', from topping the charts. Dave Dee would wiggle his finger whilst singing the suggestive lyrics. 'Bend It' had a Greek influence and the group made their singles distinctive with exotic titles and locations such as 'The Legend Of Xanadu' (with its whip-cracking sound) and 'Zabadak!'. Dee said, "We tried to make every record different from the one before, but not different from everything we had done. We kept coming back to the 'Hold Tight' sound with 'Touch Me Touch Me' and 'Hideaway'."

After going solo, Dave Dee worked in A&R, signing many well-known acts including AC/DC, Boney M, B.A. Robertson and Gary Numan: "In our day we had never heard of advances, we were just glad someone wanted us. By then, groups had decent lawyers who understood the music business law, and there was a lot of negotiation." Dave organised charity events including the two *Heroes And Villains* concerts for Music Therapy in the early Eighties. He assembled many Sixties stars, including the reclusive Scott Walker, for a TV ad for Britvic.

From time to time, Dave Dee, Dozy, Beaky, Mick and Tich play oldies shows, admittedly with a new Beaky and Mick. Touring with Peter Sarstedt and members of Marmalade and The Tremeloes, Dave is also the presenter of a musical history of the Sixties, *The Story Book Show.*

247 The Beatles
Lady Madonna

Label & Cat No.: **Parlophone R 5675**
Producer: **George Martin**
Writers: **John Lennon / Paul McCartney**
Date reached No.1: **27 March 1968**
Weeks at No.1: **2**

USUALLY WHEN THE BEATLES DID A rock'n'roll homage, they paid tribute to Chuck Berry, but with 'Lady Madonna' they doffed their hats to Fats Domino, admittedly with psychedelic lyrics. Paul said, "I wanted to pay a tribute to mothers. A lot of Catholic mothers in Liverpool see a connection between themselves and the Virgin Mary with her baby." John Lennon later said that the song "never really went anywhere", but the song is full of surprises. Could even John have anticipated that middle eight?

When the song was released, the tune was compared to Humphrey Lyttelton's 1956 hit, 'Bad Penny Blues'. Humph said, "A number of idiots came up to me and said, "They've borrowed the introduction to 'Bad Penny Blues'. What are you going to do about it?" They wanted me to sue them but I told them not to be so stupid. You can't copyright a rhythm, and a rhythm was all they'd used. Actually, we'd borrowed it from Dan Burley." As if to emphasise the jazz connection, the brass section was led by saxophonist, Ronnie Scott.

By designing the press advertisements, Paul McCartney was strongly involved in the promotion of the single. Although 'Lady Madonna' was released around Mother's Day, it remained on top for only two weeks and was out of the charts within eight. By Beatle standards, this was a poor showing. The B-side, 'The Inner Light', was George Harrison's first appearance as either a songwriter or lead vocalist on a Beatles single.

A few months later Fats Domino recorded his own version of 'Lady Madonna' and he didn't have to work hard to convert it to his style.

248 Cliff Richard
Congratulations

Label & Cat No.: **Columbia DB 8376**
Producer: **Norrie Paramor**
Writers: **Bill Martin / Phil Coulter**
Date reached No.1: **10 April 1968**
Weeks at No.1: **2**

PHIL COULTER GAVE HIS SONGWRITING partner, Bill Martin, a new melody, but Bill didn't like its title, 'I Think I Love You'. He said that you either loved someone or you didn't. He looked for a five syllable word which would fit the melody and came up with 'Congratulations'. Phil Coulter recalls, "The whole package with Cliff, that title, the brassy intro and the slow down and the key change in the middle was a good one. It was well put together for Eurovision and to be honest, we stole that slow down from Edith Piaf's 'Milord'. If you're going to steal, steal from the best!"

Cliff Richard has made better records, but he will always be remembered for entering The Eurovision Song Contest – and losing. He was the hot favourite but he came second to Massiel representing Spain with 'La La La'. Phil Coulter recalls, "We were in the Royal Albert Hall and we had a very partisan crowd supporting Cliff. It looked as though we were going to win easily but the old enmities came into play and West Germany marked us down. The song that won, 'La La La' sank without trace and 'Congratulations' has proven with time that it really was the winner of The Eurovision Song Contest. I would settle for having come second with 'Congratulations', selling six million records and writing a song that has clothed and fed and educated my children than writing a song that has won Eurovision and disappeared without trace."

'Congratulations' was recorded with the session singers, The Breakaways, who had broken away from The Vernons Girls. The bass was played by John Paul Jones, who was to join Led Zeppelin. As well as the English version, Cliff recorded it in French, German and Spanish. Undeterred, in 1973 Cliff tried again with 'Power To

All Our Friends', this time coming third.

Although 'Congratulations' was not the most sophisticated song of the year, it was the most memorable. It was played after Charles and Diana's wedding and also when the British troop ships returned from the Falklands. It is no mean achievement to have a song which is regularly sung at social gatherings – The Beatles, also in 1968, didn't quite succeed with 'Birthday', while Stevie Wonder's 'Happy Birthday', although a huge hit in 1981, has not replaced 'Happy Birthday To You'.

If you have George Harrison's 1970 album, *All Things Must Pass*, play the track 'It's Johnny Birthday'. "That really was jammy," says Phil Coulter. "George was working on his album and John Lennon arrived in the studio on his birthday. Spontaneously George and the guys in the band went into 'It's Johnny's Birthday'. They were not thinking it was 'Congratulations' but some song that had been around forever. It made its way onto the album and our publisher rang up and said, 'Is that Apple Records? We have a slight problem here, lads.' We ended up getting the lion's share of the royalties from that track."

249 Louis Armstrong What A Wonderful World / Cabaret

Label & Cat No.: **HMV POP 1615**

Producer: **Bob Thiele**

Writers: **George David Weiss / George Douglas; John Kander / Fred Ebb**

Date reached No.1: **24 April 1968**

Weeks at No.1: **4**

THE JAZZ TRUMPETER, HUMPHREY Lyttelton, says, "The first Louis Armstrong record I heard was 'Basin Street Blues', which he recorded in 1928. It was a *tour de force* – it bowled me over and it has remained a favourite of mine ever since. I don't think he took his singing very seriously at first, but when Bing Crosby came along, he started softening his voice and singing the popular songs of the day. It was still a gravel voice, but he found he could phrase in a very passionate and rhapsodic way, especially on slow ballads."

Satchmo (short for 'satchel-mouth' and a racist slur that he took in his stride) was nearly 70 years old when he had a number one with 'What A Wonderful World'. Although it was his only number one, he probably would have had several had the charts been around from the Twenties: there's 'Blueberry Hill', 'When It's Sleepy Time Down South', 'Lazy River' for starters. He continued to have hits but not number ones during the chart era – 'Mack The Knife' (1956), 'Hello Dolly!' (1964) and a reissue of a James Bond theme several years after his death in 1971, 'We Have All The Time In The World' (1994).

The world's problems were ignored in 'What A Wonderful World', written by George David Weiss whose hits include 'Wild In The Country' and 'Can't Help Falling In Love' for Elvis Presley. Weiss also has his name on 'The Lion Sleeps Tonight', aka 'Wimoweh', and a 2003 BBC documentary revealed that its original South African writer had been ignored, clearly not a wonderful world for him. 'What A Wonderful World' is now a standard with revivals from Nick Cave (presumably an example of post-modernist irony), Cliff Richard and Eva Cassidy.

Although 'What A Wonderful World' was receiving the airplay, the B-side, 'Cabaret', was also listed on the charts. It was the title song from the 1966 musical about an English cabaret singer (Liza Minnelli) witnessing the rise of the Nazis in pre-war Berlin. Although it was cynical in context, Armstrong omitted the contentious section and the result was a record with a similar message to 'What A Wonderful World'.

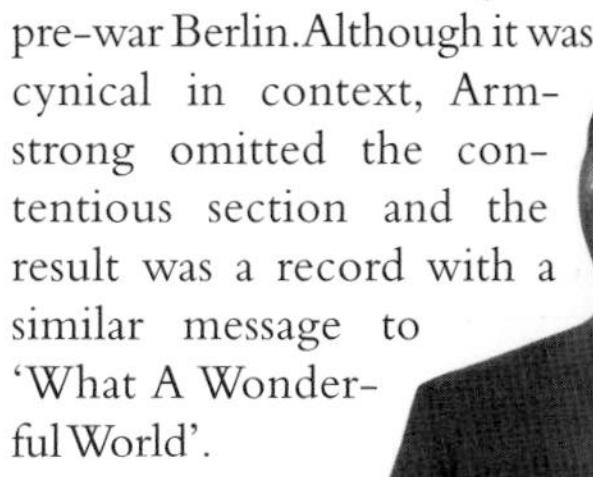

250 The Union Gap featuring Gary Puckett Young Girl

Label & Cat No.: **CBS 3365**

Producer: **Jerry Fuller**

Writer: **Jerry Fuller**

Date Reached No.1: **25 May 1968**

Weeks at No.1: **4**

GARY PUCKETT AND HIS BACKING group, The Union Gap, were discovered by Columbia Records' staff producer Jerry Fuller when he saw them performing at a San Diego bowling lounge. Jerry, who was also a singer/songwriter, was born into a musical family. Both his parents were singers and his father once performed with the Light Crust Doughboys, before they became Bob Wills & The Texas Playboys.

In 1960 Jerry wrote 'Travelin' Man' for Sam Cooke, but Ricky Nelson's bass player, Joe Osborne, was in Sam Cooke's office and heard the track. Sneaking it out of the office, he played it to Ricky, who quickly recorded it without Jerry even knowing. He went on to write 23 other songs that Ricky recorded.

Gary Puckett was born in Minnesota in 1942. His first band was The Outcasts, followed by Gary & The Remarkables. Taking the name from a Washington State suburb, he formed The Union Gap in 1966 and came up with the gimmick of giving all the members a military moniker. There was vocalist/guitarist 'General' Gary Puckett, 'Private' Gary Withem (keyboards), 'Corporal' Kerry Chater (bass), 'Sergeant' Dwight Bement (sax) and 'Private' Paul Whitebread (drums).

Jerry explained the inspiration for 'Young Girl'. "I was on the road a lot as an artist, fronting various groups for many years. I guess every entertainer goes through a time when 14 year-olds look like 20 year-olds. That's somewhat of an inspiration…not from my own experience, but just knowing that it happens."

'Young Girl' carries a serious message

about older men falling for younger girls. With the opening lyric, 'Young girl, get out of my mind, my love for you is way out of line, better run, girl, you're much too young, girl' there is a lesson to be learnt. If the song had been around 10 years earlier, would Jerry Lee Lewis have thought twice when he married his 13-year-old cousin Myra? It obviously didn't bother Elvis Presley when he started dating 14-year-old Priscilla. As for Bill Wyman, Mandy Smith was only 13 when they first met. None of those marriages lasted.

The Union Gap had two further hits, the similar sounding 'Lady Willpower' also written by Jerry Fuller, and a reissue of 'Woman Woman', which failed to chart first time round. All three titles incorporated a female theme and all three were about relationships. 'Young Girl' went back in to the Top 10 when it was re-issued in 1974.

The band split in 1971. Chater later wrote songs for Bobby Darin and Mama Cass. Gary still tours the oldies circuit in the States with Brian Hyland, Gary Lewis and Billy J. Kramer.

Many aspiring new bands include 'Young Girl' in their set, even The Searchers perform it on tour, which, for a bunch of 60 year olds, could be worrying.

251 The Rolling Stones
Jumpin' Jack Flash

Label & Cat No.: **Decca F 12782**

Producer: **Jimmy Miller**

Writers: **Mick Jagger / Keith Richards**

Date reached No.1: **19 June 1968**

Weeks at No.1: **2**

After 'Paint It, Black', The Rolling Stones released the lack-lustre 'Have You Seen Your Mother Baby Standing In The Shadow?' and the excellent double-sider, 'Let's Spend The Night Together' / 'Ruby Tuesday'. The media spotlight fell on them in June 1967 when Mick Jagger and Keith Richards were arrested for possession of amphetamines and smoking marijuana in disorderly circumstances at Keith's Sussex home where the police claimed to have found Marianne Faithfull wandering dressed only in a towel.

The Establishment considered The Beatles to be OK but the Stones to be bad boys, as illustrated in the cops' decision to allow George Harrison to leave before the arrests were made. Unjustly, Mick and Keith were given three months in jail which prompted the *The Times* to lead a campaign against the severity of the sentence, famously headlining their editorial by William Rees-Mogg, "Who Breaks A Butterfly On A Wheel?" Mick and Keith walked free within 24 hours. It was one of the defining moments of the Sixties.

The Who, seeing The Stones as scapegoats, showed their support by releasing a single of 'The Last Time' / 'Under My Thumb'. John and Paul added their voices to complete The Stones' psychedelic single, 'We Love You'. It opened with the clanking of chains and a cell door being slammed but the song was too derivative of 'All You Need Is Love'. Reflecting badly on the Stones' run of hits, it only reached number eight, but at the time that was the least of their worries. The album, *Their Satanic Majesties Request*, despite strong moments and stunning art-work, showed that the Stones were ill-suited to psychedelia.

Mick and Keith needed a great, gutsy single to re-establish themselves and as Bill Wyman has said, "We badly needed a hit record. It had been nearly 18 months since we had a US or UK Top three single. Our reputation was now based on anything but the music." The Stones appeared at the *NME Poll Winners' Concert* in May 1968 and previewed their new single, 'Jumping Jack Flash'. Said the NME, "The Stones have a unique flair for taking a basically simply formula and turning it into a miniature epic."

Their confidence returned with this powerful single, the title being a nod to Mick's lively stage presence and 'Jumpin' Jack Flash' certainly was a gas, gas, gas. Keith's guitar was tuned to an open E, giving a piercing quality to his playing which made it cut through the airwaves. Keith also put down the bass part while Bill played organ. The record was produced by Jimmy Miller, known for his work with The Spencer Davis Group, and he gave the Stones their most powerful sound to date. The blues performer, George Thorogood, comments, "If you listen to the exotic lyrics of Bo Diddley's 'Who Do You Love' and then listen to 'Jumpin' Jack Flash', you can hear that The Rolling Stones were paying attention to Bo Diddley."

After the débâcle of *Their Satanic Majesties Request*, the Rolling Stones returned to their blues roots for the 1968 LP, *Beggars Banquet*, a contender for their greatest moment ever, which included 'Street Fighting Man', possibly their response to 'Dancing In The Street'.

The Stones made a promotional film for 'Jumpin' Jack Flash', directed by Michael Lindsay-Hogg, with Mick Jagger, heavily made up, leering into the camera. Michael also directed The Rolling Stones' TV special, *Rock'n'Roll Circus*. This extravaganza, also featuring The Who, Marianne Faithfull and John and Yoko, was shot in 1968 but remained unseen until 1996.

252 The Equals
Baby Come Back

Label & Cat No.: **President PT 135**

Producer: **Ed Kassner**

Writer: **Eddy Grant**

Date Reached No.1: **6 July 1968**

Weeks at No.1: **3**

It has often been suggested that The Equals were the first multi-racial group to top the UK charts. This is not true. Georgie Fame's Blue Flames had a black conga player in the early days and The Foundations were a mixed race group too.

Guitarist Eddy Grant was born in Plaisance, Guyana on March 5, 1948. When he was 12, the family moved to England and settled in East London, where he soon discovered rhythm and blues. He formed The Equals in 1965. The rest of the band comprised twin Jamaican brothers Derv and Lincoln Gordon on vocals and guitar respectively, and Britons John Hall on drums and bassist Patrick Lloyd.

They started touring the pubs around London and auditioned for Ed Kassner at President Records. Kassner heard them sing 'I Won't Be There' which he mistakenly thought was an Otis Redding cover. He soon discovered it was one of Eddy's own songs. Eddy recalled, "Once we'd finished rehearsing it went quiet. I was convinced we'd blown it. They didn't even look at us when we'd finished. Kassner then came over to me and asked if I had, or could write any more songs like that. At the time, it was the only one I'd written but of course I said 'yes'." Eddy then wrote and produced 'Train Tour To Rainbow City' which was recorded by The Pyramids and gave him his first chart hit as a writer.

Their debut album *Unequalled Equals* achieved the rare feat for that time of making the Top 10 before any of their singles had charted.

Their first single release was 'I Get So Excited' in early 1968, which limped to number 44. The follow-up, which was first released in Germany, was 'Hold Me Closer'. It died a death, until a radio DJ in West Germany flipped it over and began playing 'Baby Come Back'. From there, it took off all over the world.

The Equals have never really received the acclaim they deserved. Eddy left the band as a performer in 1972, although he continued writing for them, but by 1973, The Equals had drifted apart. Eddy launched a successful solo career and was back at number one in 1982 with 'I Don't Wanna Dance'.

253 Des O'Connor I Pretend

Label & Cat No.: **Columbia DB 8397**
Producer: **Norman Newell**
Writer: **Les Reed / Barry Mason**
Date Reached No.1: **27 July 1968**
Weeks at No.1: **1**

DES O'CONNOR, HE OF THE PERMA-tan and cheesy persona, was born in Stepney, East London on January 12, 1932. He started his career in show business as a Butlin's Redcoat in the early Fifties, making his professional debut shortly after. In 1958 he was the compere on Buddy Holly's only UK tour.

Des' singing career began by accident. "I remember once at Chiswick Empire with Cliff Richard it got quite dangerous," he recalled. "I got two spots. They didn't like me the first time so what chance did I have? I only sang 'cause it saved me having to think up three minutes of new jokes. I made one stupid record for Columbia in 1958 called 'Moonlight Swim' and then I did a send up of 'Big Bad John' called 'Thin Chow Min' (1962, Piccadilly) who committed chop suicide. It was a hit on *Juke Box Jury*, which was a dreadful sign. You knew it would be a flop then."

Although Des used to sing songs during his live appearances as well as on television, he didn't record anything until renewing his acquaintance with Columbia Records in 1967. His first hit 'Careless Hands', which was first recorded by Mel Tormé, reached number six.

"Des has got a very pleasant voice," said Les Reed. "We were in Wessex Studios and I was working with Quincy Jones and I had just finished the session and in walked Des O'Connor and Barry Mason was there too. He wanted to do a jingle and as he passed the piano he said, 'Why don't you two guys write me a song.' So we wrote 'I Pretend' and he came back from doing the jingle and said, 'I love this and I will do it in two nights time. I will give it to Geoff Love to do the arrangement and we will have a hit.' It had taken us an hour. We wrote another song for him called 'Remember', which was not released here but it went to number one in Australia."

Throughout the Seventies, Des was the butt of Morecambe & Wise jokes. They constantly mocked his singing and defaced his record sleeves. Eric and Ernie recorded 10 singles, none of which charted, so it was Des who had the last laugh when 'I Pretend' spent 36 weeks in the hit parade.

Des has appeared at the London Palladium over 1,000 times and has won many awards including 'TV Personality of the Year', 'Best Talk Show' and 'Show Business Personality of the Year'. At the same time 'I Pretend' was at the top of the pop charts, his *Des O'Connor Tonight* show was number one in the television ratings.

In 2003 Des began a daily lunchtime show with co-host Melanie Sykes, called *Today With Des And Mel* and includes interviews with big name guests.

Few will admit to liking Des' music. One morning when he was a guest on Chris Evans' Radio One breakfast show, even the CD player rejected his disc.

254 Tommy James & The Shondells Mony Mony

Label & Cat No.: **Major Minor MM 567**
Producers: **Bo Gentry / Richie Cordell**
Writers: **Bobby Bloom / Richie Cordell / Bo Gentry / Tommy James**
Date reached No.1: **31 July 1968**
Weeks at No.1: **3 (two runs)**

IN 1963 19-YEAR-OLD TOMMY JAMES cut 'Hanky Panky' with The Shondells at a radio station in Niles, Michigan. It was an animated dance song written by Jeff Barry and Ellie Greenwich, but it meant nothing at the time. Three years later it found popularity on a radio station in Pittsburgh, causing Tommy to move there and form a new bunch of Shondells. 'Hanky Panky' topped the US charts, but they went for a smoother sound with 'I Think We're Alone Now', which climbed to number four.

One night Tommy looked at the Mutual Of New York insurance building and saw the large, neon lettering, M-O-N-Y. He told his producers that it could make a great riff and soon they had a song, 'Mony Mony', that was even more raucous and exciting than 'Hanky Panky'. The single was released and although it stopped at number three in the US, it went all the way here.

The group had further US hits with 'Crimson And Clover' (1), 'Sweet Cherry Wine' (7) and 'Crystal Blue Persuasion' (2). Tommy James &

The Shondells performed in support of Hubert Humphrey at the 1968 Democratic National Convention, the one that was disrupted by Abbie Hoffman and his politically active hippies, The Yippies. The group split up in 1969 and Tommy James had a US Top 10 hit with 'Draggin' The Line' in 1971, before retiring to a 3,000 acre estate. Despite all the US hits, Tommy James & The Shondells only made the UK charts with this single and 'Hanky Panky' (38).

Amazulu, Billy Idol and Status Quo have all revived 'Mony Mony' and made the UK charts, while Tiffany sang 'I Think We're Alone Now' and Joan Jett & The Blackhearts, 'Crimson And Clover'.

255 The Crazy World Of Arthur Brown
Fire

Label & Cat No.: **Track 604022**

Producer: **Kit Lambert / Pete Townshend**

Writers: **Vincent Crane / Arthur Brown / Peter Ker / Michael Finesilver**

Date reached No.1: **14 August 1968**

Weeks at No.1: **1**

ARTHUR BROWN WAS BORN IN WHITBY in 1942 but he was no ordinary Yorkshireman. He had, as he put it, "1001% imagination". He rebelled against conventional education and when he was at Reading University, he ignored the set examination questions and wrote his own answers to his own questions. Whilst at Reading, he made his first recordings for a Rag Week flexidisc. He formed a band and went to Paris. In the underground clubs, he blacked out his teeth and put make-up around his eyes. He constructed a crown with candles and set fire to his head and so became 'The God of Hellfire'.

Back in London, he formed The Crazy World Of Arthur Brown with the keyboard player, Vincent Crane and impressed Pete Townshend and The Who's management, Kit Lambert and Chris Stamp. To everybody's surprise, their outlandish first album, *The Crazy World Of Arthur Brown*, stormed up the album charts, reaching number two. 'Fire' was taken off the album for a single. "We were a jazzy, R&B band with some comedy thrown in," says Arthur, "and I was definitely anti-pop and anti-Beatles. 'Fire' was the closest to a pop song on the whole album. The follow-up was 'Nightmare' and the public was not ready for a horror single."

The 'Fire' song was originally attributed to Brown and Crane, but Peter Ker and Michael Finesilver pointed out that their melody for 'Baby, You're A Long Way Behind', was similar and sued successfully for credit and royalties.

Arthur Brown played the Isle of Wight festival and was in the film, *Tommy*. He started a decorating business with Jimmy Carl Black of The Mothers Of Invention. "We were gentlemen of colour," says Jimmy Carl Black, and they must have given householders a few surprises. With a degree in counselling, Arthur Brown practised in Austin but he is now back, recreating his crazy world at a theatre near you. If you visit Lewes, East Sussex, you may even see him sauntering down the High Street.

256 Beach Boys
Do It Again

Label & Cat No.: **Capitol CL 15554**

Producer: **Beach Boys**

Writers: **Brian Wilson / Mike Love**

Date Reached No.1: **31 August 1968**

Weeks at No.1: **1**

BY 1968 THE BEACH BOYS' POPULARITY in the States had waned. The *Pet Sounds* album was a relative failure, and their approach had changed from the straightforward songs about surfing, hot rod racing and girls. Brian Wilson had instigated the changes and lead vocalist, Mike Love, was unhappy about them. He liked the old songs and wanted to 'do it again'.

Brian began work on the follow-up album *Smile* with the intention of taking the innovation of *Pet Sounds* to the next level. Many of the vocal and instrumental tracks were laid down, but due to family and record company pressures, the project was abandoned. Some of the tracks turned up on bootlegs in the Eighties, and a bootleg version of the album was released in 2001. Three years later, Brian and his musicians recreated the material for live appearances and released the *Smile* album under his own name. The first single from it was 'Wonderful', issued as a limited edition on three different seven-inch coloured vinyl singles. The next album was *Smiley Smile*, a completely different project from *Smile*, although it is rumoured that much of the material would probably have been used on *Smile* anyway. The album, described by Carl Wilson as "A bunt instead of a grand slam", missed the US Top 40 altogether, but was considerably more successful in the UK, where it reached number nine.

Although 'Good Vibrations' had topped both the UK and US charts, it was their last US Top 10 hit for almost ten years. Their American fans presumably preferred the 'surf sound' that was synonymous with The Beach Boys.

In the UK the singles 'Then I Kissed Her' and 'Heroes And Villains' made the Top 10, but 'Wild Honey' and 'Friends' failed to make the Top 20, so, 'Do It Again' was a sign of desperation. After all the clever stuff they wanted to get back to basics, in both the song and the structure of it.

Mike took on lead vocals whilst the trumpet sound during the wordless chorus is Brian using a falsetto voice. The drum intro has a unique sound and was created by adding a long echo delay.

'Do It Again' appeared on the *20/20* album, which was made to fulfil contractual obligations to Capitol Records and featured leftover tracks and singles. It also included the song 'Never Learn Not To Love', written by the notorious serial killer Charles Manson, although later pressings credited to Dennis Wilson.

In 1969 a year after the Russian invasion, The Beach Boys became the first Western group to perform in Czechoslovakia.

257 The Bee Gees
I've Gotta Get A Message To You

Label & Cat No.: **Polydor 56 273**
Producers: **Robert Stigwood / The Bee Gees**
Writers: **Barry Gibb / Robin Gibb / Maurice Gibb**
Date reached No.1: **4 September 1968**
Weeks at No.1: **1**

THE BEE GEES' FIRST FLUSH OF SUCCESS also brought some problems. Neither Colin Petersen nor Vince Melouney had work permits and they had to fight deportation. The fans' pleas on their behalf were successful, but Vince soon left and joined Ashton, Gardner & Dyke, while Colin was fired for losing interest. He was stunned, saying "I can't see how they'll get across to the public on their own."

Since their first number one, 'Massachusetts (The Lights Went Out In)', The Bee Gees had had Top 10 hits with 'World' and 'Words', but did 'Jumbo', which only made number 25, indicate the end? Evidently not as they returned to the top with 'I've Got To Get A Message To You'.

Their first hit single, 'New York Mining Disaster 1941', was a fictitious story about trapped miners facing death and 'I've Gotta Get A Message To You' was about a prisoner in a condemned cell. Possibly prompted by Tom Jones's 'Delilah', he has killed a man who had been having an affair with his wife. He talks to the preacher and wants his wife to know he is sorry. Hard to believe, but the single was controversial at the time.

Although The Bee Gees followed it with another classic, 'First Of May', family frictions were being fuelled by heavy drinking and the rock'n'roll lifestyle. After collapsing with nervous exhaustion, Robin Gibb went solo and had success with 'Saved By The Bell', while The Bee Gees – now reduced to Barry and Maurice – scored with 'Don't Forget To Remember', both records going to number two. In 1971 the three brothers were back with their US number one 'How Can You Mend A Broken Heart?' which they had considered passing to Andy Williams.

258 The Beatles
Hey Jude

Label & Cat No.: **Apple R 5722**
Producer: **George Martin**
Writers: **John Lennon / Paul McCartney**
Date reached No.1: **11 September 1968**
Weeks at No.1: **2**

THE BEATLES WERE AT A LOW POINT. The Maharishi, in their eyes, had betrayed their trust and Brian Epstein had died in mysterious circumstances, but they pulled themselves together with the formation of Apple. The Apple boutique proved another disaster (they ended up giving away the clothes) and their sponsorship of some hangers-on (the inventor Magic Alex) was ill-judged. Still, they weren't businessmen and who could advise them? Allen Klein was the answer, but that catastrophe was a few months away.

The saving grace was their record label, Apple. This was a triumph: they discovered James Taylor, Mary Hopkin, Badfinger and the classical composer, John Taverner, and recorded fine product of their own.

Apple's first single, though still given a Parlophone number because of the leasing arrangement, was 'Hey Jude', though there has been much pointless discussion as to what was Apple 1. 'Hey Jude' seems the obvious choice, especially as there was a promotional pack with 'Hey Jude' and Apple 2, 3, and 4 called *Our First Four.* However, other contenders are a test pressing of 'The Lady Is A Tramp' that Frank Sinatra had recorded for Ringo's wedding and James Taylor's 'Knockin' Around The Zoo'. To put it mildly, The Beatles numbering sequence was eccentric but was later matched by Tony Wilson's Factory Records.

Paul had written 'Hey Jude' after visiting Cynthia Lennon and her son, Julian, shortly after John had teamed up with Yoko Ono. The song is probably not about Julian and, indeed, John took it as a message to himself ('Hey Jude' being 'Hey John') with Paul telling him that he would accept their relationship. Paul wrote in his autobiography, *Many Years From Now*, that it was really about himself, but he didn't expand on this. Maybe it makes sense if Paul had been considering a relationship with John's discarded wife: "Remember to let her into your heart, Then you can start to make it better."

'Hey Jude', at seven minutes and four seconds, became the world's second longest record. They should have kept going for a few seconds longer and beaten Richard Harris' 'MacArthur Park', also from 1968, at seven minutes and 20 seconds.

259 Mary Hopkin
Those Were The Days

Label & Cat No.: **Apple 2**
Producer: **Paul McCartney**
Writers: **Gene Raskin / Alexander Vertinski**
Date reached No.1: **25 September 1968**
Weeks at No.1: **6**

ALTHOUGH MARY HOPKIN HAD already recorded Welsh songs for a specialist label, Cambrian, and had appeared on regional TV, she was allowed to participate in the ITV talent show, *Opportunity Knocks*, and the studio audience put her first. So did the Swinging Sixties model, Twiggy, who phoned Paul McCartney and said she would be ideal for The Beatles' new Apple label.

While Paul McCartney had been on holiday, he had heard a Russian folk song, 'Darogoi Dlimmoyo', first recorded in the Twenties by the cabaret singer, Alexander Vertinski and then by the gypsy singers, Rada & Nikolai Volshaninov. In 1958 Maria Schell sang it on the soundtrack of *The Brothers Karamazov*, which was directed by Richard Brooks.

In 1962 Gene Raskin, a professor of architecture who also sang in a folk duo with his wife as Gene & Francesca, wrote an English lyric. He called it 'Those Were The Days', cleverly capturing

the spirit of its mournful verses and upbeat chorus. It was recorded by the folk-cabaret group, The Limeliters, who also performed Raskin's 'That's Just The Way It Goes'.

When The Beatles were establishing the Apple label, Paul McCartney, quite by chance, heard Gene & Francesca perform 'Those Were The Days' in a London nightclub and thought it suitable for Mary Hopkin. Although the lyric was intended for older singers, 18-year-old Mary Hopkin did it justice, helped by a fine orchestral arrangement. The first Apple single, though not numbered as such, was The Beatles' 'Hey Jude' and it was deposed from number one by Apple 2, 'Those Were The Days'. She recorded the song in Spanish, French, German, Italian and Hebrew, which combined with her Welsh recordings means she has recorded in seven languages. The song has been covered by Engelbert Humperdinck, Roger Whittaker, The Three Tenors and scores of other performers.

Mary Hopkin had further hits with 'Goodbye' (written by McCartney), 'Temma Harbour', 'Knock Knock Who's There' (the UK's Eurovision entry in 1970) and 'Think About Your Children'. Since then Mary Hopkin has been reluctant to tour under her own name but she has worked as part of Oasis (with Peter Skellern and Julian Lloyd Webber) and Sundance (with Mike Hurst from The Springfields).

Mike Hurst recalls, "We toured the UK with Dr. Hook and the band and the road crew were fancying her like mad. It was very hot when we did our soundcheck at Newcastle and Mary fainted. One of the roadies shouted, 'Let me through, I was a medic in 'Nam.' He went up to her, ripped open her blouse and went 'Cor!'"

Mary also added backing vocals to several of Ralph McTell's albums as well as joining Iggy Pop on David Bowie's *Low* (1977), which included the hit single, 'Sound And Vision'. Bowie's album was co-produced by her then-husband, Tony Visconti.

Gene Raskin, who was born in New York in 1909 and died there in 2004, did not write many songs as he pursued his career in architecture. He wrote three books on his specialty and wrote a play about an atomic scientist whose experiments go wrong, *One's A Crowd*.

260 Joe Cocker

With A Little Help From My Friends

Label & Cat No.: **Regal-Zonophone RZ 3013**

Producer: **Denny Cordell**

Writers: **John Lennon / Paul McCartney**

Date Reached No.1: **9 November 1968**

Weeks at No.1: **1**

ALTHOUGH HE HAD BEEN PLAYING IN bands around his native Sheffield since the early Sixties and had released an unsuccessful cover of The Beatles' 'I'll Cry Instead' in 1964, it wasn't until 1969 that Joe finally received Stateside recognition in a New York field in front of half a million people.

Woodstock, the historic four-day extravaganza of peace, love and tie-dye was *the* concert of its time. Headlined by The Who, Jefferson Airplane and Creedence Clearwater Revival, it also featured incredible sets by Jimi Hendrix, Janis Joplin, Joan Baez, John Sebastian and a blistering performance by Joe.

With his unique raspy blues voice and distinctive stage presence, which involved him swinging his arms around like a flailing human windmill and moving his fingers as if playing an invisible guitar, Joe's performance received an enormous response from the crowd. He explained, "Moving my hands around is a subconscious thing with me. A lot of the time, I am more or less conducting the band, just keeping a feel. I don't know why I do it, it's just one of those things."

Of the 25 Lennon / McCartney penned number ones, 'With A Little Help From My Friends' achieved the notable feat three times and not one of them by The Fab Four. The track originally appeared on the Beatles' 1967 album *Sgt Pepper's Lonely Hearts Club Band,* which went on to become Britain's best-selling album. Although no singles were released from it at the time, the title track and 'With A Little Help From My Friends' charted as a medley in 1978.

Joe's inimitable rendering of the single featured session musicians Jimmy Page on guitar and Clem Cattini on drums. The song's writers were thrilled with the new version, and not only sent Joe a telegram, but placed an ad in the music papers praising it.

Joe spent much of the Seventies touring the world, all the while struggling with his escalating drug and alcohol addictions. One of these tours was the infamous *Mad Dogs And Englishmen* where he, and over 20 musicians, played nearly 60 back-to-back concerts. The tour not only spawned a double album, but a film too.

In 1983 Joe was back in the Top 10, duetting with Jennifer Warnes on a Buffy Sainte-Marie song 'Up Where We Belong'. It featured in the film *An Officer and a Gentleman* for which it won an Oscar. Five years later, Joe's version of 'With A Little Help From My Friends' was used for the opening credits in the hit series *Wonder Years*.

The late comic actor John Belushi appeared on the American TV show, *Saturday Night Live*, doing an impersonation of Joe and singing 'Lonely At The Bottom'. Whilst watching it, Joe started laughing hysterically, saying, "How can you not laugh at this? It's funny."

Joe currently lives in Colorado with his wife, Pam, where they spend a lot of their time running the 'Cocker Kids Foundation', helping local children.

261 Hugo Montenegro & His Orchestra & Chorus

The Good, The Bad And The Ugly

Label & Cat No.: **RCA 1727**

Producer: **Hugo Montenegro**

Writer: **Ennio Morricone**

Date reached No.1: **13 November 1968**

Weeks at No.1: **4**

THE ITALIAN FILM DIRECTOR SERGIO Leone loved American westerns and he

Joe Cocker was one of those rare performers who sang a Beatles song better than The Beatles themselves

created the genre of spaghetti westerns in the late Sixties, notably *A Fistful Of Dollars* (1964), *For A Few Dollars More* (1965) and *The Good The Bad And The Ugly* (1966), where the characters were tougher and more ruthless than earlier cowboy bandits. All three films starred Clint Eastwood and had music by Ennio Morricone. The three hour *The Good The Bad And The Ugly* was the most ambitious, although it was truncated for British release, and it starred Clint Eastwood as The Good (just about), Lee Van Cleef as The Bad (definitely) and Eli Wallach as The Ugly (take a look). They play bounty hunters in the American Civil War and the most memorable scene is the shoot-off where Leone concentrates on the eyes of three protagonists.

Ennio Morricone's atmospheric score is justly famous and its stirring theme merges several unexpected sounds – whistling, shrieks, grunts, the ocarina and electric guitars. The New York composer and conductor, Hugo Montenegro, realised the potential of its melody and created a more palatable version with a large string section for radioplay.

Hugo Montenegro had been the arranger and conductor for Harry Belafonte, but around this time he was making his own name as a film composer. He wrote the music for *Hurry Sundown* (with Jane Fonda and Michael Caine, 1967) and this was followed by *The Ambushers* (with Dean Martin, 1968), *Lady In Cement* (with Frank Sinatra, 1968) and *Charro!* (with Elvis Presley, 1969).

A double CD for Virgin Records in 1988 included Ennio Morricone's own selections from over 100 films which he has scored, while in the same year Virgin Venture released a recording of his classical compositions. In recent years, Morricone has been acknowledged as one of the cinema's greatest composers, although he has never won an Oscar. His scores include *The Mission* (1986) and *Cinema Paradiso* (1988) and he has been giving lavish orchestral concert performances of his work, culminating in his 75th birthday concert at the Royal Albert Hall in 2003. He is fully aware of his contribution to the cinema and, if you should meet him, you address him as "Maestro".

262 Scaffold
Lily The Pink

Label & Cat No.: **Parlophone R 5734**

Producer: **Norrie Paramor**

Writers: **John Gorman / Mike McGear / Roger McGough**

Date reached No.1: **11 December 1968**

Weeks at No.1: **4 (two runs)**

SCAFFOLD, WHO TOOK THEIR NAME from a French film, *Lift To Scaffold*, marked the crossover between the Liverpool beat scene and the bohemian Liverpool 8. Their wacky, surrealistic comedy entranced audiences at the local Everyman Theatre and the Edinburgh Festival, but, when they started having hit records, they were wrong for seaside holidaymakers who expected cheerful pop records. They never resolved the dilemma and maybe Mike McGear (Paul McCartney's brother) is right when he says they paved the way for *Monty Python's Flying Circus*.

In 1967 Mike McGear wrote 'Thank U Very Much' after Paul had given him a Nikon camera and, wisely, he never revealed what the 'Aintree Iron' represented. As a result, speculation about his nursery rhyme lyric continues to this day. The most popular is that the 'Aintree Iron' is rhyming slang for Brian, that is, Brian Epstein, the manager of both The Beatles and Scaffold. Ken Dodd, relating it to the then owner of the Aintree racecourse, says the Aintree iron refers to 'Mrs. Topham's knickers'.

The following year Scaffold took a bawdy song performed in changing rooms by rugby teams and wrote new lyrics. The verse about Mr. Frears and his sticky-out ears related to their friend, film director Stephen Frears. Jennifer Eccles and her terrible freckles were added because Graham Nash of The Hollies joined them in the studios at Abbey Road. Jack Bruce played bass and Mike covered Ringo's bass drum with his overcoat and added the thump, thump, thumps.

Roger McGough wrote a book of poems about his time in Scaffold, *gig* (1973): his memories of Birmingham include:

"I remember the days we stayed
At the Albany. Five Ten a night.
I was somebody then (the one on the right
with glasses singing Lily The Pink).
The Dolce Vita."

The zaniest member of the group, John Gorman joined the cast of ITV's children's show *TISWAS* and was part of The Four Bucketeers who had a chart single with 'The Bucket Of Water Song' in 1980.

In 2000 Scaffold reformed for a tribute concert for the Liverpool painter and poet, Adrian Henri, and sang a new verse to 'Lily The Pink' in his honour. Mike and John Gorman still work as a duo, but most of Roger's time is taken up with poetry readings. "No problem," says Roger. "We'll reform at the drop of a cheque."

263 Marmalade
Ob-La-Di, Ob La-Da

Label & Cat No.: **CBS 3892**

Producer: **Mike Smith**

Writers: **John Lennon / Paul McCartney**

Date reached No.1: **1 January 1969**

Weeks at No.1: **3**

DEAN FORD & THE GAYLORDS FORMED in Glasgow in 1961, but, despite being popular, the hit records were not forthcoming. In 1966 their manager, Peter Walsh, thought a change of name was called for and when he was having breakfast, the new name was staring him in the face – Marmalade. They secured a new recording contract with CBS and had a Top 10 single with 'Lovin' Things' in 1968. The follow-up, 'Wait For Me Marianne', only nudged into the Top 30.

Marmalade were an excellent close harmony band featuring Dean, the guitarist Junior Campbell and the bassist Graham Knight, a good example of those harmonies being 'Ob-La-Di,

Ob-La-Da'. Graham recalls, "The Beatles' music publisher, Dick James, played us the acetate of The Beatles' 'Ob-La-Di, Ob-La-Da' and we thought it was great. He said, 'You can have it, I won't give it to anyone else,' but of course he passed it to another 27 acts. We rush-recorded it in the middle of the night during a week of cabaret in the north-east. Our manager, who was in America at the time, kept sending us telegrams telling us not to do it. He didn't think that we should record a Beatles' song. We expected it to do well, but we didn't think it would go to number one. We got no feedback from The Beatles at all. There had been so many covers by that time that I shouldn't think they'd have been very interested." Another version by The Bedrocks also made the Top 20.

The Beatles' own version of 'Ob-La-Di, Ob-La-Da' can be found on *The White Album*. John Lennon said it was Paul's song, "I might have given him a couple of lines, but it's his song, his lyrics." It was, however, John's tempo. The Beatles' original takes were much slower and John, both bored and stoned out of his mind, said, "Come on Paul, this is how to do it" and started playing the piano twice as fast as before. This was the take they used despite the fact that Paul sang by accident "Desmond stays at home and does his pretty face" instead of Molly.

Despite his lack of cooperation, John got half the songwriting royalties, but Paul had taken his title from the reggae group, Jimmy Scott & His Obla Di Obla Da Band. Scott was indignant and wanted a cut and Paul responded, "Come on, Jimmy, it's just an expression. If you'd written the song, you could have had a cut."

'Ob-La-Di, Ob-La-Da' did Marmalade no harm at all as they followed it with further Top 10 hits including 'Baby Make It Soon', 'Reflections Of My Life', 'Rainbow' and 'Cousin Norman'. It looked as though 'Radancer' would be their final hit in 1972 but they bounced back with 'Falling Apart At The Seams' in 1976. Junior Campbell, the guitarist and vocalist, left the band in 1971 and had his own hits with 'Hallelujah Freedom' and 'Sweet Illusion'.

264 Fleetwood Mac
Albatross

Label & Cat No.: **Blue Horizon 57-3145**

Producer: **Mike Vernon**

Writer: **Peter Green**

Date Reached No.1: **1 February 1969**

Weeks at No.1: **1**

DJ TONY BLACKBURN ONCE SAID Peter Green's haunting 'Albatross' was "The most crushingly boring tune in the world. It just drones on. It starts, then it continues and then doesn't go anywhere." Peter once admitted later that 'Albatross' may have been drug influenced, he said, "I took two big LSD trips that went on forever and ever and ever."

In the late Sixties and early Seventies, Peter Green was ranked as one of the great guitar heroes alongside Eric Clapton, Jeff Beck, Jimmy Page and Jimi Hendrix. B.B. King once admitted that Green was "the only guitarist in the world who could make me sweat." The first time George Harrison heard 'Albatross' he said "it knocked me sideways".

"I heard John Mayall's Bluesbreakers' cover of Jimmy Rogers' 'The Last Meal' – that's the blues singer not the country and western one. I thought I would take it and develop it," explained Peter. "I called it that because of that reference to the 'back of a giant albatross' on the Traffic record 'Hole In My Shoe'."

'Albatross' bears more than a passing resemblance to Chuck Berry's 1957 instrumental 'Deep Feeling'. However, Chuck made no attempts to sue for plagiarism as 'Deep Feeling' was, in turn, based on the 1939 country-tinged, 'Floyd's Guitar Blues' by Andy Kirk & his 12 Clouds Of Joy.

Fleetwood Mac were formed in 1967 and comprised Peter Green, Mick Fleetwood, John McVie and Jeremy Spencer. In August 1968 another lead guitarist, Danny Kirwin, was drafted in to give the group a jazzier feel. Although not evident on 'Albatross' he is prominently featured on the B-side 'Jigsaw Puzzle Blues'.

By 1970 Peter Green's health was failing following his involvement with LSD and both he and Spencer quit. With various personnel changes including the subsequent recruitment of Stevie Nicks, Christine Perfect (later McVie) and Lindsey Buckingham, the group were elevated to supergroup status during the Seventies and Eighties.

In an interview in 2003, Peter Green said of 'Albatross', "I'd like to do that again on Hawaiian guitars with Eric Clapton. I always liked Eric's playing: he was much better than Hendrix, although I thought Jimi was a great person."

In 1989 Mick Fleetwood, along with former Page Three model Samantha Fox, was asked to present the British Rock and Pop Awards (Brits). The show went out live and the consequences were disastrous. Both Mick and Samantha kept announcing the same thing at different times and interrupting each other. They introduced acts that were not ready to perform and Samantha, unable to read the autocue fluently, kept tripping over her words. It was the deciding factor for the show's producers to never to broadcast the show live again.

265 The Move
Blackberry Way

Label & Cat No.: **Regal Zonophone RZ 3015**

Producer: **Jimmy Miller**

Writer: **Roy Wood**

Date reached No.1: **5 February 1969**

Weeks at No.1: **1**

THE BIRMINGHAM BAND, THE MOVE, comprised Carl Wayne (lead vocals), Roy Wood (vocals, lead guitar), Trevor Burton (rhythm guitar) Ace Kefford (bass) and Bev Bevan (drums). They were signed by the London manager, Tony Secunda, who dreamed up outrageous, and wholly unnecessary, stunts to secure publicity. "We were a pretty wild band," admits Carl Wayne, later the lead singer of The Hollies and who died in 2004. "We smashed up TVs and we had a bogus H-bomb in Manchester, but it worked against us. If we had had the guts to carry on with the infamy like the Stones, it might have worked but the Stones didn't give a damn and we were frightened young boys from Birmingham. The Move was a very very good pop band, but we had to live up this myth that we were aggressive louts."

"This worked against us," agrees Roy Wood. "We'd smash up TVs on stage and then the promoters would ring up the agent and say that we had smashed up the dressing room so they didn't have to pay us."

The Move had their first hits with 'Night Of Fear' and 'I Can Hear The Grass Grow' and then, quite by chance, their 'Flowers In The Rain' was the first record to be played on Radio 1. However, they were sued by the Prime Minister, Harold Wilson, for a publicity cartoon which showed him in a compromising position with his secretary. Wilson won the case and to this day all royalties from 'Flowers In The Rain' are sent to the charity of Wilson's choice. 'Fire Brigade' was their fourth hit, but they thought of disbanding when 'Wild Tiger Woman' failed to connect.

Then came The Move's only number one, 'Blackberry Way', which was written by Roy Wood and resembles a Birmingham version of 'Penny Lane' with a little of 'Strawberry Fields Forever' thrown in: "I suppose it could have been," says Roy now. "We were all very influenced by what The Beatles were doing because they were the best songwriters around." Richard Tandy, a future member of ELO, played an electronic harpsichord on the song and musicologists have praised the E minor augmented ascent, which is the first sound we hear.

Ace Kefford left the band as he couldn't stand the publicity and Carl Wayne moved out after a disagreement over bookings into cabaret clubs. Jeff Lynne came in, and then Roy, Jeff and Bev formed The Electric Light Orchestra. Wood soon moved on and led another hitmaking band, Wizzard. "I wish that Jeff and Roy had done more together," says Carl Wayne, "I think that the best Move records were after I left when they did 'Chinatown' and 'Tonight'. Lennon and McCartney were double genius, God's talent, but Jeff and Roy together could have come close."

The publicity for 'Blackberry Way' was more restrained than usual as the press were sent blackberry pies with champagne. And was there a Blackberry Way? "Well, I've never spotted one," says Roy Wood. "It would be nice to find one."

266 Amen Corner (If Paradise Is) Half As Nice

Label & Cat No.: **Immediate IM 073**

Producer: **Shel Talmy**

Writers: **Lucio Battisti / Jack Fishman**

Date reached No.1: **12 February 1969**

Weeks at No.1: **2**

Having seen John Mayall's Bluesbreakers with Eric Clapton, Andy Fairweather-Low wanted to be in a band that played both blues and beat music. The line-up eventually became the seven-piece Amen Corner, the Cardiff group taking the name from a play by the civil rights author, James Baldwin. They were signed to Decca's hip subsidiary, Deram, and had their first hit with 'Gin House Blues' in 1967. They had further hits with 'The World Of Broken Hearts', 'Bend Me, Shape Me' and 'High In The Sky'. The public was mesmerised by the strangulated, soulful vocals of Andy Fairweather-Low, who hardly opened his mouth when he sang.

Amen Corner returned from a tour with the Jimi Hendrix Experience to find that their new manager was Don Arden, their new record label, Immediate, and their new record producer, Shel Talmy. '(If Paradise Is) Half As Nice' was an Italian song with an English lyric that had been turned down by The Tremeloes. They worked out an arrangement and recorded the song within two hours. Andy's friend, Roy Wood, sent them a new song, 'Hello Susie', and that was the follow-up, going to number four.

Their 1969 live album, awkwardly titled *The National Welsh Coast Live Explosion Company*, was a hit album and shows how much the band loved soul music – they can be seen as the Welsh Commitments. With Immediate in financial difficulties, Amen Corner split up, recording 'Farewell To The Real Magnificent Seven' for their final single, which was also Immediate's final release. Some of the band emerged in Fairweather, who had a Top 10 in 1970 with 'Natural Sinner'.

Andy Fairweather-Low had solo hits with 'Reggae Tune' (1974) and 'Wide-Eyed And Legless' (1975). He is now a journeyman musician, having worked and toured with Van Morrison, Eric Clapton, George Harrison and Bill Wyman's Rhythm Kings.

267 Peter Sarstedt Where Do You Go To (My Lovely)

Label & Cat No.: **United Artists UP 2262**

Producer: **Ray Singer**

Writer: **Peter Sarstedt**

Date reached No.1: **26 February 1969**

Weeks at No.1: **4**

Peter Sarstedt played bass for his brother, Eden Kane, but when Eden emigrated to Australia in 1965, he was without a job. He went to Copenhagen and started writing songs. He says, "The message I got from Bob Dylan was to be as unlike him as possible. A Dylan imitator is nothing like Bob Dylan because he would never imitate." In so doing, Sarstedt came up with a highly original debut single, 'I Am A Cathedral'. This cryptic song was arranged by Ian Green and produced by Ray Singer, who worked on his two 1969 albums, *Peter Sarstedt* and *As Though It Were A Movie*.

The talents of Sarstedt, Green and Singer were best heard on the atmospheric, accordion-based 'Where Do You Go To (My Lovely), a five minute track on the first album which was not intended as a single. Peter comments, "I wanted to write a long, extended piece because I was working in folk clubs and universities, and Al Stewart had something that was half an hour long and Bob Dylan's 'Sad Eyed Lady Of The Lowlands' took a whole side of an album. 'Where Do You Go To (My Lovely)?' was my first attempt at writing something longer than my normal three minutes. It was amazingly easy to write, but I knew what I wanted to say. I wanted to say something about this particular person, although it wasn't about anyone specific."

The song is about a boy and girl who grew up in the back streets of Naples: now grown up, she wants to forget her past: "He knows her, he's the voyeur. He knows she goes back to her roots when she is alone." The song is full of colourful references: "Zizi Jean Maire was a cabaret star in France and the best dancer of her generation and so when I say, 'You dance like Zizi Jean Maire', I mean you can really dance."

At first, United Artists did not think it was a single: "They said it has no drums, it is too long and there are only three instruments." The label relented and the song has become a standard, being parodied on different occasions by Roger McGough, John Otway and Craig Ferguson. Peter often performs on oldies tours and he still performs on his own or with his brother, Clive, around Europe. "I reckon that I can pull in 250 people wherever I'm booked," he says, "and that isn't bad." Evidently, Peter Sarstedt has the last ha-ha-ha!

268 Marvin Gaye
I Heard It Through The Grapevine

Label & Cat No.: **Tamla Motown TMG 686**
Producer: **Norman Whitfield**
Writers: **Norman Whitfield / Barrett Strong**
Date reached No.1: **26 March 1969**
Weeks at No.1: **3**

BARRETT STRONG RECORDED THE original version of Berry Gordy's 'Money (That's What I Want)' in 1959. He maintained his friendship with Gordy and preferred to have a backroom role, writing and producing at Tamla-Motown. He heard the phrase, "I heard it through the grapevine", and he was surprised no one had used it in a song. He developed the riff and took it to his songwriting partner, Norman Whitfield, and they completed it.

In 1967 the song was first recorded for an album, *Special Occasion,* by Smokey Robinson & The Miracles and then it was cut by The Isley Brothers, whose version was not released. It became a single for Gladys Knight & The Pips. They gave it a gospel arrangement and the record went to number two in America , but it was only in the UK Top 50 for one week.

Tamla Motown was very productive – they had a lot of acts and as the top ones all had regular releases, it meant that songs would be recorded and re-recorded. Marvin Gaye was asked to record 'I Heard It Through The Grapevine' for his album, *In The Groove*, and Whitfield decided on a sinuous arrangement that would allow Marvin to stretch his vocal muscles. His performance is extraordinary – pleading, hollering, cajoling, screaming – and despite being smooth one second and hoarse the next, he has perfect vocal control.

Even though the song had been a hit a year earlier, Marvin's version was released as a single and it topped the US charts and then did the same in the UK. Despite Marvin Gaye's ability to take instructions on 'I Heard It Through The Grapevine', he wanted to produce himself and he took both his vocals and his songwriting to new levels on the albums, *What's Going On* (1971) and *Let's Get It On* (1973). In 1986 following its appearance in a Levi's commercial, 'I Heard It Through The Grapevine' was again a hit.

To many people, Marvin Gaye's 'I Heard It Through The Grapevine' is the greatest record ever made. "'I Heard It Through The Grapevine' isn't a plea to save a love affair; it's Marvin Gaye's essay on salvaging the human spirit," writes the rock critic, Dave Marsh in his book, *The Heart Of Rock And Soul.* "The record distils 400 years of paranoia and talking drum gossip into three minutes and 15 seconds of anguished soul-searching." Maybe – Marvin Gaye was certainly paranoid, and that was a contributory factor in his death, shot by his father in 1984 with a gun Marvin had given him.

269 Desmond Dekker & The Aces The Israelites

Label & Cat No.: **Pyramid PYR 6058**

Producer: **Leslie Kong**

Writers: **Desmond Dekker / Leslie Kong**

Date reached No.1: **16 April 1969**

Weeks at No.1: **1**

IRONICALLY, THE COD REGGAE OF 'OB-La-Di, Ob-La-Da' made the top before the real thing – Desmond Dekker & The Aces' 'The Israelites'. Desmond Dekker, who was born Desmond Dacris in 1942 in Kingston, Jamaica, was known as the King of Blue Beat in Jamaica and he and his group, The Aces, made many successful singles for the noted producer, Leslie Kong.

They broke through in the UK with '007 (Shanty Town)' in 1967. The following year 'The Israelites' was a hit in London clubs, and who can forget its opening line, "Get up in the morning, slaving for bread, sir"? Rastafarians believe that they are the lost tribe of Israel, being sold into slavery in the Caribbean. Desmond Dekker's lyric suggests that little has changed. 'The Israelites' became a national hit in 1969.

Although the lyric of 'The Israelites' was inspired by *Exodus*, there was much debate as to whether Desmond was actually singing, "My wife and my children, they fuck off and leave me", which certainly would have been a first for a hit record. Also in 1969, Max Romeo was in the Top 10 with another reggae song, 'Wet Dream', which was so controversial that Radio1 DJ's were not even allowed to say its title.

Desmond almost made it a double-Dekker when the follow-up, 'It Miek', went into the Top 10. 'It Miek' was also controversial as it was said to be rude Jamaican patois, but it was simply a reference to fate. In 1970 he went to number two with 'You Can Get It If You Really Want', which was written by Jimmy Cliff, and then a reissue of 'The Israelites' made number 10 in 1975. Enjoying the puns on his name, he released an album, *Black And Dekker,* in 1980.

Despite his success, Desmond Dekker has been underrated, largely because he was eclipsed by two giants, Jimmy Cliff and Bob Marley. Neither of them, however, has had a number one.

270 The Beatles with Billy Preston Get Back

Label & Cat No.: **Apple R 5777**

Producer: **George Martin**

Writers: **John Lennon / Paul McCartney**

Date reached No.1: **23 April 1969**

Weeks at No.1: **6**

THE FILM OF *MAGICAL MYSTERY TOUR* had been panned (albeit unfairly), Apple was a national joke and The Beatles were falling apart. So what do they do? They turn away from psychedelia and get back to Chuck Berry riffs for some barnstorming rock'n'roll with Billy Preston on keyboards,'

In order to fulfil a movie commitment, The Beatles agreed to be filmed writing and recording an album. Rather like a prototype for *Big Brother*, they spent much of January 1969 on a soundstage at Twickenham Film Studios, outside of London. They often resented each other's company and there were few days when all four musicians worked happily together.

George Harrison hated the atmosphere and thought that if he brought in an outsider whom they all respected, something good might happen. He asked the organist Billy Preston to join them which resulted in Preston becoming the only musician ever to credited alongside The Beatles on one of their records. They had first met Billy when he was backing Little Richard at the Star-Club in Hamburg in 1962 and then later when he was with Ray Charles. He made a number of solo albums in the Sixties and one of them was called *The Wildest Organ In Town!*

Evidently, Paul McCartney intended "Get back to where you once belonged" as a message to himself and the other Beatles, and John, always paranoid, thought that the phrase was directed at Yoko Ono. The song was tried in several forms and Paul wrote several satirical verses, one of which started "Don't dig no Pakistanis taking other people's jobs." This has been cited as racism but heard in context, Paul is criticising the right wing opinions of the MP Enoch Powell.

The Jo Jo of the song was no one in particular. Paul said, "Jo Jo was a fictional character, half man, half woman, all very ambiguous." It is not a reference to Denny Laine's wife, Jo Jo, whom Denny hadn't even met at the time. The reference to Tucson, Arizona is a nod to Linda McCartney who lived there from 1962 to 1965 with her first husband: their daughter, Heather, was born there.

The B-side, which picked up sales in its own right, was an intense R&B ballad written by John Lennon and dedicated to Yoko, 'Don't Let Me Down'. The sessions ended with The Beatles and Billy Preston performing a set of new songs including these two on the roof of their Apple headquarters.

In April 1969 Billy Preston had a hit on Apple with the gospel-styled 'That's The Way God Planned It' and George Harrison produced his two Apple albums, *That's The Way God Planned It* and *Encouraging Words*. Joining Herb Alpert's A&M label, he had US number ones with 'Will It Go Round In Circles?' (1973) and 'Nothing From Nothing' (1974). In 1980 he and Stevie Wonder's former wife, Syreeta, had international success with the ballad, 'With You I'm Born Again', from the film *Fast Break*.

The single version of 'Get Back', which was produced by George Martin, differs from the LP version, which was remixed from the session tapes by Phil Spector. In 2003 a remixed, deSpectorised CD, *Let It Be...Naked*, was released. The single, 'Let It Be', does not appear in this book because it only reached number two in 1970.

The song was played live by The Beatles during the Apple 'rooftop' concert on January 30, 1969, when John famously ended the set, and The Beatles' live career, with the words: "I'd like to say thank you on behalf of the group and ourselves and I hope we passed the audition."

Passing the audition: the final Beatles concert, on the roof of the Apple HQ in London's Savile Row, January 30, 1969

271 Tommy Roe
Dizzy

Label & Cat No.: **Stateside SS 2143**

Producers: **Steve Barri**

Writers: **Tommy Roe / Freddy Weller**

Date reached No.1: **4 June 1969**

Weeks at No.1: **1**

ATLANTA-BORN TOMMY ROE HAD AN international hit in 1961 with 'Sheila', very much a cousin of Buddy Holly's 'Peggy Sue', and he also scored with the poignant saga of 'The Folk Singer'. In 1963 he toured the UK with Chris Montez and The Beatles, who were enjoying their first successes and on his return home, he wrote 'Everybody', one of the few hit records to be written in blank verse. The most famous song to be written without rhyming is the standard, 'Moonlight In Vermont'. Tommy had further US hits with 'Sweet Pea' and 'Hooray For Hazel', but by 1969, the hits had dried up – or so everybody thought.

Tommy Roe recalls, "Freddy Weller and I had known each other in Atlanta. I was on a TV show with Paul Revere & The Raiders. They had lost their guitarist and I suggested Freddy as a replacement. He moved to California to be with them, and we started writing together. I showed him 'Dizzy'. I had written the chorus but I couldn't complete it. Freddy loved it and said, 'Let's finish it', and we did that on a tour bus late at night. Jimmie Haskell wrote the string arrangement and we had Hal Blaine on drums, Joe Osborne on bass, Ben Benay on guitar and Larry Knechtel on keyboards. You can't get better than that. It sold six millions copies, four million of them in the States, and it was my biggest hit of all."

'Dizzy' is the ultimate bubblegum record. Tommy followed it with 'Heather Honey' and since then, he has been performing his hits quite contentedly on the oldies circuit, touring the UK with Duane Eddy and The Crickets. Starting in 1969, Freddy Weller found a way of recording country versions of Joe South and Chuck Berry songs and had several US country hits.

272 The Beatles
The Ballad Of John And Yoko

Label & Cat No.: **Apple R 5786**

Producer: **George Martin**

Writers: **John Lennon / Paul McCartney**

Date reached No.1: **11 June 1969**

Weeks at No.1: **3**

JOHN LENNON LIKED INSTANT SONGwriting – writing a song one day, recording it the next and releasing it as soon as possible. By 1969, he and Yoko were self-absorbed and he wrote about their life in 'The Ballad Of John And Yoko', wittily calling themselves "two gurus in drag" and once again leaning heavily on Chuck Berry's style.

As George Harrison was on holiday and Ringo Starr was filming *The Magic Christian*, John asked Paul McCartney to record it with him. Although Paul had his differences with John at this time, he was a working musician and readily agreed. They enjoyed recording the song with John urging the drumming Paul to "Go a bit faster, Ringo" and Paul responding to John playing lead guitar, "OK, George." Paul also plays bass, piano and maracas on the track.

The single was released on top of 'Get Back' and both songs were in the Top five together. The song was controversial as it used "Christ!" as invective and, almost certainly, the record would have been banned if he had come from a lesser act than The Beatles. Instead, the *Top Of The Pops* film, which used news footage of John and Yoko, made great play of the word "Christ!" by flashing it on the screen each time that Lennon sang it.

'The Ballad Of John And Yoko' was The Beatles' 17th and final number one as 'Something' and 'Let It Be' and, for that matter, 'Free As A Bird', didn't make it. A few weeks after 'The Ballad Of John And Yoko', John had the idea for 'Give Peace A Chance', but this time he used the pseudonym, The Plastic Ono Band. In 1971 John's 'Instant Karma' was written, recorded and released within a week.

We know now that John Lennon had something of a Messianic complex. Only a few weeks after making this single, he called his associates into the board room at Apple and told them that he was Christ reincarnated and was going to announce it on the evening news. They agreed to have a drink first and by night-time, John's claim had been forgotten. Pity really – it would have made great TV, followed, one suspects, by John's arrest for taking mind-bending drugs.

273 Thunderclap Newman
Something In The Air

Label & Cat No.: **Track 604 031**

Producer: **Pete Townshend**

Writer: **Speedy Keen**

Date Reached No.1: **5 July 1969**

Weeks at No.1: **3**

"I WOULD LIKEN HAVING A NUMBER ONE hit the way we did, rather like Haley's Comet," said Andy Newman. "It's rather like walking down the street and having your attention distracted and suddenly finding you've fallen down an open, unprotected man-hole."

A former post office engineer, Andy Newman was short and dumpy with thinning greased-back hair and a full beard. The unlikely looking pop star said of his brief chart success, "I suppose it had its beautiful side and it had its absurd side. A door would open and we'd walk out on to the stage and be surrounded by all these lovely women. Unfortunately I never had any sex appeal. They used to call me Thunderclap because of my heavy-handed style of playing. Basically I didn't know how to play the piano."

Who guitarist Pete Townshend knew Andy from art school, assembled the group as a side project and played bass on 'Something In The Air', using the pseudonym Bijou Drains. It is the only time an original member of The Who was involved in a number one hit.

Singer and drummer Speedy Keen worked as Townshend's chauffer and he gave Pete a tape of a song he'd written called 'Armenia City In The Sky'. Pete was impressed and it appeared on the 1967 album *The Who Sell-Out*. Although The Who recorded a few cover versions (notably 'Summertime Blues' and 'Shakin' All Over'), this song is the only instance of their recording an original song by someone outside the group. Pete Townshend said of his former chauffeur, Speedy Keen, "He was a talented drummer and has emerged as a great songwriter."

"The release coincided with the 1969 moon landing so everyone just went for it," explained Andy. "The original title was called 'Revolution' but The Beatles had not long done a song with that title, so we changed it to 'Something In The Air'."

'Something In The Air' was featured in the 1970 film *The Magic Christian*, based on a novel by Terry Southern, which starred Peter Sellers, Ringo Starr, Raquel Welch, Richard Attenborough and Spike Milligan.

After the group disbanded in 1970, guitarist Jimmy McCulloch joined Wings and Speedy recorded two solo albums, as well as producing albums for Motorhead and The Heartbreaker, Johnny Thunders' post New York Dolls band.

In March 2002 'Something In The Air' was used to launch a television advertising campaign for British Airways. In the same month, Speedy Keen died of heart failure. McCulloch died from a drug overdose in 1979.

274 The Rolling Stones
Honky Tonk Women

Label & Cat No.: **Decca F 12952**

Producer: **Jimmy Miller**

Writers: **Mick Jagger / Keith Richards**

Date reached No.1: **23 July 1969**

Weeks at No.1: **5**

THE ROLLING STONES' PROBLEMS weren't over when Mick and Keith were released from prison. Brian Jones was arrested for possession and was treated in hospital for both mental and physical exhaustion. Then Keith fell out with Mick when his love scenes with Keith's girlfriend, Anita Pallenberg, in the film *Performance* seemed rather too real. The Rolling Stones' TV special, *Rock And Roll Circus*, directed by Michael Lindsay-Hogg was made but not shown: it was considered sub-standard and a recent TV showing confirms it to be self-indulgent but with some good performances by other acts on the bill, notably The Who.

Brian Jones, in total disarray, left in June 1969 and his replacement was Mick Taylor, a fine guitarist from John Mayall's Bluesbreakers. Both he and Keith played guitar, which gave the Stones a very forceful sound. "We never thought of ourselves as lead guitarists, we thought of ourselves as guitar-players who played together," says Mick now. "Our styles were very different – Keith was influenced by Chuck Berry and me by B. B. King – and it worked really well. During a song we would switch back and forth between rhythm and lead and we were very supportive of each other."

Mick and Keith had written 'Honky Tonk Women' while they were in South America. They had befriended the country musician, Gram Parsons, and the song had been written as a tribute to old-time country songs, but with lyrics that could never be sung at the Opry – "She blew my nose and then she blew my mind". They changed their minds when Mick Taylor showed how their riff could be played explosively on guitar and they had a winning single. To make the sound more powerful, Jimmy Miller had found a new way to mike up Charlie's drums. They also recorded a country version of 'Honky Tonk Women' with Byron Berline on fiddle: this was included on their 1969 album, *Let It Bleed*.

The Stones were to star in a free concert in Hyde Park on July 5, 1969 with the single following a few days later. Brian Jones died in his swimming-pool on July 3 and even now, no one knows for certain what happened. The concert, now dedicated to Brian Jones, may be seen as the Stones' finest hour. Altamont, with the violent death of a young spectator by security guards, was just a few months away.

Oddly, the Stones never repeated their success in the singles chart. Only 'Brown Sugar' (1971) and 'Miss You' (1978) made the Top three, and at the time of writing, they haven't had a Top 10 single for over twenty years. Perhaps the B-side of 'Honky Tonk Women', 'You Can't Always Get What You Want', should have been reissued as a single following its use in a very popular campaign for Allied Dunbar insurance.

275 Zager & Evans
In The Year 2525 (Exordium And Terminus)

Label & Cat No.: **RCA 1860**

Producers: **Denny Zager / Rick Evans**

Writer: **Rick Evans**

Date Reached No.1: **30 August 1969**

Weeks at No.1: **3**

IN THE YEAR 1964 RICK EVANS WROTE 'In The Year 2525', a prophetic tale, highlighting a future of doom and gloom. The Transatlantic one-hit wonder was written in 30 minutes and promptly put in the bottom drawer. He was then a guitarist in a local band, The Eccentrics, formed by fellow Nebraskan, Denny Zager.

Shortly after writing the future and futuristic classic, Evans left The Eccentrics to start his own band, The DeVilles. By 1968 Zager had broken up his group, so they joined forces as Zager & Evans.

Rick Evans re-wrote the arrangement for 'In The Year 2525' for a duo and were soon including it in their live shows. Denny said, "We had so many requests for the song that we decided to record it." They invested $500 and, after recording it at ex-Cricket Tommy Allsup's studio, pressed 1,000 copies for their own Truth record label.

A radio station in Texas began playing the song, which came to the attention of promoter and producer, Jerry Weintraub. Jerry flew to Nebraska to meet both Zager and Evans and negotiated a recording contract with RCA Records.

The song topped the American chart for six weeks in the summer of 1969, eventually selling more than five million copies. Whilst it was still on the chart, Evans decided that he didn't want to be remembered for that type of song, so a follow-up, 'Mr Turnkey' a tune about a man sent to prison for his 'crimes against women', was hastily recorded. When that failed to make any impact, Zager broke up the duo.

Few artists have attempted a cover of 'In The Year 2525', but a new romantic version was recorded by Visage's Steve Strange, and R.E.M. have included it in their stage show.

Denny still lives in Lincoln, Nebraska where he teaches music and makes string instruments. Rick lives in Arizona and is now an estate agent.

276 Creedence Clearwater Revival
Bad Moon Rising

Label & Cat No.: **Liberty LBF 15230**
Producer: **John Fogerty**
Writer: **John Fogerty**
Date Reached No.1: **20 September 1969**
Weeks at No.1: **3**

ALTHOUGH THEIR BLEND OF ROCKA-billy, R&B and country music conjured up a sound more suited to the Southern States, brothers Tom and John Fogerty were raised in the San Francisco Bay area.

In 1959, along with bass player Stu Cook and drummer Doug Clifford, they formed a group called The Blue Velvets. During the British invasion, an executive at the label they were signed to, Fantasy Records, changed their name to The Golliwogs.

In 1968 they changed their name again, to Creedence Clearwater Revival. The first part after a friend of a friend of Tom's, Credence Nuball, as Tom thought it invoked feelings of integrity. Clearwater originally came from a beer commercial, but it also mirrored the surging environmental development of the time. Revival was chosen for their goals and aspirations, that, after a decade of playing together, they could take themselves to new and greater musical heights.

'Bad Moon Rising' is a homage to the echo-drenched sound created by Sam Phillips at Sun Records in the Fifties. Although, John Fogerty admitted later, "I really couldn't do it like Scotty Moore did it."

Whilst at college, Doug showed an interest in nature and ecology and was nicknamed Cosmo. At his home in California he had a back yard where the band used to rehearse. The area, which was cramped as well as smoky, was known as the factory because Doug once complained that, although it was smoky and cramped, it was better than working in a factory. Doug's nickname and the rehearsal area gave their biggest selling album, *Cosmo's Factory*, its name.

The inspiration for the song came from the 1941 film, *The Devil And Mrs Webster*, the story of a struggling farmer who makes a deal with the devil, Mr Scratch, to sell his soul in exchange for fame and prosperity. John Fogerty, who wrote the song the day Richard Nixon was elected, said in an interview with *Rolling Stone*, "'Bad Moon Rising' wasn't written about the devil or the deal itself, but about the apocalypse that was going to be visited upon us."

Film director John Landis felt the connotations of the song were perfect for some of the scenes in his 1981 comedy/horror movie *An American Werewolf In London*.

Tom Fogerty left the band in 1971 and the group disbanded 18 months later. Much to John Fogerty's annoyance, Fantasy Records continued to release old tracks, so in order to prevent this, and to be released from their contract with the label, John was forced to sign away royalties from their catalogue to label boss Saul Zaentz. In 1985 John released a solo album called *Centrefield* in which he vented his anger towards Zaentz on a track called 'Zanz Kan't Danz'. The title was later amended to 'Vanz Kan't Danz' when Zaentz threatened to sue for defamation. Zaentz filed another lawsuit claiming that the lead track on the album, 'The Man Down The Road', was a rip-off of a Creedence album track 'Run Through The Jungle'. Effectively, John was accused of plagiarising himself. John was angry and in turn, he sued Fantasy Records to re-claim his legal costs and to prove that you cannot plagiarise yourself. John appeared in court with a guitar, he played both songs and the jury agreed that 'The Old Man Down The Road' sounded nothing like 'Run Through The Jungle'. 'Mr Greed', another track on the album, was also directed at Zaentz.

Tom died of respiratory failure in 1990. John continued with a solo career and continues to perform his own songs on tour. In 1975 he wrote and recorded the original versions of 'Rocking All Over The World' and 'Almost Saturday Night', which were hits for Status Quo and Dave Edmunds respectively.

Zaentz has also made a name for himself as a film producer. His credits include *One Flew Over The Cuckoos Nest*, *Amadeus* and, in 1997, *The English Patient*, which received nine Academy Awards. He also received the Irving Thalberg Award for lifetime achievement.

277 Jane Birkin & Serge Gainsbourg
Je T'Aime...Moi Non Plus

Label & Cat No.: **Major Minor MM 645**
Producer: **Serge Gainsbourg**
Writer: **Serge Gainsbourg**
Date reached No.1: **11 October 1969**
Weeks at No.1: **1**

SERGE GAINSBOURG WAS BORN IN THE red light district of Paris in 1928 and much of his work (and life!) revealed his fascination with the area. He began performing in 1958 and acquired a cult following in France with his quirky songs about ticket collectors and cabbages. In 1965 he wrote the Eurovision winner, 'Poupée De Cire, Poupée De Son', but its singer, 16-year-old France Gall, fell out with Gainsbourg when she discovered that her follow-up, 'Les Sucettes', was really about fellatio.

In 1967 Serge persuaded Brigitte Bardot to

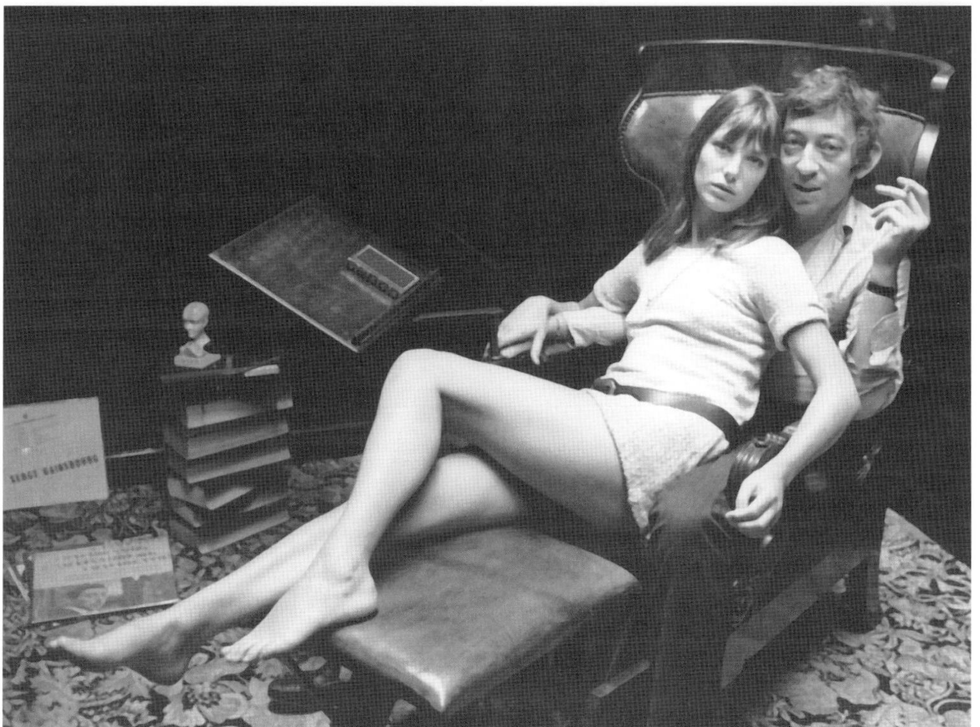

record 'Je T'Aime..Moi Non Plus', a sex-drenched duet inspired by 'A Whiter Shade Of Pale'. Bardot, although famed for taking her kit off, decided that it would destroy her relationship with the industrialist, Gunther Sachs. Being a gentleman, Serge withdrew the song but, not being a fool, he looked for a new partner. He came upon Jane Birkin, the former wife of film composer John Barry and noted for getting her kit off in the Antonioni film, *Blow-Up*.

Jane Birkin recalls, "Bardot had said to Serge, 'Will you write me the most beautiful love song that you can think of?', and he made up this love song which means 'I love you, nor do I'. The 'nor do I' refers to a conversation with Salvador Dali. Dali said, 'Picasso is a genius, so am I. Picasso is Spanish, so am I. Picasso is a Communist, nor am I.' Serge asked me to sing 'Je T'Aime, Moi Non Plus' an octave higher than Bardot so I would sound like a choirboy and I said, 'Yes' because I was far too affeard that some other beautiful girl would be singing it in my place."

'Je T'Aime…Moi Non Plus' was not among Gainsbourg's best songs, but then the record was really an event – were this couple having it off on the studio floor? (Sadly, no.) The Vatican denounced the record and although banned by the BBC, they played an instrumental cover by Sounds Nice, retitled 'Love At First Sight' and featuring Tim Mycroft's organ. The general public, however, preferred Serge Gainsbourg's organ but Fontana Records was forced to withdraw the single. Fontana was a subsidiary of Philips Records: Queen Juliana of the Netherlands was a substantial shareholder and she demanded that it be withdrawn. None of the major labels wanted to release such a controversial record, but Major Minor, an independent label (and an Irish one to boot!) agreed and soon had a number one record.

The British took the record as good fun and a *Carry On*-styled parody by Frankie Howerd and June Whitfield, 'Up Je T'Aime', was a typical response. Serge Gainsbourg, however, was genuinely debauched, falling into the Lord Byron category. Next up came *Histoire De Melody Nelson*, a concept album about a middle-aged Frenchman's passion for an underage English girl. In 1975 he wrote and directed the film, *Je T'Aime, Moi Non Plus* in which Jane played a boy who became the love interest of a homosexual trucker. Said Jane, "No one but Serge could have written this film."

In 1979 Serge gave the French national anthem a reggae treatment, 'Aux Armes Et Caetera', and in 1984 he stunned France with 'Lemon Incest', a duet with his daughter, Charlotte. In the same year he told Whitney Houston on a live TV show that he would "like to fuck her". Serge Gainsbourg died in Paris in 1991 and fans still leave mementos of cabbages and train tickets at his graveside. Jane Birkin presents his songs in concerts, but has never performed 'Je T'Aime…Moi Non Plus' live.

278 Bobbie Gentry
I'll Never Fall In Love Again

Label & Cat No.: **Capitol CL 15606**

Producer: **Kelso Hurston**

Writers: **Burt Bacharach / Hal David**

Date reached No.1: **18 October 1969**

Weeks at No.1: **1**

NOWADAYS FAMOUS FILMS ARE OFTEN transformed into stage musicals, but the announcement that the 1960 Oscar-winning Jack Lemmon and Shirley MacLaine comedy, *The Apartment*, was going to be on stage with a script from Neil Simon and songs by Burt Bacharach & Hal David was greeted with surprise. The musical, renamed *Promises, Promises*, was very successful on both Broadway and in the West End.

The score of *Promises, Promises* is not vintage Bacharach & David, though it does contain the plaintive ballad 'Wanting Things' and the punchy title song. The key song is 'I'll Never Fall In Love Again'. This song had been added at the last minute in Boston and at a time when Burt had flu: hence, Hal David's little joke of rhyming 'pneumonia' with 'phone ya'. Because there was no time to work up a full arrangement, the song, very unusually for Burt, was performed to a solitary guitar accompaniment. The US hit record was by Dionne Warwick, but in the UK it was Bobbie Gentry's version which took off. Like many Burt Bacharach songs, the melody shows his love for Latin rhythms, particularly the bossa nova.

The raven-haired beauty, Bobbie Gentry, who was born in Mississippi in 1944, began by performing songs about her upbringing and her surroundings. Her drama about country life, 'Ode To Billie Joe', topped the US charts for four weeks, and she was soon presenting TV variety shows and recording more middle-of-the-road material. After 'I'll Never Fall In Love Again', she sang another Bacharach & David song, 'Raindrops Keep Falling On My Head' from the film, *Butch Cassidy And The Sundance Kid*, but lost out to Sacha Distel. She had a Top 10 revival of 'All I Have To Do Is Dream' with Glen Campbell. Once the hits stopped coming, Bobbie Gentry became a high-earning act in Las Vegas, but she has not made any public appearances for many years.

Tommy Steele was not so fortunate with his musical version of another Billy Wilder film, *Some Like It Hot* (1959) as it lasted only a few months in 1992. Two years later, Andrew Lloyd Webber converted Billy Wilder's *Sunset Boulevard* (1950) into one of the great stage musicals. As for 'I'll Never Fall In Love Again', Burt Bacharach and Elvis Costello perform it on the soundtrack of *Austin Powers: The Spy Who Shagged Me* (1999).

279 The Archies
Sugar Sugar

Label & Cat No.: **RCA 1872**

Producers: **Jeff Barry**

Writers: **Jeff Barry / Andy Kim**

Date reached No.1: **25 October 1969**

Weeks at No.1: **8**

The Archies – Archie Andrews, Betty Cooper, Veronica Lodge, Jughead Jones, Reggie Mantle and Mr. Weatherbee – were a comic strip created by John Goldwater in 1942. In 1968 it was converted into an animated series by CBS and, as with *The Monkees* TV series, the music publisher Don Kirshner commissioned the music. He asked his key writers, including Jeff Barry of Barry & Greenwich, for songs and Barry wrote a bubblegum song with Andy Kim, 'Sugar Sugar'.

The vocalists on 'Sugar Sugar' were Ron Dante and Toni Wine, who double-tracked their voices so they sounded like the whole family. At the same time, Dante was also the lead vocalist with The Cuff Links, who had a Top 10 record with 'Tracy'. He subsequently produced Barry Manilow including his hit single, 'Mandy'. Toni Wine was a Brill Building writer, best known for 'A Groovy Kind Of Love'. Co-writer Andy Kim, who also sang on some Archies' records, had a UK Top 10 in a Neil Diamond vein with 'Rock Me Gently' in 1974.

Both 'Sugar Sugar' and 'Jingle Jangle' were US hits, but only 'Sugar Sugar' succeeded here. This in itself is impressive as the cartoon series was not screened in the UK. 'Sugar Sugar' may be dismissed as bubblegum, but Wilson Pickett recorded a fine soul version. In the UK, it has also been a hit for Sakkarin (one of Jonathan King's many pseudonyms) (1971) and Duke Baysee (1994).

280 Rolf Harris
Two Little Boys

Label & Cat No.: **Columbia DB 8630**

Producer: **Alan Braden**

Writers: **Alan Braden / Edward Madden / Theodore Morse**

Date Reached No.1: **20 December 1969**

Weeks at No.1: **6**

Shortly after his arrival in England at the age of 25, Rolf Harris made a huge impression on the British public with his sketching, painting and ability to lend his voice to parody as well as serious songs. He was here to

seek fame and fortune and it wouldn't be long before he succeeded.

In the late Sixties having spent 13 years in the UK, Rolf went back home for a four month working holiday. During this break, an old friend invited him over for dinner. He explained how he came by the song: "Once the meal was over, my friend, Ted Egan, who was a frustrated entertainer, said to me 'Here's a song you could sing on your television show in England'. He started beating his fingers on the table top and burst into 'Two little boys had two little toys'. He said, 'My mother sang it to me when I was four years old and I've never forgotten it'. I was so worried about what I was going to tell him, because it was such a namby-pamby song. All of a sudden, he got to the next part where it went, 'Did you think I would leave you dying', the hair on my arms and the back of my neck stood up and all of a sudden the story got to me."

Originally recorded by Harry Lauder in 1903, 'Two Little Boys', was the story of friendship in battle, during the American Civil War. The blue referred to the Union forces, and the grey to the Confederates. It topped the chart in Australia. "It was helped by two rival radio DJs, who had an acrimonious feud going on about what the song was all about", explained Rolf. "One said that the two boys, Jack and Joe, were a homosexual couple, the other disagreed and realised it was an anti-war song. However, the feud lasted four weeks and helped to sell a lot of records. It's a great song and it's a great story, and children learn it instantly. Blokes enjoyed it as they could whistle it down the street, women liked the emotion of it, and it's just a marvellous song."

1970-1979

ISLE OF WIGHT FESTIVAL

AUGUST 26-30 1970 Weekend £3

Friday 20/- Saturday 35/- Sunday 40/-

FRIDAY	SATURDAY	SUNDAY
CHICAGO	DOORS	JIMI HENDRIX EXPERIENCE
FAMILY	JONI MITCHELL	JOAN BAEZ
TASTE	WHO	LEONARD COHEN
JAMES TAYLOR	SLY AND THE FAMILY STONE	RICHIE HAVENS
ARRIVAL	CAT MOTHER	MOODY BLUES
LIGHTHOUSE	FREE	PENTANGLE
	JOHN SEBASTIAN	GOOD NEWS
	EMERSON, LAKE AND PALMER	
	MUNGO JERRY	
	SPIRIT	

Australia 40c South Africa 32c

MARC BOLAN BACK ON THE ROAD!

SEE PAGE 3

David Cassidy

The monster on the patio — page 7

T.Rextasy!

EXIT ROD THE ROCK STAR

MILLIONAIRE pop singer Rod Stewart has quit Britain for good. He says the taxman has forced him out.

"Much as I love the old country, I just can't afford to live there any more," he said last night.

"Taxation for me in Britain, at 83p in the £, is absolutely crippling."

Rod was speaking from his new home in Beverly Hills's famous Sunset Boulevard.

The 30-year-old leader of The Faces group added: "I have lived in California a month now to see if I like it here.

"Well, I do.

"I have reluctantly made up my mind to stay, and I am applying for American citizenship.

"I have also told my manager to sell up everything I own in Britain."

This will include Rod's magnificent mansion in Windsor, Berks. It's up for sale at £300,000.

The star's manager, Billy Gaff, who is in London, said: "Britain is going to lose a lot of money-making brains and talent because of its archaic tax system.

"The country will suffer . . . it needs the revenue that people like Rod bring in."

By STAN SAYER

Fans

Back to Rod, whose next visit to Britain will be next year, when he hopes to make a tour

still the greatest in the world, and I am looking forward to meeting them next year."

Actress Britt Ekland, his current girl friend, said: "Rod is very unhappy about having to stay away from Britain.

71's BEST SELLING SINGLES

1 **MY SWEET LORD,** George Harrison, **Apple**
2 **MAGGIE MAY,** Rod Stewart, **Mercury**
3 **CHIRPY CHIRPY CHEEP CHEEP,** Middle of the Road, **RCA**
4 **KNOCK THREE TIMES,** Dawn, **Bell**
5 **HOT LOVE,** T Rex, **Fly**
6 **THE PUSHBIKE SONG,** Mixtures, **Polydor**
7 **NEVER ENDING SONG OF LOVE,** New Seekers, **Philips**
8 **I'M STILL WAITING,** Diana Ross, **Tamla Motown**
9 **HEY GIRL DON'T BOTHER ME,** Tams, **Probe**
10 **GET IT ON,** T. Rex, **Fly**
11 **COZ I LUV YOU,** Slade, **Polydor**
12 **AMAZING GRACE,** Judy Collins, **Elektra**
13 **GRANDAD,** Clive Dunn, **Columbia**
14 **DOUBLE BARREL,** Dave & Ansil Collins, **Technique**
15 **ROSE GARDEN,** Lynn Anderson, **CBS**
16 **BABY JUMP,** Mungo Jerry, **Dawn**
17 **DID YOU EVER,** Nancy & Lee, **Reprise**
18 **FOR ALL WE KNOW,** Shirley Bassey, **United Artists**
19 **BROWN SUGAR,** Rolling Stones, **Rolling Stones Records**
20 **STONED LOVE,** Supremes, **Tamla Motown**
21 **COCO,** The Sweet, **RCA**
22 **IT'S IMPOSSIBLE,** Perry Como, **RCA**
23 **ERNIE (THE FASTEST MILKMAN IN THE WEST),** Benny Hill, **Columbia**
24 **RESURRECTION SHUFFLE,** Ashton, Gardner & Dyke, **Capitol**
25 **ANOTHER DAY,** Paul McCartney, **Apple**
26 **WITCH QUEEN OF NEW ORLEANS,** Redbone, **Epic**
27 **TWEEDLE DEE TWEEDLE DUM,** Middle of The Road, **RCA**
28 **I DID WHAT I DID FOR MARIA,** Tony Christie, **MCA**
29 **BRIDGET THE MIDGET,** Ray Stevens, **CBS**
30 **THE BANNER MAN,** Blue Mink, **Regal Zonophone**
31 **TILL,** Tom Jones, **Decca**
32 **YOU'VE GOT A FRIEND,** James Taylor, **Warner Bros.**
33 **MOZART SYMPHONY No. 40,** Walde de los Rios, **A&M**
34 **JEEPSTER,** T. Rex, **Fly**
35 **INDIANA WANTS ME,** R. Dean Taylor, **Tamla Motown**
36 **I'M GONNA RUN AWAY FROM YOU,** Tammi Lynn, **Mojo**
37 **DON'T LET IT DIE,** Hurricane Smith, **Columbia**
38 **HE'S GONNA STEP ON YOU AGAIN,** John Kongos, **Fly**
39 **BACK STREET LUV,** Curved Air, **Warner Bros.**
40 **TOM-TOM TURNAROUND,** New World, **RAK**
41 **WHAT ARE YOU DOING SUNDAY,** Dawn, **Bell**
42 **IT DON'T COME EASY,** Ringo Starr, **Apple**
43 **ME AND YOU AND A DOG NAMED BOO,** Lobo, **Philips**
44 **IN MY OWN TIME,** Family, **Reprise**
45 **JOHNNY REGGAE,** Piglets, **Bell**
46 **NO MATTER WHAT,** Badfinger, **Apple**
47 **GYPSIES, TRAMPS & THIEVES,** Cher, **MCA**
48 **I BELIEVE (IN LOVE),** Hot Chocolate, **RAK**
49 **DEVIL'S ANSWER,** Atomic Rooster, **B&C**
50 **BANKS OF THE OHIO,** Olivia Newton-John, **Pye**

Supplied by: British Market Research Bureau/Record Retailer

Disco TOP 40

THIS WEEK	TWO WEEKS AGO	TITLE/ARTIST	LABEL	BPM
1	2	HE'S THE GREATEST DANCER SISTER SLEDGE	Atlantic	116
2	15	SHAKE YOUR BODY JACKSONS	Epic	122
3	3	IN THE NAVY VILLAGE PEOPLE	Mercury	127
4	7	THE RUNNER THREE DEGREES	Ariola	
5	21	HAVEN'T STOPPED DANCING YET GONZALEZ	Sidewalk	135
6	4	I WILL SURVIVE GLORIA GAYNOR	Polydor	117
7	5	I WANT YOUR LOVE CHIC	Atlantic	116
8	12	CUBA GIBSON BROTHERS	Island	122
9	1	TURN THE MUSIC UP PLAYERS ASSOCIATION	Vanguard	115
10	39	KNOCK ON WOOD AMII STEWART	Atlantic	
11	27	LOVE BALLAD GEORGE BENSON	Warner Bros.	112
12	6	CAN YOU FEEL THE FORCE? REAL THING	Pye	132
13	9	DISCO NIGHTS (ROCK FREAK) G.Q.	Arista	123
14	11	MONEY IN MY POCKET DENNIS BROWN	Lightning	REGGAE
15	NEW	AIN'T NO STOPPING MCFADDED + WHITEHEAD	Phil Int.	
16	22	HERE COMES THE NIGHT BEACH BOYS	Caribou	134
17	NEW	BY THE WAY YOU DANCE BUNNY SIGLER	Salsoul	
18	10	KEEP YOUR BODY WORKING KLEEER	Atlantic Imp.	129
19	20	I (WHO HAVE NOTHING) SYLVESTER	Fantasy	132
20	NEW	THE DANCER GINO SOCCIO	Warner Bros.	
21	NEW	LOVE CRUSADER SARAH BRIGHTMAN	Ariola	
22	16	LOVE AND DESIRE ARPEGGIO	Polydor	
23	NEW	CAPTAIN BOOGIE WARDELL PIPER	Midsong	
24	8	KEEP ON DANCING GARY'S GANG	CBS	126
25	13	DANCE LADY DANCE CROWN HEIGHTS AFFAIR	Mercury	113
26	NEW	LOVIN IS REALLY MY GAME BRAINSTORM	Miracle	
27	NEW	GOT TO HAVE LOVING DON RAY	Polydor	
28	23	FIRE POINTER SISTERS	Planet	119
29	NEW	I DON'T WANT NOBODY ELSE MICHAEL WALDEN	Atlantic	
30	30	LIVIN' IT UP BELL AND JAMES	A&M	119
31	24	BOOGIE TOWN FLB	Fantasy	126
32	NEW	PICK ME UP I'LL DANCE MELBA MOORE	Epic	
33	NEW	ROCK YOUR BABY FORCE	Phil Int.	
34	NEW	LET'S FLY AWAY VOYAGE	GTO	
35	26	SWINGIN' LIGHT OF THE WORLD	Ensign	132
36	NEW	REUNITED PEACHES AND HERB	Polydor	
37	NEW	JAMMIN AT THE DISCO PHILLY CREAM	Fantasy	
38	NEW	MAGNETISM EUGENE RECORD	Warner Bros.	
39	14	EVERYTHING IS GREAT INNER CIRCLE	Island	122
40	17	CONTACT EDWIN STARR	20th Century	134

Imp = Import. BPM = Beats per minute.

ELTON ON ROAD AGAIN

ELTON JOHN fans will be pleased to hear that the cuddliest club manager in football has reversed his decision to retire from the stage to do his first concert tour of Britain since 1976.

BOWIE FIASCO

BEST OF 1978

78s Top 45s

In no particular order of preference

PICTURE THIS Blondie
DENIS Blondie
EVER FALLEN IN LOVE Buzzcocks
STAYIN' ALIVE Bee Gees
NIGHT FEVER Bee Gees
WHITE MAN AT THE HAMMERSMITH PALAIS The Clash
DOWN IN THE TUBE STATION AT MIDNIGHT The Jam
ONLY YOU Teddy Prendergrass
SHAME Evelyn 'Champagne' King
HOT SHOT Karen Young
I LOVE THE NIGHTLIFE Alicia Bridges
NOW THAT WE'VE FOUND LOVE Third World
RADIO RADIO Elvis Costello & The Attractions
I DON'T WANT TO GO TO CHELSEA Elvis Costello & The Attractions
MISS YOU Rolling Stones
YOU'RE THE ONE THAT I WANT John Travolta/Olivia Newton-John
SUMMER NIGHTS John Travolta/Olivia Newton-John
YMCA Village People
IN THE BUSH Musique
ONE NATION UNDER A GROOVE Funkadelic
LOVE DON'T LIVE HERE ANYMORE Rose Royce
TONIGHT'S THE NIGHT Charles Jackson
YOU MAKE ME FEEL (MIGHTY REAL) Sylvester
USE TA BE MY GIRL O'Jays
THREE TIMES A LADY Commodores
HIT ME WITH YOUR RHYTHM STICK Ian Dury & The Blockheads
WHAT A WASTE Ian Dury & The Blockheads
FLASH LIGHT Parliament
SATISFACTION Devo
BOOTZILLA Bootsy's Rubber Band
DISCO TO GO Brides Of Funkenstein
THE DAY THE WORLD TURNED DAY-GLO X-Ray Spex
GERM FREE ADOLESCENTS X-Ray Spex
JILTED JOHN Jilted John
UP TOWN TOP RANKING Althia & Donna
DO YA THINK I'M SEXY Rod Stewart
RAT TRAP Boomtown Rats
PUBLIC IMAGE Public Image Ltd

BRITAIN'S BIGGEST DAILY SALE

6p Thursday, December 2, 1976 No. 22,658

TV's Bill Grundy in rock outrage

Judge in 'murder' pardon shocker

By ARNOT McWHINNIE

A JUDGE made an astonishing attack yesterday on the way a man convicted of murder was given a royal pardon.

He told a jury: "You may well have come to the clear conclusion that he was rightly convicted."

The man at the centre of the storm is 48-year-old Patrick Meehan, who was freed from jail in May after serving nearly seven years.

The judge, Lord Robertson, said: "There is no legal justification whatsoever for saying that Meehan was wrongly convicted."

He went on to suggest that Meehan's conviction for killing elderly Mrs.

Meehan yesterday

Rachel Ross still stood, despite the pardon.

The judge spoke out at the end of a second trial over the same murder.

This time, 38-year-old Ian Waddell was in the dock. He [illegible]

The judge said of the pardon: "In the ordinary use of language, if you pardon someone you pardon them for something they have done—not for something they haven't done.

"It certainly doesn't quash the conviction."

● Who killed Rachel Ross?—Centre Pages

THE GROUP IN THE BIG TV RUMPUS

Johnny Rotten, leader of the Sex Pistols, opens a can of beer. Last night their language made TV viewers froth.

When the air turned blue . .

INTERVIEWER Bill Grundy introduced the Sex Pistols to viewers with the comment: "Words actually fail me about the next [illegible]

[illegible]

GRUNDY: Beethoven, Mozart, Bach?

PISTOL: They're wonderful people.

GRUNDY: Are they?

PISTOL: Yes they really turn us on. They do.

GRUNDY: Suppose they turn other people on?

PISTOL (in a whisper): That's just their tough s——.

GRUNDY: It's what?

[illegible] Nothing—a rude word. [illegible]

[illegible] No, no. What was [illegible] word?

[illegible] S——.

[illegible] Was it really? Good [illegible] What about you girls [illegible] Are you married or [illegible] yourself?

[illegible] always wanted to [illegible]

[illegible] Did you really? We'll [illegible] afterwards, shall we?

[illegible] you dirty old man. [illegible] old man.

[illegible] Go on, you've got a [illegible] You've got another [illegible] Say something outrageous.

PISTOL: You dirty sod. You dirty bastard.

GRUNDY: Go on. Again.

PISTOL: You dirty f——er.

GRUNDY: What?

PISTOL: What a f——ing rotter.

GRUNDY: Well, that's it for tonight . . . I'll be seeing you soon. I hope I'm not seeing YOU again. Goodnight.

THE FILTH AND THE FURY!

A POP group shocked millions of viewers last night with the filthiest language heard on British television.

The Sex Pistols, leaders of the new "punk rock" cult, hurled a string of four letter obscenities at interviewer Bill Grundy on Thames TV's family teatime programme "Today."

The Thames switchboard was flooded with protests.

Nearly 200 angry viewers telephoned the Mirror. One man was so furious that he kicked in the screen of his £380 colour TV.

Grundy was immediately carpeted by his boss and will apologise in tonight's programme.

Shocker

A Thames spokesman said: "Because the programme was live, we could not foresee the language which would be used. We apologise to all viewers."

The show screened at peak children's viewing time turned into a shocker when Grundy asked about £40,000 that the Sex Pistols received from their record company.

By STUART GREIG, MICHAEL McCARTHY and JOHN PEACOCK

One member of the group said: "F——ing spent it, didn't we?"

Then when Grundy asked about people who preferred Beethoven, Mozart and Bach, another Sex Pistol remarked: "That's just their tough s——."

Later Grundy told the group: "Say something outrageous."

A punk rocker replied: "You dirty sod. You dirty bastard."

"Go on. Again," said Grundy.

"You dirty f——er."

"What?"

Uproar as viewers jam phones

"What a f——ing rotter."

As the Thames switchboard became jammed, viewers rang the Mirror to voice their complaints.

Lorry driver James Holmes, 47, was outraged that his eight-year-old son Lee heard the swearing . . . and kicked in the screen of his TV.

"It blew up and I was knocked backwards," he said. "But I was so angry and disgusted with this filth that I took a swing with my boot.

"I can swear as well as anyone, but I don't want this sort of muck coming into my home at teatime."

Mr. Holmes, of Beechfield Walk, Waltham Abbey, Essex, added: "I am not a violent person, but I would like to have got hold of Grundy.

"He should be sacked for encouraging this sort of disgusting behaviour."

WHO ARE THESE PUNKS? PAGE NINE

Boots cut singles to 79p.

If you come to Boots between 30th July and 25th August you can buy singles for only 79p. That's 10p less than our normal selling price of 89p. It's just one part of our exciting new Disc Deal – the new music package from Boots.

Better value than ever

You see, although we normally sell singles way below the recommended price, Disc Deal means you get even better value than you bargained for.

JUKE BOX JURY

"JUKE Box Jury", the '60s TV show on which a panel of 'personalities' passed comment on new singles, is to be revived on BBC 1 for early Saturday evening screenings starting June 16. Host will be Noel Edmonds.

VINYL NEWS RATS, QUO SHAM, SEX PISTOLS etc

281 Edison Lighthouse
Love Grows (Where My Rosemary Goes)

Label & Cat No.: **Bell 1091**

Producer: **Tony Macaulay**

Writers: **Barry Mason / Tony Macaulay**

Date reached No.1: **31 January 1970**

Weeks at No.1: **5**

IN 1970, IN THE UK, THERE WAS growing conflict between the artists and the producers. The producer, Tony Macaulay, remembers, "We were very tired of how the artists used to treat us. People think that the producers treat the artists badly, and I can tell you it was the other way round. We were always being slagged off in the press and being told that our stuff was manufactured. What's more, the artists would turn up late or they wouldn't learn the songs properly. It got to the point where a number of us were thinking, 'It's the record that matters. We'll make a record and if it's a hit, we'll worry about who goes on the road later.' I suppose you could say I was anti-artist."

An excellent example is the melodic, easy-paced 'Love Grows (Where My Rosemary Goes)', written by Tony Macaulay and Barry Mason. Tony recorded it with session musicians, one of them being the vocalist Tony Burrows. In the early Sixties, Tony Burrows had been a member of The Kestrels and now he sang backing vocals on sessions in the studios around London. There could be three sessions a day and it was good, regular money.

'Love Grows' was released under the name of Edison Lighthouse and when it entered the charts, a group had to be found for *Top Of The Pops*. A group called Greenfield Hammer was up for it but the lead vocalist couldn't match Tony Burrows' performance, so Tony sang with the group.

Tony Burrows says, "I told Tony Macaulay that I didn't want to be in a group anymore, but I agreed to do TV but no touring. I never made a secret of what I did, but the BBC banned me from *Top Of The Pops* because I was also on The Flowerpot Men's 'Let's Go To San Francisco', White Plains' 'My Baby Loves Lovin'', The Pipkins' 'Gimme Dat Ding' and Brotherhood Of Man's 'United We Stand'. They thought audiences might feel it was a con if I was singing on half the programme."

We hear you, Tony, but they would think it even more of a con if someone else was performing the songs. Flash forward to the fiasco that was Milli Vanilli.

282 Lee Marvin
Wand'rin' Star

Label & Cat No.: **Paramount PARA 3004**

Producer: **Tom Mack**

Writers: **Alan Jay Lerner / Frederick Loewe**

Date reached No.1: **7 March 1970**

Weeks at No.1: **3**

FOLLOWING THE SUCCESS OF RODGERS & Hammerstein's *Oklahoma!* Lerner and Loewe wrote a light-hearted Broadway musical, *Paint Your Wagon*, about a gold rush town in California in 1853 and the problems of bigamy. The songs included 'I Talk To The Trees', 'They Call The Wind Maria' and 'Wand'rin' Star'.

The show opened on Broadway in 1951 and ran for a year but it was not filmed until 1970. Joshua Logan's casting was bizarre as the leading roles in this musical were going to non-singers, Lee Marvin as the drunken Ben Rumson (the town's sheriff, judge and mayor) and Clint Eastwood (as 'Pardner', another man with no name). Effectively, Lee Marvin is reprising his role in *Cat Ballou,* but this time with songs.

Nelson Riddle arranged the score and conducted the orchestra, and his son, Christopher, remembers the fun that he had: "Lee Marvin had a wonderful sense of humour and he thought it was hilarious that he was starring in a musical. My father said it would be ridiculous to have him mime to somebody else's voice as the role wasn't meant to be sung by a great singer. He gave him some voice lessons and got him to gravel voice, 'I was born under a wand'rin' star'. My father was very happy with the result and also with Clint Eastwood doing 'I Talk To The Trees'."

No one could have predicted that the single, which housed both the Marvin and Eastwood songs, would get to number one. The album, which also featured The Nitty Gritty Dirt Band, climbed to number two and was on the charts for 102 weeks. If the film-makers had really wanted a challenge, why didn't they get Lee and Clint to dance?

283 Simon & Garfunkel
Bridge Over Troubled Water

Label & Cat No.: **CBS 4790**

Producers: **Paul Simon / Art Garfunkel / Roy Halee**

Writer: **Paul Simon**

Date reached No.1: **28 March 1970**

Weeks at No.1: **3**

THE KEY SONGS OF 1970 – THE TWO Paul's 'Bridge Over Troubled Water' and 'Let It Be' – were written with Aretha Franklin in mind. Both have strong gospel overtones in their music and imagery, and Aretha was to record them to perfection. The novelist Martin Amis described 'Bridge Over Troubled Water' as therapy and Leonard Cohen said, "That might be the song that gets someone through a dark hour."

Paul Simon's song was triggered by a record from The Swan Silvertones, 'Oh Mary Don't You Weep', in which the lead singer Claude Jeter's improvisation caught the composer's ear. "Had it not been for him, I would never have written 'Bridge Over Troubled Water'," admitted Simon. Indeed, Simon's original title was 'Hymn'.

The song was written in the summer of 1969 when Paul Simon and his then wife, Peggy, rented a house on Blue Jay Way in Los Angeles – the house in which George Harrison had written 'Blue Jay Way'. Written on guitar, Paul Simon passed his song to the arranger Jimmie Haskell. When he transposed it for piano, he misheard the

Simon & Garfunkel, the eternally quarrelling duo from New York, with a clutch of Grammy Awards for their Bridge Over Troubled Water *album*

title and headed his sheet music, 'Like A Pitcher Of Water', which amused Simon so much that he had it framed.

The instrumental track, dominated by Larry Knechtel's piano, was laid down in Los Angeles and the vocals were added when the duo returned to New York. The slowly building arrangement was following Phil Spector's 'Ol' Man River' for The Righteous Brothers, which uses a gospel chorus but holds it back until the end for maximum impact. Simon thought that the first two verses should be sung solo and he later regretted giving this gem to Art Garfunkel, although he had nothing but compliments for his performance.

Simon was never happy with the third verse –"I always felt that you could see that it was written afterwards. It doesn't sound like the first two verses."Yet isn't the line that everyone remembers from the third verse, "Sail on silver girl"? Paul was offering sympathy to his wife, Peggy, who had grey hairs, although, actually, he was drawing attention to them.

The resulting album was also called *Bridge Over Troubled Water* and it became the first time a single and an album with the same title topped both the UK and US charts simultaneously. Although the song is about peace and tranquillity, Simon & Garfunkel split up acrimoniously shortly after the album was released. Since then, their relationship has blown hot and cold, with plenty of making up and falling out. They have had long and successful solo careers, but now, in 2004, with them touring again in harmony, the follow-up album to *Bridge Over Troubled Water* looks a possibility.

284 Dana
All Kinds Of Everything

Label & Cat No.:	**Rex R 11054**
Producer:	**Ray Horricks**
Writers:	**Derry Lindsay / Jackie Smith**
Date reached No.1:	**18 April 1970**
Weeks at No.1:	**2**

Dana was born Rosemary Brown in London to Irish parents in 1951. The family returned to Ireland and as a teenager, she was singing in Dublin folk clubs and signed with the Rex label. They entered her for the National Song Contest and she came second. The following year she was invited back to perform 'All Kinds Of Everything' and it was chosen to represent Ireland in Eurovision. "I remember thinking that it was pretty," says Dana, "and I liked it very much as it had a folky quality about it."

The music had been written by Derry Lindsay, a member of the Dublin showband, The Kamels, and his friend, Jackie Smith had written the words. It seems odd that a man should write about snowdrops and daffodils, butterflies and bees but there you are.

Feeling like Alice in Wonderland, Dana went to Amsterdam to take part in the contest: "I didn't watch any of the other artists rehearse. I felt that if I compared myself to them, I would completely disintegrate, so I looked upon it as a week's holiday as I had never been abroad before. Mary Hopkin was singing for the United Kingdom and Julio Iglesias was there for Spain. He was very handsome and he would practise his scales at the back of the stage. I think he expected to win. I never dreamt that I would win but then Mary Hopkin gave me a big hug as the scores were coming in and I knew I had a chance."

Dana came first with 'All Kinds Of Everything', Mary second with 'Knock, Knock – Who's There?' and Julio was fourth with 'Gwendolyne'. After winning Eurovision, Dana became a popular TV artist and concert performer, having further hits with 'Who Put The Lights Out?', 'Please Tell Him I Said Hello' and 'It's Gonna Be A Cold, Cold Christmas'.

In 1978 Dana married the hotelier Damien Scallon and after raising a family, entered Irish politics. Following an unsuccessful bid for the Presidency, she stood for the European Parliament and won. Politicians promise all kinds of everything, so she had the perfect calling-card. She still performs on occasion and she hosted the US religious series, *Say Yes*, which was produced by her husband.

In 1997 The Edge encouraged the audience to sing 'All Kinds Of Everything' when U2 performed in Dublin, and the following year Terry Hall and Sinead O'Connor performed it as a duet on the Channel 4 send-up, *A Song For Eurotrash*. The song's more regular home is in the repertoire of Foster & Allen.

285 Norman Greenbaum
Spirit In The Sky

Label & Cat No.:	**Reprise RS 20885**
Producer:	**Craig Leon**
Writer:	**Norman Greenbaum**
Date Reached No.1:	**2 May 1970**
Weeks at No.1:	**2**

How ironic that a nice Jewish boy like Norman Greenbaum, who, by his own admission, did not believe in Jesus, should write a Christian based song about the Son of God himself – and make a fortune out of it.

Norman was born in Malden, Massachusetts on November 20, 1942. He had a traditional Jewish upbringing by his parents who ran a bakery. He attended Boston University but soon dropped out to pursue a musical career. In 1965 he moved to Los Angeles and formed the Dr West's Medicine Show and Jug Band. Their only chart appearance in America was the curiously titled 'The Eggplant That Ate Chicago'. By 1968 they had broken up and Norman attempted a solo career.

The inspiration for 'Spirit In The Sky' came from country singer Porter Wagoner. Norman explained, "He had a regular television show in Los Angeles. About 20 minutes into the show he'd always perform a religious song. One particular time, he had a stained glass window backdrop. He did a Mel Tillis song called 'Pastor's Absent On Vacation', about a man who lived in the mountains who hadn't been to church in over twenty years. He'd been out with his mule prospecting for gold. He realised he hadn't been to church for so long and decided to head across town to church. When he got there, there was a sign that said 'The Preacher is on vacation'. At that point I realised I needed a religious song."

He said, "The thing that amazes me is, that after all these years, you never get tired of it, it just rings out and I just think, yeah, I wrote that." He followed 'Spirit In The Sky' with 'Canned Ham'. It sparked no interest from the British public, but as Norman admitted, "It wasn't 'Spirit In The Sky' and that was the downfall."

Norman once played a gig in the Santa Cruz area of California, which consisted of 40 minutes of 'Sprit In The Sky'. The crowd were so happy they wanted an encore, which comprised a further 15 minutes of the same song.

Rumours circulated that it was The Band's Robbie Robertson who played the distinctive rasping intro on the single, but as Norman confirmed, "I've never met Robbie Robertson. My friend, Robbie Robinson, played on a few tracks of my *Spirit* album and he was also the genius behind building the fuzz box into the body of my Fender Telecaster. It was me and that guitar that played that intro."

286 The England World Cup Squad Back Home

Label & Cat No.:	**Pye 7N 17920**
Producers:	**Bill Martin / Phil Coulter**
Writers:	**Bill Martin / Phil Coulter**
Date reached No.1:	**16 May 1970**
Weeks at No.1:	**3**

ENGLAND WON THE WORLD CUP IN 1966, but no one paid much attention to Lonnie Donegan's single, 'World Cup Willie'. Prior to 1970, no sporting single had done well, but everything changed and a whole new market developed with the runaway success of 'Back Home' by the next England World Cup Squad. Nowadays there are both official and unofficial singles for all the major soccer competitions.

A Scot and an Irishmen, Bill Martin and Phil Coulter, who had written 'Puppet On A String' and 'Congratulations', wrote 'Back Home' and played it to the BBC executive, Bill Cotton Jr. It was not a good demo as Phil played the piano badly as the result of a broken arm. Bill Martin, being something of a salesman, thought that it would be novel to have a football song performed by the actual team. England's manager, Alf Ramsey, had no interest in the project but said he would spare the boys for a few hours if they agreed. Bill persuaded them that it could be good money for little effort and so, unlike many subsequent football records, the team is actually singing.

Phil Coulter recorded backing tracks for an entire album and the vocals were added one Sunday afternoon. Phil says, "We knew of course that the single had to be a song that every Joe Soap had to be able to sing and it had to have that instant appeal that could transfer onto the terraces. The 'back home' bit was smart as I knew they shouldn't sing, 'We are going to kick the lining out of everybody in South America, We are the boys'. It would have been too arrogant. The way to do it was 'Back home they'll be thinking about us' – in other words, they are talking about the supporters, not themselves."

For the record (in both senses), the team was Jeff Astle (West Brom), Alan Ball (Everton), Gordon Banks (Stoke City), Colin Bell (Manchester City), Peter Bonetti (Chelsea), Bobby Charlton (Manchester Utd), Jack Charlton (Leeds Utd), Allan Clarke (Leeds Utd), Terry Cooper (Leeds Utd), Emlyn Hughes (Liverpool), Norman Hunter (Leeds Utd), Geoff Hurst (West Ham), Brian Labone (Everton), Francis Lee (Manchester City), Bobby Moore (West Ham), Alan Mullery (Spurs), Keith Newton (Everton), Peter Osgood (Chelsea), Martin Peters (West Ham), Alex Stepney (Manchester Utd), Nobby Stiles (Manchester Utd) and Tommy Wright (Everton).

Phil Coulter says, "They were all dressed up to go to a Football Association dinner and Alf Ramsey said we could only have them for half an hour for *Top Of The Pops*. Half an hour! A coach brought them into the TV Centre in Wood Lane and remember they had only sung the song once in the recording studio. My fear was that they would have forgotten it. I was standing beside the camera with the words and it was like 'Follow the bouncing ball.' If you look at the film, you will see that some of them are paying attention and some are looking around to see where Pan's People are."

'Back Home' went to number one and might have been on top for longer if England had fared better on the pitch. They were hampered by injuries, illness, the altitude and an accusation of theft against their captain, Bobby Moore. On June 14, 1970, they lost in the quarter-final 2-3. to West Germany.

In 1966 the Prime Minister Harold Wilson, had claimed England's success as a victory for Labour and presumably the electorate now blamed him for England's performance. Four days later, Labour lost the general election, the first election, incidentally, in which the 18 to 21 year olds could vote.

The England World Cup Squad admitted their failings in 'This Time (We'll Get It Right)', a number two in 1982, and then scarcely got into the Top 75 with 'We've Got The Whole World At Our Feet' in 1986. They were back at the top in 1990 with 'World In Motion', the only group to return to number one with a completely new line-up. Jeff Astle kept singing though and at Frank Skinner's request, he sang at the end of the *Fantasy Football* series.

'Back Home' was also used for the TV coverage when the British troops returned victorious from the Falklands in 1982. "We had taken the World War II songs as our inspiration – they're thinking of us, we're thinking of them – so I wasn't surprised," says Bill Martin.

287 Christie
Yellow River

Label & Cat No.: **CBS 4911**
Producer: **Mike Smith**
Writer: **Jeff Christie**
Date Reached No.1: **6 June 1970**
Weeks at No.1: **1**

FORMER ACID GALLERY MEMBER, Jeff Christie, wrote 'Yellow River' for The Tremeloes and in hindsight must have been delighted when they rejected it. It gave Jeff the opportunity to put it out himself as a single and have a number one hit with it.

Mike Blakely's brother, Howard, who was rhythm guitarist with The Tremeloes, suggested that Mike should form a band. He brought in guitarist Vic Elmes and called themselves The Epics. He then recruited lead singer and bass player Jeff Christie and renamed themselves Christie.

The Tremeloes first recorded 'Yellow River' as a demo with drummer Dave Munden on lead vocals. They weren't too keen on the song and passed it back to Jeff. As Vic Elmes recalled, "The Tremeloes had a change of heart, but they gave us their version fully recorded, to release under the name of a new band, hence Christie. All Jeff and I had to do was record our vocals to their backing track, and a new band was born." Because both groups were signed to CBS records, they were happy to let new vocals be added to the existing backing track.

The Tremeloes' producer Mike Smith saw the potential of the song and felt rather guilty when his group turned it down, so he agreed to produce Christie's version. It gave Mike his sixth and final chart topper as a producer.

The follow-up, the similar sounding 'San Bernadino', made the UK Top 10 and number one in Germany. They began touring to promote the new eponymous album, but when that failed to chart, cracks began to show which resulted in Mike Blakely being sacked and replaced by Paul Fenton. Soon after, the band split.

Vic Elmes became involved in writing TV scores, most notably *Space: 1999* and still occasionally tours as Christie. In the Nineties, Jeff 's income got a boost when Yellow Pages substituted the word 'river' for 'pages' for their TV ad campaign.

288 Mungo Jerry
In The Summertime

Label & Cat No.: **Dawn DNX 2502**
Producer: **Barry Murray**
Writer: **Ray Dorset**
Date Reached No.1: **13 June 1970**
Weeks at No.1: **7**

"PYE RECORDS WANTED TO GET HIP," says Mungo Jerry's lead singer, Ray Dorset. "The label was a mishmash and they wanted something that was more offbeat. They started Dawn Records which was run by a friend of mine, Barry Murray. He asked us to make an album, which we did in a couple of afternoons and evenings."

Ray Dorset, who was born in 1946, had seen The Rolling Stones and The Yardbirds at the Station Hotel, Richmond: "I was still at school but my uncle won the football pools and gave everyone a load of money. I bought some strange clothes and I had long hair and the headmaster said, 'You're a spiv. You'd better leave.' I had a group and we backed Jackie Edwards for a while, and Dawn were going to call us The Incredible Shark. They changed it to Mungo Jerry, which came from *Old Possum's Book Of Practical Cats*, but they got the spelling wrong." T.S. Eliot wrote Mungojerrie, but possibly only Andrew Lloyd Webber noticed the misspelling at the time.

According to Ray, 'In The Summertime' was born out of necessity: "I had bought a maisonette and it was costing me £7 a week and as I was only earning £13, I didn't have the money to buy records and learn new songs. I was writing songs that sounded like old ones and 'In The Summertime' was me trying to write a Canned Heat song, but it came out totally different. It wasn't a long record but Barry Murray said, 'If we can make it a bit longer, we can go over three minutes and get double royalties.' I said, 'Well, get the sound of a car revving off and then start the song over again.' The studio engineer drove his car past the studio and we recorded it. We joined it together and it worked out okay."

Dawn Records broke the standards of conventional record releases by making 'In The Summertime' a maxi-single, and the three tracks were on sale at a very reasonable 10 shillings (50p). "At the time I was working for Timex," says Ray, "and I asked my boss for the afternoon off to do *Top Of The Pops*." In the Nineties, 'In The Summertime' was part of a drink-driving campaign.

289 Elvis Presley
The Wonder Of You

Label & Cat No.: **RCA 1974**
Producers: **Felton Jarvis / Elvis Presley**
Writer: **Baker Knight**
Date reached No.1: **1 August 1970**
Weeks at No.1: **6**

HARD TO BELIEVE BUT TRUE – THE world's greatest entertainer, Elvis Presley, did not make a concert appearance between March 1961 and July 1969. His return in bejewelled white jump suits in a Nevada showroom could have made him a laughing stock but he became a trendsetter and numerous performers copied his lead. His lavish costumes were typical of the time: the Seventies was The Decade That Fashion Forgot.

Elvis also started recording in earnest again and 'The Wonder Of You' was captured live at the International Hotel, Las Vegas in February 1970. "Elvis had a huge range and sometimes I didn't know what key he might do a song in," says his pianist and arranger, Glen D. Hardin. "I could sit and think about it for a few minutes and touch on his highest note and his lowest note and I would figure it out and I don't think I ever missed. He would call me and say, 'Do you remember that old song, 'The Wonder Of You'? I want to do it tomorrow night, first show.' And I would say, 'Okay.' (Laughs) I worked all night on the arrangements many, many times."

'The Wonder Of You' had been written as a gentle ballad for Perry Como, but it was given to Ray Peterson who recorded it in 1959. There were UK cover versions from the two Ronnies (Hilton and Carroll), and although both Ray Peterson and Ronnie Hilton made the Top 30, their versions were soon forgotten when Elvis sang it. Glen D. wrote a very powerful arrangement on which Elvis is backed by a full orchestra as well as The Imperials Quartet and The Sweet Inspirations.

Glen D. Hardin enjoyed his years with Elvis. "We had a set list but you could never know what he was going to do. Well, we knew that he wouldn't stick to the list! He used to throw water in my direction, but I never let it bother me. One time I brought an umbrella to the second show and he got a kick out of that."

290 Smokey Robinson & The Miracles The Tears Of A Clown

Label & Cat No.: **Tamla Motown TMG 745**

Producers: **Henry Cosby / Smokey Robinson**

Writers: **Henry Cosby / Smokey Robinson / Stevie Wonder**

Date reached No.1: **12 September 1970**

Weeks at No.1: **1**

The Miracles were the first group to be signed to Tamla Motown and although they had a succession of hits in America, ('Shop Around', 'You Really Got A Hold On Me', 'Mickey's Monkey', 'I Second That Emotion'), they did not make the UK Top 20 until 1969 with 'The Tracks Of My Tears'. The British UK record-buyers preferred the harder edge of The Four Tops and The Supremes.

In 1967 Stevie Wonder and his songwriting partner, Henry Cosby, had written a melody but they weren't happy with their lyrics. They put the tune on tape and asked Smokey to come up with something. When they had recorded the tune, they had included a fairground calliope and this made Smokey think of the circus and how he might do a pop version of the Italian opera about clowns, *Pagliacci*. He wrote a new lyric, 'Tears Of A Clown', and The Miracles included it on their 1967 album, *Smokey Robinson & The Miracles Make It Happen*.

When 'The Tracks Of My Tears' eventually broke The Miracles in the UK, their British representatives were wondering what to release next. They continued the lachrymose theme with 'The Tears Of A Clown'. The record went to number one and as a result it was issued as a single in the US, becoming their Christmas number one.

Smokey Robinson left to go solo in 1972 and the similar-sounding Billy Griffin joined Ronnie White, Pete Moore and Bobby Rogers in The Miracles. The Miracles had a Top 10 disco single with 'Love Machine' in 1976.

291 Freda Payne Band Of Gold

Label & Cat No.: **Invictus INV 502**

Producers: **Brian Holland / Lamont Dozier / Eddie Holland**

Writers: **Ron Dunbar / Edith Wayne**

Date reached No.1: **19 September 1970**

Weeks at No.1: **6**

The Detroit singer, Freda Payne, is the sister of Scherrie Payne from The Supremes, but she did not record for Motown herself. "I was Berry Gordy's first female protégé, but there was a dispute between him and my mother and so I never went there."

Instead, Freda became part of the CBS radio show, *Make Way For Youth*, and then joined Pearl Bailey's roadshow. Freda recorded for various labels without much success until she met up with the production team, Holland / Dozier / Holland, who had left Motown. They signed Chairmen Of The Board and Freda Payne, and the first song they found for her was 'Band Of Gold'. The lead guitarist was Ray Parker Jr, later to find fame with 'Ghostbusters'.

Freda says, "It is about a wedding night that didn't work out. I wondered why a girl would have a problem on her wedding night and why they would be in separate rooms, but they said, 'Just learn it.' I had no idea that it would be such a big hit."

It was followed by the whispered 'Deeper And Deeper' and then 'Bring The Boys Home'. "That was a good song and it was played in South Vietnam," says Freda, "but the US Government was not happy about that as they thought it wasn't suitable for their soldiers." Freda has been on Broadway in the Duke Ellington musical, *Sophisticated Ladies* and was recently in the UK as part of the *Dancing In The Streets* ensemble.

292 Matthews' Southern Comfort Woodstock

Label & Cat No.: **Uni UNS 526**

Producer: **Iain Matthews**

Writer: **Joni Mitchell**

Date reached No.1: **31 October 1970**

Weeks at No.1: **3**

Although not scheduled to perform, Joni Mitchell intended to go to the three-day celebration of peace and music that was Woodstock, or at least on the day that her friends, Crosby, Stills & Nash, were performing. However, the traffic was so congested that she had to cry off as she had an appearance on *The Dick Cavett Show* the following day. She went to New York and watched the festival from her hotel room. She felt isolated and that she was missing the event of her generation. Her emotions were poured into 'Woodstock', which appeared on her album, *Ladies Of The Canyon*: she sings, "Maybe it is just the time of year / Or maybe it's the time of man." The song was rocked up by Crosby, Stills, Nash & Young on their *Déjà Vu* album. It became a US hit, but it was Matthews' Southern Comfort who were stardust and golden here.

Iain Matthews had been the lead singer with Fairport Convention, leaving in 1969 to form his own band, Matthews' Southern Comfort. The band included Gordon Huntley on steel so their version of 'Woodstock' had a country-rock flavour. Iain Matthews says, "I had bought Joni Mitchell's album and we had to do four songs on a BBC lunchtime show. We worked up an arrangement for 'Woodstock' and the response was so good that we put it out as a single. Crosby, Stills & Nash's record had just come out and so we waited to see what happened to that first." Although Matthews' Southern Comfort reached the top, the band soon split up: "I thought we'd gone as far as we could," says Iain.

This restlessness remains with Iain Matthews to this day and his career is scattered with one project after another. He had a US Top 20 hit with 'Shake It' in 1978 and he is also known for his work as part of Plainsong, a band he has reformed with Andy Roberts, Julian Dawson and Mark Griffiths, who is also from Matthews' Southern Comfort. Iain doesn't shut the door to anything and he has performed with Fairport Convention at their Cropredy Festivals.

An extraordinary fact: only two of the acts at Woodstock – Joe Cocker and Jimi Hendrix – had UK number ones. Why should that be?

293 Jimi Hendrix Voodoo Chile

Label & Cat No.:	**Track 2095 001**
Producer:	**Jimi Hendrix**
Writer:	**Jimi Hendrix**
Date reached No.1:	**21 November 1970**
Weeks at No.1:	**1**

Jimi Hendrix wanted his own studio, Electric Lady, in New York, but when it wasn't ready, he settled for sessions at the Record Plant in New York with the engineer Eddie Kramer. Jimi had written some songs, but it was his intention to jam the arrangements with good musicians who could keep up with him. In May 1968 he did an extended blues piece, 'Voodoo Chile', with Steve Winwood on Hammond organ, Jack Casady on bass and Mitch Mitchell on drums. Winwood remarked, "There were no chord sheets, no nothing. Jimi just started playing. It was a one-take job, with him singing and playing at the same time."

Despite its contemporary sound, the song was effectively a Delta blues, a tribute to the connections between voodoo and the blues, and it is in line with Muddy Waters' 'Got My Mojo Working' and the work of Robert Johnson, the first great blues singer and a man who was plagued by demons.

The next day ABC-TV wanted to film Hendrix for a news feature and he proposed a shortened version of 'Voodoo Chile', now called 'Voodoo Child (Slight Return)', on which he would be supported by The Experience – Noel Redding on bass and Mitch Mitchell on drums. This jam session, top heavy with feedback, proved to be one of Hendrix's key recordings. It is mostly instrumental but it does contain a memorable metaphor, "I'm standing next to a mountain and chop it down with the edge of my hand." Both versions were included on the double album *Electric Ladyland*, a record infamous for its cover photograph of naked women. WHSmith refused to stock it, and another cover appeared on the American release.

Jimi lived at 14 Brook Street in London's Mayfair and it is one of the few buildings with two English Heritage plaques, one for Hendrix and one for a previous occupant, George Frideric Handel. Kathy Etchingham, Hendrix's girlfriend, said at the ceremony in 1997, "It is right that the street should honour both Handel and Hendrix. They were both at the cutting edge, they both liked their music to be played loudly, and they both came to find fame in London."

Jimi Hendrix died in a flat in London's Notting Hill in 1970, a few days after his triumphant appearance at the Isle of Wight Festival. 'Voodoo Chile' was released as a single and as Lenny Kravitz remarked, "It just howls from the soul. It's so intense. Sometimes I put it on and I can't even take it."

As Jimi sings, "If I don't meet you no more in this world / I'll meet you in the next one, don't be late."

294 Dave Edmunds I Hear You Knockin'

Label & Cat No.:	**MAM 1**
Producer:	**Dave Edmunds**
Writers:	**Dave Bartholomew / Pearl King**
Date reached No.1:	**28 November 1970**
Weeks at No.1:	**6**

Although not so well known as Fats Domino, Smiley Lewis was a New Orleans R&B artist with Fats Domino's co-writer, Dave Bartholomew playing trumpet in his band. He recorded 'I Hear You Knockin'' in 1955. It was an R&B hit but a white cover version by Gale Storm climbed the US pop charts. Fats didn't record 'I Hear You Knockin'' until 1958, but the song, which was written by Bartholomew and his wife, Pearl King, remained unknown in the UK. Until Dave Edmunds in 1970.

Dave Edmunds had been part of the Cardiff band, Love Sculpture and his frenzied guitar work on 'Sabre Dance' had taken the single into the Top 10 in 1968. Two brothers, Kingsley and Charles Ward, had converted a barn in Monmouth into a recording studio, Rockfield, and Edmunds was to work there, either producing himself or others in a neo-rock'n'roll style.

He says, "I'd heard 'Let's Work Together' by Wilbert Harrison while I was in America, but Canned Heat beat me to it. Instead, I went for 'I Hear You Knockin''. I was absolutely amazed when it got to number one because it had nothing going for it at all. I didn't have a band or a manager and the only publicity was a quarter-page ad in *Melody Maker*. Number one around

Jimi Hendrix, still the most revered guitarist in the history of rock

the world, amazing."

Dave had the problem of following it up: "Well, it's a great problem to have. The next couple of records didn't do anything and then I did some Phil Spector-type things, 'Baby I Love You' and 'Born To Be With You' and I was all right then."

Dave Edmunds has often been associated with Nick Lowe and it is a pity that their collaboration as Rockpile in 1980 with Billy Bremner and Terry Williams was not more acclaimed. Dave Edmunds' subsequent hits include 'I Knew The Bride' (1977) and 'Girls Talk' (1979). He has produced The Stray Cats, Everly Brothers, Chet Atkins, Carl Perkins, and Shakin' Stevens' 1985 number one, 'Merry Christmas Everyone'. In recent months, Dave has been touring with his guitar in a one-man show but admits that he needs accompaniment on a backing-track if he is to tackle 'Sabre Dance'.

295 Clive Dunn
Grandad

Label & Cat No.: **Gull GULS 14**

Producers: **John Cameron / Clive Dunn**

Writers: **Herbie Flowers / Kenny Pickett**

Date reached No.1: **9 January 1971**

Weeks at No.1: **3**

THE BBC-TV COMEDY SERIES, *DAD'S Army*, was created by Jimmy Perry and David Croft around the adventures of the Local Defence Volunteers, a group of men who were prevented by age or disability from joining the regular services. The brilliant casting included Arthur Lowe as the pompous Captain Mainwaring, John Le Mesurier as Sgt. Wilson and Clive Dunn as Lance-Corporal Jack Jones, the local butcher. One of Dunn's catch-phrases was "Permission to speak, sir." His solo album was to be called *Permission, To Sing, Sir!*

Clive Dunn, who was born in 1920, had seen action in the Second World War and he came to the public's attention as a supporting actor in *Bootsie And Snudge*. He built up a reputation playing older men.

Herbie Flowers, a member of Blue Mink and Sky, met Clive Dunn at a party and Clive, thinking of a single, asked him for a song. As Herbie was writing the song, Kenny Pickett from The Creation, called round and the chimes gave him the two notes that became 'Grandad'. He passed his melody to Kenny, who used the outdated images on a tin of *Quality Street* as the starting point for the words.

Looking like a benign, doting senior citizen, Clive sat in a rocking chair with his cap and scarf and was surrounded by children while he performed 'Grandad' on *Top Of The Pops*. We can reveal the extraordinary history of that rocking chair. It began its service as part of the TV series, *Relax With Michael Holliday*. After Holliday's death in 1963, the BBC commissioned a similar easy listening show from Val Doonican. So similar that Val used the same rocking chair and he was to make the album, *Val Doonican Rocks, But Gently*. The rocking chair also did service in *The Morecambe And Wise Show*. In the Seventies, the producer John Ammonds presented the chair to Mike's widow. It is now in the home of Mike's son, Michael Holliday Jr, on the Wirral. He says, "Whenever I sit in it and rock back and forth, I can't help myself. I start singing."

In 1974/5, Clive Dunn played another old codger, Sam Cobbett, in the sitcom, *My Old Man*, and, with shades of Old Mother Riley, his screen daughter was played by his wife, Priscilla Morgan. The hit single led to his own TV series, *Grandad*, from 1979 to 1984 in which he played the caretaker of the Parkview Rehearsal Hall and, naturally, everything went wrong.

Clive Dunn

296 George Harrison
My Sweet Lord

Label & Cat No.: **Apple R 5884**

Producers: **George Harrison with Phil Spector**

Writer: **George Harrison**

Date reached No.1: **30 January 1971**

Weeks at No.1: **5**

THROUGHOUT THE BEATLES' CAREER, and especially in the final years, George Harrison felt that his songwriting deserved more credit from John, Paul and George Martin. Even though he had written the best tracks ('Here Comes The Sun' and 'Something') on their last album, *Abbey Road*, he was permitted only two songs. When The Beatles disbanded, all his frustrations came tumbling out in a flurry of songs that made up his triple album, *All Things Must Pass*, produced by Phil Spector. Twice as expensive as a single album, it nevertheless reached number four in the UK and number one in the US. The third album was a rambling jam session, but otherwise it was packed with excellent material.

The key single was the inspirational 'My Sweet Lord', which George described as "a song to live up to". He was thrilled to be singing both 'Hallelujah' and 'Hare Krishna' in the same song. Although his inspiration had been the 1969 hit by The Edwin Hawkins Singers, 'Oh Happy Day', he was accused of plagiarising a 1963 hit by The Chiffons, 'He's So Fine'. It seems odd that Spector, who was well acquainted with the New York girl group scene, hadn't drawn attention to the similarity. Joey Molland of Badfinger who played rhythm guitar and sang backing vocals on the session says, "I was struck by the similarity but I didn't feel it was my place to say anything. We relied on The Beatles for work."

A few years later, Allen Klein's management contract with The Beatles was terminated and back in New York, he acquired the rights to Ronnie Mack's song, 'He's So Fine' – Mack himself had Hodgkins' disease and died in 1963. Was it revenge that prompted Klein to sue George? In 1976 a judge ruled that George was "not guilty of stealing the tune but there was a copyright infringement". His unconscious plagiarism cost him £1m. George responded by writing and recording the witty 'This Song'.

297 Mungo Jerry Baby Jump

Label & Cat No.: **Dawn DNX 2505**

Producer: **Barry Murray**

Writer: **Ray Dorset**

Date Reached No.1: **6 March 1971**

Weeks at No.1: **2**

ONE OF MUNGO JERRY'S REGULAR gigs was at The Northcote Arms in Southall. "A lot of Hell's Angels and Teds used to go there," says the group's hirsute lead singer, Ray Dorset, "and all the girls used to wear tiny little jumpers with leather skirts, and that gave me the idea for 'Baby Jump'. It was an aggressive, simple riff – (sings) 'Baby jump into my dreams'. Like 'In The Summertime', the single was too short and Barry Murray joined two bits together."

Within a few months, Mungo Jerry were playing The Fillmore East and West rather than The Northcote Arms. They became a major concert attraction and they could have been the first act since Gerry & The Pacemakers to go to number one with their first three releases, but something went wrong. One of the tracks was a Leadbelly song about cocaine, 'Have A Whiff On Me'. "It was an anti-drug song, but people thought it was a celebration of drugs," says Ray, "The Director of Public Prosecutions visited Dawn's offices and the single had to be repressed with a different title. 'Lady Rose' was selling well and we would have had our third number one without that trouble."

Tensions flared within the group as it became more and more a showcase for Ray Dorset's singing and songwriting. The guitarist Paul King and the pianist Colin Earl sacked Dorset, only to learn that Mungo Jerry had been registered in his name and they'd have to leave instead. They formed the Earl King Boogie Band but their witty 'Plastic Jesus' was banned by the BBC and the new group never got off the ground.

298 T. Rex Hot Love

Label & Cat No.: **Fly BUG 6**

Producer: **Tony Visconti**

Writer: **Marc Bolan**

Date reached No.1: **20 March 1971**

Weeks at No.1: **6**

MARK FELD WAS BORN IN HACKNEY, London on September 30, 1947 and, from the age of 12, he was obsessed with clothes. "I would steal or hustle to get them," he said. "All that mattered to me were clothes and I used to change about five times a day." He became the cardboard cut-out in John Temple's windows and, in 1962, his photograph appeared in a *Town* magazine article about mods.

Mark had been in a group at school, Susie & The Hula-Hoops, with Helen Shapiro, and now he was singing his quirky songs around folk clubs. In 1965 he recorded 'The Wizard' for Decca and became Marc Bolan. As part of John's Children, he achieved notoriety with the banned 'Desdemona' ("Lift up your skirt and fly"). He reflected, "John's Children was an electric group and I joined them because they needed a song-writer. You'll laugh at this but I left them because I thought they were getting too commercial."

Bolan formed an acoustic duo, Tyrannosaurus Rex, with the percussionist, Steve Peregrine Took. They played hippie hang-outs and were championed by John Peel. He wrote mystical songs with mystical titles – 'Salamanda Palaganda', 'Pewter Suitor', 'King Of The Rumbling Spires' – and had minor hits with 'Debora' and 'One Inch Rock'. Marc concluded, "Hippies don't buy records and I was bored with not being recognised."

In 1970 Marc found a new partner (Mickey Finn), switched to electric guitar, shortened the name to T. Rex and worked with the producer, Tony Visconti. T. Rex broke through with 'Ride A White Swan' and, augmenting the band with Steve Currie (bass) and Bill Legend (drums), 'Hot Love' followed. Like many T. Rex songs, 'Hot Love' was a nursery rhyme lyric about sex which leant heavily on his rock'n'roll favourites, borrowing 'uh, uh, uh' from 'All Shook Up' and a guitar riff from 'Heartbreak Hotel' as well as a 'Hey Jude'-styled coda.

With rouge, mascara and painted teardrops, Glam Rock – and Bolanmania – had arrived.

299 Dave & Ansil Collins Double Barrel

Label & Cat No.: **Technique TE 901**

Producer: **Winston Riley**

Writer: **Winston Riley**

Date reached No.1: **1 May 1971**

Weeks at No.1: **2**

DAVE BARKER WAS A SESSION VOCALIST on ska and reggae records in Kingston, Jamaica. He had local success with 'Shocks Of A Mighty' in 1970 and he made an album, *Dave Barker Meets The Upsetters*. Meanwhile, Ansil Collins had played Hammond organ on the backing track that was to become 'Double Barrel' for the writer and producer, Winston Riley. Dave was asked to do the vocal but found the music too lightweight. Winston's brother, Buster, encouraged him: "Think big, think Hercules or James Bond – 007" and from that, the record emerged.

Sly Dunbar plays drums on his first recording. As well as being a popular reggae record, it was also a skinhead anthem, hence its high chart position. Indeed, Dave & Ansil Collins were only the second reggae act to top the UK charts, the first being Desmond Dekker. 'Double Barrel' was also the first reggae record to make the US Top 30.

Promoting their record in the UK, Dave & Ansil Collins had a further Top 10 hit with 'Monkey Spanner', but 'Ton Up Kids' failed to make any impact. Ansil Collins has continued as a session musician, appearing on records by U Roy, Toots & The Maytals and Yellowman. Dave, now living in the UK, has made many reggae and soul records, and the duo have worked together including the 7-inch, 'Single Barrel', in 1975.

'Double Barrel' was sampled on the 1994 hit single by Chaka Demus & Pliers, 'Gal Wine', and Dave Barker appeared on an album with The Selecter, *Cruel Britannia*, in 1999.

300 Dawn
Knock Three Times

Label & Cat No.: **Bell 1146**
Producers: **Dave Appell / Hank Medress**
Writers: **Irwin Levine / Larry Russell Brown**
Date reached No.1: **15 May 1971**
Weeks at No.1: **5**

IN 1961 17-YEAR-OLD TONY ORLANDO, a Greek and Puerto-Rican American singer from New York, made the UK Top 10 with 'Bless You', a Barry Mann and Cynthia Weil song which was arranged by Carole King. He was given fine songs by the top Brill Building writers, but was unlucky as both 'Halfway To Paradise' and 'I'd Never Find Another You' were covered very successfully for the UK market by Billy Fury. His spooky and insidious 'Chills' failed to connect and can be viewed as a companion to Fury's 'Wondrous Place'.

As Tony wasn't able to maintain his career like his close friend Bobby Vee, he returned to the Brill Building and become an executive for a music publishing company, singing on demo records and commercials in his spare time. In 1970 the producers, Dave Appell (who recorded 'Applejack' in 1957) and Hank Medress (of The Tokens) made a record, 'Candida', but their record company, Bell, wanted a different lead singer. They asked Tony Orlando to supply a new vocal, which he did. The record, released under the name of Dawn, became a Top 10 in both the US and the UK. The group was named Dawn after the daughter of The Tokens' Jay Siegal.

The next song, 'Knock Three Times', was very much in The Drifters' style. This time the single went to number one in both countries and Tony realised that he would have to tour to avoid fake Dawns. It was only then that he met the backing vocalists on 'Candida' and 'Knock Three Times', Joyce Vincent and Telma Hopkins, who had also sung on The Four Tops' 'Reach Out I'll Be There' and Marvin Gaye's 'I Heard It Through The Grapevine'. Now slim and with long hair and a moustache, Tony Orlando became more successful than he had been in the Sixties.

Tony Orlando has performed over 2,000 times in Branson, Missouri. You may not think of this as a holiday destination but many chart performers end up there which makes it a paradise for record collectors.

301 Middle Of The Road
Chirpy Chirpy Cheep Cheep

Label & Cat No.: **RCA 2047**
Producers: **Giacomo Tosti / Ignacio Greco**
Writer: **Lally Stott**
Date reached No.1: **19 June 1971**
Weeks at No.1: **5**

THE CHIRPY 'CHIRPY CHIRPY CHEEP Cheep' was originally recorded by its composer, Liverpudlian Lally Scott, a former member of Denny Seyton & The Sabres. Neither that nor a cover version by Mac & Katie Kissoon attracted much attention.

A Glasgow band, Los Caracas, who played Latin-American music and had some popularity in Europe, were signed in Rome by Giacomi Tosti to RCA Records. He recommended the song and they recorded it under the name of Middle Of The Road. The group consisted of lead singer Sally Carr, Ken Andrew (drums), Eric Lewis (bass, piano) and his brother, Ian (guitar, bagpipes). The song became a hit in Spain and Belgium and then, with support from Tony Blackburn, soared up the UK charts. The song appeared to be about baby Don, who had been abandoned by his parents, but was it social comment? Don may have been a bird.

The follow-up, 'Tweedle Dee, Tweedle Dum', also written by Lally Stott and about fighting Scottish clans, went to number two. Middle Of The Road had further hits with the Spanish song 'Soley Soley' (5) and then finally with 'Sacramento' (23) and 'Samson And Delilah' (26).

The group disbanded in 1976 and Ken Andrew went into video production. He reformed the band with its original line-up in 1991, but Eric dropped out due to ill health and Ian set up a rival group with his son and daughter-in-law. As for Lally Stott, he was killed in a motorbike accident in 1977 on the day of the Queen's Silver Jubilee.

302 T. Rex
Get It On

Label & Cat No.: **Fly BUG 10**
Producer: **Tony Visconti**
Writer: **Marc Bolan**
Date reached No.1: **24 July 1971**
Weeks at No.1: **4**

THE OPENING RIFF ON 'GET IT ON' WAS reminiscent of 'Honky Tonk Women', the whole song reeked of Chuck Berry with even a 'Meanwhile, I'm still thinking' lifted directly from 'Little Queenie', but somehow Marc Bolan managed to sound original. He admitted, "I don't sing the old rock'n'roll songs myself. I prefer to change the words and make new songs out of them. That's all 'Jeepster' is." 'Get It On' was the same, but it added sex, 'You're dirty sweet and you're my girl.'

Marc Bolan said, "My music is all about sex. 'Get It On' is a great screwing record. I bet over 20,000 kids have been conceived to that one.

'Hot Love' is another and so is 'New York City'. People write in and tell me their experiences. I think that's great. I like to think of my records being used for other purposes than listening and dancing. I think of myself as a utensil like a non-stick pan."

'Get It On', which featured backing vocals from Howard Kaylan and Mark Volman of The Turtles, was also featured on T. Rex's *Electric Warrior*, which topped the album charts, but there was difficulty in establishing T. Rextasy in the States. 'Ride A White Swan' and 'Hot Love' were only minor hits, and then Marc broke through with 'Get It On'. "There was an American group which already had a song out called 'Get It On In The Morning'," he recalled, "and it had been banned for being too suggestive. We therefore changed the title to 'Bang A Gong'. We sold a million but it did take the record nine months to go gold." The song returned to the US Top 10 in 1985 with a version by The Power Station featuring Robert Palmer.

303 Diana Ross
I'm Still Waiting

Label & Cat No.:	**Tamla Motown TMG 781**
Producer:	**Deke Richards**
Writer:	**Deke Richards**
Date Reached No.1:	**21 August 1971**
Weeks at No.1:	**4**

BERRY GORDY WANTED TO MAKE Diana Ross the star of The Supremes, so in the summer of 1967 he amended the group name to Diana Ross & The Supremes. Diana recalled, "I felt separated from the group, still part of the group and, at the same time, not part of the group."

By the end of the Sixties, The Supremes and Diana Ross went their separate ways. Their final hit together was 'Someday We'll Be Together'. Seeing as Diana and The Supremes were getting fed up, it seemed unlikely that this would ever be the case.

Motown kept on promoting both acts with The Supremes getting off to the better start with five Top 10 hits in a row. Diana's solo career was a little more shaky. Her first project was supposed to be a duet with Bones Howe on Laura Nyro's 'Time And Love' but that was shelved when she was teamed with Motown staff writers Nick Ashford and Valerie Simpson. Her first hit 'Reach Out And Touch (Somebody's Hand)' failed to make the Top 30 and the accompanying album *Everything Is Everything* wasn't well received either. Apart from impressive covers of 'The Long And Winding Road' and '(They Long To Be) Close To You', it featured a new track entitled 'I'm Still Waiting'.

Radio One DJ Tony Blackburn, a Motown and Diana fan, was given an early pressing of the album. He started championing 'I'm Still Waiting' and told Motown that he would play it every day until they released it as a single. When they realised there was nothing to lose, Motown agreed.

Diana's next album was released in America as *Surrender*. But to capitalise on the success of the single, in the UK it was re-titled *I'm Still Waiting* and had the track tagged on.

For Diana, 1971 was a mammoth year. In January she married Robert Silberstein. Three months later she was given her own television show, *Diana!,* in which she introduced the world to The Jackson 5 and in August, she gave birth to her daughter, Rhonda.

'I'm Still Waiting' only reached number 63 in the US, so when Diana performed the song on her UK tour, she was amazed at the reaction of the British public and even more astounded when she received standing ovations. It became her anthem for years.

Diana Ross

304 The Tams
Hey Girl Don't Bother Me

Label & Cat No.:	**Probe PRO 532**
Producer:	**Rick Hall**
Writer:	**Ray Whitley**
Date reached No.1:	**18 September 1971**
Weeks at No.1:	**3**

THE SOUL GROUP, THE TAMS, STARTED as schoolboys in the Fifties in Atlanta, Georgia, and, by 1960, the line-up was Floyd Ashton, Horace Key, Robert Smith and the Pope brothers, Joe and Charlie. They wanted to look a little different so they bought tam-o'-shanter hats, hence their name. Their 1962 single, 'Untie Me', produced by Joe South, became an R&B success and, shortly after Al Cottle had replaced Floyd Ashton, they started recording for Rick Hall in Muscle Shoals. In 1964 The Tams made the US Top 10 with 'What Kind Of Fool (Do You Think I Am)', which featured lead singer Joe Pope and bass singer Robert Smith. The follow-up, which did well and was also written by one of the musicians Ray Whitley, was 'You Lied To Your Daddy'.

The Tams had several US R&B hits in the Sixties, notably 'Hey Girl Don't Bother Me' (1964) and 'Be Young Be Foolish Be Happy' (1968), but nothing happened on the UK charts. However, their records became Northern soul favourites and in 1970, a reissue of 'Be Young, Be Foolish, Be Happy' made the UK Top 40. Much to The Tams' surprise, 'Hey Girl Don't Bother Me' then went to number one.

In 1987 their dance record 'There Ain't Nothing Like Shaggin'' became a hit record, largely because the phrase meant something different here. On the Virgin label, incidentally.

305 Rod Stewart
Maggie May

Label & Cat No.: **Mercury 6058 097**
Producer: **Rod Stewart**
Writers: **Rod Stewart / Martin Quittenton**
Date reached No.1: **9 October 1971**
Weeks at No.1: **5**

RODERICK DAVID STEWART WAS BORN on January 10, 1945, in London where his Scottish father owned a newsagent's shop in Holloway. The young Rod was preoccupied with football and had a successful trial with Brentford FC, but he left when he was given menial jobs. Turning his attention to music, he played folk clubs with Wizz Jones then tried his luck in Spain but was deported for busking. His break came in January 1964 when Long John Baldry heard him playing the harmonica at Twickenham railway station. This brief encounter led to him joining Baldry's Hoochie Coochie Men, and his debut single, 'Good Morning Little Schoolgirl' was released by Decca. In 1965 a documentary about him, *Rod The Mod*, was screened on BBC-TV, but he was not a star like Eric Burdon or Mick Jagger, and he would think, "I know I can sing as well as these guys. When is it going to be my turn?" He has told reporters, "You won't ever hear me being humble about the voice 'cos I know it's brilliant."

A restless spirit, Rod The Mod moved from the Hoochie Coochie Men to Steampacket, Shotgun Express and The Jeff Beck Group. In 1969 he was invited to join The Small Faces, now renamed The Faces after the departure of Steve Marriott. The line-up consisted of Stewart, Ronnie Lane, Ron Wood, Kenney Jones and Ian McLagan. They signed with Warners and he also signed a solo contract with Phonogram. Rod received excellent reviews for his solo albums, *An Old Raincoat Won't Ever Let You Down* and *Gasoline Alley*. If 'Handbags And Gladrags' had been released as a single, would it have been his first number one?

Martin Quittenton thought of the melody for 'Maggie May' whilst taking the underground to the studio for Rod's third solo album, *Every Picture Tells A Story*. Rod wrote the lyrics, thinking back to when he was a schoolboy and had a sexual initiation from an older woman. He said, "I gave her a damn good shagging actually, but it wasn't a good innings for me so I'd better not go on about it. Very messy, if I remember rightly."

Rod wanted the album to have the feel of Bob Dylan's *Blonde On Blonde*, but he was relaxed about it as he and his musicians spent plenty of time in the pub. The drummer, Micky Waller, would only bring his sticks to the session and would play whatever was around. For 'Maggie May', there was only half a kit, but he turned that to the song's advantage. Ian McLagan and Ron Wood from The Faces were on the record, Martin Quittenton played classical guitar, Pete Sears celeste and Ray Jackson from Lindisfarne mandolin. The name, Maggie May, does not occur in the song, and Rod had borrowed the title from a Liverpool folk song about a Lime Street prostitute.

The official A-side was 'Reason To Believe', a gravel-voiced version of Tim Hardin's laconic love song. It entered the Top 20 in September 1971 but soon everyone was asking for 'Maggie May'. When Ray Jackson was unavailable for *Top Of The Pops*, John Peel mimed to his playing. Both the single and the album topped the UK and US charts simultaneously and Rod became the most familiar Face. This, as we will see, caused considerable friction.

306 Slade
Coz I Luv You

Label & Cat No.: **Polydor 2058 155**
Producer: **Chas Chandler**
Writers: **Noddy Holder / Jim Lea**
Date reached No.1: **13 November 1971**
Weeks at No.1: **4**

WOLVERHAMPTON BASED NEVILLE 'Noddy' Holder (lead vocals, guitar), Jim Lea (bass guitar, violin), Dave Hill (lead guitar) and Don Powell (drums), began life as a hard working covers band, The 'N Betweens, recording a single for EMI in 1966, 'You Better Run', produced by Kim Fowley. They became Ambrose Slade and released an album, *Beginnings*, in 1969. Newcastle born Chas Chandler, the former Animal who had managed Jimi Hendrix, saw them in the studio and suggested that they played a London club, Rasputin's. Noddy Holder recalls, "There were only 20 people in the place but we were doing audience participation when everybody else was doing long solos and very introverted music. He loved us and signed us the next day."

Chas Chandler became their manager and record producer and, liking their lack of sophistication, thought he would market them as a skinhead band, now called Slade. The Doc Martens and closely cropped hair didn't work, so they grew their hair but still retained a rebellious stance. "It didn't work because skinheads liked reggae and we played rock with a violin player," says Dave Hill, "but it was important to have a look. When people talk about Slade, they remember the way we looked. The visual image was as important as the music. I once shaved my head because I thought it would help the group."

Their revival of Little Richard's little known 'Get Down And Get With It' established Noddy's rasping vocals (not a long way, incidentally, from John Lennon's on 'Instant Karma'), and Chas encouraged them to write their own material. Noddy Holder says, "He told us to write a hit song, just like that, and that's not very easy to do. Me and Jimmy wrote 'Coz I Luv You' in 20 minutes and Chas was raving about it. We felt that it wasn't rocky enough for Slade so we added all the handclapping and boot-stomping, which made it much more commercial and became our trademark."

The record also featured Jim Lea's electric violin, which he'd played in a youth orchestra, and the title was misspelt as 'Coz I Luv You'. Noddy Holder: "We thought 'Because I Love You' was a wet title for a song and so we used the spelling that would be on toilet walls in the Midlands and that made it more hard-hitting."

Noddy adds, "When it went to number one, it gave us an enormous amount of confidence in our writing abilities. We had the courage of our

Rod Stewart topped the UK and US single and album charts simultaneously in 1971 with 'Maggie May' and Every Picture Tells A Story

convictions that we could keep on doing it." All six of Slade's number ones were written by Noddy and Jim.

307 Benny Hill
Ernie (The Fastest Milkman In The West)

Label & Cat No.: **Columbia DB 8833**

Producer: **Wally Ridley**

Writer: **Benny Hill**

Date reached No.1: **11 December 1971**

Weeks at No.1: **4**

IN 1940 THE 16-YEAR-OLD BENNY HILL had a job as a milkman, riding a horse and cart around Eastleigh in Hampshire. In 1956 he returned with a film crew for a spoof on a western song, 'Ernie (The Fastest Milkman In The West)'. And that, it would seem, was that. Between 1956 and 1971 he made numerous television appearances and yet he never performed the pastiche. Many people have assumed that 'Ernie' was a parody of Lorne Greene's US number one, 'Ringo', but it was written eight years earlier. By coincidence, there is also a parody of 'Ringo' 'The Ballad Of Irving (The 142nd Fastest Gun In The West)' by Frank Gallop.

Benny Hill used comic songs in his shows. His Sixties record producer, Tony Hatch says, "All Benny's tunes sounded the same which didn't matter in a television series. He would sing a different lyric to the same tune a week later. This wouldn't work for records and so I would polish up his tunes and or write entirely different ones. He didn't mind me doing it at all. He knew he couldn't write new tunes himself." Under Hatch's guidance, Benny Hill did well with 'Gather In The Mushrooms', 'Transistor Radio' and 'Harvest Of Love' but his wittiest record was 'Pepys' Diary': "Lord Clarendon walks swiftly on, But naughty Samuel peeps."

In 1971 he dusted down 'Ernie' and recorded it at Abbey Road for a Christmas single. The promotional film for *Top Of The Pops* had him battling with his rival for Sue's affection, Two-Ton Ted From Teddington. Although Benny did not have a follow-up hit, 'Ernie' led to something far more lucrative – TV commercials for Unigate.

Unfortunately for Benny Hill, not only did he become unfashionable, he became objectionable, and in 1987, Ben Elton launched this tirade against him: "You have Benny Hill in the late Eighties, chasing half-naked women around a park when we know in Britain, women can't even walk safe in a park any more. I could say 'fuck' 1,000 times on telly and I wouldn't be nearly as offensive as that." Benny was stunned – he had been brought up in a world where entertainers didn't criticise each other.

In 1989 Benny Hill's TV series with Thames Television was cancelled and although he achieved enormous popularity in the States, he was a broken man. And a lonely one. When Frankie Howerd died in April 1992, Benny's agent released a statement saying that Benny was very upset by the news, little knowing that Benny already lay dead from a heart attack in his Teddington flat. Not having left a will, his £7million fortune went to nephews and nieces he barely knew.

308 The New Seekers
I'd Like To Teach The World To Sing (In Perfect Harmony)

Label & Cat No.: **Polydor 2058 184**

Producer: **David Mackay**

Writers: **Roger Cook / Roger Greenaway / William Backer / Billy Davis**

Date reached No.1: **8 January 1972**

Weeks at No.1: **4**

THE SEEKERS DISBANDED WHEN Judith Durham left in 1968 but one of the group, Keith Potger, felt that there was still a market for a mixed-sex harmony group singing

cheerful, commercial, wholesome songs and he formed The New Seekers. He teamed Lyn Paul and Eve Graham from The Nocturnes with Peter Doyle, Marty Kristian and Paul Layton. They had a small hit with Melanie's 'What Have They Done To My Song, Ma?' in 1970 and followed it with Delaney & Bonnie's 'Never Ending Song Of Love', which went to number two.

The songwriter, Roger Cook, recalls, "Roger Greenaway and I wrote a song – well, he wrote most of it – called 'True Love And Apple Pie', which, let's face it, is a terrible title. We knew a singer called Susan Shirley, who was managed by her husband, and they loved the song. They put it out as a single but it did nothing."

A few months later, the two Rogers met the Coca-Cola's marketing team with a view to writing a jingle. "They wanted us to write a tune that would incorporate their jingle 'It's the real thing'. They wanted a tune that went from the C chord to the D and we already had 'True Love And Apple Pie'. We changed it to 'I'd like to buy the world a Coke', collected $5,000 and thought no more about it until the ad was broadcast."

Fellow songwriter Roger Greenaway explains, "'I'd Like to Buy The World A Coke' started out as a radio commercial. It wasn't very successful, but then somebody had the bright idea of using it as the music for a television commercial showing some kids on a hill. The commercial was so popular that Coca-Cola was getting thousands of letters a week. We amended the lyrics to remove all references to Coca-Cola, and 'I'd Like To Teach The World To Sing (In Perfect

The New Seekers

Harmony)' was a number one hit throughout the world for The New Seekers."

Lyn Paul says, "It would have been a boring song if it had been recorded by a solo singer, but all the counter-melodies make it." Lyn was doing cabaret once and someone requested 'I'd Like To Teach The World To Sin'.

309 T. Rex
Telegram Sam

Label & Cat No.: **T. Rex 101**

Producer: **Tony Visconti**

Writer: **Marc Bolan**

Date reached No.1: **5 February 1972**

Weeks at No.1: **2**

After the chart-topping albums, *Electric Warrior* and *Bolan Boogie*, Marc Bolan released his third album in a year, *The Slider*, complete with cover photographs by Ringo Starr. The album only went to number four, possibly because there was too much T. Rex product around. Marc would boast that he could write 10 albums in a year, which isn't difficult when you're basing so many of the songs on rock'n'roll favourites or what you have previously done. 'Telegram Sam' sounds like 'Get It On, Part 2'.

Just who is Marc Bolan's 'main man', Telegram Sam? "Someone who used to do little services for me," he announced, cryptically suggesting it might be a song about drug-dealing. However, the most likely candidate is Tony Secunda who was brought in to set up his new record label, T. Rex. With no thought of political correctness, Jungle Faced Jake would be his black assistant, Sid Walker. Golden Nose Slim and Purple Pie Pete remain a mystery, but Bobby, the 'natural born poet' is Bob Dylan. The blues singer, Howlin' Wolf, gets a namecheck at the end and Bolan refers to himself with "Ain't no square with my corkscrew hair".

As Marc said, "I like my songs to be durable to the ear and exciting to the mind."

310 Chicory Tip
Son Of My Father

Label & Cat No.: **CBS 7737**

Producers: **Roger Easterby / Des Champ**

Writers: **Giorgio Moroder / Peter Bellotte / Michael Holm**

Date reached No.1: **19 February 1972**

Weeks at No.1: **3**

The bass player Barry Mayger and the guitarist Rick Foster were schoolboy friends in Maidstone, Kent and they formed their first band, The Sonics, in 1971 when they were 15. Members came and went but by 1967, they were Chicory Tip with Peter Hewson as their lead vocalist and Mick Russell on drums. When Mick married and moved to Wales, Brian Shearer took over and they were signed by CBS in 1970. Their first four singles – which included 'I Love Onions' (presumably another component of the Chicory Tip salad) – flopped, but a cover version of Giorgio Moroder's US hit, 'Son Of My Father', took them to the top. Like Moroder, they featured a synthesiser, here played by Chris Thomas, who became a leading record producer.

Their follow-ups, 'What's Your Name' and 'Good Grief Christina', made the Top 20 but their next release, 'Cigarettes, Women And Wine', was banned by the BBC for fear of leading teenagers into bad habits.

Rick Foster left the band in 1972 to join Edison Lighthouse, hardly the best career move you might think, but he was with them for 25 years and Chicory Tip disbanded in 1975. In 1997 Chicory Tip reformed in their hit-making line-up and they released the CD, *Chicory Tip In 2000*.

Co-writer Roger Easterby managed Kent-based Vanity Fare, who had three UK Top 20 hits in the late Sixties.

311 Nilsson
Without You

Label & Cat No.: **RCA 2165**

Producer: **Richard Perry**

Writers: **Pete Ham / Tommy Evans**

Date reached No.1: **11 March 1972**

Weeks at No.1: **5**

Badfinger were part of the Beatles' Apple label and while they were working on an album, Pete Ham promised his girlfriend, Beverley, that they would enjoy an evening out together. In the event, he decided instead to stay in the studio. When he said he would make it up to her, Beverley said it was okay, and Pete replied, "Your mouth's smiling but your eyes are not." This became the line, "You always smile but in your eyes your sorrow shows" and the song, with a chorus from Tommy Evans, became 'Without You'.

The song was included on Badfinger's 1970 album, *No Dice*. Harry Nilsson heard it and thought it was by The Beatles. He was very impressed and so was his producer, Richard Perry, who provided an achingly sad arrangement to showcase his voice. The song, with its repeated line, "I can't live if living is without you", sounds like a suicide note.

Nilsson's recording was so extraordinary that the record was a transatlantic number one. It was his only UK Top 20 hit, and it is surprising that his equally strong interpretative performance on Fred Neil's 'Everybody's Talkin'' for the film *Midnight Cowboy* only made number 23. He would go on to befriend The Beatles, especially John Lennon, who produced his album *Pussycats* in 1974. He died on January 15, 1994.

Badfinger, who had their own hits with 'Come And Get It' (1970), 'No Matter What' (1971) and 'Day After Day' (1972), were a popular touring band, but their affairs were a mess – this is no fault of Apple's – and they never received monies due to them. In 1975 Pete

Harry Nilsson

Ham told Tommy Evans, "I know a way out. I'll see you again." The next morning he was found hanged in his garage.

Completely distressed, Tommy Evans quit the music business but he reformed Badfinger in 1978. The royalties for 'Without You' still weren't forthcoming, his new band fell apart acrimoniously and he wished Pete was still around. In 1983 after singing some Everly Brothers songs with his wife, Marianne, Tommy Evans hanged himself.

The popularity of 'Without You' was strengthened in 1994 by Mariah Carey's revival, which again was a transatlantic number one. The senior US publishing organisation, ASCAP, certified it as the most played song of the year and two Badfinger members (Joey Molland and Mike Gibbins) and their UK manager, Bill Collins, the father of actor Lewis Collins, received the award.

312 The Pipes & Drums & Military Band Of The Royal Scots Dragoon Guards Amazing Grace

Label & Cat No.: **RCA 2191**

Producer: **Peter Kerr**

Writer: **John Newton**

Date reached No.1: **15 April 1972**

Weeks at No.1: **5**

When a slave ship ran into a storm in 1748, its captain John Newton promised to give up the trade and dedicate his life to God if they survived. They did survive and, true to his word, he became a clergyman, writing 'Amazing Grace' about his experience in his rectory in the Buckinghamshire village of Olney. John Newton indicated the shame of what he had been doing by referring to himself as a 'wretch' in the song. He befriended the MP William Wilberforce and they did much to abolish slavery. Newton wrote, "I hope it will always be a subject of humiliating reflection to me, that I was once an active instrument in a business at which my heart now shudders."

John Newton wrote many well-known hymns including 'Glorious Things Of Thee Are Spoken' and 'How Sweet The Name Of Jesus Sounds', although before 1972, 'Amazing Grace' was rarely sung in UK churches. It was, however, very popular in America.

In 1969 the American folk singer Judy Collins was at a social gathering and they wanted to end it with a song. Everybody knew at least part of 'Amazing Grace' and she led the singing. Her record producer, Mark Abramson, asked her to record it and she thought it would be a wonderful response to the war in Vietnam. She wrote in her 1998 autobiography, *Singing Lessons*, "The war was still raging. There was nothing to do, I thought, but to pray and sing hymns to life. Nothing left but to sing 'Amazing Grace'."

'Amazing Grace' was a Top 10 hit for Judy Collins in December 1970 and it was to spend 67 weeks on the charts. In 1971 a tribute LP, *Farewell To The Greys*, paid tribute to the Royal Scots Greys (2nd Dragoon), who had amalgamated with the 35th Carabiniers (Prince Of Wales Dragoon Guards). Their bandmaster was W.O.I.C.I. Herbert and their Pipe Major, W.O.I.I.J.Pryde. The record was produced by Peter Kerr, who had played with the early Sixties trad jazz band, The Clyde Valley Stompers. Peter Kerr was to give up record production to become an orange farmer in Majorca and he has written the books, *Snowball Oranges* and *Mañana Mañana*.

"I loved that version," said Judy Collins in 2004 of The Royal Scots Dragoon Guards, "and I also got paid for it. I owned the publishing on my version and they used the harmony. The duo that recorded it here a couple of years ago (Robson & Jerome) also used my version, which is nice."

The Dragoon Guards were stationed in West Germany when 'Amazing Grace', which strongly featured the bagpipes, was released as a single. The DJ, Keith Fordyce played it regularly on his *Late Night Extra* on BBC Radio 2 and soon it was taken up by other programmes and other stations. It topped the charts within three weeks and remained on the listings for a total of 27 weeks.

The director of bagpipe music at Edinburgh Castle thought that the instrument was being demeaned, but he had misjudged the situation as one million people were buying a bagpipes record for the first time. 'Amazing Grace' has become a mainstay of the repertoire for bagpipe bands and Glen Campbell closes his act with 'Amazing Grace' on the pipes.

Among the many parody versions is The Putnam String County Band with "Amazing grass, How sweet the smell, That stoned a wreck like me."

313 T. Rex Metal Guru

Label & Cat No.: **EMI MARC 1**

Producer: **Tony Visconti**

Writer: **Marc Bolan**

Date reached No.1: **20 May 1972**

Weeks at No.1: **4**

T. Rex had switched from the independent Fly label to EMI and Marc was given his own label for the first single, 'Telegram Sam'. It turned out to be short-lived as EMI was reviewing its practices, and all subsequent releases, starting with 'Metal Guru', were on EMI with a MARC prefix.

'Metal Guru' was recorded outside Paris at the 'honky chateau', Château D'Hiérouville. The song was repetitive even by Marc Bolan standards. He remarked, "My lyrics always come before the music. Repetition comes into my songs a lot because I think my lyrics are so obscure that they need to be hammered home. You need to hear them eight or nine times before they start to make sense. I don't see anything wrong with that. Some artists repeat the most simple lyrics 40 times over. Look at 'I Want To Hold Your Hand' or 'All You Need Is Love'."

The lyric was about one of Marc's preoccupations, cars, although he didn't drive, but he added a mystic dimension, saying, "'Metal Guru' is a festival of life song. I believe in a god, but I have no religion, and I thought God would

Marc Bolan, the bopping elf, in the studio with his American producer Tony Visconti

be all alone without a telephone." Rather like Marc in fact – "I don't answer the telephone anymore. I have codes where people ring me at certain times."

'Metal Guru' was T. Rex's final number one but they continued with 'Children Of The Revolution', 'Solid Gold Easy Action', '20th Century Boy' and 'The Groover'. By 1974 the glory days were over and Bolan split with his producer, Tony Visconti. Mickey Finn left and he had changing line-ups for T. Rex after that. He also split with his wife, June, and had a new partner, Gloria Jones, who gave him a son, Rolan Bolan. (Is that a better or worse name than Zowie Bowie?)

Attempting to reinvent himself Bolan did a tour with The Damned in 1977 and hosted a hip TV series, *Marc*, with David Bowie, The Jam and The Stranglers. When Elvis died on August 16, he said, "I certainly hope I don't pop off in the next few weeks as I'll only get page three coverage." Marc Bolan was killed a month later, on September 16, when his car hit a tree on the southern side of Barnes Common, a mile from his London home. Gloria Jones, who was driving, left the country, seemingly to avoid prosecution. Every year on the anniversary of his death, fans gather round the tree in Gypsy Lane which has been turned into a shrine for the corkscrew-haired pop star.

314 Don McLean
Vincent

Label & Cat No.: **United Artists UP 35259**

Producer: **Ed Freeman**

Writer: **Don McLean**

Date Reached No.1: **17 June 1972**

Weeks at No.1: **2**

THE FIRST SINGLE LIFTED FROM DON McLean's *American Pie* album was the title track and a tribute to Buddy Holly. The next track released from it, 'Vincent', was another tribute song; this time to the 19th Century Dutch artist Vincent Van Gogh. McLean got the inspiration after reading a book about his life.

Don was born in New York on October 2, 1945. He had aspirations of making a living in the sports world, but asthma put paid to those dreams. Instead, he turned to music and learned to play the banjo and guitar. When he was 15, his father died and that was when he decided he wanted to be a musician.

The opening line, 'Starry starry night' refers to one of Van Gogh's better-known paintings, *The Starry Night*, which is housed in the Museum of Modern Art in New York.

When it was first released, 'Vincent' so impressed the directors and staff at the Vincent Van Gogh Museum in Amsterdam that they played the track on a daily basis. The original sheet music is buried in a time capsule in the bowels of the Museum.

In 1973 Don learned that he himself was the inspiration for a song. Singer Lori Leiberman had attended a Don McLean concert in Los Angeles. She wrote a poem expressing her feelings about it and asked songwriters Norman Gimbel and Charles Fox to write a tune to accompany it. The result was 'Killing Me Softly With His Song'.

When Don McLean heard that Madonna had recorded a version of his 'American Pie' for her album *Music* in 2000, he responded: "Great, I won't ever have to work again."

315 Slade
Take Me Back 'Ome

Label & Cat No.: **Polydor 2058 231**

Producer: **Chas Chandler**

Writers: **Noddy Holder / Jim Lea**

Date reached No.1: **1 July 1972**

Weeks at No.1: **1**

THERE WAS NO SUBTLETY ABOUT SLADE. They sang raucous songs and wore loud clothes, especially Noddy Holder with his chequered trews, top hat and Dickensian sideburns, who, in another life, would have been a circus clown or even Harry H. Corbett in fancy dress. The pixie-like Dave Hill wore a suit of gold leather or a nun-like outfit in white satin with gold trim. By contrast Jim Lea and Don Powell were relatively restrained in bright satin. Their platform shoes made it difficult for them to escape from fans, and Dave Hill fell and broke his ankle at Liverpool Stadium.

Slade's follow-up to 'Coz I Luv You', 'Look Wot You Dun' reached number four but they returned to the top with 'Take Me Back 'Ome'. Noddy Holder explains how his songwriting partnership with Jimmy Lea worked: "Jim was more the melody man and me the lyric man. We would not present a song to the band until we had a finished song that sounded good on guitar or piano. Unless the song sounded good without the arrangement, it went in the bin. Then we put the Slade stamp on it, if you like."

'Take Me Back 'Ome' is typical of Slade's style. Noddy, with plenty of echo on his voice, sings raucously as he asks a girl to take him home for the night. The chorus is very catchy but the whole arrangement owes something to Free's 'All Right Now'.

There was no sleeping while Slade was around so it was amusing that Neville Holder's nickname was Noddy. "I got that at school when I was seven," he says. "I was always dropping off to sleep. I even remember the guy who gave me the name, John Robbins."

316 Donny Osmond
Puppy Love

Label & Cat No.: **MGM 2006 104**

Producers: **Mike Curb / Ray Ruff**

Writer: **Paul Anka**

Date reached No.1: **8 July 1972**

Weeks at No.1: **5**

SINGING FAMILIES HAVE BEEN AROUND since the dawn of time, but in the Seventies they enjoyed more success than ever before. Leading the pack were The Jacksons, The

Don McLean is probably more famous for 'American Pie' – which reached number two – than for his number one hits 'Vincent' and 'Crying'

Osmonds and The Nolans.

George and Olive Osmond were devoted Mormons based in Ogden, Utah. Their first two children, Viri and Tommy, had hearing difficulties, but all the rest became musicians: Alan (born 1949), Wayne (1951), Merrill (1953), Jay (1955), Donny (1957), Marie (1959) and Jimmy (1963). Alan, Wayne, Merrill and Jay formed a harmony quartet in 1960 and, following a trip to Disneyland, they appeared on one of their TV specials. As a result, they became a regular part of *The Andy Williams Show* from 1962 to 1967 with Donny joining them when he was six. The Osmonds then spent two years on *The Jerry Lewis Show*. "Our father was an army sergeant and so we got our discipline from him," says Jimmy today. "We were always having to learn something new. Ice-skating, playing banjos, pianos or dancing."

The Osmonds recorded for Williams's label, Barnaby, and MCA, but the hits started coming when they signed with MGM. In 1971 the wizards of Os had a US number one with 'One Bad Apple', which was very much in the same vein as The Jacksons. Donny topped the US charts with a revival of the Gerry Goffin and Carole King song, 'Go Away Little Girl'.

The breakthrough in the UK came the following year. The Osmonds had a minor hit with their song, 'Down By The Lazy River' and then Donny revived Paul Anka's US hit, 'Puppy Love'. Although the song had been a big hit for the then-teen idol Paul Anka in 1960, it had only made the UK Top 40 and so 'Puppy Love' was unknown here. What sold the record was Donny's supercharged emotion on "Someone help me, help me, help me please." "Mike Curb told me to give it my all on 'Puppy Love'," says Donny now, "so I suppose it worked. Paul Anka said he would write me some new songs and I'm still waiting."

Donny Osmond

317 Alice Cooper
School's Out

Label & Cat No.: **Warner K 16188**

Producer: **Bob Erzin**

Writers: **Alice Cooper / Michael Bruce**

Date reached No.1: **12 August 1972**

Weeks at No.1: **3**

In the mid-Sixties, Vincent Furnier formed a band to play Rolling Stones covers. The group had various names but when they chose The Nazz, they discovered that Todd Rundgren had a band of the same name. At a séance with an Ouija board, their new name came to them – Alice Cooper – well, it did if you believe the hype. Initially, Alice Cooper related to the whole band – Furnier, Glen Buxton (guitar), Michael Bruce (keyboards), Dennis Dunaway (bass) and Neal Smith (drums) – although Furnier soon took the name for himself.

Frank Zappa, who also discovered Captain Beefheart and Wild Man Fischer, had them open for The Mothers Of Invention. Alice Cooper appeared in the film, *Diary Of A Mad Housewife*, and were part of The Toronto Rock'n'Roll Festival in 1969 with John Lennon, Bo Diddley and Gene Vincent. Alice threw a hen into the audience, evidently unaware that hens couldn't fly.

By 1972 Alice Cooper had an elaborate stage presentation with an electric chair, a guillotine and a boa constrictor. There have been many mishaps since – Furnier has nearly died a couple of times and one snake was fatally bitten by his lunch, a rat. In order to give himself a demonic look, Furnier applied black make-up to his face.

Alice Cooper had his / their first US hit with 'Eighteen' in 1971 and then came 'School's Out', the perfect record for the summer holidays. The anthem contained a neat line in irony: "Well we got no class / And we got no principles / And we got no innocence / We can't even think of a word that rhymes." The album of the same name made number four and then Alice Cooper topped the album charts with *Billion Dollar Babies*. Following 'School's Out', Alice Cooper had a succession of hit singles – 'Elected', 'Hello Hurray', 'No More Mr. Nice Guy' and 'Teenage Lament '74'.

Furnier, a sharp operator, has managed to retain the public interest in a clown like Alice. He had a number two hit with 'Poison' in 1989, and was Freddy Krueger's father in *Freddy's Dead: The Final Nightmare* (1991). Taking time out from playing golf (A round with Alice?), he toured the UK in 2003 and said, "I thought I'd be tired of doing it by now, but I'm not. I love Alice. I'm Alice's biggest fan."

318 Rod Stewart
You Wear It Well

Label & Cat No.: **Mercury 6052 171**

Producer: **Rod Stewart**

Writers: **Rod Stewart / Martin Quittenton**

Date reached No.1: **2 September 1972**

Weeks at No.1: **1**

Effectively, the follow-up to 'Maggie May' was The Faces' 'Stay With Me'. This anthem-like song went to number six. Rod's fourth solo album, *Never A Dull Moment*, was released in the summer of 1972 and the first single was 'You Wear It Well'. To a degree, Rod was treading water as in both structure and arrangement the song is similar to 'Maggie May', but it had charm in its own right and contained Rod's wonderful rhyme, "Your basement parties and your brother's karate". Ron Wood from The Faces was featured on guitar.

Never A Dull Moment was another chart-topping album and it included the Jimi Hendrix song, 'Angel', which was coupled with 'What Made Milwaukee Famous (Has Made A Loser Out Of Me)' for another Top 10 single. Before his next number one in 1975 with 'Sailing', Rod had further Top 10 hits with 'Oh No Not My Baby' and 'Farewell', which was backed with a Sam Cooke medley of 'Bring It On Home To Me' and 'You Send Me'. With The Faces, he was charting with 'Cindy Incidentally', 'Pool Hall

Richard' / 'I Wish It Would Rain (With A Trumpet)' and 'You Can Make Me Dance, Sing Or Anything (Even Take The Dog For A Walk, Mend A Fuse, Fold Away The Ironing Board, Or Any Other Domestic Short Comings)'.

As if that wasn't enough, a vocal he had recorded on 'In A Broken Dream' to help out Python Lee Jackson in 1970 and a single he made with The Jeff Beck Group in 1968, 'I've Been Drinking', also made the charts.

The animosity with the other Faces was growing. Rod did not turn up for some sessions on their 1973 album, *Ooh-La-La*, and they felt he was holding songs back for his solo records. Rod publicly dismissed the album on release. Wonder what he really thought of his duet of 'Angel' with Denis Law for The Scotland World Cup Football Squad's album.

319 Slade
Mama Weer All Crazee Now

Label & Cat No.: **Polydor 2058 274**

Producer: **Chas Chandler**

Writers: **Noddy Holder / Jim Lea**

Date reached No.1: **9 September 1972**

Weeks at No.1: **3**

SLADE HAD CONSECUTIVE NUMBER ONES with 'Take Me Bak 'Ome' and 'Mama Weer All Crazee Now'. Noddy Holder: "Nowadays people think that all our records were along the lines of 'Mama Weer All Crazee Now' and 'Cum On Feel The Noize', but we recorded in a lot of different styles. We did acoustic, ballady tracks, and 'Everyday', 'Look Wot You Dun' and 'Far Far Away' weren't ballsy, out and out rock'n'roll. We have always taken risks because we needed some excitement for ourselves. We slipped things in when people weren't expecting it."

As Noddy suggests, 'Mama Weer All Crazee Now' is your archetypal Slade – brash, noisy, sloganeering. "In one respect, yes," says Noddy, "but you can look at our records in two ways. They were always done a little tongue-in-cheek. We wanted to put a smile on people's faces as well as making a statement of what we were going through at the time." That statement was about not conforming and loving excess.

Slade failed to make it a hat-trick of number ones when 'Gudbuy T'Jane' stuck at number two. That song had originally been presented as 'Hello T'Jane', but wanting something sadder, Noddy quickly reversed it.

320 David Cassidy
How Can I Be Sure?

Label & Cat No.: **Bell 1258**

Producer: **Wes Farrell**

Writers: **Felix Cavaliere / Eddie Brigan**

Date reached No.1: **30 September 1972**

Weeks at No.1: **2**

FOLLOWING THEIR SUCCESS WITH *THE Monkees*, Screen Gems established another US TV series with *The Partridge Family*. The casting was equally effective – Shirley Jones, who had appeared in the musicals, *Oklahoma!*, *Carousel* and *April Love*, played the mother and David Cassidy, the son of actor Jack Cassidy (*The Eiger Sanction*, *W.C. Fields And Me*), played Keith Partridge. "She was hardly old enough to be my mother," says David, "but I looked younger than I was. I was 21, playing 16." In a curious twist, she was David's real stepmother as she had married Jack Cassidy, although David had not grown up with them.

The Partridge Family was first screened by the BBC in 1972, and when they dropped it, ITV picked up the option. They made records from the start with the curious billing, "The Partridge Family starring Shirley Jones and featuring David Cassidy" "That was contractual," says David, "She was not a pop singer and they never used her voice. I made the records with background singers and there wasn't much difference between them and my solo records."

The Partridge Family had their first hit with 'I Think I Love You' (UK 18) and followed it with 'It's One Of Those Nights (Yes Love)' (UK 11) and the first slow version of 'Breaking Up Is Hard To Do' (UK 3). In April 1972 David got to number two with the double-sided 'Could It Be Forever' and 'Cherish'.

Felix Cavaliere was a member of the New York band, The Young Rascals, who were managed by Sid Bernstein, promoter of The Beatles' concerts at Carnegie Hall and Shea Stadium, and he set up the group as America's answer to The Beatles. They had considerable success with 'Groovin'' (a US number one) and 'People Got To Be Free' (as The Rascals and another US number one). Cavaliere, their lead vocalist and keyboard player, wrote the plaintive ballad, 'How Can I Be Sure?', which made number four on the US charts in 1967. The song meant nothing in the UK and even a revival by Dusty Springfield in 1970 only scraped into the charts. David Cassidy's version only made number 25 in the US, but it topped the UK charts.

321 Lieutenant Pigeon
Mouldy Old Dough

Label & Cat No.: **Decca F 13278**

Producer: **Stavely Makepiece**

Writers: **Nigel Fletcher / Robert Woodward**

Date reached No.1: **14 October 1972**

Weeks at No.1: **4**

THE PIANIST AND SINGER, ROB Woodward, recorded first under the name of Shel Naylor and one of the songs, 'One Fine Day', was written by Dave Davies from The Kinks. With his friend, the drummer Nigel Fletcher, he converted his front room into a makeshift recording studio. Adding Stephen Johnson on bass, they became Stavely Makepeace and recorded for Pyramid Records.

When they had an idea for an instrumental, 'Mouldy Old Dough', they needed a second keyboard and so Rob asked his 59-year-old mum, Hilda, a piano teacher, to join them. Decca released the single and called the band

Lieutenant Pigeon. The title, 'Mouldy Old Dough' comes from the Twenties phrase, 'Vo-Do-De-O', a nonsensical phrase used in dance records of the period. The Savoy Orpheans recorded 'Vo-Do-De-O Blues' in 1927, and you can hear variations on Marilyn Monroe's 'I Wanna Be Loved By You' and on some Temperance Seven records.

Lieutentant Pigeon followed it with 'Desperate Dan', which made the Top 20, but the next one, 'And The Fun Goes On', bombed. Surprisingly, the group made three albums and even had an Australian number one with a revival of 'I'll Take You Home Again Kathleen' from their album, *Pigeon Party*.

Steve Johnson reformed the band for oldies shows in 1992, but he is the only original member. Hilda Woodward died in 1999. Oh, and Charlie Watts called his racehorse, Mouldy Old Dough.

322 Gilbert O'Sullivan
Clair

Label & Cat No.: **MAM 84**

Producer: **Gordon Mills**

Writer: **Gilbert O'Sullivan**

Date reached No.1: **11 November 1972**

Weeks at No.1: **2**

GORDON MILLS FROM THE VISCOUNTS went into management and found that lightning struck three times – first with Tom Jones, then Engelbert Humperdinck and finally Gilbert O'Sullivan. His methods were questionable, his habits odd (he was obsessed with Hitler and had his own private zoo) and he ended up being sued for unfair contracts, but he certainly knew how to bring his artists to public attention.

Gilbert O'Sullivan, named after Gilbert & Sullivan, came to prominence in his pudding-basin haircut, cloth cap and short trousers. "I regret it now," says Gilbert, "because it worked against me, and at the time I wanted to be like James Taylor with jeans and long hair. It was a lightweight image and it implied my songs were lightweight too."

As it happened, 'Nothing Rhymed' was a thoughtful, provocative song about poverty and he followed it with the conversational 'We Will' and the tale of a boy being left at the altar, 'Alone Again (Naturally)', which made number three and was also a US chart-topper. "'Alone Again (Naturally)' has no comic purpose at all," says Gilbert, "and it is not a song that people can dismiss like 'Get Down' or 'Clair'. Because it means so much to some people, I will not allow it to be used for karaoke or commercials."

Gilbert, who lived in the grounds of the Mills' Weybridge mansion, found himself babysitting for them. He liked the baby's name, Clair, and a song took shape. He called Gordon and asked him to hear it. Clair Mills recalls, "My dad knew it was a great song. They recorded it the next day and they needed a laugh at the end. We were out at the pool and they started tickling me. I love the song, but I don't remember proposing to him, as it says in the song."

"I might regret it now with all that has happened," says Gilbert, thinking of the acrimonious law suit, which he won, "but I wanted to say thank you to them. We put Clair's laugh on the record and Gordon is playing harmonica."

323 Chuck Berry
My Ding-A-Ling

Label & Cat No.: **Chess 6145 019**

Producer: **Esmond Edwards**

Writer: **Chuck Berry**

Date reached No.1: **25 November 1972**

Weeks at No.1: **4**

NO ONE HAS LINKED BRITISH MUSIC hall to New Orleans R&B, but there is a connection. Both audiences like ribald songs, full of sexual innuendoes. 'My Ding-A-Ling', a cheerful, jokey, almost blue beat song about playing with your penis, is close to George Formby's 'With My Little Stick Of Blackpool Rock'. 'My Ding-A-Ling' was written by Fats Domino's co-writer, Dave Bartholomew, who recorded it in 1952. He also produced a new version called 'Toy Bell' for The Bees in 1954. Fats Domino himself showed no interest in the song, but it appealed to Chuck Berry.

Many rock'n'roll fans think it is tantamount to sacrilege that Chuck Berry reached the top with such nonsense, but it is a witty performance and what they are really complaining about is the fact that 'My Ding-A-Ling' reached the top while many of his classic rock'n'roll songs were largely ignored on release. Chuck Berry is today regarded as *the* rock'n'roll songwriter, but why did no one buy his songs in the Fifties? His only showings on the UK charts were 'School Day' (24, 1957) and 'Sweet Little Sixteen' (16, 1958). 'Johnny B. Goode', 'Roll Over Beethoven', 'Little Queenie' and 'Rock And Roll Music' did nothing, and very few artists covered the songs at the time. Mind you, it was difficult to promote some of these records as Chuck was doing time.

In the end, Chuck Berry was fêted by British beat groups and had Top 10 hits with 'Memphis Tennessee' (6, 1963) and 'No Particular Place To Go' (3, 1964). In-between developing his own amusement park, he toured the globe and although he is often criticised for not giving his all, it is intriguing to see how 'My Ding-A-Ling' develops. He first recorded it, rather staidly, as 'My Tambourine' in 1966 and the audience was lifeless when he recorded it at the Fillmore in San Francisco the following year.

In 1972 a performance for the Lanchester Arts Festival at the Locarno Ballroom in Coventry was recorded for a live LP, inexplicably called *The London Sessions*. That night Chuck Berry used Roy Young's band which included Owen McIntyre and Robbie McIntosh, later of the Average White Band.

Chuck's set included a 12-minute version of 'My Ding-A-Ling', which should be heard in its entirety as the audience reaction is brilliant. It was edited into a four minute single and it is unlikely that it would have done so well if Mary Whitehouse and her Festival Of Light had not objected to it so vehemently. Inevitably, such attention gave it valuable publicity and assured its success. As Chuck says, "There's nothing wrong with sex. It's just the way you handle it."

Gilbert O'Sullivan's unlikely image certainly got him noticed, but it took him years to shake off the horrors of short trousers, cloth cap and pudding basin haircut

324 Little Jimmy Osmond Long Haired Lover From Liverpool

Label & Cat No.: **MGM 2006 109**
Producers: **Mike Curb / Perry Botkin**
Writer: **Christopher Dowden**
Date reached No.1: **23 December 1972**
Weeks at No.1: **5**

By the end of 1972, anything with the name Osmond on it was selling well. Donny Osmond had had solo hits with 'Puppy Love' (1), 'Too Young' (5), 'Why' (3) and The Osmonds took 'Crazy Horses' to number two. There had also been the hit albums, *Portrait Of Donny*, *Too Young*, *The Osmonds Live* and *Crazy Horses*, and now Jimmy and then Marie were issuing records as well. Quite possibly, the Osmonds would have amassed more than five number ones if they had released fewer records – many of their young fans couldn't afford to keep up with them.

Jimmy Osmond was not even 10 years old when he had a number one record with 'Long Haired Lover From Liverpool'. He had further hits with 'Tweedlee Dee' (4) and 'I'm Gonna Knock On Your Door' (11). "To be honest, I was at the shallow end of the gene pool," says Jimmy today. "I was the comic relief and it couldn't last because I was singing the sugar hits. I think we had some great writers in The Osmonds. 'Crazy Horses' is a wonderful song, but it was banned in South Africa because they thought it was about heroin."

Asked where 'Long Haired Lover From Liverpool' came from, Jimmy says, "I don't know, but can we put it back? Mike Curb suggested the song, and a song about The Beatles made sense. Paul McCartney brought his daughter to meet us and wanted our autographs." It was an unnatural childhood: "I only spent one day in school as the kids came at me with switchblades."

Even when he was young, Jimmy Osmond had a healthy attitude to fame: "They marketed Little Jimmy Osmond dolls and I had a lot of them. I liked to line 'em up and shoot 'em down. My weakness was eating too much food. I was in Vegas and I was sick on someone in the front row. One of my brothers picked me up and I kept on going."

325 Sweet Block Buster!

Label & Cat No.: **RCA 2305**
Producer: **Phil Wingman**
Writers: **Nicky Chinn / Mike Chapman**
Date reached No: **27 January 1973**
Weeks at No: **5**

The glam rock band, Sweet, had a solitary number one, but they could so easily have had six – 'Co-Co', 'Hell Raiser', 'Ballroom Blitz', 'Teenage Rampage' and 'Fox On The Run' were number twos, and 'Ballroom Blitz', in particular, is remembered as fondly as any chart-topper. The songwriter Nicky Chinn comments, "I like to think that our lyrics were interesting and different. I liked a title that conjured up a picture. With 'Ballroom Blitz', you can imagine the kids dancing and going crazy. 'Block Buster!' had a darker image.' Or comic as John Otway sings a novelty version without changing the words at all – "You better beware, You better take care, You better watch out if you got long black hair."

The vocalist and guitarist, Brian Connolly, formed Wainwright's Gentlemen with the drummer, Mick Tucker, in 1968. They performed a mixture of hit songs and psychedelia and then formed Sweetshop and finally, Sweet with the line-up of Connolly, Tucker, Andy Scott (lead guitar, keyboards) and Steve Priest (bass). The producer, Phil Wingman, wanted to record them and, running into Nicky Chinn and Mike Chapman, he was given 'Funny Funny'.

At first, Sweet's hits had little substance but they developed an attitude and a harder edge with 'Block Buster!', although the arrangement owed something to The Yardbirds' version of Bo Diddley's 'I'm A Man' (1965). Nicky Chinn says, "Every part of a song is important and how you get into it is especially important. You have to catch the public's attention the second that the record comes on. Look at 'Block Buster!' with its siren. You catch the attention immediately."

Sweet were banned from Mecca Ballrooms for their sexual posturing and were arrested in Belgium for an obscene stage show, though such antics would be regarded as mild today. Belgium didn't bother them as they were big in Australia and the States. After a succession of raucous hits, Sweet wanted to break away from Chinn and Chapman and record their own songs. They had a fine start with 'Fox On The Run' but their subsequent records were less successful. They had an Indian summer with 'Love Is Like Oxygen' in 1978.

In the Nineties two versions of Sweet were touring, Andy Scott's and Brian Connolly's, but Brian's speech was slow and slurred like Ozzy Osbourne's and for the same reasons. A Channel 4 documentary did him no favours at all and he died in 1997. The other Wainwright's Gentleman, Mick Tucker, died in 2002.

326 Slade Cum On Feel The Noize

Label & Cat No.: **Polydor 2058 339**
Producer: **Chas Chandler**
Writers: **Noddy Holder / Jim Lea**
Date reached No.1: **3 March 1973**
Weeks at No.1: **4**

Slade's 'Cum On Feel The Noize' was the first single since 'Get Back' to enter the charts at number one. In it, Noddy Holder replies to his critics, who accuse him of having a dirty mind and a funny face and singing out of time. He admits he's making money and as the girls rock the boys, he'll be all right. Or, as one headline put it, 'Cum On Feel The Boyz'.

"People used to tell us that we would never get anywhere with a singer like Nod," says Dave Hill, "but we got everywhere."

The energetic and enthusiastic single was performed even more ferociously on stage. "Don Powell was a very powerful drummer," says Dave Hill, "as powerful as John Bonham. He would break sticks and there aren't many drummers who do that."

Slade's stage personality and foot-stomping music encouraged raucous fans and Noddy Holder injured his arm in Brussels when a brick was thrown at the band. The band was also living the rock'n'roll lifestyle and drinking hard. Noddy Holder recalls one late-night session where the hotel porter greeted him in the lobby with the words, "This is your nine o'clock call, Mr. Holder."

Oddly, Slade did not have any success in the US during their heyday, but the heavy metal band Quiet Riot took 'Cum On Feel The Noize' to number five in 1983. Shortly afterwards, Slade had their first US Top 40 hits with 'Run Runaway' and 'My Oh My'. In 1994 Oasis included 'Cum On Feel The Noize' on their CD single, 'Don't Look Back In Anger'.

327 Donny Osmond
The Twelfth Of Never

Label & Cat No.: **MGM 2006 199**

Producers: **Mike Curb / Don Costa**

Writers: **Jerry Livingston / Paul Francis Webster**

Date reached No.1: **31 March 1973**

Weeks at No.1: **1**

The folk song, 'I Gave My Love A Cherry', can be traced back to 1680. It is also known as 'The Riddle Song' and its melody was used for 'The Twelfth Of Never'. The song was written by the sometime team of Jerry Livingston (music) and Paul Francis Webster (lyrics). Livingston had little to do on this occasion, but Webster's dictionary included a magical phrase for 'eternity', 'The Twelfth Of Never'. Livingston's hit songs stretch back to 'Under A Blanket Of Blue' in 1933 and include "Mairzy Doats' and 'It's The Talk Of The Town'. Webster, working with Sammy Fain, wrote several Fifties hits – 'A Very Precious Love', 'A Certain Smile', 'Man On Fire' and 'April Love'.

'The Twelfth Of Never', was a US Top 10 hit for Johnny Mathis in 1957, the other side being the equally successful 'Chances Are', but the British public showed no interest in the song until Cliff Richard recorded it in 1964.

You can tell that Donny Osmond's career was manipulated because his solo hits were with revivals of ballads that were usually hits before he was born – 'Puppy Love', 'Too Young', 'Why', 'The Twelfth Of Never', 'Young Love' and 'When I Fall In Love'. "Sometimes I didn't even know the songs," says Donny today, "I was given a copy of 'Too Young' and listened to it for 10 minutes. Then I went in the studio and recorded a million seller. Looking back, I wish we had pursued rock a little more. One of my favourite records is 'Crazy Horses' and we should have continued in that direction."

Johnny Mathis' recording of 'The Twelfth Of Never' was included on the soundtrack on *Close Encounters Of The Third Kind* (1977) and a version by Elvis Presley from 1974 was finally issued in 1995.

328 Gilbert O'Sullivan
Get Down

Label & Cat No.: **MAM 96**

Producer: **Gordon Mills**

Writer: **Gilbert O'Sullivan**

Date reached No.1: **7 April 1973**

Weeks at No.1: **2**

Gilbert O'Sullivan, actually Raymond O'Sullivan, is known for his gentle, conversational songs like 'We Will' and 'Alone Again (Naturally)'. "That's really because I have very little vibrato in my voice," he says. "I can't hold the notes the way that Tom Jones and Engelbert Humperdinck can. I can't show off my voice and so my songs are full of 'ands' and 'buts', which take me into the next line. Jack Jones and Andy Williams have done my songs, but I should imagine that they think the songs are too wordy."

Like 'Clair', 'Get Down' was something of a novelty song. 'Clair' was about babysitting for a young child and 'Get Down' was about trying to stop the family dog jumping all over you. 'Get Down' marked a change in direction as it was more rock-oriented than previous singles and the musicians supplementing Gilbert's piano included Chris Spedding (guitar) and Herbie Flowers (bass).

After consecutive number ones, Gilbert O'Sullivan's career lost momentum. 'Ooh Baby' only scraped into the Top 20 and he only had one more Top 20 hit, 'Why Oh Why Oh Why'. 'Matrimony' (1976) is one of his best-known songs but it didn't make the charts. His first four albums all did well, *Himself* (number five and 82 weeks on the chart), *Back To Front* (1), *I'm A Writer, Not A Fighter* (2) and *Stranger In My Own Back Yard* (9). When Gilbert O'Sullivan came to sue his manager, Gordon Mills, the judge was surprised to learn that he had been living off £10 a week pocket money.

329 Dawn
Tie A Yellow Ribbon Round The Old Oak Tree

Label & Cat No.: **Bell 1287**

Producers: **Dave Appell / Hank Medress**

Writers: **Irwin Levine / Larry Russell Brown**

Date reached No.1: **21 April 1973**

Weeks at No.1: **4**

In medieval times, a knight would give a pennant or a scarf to a loved one as he left for battle, and from this, wearing coloured ribbons became a popular way of showing support. The civil war film, *She Wore A Yellow Ribbon* (1949), starring John Wayne, underscores the lineage. Yellow was the official colour of the US cavalry and used in the piping on uniforms and regimental standards. Curiously, yellow has also become the colour of cowardice.

In the Sixties, a prisoner who had served time for writing bad cheques was returning home on a bus to White Oak, Georgia. He told the passengers that he didn't know if his girl would be waiting. If she still wanted him, she had to tie a yellow ribbon on the old oak tree in the centre of town and if he didn't see one, he would stay on the bus. Everyone on board heard the story and they were all counting the miles to White Oak. When they saw the tree, it was covered with ribbons and "the whole damn bus" was cheering.

The journalist, Pete Hamill, wrote about it in the *New York Post* and this was made into a TV drama starring James Earl Jones. Next came the hit song that we know and (maybe) love. Like 'Knock Three Times', the song topped both the UK and US charts, and although Dawn's popularity waned in Britain after that, they had a further US number one with 'He Don't Love You (Like I Love You)'. As a result of the song's popularity, yellow ribbons were seen across the US to welcome home the hostages from Iran.

Many of the old-time artists – Perry Como, Bing Crosby, Kay Starr – put the song into their repertoire, and Connie Francis recorded 'The Answer (Should I Tie A Yellow Ribbon Round The Old Oak Tree?)'.

330 Wizzard
See My Baby Jive

Label & Cat No.: **Harvest HAR 5070**
Producer: **Roy Wood**
Writer: **Roy Wood**
Date reached No.1: **19 May 1973**
Weeks at No.1: **4**

After The Move, Roy Wood formed the Electric Light Orchestra with Jeff Lynne but he left after one album, *Message From The Country*, and two hit singles, '10538 Overture' and 'Roll Over Beethoven'. He reflects, "I had felt I had gone as far as I could with The Move with just guitar and drums on my songs. A few of the songs were orchestrated for us and we had to use session men, and so I thought, 'Why not form a band with these people in?' I was talking to Jeff Lynne about it and we formed ELO. It took us 18 months to get the band on the road because we had problems in balancing the sound, and by then both Jeff and I had stockpiles of material and we were giving in to each other all the time. It was a bit fraught, so I thought I would leave and form Wizzard, but there were no problems really. We've always been good friends."

Within a fortnight of being formed, Wizzard made its debut at a rock'n'roll festival with Little Richard and Chuck Berry at Wembley. "There were a lot of people in Wizzard and half of them had never done anything bigger than The Queen's Arms," says Roy. "It is very funny in retrospect. We weren't allowed to use our own equipment and it was dreadful – my amp blew up in the first song and when another amp blew up, I performed, for the first and only time in my life, without my guitar. The sax players hadn't wanted to use music stands and they put their music on the floor, where it blew all over the place. We were lucky, we weren't booed like Gary Glitter, so we must have appealed to them."

In December 1972 Wizzard made the Top 10 with 'Ball Park Incident' and then went to number one with 'See My Baby Jive'. Roy again: "At the beginning of Wizzard, the line-up was two cellists, two drummers, two saxophone players plus guitar, bass and keyboards. What else can you do with that line-up but create a Phil Spector sound? I wrote a lot of songs around his influence, and that feel and atmosphere paid off for us. They were hellish to record though."

Roy Wood

331 Suzi Quatro
Can The Can

Label & Cat No.: **RAK 150**
Producers: **Nicky Chinn / Mike Chapman**
Writers: **Nicky Chinn / Mike Chapman**
Date reached No.1: **16 June 1973**
Weeks at No.1: **1**

Being the daughter of a professional jazz musician, Suzi Quatro has been involved with music all her life. She was born in Detroit in 1950 and she was in a group, The Pleasure Sisters, with her elder sisters, Patti and Nancy from 1964 to 1970. "Someone gave me a leather jacket when I was 12," says Suzi, "and I've worn it ever since. I've always been extremely rock'n'roll." As indeed has Patti, who went on to form the female rock group, Fanny.

In 1970 the record producer, Mickie Most, was visiting Detroit and saw the Quatros. He invited Suzi to the UK, but their album together lacked conviction. Nicky Chinn and Mike Chapman were asked for a song and when they came up with a powerful, aggressive rocker, 'Can The Can', Mickie Most asked them to produce it as well. "I can hear a record for the first time and know whether it will be a hit," says Suzi, "and I knew as soon as we had finished recording that we had a big hit on our hands."

Suzi Quatro was the only successful girl amongst the Glam Rockers, although she says she was more rock'n'roll than Glitter. Both sexes loved her image of a small girl playing bass in tight, black leathers. And just what does 'Can The Can' mean? Nicky Chinn: "It means something that is pretty impossible, you can't get one can inside another if they are the same size, so we're saying you can't put your man in the can if he is out there and not willing to commit. The phrase sounded good and we didn't mind if the public didn't get the meaning of it."

Suzi married her lead guitarist, Lenny Tucker: they had two children and divorced in 1992. "We celebrated our number one by doing *Top Of The Pops* followed by a gig," says Suzi, "and then Lenny and I got drunk in our bedsit."

332 10cc
Rubber Bullets

Label & Cat No.: **UK UK 36**

Producer: **10cc**

Writers: **Kevin Godley / Lol Creme / Graham Gouldman**

Date Reached No.1: **23 June 1973**

Weeks at No.1: **1**

GUITARIST GRAHAM GOULDMAN HAD already written hits for The Hollies ('Look Through Any Window' and 'Bus Stop'), The Yardbirds ('For Your Love', 'Heart Full Of Soul' and 'Evil Hearted You') and Herman's Hermits ('No Milk Today'), when in 1969, he, along with keyboardist Lol Creme, drummer Kevin Godley and erstwhile fellow Mindbender, vocalist Eric Stewart, formed Hotlegs. They scored one hit with 'Neanderthal Man' and toured with the Moody Blues on the strength of it.

In 1972 Jonathan King signed the Manchester band to his newly formed UK record label and promptly christened them 10cc. He claimed he saw the name in a dream, although it has been strongly alleged that it represents the average count of the male ejaculation: nine cc and they added the extra one to signify they were above average.

At the time of the release of 'Rubber Bullets', there was trouble in Northern Ireland and also controversy over the British Army's use of rubber bullets. Eric Stewart recalled, "I was amazed, but pleased that the BBC never banned the track, although they limited its airplay, because they thought it was about the ongoing Northern Ireland conflicts. It fact, it was about an Attica State Prison riot like the ones in the old James Cagney films."

"Kevin and Lol had the chorus and part of the verse, but then got stuck," remembered Graham. "We all loved the chorus and realised that it was a hit in itself, so we wanted to persist with it. I chipped in the line 'we've all got balls and brains, but some's got balls and chains'. One of my finer couplets." The song won an *Ivor Novello* Award for Best Beat Song.

The police sirens in the song are such an integral part, that to keep its authenticity, the band use a backing track of the original sirens when they perform it live.

In 1976 Kevin Godley and Lol Creme left to continue as a duo. They created the 'Gizmo', a guitar attachment that sustains notes as well as creating orchestral sounds. A good example of its haunting sound can be heard on 'It'll End In Tears', the B-side of This Mortal Coil's 1984 single 'Kangaroo'.

In the early Eighties, as well as top 10 hits with 'Under Your Thumb' and 'Wedding Bells', Godley & Creme began working on video production and have produced videos for Toyah ('Thunder In The Mountains'), Visage ('Fade To Grey'), Culture Club ('Victims') and Duran Duran ('Girls On Film').

333 Slade
Skweeze Me Pleeze Me

Label & Cat No.: **Polydor 2058 377**

Producer: **Chas Chandler**

Writers: **Noddy Holder / Jim Lea**

Date reached No.1: **30 June 1973**

Weeks at No.1: **3**

LIKE 'CUM ON FEEL THE NOIZE', 'Skweeze Me Pleeze Me' entered the charts at number one while Slade were at the height of their fame. On July 1, 1973, the Wolverhampton band gave a triumphant performance at Earl's Court to 20,000 fans, but tragedy was waiting around the corner. Three days later, after visiting a club in Wolverhampton, Don Powell drove his Bentley into a wall. His fiancée, Angela Morris, was killed and he suffered serious brain damage. He returned to playing in August 1973 but his memory was gone. He had to write down where he was before he went to sleep so that he could read it in the morning.

Although 'Skweeze Me Pleeze Me' was so successful, it is one of the hits that is forgotten now. It was followed by a number two, 'My Friend Stan', and then the third Slade single to enter at number one, 'Merry Xmas Everybody'. Noddy Holder: "I can sing properly when I want to, if that's the word for it. One reviewer likened my voice to fingernails going down a blackboard." Only one?

Slade were just as successful with albums. *Slade Alive* reached number two and spent over a year on the charts. This was followed by three number one albums, *Slayed?, Sladest* and *Old New Borrowed And Blue.* Noddy Holder: "Don had his accident while we were making *Old New Borrowed And Blue* and he couldn't remember anything from one minute to the next and he had no sense of taste or smell. I thought that he would never play the drums again but he pulled through really well."

334 Peters & Lee
Welcome Home

Label & Cat No.: **Philips 6006 307**

Producer: **Johnny Franz**

Writers: **Jean-Alphonse Dupre / Stanislas Beldone / Bryan Blackburn**

Date reached No.1: **21 July 1973**

Weeks at No.1: **1**

THE EAST ENDER, LENNIE PETERS LOST his eyesight as a result of two separate accidents – the first in a car accident when he was six and the second in a street fight when he was 16. "I got a brick pushed between my eyes and that done the other one," he said. "I said to the doctor, 'What's the chances of me getting my sight back?' and he said, 'None at all', so I had to accept it. My father died the next year, leaving my mum with six kids. By the time I was 18, I was playing the piano in pubs and earning my own living."

Lennie formed various pub bands, dismissing his nephew Charlie Watts along the way for playing too much jazz. Eventually, they became The Migil Five, but Lennie left before 'Mockingbird Hill'. By 1970 he was singing with the dancer, Dianne Lee, from The Halley Twins and they

sensed their potential after appearing on stage with Rolf Harris. They worked the cabaret circuit and then, in 1973, they won ITV's *Opportunity Knocks* for seven consecutive weeks.

Johnny Franz gave them a recording contract with Philips and played them a romantic French ballad, 'Welcome L'Ami' by Les Compagnons De La Chanson, which they liked. Franz asked Bryan Blackburn, who normally wrote comic songs, for an English lyric, hence 'Welcome Home'. "We thought it was too simple," says Dianne, "you know, 'Welcome home, come in and close the door'. We couldn't see that we could do anything with it, but it felt like a hit when we recorded it."

Peters & Lee had further hits with 'Don't Stay Away Too Long' (3, 1974), 'Rainbow' (17, 1974) and 'Hey Mr. Music Man' (16, 1976), which were German songs with Blackburn's lyrics. However, it was as album sellers that Peters & Lee excelled, having Top 10 LPs with *We Can Make It, By Your Side, Rainbow* and *Favourites*. *We Can Make It* topped the album charts and remained on the list for 55 weeks.

Totally exhausted, the duo split up in 1980 but returned to working together in 1986. In 1992 Lennie Peters contracted cancer and died. Diane has a cabaret act with her partner, Rick Price from Wizzard and she appeared in Jim Davidson's adult pantomime, *Sinderella*.

335 Gary Glitter
I'm The Leader Of The Gang (I Am)

Label & Cat No.: **Bell BELL 1321**

Producer: **Mike Leander**

Writers: **Mike Leander / Gary Glitter**

Date Reached No.1: **28 July 1973**

Weeks at No.1: **4**

GALLOPING GORMAY, HORACE HYDROgen, Stan Sparkle, Terry Tinsel and Vicki Vomit were just some of the alliterated names that Paul Gadd, born May 8, 1944, in Banbury, Oxfordshire, rejected before settling on Gary Glitter.

A decade earlier, he had tried his luck in the music world fronting a skiffle group called Paul Russell & The Rebels, adopting his stepfather's surname. He left the band to go solo, changed his name again to Paul Raven and released five unsuccessful singles for Decca, Parlophone and MCA.

By now it was the mid-Sixties and he was appearing as a warm-up act on the television show *Ready Steady Go!* As a producer for Decca Records, Mike Leander, who had worked with Paul Jones, John Rowles and Marianne Faithfull, began writing songs as well as running his own orchestra. He recalled, "I first saw Gary when he used to warm up the kids by singing and dancing on *Ready Steady Go*! I thought he was fantastic and a great figure, often better than some of the acts on the programme." Leander asked Glitter to join his outfit as lead vocalist. The band soon split, but Glitter and the band's trombonist, John Rossall, carried on working together and formed a new eight-piece group. They did an extensive tour of Germany and Scandinavia.

In 1972 Leander and Glitter decided to return to their rock'n'roll roots and started writing songs together. His stage act was getting wild and his Bacofoil costumes complete with platform boots, obligatory hairy chest and medallion were outrageous. He was the rock'n'roll equivalent of Liberace.

A few months later, the newly dubbed Gary Glitter's career started to take off. In January 1973, once established, he launched a massive publicity stunt, which involved burying his Paul Raven persona by putting his old records and photographs in a coffin and attempting to sink it in the River Thames. Unfortunately, the coffin failed to submerge and floated off downstream.

'I'm The Leader Of The Gang', with its motorbike revving at the beginning, was originally written as the opening song of Glitter's stage show, when the band would come on posing as rockers, with their backs to the audience. Many parents nursed doubts about the lyric, 'I'm the man who put the gang in bang'.

In an interview in the late Eighties, Glitter claimed that "'Leader' is still my favourite of all my hits because of the way the fans chant 'leader, leader, leader' when I walk on stage."

These days, many of his former fans chant something rather different.

336 Donny Osmond
Young Love

Label & Cat No.: **MGM 2006 300**

Producers: **Mike Curb / Don Costa**

Writers: **Carole Joyner / Ric Cartey**

Date reached No.1: **25 August 1973**

Weeks at No.1: **4**

DONNY OSMOND RECORDED ANOther cover, this time Tab Hunter's 'Young Love' from 1957, and it is another example of a song making the top in two different versions. Donny followed it with a revival of Nat 'King' Cole's 'When I Fall In Love', which made number four, and at the same time his sister, Marie, was making her chart debut with a revival of Anita Bryant's 'Paper Roses'. The two of them teamed up for a new version of Dale & Grace's 'I'm Leaving It (All) Up To You', which made number two.

They had other duet hits with 'Morning Side Of The Mountain', 'Make The World Go Away' and 'Deep Purple'. They became a popular combination in the States and *The Donny And Marie Show* was screened from 1976 to 1979. Those programmes now have a certain camp following.

Donny has had his disappointments – the Broadway musical, *Little Johnny Jones*, closed after its opening night on Broadway, although it had done well on tour. Donny signed with Virgin Records in the late Eighties and had a US number two with 'Soldier Of Love'. He has starred very successfully in a North American tour of *Joseph And The Amazing Technicolor Dreamcoat* and in 2001, he released a highly-acclaimed album of show songs, *This Is The Moment*. Like Cliff Richard, Donny's popularity has lasted: he played sold-out concert dates in the UK in 2004 and returned to the Top 10 with 'Breeze On By'.

Although the songwriters, Ric Cartey and

Gary Glitter, the UK's best known pantomime rocker, was born Paul Gadd, then became Paul Russell, then Paul Raven and finally Mr Glitter

Carole Joyner, had a major success with 'Young Love', they never wrote another hit record. Ric Cartey also wrote with Freddy Weller and Ray Stevens but neither of these hit songwriters could return him to the charts.

337 Wizzard
Angel Fingers

Label & Cat No.: **Harvest HAR 5076**

Producer: **Roy Wood**

Writer: **Roy Wood**

Date reached No.1: **22 September 1973**

Weeks at No.1: **1**

ROY WOOD HAD MUSICAL AMBITION in ELO, but, although that continued in Wizzard, Wizzard was essentially a fun band. Roy had started to paint his face in The Move, but in Wizzard, he had a succession of fully-painted visages, which with frizzed-out hair and colourful, uncoordinated clothes, gave him the appearance of a spaced-out wizard. The rest of the band appeared more conventionally – Rick Price (bass, from The Move), Bill Hunt and Hugh McDowell (cellos, from ELO), Mike Burney and Nick Pentelow (saxes) and Charlie Grima and Keith Smart (drums).

The grandiose production of 'See My Baby Jive' continued with 'Angel Fingers' and the chorus, incidentally, includes one of Roy's Birmingham compadres, Raymond Froggatt. They should have had a hat-trick of number ones with 'I Wish It Could Be Christmas Everyday'. Any other year Wizzard would have been up there, but they had the misfortune to compete with Slade's 'Merry Xmas Everybody'. "I would hate to be a writer," says Carl Wayne, who had been in The Move with Roy Wood, "because you never know what might influence you subconsciously. I'm sure Roy never thought of Donald Peers when he was writing 'Angel Fingers' but you try singing 'By A Babbling Brook' to it!"

The unwieldy band continued to have hits with a label change to Warners, although releasing 'Rock'n'Roll Winter' in April defies logic. The band, who were managed by Don Arden, split in 1975 over earnings for an American tour. Today, Roy fronts The Roy Wood Big Band with eight girls and performs songs from The Move, ELO, Wizzard and his solo records.

When asked for this book for the highlight of his musical career, Roy Wood said, "Playing the saxophone with Sooty. Good player, old Soot. I think you'll find that most musicians would want to play with Sooty. He's really in, mate."

338 The Simon Park Orchestra
Eye Level

Label & Cat No.: **Columbia DB 8946**

Producer: **Simon Park**

Writers: **Simon Park / Jack Trombey (Jan Stoeckhart)**

Date reached No.1: **29 September 1973**

Weeks at No.1: **4**

SIMON PARK, BORN IN MARKET HARborough in 1946, has been playing the piano since he was five. He graduated in music from Winchester College in Oxford.

In 1972 Thames TV commissioned him to write the theme music for a new detective series, *Van Der Valk*, starring Barry Foster as Nicholas Freeling's blond and moody detective, Piet Van Der Valk. Nigel Stock, who was noted for playing Dr. Watson, played his superior, Superintendent Samson. Simon wrote the music with a Dutchman, Jan Stoeckhart, who used the pseudonym, Jack Trombey. It was recorded in France.

The first series was popular and the theme music made number 41. However, it was during the second series that *Van Der Valk* became a major success and, as a result, the theme music went to the top of the charts. It was the first time that a TV theme had topped the charts. The series continued until 1977, but was revived in 1991.

Simon Park also wrote the music for *Danger UXB* in 1979, a series about a bomb disposal squad in London during World War II and starring Anthony Andrews.

339 David Cassidy
Daydreamer / The Puppy Song

Label & Cat No.: **Bell 1334**

Producer: **Rick Jarrard**

Writers : **Terry Dempsey; Harry Nilsson**

Date reached No.1: **27 October 1973**

Weeks at No.1: **3**

DAVID CASSIDY WAS ALWAYS UNEASY at being a teen idol and, in the US, he pressed the self-destruct button with a frank interview to *Rolling Stone* and photographs which made his pubic hair public. As few people read *Rolling Stone* in the UK, *The Partridge Family* continued as normal. Since his number one with 'How Can I Be Sure?', David had had hits with 'Rock Me Baby' (11) and 'Some Kind Of A Summer' / 'I Am A Clown' (3). As part of The Partridge Family, he was featured on 'Looking Through The Eyes Of Love' (9) and 'Walking In The Rain' (10).

His third double-sided hit and his second number one came when a new song, 'Daydreamer', was combined with Nilsson's whimsical 'Puppy Song'. This was originally recorded by Mary Hopkin on her 1969 album, *Post Card*, but Nilsson released his own version a few months later on a B-side. Both songs were on David's number one album, *Dreams Are Nuthin' More Than Wishes.*

After that, David had a Top 10 hit with 'If I Didn't Care', but an 'in concert' version of 'Please Please Me' only made number 16. He recorded the emotional ballad 'I Write The Songs' (11) and his final hit was with a revival of The Beach Boys' 'Darlin'' (16) in 1975 and by then, the series had been cancelled. David didn't mind: he came out of the business and concentrated on breeding horses.

David Cassidy fans congregate to worship in London, though the man himself was torn between his teen idol image and ambition to become known as a 'serious artist'

I LOVE DAVID
CASSIDY
I LOVE DAVID
DAVID

SUPER YOB

In 1985 David Cassidy returned to the Top 10 with 'The Last Kiss', which had backing vocals from George Michael. In 1987 he took over the lead from Cliff Richard in the West End musical, *Time*, and in 1993, he starred on Broadway in *Blood Brothers*.

340 Gary Glitter
I Love You Love Me Love

Label & Cat No.: **Bell BELL 1337**

Producer: **Mike Leander**

Writers: **Mike Leander / Gary Glitter**

Date Reached No.1: **17 November 1973**

Weeks at No.1: **4**

"I WANTED TO BE LIKE ELVIS", SAID THE man who put the glitter into glam.

In 1973 Glitter embarked on a tour that included Australia but it was not very successful. He claimed later, "They never knew what to make of me. They thought I was some sort of poof."

Before 'I'm The Leader Of The Gang' had dropped out of the chart, Bell Records were eager to promote another single and were soon pestering Gary and Mike for a title. Glitter said, "I'd always been fascinated by the title of the Elvis record, 'I'm Left, You're Right, She's Gone' and had been playing around with phrases like that for a while. I suggested to Mike Leander, 'How about 'I Love You Love Me Love"? He loved it and phoned it straight through to the head of Bell Records, Dick Leahy. Then we panicked. With a title like that, it had to be a ballad, but we'd never had one out as a single. We got to work writing a song around the vague title." As Mike recalled, "Everyone was getting ready to release Christmas records and we didn't have one, so I thought 'let's release it a month earlier"'. It paid off when the song crashed into the chart at number one.

With each tour came a new stage set and for each single, a new outfit. Such was the impact of Glittermania that Glitter starred in his own movie called '*Remember Me This Way*'. It was not a roaring success.

As soon as 'I Love You Love Me Love' topped the chart, Glitter headed to America. He turned up at Los Angeles airport dressed in the full regalia. It raised a few eyebrows from US custom officials who immediately took him away and searched him for drugs. Glitter later said, "Only an idiot would try to smuggle drugs into Los Angeles because everything you would ever need is there 24 hours a day."

Glitter once said, "Most of my songs are nonsense nursery rhymes. I was once voted Best Songwriter Of The Year for a song that went `hey hey ugugug shshs fartfart' and they haven't got much better since."

341 Slade
Merry Xmas Everybody

Label & Cat No.: **Polydor 2058 422**

Producer: **Chas Chandler**

Writers: **Noddy Holder / Jim Lea**

Date reached No.1: **15 December 1973**

Weeks at No.1: **5**

PRIOR TO 'MERRY XMAS EVERYBODY', Christmas singles had not been selling. Noddy Holder: "It was obviously a risk but we had enough confidence in the song to know that it was going to do well. We loved the song right from the minute we had written it. We wrote it in England, but we recorded it in the middle of a blazing hot summer in New York. When we did the vocals, we sang the chorus on the stairs to get the echo that we wanted. Anyone who saw us would have thought, 'Ah, the crazy English'."

'Merry Xmas Everybody' sold 300,000 on its first day of release, went straight in at number one and won a gold disc on British sales alone. It has become a standard, usually reissued in its original form each Christmas, although there has been a concert version from Reading (1980) and a remix (Slade vs. Flush, 1998). The original is still the greatest and nothing can top Noddy Holder's yell at the end.

In 1974 Slade had hits with 'Everyday' (3), a story about groupies 'The Bangin' Man' (3) and 'Far Far Away' (2), but their success was waning at the time of their film, *Slade In Flame*. This film, written by Jane Birkin's brother, Andrew, showed the seediness of the music business, and its violence was cut to prevent an X certificate. The film featured Tom Conti, Alan Lake and the DJs, Emperor Rosko and Tommy Vance, but strangely, 'How Does It Feel' (Slade plus brass) only made number 15. "I was really surprised about that as I'm really proud of that track," says Noddy Holder. "It showed that you never are certain to have a hit record no matter how big you are."

Slade had an on / off relationship with the charts for many years and they had subsequent hits with 'We'll Bring The House Down' (1981), 'My Oh My' (1983) and 'Run Runaway' (1984). Noddy no longer performs with Slade and has been a radio presenter in Manchester and then Birmingham. Jim Lea went into record production, while both Dave Hill and Don Powell have played in Slade II, the name being Noddy's idea. "I loved playing the old songs," says Dave Hill. "I feel that the music never dates – it's like Beethoven and Bach in that respect."

342 The New Seekers
You Won't Find Another Fool Like Me

Label & Cat No.: **Polydor 2058 421**

Producer: **Tommy Oliver**

Writers: **Tony Macaulay / Geoff Stephens**

Date reached No.1: **19 January 1974**

Weeks at No.1: **1**

AFTER 'I'D LIKE TO TEACH THE WORLD To Sing', The New Seekers came second to Vicky Leandros in The Eurovision Song Contest with 'Beg, Steal Or Borrow' (2). They covered Harry Chapin's 'Circles' (4) and revived The

Statistically, Slade were far and away the most successful of all the UK glam bands; left to right: Jim Lea, Dave Hill, Noddy Holder and Don Powell

Fleetwoods' 'Come Softly To Me' (20). As they were a middle-of-the-road pop group, their choice of 'Pinball Wizard' and 'See Me, Feel Me' in a medley from The Who's rock opera *Tommy* was seen, by their standards, as adventurous.

When the next single, 'Nevertheless', was billed as Eve Graham & The New Seekers, Lyn Paul thought of leaving. "I just didn't want to be oohing and aahing all the time," says Lyn. "Fortunately, they could see my point of view and they gave me 'You Won't Find Another Fool Like Me' and 'I Get A Little Sentimental Over You' to get me to stay."

The songwriter Geoff Stephens recalls, "When I was living in Switzerland, I had an office in the house. One morning I went there to start work and my secretary Roxanne was crying. Her boyfriend had been bad to her, and she had said, 'You leave, but you won't find another fool like me'. I hope I had the good grace to comfort her before dashing away to write the song. The title was so right. The record came out before Christmas and mothers would buy it for their daughters and the other way round, and it was a way of saying, 'I love you'. No doubt about it, that song touched a lot of people."

343 Mud
Tiger Feet

Label & Cat No.: **RAK 166**
Producers: **Nicky Chinn / Mike Chapman**
Writers: **Nicky Chinn / Mike Chapman**
Date reached No.1: **26 January 1974**
Weeks at No.1: **4**

"I DON'T KNOW WHY WE CALLED OURSELVES Mud," said their lead singer, Les Gray. "I know we wanted one short word like Who or Them because it looks so good on posters. If we're on a festival with a lot of acts, we get the big lettering. It was also a funny name and we knew we would get all the 'your name is Mud' jokes."

Mud appeared on *Opportunity Knocks* but were beaten by a juggler. Mickie Most of RAK Records caught them at The Revolution backing Linda Kendrick and wanted to sign them, but they had a contract with CBS. They made some unsuccessful singles and once they were free, they called Mickie Most. He asked Nicky Chinn and Mike Chapman to see them.

"We didn't get it right at first with 'Crazy' and 'Hypnosis' although they were hits," says Nicky Chinn. "They had tango beats and they would not have been a big band if we had continued like that. When Sweet turned down 'Dyna-Mite', we gave it to Mud and that went to number four and established the style."

Then came 'Tiger Feet'. Mickie Most's brother, Dave worked as a promotions executive for RAK Records. He remembered, "Mike Chapman asked me over to his house one day whilst he was doing some wallpapering. He put this piece of wallpaper against the wall and moved it across to match the previous piece and said 'That's neat, that's neat, that's neat'". Mike added, "There were stripes of my wallpaint on my feet and indeed, that's where the 'Tiger Feet' came from. Suddenly it dawned on me that 'that's neat' rhymed with 'Tiger feet', and a song was born."

"Mike Chapman played it to us on an acoustic guitar and I thought it was a terrible song," says Les, "It was just 'That's right, that's right, that's right', but by the time we had worked out the arrangement, it was very strong. That riff at the start has a jazzy feel to it: it was played on a fuzz guitar but a trad band could play it. When we did it on stage, the reaction was incredible."

Nicky Chinn says, "Of course it is repetitive but it sounds so good and it was so memorable that it made the song. Sometimes you repeat things because there is nowhere else to go and that is what happened there. Amateur songwriters often write too many lyrics, which is a big mistake because the public don't remember many words."

The easy-going Mud would go on to enjoy 14 Top 20 singles, including two more number ones.

344 Suzi Quatro
Devil Gate Drive

Label & Cat No.: **RAK 167**
Producers: **Nicky Chinn / Mike Chapman**
Writers: **Nicky Chinn / Mike Chapman**
Date reached No.1: **23 February 1974**
Weeks at No.1: **2**

AFTER 'CAN THE CAN', SUZI QUATRO almost made the top with a song about the male menopause, '48 Crash', but 'Daytona Demon' only made the Top 20. Her fourth raucous single, 'Devil Gate Drive' restored her to the top. Nicky Chinn says, "Not many people were using alliteration in their titles, but I think it sounds very good when you do it. 'Devil Gate Drive' is a good title and it was about meeting the bikers at the local caff."

"I did some ballads on my albums," says Suzi Quatro, who won a Rear Of The Year award, "but we didn't think slow songs were right for singles. I didn't have a laid-back hit single until 'If You Can't Give Me Love' in 1978." Although her duet with Chris Norman from Smokie, 'Stumblin' In' was only a Top 50 hit in the UK, it was her only US Top 10 single.

Although Suzi still performs her hits, she has shown herself capable of many other roles. She started acting when she was Leather Tuscadero in *Happy Days* and then appeared in *Minder* and *Dempsey And Makepeace*. She starred in a West End revival of *Calamity Jane* and she has produced her own show, *Tallulah Who?*, about the life of silent movie star, Tallulah Bankhead. Suzi is also known as one of Radio 2's rock'n'roll presenters.

Suzi Quatro

345 Alvin Stardust
Jealous Mind

Label & Cat No.:	**Magnet MAG 5**
Producer:	**Peter Shelley**
Writer:	**Peter Shelley**
Date reached No.1:	**9 March 1974**
Weeks at No.1:	**1**

THE NOTTINGHAM SINGER, BERNARD Jewry, became Shane Fenton and, with The Fentones, was a popular UK beat act before The Beatles. They had hits with 'I'm A Moody Guy' and 'Cindy's Birthday' and were regulars on BBC's *Saturday Club* and *Pop Go The Beatles*. Fenton married Iris Caldwell, the sister of Liverpool singer, Rory Storm, and in the late Sixties, he was often working with her as a double-act on cruises.

In 1973 the Magnet label decided that its initial release should be Fenton's version of an atmospheric rock'n'roll song, 'My Coo-Ca-Choo', written and produced by Peter Shelley. Shane Fenton was old-hat, so he dyed his blond hair, bought black leathers and became Alvin Stardust. "I didn't talk to anybody and I didn't smile, so I was the moody, untouchable Alvin Stardust," he says now. "I didn't dare do interviews in case I gave the game away and I had to ignore Tony Blackburn on *Top Of The Pops* when he recognised me. The image was an amalgam of things – certainly Lee Marvin in *Cat Ballou*, a bit of Gene Vincent and some of Dave Berry. I loved the way Dave used his hands, so I just pinched a bit from everybody."

The result was sensational and the single went to number two. "Peter Shelley was a brilliant producer and a brilliant songwriter. The minute 'My Coo-Ca-Choo' charted, he knew he had to have another one and he came up with 'Jealous Mind'." In a sense, it was the wrong song at number one as 'My Coo-Ca-Choo' is the classic Alvin Stardust record.

Peter Shelley found himself a pop star with 'Gee Baby' and 'Love Me, Love My Dog'. He said, "I was glad when it was all over because I was not comfortable on stage and I saw the strain that Alvin went through with photogaphs, interviews and getting ready for personal appearances. I got my kicks out of writing very simple songs and taking tremendous care with the production. Who wants serious stuff at the club or the disco?"

Alvin Stardust had several more hits in this vein including 'Red Dress' and 'You You You'. In 1981 he revived 'Pretend', basing his arrangement on Carl Mann's Sun recording, and in 1984 sang Mike Batt's 'I Feel Like Buddy Holly'. He still works as Alvin Stardust but, on one tour, performed with a giant wig and huge platform shoes. He had an accident when he fell off these shoes and had to cancel a few dates, this from a man who was promoting the Green Cross Code. Alvin now has two touring stage shows, one for Christmas and the other a tribute to rock'n'roll.

346 Paper Lace
Billy – Don't Be A Hero

Label & Cat No.:	**Magnet MAG 5**
Producers:	**Mitch Murray / Peter Callander**
Writers:	**Mitch Murray / Peter Callander**
Date reached No.1:	**16 March 1974**
Weeks at No.1:	**3**

IN 1972 THE SONGWRITERS, MITCH Murray and Peter Callander, formed their own label, Bus Stop, but they didn't pick up passengers with their first releases. In line with their story-songs 'The Ballad Of Bonnie And Clyde' and 'I Did What I Did For Maria', they wrote one about a cabin boy, 'Billy – Don't Be A Hero', but then changed the setting to the American Civil War. Mitch Murray wanted to give the song to a major artist, but Peter Callander's wife, Connie, saw Paper Lace win *Opportunity Knocks* and told Peter about them.

Paper Lace had been formed by the lead singer and drummer, Phil Wright, and the bassist, Cliff Fish, in 1969. The other members were the guitarists, Michael Vaughan, Chris Morris and, sounding like a tribute act, Carlo Santanna. They were the house band at Tiffany's in Rochdale and had had considerable experience before they appeared on the TV talent show.

'Billy – Don't Be A Hero' carried a powerful, anti-war message. The comedian and campaigner Spike Milligan made media appearances saying how significant this record was and how he admired the poignancy of its pay-off, "I heard she threw the letter away".

A cover version by Bo Donaldson & The Heywoods topped the US charts, but 'The Night Chicago Died', although number three here, was a US number one for Paper Lace. 'The Black Eyed Boys' was their third hit, but law suits followed as Paper Lace objected to Mitch and Peter's control. Paper Lace went to Warners and had a further chart single with 'We've Got The Whole World In His Hands' with Nottingham FC.

347 Terry Jacks
Seasons In The Sun

Label & Cat No.:	**Bell 1344**
Producer:	**Terry Jacks**
Writers:	**Jacques Brel / Rod McKuen**
Date reached No.1:	**6 April 1974**
Weeks at No.1:	**4**

THE SINGER AND SONGWRITER, Jacques Brel, made a huge impact in France and Belgium, but had to wait 10 years until he found sympathetic lyricists in Rod McKuen and Mort Shuman. He wrote 'Le Moribund (The Dying Man)' in 1961 and it was given English words by Rod McKuen in 1964 for a US single, 'Seasons In The Sun', by the campus heroes, The Kingston Trio. An excellent cover by The Fortunes just missed the UK charts.

The Canadian couple, Terry & Susan Jacks, had had a Top 10 hit with 'Which Way You Goin', Billy' as The Poppy Family in 1970. The follow-up, 'That's Where I Went Wrong', was prophetic as the couple divorced in 1973.

Terry Jacks was one of many producers asked to work with The Beach Boys, and he suggested

'Seasons In The Sun'. They recorded it but when they didn't release it, Terry reclaimed his arrangement and did it himself, thinking of a friend who had recently died as he put his vocal down. 'Seasons In The Sun' went to number one in Canada and then the US and the UK, selling nine million copies. "It's no secret that I didn't like Terry Jacks' version," said Rod McKuen, "because he changed some of my words."

Terry Jacks followed the single with another Jacques Brel & Rod McKuen song, 'If You Go Away', which made the Top 10.

348 Abba
Waterloo

Label & Cat No.: **Epic EPC 2240**

Producers: **Björn Ulvaeus / Benny Andersson**

Writers: **Björn Ulvaeus / Benny Andersson / Stig Anderson**

Date Reached No.1: **4 May 1974**

Weeks at No.1: **2**

It was the Eurovision Song Contest that eventually broke Abba, but not on their first attempt.

During the Sixties Benny Andersson and Björn Ulvaeus were the leading lights in top Swedish groups The Hep Stars and The Hootenanny Singers respectively. It was inevitable that they should meet along the way and fortunate that they became friends and songwriting partners under the stewardship of Stockholm song publisher Stig Anderson's Polar Music company. Around the same time, Anni-Frid Lyngstad, who until then had sung standards with a semi-pro jazz band, launched a solo career. She entered *Melodifestivalen*, the Swedish selections for the Eurovision Song Contest, with a song entitled 'Härlig är vår Jord' ('Our Earth Is Wonderful') and finished fourth. Meanwhile Agnetha Fältskog was beginning a career as a lightweight pop singer.

By 1972 Agnetha (pronounced Anyetta) had married Björn and Benny was living with Anni-Frid (known as Frida), so it was only natural that the two boys would bring in their partners to provide vocals on songs they wrote and recorded. Among the first was a track called 'People Need Love', under the rather unimaginative group name Björn, Benny, Agnetha & Frida. In 1973 they decided to simply use the first letters from each of their forenames, thus becoming ABBA. What they hadn't realised was that Abba was also the name of a canned fish company in Sweden. After some sweet-talking, an agreement was made that allowed them use of the name as well.

In 1973 Abba submitted a song for Sweden's Song For Europe. The song was 'Ring Ring', with English lyrics written by Neil Sedaka and a title that Benny and Björn thought had a 'bell' feeling to it. It lost out to 'You're Summer' by The Nova and eventually finished third.

The following year they considered two more songs for Eurovision: 'Waterloo' and 'Hasta Manana'. In the end they chose the former which ingeniously compared romantic surrender to Napoleon Bonaparte's defeat by British and German forces at the battle in the Belgian town.

The contest was held in the UK at The Dome in Brighton and watched by an estimated 250 million viewers worldwide. Stig Anderson, now also their manager and occasional song-writing collaborator, thought that people might feel that 'Waterloo' was too aggressive for Eurovision, but he didn't care. He knew that millions of people would see Abba and that was enough for him. They dressed in glittery costumes created by the Swedish designer Inger Svenneke, with epaulettes that emphasised the military concept, an effect heightened when their conductor, Sven-Olof Waldoff, came out wearing a Napoleon outfit. They won by six points, beating Italy into second place. Olivia Newton-John, who represented the UK with 'Long Live Love', came 11th.

Stig Anderson was so confident they would win that he had placed a bet, even though the bookies' odds were 20-1. Like many of Abba's subsequent hits, 'Waterloo' was also recorded in various foreign languages, in this case French, German and, of course, Swedish. It was re-issued in May, 2004 to commemorate the 30th anniversary of Abba winning Eurovision on 7" and CD single with the original B-Side, 'Watch Out', and reached number 20.

349 The Rubettes
Sugar Baby Love

Label & Cat No.: **Polydor 2058 442**

Producer: **Wayne Bickerton**

Writers: **Wayne Bickerton / Tony Waddington**

Date reached No.1: **18 May 1974**

Weeks at No.1: **4**

The Liverpool musicians, Wayne Bickerton and Tony Waddington, toured the world in The Pete Best Four, but the former Beatle didn't sell records. Still, it was a foot in the business and Wayne Bickerton was one of the first producers at Decca's more experimental label, Deram.

In 1974 Wayne and Tony hired session men to play 'Sugar Baby Love', a rock'n'roll pastiche which owed something to Phil Spector, The Four Seasons and The Diamonds. "We had Paul Da Vinci singing in that incredibly high falsetto voice," says Wayne, "and then a vocal group sings 'bop-shu-waddy' over and over for about three minutes. Gerry Shury, who did the string arrangements, said, 'This is not going to work: you can't have a vocal group singing 'bop-shu-waddy' non-stop. A lot of people said the same thing to us and the more determined I became to release it. Democracy doesn't work in a creative environment! The record was dormant for six or seven weeks and then we got a break on *Top Of The Pops* and it took off like a rocket and sold six million copies worldwide. Gerry said to me, 'I'm keeping my mouth shut and will concentrate on conducting the strings.' But he could have been right. I didn't really know that it was going to work."

The single had been released under the name of The Rubettes, who were Alan Williams (lead vocals, guitar), Bill Hurd and Peter Arnisson (keyboards), Tony J. Thorpe (guitar), Mick Clarke

Abba, the only Eurovision Song Contest winners to develop a lasting and successful international career; left to right: Benny, Anni-Frid, Agnetha and Björn

(bass) and John Richardson (bass). All had played on the record except Alan Williams, who was replacing Paul DaVinci.

Taking a lead from Gene Vincent's Blue Caps, The Rubettes wore white caps and also had white suits. "I think our image really sold that record," says Tony J. Thorpe, "and we were very lucky to get on *Top Of The Pops*. We were only at number 51, but the work permits for Sparks fell through at the last minute and we got on in their place. Our hats became bigger than the band. If we turned up to a TV show without the hats, the producers would go crazy."

The Rubettes had further hits with 'Tonight' and 'Juke Box Jive', and then Bickerton and Waddington formed their own record label, State, where The Rubettes had further Top 20 hits with 'I Can Do It', 'Foe-Dee-O-Dee' and 'Baby I Know'. Alan Williams leads a version of The Rubettes which tours to this day – you may not know the personnel but you'll recognise the hats. As for Tony J. Thorpe, he was the guest vocalist on The Firm's 1982 hit, 'Arthur Daley ('E's Alright)'.

350 Ray Stevens
The Streak

Label & Cat No.: **Janus 6146 201**
Producer: **Ray Stevens**
Writer: **Ray Stevens**
Date reached No.1: **15 June 1974**
Weeks at No.1: **1**

BY SPECIALISING IN ONE-OFF NOVELTIES as well as straight country songs, Ray Stevens defies categorisation. 'Ahab The Arab' would be criticised for political incorrectness now but it made number five on the US charts in 1962. He had further US hits with the social drama of 'Mr. Businessman', the saga of a guitar playing jungle king 'Guitarzan', and 'Bridget The Midget (The Queen Of The Blues)', which was a UK number two. Another hit, 'Everything Is Beautiful', was a children's hymn. After 'The Streak', he did a country styling of the jazz ballad, 'Misty', and a chicken-clucking version of Glenn Miller's 'In The Mood'.

Although there is nothing predictable about Ray Stevens' records, most of the time he is not funny and adding canned laughter and audience applause only underlines the problem. Is there anything more annoying than 'Shriners Convention', 'Your Bozo's Back Again', 'It's Me Again, Margaret', 'I Saw Elvis In A UFO' or 'Would Jesus Wear A Rolex?' On the other hand, his 'Sunday Mornin' Comin' Down' is as good as anyone's and his depiction of a shotgun marriage in 'Isn't It Lonely Together?' gets to the heart of the problem.

Streaking as such started in Los Angeles in 1974 and Ray started to write a song about it, but then moved on to something else. When he saw that other artists were releasing streaking songs, he thought he had better complete it and he took his record to the top radio station in Nashville. They played it and the reaction was instantly favourable. Five days after the record was released, a streaker ran past David Niven at the Oscars ceremony. This made front page news and Ray's record was perfect timing.

Although the weather would not usually encourage streaking in the UK, it was a hot summer and John Arlott's understated comments when a streaker stopped a Test Match cannot be bettered – "And I think he has seen the last of his cricket for the day." Over a typical weekend, arrests for offending public decency were made in Belfast, Derby, Hull, Wisbech and Speaker's Corner. For once, British and American humour came together and the phrase, "Don't look, Ethel", passed into the language.

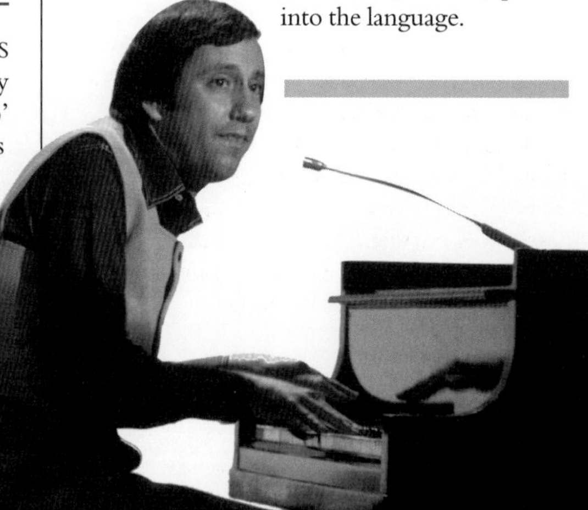

351 Gary Glitter
Always Yours

Label & Cat No.: **Bell BELL 1359**
Producer: **Mike Leander**
Writers: **Mike Leander / Gary Glitter**
Date Reached No.1: **22 June 1974**
Weeks at No.1: **1**

MANY OF GARY GLITTER'S SONG titles acknowledged the importance of his fans. After 'I Love You Love Me Love' came the number three ballad 'Remember Me This Way', an expression he may have come to regret in light of more recent events.

Mike and Gary decided it was time for another upbeat song and so, following an expression Glitter used to use on stage, "I'm yours, always yours", they wrote what was to be Glitter's last number one.

Glitter often affected a startled look, complete with bulging eyes. The eye expressions came naturally, because as a child he squinted a lot. Glitter recalled, "When I used to go and visit my nan, she used to always yell at me 'open your eyes'."

By November 1975 his run of 11 consecutive Top 10 hits came to an end when his cover of The Rivingtons' 'Papa Oom Mow Mow' stalled at number 38. Glitter soldiered on, appearing in pantomimes and attempting several comebacks. The only successful one was in Christmas 1984, when 'Another Rock And Roll Christmas' restored him to the Top 10. For a while his annual Wembley Christmas shows became gatherings of the faithful, many of whom would wear silver glitter costumes.

When Glitter was arrested in 1997 for downloading child pornography on his computer, many unflattering photographs of him, which revealed that he wore a wig to disguise his baldness, appeared in the tabloids. Two years later he was found guilty and sentenced to four months in prison. Glitter now lives abroad, but such is his disgrace that his hits no longer appear on compilations. He now uses the internet to keep in touch with his fans and sell his music. So

Ray Stevens

unpopular is he with the British press that if he returned to Britain he would certainly become a target for unwelcome coverage.

352 Charles Aznavour
She

Label & Cat No.:	**Barclay BAR 26**
Producer:	**Eddie Barclay**
Writers:	**Charles Aznavour / Herbert Kretzmer**
Date reached No.1:	**29 June 1974**
Weeks at No.1:	**4**

"THE FRENCH APPROACH TO WRITING songs is much more serious than in the English-speaking world," says Charles Aznavour, who was born in France in 1924 to Armenian parents. "A song is more than just an entertainment. Writing is a serious matter and listening is a serious matter too. Jacques Brel's songs are about death, George Brassens' are about death, Leo Ferré's are about the past and I am about the past too. But my background is not French. My background comes from Oriental poetry mixed with French poetry."

London Weekend Television were filming a drama series, *The Seven Faces Of Woman*, and they asked the lyricist, Herbert Kretzmer, for a suitable theme song. He says, "What they needed was a song to link the seven plays and the producer thought I might write something for Marlene Dietrich as she represented the ageless woman. I didn't like that idea much as if you're going to write about a woman's mystique, it would be better if it were not sung by a woman. If she sang about her own mystery, the song would be too calculated and knowing. I said, 'It should be a song about a woman as seen by a man, and what better man than Charles Aznavour, who sings about love and romance? I brought him into the project and it turned out terribly well."

Writing a theme song is by no means an easy ride: "The first verse could only run for 35 seconds," continues Herbert Kretzmer. "The time before the play began, and it had to run over the main titles and be complete in itself. Then it had to be stretched out to a record so that it did not sound like padding. At the time Aznavour was touring all over the place and it took some time to get a melody from him. The moment he played me that long, opening note, the word 'She' jumped into my mind and I knew we had the song."

The song was returned to the Top 20 in 1999 by Elvis Costello for the opening credits of the film, *Notting Hill*. Charles Aznavour, now 80 and parodied by The Goodies as Charles Aznovoice, has given his farewell concerts and the song will never again be sung as intensely again. He comments, "People say I am sad and never smile, but if I sing a happy song, I smile. I do not follow the practice of some singers who stretch their faces even though the song they are singing is of unhappy love."

353 George McCrae
Rock Your Baby

Label & Cat No.:	**Jay Boy BOY 85**
Producers:	**Harry Casey / Richard Finch**
Writers:	**Harry Casey / Richard Finch**
Date Reached No.1:	**27 July 1974**
Weeks at No.1:	**3**

ALTHOUGH TAMLA MOTOWN HAD released many 'dance' records, it was the heavy brass sound, as employed by Sly & The Family Stone on 'Dance To The Music' (1968) and James Brown on 'Get Up I Feel Like Being A Sex Machine' (1970), that signalled the arrival of disco music. George's 'Rock Your Baby' is generally accepted as the first disco number one.

Born in Florida in 1944, George, during his school years, was a member of The Fabulous Stepbrothers and then The Jiving Jets. In the Sixties, he married Gwen Mosley and they recorded as a duo. Gwen soon signed a deal with Columbia Records and George became her manager.

Prior to forming his Sunshine Band, Harry 'KC' Casey was a warehouse worker and budding songwriter. Richard Finch, who later became a member of the Sunshine Band, was an apprentice engineer at TK Studios. They wrote an instrumental disco track in 45 minutes and took it to TK Records founder, Henry Stone, who agreed they had something but felt it needed lyrics. Immediately, Harry and Richard came up with some lyrics, but in the process, Harry felt the key was too high to sing himself. Henry recalled, "I suggested to Harry that Gwen McCrae might be a good contender to cut the track, but just then George walked in and I then told Harry to let George have a go first."

The track was cheap to make. They used second hand tape in the studio and only paid one musician, Jerome Smith, for his guitar work. Harry played keyboards and Richard provided bass and drums.

Gwen and George contributed backing vocals to Bill Wyman's 1974 album *Monkey Grip*. Gwen, with George on backing vocals, had a Top 10 US hit with 'Rockin' Chair'. Her only UK hit, 'All This Love That I'm Giving' reached a disappointing number 63 in 1988, but made the Top 40 when re-recorded five years later. Gwen and George split in 1977.

In the late Nineties, London's Capital Radio organised a Seventies disco revival night which was to include George McCrae, but it was postponed when the station erroneously announced that George had died. George is, however, alive and well and still touring in the 2000s.

354 The Three Degrees
When Will I See You Again?

Label & Cat No.:	**Philadelphia International PIR 2155**
Producers:	**Kenny Gamble / Leon Huff**
Writers:	**Kenny Gamble / Leon Huff**
Date reached No.1:	**17 August 1974**
Weeks at No.1:	**2**

LIKE FRANKIE LYMON & THE TEENAGERS, the Philadelphia girl group, The Three

Degrees, was discovered by Richard Barrett. They first recorded in 1963, but it was seven years before they started to have even small hit records in the States – 'Maybe' and 'You're The One' amongst them. They appeared in *The French Connection* (1971) and became Engelbert Humperdinck's opening act. "The Three Degrees' harmonies were different to the black artists out of Motown," says lead singer, Sheila Ferguson who joined in 1966. "Richard Barrett made us listen to The Beatles, Jimmy Webb songs and The Swingle Singers and said we shouldn't listen to Motown. It gave us a distinctive sound."

In 1971 when Kenny Gamble and Leon Huff set up Philadelphia International Records (PIR), they, on the other hand, wanted to be exactly like Motown where, in the best moments, the artists, the musicians and the songwriters worked together to create many classic recordings. PIR's house band, led by Dexter Wansel, was called MFSB, which, to emphasise the camaraderie, stood for Mother, Father, Sister, Brother. Richard Barrett persuaded Gamble and Huff to sign The Three Degrees and the group joined MFSB for TSOP (The Sound Of Philadelphia). This was the theme music for the TV show, *Soul Train*, and a US number one.

In the summer of 1974, The Three Degrees (Sheila Ferguson, Valerie Holiday, Helen Scott) recorded their own breakthrough single, 'When Will I See You Again?' Sheila Ferguson says, "The song was played to me by Kenny Gamble at the piano in 1973 and I threw a tantrum. I screamed and yelled and I said that I would never sing it. I thought it was ridiculously insulting to be given such a simple song and that it took no bloody talent to sing it. We did do it and several million copies later, I realised that he knew more than me."

A series of hit singles followed, first for PIR ('Take Good Care Of Yourself') and then for Ariola ('Woman In Love', 'The Runner', 'My Simple Heart'). The group was very popular in the UK and performed at Prince Charles' 30th birthday party, acquiring the sobriquet of Charlie's Angels. The Three Degrees looked glamorous in identical spangled gowns and jewellery, and as Sheila Ferguson jokes, "Nobody saw my legs until I left The Three Degrees." In 1999 Sheila toured the UK in the musical, *Soul Train*.

355 The Osmonds
Love Me For A Reason

Label & Cat No.: **MGM 2006 458**

Producers: **Mike Curb**

Writer: **Johnny Bristol**

Date reached No.1: **31 August 1974**

Weeks at No.1: **3**

THE OSMONDS HAD THREE TOP 10 HITS in 1973 – 'Crazy Horses', 'Going Home' and 'Let Me In' – and, following a Top 20 entry with an old track, 'I Can't Stop', they went to the top with 'Love Me For A Reason'. The song was written by the Tamla-Motown writer and producer, Johnny Bristol, who at the time had his own Top 10 hit with 'Hang On In There Baby'. The romantic ballad was ideal for The Osmonds, but it could just as easily have been recorded by The Supremes or The Four Tops.

The Osmonds had a further Top 10 with 'The Proud One' in 1975, but, as so often happens with acts whose following is comprised almost wholly of young girls, the public lost interest and they stopped selling. The group split up in 1980, but returned two years later having repositioned themselves as a country music act, and played the Wembley C&W Festival. The Osmonds had little luck on the US country charts, but Marie did have three chart-toppers in 1985/6 with 'Meet Me In Montana', 'There's No Stopping Your Heart' and 'You're Still New To Me'.

Eventually, The Osmonds bought their own theatre in Branson, Missouri and now perform there regularly alongside regular tours. They came to prominence on *The Andy Williams Show* and now Andy Williams' Moon River theatre is on the next block. "We're still very popular," says Jimmy Osmond, who is part of the group. "The Osmonds' website has four million hits a week." In 1994 Boyzone revived 'Love Me For A Reason' and took it to number two.

Johnny Bristol returned to Motown in 1985 to work with The Four Tops and then he produced and recorded in the UK for Ian Levine's ersatz Motown label, Motor City. He died in Michigan in 2004, the same year that Merrill Osmond toured the UK, performing 'Love Me For A Reason' as the highlight of his act.

356 Carl Douglas
Kung Fu Fighting

Label & Cat No.: **Pye 7N 45377**

Producer: **Biddu**

Writer: **Carl Douglas**

Date reached No.1: **21 September 1974**

Weeks at No.1: **3**

THE INTEREST IN THE MARTIAL ART, Kung Fu, came about through the films of Bruce Lee and then the TV series, *Kung Fu*, with David Carradine. Thousands of people were learning the art and as Carl Douglas observed, "Everybody was Kung Fu fighting."

Carl Douglas was born in Kingston, Jamaica in 1962, but he came to the UK and obtained a degree in engineering. He sang soul music with The Charmers and built up a following around the London clubs. For over 10 years, Douglas released singles from time to time and was tantalisingly close to the big break. In 1972 he sang the title song from the 1972 espionage thriller, *Embassy*, starring Richard Roundtree and Chuck Connors.

Embassy's score was written by an Asian producer Biddu, who wanted to make some disco records. In 1974 he asked Carl Douglas to record a new American song, 'I Want To Give You My Everything', and Carl asked if he could put his own 'Kung Fu Fighting' on the B-side. The track was recorded in 15 minutes and the hoo's and the ha's in the production bring to mind the sound of Sam Cooke's *Chain Gang*. No one took it seriously until a Pye executive thought it should be the A-side.

'Kung Fu Fighting' topped both the UK and US charts, but his follow-up, 'Dance The Kung Fu', was ignored. Biddu had his own success with 'Summer Of '42' in 1975 and with writing and producing for Tina Charles. Carl Douglas

The Osmonds, the clean-cut family group of Mormons from Utah. Left to right: Jay, Merrill,, Jimmy, Donny, Wayne and Alan

returned to the Top 10 as part of a 1998 re-mix of 'Kung Fu Fighting' by Bus Stop, complete with rap and oriental sounds.

357 John Denver
Annie's Song

Label & Cat No.: **RCA APBO 0295**

Producer: **Milt Okun**

Writer: **John Denver**

Date reached No.1: **12 October 1974**

Weeks at No.1: **1**

CONSIDERING THE SUCCESS HE enjoyed in America, it is surprising that John Denver had only one UK Top 30 hit and that was a number one, 'Annie's Song'. Despite numerous tours and TV appearances, the British public ignored all his other US No 1's – 'Sunshine On My Shoulders', 'Back Home Again', 'Thank God I'm A Country Boy', 'Calypso' and 'I'm Sorry'. In the same way that the British public never took to surf records, maybe his Johnny One Note theme of the rocky mountains was too alien for us. Most of us thank God we're city boys and if we had all followed John Denver into the wilderness, there would have been no wilderness left.

He was born Henry John Deutschendorf, the son of an air force pilot, in Roswell, New Mexico on New Year's Eve 1943. At first he thought of being an architect, but he got drawn into the folk scene in Los Angeles. Randy Sparks of The New Christy Minstrels suggested a change in name and, "I chose Denver because my heart longed to live in the mountains."

John Denver became part of The Chad Mitchell Trio, and in 1967 they recorded his composition, 'Leavin' On A Jet Plane'. Denver wrote it in Washington "not so much from feeling that way for someone, but from the longing of having someone to love." He soon did have someone to love as he met Ann Martell and followed her on a skiing trip to Aspen. They were married, also in 1967.

Without Chad Mitchell, The Chad Mitchell Trio floundered and John found himself with debts of $40,000. This put a strain on the marriage, which he articulated in 'Goodbye Again'. Fortunately, Peter, Paul & Mary turned 'Leavin' On A Jet Plane' into an international hit.

Even though he was unknown, John Denver was given a six-week television series on BBC-2. The public warmed to his million-watt smile, slightly goofy personality, cowboy shirts, granny glasses, Dutch haircut, his valiant attempts at juggling and catchphrase, 'Far-out'. Sure, he was a hippie but he was one the whole family could identify with.

Denver's melodic, light voice was well suited to his songs which reflected his love of the mountains and his love of his wife. It contrasted with the cynicism of urban songwriters like Paul Simon, Bob Dylan and John Lennon. Denver's songs were seen as naïve, which was partly true – he was a mother nature's son and even when depressed, his feelings emerged in positive songs like 'Sunshine On My Shoulders'.

Although Denver's albums sold in the UK, his singles failed to have the same success as in America, but this changed in 1974 when he released 'Annie's Song'. It topped the UK charts and in 1978 became an instrumental success for the classical flautist James Galway.

The Rocky Mountain hype went into operation when Denver split with Annie in 1975. They patched up their marriage, but divorced in 1983. An album and a single, both called *Seasons Of The Heart*, captured the strain of the relationship. Denver married Cassandra Delaney, who had sung backing vocals on his albums. Much to Denver's surprise as he thought he was sterile, they had a daughter, Jesse Belle.

Denver founded an environmental group, Windstar, and visited Russia and China to discuss the preservation of the planet. He loved both undersea studies and space exploration and even applied to become an astronaut. He sang about Jacques Cousteau's boat Calypso and the space shuttle disaster in 'Flying For Me'. He died in October 1997 when the experimental, lightweight aeroplane he was flying plunged into the Monterey Bay, just off the California coast near Monterey. John Denver will be remembered as a singer-songwriter who told us that life was perfect. And maybe that's no bad thing. As he said, "I'm a kind of Everyman. I epitomise America."

358 Sweet Sensation
Sad Sweet Dreamer

Label & Cat No.: **Pye 7N 45385**

Producers: **D. E. S. Parton / Tony Hatch**

Writer: **D. E. S. Parton**

Date reached No.1: **19 October 1974**

Weeks at No.1: **1**

FIFTEEN-YEAR-OLD MARCEL KING worked in a delicatessen in Manchester. He was singing to the customers and one of the staff introduced him to the keyboard player, Leroy Smith, who played in a club band, Sweet Sensation, with three vocalists (St. Clair Palmer, Vincent James, Junior Daye), guitar (Garry Shaughnessy), bass (Barry Johnson) and drums (Roy Flowers).

They auditioned for the ITV talent show, *New Faces* and, like Showaddywaddy, they won. Tony Hatch, a judge usually regarded as the 'Hatchet Man', thought they were excellent and signed them to Pye Records. Their first single, 'Snow Fire', did very little, but the next, written by David Parton (as D.E.S. Parton) and published by Tony Hatch, was 'Sad Sweet Dreamer'. The single topped the UK charts and also made the US Top 20.

Sweet Sensation made number 11 with the follow-up, 'Purely By Coincidence', but the next record, 'Boom Boom Boom' went boom boom boom. None of their subsequent singles did any business – 'Mr. Cool', 'Sweet Regrets', 'Mail Train', 'You're My Sweet Sensation' (!) and 'Wake Up And Be Somebody'. It's just one of those things you put down to experience. David Parton, however, had his own Top 10 hit with his version of Stevie Wonder's 'Isn't She Lovely?' in 1976.

There is a coda to this story. Marcel King was signed to the ultra-hip Manchester label,

In his home country of America, his Rocky Mountain Highness John Denver was among the best selling artists of the mid-Seventies

Factory, in 1991 but his drug habit proved to be too much of a problem for the owners. This from a label with Happy Mondays and Joy Division on its books! Shaun Ryder has said that King's 'Reach For Love' was one of his favourite records.

359 Ken Boothe
Everything I Own

Label & Cat No.:	**Trojan TR 7920**
Producer:	**Lloyd Charmers**
Writer:	**David Gates**
Date Reached No.1:	**26 October 1974**
Weeks at No.1:	**3**

DAVID GATES' FATHER SAID TO HIS SON, "You can do music as a hobby, but it is hard to make a living from it." David was determined to prove his dad wrong. David explained, "I made a deal with my dad that if I didn't make any progress in the business within two years, I would return and finish college."

David's girlfriend was the sister of singer/songwriter Leon Russell. Once he'd heard Leon's material, he was inspired to write songs himself. He became a session musician and played on Jackie De Shannon demos. Six months had passed and he wasn't making much headway until Johnny Burnette recorded 'The Fool Of The Year' in 1962 and that was enough for him to keep writing.

Two years after making the deal, his father died. At the funeral, a friend took David aside and said, "Your dad was so proud of what you were doing." David agreed by replying, "My success would have been so special to him as he was my greatest influence. So I decided to write and record 'Everything I Own' about him. If you listen to the words, 'You sheltered me from harm, kept me warm, gave my life to me, set me free', it says it all." Jack Jones was such a fan that he recorded a whole album of Gates' compositions and called the album *Bread Winners*.

Ken Boothe was born in Denham Town, near Kingston, Jamaica in 1948. In his teens he met a local singer, Winston 'Stranger' Cole. Cole was so impressed with Ken's voice that the two formed a duo, which lasted a couple of years. Ken's deep gritty voice earned him the reputation as Jamaica's answer to Wilson Pickett. In 1967 Ken he cut a ska version of Sandie Shaw's 'Puppet On A String', which was huge in Jamaica.

In 1971 he signed with Trojan records and was teamed with producer Lloyd Charmers. It was Charmers' suggestion that he cover 'Everything I Own'. The follow-up, 'Crying Over You', reached number 11 in the chart and both tracks were taken from the album *Everything I Own*. In 1996 he contributed to Shaggy's single 'The Train Is Coming', which was featured in the film *Money Train*. Ken says, "I sing for God, I don't sing for money. I love making music and that's what I do best, so whenever you don't see me, that's what I'm doing."

360 David Essex
Gonna Make You A Star

Label & Cat No.:	**CBS CBS 2492**
Producer:	**Jeff Wayne**
Writer:	**David Essex**
Date Reached No.1:	**16 November 1974**
Weeks at No.1:	**3**

"I'VE ALWAYS FELT LIKE A MUSICIAN WHO acts, rather than an actor who sings now and then," says David Essex, the boy with the twinkle in his eye and cheeky grin who never failed to have women falling at his feet.

David Cook was born in Plaistow in London's East End in 1947. He recalled, "I just wanted to play blues music. Well, that was after I wanted to be a footballer. When I was 13, I had a promising career as a footballer. I played for West Ham Boys but then I got interested in urban blues and got into people like Buddy Guy, Muddy Waters and John Lee Hooker."

When he began to show an interest in the drums, his parents encouraged him by buying him a kit and, much to the annoyance of the neighbours, let him practise in their council flat. He joined a local band The Everons as their drummer. David said, "The guitarist kept moaning about having to sing and play at the same time, so because I was the youngest, they turned to me and almost forced me to sing." When the band fell apart, their manager and *Daily Telegraph* theatre critic, Derek Bowman, recognised David's talent and asked him if he wanted to become a solo singer, David agreed. Derek also helped David's film career after he had arranged an interview for him with a repertory agency.

David wrote his first hit 'Rock On' for the film *That'll Be The Day* in which he also appeared. He said, "I tried to combine Americana imagery with something quite different in recording techniques. When it was a hit all over the world, I thought to myself, 'well I must be a songwriter', and it gave me confidence."

Jeff Wayne, who was born in New York, studied at the Juilliard School Of Music and after a stint with an early incarnation of The Sandpipers, went on to work as an arranger for the Righteous Brothers before coming to London in the mid-Sixties. David met Jeff via Liz Whiting, an understudy in *Godspell* in which David appeared. She had started dating Jeff. David said, "Jeff was a fan of the show and one evening whilst visiting England he came to the show and afterwards asked me if I would like to sing on an advert. I agreed and ended up recording the Pledge polish commercial."

In 1974 David was holidaying in the South of France with his close friend Steve Collier. David remembered, "Steve had brought his guitar along and I was sitting by the pool strumming away when this tune popped into my head. It later turned out to be 'Gonna Make You A Star'.

David Essex

361 Barry White
You're The First, The Last, My Everything

Label & Cat No.: **20th Century BTC 2133**
Producer: **Barry White**
Writers: **Barry White / Tony Sepe / Peter Sterling Radcliffe**
Date Reached No.1: **7 December 1974**
Weeks at No.1: **2**

During the halcyon disco era of the Seventies, Barry White, with his deep, sexy baritone voice booming gently out of the speakers, seemed to hit the right chord with lovers everywhere.

Born Barry Carter on September 12, 1944 in Galveston, Texas and raised in Los Angeles, he grew up singing gospel songs as well as teaching himself piano and drums. He hated school, got involved with local gangs and ended up a thief. Barry recalled, "I burgled, I stole and I was always fighting. I may have burgled houses, but all I took was the record collection." In 1960 he was caught stealing car tyres and was jailed for four and a half months. "Jail was horrible, so I decided that when I get out of prison, I'm gonna make something of my life," he insisted.

In the mid-Sixties, Barry undertook an abundance of session work and did some production work with Bob & Earl and The Bobby Fuller Four. He worked for a number of local record labels before landing a job in A&R for Bob Keane. Bob owned the Mustang, Del-Fi and Bronco record labels and was responsible for Sam Cooke's early recordings. In 1968 he discovered the female trio Love Unlimited and became their manager, writer and producer.

Barry, who suffered from weight problems had a number of nicknames, including The Walrus Of Love, The Maestro, and The King Of Love. Barry said, "I think the term 'The Walrus Of Love' is not only stupid, but also a kind of negative statement that comes from people who are either envious or jealous."

Barry White

In 1956 Peter Radcliffe wrote and recorded a demo of a country and western song called 'You're The First, The Last, The In-Between'. He tried for over 20 years to get someone to record it. But no one was interested.

"One year, I had no money and Peter went out and bought my kids some Christmas presents," Barry recalled. "I was grateful for that and said I would pay him back one day." Peter told Barry he had written a song and wanted Barry to listen to it with a view to recording it. When Barry heard it he knew it was a smash. Barry remembered, "I changed some words, part of the melody and some of the title, but kept the chord structure."

Barry, whose sound owes no small debt to Issac Hayes, had a fondness for long song titles and in the Seventies, clocked up 14 hits, including 'I'm Gonna Love You Just A Little Bit More Baby', 'It's Ecstasy When You Lay Down Next To Me' and a sensual version of Billy Joel's 'Just The Way You Are'. The Eighties was a quiet decade for Barry, but he was back in full swing in the Nineties with appearances on top rated shows like *Ally McBeal* and *The Simpsons*.

During the Eighties, Barry's younger brother Darryl was killed in a street shooting. Barry died of kidney failure on July 4, 2003.

362 Mud
Lonely This Christmas

Label & Cat No.: **RAK 187**
Producers: **Nicky Chinn / Mike Chapman**
Writers: **Nicky Chinn / Mike Chapman**
Date reached No.1: **21 December 1974**
Weeks at No.1: **4**

After the Christmas extravaganza in 1973 with hyperactive hits from Slade and Wizzard, Mud had a Christmas number one with a ballad, 'Lonely This Christmas'. Nicky Chinn says, "It was Mud parodying Elvis Presley, and some people did think it was Elvis at first. Les did a great Elvis on that. We didn't write it that way, it was just how he saw the song."

Les Gray agrees, "I was doing an Elvis on that but it was really a send-up of all those smoochy songs. It works because it can also be taken seriously. I remember playing it at the Liverpool Empire and some of the fans were crying and others were laughing."

It rounded off a remarkable year for Les Gray (vocals), Rob Davis (guitar), Roy Stiles (bass) and Dave Mount (drums). Mud had had hits with 'Tiger Feet' (1), 'The Cat Crept In' (2), 'Rocket' (6) and now 'Lonely This Christmas'. They also had a big-selling album with *Mudrock*. Les Gray reflected, shortly before his death in 2004, "We'd been working so hard for years. We'd had daytime jobs for five years and were playing five or six nights a week, sometimes with two gigs a night. All I remember now is humping the equipment around."

363 Status Quo
Down Down

Label & Cat No.: **Vertigo 6059 114**
Producer: **Status Quo**
Writers: **Francis Rossi / Bob Young**
Date reached No.1: **18 January 1975**
Weeks at No.1: **1**

The South London band, Status Quo, first recorded as The Spectres ('I (Who Have Nothing)') and Traffic Jam ('Almost But Not Quite') and then, in 1967, chose The Status Quo instead of Quo Vadis. The following year they made the charts with the psychedelic 'Pictures Of Matchstick Men' but they quickly became a heavy metal boogie band, scoring 22 Top 10 singles.

Status Quo covered many oldies ('The Wild Side Of Life', 'The Wanderer') and discovered

John Fogerty's 'Rockin' All Over The World', but most of their songs were written by the band's mainstays, Francis Rossi and Rick Parfitt, often with their road manager and sometime harmonica player, Bob Young. 'Paper Plane', 'Caroline', 'Break The Rules', 'Roll Over Lay Down;', 'What You're Proposing' and 'Whatever You Want' were all original songs.

'Down Down' was written by Quo's lead singer, Francis Rossi, with Bob Young. "The Seventies are the definitive Quo years," says Bob, "I think 'Down Down' is a really good song and the title rolled off the tongue."

Francis Rossi remembers, "We had done the verses and we had 'Again and again and what?' and we kept thinking of Tyrannosaurus Rex's 'Deborah' and realised that we needed a 'd-d' in there. We thought of 'Down Down' which didn't make any sense with the rest of the song, but it worked. It didn't matter as we aren't trying to write deep meaningful lyrics. Nor was Marc Bolan. What is 'De-De-De-Debora' but 'P-P-P-Pick up a Penguin'?"

"We didn't celebrate our number one as we were so busy," says Bob, "We were on the road so much that we only came home to have children. They didn't seem to mind though. My son became Quo's road manager when he grew up."

364 The Tymes
M/S Grace

Label & Cat No.: **RCA Victor RCA 2493**

Producer: **Billy Jackson**

Writers: **Johanna Hall / John Hall**

Date Reached No.1: **25 January 1975**

Weeks at No.1: **1**

When John Hall and his then wife, Johanna wrote 'Miss Grace', they did so because they thought it would be cool to write a doo-wop song.

John Hall was a member of New York rock group, Orleans, and Johanna was a music journalist. After they married they started writing songs together. Johanna had grown up listening to doo-wop songs like the Dells' 'Oh What A Night' and Gene Chandler's 'Duke Of Earl'. John wrote the music and they collaborated on the lyrics.

As John described, "My demo version had no intro. The intro you hear on The Tymes version is something their musical director came up with. I never knew of it until the single came out. The same applies to the spelling of the title. The song has a real feminine feel and is set in perfume and roses. It was The Tymes' publishing company who felt it would appeal to a much wider female audience if they used the title M/s Grace instead of Miss Grace." The most likely reason for this was because it was becoming fashionable for women to conceal their marital status. "I loved what they did with it, except I felt it should be a bit slower."

The Tymes were formed in 1959 as The Latineers. They originally comprised George Williams, Donald Banks, Albert Berry, George Hilliard and Norman Burnett. In 1972 Melanie Moore and Terri Gonzalez replaced Hilliard and Berry.

Once John's demo was completed, he gave it to his publishers, Albert Grossman Music. Albert, who once managed Janis Joplin and Bob Dylan as well as co-organising the first *Newport Folk Festival* in 1959, passed it on to his in-house song plugger Linda Wortman. John explained, "Linda was brilliant, she always wanted to be first with a new song. She would want you to call her at three in the morning and play it down the phone to her and while you're playing it she's making a list of possible artists to record it. I did this and Linda suggested The Tymes as it has that old-fashioned Tymes feel."

John left Orleans in 1977, but periodically reforms the band and tours around the US. They still include 'Miss Grace' in their set and have recently issued a live CD. Two weeks after the CD came out, John received a call from The Tymes' manager saying "I love your cover of 'M/s Grace'."

The Tymes were unable to sustain their chart career beyond 1976 but remained together for several years after that. Hilliard and Berry were eventually replaced by two girls, Terri Gonzalez and Melanie Moore, bringing about a change of image.

365 Pilot
January

Label & Cat No.: **EMI EMI 2255**

Producer: **Alan Parsons**

Writer: **Dave Paton**

Date Reached No.1: **1 February 1975**

Weeks at No.1: **3**

In 1967 at the age of 16, David Paton answered an advert in the London *Evening News* for a lead guitarist with a popular band of the day, The Beachcombers. They secured a contract with CBS Records and had a regular slot at the Marquee Club in London. In 1974 David (vocals / bass), Bill Lyall (keyboards) – both early members of the Bay City Rollers – and Stuart Tosh (drums) formed a group and won a contract with EMI Records. Taking the initials of their surnames, they added a couple of vowels and came up with Pilot. Guitarist, Ian Bairnson, joined the band in the autumn.

Their first hit, 'Magic' made the Top Five in the US but only number 11 in the UK. Next came 'January'. David recalled, "My wife was reading a book and the main character was called January. She told me this and I wrote the chorus with that in mind. The verse is about how I felt at the time with the success of 'Magic'. I didn't write the song in January, it was in October, just after the release of 'Magic'. It was quickly recorded as the next single. We were recording the album, *Second Flight*, in Air Studios in London when 'January' got to number one. I didn't know the song was number one until I arrived at the studio where I was greeted with handshakes and congratulations."

Two more hits, 'Call Me Round' and 'Just A Smile' followed, but neither made much impact. A third album, *Morin Heights* (1976) and further singles, 'Running Water', 'Penny In My Pocket', 'Monday, Tuesday' and 'Ten Foot Tall' missed the chart altogether, the band split up in 1977. Tosh joined 10cc, whilst Lyall, Paton and Bairnson continued as the core of the Alan Parsons Project before pursuing solo careers.

David met Paul McCartney several times at

Pilot took their cue from Queen for this publicity photo. They are, clockwise from top: Stuart Tosh, Billy Lyall, David Paton and Ian Bairnson

Abbey Road Studios. David remembered, "Paul even showed me how to play 'Blackbird'. When he recorded 'Mull Of Kintyre' he came in to the studio where I was working with Alan Parsons and asked me to sing backing vocals on it." A few weeks later at the same studio, Paton and Bairnson played on the Kate Bush session that produced 'Wuthering Heights'.

366 Steve Harley & Cockney Rebel
Make Me Smile (Come Up And See Me)

Label & Cat No.: **EMI 2263**

Producers: **Steve Harley / Alan Parsons**

Writer: **Steve Harley**

Date reached No.1: **22 February 1975**

Weeks at No.1: **2**

"'COCKNEY REBEL' WAS THE TITLE OF A very long poem I wrote in 1973," says Steve Harley, "It was a lousy poem, but it was a good title." Grammar-school boy and journalist Steve Harley formed Cockney Rebel in 1973 and they had a successful album with *The Psychomodo* and hits with 'Judy Teen' and 'Mr. Soft'. But there was dissension within the group. "We split up because they wanted to take my leadership away," says Steve. "They wanted to dilute it and 'Make Me Smile' is saying, 'Come back one day and I'll laugh'. It was arrogant, but I knew they were wrong – they didn't understand the group like I did." In the song Steve accuses them of selling out and sings "You spoilt the game, no matter what you say, For only metal – what a bore!".

Steve Harley's new Cockney Rebel retained Stuart Elliott on drums and recruited Jim Cregan from Family on guitar, George Ford from Medicine Head on bass and Duncan Mackay on keyboards. They made the hit album, *The Best Years Of Our Lives*, which also included 'Mr. Raffles (Man It Was Mean)'.

Inspired by *Cabaret* and *A Clockwork Orange*, Steve wore greasepaint and a bowler hat and gave theatrical performances. He performs the songs more straightforwardly now: "When I do long tours, I have to make sure I'm not singing these songs on autopilot. I don't mean to, but you have to put your heart into them if you're going to sing them passionately and soulfully."

"There are 120 cover versions of 'Make Me Smile'," adds Steve, "but only The Wedding Present have done it differently. They did a punk version and made it kick. They understood the venom in the lyrics. It's good that the songs continue to mean something and they are in films like *Velvet Goldmine* and *The Full Monty* but I know I've never written anything that would stand alongside Ray Davies' 'Waterloo Sunset'. That is the perfect pop song."

Two of the original members of Cockney Rebel, keyboard player Milton Reame James and bassist Paul Jeffries played briefly in Bill Nelson's Be Bop DeLuxe before forming their own band, Chartreuse. Bill Nelson recalls that Paul's great passion in life was not music but tree preservation. In 1988 Paul died in the terrorist explosion on the Pan Am flight over Lockerbie in Scotland.

367 Telly Savalas
If

Label & Cat No.: **MCA 174**

Producer: **Snuff Garrett**

Writer: **David Gates**

Date reached No.1: **8 March 1975**

Weeks at No.1: **2**

IF A FILM DIRECTOR WANTED SOMEONE to play a detestable villain, Telly Savalas was your man, so how come he made one of the most romantic records of the Seventies?

Aristotle Savalas, born in New York in 1925 to a Greek family, had fought in the Second World War and then, with his rich speaking voice, had won awards as a broadcaster. He started as a screen heavy in the early Sixties and he can be seen in *The Birdman Of Alcatraz* (1962), *The Greatest Story Ever Told* (as Pontius Pilate) (1964), *The Dirty Dozen* (1967) and *On Her Majesty's Secret Service* (1969). He acquired a less threatening image as the tough cop from Manhattan, Theo Kojak, who sucked lollipops, wore fancy waistcoats and said, 'Who loves ya, baby?' The TV series was the Saturday night highlight of the BBC's schedules.

Although Savalas could sing, the record producer Snuff Garrett thought he had such a wonderful speaking voice that he should narrate Bread's song, 'If'. Savalas did make an album, *Telly*, but he was too immersed in *Kojak* to be concerned about following up his hit record. The follow-up as it happens was a vocal version of 'You've Lost That Lovin' Feelin'', a song that would stretch anyone vocally and the wrong choice for Telly.

When *Kojak* folded in 1978, he wasn't able to convert its success to leading roles in major films, but a tribute was paid to him by Nilsson with the song, 'Kojak Columbo'.

David Gates, the lead singer of Bread, still performs 'If' in concert and says, "I keep trying to beat 'If' but I know it's very difficult to top that song. Everything came together all at once. I sat down at my kitchen table one evening in a very peaceful frame of mind and the words and the melody started coming. I had finished it by midnight. Boy, I wish they all came as easy and were that good."

368 Bay City Rollers
Bye Bye Baby

Label & Cat No.: **Bell 1409**

Producer: **Phil Wainman**

Writers: **Bob Crewe / Bob Gaudio**

Date reached No.1: **22 March 1975**

Weeks at No.1: **6**

YOU ASSOCIATE THE BAY CITY ROLLERS with everything Scottish and yet they had an American name. Their bass player, Alan

Longmuir, says, "Motown was a big thing when we started and we thought The Rollers sounded American. We stuck a pin in a map of America and came up with Arkansas. We didn't like The Arkansas Rollers, but on our second attempt, we came up with Bay City, Michigan." As it happens, the city of Starsky and Hutch.

"I was in another band that was managed by Tam Paton," says Eric Faulkner, who played guitar and violin, "and we joined them together. We were all Slade fans and we started the Roller gang with the striped socks and rolled-up trousers, which made us different from other groups."

The Edinburgh group with Les McKeown (lead vocals), Stuart Wood (guitar) and Alan's brother, Derek, on drums had their first hit with 'Keep On Dancing' in 1971, but it was three years later that Rollermania took hold and journalists were calling them the biggest group since The Beatles. They had Top 10 hits with 'Remember (Sha-La-La)', 'Shang-A-Lang', 'Summerlove Sensation' and 'All Of Me Loves All Of You' and then in 1975, they went to the top with 'Bye Bye Baby'. "We had a definite style," says Eric. "We could have used the same drum track on those four hits and we played it safe with 'Bye Bye Baby' as that was still a shuffle."

'Bye Bye Baby', a song about divorce, had been recorded by that Catholic group, The Four Seasons, in 1965, and in retrospect, it was probably equally unsuited to The Rollers with their pre-teen fans. Oddly, The Rollers did not know The Four Seasons' version. Eric recalls, "'Bye Bye Baby' was in Woody's collection, but he had it by a British band called The Symbols."

The image of The Bay City Rollers in their tartan trews seems laughable today, but, standing on its own, 'Bye Bye Baby' is a fine pop record with strong harmonies.

369 Mud
Oh Boy

Label & Cat No.: **RAK 201**
Producers: **Nicky Chinn / Mike Chapman**
Writers: **Sonny West / Norman Petty / Bill Tilghman**
Date reached No.1: **3 May 1975**
Weeks at No.1: **2**

"WE STOLE THE IDEA COMPLETELY FROM Steeleye Span," says Les Gray. "They had recorded an acappella version of 'Rave On' which we loved. We felt we could do something like that as a relief from all the rock'n'roll stuff on our albums. One of the lads suggested another Buddy Holly song, 'Oh Boy'. We were on a roundabout on the A1 and we sang it and took harmonies, we knew instinctively what our parts should be."

So Mud recorded 'Oh Boy'. Les Gray: "'We had finished our deal with RAK and we were moving to Private Stock, and Mickie Most said, "'Oh Boy' is going to be your last single with us.' We thought he was trying to destroy us for leaving him as it didn't sound like a single. When it went to number one within a fortnight, we realised that Mickie Most knew a lot more than we did."

'Oh Boy' had been a Top 10 hit for Buddy Holly's group, The Crickets, in 1958, and was, coincidentally, written by the same writers as 'Rave On'. Nicky Chinn, adds: "It just shows that you can do Buddy Holly songs in any number of different ways. He is one of my all-time favourite performers. Who knows where he would have gone if he hadn't died?"

On Private Stock, Mud had further hits with 'L'L'Lucy' and 'Show Me You're A Woman'. Gray was disappointed that Mud's version of Bill Withers' 'Lean On Me' didn't reach the top as he thought it was a wonderful song. But by then, punk was making its presence felt, which made Mud look outdated. "That could have been a factor," said Gray, "but I think we got too big for our boots. We were thinking we were Steely Dan and we should have stuck to being a pop band. We made some records that were pretentious."

In subsequent years, Les formed Les Gray's Mud with members of Sweet and Liquid Gold and played nostalgia shows. "I don't care where I play," said Les Gray. "Gerry Marsden won't work in a club where he doesn't have his own toilet, but I couldn't care less who sees me having a pee."

Gray contracted throat cancer and he gave up performing. Eventually, the chemotherapy left him unable to sing and he died in February 2004.

370 Tammy Wynette
Stand By Your Man

Label & Cat No.: **Epic EPC 7137**
Producer: **Billy Sherrill**
Writers: **Tammy Wynette / Billy Sherrill**
Date reached No.1: **17 May 1975**
Weeks at No.1: **3**

WHETHER SHE WANTED TO OR NOT, Tammy Wynette lived her life like a country song. She grew up in poverty, had four husbands (and five weddings), was kidnapped, had a husband who sold nude pictures of her, was married to another country star (George Jones), had an affair with Burt Reynolds, and lived with drug addiction, depression, stalkers and D.I.V.O.R.C.E. Even when she died in 1998, she could not R.I.P. as her daughters contested her will and wanted her body exhumed to determine the cause of death. No wonder she is known as the First Lady of Country.

Starting in 1966, Tammy Wynette poured out emotions in song, having one US country hit after another. In 1968 her producer, Billy Sherrill, told her that he had a song title, even though he'd carried it around on a piece of paper for over a year: that title was 'Stand By Your Man'. Within an hour, she and Billy had written the lyrics. At a time when feminism was making its impact, Tammy Wynette was saying, 'No, stand by your man, no matter what', although she hadn't practised what she was preaching. The song not only topped the US country charts and crossed over

The Bay City Rollers

to the pop chart, it became the melody to Tammy's burglar alarm. It found a new audience when it was featured on the soundtrack of the 1970 Jack Nicholson film, *Five Easy Pieces*. 'Stand By Your Man', like Tammy Wynette's other records, was not a UK hit at the time, but it was regularly reissued, eventually breaking through in 1975.

The song has been used in many documentaries and campaigns. Tammy said, "I don't see anything in that song that implies a woman is supposed to sit home and have babies while a man goes out and raises hell. To me it means: be supportive of your man, show him you love him and you're proud of him, and be willing to forgive him if he doesn't always live up to your image of what he should be."

371 Windsor Davies & Don Estelle
Whispering Grass

Label & Cat No.:	**EMI 2290**
Producer:	**Wally Ridley**
Writers:	**Fred & Doris Fisher**
Date reached No.1:	**7 June 1975**
Weeks at No.1:	**3**

THE SECOND WORLD WAR HAS ALWAYS been fertile ground for comedy because it brought together servicemen with very different backgrounds. Following the success of *Dad's Army*, Jimmy Perry and David Croft created *It Ain't Half Hot Mum*, a series about the misadventures of a Royal Artillery Concert Party in India.

Windsor Davies played the bombastic Battery Sergeant Major Williams. He liked men to be men and so had little time for their main singer, the diminutive and cowardly Gunner 'Lofty' Sugden, played by Don Estelle. The record producer, Wally Ridley, recalls, "Don Estelle wanted to make some records on his own, but I couldn't see that working and I suggested that we did a record of the show with him singing and a lot of nonsense and funny bits. It cost very little to make and to my great delight, we sold 30,000 albums."

"The album started to sell well," says Windsor Davies, "and so Wally had the idea of lifting off 'Whispering Grass' as a single. Don sang it in his beautiful tenor voice and I was doing the talking bit, which was just as well because I can't sing. I felt a little odd being on *Top Of The Pops* because there are many serious musicians who wanted to get on there, and I didn't think we would get to number one because that 10cc record was so strong. EMI repeated it a few weeks later with 'Paper Doll' but that was a mistake – you can't repeat novelties too quickly. It's a pity because we did a few records that were funnier and a lot more musical like 'Do I Worry' and 'Bless You (For Being An Angel)'." From that remark, it is evident that the duo was working through The Ink Spots' repertoire. The black harmony group had recorded 'Whispering Grass' in 1940, so it fitted the period.

Don Estelle wanted to make straight records and for the last 20 years of his life, in between acting assignments, he would record his own albums, arrange their manufacture, load up his car and appear in shopping centres around the country, singing to backing tapes and happily signing autographs. His autobiography, *Sing Lofty: Thoughts Of A Gemini*, was published in 1999 and he died in 2003. Windsor Davies is a pantomime favourite and he is on the soundtrack of the puppet series, *Terrahawks*.

372 10cc
I'm Not In Love

Label & Cat No.:	**Mercury 6008 014**
Producer:	**10cc**
Writers:	**Eric Stewart / Graham Gouldman**
Date Reached No.1:	**28 June 1975**
Weeks at No.1:	**2**

IN 1975 AND EXACTLY TWO YEARS SINCE their first chart topper, 10cc began writing tracks for their new album *Original Soundtrack*. It was suggested that it was about time they wrote a ballad.

Eric Stewart explained the story: "My wife used to say, 'Why don't you say "I love you" more often? and I said, 'If I keep saying it, it is going to lose its meaning, so I shouldn't say it every day.' Graham and I were going to write a love song anyway, and we decided to turn it on its head and say 'I'm Not In Love', which would be very 10cc, but the song says, 'I do love you'. You don't want to admit it, but you keep giving all the reasons why you are in love. It is a twist on words like that country song, 'She Thinks I Still Care'."

For the middle eight, Eric explained, "There are 256 backing voices and a lead vocal so there are 257 voices on there. It was Kevin's idea to use voices instead of instruments. We originally went into the studio and recorded it as a Brazil 66 bossa nova song. It had a nice Latin feel but it didn't grab us so we left it alone and got on with the rest of the album. It kept coming back to us and Kevin said, 'Let's use voices, no instruments.' There are a few instruments on the record, but all the movements in the song are vocal."

Eric also felt that they needed a spoken voice during the break, and preferably a female one. He wrote the line, "Be quiet, big boys don't cry, big boys don't cry." Just at that moment, the secretary at 10cc's Strawberry Studios, Kathy Redfern, walked in with a message. Eric asked her to whisper the words and the record was complete. Kathy says, "Every time I hear the song, I'm still surprised that they kept my voice on it."

'I'm Not In Love' has been adapted to many different styles. Acker Bilk, Tony Christie, Sasha Distel, Johnny Logan and The Fun Lovin' Criminals are amongst the many covers. Possibly the contender for the most bizarre version is Petula Clark's attempt at a disco version in 1978.

With over one million radio plays, 'I'm Not In Love' regularly features in the upper echelon in polls of listeners' favourites. It caused Kevin Godley to remark, "It broke my heart because I didn't write the fuckin' thing."

Kevin had bought Who drummer Keith Moon's celebrated Tara House in Chertsey the previous year. The royalties may have been useful to pay for refurbishing the property, since Moon was unlikely to have left it in tip-top condition.

10cc were Manchester's very own 'supergroup'; left to right: Lol Creme, Eric Stewart, Graham Gouldman and Kevin Godley

373 Johnny Nash
Tears On My Pillow (I Can't Take It)

Label & Cat No.: **CBS CBS 3220**

Producers: **Johnny Nash / Ken Khouri**

Writer: **Ernie Smith**

Date Reached No.1: **12 July 1975**

Weeks at No.1: **1**

"MY AMBITION WAS TO BE A RADIO announcer, but somehow I got into recording by accident," said Ernie Smith, one of Jamaica's legendary singer/songwriters.

In 1967 after an audition for the Jamaican Broadcasting Company, he was told, "Don't call us, we'll call you" remembered Ernie. "As I had taken the whole day off, I didn't want to waste it, so I took this song that I'd written and I went down to Federal Records. When I got there the piano player was in the studio and I told them maybe they can get somebody to sing it because I went there as a writer. They told me there was a band coming in at two o'clock and that I should wait and record it with them, so that's how I recorded my first song, 'I Can't Take It'".

Johnny Nash took the song and re-titled it 'Tears On My Pillow'. Surprisingly it failed to chart in the US. However, he did have a US number one in 1972 with the self-penned 'I Can See Clearly Now', backed by Bob Marley's Wailers.

Johnny was born in 1940 in Houston, Texas. He had sung in the choir at the local Baptist Church before entering a talent show and losing out to Joe Tex. In the late Fifties Johnny had US hits with 'A Very Special Love' and 'The Teen Commandments', a collaboration with Paul Anka and George Hamilton IV. He began writing his own songs in the early Sixties.

In 1968 he had a Top 10 hit on both sides of the Atlantic with 'Hold Me Tight'. When the follow-up singles, a cover of Bill Johnson's 'You Got Soul' and Sam Cooke's 'Cupid', charted higher in Britain, Johnny came to live in this country. In 1972 having spent a year here, he decided that to maintain the reggae sound, he would fare better in Jamaica, so was on the move again. Once there, he teamed up with a then unknown Bob Marley and they began writing songs together. He later had a Transatlantic hit with a cover of Marley's 'Stir It Up'.

By the end of the Seventies, the hits stopped and Johnny channelled his energy into his West Indian recording studio complex.

374 Bay City Rollers
Give A Little Love

Label & Cat No.: **Bell 1425**

Producer: **Phil Wainman**

Writers: **Johnny Goodison / Phil Wainman**

Date reached No.1: **19 July 1975**

Weeks at No.1: **3**

ERIC FAULKNER FROM THE BAY CITY Rollers recalls, "In 1975 we started working with Phil Wainman who produced The Sweet and in the first four days we did 'Bye Bye Baby', 'Give A Little Love' and 'Money Honey', all of which were hit singles, and he also let us develop and record our own songs. We took a chance with 'Give A Little Love' as it was an out and out ballad and it worked."

Phil Wainman's writing partner was Johnny Goodison, who had written 'United We Stand' for Brotherhood Of Man and ran Big John's Rock'n'Roll Circus. The Rollers looked set for a succession of hits but things started to go wrong. A fan was shot with an air gun outside of Les McKeown's house and their ruthless manager, Tam Paton, lost his edge after a breakdown.

The merchandising got in the way of the music and the public tired of Rollermania. In essence, their young fans were growing up and the new, young fans wanted something else. Still, The Rollers found success in America with 'Saturday Night' (a US number one), 'Money Honey' and 'You Make Me Believe In Magic'. Stuart Wood says, "I felt that we made some really good records and some of them were overlooked. 'Shoorah Shoorah For Hollywood' and 'Turn On The Radio'."

In 1978 The Rollers sacked their lead singer, Les McKeown, when he insisted on recording a solo album. A few months later, *Sunday People* had a front cover story about *Pop Idols Who Lived A Lie*, itemising the sex, booze and rock'n'roll in The Rollers, and possibly the story was released in the hope that would gain them street cred. Still, The Rollers have continued, in one form or another, until today. "Yes," says Eric, "the Roller credibility may be zilch, but we have survived and we are still playing. We haven't survived this long by being a load of dummies."

375 Typically Tropical
Barbados

Label & Cat No.: **Gull GULS 14**

Producers: **Jeff Calvert / Max West**

Writers: **Jeff Calvert / Max West**

Date reached No.1: **9 August 1975**

Weeks at No.1: **1**

MAX WEST WAS PART OF THE BAND, Quasar, and he met Jeff Calvert, who knew the lead singer and would watch them rehearse. Jeff worked with his father at Morgan Studios and they thought they would write some songs and record them when nobody else was around. Jeff went on holiday to Barbados and he liked it so much that they soon had the idea for a song. They recorded it with session musicians who included Chris Spedding on guitar.

A small label, Gull, liked 'Barbados', but wanted to hear some more material before they signed them. They were given £1,500 to finish 'Barbados', cut a B-side, 'Sandy', and record a new track, which was 'Ghost Song'. 'Barbados' was ready in November 1974, but the label thought it best to wait until summer before they released it. The cod reggae record was an instant hit and the duo, to their surprise, were invited on *Top Of The Pops*, but they felt that even with backing musicians, they could not tour.

The follow-up singles, 'Rocket Now' and

'Ghost Story', failed to chart. Possibly the change of name to Calvert & West didn't help. They tried for a summer hit in 1976 with 'Everybody Plays The Fool' and then one for The Queen's silver anniversary in 1977, 'Jubilee', but to no avail. And Quasar split up as well. Max West is now an experienced pilot, but not with Coconut Airways.

In 1999 The Vengaboys based their number one single, 'We're Going To Ibiza!", around Typically Tropical's record.

376 Stylistics

Can't Give You Anything (But My Love)

Label & Cat No.: **Avco 6105 039**

Producers: **Hugo Peretti / Luigi Creatore**

Writers: **Hugo Peretti / Luigi Creatore / George David Weiss**

Date Reached No.1: **16 August 1975**

Weeks at No.1: **3**

THE ORIGINS OF THE STYLISTICS stretch back to 1968 when baritones Herb Murrell and James Dunn from The Percussions, along with Russell Tompkins Jr, Airrion Love and James Smith from The Monarchs, two Philadelphia-based doo-wop groups, joined forces.

The name was suggested by the group's guitar player, Robert Douglas, who wrote their first song, 'You're A Big Girl Now' and released it on Philadelphia's Sebring label. On the strength of local sales, they were picked up by Avco Embassy Records. They re-distributed the single and gave the Stylistics their first US hit.

Initially everyone took lead vocals. "We were singing Motown and Stax songs, songs from Aretha Franklin, Gladys Knight and The Temptations," recalled Herb. "When we got with Thom Bell, he wanted to use the tenor that Russell had and he brought Airrion in as co-lead on 'You Are Everything' and 'You Make Me Feel Brand New', but the sound was refined by Thom". 'You Are Everything' was a Top Five hit for Marvin Gaye and Diana Ross in 1974.

Even though three of their four biggest hits were upbeat songs, the band weren't too happy. James Dunn recalled, "We had become labelled as a soft group because of our ballads and we needed a change. We had done a few up-tempo songs but always reverted to ballads." So in late 1974 they began working with another songwriter/producer duo, Hugo Peretti and Luigi Creatore who had produced songs for Sam Cooke and The Tokens. As recording artists, the pair had one minor hit in 1959, 'La Plume De Ma Tante'. George David Weiss had co-written 'Can't Help Falling In Love', which The Stylistics would later cover, and 'Wild In The Country' for Elvis. Herb said, "During the disco era, 'Can't Give You Anything (But My Love)' kept us right in the pocket. We were noted for love songs and we had moved into a dancing thing. The lyric was also good."

In the early Eighties, both Dunn and Smith left, Van Fields joined the group and Harold Brown replaced Russell Tompkins Jr as lead singer. They still tour America and Britain. As Herb Murrell said, "Most of the UK clubs that book us have been booking us for years and know we put on a good show and pull a good crowd."

377 Rod Stewart

Sailing

Label & Cat No.: **Warner K 16600**

Producer: **Tom Dowd**

Writer: **Gavin Sutherland**

Date reached No.1: **6 September 1975**

Weeks at No.1: **4**

ROD STEWART'S LIFE CHANGED IN 1975. Stung by the 83 per cent rate of income tax, he decided he had had enough and moved to America, applying for US citizenship. This ended his on-off relationship with The Faces and as he had met the glamorous Swedish actress, Britt Ekland, at a party in Los Angeles, he had another reason to remain there. On a visit to the UK, he refused to move from the airport on the grounds that he would be liable for further tax if he did.

Rod Stewart used his temporary exile to good effect as he made a fine album, *Atlantic Crossing*, in Muscle Shoals with Tom Dowd, the engineer and producer from so many great Atlantic soul records. Rod was surprised to find that some of his favourite Muscle Shoals sessionmen – Steve Cropper and Donald 'Duck' Dunn – were white.

Those *Old Grey Whistle Test* favourites, The Sutherland Brothers & Quiver recorded their song 'Sailing' in 1972. Rod related to its theme of homesickness and recorded it in Muscle Shoals with a choir assembled by Bob Crewe, the Four Seasons' producer.

'Sailing' stayed on the UK charts for 11 weeks, making the top for four of them, and then it returned for another 20 and a high of number three in 1976 after it was used as the theme music for a BBC-TV series about HMS Ark Royal. The single had a new lease of life in 1982 when it became associated with British forces sailing to the Falklands and it also complemented the Ferry Aid single in 1987 when it was reissued for the Zeebrugge disaster fund.

'Sailing' has been sung at Wembley by the crowds for England and Scotland matches, but often the words have been changed for the terraces. Try this:

"No one likes us, no one likes us
"No one likes us, we don't care,
"We are Millwall, super Millwall,
"We are Millwall from the Den."

The song has been given a boost as part of the *Tonight's The Night* musical, written by Ben Elton and based on Rod's catalogue.

Rod left The Faces at the end of 1975, effectively bringing the group to an end. Ronnie Wood joined The Rolling Stones, while Ronnie Lane, Kenny Jones and Ian McLagan teamed up with Steve Marriott for a short-lived Small Faces reunion. In the coming years, Lane, Jones and McLagan all found themselves tangled up with The Who in various ways. Lane recorded an album with Pete Townshend, Jones became their drummer after Keith Moon died in 1978, and McLagan married Moon's ex-wife.

378 David Essex
Hold Me Close

Label & Cat No.: **CBS CBS 3572**
Producer: **Jeff Wayne**
Writer: **David Essex**
Date Reached No.1: **4 October 1975**
Weeks at No.1: **3**

DAVID NEVER DREAMED OF BECOMING a pop idol. He just wanted to make creative music, but when his popularity began to rise in America, his record company tried to turn him into another Elvis Presley.

His film career began to take off too. He landed the part of pop star Jim MacLaine in *That'll Be The Day* and its sequel *Stardust*, the title of which was a Top 10 hit. The reviews were generally favourable, although certain critics felt that David should stick to the pop chart.

David began work on his third album *All The Fun Of The Fair*. The first single 'Rolling Stone' made the Top Five both here and in the US. David recalled, "We were having so much fun making the album that we went past our deadline. We were being hounded by record executives from all over the world who were anxious to hear a playback. We were so up against it that I was still doing the vocals for 'Hold Me Close' as record company hierarchy were sitting in the studio reception. I did two vocal takes followed by a quick half hour mix and the track was finished. After an hour and a half wait, the record company guys were led in, we offered our apologies and played them the track. They got their own back by keeping us waiting for a reaction to the song, but eventually the chief said he liked it and the compliments started to flow."

The next few hits didn't perform as well, but he continued to play to packed houses. David hadn't acted since 1974, but Jeff Wayne's *War Of The Worlds* had whetted David's appetite to get back into acting. Coincidently, at that time his agent received a call with an offer for David to appear as Che Guevara in Tim Rice and Andrew Lloyd Webber's new Musical *Evita*. It also restored David to the chart when 'Oh What A Circus' reached number three.

In 1994 David and Catherine Zeta-Jones teamed up for a duet of 'True Love Ways'. David also spends six months of the year touring the UK.

379 Art Garfunkel
I Only Have Eyes For You

Label & Cat No.: **CBS 3575**
Producer: **Richard Perry**
Writers: **Harry Warren / Al Dubin**
Date reached No.1: **25 October 1975**
Weeks at No.1: **2**

'I ONLY HAVE EYES FOR YOU' WAS written for one of Busby Berkeley's film extravaganzas *Dames* in 1934. In the film, Dick Powell serenades Ruby Keeler with the song on the Staten Island ferry. When they fall asleep in New York, a dream sequence takes over in which Ruby's face is seen on hundreds of girls. The girls group together and bending over with boards on their backs, they complete a jigsaw of Ruby's face – just like the start of *Parkinson*. Harry Warren, who wrote the music, said, 'It seems like they go through the song 25 times. I got sick of hearing the melody but Buzz never knew when to quit.' (Incidentally, one of the forgotten songs in the film has the title, 'Try To See It My Way'.)

The American doo-wop groups of the Fifties often reworked standards and in 1959 The Flamingos from Chicago took their intricate arrangement of 'I Only Have Eyes For You' into the US Top 20. Art Garfunkel was entranced by doo-wop as he grew up and once freed of the Simon & Garfunkel shackles, he found he could record what he liked. Working with the producer, Richard Perry, he recreated The Flamingos' arrangement, both lovingly and effectively – doo-bop-she-bop anyone?

The album, *Breakaway*, was only Art's second album in five years and it also included a one-off reunion with Paul Simon, 'My Little Town'. A 1934 version of 'I Only Have Eyes For You' by Scott Wood and his Orchestra and sung by Jack Plant was used in the BBC-TV series, *Pennies From Heaven* (1978), which starred Bob Hoskins as the frustrated sheet music salesman. In 1999 the US performing rights organisation ASCAP listed 'I Only Have Eyes For You' as one of the 25 most played songs of the 20th century.

380 David Bowie
Space Oddity

Label & Cat No.: **RCA 2593**
Producer: **Gus Dudgeon**
Writer: **David Bowie**
Date Reached No.1: **8 November 1975**
Weeks at No.1: **2**

NOTED PRODUCER, TONY VISCONTI, hated 'Space Oddity'. He saw it as 'a cheap shot – a gimmick to cash in on the moon landing'. He refused to produce it and recommended Gus Dudgeon.

But after five years of recording under various guises – The Konrads, The King Bees, Manish Boys and Davy Jones & The Lower Third – it was the 'cheap shot' that landed David Bowie a contract with Mercury Records in America.

Contrary to popular belief, 'Space Oddity' was not originally written to coincide with Neil Armstrong's moon landing expedition. In 1968 Rolf Harris was advertising a new pocket-sized keyboard instrument on television called a Stylophone. David had just received one of these as a present from his friend, Marc Bolan, and having just seen Stanley Kubrick's film *2001 – A Space Odyssey*, he composed 'Space Oddity' on it for a German TV programme, *Love You 'Til Tuesday*. *2001 – A Space Odyssey* told of an astronaut lost in space, so David wrote a song about one who had left his 'tin can' thousands of miles above the earth and refused to return.

Gus Dudgeon recalled, "The song was so drop-dead great, that all I had to do was hire the session musicians." He recruited a young keyboard player, Rick Wakeman and drummer

David Bowie in 1969, when 'Space Oddity' was first released, commencing countdown to a spectacular career in music

Terry Cox. Terry remembered, "It was a pretty loose session, with David playing a basic riff and then telling us to get on with it." The promotional video used on *Top Of The Pops* showed David dressed as an astronaut spinning around inside the cockpit.

On July 21, 1969 Apollo 11, captained by Neil Armstrong, landed on the moon. The song was first issued in June and used by the BBC for their television coverage of the historic landing. It eventually entered the chart in September and climbed up to number five. It never initially charted in the US. The patriotic people of America possibly viewed it as a pessimistic song and obviously wanted the best for their crew. However, as part of an RCA re-issue campaign it finally made the US chart in 1972, peaking at number 15.

It has been suggested that 'Space Oddity', which was re-issued to tie-in with the release of the greatest hits album, *Changesonebowie*, was about drugs, with the dealer, Ground Control, selling them to Major Tom. The line, 'And I'm floating in a most peculiar way, and the stars look very different today' confirmed their suspicions. Five years later, in 'Ashes To Ashes', he continued the story, stating, 'We know Major Tom's a junkie'.

381 Billy Connolly
D.I.V.O.R.C.E.

Label & Cat No.: **Polydor 2058 652**

Producer: **Phil Coulter**

Writers: **Curly Putnam / Bobby Braddock / Billy Connolly**

Date reached No.1: **22 November 1975**

Weeks at No.1: **1**

TAMMY WYNETTE TOPPED THE US country charts in 1968 with 'D.I.V.O.R.C.E.', an ingenious song in which the fateful word was spelt out so that their child couldn't appreciate what was happening. The follow-up was 'Stand By Your Man'. When Tammy had an unexpected UK number one with 'Stand By Your Man' in 1975, her record company chose 'D.I.V.O.R.C.E.' for the follow-up and it made the Top 20.

The Glaswegian comic, Billy Connolly, started his career as a musician, playing banjo and singing with Gerry Rafferty in The Humblebums. He was nicknamed The Big Yin after a comic strip that he wrote. At first his humour and his language was thought too strong for television, but Michael Parkinson took a chance on him and the rest, as they say, is hysterics. He told the story of a husband who buried his wife in the garden with her bottom sticking up so that he would have somewhere to park his bike.

Billy Connolly thought 'D.I.V.O.R.C.E.' had rich comic potential and set about rewriting it. His comedy treatment went to number one, a rare example of a parody outselling the original. His outtakes, which are way over the top and hilarious, have not been released. The Big Yin had further hits when he parodied 'No Charge' as 'No Chance (No Charge)' and 'In The Navy' as 'In The Brownies', but it is on albums, videos and DVDs that he is a big seller: *Solo Concert* (1974), *Cop Yer Whack For This* (1975) and *Get Right Intae Him* (1975) were all Top 10 albums. He was awarded the CBE in 2003.

382 Queen
Bohemian Rhapsody

Label & Cat No.: **EMI 2375**

Producer: **Roy Thomas Baker**

Writer: **Freddie Mercury**

Date Reached No.1: **29 November 1975**

Weeks at No.1: **9**

HOW CAN SUCH A MEANINGLESS SONG mean so much to so many people? It is consistently voted number one on music polls and is one of the most complex singles ever recorded.

Queen's first release 'Keep Yourself Alive' in 1973 failed to chart. The follow-up, 'Seven Seas Of Rhye', reached number 10 the following year and the next single, 'Killer Queen' climbed to number two. Work had begun on what was to be their first number one album, *A Night At The Opera* and the first track from it was to be 'Bohemian Rhapsody'.

Freddie's 'baby', as Brian May described it, is almost six minutes long. Roger Taylor: "Record companies on both sides of the Atlantic tried to cut the song, they said it was too long and wouldn't work. We thought, 'well we could cut it, but it wouldn't make any sense', it doesn't make much sense now and it would make even less sense then: you would miss all the different moods of the song. So we said no. It'll either fly or it won't." And it flew, like no other single in chart history.

"Freddie had the bare bones of the song, even the composite harmonies, written on telephone books and bits of paper, so it was quite hard to keep track of what was going on," said Roger. Freddie loved opera and one day, he was in his flat trying to explain the song to the band, and said, "Now my dears, this is where the opera section comes in." The look of astonishment on the group's faces must have been a picture. The recording included 180 overdubs, the operatic parts took over 70 hours to complete and the piano Freddie played was the same one used by Paul McCartney on 'Hey Jude'.

Roger recalled, "We were trying to be a heavy rock band, then Freddie came to us with this outrageous concoction that turned out to be 'Bohemian Rhapsody'."

Once the song was finished, Freddie took it to his best friend, DJ Kenny Everett, at London's Capital Radio. Kenny initially agreed that it wouldn't work because of its length, but after hearing it, he said, "Forget it, it could be half an hour long, it's going to be number one for centuries!" Following its first airing, the switchboard went into meltdown and that was enough to convince EMI to release the full-length single.

July 13, 1985 was the biggest day in Queen's career. They stole the show at *Live Aid* in front of 1.4 billion people from over 170 countries – twice the size of the audience that turned on to Neil Armstrong's walk on the moon some 16 years earlier – who tuned in to watch the world's biggest concert. Concert organiser, Bob

Queen's 'Bohemian Rhapsody' is one of the UK's best loved singles; clockwise, from the top: Brian May, John Deacon, Freddie Mercury and Roger Taylor

Geldof said, "Queen were absolutely the best band on the day."

The song, in its complete form, is difficult to perform live, so the band used a pre-recorded tape for the middle section. The same applied to television, this being the main reason the band recorded a £5,000 promotional clip, which has come to be regarded as the birth of the video age.

'Bohemian Rhapsody' was Freddie's most creative statement and he got fed up with people asking him to explain its meaning. He just used to say, "It means whatever you want it to mean."

383 Abba
Mamma Mia

Label & Cat No.: **Epic EPC 3790**

Producers: **Björn Ulvaeus / Benny Andersson**

Writers: **Björn Ulvaeus / Benny Andersson / Stig Anderson**

Date Reached No.1: **31 January 1976**

Weeks at No.1: **2**

After 'Waterloo' won Eurovision in 1974, it went on to top the chart in several European countries, and looked set to launch ABBA as a major recording act. In the UK things didn't look too rosy with the follow-up 'Ring Ring' peaking at number 32. 'I Do, I Do, I Do, I Do, I Do', a tribute to Fifties orchestra leader, Billy Vaughn, fared slightly worse at number 38. However, 18 months later the palindromic 'SOS' restored them to the Top 10. Whilst 'SOS' was in the chart, Benny Andersson explained how he felt about their absence from the British scene. "In England, we didn't get the image we deserved. Because we won Eurovision, we got the image that goes with Eurovision, and it's not really correct. We just happened to be in the contest – for example, I think we'd prefer the reputation that The Mamas & The Papas had."

"Stig Anderson would come up with titles and I'd write a lyric round them," recalled Björn Ulvaeus. "'Mamma Mia' was one of them." It was the last song to be written and recorded for their third album, *Abba*. In the studio was a marimba, an instrument of African origin, similar to the xylophone, but with wooden bars, which Benny began playing it to see what it sounded like. He liked the sound it made and began using it with a tick-tock effect.

In 1976 Abba emerged as world superstars. It was the first of their three chart toppers that year, the first time any non-British or American act had achieved the feat.

On April 6, 1999, on the 25th anniversary of winning *Eurovision*, *Mamma Mia – The Musical* opened in London. It features 27 Abba songs and has been seen by more than 10 million people in productions around the world.

384 Slik
Forever And Ever

Label & Cat No.: **Bell 1464**

Producers: **Bill Martin / Phil Coulter**

Writers: **Bill Martin / Phil Coulter**

Date reached No.1: **14 February 1976**

Weeks at No.1: **1**

"The Small Faces wrote brilliant songs and were natty little dressers," says Midge Ure of the band that inspired him most. The singer and guitarist formed a group in Glasgow with Billy McIsaac (keyboards), Kenny Hyslop (drums) and Jim McGinlay (bass), and they called themselves Slik. "We were the top band in Scotland," Midge continues. "We were doing the Scottish scene, but Scotland itself at the time was a musical desert. There were no management companies, no recording studios or no record companies to speak of. You either had to pack your bags and move to London and risk falling by the wayside or you had to accept a poor deal. The deal we got wasn't brilliant but it was the only one we had. We thought we would do the pop Bay City Rollers thing for a while and then put in our own material, but once you are tarred with that brush it is very difficult to get away from it."

Bill Martin and Phil Coulter, who had written and produced some of the first hit records for The Bay City Rollers, wanted to do the same for Slik. The proposed song was 'Forever And Ever', which had originally been recorded on an album by another Martin and Coulter group, Kenny. Midge Ure again: "We had driven down from Glasgow with a seven ton truck full of equipment, all ready to make our first record. We sat in the waiting room outside the studio and we could hear this very dodgy Bay City Rollers backing track being played and we sniggered and thought it was their next single. It turned out to be our backing track. The session musicians had done it that morning and we were so despondent and downhearted. We were genuine *bona fide* musicians and when we added our voices, we felt it so far removed from anything we had done before."

Midge, despite his reservations, could appreciate the song's commerciality, "Oh, it is a great pop song and incredibly well put together. It just wasn't us."

Their producer, Phil Coulter, tends to agree. "I had also been producing the Bay City Rollers and Kenny, but I felt that Slik had more substance and could go far. They were capable of far more than teenybopper, three chord tricks. Queen was coming along then with very complex production, very complex harmonies and very complex songs. I read the critics who were saying, 'Bill Martin and Phil Coulter can do nothing complicated' and I thought, 'We'll show the buggers, we'll make a complicated record.' We did 'Requiem' which borrowed from Queen but I thought it was a great record. It only staggered into the Top 30 and it proved beyond doubt that you should not make records for critics. You should make records for record buyers. The Slik fans who bought 'Forever And Ever' were confused as it was too sophisticated and there was too much going on."

'Requiem' was effectively a requiem as the group disbanded: Midge Ure played with Glen Matlock in The Rich Kids and Steve Strange in Visage. He led Ultravox whose 'Vienna' is one of those singles that everyone thinks was number one when it never was.

385 The Four Seasons
December '63 (Oh What A Night)

Label & Cat No.: **Warners K 16688**

Producer: **Bob Gaudio**

Writers: **Bob Gaudio / Judy Parker**

Date reached No.1: **21 February 1976**

Weeks at No.1: **2**

CONSIDERING THE CLASSIC SINGLES HE has made, it is astonishing that Frankie Valli and his group, The Four Seasons, have only had one UK number one. 'Sherry', 'Big Girls Don't Cry', 'Walk Like A Man', 'Rag Doll', 'Let's Hang On' and 'I've Got You Under My Skin' were big hits that didn't go the whole way, while 'Silence Is Golden', 'The Sun Ain't Gonna Shine Anymore', 'Bye Bye Baby' and 'Working My Way Back To You' became number ones for other performers. Despite so much airplay on Radio Caroline, why did hardly anyone in the UK buy 'Dawn (Go Away)'?

The mainstays of The Four Seasons are Frankie Valli and Bob Gaudio, originally part of the quartet and then having a writing and producing role, rather like Brian Wilson with The Beach Boys. In the early Seventies, the group revitalised itself by signing with Tamla-Motown, but their key song, 'The Night', was not a UK hit until 1975. By then The Four Seasons had been reconstituted and in addition to Valli, there was Gerry Polci, Don Ciccone, John Piava and Lee Shapiro. The intention was to make harmony records that would still feature Valli, but not necessarily so prominently.

The Four Seasons went Top 10 with a song based on Kojak's catchphrase, 'Who Loves You', but 'December '63 (Oh What A Night)' was almost abandoned. Bob Gaudio recalls, "The song was originally about the repeal of prohibition. It was called 'December '33' and it was a goofy, fun lyric. The track was so strong and so infectious that Judy Parker, whom I later married, said, 'Let me fool around with this a bit.' She changed it round and it wound up on the album, thank god." The song was now about losing your virginity, something everyone (or nearly everyone) could identify with. Gerry Polci sang the lead vocal with Valli soaring in for the middle eight.

After 'December '63', Valli and his friends went to number three with 'Silver Star' but even Barry Gibb's song, 'Grease', in 1978 couldn't give Frankie a solo chart-topper.

386 Tina Charles
I Love To Love (But My Baby Loves To Dance)

Label & Cat No.: **CBS 3937**

Producer: **Biddu**

Writers: **Jack Robinson / James Bolden**

Date reached No.1: **6 March 1976**

Weeks at No.1: **3**

WHEN SHE WAS ONLY A CHILD, TINA Hoskins (later Tina Charles) was singing in front of the mirror with her hairbrush in her hand, and her parents encouraged her ambition. In 1969, when she was 15, she was singing with Tony Evans and his Orchestra at the Empire, Leicester Square and the following year, she made a single, 'Good To Be Alive', with backing vocals from Elton John. She was given a residency on *The Two Ronnies* and sang backing vocals on tour for Tom Jones and Engelbert Humperdinck.

In the early Seventies, Tina was a session singer: she and Linda Lewis supply the backing vocals on Steve Harley & Cockney Rebel's 'Make Me Smile (Come Up And See Me)'. She sang the lead vocal on 5000 Volts' Top Five hit, 'I'm On Fire', but had accepted £200 in lieu of royalties.

Her first single with the disco producer, Biddu, 'You Set My Heart On Fire', was not a hit, but their second attempt was the highly infectious 'I Love To Love (But My Baby Loves To Dance)'. Tina toured the world promoting it and it sold several million copies. The follow-up, 'Love Me Like A Lover', was only a minor hit, but she returned to the UK Top 10 with 'Dance Little Lady Dance' and 'Dr. Love'.

In 1977 she and her husband, Bernard Webb, had a son, Max. In order to look after Max, Tina wanted to stay in London so she returned to session work and jingles. The couple divorced in 1979 and Tina remained a background singer for some years.

In 1986 a remix of 'I Love To Love' with Disco Mix Club made number two in France, and she is now back performing again. Her reunion with Biddu, 'It's Friday Night', was released in 2003. Tina is a disco diva who has become a disco granny.

387 Brotherhood Of Man
Save Your Kisses For Me

Label & Cat No.: **Pye 7N 45569**

Producer: **Tony Hiller**

Writers: **Tony Hiller / Martin Lee / Lee Sheriden**

Date reached No.1: **27 March 1976**

Weeks at No.1: **6**

BROTHERHOOD OF MAN WAS the name given to a session group by the producer, Tony Hiller. They included Johnny Goodison, Roger Greenaway, Tony Burrows and Sue & Sunny, and they performed 'United We Stand', which was written by Goodison and Hiller. The song was a hit in both Britain and America and was adopted as an anthem by the Gay Liberation Front.

When Brotherhood Of Man was wanted for a performance or a recording, Hiller selected singers to participate. In 1974 he decided on a permanent line-up, Lee Sheriden, Martin Lee, Nicky Stephens and Sandra Stephens (who were not related), and they took part in a song contest in Belgium, which led to a European hit with 'Lady' and then 'Kiss Me Kiss Me Baby'.

Abba's Eurovision win transformed the contest and good-looking, two boy, two girl groups became the order of the day. Sheriden, Lee and Hiller wrote a catchy song about a man going to work and missing what you think is his girlfriend, but, in the final line, it turns out to be his three-year-old daughter. Hiller admits that his pay-off was a homage to Alma Cogan's 'The Naughty Lady Of Shady Lane' (1955).

Brotherhood Of Man only just won the UK heat but the song captivated the Eurovision judges in Le Hague (except those from Italy and, surprise, surprise, Ireland), although it was a strange year in which the Greek song protested against the Turkish invasion of Cyprus. Lee Sheriden says, "It's a catchy song, simple, easy to remember and well arranged. The presentation was part of it. We did a little dance – we foreshadowed the likes of Steps by a few years with that. It all seemed to come right for Eurovision."

388 Abba
Fernando

Label & Cat No.: **Epic EPC 4036**

Producers: **Björn Ulvaeus / Benny Andersson**

Writers: **Björn Ulvaeus / Benny Andersson / Stig Anderson**

Date Reached No.1: **8 May 1976**

Weeks at No.1: **4**

'FERNANDO' IS THE ONLY ABBA NUMBER one not to appear on any studio album (apart from greatest hits collections) and is also older than most people realise. Norwegian-born Frida originally recorded the song on her solo album *Frida Ensam* (meaning *Frida Alone*) in her native language in 1975. It was not released as a single but heavy airplay determined that it was the most popular track on the album. As a result, the album spent six weeks at number one on the Swedish chart. The writers all realised it had more potential than being merely a Swedish-language album track, so it was agreed that Abba would record it in English. Abba's version was Australia's biggest selling single of all time until it was overtaken by Elton John's 'Candle In The Wind 97'.

The Latin tinged 'Fernando', whose original working title was 'Tango', was not written about a person. "That lyric is so banal and I didn't like it," explained Björn. "It was a love lyric, someone who loved Fernando, but I inherited the word 'Fernando' and I thought long and hard, what does Fernando tell me?" He went on: "I was in my summerhouse one starry evening and the words came, 'There was something in the air that night' and I thought of two old comrades from some guerrilla war in Mexico who would be sitting in the porch and reminiscing about what happened to them back then, and that is what it is all about. Total fiction."

Abba re-recorded the song with new lyrics for the Japanese company 'National' for a massive advertising campaign in Australia, a country where their popularity rivalled that of the Beatles during the mid-Seventies.

389 J. J. Barrie
No Charge

Label & Cat No.: **Power Exchange PX 209**

Producer: **Bill Amesbury**

Writer: **Harlan Howard**

Date reached No.1: **5 June 1976**

Weeks at No.1: **1**

IN 1974 THE US COUNTRY SINGER, Melba Montgomery, was given a new song, 'No Charge', and she says, "Harlan Howard wrote that song for me and gave it to myself and my producer, Pete Drake. I didn't think I could do it because of my southern accent and I had never done a recitation before. It came off so naturally in the studio that everybody loved it. I knew we would get plays on country stations, but it crossed over to rock stations because it was a song that everybody could relate to. It is a very emotional song, especially for anyone like myself who has kids."

'No Charge' topped the US country chart and also made the US Top 40, but Melba's single

meant nothing in the UK; nor did a cover version from Tammy Wynette and her daughter, Tina, nor the Irish Guinness mix from Val Doonican.

Enter the Canadian Barrie Authors, the former manager of Blue Mink, who wanted to interest Glen Campbell in his song, 'Where's The Reason?'. His demo worked out well and Power Exchange released it under the name of J.J. Barrie, J.J. being his son's nickname. The single did not sell but his wife, Kristine, had heard 'No Charge' in Toronto and recommended it to him. Barrie thought it would only work if it was done straight. Although a fine vocalist in the Perry Como style, he asked Vicki Brown from The Breakaways to sing the choruses, but she was not credited on the single. Vicki sang backing vocals on many other hit singles and performed live with her husband, Joe Brown. She died in 1991 and her daughter, Sam, wrote an album about their loss, *43 Minutes*.

Dave Cash at Capital Radio pushed 'No Charge' and soon everyone was playing it and, defying all expectations, 'No Charge' made the top. A comedy version by Billy Connolly, 'No Chance (No Charge)', made the Top 30, but J. J. Barrie's subsequent singles failed to sell. 'So Long Bing', anyone? Or his duet with England FC manager, Brian Clough, 'You Can't Win 'Em All'? Indeed.

J. J. Barrie

390 The Wurzels
Combine Harvester (Brand New Key)

Label & Cat No.: **EMI 2450**
Producer: **Bob Barratt**
Writer: **Melanie Safka**
Date reached No.1: **12 June 1976**
Weeks at No.1: **3**

THE PHRASE, 'OOOO...AARRR', IS associated with the Somerset group, Adge Cutler & The Wurzels. Dressed as farm labourers, they embodied English Heritage, but they sang new comic material and indulged in witty banter. Audiences would sing along with 'Drink Up Thy Zyder', 'Twice Daily' (which was banned by the BBC for its sexual innuendo) and 'Don't Tell I, Tell 'Ee'. Adge, a West Country poet, was no musician but he was a good lyricist and he saw the potential in 'beet music', forming the scrumpy & western group at Royal Oak in Nailsea in 1966. "I want to create some new west country songs," he said. "We're fed up singing 'Maybe It's Because I'm A Londoner'."

In 1972 the American singer/songwriter, Melanie, had written 'Brand New Key' as a light-hearted novelty to perform in-between her more intense material. The song about a new pair of roller skates only took 15 minutes to write, but it became her most successful song, topping the US charts and making number four here.

After Adge Cutler was killed in a car accident in 1974, the group (accordionist Tommy Banner, bass and sousaphone player Tony Baylis and guitarist Pete 'Rose' Budd) continued without him. Their EMI producer, Bob Barrett suggested that they rewrote 'Brand New Key' for a single, although they were not allowed a songwriting credit or royalties. When it made the charts, the yokels appeared on *Top Of The Pops* with a combine harvester, which didn't have much real work because of the drought.

The follow-up, 'I Am A Cider Drinker', a parody of 'Una Paloma Blanca', made number three, but enough was enough. The Wurzels remain a popular variety act to this day, recording a new version of 'Combine Harvester' every few years. The last one, a remix by Humpafunk in 2001, made the Top 40. The following year, The Wurzels released their west country version of 'Don't Look Back In Anger'.

391 The Real Thing
You To Me Are Everything

Label & Cat No.: **Pye International 7N 25709**
Producer: **Ken Gold**
Writers: **Ken Gold / Mickey Denne**
Date reached No.1: **26 June 1976**
Weeks at No.1: **3**

THE CHANTS WERE A BLACK DOOWOP group in Liverpool during the Merseybeat era. Their falsetto singer, Eddy Amoo, then joined his brother, Chris, in a new band in the early Seventies. They needed a name for the TV talent show, *Opportunity Knocks*. Cue to their manager and veteran music business executive, Tony Hall, staring at a Coca-Cola ad, "It's the real thing", during a traffic jam. His group, now called The Real Thing, won the contest, made some singles and worked as a backing group on record and stage for David Essex including his hit single, 'Me And My Girl (Night-Clubbing)'.

When the songwriter, Ken Gold, played Tony Hall two songs he had written with Mickey Denne, 'You To Me Are Everything' and 'Can't Get By Without You', he knew he had found their hit singles. The first went to number one and the second to number two.

In 1977 Chris and Eddy together with Dave Smith and Ray Lake recorded their tribute to Liverpool, *4 From 8*, and they wrote the hits, 'You'll Never Know What You're Missing' (16) and 'Can You Feel The Force?' (5). Remixed, tenth anniversary versions of their first two successes were also Top 10 hits. In 1986, Chris Amoo won Cruft's Pup of the Year with his Afghan hound, Gable.

The Real Thing remain a popular touring act and, unlike most nostalgia acts, they perform long, really long, contemporary versions of their hits, complete with rapping.

392 Demis Roussos
The Roussos Phenomenon (EP)

Label & Cat No.: **Philips DEMS 1**
Producer: **Demis Roussos**
Writers: **Stylianos Vlavianos / Robert Constandinos; (Sing An Ode To Love): Stylianos Vlavianos / Robert Constandinos / Charalampe Chalkitis**
Date reached No.1: **17 July 1976**
Weeks at No.1: **1**

WAS IT RIGHT TO ALLOW AN EP INTO the singles chart? Probably not, but a record that contained twice as much music as normal was in keeping with Demis Roussos' 18 stone. It seemed generous to be given 15 minutes of music for the price of a single, but then beware of Greeks bearing gifts...

Actually, Demis was born in Egypt in 1947, but his parents were Greek. He and Vangelis were part of Aphrodite's Child, who recorded the million-selling 'Rain And Tears' in 1968, but Demis left the group thinking it did not have enough commitment. He became a solo star in the Mediterranean countries with the million-selling 'We Shall Dance' in 1972. An album of his solo hits, *Forever And Ever,* made number two on the UK albums chart in 1974 and his quavering tenor entered the UK Top 10 in 1975 with 'Happy To Be On An Island In The Sun'.

When BBC-TV recorded the documentary, *The Roussos Phenomenon*, it was clear that Demis Roussos' number one fan was himself. An EP was issued to coincide with the broadcast, the key tracks being the ballads, 'Forever And Ever' and 'My Friend The Wind'. The public warmed to Demis and his amazing Technicolored kaftans – he even had a fur-trimmed one for Christmas. The kaftans emphasised his splendour, whilst conveniently hiding his belly. He loved kaftans, saying, "I feel completely free inside because I am nude underneath."

Perhaps because he became a figure of fun and it was not cool to like him, Demis Roussos had only one more Top 10 hit ('When Forever Has Gone') and one more big album (*Happy To Be Demis Roussos*).

In 1985 Demis Roussos was a passenger on a plane that was hijacked at Beirut airport, but he survived unharmed. In recent years, he has toured the UK and found that he still has an adoring public. He sings in Greek, French, Italian and English and if you go and see him, he is likely to invite you to do Zorba's dance.

393 Elton John & Kiki Dee
Don't Go Breaking My Heart

Label & Cat No.: **Rocket ROKN 512**
Producer: **Gus Dudgeon**
Writers: **Ann Orson & Carte Blanche**
Date Reached No.1: **24 July 1976**
Weeks at No.1: **6**

In 1970 Bradford born singer Kiki Dee got a call from her manager saying that Tamla-Motown Records had called and wanted her to go to Detroit to record an album. Kiki's initial reaction was, "I just laughed, but then I thought, this is it, I'm gonna be a big star."

Kiki was the first British singer to sign with Motown. She recorded the album *Great Expectations* and that's exactly what it was, because things just didn't happen, so she returned to England. She said, "I was a bit disappointed by my time in Detroit. If I stayed longer we could have come up with some really magic things. They had just lost Holland / Dozier / Holland and were about to move to Los Angeles, so I got lost really."

John Reid, who was an executive at Motown in England, called her and said, "I'm managing a guy called Elton John and we're launching a new record label, would you like to be involved?" Kiki recounted. "Meeting Elton and working with Rocket Records was so different from Motown, at least I was working with people my own age." Elton said, "Kiki was the first person we signed to the label and it just seemed natural that we should try and write something for her. I was very proud to write for her – she really is an incredible singer." But it was Kiki's cover of Veronique Sanson's 'Amoureuse' that gave the label its first hit.

Elton John and Bernie Taupin occasionally used pseudonyms for writing purposes. They wrote this song as Ann Orson and Carte Blanche and a Kiki Dee B-Side, 'The Man Who Loved To Dance', under the guise, Tripe and Onions.

"Both Elton and I were big fans of those duets on Motown by the likes of Marvin Gaye and Tammi Terrell and as there hadn't been any around for a bit, we thought we'd do one ourselves," Kiki explained.

The song came together in a rather unusual way. Producer Gus Dudgeon: "I was with Elton in Canada and he actually sang about three quarters of the song and gave Kiki about four lines. I said 'Hang on a minute, is this supposed to be a duet or a guest appearance?' Elton replied, 'A duet'. Then you've got to give her at least 50 per cent of the song." The tapes were then sent to London and when Kiki got them she remembered, "Elton had recorded the song abroad and also did my vocals in a high pitched voice which was quite funny, so I knew which lines to sing."

The accompanying video was simply Elton and Kiki standing around a microphone. Kiki said, "I don't think Elton's ever recorded standing up and I don't think he quite knew what to do with his hands. When you consider all the cross-cutting in today's video's I think our video is quite sweet. It's just us in a TV studio."

Over the years, Elton has performed 'Don't Go Breaking My Heart' as a duet with a number of other partners including, Miss Piggy from The Muppets, comedian Steve Coogan under his alter-ego guise, Alan Partridge, and with The Spice Girls on the TV show, *An Audience With Elton John*, in which Kiki Dee was a member of the audience.

"The great thing about the song is that I think people actually sensed that Elton and I actually care about each other and that it's not manufactured," said Kiki. "It goes to show that when you record a duet, you don't need to be madly in love with each other." They proved this in 1993, when they returned to the chart singing 'True Love'.

By the time 'Don't Go Breaking My Heart' reached number one Elton John was an international superstar with 13 UK and 15 US (including five number ones) Top 20 hits to his credit. It was somewhat ironic, therefore, that he should have to wait so long for a UK number one, and only then as the senior partner in a duo.

394 Abba
Dancing Queen

Label & Cat No.: **Epic EPC 4499**
Producers: **Björn Ulvaeus / Benny Andersson**
Writers: **Björn Ulvaeus / Benny Andersson / Stig Anderson**
Date Reached No.1: **4 September 1976**
Weeks at No.1: **6**

Abba were never keen on touring and seemed particularly reluctant to tour the US where their promotional films didn't have the same impact they did elsewhere in the world. Indeed, Benny Andersson once said, "We will not tour America until we have a number one hit there." When 'Dancing Queen' finally hit the top in April 1977, they gave in to record company pressure. But of all Abba's 20 US hits, this was their only chart topper.

The recording of 'Dancing Queen' began at the same time Frida recorded 'Fernando', but it wasn't released until a full year later. They had been invited to perform for Sweden's King Carl XVI Gustaf and the future Queen, Silvia Sommerlath. At first, they were unsure which song to perform but in the end the choice was obvious. Benny said, "If you have a song called 'Dancing Queen', you naturally choose to perform it on an occasion like the gala." Over the years, many have concluded that the song was written about Queen Silvia but this wasn't so. Besides which, at the time, she was 33 not 17. The event was

Elton John with Bradford-born singer Kiki Dee. Their duet on 'Don't Go Breaking My Heart' provided Elton with his first UK number one

recorded and televised shortly before the royal couple's wedding.

James Dean Bradfield from The Manic Street Preachers has said that 'Dancing Queen' is his all-time favourite song (something he shares with Tina Turner) and has wanted to record a song that sounded like it. The attempt was 'The Girl Who Wanted To Be God' from the *Everything Must Go* album. James said "Although it sounded nothing like it, we were happy with the end result. That's the sign of a truly great band, it's difficult to replicate the essence of their music." Abba's version was used to great effect in the 1994 film, *Muriel's Wedding*.

'Dancing Queen' topped the charts around the world and is their biggest selling single and likely to remain so. A perennial favourite in gay clubs, it was also the first single whose packaging incorporated the now famous copyrighted ABBA logo with the first 'B' reversed.

In 1992 Mike Stock and Pete Waterman released a cover of 'Dancing Queen' by British dance act Abbacadabra. Epic Records shrewdly re-issued Abba's version and were rewarded with a number 16 hit, some 41 places higher than the cover.

395 Pussycat
Mississippi

Label & Cat No.: **Sonet SON 2077**

Producer: **Eddy Hilberts**

Writer: **Werner Theunissen**

Date reached No.1: **11 October 1976**

Weeks at No.1: **4**

A POLISH MINER EMIGRATED TO Holland and set up home in Limburg. His daughters, Toni, Betty and Marianne Kowalczyk, worked as telephone operators but wanted to be singers, working first as The Zingende Zusjes (The Singing Sisters). They added a female drummer and became The BG's From Holland (that's Beat Girls). Toni married Lou Willé, who played with his brothers in Ricky Rendell & The Centurions, and he established a new band, Sweet Reaction. They completed the seven-piece line-up with Theo Wetzels, Theo Coumans and John Theunissen, who all came from the heavy metal band, Scum, undoubtedly a name that was ahead of its time.

Early in 1975 the producer Eddy Hilberts changed their name to Pussycat and asked them to record a country-rock song, 'Mississippi', written by the girls' guitar tutor, Werner Theunissen, who was no relation to John Theunissen. It became an international hit, selling five million copies.

The follow-up, 'Smile', although successful elsewhere, only made the UK Top 30. The group had many continental hits including 'Georgie', 'My Broken Souvenirs', 'If You Ever Come To Amsterdam', 'Wet Day In September' and 'Doin' La Bamba'. Economics forced the sisters into using backing tapes in 1980 and they split up in 1985. Toni made a solo album, *Privilege*, and in 1989, *New Words To An Old Love Song*, was one of the top albums in The Netherlands. Toni, now divorced, recently released a single, 'Girls In Their Fifties', and, as the song said, the cat came back as the three sisters have reformed Pussycat with new backing musicians.

396 Chicago
If You Leave Me Now

Label & Cat No.: **CBS 4603**

Producer: **James William Guercio**

Writer: **Peter Cetera**

Date reached No.1: **13 November 1976**

Weeks at No.1: **3**

THE ORIGINS OF CHICAGO GO BACK TO DePaul University in the US city of the same name in 1966. Three students and two friends became The Missing Links and then The Big Thing. They were spotted by James William Guercio, who produced The Buckinghams, and the band became Chicago Transit Authority. They made their first album in 1970, but the Mayor of Chicago was horrified and threatened to sue them for using the name of a public company in that way. They shortened it to Chicago and so initiated a trend for naming bands after US cities – Boston and Kansas, amongst them.

Although Chicago were a jazz-rock ensemble, they were more rock and less jazz than Blood, Sweat & Tears, also produced by Guercio. The seven-piece band featured Peter Cetera (lead vocals, bass), Terry Kath (guitar), Robert Lamm (keyboards) and Danny Seraphine (drums), together with a brass section of Lee Loughnane (trumpet), Jimmy Pankow (trombone) and Walt Parazaider (reeds).

Chicago were favourites on *The Old Grey Whistle Test* and their LPs, all given a numeric sequence in their title, made the albums chart. Their first UK hit was with a revival of The Spencer Davis Group's 'I'm A Man' and then an original, '25 Or 6 To 4', both in 1970.

In 1976 the prolific group was recording *Chicago X* when Peter Cetera asked if he could record a new song he had written, 'If You Leave Me Now', at the last minute. This muted, middle-of-the-road ballad, arranged by veteran Jimmie Haskell, was different from anything that Chicago had done and it became a transatlantic number one.

It looked as though the band would break up when Terry Kath died in a shooting accident in 1978, but the band got over this tragedy and had further UK hits with 'Hard To Say I'm Sorry' from the film, *Summer Lovers* (1982) and 'Hard Habit To Break' (1984). Peter Cetera, who left Chicago in 1985, went to number three with 'Glory Of Love' in 1986. Chicago continues with Robert Lamm and the original brass section and their latest album, one of Christmas songs, is *Chicago 25*.

Chicago

397 Showaddywaddy
Under The Moon Of Love

Label & Cat No.: **Bell 1495**
Producer: **Mike Hurst**
Writers: **Tommy Boyce / Curtis Lee**
Date reached No.1: **4 December 1976**
Weeks at No.1: **3**

IN 1973 TWO LEICESTER ROCK'N'ROLL bands, The Hammers and The Choice, amalgamated. There were two vocalists (Dave Bartram, Buddy Gask), two guitarists (Trevor Oakes, Russ Field), two bassists (Rod Deas, Al James) and two drummers (Romeo Challenger, Malcolm Allured). The showband, all crepes and drapes, spent a year touring the clubs and got their break on the ITV talent show, *New Faces*. Almost uniquely, both Mickie Most and Tony Hatch loved them. They recorded for Bell and their producer was Mike Hurst, formerly with The Springfields.

Showaddywaddy began with their own songs, 'Hey Rock And Roll' going to number two, but their fifth single, a revival of Eddie Cochran's 'Three Steps To Heaven', set the course for the next five years. Dave Bartram recalls, "We got our songs from all over the place. One DJ in Leicester was a rock'n'roll fanatic and he came up with some really obscure things like 'Under The Moon Of Love' and 'You Got What It Takes'. There was a wealth of material to go at, no doubt about that, and we did them in our own fashion. Our version of 'Under The Moon Of Love' is far superior to Curtis Lee's, but not many people know that anyway and they think of it as a Showaddywaddy original. I thought we improved on Dion & The Belmonts' 'I Wonder Why', but Eddie Cochran's own version of 'Three Steps To Heaven' was sacred to me, although it was well worth covering."

Curtis Lee, whose name had been purloined by a Merseybeat singer Lee Curtis, also did the originals of 'Pretty Little Angel Eyes' and 'A Night At Daddy Gee's', both singles for Showaddywaddy. Dave says, "Tommy Boyce, who co-wrote 'Under The Moon Of Love' and had written for The Monkees, came to see us and it was like winning the pools for him. He gave us a load of new material but he had lost his touch. We had so much success with covers that there were people in the band and at the record company who thought it was a winning formula. We stuck with it for rather too long, in my view."

Maybe the public had tired of the group rather than the music because, once they had faded from the charts, Shakin' Stevens hit home with his rock'n'roll revivals. Showaddywaddy still has six originals in its line-up: they toured the UK with their musical, *Hey Rock'n'Roll*, in 2002.

398 Johnny Mathis
When A Child Is Born (Soleado)

Label & Cat No.: **CBS 4599**
Producer: **Jack Gold**
Writers: **Fred Jay / Ciro Dammico**
Date reached No.1: **25 December 1976**
Weeks at No.1: **3**

ALTHOUGH JOHNNY MATHIS IS AN international superstar, he hasn't had many UK hits: there's a number one and five Top 10 singles. Even his signature tune, 'Misty' (1960) only reached number 12, and his major US hits, 'It's Not For Me To Say', 'Chances Are' and 'The Twelfth Of Never' missed out completely. His album *Johnny's Greatest Hits* (1958) was on the US charts for over three years and made number one, and although he has not had such success here, he has topped the UK album charts with the compilations, *The Johnny Mathis Collection* (1977) and *Tears And Laughter* (1980).

Johnny Mathis was known as an MOR singer and so the public was surprised when he went disco for a smooth cover version of The Stylistics' 'I'm Stone In Love With You'. It was a Top 10 single in 1975 and three years later, he was teamed with Deniece Williams for 'Too Much Too Little Too Late', a number three and a US number one. In between was 'When A Child Is Born'.

In 1973 an Italian artist, Ciro Dammico, had a hit in his home country with his song, 'Soleado'. It was given an English lyric, 'When A Child Is Born', by Fred Jay, an American living in Germany, and it was then an international success for Michael Holm. Some 120 artists recorded the song before Johnny Mathis, including Barbra Streisand, Vince Hill and Bing Crosby.

Johnny Mathis has often recorded seasonal songs, and one of his first chart entries was with 'Winter Wonderland' (1958). In 1976 he recorded 'When A Child Is Born'. On first hearing, it could be a celebration of any baby being born, but the narration refers to a child who will end misery and suffering forever, so it can only be Jesus.

Johnny Mathis secured the Christmas number one and as the DJ Alan Freeman commented, "Johnny Mathis has put some reality into Christmas and made people feel religious again." In 1981 Johnny recorded the song as a duet with Gladys Knight, but the new version barely made the charts.

399 David Soul
Don't Give Up On Us

Label & Cat No.: **Private Stock PVT 84**
Producer: **Tony Macaulay**
Writer: **Tony Macaulay**
Date reached No.1: **15 January 1977**
Weeks at No.1: **4**

DAVID SOLBERG WAS BORN INTO A Norwegian family in Chicago in 1943 and reducing his name to David Soul, he recorded several folk and pop singles. Although blond, blue-eyed and extremely good-looking, he covered his face for a series of routines and songs as The Covered Man on the late night *Merv Griffin Show*. In 1973 he appeared in the Clint Eastwood film, *Magnum Force*, and the producers of a new TV cop show, *Starsky And Hutch*, saw the film and decided he was right for Ken Hutchinson, usually known as Hutch.

David Soul recalls, "I had to read with about 200 actors who might be Starsky and in walks Paul Michael Glaser, whom I'd known from New York. We had both been in off Broadway productions and it was like magic. We had no idea how the pilot would work out, but it led to the series. The fact that we were such good friends helped to bring some compassion and humour to the roles – otherwise, we would have just been two hard-hitting womanising cops."

It was inevitable that David Soul would make records, but not to him. "No, I have never been opportunistic and I did not want to make a record just because people knew me as Hutch. I do what I love and believe in and music was something I did. I made an album in San Francisco for Private Stock but there was nothing suitable for a single. The company told me that Tony Macaulay had some good tunes and he came over and played me 'Don't Give Up On Us' and 'Going In With My Eyes Open'. Within 10 days, I had learnt the songs and recorded them and Tony had mixed them and taken them back to England. They bazoomed to the top and they are two songs which have stood the test of time."

'Don't Give Up On Us' was a number one but Norway lost out to Sweden as 'Going In With My Eyes Open' couldn't dislodge Abba's 'Knowing Me Knowing You'. David Soul was not happy about Owen Wilson singing 'Don't Give Up On Us' in the 2004 revival, *Starsky And Hutch*, as his screen character never sang. At least they got the Gran Torino right.

400 Julie Covington
Don't Cry For Me Argentina

Label & Cat No.: **MCA 260**

Producers: **Tim Rice / Andrew Lloyd Webber**

Writers: **Tim Rice / Andrew Lloyd Webber**

Date reached No.1: **12 February 1977**

Weeks at No.1: **1**

When Tim Rice and Andrew Lloyd Webber wrote a musical about the Argentinian politician, Eva Peron, they decided, as with *Jesus Christ Superstar*, to make the album first. They cast the album as they would a stage musical and Julie Covington sang the title role. She was a fine actress with an excellent voice and she had recorded an album of songs by Pete Atkin and Clive James, *The Beautiful Changes*, in 1970. She also starred alongside Charlotte Cornwell and Rula Lenska in the ITV series, *Rock Follies*. A song from the second series, 'OK?', was to make the Top 10 in May 1977.

Both Tim and Andrew recognised the potential of 'Don't Cry For Me Argentina' but Tim thought that his lyric might be too obscure for a pop single. He did rework it as 'It's Only Your Love Returning', but they still preferred 'Don't Cry For Me Argentina'.

The fact that this was such an unusual song worked in its favour but it made number one against the odds as Julie Covington refused to promote it, not even appearing on *Top Of The Pops*. Tim Rice recalls, "When the single began to show signs of being a hit, she got less and less interested in the project. She backed away from it and began to feel that it was a fascist plot, that we were exploiting the workers. I'm exaggerating a bit but she definitely disapproved of the success of 'Don't Cry For Me Argentina'."

Julie Covington had been the apparent choice for the stage musical itself and a frantic search, highlighted by the media, took place to find a stage *Evita*. The role was a triumph for Elaine Paige. In 1978 Julie Covington was persuaded to make an album for Virgin and the folk-rock collection, *Julie Covington*, featured Richard Thompson. She also had a Top 20 single with the Alice Cooper song, 'Only Women Bleed'.

An instrumental version of 'Don't Cry For Me Argentina' by The Shadows reached number five in 1978 and the song returned to the top three in 1996 when Madonna sang it in the film. It has also been a chart entry for Sinead O'Connor (1992) and The Mike Flowers Pops (1996). However, Rice would not allow The Barron Knights to record a parody as he felt that theatregoers might recall that when they saw the musical and it would lessen the impact.

401 Leo Sayer
When I Need You

Label & Cat No.: **Chrysalis CHS 2127**

Producer: **Richard Perry**

Writers: **Albert Hammond / Carole Bayer Sager**

Date reached No.1: **19 February 1977**

Weeks at No.1: **3**

Leo Sayer's talents were recognised by Adam Faith, who produced his first hits ('The Show Must Go On', 'One Man Band', 'Long Tall Glasses') and albums (*Silverbird*, *Just A Boy*) as well as Roger Daltrey's first solo album which included a version of Sayer's 'Giving It All Away'. At first Leo Sayer, like Gilbert O'Sullivan, appeared as a novelty act, dressed as a clown, and, like O'Sullivan, he was then able to establish his credibility. He missed out on the top when the Gretna Green song, 'Moonlighting', couldn't dislodge 'Sailing' and his move to disco, 'You Make Me Feel Like Dancing' came up against 'If You Leave Me Now'. However, 'You Make Me Feel Like Dancing' was a US number one.

The New York producer, Richard Perry, who had made *Nilsson Schmilsson* and Carly Simon's *No Secrets,* made three big-selling albums with Leo Sayer, *Endless Flight* (1976), *Thunder In My Heart* (1977) and *Leo Sayer* (1978). Although he liked Sayer's own songs, he told him that he had a versatile voice and could interpret other material. What he had in mind was 'When I Need You', which Albert Hammond had recorded in 1976. Hammond had written the song with the lyricist, Carole Bayer Sager, to convey how he felt when he was away from home. When we spoke to Leo Sayer, he hadn't realised that Albert Hammond's version had been released.

"I was still a singer / songwriter and so I had to find something that I could really believe in," says Leo today. "Then cool, it would no problem. There was a lot of compromising but I liked Albert Hammond's songs and, of course, Carole wrote 'A Groovy Kind Of Love'. '99 Miles From LA', 'The Air That I Breathe' and 'It Never Rains In Southern California' were all great songs, so I

Leo Sayer began his career in spectacular style, dressed as a Pierrot-style clown. This was followed by some ill-advised perms

put on 'When I Need You' and wow! My wife, Janice, was home in England and those were the words I wanted to say on the phone. To me it was like a blues, and we recorded it first with Booker T on organ and I did it like Otis Redding doing 'I've Been Loving You Too Long'. It was completely wrong for the song, and we went back to how it was on the demo. Everyone does it now from Celine Dion and Julio Iglesias to someone in *Hollyoaks*. It has even been used for a cat food commercial."

Booker T is not on the hit version – the keyboards are played by James Newton and Michael Omartian – and the saxophone solo comes from one of America's top session men, Bobby Keyes, who has played with John Lennon, George Harrison and The Rolling Stones.

402 The Manhattan Transfer Chanson D'Amour

Label & Cat No.: **Atlantic K 10886**

Producer: **Richard Perry**

Writer: **Wayne Shanklin**

Date reached No.1: **2 April 1977**

Weeks at No.1: **5**

ALTHOUGH THE NEW YORK DOO-WOP vocalist, Tim Hauser, formed The Manhattan Transfer in 1969, members came and went and he reformed the group in 1972 with Laurel Masse, Alan Paul and Janis Siegel, and they developed a very tight, close harmony sound. Their act included doo-wop songs, swing favourites and acappella ballads from previous decades and, like Barry Manilow and Bette Midler, they acquired a cult following in New York's gay clubs and bath houses. "We loved the vocal groups which go all the way back to the Twenties," said Tim Hauser. "It pretty much ended when the British invasion happened, except for Motown, but that was more of a producer's medium."

In 1975 they released their first album, *The Manhattan Transfer*, and hosted their own US TV series. Their first US hit was with 'Operator' and their first UK chart entry was with 'Tuxedo Junction'. Much to their annoyance, the New York newspaper, *Village Voice*, accused them of racism. Tim Hauser commented, "Why put down white people who have a background in black music and are trying to bring it forward?"

In 1958 and clearly inspired by the sounds of Les Paul & Mary Ford, Art & Dotty Todd recorded 'Chanson D'Amour'. It won them a gold disc but it did not make the UK charts. It was an inspired choice for The Manhattan Transfer's harmonies and the record was produced by Richard Perry, who had also produced the previous number one by Leo Sayer. Quite appropriately 'Chanson D'Amour' was also a number one in France, but it was not a big hit in the US. Their biggest US hit was with 'The Boy From New York City' in 1981. The Manhattan Transfer became regulars on *The Two Ronnies* and recorded an album, *Live*, on a UK tour. The group continues to this day but many of their releases have been specialist jazz albums.

403 Abba Knowing Me Knowing You

Label & Cat No.: **Epic EPC 4955**

Producers: **Björn Ulvaeus / Benny Andersson**

Writers: **Björn Ulvaeus / Benny Andersson / Stig Anderson**

Date Reached No.1: **2 April 1977**

Weeks at No.1: **5**

BJÖRN AND AGNETHA HAD BEEN married since 1971 and cracks were opening in their relationship, although it wasn't public at this stage. The title had been suggested once again by Stig Anderson, but it was Björn who wrote the lyrics. This was the first Abba hit to acknowledge that the group consisted of four mature adults in that it dealt with the breakdown of a marriage, but in their unique fashion the four of them somehow managed to set down this melancholy theme within the framework of an immensely catchy pop song.

The best songs are usually written from a writer's own experiences. The opening verse, "No more carefree laughter, silence ever after. Walking through an empty house, tears in my eyes, here is where the story ends, this is goodbye", seems to say a great deal about a relationship, even though Björn has since denied that the lyrics had any bearing on his own situation. He claims, "Even if the roots are somewhere deep inside, from something that has happened to you, it's still 90% fiction. I just work from images. I saw a man walking through an empty house for the last time as a symbol of divorce."

At the beginning of 1977 Abba set off on the first of their two major worldwide tours. The first took in Europe and kicked off in Oslo, the capital of Frida's native Norway. The 12,000 tickets for their Valentine's Day shows at London's Royal Albert Hall show sold out in hours, the box office having received three and a half million requests in the mail. The second saw them conquer Australia, visitng Sydney, Melborne, Adelaide and Perth on a tour that has become legendry in the group's history.

British comedian Steve Coogan invented a character called Alan Partridge and, in 1995, was given his own BBC television series called *Knowing Me Knowing You with Alan Partridge*. There was also a Christmas special, which was cleverly renamed *Knowing Me Knowing Yule*. At the end of the show he would finish with a rendition of the Abba song adding extra emphasis to the 'ah-hah' parts.

The Manhattan Transfer

404 Deniece Williams
Free

Label & Cat No.: **CBS 4978**

Producers: **Maurice White / Charles Stepney**

Writers: **Deniece Williams / Hank Redd / Nathan Watts / Susaye Green**

Date reached No.1: **7 May 1977**

Weeks at No.1: **2**

DENIECE CHANDLER'S MOTHER HAD a collection of Nancy Wilson albums, which Deniece loved. The young girl would sing along and she cites Nancy's 'Moon River' as her all-time favourite record. She was born in Gary, Indiana in 1951 but she was much shyer than Gary's other musical residents, the Jackson family. She did not often sing publicly but she made her first record, 'Love Is Tears', when she was 16. However, she wanted to be an anaesthetist and she was married, becoming Deniece Williams. She continued to sing from time to time.

When Stevie Wonder heard one of her records, he asked her to join his touring band. Deniece was with Wonderlove for four years and Stevie encouraged her songwriting – 'Slip Away' was recorded by Merry Clayton and Frankie Valli. One day when she was rehearsing with Wonder's bass player Hank Redd and his pianist Nathan Watts, and they hit upon the idea for 'Free'. They developed the verse and chorus and Susaye Green of The Supremes, who happened to be around, completed the lyric.

Deniece sent her songs to Maurice White of Earth, Wind & Fire. He offered to produce her first album, which was *This Is Niecy*. The LP contained a six-minute, slow-building 'Free', which was edited for single release. 'Free' reached the US Top 30 and topped the UK chart. Deniece's wide-ranging voice was in the style of Syreeta's 'Spinnin' And Spinnin'' (1974) and Minnie Riperton's 'Lovin' You' (1975). Russell Harty introduced Deniece Williams as 'the thinking man's Diana Ross' (whatever that might mean), and Deniece was seen as the next soul diva.

Deniece Williams

She followed 'Free' with the Top 10 hits – 'That's What Friends Are For' and 'Too Much Too Little Too Late', a duet with Johnny Mathis. 'Let's Hear It For The Boy' from the film *Footloose* starring Kevin Bacon went to number two in 1984.

Coming from a religious background, Deniece nursed doubts that she was doing the right thing and for some time she made gospel records. In recent years, she has presented soul programmes on BBC Radio 2.

405 Rod Stewart
I Don't Want To Talk About It / The First Cut Is The Deepest

Label & Cat No.: **Riva 7**

Producer: **Tom Dowd**

Writers: **Danny Whitten; Cat Stevens**

Date reached No.1: **21 May 1977**

Weeks at No.1: **4**

NILS LOFGREN AND DANNY WHITTEN were part of Neil Young's band, Crazy Horse. Neil had a hit album with *After The Gold Rush* in 1969, but the next album fell to pieces as Danny Whitten was a drug addict. Nils recalls, "Danny was a very soulful man and a good man and he was the one who got me in Crazy Horse. I loved his song, 'I Don't Want To Talk About It', and I think it is one of the greatest ballads ever. It has a very haunting lyric and I put two lines into the song because Danny was so ill when he recorded it. He could still sing and play but he wasn't bothered with much else. We said, 'Danny, we've got to do this song, it's a great song' and he said, 'It needs a second verse' and this went on for months. He never could get it together and then we were in the studio and got in an argument, and he said, 'Okay, well, one of you write it'. I left the studio and wrote a couple of lines quickly and I said, 'What about these?' and he said, 'Fine, let's do it.' Danny and I sat opposite each other with acoustic guitars and Ry Cooder was playing slide on his lap and it came out beautifully." Danny's downward spiral continued and he died in November 1972, never realising what he had created.

Atlantic Crossing, Rod Stewart's 1975 album, had already garnered the hit singles, 'Sailing' (1) and 'This Old Heart Of Mine' (4). The LP included 'I Don't Want To Talk About It', and Rod found that when he performed it in concert, the audiences were singing along. Rather late in the day, he realised its commercial potential and selected it for an A-side.

When Rod tried to record his new album, *A Night On The Town*, in Los Angeles, he found that the smog affected his voice, so he moved to another studio in Colorado. This time the altitude made singing difficult, but his third choice, Miami, was perfect. The first single from the album, 'Tonight's The Night', made number five and attracted controversy for its explicitness – one line went "Spread your wings and let me come inside." The second single, 'The Killing Of Georgie', an account of a homosexual being murdered, went to number two.

The album included a revival of Cat Stevens' bitter-sweet 'The First Cut Is The Deepest', which, like Mike D'Abo's 'Handbags And Gladrags' showed that the Brits could write convincing soul ballads. The song had been a Top 20 hit for P.P. Arnold, a former member of Ike & Tina Turner's Ikettes, in 1967. Pat, or P.P. said in 2003, "Cat Stevens only lived round the corner from Immediate Records. He came in with the song and my record was produced by Mike Hurst from The Springfields. I am certain that I released the first version of the song and not Cat Stevens."

While Rod was at the top of the charts, The Sex Pistols' 'God Save The Queen' languished at number two. The chart compilers were horrified by the thought that 'God Save The Queen' might be number one for the week of the Silver Jubilee and wondered how they might stop it. Their solution was surprising and should never have been permitted: for one week only, shops were not allowed to submit returns for releases on their own labels. Hence, Virgin could not submit its sales for 'God Save The Queen' and Richard Branson did not publicly object to this. Her

Majesty had endured much worse criticism than the teenage angst of 'God Save The Queen' and anyone with any sense would realise that England could never ever be described as "a fascist regime". This meant that Rod Stewart had an extra week at number one and what could be a better title in the circumstances than 'I Don't Want To Talk About It'?

406 Kenny Rogers
Lucille

Label & Cat No.:	**United Artists UP 36242**
Producer:	**Larry Butler**
Writers:	**Roger Bowling / Hal Bynum**
Date Reached No.1:	**18 June 1977**
Weeks at No.1:	**1**

"COUNTRY MUSIC IS ABOUT PEOPLE and about people's problems. Every person has a story and every story is potentially a song," said Kenny Rogers. In 1969 he just missed out on the top spot with 'Ruby, Don't Take Your Love To Town', a story of a crippled Vietnam War veteran whose main worry was that his wife was sleeping with someone else because he had lost the use of his legs. 'Lucille' tells the story of a woman who walks out on her husband and their four children at a most inopportune moment.

Kenny Rogers has been through so many changes of music style that his adaptability is enough to make any chameleon jealous. His first high school band was The Scholars, at 19 and singing doo-wop, he had a hit in his hometown, Houston, Texas, with 'That Crazy Feeling'. Influenced by Elvis, he dabbled in rock'n'roll, but soon turned to jazz where he spent five years playing stand-up bass in the Bobby Doyle Trio. In the mid-Sixties, he joined The Kirby Stone Four and then The New Christy Minstrels, which at one time featured Barry McGuire and Kim Carnes. Then he took three of the Minstrels and formed The First Edition with Kenny on lead vocals and had their first hit with a song that Jimi Hendrix once told Kenny was his all-time favourite, 'Just Dropped In (To See What Condition My Condition Was In)'. They proved successful and the group name was soon amended to Kenny Rogers and The First Edition.

In 1975 the group disbanded and Kenny signed a solo deal with United Artists Records in Nashville. Hal Bynum's marriage was beginning to fall apart when he started writing the song. One of his wife's best friends wanted to have an affair with him. Bynum realised that if he didn't give in to an affair, he would probably give in to alcohol. His wife was preparing herself for a trip away, at which point Hal said, "You picked a fine time to leave me." Roger Bowling assisted in altering the song to a barroom situation before they took the song to producer, Larry Butler. After two label-mates turned it down, Larry submitted it to Kenny for his next album. 'Lucille' was the first of 20 country number ones, it earned him a Grammy Award for Best Country Vocal Performance and the CMA award for Single Of The Year. Ironically, Kenny's mother's name was Lucille.

A year later a Nashville songwriter, Don Schlitz, pitched a 'story' song to Kenny, which he loved. 'The Gambler' gave Kenny another US country number one, but failed to interest the British public.

Roger Bowling made little impact as a singer, but as a writer, his first big success was with 'Blanket On The Ground' (Billie Jo Spears). He died on Christmas Day 1982, aged 37.

407 Jacksons
Show You The Way To Go

Label & Cat No.:	**Epic EPC 5266**
Producers:	**Kenny Gamble / Leon Huff**
Writers:	**Kenny Gamble / Leon Huff**
Date Reached No.1:	**25 June 1977**
Weeks at No.1:	**1**

WHEN THE JACKSON BROTHERS LEFT Motown for Epic Records in 1975, they weren't allowed to keep their family group name, Jackson 5, because Berry Gordy had patented it.

The brothers, Michael, Jermaine, Jackie, Tito and Marlon, formed the group in 1966 and were managed by their father Joe. They signed to Motown in 1969 and, within a year, had their first four singles all top the US chart. Michael was the youngest at eight, Jackie was the eldest at 15.

During their time with Motown, Jackson 5 recorded 469 songs of which only 174 were released. They were not allowed to write their own material and subsequently received only 2.7 per cent of the royalties. They wanted more freedom and better pay, so decided to break away from Motown. In doing so, Berry Gordy filed a five million dollar lawsuit for breach of contract. In turn, the brothers countersued because they were owed half a million dollars on tracks not issued. The boys refused to record anything more for the label. The dispute was finally resolved with Gordy receiving $600,000.

They signed a contract with Epic Records and had to change their name to The Jacksons. Michael, who had had a concurrent solo career since 1971, was offered an additional separate contract.

Jermaine married Berry Gordy Jr's daughter, Hazel. Perhaps out of a sense of loyalty, he decided to remain with Motown. His place was taken by another brother, Randy.

The Jacksons released their eponymous album which was written, produced and recorded by Gamble & Huff in their hometown of Philadelphia. The first single from it, 'Enjoy Yourself' didn't even make the Top 40. 'Show You The Way To Go' was the second single and was released to promote their first UK tour for five years. Michael said, "It showed the good regard Epic had for our singing, it was one of the best records we did"

In 1984 Jermaine was reunited with his brothers for the much-publicised *Victory* album and associated tour. Marlon left in 1987, which left The Jacksons as a quartet of Jermaine, Randy, Tito and Jackie who still tour the United States.

Michael, meanwhile, was gearing up for a spectacular solo career which would see him eclipse not only his brothers but virtually ever other pop performer on the planet.

The Jackson 5 briefly adopt an unwise biker image, from top left: Michael, Randy, Marlon, Tito & Jackie

408 Hot Chocolate
So You Win Again

Label & Cat No.: **RAK 259**
Producer: **Mickie Most**
Writer: **Russ Ballard**
Date reached No.1: **2 July 1977**
Weeks at No.1: **3**

ERROL BROWN FORMED HOT Chocolate in 1969. "A girl in an office came up with the name, Hot Chocolate," says Errol Brown, "and I thought it was a positive name for a black face because hot chocolate is a nice thing." The group's first release, a reggae 'Give Peace A Chance' for The Beatles' Apple label, failed to sell but they were quickly signed by Mickie Most to RAK.

Many of their early hits were written by Errol Brown with his bass player, Tony Wilson. Wilson left in 1975 and the line-up at the time of 'So You Win Again' was Harvey Hinsley (guitar), Patrice Olive (bass), Larry Ferguson (keyboards) and Tony Connor (drums). These names are hardly known because Errol's image was so dominant. Especially that bald head: "I began to lose my hair when I was 18 and my father was bald by the time he was 30. When I started to be successful, I thought it would look really bad in five years' time, so why not be the first singer in the world to shave my head? I thought I was the first and then I saw Isaac Hayes."

Hot Chocolate had their first hit with 'Love Is Life' in 1970 and did well throughout the Seventies. Their key records include 'Brother Louie' (7, 1973), 'Emma' (3, 1974) and 'You Sexy Thing' (2, 1975). Despite huge success, their only chart-topper was with a song they didn't write, Russ Ballard's 'So You Win Again'. "My inspiration was quiet at the time," says Errol quite poetically, "and Mickie Most thought this would be a big song. I didn't like it in its original form but we rehearsed in a more soulful way and it worked. Mickie Most told us it would be a number one and it was." The song, like Hank Williams' country music standard 'You Win Again' (1952), is about how someone can have control over you, no matter what.

Russ Ballard is one of rock's journeymen. He played in Adam Faith's Roulettes, Argent and made solo albums. Among his many songs are 'God Gave Rock And Roll To You' (Argent, Kiss) and he has been a session guitarist on hundreds of records. He says of 'So You Win Again', "I had written 'So You Win Again' like a soul tune and I played it to Maurice Oberstein, the head of CBS and I told him that I had a great song and I wanted to do it as a single. Maurice heard it and said, 'No, you must give that to a black band.' Mickie Most recorded it straight away with Hot Chocolate. I didn't like their version at the time: it seemed too slow and too English to me, but I got used to it. I wanted it more like Boz Scaggs, but Mickie was right and I was wrong."

After 'So You Win Again', Hot Chocolate had hits with 'Put Your Love In Me' (10, 1977), 'No Doubt About It' (2, 1980) and 'It Started With A Kiss' (5, 1982). A remix of 'You Sexy Thing' made number 10 in 1987 and the original version was number six in 1997 following its inclusion in *The Full Monty*. By then Errol Brown had gone solo and now audiences were shouting out for him to strip. Errol still tours but his main love is horse-racing. He says, "I've been lucky. I managed Hot Chocolate myself so I never got ripped off."

409 Donna Summer
I Feel Love

Label & Cat No.: **GTO GT 100**
Producers: **Giorgio Moroder / Pete Bellotte**
Writers: **Giorgio Moroder / Pete Bellotte / Donna Summer**
Date reached No.1: **23 July 1977**
Weeks at No.1: **4**

AFTER TOURING EUROPE IN *HAIR*, 22-year-old LaDonna Andrea Gaines arrived in Munich in 1970. She married an Austrian actor, Helmut Somner: their marriage didn't last but she retained an anglicised version of his name, Donna Summer. Whilst appearing in shows and singing around Munich, she met the Italian record producer, Giorgio Moroder, and the English guitarist, Pete Bellotte, who had been with The Sinners. In the same way that cinema was transformed by spaghetti westerns, German disco music was set to dominate the charts and the key players included Summer, Moroder and Bellotte. In more ways than one, here comes Summer.

In 1975 Donna Summer moaned in orgasmic delight on the 17-minute 'Love To Love You Baby', which was edited for radio but retained its sexiness for single release. Her techno-sleaze was as controversial as 'Je T'Aime, Moi Non Plus'. Church authorities condemned it, the BBC restricted its airplay, and naturally, it soared into the charts.

Two years later and by now a disco star, Donna Summer covered several different styles (Crystals to Kraftwerk) on her album, *I Remember Yesterday*. One track, 'I Feel Love' was structured around electronic sequencing and it was her only UK number one. She recalled, "Giorgio brought me this popcorn track he had recorded and I said, 'What the hell is this, Giorgio?' I finished as a sort of a joke."

And that joke continues. In 1982 Donna's record was re-mixed by Patrick Cowley and made number 21. Then three years later, Marc Almond with Bronski Beat with their 'I Feel Love (Medley)', which included 'Love To Love You Baby' and 'Johnny Remember Me', reached number three. The masters of Donna Sumner's orginal had been lost by 1995 and she recorded a new version, which made number eight.

Donna Summer had many more hits, usually of a disco nature. She revived 'MacArthur Park'(1978), sang about 'Bad Girls' (1979), had more sexual innuendo with 'Hot Stuff' (1979) and recorded a duet with Barbra Streisand, 'No More Tears (Enough Is Enough)', again in 1979. All four records were US number ones. In 1989 she had UK Top 10 hits with 'This Time I Know It's For Real' and 'I Don't Wanna Get Hurt',

Donna Summer

which were produced by Stock, Aitken & Waterman. She says, "It's in every woman to be seductive, be she a teacher or a whore."

410 Brotherhood Of Man
Angelo

Label & Cat No.: **Pye 7N 45699**

Producer: **Tony Hiller**

Writers: **Tony Hiller / Martin Lee / Lee Sheriden**

Date reached No.1: **20 August 1977**

Weeks at No.1: **1**

After the young girl in 'Save Your Kisses For Me', Brotherhood Of Man turned to animals with 'My Sweet Rosalie', but this time the magic wasn't working and the record only reached number 30. Not to worry, they covered a little-known US country song from Diana Trask, 'Oh Boy (The Mood I'm In)', written by Tony Romeo, which returned them to the Top 10.

They returned to number one with a song about a Mexican shepherd boy, 'Angelo', and Tony Hiller says, "Although it took place in Mexico, Angelo felt European, the poor shepherd boy and all that, and the name fitted perfectly. The Barron Knights asked me if they could do a funny version of it and I said, 'Okay, so long as it's not filthy'. (sings) 'Long ago outside a chip shop in Walthamstow'. It was hilarious. Bob Williamson did 'Kippers For Tea' after 'Save Your Kisses For Me', and it is great when that happens. It means that everybody knows your song."

Tony Hiller continues, "It was wonderful to sit down with Martin Lee and Lee Sheriden and write album after album for Brotherhood Of Man, and because of that success, various managers were sending me their artists. In one year, I produced 88 tracks – Peter Knight Orchestra, Harry Secombe, Moira Anderson – they just kept coming."

411 The Floaters
Float On

Label & Cat No.: **ABC 4187**

Producer: **Woody Wilson**

Writers: **Arnold Ingham / James Mitchell Jr / Marvin Willis**

Date reached No.1: **27 August 1977**

Weeks at No.1: **1**

The Detroit Emeralds, who had a Top 10 hit with 'Feel The Need In Me' in 1973, purchased a club The Emerald Lounge in Detroit and used it as a showcase for new talent. Their lead singer was James Mitchell, and his brother, Paul, had a vocal group, The Floaters. They played at the Lounge and supported The Emeralds on tour.

The Floaters were making their first album at a studio in a converted garage in 1977. They had recorded an instrumental with occasional vocals, 'Float On', which would link the tracks. James Mitchell suggested that they turn it into a song in which the members could introduce themselves. As one of the fads of the late Seventies was to ask people for their star sign, The Floaters introduced themselves that way.

First off, we have Ronnie (actually Ralph Mitchell), an Aquarian who likes 'a woman who loves her freedom', and then comes Mr. Libra, Charles Clark, who only wants 'a woman who carries herself like Miss Universe'. Larry Cunningham, who is Cancer, needs 'a woman that loves everything and everybody' and our Leo, Paul Mitchell, likes 'all women of the world'. The record itself has the same feel as The Four Tops' 'Still Water (Love)'.

After the single, The Floaters floated on and never had another hit. Mercifully, the fad for asking people for their sign also passed – and the record might have helped to bring that about! Cheech y Chong recorded a stoned parody, 'Bloat On', featuring The Bloaters.

412 Elvis Presley
Way Down

Label & Cat No.: **RCA PB 0998**

Producers: **Elvis Presley / Felton Jarvis**

Writer: **Layng Martine Jr**

Date reached No.1: **3 September 1977**

Weeks at No.1: **5**

The country songwriter, Layng Martine Jr, felt he had written a good song for Elvis Presley and he asked his publisher, Ray Stevens, to help him cut a demo. They recorded it as close to Elvis's style as possible with Stevens slowing down the tape to emulate the deep voice of J.D. Sumner of The Stamps. Layng sent it to Elvis's producer, Felton Jarvis, and heard nothing. Having faith in it, he submitted it again a few months later, only to be told, "Y'know, Elvis has already recorded this." Layng went to the mixing session and Felton Jarvis told him, "We're selling excitement here."

The track featured Elvis' road band including James Burton on lead guitar, Jerry Scheff on bass and Ronnie Tutt on drums. All three toured the UK in 2004 as part of the Elvis TCB Band. Charlie Hodge, who plays rhythm, is the one who also hands Elvis his scarves and has done much to keep Elvis' memory alive. Tony Brown who played piano became one of Nashville's hottest producers in the Eighties. 'Way Down' was laid down in Memphis and then Elvis, who couldn't be bothered to visit a studio by this time, added his vocal from the Jungle Room at Graceland.

'Way Down' was released in June 1977 and Layng said, "To see my name on a record with Elvis seemed completely impossible." It was a good single with some similarities to 'Burning Love' in that it combined a contemporary sound with a Fifties feel. Elvis was by no means a consistent hitmaker at the time, but 'Way Down' looked as though it would be a moderate hit.

August 16, 1977 changed all that. Elvis had left the building for the final time and the British public rushed to buy the single. 'Way Down' became Elvis' 17th number one, putting him on a par with the Beatles. Until 2002, that is.

413 David Soul
Silver Lady

Label & Cat No.: **Private Stock PVT 115**
Producers: **Tony Macaulay / Geoff Stephens**
Writer: **Tony Macaulay**
Date reached No.1: **8 October 1977**
Weeks at No.1: **3**

After 'Don't Give Up On Us' and 'Going In With My Eyes Open', David Soul had his third hit and second number one with 'Silver Lady'. "It was an excllent song," says David Soul. "I always enjoyed working with Tony Macaulay and I wish that we had continued together. 'Silver Lady' is a brilliant song, very well written, like a standard."

David Soul had further hits with 'Let's Have A Quiet Night In' and 'It Sure Brings Out The Love In Your Eyes', and there could have been more: "It turned into a horror story as Private Stock went bankrupt. I couldn't get my back payments and I spent three years in litigation when I wasn't able to record. I won the case and got my masters, but I got no money."

In recent years, David has become an Anglophile, appearing in West End plays and campaigning to get the BBC reporter and man in white suit, Martin Bell, elected to Parliament. David Soul says, "I saw him on *Newsnight* and I was impressed by his principles. I wanted to talk to him about a role I was playing and we became good friends. When I heard he was standing in Tatten, I offered to help him out and I ended up knocking on doors. He won overwhelmingly and I don't think I had much to do with it."

David Soul

414 Baccara
Yes Sir I Can Boogie

Label & Cat No.: **RCA PB 5526**
Producer: **Rolf Soja**
Writers: **Frank Dostal / Rolf Soja**
Date reached No.1: **29 October 1977**
Weeks at No.1: **1**

Two Spanish ballet dancers, Mayte Matee and Maria Mendiolo, were dancing flamenco and singing traditional songs for tourists on the island of Fuerteventura. An Englishman, Leon Deane, who was working for the German branch of RCA, heard them and contacted the songwriters and producers, Frank Dostal and Rolf Soja. Dostal had known success in the German beat group, The Rattles, and he remembers, "He told us that he was coming to Hamburg with them on Sunday morning but they had to fly back later in the day because they were dancing on Spanish TV. We recorded the backing tracks and I wrote the lyric the night before they came. They sang two songs on the Sunday morning and then went back."

'Yes Sir I Can Boogie' was seen as instantly commercial. Frank continues, "The record was number one in every record market except the US. It wasn't released there because the record company didn't like it and we were foolish in not looking for another company. The English company did not believe in it either but the music publisher took 100 records from Germany and drove all over England and convinced the DJs at radio stations to play the song. When it was played, RCA released it."

'Sorry I'm A Lady' also made the UK Top 10 and Baccara had European hits with 'Darling', 'The Devil Sent You To Loredo', 'Body Talk' and 'Ay, Ay, Sailor'. They represented Luxembourg in the 1978 Eurovision Song Contest with 'Parlez-Vous Francais?': it only came seventh, but Dostal and Soja's song was too close to 'Yes Sir I Can Boogie' for comfort.

Both artists released solo albums in 1983 and both tour with versions of Baccara. Maria's New Baccara, but now also called Baccara, released six mixes of a new version of 'Yes Sir I Can Boogie' in 1997.

415 Abba
The Name Of The Game

Label & Cat No.: **Epic EPC 4955**
Producers: **Björn Ulvaeus / Benny Andersson**
Writers: **Björn Ulvaeus / Benny Andersson / Stig Anderson**
Date Reached No.1: **5 November 1977**
Weeks at No.1: **4**

At the end of March 1977, Abba had completed their tour, with the final concert performed in Perth, Western Australia. They were taking a break as Agnetha had fallen pregnant. As Björn explained in author Paul Snaith's 1994 book, *The Music Still Goes On*, "We are not toys, we have a desperate need to have peace and quiet". After explaining they would be back towards the end of the year, they refused all media interviews.

Benny and Björn were both admirers of Stevie Wonder and had been listening to his then-current album *Songs In The Key Of Life*. In May 1977, just a few weeks after completing their tour, they began work on a new song, with the working title 'A Bit Of Myself'. The bass line was reminiscent of a slowed down version of Stevie's 'I Wish'. This formed the nucleus and the rest of the song was then built up as a six-part harmony structure, which was a new idea Benny employed. When Stig heard the backing track, he suggested 'The Name Of The Game' as the song's new title.

Both Frida and Agnetha had their own parts to sing as well as drifting in and out of joint sequences. Benny has always admitted to being influenced by The Beatles, and the synthesized piccolo trumpet sound is very reminiscent of 'Penny Lane'.

The cinematic release of *Abba – The Movie* mainly contained footage of the recent tour of Australia with scenes from Melbourne, Perth and

Sydney. The somewhat thin plot involved a local DJ – named Ashley – who has to try and get interviews with each member of the group, but was constantly hindered when he kept forgetting his press pass and by their bodyguard who was determined to stop him getting his interviews.

In a rare move, Benny and Björn granted The Fugees permission to sample the bass and synthesizer riff from 'The Name Of The Game' for their 1997 hit 'Rumble In The Jungle'.

416 Wings
Mull Of Kintyre / Girls' School

Label & Cat No.: **Capitol R 6018**

Producer: **Paul McCartney**

Writers: **Paul McCartney / Denny Laine; Paul McCartney**

Date reached No.1: **3 December 1977**

Weeks at No.1: **9**

Wings' most successful moments were as a trio – Paul & Linda McCartney and Denny Laine, formerly of The Moody Blues. They recorded their best-known album, *Band On The Run*, together in 1974 and Wings' only number one single, 'Mull Of Kintyre', featured just the three of them in 1977.

Paul & Linda McCartney owned a farm in Campbeltown on a Scottish peninsula and the Mull of Kintyre referred to its southern tip. Paul and Denny honoured the place with a song that could have been written 200 years earlier. The song described how the place brought them solace and comfort. Wings recorded it in a barn, adding the bagpipes and drums of the 21-piece Campbeltown Pipe Band. They were also featured in the video and, when the record was a hit, they complained about not being sufficiently well paid.

The single was a double A-side with a rocking song about porno film titles, 'Girls' School', written after Paul had seen a listing in an American newspaper. Although both sides were listed, most people bought the record for 'Mull Of Kintyre' as 'Girls' School' had little radioplay.

'Mull Of Kintyre' became the first single to sell two million copies in the UK alone, but McCartney thought that Americans would not understand the song and made 'Girls' School' the US A-side. The single was only a Top 40 hit and McCartney was surely wrong – the Brits had bought 'Cumberland Gap' and the Americans had made 'Penny Lane' a number one hit.

One of the first Americans to record 'Mull Of Kintyre' was the country singer, George Hamilton IV. As he was about to cut the song in Nashville, one of the musicians said, "Hey, isn't there a mistake here? Shouldn't this be 'Mule Of Kintyre'?"

417 Althia & Donna
Uptown Top Ranking

Label & Cat No.: **Lightning LIG 506**

Producer: **Joel Gibson (Joe Gibbs)**

Writers: **Althia Forest / Donna Reid / Errol Thompson**

Date reached No.1: **4 February 1978**

Weeks at No.1: **1**

Joe Gibbs worked in an electronics store and made his first records, usually with Lee Perry, almost as a hobby at his Retirement Crescent premises. He had UK success in 1969 with The Pioneers' horse-racing tale, 'Long Shot Kick De Bucket'. When he fell out with Perry, he teamed up with the engineer, Errol Thompson, and they became known as The Mighty Two. They made hundreds of reggae records including work with Dennis Brown ('Money In My Pocket'), Nicky Thomas ('Love Of The Common People'), Peter Tosh ('Maga Dog'), Harry J. All Stars ('Liquidator'), Freddie McGregor, Prince Mohammed and Sly & Robbie.

The Jamaican DJ, Trinity, made a record about the pleasures of women, 'Three Piece Suit An T'ing', and Gibbs wanted a female response as a companion. Errol Thompson came up with the backing track, and two girls, Althia Forest (17) and Donna Reid (18), were asked to write and record the song, which became 'Uptown Top Ranking'. Mikey Dread featured the record on his programme, *Dread At The Controls*, and it was a hit in Jamaica.

The bitchy lyric was in English but the Jamaican patois was as strange as a foreign language to many listeners: 'See me in me heels an t'ing, Dem check sey we hip an t'ing.' That added to its mystique and hence, selling-power.

Despite this success and their obvious confidence, Althia & Donna made only a few more records ('Love One Another', 'The Puppy Dog Song', 'Going To Negril') and never had another hit. 'Uptown Top Ranking' was revived by another female duo, Ali & Frazier, in 1993. Althia & Donna's record has been widely sampled including 'What You Got' by Abs, the first solo release by a member of Five in 2002.

418 Brotherhood Of Man
Figaro

Label & Cat No.: **Pye 7N 46037**

Producer: **Tony Hiller**

Writers: **Tony Hiller / Martin Lee / Lee Sheriden**

Date reached No.1: **11 February 1978**

Weeks at No.1: **1**

"You hear all these stories about Spanish and Italian waiters being so romantic and pulling the English birds," says Brotherhood Of Man's songwriter and producer, Tony Hiller, "and 'Figaro' came about because of that. It was very, very big in Europe as everyone got the joke." Whilst that is true, the clear inspiration for both its structure and its tempo is Abba's 'Fernando'.

Brotherhood Of Man had only one more Top 20 hit ('Beautiful Lover') and in 1982, Barry Upton replaced Lee Sheriden and they had their last chart entry with 'Lightning Flash'. The original line-up of Lee Sheriden, Nicky Stevens and the married couple, Martin Lee and Sandra Stevens was restored in 1984. Brotherhood Of Man are going to this day, usually touring with *The 70s Story* in which they recreate their Eurovision win, and they are also in great demand for oldies weekends at holiday camps.

The vocal group re-recorded 'Save Your Kisses For Me' for their album, *Greenhouse,* in 1997. With two industry friends, Paul Curtis and David Kane, Martin Lee has written a musical based on the series of books about The Butterfly Children. Barry Upton has had the most success as he created the singing and dancing group, Steps, and wrote their first hit, '5,6,7,8' and has recently been working with Shane Richie and John Otway.

419 Abba

Take A Chance On Me

Label & Cat No.: **Epic EPC 4955**

Producers: **Björn Ulvaeus / Benny Andersson**

Writers: **Björn Ulvaeus / Benny Andersson**

Date Reached No.1: **18 February 1978**

Weeks at No.1: **3**

By 1976 manager Stig Anderson, who had co-written the early Abba material, was only suggesting the songs' titles. By the time 'Take A Chance On Me' was recorded, he was no longer involved with their songwriting.

Two days before hitting the top spot, the group attended the London première of *Abba – The Movie*. It was well received and became the sixth biggest grossing movie of the year.

Björn, by his own admission, was contributing less and less of the musical ideas, but still played an integral part of assessing and editing what Benny produced. Occasionally if one had an opinion of something that the other didn't share they employed a technique. "We would bring it up again and again and again," said Björn. "In the end we would discard it or agree that it may work and try it. I remember that Benny didn't like the line, 'We could go dancing, we could go walking', but in the end we went with it." Although 'Take A Chance On Me' was Abba's second biggest hit in the US, reaching number three, it sold more than the chart-topping 'Dancing Queen'.

In private, things were getting worse for Agnetha and Björn. Their marriage was breaking down but Björn often admitted that "It had nothing to do with the group. Whatever jobs we were doing the split would still have happened". However, on the other side of the coin, Benny and Frida were growing closer and having been engaged for nine years, they eventually married on October 6, 1978 in Stockholm. Such was the secrecy surrounding the event that not even Björn and Agnetha were told. The week of the wedding, their follow-up 'Summer Night City', a song written about Andersson's native Stockholm, peaked at number five.

On Christmas Eve 1978 Agnetha and their two children finally moved out of the house she shared with Björn. "I was a bachelor for a week," he said. Nevertheless all four members agreed to stay together as Abba. Without doubt, Björn and Agnetha's split was reflected in the lyrics of the songs 'The Winner Takes It All' and 'One Of Us'.

420 Kate Bush

Wuthering Heights

Label & Cat No.: **EMI 2719**

Producer: **Andrew Powell**

Writer: **Kate Bush**

Date Reached No.1: **11 March 1978**

Weeks at No.1: **4**

"Kate couldn't be ignored. She was obviously a great talent and it would have been criminal to have ignored her," said Pink Floyd singer and guitarist, David Gilmour.

She wrote 'Wuthering Heights' when she was 15, having read the book. It all started in 1973 when a family friend called Ricky Hopper taped Kate singing. He then took the tape to another friend, David Gilmour. As Kate remembered, "Dave was like a guardian angel and was scouting for talent. He had already found a band called Unicorn and was helping them. He came to see me and he was great, such a human, kind person – and genuine."

Gilmour did some recordings at both Kate's and his own house. He employed the drummer and bass player from Unicorn on the sessions. He then took some songs to the EMI managing director, Bob Mercer. The first track he heard was 'The Man With The Child In His Eyes'. As soon as he learned that Kate had written it herself when she was 14, he arranged for Kate and her father to come in and see him. Bob told her father he wanted Kate to finish school and then he would consider signing her. She left school with 10 O-levels and moved into her brother's home.

In August 1977 producer Andrew Powell booked Kate into Air Studios in London. As well as David Gilmour, he brought in Dave Paton (bass) and Ian Bairnson (guitar) from Pilot and Duncan Mackay (keyboards) and Stuart Elliot (drums) from Steve Harley's Cockney Rebel. As Andrew Powell recalled, "I chose those musicians because I knew they would listen to her. I didn't want musicians who would say 'Shut up, we know what we're doing.'" Once in the studio, Kate sat down at the piano and said to the guys, "I've written this song, what do you think?" It was 'Wuthering Heights', the musical tribute to Emily Bronte that she had composed one full-moonlit night. Kate said, "I deliberately wrote the song by talking about the main character as 'I'." When the song topped the chart, Kate, who shares the same July 30 birthday as Emily Bronte, became the first female artist to solely write her own number one.

Kate's adroit songwriting was highlighted when she penned all 13 tracks on the parent album, *The Kick Inside*.

Some 25 years after the song topped the chart, it is still held in high esteem. *The Guardian's* arts critic David McAllister wrote: "Kate Bush's 'Wuthering Heights' is an improvement on Bronte's original. Three and a half minutes of melodramatic caterwauling is always better than 300 pages of melodramatic prose."

Kate Bush, a doctor's daughter from Kent, was discovered by David Gilmour of Pink Floyd

421 Brian & Michael
Matchstalk Men And Matchstalk Cats And Dogs

Label & Cat No.: **Pye 7N 46035**
Producer: **Kevin Parrott**
Writer: **Michael Coleman**
Date reached No.1: **8 April 1978**
Weeks at No.1: **3**

THE MANCHESTER ARTIST LAURENCE Stephen Lowry (L.S. Lowry) had a full-time job as a rent collector, and this inspired bleak, industrial landscapes of northern England in which everyone is depicted as tiny matchstalk figures hurrying about their business. Many art critics dismissed his work as naïve and he certainly lacked the reputation of Francis Bacon or David Hockney. However, the public at large knew his distinctive style and it was front-page news when he died in 1976.

The songwriter, Michael Coleman, read the obituaries and wrote 'Matchstalk Men And Matchstalk Cats And Dogs'. He took it to the producer, Kevin Parrott, and they recorded it themselves. Kevin had a very uncool name so he became Brian (surely only marginally less cool – think of *Monty Python's Life Of Brian*) and Brian & Michael were born. They were backed by St. Winifred's School Choir, who had their own number one in 1980, and the record also dipped into Northern heritage by basing its introduction on William Rimmer's brass band march, 'Punchinello'.

To Brian and Michael's surprise, 'Matchstalk Men And Matchstalk Cats And Dogs' became controversial. Instead of being delighted that Lowry was being recognised in such a populist way (which Lowry would have loved), many pundits took the opportunity to dismiss both Lowry and the song.

The duo performed as Brian & Michael for some time, and when 'Brian' left, Michael continued with a replacement. Michael also wrote Ken Dodd's 1981 minor hit, 'Hold My Hand' and he has written a musical about Lowry. The painter's reputation has increased with the years, especially since the opening of the Lowry Centre at Salford Quays in 2000. Their website chronology of Lowry's career does not include Brian & Michael, but the duo did a reunion show there with St. Winifred's School Choir in 2002.

422 The Bee Gees
Night Fever

Label & Cat No.: **RSO 002**
Producers: **Barry Gibb / Robin Gibb / Maurice Gibb / Karl Richardson / Albhy Galuten**
Writers: **Barry Gibb / Robin Gibb / Maurice Gibb**
Date reached No.1: **29 April 1978**
Weeks at No.1: **2**

FOLLOWING A SUGGESTION FROM ERIC Clapton, The Bee Gees went to Criteria Studios in Miami and made an album, *Mr. Natural* (1974), with the producer, Arif Mardin. Mardin, was noted for his work with both Clapton and Aretha Franklin, and he gave The Bee Gees a more contemporary, disco-based sound.

In 1975 The Bee Gees changed labels to RSO and because Mardin was attached to the Atlantic / Atco record group, they could no longer work with him. They produced the next album, *Main Course*, themselves, alongside two engineers from Criteria, Karl Richardson and Albhy Galuten. The album included 'Jive Talkin'' and 'Nights On Broadway'. Whilst recording 'Nights On Broadway', Barry became Mr. Unnatural by singing higher and higher to make the track more exciting, eventually singing it in a falsetto that was unexpectedly powerful. This gave The Bee Gees a new sound and the following album, *Children Of The World* (1976), included another disco favourite, 'You Should Be Dancing'.

Their manager, Robert Stigwood, wanted to make a feature film from an article written by rock writer, Nik Cohn, about the disco scene in New York. He asked The Bee Gees to contribute to the soundtrack. The film was to be called *Saturday Night* and Stigwood asked for a new song with that title. The Gibb Brothers thought it was a corny title but they already had a song called 'Night Fever', hence the film's eventual title, *Saturday Night Fever*.

The film starred John Travolta as Tony Manero but The Bee Gees themselves did not appear in the film. They performed several songs on the soundtrack and wrote 'If I Can't Have You' for Yvonne Elliman. The double-album included both their version of 'More Than A Woman' and a cover by Tavares.

Saturday Night Fever became the biggest-selling album of all-time with sales of over 30 million, though it would eventually be overtaken by Michael Jackson's equally disco-orientated *Thriller*. As a result, The Bee Gees had a run of six consecutive number ones in the US, the first three coming from *Saturday Night Fever* – 'How Deep Is Your Love', 'Stayin' Alive' and 'Night Fever'.

Robin Gibb says, "*Saturday Night Fever* was a good film for what it represented, good for its time, but I thought the music transcended the film. I never saw the film until it came out and the combination of sound and music in that way was something of a novelty then. The sequel was all right, but it should have been left alone as it was a great moment in history.

The Bee Gees

423 Boney M
Rivers Of Babylon

Label & Cat No.: **Atlantic / Hansa K 11120**

Producer: **Frank Farian**

Writers: **Frank Farian / Hans Joerg Mayer / Brent Dowe / James McNaughton**

Date reached No.1: **13 May 1978**

Weeks at No.1: **5**

WHEN THE GERMAN RECORD producer Frank Farian created Boney M, he wasn't particularly concerned about vocal ability. True, both Liz Mitchell and Marcia Barrett from Jamaica could sing, but Bobby 'Legs' Farrell from the Antilles, an excellent dancer and front man, was a poor vocalist, and Mazie Williams from Montserrat was a model with stunning looks. He took the name Boney M. from the Australian TV series, *Boney*, which had an aborigine dancing on its credits and the M from the names of the three girls.

Boney M had their first hit with 'Daddy Cool' in 1976 and then came a revival of Bobby Hebb's 'Sunny' followed by 'Ma Baker' and 'Belfast'. All the singles went Top 10 but they broke through with 'Rivers Of Babylon'. It was a disco interpretation of Psalm 137: the opening verse being "'By the rivers of Babylon, there we sat down, yea, we wept, when we remembered Zion" and a little later, "How shall we sing the Lord's song in a strange land?"

'Rivers Of Babylon' was an enormous hit but as it started to go down the charts, DJs started playing the equally infectious B-side, 'Brown Girl In The Ring', an update of a Caribbean nursery rhyme. Their record company delayed issuing the follow-up 'Rasputin' and concentrated on promoting 'Brown Girl In The Ring'. The single climbed back to number two and you wonder how many record-buyers found that they already had the track in their collections.

Their number one album, *Nightflight To Venus*, included both sides of that single and their subsequent hits, 'Rasputin' and 'Painter Man'. Farian scored an own goal on their next album, *Oceans Of Fantasy* (1979): he called himself 'the fifth member of Boney M' and listed the performers on each track. Mazie and Bobby did nothing and the male vocals were sung by Farian himself. The entire personnel of Boney M was missing on several tracks (excepting the fifth member, of course). Precious Wilson, taking lead vocals, was listed as "special guest star of Boney M". In 1988 Farian created Milli Vanilli, not allowing the duo to perform on their own records. Two years later, when they insisted, Farian refused: the deception came to light and the group was stripped of their Grammy for Best New Artist. The duo said that they had made a pact with the Devil.

424 John Travolta and Olivia Newton-John
You're The One That I Want

Label & Cat No.: **RSO 006**

Producer: **John Farrar**

Writer: **John Farrar**

Date Reached No.1: **17 Jun 1978**

Weeks at No.1: **9**

"I ENTERED A GONG SHOW CONTEST when I was 15," recalled Olivia. "You show up early in the morning and perform something. I performed 'Summertime' and I got three gongs." On that show she met songwriter, John Farrar. Her performance got her noticed by a host of talent agencies, but her mother refused to let any of them handle her, insisting that if anyone was going to be her manager, she was.

Cambridge-born singer Olivia Newton-John had grown up in Melbourne, Australia and returned to Britain in the mid-Sixties. Her solo recording career took off in 1971. Through her then-boyfriend, The Shadows' Bruce Welch, she met Cliff Richard and they soon began singing together. For her first UK release, John Farrar suggested that she covered Bob Dylan's 'If Not For You'. Olivia said, "I wasn't keen on that song at all, but I'm so glad John chose it because it's not one that I would have picked."

She was chosen to represent the UK at the 1974 Eurovision Song Contest. Her entry, 'Long Live Love' finished fourth. By the mid-Seventies she was having more success in America, so she ended her relationship with Bruce and decided to move there. It was whilst out to dinner one evening with singer Helen Reddy she met Allan Carr. He talked about his new film version of the stage musical, *Grease*. "I've seen the London stage version with Richard Gere as Danny," Olivia told Carr. Carr asked her if she fancied playing the lead role of Sandy. Olivia's reply of "Are you serious?" was acknowledged in the affirmative and the part was hers. The film's director, Randal Kleiser agreed, "Olivia was always first choice for Sandy."

The filming for the fairground scene where they sung 'You're The One That I Want' took the best part of a day and the skin tight outfit Olivia wore restricted her. As Olivia recalled, "It was a hot day, and I wasn't allowed to drink because I wasn't allowed to go to the toilet and as they had to sew me into that outfit, it would take too long to get in and out of."

Grease, which spawned six hit singles, five of them Top 10, was set in 1959 at Rydell High School and centred around the heartthrob, Danny Zuko (John Travolta) and the innocent Sandy Olsson (Olivia Newton-John).

In 1975 John was cast as Vinnie Barbarino in the TV sitcom, *Welcome Back Kotter*. It was his popularity, largely due to his engaging smile and cheeky boyish looks, that led to him being offered his first major film role as Tony Manero in *Saturday Night Fever*.

Following his success in *Saturday Night Fever*, John would have been the obvious choice but he was not offered the part first. The film's producer, Allan Carr remembered, "We originally offered the role of Danny Zuko to Henry Winkler because of his phenomenal success as The Fonz in *Happy Days*. Henry turned us down because he felt he had played the ultimate greaser on TV for too long to repeat himself in our movie."

The single has sold almost two million copies in Britain alone and is the sixth biggest selling record of all time in the UK. *Grease* – the soundtrack, like *Saturday Night Fever*, is a double album and has sold over 24 million copies to date and is now the second biggest selling musical soundtrack of all time behind *Saturday Night Fever.*

425 The Commodores
Three Times A Lady

Label & Cat No.: **Motown TMG 1113**
Producers: **James Anthony Carmichael / The Commodores**
Writer: **Lionel Richie**
Date reached No.1: **19 August 1978**
Weeks at No.1: **5**

IN TUSKEGEE, ALABAMA, VARIOUS members of The Mighty Mystics and The Jays combined their talents and became The Commodores. They took their name from the dictionary and Lionel Richie is glad that William King's finger didn't alight on the nearby 'commodes'.

Berry Gordy Jr, the owner of Tamla-Motown, was impressed when they supported The Jackson Five and signed them to the label. They had their first hit with the instrumental 'Machine Gun' in 1974 and their hit-making line-up became Lionel Richie (vocals, keyboards), Thomas McClary (guitar), Milan Williams (keyboards), Ronald LaPread (bass), William King (trumpet) and Walter Orange (drums). Several of the band wrote songs and Lionel found there was less competition for the slow tracks on the album. He scored with 'Easy' in 1977, and the phrase, "I'm easy like Sunday morning" passed into the vernacular. Lionel Richie did not feel easy when his song was beaten by Leo Sayer's 'You Make Me Feel Like Dancing' as the Best Rhythm & Blues Song at the Grammys as he did not regard Sayer's song as R&B.

In 1978 Lionel Richie was at a party for his parents' wedding anniversary. His father gave a speech to thank his wife for standing by him all these years. Lionel was so impressed that he set his father's thoughts to music in 'Three Times A Lady'. The song was included on The Commodores' *Natural High* album, and as a single, it topped the charts in both Britain and America. Although a hit for The Commodores, the song established Lionel Richie as a solo force and when he left the group in 1982, he emerged as Tamla-Motown's successor to Smokey Robinson. J.D. Nicholas replaced Lionel as the lead vocalist but only 'Nightshift', a tribute to Marvin Gaye and Jackie Wilson, was a major hit.

426 10cc
Dreadlock Holiday

Label & Cat No.: **Mercury 6008 035**
Producer: **10cc**
Writers: **Eric Stewart / Graham Gouldman**
Date Reached No.1: **23 September 1978**
Weeks at No.1: **1**

WITH KEVIN GODLEY AND LOL CREME having departed two years earlier, 10cc now comprised Eric Stewart and Graham Gouldman with various session musicians. All three 10cc number ones feature different lead singers: Kevin Godley on 'Rubber Bullets', Eric Stewart on 'I'm Not In Love' and Graham Gouldman on 'Dreadlock Holiday'.

"Justin Hayward (from The Moody Blues) and I had both gone on holiday with our families to Barbados," explained Eric Stewart. "The song comes from different sources. Firstly I saw this white guy trying to 'truck' down the street. The expression 'Don't you walk through my words' came from a radio DJ in Newcastle who was challenged when he walked through a group of black guys talking together."

"The line 'I don't like cricket, I love it' came about when I was talking to this Jamaican guy. I said to him 'You must like cricket'. He replied, 'I don't like cricket, I love it', explained Graham.

Eric continued, "Justin and I were on a parasailing raft in the middle of the ocean and I was strapped into this parachute gear. I was towed behind a speedboat at high speed. I took off and waved goodbye to Justin. He was then left on the raft with three black guys; one Jamaican and two from Barbados. The Jamaican guy said to Justin, 'I like your silver chain, man, I'll give you a dollar for it'. Justin replied, 'come on, it's worth a lot more than that and it's a present from my mother'. And this guy said, 'If this was Jamaica, I would cut your hand off for that'. I came back and asked Justin if he wanted to have a go. He said, 'No, let's get off this raft as quick as we can, I have had some problems'. When we got back to England, I relayed the story to Graham and we wrote a song around it."

Although by 1979 10cc had not officially split, both Graham and Eric became involved in other projects. Graham had a solo hit with the theme from the film *Sunburn* and Eric went on to produce all Sad Café's hits.

In 1982 10cc were back in the chart with 'Run Away'. It only reached number 50 and thus signalled the end for the group. Paul McCartney recruited Eric for his *Tug Of War*, *Pipes Of Peace* and *Press To Play* albums whilst Graham teamed up with Andrew Gold to form Wax in 1987. In the late Nineties Graham began a songwriting partnership with Kirsty MacColl, which was cut short by her tragic death in 2000. In 2002 he released a solo album called *And Another Thing.*

427 John Travolta and Olivia Newton-John
Summer Nights

Label & Cat No.: **RSO 18**
Producer: **Louis St Louis**
Writers: **Jim Jacobs / Warren Casey**
Date Reached No.1: **30 September 1978**
Weeks at No.1: **7**

IN 1953, A YEAR BEFORE JOHN TRAVOLTA was born, his mother, Helen and sister, Ellen visited a clairvoyant. When Helen asked how her daughter would get on, the mystic said, "Fine, but your next baby will be a phenomenon."

At the age of 12, John joined a drama group and learned tap dancing from Gene Kelly's brother, Fred. At 18, he made his stage debut in the off-Broadway show *Rain*. A year later he landed a minor role as Doody in the touring company of the hit musical *Grease*. In 1973 he appeared opposite The Andrews Sisters in the Broadway musical *Over Here!*

A new soundtrack was being compiled for the film version of the stage show, *Grease*. Producers Robert Stigwood and Allan Carr had everything ready except for the title song. Having achieved great success in *Saturday Night Fever*, Robert called Barry Gibb and asked him to come up with something. An hour later, Barry called Robert and sang him what he had written. Although Allan wasn't keen, Robert loved it and suggested Frankie Valli sing it because, as a member of The Four Seasons, he reflected the era well.

Although sung as a duet, John and Olivia were not seen singing it together in the film. Sandy told her story to her surrounding girl friends, whilst Danny did likewise to the boys.

In 1982 a sequel, *Grease 2* was released and centred around a graduating class of 1961. It starred Michelle Pfieffer and Maxwell Caulfield, but made no great impact. *Grease* returned to the London stage in 1993 with Craig McLachlan and Debbie Gibson taking up the lead roles.

The week 'Summer Nights' topped the chart, a witless cover version of 'You're The One That I Want' by veteran comedy actors Hylda Baker and Arthur Mullard reached number 22. Thankfully it received little airplay.

428 The Boomtown Rats Rat Trap

Label & Cat No.:	**Ensign ENY 16**
Producer:	**Robert John 'Mutt' Lange**
Writer:	**Bob Geldof**
Date reached No.1:	**18 November 1978**
Weeks at No.1:	**2**

UNTIL ITS CLOSURE WAS ANNOUNCED in October 2004, musicians would congregate in Bewley's Coffee House in Dublin's Grafton Street. In this respectable, old-fashioned café, the music journalist Bob Geldof planned to change the music world with his friends, Gary Roberts (guitar), Gerry Cott (guitar), Pete Briquette (bass), Johnnie Fingers (piano) and Simon Crowe (drums). They became The Boomtown Rats after Geldof alighted on the name in Woody Guthrie's novel, *Bound For Glory*.

The Boomtown Rats were signed to the London label, Ensign, and spent some months touring the UK, including support for Tom Petty & The Heartbreakers. In 1977 their debut album, *The Boomtown Rats*, made the charts as did their singles, 'Looking After No.1' and 'Mary Of The 4th Form'. In 1978 they consolidated their success with 'She's So Modern' (about the girls, including Mariella Frostrup, in the Polygram press office) and their first Top 10 single, 'Like Clockwork'.

Their second album, *A Tonic For The Troops*, included 'Rat Trap'. It was as defiant as punk, but the song was rather more structured and owed much to Bruce Springsteen. The ever-quotable Geldof told *Word* magazine about the band living together in London's Chessington Road and learning they were number one, "The whole band were in the hall, we were just fucking running around, like children run around when they're excited, there was champagne, it was fucking madness. For me, it lasted for two hours and then the panic set in, and I started thinking: is it downhill from now on? What happens next?"

When the new chart-topper was announced on *Top Of The Pops,* a still of John Travolta and Olivia Newton-John appeared on the screen. It was torn apart to reveal The Boomtown Rats. 'Rat Trap' was the first number one by an Irish group and the first new wave single to make number one. The two terms 'new wave' and 'punk' are not interchangeable – punk was inspired by negativity and a refusal to ignore anything that had gone before, the new wave singles may appear similar but the artists acknowledged their sources and where this music fitted into rock history. The Sex Pistols, despite a few covers, are decidedly punk and The Boomtown Rats, along with Elvis Costello and Nick Lowe, new wave.

Olivia Newton-John and John Travolta

429 Rod Stewart
Da Ya Think I'm Sexy?

Label & Cat No.: **Riva 17**

Producer: **Tom Dowd**

Writers: **Rod Stewart / Carmen Appice**

Date reached No.1: **2 December 1978**

Weeks at No.1: **1**

By 1978 Rod Stewart was an international playboy, hounded by the paparazzi, and he appeared to be playing into his image as a leering stud with the album, *Blondes Have More Fun*. In 'Dirty Weekend', he sings about having it away with his best friend's girl and 'Da Ya Think I'm Sexy?' could be the worst example of narcissism on record. Maybe it was intended to be ironic as Rod has said, "Everybody thought that I was singing about myself. Of course not, I'm singing in the third person." But of course, everybody has always thought Rod was singing about Rod and they continue to think that no matter what Rod might say. As the rock critic Griel Marcus remarked, "Rarely has anyone betrayed his talent so completely."

The Rolling Stones had embraced disco with 'Miss You' and Rod did the same with 'Da Ya Think I'm Sexy?' The 12-inch single was promoted as the first 48-track disco mix as if anyone was interested. Rod performed his single in spiky hair, open shirt and tight leopard skin pants, which led to Kenny Everett's sketch in ever-inflating trews. Rod's persona has been ideal for tribute acts ever since.

The song had been written with Carmine Appice from Vanilla Fudge, or had it? Jorge Ben, who had recorded 'Taj Mahal' as a tribute to the blues singer, claimed that they had taken his melody. The matter never got to court but credits on reissues now state "Inspired by Jorge Ben". Rod Stewart, in an act of extreme generosity, donated all his royalties from the song to UNICEF during a United Nations concert in January 1979. The song returned to the charts via the punk band, The Revolting Cocks, in 1993 and four years later, a revamped version by N-Trance featuring Rod Stewart made the Top 10.

Rod's previous album, *Footloose And Fancy Free*, contained his goodbye to Britt Ekland, 'You're In My Heart'. In April 1979 he married Alana Hamilton, the former wife of film star George Hamilton.

430 Boney M
Mary's Boy Child / Oh My Lord (Medley)

Label & Cat No.: **Atlantic / Hansa K 11221**

Producer: **Frank Farian**

Writers: **Jester Hairston; Frank Farian / Fred Jay**

Date reached No.1: **9 December 1978**

Weeks at No.1: **4**

Jester Hairston's West Indian carol, 'Mary's Boy Child', had been a reverential number one for Harry Belafonte in 1957. The disco group from Munich, Boney M revived it and Marcia Barrett, one of the two members allowed to sing on the records, recalled, "I always thought of Boney M as being put together by a spiritual force and we liked doing spiritual songs. When we did 'Mary's Boy Child', we added a bit spontaneously at the end. As it worked, we left it in." Hence, the record is listed as a medley of 'Mary's Boy Child' and 'Oh My Lord'.

In 1979 Boney M had a number one album with *Oceans Of Fantasy* and Top 10 singles with 'Painter Man' and 'Hooray Hooray It's A Holi-Holiday', but their subsequent singles did not sell as well. The band continued touring and Mazie Williams, Marcia Barrett and Bobby Farrell were still around in 1992 when 'Boney M Megamix' restored them to the Top 10.

Now the group has splintered into three separate versions – the official one with Liz Mitchell, and the others with Mazie Williams and Bobby Farrell. Bobby Farrell, who never performed on the records, says, "I wasn't put out about it, I just looked at the cheques. Frank Farian is not as beautiful as I am and he could not prove himself on stage like me."

431 Village People
Y.M.C.A.

Label & Cat No.: **Mercury 6007 192**

Producer: **Jacques Morali**

Writers: **Jacques Morali / Henri Belolo / Victor Willis**

Date Reached No.1: **6 January 1979**

Weeks at No.1: **3**

Village People was the name given to the men in Manhattan's Greenwich Village. The band were assembled by French producer Jacques Morali at the same time the gay disco scene was finding its feet.

Jacques was born in Morocco in 1946. In 1959 the family moved to the St Paul-Les-Durance, 35 miles north of Marseille. At the age of 31, he moved to New York and began visiting gay bars. One day he ran into a man in an Indian headdress. The next week he saw him again wearing a different outfit. He was intrigued that gay men used to dress up in macho costumes and dance together in a disco. When he realised that gay people have no group of their own and nobody to personalise the gay community, he invented one.

He brought in Felipe Rose (whom he had seen wearing the Indian headdress), Randy Jones (cowboy), Alex Briley (GI), David Hodo (construction worker) and Victor Wills (policeman) as the lead singer. He wanted a sixth member, so placed an advert in a gay magazine for a singer with a bushy moustache to join a gay group. The first man to answer it secured the job. He was Glenn Hughes, former Brooklyn tollbooth collector who dressed from head to toe in leather.

The parent album *Cruisin'* was one track short. As Glenn recalled, "One day Jacques and I were walking down the street in New York and saw the sign 'Y.M.C.A'. He asked me what that was. I told him, the 'Young Men's Christian Association'. All of a sudden he started singing 'Young Man da da da da da da." Jacques went straight home and came back 20 minutes later with the finished song.

He took the song to the studio and the band thought it was hysterical and simply an album

The Village People, from New York's Greenwich Village, dressed as gay stereotypes on stage; left to right: David Hodo, Felipe Rose, Glen Hughes and Alex Briley

filler. When the song was released, they came under fire from the Y.M.C.A. who were unhappy that they hadn't been consulted over the use of the name. As David Hodo remembered in 1999, "It's ironic really, soon after the song came out they wanted to sue us. Now they are using it as their commercial."

In 1984 Jacques moved back to Paris. He died in 1991 from complications brought on by A.I.D.S. Glenn Hughes died of lung cancer in March of 2001 and was buried in his biker outfit.

The Village People made a brief comeback in 1994, when they joined the German team on their World Cup song 'Far Away In America'. In 2003, with Jeff Olsen replacing Randy Jones and Valerie Simpson's (of Ashford and Simpson fame) brother, Ray, replacing Victor Willis, the remaining members re-formed yet again for a 25th anniversary world tour.

One thing is for sure; no wedding, party or anniversary celebration is complete without this song and it is highly amusing to observe revellers on the dance floor attempting, in unison, to spell out the title of the song with their arms... and still getting it wrong.

432 Ian & The Blockheads
Hit Me With Your Rhythm Stick

Label & Cat No.: **Stiff BUY 38**

Producer: **Chaz Jankel**

Writers: **Ian Dury / Chaz Jankel**

Date reached No.1: **27 January 1979**

Weeks at No.1: **1**

IAN DURY WOULD TELL REPORTERS THAT he was conceived at the back of The Ritz and born at the height of The Blitz. He contracted polio, which left him with a severe limp, but he made light of his disability and refused, for example, offers to play Richard III.

When he was an art teacher, Dury fronted a pub rock band, Kilburn & The High Roads. Then, with the advent of punk, he formed Ian & The Blockheads: the 'Dury' being added later. Dury said to them, 'You're all blockheads' and it stuck. The group was signed to the new wave label, Stiff, and their debut album, *New Boots And Panties!!,* was released to both critical acclaim and commercial success in October 1977. Dury delivered his songs like a Cockney comic and the album included a UK take on Barry White, 'Wake Up And Make Love With Me', the saucy adventures of 'Billericay Dickie' and a tribute to his favourite rock'n'roll star, 'Sweet Gene Vincent.'. This was followed by the single, 'Sex & Drugs & Rock & Roll', and Dury added that phrase to the English language.

As bands go, the Blockheads had a reasonably static line-up, and the mainstays included Chaz Jankel (keyboards), Mickey Gallagher (keyboards), Davey Payne (saxophone), John Turnbull (guitar), Norman Watt-Roy (bass) and Charley Charles (drums). When Chaz wrote a disco melody, Dury supplied the pastiche lyrics that became 'Hit Me With Your Rhythm Stick' - among his natty rhymes, 'Hit me with your rhythm stick / Je t'adore, Ich liebe dich.' Chaz also wrote 'Ai No Corrida', a hit single for Quincy Jones from the erotic film, *In The Realm Of The Senses.*

Dury followed with one of his many 'shopping-list songs', 'Reasons To Be Cheerful (Part 3)'. His keyboard player Mickey Gallagher recalls, "Ian did enjoy writing list songs but he didn't do them in five minutes. It could take months to get the lyric exactly how he wanted it. If a journalist said to him, 'Your lyric is nothing but a list', he would say, 'Okay. Well, you write one then.' He wrote a fantastic one that he gave to Max Wall called 'England's Glory' and he refused to release it himself. It would have been a huge hit and it's just an example as to how bloody-minded he could be."

Nearly all Ian Dury's songs are packed with very English references and, to quote one of his song titles, 'There Ain't Half Been Some Clever Bastards'. Ian Dury died from cancer in London in 2000 at the age of 57. Accolades were plentiful. Government Minister Mo Mowlam, who knew Ian personally, said: "We have all lost a wonderful man, a real human being." What a waste.

433 Blondie
Heart Of Glass

Label & Cat No.: **Chrysalis CHS 2275**

Producer: **Mike Chapman**

Writers: **Debbie Harry / Chris Stein**

Date Reached No.1: **3 February 1979**

Weeks at No.1: **4**

DEBBIE HARRY WAS THE FACE OF Blondie. She was born in Miami, Florida in 1945 and at 23 she joined folk-rock band Wind In The Willows and recorded one album in 1968. Wanting a career change, she took a job as a Playboy bunny and later became a waitress at Max's Kansas City restaurant in New York. She also worked as a beautician. Working at Max's gave her the opportunity to meet other musicians and, in turn, led to her joining Elda Gentile and Rosie Ross in a trio called The Stilettos. Soon after, an art graduate called Chris Stein joined the group. The pair became an item and when the band broke up Chris and Debbie formed their own band called Angel & The Snakes. They brought in various musicians and, using Debbie's punky image and artificial blonde hair colour, rather than her natural brunette, renamed themselves Blondie.

By 1978 their line-up comprised Debbie Harry (vocals), Chris Stein (guitar), Frank Infante (guitar), Jimmy Destri (keyboards), Clem Burke (drums) and the English-born Nigel Harrison (bass). Their first UK hit in 1978 was a cover of Randy & The Rainbows' US hit 'Denis' which Blondie retitled 'Denis (Denee)'.

British producer Mike Chapman, of Chinn & Chapman, who was associated with Mud, Suzi Quatro, The Sweet and Smokie in the Seventies, was starting to have success in the US. He had seen Blondie perform at the *Whisky* in Los Angeles and was so impressed that he offered to take over as their producer.

To help boost sales and take advantage of the relatively new 12-inch single format, the mix of 'Heart Of Glass' on the 12-inch was different from that of the 7-inch and album version.

'Heart Of Glass' was initially demoed in 1975

Former art teacher Ian Dury married imaginative lyrics to funky R&B, and emerged as an unlikely punk hero with his New Boots And Panties *album in 1977*

under the working title, 'Disco Song'. "When we did 'Heart Of Glass', it wasn't too cool in our social set to play disco," Debbie recalled. "But we did it because we wanted to be uncool. It was based around a Roland Rhythm Machine and the backing took over 10 hours to get down." Chris Stein added, "We didn't expect the song to be that big. We only did it as a novelty item to put more diversity into the album."

434 The Bee Gees
Tragedy

Label & Cat No.: **RSO 27**

Producers: **Barry Gibb / Robin Gibb / Maurice Gibb / Karl Richardson / Albhy Galuten**

Writers: **Barry Gibb / Robin Gibb / Maurice Gibb**

Date reached No.1: **3 March 1979**

Weeks at No.1: **2**

After *Saturday Night Fever*, The Bee Gees became hotter than hot. They were a major touring act (and following Travolta's lead, they wore white shirts with medallions), everything they recorded was a smash hit. There were numerous offers to write and record for other artists, which included 'Grease' for Frankie Valli and several records for their younger brother, Andy. There were mistakes – the film of *Sgt. Pepper's Lonely Hearts Club Band* featuring The Bee Gees with Peter Frampton was a disaster, though not without interest as it does contain some good performances. As an example of their generosity, they donated all the royalties from their US number one, 'Too Much Heaven', to UNICEF.

'Too Much Heaven' was one of three US chart-topping singles on their 1979 album, *Spirits Having Flown*, the others being 'Tragedy' and 'Love You Inside Out'. Maurice Gibb revealed that they wrote both 'Tragedy' and 'Too Much Heaven' in an afternoon off from making the *Sgt. Pepper* movie, and for good measure, they wrote 'Shadow Dancing' for Andy Gibb that evening. The album's title suggested that the group was moving away from disco, although it was still very dance-oriented music, and they were experimenting with Barry's falsetto – listen to the notes he reaches before the explosion.

Whilst they were recording, The Bee Gees kept themselves sane by making *The Adventures Of Sunny Jim* in odd moments. These ultra-rude adventures have been heard by no one outside The Bee Gees' circle but they are in the same vein as Peter Cook and Dudley Moore's *Derek And Clive*.

435 Gloria Gaynor
I Will Survive

Label & Cat No.: **Polydor 2095 017**

Producers: **Dino Fekaris / Freddie Perrin**

Writers: **Dino Fekaris / Freddie Perrin**

Date reached No.1: **17 March 1979**

Weeks at No.1: **4**

"'Never Can Say Goodbye' was the first disco song ever to be played on AM radio," says Gloria Gaynor with pride. "Disco music was not accepted on the radio until 'Never Can Say Goodbye' came along, so I am a pioneer."

Gloria Gaynor, who was born in Newark, New Jersey in 1949, had been singing in clubs and making records for small labels for several years. She broke through with her revival of The Jackson Fives' 'Never Can Say Goodbye' in 1974 and the accompanying album, also called *Never Can Say Goodbye*, featured three segued and extended dance tracks. Gloria became the queen of the discos but then she fell off the stage: "I fell backwards over a monitor and suffered extensive back injuries and spent six months in hospital. I had spinal surgery, came out and made 'I Will Survive'," she laughs.

'I Will Survive' was written for Gloria by her producers "... and I thought it was unbelievable. Unfortunately, the A-side was the company president's pet project so there was no way I could get the record flipped. My manager told me to start singing 'I Will Survive' and the audiences would be calling for it, and they did."

Gloria Gaynor saw herself as a woman with a mission. "I don't sing songs like 'I Will Survive' and 'I Am What I Am' to myself. I sing them to the public as encouragement. I feel that a person ought to feel good about himself and if that person cannot relate to the songs, then maybe some changes need to be made."

A few months later, a country version for Billie Jo Spears made the charts. "That is a very difficult song to sing," says Billie. "There are so many words in it and they come so fast." By the Nineties, the song had become a gay anthem and it was not surprising when a re-mix of Gloria's hit restored her to the Top 10 in 1993.

436 Art Garfunkel
Bright Eyes

Label & Cat No.: **CBS 6947**

Producer: **Mike Batt**

Writer: **Mike Batt**

Date reached No.1: **14 April 1979**

Weeks at No.1: **6**

Richard Adams wrote his first book, *Watership Down* (1972), while he was working at the Department of the Environment. It depicted a colony of rabbits, which is forced to move from their warren by building developments. Unlike many children's books, Adams did not endow them with human characteristics and took great pains to treat life in the warren seriously: in short, they behaved like rabbits.

There was much speculation as to how the book could be filmed and, after several years in the making, an animated film was released in 1979. John Hurt's voice was used for Hazel and Richard Briers' for Fiver, while Joss Ackland was the Black Rabbit and Sir Ralph Richardson the Chief. Mike Batt, whose CV included The Wombles, desperately wanted to write the score, but the work went to Angela Morley (previously known as Wally Stott) and Malcolm Williamson. Mike kept submitting ideas for songs. "Even 'Bright Eyes' wasn't going to be used," he says, "but then 'Over The Rainbow' was almost taken out of *The Wizard Of Oz*. I had two songs that were dropped, so I then recorded 'Run Like The Wind' with Barbara Dickson and 'Losing Your Way In The Rain' with Colin Blunstone." Mike Batt told the producers that Art Garfunkel would be ideal for 'Bright Eyes' "and within a week, there he was, in my home in Surbiton, routining the song."

Although 'Bright Eyes' was number one, it didn't impress Richard Adams. "I was watching *Wogan* and he asked Richard Adams what he thought of the film," says Mike Batt. "He said, 'I hated 'Bright Eyes'. He based his dislike on the assumption that it was wrong factually. He said it was about a dead rabbit – well, if he reads his own book, he'll realise that the song is sung and thought by Fiver at a time when he thinks Hazel is dead. The point is that the other rabbit thought he was dead."

437 Blondie
Sunday Girl

Label & Cat No.: **Chrysalis CHS 2320**

Producer: **Mike Chapman**

Writer: **Chris Stein**

Date Reached No.1: **26 May 1979**

Weeks at No.1: **3**

"WE WEREN'T PREPARED FOR THIS level of expertise so we learned an enormous amount about how to record from him," Debbie Harry said of *Parallel Lines* producer Mike Chapman. The album was the best seller of 1979 and 'Sunday Girl' was the fourth and final single taken from it, following 'Picture This' (12), 'Hanging On The Telephone' (5) and 'Heart Of Glass' (1).

Like the 12-inch issue of 'Heart Of Glass', which came with a previously unavailable disco instrumental B-side, the sales of 'Sunday Girl' were boosted by another previously unavailable track. In this case it was a French-language version of 'Sunday Girl' on the B-side.

Tensions were mounting within the band, so much so that when it came to designing the cover of *Parallel Lines*, their manager, Peter Leeds, was forced to come up with an idea to shoot the sleeve without the members being together. He explained, "I knew I couldn't put them in a photo session together and get a usable photo, so I came up with the idea that each of them had their own black or white stripe so that we could take the pictures individually." The song, 'Parallel Lines', which was about communications, was never completed.

The more hits Blondie had, the more the media focused on Debbie Harry, which led to an increasing amount of exposure on the front covers of magazines, the majority of which found their way on to the walls of male teenagers' bedrooms. She was the Marilyn Monroe of the punk era.

438 Anita Ward
Ring My Bell

Label & Cat No.: **TK TKR 7543**

Producer: **Frederick Knight**

Writer: **Frederick Knight**

Date reached No.1: **16 June 1979**

Weeks at No.1: **2**

DESPITE HER VOCAL TALENT, ANITA Ward is only known for one hit: "It was a disco record," she says, "and I have never been a disco fan." And, even more to the point, it was a novelty record.

Anita Ward, who was born in Memphis in 1956, received vocal tuition at Rust College and sang in their acappella choir. When she auditioned for a college production of *Godspell,* one of the teachers, Chuck Holmes, asked to manage her and said he would arrange a recording deal. She obtained a degree in psychology and was signed by Frederick Knight, who had recorded for Stax Records and is known for his 1972 hit, 'I've Been Lonely For So Long'.

Knight had written 'Ring My Bell' for 11-year-old Stacy Lattisaw, but she signed with a different label. It was a song about young girls talking on the telephone and Knight reworked it, adding sexual innuendoes. He sang backing vocals on Ward's recording, which featured a much-copied synthesised drum. 'Ring My Bell' was lifted from her album, *Songs Of Love*, as a single and various 12-inch mixes were also available. It was number one in both Britain and America. Although Anita Ward made a second album for Knight, *Sweet Surrender*, there were no further hits. She feels that 'Don't Drop My Love', could have done well if it had been recorded in a lower key.

In 1981 Anita Ward fractured her skull in a car crash and following her recovery, she became a teacher. The single retains its legendary status – Frederick Knight recorded 'Let Me Ring Your Bell Again' and there is a CD comprising solely of mixes of 'Ring My Bell'. On New Year's Eve, 2002 Anita Ward appeared in Times Square to sing her hit for the crowds. Knowing that she was going to appear, thousands of partygoers arrived with little bells, so that they could add their own percussion to the song.

439 Tubeway Army
Are 'Friends' Electric?

Label & Cat No.: **Beggars Banquet BEG 18**

Producer: **Gary Numan**

Writer: **Gary Numan**

Date reached No.1: **30 June 1979**

Weeks at No.1: **4**

YOU CAN SEE THE INFLUENCES OF Kraftwerk, David Bowie and Talking Heads, but 20-year-old Gary Webb from Ashford, Middlesex created a sci-fi original in Gary Numan. The world had ended, just Gary Numan was left and he talked to replicas of himself. All the pleasure and pain had gone out of

existence, and all that was left was an electronic, dehumanised, monotonous voice.

Gary's dad, Tony, supported his music and paid for his first recording, 'That's Too Bad', at Spaceward Studios in Cambridge. The record shop, Beggars Banquet, was planning its own label and when they released 'That's Too Bad', it sold a respectable 7,000 copies. Gary left his job in a warehouse, working for WHSmith.

Seeing a synthesiser at Spaceward, Gary played a few sounds, liked what he heard and the result was 'Are 'Friends' Electric?' which he made with his uncle, Gerry Lidyard, on drums and a friend, Paul Gardiner, on bass. There was no Tubeway Army as such, but Gary did help out on a chart entry for Gardiner, 'Stormtrooper In Drag' (1981).

A live version of 'Are 'Friends' Electric?' made the charts in 1985 and then a remix in 1987. Numan's atmospheric work may appear dated, but it's the stuff that desolate film soundtracks are made of.

440 The Boomtown Rats I Don't Like Mondays

Label & Cat No.: **Ensign ENY 30**

Producer: **Phil Wainman**

Writers: **Bob Geldof**

Date reached No.1: **28 July 1979**

Weeks at No.1: **4**

BOB GELDOF WAS IN AMERICA WHEN HE heard a news story about a girl, Brenda Spencer, in San Diego, California, who was shooting indiscriminately from her bedroom window into a school playground across the street and killing several children. She was telephoned by a journalist who asked her why she was doing it. Her reply: "I don't like Mondays."

The Boomtown Rats' record became a hit everywhere with the exception of America. Radio stations did not play the record as they feared law suits from the Spencer family and it peaked at number 73. In the UK, the song won the prestigious Best Pop Song and Outstanding British Lyric categories at The Ivor Novello Awards. Bob Geldof accepted a starring role in *The Wall*, a film based on Pink Floyd's album.

The Boomtown Rats had further hits with 'Diamond Smiles', 'Someone's Looking At You' and 'Banana Republic', but Geldof's solo career has not been as successful as he would have wished. He had a Top 20 hit with 'The Great Song Of Indifference' (1990), which was about the way the public has viewed his solo career. Of course, everything he has done since 1984 has been swamped by his extraordinary organisation of Live Aid for which he has been knighted.

441 Cliff Richard We Don't Talk Anymore

Label & Cat No.: **EMI 2975**

Producer: **Bruce Welch**

Writer: **Alan Tarney**

Date reached No.1: **25 August 1979**

Weeks at No.1: **4**

BRUCE WELCH SAW THAT HIS FRIEND, Cliff Richard, was neglecting his recording career. He was regularly recording but his heart wasn't in it. Bruce found him a batch of good new songs and they made the album, *I'm Nearly Famous*, in 1976. He was being stretched vocally, singing in falsetto and, on 'Devil Woman', sounding gruffer than usual. This led to a regeneration of his chart career and he did well with 'Miss You Nights' (15), 'Devil Woman' (9) and 'My Kinda Life' (15), even having hits in America. "I was very pleased," says Bruce Welch. "I think, without sounding flash or anything, *I'm Nearly Famous* turned his world upside down. He was back with a bang and within the industry, people were sitting up and taking notice of him again."

Alan Tarney, from the duo Tarney & (Trevor) Spencer and also one of Cliff's guitarists, used to discipline himself to write songs. He says, "I would go into a studio with a blank piece of paper and I would force myself to finish a song every day. I would make the demo as well, and at the end of a week, I would have five new songs. They weren't all good songs. 'We Don't Talk Anymore' would be a song I wrote on Tuesday, say, and on Wednesday I would be doing something else."

Bruce Welch was producing an album for Charlie Dore with Alan Tarney, which was to include the chart single 'Pilot Of The Airwaves'. He heard Alan's demo for 'We Don't Talk Anymore' and knew it would be a number one. Cliff loved it and so they finished Charlie's album on the Friday and recorded Cliff's single over the weekend. "We spent two days in the studio," says Bruce Welch, "and we sold five million records."

The public might not notice anything unusual about its structure, but Alan knew how to create tension. "If you play C, F and G7, you would normally expect to return to C, but I chose to leave it unresolved and go somewhere else. There's a lot of that in 'We Don't Talk Anymore' and it keeps the suspense going." But there was a bit of suspense which surprised Alan: "Cliff lost his place at the end, but he is such a brilliant improviser that he kept going. When he sings the bit about losing sleep and not counting sheep, he doesn't really know where he is."

Alan Tarney went on to write, and also produce, many hit records for Cliff Richard including 'A Little In Love', 'Wired For Sound', 'Some People' and 'My Pretty One'. "The most surprising moment came when we were working with Phil Everly at Hammersmith," says Alan, "He told me that he was going through a divorce and he was driving along when 'We Don't Talk Anymore' came on the radio. He said, 'I don't believe this: this is my life.' He had to pull over to the side of the road so that he could listen to the end of the song properly. He went to his wife and played her the song and they started discussing it. I was in Acton when I wrote that song and it's hard to believe that it affected someone driving along in Colorado."

The Boomtown Rats, clockwise from top left: Johnnie Fingers, Gerry Cott, Simon Crowe, Pete Briquette, Gerry Roberts and their charismatic singer Bob Geldof

442 Gary Numan
Cars

Label & Cat No.: **Beggars Banquet BEG 23**

Producer: **Gary Numan**

Writer: **Gary Numan**

Date reached No.1: **22 September 1979**

Weeks at No.1: **1**

After the fictitious Tubeway Army, Gary Numan released the album, *The Pleasure Principle*, under his own name. There was little pleasure about it: Gary appeared as a humanoid who was incapable of feelings. His Doomsday rock was perfectly captured on the album's most noted cut, 'Cars'.

With his vocals and synthesisers, Gary Numan could make records on his own but he formed a band for a UK tour in September 1979. Its success prompted appearances around the world and, on his 1980 tour, all the musicians wore boiler suits and were told to remain emotionless and static, apart from playing their instruments, throughout the performances.

A succession of hit singles followed – 'Complex', 'We Are Glass', 'I Die: You Die', 'She's Got Claws' and 'We Take Mystery (To Bed)'. He formed his own Numa label in 1984 and had further success with 'Beserker', 'Change Your Mind' and a live EP, which included 'Cars'. In 1987 a remixed 'Cars', the 'E Reg Version', made the Top 20 and further re-mixes were on the charts in 1993 and 1996. The 1996 version coincided with a TV ad for Carling Premier lager.

Numan's wealth has enabled him to indulge in his passion for flying. He has flown single-handedly around the world and performed low level acrobatics in Spitfires. However, when he had a forced landing in India, nobody knew who he was. In 1981 he recorded the track 'What's It Like To Crash?' which, indeed, he found out.

443 The Police
Message In A Bottle

Label & Cat No.: **A&M AMS 7474**

Producers: **Nigel Gray / The Police**

Writer: **Sting**

Date Reached No.1: **29 September 1979**

Weeks at No.1: **3**

"I think the lyrics are subtle and well crafted enough to hit people on a different level from something you just sing along with. It's quite a cleverly put together metaphor. It develops and has an artistic shape to it," said Sting of 'Message In A Bottle'. "It's the best track I've ever played on," added guitarist Andy Summers.

Having left his job as a teacher in his hometown of Newcastle, Sting went on the dole, realising that to pursue a full-time musical career, he would have to concentrate on it 100 per cent. He joined a local band, Last Exit. Their last exit was attended by Stewart Copeland, the drummer with art-rock band, Curved Air, who were touring in the area. He was more impressed with Sting than the band. "He had then what he has now," said Stewart, "this fantastic presence."

Sting regularly wore a black and yellow jumper and it was local jazz musician Gordon Solomon who nicknamed him Sting. The group's name was inspired by Stewart Copeland's father, who was a member of the CIA. Andy Summers, who had been a member of Zoot Money's Big Roll Band and later in Eric Burdon's New Animals, was recruited in 1977 to replace the original guitarist, Henry Padovani. The same year, they appeared on American television advertising Wrigley's Spearmint Gum.

Following the success of 'Roxanne' and 'Can't Stand Losing You', they released 'Message In A Bottle' and gave Herb Alpert and Jerry Moss' 11-year-old A&M label their first UK number one.

444 The Buggles
Video Killed The Radio Star

Label & Cat No.: **Island WIP 6524**

Producers: **Trevor Horn / Geoff Downes**

Writer: **Bruce Woolley**

Date reached No.1: **20 October 1979**

Weeks at No.1: **1**

The guitarist, Trevor Horn from Newcastle, and the keyboard player, Geoff Downes from Stockport, met as part of Tina Charles's backing band. Horn wanted to establish himself as a producer, but he couldn't find the right songs or the right artists. Teaming up with Bruce Woolley, he and Downes wrote their own songs and then recorded them as a studio band. Woolley joined The Camera Club and Horn submitted their demo of 'Video Killed The Radio Star' to Island Records. Within three months, it was number one. The female singer on the record was Linda Jardim, now Linda Allan.

The Buggles released an album, *The Age Of Plastic*, which included three more chart entries, 'The Plastic Age', 'Clean Clean' and 'Elstree'. In a curious career move, The Buggles replaced Rick Wakeman and Jon Anderson in prog-rockers Yes and they made the 1980 album, *Drama*, with them. Following Yes' demise in 1981, they made another album, *Adventures In Modern Recording*. Downes became part of supergroup, Asia, and Horn produced Frankie Goes To Hollywood.

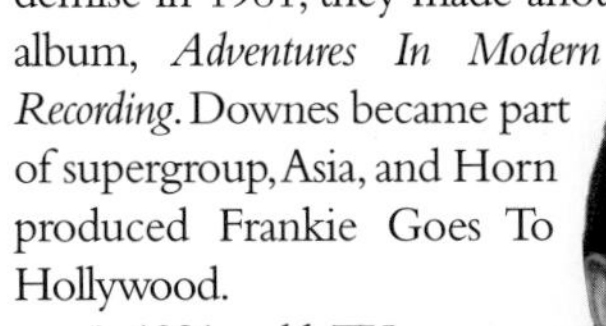

In 1981 a cable TV company, Music Television, began broadcasting from a small studio in Fort Lee, New Jersey. It was the first company to play round the clock music videos. The first video was carefully chosen, 'Video Killed The Radio Star', and the company is now known as MTV.

Gary Numan

Trevor Horn

445 Lena Martell
One Day At A Time

Label & Cat No.: **Pye 7N 46021**

Producer: **George Elrick**

Writers: **Marijohn Wilkin / Kris Kristofferson**

Date reached No.1: **27 October 1979**

Weeks at No.1: **3**

THE ACTOR AND COUNTRY SINGER Kris Kristofferson has written several country music standards ('Help Me Make It Through The Night', 'For The Good Times', 'Me And Bobby McGee') but the only number one bearing his name is 'One Day At A Time' – and he didn't write it. "To be honest, I'm kinda embarrassed about this," said Kris when asked about the song for this book. "I never sing the song because I didn't write it. Marijohn Wilkin was the first publisher I worked for and she published 'For The Good Times' and 'Darby's Castle'. She was a good songwriter herself and I was in the room when she was writing 'One Day At A Time' and I might have given her a line or two. If I studied the lyrics, I might find a phrase of mine but I think she wrote the whole song and I remember her singing it to me. Marijohn was paying me back for some of the songs I had written for her – it was her way of saying 'Thank you'. I've done it myself. I've given a lot of people who've never written a word a piece of one of my songs."

This is why you will search in vain for Kristofferson's own recording of the song. In 1974 'One Day At A Time' was a small US country hit for Marilyn Sellars, a country singer and airline stewardess from Northfield, Minnesota. It was covered by Don Gibson who took it in the US country Top Ten.

Although not up to Kristofferson's level, Marijohn Wilkin's credits are impressive – there is 'Waterloo' (Stonewall Jackson, 1959), 'Cut Across Shorty' (Eddie Cochran, 1960). 'I Just Don't Understand' (Ann-Margret, 1961) and 'P.T. 109' (Jimmy Dean, 1962). Her most impressive composition is surely 'The Long Black Veil', a country weepie first recorded by Lefty Frizzell in 1958 but then taken up by Johnny Cash, Joan Baez and The Band.

The pre-war bandleader and former presenter of *Housewives' Choice*, George Elrick, was keen to promote new talent. He managed and produced the middle of the road singer, Lena Martell, who made 13 albums for Pye Records. 'One Day At A Time' was taken from her album, *Hello Misty Morning*, but it didn't happen at first. Lena had faith: "I love that song," she says, "because it is a very simple lyric with a very big message. It appeals to people who are poorly or have just lost someone or are getting divorced. You take life one hour at a time, then one day at a time, and time does eventually heal."

One day at a time is what happened to the single. Lena used it as the theme for her television series and it went to number one. The US country market realised that a hit song had been staring them in the face, and a new version by Cristy Lane became a chart-topper there.

Lena unwisely chose to release 'Don't Cry For Me, Argentina' as its follow-up, unwise because it had only recently been a hit, and Lena's chart career was over. She retired in 1986 but she is keen to return to performing: "If you go to a theatre and people are appreciating what you do, it's very satisfying, and to find a song and make it your own is something to be proud of."

446 Dr. Hook
When You're In Love With A Beautiful Woman

Label & Cat No.: **Capitol CL 16039**

Producer: **Ron Haffkine**

Writer: **Even Stevens**

Date reached No.1: **17 November 1979**

Weeks at No.1: **3**

THE GUITARIST, GEORGE CUMMINGS, came up with the name, Dr. Hook & The Medicine Show. "We messed everything up," says lead singer Dennis Locorriere. "It came from Captain Hook in *Peter Pan* and it was some time before we realised that Captain Hook hadn't lost an eye, but an arm." Dennis is referring to the group's other lead singer, Ray Sawyer, who was injured in a car accident in 1966.

The group appeared in a dreadful Dustin Hoffman film, *Who Is Harry Kellerman And Why Is He Saying Those Terrible Things About Me?* (1971), but it led to them meeting the ultra-witty songwriter, Shel Silverstein. They broke through with 'Sylvia's Mother' and achieved notority with 'Freakin' At The Freakers' Ball', 'I Got Stoned And I Missed It' and, unbelievably, 'Don't Give A Dose To The One You Love Most'. After touring with the pretentious Emerson, Lake & Palmer, they poured their feelings into 'The Cover Of Rolling Stone'. On a more poignant note, they recorded the original versions of 'Queen Of The Silver Dollar' and 'The Ballad Of Lucy Jordan'.

Despite two gold discs and three best-selling albums in the US, Dr. Hook went bankrupt in 1973. Dennis: "It costs a lot to keep a group on the road. Most of us have families to keep and there are plane fares, hotel bills and taxi-cabs. We got the sums wrong: we should have been going out for higher fees."

Shortening their name to Dr. Hook, the group switched from Columbia to Capitol and recorded top-drawer middle-of-the-road ballads such as 'A Little Bit More' and 'If Not You'. Ray Sawyer says, "Shel was a very generous man, always recommending other writers. He said that Even Stevens and Eddie Rabbitt were really good songwriters from Nashville – Shel said that you could give them an idea and they would have a song in 10 minutes. Stevens came to Muscle Shoals and when he sang 'When You're Love With A Beautiful Woman', we said, 'Yeah, absolutely', and recorded it."

"We did it with a disco arrangement because that was the thing at the time,' says ennis, 'Play the record and you can see that glitter ball going round."

447 The Police
Walking On The Moon

Label & Cat No.:	**A&M AMS 7494**
Producers:	**Nigel Gray / The Police**
Writer:	**Sting**
Date Reached No.1:	**8 December 1979**
Weeks at No.1:	**1**

SOMEONE ONCE ASKED STING HOW long it took to write a three-minute pop song. His reply was "about 20 years."

Sting was one for keeping a notepad with him at all times. He was forever jotting down notes, lyrics and melodies and had done this for a number of years. In the early days it was not surprising to find Sting slumped over a piano at two o'clock in the morning, doodling out melodies that engineers would later transform in the studio.

Andy Summers recalled, "Nigel Gray is a great producer. Some of Sting's best songs probably emerged in the world premature. At least two or three of our big hits would have been stillborn without Nigel and the engineers."

In January 1979 Sting was visiting German *avant-garde* composer Eberhard Schoener. One night they went out on a Schnapps drinking session. The next morning, Sting awoke and tried to clear his head. He began pacing up and down the room, humming and muttering to himself, 'Walking round the room... I hope my legs don't break... walking round the room'. It wasn't unusual for Sting to start with the hook and then build a song around it.

Like 'Message In A Bottle', 'Walking On The Moon' was lifted from their second album *Regatta De Blanc* – a joke spelling of White reggae – and received rave reviews in most music magazines. Using the higher end of his range, Sting was at his best vocally and his writing never more assured. The song soon became the critics' favourite Police song and it wasn't long until Sting agreed with them.

Sting was making a name for himself in the film industry. He was cast as Ace Face in *Quadrophenia*. The film also starred Toyah Willcox, Ray Winstone, Leslie Ash and Phil Daniels as the pill-popping mod freak, Jimmy Cooper.

The accompanying video to 'Message In A Bottle' was shot on a boiling hot day at the Cape Canaveral space centre in Houston and showed Stewart Copeland drumming on the fuselage of a million-dollar rocket.

448 Pink Floyd
Another Brick In The Wall (Part II)

Label & Cat No.:	**Harvest HAR 5194**
Producers:	**Roger Waters / Bob Ezrin / David Gilmour**
Writer:	**Roger Waters**
Date reached No.1:	**15 December 1979**
Weeks at No.1:	**5**

TAKING THEIR NAME FROM TWO BLUES singers, Pink Anderson and Floyd Council, Pink Floyd had their first success in the psychedelic summer of 1967 with 'Arnold Layne' and 'See Emily Play'. When their lead singer, guitarist and visionary, Syd Barrett, was sacked for erratic behaviour, he was replaced by David Gilmour, and Pink Floyd established itself as an albums band, ignoring singles completely. *Dark Side Of The Moon* (1973) spent over 300 weeks on the albums chart and sold 13 million copies worldwide.

Their bassist, Roger Waters, felt alienated and during a concert in Montreal, he spat at his fans. Thinking it through, he realised that there was a wall between himself and the audience, and he had plans to erect a real one on stage.

In 1979 Pink Floyd released the double-album, *The Wall*, with superb packaging from the political cartoonist, Gerald Scarfe. The songs, all written by Waters, described the troubled life of a burnt-out rock star. He blamed his father for dying in the war ('Another Brick In The Wall (Part I)') and he railed against education (Part II) and being a rock star (Part III). 'Part II', which was recorded with a choir from a London school, became the first Pink Floyd single for 12 years and was accompanied by a stunning video in which Scarfe's animated teacher put his charges through a mincer.

With Scarfe's sets, Pink Floyd did concert versions of *The Wall*. Disagreements with Waters led to Rick Wright being forced from the band, and Waters split from David Gilmour and drummer Nick Mason in 1983. Wright returned and Waters tried, unsuccessfully, to prevent them from using the name, Pink Floyd.

In 1982 a film was released, *Pink Floyd The Wall*, with Bob Geldof and Bob Hoskins, directed by Alan Parker, who subsequently made *Evita*. Shortly after the Berlin Wall was demolished in 1989, Roger Waters organised an all-star performance of *The Wall* with spectacular sets at Potsdamer Platz. This time the song was performed by Cyndi Lauper dressed as a schoolgirl.

Pink Floyd would go on to make one further studio album, *The Final Cut* (1983), with Waters at the helm, before splitting up.

1980-1989

THE
NEW STANDARD

CITY PRICES

Tuesday, December 9, 1980. Price 12p — Incorporating the Evening News

Smiling gunman fires five bullets into ex-Beatle

JOHN LENNON SHOT DEAD

JOHN LENNON: Help me, he whispered . . . then Yoko screamed.

Standard Foreign News Desk

JOHN LENNON is dead. The former Beatle was shot dead at 4 a.m. today outside his New York home by a crazed, smiling gunman.

The 40-year-old superstar was rushed to hospital in a police car but died in the arms of his wife, Yoko Ono.

The Lennons had just arrived home at The Dakota, a co-operative apartment building on Manhattan's Upper West Side, from a late-night recording session when they were accosted by the gunman.

An argument broke out and the man, who had apparently been following Lennon for several days and had obtained his autograph earlier in the evening, pulled a ·38 calibre handgun from under his coat and fired five times.

Lennon staggered about five feet to a small guard's booth in the courtyard of the building.

"Do you know what you just did?" the doorman asked the man. "I just shot John Lennon," the gunman answered and threw down the gun.

[illegible]

Artery

[illegible]

Continued Page 2, Col. 1

TV 27 • Entertainment G

"There may not be another Dire Straits record"

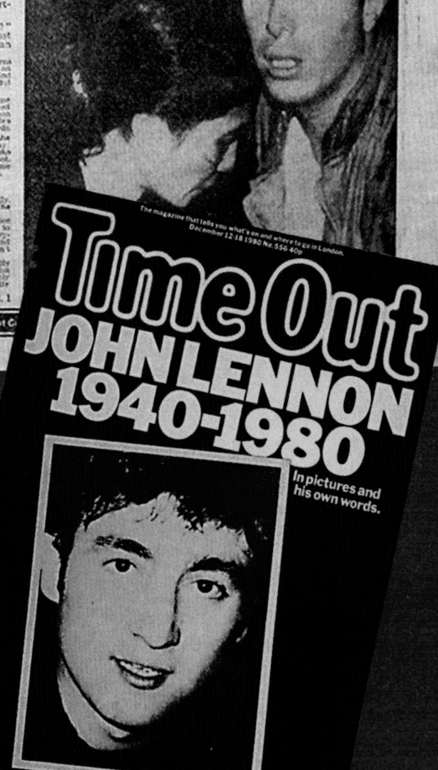

The magazine that tells you what's on and where to go in London.
December 12-18 1980 No. 556 40p
Time Out
JOHN LENNON
1940-1980
In pictures and his own words.

FEED THE WORLD
•BUY THIS RECORD•

The single by **BAND AID: DO THEY KNOW IT'S CHRISTMAS.**
All proceeds go to the famine victims of Ethiopia.

Features

BANANARAMA · BIG COUNTRY · BOOMTOWN RATS · DAVID BOWIE · PHIL COLLINS · CULTURE CLUB · DURAN DURAN · HEAVEN 17 · KOOL AND THE GANG · MARILYN · PAUL McCARTNEY · SPANDAU BALLET · STATUS QUO · STING · THE STYLE COUNCIL · ULTRAVOX · U2 · JODY WATLEY · WHAM · PAUL YOUNG

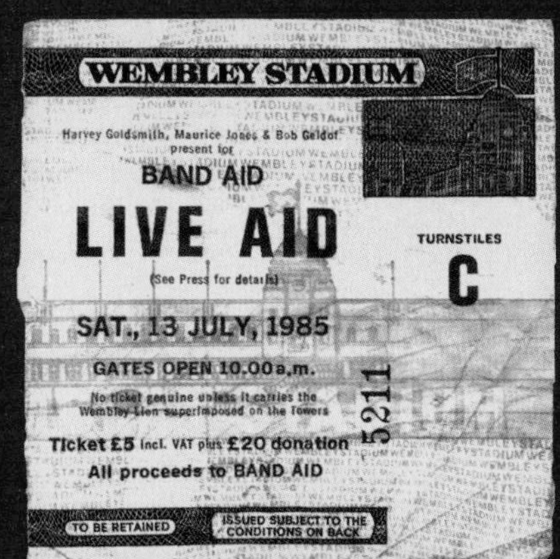

WEMBLEY STADIUM
Harvey Goldsmith, Maurice Jones & Bob Geldof
present for
BAND AID
LIVE AID
(See Press for details)
TURNSTILES
C
SAT., 13 JULY, 1985
GATES OPEN 10.00 a.m.
No ticket genuine unless it carries the Wembley Lion superimposed on the Towers
5211
Ticket £5 incl. VAT plus £20 donation
All proceeds to BAND AID
TO BE RETAINED
ISSUED SUBJECT TO THE CONDITIONS ON BACK

BRIGHTEST HOPE FOR 1980

1. MADNESS
2. THE PRETENDERS
3. JOHN FOXX
4. The Tourists
5. The Buggles
6. The Beat
7. Joe Jackson
8. The Vapors
9. The Chords
10. New Musik

Well, if you've got your hopes pinned on any of the above list you're unlikely to be disappointed. Alright, so Madness and The ... eady hit big, not to ... es, but they're nearly all ... y at the moment. Both ... pors have obviously ... deal of you with their ... cts while John Foxx is ... is due for all the influence ... amous acts.

UNEVEN

Where is Andrew Ridgeley now George Michael needs him?

Stock Aitken & Waterman's guide to writing gigantic hit singles that make you extremely rich, famous and popular. . .

OUT NEXT WEEK

I OWE YOU NOTHING

REMIX SEVEN INCH • TWELVE INCH • COMPACT DISC

SEVEN INCH AVAILABLE IN THREE DIFFERENT SLEEVES

THE IMPORTANCE OF BEING NUTTY

MIKE STAND DIAGNOSES MADNESS

“I never set out to change the world, more to change my own world. Rock ’n’ roll is a noise that has woken me up and it’s good if it wakes other people up . . .” – Bono

autonomous,” says Regine Moylett, an Island Records press officer and current

Who the hell do BANANARAMA think they are?

JULY

“I’ve come here to ROCK AND ROLL!” – Billy Idol

“As for you poor little cows who buy Duran Duran records, you need help ’cos those people are conning you.” – John Lydon

“David (Austin) just meant to cover me in ice and gave the ice bucket a good old swing. Unfortunately it slipped and hit me bang on the base of the nose . . . . It’s the truth.” – Andrew Ridgeley

AUGUST

“For the last four years he’s said he’s going to get his nose done but he kept putting it off ’cos it’s a bit of a big operation. But last week he finally found the time to go in and get it done . . . . From now on we’ll probably get loads of stories about what a fake Andrew is.” – George Michael

“It was good keeping Wham! off the top for a week. After all their boasting about how they were going to go straight in at Number One and sticking their necks out like that. There’s nothing more unattractive in an artist than a false sense of importance.” – Simon le Bon

“I’d still like to marry the Queen Mother. Then I could be the Queen Father!” – Divine

“I’m more of a greengrocer but I *am* an artist too.” – Malcolm McLaren

“I’m certainly no wild man of rock.” – Howard Jones

Once more, the garages of America are alive with the sound of Beatles’ harmonies and spangled guitars.

For The Bangles it’s been an uneasy ride from the dive bars of Los Angeles to internatio[nal] awards ceremonies.

UB 40 with CHRISSIE HYNDE

NEW SINGLE

I GOT YOU BABE

7" & 12"

What have Eric Clapton Bob Dylan Mark Knopfler Tina Turner got in common??

UK Singles

1	14	**THE POWER OF LOVE,** Frankie Goes To Hollywood, **ZTT**
2	2	**I SHOULD HAVE KNOWN BETTER,** Jim Diamond, **A&M**
3	3	**THE RIDDLE,** Nik Kershaw, **MCA**
4	5	**SEX CRIME,** Eurythmics, **Virgin**
5	1	**I FEEL FOR YOU,** Chaka Khan, **Warner Brothers**
6	10	**TEARDROPS,** Shakin' Stevens, **Epic**
7	4	**HARD HABIT TO BREAK,** Chicago, **Full Moon**
8	8	**TREAT HER LIKE A LADY,** Temptations, **Motown**
9	6	**NEVER ENDING STORY,** Limahl, **EMI**
10	16	**ALL JOIN HANDS,** Slade, **RCA**
11	22	**SHE'S FRESH,** Kool And The Gang, **De-Lite**
12	7	**CARIBBEAN QUEEN,** Billy Ocean, **Jive**
13	13	**LET IT ALL BLOW,** Dazz Band, **Motown**

449 Pretenders
Brass In Pocket

Label & Cat No.: **Real ARE 11**
Producer: **Chris Thomas**
Writers: **Chrissie Hynde / James Honeyman-Scott**
Date Reached No.1: **19 January 1980**
Weeks at No.1: **2**

IN 1971, AT THE AGE OF 20, AN AMBITIOUS Chrissie Hynde left her home in Akron, Ohio to seek fame and fortune in London. She had just £200 in her pocket, but was desperate to make things happen. Almost immediately she ran out of money, so found a job selling plastic bags on the corner of London's Oxford Street.

By January 1974 she had landed a job as music journalist with *NME*. Her first submission was a review of Neil Diamond's *Jonathan Livingstone Seagull* album. Within a few months, she had resigned and began working in a clothes shop in Chelsea, the *SEX* boutique, owned by Malcolm McLaren.

After a brief visit to Paris, Chrissie returned home and accepted an offer to sing with a Cleveland R&B group, Jack Rabbit. It wasn't her kind of scene so she left, but with her newfound confidence, formed her own band. With a love of all things French, she returned to Paris and whilst there, witnessed the emergence of punk and formed joined a local band, The Frenchies, as lead singer.

In 1977 she returned to England and within a year had formed The Pretenders, a name inspired by Sam Cooke's version of the Platters' hit, 'The Great Pretender'. Their breakthrough song was a cover of the Kinks' 'Stop Your Sobbing', which reached number 34. Two years later, she started dating the song's writer, Ray Davies.

The Pretenders came to producer Chris Thomas' attention when he saw them at the Marquee Club in London. "I especially liked 'Brass In Pocket'," he said. "I went backstage to tell Chrissie. However, Chrissie told me she didn't really like it. I insisted it was going to be a hit and if she didn't want to record it she should send it over to the producer Willie Mitchell and it would make her a fortune."

The song's title came about during a meal after their first ever UK gig, when a member of the support band, The Strangeways, (from Yorkshire) asked their manager if he had remembered to pick up a pair of trousers from the dressing room. He asked if there was any brass – a slang 16th century northern term for money – in the pockets. Chrissie fell in love with the northern expression and was inspired to write the song. Legend has it that 'Brass In Pocket' was all about a new way of movin', groovin' and being generally hip. The lyrics baffled a lot of people. After all, does anyone really know what 'Detroit leaning' means?

In June 1982 bass player Pete Farndon was fired due to 'personal differences'. The following day guitarist player James Honeyman-Scott died from a drug overdose. Billy Bremner was drafted in to replace Honeyman-Scott and ex-Big Country bassist Tony Butler temporarily replaced Farndon.

The Pretenders disbanded in 1985 but within a year, Chrissie had reformed the group with three new members Tim Stevens, Bernie Worrell and Blair Cunningham and they were back in the Top 10 with 'Don't Get Me Wrong' (1986), 'Hymn To Her' (1986) and 'I'll Stand By You' (1994).

450 The Specials
Special A.K.A. Live (EP)

Label & Cat No.: **2-Tone CHS TT 7**
Producers: **Jerry Dammers / Dave Jordan**
Writers (Too Much Too Young): **Jerry Dammers / Lloyd Charmers**
Date Reached No.1: **2 February 1980**
Weeks at No.1: **2**

THE CATALOGUE NUMBER, CHS TT 7, had already been assigned to Elvis Costello & The Attractions' 'I Can't Stand Up For Falling Down' and 13,000 copies were pressed. Costello had just signed a new contract with Warner Brothers Records and they served an injunction to stop it being released. The copies were eventually given away as a freebie at Elvis Costello gigs (a copy is now worth around £30). 'I Can't Stand Up For Falling Down' was then released on Warner Brothers' imprint F-Beat Records and TT 7 was given over to The Specials.

The group originally formed as the Coventry Automatics by Jerry Dammers, Horace Gentleman and Lynval Golding. They changed their name to the Coventry Specials when Terry Hall joined in 1978. In 1979 they had dropped the Coventry to become The Specials. At the same time, Jerry Dammers set up his own 2-Tone label, which was also home to Madness, The Beat and The Bodysnatchers. An agreement was made with Chrysalis Records for the label to produce a minimum of six singles a year.

The 2-Tone logo was designed by Dammers and showed a man dressed in a black suit, white shirt, black tie, dark sunglasses, black pork pie hat, white socks and black shoes. He was called Walt Jabsco, a name taken from an old American bowling shirt that Dammers owned. The design was inspired by Peter Tosh from the sleeve of Bob Marley & The Wailers' album, *The Wailing Wailers*. Black and white represented the whole mod revival, a plea for unity at a time when race riots and the National Front were at their peak.

'Too Much Too Young', which was issued as a live single, was based on Lloyd Tyrell's (aka Lloyd Charmers) 1969 track 'Birth Control'. Jerry Dammers sped up the tempo and updated the words. It also provided the shortest number one of the decade, clocking in at two minutes and four seconds.

The EP was only the second to top the chart after Demis Roussos' 'The Roussos Phenomenon' in 1976. The Specials' track listing, which were all ska covers, were: 'Too Much Too Young' / 'Guns Of Navarone' (The Skatalites) (both recorded at the Lyceum in London) / 'Long Shot Kick De Bucket' (The Pioneers) / 'Liquidator' (Harry J. All Stars) / 'Skinhead Moonstomp' (Symarip) (all recorded at Tiffany's in Coventry). 'Guns Of Navarone' was the first instrumental to make number one since The Simon Park Orchestra's 'Eye Level' in 1973.

The Pretenders' original line-up recorded only two albums, left to right: James Honeyman-Scott, Pete Farndon, Chrissie Hynde and Martin Chambers

451 Kenny Rogers
Coward Of The County

Label & Cat No.: **United Artists UP 614**

Producer: **Larry Butler**

Writers: **Roger Bowling / Billy Edd Wheeler**

Date Reached No.1: **16 February 1980**

Weeks at No.1: **2**

"I'VE ALWAYS BEEN DRAWN TO SONGS that tell stories that start somewhere and say something; they're like mini movies," admitted Kenny Rogers.

After having won Male Vocalist Of The Year in 1979, Kenny was an established country superstar and after the success of 'Lucille', he chose to record another Roger Bowling composition. 'Coward Of The County' was a sentimental story of Tommy, a convict's son, whose wife, Becky, was gang raped by the Gatlin boys. Tommy made a death bed promise to his father to always walk away from trouble but, on this occasion, found it too much to bear and sought revenge. Following his 1980 film appearance in *The Gambler*, Kenny appeared as Uncle Matthew in the spin-off television movie, *Coward Of The County*, a year later. Becky was played by Largo Woodruff.

When Motown Records' publishing company, Jobete Music, told Kenny that Lionel Richie wanted to write a song for him, he immediately flew to Las Vegas to meet him. Lionel played Kenny the demo of 'Lady'. Kenny loved it and within two weeks had recorded it. He said, "I love songs that are female orientated and that's the market I wanna get." The song topped the US chart for six weeks and provided a number 12 follow up to 'Coward Of The County' in the UK.

In 1986 readers of the *USA Today* newspaper, voted Kenny 'Favourite Singer Of All Time'.

The songwriter, Billy Edd Wheeler, grew up on folk music. He wrote the Kingston Trio's 1963 US hit, 'Reverend Mr. Black' and had a minor hit of his own a year later with 'Ode To The Little Brown Shack Out Back'. In 1966 he wrote and first recorded, with Gaby Rogers, 'Jackson', later made famous by Lee Hazelwood and Nancy Sinatra.

Kenny's other hobby is photography. His private collection of famous faces is, to say the least, impressive. "It brings me the same satisfaction and passion that music does," he admitted. "But if I never took another picture, it wouldn't be the end of the world, but if I never sang another song, that would really bother me."

452 Blondie
Atomic

Label & Cat No.: **Chrysalis CHS 2410**

Producer: **Mike Chapman**

Writers: **Deborah Harry / Chris Stein**

Date Reached No.1: **1 March 1980**

Weeks at No.1: **2**

'ATOMIC', LIKE 'HEART OF GLASS', WAS another disco influenced song and was the debut single from the new album *Eat To The Beat*. This was one of the first ever rock video albums, with a video to accompany each song. Following the success of *Parallel Lines*, Mike Chapman was asked to take care of production.

Blondie were flitting between the rock and disco sound. After 'Sunday Girl' came the rock orientated songs, 'Dreaming' (2) and 'Union City Blue' (13).

'Atomic', which featured King Crimson's Robert Fripp on guitar and Ellie Greenwich on backing vocals, was lyrically meaningless and was described in *Record Mirror* as 'Vapid and irritating, the best thing about this single is the live version of David Bowie's 'Heroes' on the B-side'. "Jimmy Destri wrote this song," Debbie claimed. "He was trying to do something like 'Heart Of Glass', and then somehow or another we gave it the spaghetti western treatment. Before that it was just lying there like a lox. The lyrics, well, a lot of the time I would write while the band were just playing the song and trying to figure it out. I would just be kind of scatting along with them and I would start going, 'Oooooooh, your hair is beautiful'."

Debbie Harry, who had always wanted to be a movie star, decided to pursue acting. She was cast in her first role as Lillian Harlan in Mark Reichert's *Union City*. Debbie's husband Chris Stein provided some of the music for the soundtrack, including the title track.

In 2003 Deborah, as she now likes to be called, began a new vocation, presenting a three-part documentary on Sky's Discovery Channel. The series focused on how rock'n'roll music, particularly The Beatles and the worlds of fashion and film, permeated countries outside the Western world. She recalled, "In 1980 I nearly met John Lennon. I was supposed to go and meet him the week after it happened. It was kind of awful. I mean beyond him getting shot I would have really liked to have met him."

453 Fern Kinney
Together We Are Beautiful

Label & Cat No.: **WEA K 79111**

Producers: **Carson Whitsett / Tommy Couch / Wolf Stephenson**

Writer: **Ken Leray**

Date Reached No.1: **15 March 1980**

Weeks at No.1: **1**

FERN KINNEY WAS BORN IN JACKSON, Mississippi and sowed her musical seeds in her local church. It was thanks to her minister's persuasion to take lead on the gospel songs, that Fern eventually gained the confidence to attempt a singing career.

Her local cinema would hold talent contests during the film intermissions, so her minister entered her for one. The prize was $5, which Fern won. She approached her local recording studios and offered her services as a backing singer. Two artists who were recording there at the time were soul singers Jean Carn and Floyd King. Floyd had recorded a song called 'Groove Me' which Fern later covered and released as a single.

She left school in 1967 and joined Dorothy

Moore as a backing vocalist with The Poppies replacing Patsy McClune. When The Poppies broke up in 1968, Fern pursued a solo career and released her debut single 'Your Love's Not Reliable', which went nowhere. Within a year she had married and moved to St Louis, Missouri. In the mid-Seventies she returned to Jackson and carried on working as a backing singer, this time for producer Frederick Knight.

Her next release, 'Groove Me', made little impact on the American chart, climbing no higher than number 54. The follow up, 'Baby Let Me Kiss You', failed to chart altogether. The track on the B-side was a Ken Leray song, 'Together We Are Beautiful'. Ken's version was issued as a single but it didn't connect. Surprisingly, Fern's version did likewise in the US. Fern had changed the gender and it began receiving airplay. It was re-pressed and released as the A-side.

When asked if she thought the song was going to be a hit she replied, "I don't know if I was expecting it or just hoping real hard. I've worked for 18 years and to me that's a long time. If I have to work longer then I will. But, for me, at this stage I need to see some success." Unfortunately, that success did not happen. 'Groove Me' was re-issued and, like the following releases, 'Movie Show', 'I've Been Lonely For So Long' and 'Beautiful Love Song', they all failed to chart. So Fern's success lasted just 11 weeks and she became the first one hit wonder of the Eighties.

454 The Jam
Going Underground / The Dreams Of Children

Label & Cat No.: **Polydor POSP 113**

Producer: **Vic Coppersmith-Heaven**

Writer: **Paul Weller**

Date Reached No.1: **22 March 1980**

Weeks at No.1: **3**

Paul Weller was born in Surrey but loved to write songs about London, such as 'In The City', 'Strange Town', ''A' Bomb In Wardour Street' and 'Down In The Tube Station At Midnight'. Although their 10th single 'Going Underground' appeared to refer to London's tube rail system, it wasn't. 'Going Underground' was about Paul's concerns on nuclear war and refers to Russia's invasion of Afghanistan in December 1979.

Such was the demand for the single that it became the first song to enter the chart at number one for over six years (the last being Slade's 'Merry Xmas Everybody'). Within two weeks, the song had topped the 250,000 sales mark. The tabloids remarked that the reason it entered at number one was because it was available before the official release date, a claim that Polydor product manager Denis Mundy denied. But a contributing factor might have been its availability as a limited edition double pack, containing live versions of 'The Modern World', 'Away From The Numbers' and 'Down In The Tube Station At Midnight' which Paul Weller said was "To thank the fans for three years of loyal support." The lads were on tour in New Jersey when news reached them that they were number one. In less than a minute, they made the decision to return to the UK to record *Top Of The Pops*. They never went back to finish the tour.

The title, 'The Dreams Of Children', was inspired by Liverpool writer Clive Barker's horror story, *The Forbidden*, in which the Candyman kills to preserve his reputation, so he can still haunt the 'dreams of children'. Its lyric, however, is only loosely based on the novel. It had an interesting backwards intro which, at the time Jam fans nationwide risked damaging their stereo by playing it backwards to discover what it said. Paul Weller recalled "After we'd finished recording the album *Setting Sons,* I asked the engineer if he could record the album backwards and put it on cassette. When I listened to it there was one piece of vocal that I really liked and wrote 'The Dreams Of Children' around it." The track's psychedelic feel is due to the fact that Weller had just been listening to his favourite album, The Beatles' *Revolver.*

In 2002 Paul allowed his lyrics to be rewritten for the World Cup release of 'Go England' by the England Boys which only just made the Top 30.

455 Detroit Spinners
Working My Way Back To You

Label & Cat No.: **Atlantic K 11432**

Producer: **Michael Zager**

Writers: **Sandy Linzer / Denny Randell / Michael Zager**

Date Reached No.1: **12 April 1980**

Weeks at No.1: **2**

Formed in Detroit in 1961 as The Domingoes, they were discovered by The Moonglows' lead singer Harvey Fuqua who signed them to his own Tri-Fi label and renamed them The Spinners. They were John Edwards, Bobbie Smith and Billy Henderson who all sang tenor and Henry Fambrough (baritone) and Pervis Jackson (bass). They moved to Motown Records in 1965. Their first UK hit, 'It's A Shame', came in 1970, which was produced and co-written by Stevie Wonder. They used the label name as a prefix to avoid confusion with the British folk entertainers of the same name. Two and a half years later, and after a label change to Atlantic, came their next hit 'Could It Be I'm Falling In Love' by which time they had undergone yet another name change, to the Detroit Spinners.

The New York songwriting partnership between Sandy Linzer (lyrics) and Denny Randell (music) began in the mid-Sixties. Together they had written songs for The Four Seasons, The Toys, Johnny Johnson & The Bandwagon and Limmie & The Family Cookin'.

UK pressings only credited the song as 'Working My Way Back To You'. However, the US copies showed the full title as 'Working My Way Back To You / Forgive Me Girl'. Michael Zager had already charted a couple of disco hits of his own in the late Seventies, 'Let's All Chant' being the biggest and it was his idea to combine two songs; one old, one new. 'Working My Way Back To You' had been a US Top 10 for The Four Seasons but it only reached number 50 in the UK. 'Forgive Me Girl' was a Zager original.

The follow-up, 'Body Language' only reached number 40, so Michael Zager reverted to a winning formula for the next hit, and paired Sam Cooke's 1961 song 'Cupid' with Zager's own 'I've Loved You For A Long Time'. It reached number four.

Unfortunately, Zager wasn't so lucky third time round. He'd paired The Carpenters' 'Yesterday Once More' with his own 'Nothing Remains The Same' and missed the chart completely.

456 Blondie
Call Me

Label & Cat No.: **Chrysalis CHS 2414**

Producer: **Giorgio Moroder**

Writers: **Deborah Harry / Giorgio Moroder**

Date Reached No.1: **26 April 1980**

Weeks at No.1: **1**

FOLLOWING 'UNION CITY BLUE', 'CALL Me' was Blondie's second hit from a film, this time *American Gigolo*. The film's plot centres around Julian Kaye (Richard Gere), who makes his living as an escort. He embarks on an affair with a politician's wife called Michelle Stratton (Lauren Hutton), but doesn't expect to get paid for it. Things hot up when one of Julian's clients is murdered and the police start questioning him about his other clients. Things are made worse when Michelle falls in love with him.

Giorgio Moroder originally offered the song to Stevie Nicks, but after she declined, he offered it to Debbie. Although Debbie loved the film, she didn't like Giorgio's lyrics and re-wrote them. Debbie and Chris were happy with the results, but the remaining members of Blondie thought it too commercial. It caused more tension amongst them and soon after Debbie took a break from the band. It gave all the other members a chance to either branch out on their own or collaborate with other artists.

As Debbie recalled, "Giorgio Moroder is very nice and very easy to work with, but I don't think he has a lot of patience with people who fool around or don't take what they do seriously." Harry was given complete freedom with the lyrics and both Giorgio and the film's producer, Paul Schrader, were pleased with the result. As Giorgio had already laid down the instrumental backing track, finishing the song was easy and took Debbie only a couple of hours to record the vocals.

'Call Me' gave Blondie their second US number one and was voted *Billboard*'s Number One Song Of The Year. Over here, Debbie Harry became the first woman to write three UK number ones.

457 Dexys Midnight Runners
Geno

Label & Cat No.: **Late Night Feelings R 6033**

Producer: **Pete Wingfield**

Writers: **Kevin Rowland / Al Archer**

Date Reached No.1: **3 May 1980**

Weeks at No.1: **2**

THE DUNGAREES AND GYPSY LOOK THAT is often associated with Dexys Midnight Runners didn't appear until 1982, in time for their second number one, 'Come On Eileen'. For 'Geno', however, they were still in donkey jackets and woolly hats, an image that was inspired by the Martin Scorcese film, *Mean Streets*.

Dexys Midnight Runners hailed from Birmingham and the original line-up comprised lead singer Kevin Rowland, Al Archer (guitar), Pete Saunders (keyboards), Pete Williams (bass), Andy Growcott (drums), Jimmy Patterson (trombone), J.B.Blyte (tenor sax) and Steve Spooner (alto sax). Mick Talbot from The Merton Parkas (and later, The Style Council) replaced Saunders after their first hit, 'Dance Stance' reached number 40.

Their next single, 'Geno', which begins with the crowd chanting, 'Geno, Geno, Geno', was a tribute to the soul singer Geno Washington. Washington fronted the soulful Ram Jam Band who had four hits in the Sixties, including a rather radical cover of Doris Day's 'Whatever Will Be Will Be' re-titled 'Que Sera Sera'.

Despite a strict anti-drink and drugs policy within the band, they took their name from the pep-pill Dexedrine, which was usually issued to war troops to boost energy. It was The Clash's manager Bernie Rhodes who secured them a record deal with EMI. The album *Searching For The Young Soul Rebels* was only half finished when Kevin Rowland became dissatisfied with the lack of money coming in and managed to reclaim the master tapes of the album from EMI. He wanted the contract renegotiated and, because they already had a number one hit, EMI relented.

Having got his way, Kevin's controlling nature led him to make decisions without involving other members of the band. He decided to drop 'Geno' from the live shows once it hit the top. The horn-led follow up, 'There There My Dear' also made the Top 10.

All the band members disagreed with Rowland's decision to release 'Keep It (Part 2)' as the next single. So when it missed the chart completely, everyone, except Patterson, quit.

458 Johnny Logan
What's Another Year

Label & Cat No.: **Epic EPC 8572**

Producers: **Bill Whelan / Dave Pennefather**

Writer: **Shay Healy**

Date Reached No.1: **17 May 1980**

Weeks at No.1: **2**

IN 1980 THE EUROVISION SONG CONTEST celebrated its 25th anniversary. It was staged at Congresgebouw in The Hague, Holland. This broke with tradition as the previous year's winners would normally host the following year's event. In 1979 Israel had won with 'Hallelujah' by Milk And Honey but had declined to host the show, even though they had done so the previous year when 'A-Ba-Ni-Bi' by Izhar Cohen & The Alpha-Beta triumphed in 1978.

Johnny Logan was born Seàn Sherrard in Frankston, near Melbourne in 1954. His Irish-born father, working as Patrick O'Hagan, sang tenor in a band and his work had taken him there. The family returned to Ireland in the early Sixties. On leaving school, Johnny trained to be an electrician but he always wanted to sing. He sang in bars and made a few records, coming third with 'Angie' in the National Song Contest in 1979. The winner, 'Happy Man' by Cathal Dunne, came fifth in Eurovision itself.

A young impresario, Louis Walsh, met Johnny on a bus, heard him sing and offered to take over his management, encountering rancour from the incumbent. Louis Walsh believed that Eurovision was the ideal stepping-stone for an Irish artist provided he had the right song.

Shay Healy, a press officer with the national broadcaster, RTE, had lost his mother and to comfort his father, had written an emotional ballad, 'What's Another Year" Johnny Logan recalls, "In 1980 I was voted Best New Singer in Ireland and 'What's Another Year' was up for grabs in the National Song Contest. Shay said he would like me to sing it and it was a country song. There was no sax solo and a lot of chords were different. Bill Whelen, who has done some amazing work for Kate Bush, arranged it and Colin Tolly played sax and it won."

The song had clinched Ireland's entry but then it needed to win Eurovision. The sensible money was on the Italian entry, 'Non So Che Darei' by Alan Sorrenti. However, Alan had come to The Hague with his wife and had had such an argument that she threatened to jump from the hotel window. This distracted Alan and he came in sixth with Johnny Logan emerging as the easy winner. The Dutch authorities had announced that a tulip would be named after the winner, and so, a few days later, you could buy a Johnny Logan tulip.

Following the Eurovision win, 'What's Another Year" went to number one in 11 European countries, but as Johnny Logan discovered, "I was an overnight success and then an overnight failure." The follow-ups, 'In London' and 'Save Me', failed to connect and by Christmas, Johnny was appearing in *Joseph And The Amazing Technicolor Dreamcoat* at the Opera House in Cork, not a bad gig but not what he expected.

Shay Healy wrote inspirational songs for Daniel O'Donnell, notably 'Follow Your Dream', as well as three novels, *The Stunt*, *Green Card Blues* and *It Could All Change Tomorrow*. Between 1988 and 1992 he also presented the madcap late night chat show *Nighthawks* on RTE television in Ireland.

Dutifully, Johnny Logan submitted songs to the National Song Contest each year. He almost won Eurovision itself in 1984 when Linda Martin performed his song about emigration, 'Terminal 3'. The next year his brother Mike came last in the Irish heats with another of his songs, 'Hearts'.

In 1987 Johnny returned to Eurovision itself, winning his own pop ballad, 'Hold Me Now'. This time it should have been easier to maintain his success, but he and Louis Walsh disagreed over the way his career should go. "He wanted to be Robert Palmer and I wanted him to be Cliff Richard," said Louis. He continued writing and he became the Red Rum of Eurovision when Linda Martin beat the UK's Michael Ball with his song, 'Why Me?" in 1992.

Reflecting on his success, Johnny explained in 2002, "I entered the contest with good songs that weren't written for *Eurovision*. They were written from the heart. Nowadays, I just feel that too many of the songs are contrived. When I won with 'Hold Me Now' in 1987, there were five or six other songs that were also very beautiful. Recently, I watched the 1980 *Song Contest* again on video, sitting down with a bottle of wine. I still get nervous when I watch that. It's funny, I'm still never sure I'm going to end up winning."

Johnny Logan

459 The Mash
Theme From M*A*S*H (Suicide Is Painless)

Label & Cat No.: **CBS 8536**

Producer: **Thomas Z. Shepherd**

Writers: **Mike Altman / Johnny Mandel**

Date Reached No.1: **31 May 1980**

Weeks at No.1: **3**

THE FILM M★A★S★H – AN ACRONYM for Mobile Army Surgical Hospital – was set during the Korean war of the early Fifties. Made in 1970, it was based on a book by Richard Hooker, directed by Robert Altman and starred Elliott Gould and Donald Sutherland. The spin-off television series, which featured over 250 episodes and ran for 11 years, featured Alan Alda as Captain Benjamin Franklin 'Hawkeye' Pierce. The film director's teenage son, Mike, wrote the ballad lyrics to accompany Johnny Mandel's theme. It is rumoured that Mike made more money from the song's lyrics than his father did from directing the film.

Johnny Mandel is a versatile American composer. He played trombone and trumpet in various jazz bands in the Forties and later became Artie Shaw's musical arranger. He began composing film themes in the late Fifties and won an Oscar for the Richard Burton and Elizabeth Taylor film *The Sandpiper* in 1965.

The M★A★S★H theme was unearthed in 1980 by Radio One DJ Noel Edmonds, who continually played it on his Sunday morning show. The demand was high and CBS Records were forced to release it as a single. It never received weekday radio play because the BBC management thought the line 'suicide is painless' was objectionable and might have led to listeners taking their own life.

The identity of The Mash was, for many years a mystery. In fact, they were a group of Los Angeles session musicians named The Ron Hickman Singers. They comprised Ron Hickman, John Bahler and Gene Morford who all shared lead vocals on the track. In the Sixties they had provided backing vocals on hits by Gary Lewis and in the Seventies joined David Cassidy and Shirley Jones as the other members of The Partridge Family.

The show is still regularly aired on various oldies channels and the theme went back into the Top 10 when covered by The Manic Street Preachers in 1992, so it might be time for a remake.

460 Don McLean
Crying

Label & Cat No.: **EMI 5051**
Producer: **Larry Butler**
Writers: **Roy Orbison / Joe Melson**
Date Reached No.1: **21 June 1980**
Weeks at No.1: **3**

IN 1972 DON MCLEAN WAS NOMINATED for four Grammy Awards yet didn't win any. A year later, his song 'And I Love You So' was nominated for 'Song Of The Year' but lost out to Roberta Flack's 'Killing Me Softly With His Song', a song that Don himself was the inspiration for. Roy Orbison rang Don and told him "You were robbed."

Roy explained how he came to record 'Cryin'. "I was dating a girl and we broke up," he said. "I went to the barber shop to get a haircut and I looked across the street and there was this girl that I had split up with. I wanted to go over and say, 'Let's forget about what happened and carry on'. But I was stubborn. So I got in the car and drove down the street about two blocks and said to myself, 'Boy, you really made a mistake. You didn't play that right at all'. It certainly brought tears to my eyes and that's how I came up with 'Crying'."

The original title was to be 'I Am Crying', after a casual phrase that co-writer, Joe Melson often used. It was earmarked for Don Gibson but Roy decided to cut the 'I Am' and to lose the 'g' from 'crying' to make it less 'country sounding'. However, Don wanted his interpretation to be different. Roy's had a Latin feel to it, so Don reinserted the 'g' in the title and decided it would sound good as a slow ballad.

Elvis Presley was a Don McLean fan and Don was very proud of the fact that Elvis often mentioned him on stage. Elvis' backing group, The Jordanaires, provided backing vocals on Don's 1978 album *Chain Lightning*.

Don's American record company, Millennium, deemed the song 'too slow' and refused to release it as a single. It was only when Don made a stop over for a TV appearance in Europe and performed 'Crying' that things changed. Such was the reaction that EMI were forced to issue it as a single in Britain. A year later his American record company followed suit and were awarded with a number five hit.

In an episode of the successful television comedy series, *Only Fools and Horses*, Del Boy (David Jason) booked a cabaret act – a singer with a speech impediment. When he sang Don's second chart-topper, the audience collapsed laughing when the singer blurted out 'Cwy-ing'...

461 Olivia Newton-John & Electric Light Orchestra
Xanadu

Label & Cat No.: **Jet 185**
Producer: **Jeff Lynne**
Writer: **Jeff Lynne**
Date Reached No.1: **12 July 1980**
Weeks at No.1: **2**

AFTER *GREASE*, OLIVIA SAID, "I THINK that I waited quite a long time to do anything else, but then again, maybe I didn't wait long enough."

Neither Olivia Newton-John nor Electric Light Orchestra ever had a UK number one in their own right. Electric Light Orchestra were from Birmingham and had 13 Top 10 hits in the Seventies, including; 'Roll Over Beethoven, 'Mr. Blue Sky', 'Wild West Hero', 'Sweet Talkin' Woman' and 'Shine A Little Love' which all got to number six. Olivia's hits included; 'Banks Of The Ohio' (6), 'Sam' (6) and 'A Little More Love' (4). By collaborating on the *Xanadu* film theme, they were awarded a number one hit.

Xanadu, which was loosely based on Samuel Taylor Coleridge's book of the same name, was a lightweight film with an exceptionally weak story line. Olivia said, "The music was great and the dancing was great, but the script left a lot to be desired, like it often does in musical films." The plot: Zeus's daughter Kira (Olivia Newton-John) who, for some reason, glows in various different colours, is reincarnated on earth to inspire people. She has an encounter with a down and out musician called Sonny Malone (Michael Beck). With the help of Danny McGuire (Gene Kelly), a rich businessman who is fed up with life in general, they build a roller skating arena and call it Xanadu. Olivia said, "The greatest thing was, that I got to dance with Gene Kelly."

The film itself, not surprisingly, received disastrous reviews. The strongest thing was the music and the soundtrack produced some quite wonderful songs. Six hit singles were released from the film, including the duet with Cliff Richard, 'Suddenly' (15), 'Magic' (32) (Olivia), and the three ELO hits, 'All Over The World' (11), 'Don't Walk Away' (21) and 'I'm Alive' (20). It also earned Jeff Lynne an Ivor Novello Award for Best Film Theme Song.

Matt Lattanzi was a backing dancer in the film. He asked Olivia for a date, a romance blossomed and they soon moved in together. Matt was instrumental in changing Livvy's image for the 1981 hit, 'Physical'. Their marriage in 1984 ended in divorce 11 years later.

Jeff Lynne has since concentrated more on the production side of the music business working with Dave Edmunds and The Beatles. In 1988 he was one fifth of the super group The Traveling Wilburys with Roy Orbison, George Harrison, Tom Petty and Bob Dylan. But the project was abandoned following Roy Orbison's death later that year.

A close friend of George Harrison, Jeff produced George's final album *Brainwashed* which was released posthumously. The album was completed by Jeff and George's son Dhani after the former Beatle died in December 2001.

462 Odyssey
Use It Up And Wear It Out

Label & Cat No.: **RCA PB 1962**

Producer: **Sandy Linzer**

Writers: **Sandy Linzer / Larry Russell Brown**

Date Reached No.1: **26 July 1980**

Weeks at No.1: **2**

SANDY LINZER AND DENNY RANDELL had been writing or producing hit singles since 1965, and had written a song for Frankie Valli which was included on his 1977 album *Lady Put The Lights Out*. That track was 'Native New Yorker' which Odyssey covered for their first hit later the same year. For 'Use It Up And Wear It Out', Sandy collaborated with another song-writer, Larry Russell Brown.

The three Lopez sisters, Lillian, Louise and Carmen began singing together professionally in 1968 at their local stage shows as The Lopez Sisters. This led to some tours in Europe. In the mid-Seventies Carmen left the fold and was replaced by Manila-born Tony Reynolds, but he left after just one album. Bill McEachern, a tenor formally of We The People, joined after their first hit, but left soon after. "Getting bookings was hard because Odyssey were two girls and a guy," Lillian explained. "So I said to my husband, Al Jackson, get your dancing shoes on, it looks like you're in the band."

Three years passed between their first and second hits. Louise explained, "We had problems with our management company, Champion Entertainment, and our second album, *Hollywood Party Tonight*, wasn't danceable enough and didn't really do anything. It's dodgy doing slow songs when you're just breaking through."

Lillian explains, "Use It Up And Wear It Out', is just don't get old, to me. It means just keep on going, keep on doing it and keep on enjoying until you drop."

Louise once said, "We want longevity and will go on as long as they will have us – in fact, until it's all used up and worn out." Clearly Louise became worn out rather rapidly as she left in the mid-Nineties to become an art dealer. Lillian and Al, however, did carry on touring the club circuit as Odyssey.

The B-side of 'Use It Up And Wear It Out', 'Don't Tell Me, Tell Her' was receiving more air-play on the black music stations in America than the A-side, but here copies of 'Use It Up And Wear It Out' with its disco beat, were filtering in on import. A sample of the 'Don't Tell Me, Tell Her' was used in 1999 on 'It's Over' by Rimes featuring Shaila Prospere.

463 Abba
The Winner Takes It All

Label & Cat No.: **Epic EPC 8835**

Producers: **Björn Ulvaeus / Benny Andersson**

Writers: **Björn Ulvaeus / Benny Andersson**

Date Reached No.1: **9 August 1980**

Weeks at No.1: **2**

THOUGH 'DANCING QUEEN' PROVED~ to be more popular, many fans consider 'The Winner Takes It All' to be the jewel in the crown of Abba's gilded catalogue. The opening line "I don't wanna talk about the things we've gone through, though it's hurting me now it's history," seemed to sum up Björn and Agnetha's troubled relationship. Even more poignant was the news that the other Abba couple, Benny and Frida, were now starting to have problems of their own. Their modus operandi at this point was that Benny and Björn would compose a tune, then Björn would take the song home and play it over and over again until he came up with appropriate lyrics.

'The Winner Takes It All', the first track lifted from their eighth number one album, *Super Trouper*, was written in just one hour whilst Björn was completely drunk. He had come home and opened a bottle of scotch. As he recalled "I was drunk and in a rush of emotion the words just came to me. Normally that doesn't work because they look or sound good when you're drunk and the next day they look awful, but this one actually worked."

The next day he took the song into the studio and recorded another demo. When his friends heard it they insisted that he should record it as the finished product, but Björn correctly felt that Agnetha should be the one to sing it. In a way, the song is fictitious because, as Björn explains, "In divorce, there are no winners." An accompanying video was shot in Marstrand, a town on the west coast of Sweden just 10 days after their marriage was finally dissolved in court. Things were a bit awkward, as both Björn and Agnetha had brought their new partners to the location. But it showed a genuinely heartbroken Agnetha singing to the camera while the other members of the group just stood around talking and laughing.

In a ploy to keep the song at number one, CBS Records released a limited edition 12" pressing on the second week, but the attempt failed when David Bowie dislodged them.

464 David Bowie
Ashes To Ashes

Label & Cat No.: **RCA BOW 6**

Producers: **David Bowie / Tony Visconti**

Writer: **David Bowie**

Date Reached No.1: **23 August 1980**

Weeks at No.1: **2**

AFTER HAVING SPENT 11 YEARS IN orbit, David Bowie returned to resolve the saga of astronaut Major Tom, last seen stranded in space. In what might be seen as a rare piece of autobiography, Bowie described how he had become a junkie, was strung out in heaven's high and looking down on a 'blue' planet earth.

The accompanying video was used to great effect. At times David was standing holding a portable television set portraying constantly changing scenes. It also featured Visage's Steve Strange and various others who were selected from the

crowd at Soho's Blitz Club for New Romantics. The ending shows David dressed as a glum looking clown, trekking along a jet-black sea, being lectured by his mother.

David Bowie refused to stand still, and his constant reinvention kept the fans interested. He had created the Ziggy Stardust character in 1972, he'd tried his hand at rock theatre with *Diamond Dogs*, moved into R&B and disco with *Young Americans* and rocked out on *Station To Station*. In 1977 he relocated to Berlin to make a trilogy of experimental, largely instrumental, albums produced by Brian Eno. With his latest album, *Scary Monsters And Super Creeps,* from which 'Ashes To Ashes' was taken, it seemed that David had found his own voice again.

When *Scary Monsters...* was released David was in Chicago portraying John Merrick in *The Elephant Man*, a part he played with no makeup. He received rave reviews and it later moved to the Booth Theater on Broadway. He'd already played an alien in *The Man Who Fell To Earth* (1976), and would go on to star in *The Hunger* (1983), *Merry Christmas Mr Lawrence* (1983) and *Labyrinth* (1986).

Times were changing and the New Romantic era was just beginning. David Bowie's fashion sense, his use of make-up and brightly coloured hair was enormously influential. No other rock star of his era managed to bridge generation gaps as successfully as Bowie.

465 The Jam
Start

Label & Cat No.: **Polydor 2059 266**
Producers: **Vic Coppersmith-Heaven / The Jam**
Writer: **Paul Weller**
Date Reached No.1: **6 September 1980**
Weeks at No.1: **1**

"I THOUGHT 'GOING UNDERGROUND' was a peak and we were getting a little safe with that sound, that's why we've done 'Start'," claimed Paul Weller.

In 1971 when George Harrison's 'My Sweet Lord' topped the chart, its victory was dampened by the fact he was successfully sued by the estate of Ronnie Mack, the writer of The Chiffons' hit, 'He's So Fine' for unintentional plagiarism. When The Jam released 'Start' it had so obviously 'borrowed' the bass hook from 'Taxman', the opening track on The Beatles' *Revolver* album, that you could have put money on there being an imminent court case. That never happened. Why George Harrison, who penned the song, never sued remains a mystery. OK, he didn't own the publishing, so perhaps the more pertinent question is, why didn't the publishers, Northern Songs, sue instead? Maybe George considered it a compliment and remembering how he was unfairly treated and what he went through with 'My Sweet Lord' decided not to put someone else through that. Paul Weller said, "I thought it was all a bit stupid, the riff thing doesn't bother me at all. I use anything and I don't really care whether people think it's credible or not, or if I'm credible to do it. If it suits me I do it."

Paul had recently been reading *Homage To Catalonia*, George Orwell's report from the front line in the Spanish Civil War. In it, Orwell describes his arrival in Barcelona and his own vision of democratic socialism at work. Paul related to this and said, "There is a lot of talk of an egalitarian society where all people are equal but this was it, actually in existence, which, for me, is something that is very hard to imagine." 'Start' is Paul's adaptation of Orwell's story.

Although The Jam now had a strong fan base, they were still yet to have a number one album. 'Start' was the only official single from *Sound Affects*, which crashed into the album chart at number two, but was unable to dislodge Abba's *Super Trouper*. 'That's Entertainment', which was also on the album, became the first single to chart on import and reached number 21.

The Jam

After rushing home from the record store with a copy of 'Start', some fans were a little miffed when they heard The Village People's 'Can't Stop The Music' coming from their stereo instead. This was due to a mispressing and the disgruntled fans quickly got their copies exchanged.

466 Kelly Marie
Feels Like I'm In Love

Label & Cat No.: **Calibre Plus 1**
Producer: **Peter Yellowstone**
Writer: **Ray Dorset**
Date Reached No.1: **13 September 1980**
Weeks at No.1: **2**

RAY DORSET IDOLISED ELVIS PRESLEY. He'd recorded a version of Elvis' 'Baby Let's Play House' on his eponymous album in 1970. Ray remembered, "I wrote 'Feels Like I'm In Love' in 1977 with Elvis Presley in mind and even recorded it Elvis-style on my demo. My producer, Barry Murray, was about to send it to Elvis when we got a phone call saying Elvis had died. After that, I kinda put it to bed for a while."

"Kelly Marie had a few minor hits in France and had been hanging around our office a bit. I thought she had a good voice," remembered Ray. "So I asked her if she wanted to record the song." It was issued on Pye Records in February 1979 and was a major club hit in the north of England. Ray continued, "I was in a club in Leeds and gave the DJ a copy of the track. He said he liked it and asked if he could keep it. A few weeks later it started to sell steadily."

In January 1980 Pye Records launched their imprint label, Calibre. It initially specialised in soul acts such as Freeeze, Tony Rallo & The Midnight Band and B.T.Express. After five releases, nothing had made the Top 30 so they decided to re-issue 'Feels Like I'm In Love' on that label and it went to number one.

Kelly Marie was born Jacqueline McKinnon in Paisley, Scotland on October 23, 1957. At the age of 15, she entered the television talent show *Opportunity Knocks* under the name Keli Brown and won it four times. She had success in Europe in the late Seventies and was awarded a gold disc for the single 'Who's The Lady With My Man'.

Although she had three other UK hits, 'Loving Just For Fun' (21), 'Hot Love (22) and 'Love Trial' (51), it's 'Feels Like I'm In Love' that get the crowds going in the clubs of Europe where she still performs.

467 The Police
Don't Stand So Close To Me

Label & Cat No.: **A&M AMS 7564**

Producers: **Nigel Gray / The Police**

Writer: **Sting**

Date Reached No.1: **27 September 1980**

Weeks at No.1: **4**

"IT'S AN IMAGINARY STORY, BUT IT'S A real situation. I know because I taught, briefly, in a secondary school while I was training and some of those young girls can be very attractive. The boys want to kick the shit out of you and all the young girls want to fuck you," said Sting. "Although I did think about it, I wasn't guilty of deflowering any virgins."

'Don't Stand So Close To Me' was the first track from their third album, *Zenyatta Mondatta* and gave the Police their first Top 10 hit in the US. At home, it became only the second single of the decade to enter the chart at number one, after The Jam's 'Going Underground'. The accompanying video was set in a classroom with Sting playing a teacher, wearing a black Victorian gown and angel's wings and holding a cane. The song tells the story of a schoolgirl's crush on her schoolteacher and the inspiration came from the novel *Lolita* by Vladimir Nabakov.

The working relationship between Sting and Copeland was becoming increasingly strained and they were constantly at each other's throats. It got so bad that eventually every time the two started to row, Andy Summers would hold some tape over their heads and continually chant 'I am nothing' until they stopped. Copeland admitted in an interview with *Revolver* magazine in 2000, that when he gets uptight, he just thinks about 'I am nothing' and it calms him.

In 1986 when *Every Breath You Take – The Singles* was released, The Police re-recorded the song, this time with more of an uptempo soft rock beat, and called it 'Don't Stand So Close To Me 86'. It was released as a 'new' single to promote the album, but the public weren't keen. Although the album went to number one, the single only reached number 24.

468 Barbra Streisand
Woman In Love

Label & Cat No.: **CBS 8966**

Producers: **Barry Gibb / Albhy Galuten / Karl Richardson**

Writers: **Barry Gibb / Robin Gibb**

Date Reached No.1: **25 October 1980**

Weeks at No.1: **3**

IT WAS A CASE OF BEING IN THE RIGHT place at the right time for both Barbra Streisand and Barry Gibb. Barbra had attended a Bee Gees concert at Los Angeles' Dodger Stadium. Barry, who had achieved recent success with 'Emotions' (Samantha Sang), 'If I Can't Have You' (Yvonne Elliman), 'More Than A Woman' (Tavares) and the title track from the multi-million selling film soundtrack, *Grease* (Frankie Valli), was looking for a new project. He was a Barbra Streisand fan anyway and, although nervous, relished the chance to work with her. Barry recalled, "She has a reputation as a tough lady. She knew what she wanted and I knew what I wanted. We trod on eggshells, until we got to know one another but once we began everything was OK. She's a true professional and a very nice lady."

Barbra was born in Brooklyn, New York in 1942. She got her showbiz break in 1962 in the Broadway show *I Can Get It For You Wholesale*. Two years later, she won the lead role in *Funny Girl* on Broadway and starred in the movie version (for which she won an Oscar) in 1968. She later went on to direct, produce and star in movies like *Yentl, Nuts* and *Prince Of Tides*.

As a child, her father used to tell her she couldn't sing but Barbra was determined to prove him wrong. Although she first broke into the UK charts in 1966 with 'Second Hand Rose', her biggest successes came in the Seventies with the film themes *The Way We Were* and 'Evergreen' from *A Star Is Born*. The success of 'Woman In Love' overtook most people's expectations. The album *Guilty,* which was named after a song written at the last minute to replace one that Barbra didn't think worked, became her biggest seller to date. It was number one in 12 countries and has, so far, sold over 12 million copies worldwide.

469 Blondie
The Tide Is High

Label & Cat No.: **Chrysalis CHS 2465**

Producer: **Mike Chapman**

Writer: **John Holt**

Date Reached No.1: **15 November 1980**

Weeks at No.1: **2**

IN THE SPACE OF FIVE YEARS, BLONDIE, who had started out as a new wave/punk outfit at the CBGBs club scene in New York, had moved through disco and were covering reggae songs. It also indicated that Debbie and Chris had been listening to a lot of black music, which showed on the latest album *Autoamerican*. This was proved, when the next single, 'Rapture' reflected their move into the rap scene. When 'Rapture' topped the US chart, it became the first rap record to do so.

For the next single, 'The Tide Is High', a cover of a Paragons' song from 1967, saw them reunited with producer Mike Chapman. "I first heard 'The Tide Is High' on a compilation tape that someone had given to me whilst we were in London," Debbie explained. "Chris (Stein) and I both fell in love with the song and decided it was too good to resist." They wanted to give the song a Jamaican feel, so they hired three percussion players and created a new string and horn arrangement to give it an authentic sound.

Following his own hit, 'Help Me Make It Through The Night' (6, 1974), John Holt has had more success as a writer than a performer with hits covered by Errol Dunkley ('OK Fred'), Musical Youth ('Tell Me Why') and UB40 ('Wear You To The Ball'), all of which made the Top 40.

Blondie missed out on the chance of recording a James Bond theme. They were offered 'For Your Eyes Only' but Debbie didn't like the lyrics. She then wrote her own song for the film, but Bond producer, Albert R. Broccoli, didn't like it, so the partnership ended there and Sheena Easton got the gig.

470 Abba
Super Trouper

Label & Cat No.: **Epic EPC 9089**

Producers: **Björn Ulvaeus / Benny Andersson**

Writers: **Björn Ulvaeus / Benny Andersson**

Date Reached No.1: **29 November 1980**

Weeks at No.1: **3**

ABBA'S FINAL UK NUMBER ONE CAME just as Benny and Frida were about to announce their divorce. Despite Benny and Björn having broken marriages, they continued to write and record lyrically brilliant songs. But it was looking increasingly likely that Abba's days were numbered with both couples leading increasingly separate lives.

Although the *Super Trouper* album was considered a completed project by mid-1980, there was no song on the album with that title. At the last minute, both Benny and Björn were inspired to write a song that they later considered 'a cut above the rest'. As Björn sat down to write the lyrics, he found the album's title fitted perfectly. A 'Super Trouper' is a huge spotlight used at stadium concerts.

Following 'Super Trouper' they managed just two more Top 10 hits; the disco flavoured 'Lay All Your Love On Me' and the song that was probably their most poignant insofar as it reflected the state of their relationships, 'One Of Us'. March 1980 saw their final concert appearance in Japan, followed by some TV appearances in Sweden in 1981 and '82.

After Abba's demise, Benny and Björn linked up with lyricist Tim Rice to write the successful musical *Chess*, which spawned the chart topping 'I Know Him So Well' for Elaine Paige and Barbara Dickson and the number 12 hit, 'One Night In Bangkok' by Murray Head. Agnetha loved Barbra Streisand's album, *Guilty* and there was talk of her working with its producer, Barry Gibb, but that plan fell through when she refused to work in Miami, where Barry resided. Instead, she began working with British producer Mike Chapman and released the solo album *Wrap Your Arms Around Me*. She also made her acting debut in the Swedish film *Raskenstam*. After penning a none-too revealing autobiography, she became a recluse, refusing all interview requests and dodging photographers when seen in public. Frida, the only member of Abba who genuinely loved performing on stage, sold her interest in the group and moved to the UK to pursue a solo career, releasing the album *Something's Going On*, produced by Phil Collins. A second solo album, *Shine*, only scraped into the charts and thereafter she retired from public life, appearing only at the occasional charity show in Sweden. In 1998 she suffered personal tragedy when her 31-year-old daughter, Lise-Lotte, died in a car crash. The following year, she lost her third husband, (German Prince) Ruzzo Reuss von Plauen after a long illness.

In December 1999 Westlife's chart topping cover of Abba's Christmas 1979 hit, 'I Have A Dream', gave Björn and Benny their 12th number one as song writers, putting them third on the list behind Paul McCartney (29) and John Lennon (30).

In 2004 the reclusive Agnetha announced she was making a comeback. She released *My Colouring Book*, an album of covers that included 'Sealed With A Kiss', 'Past, Present And Future' and 'What Now My Love'. The two hit singles were 'If I Ever Thought You'd Change Your Mind' (11), originally recorded by Cilla Black and 'When You Walk In The Room' (34).

It was also the year Abba celebrated the 30th anniversary of winning Eurovision. To celebrate, Polydor issued 'Waterloo' on a CD single and a limited edition seven-inch, which made number 20. Both included the original B-side, 'Watch Out'. A party was held in London, but bizarrely Agnetha did not appear. Björn said, "It's a shame, it is never going to happen again. People haven't seen us as a group since 1981 and it would come as a disappointment to them." The following week, Abba's Polar Studios in Stockholm closed and a number of items were put up for auction including two stools signed by Frida and Agnetha, a 'Chiquitita' gold disc and a mandolin that was used on 'Fernando'.

471 John Lennon
(Just Like) Starting Over

Label & Cat No.: **Geffen K 79186**

Producers: **John Lennon / Yoko Ono / Jack Douglas**

Writer: **John Lennon**

Date reached No.1: **20 December 1980**

Weeks at No.1: **1**

AFTER A FIVE YEAR ABSENCE FROM THE recording studio, John Lennon and Yoko Ono returned to public life with an album, *Double Fantasy*, which was released in November 1980. It was an optimistic, happy album featuring alternate cuts by John and Yoko as John had told the label owner, impresario David Geffen, "We have to take care of Yoko. You and I have what we set out to get, but Yoko has never got the respect she deserves."

Despite the opening Japanese wishing bell, '(Just Like) Starting Over' was one of John's tracks with a defiantly old-fashioned, rockabilly stance. John called himself Elvis Orbison when he recorded it. Maybe it was not the strongest track to release as a single but Geffen thought it best to return to the airwaves with something retro.

On the evening of December 8, 1980, as John and Yoko were returning from the Hit Factory studio to their home in the Dakota Building on New York's Westside, a deranged Beatle fan stepped out of the shadows and fired five shots into John from his .38-calibre revolver. John died in the back of a police car *en route* to the nearest emergency hospital.

'(Just Like) Starting Over' was going down the charts on at the time of the killing. The next week it was number one.

The song also reached number one in the US, again posthumously, and stayed there for five weeks. It was Lennon's second US number one as a solo artist as 'Whatever Gets You Thru The Night', which meant little in the UK, was the first in 1974. '(Just Like) Starting Over' told of a couple who wanted to recapture the love of their youth – a bit like renewing your wedding vows – but John and Yoko also considered it a song for the Eighties as men and women had been in conflict in the Seventies and this had destroyed family life.

472 St Winifred's School Choir
No One Quite Like Grandma

Label & Cat No.: **Music For Pleasure FP 900**

Producer: **Peter Tattersall**

Writer: **Gordon Lorenz**

Date Reached No.1: **27 December 1980**

Weeks at No.1: **2**

PRIOR TO THEIR CHRISTMAS NUMBER one in 1980, the children from the St Winifred's School in Stockport, Greater Manchester, had appeared on another chart-topper, backing Brian and Michael on 'Matchstalk Men And Matchstalk Cats And Dogs' in 1978.

Having had a taste of success, the headmistress, Sister Aquinas gave her consent for the children to record another song. The choir mistress, Miss Foley, rounded up the best boys and girls and set to work. The song was recorded at 10cc's Stockport's Strawberry Studios and featured Rick Wakeman on keyboards. All the royalties went to the St Winifred's school fund.

Miss Foley picked eight-year old, Dawn Ralph to be the lead singer, which was an unusual choice because most of Dawn's front teeth were missing which gave her a lisp. The group travelled to London to appear on *Top Of The Pops*. There, they met Abba, who invited them to support them on their UK tour.

"I penned the song originally for HM the Queen Mother's 80th birthday and was disappointed, to say the least, when the record company decided to delay its release until Christmas of that year," remembered the song's writer, Gordon Lorenz. "I was not to know at the time that the single would become the Christmas number one and sell one million copies, but it certainly helped to ease the disappointment at missing out on the Queen Mother's birthday."

The song entered at number 47 and surged up the chart. Tragedy struck the week it reached number two when the world learned of the murder of John Lennon. At the time, not really knowing who John Lennon was, the young performers were more concerned about not having a number one than the ex-Beatle's untimely death. It didn't look like they were going to get it. A week later, John's '(Just Like) Starting Over', which was already on the way down the chart, rebounded from 21 to number one, leaving the kids in second place. John Lennon'scomeback album, *Double Fantasy*, which had already been on the chart for five weeks, was selling well so less people bought the single. The following week was Christmas and it went to number one after children up and down the country bought a copy for their grandma. They stayed there for a fortnight. After that, the kids grew up and never troubled the chart again.

Incidentally, Sally Lindsay who plays barmaid Shelley Unwin in *Coronation Street* was a former member of the choir.

473 John Lennon
Imagine

Label & Cat No.: **Parlophone R 6009**

Producers: **John Lennon / Yoko Ono / Phil Spector**

Writer: **John Lennon**

Date reached No.1: **10 January 1981**

Weeks at No.1: **4**

THE *IMAGINE* ALBUM IN 1971 HAD followed the intense John Lennon / Plastic Ono Band, and Paul McCartney told *Melody Maker*: "'Imagine' is what John is really like. There was too much political stuff on the other album." Lennon didn't want McCartney's patronage and snarled back, "So you think 'Imagine' isn't political. It's 'Working Class Hero' with sugar on for conservatives like yourself."

The song, 'Imagine' is John's declaration of hope for himself and the world. It was based on a poem of Yoko Ono's: the words are simple, the message is strong and the short lyric is sung slowly and hypnotically. The promotional film was shot in the Lennons' white room and the piano they sat at was purchased by George Michael and presented as a permanent loan to The Beatles Experience in Liverpool.

When John performed the song at an expensive cabaret for Lord Grade and his

John and Yoko

friends, he changed the lyric from "Imagine all the people sharing all the world" to "Imagine all the people sharing all the wealth."

'Imagine', which made number five in 1975, topped the charts in 1981 and became an anthem. If any one song could sum a complicated person like John Lennon, this is it.

474 John Lennon
Woman

Label & Cat No.: **Geffen K 79195**

Producers: **John Lennon / Yoko Ono / Jack Douglas**

Writer: **John Lennon**

Date reached No.1: **7 February 1981**

Weeks at No.1: **2**

JOHN LENNON REGARDED 'WOMAN' AS the Beatle track on his LP, *Double Fantasy* and he called it the Eighties update of 'Girl', a track on *Rubber Soul*. The song and the performance were so strong that it probably would have made number one anyway, but, following John's killing, it was the third of his singles to hit the top. Paul McCartney, under the pseudonym of Bernard Webb, had written a song called 'Woman' in 1966 and given it to Peter & Gordon. What's more, in 1972, Paul's brother, Mike, had recorded his own song called 'Woman' for the title track of an album.

John felt that women had often helped him and now he was apologising for his thoughtlessness and ingratitude. He told the session musicians, "It's for your mother or your sister, anyone of the female race. That's who you're singing to." The song was based on a phrase by Chairman Mao that women were "the other half of the sky", which contrasts with John's debunking of the Communist leader in 'Revolution'.

The main apology was reserved for Yoko Ono. He said, "My history of relationships with women is a very poor one, but real changes are coming. I have come a long way. I was the pig, and it is a relief not to be a pig anymore." His contentment is revealed in 'Woman'.

475 Joe Dolce Music Theatre
Shaddup You Face

Label & Cat No.: **Epic EPC 9518**

Producers: **Joe Dolce / Ian McKenzie**

Writer: **Joe Dolce**

Date Reached No.1: **21 February 1981**

Weeks at No.1: **3**

'SHADDUP YOU FACE' IS NOT ONLY considered one of the worst records of all time, but is also remembered for having kept Ultravox's 'Vienna' off the top spot.

Joe was born to Italian-American parents in Painesville, Ohio in 1947. In the late Seventies, he had taken a train journey from Ohio to California. To pass the time, he wrote some poetry and songs based on classic verses by his favourites authors, W.B. Yeats and Dylan Thomas. He also wrote 'Shaddup You Face' and based it on a typical Italian character.

In 1979 the Dolce family emigrated to Australia. It is there that Joe invented the Dolce Music Theatre Show, which included the character Guiseppi who wore a Chico Marx hat, played a miniature mandolin and had an annoying fake Italian accent.

The song was originally released in 1979 and topped the chart in Australia, Austria, Canada, Fiji, France, New Zealand, Ireland, Germany and Switzerland and made the top 10 in seven other countries – although surprisingly, not in Italy. It went on to sell over six million copies worldwide. Such was the appeal of this novelty song that it inspired over 50 cover versions in a variety of languages, including one from Andrew Sachs in full character of *Fawlty Towers*' hapless Spanish waiter, Manuel. There is even an Aborigine version that included dingoes yelping.

Joe still performs the song that gave him his three minutes and 14 seconds of fame. But it's not the only royalty cheque Joe receives. In 1984 Joe wrote a song called 'Intimacy' which was sung by his then girlfriend, Lin van Hek, and can be heard in the film *Terminator*.

The eponymous album that accompanied the single was a prodigious waste of plastic. As far as we know, it failed to chart in any country.

In recent years Joe has turned his attention to classical music and the writings of Sappho, Albert Schweitzer and Sylvia Plath, indicating there is a serious side to Joe. He once composed a song called 'Father', which dealt with the relationship with his violent father and his determination not to let the same thing happen in his own family.

476 Roxy Music
Jealous Guy

Label & Cat No.: **Polydor ROXY 2**

Producers: **Bryan Ferry / Rhett Davies**

Writer: **John Lennon**

Date reached No.1: **14 March 1981**

Weeks at No.1: **2**

WHILE PAUL MCCARTNEY WAS warbling 'Mother Nature's Son', John Lennon was working on 'Child Of Nature' and because of the similarity between the two titles, John's song was not used on *The Beatles [White Album]* (1968). He knew he had written a strong melody and indeed some good lyrics, but he reworked the song three years later for a track on his *Imagine* album, 'Jealous Guy', which revealed the insecurity beneath his macho posturing. The song could be taken as an apology to Cynthia or to Yoko or to both of them. The producer Phil Spector gave 'Jealous Guy' a very sympathetic arrangement, but surprisingly it was not released as a single.

When Bryan Ferry was promoting his album *The Bride Stripped Bare* (1978) in Japan, John Lennon came up to him in a departure lounge and told him that he was a great fan. Bryan responded by saying that he had always enjoyed his work and they hoped to meet again.

Bryan Ferry, the guitarist Phil Manzanera, saxophonist Andy Mackay and drummer Paul Thompson reformed Roxy Music in 1979.

The following year they were scheduled to perform on a German TV show on the day after John Lennon's killing. Electing to perform one of his songs, Bryan chose one of his favourites, 'Jealous Guy', a more inspired choice than David Bowie who chose 'Imagine' for his *Serious Moonlight* tour.

'Jealous Guy' was very well received so they recorded it as a tribute single and it gave both Roxy Music and Bryan Ferry their only number one, their previous best being; 'Love Is The Drug' (2, 1975) and 'Let's Stick Together' (4, 1976). Bryan Ferry sang 'Jealous Guy' at Live Aid with David Gilmour contributing a lyrical solo, and he still includes it in his set which, in a beautiful moment, features the whole audience whistling at the close.

477 Shakin' Stevens This Ole House

Label & Cat No.: **Epic EPC 9555**

Producer: **Stuart Colman**

Writer: **Stuart Hamblen**

Date Reached No.1: **28 March 1981**

Weeks at No.1: **3**

SHAKY WAS BORN MICHAEL BARRATT IN Ely, South Wales. In the late Sixties he formed the band Shakin' Stevens & The Sunsets, turning professional in 1969. They toured the London club circuit, colleges and universities throughout the UK and Europe, and gained a strong following, which led to them signing a contract with EMI's off-shoot label, Parlophone. These sessions were produced by Dave Edmunds. In 1972 they were voted Best Live Band in an *NME* poll. The band remained together until 1977.

Prior to the band breaking up, in 1976 Stevens signed as a solo artist to Track Records, who roster included Jimi Hendrix and The Who, and released two singles and an album. Although these received good music reviews, the releases failed to chart in the UK, although years later he was to learn that one had reached the Top 40 in Australia. In late 1977 Shaky, as he came to be known, was selected alongside P J Proby and Tim Whitnall, to play a tribute, in different stages of his life, in Jack Good's multi-award winning London musical, *Elvis*. Tim played him in his early career, Shaky in mid-career, and P.J. the Las Vegas period. All three were highly praised.

Shaky was then signed to Epic on a worldwide basis, by manager Chris Brough and Mike Hurst, and he then linked up with producer and former Pinkerton's 'Assort' Colours bass player, Stuart Colman. His recordings of 'Hot Dog' (featuring Albert Lee on lead guitar) and 'Marie, Marie', originally recorded by The Blasters, had already been moderate hits. Although 'Marie, Marie' was a huge hit throughout Europe, Shaky wanted to top the chart in the UK. "I heard a version of 'This Ole House' by the NRBQ (New Rhythm and Blues Quartet)," said Stuart. "Most people think that Shaky's version is based on Rosemary Clooney's, but it isn't." Shaky heard the NRBQ version, which made him want to record the song. His rendition of this classic song stayed in the UK charts for 17 weeks, and was a huge international hit.

'The Ole House' was written in 1954 by gospel and country singer/songwriter, Stuart Hamblen. Stuart Hamblen released his recording of the song in 1954, the same year Rosemary Clooney and Billie Anthony also released their versions of this country song. Billie's version reached number four, whilst Rosemary Clooney went to number one. Jim Reeves, Johnny Cash, Elvis and Don Gibson have all recorded Stuart Hamblen's songs, and in 1970 he was inducted into the Rock'n'Roll Hall Of Fame.

Shaky's new band were: Mickey Gee (guitar), Roger McKew (rhythm guitar), Geraint Watkins (piano), Stuart Colman (bass) and Howard Tibble (drums). Although the album was originally called *Marie, Marie*, it was re-named *This Ole House*, and went to number two.

478 Bucks Fizz Making Your Mind Up

Label & Cat No.: **RCA 56**

Producer: **Andy Hill**

Writers: **Andy Hill / John Danter**

Date Reached No.1: **18 April 1981**

Weeks at No.1: **3**

ABBA DID IT FIRST IN 1974, BROtherhood Of Man did it next in 1976 and Bucks Fizz did it again in 1981. Did what, you ask? Adopt a two boy, two girl line-up, perform an upbeat song with a catchy easy-to-remember chorus, enter the Eurovision song contest, and win. At the time, Bucks Fizz were described as Britain's answer to Abba but the four individuals had nothing like the experience of Abba, nor did they write and produce their own material.

Bucks Fizz were Mike Nolan, Bobby G (born Robert Guppy), Jay Aston and Cheryl Baker (born Rita Crudgington). They were hand picked by songwriter Andy Hill and music publisher, Nichola Martin, who later became their manager. On stage, Bucks Fizz, who Nichola named after her favourite drink, were all blond, roughly the same height and dressed in bright colours.

The contest was held at the Royal Dublin Society Hall in Ireland that year. While the judges were making their minds up, the band weren't too confident. Mike Nolan recalled, "On the night, I was 100 per cent sure we were gonna walk it, until the voting started. Austria were voting first and only gave us four points: that's when my stomach just went down and I thought we'd blown it." In the end, their 136 points, just four points ahead of Germany, sealed their victory.

The most memorable part of their performance was when it came to the line, 'But if you wanna see some more'. That was when the guys ripped the girls' knee-length skirts off only to reveal mini skirts. As Bobby Gee recalled, "After that performance, I think we re-invented Velcro." Radio Two DJ, Terry Wogan, who became the BBC's official commentator for the contest a year earlier recalled, "Someone

suggested that one of the girls wasn't wearing any knickers. That is so Irish."

It was Cheryl's second stab at Eurovision. She had been a member of the 1978 UK entry, Co-Co where their song, 'The Bad Old Days', came 11th.

479 Adam & The Ants Stand And Deliver

Label & Cat No.: **CBS A 1065**

Producer: **Chris Hughes**

Writers: **Adam Ant / Marco Pirroni**

Date Reached No.1: **9 May 1981**

Weeks at No.1: **5**

At the time of their first chart topper, Adam and his Ants should have been celebrating. They were, but their joy was dampened by two impending court cases. Adam had started proceedings against his previous record company, Decca, to prevent them from releasing material recorded before they signed to CBS. Then the group's former manager, Falcon Stewart, issued a writ seeking 20 per cent of the group's earnings up until January 1981.

Adam was born Stuart Goddard in 1954. His father was a chauffeur and his mother was Paul McCartney's house cleaner in the Seventies. He said, "I decided to change my name because it suited me better. That's like Indians, too. They didn't name their children until they reached puberty. That way they would be given a name to fit their character."

In 1975, while at college, he joined Bazooka Joe & His Rhythm Hot Shots. A year later he answered an ad in *Melody Maker* to join a band called The B-Sides. They recorded a punk version of 'These Boots Are Made for Walking' then promptly disbanded. Adam then formed the first version of the Ants with ex-B-Sides members, Lester Square (guitar), Andy Warren (bass) and Paul Flanagan (drums). Adam assumed that if an insect-related name worked for The Beatles, it could work for him, too. They played their first gig at London's St Martin's School Of Art and were supported by The Sex Pistols.

He discovered Malcolm McLaren's *SEX* boutique in the King's Road and not seemingly making much headway with the band, asked McLaren for assistance. McLaren promptly sacked Adam and used the Ants for his new project, Bow Wow Wow.

Later the same month, Adam recruited a new band comprising Adam (vocals/guitar), Marco Pirroni (guitar), Merrick (born Chris Hughes) (drums) and Kevin Mooney (bass). A year later, Mooney was replaced by ex-Roxy Music bassist Gary Tibbs. Terry Lee Miall was brought in as the group's second drummer to create the African tribal rhythms. Their first CBS hit, 'Kings Of The Wild Frontier' made little impact. This was followed by the Zulu Warrior-inspired 'Dog Eat Dog' (4) and 'Antmusic' (2). "'Ant music is for sex people', was an expression Adam loved," Marco claimed. "It just rolled off the tongue. Madness invented the Nutty sound, we had the Ant sound."

A re-issue of 'Kings Of The Wild Frontier' followed and got to number two. Following that came their first number one, 'Stand and Deliver'. Adam said, "It's just stealing peoples attention. I'm a very big history fan of certainly the Georgian era and I like the flamboyance and sexuality and the bawdiness of the time. I've seen films like *Tom Jones* and I grew up going to Saturday morning pictures and seeing all these other influences. I put them all together and 'Stand And Deliver' was just purely grabbing peoples attention and using the whole sort of classical English highwayman feel as a theme."

"The idea of the 'Stand And Deliver' video was to create a Hollywood movie in three minutes," Adam explained. The Mike Mansfield-produced video contained a hanging sequence that was considered too violent by some programme producers. Most music programmes refused to show it, so an edited version was issued which excluded the scene altogether.

Adam & The Ants were the hottest band of 1981 and kids everywhere painted a white strip across their nose and crossed their arms in front of their face, in an effort to copy their idol.

In 2003 Adam joined forces with the Dian Fossey Gorilla Fund to help save mountain gorillas from extinction. He re-recorded 'Stand And Deliver' as 'Save The Gorilla' with all proceeds being donated to the fund.

480 Smokey Robinson Being With You

Label & Cat No.: **Motown TMG 1223**

Producer: **George Tobin**

Writer: **Smokey Robinson**

Date Reached No.1: **13 June 1981**

Weeks at No.1: **2**

In 1972, having spent 12 years as the lead singer of The Miracles, Smokey Robinson decided to quit. His heart was no longer in it. They had just completed a tour and Smokey had announced Billy Griffin as the new lead vocalist of The Miracles.

Smokey described his last night on stage with The Miracles; "I went out onstage and although I'd been trying to quit for years, a sadness engulfed me, an awesome feeling of loss and regret. I was being bubbly for the fans, singing and dancing, but I was dying on the inside, feeling like a character in 'Tears Of A Clown'." The last song they performed was 'Going To A Go-Go'.

Smokey took a year off before embarking on a solo career. During the Seventies 'Just My Soul Responding' was his only UK hit. In the US he had a dozen, none of which made the Top 20. The Miracles had one top 10 hit in 1976 with 'Love Machine' which was covered in 2004 by Girls Aloud.

In 1980 Kim Carnes covered an old Miracles song called 'More Love' which brought Smokey some royalties. He was pleased with the version and wrote 'Being With You' for her. After contacting her producer, George Tobin, Smokey discovered he was no longer working with her. Tobin requested a listen and on first hearing, suggested Smokey record it himself with Tobin as producer.

'Being With You' topped the UK chart but

stalled at number two in the US, ironically behind Kim Carnes' 'Bette Davis Eyes'.

In 1976 George Harrison, on his album *Thirty-Three & ⅓*, paid tribute to Mr Robinson on the track 'Pure Smokey'. In 1987, the same year he was inducted into the Rock And Roll Hall Of Fame, ABC did likewise on the hit 'When Smokey Sings'. Two years later, he received a Grammy Living Legend Award.

481 Michael Jackson
One Day In Your Life

Label & Cat No.:	**Motown TMG 976**
Producer:	**Sam Brown III**
Writers:	**Sam Brown III / Renee Armand**
Date Reached No.1:	**27 June 1981**
Weeks at No.1:	**2**

IN 1981 MICHAEL JACKSON STILL HAD black skin, an afro and his own nose. As The Jackson 5, Michael, with his brothers, recorded a plethora of material while signed to Motown in the late Sixties and early Seventies. Michael and The Jacksons signed separate contracts with Epic Records in 1976, thus allowing Michael, as he did at Motown, to record independently from his brothers. But Motown retained the rights to the Jackson 5's back catalogue.

Michael, born in Gary, Indiana in 1958, was the seventh of nine children. He had an impoverished background. His father was very strict and often beat Michael and his brothers during rehearsals when they didn't get it right. His early solo hits, 'Got To Be There', 'Rockin' Robin', 'Ain't No Sunshine' and 'Ben' all made the Top 10 but it wasn't until 1979, when he released *Off The Wall*, that his solo career really took off. 'Don't Stop 'Til You Get Enough', 'Off The Wall', 'Rock With You' and 'She's Out Of My Life' were all taken from the album and all gained high chart placings, but a fifth single, 'Girlfriend', written by Paul McCartney, missed the Top 40 altogether.

In the wake of this success, Motown Records cashed-in by remixing and re-releasing 'One Day In Your Life', a track from his 1975 album, *Forever, Michael*. It was a shrewd move as Michael's new record company had no new material scheduled and it gave Michael his long awaited first solo UK number one. Motown were happy because, by knocking Smokey Robinson's 'Being With You' out of the number one slot, it gave them back-to-back number ones.

Co-writer, Renee Armand is a Nashville-based songwriter and a former member of the white Motown trio, The Coyote Sisters with Marty Gwinn and Mama Cass' sister, Leah Kunkel. Renee recently admitted, "I've gone back to the way I started in the Sixties in San Francisco, singing jazz. I prefer live performance, and am writing a vocal piece called 'The Divine', about women's real thoughts about God."

The follow-up was another old Motown ballad, 'We're Almost There' but the label were unable to sustain the impact and it petered out at number 46. However, in 1984 Motown had another attempt at issuing Michael's old material and were awarded a Top 10 hit with 'Farewell My Summer Love'.

482 The Specials
Ghost Town

Label & Cat No.:	**2-Tone CHS TT 17**
Producer:	**John Collins**
Writer:	**Jerry Dammers**
Date Reached No.1:	**11 July 1981**
Weeks at No.1:	**3**

DURING THE SUMMER OF 1981 CIVIL unrest hit many big cities around the UK. Jerry Dammers' inspiration for the song came from scenes noted during their UK tour, as he recalled in an interview in *Mojo*, "In Liverpool, all the shops were shuttered up, everything was closing down. In Glasgow there were little old ladies on the streets selling their household goods – it was clear something was wrong." Dammers explained the wailing sirens at the start and end of the song, "They're supposed to sound a bit

middle eastern, like a prophecy of doom."

A police raid in the St Paul's area of Bristol sparked rioting which then spread to Toxteth in Liverpool, Brixton in south London and various other deprived inner city areas. Margaret Thatcher's right wing Tory government was halfway through its first term in office and while the Yuppie revolution was under way at one end of the social scale, those at the other end were already feeling the effects of Thatcher's cuts. Social unrest was everywhere, which made this Specials' single very timely indeed.

Just prior to 'Ghost Town' reaching the summit, Neville Staples, Lynval Golding and Terry Hall announced their resignation from the band. All three then formed The Fun Boy Three and notched up half a dozen hits in the early Eighties. Terry Hall then went on to form The Colourfield.

Jerry Dammers continued with Horace Panter, John Bradbury and newly recruited ex-Bodysnatchers lead singer, Rhoda Dakar. He also reverted to the band's original name, The Special A.K.A, and managed one further Top 10 hit in 1984 with 'Nelson Mandela', a song that urged for his release, before splitting up. A brief reformation in 1996 went unnoticed. Jerry Dammers was behind the free 1988 Artists Against Apartheid concert at Clapham Common and is now a DJ in the London area.

In 1995 Terry Hall released his 'Rainbows EP' with guest artists, Damon Albarn and Ian Broudie. On it there is a revamped, live version of 'Ghost Town' with rapper Tricky on lead vocals. But the eerie atmosphere of the original could not be recaptured.

483 Shakin' Stevens
Green Door

Label & Cat No.: **Epic EPCA 1354**

Producer: **Stuart Colman**

Writers: **Bob Davie / Marvin Moore**

Date Reached No.1: **1 August 1981**

Weeks at No.1: **4**

SHAKIN' STEVENS, FOLLOWED UP 'THIS Ole House' with an original song, 'You Drive Me Crazy', written by Ronnie Harwood, which went to number two and spent four weeks there behind Adam & The Ants' 'Stand And Deliver'. It was Nick Lowe, whom the band met in a pub during recording, who suggested this song could be a number one for Shaky. Shaky thought they'd had one too many, but decided to try it just for the kick. Nick Lowe was right, and it gave Shaky his second number one.

Jim Lowe was born in Missouri in 1927. In 1954 he was working as a DJ on a radio station in Chicago as well as writing and singing country songs. The following year he moved to New York where he continued his radio career, and signed with Dot Records. In 1956, in an apartment in Greenwich Village, he recorded 'Green Door'. Backed by The High Fives, and with a constant tick-tock throughout, it reached number one in the US and number eight here. The honky-tonk piano on it was played by the song's composer, Bob Davie.

Two other versions competed for chart honours: Glen Mason, who reached number 24, and Frankie Vaughan, who won by reaching number two. Frankie Vaughan's version was engineered by a young, up-and-coming Joe Meek. Vaughan gave all the royalties from his version to his favourite Boys Club Federation charity, which helped him as a boy.

How the door became green is anyone's guess. The song is based on a musician's club in Dallas, Texas, where all the young lads who weren't members and didn't have the union card couldn't get in so hung around outside, but the actual door in question was yellow.

484 Aneka
Japanese Boy

Label & Cat No.: **Hansa HANSA 5**

Producer: **Neil Ross**

Writer: **Bobbie Heatlie**

Date Reached No.1: **29 August 1981**

Weeks at No.1: **1**

IN 1981 THE *NEW MUSICAL EXPRESS*' review of 'Japanese Boy' claimed the song sounded like Neddy Seagoon with his jaws wired together. Whatever, it sold by the bucket load. Aneka, who was born Mary Sandeman, had always aspired to enter the pop music world. She loved singing and was a respected Gaelic folk singer.

Bobbie Heatlie, former member of the Scottish rock band, The Headboys, was also Aneka's arranger. He said, "'Japanese Boy' was a complete accident. I'd been working with Mary on some Scottish folk albums, when she said to me that she'd love to have a bash at some pop songs. Now keep in mind that she was almost six feet tall, spoke in a frightfully posh voice and was the respectable wife of a small town GP with two children. I never thought in a million years that she had a chance of making it in the pop world. Anyway she kept pestering me, and I kept forgetting to write something for her, until one day she called me to say that the studio had been booked to record a song...that I hadn't written yet. To cut a long story short I wrote the chorus, and I threw the whole thing together by taking bits from other songs that I had written years before. It was recorded as a demo, and was turned down by every major company. Then the German company Hansa took it on and it went straight into the charts, and eventually number one all over the world. There was a massive panic as to what to do about her image. Then someone came up with the great idea of the wig and kimono. A complete transformation." Mary and her record company decided that her real name was not a good name to sing about an old Japanese boyfriend. So, sifting though the local phone directory in search of a suitable oriental name, she came across 'Anika'. She changed the middle letter and was ready for action."

Bobbie also recalled, "During an interview on the *Russell Harty* show, he asked her how she was enjoying fame as pop star. She replied in her very posh voice, 'We all rather think it's a bit of a hoot actually.'"

At the end of the day, she only wanted to chance her arm in the pop world and was rewarded with a number one hit. She reverted to her real name and returned to Gaelic singing. In 1992 she split with her husband, Dr Angus McKinnon, and promptly took a holiday with Angus' cousin, a Catholic priest named Father John McDonald. The couple claimed they were just friends, but the tabloids suggested otherwise.

She stills tours occasionally and is the featured singer with the Scottish Fiddle Orchestra and released a new solo CD in 2004. In 2003 she revealed, "I'm now studying the art of using the singing voice to heal people."

485 Soft Cell
Tainted Love

Label & Cat No.: **Some Bizzarre BZS 2**

Producer: **Mike Thorn**

Writer: **Ed Cobb**

Date Reached No.1: **5 September 1981**

Weeks at No.1: **2**

NORTHERN SOUL MUSIC IS ONE category that rarely gets recognised in the UK singles chart. But this 1964 northern soul classic was given the new romantic, synthesiser treatment and became the biggest selling single of 1981. "A mixture of cold electronics with an over passionate, over exuberant slightly out of key vocal," is how Almond described their version of the song.

Soft Cell were Marc Almond from Southport and David Ball from Blackpool. Although they were both from Lancashire, they met at Leeds Art College and began as a duo in October 1979. Marc said, "When I first met Dave, he was

Soft Cell, featuring David Ball (left) and Marc Almond, took Northern Soul to the top of the charts

working in a little studio in the art college and he was working with experimental, electronic synthesisers and keyboards. They were quite new, exotic instruments and people were starting to realise that you could make your own records with them. We wanted to be a guitarless band, a synthesiser duo. We were laughed at by some people and dismissed by others. A lot of the other bands around Leeds and in the art college were straight faced guitar bands making political statements, and we were looked on as rubbish, but we had the last laugh."

'Tainted Love' was Dave Ball's idea. Marc continued, "Dave introduced me to the record and I loved it so much and we wanted an interesting song for an encore number in our show. Dave loved northern soul and it was a novelty to have an electronic synthesiser band doing a soul song. When we signed with our record company, they wanted us to record it. They told us to put bass, guitar and drums on it as they said it was too odd. They put it out anyway and the next thing it was gathering radioplay and then it was number one. I was fascinated that it was originally by Gloria Jones, the girlfriend of Marc Bolan and I'd always been a T.Rex fan."

Gloria Jones never commented on the record but she probably wondered why her version wasn't the hit. 'Tainted Love', which was featured on the album *Non-Stop Erotic Cabaret*, and was written by former Four Preps singer Ed Cobb, who became a multi-millionaire just on the back of that song, spent 43 weeks on the US chart, a record at the time.

In Britain, they had further Top 10 hits with, 'Bedsitter', 'Say Hello, Wave Goodbye', 'Torch' and 'What'. By 1984 their releases were barely reaching the Top 20, so they split. Almond embarked on a solo career and despite having over 20 hits, only managed one Top 10 with 'The Days Of Pearly Spencer'. Ball formed The Grid and their biggest hit was 'Swamp Thing', which made number three in 1994. Marc Almond has constantly dropped hints of a reunion, but nothing has materialised yet. 'Tainted Love' remains a timeless classic and, when reissued in 1991 – just prior to its 10th anniversary – went back in the Top 10.

"The one thing that makes Dave and I cry about that single is that we didn't write it ourselves," said Marc. "Even if I could have had a fraction of the publishing profits, I would have been able to buy a mansion."

486 Adam & The Ants Prince Charming

Label & Cat No.: **CBS A 1408**

Producer: **Chris Hughes**

Writers: **Adam Ant / Marco Pirroni**

Date Reached No.1: **19 September 1981**

Weeks at No.1: **4**

ELABORATE COSTUMES, EMBROIDERED hair decoration and a pile of extensive make-up certainly captured the imagination and caught the nation's attention in 1981 and Adam Ant was doing it in public before Boy George. The accompanying video for 'Prince Charming' featured Swindon's most famous sex-siren, Diana Dors as the Fairy Godmother, and Adam in the title role.

"I was very interested in going back," said Adam. "I'd been reading the early Brothers Grimm fairytales which had always fascinated me. 'Prince Charming' is based on Beau Brummel, the British dandy leader of fashion in the 18th century. That and the French revolution when fashion for men were just exceedingly outrageous and everything was exaggerated and I felt that the early Eighties scene could certainly do with that." The crowd in the ballroom sequence was made up of Adam's friends and the famous chandelier swing and crash through the stained-glass window was done in just two takes.

Adam liked the idea of a famous female in his videos, so he invited Scottish actress/singer Lulu to appear in the follow up 'Ant Rap'.

Adam came in for some ridicule when he was accused of stealing the tune from Rolf Harris' 'War Canoe'. Adam said, "'War Canoe' is a traditional song but I'd had never heard Rolf's version. I've got a large collection of traditional ethnic music. We spoke to Rolf about it and we came to an amicable arrangement and I think we were both satisfied with the fact that we derived the idea from an original source."

Adam Ant

Adam, whose professional acting experience had stretched only to his band's appearance in the 1977 punk movie *Jubilee*, was offered a part in the London production of Gilbert & Sullivan's *The Pirates Of Penzance*. He declined the role explaining, "I've already been through that pirate stuff once." However, he attempted to break into acting and can been seen in the 1987 film *Slam Dance* and the 1988 film *World Gone Wild*. He also made cameo appearances in the television series' *The Equalizer* and *Northern Exposure*.

In 1982 he and Pirroni were named Songwriters Of The Year for 'Stand And Deliver' at the annual Ivor Novello Awards. But the fun of the group had gone for Adam. He said, "We were all so sick of each other. All we thought about was money, we didn't do it for the music and fun anymore, rehearsals were a mess. I just had to leave." He took his best friend, Marco, with him and within nine months, had his first solo number one, 'Goody Two Shoes'.

In 2002 Ant was arrested twice in two days for brandishing a gun in a north London pub, criminal damage and ABH. He was sectioned and legally confined under the 1983 mental health act. In April 2004 plans were put in place for a comeback nostalgia tour.

487 Dave Stewart with Barbara Gaskin It's My Party

Label & Cat No.: **Stiff BROKEN 2**

Producer: **David A. Stewart**

Writers: **Herb Weiner / Wally Gold / John Gluck Jr**

Date Reached No.1: **17 October 1981**

Weeks at No.1: **4**

NOT TO BE CONFUSED WITH THE guitarist from Eurythmics, this Dave Stewart is a former member of the non-charting group, Hatfield & The North. Their backing singers were known as the Northettes, one of whom was Barbara Gaskin.

Dave Stewart was born in London and in 1967 he formed his first band, Uriel with Steve Hillage. When Hillage left a year later they changed their name to Egg, but by 1972 the band had fallen apart and Stewart then successfully auditioned for Hatfield & The North.

Barbara Gaskin was born and bred in Hatfield, but moved to Canterbury to study for a degree in Philosophy. Whilst there she got involved in the Canterbury music scene and joined a folk band called Spirogyra. When Spirogyra split she went travelling for three years to pursue her interest in Eastern Philosophy. She returned to the UK in the early Eighties and linked up with Dave Stewart who was writing songs for ex-Yes drummer, Bill Bruford.

Many artists wanted to record 'It's My Party'. Helen Shapiro was the first during the Nashville sessions of 1963. The Shirelles recorded their version a few weeks later and whilst Phil Spector was recording a version with The Crystals, he learned that Mercury Records were rush releasing a version by a new singer, Lesley Gore. Lesley was discovered by Quincy Jones who heard her sing and recommended she be signed to Mercury Records. Once that was agreed, Quincy went over to Lesley's house with over 200 demos for her to listen to. The first one he played was Helen Shapiro's version of 'It's My Party'. Lesley's version topped the American singles chart and, in doing so, gave Quincy his first number one as a producer and a young Phil Ramone his first as an engineer. Lesley followed it up with the sequel, 'Judy's Turn To Cry', which also made the US Top five. Dave and Barbara's follow-up was 'Busy Doing Nothing', which Bing Crosby had recorded in the Fifties, but it failed to make the Top 40.

Dave and Barbara currently live together in south London and Dave has written two books, *The Musicians Guide To Reading And Writing Music* and *Inside The Music*.

488 The Police Every Little Thing She Does Is Magic

Label & Cat No.: **A&M AMS 8174**

Producers: **Hugh Padgham / The Police**

Writer: **Sting**

Date Reached No.1: **14 November 1981**

Weeks at No.1: **1**

HAVING RECENTLY RETURNED FROM A four-continent tour, the boys began work on their fourth album *Ghost In The Machine*. They were looking for a change of producer and it was XTC's lead singer, Andy Partridge, who recommended that they link up with their producer Hugh Padgham. They then headed off to George Martin's Air Studios on the Caribbean island of Montserrat.

The album's lyrical content reflected some of the sights and experiences they had witnessed on tour, especially the poverty and destitution of some of the poorer Western countries. The first single, 'Invisible Sun', which, like 'Every Little Thing She Does Is Magic', was written in 1976, was inspired by the rioting in Northern Ireland. The accompanying video, which depicted some terrible scenes, was deemed by the television authorities as unfit to broadcast. Even with such little television exposure, the song climbed up to number two.

The follow up, 'Every Little Thing She Does Is Magic', was a simple love song and the only track on the album not recorded in Montserrat (it was recorded in Canada), and was the most light-hearted on the album. In 1982 it won Best Pop Song at the annual Ivor Novello Awards.

The final single from the album, 'Spirits In The Material World', seemed to express Sting's political opinion, although he had said, "My songs are apolitical. I hate politics, I hate politicians and I hate the mess they've made of the world."

In 1982 Sting starred as Martin Taylor in the film version of *Brimstone And Treacle*, a remake of a 1976 television play written by Dennis Potter. Incidentally, Denholm Elliot appears as Mr Bates in both versions. It also spawned Sting's first solo single, a remake of Binnie Hale's 1929 song, 'Spread A Little Happiness'.

489 Queen and David Bowie Under Pressure

Label & Cat No.: **EMI 5250**

Producers: **Queen / David Bowie**

Writers: **Queen / David Bowie**

Date Reached No.1: **21 November 1981**

Weeks at No.1: **2**

IN 1979 QUEEN BOUGHT THE MOUNTAIN Studio in Montreux, Switzerland, so named because of its location, which overlooks Lake Geneva on one side and mountains on the other. As bass player John Deacon recalled "We were looking for a studio in England but the right thing never came up. Then we were in Mountain Studios and found out they were selling it, so we bought it."

Over the years, David Bowie and Queen's paths had crossed and David, who had a house near the studios, popped in one night during one of Queen's recording sessions. After the session, they began playing together and the next morning, when they listened back to the tape, they picked out 'Under Pressure' as the most promising track. As it was a one-off collaboration, the record needed a B-side and being a Queen recording session, the decision was made to put a Queen track on the flip, which was the non-album track 'Soul Brother'. Fortunately both acts were signed to EMI at the time, so there were no contractual problems to prevent the record being released.

The song entered the chart the same week that Queen's *Greatest Hits* album went to number one. Although 'Under Pressure' wasn't on the *Greatest Hits* album, it did appear on the American pressing, which was delayed due to the phenomenal success of 'Another One Bites The Dust', which sold over three million copies in the States alone.

It was only the second time in chart history that two former chart-topping artists had collaborated on another number one. The first occurrence was when Frank and Nancy Sinatra took 'Something Stupid' to the top in 1967.

490 Julio Iglesias
Begin The Beguine (Volver A Empezar)

Label & Cat No.: **CBS CBS A 1612**

Producer: **Ramon Arcusa**

Writer: **Cole Porter**

Date Reached No.1: **5 December 1981**

Weeks at No.1: **1**

WHETHER SINGING IN SPANISH, English, Portuguese, French or Italian, Julio Iglesias has the voice of romance and is blessed with the ability to make any woman feel that he was singing to her alone.

Julio was born in Madrid in 1943. He trained as a lawyer but had more interest in football and turned pro. He played in goal for the Real Madrid Junior Team, but a car accident, which left him partially paralysed, put paid to his football career. Whilst recovering, he turned to singing.

Having recovered, apart from a slouch, he wrote 'La Vida Sique Igual' which he performed at the 1968 *Spanish Song Festival*. It won him first prize and resulted in a recording contract.

On the strength of that, in 1970, he was asked to represent Spain in the Eurovision Song Contest. The self-penned song, 'Gwendolyne', tied with France for fourth place, some 24 points behind the winner – Dana.

Cole Porter wrote 'Begin The Beguine' in 1935 and it was first performed by June Knight on Broadway in *Jubilee*, a musical inspired by King George V and Queen Mary's silver anniversary. Over the years many versions have been recorded, including adaptations by Spanish-born violinist Xavier Cugat, Artie Shaw, Perry Como, Frank Sinatra, Ella Fitzgerald, Bing Crosby, Tom Jones and Dionne Warwick. If you search hard enough, you'll even find versions by Pete Townshend and Des O'Connor.

As Stephen Citron, in his book *Noel And Cole – The Sophisticates* (1992) observed: "Begin The Beguine' is a minor-key melody that is unmistakably Eastern Mediterranean, although it derives its rhythmic origin from French Martinique, and its melodic one from an Indonesian island'. It is generally danced to by specialists in rhumba, cha-cha and other South American steps." Porter, who invented the word Beguine, also wrote 'Let's End The Beguine' for Beatrice Lillie in 1944.

Julio once claimed to have made love to over 3,000 women. When asked to confirm this in a 1995 interview with the *Independent On Sunday*, he said, "I have sex every day I can and I love sex like every human being, but I don't have a number. I'll love women to the day I die." In 1984 Julio collaborated with Willie Nelson on 'To All The Girls I've Loved Before', which topped the US country chart.

Julio was the second Spanish act to top the UK singles chart, after Baccara. The third Spanish artist to achieve this feat was his son Enrique in 2002 and in doing so became the only father and son act to top the chart individually.

491 Human League
Don't You Want Me

Label & Cat No.: **Virgin VS 466**

Producer: **Martin Rushent**

Writers: **Jo Callis / Phil Oakey / Adrian Wright**

Date Reached No.1: **12 December 1981**

Weeks at No.1: **5**

SOFT CELL'S MARC ALMOND DESCRIBED 'Don't You Want Me' as, "The greatest record of all time. A beautiful operetta set to

electronic music."

Phil Oakey, who, like ABC's Martin Fry, is as much remembered for his lopsided wedge haircuts as for his music, was born in Sheffield in 1955. He left his job as a hospital porter to join Martyn Ware and Ian Craig-Marsh as lead singer in their band The Future. They soon changed their name to Human League – a name taken from the computer game *Star Force*.

During 1980, Craig-Marsh and Ware had left to form Heaven 17, so Oakey recruited Adrian Wright and Ian Burden and two teenage cocktail waitresses, Joanne Catherall and Susan Sulley. A year later, ex-Rezillos guitarist Jo Callis completed the line-up. They signed with Virgin but their first three singles failed to make the Top 40.

Adopting a slightly more commercial sound, they broke into the Top Ten in May 1981 with 'Love Action (I Believe In Love)' (3) followed by 'Open Your Heart' (16). The accompanying album, *Dare,* was produced by Martin Rushent who had previously worked with The Stranglers and The Buzzcocks.

Next came what was to be the album's most successful track, the call and response story, 'Don't You Want Me', which was inspired by the film *A Star Is Born*. Susan Sulley said "We didn't want to release that song, we tried hard to get Virgin not to release the record. We thought it was too commercial." But Virgin saw its potential and released it. Their 1984 hit, 'Louise' was written about the same two characters.

In 1964 America saw its first British invasion. In 1982 it saw its second. 'Don't You Want' Me' topped the US chart for three weeks and paved the way for other New Romantic British bands like Culture Club, Eurythmics and Dexys Midnight Runners.

'Don't You Want Me' returned to the Top 20 as a remix in 1995. It was also re-done in a spoof spoken word form for a 2002 TV advert for the Fiat Punto.

492 Bucks Fizz
The Land Of Make Believe

Label & Cat No.: **RCA 163**

Producer: **Andy Hill**

Writers: **Andy Hill / Pete Sinfield**

Date Reached No.1: **16 January 1982**

Weeks at No.1: **2**

ALTHOUGH NOT WRITTEN AS A Christmas song, 'The Land Of Make Believe' had a seasonal feel. It entered the chart in November, was highly placed throughout December and made the top long after the decorations had been taken down.

Few UK artists who top the charts with a Eurovision song go on to have much of a chart career, although will often appear in panto and end up in variety shows or oldies packages. Initially, it looked that way for Bucks Fizz. They followed 'Making your Mind Up' with 'Piece Of The Action (12) and then 'One Of Those Nights' (20). But Andy Hill had got together with an old friend, Pete Sinfield, to write this magical song that rescued Bucks Fizz from falling by the wayside. Sinfield was a founding member and lyricist with King Crimson. Pete recalled, "It is 10 times more difficult to write a three minute HIT song, with a veneer of integrity, than it is to write anything for King Crimson or Emerson, Lake & Palmer. But I half succeeded, for instance 'The Land of Make Believe' beneath its Tra la la's is a virulent anti-Thatcher song. Oh yes it is, something nasty in your garden, waiting, till it can steal your heart."

In December 1981 the Labour Party began parading around with badges advertising the logo 'The Tories have a worse record than Bucks Fizz'. The group personally asked party leader Michael Foot to withdraw the badges. Had they lost their sense of humour, we wonder? It did them no harm as 'The Land Of Make Believe' topped the chart a couple of weeks later.

The yuletide feeling was enhanced by the record's final moments in which the former Minipops singer Abby Kimber narrated a poem about Santa Claus.

493 Shakin' Stevens
Oh Julie

Label & Cat No.: **Epic EPCA 1742**

Producer: **Stuart Colman**

Writer: **Shakin' Stevens**

Date Reached No.1: **30 January 1982**

Weeks at No.1: **1**

IT WAS BECOMING A HABIT THAT EVERY other single Shaky released reached number one. He followed 'Green Door' with a new arrangement of Irma Thomas' 'It's Raining', which peaked at number 10. Then came 'Oh Julie', one of four hits together with numerous album tracks and B-sides that Shaky wrote himself.

"The idea just came to me while we were rehearsing in Nomis Studios in London, in January 1982," Shaky recalls. "I said to Geraint Watkins, my keyboards player at the time, 'bring your squeeze-box in tomorrow, I've got an idea for a song.' I wanted to write something with a Cajun feel, and I think we got pretty near to that, although these days when we do it on stage we give it even more of a Louisiana feel."

For the next album, *Shaky*, the idea was to record an album of songs consisting only of girls names. The album included the self-written 'Josephine' and covers of Billy Swan's 'Vanessa', Big Danny Oliver's 'Sapphire', and John Fred & the Playboys' 'Shirley'. "The premise was to appease as many (largely female) fan club members as possible," said producer, Stuart Colman. 'Oh Julie' was chosen as a single and it went to number one. "The name was not significant, it could have been any female name, but Julie just fits," Shaky explained.

'Oh Julie' became a massive international hit, and was later covered by Barry Manilow, who took it into the US chart.

Other tracks that weren't on this album included the hit 'Marie Marie', the non-charting follow-up 'Hey Mae', 'Lawdy Miss Clawdy' from the 'Blue Christmas' EP, 'Mona Lisa' from the *Shaky* album and 'Don't Be Late, Miss Kate' which was the flip side of 'I'll Be Satisfied'.

494 Kraftwerk
The Model / Computer Love

Label & Cat No.: **EMI EMI 5207**

Producers: **Ralf Hütter / Florian Schneider-Esleban**

Writers: **Ralf Hütter / Karl Bartos / Emil Schmitt**

Date Reached No.1: **6 February 1982**

Weeks at No.1: **1**

THE NUMBER OF ARTISTS INFLUENCED by Kraftwerk has been phenomenal: Jean Michel Jarre, David Bowie, Ultravox, New Order, Gary Numan, Eurythmics, The KLF and that's just for starters. Without Kraftwerk, songs like 'Blue Monday', 'Are Friends Electric' and 'What Time Is Love' might have sounded quite different. Kraftwerk, whose own style is based on recurring themes, are the real pioneers of today's dance music.

Formed in Düsseldorf in 1969 as Organisation, Kraftwerk comprised Ralf Hütter (electric organ), Florian Schneider-Esleben (flute and echo unit), Butch Hauf (bass), Basil Hammond (percussion) and Fred Monicks (drums). After one five-track album, *Tone Float*, Butch, Basil and Fred left to be replaced by Klaus Dinger (guitar and keyboards) and Thomas Homann (percussion). Again, after one album Klaus and Thomas left and Kraftwerk became a duo. In 1974 Klaus Roeder and Wolfgang Flür were recruited and they had their first UK hit with 'Autobahn' which, in order to get the car-on-the-motorway sounds, Hütter travelled on the autobahn with a tape recorder. The following year Karl Bartos replaced Roeder and Kraftwerk's final line-up was complete.

In 1977 David Bowie and Iggy Pop went to a Kraftwerk concert in Paris. They met the band a number of times after that and there was talk that Kraftwerk might become David's backing group.

Their image since 1978 has been that of motionless dummies. Their totally digital Kling Klang recording studio in Düsseldorf accepts no mail or phone communication. Ralf said, "We have codes if people need to get in touch with us in the studio."

'The Model', inspired by the untouchable Playboy-type models who worked at The Bagel nightclub in Cologne, first appeared on their 1978 album, *The Man Machine*. It can also be found on the B-side of 'Neon Lights'. The German DJs preferred 'The Model' to 'Neon Lights', but it made no impact outside Germany. In July 1981 Kraftwerk issued a new single, 'Computer Love'. EMI remembered 'The Model's' club potential in Germany and decided to release it with 'Computer Love' and promote it as a double A-side. Only 'Computer Love' initially received airplay and the single peaked at number 36. Within a few weeks, radio stations had flipped the single and began playing 'The Model'. EMI then repackaged the sleeve to show 'The Model' as the lead track.

Kraftwerk had further hits with 'Showroom Dummies' (1982), 'Tour De France' (1983), 'The Robots' (1991) and 'Aerodynamik' (2004). They reformed for an acclaimed tour in early 2004 and, as Ralf said in one radio interview, when asked how they went about recording new material, "We just press the red button."

495 The Jam
Town Called Malice / Precious

Label & Cat No.: **Polydor POSP 400**

Producers: **Pete Wilson / The Jam**

Writer: **Paul Weller**

Date Reached No.1: **13 February 1982**

Weeks at No.1: **3**

It was the title of Nevil Shute's novel, *A Town Called Alice*, that inspired the song's title, but the inspiration for the song comes from Paul's friend Dave Waller who had a way of describing an urban lifestyle. The song is about unemployment in a working town and Paul Weller confessed, "It could have been written about any suburban town, but was in fact written about my hometown of Woking."

The story was set to a faster beat than Paul really wanted and has a bass line reminiscent of The Supremes' 1966 hit, 'You Can't Hurry Love'.

The Jam were formed in Sheerwater, Surrey in late 1973. They comprised singer/guitarist Paul Weller, bass player Bruce Foxton and drummer Rick Buckler.

With 'Town Called Malice' / 'Precious' knocking off Kraftwerk's 'The Model' / 'Computer Love', it was the only time two consecutive double A-sides headed the chart. 'Precious' was an upbeat, funky jazz song with a new horn sound that Paul had recently discovered. The backing was reminiscent of Pigbag's recent instrumental, 'Papa's Got A Brand New Pigbag'.

The single was issued in a number of different formats, some including extra tracks or new mixes, thus ensuring the die-hard fans would lap it up and it would achieve a high chart placing. It worked, as the song entered at number one. EMI were up in arms about this and promptly launched an investigation because, not only had they just relinquished the top spot, it also prevented one of their biggest hits of the year, The Stranglers' 'Golden Brown' from reaching the top. The chart compilers *British Market Research Bureau* looked into the matter and decided nothing untoward had taken place.

In November 1981 The Jam won Best Group and Paul Weller won the Best Songwriter awards at the annual *NME* readers' poll.

On its first week at the top The Jam performed both tracks on *Top Of The Pops*. The only other time this had happened was in December 1965 when The Beatles did likewise with 'Day Tripper' and 'We Can Work It Out'.

The song was introduced to a new audience when it was featured in the 2000 film *Billy Elliot*.

496 Tight Fit
The Lion Sleeps Tonight

Label & Cat No.: **Jive JIVE 9**

Producer: **Tim Friese-Greene**

Writers: **Hugo Peretti / Luigi Creatore / George David Weiss / Solomon Linda / Paul Campbell**

Date Reached No.1: **6 March 1982**

Weeks at No.1: **3**

The fact that five composers are credited as writing this song offers some clue as to its complex origins. 'The Lion Sleeps Tonight' started life in 1939 as 'Mbube' (pronounced Eem-boom-beh), which translates as 'the lion' and was first recorded by Solomon Linda's Original Evening Birds. The same year, Solomon Linda (born Solomon Linda Ntsele), sold the song outright to record producer, Eric Gallo for 10 shillings, thus forfeiting the right to future royalties.

Miriam Makeba recorded a version in the Fifties, followed shortly after by an America folk group, The Weavers. They based their version on Makeba's, but changed the title to 'Wimoweh' because, to the untrained ear, Eem-boom-beh sounded like Wimoweh. In doing so, they added their collective pen name, Paul Campbell to the credits. Wimoweh is what the refrain sounded like to a non-native, but it has no meaning and is the English equivalent to shooby-dooby-doos.

Kraftwerk

Tight Fit

In 1960 the American doo-wop group, The Tokens, auditioned for Hugo Peretti and Luigi Creatore at RCA Records and did so with 'Wimoweh'. Hugo & Luigi liked the song but decided it needed new lyrics so, with George David Weiss, they added a 16-word translation and copyrighted it as a new composition, 'The Lion Sleeps Tonight'. The Tokens' version topped the US chart for three weeks and made number 11 in the UK. British singer, Karl Denver, under the title, 'Wimoweh', made the Top five in 1962 and Dave Newman, who decided to use both titles, had a minor hit in 1972.

Tight Fit, originally a group of session musicians, were formed in 1981. Their first single, 'Back To The 60s', was a medley of Sixties hits and reached number four. The follow-up, another medley, 'Back To The 60s – Part II' missed the Top 30 altogether. For the next single, they needed a new image and so recruited Steve Grant, Julie Harris and Denise Gyngell. Denise had failed an audition for Bucks Fizz, but all three were good looking and were employed for that purpose. However, none of them sang on the records – the vocals on 'The Lion Sleeps Tonight' were provided by former City Boy drummer Roy Ward.

In 1994 the song was featured in the award winning Disney film, *The Lion King*, for which Tim Rice and Elton John supplied most of the music. To complete its appearance in every decade, the Baha Men sampled Tight Fit's version in their 2001 Top 20 hit 'You All Dat'.

Solomon Linda died in 1962, but a provision in a 1911 British imperial copyright law states that all rights to a song revert to the composer's estate 25 years after his death. The Supreme Court in Pretoria has appointed an executor to Linda's estate who will attempt to recover the royalties for his two daughters who are living in poverty in Johannesburg. So in 2004 Disney found themselves being sued for £900,000 for using the song in both the film and the stage show versions of *The Lion King* without permission. "We intend going after anyone who is using the song. We started with Disney because they are the most active of the users," said Owen Dean, the South African advocate. In 2004 the matter was resolved with annual payments awarded to the two daughters.

497 Goombay Dance Band
Seven Tears

Label & Cat No.: **Epic EPC A 1242**

Producer: **Lochen Petersen**

Writers: **Wolff Eckehardt Stein / Wolfgang Jass**

Date Reached No.1: **27 March 1982**

Weeks at No.1: **3**

SOME 18 GERMAN ACTS HAVE CHARTED since 1952, but none of them reached number one until 1982, when, like buses, two came along together.

Oliver Bendt was born Jorgen Knoch in 1947 in the East German town of Potsdam, but grew up in Munich. He began acting at the age of four and by six, had joined a children's choir. In 1967, having completed two years of army service, he joined the German production of *Hair*, where he met his wife, Alicia. In 1971, having changed his name to the more pronounceable Oliver Bendt (actually pronounced 'bent'), he recorded 'Was Ich Tat, Tat Ich Nur Für Maria', the German version of Tony Christie's 'I Did What I Did For Maria'. On a similar theme, he also charted in Germany with 'Oh Marie'.

It was while the couple were holidaying in the Caribbean island of St. Lucia, enjoying the music and watching limbo dancers, that he had the idea to form a band. He said, "It was the wonderful feeling of freedom that the music and sunshine created and something I felt I could share with the world, so that's why I formed the Goombay Dance Band."

On returning to Germany, Oliver, along with Alicia, recruited Wendy Doorsen, Dorothy Hellings and Mario Slijngaard to complete the line-up. The Goombay Dance Band's early stage acts incorporated limbo dancing and included a fire-eating act performed by Oliver.

After 'Seven Tears' fell off the chart, they followed it up with an old track, 'Sun Of Jamaica'. Although it topped the chart in a number of European countries, it peaked at a rather dismal number 50 in the UK.

In 2000 Oliver claimed he was making a comeback and when asked what he would be doing, he replied, "I'd rather not talk about it now. When it happens everyone will know about it."

We're still waiting…

498 Bucks Fizz
My Camera Never Lies

Label & Cat No.: **RCA 202**

Producer: **Andy Hill**

Writers: **Andy Hill / Nichola Martin**

Date Reached No.1: **17 April 1982**

Weeks at No.1: **1**

FOR BUCKS FIZZ'S THIRD AND FINAL number one, Andy Hill wrote the music, but asked Nichola, to whom he was now married, to write the lyrics. The song tells the story of a jealous man, who suspects his lady is having an affair and has her followed.

The parent album *Are You Ready*? was their only Top 10 album. They followed 'My Camera Never Lies' with the partly acappella 'Now Those Days Are Gone'.

In 1984 just five minutes after leaving a gig in Newcastle, the coach in which Bucks Fizz were travelling collided with an articulated lorry. All the members suffered injuries. Mike Nolan was the worst affected – he was in a coma for four days after being thrown through the windscreen. Bobby G seemed to be fine at first, but the knock on his head brought on a brain haemorrhage. Both made a full recovery and later the same year, Bobby wrote the incidental music and recorded the theme to the TV series *Big Deal*.

In 1986 Jay Aston left in a blaze of publicity. According to newspaper reports, she attempted suicide and had an affair with the group's songwriter, Andy Hill. Other reports recounted an affair with their publicist. The remaining members auditioned 2,000 girls, of which Shelley Preston was chosen as her replacement. Cheryl Baker recalled, "I never got on with Jay, we were never friends. I was so happy when Shelley joined, at last I had a girl friend in the band." Preston then left in 1989 and the group continued as a trio.

Cheryl left the band in 1993 to concentrate on a career as a television presenter. Bobby and Mike wanted to carry on, so they recruited Heidi Manton and Amanda Szwarc. Bobby later married Heidi. By 1996 Nolan had had enough and left. He was replaced by former Dollar star, David Van Day. Nolan was not happy with his replacement and promptly formed his own rival touring group, also called Bucks Fizz.

499 Paul McCartney with Stevie Wonder Ebony And Ivory

Label & Cat No.: **Parlophone R 6054**

Producer: **George Martin**

Writer: **Paul McCartney**

Date reached No.1: **24 April 1982**

Weeks at No.1: **3**

One evening Paul McCartney was watching the most inventive of all British comedians, Spike Milligan, on TV. Spike was playing a segregated piano where the black and white keys were kept apart which demonstrated how one couldn't work without the other. Paul loved the concept and developed it into a song about racial harmony.

Once he had written 'Ebony And Ivory', Paul asked Stevie Wonder to record it with him and the single, as well as Paul's album, *Tug Of War*, was produced by George Martin at the AIR studios on the island of Montserrat. All the instruments were played by Paul or Stevie and they also cut another track for the album, a joint composition entitled 'What's That You're Doing'. Rather ridiculously, Motown would not permit Wonder to share full billing on the single with McCartney, hence the linking 'with', but it turned out to be Stevie's first UK number one.

'Ebony And Ivory' sounded like a hit single and Paul and Stevie did intend to make a video together. However, events got the better of them and they couldn't coordinate their diaries. In the end, they were filmed separately and the video was put together with technical wizardry.

500 Nicole A Little Peace

Label & Cat No.: **CBS CBS A 2365**

Producer: **Robert Jung**

Writers: **Ralph Siegel / Bernd Meinunger / Paul Greedus**

Date Reached No.1: **15 May 1982**

Weeks at No.1: **2**

By 1982 the Eurovision Song Contest may have been starting to lose its edge. Both France and Greece refused to take part, citing the contest as, 'A monument to drivel and mediocrity'.

It was the UK's turn to host the contest following Bucks Fizz's win the previous year. The venue was the Harrogate Centre in West Yorkshire, and Britain's entry was 'One Step Further' by Bardo, which came seventh.

West Germany's 17-year-old Nicole Hohloch was not a sure-fire favourite to win. Firstly, since Abba's win in 1974, the contest had become dominated by boy/girl combos and secondly, Germany had never won. The song's original German title was 'Ein Bibchen Frieden' and was a Seventies-styled folksy peace song. She recorded it in six different languages with the English title translating as 'A Little Peace'. It topped the charts all over Europe. On the Danish chart, she held the top two positions with the Danish-language version at number one and the German rendition at number two. With Johnny Logan (1980), Bucks Fizz (1981) and Nicole (1982), it was the only time that three consecutive winners all topped the singles chart.

Nicole was born in Saarbrücken in 1964. She signed with Jupiter Records in 1980 and her first release, the catchy titled, 'Flieg Nicht so Hoch Mein Kleiner Freund' ('Do Not Fly High My Small Friend'), topped the German charts for several weeks. It was fourth time lucky for writers Ralph Siegel and Bernd Meinunger – they had written the German entries for 1979, 1980 and 1981, and came fourth, second and second respectively. They came close again in 1987, when the German entry, 'Lass Die Sonne In Dein Herz' by Wind came second to Johnny Logan's 'Hold Me Now'.

Nicole married at the age of 20 and continues to record. In 2000 she released the album, *Abrakadabra*, which she wrote with Ralph Siegel.

501 Madness House Of Fun

Label & Cat No.: **Stiff BUY 146**

Producers: **Clive Langer /Alan Winstanley**

Writers: **Mike Barson / Lee Thompson**

Date Reached No.1: **29 May 1982**

Weeks at No.1: **2**

Without doubt, Madness were one of the biggest success stories of the Eighties, almost an institution. Such was the success of the 'Nutty boys' that they invented their own genre – The Nutty Sound. It was pure pop and every one of Madness' singles was instantly recognisable.

All hailing from north London's Camden district, they began as a ska revival band in 1976 as The Invaders, with Dikron as lead singer, but he was replaced in February 1977 by the charismatic Suggs (born Graham McPherson). By early 1979 the full line-up comprised Mike Barson (keyboards), Chris Foreman (guitar), Bedders (born Mark Bedford, bass), Chas Smash (born Cathal Smyth, horns), Lee Thompson (sax) and Woody (born

Daniel Woodgate, drums).

It was at the Hope And Anchor pub in nearby Islington, where they had gone to see The Specials, that Suggs and The Specials' lead singer, Jerry Dammers, struck up a friendship and he signed Madness to Dammers' own 2-Tone label.

After their debut hit, 'The Prince' (16), they signed with Stiff Records and had further hits with, 'One Step Beyond' (7), 'My Girl' (3), 'Baggy Trousers' (3) and 'It Must Be Love' (4). Chas Smash explained the story behind their only chart topper: "'House Of Fun' is about when you're a teenager and coming of age. You know, the difficulty of walking into a chemist and asking for a prophylactic for the first time. Madness, I suppose, tends to write songs about normal life. We just take a segment of everyday life and blow it up to cinematic proportions. I suppose the kind of things everyone can relate to." In the Eighties, a song about buying condoms was not one that radio programmers relished, but Madness quite cunningly disguised it with the lyric 'Box of balloons with the feather-light touch'.

In 1985 they launched their own Zarjazz Record label and their first signing was Feargal Sharkey. The following year they announced their split, with various members pursuing other projects. In February 1988 Suggs, Thompson, Foreman and Smyth reformed as The Madness, but the single, 'I Pronounce You' missed the Top 40. In 1992 they reformed again for two massive sell out concerts at London's Finsbury Park. The shows were recorded and released the following year as *Madstock – The Movie*. Madness fever never went away and in 1999, they were back in the Top 10 with 'Lovestruck'.

In October 2002 *Our House* – the musical opened in London and Suggs who, from April 2003 till it closed in August the same year, appeared in the show, said, "We would never authorise a biography about the band. We never saw one that got it quite right. But *Our House* is a new story that's not about us at all and we love it! We are really proud of it." In 2003 it won the Olivier Award for Best New Musical.

They followed their number one with five more Top 10 hits: 'Driving In My Car', 'Our House' (which became their only US Top 10 hit), 'Tomorrow's (Just Another Day)', 'Wings Of A Dove' and 'The Sun And The Rain'.

502 Adam Ant
Goody Two Shoes

Label & Cat No.: **CBS A 2367**

Producers: **Chris Hughes / Adam Ant / Marco Pirroni**

Writers: **Adam Ant / Marco Pirroni**

Date Reached No.1: **12 June 1982**

Weeks at No.1: **2**

"THE KEY TO THE ANTS SPLITTING UP was when Marco said he didn't want to tour anymore," admitted Adam. "I knew I couldn't put together another Ants without him and I wanted him to be happy because he was one half of 'Antmusic'," as the writing credit confirms.

"Although Gary Tibbs and Terry Lee Miall left amicably, the two hadn't been pulling their weight. The interest wasn't there anymore. Each night the sign outside might have said 'Adam & The Ants but onstage I almost felt I was on my own," Adam continued. "I ended up talking more to their lawyers and managers than them, that's when I decided to nip it in the bud."

Because it was a sudden decision by Adam to dissolve the band, some copies of 'Goody Two Shoes' were already pressed and credited to Adam & The Ants.

It was a complete change of lifestyle for Adam who wanted to become a household name with a clean image and a new public perception. He said: "'Goody Two Shoes' was a sort of answer back manifesto and just trying to keep things level-headed, because I felt that, and still do, to a degree, that going on stage is creating an illusion. It's magical and it's wonderful and I love doing it, but off stage there has to be time out." The lyric, 'When I saw you kneeling / crying words that you mean / opening the eyeballs / pretending that you're Al Green, Al Green' stemmed from when Adam saw Dexys Midnight Runners at the Old Vic in 1981. He said, "When I saw Kevin Rowland sing those words and really get into it, I think it was more honest than anything The Clash had ever done."

In 1983 Adam, having just cracked the US chart with 'Goody Two Shoes', was invited to perform at Motown Records' 25th anniversary. The idea was to bring in some white artists like Linda Rondstadt, Jose Feliciano and Adam Ant to broaden the label's appeal. Adam performed a version of 'Where Did Our Love Go', during which, unrehearsed, Diana Ross appeared on stage. The audience burst into spontaneous, rapturous applause. Adam thought it was for his performance, only to realise moments later that the ovation was not for him. Adam said, "Being on the show was like Hollywood with people like Jack Nicholson in the front row."

Two years later he was on the world's biggest stage – the Live Aid concert at Wembley. Adam remembered, "I was given three songs originally. I was going to do 'Stand And Deliver' and 'Goody Two Shoes' and one other. 'Viva Le Rock' seemed the most appropriate for the day, but everything got cut back and suddenly we were dealing with one song. Also I had a band that didn't know all the stuff. So I came down and we just did, 'Viva Le Rock'." Most artists who performed on the day saw an increase in sales, Adam was one of the exceptions. His latest single, 'Viva Le Rock' became his lowest charting hit when it stalled at number 50.

503 Charlene
I've Never Been To Me

Label & Cat No.: **Motown TMG 1260**

Producers: **Ron Miller / Berry Gordy Jr / Don Costa**

Writers: **Ron Miller / Ken Hirsch**

Date Reached No.1: **26 June 1982**

Weeks at No.1: **1**

CHARLENE D'ANGELO WAS BORN IN Hollywood in 1950. She was discovered by the moguls of Motown Records who signed her to the label in 1973 and changed her surname to Duncan. They teamed her up with the songwriting duo, Ron Richards and Ken Hirsch, but her first single, 'All That Love Went To Waste' did just that.

In 1977 she had dropped her surname altogether and released her first album, *Charlene*, which confusingly credited her as Charlene Duncan on the sleeve. The first single from it, 'It Ain't Easy Comin' Down', barely scraped into the US chart. Now signed to Prodigal Records, a subsidiary of Motown, she released, 'I've Never Been To Me' which again made little impact. The original recording didn't have the spoken passage, which talks about unborn children.

When no more hits were forthcoming, she became disillusioned with the music business and decided to call it a day. She married and moved to England where she took a job working in a sweet shop in Ilford, Essex.

In 1981 Scott Shannon, a DJ on a WRBQ-FM in Tampa, Florida, discovered the album and began spinning the track. Motown wanted to re-promote Charlene and it took a while for the Motown staff to track her down to inform her of her belated success. Once they did, they rushed her into the studio to re-record the track. To enhance the song's female sentiment she added the narrative passage in the middle. Charlene also recorded a Spanish language version, which interestingly replaced the line 'I've been to Nice, and the isle of Greece' with 'I've been to Acapulco and Buenos Aires'.

The song reached number one exactly one year after Motown had re-issued Michael Jackson's 'One Day In Your Life'. Both songs were six years old when they hit the top. In the wake of her new-found success, Motown teamed her up with Stevie Wonder for the duet 'Used To Be'. It failed to make the Top 50 in the US and missed the chart altogether in Britain. Motown were disappointed with the lack of success and dropped Charlene from the roster.

504 Captain Sensible
Happy Talk

Label & Cat No.: **A&M CAP 1**

Producer: **Tony Mansfield**

Writers: **Richard Rodgers / Oscar Hammerstein II**

Date Reached No.1: **3 July 1982**

Weeks at No.1: **2**

"I WAS EXCEEDINGLY DRUNK WHEN I recorded that vocal," remembered Captain Sensible about 'Happy Talk', in an interview with Q Magazine.

Not many chart-topping songs have real swearing in them. Until Eamon and Frankee in 2004, there are two and neither of them were noticeable enough to get a radio ban. The first was in The Beatles' 'Hey Jude'. Listen on a quality sound system, and at two minutes and 58 seconds you might just hear John Lennon mutter "bloody 'ell" after fluffing a backing vocal. The second was on 'Happy Talk'. Captain Sensible: "I went down to the studio and the producer didn't have his Fairlight sampler working, so he sent me down to the pub until it was fixed. By the time he got it working it was about closing time, so I'd had a bit of a session." The line under scrutiny is: 'Golly baby I'm a lucky cunt' instead of 'Golly baby I'm a lucky cuss' as sung by Bloody Mary (Juanita Hall) in *South Pacific*. Based on stories from James A. Michener's book, *Tales Of The South Pacific*, the story is set during World War II and deals with racist issues in the South Sea island which is occupied by American troops. The Captain continued, "I had a bit of fun with that line, it's sort of mumbled but you can make it out on the record. Actually, the vocal is awful and I can't stand it."

Because The Captain didn't like it, he didn't want it released, but his record company did, so they tricked him. They said, "Someone from another label is recording the same song and are planning to release it. It's a sure-fire number one and if you don't let us release it they will have the number one." The captain relented. The song entered the chart at number 33 and the following week catapulted to number one, ironically breaking the previous record holders – The Beatles – when the aforementioned 'Hey Jude' leapt 27-1.

Captain Sensible was born Raymond Burns in 1955. He joined The Damned as their bass player in 1976 at the start of the punk era. By 1977 he'd switched to guitar and keyboards and they were the first punk act to chart an album in the UK.

In 1984 he was dismissed from the band and continued his solo career. He made the Top 10 with his first single, 'Glad It's All Over' which was backed with the medley, 'Damned on 45'. It looked like his music career was all over until he re-joined The Damned in 1991.

505 Irene Cara
Fame

Label & Cat No.: **RSO 90**

Producer: **Michael Gore**

Writers: **Michael Gore / Dean Pitchford**

Date Reached No.1: **17 July 1982**

Weeks at No.1: **3**

FIRST THERE WAS *FAME* THE MOVIE, then the spin-off television series. The story follows four students, Coco Hernandez (Irene Cara), Doris Finsecker, Montgomery MacNeil and Raúl García, who attend the New York City High School for the Performing Arts. The BBC obtained the rights to the TV cast album, which had Erica Gimpel playing Coco Hernandez, but had failed to release it as a single. They didn't have the foresight to release Erica's version of the TV theme, so RSO records took the opportunity to release Irene's original movie theme from two years earlier. It paid off, the song, with its hook, 'I'm gonna live forever', reached number four in the US and topped the chart in Britain.

Irene was born in New York City in 1959. She made her stage debut at the age of seven in the Jack Cassidy/Shirley Jones musical *Maggie Flynn*. Her television debut came as a member of the rock group The Short Circus, in the series *Electric Company*. At the age of 10 she appeared with Stevie Wonder and Roberta Flack at a tribute concert for Duke Ellington at New York's Madison Square Garden.

Lesley Gore was discovered in the Sixties by Quincy Jones and is best remembered for her hit, 'It's My Party'. Her brother, Michael, with Dean Pitchford wrote 'Fame'. The pair also wrote Whitney Houston's 1990 hit, 'All The Man I Need'. Both Lesley and Michael wrote Cara's follow-up 'Out Here On My Own'. It failed to make much impact on either side of the Atlantic, but did make history when, for the first time, two songs from the same movie were nominated for the same category of Best Original Song – 'Fame' won.

In 1983 Irene was invited to record the theme to another film, *Flashdance.* She co-wrote the lyrics as she wanted to describe the feeling of dance. The song reached number two in the UK and topped the US charts for six weeks. In 1998 *Fame – The Musical* opened in London and more recently was touring nationwide.

506 Dexys Midnight Runners & The Emerald Express
Come On Eileen

Label & Cat No.: **Mercury DEXYS 9**

Producers: **Clive Langer / Alan Winstanley**

Writers: **Kevin Rowland / Jimmy Patterson / Kevin Adams**

Date Reached No.1: **7 August 1982**

Weeks at No.1: **4**

Dexys Midnight Runners were formed in Birmingham in 1978 by Wolverhampton-born Kevin Rowland and guitarist Al Archer (born Kevin Archer). Rowland had cut his musical teeth in a band called Lucy & The Lovers before moving to the punk outfit The Killjoys.

By 1982 the Dexys Midnight Runners' line up was: Billy Adams (guitar), Seb Shelton (drums), Giorgio Kilkenny (bass) and the only original member Jimmy Patterson (trombone). Rowland had also brought in a trio of folk fiddlers, Helen O'Hara, Roger MacDuff and Steve Brennan, known as The Emerald Express. Kevin said, "I saw Helen one morning at a bus stop just down the road from where I live, she was carrying a violin case so I started talking to her. I'd wanted to use strings before but it never really worked out. So her and Steve came down to

rehearsals and started playing." With this new sound came a new image of baggy jeans, bandanas, dungarees and sandals. "The look was put together from different elements which was intended to convey a wild feeling, not necessarily a gypsy look," Rowland claimed.

The 'Eileen' was Eileen McClusky, an ex-girlfriend of Rowland's. Kevin was confident about the song's potential and confessed in an interview with *The Face,* "If 'Come On Eileen' didn't do well, I would find another way of making money. I don't want to be in a loser group."

'Come On Eileen' and the Top five the follow-up, a cover of Van Morrison's, 'Jackie Wilson Said (I'm In Heaven When You Smile)' were both taken from the album *Too-Rye-Ay* and it was well received. For their 'Jackie Wilson' appearance on *Top Of The Pops*, the background showed a huge mural of the darts player, Jocky Wilson. During a Jonathan Ross interview in 2003, Kevin claimed that it was all his idea and had done it for a joke.

Their last hit, in 1986, was 'Because Of You', the theme to the TV series *Brush Strokes*. After that, the band broke up again. Kevin released a solo album, *The Wanderer*, which failed to create any interest. He attempted a comeback in 1999 with *My Beauty*, an album of unusual covers, including 'The Greatest Love Of All', 'Daydream Believer' and 'Rag Doll'. The sleeve showed Rowland in stockings, a crushed velvet top and a pearl necklace. An image and sound the British public didn't favour.

507 Survivor
Eye Of The Tiger

Label & Cat No.: **Scotti Brothers SCT A 2411**

Producers: **Jim Peterik / Frankie Sullivan**

Writers: **Jim Peterik / Frankie Sullivan**

Date Reached No.1: **4 September 1982**

Weeks at No.1: **4**

"We called ourselves Survivor because we are all survivors of different bands and rock and roll situations," explained Survivor's keyboard player, Jim Peterik.

The first *Rocky* movie came in 1977 with the theme provided by Bill Conti ('Gonna Fly Now'). In 1979 *Rocky II* hit the big screen. This time it not only starred Sylvester Stallone, it was directed by him as well. 'Sly's' brother, Frank, had provided a couple of songs for the film but there was no real theme. In 1982 the third one was unleashed upon the film-going public. It's unusual that sequels and sequels to sequels do so well but *Rocky III* turned out to be the most successful one. Again it was directed by Sly who packs a mean punch with his opponent, Mr T and subsequently wanted a rockier theme. Initially Queen's 'Another One Bites The Dust' was considered, but dismissed it in favour of a new song by a relatively unknown Chicago band.

Survivor were formed in 1973. "I was singing jingles in Sunkist orange soda commercials in Chicago and found myself at a session with an amazing singer named Dave Bickler. His range was incredible, he had an interesting voice and was a very nice guy. I asked him to sing on my solo album and when I decided to put another band together I tried to find the cream of the crop," explained Survivor's Jim Peterik. Survivor were Jim Peterik (keyboards), David Bickler (vocals) and Frank Sullivan (guitar). They added Stephan Mills (bass) and Marc Droubay (drums) a couple of years later. Peterik was the only one who had had chart success as lead singer of The Ides Of March, whose sole UK hit, 'Vehicle' reached number 31 in 1970.

Sylvester Stallone had heard Survivor's 1981

album, *Premonition* and called Jim to explain that he liked the tough honesty of it. He explained that his new film, *Rocky III* was complete except for the theme song. Stallone then sent Jim a tape of the first three minutes of the film where the song would fit in and left it up to them, but requesting it was to have a 'strong beat'. The title was taken from a phrase used by Rocky's trainer Mickey, who kept saying, "Stay focused and keep the eye of the tiger." The drum stabs in the intro are meant to reflect the boxer's punch. They sent Sly the demo which only had two verses. Jim said, "He flipped over the song, but made us write a third verse and offered a few other suggestions. Due to the tightness of the schedule, the version you hear in the actual movie was the demo version."

Such was the success of 'Eye Of The Tiger' that they were asked to contribute a song for *Rocky IV*. They submitted 'Burning Heart' which reached number five in the UK. Survivor had no further hits and they split in 1989. *Rocky V* followed in 1990, but by now the plot was wearing a bit thin.

508 Musical Youth
Pass The Dutchie

Label & Cat No.: **MCA YOU 1**

Producer: **Peter Collins**

Writers: **Jackie Mittoo / Fitzroy Simpson / Lloyd Ferguson**

Date Reached No.1: **2 October 1982**

Weeks at No.1: **3**

"IF WE'D ALL BEEN 18 AND LEGALLY ABLE to cope for ourselves, Musical Youth would still be going now," said Musical Youth's lead singer, Dennis Seaton. Musical Youth were only allowed to work 39 hours a week, the legal requirement for kids their age. It was a hindrance to them because they had to cancel tours to attend school, thus there was a lack of promotion.

Freddie Waite, a former singer with Jamaican band, The Techniques, was teaching music at his local community centre in Birmingham. He began assembling a band in 1979 with his two sons Patrick on bass and Junior on drums and he named them Musical Express. He set up some auditions and found the keyboard player, Michael Grant. Michael suggested that his brother Kelvin (then only eight), who played guitar did an audition. Once Freddie saw his performance, he recruited him as well. Finally he brought in the vocalist, Dennis Seaton. In late 1979 he changed their name to Musical Youth and they showed the potential of being Britain's answer to The Jackson 5. They topped the US singles chart and won a Grammy for Best Newcomers.

Freddie had found an old Jamaican song by the little known Mighty Diamonds called 'Pass The Kutchie'. They had the foresight to realise that a song about a device for making and consuming illegal substances would not go down well with the radio authorities, or even with their fans, so they decided to change the lyric to 'Dutchie'. Whenever they were interviewed and asked what a 'Dutchie' was, they always replied, "a kitchen cooking utensil". When one BBC interviewer asked him why it had to be passed to the left, Dennis replied, "It doesn't matter, you can pass it to the right too."

Jackie Mittoo is a reggae songwriter who was the musical director at Coxone Dodd's Studio One label. Lloyd Ferguson and Fitzroy Simpson were both members of the Mighty Diamonds who had formed in 1969 and were known in their native Trenchtown as the young group with the Motown sound.

Musical Youth followed-up their chart-topper with 'Youth Of Today', with its memorable intro "Dennis, come back with my apple pie" and had one further Top 10 hit with 'Never Gonna Give You Up'. Unable to cope with the pressures, they split in early 1984. Both the Grants continued in other aspects of the music industry, Junior became a recluse, and tragedy befell Patrick. As Dennis described, "He became bored and returned to joyriding and drugs." When he turned 22, he served three years in prison for robbery and assault, and died in a car accident in 1993. Dennis however, was enthusiastic and formed a new reggae band called 'XMY' standing for Ex Musical Youth', but failed to make any impact on the UK charts. He has more recently been spotted selling second-hand cars in the Birmingham area.

509 Culture Club
Do You Really Want To Hurt Me?

Label & Cat No.: **Virgin VS 518**

Producer: **Steve Levine**

Writer: **Culture Club**

Date Reached No.1: **23 October 1982**

Weeks at No.1: **3**

"THE NEXT TIME WE FACE A FOREIGN policy crisis, I will work with John Major and Boris Yeltsin, and Bill Clinton can consult Boy George," proclaimed US President George Bush in 1992.

George (born George O'Dowd) first appeared on the music scene in 1980, when his cross-dressing attracted the attention of former Sex Pistols manager Malcolm McLaren. Matthew Ashman, Bow Wow Wow's guitarist, asked George if he wanted to audition for the band, as their lead singer Annabella wasn't pulling her weight. McLaren brought him in under the alter-ego Lieutenant Lush.

After breaking away from Bow Wow Wow, he met bass player Mikey Craig and was then introduced to drummer Jon Moss by a mutual friend. They recruited guitarist Roy Hay and set about forming a group. "We all agreed that Sex Gang Children was the wrong name. We toyed with new names, Caravan Club and Can't Wait Club," claimed George in his autobiography. "Then Jon said, 'look at us: an Irish transvestite, a Jew, a black man and an Anglo-Saxon', so that's how I came up with Culture Club."

Their first two singles, 'White Boy' and 'I'm Afraid Of Me', failed to make any impact, but during a recording session for the Peter Powell show on Radio One, they found they had some spare studio time, and filled it by writing and recording 'Do You Really Want To Hurt Me?' It was issued as a single, although George was reluctant at first claiming that "It was too personal and wasn't a dance record." However, it flew to the top of the UK chart and broke them in America, giving them their first of six consecutive Top 10 hits. George said, '"Do You Really Want To Hurt Me?' is a really well constructed song. It's probably the only proper song we've got with proper chord sequences and keyboard changes in it. It's just very musical. The most powerful songs are love songs. They apply to everyone – especially kids who fall in and out of love more times than anyone else. At the end of the day, everybody wants to be wanted."

Even though George had very quickly become a household name, many parents enquired of their son or daughter as to the gender of the character on the television. His contemporaries would mock him too and he became a target for many impressionists.

510 Eddy Grant
I Don't Wanna Dance

Label & Cat No.: **Ice ICE 56**
Producer: **Eddy Grant**
Writer: **Eddy Grant**
Date Reached No.1: **13 November 1982**
Weeks at No.1: **3**

"IT'S ALWAYS BEEN MY INTENTION TO LIVE in the sun," said Eddy Grant, who was born in Guyana in 1948. It seemed a strange thing, perhaps for a man who spent much of his career in the UK.

Eddy resided in London from 1960, when his parents decided to move to the UK. He was educated in north London's Camden district and learned a variety of instruments, including piano and guitar. He formed The Equals in 1965 and they had their first hit in 1968. Just a year later, Eddy was injured in a car accident in Germany. Despite being a vegetarian and a teetotaller, Eddy suffered a heart attack due to the pressures of recording and touring. In 1972 he pulled out of the tour and left The Equals although he did continue to write songs for them.

In the mid-Seventies, he built his own studio so he could record at his own place. It also allowed him time to encourage other artists that he had discovered. He launched his own Ice record label and began a solo career with the release of his first album, *Message Man*. In 1979 he signed a licensing deal with Ensign Records and released the single 'Walking On Sunshine' (not the Katrina & The Waves hit), which failed to chart, but was successfully covered in 1982 by Rockers Revenge featuring Donnie Calvin. The follow-up, 'Living On The Frontline', gave him the first of 12 hits over a 10-year period.

In early 1982 Eddy relocated to Barbados. "I've always been popular in the Caribbean," said Eddy. "It's a territory where they don't sell a lot of records, but it's where my whole career started after I left The Equals." He built his own studio, Blue Wave, where artists like Sting, The Rolling Stones and Elvis Costello have recorded.

The hits dried up at the end of the Eighties, but in 2001 a Hawaiian DJ, Peter Black, remixed Eddy's follow-up hit to 'I Don't Wanna Dance', 'Electric Avenue' and Eddy was back in the chart for the first time in 18 years.

511 The Jam
Beat Surrender

Label & Cat No.: **Polydor POSP 540**
Producer: **Pete Wilson**
Writer: **Paul Weller**
Date Reached No.1: **4 December 1982**
Weeks at No.1: **2**

THE JAM HAD AN IMMENSE FAN BASE, so when Paul announced that The Jam were to split, it sparked a 'Save The Jam' campaign with T-shirts and badges readily available all over London. Paul claimed his reason for the split was "I was getting frustrated with the band's sound."

For their final single, The Jam recorded two tracks, 'Beat Surrender' and 'Solid Bond In Your Heart'. After much debate, they decided to go with 'Beat Surrender', a title based on Anita Ward's 1979 disco song, 'Sweet Surrender'. The seven-inch sleeve for 'Beat Surrender' featured Paul's girlfriend, Gill, holding a white flag of surrender. 'Solid Bond In Your Heart' was eventually a number 11 hit for Paul's next group, The Style Council.

Ironically, 'Beat Surrender' was originally written with the band's split in mind. But Paul wanted it kept secret. His intention was to announce it on the debut edition of the new Channel 4 music show, *The Tube*, which The Jam had been specially invited to appear on.

Before The Jam left the building, they set one more record. On week ending 5 February 1983, all 13 re-issued Jam singles were in the Top 75 all at the same time. The highest, 'Going Underground' / 'The Dreams Of Children', was at number 21. The accompanying album, *Dig The New Breed*, was a collection of live recordings.

After The Jam's demise, Bruce Foxton went solo and scraped together three fairly minor hit singles. Rick Buckler formed Time UK and managed one hit single with 'The Cabaret' in 1983. Soon after, the pair teamed up with Time UK vocalist Jimmy Edwards to form Sharp, but they failed to chart at all. Paul Weller, however, showed them how it should be done. He formed The Style Council with ex- Merton Parkas keyboard player Mick Talbot before embarking on a solo career.

Weller has wisely resisted all calls to reform the group and by the turn of the millennium had emerged as a much respected elder statesman of the punk era, affectionately referred to by his fans as The Modfather. He topped the UK album charts with Style Council's *Our Favourite Shop* (1985), and twice under his own name with *Stanley Road* (1995) and *Illumination* (2002).
A greatest hits album, *Modern Classics*, reached number two in 1997.

512 Renee & Renato
Save Your Love

Label & Cat No.:	**Hollywood HWD 003**
Producer:	**John Edward**
Writers:	**John Edward / Sue Edward**
Date Reached No.1:	**18 December 1982**
Weeks at No.1:	**4**

If 'Save Your Love' had been released at any other time of the year it is unlikely that it would have made number one. But Christmas time has a knack of sending sentimental songs, or songs with appeal for the older generation, zooming up the chart. As Renato concurred, "It's a very romantic song and just happened to come out at the right time. At a time when the chart was full of heavy rock and bang bang music, maybe people wanted something romantic."

Renato was born Renato Pagliari in Rome, but grew up in Birmingham. He worked as a waiter in a local restaurant and got his break into showbiz by accident when a local cabaret singer failed to turn up at the restaurant. Renato filled the gap for the night and was so well received by the customers that he decided to make it more permanent.

And Renee? Well, there were two of them. The Renee that sang on the record was a 22-year-old English girl, Hilary Lester, but she was not the girl who appeared in the video. That was Val Penny. Hilary explained, "I didn't want to do the video. It was my mistake really but it just wasn't my sort of thing. So they found another girl, put a blonde wig on her and that was it. Also, you don't see her lip-synch in the video."

Renato was very proud of his romantic love song, but Hilary saw it differently. In the Nineties she said, "I think you have to laugh along with it, you have to take something for what it is. I'll never be ashamed of it, but at the end of the day it was a novelty record."

John Edward, who wrote with song with his wife, also invented the children's robot, Metal Mickey. He originally wrote a song called 'Metal Mickey' and took it to a song publisher. The publisher asked who Metal Mickey was, but John hadn't thought about that, so he was told to come back when he had the character, which is exactly what he did.

The corny video showed Renato serenading his lady who was standing on her bedroom balcony. It ends with him throwing a red rose up to her, which she catches. The video is best forgotten, and it would have been, had the late Kenny Everett not made a hilarious spoof. Kenny portrayed both characters; an enormous Renato, who kept getting fatter, splitting all his clothes, and an angelic Renee (complete with beard) who was trying to catch the rose, but kept missing and eventually falling head first over the balcony, before landing in a heap on the ground.

Renato lives and owns his own restaurant in Sutton Coldfield, near Birmingham and regularly sings to his guests.

513 Phil Collins
You Can't Hurry Love

Label & Cat No.:	**Virgin VS 531**
Producer:	**Phil Collins**
Writers:	**Brian Holland / Lamont Dozier / Edward Holland**
Date Reached No.1:	**15 January 1983**
Weeks at No.1:	**2**

Phil got his show business foot in the door in 1964 when he and 349 other teenagers went along to the Scala Theatre in London as members of the audience for a scene in The Beatles' first film, *A Hard Day's Night*. His mother, June, ran a booking agency and Phil, with his blond hair and blue eyes was in demand for modelling knitting patterns for British Home Stores.

In the summer of 1970, Phil Collins received an invitation to play percussion on the first solo album by a Beatle, George Harrison. At the studio he met Phil Spector, Ringo Starr, Billy Preston and Maurice Gibb. All had assembled to work on the triple album *All Things Must Pass*. When the album was released, Phil was disappointed. Not only was his name not on the album, his contribution had not been included.

Former Cambridge graduate, Jonathan King was working for the head of Decca Records in 1967 and received a demo tape from a band. He was instrumental in getting them signed to the label and produced their debut album *From Genesis To Revelation*. King revealed, "I christened them Genesis to celebrate the start of my serious career as a producer." When the album flopped, they ended their association with King. Their original drummer, Chris Stewart, left in 1968 and was briefly replaced by John Silver.

Whilst reading *Melody Maker*, Phil answered an advert placed by Tony Stratton-Smith, who owned the Charisma label. They had a meeting and Tony contacted his friend, Marquee Club manager Jack Barrie, who had heard Phil play and confirmed he was a 'good drummer'. Strat, as he was known, said he would forward his name to a new group, Genesis, who were auditioning.

In 1975 lead singer Peter Gabriel left and the band had trouble finding a replacement. Eventually it was suggested that Phil take over as lead singer and had their first Top 10 hit with 'Follow You Follow Me' in 1978.

In 1981 Phil released his first solo single, 'In The Air Tonight' which went to number two. He also topped the album chart with *Face Value*, *No Jacket Required* and *...But Seriously*. Phil loved the Tamla Motown sound and wanted to revive The Supremes' 1966 US chart-topper (UK number three), 'You Can't Hurry Love' for his second album, *Hello, I Must Be Going*. Eddie Holland came up with the title to Brian Holland's melody for the song. Lamont Dozier recalled, "We were trying to reconstruct 'Come See About Me' and somehow it turned into 'You Can't Hurry Love'. It was basically a gospel feel we were after."

The album title, *Hello I Must Be Going*, was inspired by the song 'Hooray for Captain Spaulding', which Groucho Marx sung in the Marx Brothers movie *Animal Crackers* (1930).

Phil's version, which was faithful to the original, inspired Andy Rourke's bass in The Smiths' 'This Charming Man'. Such was his love for the label, that Phil inscribed 'Motown, we salute you' on the album sleeve. Even the black and white video showed three Phil's standing in a line as a homage to The Supremes.

514 Men At Work
Down Under

Label & Cat No.: **Epic EPC A 1980**
Producer: **Peter Mclan**
Writers: **Colin Hay / Ron Strykert**
Date reached No.1: **29 January 1983**
Weeks at No.1: **3**

EVER SINCE THE EASYBEATS TOOK 'Friday On My Mind' to number six in 1966, there have always been Australian beat groups contending for chart places and around 1983, there was Air Supply, Little River Band, AC/DC and Men At Work. Men At Work started when Scottish-born lead singer Colin Hay met fellow student, guitarist, Ron Strykert at La Trobe University in Melbourne. They decided to form a group and added Greg Ham (keyboards, woodwind) and Jerry Spieser (drums) from other bands as well as recruiting a trained classical violinist, John Rees, to play bass. They had their first gig as Men At Work at the Cricketers Arms Hotel in Melbourne and soon had a local following.

Columbia Records recognised their potential and teamed them with the American producer, Peter McIan. They made an album, *Business As Usual*, and, following a tour on which they supported Fleetwood Mac, their single, 'Who Can It Be Now?', topped the US charts.

Their second single, 'Down Under', was about Aussies who go overseas and want to return home, and performed with an infectious reggae rhythm. The song listed things that were endemic to Australia including fried-out combies and Vegemite sandwiches. With the help of a comic video, Men At Work had the number one single and album in both Britain and America.

Although Men At Work had further hits – 'Overkill', 'It's A Mistake' and 'Dr. Heckyll & Mr. Jive' – their time was up by the mid-Eighties and the group split up. Colin Hay now fronts a version of Men At Work and he did tour with Ringo Starr's All-Starr Band in 2003.

515 Kajagoogoo
Too Shy

Label & Cat No.: **EMI 5359**
Producers: **Nick Rhodes / Colin Thurston**
Writers: **Kajagoogoo**
Date reached No.1: **19 February 1983**
Weeks at No.1: **2**

IN 1982 ART NOUVEAU FROM LEIGHTON Buzzard, Beds were looking for a lead vocalist – the various members of The Barron Knights being too old. They put an ad in *Melody Maker* and Chris Hamill, a jobbing actor, who had toured in *Murder At The Vicarage* and *Joseph And The Amazing Technicolour Dreamcoat,* applied. He chose an anagram of his surname, Limahl, and Kajagoogoo was born with Steve Askew (guitar), Nick Beggs (bass), Stuart Crawford (synthesisers) and Jez Strode (percussion).

Kajagoogoo made a demo tape and Limahl, working as a waiter, passed it to Duran Duran's Nick Rhodes. He decided to produce the group with Duran Duran's producer, Colin Thurston. The group wrote 'Too Shy' for the first single and with the support of Radio 1 DJ, Paul Gambaccini, the record went to number one. The *NME* was less impressed. Julie Birchill was of the opinion that "the singer looks like the resident rodent in a Leicester Square lavatory." Still, 'Ooh To Be Ah' was a Top 10 single, *White Feathers* was a big-selling album and girls loved Limahl's two-tone hairstyle.

It was soon Ooh To Be Out as The Kajas, in the strangest dismissal since Pete Best, complained of what Limahl was doing with his goo goos. *The Sun* claimed, "Limahl, 24, upset the rest of the band by getting closely involved with Radio 1 star, Paul Gambaccini" and, in a frantic attempt to discredit both Limahl and Gambaccini, stated that they were living together.

Limahl had solo hits with 'Only For Love' and 'Never Ending Story', which was produced by Giorgio Moroder. He moved into songwriting and production, working with Kim Wilde and Peter Andre. In 2000 Limahl starred in a nationwide tour of the musical, *What A Feeling!*

516 Michael Jackson
Billie Jean

Label & Cat No.: **Epic EPCA 3084**
Producer: **Quincy Jones**
Writer: **Michael Jackson**
Date Reached No.1: **5 March 1983**
Weeks at No.1: **1**

DURING CHRISTMAS 1982, MICHAEL Jackson rang Paul McCartney in London and suggested they write and record some songs together. Due to Michael's famous high-pitched voice, Paul originally thought it was a young female fan messing around. Once Michael had convinced him that he was the real Michael Jackson, Paul promptly boarded a plane to Los Angeles. They recorded three tracks: 'The Girl Is Mine', a story of two men playfully fighting for a girl's affection, together with 'Say Say Say' and 'The Man', both of which appeared on Macca's album, *Pipes Of Peace*.

During 1982 Michael was occupied with writing and producing songs for Diana Ross, ('Muscles' – also the name of his pet snake). He also narrated the storybook album *E.T. – The Extra Terrestrial* and began work on his next album, *Thriller*. Michael was delighted about his collaboration with producer Quincy Jones on *Off The Wall* so he chose the same team for *Thriller*. Quincy said, "I was still working with Donna Summer on her self-titled album, when I got the call to go to Tuscon, Arizona to record the Jacko/McCartney duets. It was the only time Paul could make it and we only had three days to do it in." Once that session was in the can, Jones continued his project with Donna Summer and returned to *Thriller* later that year.

In his autobiography, *Moonwalk*, Michael explained, "'Not My Lover' was a title we almost used for 'Billie Jean' because Quincy had some objections to calling the song 'Billie Jean', my original title. He felt people might immediately think of Billie Jean King, the tennis player. There was never a real 'Billie Jean'," he explained. "It's just a case of a girl who says that I'm the father of her child and I'm pleading innocence. This kind

of thing has happened to some of my brothers and I really used to be amazed by it. I couldn't understand how these girls could say they are carrying someone else's child when it wasn't true." The original album version was over six minutes. As Quincy said, "All we needed to do was cut down the intro." The song was untouched and done in one take.

Quincy Jones said, "Michael is like an Eighties Sammy Davis Jr. He's the best of Broadway, Disneyland, Vegas, Pop, rock'n'roll and R&B. He's taken us right up there where we belong. Black music had to play second fiddle for a long time, but its spirit is the whole motor for pop. Michael has connected with every soul in the world."

For the Motown 25th anniversary in 1983, Michael wasn't sure what he was going to do for the special occasion, so the day before, he decided to play the track at full volume and see what the music told him. On the night, Michael presented a new image with a new hat, one white glove and a black sparkly jacket. The added surprise was the debut of his 'moonwalking' dance, in which his feet seemed to be going one way while his body was propelled the other.

Thriller took music sales into a different dimension. The single spent only one week on top of the UK chart but seven in America. The album, which topped every European chart, spent 37 weeks at number one in the US and sold over 25 million copies there alone. Worldwide sales are currently in excess of 52 million.

517 Bonnie Tyler
Total Eclipse Of The Heart

Label & Cat No.: **CBS TYLER 1**

Producer: **Jim Steinman**

Writer: **Jim Steinman**

Date reached No.1: **12 March 1983**

Weeks at No.1: **2**

When Bonnie Tyler was singing around the Welsh social clubs in the mid-Seventies, she developed nodules on her throat. An operation to remove them altered her voice so that she sang with a rasp, rather like a female Rod Stewart, which was the making of her.

Bonnie was born Gaynor Hopkins in Skewen, near Swansea in 1953. She loved raunchy rock singers such as Janis Joplin and Tina Turner and she sang soul music in the Welsh clubs. She was spotted by Ronnie Scott and Steve Wolfe, who became her managers, songwriters and producers. Several journalists, invited on a mystery binge, found themselves 'lost in France', the title of Bonnie's first hit single in 1976. Then 'It's A Heartache' was a hit in both Britain and America.

When Bonnie stopped having hits, she realised the restrictiveness of her relationship with Scott and Wolfe as she had to choose from *their* songs. She broke with them in 1981 and signed with David Aspden. She loved Meat Loaf's *Bat Out Of Hell* and asked if his producer, Jim Steinman, was available. Steinman agreed, saying, "Bonnie could scream at the top of her lungs over an army of guitars and yet still sound musical."

She met Steinman who arranged for Rory Dodd to sing 'Total Eclipse Of The Heart' to her. She recorded it in a grandiose production which included Max Weinberg (drums) and Roy Bittan (keyboards) from Bruce Springsteen's E Street Band, Rick Derringer of The McCoys (guitars) and Rory Dodd on backing vocals. The video showed Bonnie, very glamorous and all in white, but in a menacing, gothic setting.

The album, *Faster Than The Speed Of Night*, went to number one and the single also topped the US charts. Bonnie Tyler had a Top 10 hit with a playful revival of 'A Rockin' Good Way' with another Welsh star, Shakin' Stevens, but she was back with Steinman's immense productions with 'Holding Out For A Hero', a number two single from the film, *Footloose*.

In 1995 Nicki French made the Top Five with a dance version of 'Total Eclipse of the Heart' although the introductions to the two records were similar. In 2000 Nicki French represented the UK in *The Eurovision Song Contest*, but the song title 'Don't Play That Song Again' was all too prophetic.

518 Duran Duran
Is There Something I Should Know?

Label & Cat No.: **EMI 5371**

Producers: **Duran Duran / Ian Little**

Writers: **Simon Le Bon / Andy Taylor / John Taylor / Roger Taylor / Nick Rhodes**

Date reached No.1: **26 March 1983**

Weeks at No.1: **2**

Barbarella, an astronaut from the 40th century, lands on Planet Lythion, while searching for Durand-Durand, the inventor of the Positronic Ray, which could destroy the peace of the Galaxy. The 1964 book was made into a film four years later starring Jane Fonda as the female Flash Gordon and Milo O'Shea as Durand-Durand.

Ten years later in Birmingham, some musicians started to play together at Barbarella's club. Nick Rhodes (keyboards, synths) and John Taylor (guitar) are part of a group and they think Duran Duran is a cool name. Which it is. Various changes take place with Nick playing alongside three unrelated Taylors – John (now on bass), Andy (guitar) and Roger (drums). They did not have a lead vocalist until the barmaid at The Rum Runner suggested her boyfriend, a university drama student, Simon LeBon. Thinking of Barbarella, they called themselves Duran Duran.

Right from the off, they had a very iconic, futuristic look and Andy Taylor was to marry the group's hairdresser, Tracey Wilson. Their videos, especially the one for 'Rio' which was shot in Antigua, were always stunning, making them the darlings of MTV. Godley and Creme directed the sexist and therefore controversial 'Girls On Film' (1981), while 'Hungry Like A Wolf' was filmed in Sri Lanka. 'Save A Prayer' almost took them to the top, but they succeeded with their eighth single, 'Is There Something I Should Know?'. This time the video was a stark contrast to the previous postcards from Duran Duran. It concentrated on five close-up images of their faces

The ever-elegant Duran Duran always seemed to be flying off to somewhere or other; left to right: John Taylor, Andy Taylor, Simon Le Bon, Roger Taylor and Nick Rhodes

and aimed to give clues about their individual personalities.

Duran Duran were strongly influenced by Roxy Music and David Bowie, but 'Is There Something I Should Know?' could have been a Beatles song. It was written by the entire group and told of a relationship that was going sour. It included the line, "Don't say you're easy on me: you're about as easy as a nuclear war."

519 David Bowie
Let's Dance

Label & Cat No.:	**EMI 525**
Producers:	**David Bowie / Nile Rodgers**
Writer:	**David Bowie**
Date Reached No.1:	**9 April 1983**
Weeks at No.1:	**3**

"THIS IS PROBABLY THE SIMPLEST ALBUM I've ever made," David Bowie said of *Let's Dance*, his 19th charting album. Perhaps he took the advice given to him by his co-writer on 'Fame', John Lennon, who said, "It's very easy. Say what you mean, make it rhyme and put a backbeat into it."

He had teamed up with ex-Chic guitarist, writer and producer, Nile Rodgers, for a completely new sound. It gave the track that distinctive disco sound that was synonymous with Chic. The album also featured two other Chic members, bass player Bernard Edwards and drummer Tony Thompson. The guitar solo was by Stevie Ray Vaughan, who impressed David when he saw him perform at the Montreux Jazz Festival a year earlier.

'Let's Dance' was a witty, dance record with its quirky lyrics, 'serious moonlight'. Nile Rodgers: "David got the serious bit from me. I used to say 'serious' all the time. I would say, 'man that shit is serious!' meaning it's happening. It's a disco expression. In the disco everything is serious."

Nile Rodgers replaced Tony Visconti as producer on *Let's Dance*. Nile had already achieved success with artists like Sister Sledge, Diana Ross and Carly Simon. They first met in a bar in Manhattan and Nile, who was expecting a Ziggy Stardust character, failed to recognise David. "I wasn't expecting this average looking guy." Working with David Bowie paid off as it gave him, for the first time, three Top two hits in a row, the follow-ups being 'China Girl' and 'Modern Love'. 'Let's Dance' was his only transatlantic number one and described by David as "positive, emotional and uplifting".

During the Nineties David's music seemed to change direction somewhat sporadically and he only managed one Top 10 hit with 'Jump They Say' in 1993.

In 1989 the Thin White Duke attempted the side-line project, Tin Machine. He ignored the jibes by the press and gave it two and a half years before returning to solo status again.

520 Spandau Ballet
True

Label & Cat No.:	**Reformation SPAN 1**
Producers:	**Tony Swain / Steve Jolley / Spandau Ballet**
Writer:	**Gary Kemp**
Date reached No.1:	**30 April 1983**
Weeks at No.1:	**4**

THE TERM, 'NEW ROMANTICS', described and bracketed ABC, Duran Duran and Spandau Ballet, bands who sang stylish love songs, were well-mannered and fashion-conscious, and loved being seen at trendy night-clubs. It was the antidote to punk and as Spandau Ballet's manger, Steve Dagger, said, "All you needed was a band to go on-stage wearing those clothes and they'd have it made."

The Nazi war criminal, Rudolf Hess, was the only prisoner at Spandau and, by the late Seventies, he had become a political football. In 1979 the group took their name from his prison. The lead vocalist was Tony Hadley, whose style was very close to the Old Romantic, Bryan Ferry; Gary Kemp played guitar and keyboards, and his brother, Martin, was learning bass; Steve Norman was on saxophone and John Keeble on drums. Chris Blackwell heard them at the fashionable Blitz club and offered them a contract with Island. However, they set up their own label, Reformation, which was distributed through Chrysalis. Their first single, 'To Cut A Long Story Short', went Top 10 in 1980.

Top 10 singles followed with 'Musclebound', 'Chant No.1 (I Don't Need This Pressure On)', 'Instinction' and 'Lifeline'. Gary Kemp was the group's main songwriter and a ballad with Marvin Gaye overtones, 'True', topped the UK chart. It was a class song but the line, "Take your seaside arms and write the next line", has figured in lists of the world's worst lyrics, although it was taken from a line from Nabokov's *Lolita*. The follow-up single, 'Gold', went silver, stopping at number two, but it became the theme for the BBC's Olympic coverage in 1984.

One of the producers, Tony Swain, recalls, "We made the *True* album in the Bahamas and I am sure that a lot of that place got into the album. 'True' was not a complicated song but it has really got something. There is something timeless about it: it has had over two million radioplays in America and it has been used in the wedding scenes for lots of films. It's very nice to have made a record that has lasted that long and I still feel good about it." But was it necessary to make it in the Bahamas? Couldn't Spandau Ballet have had the same results in London? "I do think it helps if groups want to go away and chill out. It didn't make any difference to me though. Wherever I am, I am simply spending time in a room with no windows."

Although 'True' was a US Top 10 hit, Spandau Ballet felt that Chrysalis were doing little to publicise them in the States. This was an own goal as the legal wrangling meant that no records could be released during 1985, the year in which they appeared at Live Aid.

The following year Spandau Ballet moved to CBS and returned to the Top 10 with 'Through The Barricades'. By then, other interests were creeping in: the Kemps starred as Ron and Reggie Kray in *The Krays*, the thugs who terrorised London's clubland in the Sixties. Gary Kemp played a rock manager in *The Bodyguard* (1992), while Martin became nationally known as the double-dealing Steve Owen in *EastEnders*.

Martin Kemp is married to Shirlie, one-half of Pepsi & Shirlie, who had a number 2 with *Heartache* (1987) and worked on Wham!'s records. He says today, "Gary was always the one into music. It was never really me. People say that 'True' is part of the soundtrack of their lives, and it's part of mine too. When I hear those songs, they don't trigger memories of making them, just of being around when that music was around."

The group broke up amidst litigation, which was resolved in Gary Kemp's favour. In 2003 Tony Hadley revitalised his career by winning the ITV talent show, *Reborn In The USA*. He toured the UK with Peter Cox of Go West performing, amongst other things, Spandau Ballet songs. Tony Swain comments, "Because of all the arguments, Spandau Ballet will never reform but Tony Hadley has a wonderful voice and it would be perfect if he agreed to do the Eurovision Song Contest. The only way we will win it again is with a great singer and if you hear 'True' in isolation, Tony Hadley is like a modern Frank Sinatra."

521 New Edition
Candy Girl

Label & Cat No.: **London LON 21**

Producers: **Maurice Starr / Michael Jonzun**

Writers: **Maurice Starr / Michael Jonzun**

Date reached No.1: **28 May 1983**

Weeks at No.1: **1**

THE FIVE MEMBERS OF NEW EDITION were under 16, but they knew that the only way out of their rough area of Boston was by singing. The group – Ralph Tresvant (the high-pitched lead vocalist), Michael Bivins, Ronald DeVoe, Ricky Bell and Bobby Brown – worked out a vocal and dance act and won a talent night at the Strand Theatre.

Picking their name from pieces of paper thrown into a hat, New Edition were spotted by Maurice Starr, who asked his brother, Michael Jonzun from The Jonzun Crew, a popular act in New York discos, to write and produce with him. They came up with 'Candy Girl', which, a decade earlier, would have suited The Jackson 5. Ronnie DeVoe said, "We might have grown up in a bad neighbourhood, but there was still some sweetness there."

'Candy Girl' was the first UK number one with rapping in it. New Edition had further UK successes with 'Popcorn Love' and 'Mr. Telephone Man' and then, in the Nineties with 'Hit Me Off' and 'Something About You'.

Ralph Tresvant was featured with Luther Vandross, Janet Jackson and BBD on the UK number two, 'The Best Things In Life Are Free' (1992). Bobby Brown had solo hits with 'My Prerogative', 'Every Little Step', 'Two Can Play That Game' and 'On Our Own' from *Ghostbusters II*. He married Whitney Houston in 1992 and their tempestuous relationship has been a gift to the tabloids.

522 The Police
Every Breath You Take

Label & Cat No.: **A&M AM 117**

Producers: **Hugh Padgham / The Police**

Writer: **Sting**

Date Reached No.1: **4 June 1983**

Weeks at No.1: **4**

"PEOPLE OFTEN CHOOSE THIS SONG AS their wedding song. They think it's a cheerful song. In fact, it's not a cheerful song at all, it's a very dark song," said Stewart Copeland whose Police colleague Sting was going through a particularly unpleasant divorce with his first wife. The song is about a fanatical and obsessive love. "Life is all messed up and that's the emotion and driving powerhouse behind it."

Sting had gone off to the Caribbean and was staying at *Goldeneye*, the Jamaican home of James Bond creator, Ian Fleming. Here he wrote 'Every Breath You Take', which was motivated by the break-up of his marriage to the actress, Frances Tomelty.

'Every Breath You Take' was the first single released from the final studio album, *Synchronicity*. "The bastards wrote us off, but I knew I had this song and I knew it would be number one," insisted Sting. The video's basic black and white image seemed to capture Sting's sinister mood accurately.

The single received a multitude of awards including: Song Of The Year, Best Pop Performance at the 1984 Grammy Awards, Best Song Musically and Most Performed Work at the Ivor Novello Awards. At the inaugural MTV Music Video Awards in 1984, it also won Best Cinematography Award. The song is one of the most played on American radio. By 2000 'Every Breath You Take' had clocked up five million plays.

The tension between Stewart Copeland and Sting was at its most rife. Producer Hugh Padgham said, "It was difficult for me to do anything about the fighting, because when I would try to say something like, 'Come on guys, do you have to kick the shit out of each other'? They would say, 'You don't know anything about us'."

Sting, Stewart and Andy got back together in the summer of 1986, with plans of a follow-up album, but the pressure was too much. It resulted in Sting's announcement that he was pursuing a solo career, and the break up of the band.

In 1996 *Regatta Mondatta*, a compilation of reggae covers of Police songs was released. The first single taken from it was Pato Banton and Sting duetting on 'Spirits In The Material World'.

In 1988 Sting took part in Amnesty International's Human Rights Now world tour which also featured Bruce Springsteen, Peter Gabriel, Youssou N'Dour and Tracy Chapman. At one point during the shows Sting and Bruce would perform a duet, with the ex-Policeman taking over from Springsteen during his anthem 'The River'. Then the Boss would return the compliment by taking over from Sting and offering his rendition of 'Every Breath You Take'.

523 Rod Stewart Baby Jane

Label & Cat No.: **Warner W 9608**
Producers: **Rod Stewart / Tom Dowd**
Writers: **Rod Stewart / Jay Davis**
Date reached No.1: **2 July 1983**
Weeks at No.1: **3**

'DA YA THINK I'M SEXY?' WAS A STEP too far. It was a huge hit but it also made Rod Stewart a figure of fun, and singles which would have been big hits floundered. During the five years that followed 'Da You Think I'm Sexy?', Rod Stewart had only one Top 10 single, 'Tonight I'm Yours (Don't Hurt Me)', in 1981.

Rod was also a casualty of the punk explosion – he was as working class as any of them but he epitomised the high life and was seen as out of touch. The fans still bought his albums – *Foolish Behaviour* (1980), *Tonight I'm Yours* (1981) and *Body Wishes* (1983) – and he remained a major concert attraction. What thought possessed him to wear full tartan regalia for the inner sleeve of *Body Wishes*?

As Rod had not been happy with the way *Body Wishes* was sounding, he asked Tom Dowd to rescue the project. 'Baby Jane' was particularly successful. In one sense, it was back to the days of 'Maggie May' and 'You Wear It Well', but the song also had the feel of Michael Jackson's 'Billie Jean'. The theme was identical to Peter Sarstedt's 'Where Do You Go To (My Lovely)?' – "Now you're movin' in high society, Don't forget I know secrets about you."

The follow-up, 'What Am I Gonna Do (I'm So In Love With You)', made number three, but Rod didn't return to the Top 10 until he recorded 'Every Beat Of My Heart' in 1986. Nowadays he is regarded as an elder statesman of rock and he returns to the charts when he has the right song – Tom Waits' 'Tom Traubert's Blues', Van Morrison's 'Have I Told You Lately' and the big ballad from *The Three Musketeers*, 'All For One', which he sang with Bryan Adams and Sting. It was no surprise when he recorded three albums of standards, *It Had To Be You* (2002), *As Time Goes By* (2003) and *Stardust* (2004).

524 Paul Young Wherever I Lay My Hat (That's My Home)

Label & Cat No.: **CBS A 3371**
Producer: **Laurie Latham**
Writers: **Marvin Gaye / Norman Whitfield / Barrett Strong**
Date Reached No.1: **23 July 1983**
Weeks at No.1: **3**

LUCKILY, FEW PEOPLE WILL REMEMBER Paul's appearance on the *Cannon & Ball* show doing a rather poor impression of Max Bygraves. The man with the golden larynx didn't make such a good impression and decided to stick to singing.

Paul first charted in 1978, when the 22 year-old talked his way through the hit 'Toast' as lead singer of Streetband. Paul remembered, "'Toast', as a debut on *Top Of The Pops* was probably one of the worst debuts you could ever have. It was giving the wrong impression as to what you want to be and where you want to be going."

Born in Luton in 1956, Paul served an apprenticeship at the Vauxhall car plant but soon realised his heart was in music. He loved soul music, so his next move was to form the soul covers band, The Q-Tips. The eight-piece extensively toured the local counties with a set that included covers of Joe Tex's 'S.Y.S.L.J.F.M. (The Letter Song)' and Smokey Robinson & The Miracles' 'The Tracks Of My Tears'. They signed a deal with Chrysalis Records but were dropped after their first two singles failed to chart. As Paul recalled, "My manager came to me and said he was having trouble getting a record deal for the band, but Muff Winwood at CBS was interested in me, so I decided it was time to move on."

His first solo release, as Paul Young & The Royal Family, was a cover of Don Covay's 'Iron Out The Rough Spots' which failed to chart. Next came his pop cover of a Four Preps original, 'Love Of The Common People', which had also been covered country style by Waylon Jennings and in a reggae version by Nicky Thomas. Paul dropped The Royal Family and had a third attempt at a cover version. The result, 'Wherever I Lay My Hat', the B-side of Marvin Gaye's 1969 hit 'Too Busy Thinking About My Baby', which were both originally recorded by The Temptations. The backing singers on the first four hits were Kim and Maz, collectively known as the Fabulous Wealthy Tarts.

His debut album *No Parlez* followed hot on the heels of the single. It went on to sell over seven million copies worldwide and spent over two years on the UK album chart.

Paul contributed the opening line on the Band Aid single in 1984 and performed 'Radio Ga Ga' at the Freddie Mercury Tribute Concert in 1992. In 2000 he was fronting his latest band, Los Pacaminos.

525 KC & The Sunshine Band Give It Up

Label & Cat No.: **Epic A 3017**
Producers: **Harry Casey / Richard Finch**
Writer: **Harry Casey**
Date Reached No.1: **13 August 1983**
Weeks at No.1: **3**

KC & THE SUNSHINE BAND DOMINATED the disco charts during the Seventies both here and in the US with songs such as 'That's The Way I Like It' and 'Get Down Tonight'. Another hit, 'Boogie Shoes' featured on the soundtrack to *Saturday Night Fever*. Their last hit came at the very end of the decade when 'Please Don't Go' reached number three.

In early 1981 Harry 'KC' Casey suffered a set back when his record company, TK Records, went bust. He spent the rest of the year looking for a new record deal, which resulted in him signing with Epic Records. He said, "I always thought 'Give It Up' was a hit but was surprised when they released it in the UK, because it had been around for quite a while."

Then, at the beginning of 1982 Harry was involved in a serious car accident. "It took me all year to recover. I suffered concussion and temporary paralysis to my right side. It's all OK now but I still have problems now and then. The hospital had me on so much medication that I didn't know if I was coming or going. So basically I passed the time by writing songs."

Despite the credit, when he returned to the spotlight he appeared alone. He had ditched the Sunshine Band. "I'm sort of fading that out, it's just me now, to update everything," says KC. He now simply relies on the help of his friend Richard Finch, who has been with him since the early Sunshine days.

The comeback was short-lived. The follow-up hit '(You Said) You'd Gimme Some More' ran out of steam just outside the Top 40. In 2001 he released a new album, *I'll Be There For You*. The proceeds of the title track, which was released as a single, were donated to the 9/11 relief effort. The following year, KC received a star on the Hollywood Walk Of Fame and made a cameo appearance in the 2003 film *Til Death Us Do Part*, starring Michael Douglas.

Harry 'KC' Casey

526 UB40
Red Red Wine

Label & Cat No.: **DEP International 7 DEP 7**
Producers: **UB40**
Writer: **Neil Diamond**
Date Reached No.1: **3 September 1983**
Weeks at No.1: **3**

IN 1969 A ONE-HIT WONDER JAMAICAN act, Tony Tribe, took 'Red Red Wine' into the lower end of the chart. It was their version that inspired UB40's lead singer Ali Campbell to cover the song, totally unaware that the song was already a cover.

UB40, who took their name from the number of the unemployment benefit form, were predominantly a white band from Birmingham playing reggae music. Something that doesn't sound like it should work but Astro, the only black member of the band recalled, "We always thought that if reggae was given the same shot as mainstream pop music it would stand a good chance in the marketplace. But unless people hear it, they're not gonna know."

Lead singer Ali Campbell remembered, "The funny thing about the song is we only knew it as a reggae song. We had no idea Neil Diamond had anything to do with it." Astro confirmed: "Even when we saw the writing credit which said N. Diamond, we thought it was a Jamaican artist called Negus Diamond or something."

Neil Diamond released his country-tinged version in 1968. It was produced by Ellie Greenwich and Jeff Barry but stalled at number 62 on the US charts. A year earlier, Neil had his first success in the UK as a songwriter when The Monkees took 'I'm a Believer' to the top.

It was only after UB40 had charted the song that Neil included it in his own concerts, performing it reggae style and occasionally attempting Astro's rap.

Having reached number 34 in America in 1984, the song got a second lease of life in 1988 when Guy Zapoleon at KZZP-FM in Phoenix included the song on his 'Would've Been, Should've Been' feature. He knew the song had been a minor hit four years earlier but didn't think it had reached its potential, so he gave it a spin. The requests came fast, so he urged the record company to re-issue the single. Within a few weeks the song was a Stateside number one.

527 Culture Club
Karma Chameleon

Label & Cat No.: **Virgin VS 612**
Producer: **Steve Levine**
Writers: **Boy George / Mikey Craig / Roy Hay / Jon Moss / Phil Pickett**
Date Reached No.1: **24 September 1983**
Weeks at No.1: **6**

OVER THE YEARS, 'KARMA CHAMELEON' has been dismissed as a nonsensical song, but as George explained in the *Billboard Book Of Number One Hits*, "The song is about the terrible fear of alienation that people have, the fear of standing up for one thing. It's about trying to suck up to everybody. Basically, if you aren't true, if you don't act like you feel, then you get Karma – Justice, that's nature's way of paying you back."

In a similar way that teenagers had copied Adam Ant two years earlier by dressing up and painting their faces, they were now imitating Boy George. Kids nationwide were emulating George's outrageous and oft-changing style which usually involved long white gowns and multi-coloured plaits. Even children's television favourite, *Grange Hill,* jumped on the bandwagon, when in one episode, Suzanne Ross, played by Susan Tully, went to a fancy dress party as Boy George. George once said, "I'd like the band to be remembered as a good band, not as a funny old drag queen with some silly hat on."

'Karma Chameleon', co-written by erstwhile member of Seventies band Sailor, Phil Pickett, topped the Canadian chart for seven weeks; it also gave Culture Club the distinction of being the first group to sell a million copies of a single in Canada.

Back home more hits followed – 'Victims' (5), 'It's A Miracle' (4), 'The War Song' (2) and 'Move Away' (7) – but cracks were beginning to appear within the band. 1986 was not a good year for Culture Club. George and Jon Moss were constantly fighting and arguing, and George was publicly exposed by his brother as a heroin addict which prompted *The Sun* newspaper to carry the headline 'Junkie George has eight weeks to live'. More controversy followed when keyboard player Michael Rudetski, who had contributed to Culture Club's 1986 album *From Luxury To Heartache,* was found dead from a drug overdose in George's London home.

George managed to pull himself through, clean himself up and began following Buddism. But by 1987 he had had enough of the band and broke it up. He immediately embarked on a solo career and his first release, a cover of Ken Boothe's 'Everything I Own'(see entry 586), went to number one.

By 1998 all the rifts had been healed and Culture Club were friends again. They reformed and toured with the original line-up and had a return-to-form, reggae-flavoured Top five hit 'I Just Wanna Be Loved'.

528 Billy Joel
Uptown Girl

Label & Cat No.: **CBS A 3775**

Producer: **Phil Ramone**

Writer: **Billy Joel**

Date reached No.1: **5 November 1983**

Weeks at No.1: **5**

New York's Billy Joel, has had enormous success in America, scoring number one hits with 'It's Still Rock And Roll To Me' (1980), 'Tell Her About It' (1983) and his justification of American foreign policy, 'We Didn't Start The Fire' (1989). He nearly made the top with 'Just The Way You Are' (1977), 'My Life' (1978), 'Uptown Girl' (1983) and 'The River Of Dreams' (1993). His tally of five UK Top 10 singles is not so impressive, possibly because we already have our own much loved singer, pianist and songwriter in Elton John.

Billy Joel's 1983 album, *An Innocent Man,* was a tribute to the music he loved as he was growing up in the early Sixties. He wrote the songs himself but they captured the style of those performers – he said, "Usually I agonise over every note, but this time the songs came pouring out of me." 'Tell Her About It' was a tribute to Martha & The Vandellas, 'An Innocent Man' evoked Ben E. King and The Drifters, and 'Uptown Girl' was modelled on both The Four Seasons' style and their subject-matter: poor boy loving rich girl, or vice versa. "It was very flattering," says their lead singer, Frankie Valli, "but I wish he'd given the song to me as we needed it at the time."

The video, shot in a rough part of New York, showed Billy Joel and his workmates in a garage, ogling a pin-up of model Christie Brinkley, and being amazed when she drives in to have her car serviced. Billy said, "She's my girlfriend and she's the sexiest, most wonderful woman in the world. I'm five foot seven and balding and definitely not as pretty as Simon LeBon. The song is saying, 'What is a stunning girl like you doing with a guy like me?'" Billy and Christie were married in 1985, but divorced in 1994.

529 Flying Pickets
Only You

Label & Cat No.: **10 Records TEN 14**

Producers: **Flying Pickets / John Sherry**

Writer: **Vince Clarke**

Date reached No.1: **10 December 1983**

Weeks at No.1: **5**

As seven per cent of the population own 84 per cent of the wealth, a Socialist theatre company that called itself 7:84 was formed by director John McGrath. During the miners' strike, the group toured the UK with a play, *One Big Blow*, which involved acappella singing, written and arranged by Rick Lloyd. As they toured in a transit, they created arrangements for their favourite songs, more to amuse themselves than anything else. At short notice, they did a concert at Albany Empire in Deptford, and when the play finished, they thought that they would do some concerts rather than return to the dole. Calling themselves, with political connotations, The Flying Pickets, they had a successful fortnight at The Edinburgh Festival.

Part of The Flying Pickets' appeal was that they didn't select the obvious songs for acappella treatment. They took Talking Heads' 'Psycho Killer', Bob Marley's 'Buffalo Soldier' and they included new songs from Rick Lloyd like 'Remember This' and 'So Close'. One of their surprising choices was Yazoo's 'Only You'. The 1982 single by Vince Clarke and Alison Moyet made number two and The Flying Pickets revived it on Virgin's 10 label, also recording versions in Spanish, German and Italian. It was the first acappella single at number one, although 'Amazing Grace' (Judy Collins, 1970), 'Gaudete' (Steeleye Span, 1973) and 'After The Goldrush' (Prelude, 1974) had been hits. Subsequent acappella hits include 'Caravan Of Love' (Housemartins, 1986), 'Tom's Diner' (Suzanne Vega's original version, 1987) and 'Don't Worry, Be Happy' (Bobby McFerrin, 1988).

Although The Flying Pickets' harmonies were spot on, the 30-somethings resembled *The Usual Suspects*. The lead singer on 'Only You', Brian Hibbard, dressed like an ageing Teddy Boy, the shaven-headed Red Stripe, a former fire-eater, wore a donkey-jacket, the diminutive, tousled-haired David Brett had a long scarf and a fedora, Rick Lloyd was Harvey Keitel, Ken Gregson in his shiny blue suit was a 'Mr. Blonde', and Interpol might have been chasing the mysterious bassman Gareth Williams. The day the single entered the charts, Brian and Stripe received notice to quit their Deptford Housing Association home.

Like Scaffold, The Flying Pickets found it hard to adapt to family audiences and they created controversy on the children's programme, *Saturday Superstore*, by offering Karl Marx tea-towels as prizes. That was the producer's fault for having them on live: their 'fan club' was after all called The Picket Line.

The Flying Pickets had a further hit with

Ruby & The Romantics' 'When You're Young And In Love' and their stage favourites included 'Summertime' with its reference to *Reach For The Sky*, their John Otway-styled 'Get Off Of My Cloud', and their gay duet of 'I Got You Babe'. "We found that there weren't many good songs that had a political message," says Stripe, "and we worked more in an ironical way. Songs that were heavily romantic sounded strange when coming from six blokes, you know."

530 Paul McCartney Pipes Of Peace

Label & Cat No.: **Parlophone R 6064**

Producer: **George Martin**

Writer: **Paul McCartney**

Date reached No.1: **14 January 1984**

Weeks at No.1: **2**

After chart-toppers as a part of a duo (with Stevie Wonder), a trio (Wings), a quartet (Beatles) and a quintet (Beatles with Billy Preston), Macca finally made it on his own with 'Pipes Of Peace'. It was back to his old team as the record was produced by The Beatles' producer, George Martin and engineered by Geoff Emerick.

Paul's songs, 'Tug Of War', 'Tug Of Peace' and 'Pipes Of Peace' can be taken as a trilogy. They are anti-war songs and the poignant, award-winning video for 'Pipes Of Peace' showed Paul portraying soldiers on opposite sides in the trenches during the First World War. The video recreated the incident where the opposing sides played a football match in No Man's Land on Christmas Day, 1914.

The key line of the song, 'In love our problems disappear' is taken from India's greatest poet, the 1913 Nobel prize winner, Rabindranath Tagore: 'In love all of life's contradictions dissolve and disappear.'

The album was going to be called *Tug Of War II* but, because of the strength of his new composition, Paul switched it at the last minute to *Pipes Of Peace*. It was the first album by a Beatle to be issued on CD and it included a hit duet with Michael Jackson, 'Say Say Say'. 'Pipes Of Peace' was Paul McCartney's 25th number one as a songwriter, but the B-side, a high-pitched soul ballad 'So Bad', was the hit in the US.

531 Frankie Goes To Hollywood Relax

Label & Cat No.: **ZTT ZTAS 1**

Producer: **Trevor Horn**

Writers: **Peter Gill / Holly Johnson / Mark O'Toole**

Date reached No.1: **28 January 1984**

Weeks at No.1: **5**

Frankie Goes To Hollywood took their name from an illustration by Guy Peellaert in his 1974 book, *Rock Dreams*, which showed Sinatra going to the film capital. Whilst performing in Liverpool clubs, the band wrote 'Relax' and 'Two Tribes' and the versions recorded for John Peel's Radio 1 programme are not far from the finished versions.

The song was given a bulldozing production by Trevor Horn, who had been a member of Buggles and Yes. There was to be much debate, even in court, over who had played on the record and what Horn had created on his electronic equipment. Whatever, 'Relax' was a remarkable record, although its controversial lyric owes as much to Shakespeare as Holly Johnson as he wrote in *Hamlet* in 1602, 'Young will do't, If they come to't, By cock, They are to blame.'

Mike Read criticised the song on his breakfast show for its message of gay sex and the record, which had been on Radio 1's playlist, was banned. This doubtless helped it to spend 48 consecutive weeks on the charts, thereby outlasting the follow-ups, 'Two Tribes' and 'The Power Of Love'. The two million plus UK sales were helped by a brilliant but cynical marketing campaign, spearheaded by Paul Morley, which involved numerous remixes, T-shirts, slogans and an infamous video modelled on Fellini. Morley later said, "It's easy to get publicity if you annoy people", and he was right.

The B-side on the 12-inch version was 'Ferry Cross The Mersey' and they included covers of Edwin Starr's 'War' and Bruce Springsteen's 'Born To Run' on their double-album, *Welcome To The Pleasuredome*. The album was as brash and provocative as their single and it topped the albums chart.

532 Nena 99 Red Balloons

Label & Cat No.: **Epic A 4074**

Producers: **Reinhold Heil / Manne Praeker**

Writers: **Joern-Uwe Fahrenkrog-Peterson / Carlo Karges / Kevin McAlea**

Date reached No.1: **3 March 1984**

Weeks at No.1: **3**

Nena was both the name of the group and the name given to the lead singer, Gabriele Kerner, who was born in Hagen, West Germany in 1960. She formed a Blondie-styled band, The Stripes, in 1979 with the drummer, Rolf Brendel. When the group folded in 1982, they went to Berlin and formed Nena, which became an integral part of NDW (Neue Deutsche Welle, which is German New Wave). They recorded rock-based, cheerful tunes, often with ridiculous lyrics. They had a German hit with 'Nur Getraeumt (Just A Dream)' and then came '99 Luftballons'. It was inspired by seeing The Rolling Stones release hundreds of balloons during their concert at the Waldbühne Arena in Berlin.

In the song, two youths buy a bag of balloons. They inflate and release them, but military surveyors mistake them for the enemy and begin a nuclear attack. The singer has one balloon left and seeing the world in ruins around her, lets it go. A Los Angeles DJ loved the song's dance rhythm and started playing it. Epic rush-released the single and it climbed to number two, a rare acheivement for a foreign language single in the States.

Epic had been taken by surprise in the US, but they had time to commission and record an English lyric for the UK. The single went to the top, and Trekkies everywhere loved the line, 'Everyone's a superhero, Every one's a Captain Kirk', a direct translation from the German. Actually, Dr. Strangelove would have been a closer comparison.

Nena, the band, had 13 chart singles in Germany, but just the one in the UK: when they folded in 1987, Nena, the soloist, had a further six hits. Now she is a mother of five children and although in her forties, she looks much younger. In 2002 she recorded a big-selling live album in Germany, and she and Kim Wilde had a number one in Austria with one of the tracks, 'Anyplace Anywhere Anytime'.

533 Lionel Richie
Hello

Label & Cat No.: **Motown TMG 1330**

Producers: **James Anthony Carmichael / Lionel Richie**

Writer: **Lionel Richie**

Date reached No.1: **24 March 1984**

Weeks at No.1: **6**

After 'Three Times A Lady', Lionel Richie still worked with The Commodores, but he undertook solo projects. He wrote and produced an album for Kenny Rogers, *Share Your Love*, and their single, 'Lady', topped the US charts for six weeks. Another of his songs, 'Endless Love', was a film theme and an international hit for himself and Diana Ross.

Lionel Richie left The Commodores in 1982 and immediately had a hit album, *Truly*, which included the singles, 'Truly', 'You Are' and 'My Love'. He had written 'Hello' for the album, but he felt its mood was too similar to 'Truly' and he left it off.

His second solo album, *Can't Slow Down*, was even more successful. It contained five hit singles – 'All Night Long (All Night)' (2), 'Running With The Night' (9), 'Hello' (1), 'Stuck On You' (12) and 'Penny Lover' (18) – and this number one album remained on the UK charts for three years. During 1984 Lionel Richie wrote and recorded Pepsi ads for an astonishing $8.5m. He did, however, have to challenge an allegation from Marjorie White that 'Hello' was based on her song, 'I'm Not Ready To Go', but he won.

The sentimental song, 'Hello', was promoted with a distinctive but cringe-inducing video, which included dialogue. Lionel Richie plays a teacher who falls in love with a blind student. When he looks in at her sculpture class, he finds that she has made a perfect model of him.

534 Duran Duran
The Reflex

Label & Cat No.: **EMI DURAN 2**

Producers: **Duran Duran / Ian Little / Alex Sadkin**

Writers: **Duran Duran**

Date reached No.1: **5 May 1984**

Weeks at No.1: **4**

Duran Duran epitomised the glamorous rock star life, plenty of girls and jet-setting, and, with Simon Le Bon, his passion for sailing. In 1985 this would catapult him into the headlines when his boat capsized in a force eight gale during The Fastnet Race.

Their 1983 album, *Seven And The Ragged Tiger*, had done well, spawning two hit singles. They felt that 'The Reflex' also had potential and they invited Nile Rodgers of Chic, who had worked with David Bowie on 'Let's Dance', to remix it. The result was a single that went to number one in both Britain and the USA.

There had, however, been dissatisfaction in the Duran Duran camp over *Seven And The Ragged Tiger* and, in 1985, the group split into two. Both factions had hit singles – Arcadia (Simon LeBon, Nick Rhodes and Roger Taylor with Grace Jones) made 'Election Day' and Power Station (Andy Taylor and John Taylor with Robert Palmer) offered 'Some Like It Hot'. They returned with one of the most successful James Bond themes, *A View To A Kill,* which made number two. Surprisingly, no Bond theme has ever topped the UK charts.

Duran Duran outlasted its New Romantics tag by having hits in 1989 with 'All She Wants Is' and in 1993 with 'Ordinary World'. The Duranies were out in full force for the band's sell-out stadium tour in 2004, and they were back in the Top five with '(Reach Out for The) Sunrise'.

535 Wham!
Wake Me Up Before You Go-Go

Label & Cat No.: **Epic A 4440**

Producer: **George Michael**

Writer: **George Michael**

Date reached No.1: **2 June 1984**

Weeks at No.1: **2**

George Michael's father was a Greek-Cypriot restaurateur who settled in the affluent suburb of Bushey, Herts. In 1975 when Georgios Kyriacos Panayiotou was 12, he went to Bushey Meads Comprehensive School where another pupil, Andrew Ridgeley, was asked to look after him. Soon they were discussing records and, given a couple of years, they were playing ska in a local band, The Executive.

In 1982 George and Andrew hired a portastudio for £20 and made a demo, 'Wham Rap! (Enjoy What You Do)', with George on vocals and bass and Andrew on guitar and drum machine. They hawked it around London and got a £500 advance from a new label, Innervision. The single wasn't a hit, but their second one, 'Young Guns (Go For It)' made number three in 1982. 'Wham Rap!' was reissued, making number eight, and then they scored with 'Bad Boys' (2) and 'Club Tropicana' (4), which was a close cousin to Club 18-30. Their album, *Fantastic!*, entered the album charts at number one and they hit the road with their Club Fantastic Tour, featuring Pepsi & Shirlie as backing singers and dancers.

In reality, not everything was so carefree. Wham! realised that they had signed a mean-spirited and demanding contract with Innervision and they asked Simon Napier-Bell, who had managed The Yardbirds and Marc Bolan, to resolve it. As a result, they moved to the CBS label, Epic, and realising that they were getting no new product, Innversion released 'Club Fantastic Megamix', which Wham! disowned but it still made the Top 20.

When George was at the Ridgeley family home, he saw that Andrew had written a message for his mother, who was working in the morning, 'Wake me up-up before you go-go'. George Michael developed this into a party song with the much-ridiculed couplet, 'Wake me up before you go-go, Don't leave me hanging on like a yo-yo', and it was recorded quickly around a drum track at the Sarm West studio in London. The lyric also contained the line, 'I'm not planning on going solo.' Well, not for a couple of months anyway.

536 Frankie Goes To Hollywood Two Tribes

Label & Cat No.: **ZTT ZTAS 3**
Producer: **Trevor Horn**
Writers: **Peter Gill / Holly Johnson / Mark O'Toole**
Date reached No.1: **16 June 1984**
Weeks at No.1: **9**

It is always difficult to follow a truly unique record but Frankie Goes To Hollywood did remarkably well by moving from gay sex to the Cold War for 'Two Tribes'. The whole song was written around one of Mark O'Toole's bass lines. "Trevor Horn wasn't too sure about the single," reveals their guitarist Brian Nash (Nasher). "He wanted us to do 'Slave To The Rhythm' but then he changed his mind and gave the song to Grace Jones."

During the summer, numerous remixes of 'Two Tribes' were put into the shops – some devotees bought all nine versions! – and again FGTH were helped by a controversial video. This one, made by Godley & Creme featured a wrestling match between look-alike American and Soviet presidents, Reagan and Chernenko. "I don't think the single went down very well in Russia," quips Nasher. As well as Frankie Goes To Hollywood, the actor, Patrick Allen, read extracts from civil defence leaflets.

With two groundbreaking number one singles, Holly Johnson was becoming a major celebrity and naturally his sexuality was a source of media interest. "I don't count myself as the first openly gay pop star," says Holly. "What about Little Richard, and he was queer in both senses of the word. I loved the make-up and the glamour and the androgyny of what he did."

The technology was backfiring on Frankie as some maintained that the group was created in the studio. However, they played hugely successful concerts in which it was clear that the five members – Holly, Mark Rutherford, Nasher (guitar), Mark O'Toole (bass) and Peter Gill (drums) could play and sing.

537 George Michael Careless Whisper

Label & Cat No.: **Epic A 4603**
Producer: **George Michael**
Writers: **George Michael / Andrew Ridgeley**
Date reached No.1: **18 August 1984**
Weeks at No.1: **3**

In 1979 George Michael was dreaming of stardom, but working as an usher in a cinema. As he travelled on the bus, he worked out a lyric about one of his relationships, 'Careless Whisper' – note the reference to 'the silver screen' in the first verse. He has said since, "I wasn't secure enough to write something that would expose my feelings, so it's very clichéd in a lot of its terms." He completed the song, which could have been called 'I'm Never Gonna Dance Again', with his partner in Wham!, Andrew Ridgeley.

When Wham! started having hits, George Michael recorded the song in Muscle Shoals, Alabama with the noted soul producer, Jerry Wexler. Oddly, he felt that the version lacked soul and he recorded it again at his usual Sarm Studio, West London with Andy Richards on keyboards. Jerry Wexler commented in his autobiography, *Rhythm And The Blues*, "Our version came out only in Japan, though some think, because of the live fiddles, the American rendition has the edge."

The single was issued under George's name alone and he dedicated the ballad to his mother and father saying it was "five minutes in return for 21 years". While he was promoting the single, Andrew Ridgeley was having plastic surgery on his nose. The record was an international number one, but in America it was released with the billing, 'Wham! featuring George Michael'. It was also included as a track on Wham!'s number one UK album, *Make It Big*.

As a result of 'Careless Whisper' and other songs, George Michael became, at the age of 21, the youngest recipient of the Ivor Novello Songwriter Of The Year award, and the song itself received an award for being the Most Performed Work that year. George has said, "It disappoints me that you can write a lyric very flippantly and it can mean so much to so many people."

538 Stevie Wonder I Just Called To Say I Love You

Label & Cat No.: **Motown TMG 1349**
Producer: **Stevie Wonder**
Writer: **Stevie Wonder**
Date Reached No.1: **8 September 1984**
Weeks at No.1: **6**

Stevie Wonder's first solo number one, 'I Just Called To Say I Love You' came

18 years after his first chart appearance with 'Uptight (Everything's Alright)' in 1966. He had come close a few times; 'Yester-Me, Yester-You, Yesterday', 'Sir Duke', 'Masterblaster (Jammin')' and 'Happy Birthday' all reached number two.

Stevie was born Steveland Judkins in 1950 in Saginaw, Michigan. He had been blind since birth, due to accidentally being given too much oxygen in an incubator, but Stevie didn't let his handicap hinder him. In 1954 the family moved to Detroit where, after becoming influenced by Sam Cooke and Ray Charles, he joined a local choir. He learned to write songs and by seven he had learned to play the piano. Within two years, he had also mastered the harmonica and drums.

In 1960 he was discovered by Ronnie White of The Miracles, who arranged an audition with a small up and coming label, Tamla Motown. The label owner, Berry Gordy was too busy at the time and arranged for Brian Holland, of Holland / Dozier / Holland fame, to see him. Brian realised his potential and recommended Gordy sign him. The first year was spent grooming Stevie. Gordy renamed him 'Little Stevie Wonder'. His first hit, 'Fingertips – Part 2' went to the top of the US chart, as did his first album, *Little Stevie Wonder/The 12 Year Old Genius*. He was allowed to work to his own schedule and by his own rules.

Throughout the Seventies, Stevie was a mainstay in both the UK and US charts. His albums, *Innervisions* (1974), *Fulfillingness' First Finale* (1974) and *Songs In The Key Of Life* (1976) were all Album Of The Year Grammy winners. In 1970 he married fellow Motown singer, Syreeta Wright. Together they wrote 'Signed, Sealed, Delivered (I'm Yours)' and 'It's A Shame', for the Motown Spinners. Two years later they divorced.

In 1984 Dionne Warwick suggested to the producers of a new film, *The Woman In Red*, that Stevie could score it. Stevie was invited to 'see' the film, starring Gene Wilder, and Kelly LeBrock as the woman in red. Dionne Warwick confirmed, "Stevie must have seen that film. There's no way in the world that you could write the pieces of music that he wrote so directly." When the song topped the UK chart, it became the first number one to be written, produced, performed, arranged and all instruments played by the same person.

In 1984 'I Just Called To Say I Love You', which had been written in the late Seventies, but hadn't yet made it onto an album, was nominated in the Best Song category at the Grammy Award, but was up against 'Footloose' and 'Let's Hear It For The Boy', both from *Footloose*, 'Against All Odds (Take A Look At Me Now)' from *An Officer And A Gentleman* and, 'Ghostbusters' from the film of the same name.

Stevie won and collected his first Oscar on behalf of the imprisoned ANC leader, Nelson Mandela. News travelled fast – the very next day the South African Broadcasting Company banned all Stevie Wonder songs from their airwaves. Stevie reacted by declaring, "If my being banned means people will be free, then ban me mega-times."

539 Wham!
Freedom

Label & Cat No.: **Epic A 4743**

Producer: **George Michael**

Writer: **George Michael**

Date reached No.1: **20 October 1984**

Weeks at No.1: **2**

ALTHOUGH GEORGE MICHAEL WAS THE dominant partner in Wham!, Andrew Ridgeley played his part and he did much work on Wham!'s image and 'casual chic' look – remember the white T-shirts and trousers? As a result, Wham! mania was everywhere and 'Freedom' was released in two versions – you could choose between a George or Andrew shaped single. Many fans bought both which only increased the sales.

'Freedom' retained the catchiness of 'Wake Me Up Before You Go-Go', although the lyric was more of a soap opera. George is coming to terms with his girlfriend's promiscuity but he has no intention of being promiscuous himself. There was nothing personal about the song – he wrote it to pass the time while being driven to an airport in France.

Through skilful negotiations by their manager, Simon Napier-Bell, in 1985 Wham! became the first western group to perform live in China, entertaining 10,000 fans at the Workers' Gymnasium in Beijing. In his solo career, George has taken up many political causes. As an early example, he announced in Beijing: "This is a number one hit in our country, and I hope one day it will be number one in China with your help. It is called 'Freedom'."

Not everyone loved Wham! though and George Michael was to sympathise with his detractors, "I understand completely why some people hated us, we were so cocky and so childish." In 1990 George Michael wrote a response to his days in Wham! with another 'Freedom' song, this time called 'Freedom '90': "Just my buddy and me, We had every big shot, good-time band on the run, boy."

540 Chaka Khan
I Feel For You

Label & Cat No.: **Warners W 9209**

Producer: **Arif Mardin**

Writer: **Prince**

Date reached No.1: **10 November 1984**

Weeks at No.1: **3**

IT COMES IN LIKE A DRUMBEAT – "Chaka Chaka Chaka Chaka Khan" – it's the riveting, rapping start by Melle Mel to the number one single, 'I Feel For You'. "I was so embarrassed when I first heard it," says Chaka about that introduction. "I thought it was horrible and Arif Mardin said that I would have to trust him on this one."

Chaka Khan, born Yvette Marie Stevens in 1953 in Grand Lakes, Illinois, was the lead singer of the rock and soul band, Rufus. They had only a cult following in the UK, but they had US hits with the Stevie Wonder song, 'Tell Me Something Good' and 'Sweet Thing'. Chaka left in 1978 but, on their reunion in 1984, they scored with 'Ain't Nobody'.

In both Britain and America, Chaka's solo career had a fine start with a song about independence, 'I'm Every Woman' (1978), written by the Motown writing team of Nick Ashford and Valerie Simpson. She had big selling albums with *Chaka* (1978) and *What Cha' Gonna Do For Me* (1981), but received only critical praise for *Chaka Khan* (1983). She and her producer, Arif Mardin, won a Grammy for their 'Bebop Medley' but Warners felt that she was being self-indulgent: she was recording jazz songs and ignoring contemporary sounds. The next album would have to be aimed at the charts.

Prince's 1980 album, *Prince*, included 'I Feel For You' and Chaka Khan thought it would make a good single. Prince agreed to play guitar, but, in the end, he couldn't fit it into his schedule. Stevie Wonder played harmonica and Mardin flew from New York to Los Angeles to record his contribution on the same day as Marvin Gaye's funeral.

With the addition of Melle Mel, the record sounded very contemporary, but at its heart was an excellent vocal from Chaka herself. The record had cost $30,000 but it would be an international hit. The whole album, *I Feel For You*, found Chaka working effectively in electro-funk rhythms and it also contained 'This Is My Night', 'Eye To Eye' and 'Through The Fire'.

Since then, Chaka Khan has had sporadic success in the UK charts including remixes of 'I'm Every Woman', 'Ain't Nobody' and 'I Feel For You' in 1989. The following year she made the Top 30 with 'I'll Be Good For You' with herself, Ray Charles and Quincy Jones.

In 1995 Chaka Khan starred as Sister Carrie in the West End musical about Doris Troy's life, *Mama, I Want To Sing.*

Chaka Khan

541 Jim Diamond
I Should Have Known Better

Label & Cat No.: **A&M AM 200**

Producer: **Pip Williams**

Writers: **Jim Diamond / Graham Lyle**

Date reached No.1: **1 December 1984**

Weeks at No.1: **1**

JIM DIAMOND, WHO WAS BORN IN GLASgow in 1951, is a good example of a journeyman musician who eventually breaks through. He had started his professional career playing guitar and singing in a Glasgow band, Jade, and then performing around Europe in a soul and blues band, Gully Foyle. He formed Bandit and although they recorded melodic singles for Arista in the late Seventies, they had little success as punk had become the order of the day. Jim moved to Alexis Korner's blues band and then formed Slick Diamond with Earl Slick, who had played on David Bowie's *Young Americans*. Jim and the French composer, Michel Legrand, wrote 'Lady Oscar' for Merry Clayton and Jim also produced Zoot Money's album, *Mr. Money*.

In 1981 Jim Diamond teamed up with the keyboard player, Tony Hymas, and the drummer, Simon Phillips, to form the synth-based PhD. They had a Top 10 with 'I Won't Let You Down' as well as a European hit with 'I Didn't Know', featuring Jeff Beck, but PhD never played live.

Written with Graham Lyle of Gallagher & Lyle, 'I Should Have Known Better' was the first number one for Rondor Music. Graham recalls, "We knew it was good and very commercial. We also thought it could buried as it wasn't danceable, it was slow, it was sentimental, and none of those things were commercial at the time. Jim did a great job, here is a man who knows how to communicate a lyric." Jim's follow-ups, 'I Sleep Alone At Night' and 'Remember I Love You', hardly registered, but in 1986 he was back with the theme song for the crime series, *Boon*, starring Michael Elphick, 'Hi Ho Silver'. In 1993 his album, *Jim Diamond*, was produced by Graham Lyle and he recorded a new version of 'I Should Have Known Better'.

542 Frankie Goes To Hollywood
The Power Of Love

Label & Cat No.: **ZTT ZTAS 5**

Producer: **Trevor Horn**

Writers: **Peter Gill / Holly Johnson / Brian Nash / Mark O'Toole**

Date reached No.1: **8 December 1984**

Weeks at No.1: **1**

FRANKIE GOES TO HOLLYWOOD HAD their third number one with 'The Power Of Love', this time moving from sex and politics to religion, although the song was not controversial. "We weren't helped by the video," says Holly Johnson. "It was naff and it was made by Godley & Creme while we were away. I love the song though and people have told me that they fell in love to it."

With 'The Power Of Love', FGTH equalled Gerry & The Pacemakers' achievement of making number one with their first three releases. And, just like Gerry, their fourth single, 'Welcome To The Pleasuredome', made number two.

Their success ended in tears as the group sued their record label, ZTT, for non-payment of royalties and breaking contractual obligations. Holly Johnson has had a successful but sporadic solo career, the high point being a number one album, *Blast*, in 1989. His biggest singles, also in 1989, have been 'Love Train' (with Brian May on guitar) and 'Americanos'. Being HIV positive, he lost his fixation with being in the public eye and has concentrated on art, having his tribute to Elvis Presley displayed at the Tate and a 2004 exhibition, *Hello Sailor*, in Liverpool.

Nasher wrote several songs on his own CD, *Le Grande Fromage* (2002), which illustrated that he felt bitterly about the way they had been treated, particularly by ZTT. In 2000 Rob Searle remixed 'The Power Of Love' and the single restored them to the Top Ten. Frankie Goes To Hollywood, with Ryan Malloy replacing Holly Johnson, performed at a homage to Trevor Horn at Wembley Arena in November 2004.

543 Band Aid
Do They Know It's Christmas?

Label & Cat No.: **Phonogram FEED 1**
Producer: **Midge Ure**
Writers: **Bob Geldof / Midge Ure**
Date reached No.1: **15 December 1984**
Weeks at No.1: **5**

ALL-STAR CHARITY SINGLES DATE BACK to the Fifties, but Bob Geldof of The Boomtown Rats organised one on an unprecedented scale. He saw a BBC-TV report by Michael Buerk about the famine in Ethiopia and became determined to do something about it straightaway: "I'm not interested in the bloody system," he said. "Why has he no food? Why is he starving to death?" He rang his wife, Paula Yates, who was hosting *The Tube* in Newcastle and asked her to put one of the guests, Midge Ure of Ultravox, on the line. They concluded that the only thing they knew about was making records and as 50 per cent of the monies generated on a single went to the songwriters, they had better write a new one. "We knew if we made it a Christmas song, we would pull at the purse strings as well as the heartstrings," says Midge Ure.

Bob Geldof acquired a major studio for a day and requested one chart act after another to take part. Bob asked the stars "to leave their egos outside the studio" and they recorded the song with no hassle. The single featured David Bowie, Boy George, Marilyn, George Michael, Sting, Paul Weller, Paul Young and members of Bananarama, The Boomtown Rats, Duran Duran, Frankie Goes To Hollywood, Heaven 17, Kool & The Gang, Shalamar, Spandau Ballet, Status Quo, U2 and Ultravox.

The vocalists were adding their voices to a track laid down by Midge Ure with Phil Collins on drums. Midge recalls, "I sang my guide vocal in middling keys with no extremes, which meant that nobody would be given anything that they couldn't sing. I was standing next to Bono when he got the line, 'Tonight, thank God, it's them instead of you', a controversial line that Bob

insisted should be included. They ran the track and Bono took that line up an octave and belted it out like you wouldn't believe. It was like standing next to a wonderful opera singer, and it was absolute magic."

The picture sleeve was designed by Peter Blake, who was famous for his package for *Sgt. Pepper's Lonely Hearts Club Band*. The Band Aid single sold 3.5m copies, easily becoming the biggest-selling single in the UK to date: "Bob and I hoped we would make about £100,000, but it is now around £10m. It is included every year on *This Is What I Call Christmas, 2,000,000* and the like, and it will be making money for charity long after Bob and I have gone."

The artists, the musicians, the record companies and the distributors had agreed to forgo their profits, but Bob Geldof was less successful with the Government, who insisted on the payment of VAT.

And it shouldn't be overlooked that Bob Geldof and Midge Ure wrote a classic Christmas song.

544 Foreigner
I Want To Know What Love Is

Label & Cat No.: **Atlantic A 9596**
Producers: **Alex Sadkin / Mick Jones**
Writer: **Mick Jones**
Date reached No.1: **19 January 1985**
Weeks at No.1: **3**

THE ROCK BAND FOREIGNER WAS formed in New York in 1976. It included the Londoners, Mick Jones (guitar, ex-Nero & The Gladiators, Johnny Hallyday, Spooky Tooth) and Ian McDonald (guitar, keyboards, ex-King Crimson) and Dennis Elliott (drums) with the New Yorkers, Lou Gramm (vocals, ex-Black Sheep), Al Greenwood (keyboards) and Ed Gagliardi (bass). In view of their nationalities, they called themselves Foreigner. Signed to Atlantic and starting in 1977, they had a succession of US hit singles – 'Feels Like The First Time', 'Cold As Ice', 'Hot Blooded' and 'Double Vision' – although they were only minor successes in the UK.

The personnel changed in 1980 and Foreigner became Jones, Gramm and Elliott with Rick Wills (bass, ex-Roxy Music). They had a change of direction with a powerful ballad, 'Waiting For A Girl Like You', which gave them their first UK Top 10 hit and was also number two in America for 10 weeks.

In 1984 they made their album, *Agent Provocateur*, and chose another ballad as the first single, 'I Want To Know What Love Is'. The group was split over this decision as they thought they might lose some of their hard rock credentials – which they did, but it was a US number one.

'I Want To Know What Love Is' featured Tom Bailey from The Thompson Twins and Jennifer Holiday from *Dream Girls* and it developed into a gospel song as Lou Gramm was supported in the final chorus by The New Jersey Mass Choir. Foreigner had one other Top 30 hit in the UK ('That Was Yesterday') but other huge US singles in the same style, 'Say You Will' and 'I Don't Want To Live Without You', meant nothing here. Foreigner still tours, playing a nudist festival in 1995. Lou Gramm has been in and out of Foreigner: he stopped touring because of a brain tumour in 1997 but now fronts his own band.

Mick Jones of Foreigner

545 Elaine Paige & Barbara Dickson I Know Him So Well

Label & Cat No.: **RCA CHESS 3**

Producers: **Benny Andersson / Tim Rice / Björn Ulvaeus**

Writers: **Benny Andersson / Tim Rice / Björn Ulvaeus**

Date reached No.1: **9 February 1985**

Weeks at No.1: **4**

IN 1982 BENNY ANDERSSON AND Björn Ulvaeus teamed up with Tim Rice to write the musical, *Chess*, which took two years to complete. Björn says, "We were very pleased as we had something longer to work on, both the bigger format and the concept of drama and music together. I can see now that there is quite a lot of that in the later Abba songs, so we were working towards that. 'One Night In Bangkok' and 'I Know Him So Well' could easily have been Abba songs."

'I Know Him So Well', a beautifully crafted song about two disillusioned lovers of the same man, was performed by Elaine Paige and Barbara Dickson. Elaine Paige had starred in *Evita* and had had a Top 10 single with 'Memory' from *Cats* in 1981. Barbara Dickson was a folk singer, performing traditional Scottish material, until Willy Russell asked her to perform in his 1974 musical, *John Paul George Ringo...And Bert*. Her hits included a revival of 'Answer Me' (1976), 'Another Suitcase In Another Hall' from *Evita* (1977) and 'January February' (1980). "We had Elaine Paige in mind from the start," says Björn. "She was with Tim at the time and she was the best theatre singer in the world. When we heard Barbara Dickson, we realised that she was wonderful too. She retained that folky quality even when she did *Chess* and that really attracted me."

Barbara Dickson says, "It sounded to the average person in the street like a fantastic new Abba record and they loved the chance of buying an Abba record again. It was a sophisticated song – two women singing different things about the same man. We didn't record it together. Elaine had been to Stockholm and done the recording and I was brought in much later. When the record came out, we promoted it together of course."

The musical, which featured a chess match between Russia and America, was reasonably successful but many found it too demanding. "I think the same," said Björn in 2004. "The new version, which is running in Stockholm, is much less about chess and is much clearer. We are planning to bring it to London."

Because of the song's unusual lyric, it is not covered as much as it might be. One cover comes from the mother and daughter partnership of Cissy and Whitney Houston on the *Whitney* album in 1987. And was Barbara and Elaine a one-off partnership? "Yes, says Barbara, "although it was mooted that Elaine and I should make an album together. We have become very good friends and there have been times where we have thought of making that album. I think we have missed the time now."

546 Dead Or Alive You Spin Me Round (Like A Record)

Label & Cat No.: **Epic A 4861**

Producers: **Mike Stock / Matt Aitken / Pete Waterman**

Writers: **Pete Burns / Stephen Coy / Tim Lever / Michael Percy**

Date reached No.1: **9 March 1985**

Weeks at No.1: **2**

THE RECORD SHOP DEPICTED IN *High Fidelity* had nothing on Liverpool's Probe Records, which was mostly staffed by eccentrics and misfits. An alien couldn't have looked stranger than Pete Burns, a tough guy with outlandish clothes, coloured dreadlocks and much mascara and make-up. If you wanted a record he disapproved of, he wouldn't sell it to you – and that included everything by Boy George. He was as much a mouth of the Mersey as Derek Hatton.

As Pete also sang in the evenings with Dead Or Alive, everyone wondered how he found the time to dress so beautifully. Dead Or Alive also featured Stephen Coy (drums), Tim Lever (keyboards) and Michael Percy (bass). The dance song, 'You Spin Me Round (Like A Record)', which they wrote together, was inspired by Pete's days of selling vinyl.

Pete Burns was impressed by Stock Aitken & Waterman's techno sound for Hazell Dean and Devine and he approached the production team about taking him on.

The record became the first number one record by the production team of Mike Stock, Matt Aitken and Pete Waterman. In a very revealing interview for *BBC Music* magazine in 2002, Pete Waterman told Adam Sweeting, "That had *Ride Of The Valkyries* all over it. I've stolen from Wagner about 20 times and what I take from him is pathos, string runs and harmonies. My job is to make sure you don't spot it. We changed a few things around, but if you listen to 'You Spin Me Round', the strings are straight off *Valkyries* – they do all the glissandos and the wind-ups."

Dead Or Alive had other Top 20 records ('Lover Come Back To Me', 'In Too Deep', 'Something In My House') and they are one group who can genuinely boast of being big in Japan.

In recent years, Pete Burns has become a joke figure with his collagen implants to his lips and his desire to dress and look like Cher. A BBC

Pete Burns

series, *Diners*, made fun of him, but he had the last laugh as a new version of 'You Spin Me Round' restored Dead Or Alive to the charts in 2003.

547 Philip Bailey (Duet with Phil Collins) Easy Lover

Label & Cat No.: **CBS A 4915**
Producer: **Phil Collins**
Writers: **Phil Bailey / Phil Collins / Nathan East**
Date Reached No.1: **23 March 1985**
Weeks at No.1: **4**

During the Seventies, Earth Wind And Fire, who took their name from the three elements in Maurice White's astrological sign, had established themselves as one of the great American soul/funk bands. They were formed in 1969 as The Salty Peppers by multi-talented singer/ songwriter/producer White who had been a session drummer for Chess Records and a member of the Ramsey Lewis Trio. He brought in his bass-playing brother, Verdine and after two years of using a line-up of session musicians, they formed a new permanent line-up comprising: Philip Bailey (co-lead vocals), Larry Dunn (keyboards), Al McKay (guitar), Andrew Woodfolk (saxophone) and Ralph Johnson (drums). Their Top 10s included, 'September' (3, 1978), 'Boogie Wonderland' (4, 1979) and 'Let's Groove' 3, 1981).

Like Phil Collins in 1981, Philip Bailey began a solo career in 1983 whilst both remained lead singers of Genesis and Earth Wind And Fire respectively. The following year Bailey asked Phil Collins to produce and play drums on his second solo album, *Chinese Wall*. Collins, who had produced albums for Adam & The Ants and Eric Clapton, agreed and they met in London with bass player, Nathan East. Once the album was finished, Bailey, Collins and East all agreed that it didn't have a commercial enough song to release as a single, so they sat down and wrote, 'Easy Lover'.

As Philip Bailey recalled in *Musician* magazine, "Phil and Nathan were playing around with a riff on the piano and I was walking around singing 'Choosy Lover' over the piano chords. We worked on it all day and put a rough version of it down on tape. The next day we said, 'let's check it out so we can go in and record it.' When we heard it, we realised there was nothing wrong with it. We tried doing it again, but we kept the original."

Phil Collins was just about to release his new solo album, *No Jacket Required*, and as the first single from it, 'One More Night' was a ballad, there was no reason not to release the uptempo 'Easy Lover'.

The video was unusual. It showed the two Phils in the studio learning a dance routine and picking out costumes. It was more like a fly-on-the-wall documentary than a music clip. But, if nothing else, it was original and won the 1985 MTV award for Best Overall Performance. Their theory that the album lacked commerciality was proved when the follow-up, 'Walking On The Chinese Wall' failed to make the Top 30.

548 USA For Africa We Are The World

Label & Cat No.: **CBS US AID 1**
Producer: **Quincy Jones**
Writers: **Michael Jackson / Lionel Richie**
Date reached No.1: **20 April 1985**
Weeks at No.1: **2**

America responded to the Band Aid single with USA For Africa (United Support of Artists For Africa), the prime movers being Harry Belafonte, Michael Jackson and Lionel Richie. After three days of individual preparation, Michael Jackson and Lionel Richie wrote the song together in a few hours. – "I'd throw out a line and Michael would come back with a greater one," said Lionel. Unlike the sadness of the British song, 'We Are The World' could be regarded as tub-thumping for America.

'We Are The World' was recorded after the Grammys ceremony on January 28, 1985. The performers went to the A&M studios in Hollywood. The soloists were Lionel Richie, Stevie Wonder, Paul Simon, Kenny Rogers, James Ingram, Tina Turner, Billy Joel, Michael Jackson, Diana Ross, Dionne Warwick, Willie Nelson, Al Jarreau, Bruce Springsteen, Kenny Loggins, Steve Perry, Daryl Hall, Huey Lewis, Cyndi Lauper, Kim Carnes, Bob Dylan and Ray Charles. Not to mention Bette Midler, Smokey Robinson, Waylon Jennings and several others, who sang in the background. Bob Geldof, although not American, was invited to join the recording. The video is a remarkable piece of pop history and as Ben Elton remarked, "You must know who Bob Dylan is. He's the one who can't sing in the 'We Are The World' video."

Because it was not a seasonal song like 'Do They Know It's Christmas?', 'We Are The World' has not been revived in the same way. The Canadian Band Aid single, 'Tears Are Not Enough' by Northern Lights (Bryan Adams, Gordon Lightfoot, Joni Mitchell, Neil Young) was not released as a single in the UK, although it, too, is an excellent song.

On July 13, 1985 the world stopped to watch Live Aid with its stages in London and Philadelphia. Phil Collins, with the help of Concorde, appeared on both stages, and the day was full of triumphs – Queen above everyone else, U2, David Bowie, Madonna, Neil Young, Mick Jagger and Tina Turner together, three-quarters of Led Zeppelin reunited and Elvis Costello singing 'All You Need Is Love'. Paul McCartney was hampered by a faulty mike and Bob Dylan by the chorus assembling for 'We Are The World' behind him.

Live Aid raised £50m in pledged donations. Bob Dylan, in an extraordinary moment (it was not his day), suggested that some of the monies should be given to American farmers, thereby failing to appreciate the difference between poverty and starvation. His remarks did, however, prompt Willie Nelson to start the Farm Aid concerts which have raised over $15 million for more than a hundred farm organizations, churches, and service agencies in forty-four states.

549 Phyllis Nelson
Move Closer

Label & Cat No.:	**Carrere CAR 337**
Producer:	**Yves Dessca**
Writer:	**Phyllis Nelson**
Date Reached No.1:	**4 May 1985**
Weeks at No.1:	**1**

In 1985 Phyllis said of her album, "Apart from the single, I'm not too fond of the rest of the album. I'm hoping to go home and do another one with more of me on it."

Phyllis' producer, Yves Dessca, didn't have much money, so the album was recorded on a shoestring budget. As Phyllis recalled in *Record Mirror* in 1985, "Most of the songs on the album were tracks I'd already recorded and I did new vocals on top of those just to keep recording costs down." Curiously, with the rapid emergence of the video, 'Move Closer' was the only chart topper of the year that didn't have one.

She was the first black female artist to write and record her own number one. Her style at the time was compared to Deniece Williams. Coincidently, both singers were born in Gary, Indiana.

Pirate radio stations in the London area first picked up on the song in 1984. Nothing happened at first, but when BBC Radio London jumped on board six months later, the song was re-issued. It took 11 weeks to reach the chart summit, but Phyllis wasn't complaining, especially as the song had failed to chart in her native country.

"That song was really written with people in mind," explained Phyllis. "I had the idea back in 1979. I thought about the public and it seemed to me that people had drifted apart physically and musically. Not much music lets you dance close anymore so I thought I'd write a song you could really dance close to. But I was also thinking about my husband as well, because with the job he had and me being away a lot, we don't see each other too often. It came so easily and weird how the lyrics just fell out of my mouth, it was like the song had been written by someone else."

Two further singles, 'I Like You' and 'Chemical Reaction', both failed to chart and Phyllis remained a one-hit wonder. However, 'Move Closer' was re-issued and spent three weeks in the Top 40 in 1994 after its inclusion in the Soft and Gentle anti-perspirant commercial. Phyllis died on 18 January 1998.

550 Paul Hardcastle
19

Label & Cat No.:	**Chrysalis CHS 2860**
Producer:	**Paul Hardcastle**
Writers:	**Paul Hardcastle / William Coutourie / Jonas McCord**
Date reached No.1:	**11 May 1985**
Weeks at No.1:	**5**

A common theme of the protest songs of the Sixties was that the warmongers were much older than the soldiers – in 'Masters Of War', Bob Dylan refers to "young people's blood' and in 'I Ain't Marching Anymore', Phil Ochs sings, "It's always the old who lead us to the wars, Always the young who fall."

In 1985 the London record producer, Paul Hardcastle, was watching a TV programme: "It was called *Vietnam Requiem* and I wondered if I could make a record about it. I had a keyboard that was one of the first samplers and I put the word 'nineteen' into it, and got the n-n-n. Everytime you hit that key, you would get a n, and I kept tapping that and realised I had the chorus. I am very proud of that record as it is a musical documentary. It was very in your face and although a couple of the tabloids were negative about it, I got loads of letters from Vietnam vets thanking me for making that record."

To electro-funk dance rhythms, the record emphasised that the average age of combatants in the Second World War was 26 and in Vietnam was only 19.

A parody record by The Commentators, 'N-N-N-Nineteen Not Out', also made the Top 20. "Rory Bremner liked the original," says Paul, "and he got in contact with me. The record company didn't want me to do it as they felt that a serious record shouldn't be followed by a silly one. I liked his idea and I did it with him anyway and didn't tell anyone."

Paul Hardcastle was managed by Simon Fuller, who later managed The Spice Girls and masterminded *Pop Idol*, and in a nod to his first managerial number one named his company 19 Management. Paul had further hits with 'Don't Waste My Time' and 'The Wizard', which was his theme music for *Top Of The Pops*. He says, "I feel that sampling has had its day and I prefer to work with proper instruments, but I am very pleased that 'N-n-n-nineteen' is such a catch-phrase."

551 The Crowd
You'll Never Walk Alone

Label & Cat No.:	**Spartan BRAD 1**
Producer:	**Graham Gouldman**
Writers:	**Richard Rodgers / Oscar Hammerstein II**
Date reached No.1:	**15 June 1985**
Weeks at No.1:	**2**

On May 11, 1985 a stand packed with football fans caught fire at the Valley Parade ground, the home of Bradford City Football Club. Some 56 fans died and hundreds more were injured, both physically and mentally. Gerry Marsden's manager, Derek Franks, lived in Bradford and could see the flames from his house. He and Gerry decided to make a charity song, but the original plan to re-record the uplifting 'You'll Never Walk Alone' with the team was not possible because many of the players were too distressed. Instead a record was made with various showbiz personalities.

Gerry took the lead vocal and the talent on the record could hardly be more varied – The Barron Knights, Colin Blunstone, Keith Chegwin, Tony Christie, Jess Conrad, Peter Cook, Kiki Dee, John Entwistle (Who), Joe Fagin, Bruce Forsyth, Rolf Harris, Tony Hicks (Hollies), Denny Laine, Kenny Lynch, Phil Lynott, Motorhead, The Nolans, John Otway,

Smokie, Zak Starkey, Dave Lee Travis, Rick Wakeman and Bernie Winters. Besides Gerry, only five of those performers had been on a number one before. Paul McCartney wasn't available for the recording but a telephone message from him was added to various greetings from the ensemble for the B-side. The record was produced by Graham Gouldman of 10cc.

The single made £132,000 but when Gerry was ready to present the cheque, he was told that the Disaster Appeal had closed. Instead, the money was given to a burns research unit which had opened in Bradford and also to support the manufacture of the Bradford Sling; a support for broken arms and wrists.

552 Sister Sledge
Frankie

Label & Cat No.: **Atlantic A 9547**
Producer: **Denise Rich**
Writer: **Denise Rich**
Date Reached No.1: **29 June 1985**
Weeks at No.1: **4**

THE PHILADELPHIAN SISTERS, KATHY, Debbie, Joni and Kim, were born into a musical family and were encouraged by their grandmother, Viola, who was an opera singer. The girls began recording together in 1971 as The Sisters Sledge.

In 1979 the siblings dominated the disco and pop charts with the songs, 'He's The Greatest Dancer', 'We Are Family' and 'Lost In Music'. In the early Eighties, they found themselves struggling for a chart placing. In 1984 an old song, 'Thinking Of You', was re-issued and went to number 11 and a remix of 'Lost In Music' put them back in the Top 10. A new song, 'Frankie', was offered to them, but the girls were sceptical about recording it as they thought it was naff.

In 1985 Sister Sledge arrived for a UK tour. Whilst here, Elton John invited them to record backing vocals on 'This Town', a song on his new album *Ice On Fire*.

"A lot of people think the song was written about Frankie Goes To Hollywood, but Denise Rich actually wrote it about Frank Sinatra," recalled Kathy Sledge. A glance at the lyrics, however, wouldn't tell you that. Denise claimed the song came to her in a dream on an aeroplane on the way back from visiting her sister. Kathy continued, "We had almost finished our latest album, *When The Boys Meet The Girls*, when we heard the song. We all said we didn't know if it was the song for us or not, but we gave it to our producer Nile Rodgers who listened to it and hated it said 'I don't believe this, you can't be serious'. He came back to us a week later and said 'I can't stop singing that damn song, you've got to record it'".

They performed the song live for the first time on the opening night of their tour in Huddersfield and as Kim remembered, "It was nice to be there when the record was climbing the chart. It took off so fast and was nice to see everybody singing it on our tour."

Denise Rich first came to prominence as the wife of a billionaire commodities trader. Her original intention for taking up songwriting was to address her failing marriage. She has since written songs for Aretha Franklin, Celine Dion, Diana Ross, Patti LaBelle, Johnny Mathis and Mandy Moore's 2000 UK Top 10 hit 'Candy'.

553 Eurythmics
There Must Be An Angel (Playing With My Heart)

Label & Cat No.: **RCA PB 40339**
Producer: **Dave Stewart**
Writers: **Annie Lennox / Dave Stewart**
Date Reached No.1: **27 July 1985**
Weeks at No.1: **1**

STEVIE WONDER WAS ANNIE LENNOX'S idol so, when he agreed to appear on the Eurythmics' latest single, she was delighted. After all, his music was her inspiration to write songs in the first place.

Dave Stewart was born in 1952 and Annie Lennox was born on Christmas Day, 1954 in Aberdeen. They met at Pippins restaurant in north London, where Annie worked as a waitress. They fell in love but, although Dave proposed, they didn't marry. In 1977 they joined forces with Dave's friend Pete Coombes, signed to Logo records and became Catch 22. After 18 months, Eddy Chin and Jim Tooney joined the band and they underwent a name change to The Tourists.

In December 1980 they were involved in a legal wrangle with their label, which led to the breaking up of the band and the end of Annie and Dave's romance. One week later, they formed a new band, Eurythmics, taking their name from a system of rhythmical body movements known as eurythmics, which was developed in the early 20th Century by Professor Emil Jacques-Dalcrose, and based on a Greek method of teaching children music by movement. Most of the Eurythmics' hits reflected the trials and tribulations of their own relationship.

During the mid-Eighties, Annie was having problems with her voice. Nodules were discovered on her throat and she was admitted to a Nashville hospital for surgery. Annie said, "It's like trying to run with a broken leg," and it upset her. "Talking about my voice being fucked is the worse thing I can do, it's too depressing." She was ordered to rest. During this time Dave carried on working with a change of direction. He started directing videos and producing tracks for Bob Dylan.

Annie and Dave went to Los Angeles to record 'There Must Be An Angel (Playing With My Heart)'. Annie recalled, "We were booked into this studio and rumour had it that Stevie Wonder didn't really know what time it is and we'd have to wait and see if he turned up. Eventually he did show up and was a really adorable person. He had his hair in braids with beautiful gold beads, and when he plays he shakes his head so the beads make a loud noise."

It was his brilliant harmonica solo that inspired Annie to dedicate the song to Stevie. "To hear Stevie Wonder playing on a song that was dedicated to him anyway was just heaven."

554 Madonna Into The Groove

Label & Cat No.: **Sire W 8934**
Producers: **Madonna / Stephen Bray**
Writers: **Madonna / Stephen Bray**
Date Reached No.1: **3 August 1985**
Weeks at No.1: **4**

SO HOW DID THE BIGGEST-SELLING female artist in the world get her break? Madonna was one of eight children, whose mother died when she was six. Madonna was persuaded to take piano lessons, which she hated, but she insisted her father let her have dancing and ballet lessons. It was at ballet school that her tutor, Christopher Flynn, persuaded her to make the most of her talent and to seek fame and fortune. She never looked back.

In 1978 she headed for New York from her Detroit home and found somewhere to stay in Times Square. To make some money, she appeared in a soft porn film, *A Certain Sacrifice*, for which she was paid $100. It came back to haunt her in the early days of her success, when it was released on video.

In 1979 she successfully auditioned for two Belgian television producers, Jean-Claude Pellerin and Jean van Lieu. They were managing a new French disco singer, Patrick Hernandez, and she was invited to Paris to record backing vocals for his *Born To Be Alive* album. After six months, when no more work was forthcoming, she returned to New York, where she met a Dutch bass player, Angie Smit. Angie introduced Madonna to her friends, Ed and Dan. With Madonna on drums, they began playing and often rehearsed during the night, after which they would go for breakfast, so they named themselves The Breakfast Club.

After their demise, she met a club DJ, Mark Kamins, who was also an A&R man for Island Records. She passed a demo to him and began flirting in an effort to get him to listen and play the track. The song was 'Everybody'. He played it and the crowd loved it, so Mark signed her to a two-single deal. Madonna was so excited that she immediately sat down and started scribbling some lyrics on the back of a piece of paper. That song was 'Lucky Star'. 'Everybody' failed to make any impact on either side of the Atlantic. A few years later, Madonna had become one of the most collectable artists and seven-inch copies of 'Everybody' are worth around £150.

The hits started to flow, 'Holiday' (6), 'Like A Virgin' (3) and 'Material Girl' (3), and her second album, *Like A Virgin*, went to number one. In 1985 Madonna appeared as a nightclub singer in *Vision Quest*. The film spawned the hit single 'Crazy For You' which went to number two. Then came the hit comedy *Desperately Seeking Susan*, from which came 'Into The Groove'.

The song was co-written with Stephen Bray. Bray was having trouble with the bridge when Madonna walked into the studio, stepped up to the microphone and sang, "live out your fantasy here with me."

In 2003 Madonna signed a deal with the GAP clothing company to appear in their latest commercial. Although her 2003 hit 'Hollywood' was playing in the background, the ad also shows rapper Missy Elliot singing alternate lyrics to 'Into The Groove', cleverly amended to 'Into The Gap'.

555 UB40 with guest vocals by Chrissie Hynde I Got You Babe

Label & Cat No.: **DEP International:/Virgin DEP 20**
Producer: **UB40**
Writer: **Sonny Bono**
Date Reached No.1: **31 August 1985**
Weeks at No.1: **1**

IN 1965 THE IAN CAMPBELL FOLK Group scraped into the Top 50 with a cover of Bob Dylan's 'The Times They Are A Changin'. Ian had always hated reggae music, yet his sons Ali and Robin are members of the most successful predominately white reggae band in the world. Ali recalled, "Dad never understood. I remember listening to Bob Marley's album *African Herbsman* when I was 13 and him asking how I could listen to that rubbish. Dad occasionally listens to Bob Marley now, because a folk singer friend of dad's once recorded a version of 'Get Up Stand Up'."

As Bob Geldof was preparing the mammoth Live Aid concert, other acts not involved with Bob's project were keen to do their own bit to raise money for the African famine relief.

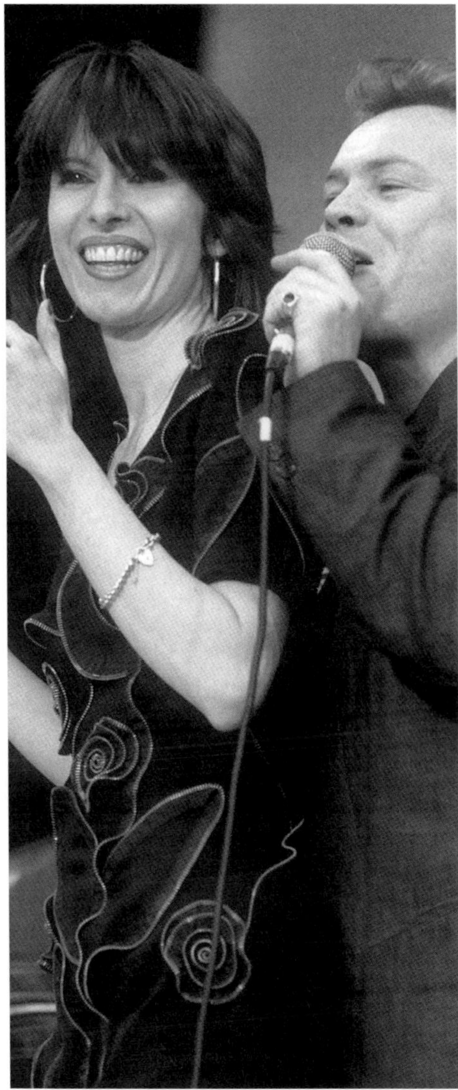

Chrissie Hynde and Ali Campbell

A collective called Starvation, comprising members of Madness, General Public and The Pioneers, as well as Jerry Dammers (from The Specials) and Robin and Ali from UB40, gathered to record a cover of The Pioneers' 'Starvation' on Madness' Zarjazz label. It was issued as a double A-side with 'Tam-Tam Pour L'Ethiope' by several African musicians and reached number 33.

UB40 had set their sights on breaking America. Their only hit had been 'Red Red Wine', which peaked at number 34. They made three separate visits to the States and they were well received. At one particular show at Jones Beach in Long Island, they were joined on stage by Chrissie Hynde who accompanied Ali on 'I Got You Babe'.

The single reached the top exactly 20 years after Sonny and Cher's original. It also took off in America where it became their first Top 30 hit. To help boost sales, a special limited edition four-track 12-inch version was also released that included 'Mi Spliff' and their next hit single, 'Don't Break My Heart'.

556 David Bowie & Mick Jagger Dancing In The Street

Label & Cat No.: **EMI America EM 204**
Producers: **Clive Langer /Alan Winstanley**
Writers: **Marvin Gaye / Ivy Hunter / William Stevenson**
Date Reached No.1: **7 September 1985**
Weeks at No.1: **4**

When two superstars get together to record an all-time Motown classic for charity, the odds are it's going to be a number one.

Marvin Gaye, as a performer, only had one number one. As a writer he had two. The first was Paul Young's 'Wherever I Lay My Hat (That's My Home)'. This was the second, but sadly Marvin never got the chance to celebrate it as he'd died after being shot by his father just 17 months earlier.

The song was first recorded by Marvin as a demo, but he hated it and suggested Martha & The Vandellas cover it. It had been a hit twice, firstly in 1964, peaking at number 28 and then reaching number four when re-issued five years later.

It was David's musicians who performed on the track. He told them that he'd been out the night before with Mick Jagger and they'd had the idea to record 'Dancing In The Street' together. Drummer Neil Conti remembered, "It was a huge ego trip for Mick, he kept trying to upstage David." David was happy with the first take, but Mick wasn't. He kept insisting that the bass and drum parts be re-done. The next job was a video. David Mallet shot the video at London's Docklands, which showed them, as one newspaper critic put it, "mincing and jiggling about like two old music-hall artistes."

Bowie and Jagger's collaboration was for the Band Aid Trust charity. The accompanying video was shown twice during the Live Aid concert. To endorse its world awareness the song begins; "OK, talk to you South America, Australia, France, Germany, UK, Africa". Both artists performed live on the day as well; Bowie at London's Wembley Stadium and Jagger, with Tina Turner, at the JFK Stadium in Philadelphia.

Producer Clive Langer said, "We were working on 'Absolute Beginners' with Bowie. We were doing the backing track and David said, 'Do you mind if we do a charity single tonight?' I said, not at all, we'll help you. David said, 'Mick will be coming down'. Mick came in the studio and was twiddling his arms around and everything and we knocked the backing track down. We recorded most of it, I think they did the horns in America and somebody else mixed it. It was nice of David to put our names on it because it was really produced by a lot of people."

Both artists were delighted to have another number one, especially Mick Jagger, who hadn't visited the top spot for exactly 16 years, when The Rolling Stones' last chart topper, 'Honky Tonk Women' was knocked off by Zager & Evans.

557 Midge Ure If I Was

Label & Cat No.: **Chrysalis URE 1**
Producer: **Midge Ure**
Writers: **Midge Ure / Danny Mitchell**
Date reached No.1: **5 October 1985**
Weeks at No.1: **1**

A contender for the greatest number one that never was is 'Vienna' by Ultravox from 1981. "We were kept from the top by 'Shaddup You Face'," says Midge Ure, "which is one of the worst records ever made, and everyone in the industry was sorry for us."

The following year Midge Ure had his first solo with 'No Regrets': "I loved Scott Walker's voice and The Walker Brothers were in the charts with that song when I did my first *Top Of The Pops* with Slik. I'd always wanted to give that song a crack, and my version starts very quietly and ends up with the kitchen sink. That was how I remembered The Walker Brothers' version but when I heard it again, it was very laidback, almost like a country song, so memory plays tricks on you."

Ultravox never repeated the success of 'Vienna' although they had Top 10 singles with 'All Stood Still' (1981) and 'Dancing With Tears In My Eyes' (1984). They took part in Band Aid in 1985 and then decided to have a year's break.

Midge Ure made his solo album, *The Gift*, and the number one ballad, 'If I Was', synth-driven like Ultravox but featuring Mark King from Level 42 on bass. Midge says, "Danny Mitchell is a brilliant songwriter and a good friend from Glasgow. We decided to do a Lennon & McCartney on that particular album: we said that it doesn't matter who writes what, it is 50-50. Danny had sent me a demo of 'If I Was' and I altered it a little and recorded it without him knowing. He was gobsmacked when he heard it, he loved it and I have to give him credit for most of that song."

The Gift was released shortly after the single and was a number two album, being kept from the top by something more substantial

David Bowie and Mick Jagger square off to one another for the video of their 'Dancing In The Street' duet

than Joe Dolce, Kate Bush's *Hounds Of Love*. Ultravox made a final album, *U-Vox*, in 1986 and then disbanded.

Midge Ure is still performing 'If I Was' and many of his other successes: "You're only as big as your last record, so I play the theatres rather than the stadiums and I like that very much. The economics of having a full-blown band can be difficult but I still love to strap on my guitar and go kerrang from time to time."

558 Jennifer Rush
The Power Of Love

Label & Cat No.: **CBS A 5003**

Producers: **Gunther Mende / Candy de Rouge**

Writers: **Gunther Mende / Candy de Rouge / Jennifer Rush / Mary Susan Applegate**

Date reached No.1: **12 October 1985**

Weeks at No.1: **5**

THE NEW YORK OPERA SINGER, Maurice Stern accepted a job in Germany in 1982 and took his family with him. His daughter, Heidi, pursued her own career, first under her own name and then as Jennifer Rush. In 1984 she had European hits with '25 Lovers' and 'Ring Of Ice' and a hit album with *Jennifer Rush*. Her producers wrote a big-voiced ballad, 'The Power Of Love' and it became a hit across Europe. At first, the record made little headway in the UK. With such compliant lyrics as "Whenever you reach for me, I'll do all that I can", the song could have been criticised on the same grounds as 'Stand By Your Man'.

In old copies of *Billboard,* you will see the US charts as well as the regional breakouts, that is, records that were popular in one area and had the potential to go further. Similar breakouts in the UK are rarely mentioned but 'The Power Of Love' is a good example. Billy Butler, the morning presenter at BBC Radio Merseyside, says, "People in this area go for big love songs that build to a climax. I was playing 'The Power Of Love' every day and the shops were stocking it, which is something they wouldn't do now as the ordering comes from head office. The record was so popular that other stations picked up on it and it went to number one. CBS was so pleased that they gave me a gold disc and Jennifer sang me a song at the Manchester Apollo. She knew I loved rock'n'roll and so she threw 'Great Balls Of Fire' into the act. Great version, too."

'The Power Of Love' was not a major hit in the US until Celine Dion recorded it in 1993. Jennifer Rush has failed to have major UK successes since 'The Power Of Love', although her hits have continued in Europe. She has often recorded duets with established artists such as 'Flames Of Paradise' (with Elton John), 'Till I Loved You' (with Placido Domingo), 'Same Heart' (with Michael Bolton) and 'Who Wants To Live Forever?' (with Brian May). In 1998 she recorded *Classics*, which included a classical arrangement of 'The Power Of Love'. The record was featured in the hit film, *Bend It Like Beckham* (2002).

Jennifer Rush

559 Feargal Sharkey
A Good Heart

Label & Cat No.: **Virgin VS 808**

Producer: **David A. Stewart**

Writer: **Maria McKee**

Date Reached No.1: **16 November 1985**

Weeks at No.1: **2**

VINCE CLARKE ONCE SAID OF FEARGAL Sharkey, "He sings a nifty song." When told this, Feargal replied, "Coming from Vince, that's a hell of a compliment." As frontman of The Undertones between 1976 and 1983, the band carved out their own niche in the UK pop charts. Even respected DJ John Peel cited the adolescent angst anthem 'Teenage Kicks' as his all-time favourite single.

Feargal split the band in 1983. He explained why, "One of the reasons I left when I did was that I wanted to preserve The Undertones for people as something special. Listening to people saying 'I was in a bad part of my life and listening to your album helped me through it' is a great feeling."

Feargal, who was born in Londonderry, Northern Ireland, embarked on a solo career in 1984 and his first hit, 'Listen To Your Father', was written by Madness' Cathal Smyth. It also became the first hit on Madness' own Zarjazz label. After one hit, he signed a long-term deal with Virgin Records.

In 1984 Californian-born Maria McKee formed Lone Justice and supported U2 on tour. It was there that she and her boyfriend – Benmont Tench, keyboard player with Tom Petty's Heartbreakers – met and became friends with Feargal Sharkey. When the pair split, she wrote a song about it with Feargal as her shoulder to cry on. Benmont was heartbroken and responded by also writing a song, although he dropped more subtle references about the break-up. The song, 'You Little Thief', was recorded by Feargal later the same year.

When Virgin Records were trying to break Feargal in America, they discovered Stateside folk had trouble pronouncing his name

correctly. Their cunning ploy of placing advertisements on billboards showing a fur coat (for Fear), and gull (for gal), a shark followed by a key, unfortunately failed when people went around asking 'what in hell is a coat bird fish lock?'

560 Wham! I'm Your Man

Label & Cat No.: **Epic A 6716**

Producer: **George Michael**

Writer: **George Michael**

Date reached No.1: **30 November 1985**

Weeks at No.1: **2**

WHAM!'S 'LAST CHRISTMAS' / 'EVERYthing She Wants' was released in 1984 and although it didn't dislodge Band Aid, it was the first single to sell a million copies in the UK without making the top. With total sales of 1.4m, it is the UK's biggest selling single which did not make the top. Dick James Music claimed that the song was similar to Barry Manilow's 'Can't Smile Without You' but as Wham! were adding their royalties to the Band Aid fund, the matter was dropped. Both group and song made the Top 10 the following year and George Michael found himself featured on four records in the Top 20 – those two plus Wham!'s 'I'm Your Man' and Elton John's 'Nikita'.

By now Wham! had become a vehicle for George Michael and his songs while Andrew Ridgeley's role seemed to diminish accordingly. He remarked, "The guy's a brilliant songwriter. If I write a song, he'll come up with a better one, so why bother?" At the 1985 Ivor Novello Awards, Elton John called George "the greatest songwriter of his generation."

For all that, the lyrics of 'I'm Your Man' are banal but they contain indications that George Michael wanted to get away from bland disco music with the line, "I'll be your sexual inspiration, And with some stimulation, We can do it right." The single was also issued in a 12-inch 'Extended Stimulation' mix and the B-side was an instrumental, 'Do It Right'.

561 Whitney Houston Saving All My Love For You

Label & Cat No.: **Arista ARIST 640**

Producer: **Michael Masser**

Writers: **Michael Masser / Gerry Goffin**

Date reached No.1: **14 December 1985**

Weeks at No.1: **2**

THE PRESIDENT OF ARISTA RECORDS, Clive Davis, said on a nationwide US TV programme in 1985, "For the next generation, there's a singer who combines the fiery gospel of Aretha Franklin with the stunning elegance and the beauty of lyric phrasing of Lena Horne, and she is Whitney Houston." He was biased – Whitney was on his record label – but he was also right.

It was no surprise that Whitney Houston should be such an extraordinary singer. Her mother was Cissy Houston, whose R&B vocal group, The Sweet Inspirations, backed Aretha and Elvis Presley. Her aunts included Dionne and Dee Dee Warwick, and Aretha was her godmother when she was born in New Jersey in 1963.

When Whitney was only eight, she was singing gospel music with her mother. She became a teenager with stunning looks and accepted modelling assignments, appearing on the cover of US *Seventeen* magazine, acting in several TV shows, and supplying backing vocals for Chaka Khan and Lou Rawls. In 1984 Whitney sang a duet with Teddy Pendergrass, 'Hold Me', which made the US R&B charts. It was part of Teddy's recuperation after he had been paralysed following an automobile accident in 1982.

Clive Davis wanted a stunning debut album and he assigned many musicians, songwriters and producers to the project. One of the producers, Michael Masser, heard her at Sweetwater's in New York and was mesmerised by the way she performed one of his songs, 'Greatest Love Of All', which had originally been recorded by George Benson. He suggested another of his songs, 'Saving All My Love For You', which had been recorded by Marilyn McCoo and Billy Davis Jr. from Fifth Dimension in 1978. He told Whitney, "This is going to make women cry. It is a woman's song", but Cissy Houston was unsure, unwilling for her daughter to sing about adultery. Eventually, Whitney agreed to do the song, though the subject-matter was even clearer in the video. Davis had instructed Masser not to make the record 'too black', so that it would appeal to black and white audiences. Masser included a sax solo from the veteran Tom Scott, but he did not complicate the arrangement as he wanted to showcase Whitney's remarkable voice.

The album, *Whitney Houston*, was released in 1985 and Whitney had her first US hit with 'You Give Good Love'. Then came 'Saving All My Love For You', which topped both the US and UK charts. The album also included 'How Will I Know' and 'Greatest Love Of All' and sold 13 million copies worldwide, making it the most successful debut album ever. Whitney received a Grammy for Best Female Pop Vocal for 'Saving All My Love For You'. "I loved the melody," says the lyricist Gerry Goffin. "It's a great tune and it could have been written in the Thirties."

Feargal Sharkey

562 Shakin' Stevens Merry Christmas Everyone

Label & Cat No.: **Epic A 6769**
Producer: **Dave Edmunds**
Writer: **Bobbie Heatlie**
Date Reached No.1: **28 December 1985**
Weeks at No.1: **2**

SHAKY ALMOST HAD HIS FOURTH number one at Christmas 1982 with 'Blue Christmas', from the *Shakin' Stevens* EP. But it was unable to dislodge Renee and Renato's sentimental 'Save Your Love'.

In 1983 Scottish songwriter Bob Heatlie, who had written 'Japanese Boy' for Aneka, said, "I wrote a song for Elkie Brooks called 'Cry Just A Little Bit'. However, it was played to Shaky's producer who thought it would be ideal for him." It was, and it went to number three. Shaky had further Top five hits with 'A Rockin' Good Way' – a duet with fellow Welsh star Bonnie Tyler, 'A Love Worth Waiting For' and 'Teardrops'.

"I'd always wanted to have a big Christmas hit, because if and when it all ends, it's something that would go on forever you know! The grandchildren and all that sort of stuff," commented Bob. "'Merry Christmas Everyone' was written and a demo made in my garage studio in Edinburgh. I'll never forget that. It was in the summer of 1984, and with no ventilation in the studio, I was sweating like a pig! It was quite weird; there I was wearing nothing but a pair of shorts, shaking sleigh bells, and singing about snow falling. Everything was in place ready for Christmas 1984 when the Band Aid release was announced. So Shaky decided that it should be held back, and indeed it was, until the following year and became a Christmas classic.

Although Bob never actually got to work with Dave Edmunds, he said, "The production he did was exactly copied note for note from my demo." As Shaky always says about demos, "If it ain't broke, don't fix it, just try and get more from the desk, sound-wise". Bob, who now mainly writes music for TV animation, has just had a new song, 'Talk To Me', recorded by Tina Arena, due for release late in 2004.

Shaky, like Cliff Richard, was becoming a Christmas chart regular when 'Merry Christmas Everyone' returned to the chart in 1986, 'What Do You Want To Make Those Eyes At Me For' (1987), 'True Love' (1988), 'The Best Christmas Of Them All' (1990) and 'I'll Be Home For Christmas' (1991).

Although he had hits into the early Nineties, in 1993 Shaky stopped recording. However, he continued to receive awards and to tour, playing to festival audiences of up to 200,000 people. Shaky has now been ranked as the 16th highest selling artist in the UK and in 2004 was back in the studio recording new material.

563 Pet Shop Boys West End Girls

Label & Cat No.: **Parlophone R 6115**
Producer: **Stephen Hague**
Writers: **Neil Tennant/Chris Lowe**
Date Reached No.1: **11 January 1986**
Weeks at No.1: **2**

LIKE CLIFF RICHARD IN *SUMMER Holiday*, the idea of travelling around in a London bus appealed to Neil Tennant. When The Beatles came along he decided on a career in music, but after seeing The Sex Pistols and watching Sid Vicious beat up a hippy with a bicycle chain, he became disenchanted.

That changed again in 1981 when Neil was in a hi-fi shop in Chelsea getting a lead made up for his new synthesiser, and Chris Lowe walked in. The pair got talking. Chris loved disco music and he invited Neil to a club called Shagarama's where they had just started playing hip-hop and electronic music.

By this time Neil was the assistant editor at the pop magazine, *Smash Hits*. In 1983 he had the opportunity to go to New York to interview The Police. Whilst there, he arranged to meet Bobby 'O' Orlando, whose music he had admired. In Bobby's studio, Neil played him a demo of 'Opportunities (Let's Make Lots Of Money)', which Bobby liked. As he should have; Neil admitted he had ripped it off from Bobby in the first place. Bobby invited Neil and Chris back to New York to make a record.

"We arrived in the studio and Bobby had programmed Michael Jackson's 'Billie Jean' drum pattern", said Neil. "Chris started to play along and I started playing chords. In terms of the lyrics, the inspiration for 'West End Girls' came from 'The Message' by Grandmaster Flash. I remember once staying at my cousin's house in Nottingham and we were watching some kind of a gangster film with James Cagney, and just as I was dropping off to sleep the lines 'Sometimes you're better off dead, there's a gun in your hand and it's pointing to your head' came into my head and I thought 'that's quite good' so I went off to find a pen."

Another big influence for the song came from *The Waste Land* by T.S.Eliot. "What I like about it is, it's the different voices, almost a sort of collage. All the different voices and languages coming in and I've always found that very powerful. So on 'West End Girls' it's different voices. The line, 'Just you wait till I get you home' is a direct quotation."

The song was recorded in one take in about 45 minutes. When first released in 1985 it failed to make the chart, although it had been a number one in Belgium. Tom Watkins became their manager and secured a deal with EMI Records. The song was re-recorded with producer Stephen Hague. As Stephen explained, "I heard the Bobby O version and thought it had potential. I felt it should be slowed down and the story told a little clearer. Neil and Chris agreed once they'd heard it."

It was also agreed that the beginning needed something different, so Stephen took a tape recorder onto the street outside the studio and began recording traffic noises and the sound of people walking around. As Stephen played the sounds back, the engineer hit the record button and the new introduction was born.

564 A-Ha
The Sun Always Shines On T.V.

Label & Cat No.: **Warner Brothers W 8736**

Producer: **Alan Tarney**

Writer: **Pal Waaktaar**

Date Reached No.1: **25 January 1986**

Weeks at No.1: **2**

Up until the mid-Eighties, it's unlikely that anyone would associate Norway with pop music other than for their disastrous 'nul points' score in the Eurovision Song Contest in 1978, a distinction they would go on to achieve on a record four occasions.

But suddenly in 1985 all that changed. Not only did A-Ha, a fully-fledged Norwegian pop group, crack the British chart when 'Take On Me' reached number two, but Norway, for the first time, won the Eurovision Song Contest. It was the female duo, Elisabeth Andreasson and Hanne Krogh, known as Bobbysocks that led their country to victory with the song, 'Let It Swing'. It did so in style, with an 18-point lead over Germany who were pushed into second place.

"'The Sun Always Shines On TV' was written on one of those down days," says Pal Waaktaar, A-Ha's guitarist. "Me and Mags (Furuholmen, keyboards) were in a hotel watching English television on a rainy day and the guy announcing the programme says 'It's a rainy day but, as always, the sun always shines on TV'. The song is about the power of television and the way that television presents life."

Their debut album, *Hunting High And Low* sold well and in addition to 'Take On Me' and 'The Sun Always Shines On TV', spawned 'Train Of Thought' and the title track, both of which made the Top 10.

The video for the first single, 'Take On Me' was revolutionary for its time. Incorporating a mixture of pencil-drawn cartoons with live colour action, it showed lead singer, Morten Harket pursuing the girl of his dreams by reaching his animated hand out to her through a comic. He then pulls her into his black and white surroundings and changes her life forever. 'The Sun Always Shines On T.V.' video wasn't nearly as exciting. It was filmed at St Albans Cathedral in Hertfordshire and showed the band playing in a church surrounded by hundreds of plastic dummies, all playing violins.

565 Billy Ocean
When The Going Gets Tough, The Tough Get Going

Label & Cat No.: **Jive JIVE 114**

Producers: **Wayne Braithwaite / Barry Eastmond**

Writers: **Wayne Braithwaite / Barry Eastmond / Billy Ocean / Robert John 'Mutt' Lange**

Date Reached No.1: **8 February 1986**

Weeks at No.1: **4**

In 1984 Eddy Grant was asked to write the theme song for a new film *Romancing The Stone*. Eddy wrote, produced and recorded the title song, but was disappointed when film's producer didn't include it. However, it was released as a single but fell short of the UK Top 50.

The sequel, *The Jewel Of The Nile*, was released two years later and featured the same three stars as the in the original movie, Michael Douglas, Kathleen Turner and Danny DeVito. Even though not one of them could sing, they appeared in the video next to Billy Ocean, miming as backing singers.

The storyline focused on Joan Wilder (Kathleen Turner) and Jack Colton (Michael Douglas) who embark on a romantic escapade, when Joan is invited to a middle-eastern country as a guest of the Sheik, and is then abducted. In one scene when Joan and Jack are discussing their future, Joan turned to Jack and said, 'When the going gets tough, the tough... well, I don't know what the tough do', that inspired Billy to find an answer and turn the phrase into a song.

Billy was born Leslie Charles in Trinidad on January 21, 1950. At the age of eight, the family moved to North London, where they have remained ever since.

"The album, *Love Zone*, was predominately written at Battery Studios in Willesden in north London," explained producer Barry Eastmond. "We then flew to New York and did the guitar overdubs and backing vocals, then brought the tracks back for Billy to add his vocals." Billy added, "For them, it was a change of environment. It wasn't a change for me, because I live here." Barry continued, "It was great fun working with Billy, but hard too. Billy loves late nights and could be doing a vocal at four in the morning, but I was falling asleep at the mixing desk. The other producer, Wayne Braithwaite, and I took it in turns to make the coffee."

Billy Ocean

566 Diana Ross
Chain Reaction

Label & Cat No.: **Capitol CL 386**

Producers: **Barry Gibb / Karl Richardson**

Writers: **Barry Gibb / Maurice Gibb / Robin Gibb**

Date Reached No.1: **8 March 1986**

Weeks at No.1: **3**

In 1981 after two decades with Motown Records, Diana Ross changed labels. She signed a $20m contract with RCA in America and an international deal with Capitol/EMI.

In the early Eighties, Barry Gibb, alongside producers Karl Richardson and Albhy Galuten, discussed working on some songs for Diana. They finally got around to it in 1985, which resulted in the album *Eaten Alive*. The title track, co-written with Michael Jackson, was the first single released from it and stalled at number 71.

As Barry Gibb said, "Diana Ross is a woman of many parts, and she concentrates on about a dozen things at once. She might be hosting the Academy Awards the same week as she's doing her vocals."

'Chain Reaction' was never originally meant to be on the album. Barry Gibb explains, "'Chain Reaction' was the last song we cut. We'd done the whole album and Diana said, 'Well, we still need one more song from somewhere'. We had 'Chain Reaction' all along but didn't have the nerve to play it to her because it was so Motown-ish that we were scared she wouldn't want to go back there. Robin Gibb persuaded her by saying, 'We think it's time you did something that you would have done with The Supremes and not just Diana Ross'. Once Diana had recorded it, she sat down and heard the playback and realised it was a credible tribute to her past."

To accompany The Supremes' sound that The Bee Gees had created, the video showed Diana as a Sixties recreation of herself in a modern style dance show.

Diana's biggest selling UK hit was back in the chart in October 2001 when Steps' cover reached number two.

567 Cliff Richard & The Young Ones, featuring Hank Marvin Living Doll

Label & Cat No.: **WEA YZ 65**

Producer: **Stuart Colman**

Writer: **Lionel Bart**

Date reached No.1: **29 March 1986**

Weeks at No.1: **3**

In 1982 four members of London's alternative comedy scene, Rik Mayall, Adrian Edmondson, Nigel Planer and Christopher Ryan, assembled together as The Young Ones for a BBC series. Their rude, violent, anarchic comedy proved very successful and, in 1984, Nigel Planer (as Neil, the 'hippy' character) reached number two with a surprisingly straight retread of Traffic's psychedelic hit, 'Hole In My Shoe'.

Comic Relief was launched by their friend Lenny Henry in 1985 to help combat poverty and social injustice in the UK and in third world countries. Every March it provides a whole night's viewing on BBC1 and every major comedian and many key musicians have been involved. Over £60m has been raised from the viewing public. There is always a spin-off single and in 1986 the organisers asked The Young Ones to make a single with Cliff Richard.

The record producer Stuart Colman was asked to participate: "After I'd worked with Cliff on 'She Means Nothing To Me', I was approached by the Comic Relief team to discuss doing a single with The Young Ones. Richard Curtis and Ben Elton came up with both the concept and the song. I remember very well the afternoon we all got together to discuss the outline, and we never stopped laughing at the prospect of how the imagery 'twixt Cliff and these snotty yobs would work out. Richard and Ben wrote the basis of the new lyric and I added bits along the way. Having worked with both Cliff and The Shadows, I suggested that Hank Marvin was involved, and it all fell into place very quickly. The Young Ones were more worried about working with Cliff, than he was with them. They were in awe of him and he was a true professional. Everybody had a ball and we loved every minute of making it, although it was one of the most complicated records I have ever made."

The record enhanced Cliff's reputation – the video showed him picking his nose! – suggesting another side to him than the somewhat conservative, holier-than-thou image he'd been saddled with in recent years. He also became the only solo artist to have the same song in two different versions at number one.

Cliff and the Young Ones

568 George Michael A Different Corner

Label & Cat No.: **Epic A 7033**

Producer: **George Michael**

Writer: **George Michael**

Date reached No.1: **19 April 1986**

Weeks at No.1: **3**

As George Michael was much the dominant partner in Wham!, it was inevitable that they would break up. This was announced in 1986 with George calling it, "The most amicable split in pop history". Less amicably, George Michael also split with their manager, Simon Napier-Bell, over a decision to sell the management company to the notorious Sun City in South Africa.

'A Different Corner' was the perfect way for George Michael to launch his solo career, although he had had a UK number one. It was a strong, reflective ballad, quite different from the disco sounds of Wham! It was also very much George the solo artist as he wrote, arranged, produced, sang and played all the instruments on the track. He may have made the tea as well.

George Michael's first solo album, *Faith*, was released in 1987 with its unexpected cover photograph in which George appears to be sniffing his own armpit. The biker look of his black leather jacket was enhanced by his designer stubble. The album sold 15 million copies and was full of hit singles – *I Want Your Sex* (3), *Faith* (2), *Father Figure* (11), *One More Try* (8), *Monkey* (13) and *Kissing A Fool* (18). Very influenced by Prince, George's 'I Want Your Sex' was a steamy single that was included on the soundtrack of *Beverly Hills Cop II*.

569 Falco
Rock Me Amadeus

Label & Cat No.: **A&M AM 278**
Producers: **Rob Bolland / Ferdi Bolland**
Writers: **Rob Bolland / Falco / Ferdi Bolland**
Date Reached No.1: **10 May 1986**
Weeks at No.1: **1**

MANY CLASSICALLY-BASED SONGS have made an impact on the singles chart over the years. But only a few classical composers have been mentioned in song. Not including Walter Murphy's instrumental, 'A Fifth Of Beethoven', Ludwig Van Beethoven has been the subject of two hits, 'Roll Over Beethoven' (ELO), 'Beethoven (I Love To Listen To)' (Eurythmics). In addition, Second City Sound took 'Tchaikovsky One' to number 22 in 1966 and Italian trance DJ, Mauro Picotto scraped into the bottom end of the chart in 2001 with 'Verdi'. Only Wolfgang Amadeus Mozart has made it to the top.

The Austrian composer was born in 1756 and died in 1791. He began composing when he was five. At the age of seven, his father took him to Paris and London where he played in various courts, and even performed for the English and French Royal families. His contemporaries respected him. Joseph Haydn told Mozart's father, Leopold, that his son was "The greatest composer known to me in person or by name. He has taste and, what is more, the greatest knowledge of composition."

Although Falco's song was sung in German, the opening lines when translated, are 'He was the first punk ever to set foot on this earth. He was a genius from the day of his birth. He could play the piano like a ringing a bell'. Falco explained his interpretation of the word punk, "It's just a word – to me it means a kind of intellectual working class feeling."

Falco, who was born Johann Hoelzel in Vienna in 1957, called himself Falco because as he said, "It sounds better than Johann Hoelzel, also it means the falcon, or two vocals." He teamed up with brothers Rob and Ferdi Bolland to write a song about Mozart because they felt he was Austria's son. In an interview, Falco joked, "He's a very good friend of mine. I met him last week in a bar. He's 200 years older than me and he's got a really good job in Vienna at the Royal Empire Opera House playing Midnight Showtime for the next 250 years. He plays all his hits. One of the highlights of the show though is him doing a perfect cover version of 'Rock Me Amadeus'." The Bollands wrote and recorded 'In The Army Now', later covered by Status Quo, and 'Love House', which was a Top 40 hit for ex-Page three girl, Samantha Fox.

The trio had another hit about their homeland, the follow-up, 'Vienna Calling', which reached number 10. After two more minor hits, Falco's chart days were confined to 1986, but he remained a star in his native Austria. He died in a car crash on February 6, 1998.

570 Spitting Image
The Chicken Song

Label & Cat No.: **Virgin SPIT 1**
Producer: **Philip Pope**
Writers: **Rob Grant / Doug Naylor**
Date Reached No.1: **17 May 1986**
Weeks at No.1: **3**

SPITTING IMAGE'S FOUR MOST REGULAR writers were Rob Grant, Doug Naylor, Nick Newman and *Have I Got News For You* team captain, Ian Hislop. They were collectively known as KTB, which was short for Keep That Bloody Noise Down In Here.

The voices for many of the characters were provided by another host of well-known names including; Chris Barrie, Steve Coogan, Rory Bremner, Adrian Edmondson, Harry Enfield and Pamela Stephenson. Some of the public figures immortalised in gross rubber caricatures included numerous members of the Royal family, politicians – a speciality being Ronald Reagan – and personalities like Oliver Reed, John McEnroe, Dustin Hoffman and Lester Piggott. Among the many pop stars were Kylie Minogue, Paul McCartney, Boy George, Mick Jagger, Bruce Springsteen, Tina Turner and Madonna.

Spitting Image ran between 1984 and 1996, so to cash in on the show's success, a 40-track album was released. Some of the satirical numbers included 'One Man And His Bitch' by 'Ronald Reagan & Margaret Thatcher', and 'We've Got Beards' by The Mike Fenton Singers as ZZ Top. The first single released, 'Da Doo Run Ron' by Nancy (Louise Gold) and Ronald Reagan (Chris Barrie), failed to chart. The song's co-writer, Doug Naylor, was also the creative force behind another successful BBC comedy show, *Red Dwarf*.

'The Chicken Song', which featured second cousin to Paul McCartney, Kate Robbins on lead vocals, was a deliberately cruel parody of the myriad disposable catchy singalongs invariably released each summer.

The puppets' inventors were Roger Law and Peter Fluck, who both began their 'modelling' career by making sculpted caricatures for Sunday supplement magazines. The only problem they had when it came to making the puppets were the pop stars. As Roger admitted, "We're a couple of old dinosaurs." Peter added, "We're not familiar with most of the pop stars of today, what we're after is the pop star who has an image and sticks with it. What annoys me is all this business of flitting from one image to another."

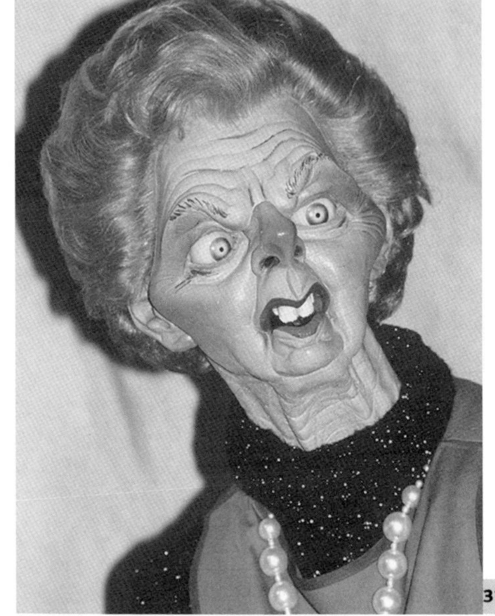

The Spitting Image puppet of Margaret Thatcher

571 Doctor & The Medics Spirit In The Sky

Label & Cat No.: **IRS IRM 113**

Producer: **Erik Jacobson**

Writer: **Norman Greenbaum**

Date Reached No.1: **7 June 1986**

Weeks at No.1: **3**

NORMAN GREENBAUM WAS UNABLE TO repeat the success he had had with 'Spirit In The Sky'. He and his wife went into the dairy business and began marketing their own Velvet Acres goat's milk for health food stores.

However, in 1986 Norman started receiving increased royalty cheques when an unknown band called Doctor & The Medics took his song to number one.

The band, who were formed in 1981, were The Doctor – the six foot six lead singer, Clive Jackson – together with Steve McGuire (guitar), Richie Searle (bass), Vom (born Robert Morris, drums) and two backing singers, Clive's wife, Wendi and her sister Collette who, for reasons best known to themselves, were called The Anadin Brothers. For many years Clive was a DJ in a club called The Surgery and was known to the crowd as 'the Doctor'.

Clive has always been the spokesman for the band and once described themselves as a cross between Valerie Singleton and a slug. Obviously not having a very high opinion of themselves, in 1999, Clive said, "The look of the band at present is influenced by age and at the moment we look like a bunch of cunts."

"We love Norman and 'Spirit In The Sky' although it was very hippy dippy, so we just cranked it up a bit," admitted Clive. "We knew at the time that nothing much was gonna happen after 'Spirit In The Sky' so we just enjoyed it for what it was at the time."

They did follow it up with 'Burn' (29) and then a cover of Abba's 'Waterloo' (45) which featured Roy Wood. But, with no more chart success, the band soon broke up. A few years later, Clive assembled a new line-up of Medics, which comprised Jon Morgans, Carl Axon and John Randle, Gabby Appleby and Fay Jackson, alongside original members Colette and Wendi.

According to the Doctor & the Medics website, Clive, who was born in Liverpool 1962, vowed never to be seen on stage when he was 40. So subsequently he took 2002 off and reappeared in 2003 and has continued touring.

572 Wham! The Edge Of Heaven

Label & Cat No.: **Epic FIN 1**

Producer: **George Michael**

Writer: **George Michael**

Date reached No.1: **28 June 1986**

Weeks at No.1: **2**

WHAM!'S FINAL SINGLE WAS A TWIN-pack; two singles sold together with the A-sides being George Michael's song ,'The Edge Of Heaven', and a cover of Was (Not Was)'s 'Where Did Your Heart Go?'. The other titles were a new song, 'Battlestations', and a remake of their first hit, 'Wham! Rap 86'.

Elton John and George were taken to appearing with each other. George was on Elton's hit singles, 'Nikita' and 'Wrap Her Up' and Elton played piano on Wham!'s farewell concert at Wembley Stadium in front of 72,000 fans. The supporting act at the concert was Gary Glitter, by then the campest of camp acts.

As well as a best-selling single, Wham! also had a number two album with *The Final* (great title!) and topped the video charts with, yes, you've guessed it, *Wham! The Videos*.

George Michael recorded a number one album in 1987, *Faith*, which remained on the album chart for 72 weeks, but what of Andrew Ridgeley? He wasn't bothered, spending his time motor-racing and with his wife, Keren Woodward from Bananarama, moved to Cornwall.

Andrew didn't make a solo album until *Son Of Albert* in 1990. It was swiftly remaindered and the single, 'Shake', could only manage a high of number 58. Intriguingly, an earlier unreleased version of this song included George's vocals. George and Andrew remained good friends and they did perform a few songs together in Rio in 1991.

573 Madonna Papa Don't Preach

Label & Cat No.: **Sire W 8636**

Producers: **Madonna / Stephen Bray**

Writers: **Madonna / Brian Elliot**

Date Reached No.1: **12 July 1986**

Weeks at No.1: **3**

WHEN 'LIKE A VIRGIN' WAS RELEASED in 1984, some American radio stations banned it because they thought is was about sex. It was only after Madonna explained that it was actually about a woman finally finding someone who made her feel special and brand-new, and that it was like the first time all over again, that stations started playing it. She had similar problems with 'Papa Don't Preach'. It contained a message which people misunderstood.

Before anybody had heard the song, Madonna envisaged that people would take it the wrong way. In an interview with the *New York Times*, she stated, "Immediately they're going to say I am advertising every young girl to go out and get pregnant. This song is really about a girl who is making a decision in her life. She has a close relationship with her father and wants to maintain that closeness. To me it's a celebration of life." For the accompanying video, a 28-year old Madonna convincingly played a pregnant teenager. She had ditched the glamour look and was now sporting a mixture of denim and leather and a bleached blonde crop. Her father in the video was portrayed by Danny Aiello.

The song wasn't originally intended for Madonna. Brian Elliot, a singer/songwriter who had a recording contract with Warner Brothers, was working with a new artist called Cristina

Madonna underwent a complete make-over when 'Papa Don't Preach' was released, the first of many in her long career

ITALIANS
DO IT BETTER

Dent. Once he had written the song, he took it to Mo Ostin in the A&R department to get his opinion on it. He was sceptical at first, but then suggested it would be better for Madonna and would like to play it to her. When Madonna heard it, she jumped at it. Brian was still keen to let Cristina record it first, but was soon persuaded that to let Madonna record it, made for a wise career move.

Madonna had yet to realise that she acted best when she was placed in a musical setting as with *Evita*. Because of its good script, Madonna was okay in *Desperately Seeking Susan* but the disaster of *Shanghai Surprise* was about to follow.

574 Chris de Burgh The Lady In Red

Label & Cat No.: **A&M AM 331**

Producer: **Paul Hardiman**

Writer: **Chris de Burgh**

Date reached No.1: **2 August 1986**

Weeks at No.1: **3**

In Shakespeare's *King John*, Hubert de Burgh disobeys the King's orders by refusing to burn out the eyes of the Duke of Bretagne. "That's one of my ancestors," says Chris de Burgh. "They've been involved in the running of the country since William the Conqueror, and Elizabeth de Burgh married Robert the Bruce." Chris was born, the son of a diplomat, in Argentina in 1948.

In 1960 Chris de Burgh's family bought a castle in Ireland and converted it to a hotel. He graduated from Trinity College, Dublin in 1973 and started singing for the guests, his first album being *Far Beyond These Castle Walls* (1975). His albums attracted critical popularity and he had hits in Europe and South America, but only a cult following here. *Spanish Train And Other Stories* (1976) included his inventive take on the Christmas story, 'A Spaceman Came Travelling', and *Crusader* (1979) followed his research into the Crusades.

In 1986 Chris de Burgh was stunned by the way his wife looked and wrote 'The Lady In Red', which he included on his album, *Into The Light*. At last, he had a best-selling UK single, and the album went to number two and stayed on the charts for over a year. Prince Andrew, who married the redhead, Sarah Ferguson, said it was their song. De Burgh's declaration of love turned sour when he wrote of his affection for the family nanny in 1994, 'Blonde Hair, Blue Jeans', on the album, *This Way Up* – by any standards, an extraordinary thing to do. The tabloids had a field day but the de Burghs did manage to save their marriage.

"It is every songwriter's dream to come up with a song that everybody loves," says Chris de Burgh, "and I'm so glad that I did it with 'The Lady In Red' rather than a novelty like 'Patricia The Stripper'. I can see why everybody likes 'The Lady In Red' – it's got a lovely, warm feeling to it and it's like putting on a coat when you hear it. I've got a forever classic almost by default."

575 Boris Gardiner I Wanna Wake Up With You

Label & Cat No.: **Revue REV 733**

Producer: **Willie Lindo**

Writer: **Mac Davis**

Date Reached No.1: **23 August 1986**

Weeks at No.1: **3**

Some 16 years had passed since Boris Gardiner first graced the UK chart (although, due to a record label misprint, he was credited as Boris Gardner on some copies). You could be forgiven for not remembering his name for two reasons. Firstly some pressings of his only previous chart hit, 'Elizabethan Reggae' in 1970 was erroneously credited to Byron Lee and the other reason was that it was an instrumental.

Boris was born in Kingston, Jamaica in 1946. He joined The Upsetters as bass player and had one double A-sided hit in 1969 with 'Return of Django' / 'Dollar In The Teeth'. In 1970 he was a session player with other reggae groups, The Aggrovators and The Crystalites before becoming a member of Byron Lee's Dragonaires. It was that band that featured on the B-side of 'Elizabethan Reggae' with 'Soul Serenade'. In the same year, he contributed bass guitar on Bob & Marcia's Top 10 hit 'Young, Gifted And Black'.

Mac Davis was a Texas-born singer/songwriter. He had written hits for Elvis Presley – 'In The Ghetto' and 'Don't Cry Daddy' (the latter under his pen name Scott Davis), Kenny Rogers – 'Something's Burning' and Glen Campbell – 'Everything A Man Could Ever Need'. 'I Wanta Wake Up With You', as it was credited, first appeared on Davis' 1980 album *It's Hard To Be Humble*, for which the title track was a minor hit.

Two further hit singles followed in 1986; 'You're Everything To Me' reached number 11 and then in an attempt to cash in on the festive season, Boris' self-penned 'The Meaning Of Christmas', ground to a halt at number 69.

576 Communards with Sarah Jane Morris Don't Leave Me This Way

Label & Cat No.: **London LON 103**

Producer: **Mike Thorne**

Writers: **Kenny Gamble / Leon Huff / Cary Gilbert**

Date Reached No.1: **13 September 1986**

Weeks at No.1: **4**

"I don't want to play pop music anymore," declared Jimmy Somerville when he stormed out of Bronski Beat in the summer of 1985. "It's because of differences about what we wanted."

That retirement lasted a matter of weeks. By December that same year, he teamed up with a classically-trained pianist, Richard Coles, as The Committee. Realising a group of that name already existed, they renamed themselves

The Communards. It looked a bit dubious at first as to whether the partnership would last. Richard explains, "Jimmy was a bit of a basket case then, whenever we went away anywhere to play, come two in the morning we'd be scooping him out of some dive."

The Communards, who named themselves after the French Revolutionaries who ruled Paris between March and May 1871, decided to cover 'Don't Leave Me This Way' because Jimmy loved Thelma Houston's disco version, although Richard preferred the Harold Melvin & The Bluenotes' original. Both versions charted within two weeks of each other in early 1977.

"I hate music snobs who resent you doing a totally different, off-the-wall electro-dance cover of an old song," explained Richard. "People might throw their hands up in horror when they hear it, but we're not James Last."

British-born singer Sarah Jane Morris has had quite a varied career. She loved disco music and scored a number one hit in Italy and Greece with a cover of Barry White's 'Never Never Gonna Give You Up'. She loves jazz music and has performed Bertolt Brecht and Kurt Weill classics with the Royal Liverpool Philharmonic Orchestra. In 1991 she co-wrote 'I'm Missing You' which went on to win the San Remo festival.

After topping the chart, Jimmy had another ambition. "I've got my heart set on doing the ultimate disco megamix version of The Sex Pistols' 'Pretty Vacant', with backing vocals and screaming from beginning to end." Thankfully, that hasn't materialised yet. However his solo career in the Nineties has included the Top 10 hits, 'You Make Me Feel (Mighty Real)' and 'To Love Somebody'.

Communards

577 Madonna
True Blue

Label & Cat No.:	**Sire W 8550**
Producers:	**Madonna / Stephen Bray**
Writers:	**Madonna / Stephen Bray**
Date Reached No.1:	**11 October 1986**
Weeks at No.1:	**1**

IT WAS ONLY HER SECOND YEAR OF chart action, but 1985 was Madonna's most successful year, in terms of sales and breaking new records.

'Into The Groove' is still Madonna's biggest selling UK hit single. Here are the facts: she was the only artist to have eight Top 10 hits in a one year; in America she was the first woman to sell three million singles in a calendar year, the first woman to take five Top five singles off one album, the only woman to hold the top two places on the UK singles chart and the first female artist to enter the singles chart in the Top three; in Australia, she is the only woman to replace herself at the top of the chart.

Madonna's third album, *True Blue*, took its title from a favourite expression of her then husband Sean Penn. "To my husband's very pure vision of love," exclaimed Madonna. All the other tracks, which Madonna co-wrote, were inspired by her feelings for him at the time. As producer Steve Bray said, "She was very much in love with Sean. When she's in love, she'll write great love songs. If she's not, she won't."

Despite the album's slating by the critics, it went on to sell over 12 million copies worldwide, but Madonna was more concerned with getting her film career off the ground. She was desperately seeking movie stardom. John Kohn, a film producer and a friend of Sean's, sent Madonna a script for a new comedy called *Shanghai Surprise*. She loved the plot and was cast as Gloria Tatlock, opposite Sean.

The film, which cost around $17million, was a spectacular failure. Madonna was extremely disappointed as she felt it had so much potential. George Harrison's Handmade Film Company, who had backed the project, only managed to claw back around $2 million. George later admitted that he "walked away from the experience hating Madonna."

578 Nick Berry
Every Loser Wins

Label & Cat No.:	**BBC RESL 204**
Producer:	**Simon May**
Writers:	**Simon May / Stewart James / Bradley James**
Date Reached No.1:	**18 October 1986**
Weeks at No.1:	**3**

"MY AGENT PHONED ME UP AND SAID, 'I don't think you're right for the job, but go along anyway'. To me it was just another audition, but they wanted someone who could play the piano," explained Nick Berry on how he won his role in *EastEnders*. "I didn't have any aspirations to be a pop star, I never fancied it. I told them that I used to play in a band and I got the job."

EastEnders first hit the UK screens in 1985. Over 17 million viewers tuned into the first episode and 20 years on, audience figures are still high. They do have, however, an ongoing ratings battle with the Britain's longest running soap, *Coronation Street*.

Nick, who once appeared as a rat in the children's Christmas drama *The Box of Delights*, played Simon Wicks but is not the first member of the cast to make the charts. That honour goes to Wendy Richard, who, with Mike Sarne, took 'Come Outside' to the top in 1962, though this was many years before she appeared in *EastEnders*. But even before Nick, Anita Dobson, who played landlady Angie Watts, had a Top five hit with a vocal version of the theme, retitled 'Anyone Can Fall In Love' and Angie's daughter, Sharon Watts (Letitia Dean), teamed up with

Kelvin Carpenter (Paul Medford), for a number 12 hit 'Something Outta Nothing'. Let's be grateful that Peter Dean's 'Can't Get A Ticket' and Tom Watt's horrendous cover of Bob Dylan's 'Subterranean Homesick Blues' never troubled the charts.

BBC Records was formed in 1970. The 26 hits prior to Nick Berry were mainly television theme hits, the exceptions being Keith Harris and Orville's two hits, 'Orville's Song' and 'Come To My Party', *Grange Hill* Cast's 'Just Say No' and Claire and Friends' 'It's 'Orrible Being In Love When You're 8½'. Nick Berry not only gave the label their first number one, he also set a new record of the highest climb within the published Top 75 chart when he catapulted 66-4.

Nick left the soap after five years and almost immediately landed the job of PC Rowan in *Heartbeat*. Its theme was the Buddy Holly song of the same name, which Nick covered and took to number two in 1992.

579 Berlin

Take My Breath Away (Love Theme From 'Top Gun')

Label & Cat No.: **CBS A 7320**

Producer: **Giorgio Moroder**

Writers: **Giorgio Moroder / Tom Whitlock**

Date Reached No.1: **8 November 1986**

Weeks at No.1: **4**

One of the top films of 1986 was *Top Gun* starring Tom Cruise, Val Kilmer and Kelly McGillis. The story centres around the romance between up and coming fighter pilot Lt Pete Mitchell (Tom Cruise) and his instructor, Charlotte Blackwood (Kelly McGillis) and his rivalry with fellow cadet, Iceman (Val Kilmer).

Berlin were originally formed in 1979 by bass player, John Crawford. He had advertised for a lead singer and, after one audition, recruited a former teenage actress, Terri Nunn. To give the band a wider appeal he wanted an international name, so he chose Berlin. Terri left within a year and was replaced by Virginia Macalino. But John wasn't happy and disbanded the group. He then formed Fahrenheit but again was dissatisfied. In 1981 he re-formed Berlin with a new line-up of Rik Olsen (guitar), David Diamond and Matt Reid (keyboards) and Rob Brill (drums). He also invited Terri back to the group. By 1985 Reid, Diamond and Olsen had left and the group remained a trio.

CBS originally wanted Aimee Mann to record 'Take My Breath Away'. Terri recalled how they came to record the song instead: "Giorgio Moroder wanted us to do it and gave us the choice of 'Danger Zone' or 'Take My Breath Away'. He originally intended 'Danger Zone' to be a duet between us and Kenny Loggins, but I preferred 'Take My Breath Away'. I know it was not a typical Berlin song, but I liked it. When we first heard the song, it was in such an early phrase and we didn't know anything about the movie." John Crawford added, "To be honest, we did it because we needed a little bit of money." Tom Whitlock told American author, Fred Bronson, how he came to write the lyrics, "I hopped in my car and was driving home into Hollywood. By the time I got home, I had written the lyric. The title was a phase that had been running through my mind, in terms of asking for that kind of awe, something so striking that you can't breathe."

'Take My Breath Away', which was featured during a sensual lovemaking session between Tom Cruise and Kelly McGillis, went to number one in both the UK and US and won an Oscar for the Best Song and a Golden Globe award for Best Original Song. Kenny Loggins performed 'Danger Zone' as a solo and other songs included on the nine million-selling soundtrack were '(Sittin' On) The Dock Of The Bay' (Otis Redding), 'You've Lost That Lovin' Feeling' (Righteous Brothers) and 'Mighty Wings' (Cheap Trick).

The follow-up, 'You Don't Know' barely made the UK Top 40. The next single, 'Like Flames', did even worse. However in 1990, when *Top Gun* had its first airing on British television, 'Take My Breath Away' was re-issued and went back to number three. In 2002 Soda Club featuring Hannah Alethea took a dance version of it into the Top 20.

580 Europe

The Final Countdown

Label & Cat No.: **Epic A 7127**

Producer: **Kevin Elson**

Writer: **Joey Tempest**

Date Reached No.1: **6 December 1986**

Weeks at No.1: **2**

Abba were unquestionably Sweden's biggest musical export, with Roxette not far behind. Like Abba, Europe, under their original name, The Force, had tried their hand at Eurovision.

The Force were assembled near Stockholm in 1978 by bass player, Peter Olsson, guitarist John Norum and drummer Tony Reno. Having spotted Joey Tempest (born Joakim Larsson) who was then a member of Roxanne, they persuaded him to join the band as lead singer. In 1981 Olsson left and was replaced by John Levén. The following year they submitted a song for Europe to represent Sweden in the Eurovision Song Contest, but failed to make the final three.

In 1985 Ian Haugland was brought in to replace Reno, Kee Marcello replaced John Norum and Mic Michaeli was brought in as the new keyboard player. Joey changed their name to Europe. They tried to portray an image as a hard rock band, but Joey's pretty boy looks and his long flowing blonde locks weakened their appearance somewhat.

'The Final Countdown' was written in 1985 and was included in the Sylvester Stallone film, *Rocky IV*. It went to number one and brought Europe instant fame. Joey Tempest recalls, "We were 20 years old and very inexperienced. We were carried away with success, shows, money and crazy women crowded everywhere."

The debut album, *The Final Countdown*, made the Top 10 and spawned the follow-up hits, 'Rock The Night' (12) and 'Carrie' (22). 'Superstitious' was released in 1988 but missed the Top 30. They took a break and, after a four-year hiatus, the band returned in 1992 with 'I'll Cry For You' (28). The next hit, 'Halfway to Heaven' made little impact and tension was mounting.

Joey Tempest again: "In the end, I couldn't stand it no more and in 1992, I decided to leave the band. We hadn't anything to say and people were aware of it."

As the millennium approached, record companies were cashing in on songs appropriate for the situation. So, when Warner Brothers reissued Prince's '1999', Epic did likewise with 'The Final Countdown'. This time it was re-recorded with a dance beat behind it, perhaps explaining its reason for barely making the Top 40. Initial copies were issued in picture sleeves with a printing error wherein the first 'o' in 'countdown' was omitted!

581 The Housemartins
Caravan Of Love

Label & Cat No.: **Go! Discs GOD 16**

Producer: **John Williams**

Writers: **Ernie Isley / Chris Jasper / Marvin Isley**

Date Reached No.1: **20 December 1986**

Weeks at No.1: **1**

"MY INITIAL INTEREST IN ACAPPELLA was in gospelmusic and things like that, The Persuasions especially," said The Housemartins' lead singer Paul Heaton. "The Housemartins performing acappella seems to have stemmed from the increasing use of backing vocals. We aren't great musicians or wonderful soloists, or anything like that, so it seems to have helped the set from all sounding the same."

The Housemartins were formed in 1983 in Hull by singer Paul Heaton and guitarist Stan Cullimore. Ted Key (bass) and Chris Lang (drums) were soon recruited to complete the line-up. Their early gigs carried political messages supporting the miners and CND. Just prior to signing a deal with Go! Discs, Hugh Whitaker replaced Lang and Norman Cook replaced Key. They were promoted as Hull's fourth most popular band, which got people thinking as to who the first three were...

Their first single, the political 'Flag Day' failed to chart. The follow-up, 'Happy Hour' reached number three, as did the parent album, *London 0 Hull 4*, which continued the promotional theme of being Hull's fourth most popular band.

Ernie Isley, Chris Jasper and Marvin Isley were the rhythm section of The Isley Brothers and had recorded their version in 1985 under the name Isley Jasper Isley. "I had been looking at the world scene quite a bit and I wasn't pleased with what I was seeing. I just felt that we all needed a positive message. I had the melody in my head for about four months before I put pen to paper. When I did, I wrote the song in 20 minutes and those lyrics just poured out," explained Chris Jasper.

The Housemartins viewed 'Caravan Of Love' as a religious song. But as Norman Cook explained, "I draw a distinction between being a Christian and being religious. You don't have to be a Christian to be religious. It's like saying to be a political person you have to be a member of a party."

They split up in 1988. Norman Cook went solo and recorded under various guises including Freak Power, Pizzaman, Mighty Dub Kats and most famously, Fatboy Slim. Paul Heaton formed The Beautiful South and Stan Cullimore went on to write and illustrate many children's books including: *Tabby's Cat, Where's Blinky* and *Henrietta And The Magic Trick*. As for Hugh Whittaker, he lent a friend £10,000 which he never got back. In an attempt to recover the money, he firebombed his house then planted an axe in his friends forehead, for which he received a five-year jail sentence.

The Housemartins

582 Jackie Wilson
Reet Petite (The Sweetest Girl In Town)

Label & Cat No.: **SMP SKM 3**

Producer: **Carl Davis**

Writers: **Berry Gordy Jr / Tyran Carlo (Billy Davis)**

Date reached No.1: **27 December 1986**

Weeks at No.1: **4**

THERE WAS NO HEADSTONE, JUST THE marker B261. It was Detroit in 1984 and one of America's greatest entertainers, Jackie Wilson, was being buried like a pauper. What had gone so dreadfully wrong with his career? The answer is, just about everything.

Jackie Wilson was born in Detroit in 1934 and he would have been a boxer if he'd won more fights. He joined the doo-wop group, Billy Ward & The Dominoes, and although he and Ward had disagreements (Jackie slept with Ward's fiancé), he displayed his vocal gymnastics on the US hit, 'St. Therese Of The Roses' (1956).

When Jackie left The Dominoes, he befriended Berry Gordy Jr and his cousin, Billy Davis, who gave him songs. 'Reet Petite (The Sweetest Girl In Town)' was Davis' first song, being a contemporary phrase for a good-looking girl. It had been written as a simple boogie-woogie but Dick Jacobs's colourful orchestration added brass passages and horn stabs. "It didn't bother Jackie," said Billy, "There was no way of overpowering him." The rolling of the R's was particularly distinctive but when Jackie did it on stage, he blew his front teeth out: "I'll never sing that again," he said, "and he never did."

Berry Gordy Jr and Billy Davis wrote many of Jackie Wilson's first hits – 'To Be Loved', 'Lonely Teardrops', 'I'll Be Satisfied' – but they were cheated out of royalties and decided to start their own projects. Gordy Jr started Tamla-Motown, and though Billy Davis worked with him from time to time, he established his own career, producing Fontella Bass' 'Rescue Me' and co-writing 'I'd Like To Teach The World To Sing'.

Wilson, however, remained with Brunswick

(Coral in the UK) and had hits based on the classics with 'Night', 'Alone At Last' and 'My Empty Arms'. His 'Baby Workout' with The Count Basie Orchestra rivalled 'Reet Petite' for enthusiasm. He turned to soul music and made 'Higher And Higher' and 'I Get The Sweetest Feeling'.

But there were countless problems. In 1961 he was shot by a former girlfriend while on stage and his personal life included three marriages and numerous affairs. He was fuelled by amphetamines and alcohol, he didn't pay his taxes or child support, and he was hounded by the Mafia because of some suspect management deals. In 1975 he suffered a heart attack on stage, fell down and hit his head. He never regained consciousness and died in 1984.

In 1986 a very amusing video for 'Reet Petite' was shot using plasticine models. The record went to number one and there is now a headstone with the epitaph, 'No More Lonely Teardrops'.

583 Steve 'Silk' Hurley
Jack Your Body

Label & Cat No.: **London LON 117**
Producer: **Steve 'Silk' Hurley**
Writer: **Steve 'Silk' Hurley**
Date Reached No.1: **24 January 1987**
Weeks at No.1: **2**

When Steve 'Silk' Hurley reached number one on the UK, it indicated that house music had finally broken out of its home city, Chicago. As DJ Pete Tong recalled, "It was the first time daytime radio had played a house record. I think they had to check it wasn't April Fool's Day, because it sounded like the most alien thing."

House music was originally a monotonous electro beat with a Hi NRG feel and was still making its mark on the UK music scene. The only real house track to breach the chart was in the summer of 1986, when Farley 'Jackmaster' Funk's 'Love Can't Turn Around', which itself was heavily sampled from J. M. Silk's 'I Can't Turn Around', reached number 10. Steve 'Silk' Hurley was now one half of the duo J. M. Silk.

Jackin' is a frenzied dance that looks like someone had plugged themselves into the mains. One American dance DJ described jackin' as 'Like having sex standing up with your clothes on'.

'Jack Your Body', originally released in April 1986, was a simple repetition of the phrase 'Jack, jack, jack, jack, jack your body' over a looped bassline plundered from The Philly soul group First Choice's, 1986 disco anthem, 'Let No Man Put Asunder'. Kym Sims sampled the same track for 'Too Blind To See' and Break Of Dawn did likewise for 'Rhythm On The Loose'.

Steve refused to promote the track, as he was now a member of J. M. Silk. Instead the video used clips from the Thirties slapstick comedy dancing including an appearance by Charlie Chaplin. It could also have doubled as a karaoke video because whenever the repetitive title was heard, the words were flashed up all over the screen.

584 George Michael & Aretha Franklin
I Knew You Were Waiting (For Me)

Label & Cat No.: **Epic DUET 2**
Producer: **Narada Michael Walden**
Writers: **Simon Climie / Dennis Morgan**
Date reached No.1: **7 February 1987**
Weeks at No.1: **2**

In 1983 country songwriter Dennis Morgan came to the UK to see The Everly Brothers' reunion at the Royal Albert Hall. After the show, he went to Peter Stringfellow's club with Phil Everly and was introduced to Simon Climie of the soul band, Climie Fisher, and they decided to write songs together.

Sometime later, Dennis Morgan was in Salisbury Cathedral and he prayed for a good song to take to MIDEM, the industry's musical festival in Cannes. Not surprisingly, he hit upon a song of hope with a strong Christian feeling, and he and Simon completed 'I Knew You Were Waiting (For Me)'. They made a demo and pitched it to Tina Turner and Aretha Franklin. Clive Davis, the president of Arista Records, agreed that the song was perfect for Aretha but wanted to team her with George Michael.

Considering her eminence as possibly the greatest soul singer, Aretha Franklin has not had many UK Top 10 hits – 'Respect' (10, 1967), 'I Say A Little Prayer' (4, 1968) and 'Sisters Are Doin' It For Themselves' (with Eurythmics) (9, 1985). The sublime '(You Make Me Feel Like) A Natural Woman' (1967) didn't even make the UK Top 50.

This was George Michael's third single under his own name so he completed a hat-trick of number ones. His next record, 'I Want Your Sex', stalled at number three. George has had other successful collaborations – number ones with Elton John and Queen / Lisa Stansfield and hits with Toby Bourke ('Waltz Away Dreaming'), Mary J. Blige ('As') and Whitney Houston ('If I Told You That').

585 Ben E. King
Stand By Me

Label & Cat No.: **Atlantic A 9361**
Producers: **Jerry Leiber / Mike Stoller**
Writers: **Jerry Leiber / Mike Stoller / Ben E. King**
Date reached No.1: **21 August 1987**
Weeks at No.1: **3**

In 1960 Ben E. King left The Drifters and set about a solo career with the same producers, Jerry Leiber and Mike Stoller. The first single was the stunning 'Spanish Harlem', written by Leiber with Phil Spector, and the second was 'Stand By Me'.

Ben E. King had updated a gospel song and

he says, "I took it from an old spiritual that The Soul Stirrers did, (sings) 'Oh Lord stand by me', but in the end my tune was nothing like that, and all the romantic bits came from me. Many times I have heard my song, 'Stand By Me', being done by gospel groups, which is very pleasing to me." Although 'Stand By Me' is such a mesmerising, atmospheric record, it only made number 27 on the UK charts. Still, it was appreciated by John Lennon, who recorded it as a single in 1975.

In 1987 the director Rob Reiner was making a film, based on a Stephen King novel, about four 12-year-old boys who found a corpse and how it affects their lives. The music was by Jack Nitzsche, but Reiner wanted a song for the title sequence. Ben E. King says, "The movie was going to be called *The Body* but the title was too heavy for the kids. Rob Reiner was going through his old records and he rang up the producers and he said, 'Here it is, the title of the movie, *Stand By Me*.' It was breathtaking to see *Stand By Me* on a marquee. It was nice to bounce back into life like that and it gave me a whole new audience of kids to sing to. All of a sudden I was doing concerts instead of nightclubs. The angels above were watching over me."

586 Boy George
Everything I Own

Label & Cat No.: **Virgin BOY 100**

Producer: **Steve Levine**

Writer: **David Gates**

Date Reached No.1: **14 March 1987**

Weeks at No.1: **2**

IN 1987 GEORGE O'DOWD, BORN IN Eltham, Kent, was getting his life back on track after a drug habit had pushed him over the edge the previous year. "Numerous jokes were going round about me," remembered George. "What does Boy George have for breakfast? Smack, Crackle and Pop, was one. How can you tell which Christmas tree is Boy George's? The one without any needles. The thing that people really love is other people's misery, but it doesn't bother me. I just think, stuff it."

In 1987 he had sorted himself out enough to embark on a solo career, and his first hit was this rather tame, reggaefied cover of Bread's, 'Everything I Own'. The video showed George alone on a stage with a complete band set-up, but without a band. He looked pale but reasonably healthy, bearing in mind what he had gone through.

In the background was a bank of television screens flashing images of a young painter friend, Trojan, who had died of a drugs overdose the previous August. The images were from a film that George's boyfriend John Maybury had made. "Trojan was one of those people who defied description in a lot of ways and would never want to be forgotten," explained George. George dedicated the song to him.

Other hits followed: 'Sold', 'To Be Reborn', 'Live My Life', which was featured in the film *No Hiding*, 'No Clause 28' – a protest song against the Government bill banning the promotion of homosexuality – and 'The Crying Game' from the film of the same name.

Between 1989 and 1991 he recorded under the moniker Jesus Loves You, but after four singles – none of which made any great impact ('Bow Down Mister' being the biggest seller, reaching number 27) – he continued as Boy George. He was also making a name for himself as a nightclub DJ.

In 2001 *Taboo – The Musical* opened in London. It portrayed London in the early Eighties and focused on two young men, an artist and designer, Leigh Bowery (played by Boy George) and Boy George (played by Euan Morton). It ran for 15 months before moving to New York, where it's been running since November 2003.

587 Mel & Kim
Respectable

Label & Cat No.: **Supreme SUPE 111**

Producers: **Mike Stock / Matt Aitken / Pete Waterman**

Writers: **Mike Stock / Matt Aitken / Pete Waterman**

Date Reached No.1: **28 March 1987**

Weeks at No.1: **1**

"BONEY M WITH A 36B CUP. HORRIBLE," was how Eleanor Levy described 'Respectable' in a *Record Mirror* singles review.

The gorgeous Appleby sisters were born in London's East End; Kim in 1961 and Melanie in 1966. Mel, with her mother's encouragement, began modelling and eventually made it to page three of *The Sun*. Mel later agreed that it probably helped her move into the music industry.

Boy George

Their entrance happened in a rather unusual way. Kim recalled, "We'd sent off a tape to one of the record companies but nothing happened. So we went down there and it was the usual story, 'He's in a meeting' or 'He's out of the office today'. So we just started singing and dancing outside the office. A man who must have heard the commotion came out. We were showing him we had rhythm and voices to go with it, so he took us into the office for a chat." But nothing more came of it.

The sisters met Pete Waterman at London's Hippodrome nightclub. After explaining who they were, Pete invited them to the studio the next day. "As soon as I heard them, I knew they were really good and the best thing about them was their personalities."

Stock, Aitken & Waterman wrote their first hit, 'Showing Out (Get Fresh At The Weekend)' after a comment the girls made about going out for the night and showing out. Kim explained, "Showing out is when you go out and kiss frogs, seeing if they turn into princes." "The follow-up, 'Respectable' became an anthem, not just for them and their image, but also for the company itself," said Pete Waterman. "The lyrics came from an ad we took out in the trade press that used the lines, 'You can love or hate us, you ain't gonna change us... we ain't ever going to be respectable." It was Mike Stock's idea to add the gimmicky, 'Tay-tay, tay, tay, t-tay' at the beginning, but Mel and Kim hated that bit. Nonetheless, they took the track away with them to a gig they were doing in Holland that evening. Later that night, Pete got a call from the girls saying that the Dutch audience went wild for that intro and it should not be taken out.

Mel and Kim had two further Top 10 hits, 'F.L.M.' and 'That's The Way It Is'. Christmas 1987 saw another Mel and Kim in the chart. It was comedian Mel Smith who had teamed up with Kim Wilde for a comedy cover of 'Rocking Around The Christmas Tree'.

In 1988 the girls attended the Montreux festival, but Mel was taken away in a wheelchair. Despite press reports claiming it was a slipped disc, Mel was receiving treatment for spinal cancer. She died in January 1990 of pneumonia. Later the same year Kim began a solo career and her first single, 'Don't Worry' got to number two.

588 Ferry Aid
Let It Be

Label & Cat No.: **Sun AID 1**
Producers: **Mike Stock / Matt Aitken / Pete Waterman**
Writers: **John Lennon / Paul McCartney**
Date reached No.1: **4 April 1987**
Weeks at No.1: **3**

On March 6 1987, the Townsend Thorensen ship, Herald Of Free Enterprise, capsized and 197 people were killed. It became known as the Zeebrugge Ferry disaster and it was soon evident that the bow doors had been left open and water had flooded in. Several of *The Sun*'s readers were on board as they had taken up an offer from the newspaper. *The Sun* set up a disaster fund and announced a charity single.

In wake of Band Aid, Stock, Aitken & Waterman were asked to produce a new, all-star version of 'Let It Be'. Paul McCartney gave his support but he was unavailable on the day of recording so the first line of his single with The Beatles (which had only made number two) was used instead. The other participants included Boy George, Kate Bush, Mel & Kim, Nik Kershaw, Mark Knopfler, Suzi Quatro, Alvin Stardust, Edwin Starr, Ruby Turner, Bonnie Tyler and Kim Wilde as well as members of Bucks Fizz, The Christians, Dr. & The Medics, Frankie Goes To Hollywood, The New Seekers and The Nolans. Not to mention some Page 3 girls who could sing in tune. 'Let It Be' made £700,000 for the charity.

Paul McCartney had written 'Let It Be' in 1969 as a message of hope to himself. He was having a restless night in which he was worried about the break-up of The Beatles. When he drifted off to sleep, he had a dream in which his mother, Mary, came to him "speaking words of wisdom". The song was written around the same time as Paul Simon's 'Bridge Over Troubled Water' and, intriguingly, both songwriters wanted Aretha Franklin to give the song a gospel treatment, which she did. The B-side of the Ferry Aid single is titled 'Let It Be (Gospel Mix)', but it is a lost opportunity, being little more than caterwauling. At the very end, Radio 1 DJ Steve Wright hopes that "everyone who lost relatives will be able to have a great life as a result of this record." Pardon?

In 1989 charges of both corporate manslaughter and individual manslaughter came to court, but the case collapsed.

589 Madonna
La Isla Bonita

Label & Cat No.: **Sire W 8378**
Producers: **Madonna / Patrick Leonard**
Writers: **Madonna / Patrick Leonard / Bruce Gaitsch**
Date Reached No.1: **25 April 1987**
Weeks at No.1: **2**

Producer Patrick Leonard first came to prominence in 1984 when he worked with The Jacksons on their *Victory* tour and the accompanying live album. Two years later, he wrote 'La Isla Bonita' for Michael Jackson, but he turned it down claiming he didn't like the title. He then offered it to Madonna who rewrote some of the lyrics to make the song her own. Interestingly, the seven-inch single erroneously credits Stephen Bray as the co-writer instead of Leonard.

Madonna had clearly developed a love for the Latin way of life. 'La Isla Bonita' is a lament for the fictitious island of San Pedro. "The song is a tribute to the beauty and mystery of Latin American people," Madonna once said in an interview with the *New York Times*. Many fans were having trouble keeping up with Madonna's ever changing images. The video, which was shot in a Latin district of Los Angeles, has, in one section, Madonna dressed as a flamenco dancer complete with a wide-brimmed Spanish hat and a bolero jacket. She had started another fashion craze. In 1998 during her *Drowned World* tour, she held her own flamenco parties. In 2002 she recorded a Spanish version of 'What It Feels Like

For A Girl'. In 2003 a missable version of 'La Isla Bonita' was recorded by *Baywatch* star, David Hasselhoff, for his album, *David Hasselhoff Sings America.*

In 1987 Madonna began her 'Who's That Girl?' world tour, including one night in Leeds and two at London's Wembley Stadium. Unsurprisingly, the 150,000 tickets for Wembley sold out in just 18 hours, so the promoters added an extra date.

Whilst Madonna was touring, she was surprised to learn from a British tabloid that her husband, Sean Penn, was in trouble with the law. He had been arrested on a reckless driving charge and was facing a jail sentence. Equally, Sean had a surprise when he learned that the latest issue of *Penthouse* magazine carried nude pictures of his wife inside. Unbeknown to Sean, the pictures of Madonna were taken a number of years before and she had no control over their publication.

590 Starship
Nothing's Gonna Stop Us Now

Label & Cat No.: **Grunt FB 49757**

Producers: **Narada Michael Walden**

Writers: **Albert Hammond / Diane Warren**

Date Reached No.1: **9 May 1987**

Weeks at No.1: **4**

In 1986 Patti LaBelle and Michael McDonald teamed up to record 'On My Own' which went to number one in the US and number two in the UK. Film director, Michael Gottlieb sent Diane Warren and Albert Hammond a script for his new film, *Mannequin*, and asked them to write a song for the wedding scene.

"I had lived with my girlfriend Claudia for seven years. I had finally gotten divorced from my other marriage and was thinking of writing a song for me to sing and make a demo for our wedding, so I combined the two," explained Albert Hammond. "What we thought of, what I said to Diane was 'it's almost like they've stopped me from marrying this woman for seven years, and they haven't succeeded. They're not gonna stop me doing it'. That's when suddenly 'Nothing's Gonna Stop Us Now' came up."

Neither Diane nor Albert had any particular artist in mind to record the song, but the film-makers did. They liked the idea of a duet and suggested pairing Laura Branigan with John Parr or even getting Patti and Michael together again. But Diane took the song to an A&R friend, Teri Muench, at RCA Records who thought Grace Slick of Starship would make a nice job of it. Teri sent Grace the demo and she agreed to record it.

Starship were formed as Jefferson Airplane in 1965 by Paul Kantner and Marty Balin. Grace Slick (born Grace Wing) joined in 1966 and they had US Top 10 hits with 'Somebody To Love' and 'White Rabbit'. They were an integral part of the San Francisco scene and were the only band to play all three major Sixties pop festivals, Monterey, Isle Of Wight and Woodstock. In 1971 after a change in the line-up they renamed themselves Jefferson Starship and had US Top 10 hits with, 'Miracles' and 'Count On Me'. By 1985 they had dropped the Jefferson, due to Kantner's departure and legal problems and were rewarded with the US number ones, 'We Built This City' and 'Sara'.

In 1987 the line-up comprised Slick (vocals), Mickey Thomas (vocals), Craig Chaquico (guitar), Don Baldwin (drums) and Pete Sears (bass). Starship were on tour at the time of the recording, so Narada Michael Walden, brought in some guest musicians he had used while working with Whitney Houston to lay the track down and got Grace to add the vocals on their return. He loved the echo he heard on the demo and thought it sounded like Phil Spector's Wall Of Sound. Walden said, "I thought this was my big chance to impress the world with my Phil Spector imitation, so that's why I agreed to do it."

"Initially I had Grace singing the low parts," added Walden. Donny Baldwin was in the studio and suggested that it was too low for her and that she should sing the high parts. Walden agreed, and asked Thomas to sing the low parts.

When the song reached number one, Slick was 47, which at the time made her the oldest female singer on a UK number one hit. They were inducted into the Rock And Roll Hall Of Fame in 1996.

591 Whitney Houston
I Wanna Dance With Somebody (Who Loves Me)

Label & Cat No.: **Arista RIS 1**

Producers: **Narada Michael Walden**

Writers: **George Merrill / Shannon Rubicam**

Date reached No.1: **6 June 1987**

Weeks at No.1: **2**

George Merrill and Shannon Rubicam, who together form Boy Meets Girl, wrote 'How Will I Know' for Janet Jackson. She turned it down so they passed the song to Whitney Houston, and it became a US number one and was also part of her mult-million selling album, *Whitney Houston.*

Merrill and Rubicam were asked to write for Whitney's second album and submitted 'Waiting For A Star To Fall'. The standards were extremely high and the song was rejected. Not to worry as they recorded it themselves and it became both a UK and US hit in 1988.

The couple thought they would try again and 'I Wanna Dance With Somebody (Who Loves Me)' describes a girl who is tired of dancing aimlessly. She wants someone who loves and appreciates her. She submitted it to Clive Davis, the head of Arista, who loved it, but her producer, Narada Michael Walden, felt it sounded more like a country song for Olivia Newton-John.

Narada worked out an arrangement to make it funkier, and the song was included on *Whitney*, the first album to go straight into the charts at number one in both the US and the UK. The album also included a duet of 'I Know Him So Well' with her mother, Cissy.

'I Wanna Dance With Somebody (Who Loves Me)' included Jim Gilstrap on backing vocals and Randy Jackson from the Jackson family on bass synth. The producer, Narada Michael

Walden, played drums. The song had a very bright sound and, unusually for the Eighties, a calypso feel.

592 The Firm
Star Trekkin'

Label & Cat No.: **Bark TREK 1**
Producers: **Grahame Lister / John O'Connor**
Writers: **Grahame Lister / John O'Connor / Rory Kehoe**
Date Reached No.1: **20 June 1987**
Weeks at No.1: **2**

In 1982 John O'Connor and Grahame Lister, as The Firm, wrote 'Arthur Daley (E's Alright)', a song paying homage to the lovable rogue Arthur Daley from TVs *Minder*, played by George Cole. The song went to number 14, after which The Firm seemingly disappeared. The follow-ups, 'Cash In Hand' and 'Bravo Costa Brave' failed to connect. Five years later, they returned with another novelty song, 'Star Trekkin'.

The song had its origins among a group of people known as The Sealed Knot, who held weekend jamborees recreating English Civil War battles. Part of the entertainment was to gather around the campfire at night and sing songs. One of the favourites was a parody of 'I Am The Music Man' from the Sixties musical *The Music Man*, recast as 'I am the Star Trek Man' featuring the five 'spoken' lines used in Star Trekkin', ie. 'It's life Jim, but not as we know it', 'There's Klingons on the starboard bow' etc. Grahame heard folk singer Chris Steinhauer perform a version of the song one evening at a local folk club and was struck by its good humour. Grahame asked Chris to record his version onto cassette, which he then took to his writing partner John O'Connor.

John, a guitarist who had worked with Steeleye Span in the Seventies and Bucks Fizz in the Eighties, owned Bark Studio in Walthamstow, London, and the two of them began playing around with the idea. They decided to abandon the *Music Man* parody, write a new melody and chorus, and use the tongue-twisting, ever-increasing tempo format pioneered by Rolf Harris with his tune 'The Court Of King Caractacus'. Rory Kehoe, a member of The Sealed Knot, was eventually identified as the author of the five 'spoken' lines, and duly credited as co-writer. The Firm were never a proper gigging band but for the recording of 'Star Trekkin', Bill Martin played keyboards, Dev Douglas voiced Spock, John provided the voice of Kirk and McCoy, studio engineer Brian O'Shaughnessy was Scotty, Grahame's wife Kathy and Karen Turney were the female backing singers with Grahame and Dev supplying the male backing voices. John's wife Shelley was the distinctive voice of Lt. Uhuru. Shelley, a native Californian, was at first embarrassed about her singing and didn't want her vocal used, but was eventually persuaded otherwise by John and Grahame. Fortunately so, for Shelley's 'Klingons on the starboard bow' contribution turned out to be the most memorable and most quoted part of the record.

They had trouble getting the record released, as John explained: "We approached a few record companies who said, 'You must be joking, we're not going to release this as a single!' But we believed in it so much that we started our own label Bark, named after my studio, pressed 500 copies and sent them to radio stations in England. Then, suddenly everything went haywire."

"It started selling fast and we knew it was going to be a hit, but John and I decided not to do personal TV appearances – we were a bunch of balding 30-somethings and we figured us doing *Top Of The Pops* would kill the whole fun element of the thing stone dead! So we decided to do a claymation / cartoon type video as the song's 'image'. We approached the *Spitting Image* team among others, but all the quotes were far too expensive and most required months of preparation time, whereas we had exactly one week to have it ready for *Top Of The Pops*," remembers Grahame. "So we gave the project to a group of young art school graduates called The Film Garage who performed miracles with potato heads, stick-on mouths, cardboard cut-outs and a minimal budget, finishing the video with just hours to spare."

The Firm's follow-up, 'Superheroes', duly bombed, and John soon moved to America where he pursued a successful career as an acoustic guitarist specialising in new-age music (recording under the name EKO). He also writes incidental music for the Channel 4 series *King Of The Hill*. Grahame still lives in Essex, still writes and records original songs, and performs locally, in addition to pursuing a parallel career as a tennis coach. In the early Eighties, he wrote and recorded a solo acappella doo-wop single called 'Automobile' released under the name of The Stick Shifts which was a turntable hit and later used as the basis of a Lurpak butter commercial.

593 Pet Shop Boys
It's A Sin

Label & Cat No.: **Parlophone R 6158**
Producer: **Julian Mendelsohn**
Writers: **Neil Tennant / Chris Lowe**
Date Reached No.1: **4 July 1987**
Weeks at No.1: **3**

Any songs with religious connotations attract their share of controversy, and The Pet Shop Boys' second number one was no exception.

'It's A Sin' is ostensibly about Neil Tennant's experiences at St Cuthbert's School in Newcastle. He said, "It was really about guilt. When I was growing up I thought everything that was any good was a sin. When people ask me, 'Do you believe in God?' I always say 'No'. That's my stock answer. But, deep down, I think I'm lying."

The Derek Jarman-directed video showed Neil dressed as a Bishop, which caused one of Neil's old teachers to complain to the press about the image Neil was portraying. As always happens when juicy controversial gossip is featured in the tabloids, it helped the song to climb the chart.

Then came more bad press. Jonathan King, who had a regular gossip column in *The Sun*, as well as a show on London's Capital Radio, began a vicious attack and started accusing The Pet Shop Boys of stealing the song from Cat Stevens'

'Wild World'. As Neil recalled, "When it got to number one, it was ruined for us. *The Sun* was a very influential paper then, but nothing came of it and they actually settled out of court and paid us damages. If there was a similarity, it certainly wasn't any intention. Cat Stevens wrote to me, because he knew Jonathan in the Sixties and wanted to help resolve the situation."

For the next single, 'What Have I Done To Deserve This', which reached number two, Neil wanted to collaborate with one of his childhood heroes and succeeded when Dusty Springfield agreed to record with them.

EMI were contemplating one more single from the album. The album's last track, 'King's Cross', was scheduled but the idea was halted when, on Wednesday November 18, one of London's worst disasters occurred. A discarded cigarette end started a fire on an escalator at London's King's Cross Underground Station. Within minutes, the whole concourse area was ablaze and 31 lives were lost.

594 Madonna
Who's That Girl?

Label & Cat No.: **Sire W 8341**

Producers: **Madonna / Patrick Leonard**

Writers: **Madonna / Patrick Leonard / Bruce Gaitsch**

Date Reached No.1: **25 July 1987**

Weeks at No.1: **1**

FOLLOWING THE SUCCESS OF *TRUE BLUE*, Madonna decided to continue working with Patrick Leonard. Although she had come to terms with the fact that none of her movies had been a major success, she was, if nothing else, determined to make at least one successful movie. So, in June 1987 she began working on her role as Nikki Finn in her latest film, *Who's That Girl?* Its original title, *Slammer*, was changed when it coincided with Sean Penn's 60-day jail sentence, this time for violating a probation order imposed on him after he assaulted a friend of his wife.

"Madonna rang me up one night and told me she wanted an uptempo song and a downtempo song," explained producer, Patrick Leonard. "She came over one night. I had already put down the chorus for a song on a cassette, she took it into the back room while I worked on the rest of the lyrics. Soon after, she came out and said 'We'll call it, 'Who's That Girl?'" The backing track was recorded in one take and Patrick added the guitars and percussion the next day.

In 1989 Madonna began work on her next movie, *Dick Tracy*. The Disney film starred and was directed by Warren Beatty who cast Madonna as Breathless Mahoney. During the filming, Madonna and Warren became an item and he said of her, "She is funny, smart, beautiful and musical. She has everything, she's an actress, a singer and she's great at it all." He also went on to say, "One day, she is going to be a huge movie star."

Madonna still wanted to get her film career off the ground. In 1988 she was cast as Hortense Hathaway in a remake of *Bloodhounds Of Broadway*. There were no songs in the film, but she took the role in the hope that her fans would take her acting more seriously. The film version, which starred Matt Dillon, Jennifer Grey and Randy Quaid, was based on short stories by Damon Runyon and was rated by neither the reviewers nor cinemagoers. It was so boring that during its two-week run in New York, one of the film reels went missing and no-one in the audience even noticed.

595 Los Lobos
La Bamba

Label & Cat No.: **Slash / FFRR / London LASH 13**

Producer: **Mitchell Froom**

Writers: **Traditional, arranged by Ritchie Valens**

Date reached No.1: **1 August 1987**

Weeks at No.1: **2**

"ELVIS PRESLEY MAY HAVE BEEN THE king of rock'n'roll," says Chris Montez, "but Ritchie Valens was the king on our block. I was in Los Angeles but my parents are from Mexico, and it gave us tremendous pride when someone from our background made it." Ritchie Valens scored with the rock'n'roll hits, 'Come On, Let's Go' and the double-sider, 'Donna' / 'La Bamba', but he died in the 'plane crash which killed Buddy Holly and The Big Bopper. He was only 17, though he looked much older, and his potential had been enormous.

The slaves who came from Africa were homesick, and to retain their memories of home, they might chant the name of their village over and over. One of the villages was called Mamamba and this chant became, the wedding song, 'La Bamba'. In time, it travelled to Mexico and wedding guests would dance around their hats. Ritchie learnt the song from a cousin but when he converted it to rock'n'roll, he was unsure about recording it in case some might think he was mocking his culture. His producer, Bob Keane, encouraged him and even though it was sung in Spanish, the song was a US hit. The lyric refers to the slave ships – "Yo no soy marinero, Yo soy capitan" means "I am not a sailor, I am the captain." In 1964 an English version with surf lyrics by The Crickets and arranged by Leon Russell made the Top 30. The tune was the inspiration for 'Twist And Shout' and, as Bob Dylan has said, "It's always fun to rewrite 'La Bamba'."

In 1987 Lou Diamond Phillips played Ritchie Valens in the bio-pic, *La Bamba*. Rather than mime to Valens' recordings, a band from the same LA community, Los Lobos, was asked to perform on the soundtrack and David Hidalgo's lead vocals were sped up to match Valens' voice. In the film, Ritchie Valens goes to a brothel with his brother and hears 'La Bamba' being performed in its original setting by Los Lobos. He rocks it up and the colourful video publicised both the film and the record. Los Lobos had another Top 20 hit with 'Come On Let's Go', but they are more of an albums band with such excellent work as *How Will The Wolf Survive?*, *The Neighbourhood* and their own album of Mexican songs, *La Pistola Y El Corazon*.

596 Michael Jackson with Siedah Garrett I Just Can't Stop Loving You

Label & Cat No.: **Epic 650 202 7**

Producer: **Quincy Jones**

Writer: **Michael Jackson**

Date Reached No.1: **15 August 1987**

Weeks at No.1: **2**

AFTER THE EUPHORIA SURROUNDING *Thriller* had died down, Michael got to work on his next album. How do you attempt to follow a 50 million selling album? The answer was *Bad*. *Thriller* had spawned six hit singles, five of which made the Top 10. But *Bad* did even better. Eight of the album's 10 tracks on the vinyl (or nine of the 11 tracks, if you had the CD) reached the Top 20. The number two hit, 'Leave Me Alone' only appeared on the CD. In the end, *Bad* almost became a greatest hits package and sold over 30 million copies worldwide.

Like *Thriller*, only the first single topped the chart. 'I Just Can't Stop Loving You' was a duet with soul singer Siedah Garrett (although she was credited only on the sleeve). It was difficult to tell who was singing which part because Michael and Siedah's voices were very similar. Siedah said, "Michael is like a vocal chameleon, he can sound like anybody." Siedah was unlucky when it came to credits. She sang uncredited lead vocals on Dennis Edwards' 1984 hit 'Don't Look Any Further', which was later covered by M People, and also provided backing vocals on Madonna's 'Papa Don't Preach', 'True Blue', 'La Isla Bonita' and 'Who's That Girl'. When Quincy Jones was looking for songs for *Bad*, he suggested that Siedah write something, so she teamed up with Mississippi songwriter, Glen Ballard and penned, 'Man In The Mirror'.

The press, obsessed with his weird habits, his odd looks, and his peculiar practice of sleeping in an oxygen tank, were unable to leave Michael Jackson alone. He had a bizarre fascination with children, which probably stemmed from the fact that he never had a childhood of his own as he was constantly in the spotlight. He would frequently ask young children to stay at his house overnight and, astonishingly, their parents permitted it. Things went too far in 2002, when he dangled his baby son over the balcony of a Berlin hotel room. He later apologised claiming he made a 'terrible mistake'.

Whatever stories the tabloids ran about 'Wacko Jacko', as they christened him, he kept making catchy songs and appealing to all age groups. He had a subtle dig at the tabloids as the video for the hit single 'Leave Me Alone' will testify.

597 Rick Astley Never Gonna Give You Up

Label & Cat No.: **RCA PB 41447**

Producers: **Mike Stock / Matt Aitken / Pete Waterman**

Writers: **Mike Stock / Matt Aitken / Pete Waterman**

Date Reached No.1: **29 August 1987**

Weeks at No.1: **5**

"HE HAS A MARVELLOUS VOICE AND I rate him as one of the greatest British singers of all time," said Pete Waterman. "But he's a singer rather than a pop star; he's Frank Sinatra rather than Elvis Presley."

Rick was born in 1966 in Warrington and grew up in nearby Newton-le-Willows. After a stint in a local church choir, he developed an interest for the drums and joined his first band, Give Way. Soon after, he and four other school friends formed a new band, FBI. They became noted for writing their own material and built up a local fan base. After a few months, FBI's lead singer left and Rick offered to take over the role. Pete Waterman was invited to a gig and was impressed with Rick's mature voice and realised that he could be a star.

Legend has it that Rick began at the S/A/W studios as a tea-boy. "Rick didn't like anybody saying that because he thinks it's insulting," says Mike Stock, "but we mean it as a great tribute. He came down and mucked in with us while he waited for us to get our shit together and make a record with him. It wasn't beneath his dignity. Matt and I weren't entirely convinced about his voice. It was a very powerful voice – coming out of his frame it was quite unnerving – but it was very difficult to get him to sing quietly. Pete wanted him to do songs like 'Ain't Too Proud To Beg' but he needed songs that had to be projected like 'Together Forever' and 'Never Gonna Give You Up' and he did that brilliantly."

Once 'Never Gonna Give You Up' was released, Rick Astley became an overnight star and it became the biggest selling single of 1987. It was also a US number one, but there was a problem brewing. Rick didn't want to be a star; he just enjoyed singing. "One day I turned up for a rehearsal, but there was no sign of Rick, he'd disappeared," said Pete Waterman. "His manager didn't know where he was and neither did his record company. He wasn't at home and we were told that he hadn't been in touch with anybody. Then I heard on the grapevine that he didn't want to record and that we had forced him into it. We spoke to his management and sorted things out and then the relationship between Rick and us started to change."

The album, *Whenever You Need Somebody*, shot to number one. Stock Aitken and Waterman wrote only four of the 10 tracks, Rick wrote five. The title track, 'Together Forever' (which was another US chart-topper) and a cover of Nat 'King' Cole's 'When I Fall In Love' all made the Top three. Rick came under criticism for his dancing, reminiscent of your favourite uncle at a wedding, but as Rick explained in *Smash Hits*, "I haven't really got a dancing style at all. I just get up and do whatever I feel. I enjoy dancing and am a bit of a bopper, but I'm not a brilliant dancer."

By the summer of 1988 Rick had split with Stock, Aitken & Waterman. Pete recalled, "It was a shame, we had a great song lined-up for Rick but he could no longer do it. It was 'Nothing Can Divide Us', so we gave it to Jason Donovan who we had just signed."

Rick still doesn't have any desire to be famous. He lives in Surrey with his Danish wife, Lene, and daughter, Emilie. In 2002, some 11 years after his last hit single, RCA released a greatest hits album, which made the Top 20, and he returned to public performance with a low-key tour in September 2004.

598 M/A/R/R/S

Pump Up The Volume / Anitina (The First Time I See She Dance)

Label & Cat No.: **4AD AD 707**

Producer: **Martyn Young**

Writers: **Steve Young : A.R. Kane / Colourbox**

Date Reached No.1: **3 October 1987**

Weeks at No.1: **2**

'PUMP UP THE VOLUME' HAD A shorter two weeks at number one than any other two-week chart topper. It was the week Radio One changed the day they revealed the UK Top 40. Up until October 1987, the official chart show, as broadcast by the BBC, had been announced on a Tuesday. Now it had changed to a Sunday, effectively making M/A/R/R/S' first week at the top only five days long.

Like Abba, M/A/R/R/S, took their name from the initials of the members. An amalgamation of 4AD label acts, Colourbox (Martin and Steve Young) and A. R. Kane (Alex & Rudi) and it was the label's owner, Ivo Watts-Russell, who suggested the collaboration.

London DJs, Chris 'CJ' Mackintosh and Dave Dorrell were recruited by M/A/R/R/S to take care of the crucial sampling. CJ recalls, "It was all done very quickly. They called me in the morning, we went to Blackwing Studios at London Bridge and stuck all the samples on that day and I got a £200 fee." Dave Dorrell said, "'Pump Up The Volume' provided a link between the retro sound of rare groove and the sample-heavy nature of much of the new US dance music. Everyone was listening to Maceo & The Macs' 'Cross The Track' and The Jackson Sisters' 'I Believe In Miracles'. Those tunes would fill any dance floor in London." In Manchester, the main champions of house music were DJs Mike Pickering and Graeme Park.

The breakbeats were sampled from various James Brown tracks, as well as Eric B. & Rakim's 'I Know You Got Soul' and Stock, Aitken & Waterman's own song, 'Roadblock'. Unfortunately they failed to get official clearance from Stock, Aitken & Waterman and were soon served with a high court injunction over its illegal use. "It got very bitter," said Mackintosh, "but these are the hazards of the gentleman's agreement." The video consisted of archive footage of various space scenes and moon landings as well as high speed motorway driving.

'Anitina (The First Time I See She Dance)' was only listed as a double A-side at the record company's insistence. It was only 'Pump Up The Volume' that received any radio and nightclub exposure. CJ and Dave produced Tina Turner's 1991 re-recorded version of 'Nutbush City Limits'. CJ returned to the club circuit and Dave went into production.

599 The Bee Gees

You Win Again

Label & Cat No.: **Warner Brothers W8351**

Producers: **Arif Mardin / Barry Gibb / Robin Gibb / Maurice Gibb**

Writers: **Barry Gibb / Robin Gibb / Maurice Gibb**

Date reached No.1: **17 October 1987**

Weeks at No.1: **4**

AFTER THE ASTONISHING SUCCESS of *Saturday Night Fever*, it was inevitable that there would be a backlash. The Bee Gees, both collectively and individually, recorded solo albums in the Eighties but no one paid much attention to them. They were, however, still hot as producers and writers and they had success with Barbara Streisand ('Woman In Love', 1980), Dionne Warwick ('Heartbreaker', 1982), Kenny Rogers and Dolly Parton ('Islands In The Stream', 1983) and Diana Ross ('Chain Reaction', 1986). However, as Barry Gibb said, "We want to be The Bee Gees, we enjoy being The Bee Gees."

In 1987 they were reunited with the producer, Arif Mardin, for the *E.S.P.* album. The key track was 'You Win Again', a title borrowed from Hank Williams although Robin Gibb said he had not heard that song and had wondered if the title was too close to Hot Chocolate's 'So You Win Again'. He added, "We absolutely thought that 'You Win Again' was going to be a big hit. It took us a month to cut it and get the right mix." Listen to that drum sound and you'll see what he means. Those stomping beats come from Maurice Gibb and Rhett Lawrence.

In 1988 Andy Gibb, a singer in his own right, died from heart failure, which caused Maurice Gibb to resume his heavy drinking, and they recorded a tribute to Andy, 'Wish You Were Here' the following year. The Bee Gees continued to tour but Barry's arthritis and back pain limited their commitments. The three Bee Gees were each appointed CBE in the 2002 New Years Honours, but Maurice Gibb died suddenly the following January following a hospital operation.

600 T'Pau

China In Your Hand

Label & Cat No.: **Siren SRN 64**

Producers: **Ronnie Rogers / Tim Burgess**

Writers: **Carol Decker / Ronnie Rogers**

Date Reached No.1: **14 November 1987**

Weeks at No.1: **5**

JUST TWO MONTHS AFTER THE FIRM had immortalised *Star Trek* characters in their chart topping hit, 'Star Trekkin", along came T'Pau, taking their name from a stateswoman who appeared in the episode *Amok Time* and was from the planet Vulcan, also home to Second Officer Mr Spock.

T'Pau's lead singer, Liverpool-born Carol Decker, began as a member of a ska band, The Lazers at Shrewsbury art college. Ronnie Rogers was a guitarist of a band called The Katz. In 1982 Carol attended a Katz gig where Ronnie threw his guitar into the audience, which hit Carol and cut her finger. She used it as an opportunity to get backstage and meet Ronnie, whom she fancied. She successfully poached him for her own band, but just three weeks later, the band split. Carol and Ronnie put together a new band and won a couple of support slots at London's Marquee Club with a repertoire that included cover versions of 'Save Your Kisses For Me' and 'Ob-La-Di, Ob-La-Da'. After being spotted by former Curiosity Killed The Cat manager, Chris Cooke, he offered to oversee Carol's career. "I was very taken with Carol's voice, so we struck a kind of agreement and the first thing I did was fire most of the band," revealed Chris in an interview with Q magazine. "The songs were all there but the band just weren't cutting it."

They recruited guitarist Taj Wyzgowski, bass player Paul Jackson, keyboard player Michael Chetwood and London-born drummer, Tim Burgess to form T'Pau. They recorded some demos, got a contract with Siren Records and were offered a support slot on Nik Kershaw's UK tour.

Their debut album, *Bridge Of Spies*, was released in September and the first single from it was 'Heart And Soul' which reached number four in both the UK and the US. Taj, who was more of a jazz guitarist, didn't feel comfortable with T'Pau's rock style, so he left and Dean Howard was his replacement.

The next release, 'China In Your Hand', failed to chart in the US but went all the way in the UK. It was re-recorded for the single version. Carol explained why: "We recorded the song in one passionate take and we were happy with it for the album. Although it wasn't noticeable enough to mar the enjoyment of the track, the tempo fluctuated so much that we could not edit the album version successfully for the single, besides which, the record company thought it was too long. So we went to the Workhouse Studio in London and re-recorded it as faithful to the production as possible in a three-minute format. Roy Thomas Baker was not available so as Ronnie and Tim worked into the wee small hours to get it right, we agreed they should get the production credit. We originally intended to have David Sanborn do the sax solo on the album, but due to a fear of flying, he wasn't able to make it to Chicago on time." For the single version, Gary Barnacle did the honours.

The inspiration for 'China In Your Hand' came from Frankenstein's creator, Mary Shelley. "I was watching a documentary on the whole Mary Shelley and Byron and Keats gang and was enthralled by how, at 19, she outsold both noted poets," revealed Carol. "But her success caused much dissent and jealousy in her marriage and friendships, so created her own monster. It is a story within a story, be careful what you wish for in case you get it. Ronnie's mother gave us a china tea-set and if you lifted the cups up to the light you can see a woman's face in the bottom. The cups were paper thin and so fragile when you held it in your hand. I guess subconsciously that's how I got the title."

Other Top 20 hits followed: 'Valentine', 'I Will Be With You', 'Secret Garden' and 'Whenever You Need Me'. The band split in 1991 with Ron returning to production. Carol launched a solo career but in 1997 assembled a new T'Pau and the following year performed 'China In Your Hand' with the BBC Concert Orchestra at the Princess Diana Tribute Concert at Althorp House.

In the summer of 2003 Carol appeared in the all-star, all-female hit show, *Mum's The Word* in London's West End. Later the same year she appeared in the film *Nine Dead Gay Guys* as the wife of Steven Berkoff.

T'Pau

601 Pet Shop Boys
Always On My Mind

Label & Cat No.:	**Parlophone R 6171**
Producer:	**Julian Mendelsohn**
Writers:	**Wayne Thompson / Johnny Christopher / Mark James**
Date Reached No.1:	**19 December 1987**
Weeks at No.1:	**4**

"WE WERE APPROACHED BY CENTRAL TV to be on a programme called *Love Me Tender*, commemorating the 10th anniversary of the death of Elvis Presley, and for some reason we agreed to do it," explained Neil Tennant. "Rob Holden, who worked with our manager, Tom Watkins, got us a load of Elvis cassettes and the first track on the first one Chris picked up, *Magic Moments With Elvis*, was 'Always On My Mind'. We were originally going to do a house version of 'Baby Let's Play House' but there wasn't time.

We wouldn't have done 'Always On My Mind' unless it was going to be very different from the original, so we added an extra chord to it. There's a B flat at the end of each chorus that wasn't in the original. It makes it far more like a pop song."

The sales of CD singles were introduced to the chart in January 1986 and instantly became a recognised format. However, from June 13 1987, CD singles, double pack 7" singles and any format featuring more than 20 minutes of music were disqualified from the chart. The record industry hadn't banked on the CD format taking over from vinyl.

Thankfully by November, CD sales were eligible again and counted towards the chart. 'Always On My Mind' became one of the biggest selling CD singles of the Eighties. It was also the only Pet Shop Boys single issued in a jewel case as opposed to the card sleeves in which all previous singles were distributed.

In 1972 Elvis who had recently split from Priscilla, was looking for songs about broken relationships. Although 'Always On My Mind' wasn't actually written for him, it was appropriate to the situation, so he recorded it just days before Brenda Lee recorded her version. The songwriters had given this new song to both artists and although Brenda's was issued first, it was only a minor success on the US country chart.

Stateside, Elvis' version was relegated to the B-side of 'Separate Ways', another song that was submitted to him after his break-up with Priscilla, which reached number 16 on the country charts.

In 1982 Willie Nelson, unaware that Elvis had recorded it originally, released his own version giving him another number one on the US country chart. The single and album of the same name were voted both single and album of the year at the annual CMA Awards.

Because the Pet Shop Boys' version was originally recorded for the television tribute, it did not appear on their then current album, *Actually*. Instead it was added to the follow-up, *Introspective*. Incidentally, the cover of *Actually* shows both Neil and Chris Lowe dressed in dinner suits and bow ties. Neil looked particularly dishevelled with his hair in a mess, displaying a considerable yawn. When asked why, he replied, "I was tired."

602 Belinda Carlisle
Heaven Is A Place On Earth

Label & Cat No.: **Virgin VS 1036**

Producer: **Rick Nowels**

Writers: **Rick Nowels / Ellen Shipley**

Date Reached No.1: **16 January 1988**

Weeks at No.1: **2**

BACK IN 1977, AT THE AGE OF 19, Belinda Carlisle left home, changed her name to Dottie Danger and joined a punk commune. Although she was never officially a member, Belinda performed with the seminal Los Angeles punk group, The Germs. The following year she teamed up with Jane Wiedlin (guitar), Charlotte Caffey (guitar), Margot Olaverra (bass) and Elisa Bello (drums) to form The Go-Go's who were invited to open for The Dickies on their US tour. Within a couple of years Gina Schock had replaced Bello, Kathy Valentine took over from Olaverra and they signed a contract with Miles Copeland's I.R.S. record label.

The Go-Go's broke up in 1984. Belinda had been involved with drugs and was at a low point. By her own admission she said, "I was being a loud obnoxious brat and my character changed completely." But she had determination. She sought help and very quickly got her life, career and health back on track. She married Morgan Mason (son of James) who had his own PR company and released her first solo album, *Belinda*, in 1986. The first single, 'Mad About You' featured Andy Taylor of Duran Duran on guitar and reached number three in the States.

For her second album, Belinda wanted to select her own team. She interviewed several producers and chose Rick Nowels, a San Francisco songwriter who began writing songs at 13. His first success was as writer and producer of Stevie Nicks' first solo single, 'I Can't Wait'. His writing partner, New York-based Ellen Shipley, was a former RCA recording artist. The pair eventually wrote 11 hits for Belinda Carlisle.

Rick recalled, "We started brainstorming concepts. Ellen mentioned the title 'Heaven On Earth' and I thought it was a good concept for Belinda. I started singing 'Heaven is a place on earth', which I thought was a fresher title and before long we had finished the song." After a month of recording, Rick loved the hook but was uncomfortable with the verse. He asked Ellen back to Los Angeles to re-write the song. Three days later it was complete. The new version was played to Belinda who loved it, so it was recorded with Rick, Ellen, Michelle Phillips (of The Mamas & The Papas) and songwriter Diane Warren on backing vocals. "'Heaven Is A Place On Earth' is a kind of hopeful song," says Belinda. "I think it's saying you can create your own piece of heaven on your own patch. It's a song about peace of mind and it's also partly a love song." The accompanying video was produced by actress, Diane Keaton.

Belinda notched up over 20 hits including the Top 10s 'I Get Weak', 'Circle In The Sand', 'Leave A Light On' (featuring George Harrison on slide guitar), '(We Want) The Same Thing' and 'In Too Deep'. Former Go-Go, Charlotte Caffey is still a member of Belinda's band. The Go-Go's periodically reform and were back in the chart in 1995 with 'The Whole World Lost Its Head'.

In August 2000 Belinda posed naked for *Playboy*. Her reason, she exclaimed, was "I'm really fed up with the whole media thing where you have to be 20 years-old, a size zero and blonde with plastic tits to be sexually viable."

603 Tiffany
I Think We're Alone Now

Label & Cat No.: **MCA MCA 1211**

Producer: **George E. Tobin**

Writer: **Richie Cordell**

Date Reached No.1: **30 January 1988**

Weeks at No.1: **3**

THE WEEK 'I THINK WE'RE ALONE Now' hit the number one slot, the newspapers reported that 2000 children skipped school to watch Tiffany perform the song live at the Trocadero shopping centre in London's

Piccadilly Circus.

Tiffany Darwisch, who was born in Norwalk, California in 1971, was taught to sing when she was two, by her cousin, Darla. By the age of five she knew that she wanted to be a singer. At nine she made her first public performance when her stepfather took her to a barbeque where a local band invited her on stage. They were so impressed that they asked her to join them at weekends when they were performing locally.

She sent a demo tape to George Tobin's studios in the San Fernando Valley and was soon invited to record some more demos there. George was impressed by the power of the 12 year old's voice and had her signed to MCA Records. They started recording her when she was 14. It was Tiffany's suggestion to do the shopping malls. She said to MCA's vice chairman, Larry Solters, "There are three things most human beings have in common. One, they pick their noses, two, they go to the toilet and three, they go shopping."

Over 40 tracks were recorded for the first album, *Tiffany*, including 'I Think We're Alone Now', which was first recorded by Tommy James & The Shondells. As George Tobin recalled, "'I Think We're Alone Now' is one of my five favourite records of all time. I've always loved that song and I wanted to do it because I was making records in that time period and knew Richie Cordell, we all worked in the Brill Building."

Tiffany's follow-up, 'Could've Been' topped the US chart and made number four in the UK. The gentle ballad showcased the quality of Tiffany's voice. She had further hits with a gender-altered remake of The Beatles', 'I Saw Him Standing There' and 'Radio Romance'. But by the end of the Eighties, the hits had dried up. In the early Nineties she toured Asia extensively where she was still successful. "Pop seemed to be going more R&B and dance which I wasn't convinced was what I wanted to do. I'd always wanted to do rock – my idol was Stevie Nicks. I then took a couple of years off to learn how to write songs, plus I'd just had a little boy so I wanted to be mom."

In 2001 Tiffany released a solo album, *The Color Of Silence*. Her new style resembled Sheryl Crow, but she was unable to shake off her original teeny-bop image of the shopping mall singer with the bright red hair, and despite good reviews, it failed to sell. So in order to show the world that she had grown up, she posed naked for *Playboy*. She occasionally presents VH1 in the States. Richie Cordell died on April 13, 2004.

604 Kylie Minogue I Should Be So Lucky

Label & Cat No.: **PWL PWL 8**

Producers: **Mike Stock / Matt Aitken / Pete Waterman**

Writers: **Mike Stock / Matt Aitken / Pete Waterman**

Date Reached No.1: **20 February 1988**

Weeks at No.1: **5**

Many soap stars have had a crack at the pop music scene, but none have come close to matching the success of Kylie Minogue.

Kylie was born in 1968 in Melbourne, Australia. Showing no aspirations to be a star, it was only whilst watching *Grease* – when Sandy transforms from the shy, girl-next-door to the confident woman in black leather – that the 10-year-old Kylie realised what she wanted to do. Her aunt Suzette, who had worked in the acting profession, heard of a small part for a youngster in Australia's most popular soap, *The Sullivans*, but it was her sister Dannii she had in mind for the part. Kylie's mother Carol took both girls along for the audition where Kylie won the role of a Dutch war orphan called Carla. Ironically, when Kylie left, Dannii was brought in to continue the role.

Kylie moved onto other soaps including; *Skyways, The Henderson Kids* and *Fame and Misfortune*. In 1986, a year after its debut, she was cast as the outspoken, tomboy mechanic Charlene Mitchell, in *Neighbours*. With their good looks and endearing personalities, she and Scott Robinson (Jason Donovan) soon became the programme's most popular characters and the show was well received when first aired on British television in October 1986.

Now that she had established herself as a successful actress it wasn't hard to get a record deal. She recorded a version of Little Eva's 'Locomotion' in 1987, which was issued on Mushroom Records. It went to number one in Australia and became the biggest selling single that year.

Mike Duffy, an engineer who worked for British producers Stock, Aitken & Waterman, went to Australia to help out at Mushroom. A few weeks later he sent a copy of Kylie's 'Locomotion' to Pete Waterman who ignored it. He called Pete at three in the morning to tell him it was number one in Australia. Pete got out of bed, put the record on, told Mike it was rubbish and went back to sleep. A few weeks later Mike called again to say Kylie was still number one and that Pete should produce her in the UK. He eventually agreed.

Pete recalled, "I was at home one Friday afternoon when I got a phone call from Mike Stock at the office who asked if there was something I had forgotten to tell him. 'A small Antipodean called Kylie Minogue?' prompted Mike, 'Oh yes, I forgot, she's in town'. Mike said, 'No, she's in reception.' I apologised for messing up and said we'll have to drop the whole project. Mike said, 'We can't, she's expecting to do something with us.' 'She should be so lucky,' I replied. 'Great', Mike said, 'That'll do. 'I Should Be So Lucky'. Can we write some lyrics?" Mike and Pete began faxing lyrics back and forth and within an hour, the song was finished.

The song was recorded with Mike and Matt. The first time Pete heard it was at the 1987 staff Christmas party, when their guest DJ, Lenny Henry, played it. The following weekend, Pete went to Liverpool to present his new show on Radio City. When the producer saw the Kylie record he instructed Pete to only play a few bars then take it off. He told him to announce that he wouldn't play any more until people rang in to request it. Within minutes, the switchboard had gone into meltdown.

The accompanying video of 'I Should Be So Lucky', which reached number one in 18 countries, showed Kylie in the bath engulfed in bubbles, with every hot-blooded male trying to get a glimpse of what Kylie wasn't going to let you see.

In 1996 Kylie went on stage at the Royal

Kylie in her early incarnation as Charlene, the curly-haired but tomboyish car mechanic in TV soap Neighbours

Albert Hall on Poetry Day and recited the lyric to 'I Should Be So Lucky' as if it was a serious verse. "It was Nick Cave who told me to do that. It would never have crossed my mind, but it turned out to be genius."

605 Aswad
Don't Turn Around

Label & Cat No.:	**Mango IS 341**
Producer:	**Chris Porter**
Writers:	**Diane Warren / Albert Hammond**
Date Reached No.1:	**26 March 1988**
Weeks at No.1:	**2**

IN 1971 SCOOPER, BILLIE, BRAINS, Doughnut, Spring, Sticks and Tiger were collectively known as The Double Deckers. The BBC children's programme involved seven do-gooder children who got mixed up in crazy escapades and used a London double-decker bus in a junk yard as their headquarters. Spring was played by a teenage Brinsley Forde, who a few short years later would become the lead singer of reggae band, Aswad.

Aswad, meaning black in Arabic, came out of London's Ladbroke Grove in 1974 and are dreadlocked singer and guitarist Brinsley, bass guitarist Tony Gad and drummer Angus Zeb, whom Brinsley renamed Drummie when they first met. Drummie had been a session musician and has played with artists as diverse as Bob Marley and Johnny Hates Jazz.

"In the early Seventies there were a lot of reggae bands coming through," explained Drummie. "We wanted to make music that identified with Britain because we live here. The punk thing came along and people said they could identify reggae music with punk. But punk died and we kept on."

In 1980 Aswad provided some of the music for *Babylon*, a movie that focused on the problems young black people faced living in London. *Babylon*, which is a slang term for the police, starred Brinsley, Karl Howman and Mel Smith.

Their earlier releases, 'Back To Africa' (1976), 'Three Babylon' (1976), and 'Warrior Charge' (1980), were all anthems within the British black community, but failed to chart. However, 'Chasing The Breeze' and '54-46 (Was My Number)' were both minor hits in 1984.

Californian songwriter Diane Warren and London-born singer/songwriter Albert Hammond began writing songs together in the mid-Eighties. "I wrote 'Don't Turn Around' as a rock ballad," explained Diane. "Aswad heard a version of it that Tina Turner had done as a B-side on 'Typical Male'. I remember being so depressed because it wasn't on her album and I remember hearing her album and thinking that my song is better than anything on the album. When Aswad heard it and did it reggae style, you could say they screwed around with it, but my God, what they did with it was great. I love it when someone can take a song and make it something else." Aswad's album, *Distant Thunder* reached number 10 and also contained the next single, a cover of 'Give A Little Love' also written by Hammond and Warren.

Aswad only visited the Top 10 on one further occasion when 'Shine' reached number five in June 1994. That same week, 'Don't Turn Around' was back in the chart after being covered by Ace Of Base. The following year Aswad split up and Brinsley returned to television as a presenter on VH1.

606 Pet Shop Boys
Heart

Label & Cat No.:	**Parlophone R 6177**
Producer:	**Andy Richards**
Writers:	**Neil Tennant/Chris Lowe**
Date Reached No.1:	**9 April 1988**
Weeks at No.1:	**3**

STOCK, AITKEN AND WATERMAN WERE offered the chance to produce the Pet Shop Boys' second number one 'It's A Sin'. It didn't happen because Pete Waterman didn't like the song.

"The inspiration for 'Heart', which was originally called 'Heartbeat', was Phyllis Nelson's minor American hit 'I Like You'," explained Neil Tennant. "It was produced by Shep Pettibone whom I've always wanted to work with." 'Heartbeat' was scrapped because Culture Club's Jon Moss, had just started a band called Heartbeat UK.

After hearing the first playback, Chris Lowe didn't care too much for the song and stuck it on the back burner. Neil, however, knew it had potential and would one day rework the chord structure. He then asked producer Andy Richards if he was interested in doing a song with them. He agreed. Neil explained, "Firstly, we reworked 'Heart'. The first version we did with him, with the syn drum on it, ended up being the seven-inch and has J.J. Belle playing guitar on it, but for some reason we went off that and then asked Julian Mendolsohn to mix the song for the album. He took out the guitar

Pet Shop Boys

because he said it was too complicated, and he accidentally wiped a bit off the track – that's why it comes in going 'beat… beat… heartbeat'."

"This is the song we wanted to give to Madonna, but we never even tried," said Neil. "Then I thought about giving it to Hazell Dean, but after Pete Waterman's negative comments about 'It's A Sin', Neil decided against giving the song to one of his artists."

After nearly three years of chart success, the Pet Shop Boys still refused to go out on tour. They preferred to rely on radio, video coverage and media interviews to promote their songs.

Neil and Chris liked working with actors in their videos. The Jack Gold-directed video, which retold the story of Dracula, featured Ian McKellen as the vampire.

607 S-Express Theme From S-Express

Label & Cat No.: **Rhythm King Mute LEFT 21**
Producers: **Mark Moore / Pascal Gabriel**
Writers: **Mark Moore / Pascal Gabriel**
Date Reached No.1: **30 April 1988**
Weeks at No.1: **2**

WITH SO MANY DJS TRYING TO MAKE a name on the chart, it helped to have a job within the music industry. It certainly benefited DJ Mark Moore, who was the A&R man at Rhythm King Records.

Mark first started DJing at Philip Salon's Mud Club in London. The resident DJ, Tasty Tim, asked Mark to fill in one night. He performed such a good set that he was offered a residency, which lasted five years.

He was then offered a job at London's premier gay club, *Heaven*. He was one of the first supporters of Chicago house music and regularly mixed it with European electro music such as Soft Cell, Yello and Cabaret Voltaire. The club used to attract remixers, producers and the occasional celebrity. The Pet Shop Boys and DJs Pete Tong and Paul Oakenfold were often in attendance. One night Liza Minnelli turned up.

The natural progression was to make a record. By taking the bass and brass sections from Rose Royce's 1979 hit 'Is It Love You're After' and 'Rose Royce Express' and interspersing it with the brass stabs from Crystal Grass' 1975 funk anthem, 'Crystal World', he came up with this chugging floor filler. He brought in a singer called Michelle, and Chilo Harlo who provided the 'Enjoy this trip, enjoy this trip and it is a trip' intro. Mark said, "I wanted the song to be a disco record with Seventies influences but with an Eighties feel."

More dance hits followed: 'Superfly Guy' (5), Hey Music Lover (6), which featured future star Billie Ray Martin on vocals. In 1992 he covered Dobie Gray's 'Find 'Em, Fool 'Em, Forget 'Em' that introduced the future number one hit-maker on vocals, Sonique. A remix by Tony De Vit and Simon Parkes, with the amended title 'Theme From S-Express: The Return Trip' brought Mark back to the chart in 1996, when it reached number 14.

608 Fairground Attraction Perfect

Label & Cat No.: **RCA PB 41845**
Producer: **Kevin Moloney**
Writer: **Mark Nevin**
Date Reached No.1: **14 May 1988**
Weeks at No.1: **1**

SADENIA READER, THE GLASWEGIAN-born lead singer with Fairground Attraction, never craved the limelight. "I used to hide behind big glasses, wear wigs and silly plastic skirts. The idea was to distract attention from me, but of course it did exactly the opposite," she admitted.

The daughter of a welder, Eddi grew up listening to The Beatles and Elvis. It was only when the family moved to Irvine, that she realised what she wanted to do. "When I was 17, I went to an Irvine folk club. I had never heard folk music before. I had never heard unaccompanied singing and storytelling songs, certainly not in a Scottish accent. That's when I realised it was something I could do."

After studying at Glasgow Art School, she became a busker and travelled around Europe with a circus. On her return she moved to London and became a backing singer for the Eurythmics and Alison Moyet before meeting guitarist Mark Nevin. Mark recalled, "I was in a band called Jane Aire & The Belvederes and one night there was a fight at this club and all the band got beaten up except me and the singer. We then needed a new backing singer, so Eddi turned up, but she was better than our lead singer." The pair then left to form Fairground Attraction and completed the line-up by recruiting Simon Edwards (bass) and Roy Dodds (drums).

They recorded the album, *The First Of A Million Kisses* in 1987, which went to number two, and spent a lot of time touring the UK. Mark, who wrote 'Perfect', was surprised it became so popular. "It's just about having girlfriends that haven't really worked out. You get into a relationship and go along with it in a half-hearted attitude and then you think, well, it's time to stop messing about and get it right this time. Find that perfect one."

"We used 'Perfect' at the end of the set to cheer everyone up because the rest of the songs were full of angst, break-up and love gone wrong, so 'Perfect' was thrown in at the end of the hour to make everyone dance a little bit," Eddi explained.

The next single, 'Find My Love' reached number seven but 'A Smile In A Whisper' and 'Clare' went nowhere. When the next album, *Any Fond Kiss*, failed to make the Top 50, the band broke up. Mark Nevin, adding his middle initial 'E' to his name, returned to writing songs and Eddi had two children before launching a solo career. She had two Top 40 hits, 'Patience Of Angels' (1994) and 'Town Without Pity' (1996). In 2003 she moved back to Glasgow declaring she was sick of the music business.

609 Wet Wet Wet / Billy Bragg featuring Cara Tivey
With A Little Help From My Friends / She's Leaving Home

Label & Cat No.: **Childline CHILD 1**

Producers: **Wet Wet Wet : John Porter / Kenny Jones**

Writers: **John Lennon / Paul McCartney**

Date Reached No.1: **21 May 1988**

Weeks at No.1: **4**

IN 1988 THE NME REMAKE OF THE Beatles' *Sgt Pepper's Lonely Hearts Club Band* album, retitled *Sgt Pepper Knew My Father* was released with 12 different artists covering all 13 tracks of the original record, in sequence. All the profits were donated to Childline, the first free national helpline for abused and troubled children.

'With A Little Help From My Friends', (originally titled 'Bad Finger Boogie'), was the official A-side because Wet Wet Wet had a greater chart profile than Billy Bragg. Billy chose to record 'She's Leaving Home' because he felt the lyrics were very relevant to the message of the charity. Billy saw Cara Tivey playing keyboards for Everything But The Girl and she joined him for *Workers Playtime*. She played 'She's Leaving Home' while they were recording the album and Billy put his vocal on in three takes. Billy gave Cara the credit for the arrangement. She also toured with Billy, taking her baby with her.

On February 27, 1967 the *Daily Mail*'s headline read: 'A-level girl dumps car and vanishes'. That girl was 17-year-old Melanie Coe who had ran away from home leaving everything behind. Her father was quoted as saying, 'I cannot imagine why she should run away, she has everything here.' "We'd seen that story and it was my inspiration," said Paul McCartney. "There was a lot of these at the time and that was enough to give us the storyline. So I started to get the lyrics: she slips out and leaves a note and the parents wake up, it was rather poignant. I like it as a song and when I showed it to John, he added the Greek chorus and long sustained notes. One of the nice things about the structure of the song is that it stays on those chords endlessly."

In June 1988 the sixth annual Prince's Trust Rock Gala took place at the Royal Albert Hall and featured, among others, Elton John, Mark Knopfler, Brian May and Phil Collins. During the concert, Wet Wet Wet's lead singer, Marti Pellow and Joe Cocker performed a duet of 'With A Little Help From My Friends', which received a standing ovation. Elton John was so impressed that he asked the Wets to support him on his next tour.

610 The Timelords
Doctorin' The Tardis

Label & Cat No.: **KLF Communications KLF 003**

Producer: **The Timelords**

Writers: **Nicky Chinn / Mike Chapman / Ron Grainer Gary Glitter / Mike Leander / Timelords**

Date Reached No.1: **18 June 1988**

Weeks at No.1: **1**

AFTER GARY GLITTER'S SURPRISE comeback in 1984 with 'Another Rock And Roll Christmas' things went quiet again for four years. By 1988 Glitter was ready for yet another return; this time as a TV chat show host.

As Glitter recalled, "I got my own chat show on LWT's Night Network and we called it *The Leader Talks*. It was great fun. I had a big throne and wore 'Leaderish' gear. I had a hand in selecting some unusual guests. We had Noddy Holder on talking about the good old days, Richard O'Brien on promoting *The Rocky Horror Show* and even gave Julian Clary his first-ever TV appearance."

"The KLF, calling themselves The Timelords for this particular record were Glitter fans and really wanted to work with me," Gary recalled. "They came to me and played me a rough mix, which I liked. I was so fascinated by their idea of using a police car in the video that I had to be in it too." The collaboration not only got Gary back on *Top Of The Pops*, but the *NME* gave him the front cover for the only time in his career.

The Timelords were Lord Rock and Timeboy; pseudonyms for KLF duo Jimmy Cauty and Bill Drummond. The third member was Ford Timelord – an American Ford Galaxy police car, the same one used in the film *Superman 3*.

The hook line, 'Doctor Who, hey Doctor Who, Doctor Who, hey, the Tardis' was sung to the chorus of Gary Glitter's 'Rock And Roll Pt. 2'. It was interspersed with the new heavier drum version of the *Dr Who* theme used from 1980 and incorporated the American police siren. The lines 'We obey no one' and 'We are the supreme beings' were taken from the episode *Genesis Of The Daleks*.

611 Bros
I Owe You Nothing

Label & Cat No.: **CBS ATOM 4**

Producer: **Nicky Graham**

Writers: **Luke Goss / Matt Goss**

Date Reached No.1: **25 June 1988**

Weeks at No.1: **2**

THE BROS TWINS, LUKE AND MATT Goss were born 20 minutes apart on September 26, 1968 in Lewisham, South London. At school they formed Caviar and invited school friend Craig Logan to join them. The twins had long curly blond hair and would have easily fitted into the new romantic genre had they been a tad older. In 1984 they left school and having changed the band name to Gloss, they began performing in clubs in south London. The following year they met songwriter and producer, Nicky Graham. Graham in turn introduced them to the Pet Shop Boys' manager, Tom Watkins.

Tom secured them a deal with CBS and everyone got to work on their image before a song was even released. For the new look, gone was the long hair and in its place were ripped jeans, black leather jackets, a number of gold chains and the new name Bros. Now they were ready to be unleashed on the teenage market. In August 1987 their debut single 'I Owe You Nothing', bombed. They quickly followed it with the Nicky Graham-penned 'When Will I Be Famous', which fared slightly better by reaching number 62. Teenage magazines started taking an interest and suddenly the boys were in demand. On the strength of that, the appropriately named 'When Will I Be Famous' shot up to number two. Their debut album, *Push* and the next single from it, 'Drop The Boy' both reached number two, so CBS decided to give 'I Owe You Nothing' a second shot. The song was voted number one in an annual poll conducted by Radio 1 listeners' 100 favourite songs. The following year, it didn't even make the Top 100.

When Bros made an appearance at HMV in London in September 1988, there were scenes of mass hysteria to rival The Osmonds and the Bay City Rollers. The police had to close parts of Oxford Street, which generated all around chaos. But it was short lived: within two years they had fallen out of favour.

"Matt was great with the vocals licks," remembered Nicky Graham. "But Luke, he didn't really do anything. He'd come in the studio and hear how things were going, then get into his jeep and go down the King's Road and pose for a bit, then come back to the studio and say, 'Wow!'"

They had further hits with, 'I Quit' (4), 'Cat Among The Pigeons' / 'Silent Night' and 'Too Much' (both 2). In 1989 they won Best British Newcomer at the Brit Awards. Their last Top 10 hit, 'Sister', in 1989, was dedicated to the twins' sister, Carolyn, who had died in a car crash. The same year, Craig announced he was leaving the band claiming he was unhappy.

They made a fortune in two years but somehow it all slipped through their fingers. Craig, who sued the brothers for unpaid royalties and was awarded £1 million, was the only member of Bros to come out on top. He dated Kim Appleby and then Dannii Minogue and joined EMI as a marketing manager. He now manages Pink. Luke married Shirley Holliman (of Pepsi & Shirley), played the role of Danny in the West End production of *Grease* and made a comeback in 1993 with his new group, The Band Of Thieves. In 1996 Matt returned under the guise MG and managed two Top 40 hits, then a second comeback in 2003 when 'I'm Coming At Ya' just missed the Top 20. In 2004 Matt was picked to appear on *Hell's Kitchen*, a show where 10 celebrities were thrown together to run a restaurant under the infamous chef, Gordon Ramsey. He came third.

612 Glenn Medeiros
Nothing's Gonna Change My Love For You

Label & Cat No.:	**London LON 184**
Producer:	**Jay Stone**
Writers:	**Michael Masser / Gerry Goffin**
Date Reached No.1:	**9 July 1988**
Weeks at No.1:	**4**

GLENN MEDEIROS WAS BORN TO Portuguese parents in June 1970 in Lawai, a tiny village on the island of Kauai in Hawaii. In 1986 his school teacher entered him in a talent contest, *Brown Bags For Stardom*, run by a local radio station. Glenn had been listening to George Benson's 1984 album, *20/20*, and as he could choose his own song, he picked 'Nothing's Gonna Change My Love For You', written by legendary songwriters, Gerry Goffin and Michael Masser.

Glenn was a good-looking lad with a clean-cut image. He didn't drink or smoke and, despite his roots, didn't surf either. He won the talent show and the prize of $500 and a chance to record a single. He decided to record the track he had won the contest with. The radio station, KMAI-FM, playlisted the song and within a couple of weeks, it was number one on the local chart.

During the summer, Guy Zapoleon, a radio DJ from Phoenix, Arizona – the same guy who had UB40's 'Red Red Wine' reissued in the States – was on holiday in Hawaii and heard Glenn's song. He took it back to his radio station and incorporated it into a feature called *Make It Or Break It*. Within a few hours, the telephones had gone mad.

Leonard Silver, the owner of New York's Amherst label, was attending a record convention in Phoenix when he heard the song but was unable to get hold of a copy. Undeterred, he flew to Hawaii and signed Glenn Medeiros to his label. The self-titled album made little impact in the States and missed the UK chart altogether. The next album, *Not Me*, fared slightly better in the UK, but did achieve double platinum status in Spain and Taiwan.

Motown singer Rick James used to include 'Nothing's Gonna Change My Love For You' in his live set. When he heard Glenn's version and realised he could sing, he asked to work with him. Glenn had one further Top 20 hit, 'She Ain't Worth It', a duet with Bobby Brown, a pairing suggested by James.

Glenn is married, still lives in Hawaii and tours locally. His last album, *Captured* was released in 1999.

613 Yazz & The Plastic Population
The Only Way Is Up

Label & Cat No.:	**Big Life BLR 4**
Producer:	**Coldcut**
Writers:	**George Jackson / Johnny Henderson**
Date Reached No.1:	**6 August 1988**
Weeks at No.1:	**5**

YAZZ WAS BORN IN LONDON IN 1960 to a Jamaican father and an English mother. After leaving school she joined a local band as keyboard player. "One day the singer didn't turn up and I started singing instead and decided I quite enjoyed it." The group performed one concert then broke up. Yazz began a modelling assignment and met Austin Howard, later of Ellis, Beggs and Howard. They both signed with a management company and formed a band called The Biz. Their one single, 'Falling', failed to chart, and being unhappy with the management company, they quit.

Yazz, with her bleached blonde hair, first burst onto the charts in 1987 as the featured lead singer on Coldcut's number six hit, 'Doctorin' The House'. The song went into the Top 10 despite no airplay on Radio 1, the reason being that Coldcut and, for that matter, the Plastic Population – Jonathan Moore and Matthew Black – were both DJs on the London pirate station Kiss FM.

She started dating Jazz Summers, who owned the Big Life record label and was soon signed to it. The first song they chose was 'The Only Way Is Up', which was originally recorded by American soul singer Otis Clay on his 1982 album of the same name. "There is a really heavy sentiment to that song," explained Yazz at the time. "It's about being down-and-out and on the dole but not worrying about it; keep on doing what you want to do because you can get through in the end. It's exactly what I've done to get where I am now."

Her debut album, *Wanted*, went to number three and spent 30 weeks on the chart. Three more singles were lifted from it; 'Stand Up For Your Love Rights' (2), 'Fine Time' (9) and 'Where Has All The Love Gone' (16). In 1990 'Treat Me Good' gave Yazz her last solo Top 20 hit. Three years later she teamed up with Aswad for a reggae cover of Ace's 'How Long'.

614 Phil Collins
A Groovy Kind Of Love

Label & Cat No.: **Virgin VS 1117**

Producer: **Phil Collins**

Writers: **Toni Wine / Carole Bayer Sager**

Date Reached No.1: **10 September 1988**

Weeks at No.1: **2**

Like Bryan Ferry and Roxy Music in the Seventies, Phil Collins ran a concurrent solo career alongside Genesis throughout the Eighties.

In 1985 he was nominated for a Grammy for Best Original Score for *Against All Odds* but lost out to Prince's *Purple Rain*, although he did win Best Male Pop Vocal with the title song. The same year Phil performed twice at the Live Aid concert. After performing 'Against All Odds (Take A Look At Me Now)' and 'In The Air Tonight', he joined Sting on 'Long, Long Way To Go' followed by 'Every Breath You Take' at Wembley Stadium before racing to Heathrow and taking to the air via Concorde, to be greeted by Eric Clapton and Robert Plant in Philadelphia. He then took the stage for another rendition of 'In The Air Tonight'. He also drummed with Led Zeppelin during the evening. He finished 1985 playing a cameo role in the US television series, *Miami Vice*. It was his first acting experience since he played the Artful Dodger in the West End production of *Oliver!* in 1965.

In 1987 Phil attended the Cannes Film Festival where he announced that he was to star as one of the Great Train Robbers, Ronald 'Buster' Edwards in the film *Buster*. He claimed that it was the romantic side of the story of the love between Buster and his wife June that attracted him to the script.

He didn't initially intend to get involved with the soundtrack, but changed his mind when one of his heroes, Lamont Dozier, agreed to write some songs with him. American singer/songwriter, Stephen Bishop had intended to revive 'A Groovy Kind Of Love, which Toni Wine and Carole Bayer Sager had recorded originally under the pseudonyms, Diane and Anitta. He asked Phil to produce his version, but when Phil heard his demo, he told Stephen that he really wanted to record it in a new film he was starring in. Stephen agreed and Phil told Toni Wine, "I love Stephen Bishop and I give him a million kisses and thank him every day." Toni Wine recalled, "It took Carole and I about 20 minutes to write the song. We were chuckling about the word 'groovy'. It was a new word and we just jumped on it." It was American producer, Don Kirshner who submitted it to The Mindbenders who took it to number two in 1966. Les Gray, after he split from Mud, had a minor hit version in 1977 but Phil took it to number one on both sides of the Atlantic.

Phil travelled all over the world to promote the film and was well received everywhere. The soundtrack also spawned 'Two Hearts' which won an Oscar in the category Best Song Written Specifically For A Motion Picture Or Television, and 'Loco In Acapulco' which was recorded by The Four Tops.

After his release from jail in the late Eighties Buster Edwards became a flower seller outside Waterloo Station until his death in 1994. Phil Collins sent flowers but did not attend the funeral. As the mourners entered the chapel, it was Phil's version of 'A Groovy Kind Of Love' that filtered from the loudspeakers.

615 The Hollies
He Ain't Heavy, He's My Brother

Label & Cat No.: **EMI EM 74**

Producer: **Ron Richards**

Writers: **Bob Russell / Bobby Scott**

Date Reached No.1: **24 September 1988**

Weeks at No.1: **2**

The Hollies nearly missed out on the chance to record 'He Ain't Heavy, He's My Brother'. As Tony Hicks recalled, "We were looking for new material so I visited London-based music publisher Cyril Shane in early 1969. He played me some songs that had recently been submitted, but skipped past the song 'He Ain't Heavy, He's My Brother', saying it was not suitable, but I insisted on hearing it and realised its potential."

'He Ain't Heavy, He's My Brother' was written by New York jazz pianist Bobby Scott and the L.A. songwriter Bob Russell. Over the years, many versions have been recorded including, Matt Monro, Joe Cocker, Olivia Newton-John, The Housemartins, Neil Diamond and Brother-

Phil Collins with Great Train Robber Ronald 'Buster' Edwards, who ran a flower stall at Waterloo Station for many years after his release from jail

hood Of Man, but The Hollies' version, which featured Elton John, then a session player, on piano is definitive.

The song takes its title from an expression used in the 1938 film *Boys Town*, starring Mickey Rooney and Spencer Tracy. It was about a shelter for homeless boys in Omaha, Nebraska. One of the boys was carrying a crippled man in his arms and Father Flanagan (Tracy) asked him if he was a heavy load. His reply was "He ain't heavy, he's my brother." In 2003 Bobby Elliott said, "On a recent visit to the States, I found out that the home is still there and now incorporated a home for homeless girls as well."

In 1988 another version of the song was recorded by former Righteous Brother, Bill Medley. It was featured in the Sylvester Stallone movie *Rambo III* and released as a single but reached only number 25. Within a couple of weeks, The Hollies' version was re-released following its use in a Miller Lite beer television commercial. In 1999, the song was back on television when Miller Lite decided to re-use the track. It was also used to help sell Panadol Extra.

616 U2
Desire

Label & Cat No.:	**Island IS 400**
Producer:	**Jimmy Iovine**
Writers:	**Bono / Larry Mullen / The Edge / Adam Clayton**
Date Reached No.1:	**8 October 1988**
Weeks at No.1:	**1**

In 1976 Larry Mullen Jr left a message on the school notice board at Dublin's Mount Temple High School advertising for anyone interested in forming a band. He held the auditions at his parents' house and recruited school buddies, Paul Hewson, David Evans, Dik Evans and Adam Clayton. It was Bono who nicknamed David 'The Edge' because of the sharp features of his face, but it also applied to his sharp mind. Collectively they

called themselves Feedback and their early gigs consisted mainly of Beatles and Rolling Stones covers.

The following year Hewson saw a poster promoting the *Bono Vox* hearing aid and decided to adopt Bono as his new name. Around the same time, Dik Evans left to form The Virgin Prunes and Feedback changed their name to Hype.

Adam approached his friend Steve Averill of the punk group The Radiators for advice on how to get the band started properly. Both thought Hype was an unsuitable name. Adam had mentioned that he liked the pun of XTC, so Steve suggested something similar like U2, a suggestion that everyone (you too) could share the excitement of this new band. In 1979 they came to the attention of a young Dublin-based advertising executive, Paul McGuinness, who became their manager, and A&R man Jackie Hayden. It was Jackie who obtained a record deal with CBS in Ireland. U2, whose first two releases 'U2-3' and 'Another Day', reached the Top 10 on the Irish chart, were soon poached by Island Records for a worldwide deal.

Their first Island single, '11 O'Clock Tick-Tock' failed to chart, but once their debut album, *Boy*, produced by Steve Lillywhite, was released, U2's career began to take off. Their greatest moment was at Live Aid in 1985, where, like Queen, they led the crowd in song and had them eating out of the palm of their hand and took their career to new heights.

They had UK Top 10 hits with, 'New Year's Day' (1983), the Martin Luther King tribute 'Pride (In The Name Of Love)' (1984), 'The Unforgettable Fire' (1985), 'With Or Without You' and 'I Still Haven't Found What I'm Looking For' (both 1987), with the latter two topping the US chart. They also had Top 10 albums with *War*, *Under A Blood Red Sky*, *The Unforgettable Fire* and *The Joshua Tree*.

The band had an obsession with America and extensively toured there, so much so that they made a rockumentary called *Rattle And Hum*. That name also lent its title to the next album and the first single from it was 'Desire', a story of sex, guns and drugs. "We talked about getting some songs with interesting drum lines, so instead of spending time jamming as we used to, we each went away and did research and came back and 'Desire' is what we came up with," Larry explained. The demo of 'Desire' was recorded at STS Studios in Dublin. It was re-recorded in the A&M Studios in Los Angeles, but as The Edge expressed, "It was much tighter and more accurate but it lacked feel, so we went back to the original two minutes and 58 seconds of it, in all its dirty magnificence."

617 Whitney Houston
One Moment In Time

Label & Cat No.:	**Arista 111613**
Producers:	**Narada Michael Walden**
Writers:	**Albert Hammond /John Bettis**
Date reached No.1:	**15 October 1988**
Weeks at No.1:	**2**

The President of Arista Records, Clive Davis, obtained the rights to release an album to celebrate The Olympic Games in Seoul, South Korea. The album, *One Moment In Time*, included new and uplifting songs from Eric Carmen ('Reason To Try') and The Four Tops ('Indestructible'). Albert Hammond, known for 'It Never Rains In Southern California' and 'The Free Electric Band', teamed up with The Carpenters' lyricist, John Bettis, to write 'One Moment In Time'.

The music from the album was heard throughout NBC's transmission of the Games. The torch was carried into the stadium by 76-year-old Sohn Kee-chung, the winner of the 1936 marathon. In that year, he had competed using a Japanese name because Korea was occupied by Japan. Christa Luding-Rothenburger, who was also a speed skater, earned a silver medal in cycling to become the only person in history to win Winter and Summer medals in the same year. The tennis star, Steffi Graf, concluded her Grand Slam season by winning Olympic gold. However, the Games are best remembered for the disqualification of sprinter Ben Johnson following a drugs test.

Whitney Houston's single 'One Moment In Time', although stopping at number five on the US charts, won the UK Gold. It was the first Top 10 single celebrating a sport other than football.

618 Enya
Orinoco Flow (Sail Away)

Label & Cat No.: **WEA YZ 312**

Producer: **Nicky Ryan**

Writers: **Enya / Rona Ryan**

Date Reached No.1: **29 October 1988**

Weeks at No.1: **3**

CLANNAD AND ENYA ARE THE ONLY two Gaelic acts to have achieved a successful crossover to the mainstream pop charts. Enya first hit the chart in 1982 alongside her siblings as a member of Clannad who are best remembered for their hit television themes, *Harry's Game* and *Robin Of Sherwood*. They also collaborated with Bono on the single, 'In A Lifetime'.

She was born Eithne Ni Bhraonain (the Gaelic spelling of Enya Brennan) in County Donegal, Ireland in 1961. Enya didn't care much for pop music. She said, "People never believe me when I say it, but it's true. I have *never* bought a pop record. It's never been something that has interested me. My father was a member of Slieve Foy who performed hits of the Forties and Fifties, and my mum often entertained the family with traditional Irish songs. If we did listen to music, it was classical or authentic folk."

In 1980 Enya was commissioned by the BBC to provide a soundtrack to the series *The Celts*. Two years later she left Clannad and started working with producer Nicky Ryan and his wife, lyricist, Roma. "'Orinoco Flow' was a very difficult song to work on, because we had it shelved a few times. We would work on it for a while, leave it, then go back to it again, but in the end we said 'this is good'. All the time it was an album track and only at the very end was it decided this might be good as a single."

It was Warner Brothers' chairman, Rob Dickins, who signed Enya to the label and to show her appreciation, she name-checked Rob in the lyric, "We can steer, we can near with Rob Dickins at the wheel". The parent album, *Watermark* went to number five and spent over 18 months on the chart. However, the follow-up album *Shepherd Moons*, did go to number one.

The video was an extension of the *Watermark* album sleeve. "We were so happy with the cover which was basically a picture of me," described Enya, "but there were layers and layers of beautiful imagery revolving around me that were hand painted on, and this is what we achieved with the video."

"If the record company were looking for 'Orinoco Flow Part Two', they certainly didn't get it. No, I do my best to keep my work fresh. I'm very much aware of the traps where other groups have stumbled into."

619 Robin Beck
The First Time

Label & Cat No.: **Mercury Mer 270**

Producer: **Gavin Spencer**

Writers: **Gavin Spencer / Tom Anthony / Terry Boyle**

Date Reached No.1: **19 November 1988**

Weeks at No.1: **3**

THE FIRST TIME MOST PEOPLE IN Britain came across Robin Beck was when she started climbing the chart after her song was heard in a Coca-Cola television commercial.

Coca-Cola was invented in 1886 by pharmacist John Smyth Pemperton and first advertised on American television in 1958 by the all-girl group, The McGuire Sisters with the song 'Pause For A Coke'. During the Sixties, TV and radio ran separate commercials: for television, Connie Francis, Anita Bryant and the Brothers Four all recorded 'Refreshing New Feeling', and for radio, 'Things Go Better With Coke' was recorded by The Four Seasons, Jan & Dean, Tom Jones, Petula Clark, the Everly Brothers, Marvin Gaye and Roy Orbison. The Who recorded a spoof Coke commercial for their *Sell Out* album in 1967 but it wasn't released until a de-luxe *Sell Out* with bonus tracks appeared in 1995.

The New Seekers achieved huge success with 'I'd Like To Teach The World To Sing (In Perfect Harmony)'. The only other hits to promote Coca-Cola were: 'Hello Summertime' (Bobby Goldsboro, 1974), 'It Oughta Sell A Million' (Lyn Paul, 1975), 'Eat My Goal' (Collapsed Lung, 1996) and 'I Wish I Knew How It Would Feel To Be Free' (Sharleen Hector, 2004). However in 1970, Coca-Cola received a massive amount of free publicity when The Kinks released 'Lola'. Ray Davies' original line, 'you drink champagne and it tastes like Coca-Cola' had to be altered to 'cherry cola' when the BBC refused to play it, citing it as advertising. Years later the Coca-Cola company invented a cherry-flavoured Coke drink, but by then the BBC had probably forgotten the lyric to the Kinks' song.

Robin Beck was born in Montreal but moved to Florida as a child. She left home at 16 and worked in McDonald's, then as a cocktail waitress. In 1979 she signed with Mercury records and released the single, 'Sweet Talk'. She loved to sing and became a backing vocalist for David Bowie, Leo Sayer and Chaka Khan. 'The First Time', which never charted in America, was originally a jingle for Coca-Cola, which Robin re-recorded for a single.

In 1989 she recorded the first version of the Desmond Child and Diane Warren-penned song, 'Save Up All Your Tears', which featured Paul Stanley from Kiss on backing vocals. It missed both the UK and US charts, but Cher turned it into a hit two years later. In 1992 Robin's single 'In My Heart To Stay' became a hit in Germany, but she garnered further publicity in 1994 when her single 'Close To You' was used to advertise the McDonald's food chain, and certainly earned her more money than all her time spent working there in her teens.

620 Cliff Richard Mistletoe And Wine

Label & Cat No.: **EMI EM 78**

Producer: **Cliff Richard**

Writers: **Leslie Stewart / Jeremy Paul / Keith Strachan**

Date reached No.1: **10 December 1988**

Weeks at No.1: **4**

IN 1977 HANS CHRISTIAN ANDERSEN'S *The Little Match Girl* was made into a musical with lyrics by Leslie Stewart and Jeremy Paul and music by Keith Strachan. It was staged at a fringe theatre in Richmond, Surrey and was then made available to theatres and schools. "I felt all along that 'Mistletoe And Wine' could be a hit," says Keith Strachan, "and I tried to get people to record it without any success."

The Little Match Girl became a TV production in 1986 starring Twiggy and Roger Daltrey, with Twiggy performing 'Mistletoe And Wine'. Its producer thought that the song would be ideal for Cliff, and so Keith did a demo in his key. Cliff loved the song but he wanted to amend the lyric, bringing out a religious message. The song reached number one within a fortnight and Keith was delighted. "I went to see him at Hammersmith Odeon and he did it as an encore. It was great to see everybody swaying as they sang the song."

Keith Strachan has been the musical director for numerous touring and West End musicals including *Elvis*, *Only The Lonely* and *The Sound Of Fury*. In 1999 he directed the rock'n'roll musical, *Harry's Web*, which was billed as 'Devil Woman vs. The Young Ones'.

As successful as Cliff Richard's Christmas singles have been, they have destroyed his credibility. It becomes increasingly difficult for Cliff to be accepted for something that is artistically valid.

621 Kylie Minogue & Jason Donovan Especially For You

Label & Cat No.: **PWL PWL 24**

Producers: **Mike Stock / Matt Aitken / Pete Waterman**

Writers: **Mike Stock / Matt Aitken / Pete Waterman**

Date Reached No.1: **7 January 1989**

Weeks at No.1: **3**

IN 1988 KYLIE FOLLOWED 'I SHOULD BE So Lucky' with three number two hits, 'Got To Be Certain', a re-recorded version of 'The Locomotion' and 'Je Ne Sais Pas Pour Quoi', which were all lifted from her debut album, *Kylie*. When the album made number one, Kylie set two new records. She became the youngest female artist to have a number one album and, with its sales of 1.8 million, the biggest selling debut album by a female.

In the UK, *Neighbours* was 18 months behind Australia and the UK viewing figures were phenomenal which, in turn, helped Kylie's pop career. But the pinnacle of their acting careers came in October 1988, when Charlene (Kylie) married Scott Robinson (Jason Donovan) in what was publicised as 'The wedding of the year'. The kissing scenes came naturally as the couple were dating in real life. Accompanying the pair down the aisle was the song 'Suddenly', performed by Angry Anderson. Such was the demand for the record, that it was released as a single giving the former lead singer with Aussie hard rockers, Rose Tattoo, a number three hit. The wedding made such an impact that Kylie's wedding dress was put on display in London's Museum Of The Moving Image.

"Because we were working with both Kylie and Jason, who were romantically linked, there was inevitably a feeling amongst the public that we'd have them do a romantic duet together," wrote Pete Waterman in his autobiography, *I Wish I Was Me*. "We'd known from the beginning that they were going out, but the idea seemed a sickly proposition." Pete met Matt at Heathrow Airport and the pair flew to Sydney and sat up all night writing the lyrics. "We didn't actually sing the duet together," recalled Jason. "We had to learn the song very quickly and recorded our parts separately." After 10 hours of recording, Pete and Matt flew straight back to London.

"When I heard the finished version, I hated it. It had absolutely no passion. Mike hated it and everybody I played it to in the office hated it," admitted Pete. "But it was going to be a smash because of who was singing it." Mike Stock spent four hours remixing it, but they still weren't happy. Then Pete had a go and as he remembered, "somehow it came together at the last moment; so we rushed to the pressing plant and got it out in time for Christmas."

It became Stock, Aitken & Waterman's biggest selling single and was the 15th best selling single of the Eighties. In 1998 Johnny Vaughan and Denise van Outen, with Steps on backing vocals, recorded a cover for the BBC's Children In Need appeal, which went to number three.

On her 2001 show *An Audience with…* Kylie, after giving the song a big build up, asked the audience to welcome an old friend. As the orchestra played the opening bars of 'Especially For You', the audience found themselves applauding Kermit the Frog.

622 Marc Almond featuring special guest Gene Pitney Something's Gotten Hold Of My Heart

Label & Cat No.: **Parlophone R 6201**

Producer: **Bob Krauushaar**

Writers: **Roger Cook / Roger Greenaway**

Date reached No.1: **28 January 1989**

Weeks at No.1: **4**

Possessing a superb, wide-ranging and very distinctive voice, Gene Pitney was a song's best friend. He recorded class songs by American writers from the Brill Building and although he did not have a UK number one in the Sixties, he scored heavily with '24 Hours From Tulsa' (Bacharach / David), 'I'm Gonna Be Strong' (Mann / Weil) and 'Nobody Needs Your Love' (Randy Newman) amongst others. When he toured the UK, he was impressed by British writers and he added 'That Girl Belongs To Yesterday' (Jagger/Richards) and 'Something's Gotten Hold Of My Heart' (Greenaway/Cook) to his repertoire.

"When you get a great song, you grab it," says Gene. "I don't care where it's come from or who's written it. This is quite different from today where the music business is so money-orientated and everybody wants to publish everything themselves. The quality gets overlooked."

The songwriter Roger Cook recalls, "I did the demo for 'Something's Gotten Hold Of My Heart' in 1967 at New Regent Sound, a four track studio in Tottenham Court Road, with Clem Cattini on drums, and one day Ron Richards told me that Gene Pitney wanted to cut it. I thought, 'That's wonderful. Gene Pitney had been cold for a year but he could have a big hit with that.' I heard nothing for a while and then I got a call from Gene who said, 'What have you done with that demo track? We've tried very hard to come up with something that has the same magic but we can't come up with anything. Can we use your demo and put some strings on it?' I said, 'Sure, anything you want.' They put strings and cellos on it and added Gene's voice and it was a big hit."

Gene Pitney's record reached number five in November 1967 and was on the charts for three months. It was a golden oldie that Gene would sing on his concert tours: "I was in the UK and my agent asked me if I would like to re-record one of my hits with Marc Almond. I was happy about that because 'Tainted Love' is a classic. I was playing in Bristol and I had to be in London for ten in the morning to record my vocal three or four times. Then I went up north for another show. Marc's arrangement was very different from mine, so I was singing it one way in the morning and a different way that night! Our two vocals were edited together and I couldn't believe the result because it sounded like we were standing next to each other, and I had never met him."

They met up for a video at the Neon Junkyard in Las Vegas. "It was the only place in the world where you could have a neon junkyard," says Gene, "It was full of old neon signs and they wired up these old signs and parts of them lit up. It freezes out there at night in the wintertime and the cameramen were wearing blankets and coats, but the record was booming across the desert and it sounded great."

623 Simple Minds
Belfast Child

Label & Cat No.:	**Virgin SMX 3**
Producers:	**Steve Lipson / Trevor Horn**
Writers:	**Traditional: lyrics by Simple Minds**
Date Reached No.1:	**25 February 1989**
Weeks at No.1:	**2**

In 1977 singer Jim Kerr, guitarist Charlie Burchill and drummer, Brian McGee formed a band in Glasgow called Johnny & The Self Abusers. They released one single on Chiswick Records, 'Saints And Sinners' but when it failed to connect with the British public, the three had a rethink. They recruited Mick McNeill (keyboards) and Derek Forbes (bass) and, taking their name from the line 'He's so simple-minded he can't drive his module' in the David Bowie song 'The Jean Genie', they called themselves Simple Minds.

Signing with Virgin Records in 1981, they released a string of hit singles including the Top 10s 'Don't You (Forget About Me)', 'Alive & Kicking', 'Sanctify Yourself' and 'All The Things She Said'. They also topped the album chart with *Sparkle In The Rain* (1984), *Once Upon A Time* (1985), '*Live In The City Of Light* (1987) and *Street Fighting Years* (1989). Mel Gaynor joined as their new drummer in 1982 and three years later John Gibling replaced Derek Forbes. Jim Kerr's profile, meanwhile was raised when he married Pretenders' lead singer, Chrissie Hynde in 1984.

'Belfast Child' is an anti-war song with a tune based on the traditional folk song, 'She Moved Through The Fair'. Jim Kerr recalled, "I first heard the melody a few days after the Enniskillen bombing and like everybody when you see the images I was just sick. In the second part of the song, I'm trying to relate to people in Northern Ireland who lost loved ones. I'm trying to talk about the madness, the sadness and the emptiness. I'm not saying I have any pearls of wisdom, but I have a few questions to ask."

In 1988 Simple Minds played at Nelson Mandela's 70th birthday party concert much to the distress of Scottish Tory MP Nicholas Fairburn who called them and Annie Lennox, who also performed, 'Left-wing Scum'. They recorded 'Mandela Day', especially for the event but refused to release it as an A-side. Instead it appeared on the flip side of 'Belfast Child' and did receive some radio play. When 'Belfast Child' topped the chart, it was, at six minutes and 39 seconds, the second longest song to make number one after The Beatles' 'Hey Jude'.

624 Jason Donovan
Too Many Broken Hearts

Label & Cat No.:	**PWL PWL 32**
Producers:	**Mike Stock / Matt Aitken / Pete Waterman**
Writers:	**Mike Stock / Matt Aitken / Pete Waterman**
Date Reached No.1:	**11 March 1989**
Weeks at No.1:	**2**

Once Kylie Minogue had successfully made the transition from *Neighbours* to pop star, it seemed inevitable that her screen husband was going to follow suit.

Jason Donovan was born four days after Kylie in 1968. His mother, Sue, was a television presenter and his dad, Terence, a successful actor in Australia. Jason was brought up by his father after his parents split when he was five. He spent a lot of time watching his father on film sets and in television studios and decided he wanted to be actor too. He made his first television appearance at the age of 11 in *Skyways*.

In 1985 he received a message that Grundy Television were interested in him for the part of Scott Robinson in *Neighbours*. He had previously turned down the part of Danny in order to finish his education. Jason, with his clean-cut image was the boy every girl-next-door wanted to meet, and it was one particular girl-next-door with whom he had an on-screen affair which spilt over into real life. However, Kylie and Jason managed to keep their relationship secret for months. Perhaps it was ironic that later Kylie would ditch this clean-cut boy-next-door for a rather more explosive model in the form of INXS singer Michael Hutchence.

Following Kylie's lead, Mushroom Records in Australia contacted Jason with a view to recording some songs and they then approached Stock, Aitken & Waterman. Pete Waterman recalled, "Our first reaction was to have nothing to do with it as the whole idea seemed too tacky but I suggested that he go into the studio with Pete Hammond." When things didn't go to plan, Jason again turned to Pete Waterman. Pete took Kylie and Jason out for a Chinese meal where he said to Kylie, "If you want me to work with Jason, I will." Kylie agreed that he should.

Matt Aitken adds, "We knew 'Nothing Can Divide Us' would be a number one for Rick Astley but he didn't want to know. Bosh. So that was the end of our relationship with Rick. We got Jason Donovan to sing it instead but we didn't know until about two years in that he had some blockage between his ears and his sinuses that made it very difficult for him to pitch. He had an operation and singing went up at that point so he could then do *Joseph And The Amazing Technicolor Dreamcoat*."

'Nothing Can Divide Us' reached number five. The Kylie/Jason duet, 'Especially For You' followed and went to number one. Jason felt more at ease singing 'Too Many Broken Hearts'. He said, "I think it shows in my voice that I'm more comfortable with the style and I'm starting to relax." The lyrics, 'I'll be hurt, I'll be hurt if you walk away' must have seemed more poignant as Kylie was splitting up with Jason and seeing Michael Hutchence. The video was somewhat amusing as it showed Jason strumming a guitar that no one had bothered to plug in. The fact that a guitar wasn't actually featured in the song, only made it more comical.

Jason's debut album, *Ten Good Reasons* sold over a million copies and was the biggest selling UK album of 1989.

A recent book, *The Guys Who Wrote 'Em* by Sean Egan (Askill Publishing) casts doubts on the role Pete Waterman played in the S/A/W partnership. Both Mike Stock and Matt Aitken regard his creative input as minimal; that is, he did much to promote the records but most of the time he wasn't in the studio. Mike Stock says, "For about three years, he turned up on Thursday afternoons for about an hour. He did come up with the title 'Never Gonna Give You Up' for Rick Astley but sometimes his titles were too verbose like 'There Are Too Many People Walking Around With Broken Hearts', which became 'Too Many Broken Hearts'. He told people that he wrote 'Too Many Broken Hearts' sitting on the toilet, but he didn't! He came up with a title which was unusable and we turned it round. We wrote that song and made the record." Asked for further examples of Pete Waterman's input, Mike Stock says, "I begin to falter here."

Jason Donovan

625 Madonna
Like A Prayer

Label & Cat No.:	**Sire W 7539**
Producers:	**Madonna / Patrick Leonard**
Writers:	**Madonna / Patrick Leonard**
Date Reached No.1:	**25 March 1989**
Weeks at No.1:	**3**

MADONNA'S LIFE IN THE EIGHTIES WAS full of ups and downs. Her film career was a disaster, while her music career was still thriving. By the end of 1988, she had divorced Sean Penn. A few months later she signed a $5 million dollar contract to promote Pepsi-Cola in America.

'Like A Prayer' which, in its original form, contained bongos and Latin percussion similar to 'La Isla Bonita', was the first single released from her eponymous album. When Madonna was five, her mother died of cancer, and the dedication on the album's inner sleeve read, "This is for my mother who taught me how to pray." After her mother died, her father and Madonna got on badly and this sad tale she reveals on the track, 'Oh Father', which was belatedly issued as a single in 1996.

The video for 'Like A Prayer' caused much controversy. It showed Madonna watching a girl being raped by a gang of white youths with a black man looking on. When the police arrived, they arrested the black man, assuming he was involved. Not wanting to get involved, Madonna ducked into a nearby church. Inside, she was confronted by a black saint statue, which resembled the man outside. The saint comes to life and started making love to Madonna. When he had finished, she ran out of the church and straight to the police to confess what she had witnessed and the man was set free.

The video for the Pepsi advert received its only airing just a few days before the single was released. It was a completely different clip from that of the single. It was Madonna innocently reliving a childhood birthday party. Pepsi decided to pull the video following a plethora of complaints from consumers who were getting confused with the video for the single and the video for the advert.

Madonna refused to actually drink the product she was endorsing, Nonetheless, it worked wonders for the single. In an interview with *Rolling Stone*, Madonna said, "The Pepsi spot is a great and different way to advertise the single. Record companies just don't have the money to finance that kind of publicity."

626 The Bangles
Eternal Flame

Label & Cat No.:	**CBS BANGS 5**
Producer:	**Davitt Sigerson**
Writers:	**Susanna Hoffs / Billy Steinberg / Tom Kelly**
Date reached No.1:	**15 April 1989**
Weeks at No.1:	**4**

TWO ROCK'N'ROLLING SISTERS, VICKI and Debbie Peterson played guitar and drums respectively, and they put an ad in the Los Angeles newspaper, *The Recycler*, in 1980 asking for girls to contact them. It read: "Band members wanted: Into The Beatles, Byrds and Buffalo Springfield." When Susanna Hoffs replied, it was clear that they had a strong lead vocalist and they could create magical harmonies. With bass player Michael Steele (still a girl), they became The Supersonic Bangs and then The Bangs (an hilarious name for a female group!). As The Bangles, they provided a female take on the great groups of the Sixties, and there are nods to The Hollies, The Yardbirds, The Kinks and Fairport Convention throughout their work. They had a contemporary edge but you always felt that they were going down to Liverpool.

The Bangles got their jangly guitars and four-part harmonies in place on their first album, *All Over The Place* (1984), and they sharpened their sound on *Different Light* (1986). They had hits with Prince's anthem for the work-shy, 'Manic Monday' (US 2, UK 2), and the dance track, 'Walk Like An Egyptian' (US 1, UK 3), which, inexplicably, was banned by the BBC during the Gulf War.

The group performed 'A Hazy Shade Of Winter' (US 2, UK 11) on the film soundtrack for *Less Than Zero*, which marked Susanna Hoffs' acting debut. Her second film, *The Allnighter*, had appalling reviews and would she have had a leading role if it hadn't been directed by her mum, Tamar Simon Hoffs. In 2002 Susanna appeared in a hit film, the latest in the Austin Powers sequence, *Goldmember*.

Their album, *Everything* (1988), featured their own songs, but the record was as sunny and as Sixties based as ever. 'Eternal Flame', inspired by the eternal flame burning on Elvis Presley's grave, had the feel of The Beatles' 'Here, There And Everywhere'. The Bangles split up later in 1989 as Susanna was getting so much attention from the public that a solo career was inevitable. Neither her album (*When You're A Boy*) nor her singles ('My Side Of The Bed', 'Unconditional Love', 'All I Want') made much impression on the charts.

When they reformed in 2000, they found that Atomic Kitten had taken 'Eternal Flame' back to the top. "Do you think the young kids who buy it know it's our song?" Susanna Hoffs asked *The Times*.

The Bangles

627 Kylie Minogue
Hand On Your Heart

Label & Cat No.:	**PWL PWL 35**
Producers:	**Mike Stock / Matt Aitken / Pete Waterman**
Writers:	**Mike Stock / Matt Aitken / Pete Waterman**
Date Reached No.1:	**13 May 1989**
Weeks at No.1:	**1**

TAKING KYLIE AND JASON'S LEAD, IT was becoming a trend for Australian soap stars to make moves into the pop world. The week 'Hand On Your Heart' entered the chart at number two, Jason Donovan's on-screen brother Paul Robinson (Stefan Dennis) made his debut with 'Don't It Make You Feel Good'. Stefan's next single, 'This Love Affair' stalled at number 67 in late 1989, thus ending his musical career.

In 1989 Stock, Aitken & Waterman had their most successful year. They had won the Ivor Novello Songwriter Of The Year award for the third successive year and the trio, with their ability to churn out hit after hit and named themselves The Hit Factory.

Kylie had spent the first few months of 1989 recording her new album, *Enjoy Yourself*. The first single from it was 'Hand On Your Heart'. At the same time, filming began for a new movie, *The Delinquents*, starring Kylie as Lola Lovell and Charlie Schlatter as Brownie Hansen. It was set in the Fifties and followed a couple deeply in love and desperate to be together but forced apart by their parents who felt they were too young.

Kylie's private life became tabloid news as she drifted away from wholesome Jason Donovan into the arms of Michael Hutchence, INXS' decidedly unwholesome lead singer. It seemed an unlikely pairing but they hit it off and Kylie was happier than ever before. The relationship had a noticeable effect on Kylie's image, moving her away from the clean-living, girl-next-door persona towards a sexy, live-for-the-moment rock chick who dressed accordingly. "That was the time I was meant to meet him," said Kylie in retrospect. "It was like my blinkers were taken off and I entered the next stage. I was a suburban girl working in a soap opera, and then it was like 'wow! Oh my God!'"

628 The Christians, Holly Johnson, Paul McCartney, Gerry Marsden and Stock Aitken Waterman Ferry Cross The Mersey

Label & Cat No.: **PWL PWL 41**
Producers: **Mike Stock / Matt Aitken / Pete Waterman**
Writer: **Gerry Marsden**
Date reached No.1: **20 May 1989**
Weeks at No.1: **3**

ALUN OWEN WROTE A FINE FILM script for The Beatles and Tony Warren, who had created *Coronation Street*, was assigned to do the same for Gerry & The Pacemakers. He went on the road with the band and came up with a witty, knockabout script, *Ferry Cross The Mersey*.

Gerry, composer of some fine songs ('I'm The One', 'Don't Let The Sun Catch You Crying', 'Away From You'), was asked to write the score. The songs included 'It's Gonna Be All Right' and 'Ferry Cross The Mersey', which was a Top 10 single in December 1964. In 1983 the song was revived by Frankie Goes To Hollywood on the 12-inch single of 'Relax'.

Following the Hillsborough tragedy in 1989, some key Liverpool performers got together for a charity single – The Christians, Paul McCartney and Holly Johnson from Frankie Goes To Hollywood. The single was produced by Stock Aitken & Waterman.

The song, which is played endlessly on the Merseyside ferries, captures the friendly spirit of Liverpool, although you can sympathise with the crew who hear it day in and day out. The lyric is very touching and perhaps Gerry was ahead of his time with its comment on asylum seekers: "We don't care what your name is, boy, we'll never turn you away."

629 Jason Donovan Sealed With A Kiss

Label & Cat No.: **PWL PWL 39**
Producers: **Mike Stock / Matt Aitken / Pete Waterman**
Writers: **Gary Geld / Peter Udell**
Date Reached No.1: **10 June 1989**
Weeks at No.1: **2**

A MONTH AFTER 'TOO MANY BROKEN Hearts' hit the top, Jason quit *Neighbours* but, in the UK, he would still be seen in it for another 18 months. Although Jason had written three songs of his own, 'Please Come Back', 'Hold Me Now' and 'The Yellow Cab', he had no plans to release them. Instead, he personally chose his next single, 'Sealed With A Kiss'.

Composer Gary Geld and lyricist Peter Udell began their writing partnership in the early Sixties and wrote over 100 songs including three 1961 British hits 'I Told You So' (Jimmy Jones), 'Motorcycle Michael' (Jo Ann Campbell) and 'Ain't Gonna Wash For A Week' (Brook Brothers). One of their first songs was the archetypal American high-school teen love song, 'Sealed With A Kiss' which they had written in 1960 and was a hit for Brian Hyland two years later. Brian said, "'Sealed With A Kiss' was recorded about a year before I did it by The Four Voices, who had a sound like The Brothers Four. It dragged and didn't have any life in it, so it wasn't a hit. I told them that we should do it. Gary Geld was a classically trained musician and he had been inspired to write it from a finger exercise for the piano."

When Jason's version of 'Sealed with A Kiss' was released, Brian Hyland received a message from the *News Of The World*. He must have assumed it was his version. "They didn't say on their message that it wasn't by me, so I thought my luck was in. It had been on some ad and was being reissued. I rang back and they told me about Jason Donovan, but I didn't know who he was because *Neighbours* wasn't shown in the States. I didn't mind his version – he got all the chords right." When Jason crashed into the chart at number one, it deprived Cliff Richard of reaching the top with his 100th single, 'The Best Of Me' which entered at number two.

Jason had further Top 10 hits with 'Every Day (I Love You More)', 'When You Come Back To Me', 'Hang On To Your Love' and a cover of The Cascades' 'Rhythm Of The Rain'. In May 1991 Jason's manager, Richard East, contacted Pete Waterman to let him know that Jason had been offered the part of Joseph in Andrew Lloyd Webber's London production of *Joseph And His Amazing Technicolor Dreamcoat*. Pete claimed in his autobiography, *I Wish I Was Me*, "They wanted me to write five songs for it and release Jason from his contract with me. After a couple of meetings, I agreed to release Jason but decided against writing any songs because they seemed simpler songs than Stock, Aitken & Waterman ones." Tim Rice retorted, "That is completely untrue. I like what Pete does and he writes some great songs, but there is no way I would ask him to write any songs for *Joseph*."

630 Soul II Soul featuring Caron Wheeler Back To Life (However Do You Want Me)

Label & Cat No.: **10 TEN 265**
Producers: **Jazzie B / Nellee Hooper**
Writers: **Beresford Romeo / Caron Wheeler / Simon Law / Nellee Hooper**
Date Reached No.1: **24 June 1989**
Weeks at No.1: **4**

BY THE MID-EIGHTIES MUSICAL STYLES were changing at a fast pace. In 1986 the

Chicago House sound was introduced via Farley 'Jackmaster' Funk and Steve 'Silk' Hurley. By 1987 it had moved on to 'house' music with Housemaster Boyz and Royal House. A year later 'acid', the hypnotic trancy screeching sound accompanied by yellow smiley stickers, was brought to us by Swan Lake and Jolly Roger. By 1989 a new downtempo seductive R&B sound was a welcome change courtesy of Soul II Soul.

Jazzie B, born Beresford Romeo in 1963 to Antiguan parents, and his school friend Philip 'Daddae' Harvey began playing reggae music at clubs and parties in 1982. With another friend, Aiche B, they opened a shop in north London for hiring PA systems and called it Soul II Soul. The pair met Bristol-based Nellee Hooper, a member of the mixing crew Massive Attack in 1985 after he had hired one of Soul II Soul's PAs. They began working together and formed a group also called Soul II Soul. "I'm no musician. I can bang out a few chords, but the important thing is that I can interpret my ideas to other musicians," admitted Jazzie B.

They preferred using guest female vocalists. Their first hit, 'Fairplay' featured Rose Windross and their second, 'Feel Free', was performed by Do'reen Waddell who died after she was hit by a car in March 2002. For the third single, 'Keep On Moving', which featured the Reggae Philharmonic Orchestra, they brought in British soul singer Caron Wheeler. Caron had been a vocalist with reggae group, Brown Sugar, as well as a session singer for Phil Collins, Elvis Costello and Erasure. 'Keep On Moving' reached number five and became the backbeat for dozens of similar sounding songs. The debut album, *Club Classics – Volume One*, went all the way to the top. "All we had were Caron's acappella vocals for 'Back To Life'. We had to put the music to the vocals," said Jazzie B. The song won a Grammy but nothing in Britain. Jazzie B wasn't happy, "Fuck 'em!" he said. "You can't argue with hit records. Who cares about the Brits anyway. The rest of the world sat up and took notice. Neneh Cherry won one and she broke it and gave half to us."

After 'Back To Life' Caron left to pursue a solo career and had Top 40 hits with 'Livin' In The Light' and 'UK Blak'. Soul II Soul carried on with more guest vocalists and had Top 10 hits with 'Get A Life', 'A Dreams A Dream' and 'Joy'.

631 Sonia
You'll Never Stop Me Loving You

Label & Cat No.: **Chrysalis CHS 3385**

Producers: **Mike Stock / Matt Aitken / Pete Waterman**

Writers: **Mike Stock / Matt Aitken / Pete Waterman**

Date reached No.1: **22 July 1989**

Weeks at No.1: **2**

"YOU HAVE TO BE PUSHY TO GET anywhere," says Sonia. She grew up singing for friends and relations and appearing in social clubs around Liverpool. She was determined to be a professional singer and in 1989 when she was 18, she pestered the producer Pete Waterman for an audition when he was appearing as a DJ. He liked what he heard and she was signed to the production company of Stock, Aitken & Waterman.

Sonia's first hit, 'You'll Never Stop Me Loving You', topped the charts and especially appealed to the pre-teen audience. She had eight other Top 20 entries including a charity single, 'You've Got A Friend' with Big Fun for ChildLine (1990) and her UK entry for the Eurovision Song Contest, 'Better The Devil You Know' (1993). In addition, she sang on Band Aid II. "It was all great," she reflects, "but there was a backlash that said that Stock, Aitken & Waterman's artists couldn't sing and the vocals were fixed in the studio. That's certainly not true in my case because I can sing."

Lacking chivalry, Matt Aitken says, "Sonia was ordinary and wasn't particularly good-looking either. The guy that was in charge of Chrysalis said in *Music Week* that he was deeply embarrassed when she was number one. He got the sack."

Sonia starred in Olivia Newton-John's role in the West End production of *Grease*, and, in 2003, she was competing with Elkie Brooks, Peter Cox, Dollar, Hydon Eshun, Gina G, Michelle Gayle, Tony Hadley and Lee John in the TV series, *Reborn In The USA*. Sonia, despite, or perhaps because of, her eagerness to please, was one of the first to be eliminated.

632 Jive Bunny & The Mastermixers
Swing The Mood

Label & Cat No.: **Music Factory Dance MFD 001**

Producers: **Andy Pickles / Les Hemstock**

Writers: **See names in brackets below**

Date Reached No.1: **5 August 1989**

Weeks at No.1: **5**

MOBILE DJS HAVE ALWAYS INCORPorated party songs into their sets, but life was made a little easier for the DJ in 1981 (or more likely made them lazy), when a plethora of medley songs flooded the market. They included Star Sound with their various versions of 'Stars on 45', both Tight Fit's 'Back To The 60s' medleys, The Royal Philharmonic Orchestra's 'Hooked On Classics' and various group mixes by The Beach Boys, The Bee Gees, The Rubettes, The Hollies, Gary Glitter and Chas & Dave.

In 1984 John Pickles and his son, Andy, founded a subscription-only entertainment company called The Music Factory. Its function was to supply DJs with exclusive megamixes and new releases in the form of an album. "Myself and a friend did the original mix for 'Swing The Mood' as part of our mastermix subscription service," recalled Andy. "It got such a huge reaction when we sent it out that we decided to release it as a single. We didn't have a record label, so I suggested Jive Bunny, the name I'd given to a friend of mine, but dad suggested we use that name to front the act." The others Mastermixers were: Ian Morgan, Rob Adlin, Darren Ash, Rick Stuart, Martin Smith, Les Hemstock and Dave Roarthy.

The idea was easier said than done. Andy and John had trouble obtaining the rights to use some of the tracks. The medley consisted of snippets from: 'Let's Twist Again' (Kal Mann / Dave

Appell); 'In The Mood' (Joe Garland / Andy Razal); '(We're Gonna) Rock Around The Clock' (Jimmy DeKnight / Max C. Freedman); 'Rock-A-Beatin' Boogie' (Bill Haley); 'Tutti Frutti' (Dorothy La Bostrie / Richard Penniman / Joe Lubin); 'Wake Up Little Susie' (Felice Bryant / Boudleaux Bryant) ; 'C'mon Everybody' (Eddie Cochran / Jerry Capehart);'Hound Dog' (Jerry Leiber / Mike Stoller); 'Shake Rattle And Roll' (Charles Calhoun); 'All Shook Up' (Otis Blackwell / Elvis Presley); 'Jailhouse Rock' (Jerry Leiber/Mike Stoller); and 'At The Hop' (Arthur Singer / Johnny Medara / David White).

Many of these songs, and the artists that recorded them, can be found elsewhere in this book. Among the songs you won't find is the opener, 'Let's Twist Again' which was a number two hit for Chubby Checker at the end of 1961. The Twist was a popular – arguably the most popular - dance craze in an era when new dance crazes cropped up on an almost weekly basis. Chubby's hit was a follow-up to 'The Twist' which reached only number 44 on its initial release in 1960 but made number 14 immediately after 'Let's Twist Again'.

Another you won't find is the closer, 'At The Hop', a classic example of rock'n'roll singing at its best which was a number one hit for Danny & The Juniors in the US for a staggering seven weeks in 1957 and a UK number three hit the following year. Like Chubby Checker, Danny and his three Juniors jumped on the dance craze bandwagon too, recording songs about such dances as the Pony, Mashed Potato, Fish and Limbo. In 1976 a re-issue of 'At The Hop' returned the group to the UK Top 40.

"We weren't allowed to use the Elvis tracks, so we brought in Elvis impersonator Peter Wilcox," says John Pickles. Once it was finished, they re-titled it 'Swing The Mood' and within two weeks it was number one.

The imaginatively-titled release, *The Album*, featured 'Swing The Mood' with longer versions of some of the tracks and included two extra Glenn Miller numbers, 'Pennsylvania 6-5000' and 'Little Brown Jug'.

633 Black Box
Ride On Time

Label & Cat No.: **Deconstruction PB 43055**

Producer: **Groove Groove Melody**

Writers: **Dan Hartman / Mirko Limoni / Daniele Davoli / Valerio Semplici**

Date Reached No.1: **9 September 1989**

Weeks at No.1: **6**

House music had been around for a couple of years by the late Eighties, but its sound was beginning to alter slightly. Thanks to the Italians, it was becoming more piano led and more melodic. Starlight's 'Numero Uno', the Mixmaster's 'Grand Piano' and Black Box's 'Ride On Time' are good examples. It earned itself the name 'Italo-House'.

Black Box were studio engineer, Mirko Limoni, clarinet teacher Valerio Simplici and DJ Daniele Davoli. Davoli had been DJing since 1981 and was resident at the Marabou Starlight club in Rimini, playing a mix of disco and old soul tracks. He cut his first track, 'House Machine' in 1987. For 'Ride On Time' he used soul diva, Loleatta Holloway's 'Love Sensation' with the powerful hook line 'Ri-ri-ri-ri-ride, ride on time'.

Davoli said, "People were dancing to the new piano sound, even though it sounded quite different. The piano sound wasn't that big in Italy until after we had the success in England. Mirko came to the club where I was DJing. I would play the keyboard and the sampler, but it was such a small sampler, I only had space for two or three lines. The main sound I created was a Wah-wah-wah-wah-wah effect and incorporated into nearly every record I played. Mirko said to me, 'I couldn't avoid noticing that, what was it?' I said, 'It was from this acappella that I got from an old record'. Mirko said, 'Bring it in to the studio and I think we can do something with it'."

For their *Top Of The Pops* appearance, Davoli asked his ex-girlfriend, stunning Italian model Katrin Quinol, to front the act. He hadn't given Loleatta Holloway any credit and it was Katrin's poor miming that caused controversy. Loleatta said, "I've been around for years trying to get this one hit record. It annoyed me knowing that Black Box were number one for six weeks using my voice and I was not getting any credit for it. Then I found out that she couldn't even speak English." Loleatta threatened legal action and the track was quickly re-recorded with a session singer. But Loleatta did appear on *Top Of The Pops* eventually, to prove the vocals were hers.

Dan Hartman, who had written 'Love Sensation', had hits in his own right as the performer of 'Instant Replay' and 'I Can Dream About You' and as a writer of 'Work That Body' (Diana Ross) and 'Living In America' (James Brown). He died from a brain tumour in 1994. Black Box had two further Top 10 hits with 'I Don't Know Anybody Else' and a cover of Earth Wind & Fire's 'Fantasy'. As for Loleatta, she had hits in the Nineties from collaborations with Marky Mark & The Funky Bunch, Cappella and Fire Island.

634 Jive Bunny & The Mastermixers
That's What I Like

Label & Cat No.: **Music Factory Dance MFD 002**

Producers: **Andy Pickles / Ian Morgan**

Writers: **See names in brackets below**

Date Reached No.1: **21 October 1989**

Weeks at No.1: **3**

Andy Pickles was so surprised by the success of 'Swing The Mood' that while it was still at number one, they began working on the follow-up, 'That's What I Like'. Andy used more artists from the same period for his second rock'n'roll tribute.

This time they used: 'Theme from Hawaii 5-O' (Morton Stevens); 'Let's Twist Again' (Kal Mann / Dave Appell); 'Let's Dance' (Jim Lee); 'Wipe Out' (Ron Wilson / Jim Fuller / Bob Berryhill / Pat Connolly); 'Great Balls Of Fire' (Jack Hammer / Otis Blackwell); the intro to 'Johnny B. Goode' (Chuck Berry); 'Good

Golly Miss Molly' (Richard Penniman); 'The Twist' (Hank Ballard); 'Summertime Blues' (Eddie Cochran / Jerry Capehart); 'Razzle Dazzle' (Charles Calhoun); 'Runaround Sue' (Ernie Maresca / Dion DiMucci); and 'Chantilly Lace' (Jiles Perry Richardson), from which the hook line, 'Oh baby, that's what I like' gave the song its title.

The album, which at this time was still being compiled, featured eight tracks, all medleys. It contained 'Do You Wanna Rock' a glam medley consisting of Gary Glitter, Suzi Quatro, T. Rex and The Sweet songs. There was also the Forties medley, 'Swing Sisters Swing' with such gems as 'Lullaby Of Broadway', 'Chattanooga Choo Choo' and 'Boogie Woogie Bugle Boy'. It eventually reached number two when released in December 1989. Curiously, their third and final number one, 'Let's Party' wasn't on there.

635 Lisa Stansfield
All Around The World

Label & Cat No.: **Arista 112 693**

Producers: **Ian Devaney / Andy Morris**

Writers: **Lisa Stansfield / Ian Devaney / Andy Morris**

Date Reached No.1: **11 November 1989**

Weeks at No.1: **2**

LISA IS ONE OF TWO FAMOUS STANSFIELDS to come out of Lancashire. The other was the unrelated popular singer and comedienne of the Thirties and Forties, Gracie Fields (born Grace Stansfield).

Lisa, who was born in 1966, has a broad Lancashire accent but sings like the best of American soul singers. At 14 she won a talent contest sponsored by the *Manchester Evening News* and one of the judges was a Granada Television producer who invited her to appear on a programme he was involved with. "I didn't enjoy it because I couldn't have my say about what I wanted to do or look like. They made me look like Joan Collins." It served its purpose though, leading to the 16-year-old Lisa being offered a

Lisa Stansfield

job of hosting the Saturday morning children's show, *Razzamatazz*. It was hard going filming with children all day and after a few months she abruptly quit the show. By chance, Lisa met up with two old school friends and budding musicians, Andy Morris and Ian Devaney and they began writing songs together. It also led to a long-term relationship between Lisa & Ian.

They put a band together called Ede Bopp and played a couple of gigs at Rochdale Social Club. On the second night they told the 300-strong audience they were changing their name to Blue Zone. In 1987 they signed to the local Rockin' Horse label and recorded their first single, 'On Fire'. "The song was getting quite popular," recalled Lisa, "but then the King's Cross fire happened and we pulled the single in order not to offend anybody."

In 1989 Matt Black and Jonathan Moore from Coldcut invited Blue Zone to collaborate on a song they were working on. The result was 'People Hold On', which was credited to Coldcut featuring Lisa Stansfield and reached number 11. With Lisa's name on a hit single, they ditched the name Blue Zone and Matt and Jonathan returned the favour by producing Lisa's first solo single, 'This Is The Right Time'.

One day Lisa, Ian and Andy were sitting round the piano. Andy played some chords and Lisa began talking in a low voice, which later became the intro. Ian remembered, "We booked this little studio and started a really rough demo on an eight-track machine with Lisa's vocals being done in one take. When we came to the proper recording, we transferred the original vocals to 24-track, added some strings and transferred it back to eight-track which we later mixed at home." The single, 'All Around The World' went to number one nearly all around the world.

The album, *Affection*, reached number two and Lisa had further Top 10 singles with 'Live Together', 'Change', 'Someday (I'm Coming Back)', 'In All The Right Places' and 'The Real Thing'. She also had a further number one as part of the Queen Five Live EP on which Lisa sang 'These Are The Days Of Our Lives'.

In 1999 she made an appearance in the romantic comedy film *Swing*. Three years later, Lisa, who still records, made her West End debut in the *Vagina Monologues* alongside Celia Noble and Anita Dobson.

636 New Kids On The Block
You Got It (The Right Stuff)

Label & Cat No.: **CBS BLOCK 2**

Producer: **Maurice Starr**

Writer: **Maurice Starr**

Date Reached No.1: **25 November 1989**

Weeks at No.1: **3**

MAURICE STARR, WHO WAS BORN Lawrence Johnson, can be likened to Berry Gordy Jr in the way he hand picked and worked on his acts. He'd proved that with New Edition in the early Eighties but after a falling out, Maurice decided to put together a white version of the successful boy band. "I always felt I could teach anybody to sing. Anybody," said Starr. "My whole thing is promotion, strategy, marketing and management." It was his revenge and it paid off.

In 1984 he and a friend, Mary Alford, assembled his new act, the Boston-based Donnie Wahlberg, Danny Wood, Joey McIntyre and brothers Jonathan and Jordan Knight. After a brief spell as Nynuk, the youngsters renamed themselves New Kids On The Block – from the title of one of their early songs – and made their debut appearance in 1986 on the American television show *WILD Live*. To increase their status, Starr fought hard and succeeded in getting them on tour with Tiffany, where they ended up headlining.

Their debut album, *New Kids On The Block* made no impact and the first single, 'Be My Girl' fared only slightly better. However, another track from the album, a cover of The Delfonics' 'Didn't I (Blow Your Mind)' was belatedly released in 1990 and made the Top 10 on both sides of the Atlantic.

Their second album, *Hangin' Tough*, went to number one in the US and number two in Britain, eventually selling more than eight million copies. After the title track stalled at number 52 in the UK, Columbia got it right with 'You Got It (The Right Stuff)', when the boys took the tale of a young couple's first experience of falling in love, all the way to the top.

637 Jive Bunny & The Mastermixers Let's Party

Label & Cat No.: **Music Factory Dance MFD 003**
Producers: **Andy Pickles / Ian Morgan**
Writers: **See names in brackets below**
Date Reached No.1: **16 December 1989**
Weeks at No.1: **1**

When Jive Bunny & The Mastermixers reached the top of the chart for the third time with their third release, they matched a feat that had previously been achieved only by Gerry & The Pacemakers and Frankie Goes To Hollywood. Furthermore, they did it in the least amount of time.

The backing track for the Christmas medley was John Anderson's 'March Of The Mods' (Tony Carr) with snippets of Slade's 'Merry Xmas Everybody' (Noddy Holder / Jim Lea); Wizzard's 'I Wish It Could Be Christmas Everyday' (Roy Wood); Gary Glitter's 'Another Rock And Roll Christmas' (Gary Glitter / Mike Leander); and Chubby Checker's 'Christmas Rap' (Eddie Seago / Chubby Checker) played over the top of them.

The fact that 'Let's Party' spent just five weeks on the chart was an indication that the medley concept was wearing thin. The follow-up, 'That Sounds Good To Me' peaked at number four. Andy claimed, "I think it was a conspiracy. I don't believe the industry wanted a rabbit to hold the record of their first four singles going to number one." After one further Top 10 hit with 'Can-Can You Party', a few minor hits followed but then Pickles decided to call it a day. "We couldn't afford to release them any more," explained John. "The interesting thing is that it isn't the public who decide when a life has come to an end, but the retailers. The problem we had in the end is that we couldn't get our records stocked in Woolworths or Our Price, and you need a Top 20 hit to make it viable."

In 1992 The Music Factory expanded and employed their own A&R and production teams and invested in six new recording studios. Their production teams, which still include Andy, have charted under the guises of 2 In A Tent ('When I'm Cleaning Windows (Turned Out Nice Again)' 1994), Hyperlogic ('Only Me' 1995) and The Handbaggers ('U Found Out' 1996). The Music Factory umbrella is still up and home to a number of spin-off dance labels that cater for techno, hard house and drum'n'bass. The most successful is Tidy Trax with 31 hit singles to their credit. There were problems getting clearance for some of the tracks, so Noddy Holder and Roy Wood offered to re-sing their vocals and Chubby Checker recorded a special 'Christmas Rap'.

638 Band Aid II Do They Know It's Christmas?

Label & Cat No.: **PWLP / Polydor FEED 2**
Producers: **Mike Stock / Matt Aitken / Pete Waterman**
Writers: **Bob Geldof / Midge Ure**
Date reached No.1: **23 December 1989**
Weeks at No.1: **3**

The success of Band Aid in 1984 has led to numerous charity singles, which has continued to the present. The production team of Stock, Aitken & Waterman were responsible for Ferry Aid (1987) and 'Ferry 'Cross The Mersey' (1989) and they scored a hat-trick by reviving the Band Aid song with a new team.

The first Band Aid single returned to the charts in 1985 at number three but failed to chart in succeeding years. The new version took the song back to the top. Band Aid II included Bananarama, a Stock, Aitken & Waterman group, who were also on the first single. It also featured Cathy Dennis, Jason Donovan, Kevin Godley, Glen Goldsmith, Kylie Minogue, Chris Rea, Cliff Richard, Jimmy Somerville, Sonia and Lisa Stansfield as well as the groups, Big Fun, Bros, D Mob, Pasadenas, Technotronic and Wet Wet Wet.

Although the line-up would be impressive in any other setting, it lacked the star power (and truly distinctive voices) of the first Band Aid or USA For Africa singles.

Sonia and Big Fun

1990-1999

and The Rockingbirds baldly go ...

Old, gifted and back! BOB DYLAN and NEIL YOUNG LPs reviewed

Bloody hell! REM's Material World!!

NME's SUPERB 'RUBY TRAX' ALBUM: HOW TO GET IT (slowcoaches!)

9 770028 636024 44

PROPHET OR LOST?

The end of the world or the end of Sinead?

NETWORK UK TOP 50 45s

1 LOVE IS ALL AROUND .... Wet Wet Wet (Precious)
2 BABY, I LOVE YOUR WAY .... Big Mountain (RCA)
6 SWAMP THING .... The Grid (deConstruction)
10 I SWEAR .... All-4-One (Atlantic)
3 YOU DON'T LOVE ME (NO, NO, NO) .... Dawn Penn (Atlantic)
4 DON'T TURN AROUND .... Ace Of Base (Metronome)
7 ANYTIME YOU NEED A FRIEND ..... Mariah Carey (Columbia)
(—) GO ON MOVE
Reel 2 Real featuring The Mad Stuntman (Positiva)
5 NO GOOD (START THE DANCE) .... The Prodigy (XL)
8 GET-A-WAY .... Maxx (Pulse 8)
(—) CAUGHT IN THE MIDDLE – THE '94 MIXES
Juliet Roberts (Cooltempo)
(—) SHAKERMAKER .... Oasis (Creation)
11 ANY TIME, ANY PLACE .... Janet Jackson (Virgin)
26 WILLING TO FORGIVE .... Aretha Franklin (Arista)
30 SHINE .... Aswad (Bubblin')
12 U & ME .... Cappella (Internal Dance)
14 AROUND THE WORLD .... East 17 (London)
(—) BODY IN MOTION .... Atlantic Ocean (Eastern Bloc)
21 CRAZY FOR YOU .... Let Loose (Mercury)
24 I WANNA BE YOUR MAN ..... Chaka Demus & Pliers (Mango)
13 NO MORE TEARS (ENOUGH IS ENOUGH)
Kym Mazelle And Jocelyn Brown (Arista)
(—) BACK AND FORTH .... Aaliyah (Jive)
9 ABSOLUTELY FABULOUS .. Absolutely Fabulous (Spaghetti)
15 COME ON YOU REDS
Manchester United Football Squad (Polygram TV)
16 EVERYBODY'S TALKIN' ..... The Beautiful South (Go! Discs)
31 MIDDLEMAN .... Terrorvision (Total Vegas)
(—) SHUT UP AND DANCE .... Aerosmith (Geffen)
18 INSIDE .... Stiltskin (White Water)
33 MOVE YOUR BODY Anticappella featuring MC Fixx It (MCA)
19 SINCE I DON'T HAVE YOU .... Guns N' Roses (Geffen)
20 TAKE ME AWAY .... D:Ream (Magnet)
23 DO YOU WANT IT RIGHT NOW .... Degrees Of
28 DOLPHIN .... Shed Sev
(—) AIN'T NOBODY (LOVES ME BETTER)

35 (—) I CAN'T IMAGINE THE WORLD WITHOUT ME
36 22 CARRY ME HOME .... Echobelly (Fauve)
37 (—) I DON'T LIKE MONDAYS .... Gloworm (Go Beat)
38 49 THE SUN DOES RISE EP .... Boomtown Rats (Vertigo)
Jah Wobble's Invaders Of The Heart (Island)
39 45 7 SECONDS
Youssou N'Dour featuring Neneh Cherry (Columbia)
40 17 TO THE END .... Blur (Food)
41 29 CLEOPATRA'S CAT .... The Spin Doctors (Epic)
42 (—) GHETTO DAY/WHAT I NEED .... Crystal Waters (A&M)
43 37 THE ONE FOR ME .... Joe (Mercury)
44 38 FEEL WHAT YOU WANT .... Kristine W (Champion)
45 27 CRAYZY MAN .... Blast featuring VDC (MCA)
46 (—) MAYBE LOVE .... Stevie Nicks (EMI)
47 50 TWO CAN PLAY AT THAT GAME .... Bobby Brown (MCA)
48 (—) YOU MUST BE PREPARED TO DREAM
Ian McNabb (This Way Up)
49 (—) JESUS HAIRDO .... The Charlatans (Beggars Banquet)
50 (—) LOVE TOWN .... Peter Gabriel (Epic)

MRIB

PICTURE: KEVIN CUMMINS

Q

NEW ELVIS COSTELLO ALBUM His best yet?

PAUL SIMON LIVE

Q REVIEW The essential guide to over 100 new LPs

The modern guide to music and more

June 1991 £1.75 DM 11.50 US $5.95

MADONNA

IN THE Q INTERVIEW

"Everyone thinks I'm a nymphomaniac but I'd rather read a book."

Plus MC HAMMER JANE'S ADDICTION JOHNNY CASH CHARLIE WATTS

Q SLEEVENOTES Four more classic CD booklets

"You can sleep with me and Trudie tonight if you want. Come in for a few hours anyway, see if you can keep up." *Sting offers a hostly hop on the wife*

Axl Rose Starts A Riot

July 2, 1991

Having punched a snap-happy biker at a Guns N'Roses show in St Louis, Axl Rose lost his contact lens and stormed offstage in a huff. The ensuing riot left dozens of police bleeding and the band in fear for their lives.

BRITISH HEAVYWEIGHT

CHAMPIONSHIP

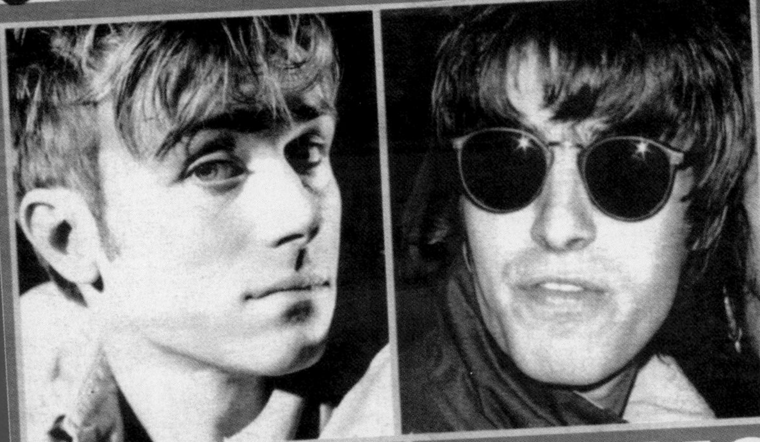

BLUR vs OASIS

AUGUST 14: THE BIG CHART SHOWDOWN

"Groups have to have that hit single quickly or the marketing budget will be applied to somebody else"

VOTE FOR THE BRATS! THE *NME* READERS POLL

23 November 1996 90p $(US)3.95

NME

NEW MUSICAL EXPRESS

PUPPET SOUNDS! The roar power of TIGER

JUST SAY FERRINO! STEVE COOGAN'S latest bluff

ZIGAZIG-HA 72 PAGES! (Whatever that means)

SEX! SUCCESS! SHOPPING! STREAKING! TONY BLAIR?!

SPICE GIRLS

The ULTIMATE rock'n'roll interview!

KISS ★ CATATONIA ★ SNOOP DOGGY DOGG ★ BJORK

DERSTICKS ★ SKUNK ANANSIE ★ JAMIROQUAI ★ ICE CUBE

n Björkland, every day is a bad hair day…

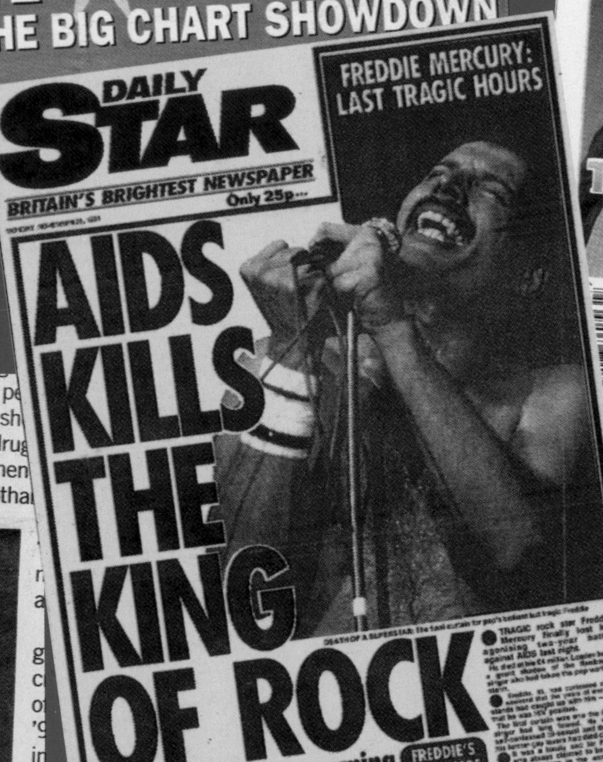

DAILY STAR

BRITAIN'S BRIGHTEST NEWSPAPER Only 25p

FREDDIE MERCURY: LAST TRAGIC HOURS

AIDS KILLS THE KING OF ROCK

FREDDIE'S NIGHTMARE Pages 2-3

Music world is in mourning for Queen's superstar singer

naked pe
other's sh
selling drug
'Recommen
Ian Botha

ey should build some
e bypasses over this
hole!' – Nicky Wire at
tonbury, 1994

ed to find
Vhen 'You

"They should build some m
over this shithole!"

BRITPOP SAVES THE WORLD!

"YOU'RE NEXT, POL POT!" SAYS BONEHEAD

Phil Collins. No Paul Young. No running six miles

FUCK
IN SHORT
LEGS

639 New Kids On The Block
Hangin' Tough

Label & Cat No.:	**CBS BLOCK 3**
Producer:	**Maurice Starr**
Writer:	**Maurice Starr**
Date Reached No.1:	**13 January 1990**
Weeks at No.1:	**2**

FOLLOWING THE NUMBER ONE SUCCESS of 'You Got It (This Right Stuff)', Columbia decided to re-release New Kids' previous single, 'Hangin' Tough'. It had failed to make the Top 50 first time round. "I think people may have taken 'Hangin' Tough' too seriously and maybe thought we wanted to be tough and beat people up," suggested Jonathan Knight. However, it paid off, reaching number one in both the US and UK.

They had had a few tough years getting things off the ground and as Maurice Starr recalled, "We needed a song that symbolised what we had been going through, so I came up with this title, 'Hangin' Tough'." The song, which also lent its name to the album, was the first of seven Top 10 hits in a year, a feat previously achieved only by Madonna.

Following the hits, 'I'll Be Loving You (Forever)' (which was originally written with Smokey Robinson in mind), 'Cover Girl', 'Step By Step', the Beatlesque 'Tonight' and 'This One's For The Children', the 'kids' started getting themselves into trouble. In 1991 Donnie Wahlberg and Joey McIntyre were involved in serious brawls and later the same year, Wahlberg was arrested for attempted arson but later claimed he accidentally let off a fire hydrant – an offence in Kentucky. Instead he was charged with second-degree criminal mischief and served community service as a punishment. They fell out with Maurice Starr who refused to let them use the name New Kids On The Block, so their next three hits went under the acronym, NKOTB.

In 1994 the group broke up. Danny Wood became a record producer in Miami, Jonathan Knight became an estate agent and Jordan's brief solo career amounted to one Top 10 hit, 'Give It To You'. Likewise, Joey has one US Top 10 with 'Still The Same' and starred in the 2004 film *Tony 'n' Tina's Wedding*. Donnie followed his brother Mark into the acting world and is best remembered for his role as Vincent Grey in the 1999 film, *The Sixth Sense*.

640 Kylie Minogue
Tears On My Pillow

Label & Cat No.:	**PWL PWL 47**
Producers:	**Mike Stock / Matt Aitken / Pete Waterman**
Writers:	**Sylvester Bradford / Al Lewis**
Date Reached No.1:	**27 January 1990**
Weeks at No.1:	**1**

IN 1955 ALAN FREED WAS THE FIRST DJ to refer to music of the time as rock'n'roll. Three years later he was also responsible for dubbing The Imperials' five foot four lead singer, Anthony Gourdine, Little Anthony.

This New York quintet were school friends who grew up in Brooklyn and although they all sung with various different groups, they occasionally sang together in church and on variety programmes. Anthony sang with The Duponts before forming The Chesters in 1957. They were spotted by Richard Barrett, who had also discovered The Isley Brothers, and changed their name to The Imperials. In addition to Anthony there was Ernest Wright, Glouster Rogers, Clarence Collins and Tracy Lord. Their first single, the million-selling 'Tears On My Pillow', with the backing based on The Penguins' 'Earth Angel', was originally released as The Imperials. Because Freed kept referring to them as Little Anthony & The Imperials, later copies credited them that way. They were one of the most successful doo-wop groups of the Fifties.

Kylie attended the première of her film, *The Delinquents* in Sydney with then-boyfriend, INXS frontman Michael Hutchence, and a new look so extreme that initially the press photographers didn't recognise her. She wore a noughts and crosses micro-dress and a blonde wig, which she named suicide blonde, later becoming the inspiration for the INXS song of the same name.

In 1989 a reader's poll of *Smash Hits* voted Kylie Best Female Singer. A year later in the same magazine, she was voted Worst Female Singer. One reason may have been due to this chart-topper which was a radical departure from the familiar uptempo and catchy pop songs that Kylie had been become known for. Kylie recalled, "It has surprised a lot of people because they didn't expect this kind of thing from me. Although I enjoyed doing it, I'm not going to become a big ballad songstress and forget dance. Maybe I'll just stay with my foot in that kind of area."

Kylie was exerting more control over her work and knew what she wanted. After dabbling in songwriting and showing signs of wanting to break away from Stock Aitken & Waterman, she expressed an interest in working with Janet Jackson's producers, Jimmy Jam and Terry Lewis. In turn, people were now beginning to show her some respect and the music press were making comparisons to Madonna. The battle for the Queen of Pop was underway.

641 Sinéad O'Connor
Nothing Compares 2 U

Label & Cat No.:	**Ensign ENY 630**
Producer:	**Sinéad O'Connor**
Writer:	**Prince**
Date Reached No.1:	**3 February 1990**
Weeks at No.1:	**4**

SINÉAD O'CONNOR, LIKE ENYA, NEVER listened to pop music until she was in her teens. "The first records I listened to were Aretha Franklin when I was 17," revealed Sinéad, "but I was only ever affected by one band and that's

Sinéad O'Connor's tough-girl image belied the romanticism of 'Nothing Compares 2 U'

The Smiths. They were the only thing that made me excited to be alive."

Born in Dublin in 1966, Sinéad's parents' divorce when she was young hit her hard and she became insecure, bitter, and very withdrawn. "The reason I shaved my head was because I just felt I didn't have anything to set me apart from the crowd."

When she was 16 she was asked to sing at her schoolteacher's wedding where she was spotted by a singer from a local band, In Tua Nua. She left school, joined the band and moved to London. The following year her mother died and Sinead turned to religion to help cope with her loss. In London, she came across a tarot card reader who told her she had a bright future as a singer, and on the strength of that, decided to go solo. She signed former *Irish Press* journalist and Boomtown Rats manager, Fachtna O'Ceallaigh as her manager and in 1987 signed a record deal with Ensign Records.

Her first single, 'Troy' didn't connect but the next, 'Mandinka', went to number 17 in January 1988. It was O'Ceallaigh who suggested the follow-up, 'Nothing Compares 2 U'. Prince had assembled a band in Minneapolis, called The Family and he wrote the song about the percussionist, Jerome Benton's break up with his girlfriend and gave them the song first. Their version was sung as a duet and had lead singers, Susannah Melvoin and Paul Peterson trading choruses. Sinéad sang it with angst, conviction and above all, emotion. So much so, that in the video, the tears she cried were real. She later admitted that her split with O'Ceallaigh just two days before the recording helped the tears flow more naturally. All this helped to push the album *I Do Not Want What I Haven't Got* to number one.

She hadn't met Prince until after the song had been a hit, but they never hit it off. She accused Prince of being jealous that she'd had a hit with one of his songs without his involvement. Prince had tried to reclaim his own song back and began including it on his 1990 European tour as a duet with his backing singer, Rosie Gaines. In conjunction, a promotional-only greatest hits album was issued to radio stations cheekily entitled *Nothing Compares 2 Him*. Sinéad said, "Prince hasn't a clue what life is like for ordinary people. He's got a huge ego."

In 1992 her appearance on *Saturday Night Live* caused controversy when, during a rendition of 'War' she ripped up a picture of the Pope when she got to the line, 'We have confidence in the victory of good over evil'. Two years later Sinéad, who occasionally claims she is a lesbian although she has two children by different men, announced that she was being ordained as a priest in the Latin Tridentine Church, claiming, "My soul is worth a lot more than money."

After contributing the song 'Harbour' to Moby's 2002 album *18*, Sinead started struggling with chronic fatigue syndrome and was advised to rest. In 2003 she declared via her website that she would 'be retiring from the music business in order to pursue a different career.'

642 Beats International featuring Lindy
Dub Be Good To Me

Label & Cat No.: **Go Beat GOD 39**

Producer: **Norman Cook**

Writers: **Norman Cook / James Harris III / Terry Lewis**

Date Reached No.1: **3 March 1990**

Weeks at No.1: **4**

During the Eighties, the Hull-based Housemartins had six Top 40 entries including 'Happy Hour' and the chart topping 'Caravan Of Love'. After they split in 1988 the bass player Norman Cook formed a new band, Beats International.

Norman brought in Luke Cresswell (drums), Andy Boucher (keyboards) and singer Lindy Layton, who had appeared in *Grange Hill* and *Casualty* as well as a number of television adverts. She had also been in a band with Daniel James from Yell and recorded one solo single, 'Wait For Love' but it was never released.

"Credit where credit's due," said Norman. "It was Lindy's idea to do a cover of the S.O.S. Band's 1984 hit 'Just Be Good To Me'. I knew it would go well with other beats because I'd tried it as a DJ. I used the bassline from The Clash song 'Guns Of Brixton', which was me tipping my hat to The Clash as I was such a big fan. I also wanted to do something slower than the current house music, yet something funky you could get into." The spoken rap 'Tank fly boss walk jam nitty gritty, you're listening to the boy from the big bad city, this is jam hot' is swiped from Double Trouble's 'Stoop Rap' which was used on the *Wild Style* soundtrack.

The follow-up, 'Won't Talk About It', reached the Top 10 and after a further four minor hits the group disbanded. Lindy launched a solo career and had Top 40 hits with 'Silly Games' and 'We Got The Love'. Norman, who continues DJing, darted between one act and another and was involved with hits under various guises such as Freak Power ('Turn On, Tune In, Cop Out'), Pizzaman ('Sex On The Streets' and 'Trippin' On Sunshine') and Mighty Dub Katz ('Magic Carpet Ride') before going completely solo and settling on the name Fatboy Slim.

643 Snap!
The Power

Label & Cat No.: **Arista 113 133**

Producer: **Snap!**

Writers: **Benito Benites / John Garrett**

Date Reached No.1: **31 March 1990**

Weeks at No.1: **2**

Just six months after Loleatta Holloway threatened Black Box with legal action for stealing her vocals for 'Ride On Time' along came Snap! who tried to get away with the same trick.

Snap! were formed in Pennsylvania by two German producers, Michael Munzing and Luca Anzilotti. They recruited rapper Turbo B and his cousin, singer Jackie Arlissa Harris. Turbo was born Durron Butler, but his friends nicknamed him Turbo because of his resemblance to the character Turbo in his favourite film *Break In*.

Snap!'s number one led to court cases over copyright infringement; foreground: Jackie Harris, and Turbo B at a London awards ceremony

HITS
HITS
HITS

They moved back to Germany and assembled a 12-inch track for Germany's Logic Records, called 'The Power'.

'The Power' heavily borrowed the rap from New York rapper Chill Rob G's song 'Let The Words Flow', whilst the song's hook line, 'I've Got The Power' was lifted from Jocelyn Brown's 'Love's Gonna Get You'. Rob G knew his song had potential and rather than instigate legal proceedings, he re-recorded his song under the pseudonym Power Jam Featuring Chill Rob B and borrowed bits from Snap!'s version. Jocelyn was not best pleased and won her case in court to get the credit she deserved. "I respect the fact that folks appreciate what we do and want to use it to collaborate. I just think they need to do the right things first. I wouldn't have minded if they'd asked first," she stated in an interview with *Billboard* magazine.

Snap! followed 'The Power' with the Top 10 hits 'Ooops Up', 'Cult Of Snap', 'Mary Had A Little Boy' and a megamix of the first four hits. The album *World Power* also made the Top 10.

To this day, Turbo B still insists that he did the first version of 'The Power' and says, "I was talked out of it at first because it was 'too hard' and wouldn't sell, and only softies like Milli Vanilli make it." And just look how well their careers turned out!

644 Madonna
Vogue

Label & Cat No.: **Sire W 9851**
Producers: **Madonna / Shep Pettibone**
Writers: **Madonna / Shep Pettibone**
Date Reached No.1: **14 April 1990**
Weeks at No.1: **4**

THE VOGUE WAS AN UNDERGROUND dance being performed in New York's gay and Hispanic nightclubs during the late Eighties. Madonna's best friend, Debi Mazar, first noticed the craze, which involved hypnotic hand movements, whilst out clubbing with Madonna. Madonna then took the idea to Shep Pettibone, a New York DJ turned producer who she had recently begun working with, and they wrote the song together.

Debi was stunned by the way these men would shout 'Strike A Pose', whilst holding their bodies in strange positions. Madonna decided to copy the posing which can be seen in the videos to both 'Vogue' and her 1989 hit 'Express Yourself'.

Sire Records wanted to release one more track from the *Like A Prayer* album and they decided it would be 'Keep It Together' with 'Vogue' as the B-side. When Shep played 'Vogue' to the executives at Sire, they flipped. Shep remembered, "The record company went bananas, her manager went bananas too. Everyone did. Everybody agreed that the song was too good to waste on a B-side." In the end 'Keep It Together was released in America in its own right with an instrumental version on the flip side and peaked at number eight. 'Vogue', which pays homage to, amongst other film greats, Marilyn Monroe, Marlon Brando, James Dean and Katharine Hepburn, was the follow-up and reached number one.

In 1990 Madonna commissioned Jean-Paul Gaultier to design clothes for her forthcoming Blonde Ambition world tour. One of her most memorable outfits was the gold basque with a pointed cone-shaped bra she wore.

When *Shanghai Surprise* bombed, Madonna vowed never to appear in a movie again, but in 1996 when offered the part, she relished the idea of portraying Argentina's first lady, Eva Peron, in the movie version of Tim Rice and Andrew Lloyd-Webber's *Evita*.

The part suited Madonna as both her and Eva Peron had a hunger for the admiration of the masses as well as a driving ambition. When the show opened, Madonna finally received some glowing reviews. By this time, Madonna wasn't too concerned. She was pregnant and was more anxious about her impending motherhood.

'Vogue' was followed by three straight UK number twos for Madonna: 'Hanky Panky', 'Justify My Love' and a remix of 'Crazy For You'. She would have to wait almost eight years for her next UK chart topper.

645 Adamski
Killer

Label & Cat No.: **MCA MCA 1400**
Producer: **Adamski**
Writers: **Adamski / Seal**
Date Reached No.1: **12 May 1990**
Weeks at No.1: **4**

IT WAS HIS FASCINATION WITH PUNK that pushed Adamski, who was born Adam Tinley in 1967 in Leamington, into music. "I can remember sitting watching *Top Of The Pops* waiting for The Sex Pistols to come on so I could see what punk looked and sounded like. Then on came Emerson, Lake & Palmer doing 'Fanfare For The Common Man' and I mistook them for The Sex Pistols. But I really got into the punk thing. I started putting food colouring in my hair and used to pogo at the school disco."

In 1978 Adam's older brother, Mark joined a group at school, so Adam began writing songs with his younger brother Dominic. They called themselves The Stupid Babies and recorded the song 'Babysitters', a protest song about, yes, you've guessed it, babysitters. During the mid-Eighties he changed his name to Adam Schmuck and joined a hip-hop group called Diskord Datkord.

Adamski became interested in house music after meeting Chicago house DJ, Jimi Polo. He also learned the basics of the sequencer from Polo. His first record was the instrumental, 'N-R-G' which reached number 12, but he ran into problems when he put a bottle of Lucozade on the sleeve and the company threatened to sue. Adamski's dog, Dis, named after Discordia, the Greek Goddess of chaos and confusion, appeared on all Adamski's record sleeves and was even allowed into the *Top Of The Pops* studio.

He had the idea of recording acid-house backing tracks and bringing in different singers to front them. The first was an instrumental called 'Killer' and the first singer he hired was Seal, although he wasn't credited on the single. Adam said, "I met him in a club when he approached me to tell me he was a singer. Just hearing the things he was talking about, I thought he was brilliant, so I became friends with him. He wrote the lyrics to the song and then recorded it in one take."The title doesn't appear in the lyrics and the words make no hint towards it either.

The next single, 'A Space Jungle' sampled Elvis Presley's 'All Shook Up and made it into the Top 10. The album, *Liveandirect*, wasn't quite as successful. It failed to make the Top 40 and spent a mere 12 weeks on the chart. Seal launched his own solo career and his first hit, 'Crazy' went to number two. In November 1991 Seal released the *Killer... On The Loose* EP and the lead track was a re-recorded version of 'Killer' which went to number eight.

646 Englandneworder
World In Motion

Label & Cat No.:	**Factory FAC 293**
Producer:	**Stephen Hague**
Writers:	**New Order / Keith Allen**
Date reached No.1:	**6 June 1990**
Weeks at No.1:	**2**

ROB GRETTON AND TONY WILSON'S Factory label in Manchester encouraged wayward but innovative (and often drug-fuelled) talent, who performed at their Hacienda club. Joy Division recorded the classic 'Love Will Tear Us Apart' in 1980 and after Ian Curtis' suicide, the band regrouped as New Order. They had Top 10 singles with 'Blue Monday' (1983) and 'True Faith' (1987). The group were so far off the main-stream that they were an unlikely choice for the official World Cup single. However, the sugges-tion came to Tony Wilson from the PR for the team, David Bloomfield.

Barney Sumner from New Order asked the anarchic, alternative actor/comedian, Keith Allen, for some lyrics. Two other members of New Order, Steve Morris and Gillian Gilbert had already written a theme for BBC2's *Reportage* and they thought the same music could be used. The single was recorded by top producer, Stephen Hague (OMD, Pet Shop Boys and 'True Faith'), at Mill Studios, owned by Jimmy Page.

The England World Cup Squad, chosen by manager Bobby Robson, was John Barnes (Liverpool), Peter Beardsley (Liverpool), Steve Bull (Wolves), Terry Butcher (Rangers), Tony Dorigo (Chelsea), Paul Gascoigne (Spurs), Steve Hodge (Notts Forest), Gary Lineker (Spurs), Steve McMahon (Liverpool), Paul Parker (QPR), Stuart Pearce (Notts Forest), David Platt (Aston Villa), Bryan Robson (Manchester Utd), David Seaman (Arsenal). Peter Shilton (Derby County), Trevor Steven (Rangers), Gary Stevens (Rangers), Chris Waddle (Olympique de Marseille, France), Des Walker (Notts Forest), Neil Webb (Manchester Utd), Chris Woods (Rangers) and Mark Wright (Derby County). When the squad arrived in Italy, the goalkeeper David Seaman injured his thumb and was replaced by Dave Beasant (Chelsea).

The England World Cup Squad duly sang 'World In Motion' with the rap performed by John Barnes, born in Kingston, Jamaica. There is an outtake featuring an unintelligible rap from another Liverpool player in the squad, Peter Beardsley. It is not the best lyric ever to reach number one as, needing a three syllable line to follow We're singing for England", the response is "Eng-er-land". Still, it helped to sell the record.

The England team went to Italy where the giant-killers, Cameroons, defeated the defending champions, Argentina, and were only beaten in extra time by England. Germany beat the hapless Argentina in the final and, losing 2-1 on penalties against Italy, England were fourth. But the single topped the charts.

One of the most replayed moments in foot-ball history follows Gazza (Paul Gascoigne) receiving his second yellow card. He wept as he realised he would not play in the final if England won the semi-final. England came third in the contest. Later that year, Gazza and his friends, Lindisfarne, revived 'Fog On The Tyne' and Alan Hull's bittersweet song about life on the dole in Newcastle made number two.

Following the success of the single, Tony Wilson became embroiled over the royalties on T-shirts. As the squad failed to qualify in 1994, there was no official single.

647 Elton John
Sacrifice / Healing Hands

Label & Cat No.:	**Rocket/Phonogram EJS 22**
Producer:	**Chris Thomas**
Writers:	**Elton John / Bernie Taupin**
Date Reached No.1:	**23 June 1990**
Weeks at No.1:	**5**

AFTER NEARLY 20 YEARS OF HIT SINGLES and albums, Elton must have wondered if he was ever going to have a solo number one hit in his own country.

Elton was born Reginald Kenneth Dwight in Pinner, Middlesex in 1947. As a young boy, he idolised Winifred Atwell and began taking piano lessons. In 1958 he joined a local band The Corvettes and three years later they changed their name to Bluesology. They expand-ed to a nine piece, which included singer Long John Baldry.

In the late Sixties, he broke away and at an audition for Liberty Records was too scared to sing his own songs so gave a rendition of two Jim Reeves hits. The audition wasn't a success but he was given some lyrics which had been submitted to the label by Bernie Taupin. The pair made contact and so blossomed a long and healthy songwriting partnership. At that time he also changed his name, taking the Elton from Bluesology sax player Elton Dean and John from Long John Baldry.

Elton had always supported his local football team and in 1974, he became a member of Wat-ford Football Club's board of directors. The club was £40,000 in debt, so Elton generously agreed to perform a benefit concert. Tickets were priced at £2 and it drew a crowd of 30,000 helping the club to get back in the black.

In the summer of 1989 'Healing Hands' hit the UK chart but stalled at number 45. Three months later, the follow-up 'Sacrifice' peaked 10 places lower. With the exception of the live version of 'Candle In The Wind' in 1988, Elton hadn't had a Top 10 hit since 1985. Bernie Taupin described 'Healing Hands' as an updated version of the Four Tops' 'Reach Out I'll Be

There', only slightly more religious. Elton noted, "The Impressions were a big influence on this album and 'Healing Hands' is probably where they made their mark".

'Sacrifice', which was about infidelity, continued to receive hefty radioplay, so Rocket decided to reissued the single with the previous single and promoted it as a double A-side and, so, after 66 releases, Elton finally got his first solo chart topper.

Just before the song reached the top, Elton decided that he wanted to do more than just donate the royalties from this single to AIDS charities, so he announced on the Terry Wogan show, that the royalties from all future UK hit singles would be spread between four different AIDS charities. He then quipped, "My manager has just fainted in the dressing room".

648 Partner In Kryme
Turtle Power

Label & Cat No.: **SBK TURTLE 1**
Producers: **James Alpern / Richard Usher**
Writers: **James Alpern / Richard Usher**
Date Reached No.1: **28 July 1990**
Weeks at No.1: **4**

THE TEENAGE MUTANT NINJA TURTLES began life as four pizza-eating cartoon characters called Michelangelo, Leonardo, Donatello and Raphael in an American comic book. They had their own 'turtle-speak' and spawned a multitude of turtle products like turtle T-shirts, turtle games, turtle pyjamas, turtle toothbrushes and even turtle breakfast cereals.

Next came the film. *Teenage Mutant Ninja Turtles* was created by the Muppets' inventor, Jim Henson and involved four actors dressing up in green, pyrotechnic turtle outfits. Apparently they mutated from ordinary reptiles when they were accidentally dropped in a New York sewer, which just happened to be full of radioactive slime. They then became talking teenage turtles. Incidentally, a 'ninja' is a Japanese shadow warrior.

DJ James Alpern and rapper Richard James were a black and white hip-hop duo from New York who used the alter-egos, Keymaster Snow and MC Golden Voice respectively and recorded under the group name Partners In Kryme. Kryme stands for Keeping Real Your Motivating Energy. "Our record company offered us the challenge and we took it on," James explained. "We were really knocked out about it. We wrote 'Turtle Power' over a weekend and everyone loved it and everything came together really quickly." The song is heard a few minutes into the movie whilst the turtles are beating up muggers, displaying their martial art skills.

"It's great having a number one with your first record," explained James, "but you run the risk of becoming a novelty act. People thought we were created for the movie, but we're a working group with our own material and we are *not* a novelty act." Maybe not, but they are one-hit-wonders.

The soundtrack album reached the Top 10 and includes the Top 20 hit single, 'Spin The Wheel' by Hi-Tek 3 featuring Ya Kid K.

649 Bombalurina
Itsy Bitsy Teeny Weeny Yellow Polka Dot Bikini

Label & Cat No.: **Carpet CRPT 1**
Producer: **Nigel Wright**
Writers: **Paul Vance / Lee Pockriss**
Date reached No.1: **25 August 1990**
Weeks at No.1: **3**

IN 1960 THE TEENAGE SINGER BRIAN Hyland would go to the New York's Brill Building hoping for a record deal. His first single for Kapp Records, 'Rosemary', did not sell but the second had more promise. Brian recalls, "We had cut 'Don't Dilly Dally, Sally' but Kapp wanted something stronger for the A-side. Paul Vance and Lee Pockriss had shown 'Itsy Bitsy Teeny Weeny Yellow Polka Dot Bikini' to a lot of singers but no one wanted to do it. Kapp thought it was right for me and got really excited about it. It was a number one hit in America which meant that I could stop riding on the subway and buy some Martin guitars."

Nowadays Brian Hyland is better remembered for his classy ballads, 'Ginny Come Lately' and 'Sealed With A Kiss' but whenever he comes to the UK for a Sixties tour, he includes 'Itsy Bitsy' in his stage act with his wife Rosemari chanting the female's part. His son, Bodi, plays the drums and Brian surprises many of the audience by playing raunchy rock'n'roll.

Timmy Mallett began broadcasting while he was studying at Warwick University and then he worked for Radio Oxford and Piccadilly Radio in Manchester. The wacky and highly excitable entertainer replaced Roland Rat as the children's favourite on TV-AM and then presented his own shows, *The Wide Awake Club* (1984-9) with Carol Vorderman and *Wacaday* (1985-92). *Wacaday* featured a word game which incorporated an oversized large pink sponge mallet, known as Mallett's Mallet. He would attack celebrities with his mallet, including Mrs. Thatcher, and he wore the most outrageous spectacles this side of Elton John.

In 1990 Andrew Lloyd Webber told Timmy to revive 'Itsy Bitsy' and he recorded the song at Nigel Wright's Scratch Studios in Chertsey, Surrey. Andrew Lloyd Webber released it under the name of Bombalurina, one of the felines in *Cats*, and a new label, Carpet, was formed. When Timmy went on location, he played the song in a nightclub in Crete and the DJ told him it would be a monster hit. He returned to the UK full of confidence.

As luck would have it, *The Sun* spotted Princess Diana in a bikini and ran the headline, Itsy Bitsy's Di's A Dream In Her Bikini', which helped Timmy into the charts. When Timmy was on *Top Of The Pops*, the two girls, Dawn and Anne (that is, the rest of Bombalurina), danced a routine based on Madonna's 'Vogue'. Dawn was to marry Gary Barlow.

When he was convinced it would be number one, Andrew Lloyd Webber threw a party at his mansion in Berkshire and everything stopped for Bruno Brookes' chart rundown on Radio 1. A few weeks later Timmy married Lynda Bingham in Wye and said, "I may be number one, but it's nothing compared to be being married to the number one girl in the world." We're glad to hear that because the follow-up, 'Seven Little Girls (Sitting in The Backseat)', only made the Top 20 and the album, *Huggin' And A Kissin'*, stiffed.

When the gloss wore off, Timmy Mallett devised a stage show for universities and he is a pantomime star who has the kids singing along to 'Itsy Bitsy'. In 2004 he was on the substitute bench for *I'm A Celebrity... Get Me Out Of Here* and although none of the celebs walked out, he generated publicity by singing 'Itsy Bitsy' from the top of Sydney Harbour Bridge.

650 Steve Miller Band
The Joker

Label & Cat No.: **Capitol CL 583**

Producer: **Steve Miller**

Writers: **Steve Miller / Eddie Curtis**

Date Reached No.1: **15 September 1990**

Weeks at No.1: **2**

SOME PEOPLE CALL HIM THE SPACE cowboy, some call him the gangster of love. Some people call him Maurice... but we know him as guitar player, Steve Miller.

Miller, who was born in Wisconsin in 1943, formed his first band, The Marksmen, with school friend Boz Scaggs. A few years later, at the University Of Wisconsin, the pair fronted a soul band, The Fabulous Night Trains. After college, Miller moved to Chicago, met keyboard player Barry Goldberg and formed a new band called The Goldberg-Miller Blues Band. Scaggs later joined them and they signed a contract with Capitol Records.

In 1968 Miller left to start his own band with a varying line-up, playing a mix of blues and rock. His first single, 'Living In The U.S.A.' only just scraped into the US chart. Two years later, his next hit, 'Going To The Country', fared a little better. He also had US hit albums with *Sailor*, *Brave New World*, *Your Saving Grace* and *Number 5*. In 1973, with a line-up of Steve Miller on vocals, guitar and harmonica, Gerald Johnson on bass and John King on drums, he released *The Joker* which shot to number two and the title track, which was the first single from it, reached number one in America and brought his music to a new audience. Miller was making his name as an albums artist, so when he landed a chart topping hit, it was the icing on the cake.

The lyric to 'The Joker' may have had some people wondering what he was singing about. The first verse credits various Miller songs over the past years: 'Space Cowboy' was on *Brave New World* (1969), 'Gangster Of Love' on *Sailor* (1968) and 'Maurice', from the track 'Enter Maurice', on *Recall The Beginning* (1972). Miller's early doo-wop influences can also be spotted in 'Enter Maurice', which lyrically bares a resemblance to the 1954 R&B song 'The Letter' by The Medallions. Another mystery was the meaning of the word 'pompitous', or 'pompatus' as it's written on The Medallions' sheet music, which also appeared in 'Enter Maurice'. The Medallions' singer/songwriter Vernon Green revealed that the actual word in question was 'puppetutes' which he invented to mean 'a secret paper-doll fantasy figure'. The Joker itself is yet another reference to 'Enter Maurice'. The line 'I really love your peaches, want to shake your tree, lovey-dovey lovey-dovey lovey-dovey all the time' can be found in the first verse of The Clovers' 1953 song 'Lovey-Dovey'. And, a 'midnight toker'? Well, that would be someone who partakes in a 'herbal jazz cigarette' late in the evening.

Steve Miller first hit the UK chart in 1976 with 'Rock 'N' Me' which reached number 11. 'Swingtown' and 'Jungle Love' were two worthy releases but failed to attract the record buying public. His next hit came six years later when 'Abracadabra' reached number two.

'The Joker', which Steve Miller professed he wrote in half an hour, was re-issued after its use in a Levi 501 television commercial. The week it reached number one, Dee-lite's 'Groove Is In The Heart' was at number two. Controversy raged at the chart compilers, Gallup, because although both songs shared equal panel sales, Dee-lite were denied a joint number one placing. A panel sale is the average figure used from all the outlets that record the sale of records. The row was fuelled by *The Sun* who carried the headline: 'Fury over top chart slot fix'. Chart manager, John Pinder at Gallup said, "The rule is: if there are equal total sales, the computer automatically promotes the act which has shown the greatest increase from its previous chart position." In reply, Dee-lite's record company chairman, Rob Dickens, issued a statement which said, "If statistics can wreak havoc with a group's career, we will seriously have to rethink our commitment to the chart." So far, there's been no reoccurrence. Chart statistician, Alan Jones explained, "Technically the report is correct. 'The Joker's' sales increased by 52% whereas 'Groove Is In The Heart' increased by only 37%. This method of tie-breaking has been used by Gallup since 1983 with the full knowledge of the British record industry, but it's the first time it's been used to determine a number one and the first time anyone has complained."

When the figures were broken down and more closely examined, it was determined that Steve Miller has sold exactly eight more copies than Dee-Lite.

651 Maria McKee
Show Me Heaven

Label & Cat No.: **Epic 656 303 7**

Producer: **Paul Staveley O'Duffy**

Writers: **Joshua Rifkin / Eric Rackin / Maria McKee**

Date Reached No.1: **29 September 1990**

Weeks at No.1: **4**

MARIA MCKEE, WHO WAS BORN IN Los Angeles in 1964, has been mixing in celebrity circles since she was a toddler. Her father, Jack, was a Hollywood film extra and her half-brother, Bryan MacLean, a member of psychedelic band, Love, was dating Liza Minnelli. As a five year-old Maria was introduced to Frank Zappa.

Maria used to sing along to Barbra Streisand songs on the radio and as Bryan remembered, "It was a friend Gabriel Ferrer who discovered

her. I didn't pick up on her until he said I should, then I listened to her and realised her voice was exquisitely brilliant." Bryan took Maria into the studio to sing some songs. "Maria had no self confidence," Bryan said, "but she did a beautiful job." So they formed a duo called The Maria McKee Band, but as Bryan said, "We changed it to The Bryan MacLean Band because my name was more well-known through Love."

After the duo split in early 1985, Maria formed her own country-rock band, Lone Justice, which included her boyfriend, keyboard player Benmont Tench. She moved to Dublin and began writing her own songs but was also given songs by Bob Dylan ('Go 'Way Little Boy') and Tom Petty ('Ways To Be Wicked'). After she and Tench split, she wrote 'A Good Heart' about their relationship which her friend Feargal Sharkey took to number one.

Lone Justice, who had one UK hit with 'I Found Love', split in 1987 and Maria began a solo career. She toured extensively impressing many, including Deacon Blue's Ricky Ross, who wrote 'Real Gone Kid' about her.

Joshua Rifkin and Eric Rackin wrote the original lyrics for 'Show Me Heaven' for the film *Days of Thunder*. However, Maria didn't like some of the lyrics and only agreed to record it if she could re-write some of them. The film tells the story of Cole Trickle (Tom Cruise) as a young inexperienced stock car driver who attempts to make it to the top, on the way falling in love with Dr Claire Lewicki (Nicole Kidman). It was that film where the couple first met and led to their own real-life marriage. In 1991 at Linda Ronstadt's recommendation, Maria signed to Geffen Records and had minor UK-only hits with 'Sweetest Child' and 'I'm Gonna Soothe You'. She recorded the album *Life Is Sweet* in 1996 but that failed to chart in both the UK and the US. After a seven-year hiatus, Maria returned in 1993 with her new album, *High Dive*.

'Show Me Heaven', which never charted in the US, was covered by Tina Arena in 1995 and a dance version by Saint featuring Suzanne Dee made the Top 40 in 2003. Maria also re-recorded the song in 1993 as a duet with Cheap Trick's Robin Zander.

652 The Beautiful South
A Little Time

Label & Cat No.: **Go! Discs GOD 47**

Producer: **Mike Hedges**

Writers: **Paul Heaton / Dave Rotheray**

Date Reached No.1: **27 October 1990**

Weeks at No.1: **1**

After The Housemartins split up in 1988, bass player Norman Cook formed Beats International and had a number one with 'Dub Be Good To Me'. Two other members, Paul Heaton and Dave Hemingway formed The Beautiful South, a wry comment about everywhere south of their home city, Hull, especially south London, and recruited guitarist Dave Rotheray, bassist Sean Welch and drummer Dave Stead. Paul brought in Irish-born, London-based singer Briana Corrigan after he heard a demo tape of her group, The Anthill Runaways, which was sent to their record company.

Their debut album, *Welcome To The Beautiful South* depicted a young girl on the sleeve with a gun in her mouth. After numerous complaints, the sleeve was redesigned and showed a bunch of cuddly toys. The first two singles lifted from it, 'Song For Whoever' and 'You Keep It All In' both made the Top 10. A third single, 'I'll Sail This Ship Alone' only reached number 35.

Work began on their next album *Choke*. The first release was a duet between Briana and Dave Hemingway, but the writers, Paul Heaton and Dave Rotheray, couldn't decide if it was a love song or not. Lyricist Heaton explained, "It's a relationship song which I probably did write from personal experience. I've been in a situation myself where I said 'I need a little time'." Songwriter Dave Rotheray, on the other hand, said, "It's still a love song, but it doesn't follow the same path as every other love song." Briana added, "'A Little Time' is a common situation. Love's not always pretty, it can be a really horrible situation and not many people sing about that."

The accompanying video opens with the pair in a very untidy living room, 'discussing' their relationship. The second scene shows Dave with a number of kitchen knives in the wall behind him, while the third scene reveals that the couple had been fighting and were left covered in feathers. It won Best Music Video at the Brit Awards in 1991.

In 1992 they recorded '36D', a song about *The Sun* newspaper's topless Page 3 models. The lyrical content upset Briana enough to leave the band. She was replaced by Jacqueline Abbott whose atmospheric voice is well demonstrated on 'Everybody's Talkin''. The 1996 single 'Don't Marry Her' was re-recorded with amended lyrics for the single as the album version contained the line 'Don't marry her, fuck me' as Terry Wogan found out to his surprise when he played it on his Radio 2 breakfast show one morning, thus proving that nobody bothered checking it beforehand.

In 2003 Jacqueline, feeling that she wasn't appreciated enough, left and the 'South' continued without a female singer. In 2004 when Paul was asked if he missed having a female singer in the band he said, "Yes. And going by the new lyrics I've written, we're gonna need one."

653 The Righteous Brothers
Unchained Melody

Label & Cat No.: **Verve/ Polydor PO 101**

Producer: **Phil Spector**

Writers: **Alex North / Hy Zaret**

Date reached No.1: **3 November 1990**

Weeks at No.1: **4**

The song is called 'Unchained Melody' because it was written for the 1955 prison drama, *Unchained*, but everybody associates it with the moulded clay scene in the 1990 film, *Ghost*. In the most erotic moment to be found in a standard, commercial film, Demi Moore's pottery wheel collapses as she is

The Beautiful South blended perfect harmony with subtle irony, left to right: Dave Rotheray, Sean Welch, Briana Corrigan, Paul Heaton and Dave Hemingway.

distracted by Patrick Swayze's intentions – and The Righteous Brothers' singing 'Unchained Melody'. Many people bought the record because they wanted some of that for themselves. It also prompted two best selling albums -the soundtrack of *Ghost* and *The Very Best Of The Righteous Brothers*.

After their number one hit with 'You've Lost That Lovin' Feelin'' in 1965, The Righteous Brothers recorded an underrated ballad by Gerry Goffin and Carole King, 'Just Once In My Life' (US 9), and then released 'Hung On You'. The high-voiced Bobby Hatfield became disillusioned with Bill Medley taking the lead vocals and Spector placated him by recording solo performances of the oldies, 'Unchained Melody' and 'Ebb Tide'. 'Unchained Melody' was placed on the B-side of 'Hung On You', but US radio stations preferred that side and it reached number four. 'Unchained Melody' was released as an A-side in the UK and made number 14.

Late in 1965 both Brothers became disillusioned with Spector claiming the credit for their successes and they moved to Verve, where Bill Medley set about duplicating Spector's sound on '(You're My) Soul And Inspiration' and doing it very effectively. The duo split in 1967 but Medley retained the name and worked with a new partner, Jimmy Walker. In 1987 Medley had a US number one with '(I've Had) The Time Of My Life', a duet with Jennifer Warnes, from the film, *Dirty Dancing*, again starring Patrick Swayze.

In recent years, the original Righteous Brothers had reformed but Bobby Hatfield died just minutes they were due to perform in Michigan in November 2003.

654 Vanilla Ice
Ice Ice Baby

Label & Cat No.: **SBK SBK 18**

Producer: **Vanilla Ice**

Writers: **Vanilla Ice / Earthquake / David Bowie / Freddie Mercury / Brian May / John Deacon / Roger Taylor**

Date Reached No.1: **1 December 1990**

Weeks at No.1: **4**

"I'M GONNA TAKE RAP INTO A NEW dimension," announced Vanilla Ice on his arrival in the UK for a tour supporting MC Hammer. Or as Ice, as he liked to be known, put it, "I'm not supporting him, we're on the same bill and it's *our* show."

Born Robert Van Winkle in Miami Lakes, Florida in 1968, he claims he got the nickname Vanilla because of his complexion and because he rapped all the time at school where he was the leader of the 2 Live Crew. "I just added 'Ice' on the end because it fitted really well."

In his hometown, he was a celebrity motocross racer. He won three national championships, but a serious accident, involving two broken ankles, put a stop to that. In 1987 while on holiday in Dallas, Texas, his friend entered him into a talent contest at the City Lights club. He walked on stage with just a microphone, rapped for half an hour and won the contest. In the audience were various record company executives, a number of whom wanted to sign him up.

Tommy Quon, who owned both the club and Ultratrax Records signed Ice the next day. He said in *Rolling Stone*, "He wasn't that great as a rapper but he had charisma and style." Quon employed some black dancers and let him open for club residents, Paula Abdul and Public Enemy.

'Ice Ice Baby' generously borrows the bass line from Queen and David Bowie's 'Under Pressure', which Queen sued him over, and was originally the B-Side of his debut single, a cover of Wild Cherry's 'Play That Funky Music'. Still unsigned, it was a DJ on a radio station in Columbus, Georgia who began playing the flip that led to Ice being signed up by SBK Records. When 'Ice Ice Baby' topped the US chart, Ice became the first rapper to achieve that status. That same week, SBK deleted the single in the hope it would increase sales of his debut album, *To The Extreme*. It did, and went on to sell over seven million copies.

Ice, who had little acting experience, appeared in the sequel to *Teenage Ninja Mutant Turtles - The Secret Of Ooze*, and re-issued 'Play That Funky Music' which went to number 10. He also achieved Top 30 hits with 'Rollin' In My 5.0' and a cover of 'Satisfaction'.

In 2004 VH1 started a new series called *Remaking Of The Artist* in which Vanilla was one of the first to be featured. His girlfriend owns a surf-shop which she called To The Extreme, after Ice's album.

655 Cliff Richard
Saviour's Day

Label & Cat No.: **EMI XMAS 90**

Producers: **Cliff Richard / Paul Moessl**

Writer: **Chris Eaton**

Date reached No.1: **29 December 1990**

Weeks at No.1: **1**

OUTSIDE OF THE ARCHBISHOP OF Canterbury, Cliff Richard may be the UK's best-known Christian, and he has been making religious records since the Sixties. He included 'When I Survey The Wondrous Cross' in his cabaret act at the Talk Of The Town and he has often appeared on gospel tours. However, until the Eighties he was against Christmas singles, taking the view that they detracted from the original meaning of the festival. His opinion evidently changed in 1982 when he made the Christmas charts by updating 'O Little Town Of Bethlehem' as 'Little Town' in a new arrangement by Chris Eaton.

Chris Eaton is a Christian songwriter from Birmingham who first recorded as part of Lyrix in 1982. Since then he has made several solo albums and has written for Sheila Walsh, Amy Grant and Vince Gill. 'Breath Of Heaven (Mary's Song)' has been recorded by several contemporary Christian artists. Since the early Eighties, Cliff Richard has regularly included his songs on albums including 'Lost In A Lonely World', 'Joanna' and 'Let Me Be The One'. Chris often performs in public but you are more likely to catch his concerts in a church than a theatre.

In 1990 Cliff planned to release Julie Gold's plea for world peace, 'From A Distance', as a Christmas single. When Chris Eaton played him his new song, 'Saviour's Day', he changed his mind. 'From A Distance' was released in the autumn and who can say why it got no higher than number 11. The song became a Top 10 hit for Bette Midler in 1991.

Cliff's instincts about this Christmas single were correct as 'Saviour's Day' reached the top. Chris Eaton's own version was included on the 1995 compilation *Christmas Carols Of The Young Messiah*. His 1997 album, *Cruisin'*, was retitled *What Kind Of Love* as the word had other connotations in America. In 2003 he wrote another Christmas hit for Cliff, 'Santa's List', although this one was considerably weaker.

656 Iron Maiden
Bring Your Daughter... To The Slaughter

Label & Cat No.:	**EMI EM 171**
Producer:	**Martin Birch**
Writer:	**Bruce Dickinson**
Date Reached No.1:	**5 January 1991**
Weeks at No.1:	**2**

TAKING THEIR NAME FROM THE medieval torture instrument – a coffin with metal spikes driven through the inside of the lid, referred to in the film *The Man With The Iron Mask* – Iron Maiden were formed in 1975 by bass player, Steve Harris. The band's original lead singer was Paul Day but he was quickly replaced

by Dennis Wilcock who had been in Smiler with Steve. Over the next six years there were a number of personnel changes and by 1981 the more permanent line-up was: Steve, Bruce Dickinson (vocals), guitarist Dave Murray and drummer Clive Burr. Burr was replaced the following year by Nicko McBrain.

"The whole essence of music is knowing when to have quiet passages and when to have loud ones," says Bruce Dickinson, "and not everything we do is completely over the top. In comparison to a lot of chart acts, it may be fearsome stuff but then so is Blaster Bates."

Derek Riggs was the man responsible for designing 'Eddie', the evil looking skeleton that appeared on everything related to Iron Maiden. Even a life-size version that walked around the stage at gigs was created.

Their early releases included 'Running Free', 'Sanctuary', the sleeve of which showed Eddie stabbing Margaret Thatcher, and 'Twilight Zone', which all barely made the Top 30. Their third album, *The Number Of The Beast*, went to number one and its first single, 'Run To The Hills' went into the Top 10, becoming their first single to receive proper daytime radio play bringing them a new audience. Their next number one album came in 1988, entitled *Seventh Son Of A Seventh Son*. It spawned four Top 10 singles: 'Can I Play With Madness', 'The Evil That Men Do', 'The Clairvoyant' and 'Infinite Dreams'.

In 1990 Bruce Dickinson – whilst not leaving the band – embarked on a solo project and wrote 'Bring Your Daughter...To The Slaughter'. It was featured in *A Nightmare On Elm Street: The Dream Child* and it received a Golden Raspberry Award as the Worst Original Song. It was to be the opening track on his album *Tattooed Millionaire*, but when Steve Harris heard it he wanted it for Iron Maiden's next album. The song was re-recorded and appeared in *No Prayer For The Dying*.

When 'Bring Your Daughter...To The Slaughter' was released in the first week after Christmas, traditionally the quietest sales week of the year, there was a strategic marketing ploy to ensure the song debuted high. It was released on six different formats, hoping that hardcore Maiden fans bought the lot. In addition to the standard 7-inch single, it came in a 7-inch picture disc 'brain pack', a 12-inch with exclusive poster, a 12-inch picture disc, a cassette and a CD single.

Dickinson quit Iron Maiden in 1994 to continue a solo career and was replaced by ex-Wolfsbane singer, Blaze Bailey. He lasted four years until the band sacked him citing the time-honoured 'musical differences'. Realising that Dickinson's solo career was not really going anywhere, Harris invited him back to the band. He accepted.

In 2002 Bruce became a commercial pilot and now works as a first officer for the new British charter airline, Astreus. The same year, 'Run To The Hills' was re-issued with all proceeds being donated to their early drummer, Clive Burr's Multiple Sclerosis Trust Fund. They continued churning out singles, each one making the Top 20 but spending an average of three weeks on the chart. This song, with only five weeks, still holds the record for the fewest weeks on the chart for a number one hit.

657 Enigma
Sadness Part 1

Label & Cat No.:	**Virgin International DINS 101**
Producer:	**Michael Cretu**
Writers:	**Curly M.C / David Fairstein**
Date Reached No.1:	**19 January 1991**
Weeks at No.1:	**1**

"I WANT PEOPLE TO LISTEN TO MY MUSIC and buy it because they like what they heard. With me, there is no image, no pictures and no video, just musical interpretation," explained Enigma when he first burst onto the music scene in 1990.

Enigma was born Michael Cretu in the Romanian capital, Bucharest in May 1957. He moved to Munich in 1975 and had European hits under the guises Moti Special and Cretu & Theirs. He also produced some hit singles, including a cover of'Everlasting Love' for Sandra, whom he later married. In 1988 he moved again, this time to Ibiza where he still lives.

"I am not Enigma," Michael insisted, "I am the man who created Enigma. It's a project not an act. I use the name writing name Curly MC because Curly is Romanian for Cretu and of course MC are my initials, so in effect Curly MC means Cretu, Michael Cretu."

The original album title 'Sadeness', pronounced 'sadness', refers to the 18th century French author, the Marquis de Sade. In Britain it was released as 'Sadness Part 1' thus indicating that a Part 2 was to follow. Not so, as Enigma explained. "The reason I used that title is that I wanted to let everyone know that Enigma will have future releases and wasn't just a one-off project." 'Sadness' contains Gregorian chants from the sixth century. "Using a flute, chants and African rhythms together meant I could create something very different," said Michael. "What I tried to do was put together the most unlikely combination and make it work. That's why I used French lyrics penned by a Parisian friend, David Fairstein and were spoken by Sandra." Despite Michael initially saying there would no video, there was, but it didn't feature Sandra. "She was too well known in Europe so we used a French model instead."

'Sadness', which topped the charts in Belgium, Germany, France, Italy and Spain, was lifted from the debut album *MCMXCAD*, which is 1990 AD in Roman numerals. Enigma chose that title for two reasons, "It was the year of its album's birth, so to speak and it contains my initials twice."

Enigma had further hits with 'Mea Culpa Part II' which again incorporated his initials, 'Return To Innocence', 'The Eyes Of Truth' and 'Age Of Loneliness' which featured in the film, *Sliver*. The follow-up album, *The Cross Of Changes*, was credited to Enigma 2.

658 Queen
Innuendo

Label & Cat No.: **Parlophone QUEEN 16**

Producers: **Freddie Mercury / Brian May / Roger Taylor / John Deacon / Dick Richards**

Writers: **Freddie Mercury / Brian May / Roger Taylor / John Deacon**

Date Reached No.1: **26 January 1991**

Weeks at No.1: **1**

DURING 1989 AND 1990 QUEEN recorded what was to be their final official studio album. Freddie had known for a few years that he had contracted AIDS and by now his condition had deteriorated so much that a bed was set up in the recording studio so he could rest during takes.

Throughout the recording, the band knew Freddie was not well, but he hadn't actually told them. Even though the tabloids carried gossip headlines, no one knew what was wrong with Freddie – not even the band, until January 1991, when Freddie called a meeting at the Mountain Studios in Montreux, near where he had bought himself a hideaway house. It was then he turned to Brian, Roger and John and said, "You probably realise what my problem is". Once Freddie realised they did know, he said, "Well, that's it, I don't want it to make any difference, I don't want it to be known and I don't want to talk about it, I just want to get on and work until I can't work any more". Brian later recalled, "None of us will forget that day. We all went off and were quietly sick somewhere."

Although they realised they would never top 'Bohemian Rhapsody', the Latin-tinged 'Innuendo' was similar in length and structure with its varying tempos and style changes. The accompanying video only featured the band in animation with some very clever editing to look like Freddie was lip-synching.

The follow-up, 'I'm Going Slightly Mad' insinuated that Freddie was going mad. For the video, which was co-directed by Freddie, he made the rest of the band portray different symptoms of madness. Such was Freddie's condition, his make-up was caked on to hide the cracks in his face, and a wig was used to hide his thinning hair.

659 The KLF featuring The Children Of The Revolution
3am Eternal (Live At The S.S.L.)

Label & Cat No.: **KLF Communications KLF 005**

Producers: **Jimmy Cauty / Bill Drummond**

Writers: **Jimmy Cauty / Bill Drummond / Ricardo Lyte**

Date Reached No.1: **2 February 1991**

Weeks at No.1: **2**

THROUGHOUT THE SEVENTIES, Jonathan King was king of the pseudonyms, having charted under 10 different guises. The KLF were heading a similar way. They have used the names Lord Rock & Timeboy, The Timelords, King Boy D & Rockman, The Justified Ancients Of Mu Mu, The Jamms and TwoK. Either way, they are London born Jimmy Cauty and South African-born, Scottish-raised Bill Drummond.

Bill moved to Liverpool and enrolled in an art school in the Seventies before becoming involved in the punk scene. He was a member of the group Big In Japan with Ian Broudie and Holly Johnson and later went on to manage Echo & The Bunnymen and The Teardrop Explodes. After a stint as an A&R man at WEA Records, he left the management side to record an album for Creation Records called *The Man*. It included the bizarre songs 'Ballad Of A Sex God', 'Julian Cope Is Dead', (in response to Julian Cope's song, 'Bill Drummond Said') and 'Son Of A Preacher Man' (not the Dusty Springfield hit), which featured his father, the Rev Jack Drummond, narrating Robert Burns' anti-English poem 'Such A Parcel Of Rogues In a Nation.' His next goal was to make a hip-hop record, so he called his old friend Jimmy Cauty, who was in a group called Brilliant, and within a week they formed the Justified Ancients Of Mu Mu.

They have made a living out of sampling other artists' work, lifting lengthy segments of tracks by The Beatles, Led Zeppelin and Abba. Of the three, only Abba publicly objected and reported it to the Copyright Protection Society who ordered Bill and Jimmy to recall and destroy all copies. The lads went to Sweden to meet Abba and try to resolve the situation. Abba refused to see them, so they decided to head into a field and set fire to all 500 copies of the track. They also filmed the event of which a photograph can be seen on the front cover of the album *History Of The Jams*. In 1988 they released a book called *The Manual: How To Have A Number One The Easy Way*. Within, it guaranteed a number one within three months, or your money back.

In 1989, using the name The KLF, supposedly standing for The Kopyright Liberation Front, they issued the novelty track, 'Kylie Said To Jason', which stiffed. The following year and with a change of musical direction into the acid house and rave scene, they issued their next single, 'What Time Is Love?' which went to number five. The parent album, *The White Room*, which reached number three, was released a month after the next single, '3am Eternal' – the title of which refers to chucking out time at the Spectrum Acid House club in London – hit the top. The money from the single didn't last long. As Bill explained, "We spent it before we saw it. We had this idea to go to Spain with a film crew, who'd just finished working with Spielberg, and began making a movie called *The White Room* that cost us £250,000."

The single is credited to The KLF featuring The Children Of The Revolution, but as Jimmy Cauty explained, "You won't hear any of them. They consist of singers, accountants, rappers, taxi drivers, lawyers, photographers and pluggers that we hired from time to time." As the title describes the song as being 'live from the S.S.L.' you could be forgiven for thinking that the song was recorded before an audience. "The S.S.L. stands for Solid State Logic, a type of mixing desk popular in the early Nineties," Jimmy revealed.

The original 7-inch version of '3am Eternal' was first issued in November 1988. The 12-inch single that accompanied it confusingly went under the title 'Blue Danube Orbital'. Neither troubled the chart. It was remixed and featured vocals by Maxine Harvey and a rap by Ricardo Lyte. In 1992 at the Brit awards, the pair performed a thrash metal version under another pseudonym, Extreme Noise Terror.

The song's co-writer, Ricardo Lyte, is a DJ and rapper. He recalled, "I met Bill and Jimmy when I was DJing in Ibiza and I was impressed by how funny they were. We got talking and I liked the way they are quite prepared to use different influences. They liked my rapping and asked me to do some stuff on their album." The KLF had two further singles, both reaching number two, with 'Last Train To Trancentral' (which Ricardo also rapped on) and 'Justified and Ancient', which featured, as the single credits, the vocals of the First Lady Of Country, Miss Tammy Wynette.

During the Eighties they had set up an art organization called The K Foundation. Having made a fortune they decided to give £40,000 to Rachel Whiteread, the Turner Prize winner in 1994. Bill said, "We phoned her up and offered her the money. When she refused it, I told her that if she didn't take it, we were going to burn it."

Bill and Jimmy have always staged weird stunts, the most bizarre was during the night of August 23, 1994 when they supposedly took £1 million in British bank notes to an abandoned Scottish boathouse on the Isle of Jura and set fire to the lot. The burning question was why? Bill's explantion: "We filmed the event and took it around to different places, to a prison to ask if it was a crime, to a mental hospital to ask if it was madness, to Eton and to an inner city public school to ask if it was educational. We wanted to know why we had done it. Someone confronted us with the fact that it was a waste of time going round talking about it because all people wanted to know was did we do it? So we ended up signing a 23-year contract with this person that we would stop talking about it. We have had five years so there is another 18 to go before I can really talk about it." Jimmy's explanation: "It wasn't really a giggle. We were deadly serious about it. It's something we've always wanted to do."

660 The Simpsons Do The Bartman

Label & Cat No.:	**Geffen GEF 87**
Producer:	**Bryan Loren**
Writer:	**Bryan Loren**
Date Reached No.1:	**16 February 1991**
Weeks at No.1:	**3**

THE SIMPSONS HAS COME A LONG WAY since its humble beginnings as a five-minute sketch between ad breaks on the *Tracey Ullman Show* in 1987. Within a couple of years this groundbreaking show had made its debut on US prime-time television. Before this, a cartoon depicting such a truly dysfunctional all-American family was virtually unheard of, but kids (and adults) globally rapidly became hooked, buying up millions and millions of pounds of merchandise and in February 2003 it became the longest-running animated series ever. In the Nineties the record companies jumped on the bandwagon inviting The Simpsons to dip a yellow toe into the music pool.

Creator Matt Groening (sounds like 'raining') was born in Portland, Oregon in 1954, and developed an interest for drawing cartoons at an early age, thanks largely to his cartoonist father. He named the show's main characters after his own family: Homer (his dad), Marge (his mother) and Lisa and Maggie after his sisters. Choosing to forego his own namesake, he decided on Bart, an anagram of 'brat'. "Our family really isn't anything like *The Simpsons*. Out of all the episodes we've done so far, my family has never been bothered by anything on *The Simpsons*, except one time my Dad called me up and said, 'When the family's car broke down in the desert, Homer shouldn't have made Marge carry that flat tyre back to the gas station.' He was really bothered by that, and I said, 'Dad, this is a show where Homer skateboards off cliffs and strangles Bart and stuff, and that's what bothers you?'"

Bryan Loren is a native of Long Island, New York and a multi-talented multi-instrumentalist, songwriter, recording artist and producer, whose songwriting and production credits include

Michael Jackson – on which he provided percussion, drums and Moog synthesiser for his album *Dangerous* (1992), and played keyboards for Barry White on the song 'The Right Night' (1987). He was also one of several producers on Sting's 1987 release, *Nothing Like The Sun*.

The album *The Simpsons Sing The Blues,* which also included the UK number seven hit, 'Deep Deep Trouble', went on to sell over two million copies in the US. However, it was still surprising that 'Do The Bartman' had proved so popular here, as the series only began on Sky in September 1990 when satellite television was in its infancy. The first showing on British terrestrial television was not until more than six years later. The amusing accompanying video to the comical rap, 'Do The Bartman' was where most people saw *The Simpsons* for the first time.

The Simpsons is renowned for having the finest cameos of any television series. Appearances by recording artists such as Paul McCartney, George Harrison, Ringo Starr, U2, Aerosmith, Britney Spears, The Who, R.E.M., Mick Jagger & Keith Richards, Elvis Costello, Tom Jones, Tony Bennett, Sting, James Brown, Red Hot Chili Peppers, Bette Midler, The Moody Blues, B-52s and Elton John. 'John Jay Smith' also appeared – as a white, 300-pound mental patient, who thought he was the 'gloved one'. His voice was generously provided by an uncredited Michael Jackson.

The instrumentation is provided by Bryan Loren and Paul Jackson Jr with Bart's voice being supplied throughout by Kettering, Ohio-born Nancy Cartwright. Nancy, who studied with Daws Butler, the voice of Yogi Bear and Huckleberry Hound, knew from an early age that she had a gift for entertaining and spent her teens acting in a variety of amateur theatre productions. Nancy also had a small role doing additional voices on the Eighties-revived *Alvin & The Chipmunks* television series in the US. Thanks to the fame she received from *The Simpsons*, the Mayor of Kettering declared that 2nd November of every year is officially Nancy Cartwright Day. "I felt like the bride," she proclaimed.

Homer's famous disgruntled cry of 'Doh!' is now listed in the *Oxford English Dictionary*. Matt Groening explained that the word 'Doh!' was initially written in the script as 'Annoyed Grunt'. It was inspired by James Finlayson, the Scottish actor famous for his exaggerated double-takes in the Laurel & Hardy films.

661 The Clash
Should I Stay Or Should I Go?

Label & Cat No.: **Columbia 6566677**

Producer: **Mick Jones**

Writers: **Joe Strummer / Mick Jones / Paul Simonon / Topper Headon**

Date Reached No.1: **9 March 1991**

Weeks at No.1: **2**

In 1976 the London punk scene was calling and The Clash were in the right place at the right time. Assembling early that year and still known as The 101ers, Joe Strummer (born John Mellor) (vocals), Mick Jones (guitar), Paul Simonon (bass) and Nicky 'Topper' Headon (drums) began writing songs about oppression and against racism. Their early gigs were supported by The Sex Pistols. Bernie Rhodes, who used to print T-shirts for Malcolm McLaren, wanted to get in on the act and manage his own band, so he approached Strummer and offered to manage them and changed their name to The Clash. Rhodes was held in high esteem, so much so that even when punk started to fade and the mod revival began in 1979, The Specials opened their debut single, 'Gangsters' with the line 'Bernie Rhodes knows, don't argue'.

Rhodes secured them a recording contract with CBS in January 1977 and they immediately began recording 'White Riot' and '1977', the A and B-Sides of their debut single. Punk had exploded and competition was fierce. The Stranglers' album *Rattus Norvegicus* and The Clash's *Clash* both charted in the same week, but it was The Damned who beat them both by six weeks when *Damned Damned Damned* entered the chart in March 1977.

Within a few months, and possibly helped by the Pistols' behaviour seeing them banned from many venues, The Clash became the most important rock group in Britain. Further hits followed, 'Complete Control', 'Tommy Gun', 'English Civil War (When Johnny Comes Marching Home)', 'I Fought The Law' and 'London Calling' which all made the Top 30. The albums *Give 'Em Enough Rope* and *London Calling* both made the Top 10.

As the Eighties came and punk went, The Clash experimented with reggae and rap. Their 1982 album, *Combat Rock* went to number two in the UK and number seven Stateside and sold over a million copies worldwide. The first single from it, 'Know Your Rights' didn't make much impact but the next two hits, 'Rock The Casbah' and 'Should I Stay Or Should I Go?' / 'Straight To Hell' were more commercial and brought them a new audience. Just prior to the album's release, a few last minute changes were made to 'Should I Stay Or Should I Go?' causing Mick and Joe to fall out. It was re-recorded with the line 'If you want me off your back' replacing the original 'On your front or round the back'. It was too late for changes to be made for the album's sleeve notes, so some early copies showed the original lyric.

"'Should I Stay Or Should I Go?' wasn't about anything specific and it wasn't pre-empting my leaving The Clash. It was just a good rocking song, our attempt at writing a classic," Mick explained. But things started to go wrong. Joe and Mick were rowing and the pressures of touring became too much. Headon left and was replaced by Terry Chimes, who had been with them in the very early days, and Mick left to form Big Audio Dynamite. He was replaced by guitarists Nick Sheppard and Vince White and a new five-man version of The Clash soldiered on for a couple of years.

After a brief attempt at a solo career in the mid-eighties, Joe turned his hand to acting and appeared in *Straight To Hell* (1986) and *Lost In Space* (1989).

In the late Eighties a Spanish whiskey company called Ballentine's wanted to use 'Should I Stay Or Should I Go?' for a television advert. It didn't happen as Joe explains: "We used to have a voting system within the band for anything we wanted to do. If there's a split decision we have an aggressive discourse! Anyway, they approached me, I called up Mick and he said 'No, I can't condone the advertising of alcohol'. Because it was more his song than mine, it was agreed that it wouldn't happen." When Levi's approached them in 1991, the decision was easier. "We were all wearing Levi's at the time." Instead they argued over something else. Strummer wanted a Clash song on the flip side, Jones wanted a Big Audio Dynamite. As it was inevitable that 'Should I Stay Or Should I Go?' would get all the airplay they agreed that 'Rush' – a new title for an old reworked Big Audio Dynamite track called 'Change Of Atmosphere' – would appear on the B-side.

In 1996 rumours spread The Clash were to reform, but The Sex Pistols got in there first, when their 1977 hit 'Pretty Vacant' was re-issued and went back in the chart at number 18, leading to a world tour.

In 1999 Joe formed a new band, Joe Strummer & The Mescaleros and three albums were released: *Rock Art And The X-Ray Style* (1999), *Global A Go Go* (2001) and *Streetcore* (2003).

Nowadays Paul Simonon is a full-time painter, Mick Jones still produces and has most recently worked with The Libertines, and Topper Headon has retired. For many years, The Clash dismissed the chance of reformation, and with the passing of Joe Strummer, from heart failure three days before Christmas 2002, all hopes of a reunion were dashed.

662 Hale & Pace & The Stonkers
The Stonk

Label & Cat No.: **London LON 296**
Producer: **Brian May**
Writers: **Joe Griffiths / Gareth Hale / Norman Pace**
Date Reached No.1: **23 March 1991**
Weeks at No.1: **1**

In the mid-Seventies, Laurel & Hardy became the first comedy duo to make the UK chart and almost made it to the top. But some 38 years after it was recorded, 'The Trail Of The Lonesome Pine' peaked at number two behind 'Bohemian Rhapsody'. Since then other comedy duos have had a bash, Morcambe & Wise issued 'Boom Ooh Ya-Ta-Ta-Ta' and their theme tune, 'Bring Me Sunshine', Little & Large unwisely released a cover of Meri Wilson's 'Telephone Man' and Cannon & Ball really shouldn't have attempted 'It's All In The Game' and 'The Wind Beneath My Wings', none of which attracted the attention of the record buying public.

Gareth Hale and Norman Pace, both born in 1953, met at a teacher training college in south London in 1971. Realising they shared the same taste in music as well as a similar sense of humour, they began playing together in a band called Daffy. In 1976 they slimmed down to a duo and incorporated comedy into their pub gigs. Noticing that their comedy was being better received than their music, they became a full-time comedy duo. Their big break came via BBC 1's *The Entertainers* in 1984 followed by Channel Four's *Pushing Up Daisies* later the same year. The icing on the cake was in 1986, when they were granted their own Christmas special on LWT.

Their shows were generally made up of sketches and favourite personas, such as the children's television presenters Billy and Johnny, cab drivers Jed and Dave and the dimwits Curly and Nige. One particular sketch caused controversy when they pretended to microwave a cat. Their best-known characters were The Two Rons – a.k.a. The Management – who dressed up in tuxedos and black bow-ties and looked like a couple of bouncers from some fictitious East-End nightclub. With their habit of not smiling they were likened to the Krays.

Lenny Henry, who launched *Comic Relief* live from a refugee camp in Sudan on Noel Edmunds' *The Late Late Breakfast Show*, asked Norman and Gareth to record for the charity in the guise of The Two Rons. He also brought in a variety of established musicians, who became knows as The Stonkers, to give the song that extra boost. They comprised Pink Floyd's David Gilmour on guitar, Queen's Roger Taylor on drums and Cozy Powell on backing vocals. The whole shebang was produced by Queen's Brian May.

Unlike 'The Twist' or 'The Mashed Potato', 'The Stonk' is not a dance. The word 'stonk' means excitable appreciation and is used in that context in the song where various well-known people are name-checked. Bruce Forsyth, George Bush, John F. Kennedy and Neil Armstrong all get a mention. The chorus was: 'S.T.O.N.K. Let's stonk, to the rhythm of the honky-tonk, stick a red nose on your conk, and let's stonk.' The B-side, which was equally as funny, was 'The Smile Song' by comedienne Victoria Wood.

Up to the end of 2003, Comic Relief had raised over £210 million.

663 Chesney Hawkes
The One And Only

Label & Cat No.: **Chrysalis CHS 3627**
Producers: **Alan Shacklock / Nik Kershaw**
Writer: **Nik Kershaw**
Date Reached No.1: **30 March 1991**
Weeks at No.1: **5**

In the Sixties Brian Poole & The Tremeloes scored Top 10 hits with 'Twist And Shout', 'I Can Dance', 'Candy Man' and the number one, 'Do You Love Me?' When The Tremeloes split with Brian Poole, singer and guitarist Len 'Chip' Hawkes became his replacement and they scored a further seven Top 10 hits including the number one, 'Silence Is Golden'. In the Seventies, his mother Carol, worked with Bob Monkhouse on the game show, *The Golden Shot*. Some 24 years later, Len and Carol's son Chesney was at the top of the chart.

In the Eighties Nik Kershaw had Top 10 hits with 'Wouldn't It Be Good', 'The Riddle', 'Wide Boy and 'Don Quixote', but the closest he came to a number one was with 'I Won't Let The Sun Go Down On Me' which peaked at number two behind 'Two Tribes'. Although he still records, Nik ventured into songwriting and production and scored his first number one with 'The One And Only'.

Chesney was born in Windsor in 1971 and named after the comedian Chesney Allen, from the comedy duo Flanagan & Allen. In 1990 he was picked to star alongside Roger Daltrey in *Buddy's Song*. "They were looking up and down the country for someone who could possibly be Roger Daltrey's son," remembered Chesney. "They wanted someone who could play guitar, play piano and sing and I got the job. I remembered being so nervous because I'd never acted before."

"I wasn't particularly precious about 'The One And Only'," said Nik Kershaw. "I've just got this affliction to write those kind of songs. I just have to write them and stick them on a shelf and get them out of the way. I really don't know why people like them." Early in 1991 Nik had submitted a number of songs to Warner Chappell music. One day Chesney's manager was in the Warner offices and heard the song and thought it would be good for Chesney to do. "I did one performance on *The Little And Large Show* and it skyrocketed from there," noted Chesney. "Two weeks later, it was number one."

'The One And Only' featured in *Buddy's Song*, and although Chesney is often unfairly classed as a one-hit-wonder, 'The One And Only' was not his one and only hit. He followed it up with two more songs also from the film, 'I'm A Man Not A Boy' (number 27) and 'Secrets of The Heart' (number 54).

Chesney's most distinctive feature was a mole on his upper lip. When he was at number one, a radio station in London ran a competition with the prize being a do-it-yourself Chesney Hawkes kit. It comprised of a brown felt-tip pen!

In 2000 Chesney started playing live again as an indie rocker. The following year he co-wrote the track 'Jane Doe' on Nik Kershaw's 2001 album *To Be Frank*.

664 Cher

The Shoop Shoop Song (It's In His Kiss)

Label & Cat No.: **Epic 6566737**

Producer: **Peter Asher**

Writer: **Rudy Clark**

Date reached No.1: **4 May 1991**

Weeks at No.1: **5**

WHO WOULD HAVE THOUGHT IT? Sonny & Cher had had a succession of hits in the Sixties, made two disastrous films – *Good Times* (1967) and *Chastity* (1969) – and then hosted the US TV variety series, *The Sonny And Cher Comedy Hour*, which was as uninspiring as it sounds. Sonny was the dominant partner and eventually Cher had had enough and left him for record executive, David Geffen. As an example of a Hollywood courtship, David Geffen confided, "I told my therapist today that I think I am in love with you." By means of celebration, Cher had a butterfly tattooed on her behind.

David Geffen wanted to establish Cher as a contemporary force but the record buyers ignored her work with the producers Phil Spector ('A Woman's Story') and Jimmy Webb (*Stars*). Cher then dated Alan Gorrie of The Average White Band. In 1975 her steamy courtship and tempestuous marriage to Gregg Allman of the Allman Brothers sold newspapers but they were soon divorced. Her next beau was Gene Simmons of Kiss.

In 1982 the director Robert Altman invited Cher to take part in a Broadway play about a reunion of James Dean fans, *Come Back To The Five And Dime Jimmy Dean, Jimmy Dean*. Its success led to a film version with Cher, Sandy Dennis, Kathy Bates and Karen Black. Cher received good reviews both on stage and in the film. In 1983 she was nominated for an Oscar as Best Supporting Actress for her role as Meryl Streep's lesbian friend in *Silkwood*, a true story about a whistleblower in a nuclear plant.

Her first starring role in a major film came in 1985 with *Mask*, which was directed by Peter Bogdanovich and told how the biker mum Rusty Dennis (Cher) coped with her son's facial deformities, the son, Rocky, being played by Eric Stoltz. Cher was very convincing, and two years later starred with Nicolas Cage in *Moonstruck*, but she was responsible for Frank Oz being replaced as a director – she told him that she wasn't a Muppet! The grouchy and abrasive Norman Jewison took over and the madcap comedy involved a dowdy girl (Cher) being given a makeover and looking sensational. Praise from *The New Yorker* critic, Pauline Kael, is hard to come by but she called Cher "devastatingly funny and sinuous and beautiful". Cher won an Oscar for the role.

Cher played a public defender in *Suspect* (1987), acting alongside Dennis Quaid and Liam Neeson. Her third key film in 1987 was *The Witches Of Eastwick,* based on a John Updike novel. It gave Jack Nicholson the chance to over-act (so what's new?) and Cher, Susan Sarandon and Michelle Pieffer did very well in being able to match his bravura performance.

Although Cher sung (uncredited) on Meat Loaf's 1981 hit, 'Dead Ringer For Love', she did not capitalise on this, preferring to show that she was dedicated to acting. In 1987, encouraged by David Geffen, her musical renaissance started with 'I Found Someone' (UK 5, US 10), which was written and produced by Michael Bolton with a video that was directed by Cher. Then came 'We All Sleep Alone' (UK 47, US 14), written and produced by Jon Bon Jovi. Then there was a duet with Peter Cetera, 'After All' (US 6), from the film *Chances Are* and 'If I Could Turn Back Time' (UK 6, US 3) and 'Just Like Jesse James' (UK 11, US 8).

In 1991 Cher starred as a wayward mother in *Mermaids*. She left whenever a relationship got serious and her children were always on the

Cher

move. They decided that Bob Hoskins was right for her and the story is about making her stay. The film, which was set in 1963, was directed by Richard Benjamin and the music was by her friend from the Sixties, Jack Nitzsche. (Jack wrote 'Needles And Pins' with Sonny.) The soundtrack incorporated records from the era and they included Betty Everett's US hit, 'It's In His Kiss (The Shoop Shoop Song)'

The R&B song was written by Rudy Clark, whose other compositions include 'If You Gotta Make A Fool Of Somebody' (Freddie & The Dreamers), 'Itty Bitty Pieces' (James Ray) and 'Got My Mind Set On You' (George Harrison), all of which had originally been recorded by James Ray. However, the original of 'The Shoop Shoop Song (It's In His Kiss)' was by one of Ray Charles' Raelets, Merry Clayton in 1963. A few months later it was recorded in Chicago by Betty Everett and the reason the shoop shoops are to the fore in the title is because the backing singers are projected as loudly as the lead vocalist. The lyric is a conversation in which Betty informs the girls how to tell if a man is sincere. (Pretty flawed advice in reality, but never mind.) Betty Everett is also known for 'You're No Good' (which was covered by The Swinging Blue Jeans) and her own UK Top 30 hit, 'Getting Mighty Crowded'. In 1968 her single of 'The Shoop Shoop Song (It's In His Kiss)' belatedly made the UK Top 40 and then, in 1975, the song as 'It's In His Kiss' was a Top 10 record for Linda Lewis.

Cher recorded her own version for the end credits of *Moonstruck* and it was produced by Peter Asher, formerly of Peter and Gordon and then the producer of James Taylor and Linda Ronstadt. The single only made number 33 in the US but it went all the way here. It was followed by another UK Top 10 single, 'Love And Understanding', but her attempt to ignite the flame of 'The Shoop Shoop Song' with another Sixties classic, 'Oh No Not My Baby', only nudged into the Top 40. She also recorded a fun single of 'I Got You Babe' with Beavis & Butt-Head.

One month after 'The Shoop Shoop Song' reached number One Cher topped the UK album charts with *Love Hurts*, which remained on the charts for 51 weeks.

665 Color Me Badd
I Wanna Sex You Up

Label & Cat No.: **Giant W 0036**

Producer: **Dr Freeze**

Writers: **Elliott Straite / Betty Wright / Willie Clarke**

Date Reached No.1: **8 June 1991**

Weeks at No.1: **3**

When Oklahoma City's Color Me Badd rose to number one, it was the first time in chart history that three consecutive chart toppers had been recorded specifically for movies.

In 1986 Bryan Abrams, Kevin Thornton, Mark Calderon and Sam Watters met at Northwest Classen High School. "Our high school was mainly a black school and we attended a black church," Sam Watters noted in *Billboard* magazine. "We were almost the only white guys there, so we got together, called ourselves Take One and started doing acappella covers of songs by Sam Cooke and The Temptations."

Their harmonies blended perfectly, reminiscent of the Fifties doo-wop groups. It also began a Nineties revival of R&B vocals group which led to success for En Vogue, SWV and Boyz II Men.

They had a knack of bumping into famous people and launching into a 'spontaneous' audition. Huey Lewis, Ronnie Milsap and The O'Jays were among people they performed for, and their first live gig came when they met Jon Bon Jovi coming out of a cinema. Jon was so impressed he invited them to perform before his support act, Skid Row, the following night. In 1987 Robert 'Kool' Bell of Kool & The Gang was in Oklahoma City and attended a gig where Color Me Badd were playing. He too was impressed, enough to find them a manager, arrange for them to move to New York and sign a deal with Giant Records. There they were invited to record a song for a new movie, *New Jack City*.

The song is heard during a strip club scene, "It's not a pervy song. 'I Wanna Sex You Up' is just a modern way of saying 'I want to romance with you," explained Bryan. "But to get people's attention, to get noticed, you have to be bold. That's what we did." The single credits the producer as Dr Freeze, which is a pseudonym for New York songwriter Elliott Straite. It also samples Betty Wright's 'Tonight Is The Night'.

The parent album, *C.M.B.*, reached number three in both the UK and US and contained the other hit singles, 'I Adore Mi Amor', 'All 4 Love' and 'Heartbreaker'. The follow-up album, *Young, Gifted and Badd* contained remixes of all the tracks on *C.M.B.* but failed to interest record buyers. Their next album, *Time And Chance*, struggled up to number 56.

Their fourth album, *Awakening*, was poorly received. Nonetheless, the group donated some of the proceeds to the memorial fund in honour of the victims of the Oklahoma bombing in April 1995.

666 Jason Donovan
Any Dream Will Do

Label & Cat No.: **Really Useful RUR 7**

Producer: **Nigel Wright**

Writers: **Andrew Lloyd Webber / Tim Rice**

Date Reached No.1: **29 June 1991**

Weeks at No.1: **2**

Jason had been released from his contract with Pete Waterman's PWL label and free to sign with Andrew Lloyd Webber's Really Useful group, enabling him to accept the part of Joseph in the West End production of *Joseph And The Amazing Technicolor Dreamcoat*. It opened at the London Palladium to rave reviews and became a box office smash.

Although the original tale of Joseph goes back to the Bible, the show's story began in 1967 when a young Julian Lloyd Webber, a pupil at London's St Paul's Junior School, was asked by the head of the music department, Alan Doggett, if his brother Andrew would compose a 20-minute pop cantata for an Easter concert. He collaborated with lyricist Tim Rice and came up with a story rooted in the Book Of Genesis. It starts with a young Joseph, son of Jacob, announcing to his father and 11 brothers that he has the power to interpret dreams. His father buys Joseph a multi-coloured coat, causing jealousy among his brothers who try to kill him. He subsequently gets sold to an Egyptian guard called Potiphar. The brothers tell their father that Joseph is dead and return the 'coat of many colours' to him. Joseph ends up in prison, but is pardoned when Pharaoh learns of Joseph's power to interpret dreams and thus predicted that Pharaoh will have seven years of plenty in a time of famine.

The first London production opened at the Albery Theatre in 1973 with Gary Bond as Joseph. It made its Broadway debut in 1981 and has been revived a number of times throughout the Seventies and Eighties. Although 'Any Dream Will Do' was in it from the beginning, Tim Rice didn't realise its potential. He said, "It was number one in Ireland and number one in Australia quite soon after the show was written. It wasn't until the Jason Donovan production in 1991 that it became a big bona fide hit single. Initially, we thought of it as a show song and put it on the studio album. Sometime later, about the middle of 1969, we recorded this choirboy called Christopher singing 'Any Dream Will Do' for a single and I changed the lyrics, not completely but I took out the references to 'Coloured Coats' and anything to do with Joseph. This was silly because that was the appeal of the song."

The 1991 two-hour show incorporated 22 songs, 14 of them sung by Jason. When *Joseph* closed in January 1994, it held the record for the longest running show at the Palladium.

Jason ran into a legal battle when he claimed *The Face* published fake photos of him and argued that he wasn't telling the truth about his sexuality, inferring he was gay. *The Sun* didn't help matters when they carried the headline, 'Jason's acting so queer'. "It started really with the Technicolor Dreamcoat, which was the gay flag," remembered Jason, "I was the perfect victim of gay militant sexism." He successfully sued the magazine and won £292,000. But in order to save *The Face* from bankruptcy, Jason, having made his point, waived the money. The whole escapade was too much for him and he turned to cocaine. "It was *The Face* that did it," he confirmed.

In 1996, cured of his addiction, he returned to the London stage in *Camelot* alongside Paul Nicholas and Samantha Janus. In 1998 he joined the UK tour of *The Rocky Horror Show* taking on the camp role Frank-n-Furter.

In 2004 Jason was back at the London Palladium appearing as Caractacus Potts in *Chitty Chitty Bang Bang*.

667 Bryan Adams
(Everything I Do) I Do It For You

Label & Cat No.: **A&M AM 789**

Producer: **Robert John 'Mutt' Lange**

Writers: **Bryan Adams / Robert John 'Mutt' Lange / Michael Kamen**

Date Reached No.1: **13 July 1991**

Weeks at No.1: **16**

During the late Eighties local radio DJs in London started calling him 'The Groover From Vancouver', but in fact husky-voiced Bryan was born in Kingston, Ontario in 1959 and is Canada's most successful male singer of all time.

Bryan was the lead singer with Canadian rock band Sweeney Todd at the age of 16 and a year later he formed a successful writing partnership with Jim Vallace. His early UK hits included 'Run To You', (UK 11, US 1), 'Somebody' (UK 35, US 11) and two of his best-known songs, 'Heaven' (UK 38, US 1) and 'Summer of 69' (UK 42, US 5). His first UK Top 10 was '(Everything I Do) I Do It For You' from the film *Robin Hood (Prince Of Thieves)*, starring Kevin Costner. It was nominated for an Academy Award for Best Song but lost out to 'Beauty And The Beast'.

Bryan was not the first choice to sing the theme. Michael Kamen, who scored the film and wrote the song, saw it as Maid Marian's (played by Mary Elizabeth Mastrantonio) song and thought it should be sung by a female and originally approached Kate Bush. He said, "Kate didn't feel it was right for her voice, so that didn't work out." His next choice was Annie Lennox. "Annie was too busy making her first solo album, *Diva*, so that didn't work out either." He approached David Kershenbaum who was overall in charge of music for the film, who suggested it be done as a duet between Julia Fordham and Peter Cetera. They recorded a demo but it was turned down. Kamen said, "Lisa Stansfield was also interested in doing it and even wanted to add some of her own lyrics, but for some reason Clive Davis at Arista Records decided that he didn't want her involved in the movie." They all had a meeting and finally came up with the suggestion of Bryan Adams. Adams and songwriter/producer, Robert 'Mutt' Lange added a new arrangement, but Kamen didn't like their piano intro because he didn't want any modern sounding instruments in the score, preferring orchestrations. Bryan told Q magazine, "We had a great deal of trouble convincing Michael and the film company that our arrangement was going to work. They wanted to have more period instruments to fit the film, I said, 'We don't want lutes and mandolins on this – this is a pop record!' I think they're probably very pleased with the way things turned out, but they still buried the song as far back in the film as possible – halfway through the credits – that's a reflection of how disappointed they were." The video showed the musicians playing in the forest interspersed with clips from the film.

The soundtrack to the film was released four weeks after the single, but contained mostly instrumentals and spent three months on the chart. The track also appeared on Bryan's album, *Waking Up The Neighbours*, but because it wasn't released until the single's 12th week at number one, the only way to get the song was to buy the single.

During its 16-week reign at the top, the follow-up, 'Can't Stop This Thing We Started' entered the chart, climbed to number 12 and dropped out of the Top 40. '(Everything I Do) I Do It For You' also spent seven weeks at number one in the US.

In November 1991 Slim Whitman, who, since 1955, with 11 weeks, had held the records for the longest continuous residency at number one, joined Bryan on stage at Wembley Arena. He

Canadian rocker Bryan Adams, who like Paul McCartney fronts his band on bass guitar, holds the record for the longest consecutive stay at number one

sang his own number one, 'Rose Marie' and then presented Bryan with a plaque for breaking his record whilst praising him quite effusively.

Bryan's other film songs include, 'All For Love' (with Rod Stewart and Sting) (*The Three Musketeers*, 1994), 'Have You Ever Really Loved A Woman?' (*Juan De Marco*, 1995), 'I Finally Found Someone' (with Barbra Streisand) (*The Mirror Has Two Faces*, 1997) and 'Here I Am' (*Spirit – Stallion Of The Cimarron*, 2002). They all made the Top 10.

668 U2
The Fly

Label & Cat No.:	**Island IS 500**
Producers:	**Steve Lillywhite / Daniel Lanois**
Writers:	**Bono / The Edge / Adam Clayton / Larry Mullen**
Date Reached No.1:	**2 November 1991**
Weeks at No.1:	**1**

WITH BRYAN ADAMS HAVING SPENT half the summer and most of the autumn at number one, whatever was going to knock it off would have been more than welcomed. 'The Fly' crashed in at number one but was this partly because of a marketing ploy by Island Records who announced that the single would be deleted on the day of issue?

Following the success of *Rattle And Hum*, which spent just over a year on the album chart and spawned the Top 10 singles, 'Angel Of Harlem', a tribute to Billie Holiday, 'When Love Comes To Town' a duet with blues guitarist B.B.King and 'All I Want Is You', U2 spent 1990 working on their new album.

The Gulf War was breaking out and it made some of the lyrics of 'The Fly' that much more poignant. The opening line, 'It's no secret that the stars are falling from the sky, It's no secret that our world is in darkness tonight' and Bono's falsetto on 'Love... we shine like a burning star, We're falling from the sky... tonight', is spine tingling.

'The Fly' was recorded in Dublin. "In the first place, it was too Leonard Cohen," admitted Bono, "but the sunglasses cured that." It was Fintan Fitzgerald, U2's wardrobe assistant, who bought Bono the mad shades. He also bought him a book of Jenny Holger's truisms. "I became very interested in these single-line aphorisms," Bono said. "I had been writing them, so I got this character who could say them all, from 'A liar won't believe anybody else' to 'A friend is someone who lets you down', and that's where 'The Fly' was coming from." Bono described the song as, "The sound of four men chopping down *The Joshua Tree*." 'The Fly' was about rebellion.

'The Fly' appeared on the band's eighth studio album, *Achtung Baby*. It was less political and, if anything showed a more personal side to the band. The title was inspired by a line in the 1968 film *The Producers*, a line their engineer Joe O'Herlihy kept repeating during the recording of the album. 'Mysterious Ways', the anthemic 'One', 'Even Better Than The Real Thing' and 'Who's Gonna Ride Your Wild Horses' were all Top 20 singles. A Paul Oakenfold and Steve Osborne remix of 'Even Better Than The Real Thing' was issued just three weeks after the single and charted four places higher at number eight.

669 Vic Reeves & The Wonder Stuff
Dizzy

Label & Cat No.:	**Sense SIGH 712**
Producer:	**Mick Glossop**
Writers:	**Freddy Weller / Tommy Roe**
Date Reached No.1:	**9 November 1991**
Weeks at No.1:	**2**

'BORN FREE' IS ARGUABLY MATT Monro's finest moment, but bizarrely it was never a UK hit, at least not until British comedian Vic Reeves covered it earlier in 1991. For the follow-up, he collaborated with one of the West Midlands' finest Britpop band, The Wonder Stuff.

Vic, who was born James Moir in Darlington, is a former pig farmer, tomato farmer, an apprentice engineer, an art student, a gallery attendant and a record shop assistant. "I was just trying to entertain myself, that's always been the criterion with me. I originally wanted to be in a band like Roxy Music, then T.Rex and Slade and then punk came along and I wanted to be in a punk band. We had the attitude but we didn't have the skills." But one thing was for sure, Vic could sing. When he did finally get a band together, they didn't rehearse. "We used to make a terrible row. We used to change our name every gig to avoid people coming to see us more than once." They Called It Rum, Hot Murder and Fantantiddlyspan were just three of the monikers they performed under.

He teamed up with Bob Mortimer and soon landed their own Channel 4 show, *Vic Reeves' Big Night Out*, later moving to BBC2 for the series *At Home With Vic And Bob*. It was that show that later turned into their best known series, *Shooting Stars*, an unconventional show which derived its humour from asking the celebrity contestants to behave ridiculously. The regular team captains were Ulrika Jonsson and Mark Lamarr and the actor Matt Lucas who, under the guise of George Dawes read the scores at the end of each round.

The Wonder Stuff formed in 1986 and comprised singer/guitarist Miles Hunt, whose uncle is Bill Hunt from Wizzard, guitarist Malcolm Treece, Rob Jones on bass and drummer Martin Gilks. Three years later they added Martin Bell on banjo and James Taylor on organ. Their early hits included 'Don't Let Me Down Gently' (19), 'Circlesquare' (20) and 'The Size Of A Cow' (15). Rob died of a heart attack in 1993.

Vic, Bob and The Wonder Stuff teamed up for a raucous cover of Tommy Roe's 1969 number one hit 'Dizzy'. Their *Top Of The Pops* appearance caused them problems. Vic recalled, "We were very drunk because The Wonder Stuff had this theory that 30 seconds before you go in, you have some tequila and you knock it back and then halfway through your song, you suddenly get your peak and your rush and then you feel great. But the problem was we had to go on five times because something kept going wrong technically, so we ended up having five tequilas and we were just pissed."

Vic recorded the album, *I Will Cure You*, which in addition to 'Dizzy' contained his hits 'Born Free', 'Abide With Me' and a cover of Deep Purple's 'Black Night'. In 1995 he and Bob teamed up with EMF for another manic cover, this time 'I'm A Believer', which got to number three.

In 2000 Vic and Bob appeared in a film remake of the Seventies TV series *Randall & Hopkirk (Deceased)*. Four year later they were seen as Chris and Carl Palmer in the TV series *Catterick*.

670 Michael Jackson
Black Or White

Label & Cat No.: **Epic 657 598 7**
Producers: **Michael Jackson / Bill Bottrell**
Writer: **Michael Jackson**
Date Reached No.1: **23 November 1991**
Weeks at No.1: **2**

SINCE 'BILLIE JEAN' IN 1983, IT APPEARed that Michael was achieving a number one hit every four years. Was this song about Michael's ever-changing skin colour? No. It was an appeal for cultural acceptance throughout the world, as emphasised in the lyric, "Where your blood comes from is where your space is / I've seen the bright get duller / I'm not going to spend my life being a colour".

Work on his next album, *HIStory: Past, Present and Future Book 1* began less than a week after he had completed *Bad* and the first track lifted from it shot to number one. The concept for 'Black Or White' came about in 1986 and was originally intended for the *Bad* album. However, it got shelved until the summer of 1989 when Michael retrieved it and played it to producer Bill Bottrell. It was Bill who arranged for Guns 'N Roses' guitarist Slash to play on the track. The rapping was provided by Bill.

The original video for 'Black Or White' was another epic lasting 11 minutes. It premièred on the *Fox Television Network, Black Entertainment Television* and *MTV* simultaneously in November 1991. But, following complaints from journalists and fans alike about the way Michael was grabbing his crotch in the last few minutes, the video was edited and Jacko offered an apology for any offence.

Within seven weeks of 'Black Or White' charting, a re-mix by producers Robert Clivilles and David Cole had found its way onto the chart and peaked at number 14.

671 George Michael with Elton John
Don't Let The Sun Go Down On Me

Label & Cat No.: **Epic 657 6467**
Producer: **George Michael**
Writers: **Elton John / Bernie Taupin**
Date Reached No.1: **7 December 1991**
Weeks at No.1: **2**

AS A CHILD, GEORGE MICHAEL IDOLISED Elton John – he collected all his albums, his favourite being *Goodbye Yellow Brick Road*. When George discovered that his school friend Andrew Ridgeley had the same album and shared the same admiration for Elton, they became closer friends and subsequently formed a musical partnership.

'Don't Let The Sun Go Down On Me' was originally recorded in 1974 and was lifted from Elton John's *Caribou* album. It peaked at number 16 and featured Captain & Tennille and Bruce Johnston (of the Beach Boys) on backing vocals.

Elton said, "I wrote the song very early in the morning, just as my drummer, Nigel Olsson, was going to bed. When he woke up, I sang it to him and he said, 'It's a number one'." Gus Dudgeon, who produced Elton's version, recalled, "When Elton sang the vocal track, he was in a filthy mood. On some takes, he'd scream it, on others he'd mumble it. Eventually he flung off his headphones and said, 'Okay, let's hear what we got'. When I played it to him, he said, 'That's a load of fucking crap. You can send it to Engelbert Humperdinck and if he doesn't like it, you can give it to Lulu as a demo'."

In 1985 George Michael, at the age of 21, became the youngest person to ever win Songwriter Of The Year at the annual Ivor Novello Awards. The award was presented by Elton John and he invited George to help him on his latest album *Ice On Fire*. George agreed and can be heard on backing vocals on the hit single 'Nikita' and more prominently on the follow-up, 'Wrap Her Up'. The following year, Elton repaid the compliment by playing piano on Wham's last number one 'The Edge Of Heaven'.

It was on 25 March 1991, during George's *Cover To Cover* tour at Wembley Stadium, that Elton turned up backstage to surprise him. Elton suggested doing a duet, George agreed and an instant decision was made to sing 'Don't Let The Sun Go Down On Me' as George had often included it in his set. The accompanying video, however, was not filmed at Wembley. Instead, it was filmed in Chicago and when George introduced Elton in the song, the place went crazy.

George joined Pavarotti on a version of the song at the Friends International Benefit concert for Tibetan and Cambodian Children in Italy in June 2000.

Vic Reeves

672 Queen

Bohemian Rhapsody / These Are The Days Of Our Lives

Label & Cat No.: **Parlophone QUEEN 20**

Producer: **Roy Thomas Baker**

Writers: **Freddie Mercury : Freddie Mercury / Brian May / Roger Taylor / John Deacon**

Date Reached No.1: **21 December 1991**

Weeks at No.1: **5**

THE GRAVITY OF FREDDIE MERCURY'S illness was one of the music industry's best-kept secrets. On Saturday November 23, Freddie released a press statement to the world admitting he had AIDS. The next day, he was gone.

That week Queen's latest single 'The Show Must Go On' had just dropped out of the Top 40. The words "Inside my heart is breaking my make-up may be flaking, but my smile still stays on" told Freddie's story from the heart. Surely the lines "I'll top the bill, I'll overkill, I have to find the will to carry on, on with the show" ensured his determination till the end.

'Bohemian Rhapsody', at the time, was the only number one single to return to the top of the chart in its original form. It was re-issued with a new song on the B-side which was the last song Freddie ever recorded. The video was released in black and white and had Freddie heavily made up to conceal his illness.

'These Are The Days Of Our Lives' was Freddie reminiscing. As Brian May said, "There are a lot of things in there which, to us, was completely about Freddie saying goodbye" and for a man who absolutely adored his audience and fans, it was no coincidence that the last line Freddie ever uttered on camera was "I still love you".

The single was the second biggest seller of 1991, behind Bryan Adams' '(Everything I Do), I Do It For You'. The band agreed that all profits would to go to *The Terrence Higgins Trust,* a charity for HIV and AIDS sufferers.

On April 20, 1992 The Freddie Mercury Tribute Concert was staged at Wembley Stadium in front of 70,000 fans. The three remaining members of Queen played while George Michael, Robert Plant, Roger Daltrey, Annie Lennox, Elton John, David Bowie, Liza Minnelli and others sang their many hits.

Throughout his life Freddie was always aping around, never took too much too seriously and was forever holding elaborate parties, so it's not unreasonable to assume that Freddie might have said, echoing the title of their 1986 hit, 'Who wants to live forever?' anyway.

673 Wet Wet Wet

Goodnight Girl

Label & Cat No.: **Precious Organisation JEWEL 17**

Producer: **Wet Wet Wet**

Writers: **Graeme Clark / Tom Cunningham / Marti Pellow / Neil Mitchell**

Date Reached No.1: **25 January 1992**

Weeks at No.1: **4**

WET WET WET, WHO WERE FORMED in Glasgow in 1982 by singer Marti Pellow (born Mark McLoughlin), bass guitarist Graeme Clark, keyboard player Neil Mitchell and drummer Tom Cunningham, took their name from the line 'His face was wet wet wet with tears', in the Scritti Politti song 'Getting Having And Holding'. Session guitarist Graeme Duffy, who has played with them from the start, is the unofficial fifth member. They met Elliot Davis who became their manager and started the record label and management company, Precious, named after Dexys Midnight Runners' hit 'Let's Make This Precious'.

Having got their career off the ground with the chart topping album, *Popped In Souled Out*, and seven Top 20 hits including the charity number one, 'With A Little Help From My Friends', Wet Wet Wet had now reached an all-time low. Their second album, *The Memphis Sessions*, was an eight-tracker in which the band wanted to work with their idol Willie Mitchell who had worked with Tina Turner and Al Green. Their record company agreed and so they travelled to Memphis where they had met Willie and told him what they wanted from him. "We wanted to write about emotions we had never really experienced. We wanted to do love songs although we'd never been in love," admitted Marti. Willie was touched they had come to him and even let Marti use the same microphone that Al Green had used. The album, which included five redone songs from *Popped In Souled Out*, did not impress the record company who felt it was not fit for release. The Memphis session had meant so much to them and they were convinced it would be big. After all, they knew how they wanted to sound. Marti even commented, "Four heads are better than one dickhead." Jonathan King praised them in his newspaper column and predicted that they were going to be one of the biggest bands in the world. Phonogram eventually relented and *The Memphis Sessions* reached number three.

The third album, *Holding Back The River*, reached number two, but two of the singles from it, 'Hold Back The River' and 'Stay With Me Heartache' / 'I Feel Fine' failed to make the Top 30 and it looked like the Wets were on a downward spiral.

In 1992 they released their fourth album, *High On The Happy Side*. It was the album that was meant to re-establish them. They tried to do what Cliff Richard and George Michael had done before and successfully cross over from teen idols to a more mature adult group. Elliot Davis said, "The Wets are a phenomenon. The Wets appeal to a large demograph. If you're a fan, *High On The Happy Side* will convince you they're the best fucking band around and if you're not a fan, you soon will be." All the tracks were written by the band, but were not of the standard of their first two albums. The first two singles 'Make It Tonight' and 'Put The Light On', both failed to make the Top 30. The third single, however, the ballad 'Goodnight Girl' exceeded everyone's expectations when it went to number one. Although admittedly the easiest time to get a number one is just after Christmas when singles sales are at their lowest.

Wet Wet Wet took their name from a line in a Scritti Politti song, left to right: Tom Cunningham, Neil Mitchell, Graeme Clark, Marti Pellow

RAAMDWARS
STRAAT

674 Shakespears Sister
Stay

Label & Cat No.: **London LON 314**

Producer: **Alan Moulder**

Writers: **Siobhan Fahey / Marcella Detroit / Guiot (aka Dave Stewart)**

Date Reached No.1: **22 February 1992**

Weeks at No.1: **8**

BANANARAMA WERE THE MOST successful British girl group, until the Spice Girls usurped them, but despite 26 UK hit singles, they never had a number one. However, their cover of Shocking Blue's 'Venus', which reached number eight in the UK, gave them their only US chart topper.

One of the trio, Siobhan Fahey, who had previously worked in the press office at Decca, left the group in early 1988. She explained, "The group changed a lot and I was no longer inspired and I wasn't able to fulfill myself. I was a bit of a fly in the ointment for the last couple of years because I would argue about everything." She had married The Eurythmics' Dave Stewart in August the previous year and it was he who encouraged Siobhan to leave the group and try again.

Marcella Detroit first came to prominence as a backing singer then a co-writer with Eric Clapton. She wrote 'Lay Down Sally' under the name Marcy Levy. She has also written songs for Al Jarreau, Chaka Khan and Belinda Carlisle. In 1980 she contributed 'Help Me' – a duet with Robin Gibb – to the film soundtrack *Times Square*.

Marcella and Siobhan met at Marcella's home in Los Angeles in 1988 and discovered they shared the same musical taste, especially The Smiths. It was The Smiths' 1985 Top 30 hit, 'Shakespear's Sister' that gave the group their name.

Their first single, 'You're History' reached the Top 10. Marcy commented, "After 'History' I really thought, Wow, there really is something here." But the follow-ups, 'Run Silent' and 'Dirty Mind', all from the debut album, *Sacred Heart*, failed to make the Top 50. In 1991 their next single, 'Goodbye Cruel World' from their second album, *Hormonally Yours*, also made little impact. The first four singles had all been credited as Shakespear's Sister. For the next single, 'Stay' the singles' sleeve was misprinted as Shakespears Sisters.

Marcy has a four-and-a-half octave voice and every squeak on the record is natural. "My voice wasn't always like that," she explained, "but I've trained it up that way. You have to work at it, keep on top of it."

The follow-up single, 'I Don't Care' also made the Top 10, but they went out in spectacular fashion the following year when live on stage, Fahey announced to an unsuspecting audience and an even more shocked Marcella that the band was being dissolved. Siobhan had a few health problems and has kept a low profile while Marcella launched a solo career and had the Top 30 hit 'Ain't Nothing Like The Real Thing', a duet with Elton John.

675 Right Said Fred
Deeply Dippy

Label & Cat No.: **Tug SNOG 3**

Producer: **Tommy D**

Writers: **Fred Fairbrass / Rob Manzoli / Richard Fairbrass**

Date Reached No.1: **18 April 1992**

Weeks at No.1: **3**

IN 1962 COMEDIAN, ENTERTAINER, actor and singer, Bernard Cribbins, scored three chart hits with the novelty songs 'The Hole In The Ground', 'Right, Said Fred' and 'Gossip Calypso'. He later appeared as the stationmaster in *The Railway Children* and as Mr Hutchinson in *Fawlty Towers*. He had spent many years writing comedy shows. In 1991 two brothers from Sussex, Fred and Richard Fairbrass, who ran their own gym in West London, decided to form a band. They recruited a guitarist from Putney, Rob Manzoli who they saw rehearing in a spare

room in their gym. "We needed a name very quickly as we had to get the info into *Time Out* for some upcoming shows. A friend of mine, Kate Randall, suggested the name as she had just heard Bernard Cribbins' song on the radio and we just liked it," remembered Richard. They donned some tight lycra and proved to the world there was still a place in the pop chart for bald men in their thirties. "We went for the name because we knew it was stupid," he admitted.

Their first single 'I'm Too Sexy' came about during a tea break from recording. They had programmed a bass-line into a computer and it kept repeating it. All of a sudden Richard began singing, 'I'm too sexy for my shirt' and he and Rob fell about laughing. Fred, however, was a bit more serious about it, but Richard soon convinced him it was OK. The song went to number one in over 25 countries including the US, but at home they were unable to get past Bryan Adams and had to make do with five weeks at number two.

For the follow-up, 'Don't Talk Just Kiss', they invited soul diva, Jocelyn Brown to help out and that song reached number three. Both tracks were featured on their debut album *Up*, which also went to number one. The third single, 'Deeply Dippy' went all the way to the top. "I'm not sure what it actually means," Richard said, "it's just an expression that came from an episode of *Jeeves And Wooster*, I think."

In 1993 they were invited to record the annual *Comic Relief* song, 'Stick It Out', which reached number four and was credited to Right Said Fred and Friends. The friends being: Jools Holland, DJ Alan Freeman, Peter Cook, Steve Coogan, Clive Anderson, Hugh Laurie, Pauline

Right Said Fred

Quirke, Linda Robson, Basil Brush and even Bernard Cribbins.

Right Said Fred broke up in 1994. Richard made regular appearances on *Never Mind The Buzzcocks* and went on to present *Gaytime TV*. In 2001 Right Said Fred were back as a duo and they had a Top 20 hit with 'You're My Mate'. Richard said, "I just wanted to write a song about being friends. There are plenty of songs about love but not many about friendships. We're doing really well in Europe, especially Germany, but the UK doesn't cherish its more idiosyncratic artists, and that's a shame."

676 K.W.S.

Please Don't Go / Game Boy

Label & Cat No.: **Network NWK 46**

Producers: **Chris King / Winston Williams**

Writers: **Harry Casey / Richard Finch : Chris King / Winston Williams**

Date Reached No.1: **9 May 1992**

Weeks at No.1: **5**

In 1992 keyboardist Winston 'Winnie' Williams and producer Chris King, both from Nottingham, were part of a struggling dance act, B-Line who were signed to the Birmingham-based label, Network. In March of that year an Anglo-Italian singer, William Moralas, who was signed to the German-based ZYX label, and recorded under the guise Double You? decided to record a dance version of KC & The Sunshine Band's 1979 ballad 'Please Don't Go', which was arranged by Robert Zanetti.

"I first heard the Double You? version in a club some months previous to us covering it," recalled Chris. "It was released in Germany and Italy but did nothing at all. Winnie and I got together and Winnie asked Delroy Joseph, whom he had worked with backing the Nottingham soul singer Wycliffe, to do the test vocal. The record company liked the demo and so we went with that as the final version." We decided to cover it just like The Love Affair covered Robert Knight's 'Everlasting Love' or David Parton covered Stevie Wonder's 'Isn't She Lovely'." Once the track was finished, they needed a name to release it under, so they took King's and Williams' initials, but added St. to Delroy's name making him Delroy St. Joseph and used the 'S' to make K.W.S.

The record was issued as a double A-side with 'Game Boy'. "We wanted something new and Game Boy was my son's favourite games console at the time. There were various mixes on the 12-inch single with silly names like Afternoon Of The Rhino, which had been the title of a northern soul single by Mike Post."

They began making personal appearances to promote the track. "We even came up with the idea that the record would be dedicated to Des Walker who was leaving Nottingham Forest to play for Italy." Chris continued, "Our local TV station picked up on it and did a piece on it. Then it got Record Of The Week on Radio One and it shot up from 30 to nine to one and then we finally got on *Top Of The Pops*."

They followed it up with another Casey and Finch composition, a cover of George McCrae's 'Rock Your Baby', and 'Hold Back The Night' which featured the originators of the song, The Trammps, on guest vocals. They had one final Top 30 hit with Rose Royce's former lead singer, Gwen Dickie covering 'Ain't Nobody'.

Once the song reached the top of the chart, a legal battle ensued when Double You?'s label, ZYX, whose version reached number 41, accused Network Records of copying Robert Zanetti's arrangement for the K.W.S. version. The proceedings lasted three years with the judge finally ruling that there was a separate copyright in an arrangement, distinct from the copyright in the original song. It opened a can of worms as record industry practice did not allow for arrangers to earn a share of the copyright when a song was covered.

Chris opened a record pressing plant in Nottingham, which is still one of the largest in Europe. Winnie went to Scandinavia teaching children how to get into the music business, then came back and worked with Chris. More recently he's returned to teaching music. Delroy turned his hand to writing songs and became a producer.

677 Erasure

Abba-esque EP

Label & Cat No.: **Mute MUTE 144**

Producer: **Dave Bascombe**

Writers (Lay All Your Love On Me): **Björn Ulvaeus / Benny Andersson**

Date Reached No.1: **13 June 1992**

Weeks at No.1: **5**

In 1985 Vince Clarke left Yazoo to embark on his new project, Erasure. The keyboard wizard, who said he chose the name because, "Erasure is more important than recording in the Studio," needed a singer, so he placed an advert in *Melody Maker*, which was answered by Andy Bell, former singer with The Void. Andy was very camp and pranced around the stage in his outrageous clothes whilst Vince remained impassive behind the keyboard.

Their first Top 10 came in 1986 when 'Sometimes' reached number two. The follow-up, 'Oh L'Amour' failed to chart, but the 12" single had an extra track – a cover of Abba's 'Gimme Gimme Gimme (A Man After Midnight)'. Although 'Oh L'Amour' was a hit for Dollar the following year, 'Gimme Gimme Gimme' was well received, especially on the gay nightclub scene. Andy was a major Abba fan and would often include their songs in their live sets.

Because the Abba songs gave their live sets an atmospheric punch, they decided to record another Abba song for single release. Unable to decide which, they chose four and released them as an EP. The tracks were: 'Lay All Your Love On Me', 'SOS', 'Voulez-Vous' and 'Take A Chance On Me' which featured a rap by MC Kinky. "The Abba EP was commercial and fun, but a throw-away project for us to do because it was only four songs. And because they were written by the same writers it was easy for us to do," admitted Andy.

"The Abba stuff was originally going to be an album project, but then we were glad we didn't do that, because we were pretty swamped by Abba anyway," Andy remembered. Vince added, "We thought about it a lot. The Abba thing was done on a whim but we ended up ditching a lot of the songs because they weren't working."

When Erasure brought Abba back to the top of the chart, it kick-started a whole Abba revival. A plethora of Abba tribute bands were coming from every corner of the globe, the most successful being Australia's Björn Again. This brought Abba a whole army of new fans, and probably helped turn *Abba Gold* into a multi-million seller. As Andy Bell said, "You didn't like admit to liking them at school unless you were a bit femme, so me and my friends did."

They followed the EP with a remix of their first hit, 'Who Needs Love Like That' which made the Top 10, as did 'Always' and 'Run To The Sun'. In 2003 they issued *Hits! – The Very Best of Erasure* and to promote it they re-released 'Oh L'Amour' which went to number 13.

Erasure continue recording and in 2003 released the covers album, *Other People's Songs*, which included: 'Solsbury Hill', 'You've Lost That Lovin' Feeling', 'When Will I See You Again' and 'Video Killed The Radio Star'.

678 Jimmy Nail
Ain't No Doubt

Label & Cat No.: **eastwest YZ 686**

Producers: **Guy Pratt / Danny Schogger / Jimmy Nail**

Writers: **Guy Pratt / Danny Schogger / Jimmy Nail / Charlie Dore**

Date reached No.1: **18 July 1992**

Weeks at No.1: **3**

A STARTER FOR TEN: WHOSE REAL NAME is James Michael Aloysius Bradford? The name of the teddy bear in *Brideshead Revisited* is hardly appropriate for the Newcastle hard man, who became Jimmy Nail after treading on a plank and putting a nail through his foot. Born in Newcastle in 1954, he did six months in Strangeways for GBH and ducked questions about his past on *The South Bank Show* on the grounds that it might incriminate him further. (Saving it for his autobiography is more likely.) He also liked music and played in local R&B bands.

Jimmy Nail made his name in the acclaimed TV socio-comedy *Auf Wiedersehen Pet*, based on the adventures of seven building workers forced to find employment in Germany when work at home became scarce during the Thatcher years. His character, Oz, loved Merle Haggard, but the title song, 'That's Livin' Alright', was a hit in 1984 for Joe Fagin. In 1985 Nail released his cover of Rose Royce's 'Love Don't Live Here Anymore', which was produced by Roger Taylor from Queen. It made number three and Nail was mystified when the follow-up, 'Laura', failed to connect.

He conceived and co-wrote the BBC TV series, *Spender*, about an unconventional Geordie policeman. As always, he played to his strength – and accent. Sample dialogue, to a waiter, complaining that his lamb is undercooked: "A good vet would have this back on its feet in no time." "I think it's the job of fuckers like me to fly the flag," he says. "I like to remind people that Newcastle's there."

In 1992 Nail made the album, *Growing Up In Public*, with guest appearances from Gary Moore, George Harrison and David Gilmour. It was produced by session players, Danny Schogger (keyboards) and Guy Pratt (bass). The three of them wrote 'Ain't No Doubt', with Charlie Dore, a British country-rock artist, whose 'Pilot Of The Airwaves' was a minor UK hit in 1979. The song, partly spoken, partly sung, included a reference to another Newcastle singer with Sting's 'If You Love Somebody, Set Them Free'. It was a theatrical record with Katie Kissoon as the female lead, and the trombone solo came from Neil Sidwell.

The Nail file continued with his cameo in *Evita* and a witty TV series about an aspiring British country songwriter, *Crocodile Shoes*. His videos for the title song and 'Cowboy Dreams' became very popular on the European transmission of CMT (Country Music Television). Nail made the Top 20 in 1995 with 'Big River', featuring Mark Knopfler on guitar, saying, "It's about me, it's the most personal song I've ever written."

Jimmy Nail

679 Snap!
Rhythm Is A Dancer

Label & Cat No.: **Arista 115 309**

Producer: **Snap!**

Writers: **Benito Benites / John Garrett / Thea Austin / Durron Butler**

Date Reached No.1: **8 August 1992**

Weeks at No.1: **6**

WITH THE SUCCESS OF THEIR FIRST album *World Power*, Snap! spent the best part of 1991 touring the US with MC Hammer. They then returned to the Master Studios in Frankfurt to record their next album. They underwent a change of singers with Jackie Harris being replaced by Sharon Redd's sister, Ohio-born soul singer, Penny Ford. She recorded a couple of tracks for the album *The Madman's Return* and then decided to pursue a solo career. Her replacement was Thea Austin. But after laying down the vocals for what was to become the first single, 'Rhythm Is A Dancer', she also left. Around the same time, Turbo B quit the band after a series of what he claimed were 'musical disagreements'. His replacement was Niki Harris, a former backing singer for Madonna.

'Rhythm Is A Dancer', with its rap lyric 'If the groove don't get ya the rifle's gonna, I'm serious as cancer when I say rhythm is a dancer', was followed by the Top 10 hits 'Exterminate', 'Do You See The Light' and 'Welcome To Tomorrow'.

Turbo B, the ex-US army vocalist, said he wanted to pursue more out and out rap. He tried to continue under the Snap! banner but was threatened with legal action by Michael Munzing and Luca Anzilotti who owned the copyright on the name. He also collaborated with Thea Austin on the German-released single, 'I'm Not Dead Yet'.

A remix by CJ Stone was back in the Top 20 in May 2003.

680 The Shamen
Ebeneezer Goode

Label & Cat No.: **One Little Indian 78 7P7**
Producer: **The Shamen**
Writers: **Colin Angus / Richard West**
Date Reached No.1: **19 September 1992**
Weeks at No.1: **4**

OVER THE YEARS, MANY SONGS HAVE had drugs references, but none so blatantly as 'Ebeneezer Goode'. The Shamen's Mr C, however, would deny this for years.

The Shamen were formed in Aberdeen in 1984 and were originally called Alone Again Or, after the Love track. The group comprised Colin Angus, Will Sinnott and Mr C (born Richard West). In 1990 they signed to One Little Indian Records, but their first hit, 'Pro-gen' failed to make the Top 50. It was remade two years later with the new title 'Move Any Mountain' and reached number four. 'L.S.I' (Love, Sex Intelligence) followed making number six. Then came 'Ebeneezer Goode'.

Mr C: "We were at the Town & Country Club in London and Colin was in the crowd. All of a sudden this black guy came up to him and put his arms on Colin's shoulders. Colin said, 'Are you all right mate?', he replied, 'Yeah man, the E's are good'. He then came up to me and said, 'Richard, I've just had this fantastic idea' and he told me about doing this track called 'Ebeneezer Goode', about E."

"It was an ambiguous song," continued Mr C." It did have two meanings, but there was never any mention of any drugs anywhere in the song. The chorus is saying 'Eezer good, Eezer good, Ebeneezer Good'. Within the first verse it says, 'His friends call him Eezer and he is a main geezer', Eezer being short for Ebeneezer which is justified for the chorus." He added, "Anyone who thinks that my song had anything to do with people taking drugs and dying from them is the most stupid accusation that any human being could put forward."

Top Of The Pops producer, Stanley Appel, was sceptical about letting The Shamen appear on the show. It was agreed that the line, 'Anybody got any Veras' (Veras being Cockney rhyming slang for Vera Lynn's – skins [tobacco paper]) was substituted with 'Anybody got any underlay'. When Mr C was asked what he meant by underlay, he replied, "Underlay, that was just a rug reference."

681 Tasmin Archer
Sleeping Satellite

Label & Cat No.: **EMI EM 233**
Producer: **Julian Mendelsohn**
Writers: **Tasmin Archer / John Beck / John Hughes**
Date Reached No.1: **17 October 1992**
Weeks at No.1: **2**

TASMIN, WHO WAS BORN IN BRADFORD in 1964 to Jamaican parents, left school at 16. She worked in a factory by day and sang with a variety of covers bands by night.

In 1983 she landed a job at Bradford's Flexible Response Studios. Initially making the tea and cleaning the toilets, she was asked to sing backing vocals on a couple of sessions. She was then introduced to John Beck and John Hughes and the trio formed a songwriting partnership. "We wrote a load of songs in 1988, which included 'Sleeping Satellite' and did some demos. We sent them to various record and publishing companies and had the usual rejections. One of the publishing companies took an interest and played the songs to a manager called Ian McAndrew. It was him who got us a contract with EMI and began representing us."

EMI spent £40,000 on advertising on a number of commercial radio stations. At the same time, EMI appointed a new MD, Jean-Francois Cecillon, who decided that Tasmin's album was a priority and sent her out on a meet-and-greet tour, where they played for company reps and record dealers.

It paid off. The introductory album, *Great Expectations*, with all tracks written by the trio, went into the Top 10 and spent almost a year on the chart. It also spawned the follow-up singles 'In Your Care' (16), 'Lords Of The New Church' (26) and 'Arienne' (30).

Tasmin was often dressed in a suit with shirt, tie and waistcoat. The song, which has been interpreted as a love song, is mainly about the waste of human resources and the money spent trying to get to discover life on other planets when the money could be used to greater effect on the starving millions. It's about man's urge to know everything there is to know before our planet disappears.

Tasmin won a Brit award for Best Newcomer. "I keep my award in the kitchen and I use it to crack nuts with," she admitted. By 1998 she had lost interest. "I've realised that the music business is a lot more to do with business than it is to do with music." In the late Nineties EMI passed on the option to renew Tasmin's contract. At the same time, "I lost all enthusiasm for music, I tried to keep writing out of habit, but my heart wasn't in it so I decided to take a year off, which turned into two years. In 2000 I felt I should write again, but both my partner and I were completely blocked." Two years later they had written some songs and were contemplating making them available for download.

682 Boyz II Men
End Of The Road

Label & Cat No.: **Motown TMG 1411**
Producers: **L.A.Reid / Babyface**
Writers: **L.A.Reid / Babyface / Daryl Simmons**
Date Reached No.1: **31 October 1992**
Weeks at No.1: **3**

THE EARLY NINETIES SAW A SURGE OF new R&B acts: Color Me Badd, En Vogue and SWV to name just a few, but none have matched the success of Boyz II Men.

Only Elvis Presley (80), Mariah Carey (61) and The Beatles (59) have spent more weeks on top of the US singles chart. But Elvis, Mariah and The Beatles did it with 18, 15 and 20 hits respectively. Boyz II Men spent 50 weeks with

just five singles, making them the most successful R&B group of all time.

Nathan Morris and Phyllis Nelson's son Marc, met at school and sang together for years. Whilst at the Philadelphia's School of Creative and Performing Arts, they tried for ages to get a group together, but it proved difficult due to various members graduating. Eventually they stabilised a line-up in 1988 when they recruited Shawn Stockman, Wanya Morris and Michael McCary. They called themselves Unique Attraction and their harmonies were reminiscent of The Five Satins in the Fifties.

They were fans of New Edition and would often cover their songs including 'Boys To Men', a track from the 1988 album *Heart Break*, which they would later adopt as their name. The following year they met former New Edition member Michael Bivins at a Bell Biv DeVoe concert and impressed him with their acappella version of New Edition's 'Can You Stand The Rain'. Michael offered to manage them and got them a recording contract with Motown. Michael Bivins and Marc Nelson never saw eye-to-eye and Marc left, leaving Boyz II Men a quartet.

Their debut album *Cooleyhighharmony* was released in 1991and reached the Top 10 in both the US and UK. The first single, the dancey 'Motownphilly', a reference to their early influences, featured a rap by Michael Bivins, and went to number three in the US. In the UK, it became the follow-up to 'End Of The Road'.

'End Of The Road' was written for the Eddie Murphy film *Boomerang*. Co-writer Babyface was going to sing it himself but he, L.A. Reid and Daryl Simmons decided Boyz II Men would do a better job, so it was offered to them. "We flew to Philadelphia to meet them and they told me they had to be back on tour the next day, so we laid down all the vocals in just three hours," Reid remembered.

When 'End Of The Road' stayed at the top of the US chart for 13 weeks, it broke a record Elvis Presley had set in 1956 when 'Hound Dog' / 'Don't Be Cruel' spent 11 weeks at the top. That record didn't last long. Two years later Boyz II Men broke their own record when 'I'll Make Love To You' took residency for 14 weeks. The following year, they teamed up with Mariah Carey for 'One Sweet Day', which yet again broke their record by spending 16 weeks at the top and became America's most successful record of all-time, eclipsing Whitney Houston's 'I Will Always Love You'.

Their next single '4 Seasons Of Loneliness' topped the US chart and became their last top 10 hit in the UK. Wanya developed a polyp on his vocal chords, which forced them to cancel a number of shows. He made a full recovery and in 1999 their contract got transferred to Universal in a major record company merger. In 2002 and now signed to Arista, the group released their latest album, *Full Circle*, which spent a mere two weeks on the UK chart.

683 Charles And Eddie
Would I Lie To You?

Label & Cat No.: **Capitol CDCL 673**

Producer: **Josh Deutsch**

Writers: **Michael Leeson / Peter Vale**

Date Reached No.1: **21 November 1992**

Weeks at No.1: **2**

A MUTUAL LOVE OF MARVIN GAYE brought black and white duo Charles Pettigrew and Eddie Chacon together. The pair met on the New York subway when Eddie spotted Charles carrying his favourite album, Marvin Gaye's 1972 *Trouble Man* soundtrack under his arm.

Charles, who had been a member of Down Avenue, and Eddie struck up a conversation. "We were both working musicians and the New York soul music community isn't that large so we started hanging together," Eddie explained in *Mojo* magazine. "But when Charles came down and sang on this project I was working on and we heard a track with both our voices on – 'Hurt No More' – it had a real uniqueness and we just took it from there."

Charles and Eddie's singing style can be likened to Sam & Dave, in as much as they both sang lead. "Voices singing in harmony are pretty much irresistible. But we're not singing lead and harmony like The Everly Brothers. Marvin Gaye did it all the time, recording himself singing two parts that backed each other up. Al Green was another," Charles explained.

British-born songwriters Michael Leeson and Peter Vale were both former school teachers who began writing in the early Eighties and had written hits for Sheena Easton ('One Man Woman'), Alvin Stardust ('So Near To Christmas'), Haywoode ('Roses') and Mica Paris ('My One Temptation').

"*Duophonic* stood out because hardly anyone was using live instruments at that moment," Eddie said of their debut album. But they found it hard to get airplay. In Britain, the charts were being filled with more electronic dance music. In the US it was also difficult. Eddie reasoned, "It's not got the hard rum sound of rap or new jack swing, so black stations ignore it. The rock stations ignore it because it's clearly not rock and the oldie soul stations won't play it, because it was made in the Nineties."

The next single, 'N.Y.C (Can You Believe This City)', which was written about their initial meeting, stiffed at number 33 and the follow up album, *Chocolate Milk*, in 1995 attracted few buyers. They decided to concentrate on songwriting and joined Leeson and Vale in writing Connor Reeves' 1998 hit 'Searching For A Soul'. That partnership came to an end when Charles died of cancer in April 2001 aged just 37.

684 Whitney Houston
I Will Always Love You

Label & Cat No.: **Arista 74321120657**

Producer: **David Foster**

Writer: **Dolly Parton**

Date reached No.1: **5 December 1992**

Weeks at No.1: **10**

FROM 1967 TO 1974, THE COUNTRY singer Dolly Parton was part of Porter Wagoner's road show, but she also made records in her own right. When she became more

As the daughter of Cissy Houston and niece of Dionne Warwick, Whitney Houston was born into a career in music and she didn't disappoint

successful than Wagoner she was determined to break away from him, but while she was loathe to destroy a very profitable relationship she disliked the way the split developed into legal wrangles. So she wrote this song to tell Porter how she felt about him, no matter what and irrespective of his indifference. The song topped the US country charts on release and again, six years later, when it was used in the film of the stage musical, *The Best Little Whorehouse In Texas*. Dolly as the madam is engaging, but Burt Reynolds is no singer.

Around the same time as Dolly was writing 'I Will Always Love You', a film script called *The Bodyguard* was written for Ryan O'Neal and Diana Ross. It was never made but it was revived in 1992 for Kevin Costner and Whitney Houston. In the script, the bodyguard takes the soul diva to a bar and Jimmy Ruffin's 'What Becomes Of The Brokenhearted?' is on the jukebox. At the end of the film, after the bodyguard has saved her life, Whitney performs the song for him.

Just before the film was made, 'What Becomes Of The Brokenhearted?' was included in another film, *Fried Green Tomatoes*, and another song had to be found at short notice. A researcher suggested Linda Ronstadt's 'I Will Always Love You'. When they looked into the song's history, they noted that Dolly Parton's original included a third, spoken verse which Linda had omitted. Whitney decided to sing the complete song very emotionally. Her *tour de force* topped the US charts for a record-breaking 14 weeks and it even outsold 'We Are The World' as America's biggest selling single to date. It topped the UK charts for 10 weeks and became the biggest-selling CD single to date.

The single was appropriate as Whitney married the bad boy rapper, Bobby Brown, at her mansion in New Jersey with Stevie Wonder singing at the wedding. Bobby topped the UK charts as part of New Edition in 1983 and, in 1994, they recorded the duet single, 'Something In Common'. Their squabbles became public property (Houston, we have a problem) and he even told the press that he had married a lesbian. Drugs busts and rehab followed, Whitney lost weight and was ditched from the 2001 Oscars when she forgot the words to 'Over The Rainbow' at rehearsals. In 2004 she made a spectacular comeback in China.

Whitney Houston's 'I Will Always Love You' is the most requested record to be played at funerals. Clearly a song to die for.

685 2 Unlimited
No Limit

Label & Cat No.: **Network NWK 46**

Producers: **Phil Wilde / Jean-Paul De Coster**

Writers: **Anita Dels / Ray Slijngaard / Phil Wilde / Jean-Paul De Coster**

Date Reached No.1: **13 February 1993**

Weeks at No.1: **5**

WHEN TWO BELGIAN WRITER/PRODUCERS, Phil Wilde and Jean-Paul De Coster assembled 2 Unlimited in 1991, they took techno to new limits, or was it no limit?

"Three years ago we were the first to pick things from the underground scene and translate them to a broader audience," Phil said in an interview with *Knack* magazine. "Ever since we were one step ahead of the competition when it comes to including new trends in techno."

Jean-Paul had already written the 1990 Top 10 hit for Bizz Nizz called 'Don't Miss The Partyline'. For 2 Unlimited they recruited a Dutch duo that comprised singer Anita Dels and keyboardist and rapper Ray Slijngaard and got a record deal with Bite Records in Holland. Pete Waterman heard their debut single, 'Get Ready For This' as an import whilst recording his television show, *The Hitman And Her* in Manchester. Pete said, "I was straight on the phone to my friend Tony in Holland and asked him to track down the band because I wanted to sign them. Tony told me that 'Get Ready For This' was actually the B-side. He played me the A-side and it was the most awful rap you've ever heard, so I told him I only wanted to buy the B-side and that he could sell the A-side to anyone he wanted. It cost me £1,000 and the whole deal was done in four hours."

'Get Ready For This' had all the makings of a number one hit, but it came up against Bryan Adams. The follow-up, 'Twilight Zone' also reached number two. After two further hits, 'Workaholic' and 'The Magic Friend', their fifth single, 'No Limit' went all the way.

It appeared a bit odd that on Valentine's week, more people would go out and buy a song called 'No Limit' rather than 'I Will Always Love You', but it seemed the public couldn't help themselves from purchasing a song with 12 consecutive 'no's in the lyric.

Things turned negative when the music journalists started calling them 2 Untalented. On top of that, 'No Limit' became referred to as 'No Lyrics'. Even so, Ray insists that despite over 50 no's, there is nothing negative about them or the song.

In 1995, after eight Top 10 hits, both Ray and Anita quit the band. Anita, who lives in Amsterdam said, "I had my own ideas which I tried to put into the group, but it became too difficult." She went on to present a television dance show called *Welcome To The Pleasure Zone* as well as her own radio show, and attempted a solo career with a more R&B style. She also runs her own production company, Unlimited Ways. Ray formed his own company, Raymar Productions and released a solo single, a cover of Rod Stewart's 'Da Ya Think I'm Sexy'. He says, "There is so much young talent in Holland and I can teach them a lot because I had done a lot." As for 2 Unlimited, they continued with two new female members, Romy and Marion and charted one hit, 'Wanna Get Up' which just scraped into the Top 40. It seemed there was no limit, at least, until Ray and Anita left!

2 Unlimited

686 Shaggy
Oh Carolina

Label & Cat No.: **Greensleeves GRECD 361**

Producer: **Sting International**

Writers: **John Folkes / Henry Mancini**

Date Reached No.1: **20 March 1993**

Weeks at No.1: **2**

BORN ORVILLE RICHARD BURRELL IN Jamaica in 1968, Shaggy earned his nickname when school friends coined it after the *Scooby Doo* character and also because of his shaggy hair. At 18 his family moved to Brooklyn, New York where Shaggy began performing with a group of Jamaican friends who called themselves Sting International. Among that group was Shaun Pizzonia who later became Shaggy's sole producer.

At 20 he joined the Marines and was stationed in North Carolina. In his spare time he continued performing, occasionally driving back to New York for recording sessions. He released his first single, 'Man In Mi Yard' which didn't sell well. The follow-ups, 'Mampie' and 'Big Up' went to number one on the New York reggae chart. He also met Brooklyn singer Rayvon, with whom he would record a cover of Mungo Jerry's 'In The Summertime' in 1995.

When he had completed a four-year stint in the Marines, in which he was involved in the Gulf War's 'Operation Desert Storm', he continued recording. He heard an old ska track from 1959 called 'Carolina' which was written by John Folkes and recorded by him and his brothers. Shaggy's version incorporated a sample from Henry Mancini's version of 'Peter Gunn'. Initially it was only a hit locally until it gained some international promotion.

Greensleeves Records, which was formed in 1978, was a specialist reggae label. Despite releasing over 300 records, they had never had a UK hit until they issued Shaggy's remake of 'Oh Carolina'. It was released in the UK in January and failed to make an impact for six weeks. It was then included in the Sharon Stone film *Sliver*, which helped it rocket to number one.

It was reggae's greatest resurgence. The second week Shaggy was at number one, Snow, a white rapper from Canada, was at number two with 'Informer' and Shabba Ranks' 'Mr Loverman' was at number three, an achievement Bob Marley would have been proud of.

A new craze was taking hold. Ragga, a dancehall variation of reggae, was characterised by its use of computerised beats and involves the singer 'toasting', which itself is a more frenzied style of talking over the backing track and first used by Jamaican disc jockeys. The patois often condoned the use of firearms and promotes homophobia and misogyny.

On the strength of his first number one, Greensleeves issued a compilation album, *Original Doberman*, which included many of Shaggy's early recordings.

In 1994 the UK female ragga duo, Louchie Lou and Michie One released a cover of the Isley Brothers' 'Shout', which sampled the rhythm of 'Oh Carolina'.

687 The Bluebells
Young At Heart

Label & Cat No.: **MCA MCSTD 40257**

Producer: **The Bluebells**

Writers: **Robert Hodgens / Bobby Valentino / Siobhan Fahey**

Date Reached No.1: **3 April 1993**

Weeks at No.1: **4**

LIKE ORANGE JUICE AND AZTEC Camera before them, Scottish quintet The Bluebells made fine feel-good pop songs.

Formed in 1982 they comprised brothers Ken McCluskey (vocals/harmonica) and David McCluskey (drums), Robert Hodgens (guitar), Lawrence Donegan (bass) and Russell Irvine (guitar). Within a few months, Craig Gannon replaced Irvine and Neal Baldwin took over from Donegan. Their first two singles, 'Cath', and 'Sugar Bridge (It Will Stand)' in 1983 made little impact. The next single 'I'm Falling' reached a respectable number 11.

In March 1983 Robert Hodgens, who was dating Siobhan Fahey from Bananarama, gave the girls a hand by co-writing a couple of tracks for their debut album *Deep Sea Skiving*. One of them, 'Cheers Then' was released as a single and reached number 45. The other, 'Young At Heart' remained an album track, which Siobhan thought The Bluebells should cover on their debut album, *Sisters*.

'Young At Heart' originally reached number eight in June 1984 and gave The Bluebells their only Top 10 hit. On the strength of that, 'Cath' was re-issued but only just dented the Top 40. By 1985 they had split up.

Ken and David formed The McCluskey brothers and released the album *Aware Of All*. Robert Hodgens formed the short-lived group, Up, and Craig became The Smiths' second guitarist having temporarily stood in for bassist Andy Rourke.

When Volkswagen began using 'Young At Heart' to advertise their various models on television in 1993, MCA re-issued it and it went to number one. The band were more surprised than anyone and had no intention of reforming the band, but did agree to get together for a *Top Of The Pops* appearance, all except for Donegan who was banned after he had a falling out with BBC staff and used the opportunity to write an exposé in *The Guardian*. Original guitarist Irvine, who had become a chef, agreed to step in.

The same week The Bluebells hit the top, Siobhan Fahey, who had now married the Eurythmics' Dave Stewart, appeared as a guest vocalist on 'Walk Into The Wind', by Vegas.

Although credited above, Bobby Valentino's name wasn't on the single. Bobby, who also records under his real name Robert Beckingham, launched a complicated high court appeal in 2002 to claim royalties for the violin solo that he claimed he wrote and played. Robert Hodgens stated in court that Bobby was paid a £75 session fee for playing on the track but insisted he wrote it. Bobby played the solo on his violin in court. Mr Christopher Floyd QC found that Bobby was the composer and was awarded a share of the music copyright. In 1996 Bobby released the solo album, *You're Telling Me*.

688 George Michael & Queen With Lisa Stansfield Five Live (EP)

Label & Cat No.: **Parlophone CDRS 6340**

Producers: **George Michael / David Richards / Queen**

Writer (Somebody To Love): **Freddie Mercury**

Date Reached No.1: **1 May 1993**

Weeks at No.1: **3**

EIGHTEEN MONTHS AFTER HIS DEATH, Freddie Mercury's memory and music was still very much alive.

For an EP to make the chart is a rare enough thing, but this was the first five tracker to make number one. The lead track on the EP was 'Somebody To Love'. The other tracks were a medley of Adamski's' 'Killer' and The Temptations' 'Papa Was A Rolling Stone' and 'Calling You', sung by George Michael, and 'These Are The Days Of Our Lives', which is sung by Lisa Stansfield.

'Somebody To Love', with its poignant opening line 'Each morning I get up I die a little, can barely stand on my feet', which originally reached number two in 1976, was a live recording from the Freddie Mercury tribute concert.

George Michael made the heartfelt plea, "I think a lot of people, not necessarily people who have anything against gay people, are probably taking some small comfort in the fact that although Freddie died of AIDS he was publicly bisexual. It's a very, very dangerous comfort. The conservative estimate for the year 2000 is that 40 million people on this planet will be infected by HIV and if you think that those are all going to be gay people or drug addicts, then you are pretty well lining up to be one of those numbers. So please, for God's sake and for Freddie's sake, and for your own sakes, please be careful."

All the proceeds and the artists' royalties were donated to The Mercury Phoenix Trust for the distribution to AIDS charities worldwide in memory of the incomparable Freddie Mercury.

689 Ace Of Base All That She Wants

Label & Cat No.: **MCA MCSTD 40257**

Producer: **Denniz Pop**

Writers: **Jonas Berggren / Ulf Ekberg**

Date Reached No.1: **22 May 1993**

Weeks at No.1: **3**

AFTER ABBA SPLIT IN 1982, SWEDEN'S musical flag fluttered in the breeze created by Europe and Roxette until Ace Of Base came together in Gothenburg in 1990. There was synthesizer player Jonas Berggren, his two sisters Jenny and Malin (known as Linn), whose only musical experiences had been singing in a local church, and two of Jonas' friends. "After our first gig Jonas' friends quit due to stage fright. We all knew Ulf Ekberg so we took him in," recalled Linn.

Jonas and Ulf started writing songs together and the quartet began playing dance music in the local pubs and clubs. They demoed two songs 'Wheel Of Fortune' and 'All That She Wants' and sent them to Mega Records who signed them immediately.

Mega Records wanted Ace Of Base to record an album of cover versions, but as Linn remembered, "We said to them, 'please, no covers because we write out own material and it's very good.'" They argued over it and eventually Ace Of Base agreed to do one cover, the Diane Warren and Albert Hammond-penned 'Don't Turn Around'.

They teamed up with DJ and producer Denniz Pop (born Dag Volle) following his success as producer and co-writer of Dr Alban's 'It's My Life'. He went on to write and produce hits for 'N Sync and Five. Denniz died of cancer in 1998, aged just 35.

Mega Records issued 'Wheel Of Fortune' in 1992 and although it went unnoticed in their homeland it topped the charts in Denmark and Norway. They re-recorded 'All That She Wants' the following year and it topped the charts all over Europe. They signed to Arista Records in the US and the song went to number two there.

"Some songs work on the dance floor and not on the radio and vice versa," Jenny explained in *Rolling Stone*. But 'All That She Wants', with its steady dance beat and hook line "All that she wants is another baby" has appeal in both places. They followed it with the debut album, *Happy Nation*, which initially peaked at number 21 in the UK.

'Wheel Of Fortune' was issued as the follow-up in the UK and faltered at number 20. The album's title track was next and that fell short of the Top 40. When their next single, 'The Sign', peaked at number two here and topped the chart in the States the following year, it prompted the record company to reissue the album adding four tracks, including 'The Sign', and it went to number one. It also earned its placed in the *Guinness World Of Records* as the biggest selling debut album of all time.

690 UB40 (I Can't Help) Falling In Love With You

Label & Cat No.: **DEP International DEPDG 40**

Producer: **UB40**

Writers: **George David Weiss / Hugo Perretti / Luigi Creatore**

Date Reached No.1: **12 June 1993**

Weeks at No.1: **2**

SINCE THEIR LAST NUMBER ONE, 'I GOT You Babe' in 1985, UB40 had scored Top 10 hits with 'Don't Break My Heart' (1985), 'Sing Our Own Song' (1986), 'Breakfast In Bed' (1988), 'Homely Girl' (1989), 'Kingston Town' and 'I'll Be Your Baby Tonight' (both 1990). Despite writing over 45 hit singles, UB40's three chart toppers were all cover versions.

In 1992 UB40, along with 200 other artists, were asked to record an Elvis tune of their choice for a new film called *Honeymoon In Vegas*. Twenty Elvis songs appeared in the film including some by the King himself. Although John

Swedish, two female vocalists, one blonde, the other brunette... Ace Of Base are, left to right: Jonas Berggren, Malin Berggren, Jenny Berggren and Ulf Ekberg

Mellencamp's version of 'Jailhouse Rock' was released, it attracted few buyers. However, Billy Joel's version of 'All Shook Up' was better received and reached number 27.

UB40's drummer, James Brown, suggested they record 'Can't Help Falling In Love', because it was one of his favourites. It was a popular song and had already been a hit for Elvis (1), Andy Williams (3), The Stylistcs (4) and Lick The Tins (42). The whole band agreed and gave it a reggae treatment, including an acappella intro. When they presented the song to the film director Andrew Bergman, they learned that a few other acts had recorded the same song, with Clarence Giddons and Bruno Hernandez's version making it into the film, whilst Bono's version ended up on the soundtrack album even though it wasn't in the film.

Around the same time, music producer Tim Sexton was working with director Philip Noyce on a new film, *Sliver*. They approached Virgin Records with a view to using some songs by artists on their roster and also hoped they would take on the soundtrack to the movie. He had already secured Enigma and Massive Attack and wanted UB40 as well. The film, an erotic thriller, starred Sharon Stone and William Baldwin.

"We weren't all that happy with the finished version," admitted Robin Campbell, of UB40. "But we thought it might have been used in *Honeymoon In Vegas*. We were going to scrap it because we were working on our new album, *Promises And Lies* at the time and were determined not to put any covers versions on it. It was all our own material." The band were unsure whether to put the track on the album or not. Most were against it because, as Robin said, "They thought it wasn't representative of the rest of the album, but I persuaded them that it would be pointless not to, as it was likely to be a smash hit."

'(I Can't Help) Falling In Love' gave UB40 their second US number one and went one better than Elvis who peaked at number two behind Joey Dee & The Starliters' 'Peppermint Twist' in 1962.

691 Gabrielle
Dreams

Label & Cat No.: **Go. Beat GODCD 99**

Producer: **Richie Fermie**

Writers: **Gabrielle / Tim Laws**

Date Reached No.1: **26 June 1993**

Weeks at No.1: **3**

LOUISE GABRIELLE BOBB WAS BORN in Hackney, East London in 1969, but spent most of her life growing up south of the river. She spent her teenage years working in an office by day and singing for free in West End clubs at night. She had suffered with a lazy right eye-lid since birth, but had refused cosmetic surgery and chose instead to wear an eye patch, using it as a fashion statement. Later in her career the patch came off after corrective eye surgery, but to avoid her eye being seen she would carefully hang her wedge haircut over it, or wear dark glasses.

In 1991 at a session produced by Victor Trim, she recorded a demo of 'Dreams' with a sample of Tracy Chapman's 'Fast Car'. The pair subsequently fell out over business matters but it received airplay on Kiss FM and began selling in dance shops in 1992.

A member of staff at Go. Beat, a subsidiary of Go! Discs Records, heard it and contacted Gabrielle with the intention of signing her. When they learned of Tracy Chapman's refusal to allow the sample they re-recorded the track.

Gabrielle topped the chart in the summer but before she could enjoy the success, she was haunted by Victor Trim. "He went to court saying that he had produced the music for 'Dreams' and that he owned the lyrics because I had assigned him my rights in a publishing deal that I was supposed to have signed, but didn't," she said in an interview with *Q* magazine. "When his own lawyers withdrew that must have told him something. We won, but it was a waste of a lot of money, it was ridiculous."

With a soulful voice reminiscent of Randy Crawford, Gabrielle recorded her debut album, *Find Your Way*, which went on to sell nearly a million copies. The album also contained the follow-up singles, 'Going Nowhere' and 'I Wish'.

The following year she won a Brit award for Best Newcomer and looked set for a long career when she fell pregnant. Her son Jordan was born in April 1995 and his father, Tony Antoniou walked out the day he was born. A few months later, Tony was arrested on suspicion of the murder of his step-father, Walter McCarthy. Gabrielle was brought in for questioning but released when the police were satisfied that she was not involved. In 1997 he admitted stabbing his step-father 52 times and then beheading him with a sword. He is now serving life in prison.

692 Take That
Pray

Label & Cat No.: **RCA 74321154502**

Producers: **Steve Jervier / Paul Jervier / Jonathan Wales / Mark Beswick**

Writer: **Gary Barlow**

Date reached No.1: **17 July 1993**

Weeks at No.1: **4**

WITH THEIR COMBINATION OF youthful good looks, melodic songs and choreographed stage performances, the US boy band New Kids On The Block were, well, the new kids of the block. In 1991 a UK manager, Nigel Martin-Smith, assembled a group of Manchester boys to appeal to the same market.

Gary Barlow, born in Frodsham, Cheshire in 1971, had played the organ at the Runcorn British Legion for Ken Dodd and been a finalist with a Christmas song in *Pebble Mill At One*. As a result, Rod Argent had been giving him advice on writing songs. The fashion-conscious and eternally smiling Mark Owen, born in Oldham in 1972, had had dreams of being a professional footballer, but his various trials had come to naught. Howard Donald, born in Droylsden, Manchester, in 1968, worked for a garage and was passionate about breakdancing. Another Mancunian, Jason Orange, born in 1970, was

Gabrielle's eye patch – worn to hide a lazy right eye-lid – made for an unusual fashion statement

also into breakdancing but was painting and decorating for a living. Martin-Smith decided they needed a fifth member and placed an advert in a local paper. Enter Robbie Williams, the most divisive member of the group, who was born in Newcastle-under-Lyme in 1974 and whose father, Pete Conway, had been a finalist on *New Faces*. Robbie had a background of juvenile roles including, rather appropriately, one as the Artful Dodger in *Oliver!*. At the audition he sang a Jason Donovan song.

Take That's first single, 'Do What U Like', was written by Barlow, on Martin-Smith's own Dance label. Then came Martin-Smith's odd plan: instead of aiming for teenage girls immediately, his plan was to break them through gay clubs and he didn't even consider events for under 18s. 'Do What You Like' didn't sell but the mooning video got attention – and we were to see a lot of Williams's bottom over the coming years – and they were signed to RCA. They had a minor hit with 'Promises' and expected big things from 'Once You've Tasted Love' which stiffed at number 47 and almost caused the group to split.

Determined to have a major hit, Take That went on their Big Schools tour, visiting three schools a day promoting safe sex and playing a club in the evening. As result, they made the Top 10 with a revival of Tavares' 'It Only Takes a Minute'. They got into the Top three with Barry Manilow's (and Chopin's) 'Could It Be Magic?', the first single to feature Robbie's lead vocal. Their debut album, *Take That And Party*, was a big seller, and Mark Owen won a *Smash Hits* award as Most Fanciable Male. 'Why Can't I Wake Up With You?', another Gary Barlow song, entered at number two, but it couldn't dislodge 2 Unlimited's 'No Limit'. A promotional T-shirt said, "Why did I wake up with you?"

Mark Owen was impressed with Gary's keyboard playing and so Gary sold him one to practice on. As Gary showed him how to use it, Gary found he was writing a song, which became the ballad of lost love, 'Pray'. 'Pray' went straight in at number one, the B-side being an acappella version. 'Pray' won both Best Song and Best Video at the Brit awards, where they sang a medley of Beatle songs. It won Best Contemporary Song at the Ivor Novello awards.

As a northern lad, Robbie Williams was once asked if he had ever eaten tripe. "No," he replied. "Tripe was when we had our first number one."

693 Freddie Mercury
Living On My Own

Label & Cat No.: **Parlophone CDR 6355**
Producer: **Serge Ramaekers / Carl Ward / Colin Peter**
Writers: **Freddie Mercury**
Date Reached No.1: **14 August 1993**
Weeks at No.1: **2**

HAVING EARNED HIMSELF A reputation as one of the world's greatest frontmen, Freddie Mercury decided to take a chance on working solo. His first hit, 'Love Kills', reached number 10 in 1984. His album, *Mr Bad Guy* also made the Top 10, but by Queen standards, these were only moderate hits. Three other singles were released from it, including the funky 'Living On My Own', which floundered at number 50. In 1987, having learned that he was HIV positive, he covered 'The Great Pretender', a song with which he could identify, especially the line, 'I'm lonely, but no-one can tell'. A more diverse venture came later the same year when he collaborated with the Spanish opera singer Montserrat Caballe on the number eight hit 'Barcelona'. The track reached number two when it was re-issued in 1992 to coincide with the Olympic Games in Barcelona.

"If you listen to 'Living On My Own', that's very me," said Freddie. "It's very characteristic of myself. I have to go around the world living in hotels. You can have a whole shoal of people looking after you, but at the end of day, they all go away. Basically, it's me living on my own, but I'm not complaining about it."

In 1989 a Belgian DJ Serge Ramaekers said, "I was asked by a nightclub owner to record a theme from for a new group called Confetti's. I recorded 'Sound Of C' which sold over 150,000 copies in Belgium." On the back of that success he turned his hand to remixing dance tracks and began collaborating with other remixers, Colin Peter and Carl Ward, who collectively used the pseudonym No More Brothers. In 1992 music producer John Becket and actor Ray Burdis were working with Serge Ramaekers and Carl Ward on a remix of a song by a German outfit called Vagen. Burdis was so impressed with Ramaekers' mixing skills that he asked Queen's manager Jim Beach if Serge could mix a Freddie song. Jim agreed they could mix 'Living On My Own'.

According to Greg Brooks' sleeve notes to Freddie Mercury's *Solo* box set, "When the remix was presented to EMI, they didn't consider it commercial enough to issue as a single, but they did agree that it could be released to clubs on an independent label controlled by the No More Brothers throughout Europe – with EMI having the option to pick up the single and make it an official release, in the event that it was a hit." 'Living On My Own' sold over two million copies worldwide and posthumously earned Freddie an Ivor Novello award.

The remix prompted others to remix Queen songs. In 1996 a previously unreleased song, 'You Don't Fool Me' was issued and contained three remixes by Dancing Divas, Jam & Spoon and David Richards. In 1998 a remix of 'Another One Bites The Dust' reached number five. Queen's own remix of 'Under Pressure' in 1999 and the Vanguard remix of 'Flash' in 2003 both made the Top 20.

Serge also made the chart as a recording artist. In 2002 under the name Orion Too he had the minor hit, 'Hope And Wait' and the following year as a member of the Supreme Dream Team they made number 23 with 'Dreamer' which sampled Supertramp's song of the same name.

Freddie Mercury

694 Culture Beat
Mr. Vain

Label & Cat No.: **Epic 659 4682**
Producer: **Torsten Fenslau**
Writers: **Torsten Fenslau / Peter Zweier / Juergen Katzmann / Jay Supreme**
Date Reached No.1: **28 August 1993**
Weeks at No.1: **4**

In October 1992 Annie Lennox's Top 30 release, 'Cold' became the first 'hit' single not commercially available on vinyl, and ever since there has been speculation about the future of vinyl. To add fuel to their argument, Culture Beat's 'Mr.Vain', although still available as a 12" single, became the first number one not available as a seven-inch single.

Frankfurt-born Torsten Fenslau was the resident DJ at the Dorian Club that became known for its all-night hard beat raves. Inspired by the atmosphere of those hot sweaty nights, Torsten recorded his first single, 'The Dream' under the pseudonym Out Of The Ordinary. In 1989 he joined forces with songwriter and engineer Peter Zweier and assembled Culture Beat comprising German keyboard player Jens Zimmerman, guitarist Nosie Katzmann, New Jersey rapper Jay Supreme and British singer Tania Evans.

Their debut single, '(Cherry Lips) Der Erdbeermund' fared well across Europe. The follow-ups, 'I Like You', 'No Deeper Meaning' and 'Tell Me What You Want' were well received in Torsten's native Germany but failed to connect in the UK. In 1993 they released the album *Serenity*, which sold 1.5 million and won Torsten an Echo prize, the highest German music industry award, for Producer Of The Year, and Culture Beat the prize of Most Successful Album Abroad. The album's first single, 'Mr Vain', which was rumoured to be autobiographical, topped the chart in 12 European countries and made the Top 20 Stateside.

The follow-up, 'Got To Get It' reached number four in the UK, but its success was overshadowed by the death of Torsten following a car accident. Determined to continue Culture Beat's success, his brother, Frank, took over.

The next album, *Metamorphosis*, saw a change of direction from the usual fast Euro-dance beat. This was attributed to Tania who left the group for a solo career and was replaced by Kim Sanders, who had worked with Torsten in the Eighties. Frank, who used five different production teams said, "Thinking it over in the short term, it would have been much simpler to continue the success of the Culture Beat formula. But we decided not to. We were seeking a musical challenge. *Metamorphosis* encompasses the entire international pop cosmos. Culture Beat's trademark used to be catchy lyrics and succinct passages of rap, but now they have been replaced by clear versatile song structures."

Culture Beat, who continued to have hits in Europe, brought in a new lead singer Jacky Sangster in 2003 and they re-recorded 'Mr Vain' as 'Mr Vain Recall'. It was released in the UK to mark the 10th anniversary of the original release, but it stiffed at number 51.

695 Jazzy Jeff & The Fresh Prince
Boom! Shake The Room

Label & Cat No.: **Jive JIVECD 335**
Producer: **Mr Lee**
Writers: **Will Smith / Lee Haggard / Walter Williams /Ken Mayberry / Leroy Bonner / Marshall Jones / Ralph Middlebrooks / Marvin Pierce / Walter Morrison / Norman Napier / Andrew Noland**
Date Reached No.1: **25 September 1993**
Weeks at No.1: **2**

In 1990 Will Smith won the lead role in the TV sitcom *The Fresh Prince Of Bel-Air* after passing an audition held at Quincy Jones' house in California. It was this role that made him a household name, but four years before that he had teamed up with DJ Jazzy Jeff (born Jeff Townes) for the hit 'Girls Ain't Nothing But Trouble'. They had further US-only hits with 'Parents Just Don't Understand', which dealt with the problems parents have understanding why teenagers spend a fortune on clothes, 'A Nightmare On My Street' and 'I Think I Can Beat Mike Tyson'. They were often criticized by other rappers for not taking rapping seriously. Their videos usually showed Will and Jeff having fun and larking about. Their breakthrough album *Rock The House* was only a moderate hit, but it was the follow-up, the three-million selling *I'm The DJ, He's The Rapper*, that won them Best Rap Album and Best Rap Artists at the 1989 National Music Awards. In the UK the Philadelphian rap duo looked set to become one-hit wonders until they returned in 1991 with the Top 10 hit 'Summertime'.

They then took two years off from recording so Will Smith could pursue his acting career. He starred alongside Whoopi Goldberg and Ted Danson in the 1993 film *Made In America*, whilst Jeff continued as a DJ. They returned the same year with the hard-hitting, yet radio-friendly, 'Boom! Shake The Room' which samples The Ohio Players' 1973 US hit 'Funky Worm'. Will and Jeff first performed the song on *The Fresh Prince Of Bel-Air* show.

The pair continued to release singles although Will was more in demand as an actor. It was his appearance in *Made In America* that landed him his next film role of Paul in the film version of the Broadway show, *Six Degrees Of Separation*, alongside Donald Sutherland and Stockard Channing.

In 1995 'Boom! Shake The Room' was remixed by Hula from The Outhere Brothers and went back to number 40 in the chart. The next single, the Bill Withers-sampled 'Lovely Daze', became their last UK hit as a duo. Jazzy Jeff again continued DJing and Will went on to star in *Bad Boys* (1995), *Independence Day* (1996), *A Thin Line Between Love And Hate* (1996) and *Men In Black* (1997) and *Men In Black II* (2002).

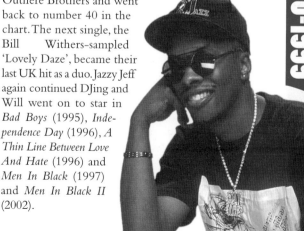

DJ Jazzy Jeff

696 Take That featuring Lulu Relight My Fire

Label & Cat No.: **RCA 74321167722**

Producers: **Joey Negro / Andrew Livingstone**

Writer: **Dan Hartman**

Date reached No.1: **9 October 1993**

Weeks at No.1: **2**

IN AUGUST 1993 TAKE THAT ASKED Lulu if she would take part in a remake of 'Relight My Fire', a disco favourite by Dan Hartman and an uncredited Loleatta Holloway. RCA had wanted to feature a black disco diva but Take That insisted on Lulu, having loved her hit single, 'Independence' (1993). Lulu said, "My cameo was about two-thirds of the way through. It was a powerful section of the song and everyone seemed happy with the result. It wasn't until I heard the final mix that I realised why the producers were so excited."

Strangely, 'Relight My Fire' was Lulu's first number one. Her recording debut, 'Shout', went Top 10 in 1964 and she also had hits with 'Leave A Little Love', 'The Boat That I Row', 'Me, The Peaceful Heart' and 'I'm A Tiger'. Although she was joint first in the 1969 Eurovision Song Contest with 'Boom Bang-A-Bang', the record fell short at number two and, for a time, this Europop confection undermined her credibility. David Bowie wrote, produced and played saxophone on her number three, 'The Man Who Sold The World', and, in 1986, she returned to the Top 10 with a remake of 'Shout'. In 1993 the disco-oriented 'Independence' had made number 11.

Lulu wrote about touring with Take That in her autobiography, *I Don't Want To Fight*: "We all looked outrageous. The boys were half naked in skimpy thongs or shorts, with devil-like horns on their heads. I wore a figure-hugging, completely see-through red lace dress and a red wig that made me look like Medusa with my hair on fire. For the finale, amid smoke and fireworks, I came up from the middle of the boys and they hoisted me high above their heads. The audience went insane."

The steamy video for 'Relight My Fire' featured Jason Orange in the shower. According to Lulu's book, Jason would flirt with her and Lulu says, "When I'm 70, I'll look back and say, 'Why didn't I sleep with him?'"

697 Meat Loaf I'd Do Anything For Love (But I Won't Do That)

Label & Cat No.: **Virgin VSCDT 1443**

Producer: **Jim Steinman**

Writers: **Jim Steinman**

Date Reached No.1: **23 October 1993**

Weeks at No.1: **7**

ON 22 NOVEMBER 1963, 16-YEAR-OLD Texan, Marvin Lee Aday witnessed the assassinated President Kennedy's limousine's arrival at Dallas' Parkland Hospital. That teenager was to adopt his nickname of Meat Loaf (partly coined by his father because of his size, even at the age of two; his classmates added the 'Loaf' in his later school years) and became one of rock's most successful artists.

In 1975 he played the roles of both Eddie and Dr Scott in a Broadway production of *The Rocky Horror Show*. Shortly after, he recreated the role of rocker Eddie in the film version. Meat also acted in many movies, including *Roadie, Wayne's World, Spiceworld* and more recently, *Fight Club.*

After meeting and befriending New York-born virtuoso pianist Jim Steinman at an audition for a part in Jim's off-Broadway play, *More Than You Deserve*, they created one of the biggest albums ever, the 30 million-selling *Bat Out Of Hell,* which has spent almost 500 weeks on the UK chart. Jim wrote and arranged the epic record with the multi-talented, singer/ songwriter Todd Rundgren in the role of producer. At almost 22 stone, Meat was an unlikely sex symbol, but *Bat Out Of Hell* turned him into a big star.

The album took some time to set the chart alight, but received a much-needed boost when BBC2's *Old Grey Whistle Test* showed a clip of 'Bat Out Of Hell' in early 1978. It eventually produced three singles, 'You Took The Words Right Out Of My Mouth' (33), 'Two Out Of Three Ain't Bad' (32) and the title track (15). These songs have become classics – more than the rather unimpressive chart positions of the first two suggest. Exhaustive world tours took their toll on Meat's voice and he took many months to fully recover.

The Eighties wasn't a particularly good decade for Meat. Being at a physical and mental low, and plagued with 22 separate lawsuits from his former manager and music publisher, Meat was advised to declare himself bankrupt. Although CBS Records claimed *Bat Out Of Hell* to be 'the most profitable record in history of the industry- more so than *Thriller*', astonishingly Meat only started receiving royalties in 1997.

Meat and Jim fell out in 1983, largely due to the album *Bad For Good*, a record meant as Meat's follow-up, but because of the problems he was experiencing with his voice, Jim had decided to sing it himself and release it as his own. He then went on to write and produce for artists such as Bonnie Tyler ('Total Eclipse Of The Heart', 1983), Air Supply ('Making Love Out Of Nothing At All', 1983), Celine Dion ('It's All Coming Back To Me Now', 1996) and a chart topper for Boyzone, ('No Matter What') in 1998.

They were reunited in 1990 when Meat invited Jim over to his house for a meal. Jim brought a new song, 'I'd Do Anything For Love (But I Won't Do That)' over for him to hear. Meat Loaf loved it but recommended they make some changes to the arrangement. Letting bygones be bygones, they agreed to record a sequel album, *Bat Out Of Hell II: Back Into Hell.* Featuring a similar bombastic and over-blown production to its predecessor, it went on to sell over five million copies worldwide. The first single released 'I'd Do Anything For Love (But I Won't Do That)' (doesn't he just love those parentheses), which was edited down from the original 12-minute album version, went to number one in a remarkable 25 countries and won him a Grammy for Best Rock Vocal. Meat Loaf

Lulu resurrected her career and hit number one for the first time by teaming up with Take That; left to right: Jason Orange, Gary Barlow, Lulu, Robbie Williams and Mark Owen

CHECKER

has always enjoyed becoming the character in his songs. "I saw myself as a 14-year-old boy, looking at this girl trying to figure out how to get the nerve to go over and ask her out," he revealed to *Billboard's* Fred Bronson. As for the song's seemingly ambiguous lyric, Meat explains: "It's so simple. The answer is right before every chorus. 'I'd do anything for love but I won't do that. I'll never stop dreaming of you every night of my life.'"

Meat Loaf began a new world tour in 2003, but had to cancel some dates after he collapsed in front of 11,000 fans at Wembley Arena. It was discovered he was suffering from Wolff-Parkinson-White Syndrome, a heart condition.

Jim Steinman and Meat are currently working on *Bat Out Of Hell 3*, which is expected to be released in 2005.

698 Mr. Blobby
Mr. Blobby

Label & Cat No.: **Destiny Music CDDMUS 104**

Producers: **Paul Shaw / David Rogers**

Writers: **Paul Shaw / David Rogers**

Date reached No.1: **11 December 1993**

Weeks at No.1: **3 (2 runs)**

NO *LET'S LOOK AT 1993* TV programmes could be comprehensive without mentioning Mr. Blobby, who lived in Noel Edmonds' fun town, Crinkley Bottom. In 1992 Mr. Blobby (we never learnt his first name) was created by TV producer, Mike Leggo, for *Noel's House Party* on BBC1 on Saturday evenings. It involved an actor, Barry Killerby, donning a pink foam rubber costume with yellow polka dot spots and wearing a ridiculous bow-tie. Ostensibly, the perambulating blancmange was there to assist celebrities in explaining their specialist subject to children – Valerie Singleton on money, Will Carling on rugby and Wayne Sleep on dance – but in every case, Mr. Blobby would become the centre of attention by falling over, creating havoc and intoning "Blobby, blobby, blobby".

Very young children loved Mr. Blobby and so they were bombarded with Mr. Blobby dolls, Mr. Blobby mugs, Mr. Blobby books, Mr. Blobby plastic suits, Mr. Blobby board games and, naturally, the Mr. Blobby single. It took talent to make a three-minute single by someone whose vocabulary was limited to "Blobby, blobby, blobby!" Mr. Blobby succeeded where Pinky and Perky, Sooty, Basil Brush, Bungle, Roland Rat and Muffin the Mule had failed – he had a number one. And Barry Killerby at nearly seven feet became the tallest artist to make number one.

The tabloids loved Mr. Blobby and it led to all manner of jokes – the Chancellor of the Exchequer, Kenneth Clarke was said to be presenting Mr. Blobby's budget. In an unexpected twist, intellectuals took Mr. Blobby seriously. Writing in *The Sunday Times*, Cosmo Landesman said, "Mr. Blobby is the first truly post-modern pop star, a simulacrum of stardom created to conceal the fact that there is no such thing as a real star anymore." Nonsense of course as there were plenty of real pop stars around – Madonna, Sting and the group who staggered Mr. Blobby's run at the top, Take That.

Lancashire County Council believed Mr. Blobby had the staying power of a Donald Duck or Bugs Bunny and they paid Noel Edmonds' Unique company £1m for the rights for a Crinkley Bottom theme park featuring Mr. Blobby in Morecambe, a town that needed to regain its tourists. It opened in July 1994 but the inflatable costumes were already letting in air. The park closed after three months and the Audit Office criticised the Council for failing to protect the interests of its taxpayers. Hindsight is a wonderful thing.

In 1995 Mr. Blobby had a mini-revival when 'Christmas In Blobbyland' made the Top 40, the only other chart single, incidentally, to feature its writers and producers, Paul Shaw and David Rogers. Mr. Blobby has not been seen since but Barry Killerby is still playing tricks on unsuspecting victims in CBBC's *Stitch Up*.

699 Take That
Babe

Label & Cat No.: **RCA 74321182122**

Producers: **Steve Jervier / Paul Jervier / Jonathan Wales / Mark Beswick**

Writer: **Gary Barlow**

Date reached No.1: **18 December 1993**

Weeks at No.1: **1**

TAKE THAT OFTEN WORKED WITH THE production team of Steve and Paul Jervier. Steve Jervier had been a key DJ at Kiss FM and when he set up Jerv Productions with his brother, they worked with Take That, Boyzone and Gabrielle.

Despite its brief title, 'Babe' is a rambling story-song, written by Gary Barlow. The record starts with a message that a telephone number is no longer available, and then Mark Owen goes to his former girlfriend's address only to be told she doesn't live there anymore. He gets her number and when he finally finds her, he learns that he has a son and all, we assume, ends happily. It took some time to get to the chorus but it was a killer hook in line with the best of The Bee Gees.

'Babe' was helped by an emotional video which added another dimension: the young man is a soldier returning from the war. The single soared straight in at number one, deposing Mr. Blobby. Unfortunately, Mr. Blobby bounced back the next week.

Robbie Williams was already showing himself to be a loose cannon. He revealed in his autobiography, *Feel* (2004), "They'd have mega meetings about tours and stuff and I just wouldn't be

Mr. Blobby

there. I couldn't give a shit. It wasn't my style of music and I would say, 'Whatever you're going to do is fine by me.'"

700 Chaka Demus & Pliers with Jack Radics & Taxi Gang
Twist And Shout

Label & Cat No.:	**Mango CIDM 814**
Producers:	**Sly Dunbar / Robbie Shakespeare / Lloyd Willis**
Writers:	**Bert Russell / Phil Medley**
Date Reached No.1:	**8 January 1994**
Weeks at No.1:	**2**

"IT'S ALWAYS FUN TO REWORK 'LA BAMBA'," said Bob Dylan, and there have been numerous variations of that exciting rhythm over the years. 'La Bamba' was an old Mexican song given a rock'n'roll workout by Ritchie Valens in 1958.

The best-known rewrite is 'Twist And Shout' put together in the twist era (although it is rarely considered a twist song) supposedly by two New York songwriters, Bert Russell and Phil Medley, but actually a pseudonym for just Bert Berns himself. The Top Notes recorded it in 1961 with the record being produced for Atlantic by Jerry Wexler and Phil Spector. Jerry recalled, "It was a horrible record. Bert was a newcomer, watching Phil and I butcher his song. Phil changed the middle around, we had the wrong tempo, the wrong feel, but we didn't realise that Bert could have produced it himself." Although an appalling record, one of The Top Notes, Derek Martin, had just recorded the fêted R&B track, 'Daddy Rollin' Stone'. The following year Bert Berns was producing The Isley Brothers. They had had a US hit with 'Shout' and Berns realised that 'Twist And Shout' would make an ideal single. They recorded it in 10 minutes at the end of a session and it is one of the best R&B records of the era.

Three weeks before the Isley Brothers charted, Brian Poole & The Tremeloes, whose first release, 'Twist Little Sister', a year earlier failed to connect, made their chart debut with the same song. The following year The Beatles, who, like Brian Poole, based their version on the Isley Brothers', included it on their debut album, *Please Please Me*. It was also used as the title track of a best-selling EP, the one that shows them jumping for joy on a derelict site. It was recorded in one take at the end of the *Please Please Me* session. John Lennon's voice was not in good shape as they had recorded the album in about 12 hours and his throat was raw. 'Twist And Shout' became a regular closing number for The Beatles although John was reluctant to sing it when there were American R&B acts on the bill, feeling that they might perform it better. John was nothing if not inconsistent: on another occasion, he said, "I could eat Chuck Berry for breakfast."

Berns continued the theme with 'Hang On Sloopy' for The McCoys. In 1988 the song was used by Sting, Peter Gabriel and Bruce Springsteen to close their Amesty International tour. In the same year the song was radically reworked by the rap duo, Salt'n'Pepa and their version went to number four.

Jamaican born duo DJ Chaka Demus (born John Walker), and Pliers (born Everton Bonner), who took his name as a tribute to another Jamaican singer called Pincers, had pursued solo careers before coming together after an impromptu jam session in Miami in 1990. The dancehall reggae duo's first single 'Gal Wine' topped the UK reggae chart, but failed to cross over into mainstream pop.

They recorded a couple of songs, 'Bam Bam' and 'Murder She Wrote' which found their way into the hands of British-based producers Sly & Robbie. They began working together and produced the debut album, *Tease Me*, which went to number one. The title track, which was co-written by Pliers' brother Spanner, gave them their first hit, which reached number three. The follow-up, a cover of Curtis Mayfield's 'She Don't Let Nobody' went to number four. When 'Twist and Shout' followed and went to the top, they became the first Jamaican act to chart three Top five hits in the UK.

"Chaka went off DJing somewhere and Pliers went back to Jamaica," remembered Sly Dunbar. "I was in a lift in New York when I heard The Beatles' 'Twist And Shout' and I was struck by the similarity of its rhythm to 'Bam Bam'. I told Pliers who recorded it in Jamaica with another reggae group, Jack Radics & Taxi Gang and set about looking for someone to do some chattering." He had tried about 10 before Chaka Demus returned and voiced the track in a couple of takes.

They released four more singles including a re-issue of 'Murder She Wrote', which only reached number 27. Then came 'I Wanna Be Your Man' (not The Beatles/Rolling Stones song) followed by cover versions of 'Every Kinda People' and 'Every Little Thing She Does Is Magic'. In 1999 the Los Angeles-based Hip-O label issued a greatest hits package which failed to chart in the UK or US.

701 D:Ream
Things Can Only Get Better

Label & Cat No.:	**Magnet MAG 1020CD**
Producer:	**D:Ream**
Writers:	**Peter Cunnah / Jamie Petrie**
Date reached No.1:	**22 January 1994**
Weeks at No.1:	**4**

A SINGER FROM DERRY, PETER CUNNAH, formed D:Ream in London with a keyboard player from Scotland, Al Mackenzie, to make dance records with a purpose. Said Cunnah, "There used to be this idea that rock music was intellectual and dance music was just a totally physical thing. I think we're one of the bands that has succeeded in breaking that down. If people just want to dance to our music, that's fine. If they want to sit down and take in some of the serious points addressed by the lyrics, that's also fine. If they want to listen to it on both levels, that's even better." These words were spoken sometime before the 1997 General Election.

From 1992 D:Ream had several minor hits:

'U R The Best Thing', 'Things Can Only Get Better', 'Unforgiven' and 'Star' / 'I Like It'. Their second single, 'Things Can Only Get Better', was remixed by Paul Oakenfold and went to number one early in 1994. This led to 'U R The Best Thing' reaching number four and they had further hits with 'Take Me Away' (18), 'Blame It On Me' (25), 'Shoot Me Up With Your Love' (7), 'Party Up The World' (20) and 'The Power (Of All The Love In The World)' (40).

And that would appear to be that. By 1995 D:Ream had had their 15 minutes of fame. Then something extraordinary happened. Political parties were known for their stuffiness and attempts to win young voters through pop and rock music often floundered: the Tories were heavily criticised when Kenny Everett spoke at their conference and Labour found that having the *agit prop* singer songwriter Billy Bragg front their Red Wedge campaign did not attract millions of new supporters.

New Labour's spin-doctors, led by Peter Mandelson, were determined to secure an election victory in 1997. 'The Red Flag' gave way to D:Ream's 'Things Can Only Get Better', which was regarded as a song of hope after 18 years of Tory rule. When their conference was televised, it was self-evident that John Prescott for one did not approve of their choice. Still, it underscored Tony Blair's dreamy smile and he was partial to transforming The Lightning Seeds' "Football's coming home" (from 'Three Lions') into "Labour's coming home". New Labour were elected, D:Ream's record returned to the Top 20 and within a few weeks, we had Cool Britannia.

If the New Labour had listened to the whole song, they would have realised that it sowed seeds of doubt. The lyric said, "I sometimes lose myself in me, I lose track of time, And I can't see the wood for the trees" and this seemed apt as problems came with NHS waiting lists, public transport, class sizes and, of course, the fiasco surrounding the Millennium Dome. Drug dependency increased indicating that many thought things only got better with coke. John O'Farrell's book, *Things Can Only Get Better*, is the *Fever Pitch* of political writing.

D:Ream are long gone, but in 1999 Peter Cunnah co-wrote the first two hit singles by A1, 'Be The First To Believe' and 'Summertime Of Our Lives', and in 2000, the TV theme from *Starstreet*, 'Best Friends' by Allstars. In 2003 he sang lead vocals on Chicane's Top 40 single, 'Love On The Run'.

702 Mariah Carey
Without You

Label & Cat No.: **Columbia 6599192**

Producers: **Walter Afanasieff / Mariah Carey**

Writers: **Pete Ham / Tom Evans**

Date reached No.1: **19 February 1994**

Weeks at No.1: **4**

In 1960 Alfred Carey, a partly black, partly Latin aerospace engineer, married Irish-American Patricia Hickey, a singer with The New York City Opera. Their third child, Mariah, named after a song in *Paint Your Wagon*, was born in Long Island on March 27, 1970.

Mariah's parents divorced when she was two and her mother became a vocal coach to support the family. As a young child, Mariah picked up her mother's cue in *Rigoletto* and she became aware that her daughter was developing a remarkable range, possibly as great as five octaves. As she grew up, Mariah loved singers with a wide range of notes including Minnie Riperton, Barbra Streisand and Nilsson.

When Mariah was 18, she was singing back-up for the New York singer, Brenda J. Starr, who was enjoying US hits with 'I Still Believe' and 'What You See Is What You Get'. When they went to a party, Mariah Carey passed a demo tape to Tommy Mottola, the 38-year-old president of Columbia Records. On his way home, he played it on his car stereo and decided he had discovered his own Whitney Houston.

The first album, *Mariah Carey*, was two years in the making and showed the strength of her songwriting as well as her voice. Mottola threatened to sack the promotions team if she did not have a number one single. With such pressure, Mariah Carey scored a US number one with 'Vision Of Love' and then with 'Love Takes Time', 'Someday' and 'I Don't Wanna Cry'. An impressive start but George Michael was not happy at the attention being lavished on his labelmate, one of many complaints he made against Columbia's owner, Sony.

Awards abounded and Mariah's second album, *Emotions*, was off to a flying start with a number one for the title track. Clearly though, Tommy Mottola did not issue such ultimatums to the UK promotions team (or they ignored him!) as the only one of Mariah's first five singles to make the UK Top 10 was 'Vision Of Love'. Mariah's turning point in the UK came with her appearance on MTV's *Unplugged* series. Her live version of The Jackson 5's 'I'll Be There' topped the US chart and made number two here.

Tommy Mottola was besotted with Mariah Carey. He left his wife and children and, in June 1993, married her in a lavish ceremony, which aped the wedding of Charles and Diana. They lived in a huge house on a 50-acre site in the Hudson River Valley.

Her album, *Music Box*, was another international best-seller with both 'Dreamlover' (with a performance inspired by Minnie Riperton) and 'Hero' (inspired by Barbra Streisand) topping the US chart. The album included a cover of Nilsson's transatlantic number one, 'Without You'. This song is as well-known as any standard but is not often covered because it calls for considerable vocal expertise. Nilsson's version opened quietly, giving no indication as to how it would end. Mariah Carey, with a surfeit of grace notes, unleashes her attack much earlier in the song, but curiously ends with a fade-out without any earth-shattering notes. 'Without You' gave Mariah Carey her only UK solo number one, but the single faltered at number two in the US.

The follow-up, 'Anytime You Need A Friend', made the UK Top 10 and Mariah had two further big records before 1994 was out – 'Endless Love', a duet with Luther Vandross (3) and 'All I Want For Christmas Is You' (2), later used on the soundtrack of *Love Actually* (2003).

The hits continued along with some major industry awards and Mariah had another big album with *Daydream* (1995). Her biggest US hit was with 'One Sweet Day' (1995) on which she shared the billing with Boyz II Men. This record topped the US charts for 16 weeks, but it peaked at number six in the UK. She had US number ones with 'Fantasy' and 'Always Be My Baby' from the same album.

By 1997 Mariah and Tommy's marriage was over and they divorced the following year. Her 1997 album was symbolically called *Butterfly*. She had further US number ones with the tracks, 'Honey' and 'My All', bringing her tally to 12. The single 'When You Believe', a duet with Whitney Houston, from the cartoon film, *The Prince Of Egypt* made the UK Top 10, and a revival of 'Against All Odds' with Westlife made number one.

Mariah Carey had relationships with the baseball star, Derek Jeter, and the Mexican Elvis, Luis Miguel. Seeking complete independence from Tommy Mottola, she left Columbia and signed with Virgin. The first public indication that things were not as they should be was when she posted rambling messages on her website, one suggesting that Marilyn Monroe was talking to her through her piano. Her sister, a prostitute, was HIV positive and she and her mother took custody of her child. In July 2001 Mariah Carey collapsed with exhaustion and there were rumours of a suicide attempt. Her PR people issued a statement that she had had 'an accident with plates'.

When Mariah recovered, she promoted her film, *Glitter*, and its soundtrack album, which gave her a much funkier sound. Unfortunately, the film – depicting the rise of a big-voiced singer from New York – was risible. Although the album contained some hit singles ('Loverboy' and 'Never Too Far' / 'Don't Stop (Funkin' 4 Jamaica)'), Virgin was disappointed and its parent company, EMI, in an extreme example of cash and Carey, terminated her contract with a $35m payout. This extraordinary move was surely not the best solution for although Mariah did very well financially, it gave the impression that she was artistically bankrupt. .

Since then, Mariah has established her own label Monarc and written a number of songs while relaxing in a catamaran off Puerto Rico. The resulting album, *Charmbracelet*, did poorly but included two hit singles, 'Through The Rain' and 'Boy (I Need You)'. She returned to the Top 10 in 2003 with 'I Know What You Want' with Busta Rhymes. A world tour in 2004 has helped to restore her reputation, but there's some way to go.

703 Doop Doop

Label & Cat No.: **Citybeat CBE 774CD**

Producer: **Ferry Ridderhof**

Writer: **Ferry Ridderhof**

Date Reached No.1: **19 March 1994**

Weeks at No.1: **3**

SEVENTY YEARS OF MUSIC CAME FULL circle when two Dutch producers and keyboard players, Ferry Ridderhof and Peter Garnefski, brought us a techno version of the Twenties dance, the Charleston.

The Charleston is thought to have originated in a small island near Charleston in South Carolina as early as 1903. It's done by performing outward heel kicks combined with an up-and-down movement achieved by bending and straightening the knees in time to the syncopated 4/4 rhythm of ragtime jazz.

The pair met at school and both studied at the Royal Conservatory in The Hague. Wanting to fulfil the ambition of making music, their first collaboration was under the name Doop. "We decided on that name because we liked the sound of it when Ferry was singing the 'Doop-be-doop-be-doop-be-doop' bits," revealed Peter. Added Ferry, "I always do the vocals. It was very funny to see how people make those kind of up-tempo moves, In the Twenties, the Charleston was a big dance craze," continued Peter. "I thought it had a similar tempo and speed to the house music scene, so I tried it and it worked."

They followed-up 'Doop' with 'Huckleberry Jam', 'Wan Too' and 'Ridin'' and although they had reasonable success across Europe, they failed to connect in the UK leaving them a one-hit-wonder. All the tracks appeared on the album *Circus Doop*, which also attracted few music collectors in the UK.

Ridderhof and Garnefski had further success in Europe under various guises including Hocus Pocus, Vicious Delicious, Boobytrax and Waxattack. In 1997 they formed two record labels, Mr. Cheng's Quality tunes and Proudly. That same year they teamed up with Hans Weekhout, who had the minor UK hit '20Hz' under the moniker Capricorn, and Edward Boellaart to form Peblab. Their first single, 'Ride The Pony' was a club favourite on the continent.

Whilst they continue to record under the moniker, Peblab, Peter and Ferry made it back into the UK chart in 2002 under another moniker, Kioki. The single 'Do & Don't For Love' reached number 66.

704 Take That Everything Changes

Label & Cat No.: **RCA 74321167732**

Producers: **Mike Ward / Eliot Kennedy / Cary Baylis**

Writers: **Gary Barlow / Mike Ward / Eliot Kennedy / Cary Baylis**

Date reached No.1: **9 April 1994**

Weeks at No.1: **2**

THE CO-WRITER AND PRODUCER OF 'Everything Changes', Eliot Kennedy, comes from Sheffield and trained as a studio engineer. His first success as a producer was with 'Independence' for Lulu in 1993. This impressed Take That's manager, Nigel Martin-Smith, who invited him to work with Gary Barlow.

'Everything Changes' was the title track from their 1993 album and it was also their fourth number one from the collection. The disco song was the only one of Take That's number ones to feature lead vocals from Robbie Williams. Not that it was Robbie's idea of stardom: he wanted to be like David Bowie, not Gary Barlow. Talking of Gary, he said, "He had a bloody leather briefcase which had song sheets for crap cabaret songs in it." He also said that Take That was only famous for being "a bunch of wankers".

Take That were pushing their luck with a

fifth single from the album, 'Love Ain't Here Anymore', but it still made number three and was certainly a summer holiday favourite. The album sold three million copies worldwide.

When Take That were featured on the *Spitting Image* ITV show, the puppets went into hysteria as their manager gave them 50 pence. *Spitting Image* made a special Gary Barlow puppet but for the rest, they put on nondescript masks on four puppets they already had. "You ask me why I've got problems," said Robbie Williams.

705 ♂ (Prince) The Most Beautiful Girl In The World

Label & Cat No.:	**NPG NPG 60155**
Producer:	**♂ (Prince)**
Writer:	**♂ (Prince)**
Date reached No.1:	**23 April 1994**
Weeks at No.1:	**2**

PRINCE ROGERS NELSON WAS BORN, the son of a jazz musician, on June 7, 1958 in Minneapolis. He was taken to see James Brown when he was 10 and was carried backstage by James's bodyguards: "The reason I liked James Brown so much is that on my way backstage, I saw some of the finest girls I had ever seen in my life."

The young boy became a teenage prodigy, learning guitar, bass, keyboards and drums, but unfortunately he developed an inflated sense of his own importance, a character weakness which was to dog, and almost destroy, his career.

When he was only 17, Prince received a contract from Warners which allowed him to perform, write and produce his own records, and his first album, *For You* (1978), went way over budget. It enjoyed moderate success but *Prince* (1979) included some minor R&B hits and featured 'I Feel For You', which was revived by Chaka Khan in 1984. Further albums, *Dirty Mind* (1980) and *Controversy* (1981), helped his ascent and emphasised the sexual content of his work. His suggestive *Black Album* (1987) was withheld by Warners for some years.

The international breakthrough came in 1984 with the film and soundtrack, *Purple Rain*, which included 'When Doves Cry' (UK 4, US 1). The Jimi Hendrix influence on that track was unmistakable and Prince, though highly original, can be seen as an amalgam of Hendrix, David Bowie, James Brown and Stevie Wonder. He became a major star, challenging Michael Jackson, and his UK hits included 'Purple Rain' (8), '1999' / 'Little Red Corvette' (2) and 'Let's Go Crazy' / 'Take Me With U' (7). He declined to take part in the all-star recording of 'We Are The World' (1985) because he did not perform with other artists – in other words, he was piqued at not being asked to write and produce the record himself.

Warners allowed Prince to establish his own label and recording studios, Paisley Park, but the records by his protégés (Sheila E, Jill Jones) and heroes (George Clinton, Mavis Staples) failed to recoup their costs. His own success continued with the adventurous double-album *Sign 'O' The Times* (1987), which is acclaimed as his best work and included 'U Got The Look' with Sheena Easton, and the score for *Batman* (1989). His disco record, 'Batdance', brought soundbites from Michael Keaton and Jack Nicholson onto the UK charts. Hit singles included 'Kiss', 'Alphabet Street', 'Thieves In The Temple', 'Gett Off' and, rather prophetically in 1992, 'My Name Is Prince'.

Prince also became a hot songwriter with Top 10 hits coming from The Bangles' ('Manic Monday', 1986), The Art Of Noise featuring Tom Jones ('Kiss', 1988), MC Hammer ('Pray', based on 'When Doves Cry', 1990). Sinead O'Connor ('Nothing Compares 2 U', 1990) and Martika ('Love... Thy Will Be Done', 1991).

Where there was Prince, there was litigation and he became involved in claims from his management team when he dismissed them in 1991. He became a control freak, involved in every aspect of his career, and he was perpetually arguing with Warners about his releases. For example, Warners refused to sanction the release of his *Graffiti Bridge* album until the sales of *Batman* had tapered off. Unlike most major artists who released an album every two or three years and then toured on it, Prince wanted to release albums when he felt like it. He said, "My problem is getting things out before another idea comes along."

On his birthday in 1993, he announced that he was no longer Prince but some unpronounceable heiroglyphic, partly formed from the symbols for gender. He was photographed with the word 'SLAVE' in eyeliner on his cheek. Maybe he expected a stand-off with Warners but they appeared to take it in fairly good nature.

Warners was disillusioned by the sales of the other Paisley Park albums and in 1994, they disbanded the label but allowed him to release product elsewhere. Prince set up his own NPG label. Around the same time, Prince had written a romantic song, 'The Most Beautiful Girl In The World', and he wanted to release it as a single. Warners opposed this as his new album, *Come,* was not ready and to release a single with no related product was not considered profitable. Prince argued his case and Mo Austin, the chairman of Warners, relented and allowed Prince to release the single on NPG.

Prince orchestrated a clever publicity campaign. Many US magazines carried his face in silhouette with his message, "Eligible bachelor seeks the most beautiful girl in the world to spend holidays with." In February 1994 he launched the song on CBS-TV's *Miss America*, a good choice as the standard 'The Most Beautiful Girl In The World' (written by Rodgers and Hart in 1935 and recorded by Frank Sinatra, Buddy Greco et al) was often performed at this pageant. The single went to number three on the US chart and, largely as a result of this, Mo Austin was forced to resign. The small Grapefruit PR company – just two people – promoted the single in the UK and it went to number one.

The single was followed by a seven-track CD, *The Beautiful Experience*, which featured seven different versions of the song. Selling at £9.99, it was promoted as a collector's item but nevertheless made the UK Top 20.

By now the public had taken to calling him The Artist Formerly Known As Prince and other, less flattering names. By coincidence, Prince Charles had painted some landscapes

Determined to emphasise the hieroglyphic he adopted as his new name, Prince even had a guitar made in that shape

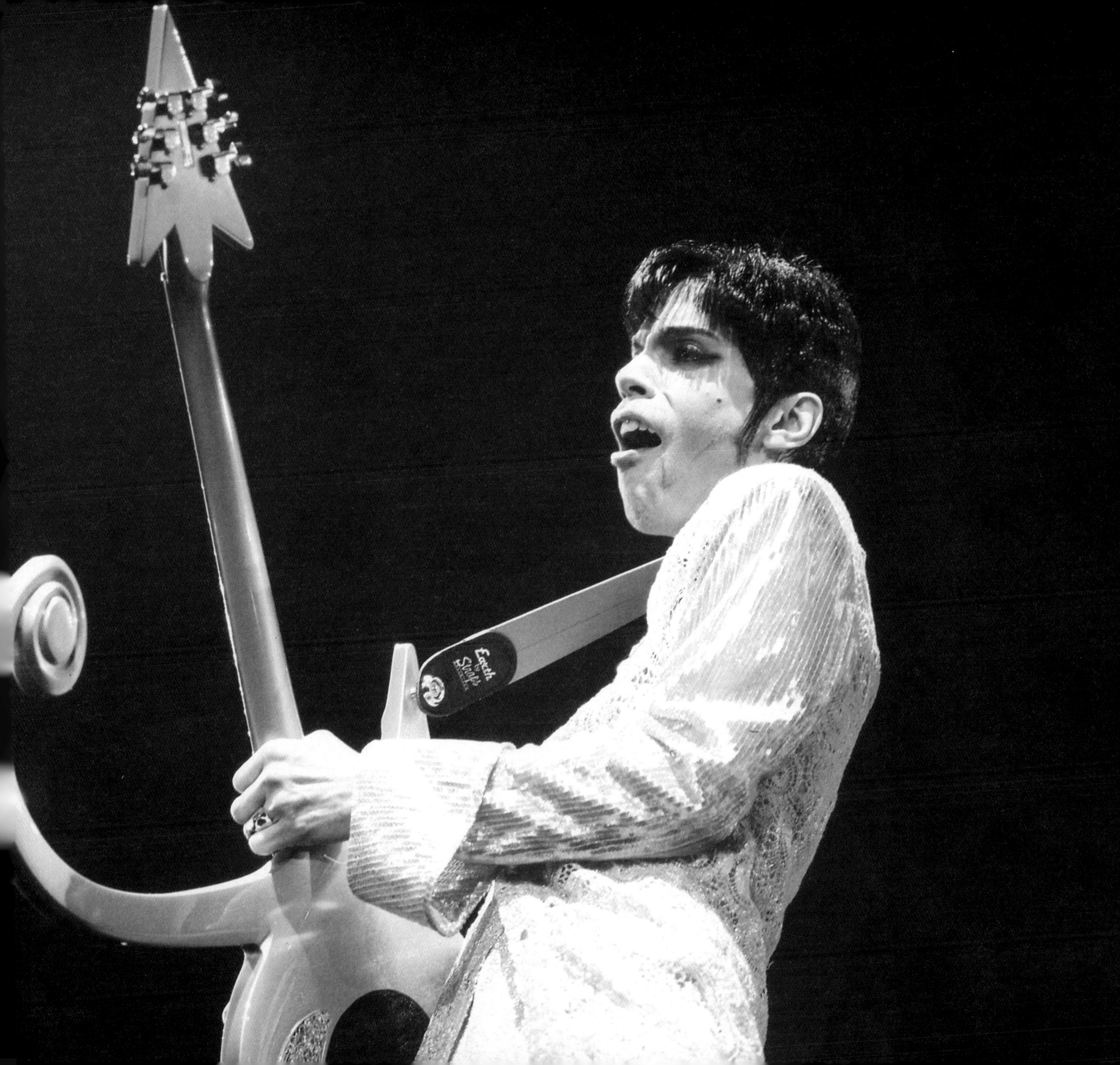
Earth

which were shown on a set of postage stamps so he became The Artist Known As Prince.

Since that time, the only records Prince has had in the Top 10 have been 'Gold' (1995) and, topically, a reissue of '1999' (1999). His triple CD, *Emancipation* (1996), although containing some good work, was quickly remaindered and could be bought for £3. His live shows are as exciting as ever but his non-appearance at Glastonbury in 2003 did him no favours. An album, *Musicology*, was issued in 2004, and only one single, 'Cinnamon Girl', just missed the Top 40. As the album climbed the US *Billboard* album charts, *Rolling Stone* reported, "Prince continues racking up big numbers – 95,000 this week" – thanks to a CD giveaway for fans who buy concert tickets. The free CDs are tallied in his overall sales.

In 2000 TAFKNAP went back to being Prince again. Current reports suggest that he is knocking on doors for Jehovah's Witnesses. Imagine opening your door and finding Prince there.

706 Tony Di Bart
The Real Thing

Label & Cat No.: **Cleveland City CCBCD 15001**
Producer: **Tony Di Bart**
Writers: **Tony Di Bart / Andy Blissett / Lucinda Drayton**
Date Reached No.1: **7 May 1994**
Weeks at No.1: **1**

TONY, BORN ANTONIO DIBARTOLOMEO in 1964 in Slough, Berks, to Italian parents, had a love of gospel music which led him to join a local church band called Oasis as a backing singer when he was 16. When they recruited a new guitarist who turned the band towards rock music, Tony left to concentrate on making soul music.

To earn a proper living, Tony trained as a plumber and then opened his own business, Cameo Bathrooms in Slough. "It wasn't like a newsagent where you've got people coming and going all day," he recalled. "I built my own studio above the shop and I often used to go and sit up there and write music. I wrote a gospel song, which I took to a gospel music company, but they said, 'it was too funky for God'. I then met two other songwriters, Lucinda Drayton and Andy Blissett via a guy called Victor Trim and we sat down and wrote 'The Real Thing' together."

"I used to play some of my tracks to my friends. One day some of my friends got back from holiday with a friend of theirs who lived in Wolverhampton. He stayed over before heading home and I played him this track. He loved it and asked if he could take a copy because he knew some DJs at Cleveland City Records in Wolverhampton. Before I knew it, Mick Evans from Cleveland City was on the phone and wanted to buy the track from me, which I sold to him for £500."

Cleveland City is a dance label that had never had a Top 20 hit. "They pressed up a 12-inch promo-only copy for club DJs, but when the DJs began playing it in the clubs, it just flew," recalled Tony. "You could hear it in the clubs but not on the radio, which is when it was decided to release it commercially.

"We were at number three in the chart, Take That came in and went straight out, we had the same distributors as Prince who was at number one, but Mick Evans had to remortgage his house so that he could pay to have enough copies pressed up. We let Prince have an extra week at the top because not only were the shops awaiting stock, it was the time when he had a slave on his face and had a point to make. The following week we did it."

Sony offered Cleveland City £1million to sign Tony but Mick refused to let him go. The follow-up single, 'Do It' failed to get any airplay and only reached number 21. He released the album, *Falling For You*, but due to a lack of commitment by Cleveland City it didn't sell many copies. After two further singles, Tony, who had sold his bathroom shop a few years earlier, returned to plumbing but continues to make music in his spare time.

Lucinda Drayton released the solo album, *Suicidal Angel*, which she had made with Andrew Blissett in 1997. Then followed a New Age album *Through These Eyes* as Bliss.

Tony has an ongoing contract with UDP Records in Italy and more recently signed a new deal with Universal in Italy. "It's the first time I've been involved with a major label," said Tony. "But let's see what happens."

707 Stiltskin
Inside

Label & Cat No.: **White Water LEV1 CD**
Producer: **Peter Lawlor**
Writer: **Peter Lawlor**
Date Reached No.1: **14 May 1994**
Weeks at No.1: **1**

HAVING YOUR DEBUT RELEASE PUT out as the supplementary music to a Levi's commercial can often be the kiss of death. 'Underwater Love' (1997) by Smoke City, 'Nanny In Manhattan' (1998) by The Lilys or 'Before You Leave' (2001) by Pepe Deluxe have all suffered the same fate with their music career both beginning and ending with their song's appearance in the ad series, never to chart a single again. They are classic one-hit wonders.

Scottish rock quartet Stiltskin were different. They became a two-hit wonder.

Stiltskin (who took their name from the children's story, *Rumpelstiltskin*) began life in 1992, when guitarist Peter Lawlor met James Finnigan at a Hue And Cry gig, where James was playing bass. Ross McFarlane joined on drums and a year later they found their singer, 25-year-old gravel-voiced Ray Wilson from Dumfries. Ray had grown up listening to David Bowie, Rush and Bob Dylan. At the age of 14, he joined his first band, Pink Gin. His first performance was in front of 800 fellow school pupils.

The accompanying ad was particularly amusing. It featured an Amish family on a trip through Yosemite National Park, complete with horses and buggy. After a picnic in the woods, the two teenage girls stumble upon a fit young man taking a dip in a lake. Spotting a pair of jeans nearby, one collects them to pass to him in order to spare their blushes. The handsome fellow comes out of the water, only to still be wearing his 'Shrink To Fit' Levi's. An old, bearded man appears. The jeans are his. No vocals are heard, just 60 seconds of grungy guitar.

Stiltskin were accused of being a rip-off of The Smashing Pumpkins. Indeed, when The Smashing Pumpkins walked onstage in Germany soon after 'Inside' was released, Billy Corgan announced, "Hi, we are Stiltskin…"

Stiltskin's second and final single, 'Footsteps' was released that September. Gracing the charts for two whole weeks, it reached the lofty heights of number 34.

In 1996 Ray Wilson was invited to step into the shoes of Phil Collins, and tour with the remaining members of Genesis. An album, *Calling All Stations,* although a UK number two, was released to a luke-warm response by the public and critics alike. The singles, 'Congo', Shipwrecked' and 'Not About Us' (numbers 29, 54 and 66 respectively) were in the charts for a collective four weeks. Ray was informed of his dismissal via a telephone call. They have no plans to record together again.

Ray, who has a small but loyal following, still occasionally tours and has released several solo albums.

708 Manchester United Football Club
Come On You Reds

Label & Cat No.: **Polygram TV MANU 2**

Producer: **Status Quo**

Writers: **Francis Rossi / Andy Bown / John Edwards**

Date reached No.1: **21 May 1994**

Weeks at No.1: **2**

FOOTBALL SINGLES HAVE A SHORT LIFE and limited sales appeal. A record by England's team is unlikely to find many takers in Scotland and if a team's performance collapses, the record is dead. Three England records have made number one, but, until 1994, it seemed unlikely that even a premiership team could garner enough sales for a chart-topping single. Still, by then Manchester United was as much a global brand as a football team and its shares were soaring on the stock market. The team boasts 50 million fans although this is impossible to verify.

In 1958 an air disaster in Munich robbed the team of eight of its players and it says much for Sir Matt Busby's resilience that he was able to rebuild the squad so successfully. The folk singer and editor of *Sing* magazine, Eric Winter, wrote the poignant *Flowers Of Manchester*, arguably the best song ever written about football. The best-known version is from Manchester's Mick Groves fronting The Spinners.

The team had had four chart entries before their number one: 'Manchester United' (50, 1976), 'Glory Glory Man. United' (13, 1983), 'We All Follow Man. United' (10, 1985) and 'United We Love You' (37, 1993). In 1994 Status Quo reworked 'Burning Bridges' (5, 1988) from their album *Ain't Complainin'* and recorded it with the team as 'Come On You Reds'.

The captain was Steve Bruce and they had a great goalkeeper in Peter Schmeichel. The Frenchman Eric Cantona had taken over from Bryan Robson in the number 7 shirt. The Red Devils won the double of the Premier League and the FA Cup that year, but effectively it was a treble with the pop chart as well.

In 1995 Eric Cantona was disciplined for a scuffle following a racist slur from a spectator at Crystal Palace. He was banned for some months and as a result the weakened team just missed out on both the league and the cup. The single, 'We're Gonna Do It Again', this time based on Quo's 'Again And Again' (13, 1978), stopped at number six and went down when fans knew they weren't going to do it again.

The following year they recaptured the double but the single, 'Move Move Move (The Red Tribe)', couldn't climb higher than number six. In 1999 MU completed the true treble of the FA Cup, Premier League and European Champions Cup, but their single at the time, 'Lift It High (All About Belief)', only reached number 11.

MU changes its song as often as its strip – well, not quite – and there are also a succession of songs sung at Old Trafford. Go along and you might hear 'Stretford End Arising' (to the tune of 'Bad Moon Rising') and 'Ryan Giggs, Ryan Giggs, Running down the wing' to the tune of 'Robin Hood'.

709 Wet Wet Wet
Love Is All Around

Label & Cat No.: **Precious JWL 23**

Producers: **Wet Wet Wet / Graeme Duffin**

Writer: **Reg Presley**

Date reached No.1: **4 June 1994**

Weeks at No.1: **15**

IN 1966 THE TROGGS HAD JUST FINISHED a nationwide tour, and their lead singer, Reg Presley, was back home. "I was living just off Oxford Street and it was a Sunday and I had eaten my lunch and I was feeling good. A Salvation Army band called The Joy Strings were on TV. They were banging their tambourines and singing about love and that gave me the idea for 'Love Is All Around'. I picked up my bass and started working on it. I wrote it within 20 minutes, probably the fastest song I ever wrote."

The Troggs' record, ideally suited to the Summer of Love or, at least, the Autumn of Love, entered the charts in October 1967 and climbed to number five. And that, it might be thought, was that. By the Nineties, The Troggs were still playing their song on oldies tours, but nobody covered it.

Then, in 1994, the song was revived by Wet Wet Wet for the soundtrack of *Four Weddings And A Funeral*, starring Hugh Grant, Andie MacDowell, Simon Callow and Kirstin Scott Thomas. As the writer Richard Curtis pointed out, it was his good fortune to have a film starring Hugh Grant, who was every girls' dream date. Hugh Grant's presence in Wet Wet Wet's video also contributed to the single's success.

'Love Is All Around' topped the charts for 15 weeks and looked set to better Bryan Adams' 16 weeks, but their record company, with a lack of sense and chart history, deleted it so they could promote The Wets' next release, 'Julia Says'.

Wet Wet Wet soon ran aground. First of all, amidst ill feeling, drummer Tommy Cunningham's split of the songwriting royalties was reduced, and then Marti Pellow's addiction to heroin made him hard to handle. Following tabloid exposures, the band split up in 1997. Marti sought rehab and then worked with Al Green's producer, Willie Mitchell, on the album, *Smile*. He also starred in the musical, *Chicago,* in London and New York and on a UK tour. The band members did not even speak to each other for five years but were reunited at the funeral for Marti Pellow's mother.

In 2004 Wet Wet Wet announced that they were back together for an arena tour and the promotion of their *Greatest Hits* CD. Their first single in over seven years, 'All I Want' reached number 14. Meanwhile, The Troggs continue as though nothing had happened and may well be appearing at a theatre near you.

710 Whigfield
Saturday Night

Label & Cat No.: **Systematic SYSCD 3**

Producers: **Larry Pignagnoli / Davide Riva**

Writers: **Larry Pignagnoli / Davide Riva**

Date reached No.1: **17 September 1994**

Weeks at No.1: **4**

SANNIE CHARLOTTE CARLSON WAS born in Skaelskor, Denmark and is known as Denmark's first pop star, although she spent little time there. She grew up in Africa with her parents and then lived in Italy and Spain. A beautiful blonde, she worked as a model for some top designers in Italy but found it frustrating. She said, "Being a model is an insult to women. It completely ignores your intellect." She studied piano with a teacher called Whigfield (and she borrowed her name as a way of saying thanks) and she played for a time in a band with her brother.

She befriended the producer Larry Pignagnoli, who had produced several successful Europop acts – Spagna, Benny Benassi and Katla among them. Her debut single, 'Saturday Night', was a huge hit on the Continent, topping the Spanish charts for 11 weeks. Clubgoers were soon devising a dance to go with the record.

UK holidaymakers heard 'Saturday Night' and loved it, so it was off to a flying start when it was released here in September 1994. Whigfield ended Wet Wet Wet's remarkable run with 'Love Is All Around' and in so doing became the first female artist to enter at number one with a debut single. Strangely, the CD did not include her picture on the cover while the CD itself featured seven versions of 'Saturday Night' – Radio Mix, Extended Nite Mix, Nite Mix, Beagle Mix, Dida Mix, Deep Nite Mix and Trance Beat Mix.

Lincoln Gordon of The Equals had written their 1970 hit, 'Rub A Dub Dub' ("Saturday night and I'm having a rub"), and the publishers sued the writers of 'Saturday Night' for plagiarism. This was audacious because even if correct, the new writers had improved the song. The judge ruled that the claim was without foundation. Lindisfarne also complained that the song was based around their 'Fog On The Tyne' but again this came to naught.

Whigfield's follow-up, 'Another Day', which reached number seven, again led to charges of plagiarism as the lead singer of Mungo Jerry, Ray Dorset claimed it was based on 'In The Summertime'. This time a settlement had to be agreed.

Whigfield had further success with songs from her album, *Whigfield*, 'Think Of You' (7), 'Close To You' (13) and 'Last Christmas' / 'Big Time' (21). She has had little UK chart success since – one week at number 68 with 'Sexy Eyes' – but she retains her popularity in Europe. The album, *Whigfield II* (1997), did well with a hit single, 'Givin' All My Love', and *Whigfield III* (2000) included her revival of The Ronettes' 'Be My Baby'. *Whigfield IV* (2003) featured 'Gotta Getcha'. A special single, 'The Battle Mix' (2003), combined Whigfield's 'Saturday Night' and Ann Lee's 'No No No'. Whiggy's latest single, 'Was A Time', was released across Europe in 2004. She is friendly with Jade Goody from *Big Brother* as they share the same management.

Whigfield

711 Take That
Sure

Label & Cat No.: **RCA 74321236622**

Producers: **Brothers In Rhythm / Gary Barlow**

Writers: **Gary Barlow / Robbie Williams / Mark Owen**

Date reached No.1: **15 October 1994**

Weeks at No.1: **2**

AFTER FIVE SINGLES FROM THE *Everything Changes* album, Take That shot to the top with a new song, 'Sure', co-written by three of the band and an indication that there wasn't always tension between Gary and Robbie. Robbie had said, "I'm starting to write music now. I'm up to M-U-S." The sound is more contemporary and American, including a cheeky rap about what Take That want from a girl – "It's gotta be social, compatible, sexual, irresistible". The single was issued and reissued in a variety of versions including 'Thumpers Club Mix' and 'Full Pressure Mix'.

In actuality, Robbie had been wanting to put his songs into Take That for some months. When he played one song to Gary, he commented, "It's all right if you're in a rock group" and refused to consider the song further. Robbie and Mark did write the middle eight for 'Sure' with each of them getting five per cent of the publishing royalties.

As well as topping the singles and albums charts, Take That had a best-selling video with *The Party / Live At Wembley*. Dressed all in white, their constant movement and dance routines resemble a Jane Fonda workout video, but compared to, say, Michael Jackson, it is routine choreography. Gary Barlow is out front and the backstage footage is illuminating as Robbie Williams is shown to be uncomfortable with this from the start. As Robbie said, "The first time Gary Barlow was on TV, he was so unsexy that they had to shoot him from the waist down."

712 Pato Banton featuring Ali & Robin Campbell of UB40 Baby Come Back

Label & Cat No.: **Virgin VSCDT 1522**

Producer: **Susan Stoker (Michael Railton)**

Writer: **Eddy Grant**

Date Reached No.1: **29 October 1994**

Weeks at No.1: **4**

BIRMINGHAM NATIVE, PATO BANTON was born Patrick Murray and began his musical career as an MC with his stepfather's V-Rocket reggae sound system. It was his stepfather who nicknamed him Pato after he heard an owl in Jamaica that spent the whole night hooting 'Patoo Patoo'. The Banton came from a heavyweight DJ friend called The Banton. He joined the Crucial Music band that later became the Bob Marley tribute band, Buffalo Shoulder.

In 1981 he won a talent contest that was judged by The Beat's Ranking Roger. The pair became friends and they recorded the song 'Pato & Roger A Go Talk' which appeared on The Beat's album, *Special Beat Service*, the following year.

Roger produced Pato's 1985 debut solo single 'Hello Tosh', which was a parody of the television ad 'Hello Tosh, got a Toshiba?' Later the same year he collaborated with fellow Brummies UB40 on the track 'Hip Hop Lyrical Robot' which turned up on their album *Little Baggariddim*. Pato's debut album, *Never Give In*, in 1987 saw collaborations with Ranking Roger and Steel Pulse. He also supported Bob Marley's son, Ziggy,on his North American Tour.

Pato regularly put songs onto the reggae charts, but his material wasn't commercial enough to cross over to the pop chart. Initially he wasn't interested in making his music commercial because he didn't want to become a mainstream pop star, but eventually he was persuaded. "This business is a thing of give and take," Pato conceded. "At the end of the day we have to make money and if I get mainstream or pop success, that's fine as far as I'm paying bills, but the main thing is to play music and spread my message."

He began working with local producer, Michael Railton and they recorded the album *Universal Love*, which featured the duet with Ranking Roger, 'Bubbling Hot'. This track was issued as a single in 1995. For his next album, *Collections*, he called in a favour from Ali and Robin Campbell to accompany him on a cover of The Equals' 1968 number one, 'Baby Come Back'. The problem was that both UB40 and Pato were touring and it was hard to get them together, so the track was recorded in Japan, America and England. The following year Railton was asked to remix an old Sting track, 'This Cowboy Song', and because it had a reggae feel to it, Railton called on Pato to provide the rap.

Pato was a fan of Sting's and asked if they could duet on a cover of The Police hit 'Spirits In The Material World'. The track featured in the Jim Carrey film *Ace Ventura – When Nature Calls*, and when released as a single in 1996 it went to number 36.

"To a lot of people, I'm just a one-hit wonder who rode on the coat-tails of UB40 and did a happy-go-lucky cover of 'Baby Come Back'" remarked Pato. But in 2002 Pato, who now runs a music technical school in Birmingham where young people can learn musicianship skills, said in his website, "I reached a point where I was fulfilled with my career and considered slowing down. My studio here in Birmingham was next to the local community centre. Every day kids would knock on the door wanting to come in and see what I was doing. I wanted to work with them, to teach them and give them opportunities to make music. It's been an amazing journey. We are tapping into what is inside the students already, bringing it out. We are working with some outstanding talent. It's so rewarding. Music gives them something to focus their energy on."

713 Baby D Let Me Be Your Fantasy

Label & Cat No.: **Systematic SYSCD 4**

Producer: **Floyd Dyce**

Writer: **Floyd Dyce**

Date Reached No.1: **26 November 1994**

Weeks at No.1: **2**

IN THE EIGHTIES PHIL FEARON LED THE disco group Galaxy and had the Top 10 hits 'Dancing Tight', 'What Do I Do?', 'Everybody's Laughing' and 'I Can Prove It'. When the hits dried up in 1986, Phil set up his own Production House record label the following year. He signed acts like Jazz & The Brothers Grimm, Acen and Baby D.

Baby D comprised Phil's wife, Dorothy on vocals, Floyd Dyce (under his stage name, Dice) on keyboards and MC Nino (born Terry Jones), although Terry did not appear on 'Let Me Be Your Fantasy'.

"I was the in-house producer for Production House," remembered Floyd. "I also wrote and performed as The House Crew, DMS and Xstatic. I was the main songwriter and I formed Baby D as a vehicle for some of the songs I was writing. It was the whole rave scene, which I was heavily involved with, that inspired me to write 'Let Me Be Your Fantasy' in 1992. I asked Dorothy to do the vocal and it became the follow-up single to 'Daydreaming', which was a massive hit on the underground scene, but didn't cross over to mainstream pop. We needed a name for the group, so it was Raj at Production House that came up with the name Baby D.

It wasn't a reference to Dorothy, It didn't actually stand for anything."

Baby D followed it up the following summer with a raved up version of The Korgis' 1980 ballad, 'Everybody's Got To Learn Sometime', mainly using the hook 'I Need Your Lovin'', which got to number three. Two further singles, 'So Pure' and 'Take Me To Heaven', followed as did the Top 10 album *Deliverance*.

"We fell out big time after that," recalled Floyd. "I'm still writing and producing and run my own Redmaster Record label. Dorothy and Terry still perform 'Let Me Be Your Fantasy' on stage somewhere."

In September 2000, 'Let Me Be Your Fantasy' was given a make-over by the remix team, Trick Or Treat and went to number 16. But it's the original that will always remain a club favourite.

714 East 17
Stay Another Day

Label & Cat No.: **London LONCD 354**

Producer: **Phil Harding**

Writers: **Tony Mortimer / Rob Keane / Dominic Hawken**

Date Reached No.1: **10 December 1994**

Weeks at No.1: **5**

TAKING THEIR NAME FROM THE POST-code of an East London district that is most famous for its dog track, East 17 put Walthamstow on the pop map and to prove they are proud of their roots, they named their first album after it.

"When we signed them, we told them to go away and teach themselves how to play music," said Tom Watkins, their first manager. Watkins, who had launched the careers of The Pet Shop Boys and Bros, added, "They were about as inexperienced as you could get. In fact two of them were asked to join as dancers initially."

The four singers were Tony Mortimer, Brian Harvey, Terry Coldwell and John Hendy. Brian recalled, "When the record company met us, they looked at us and thought, 'we've got something we can sell here'. But they didn't try and change us, they let us walk round in our baggy clothes and attitude." Tony agreed, "We weren't worried about anything, let alone image." Watkins wanted a group to rival Take That. He showed the boys a video of five guys wearing leather thongs and said, "This is your competition," to which Brian replied, "There really is *no* competition."

They portrayed a hard rap image and their first single, 'House Of Love', which reached number 10 in 1992, was written about the Gulf War. They had more Top 10 hits with 'Deep', which featured in the movie *Up 'N Under*, 'It's Alright', 'Around The World' and 'Steam'. That same year they won the *Smash Hits* award for Best New Band.

Every pop act wants to have the Christmas chart-topper, so in October 1994 Tony came up with the ballad, 'Stay Another Day' He said, "I always prefer writing ballads because they are easy to write. They're slow, there's hardly any words in them and the melody's drawn out and before you know it, you've got to the end of three and a half minutes." Their appearance on *Top Of The Pops* standing round a piano played by Tony Mortimer, wearing snow coats and the fake snow gave it that Christmas feel.

For their second album, *Steam*, they worked with songwriters Rob Keane, an old school friend of Tony's, and Dominic Hawken who was a former keyboard player for Boy George and Hayzi Fantayzee. In 1995 they were named Best Dance Act at the MTV Europe awards.

They had further Top 10s with 'Let It Rain', 'Thunder', 'Do U Still' and the number two duet with Gabrielle, 'If You Ever'.

In 1997 Brian was kicked out of the group after he claimed in an interview that he had taken 12 Ecstasy pills in one night and that drugs made 'better people'. Watkins was dismayed at his revelation and gave the band the ultimatum, "either he goes or I do". Harvey went, but was re-instated a year later. It prompted Frank Skinner to comment, "A pop star who does drugs – how unusual." The following year Tony left to pursue a solo career and the group had two further hits, 'Each Time' and 'Betcha Can't Wait' under the amended name E-17, before splitting in 1999.

In 2000 Brian was a guest vocalist with The Truesteppers on their number 25 hit 'True Step Tonight'. The following year he signed a deal with Edel records and scored two solo hits 'Straight Up (No Bends)' and 'Loving You (Ole Ole Ole)'.

715 Rednex
Cotton Eye Joe

Label & Cat No.: **Internal Affairs KGBCD 016**

Producer: **Pat Reiniz**

Writers: **Jan Eriksson / Oerjan Oeberg / Pat Reiniz**

Date reached No.1: **14 January 1995**

Weeks at No.1: **3**

'COTTON EYE JOE' WAS WRITTEN BY Jim Rivington, who worked in the Lancashire cotton mills with his brother, Joe. Their job was to thread the needles so that the millworkers could sew the buttons onto the coats, and Joe was so good that he became known as Cotton Eye Joe. Jim's song was stolen by a tough, cigar-chomping American publisher and although he is 95, Jim is still fighting for his royalties. Not. We've made that up but nobody really knows the origins of the song.

The phrase, Cotton Eye Joe or Cotton Eyed Joe, goes back to the plantations in the southern states of America. Possibly to be cotton-eyed was to have the whites of your eyes prominent and John Steinbeck's *East Of Eden* refers to "The crooked little cotton-eyed piano player." It could also refer to a charmer with light blue eyes, which would tie in with the lyric of 'Cotton Eye Joe'.

'Cotton Eye Joe' was originally a lullaby, being discovered in the hills of Tennessee by the collector, Margaret Valliant. Around 1935 the German/Czech musician, Adolph Hofner, was the first to record it with his polka band in Texas and there are numerous versions of 'Cotton Eye Joe', usually as a dancing tune with a fiddle solo. It has been recorded by Woody Guthrie, Bob Wills & His Texas Playboys, Uncle Dave Macon,

East 17's career never really recovered from Brian Harvey's admission over drug taking, left to right: Harvey, John Hendy, Tony Mortimer and Terry Coldwell

Red River Dave, Don Reno and Red Smiley, Nina Simone and Vanessa-Mae.

In 1992 in Stockholm, a team of performers, writers, producers, programmers and art designers banded together to create entertainment around the wild west. They combined hillbilly with techno for their 'country house' version of 'Cotton Eye Joe' and called the band Rednex (great name!). Most adolescents think that country music has nothing to say to them, yet country music, albeit in a very contemporary form, was appealing to them via Rednex and similar bands such as Swamp Fever and The Grid. By way of contrast, 'Cotton Eye Joe' was also a favourite with senior citizens at line dancing clubs.

Rednex had further UK chart entries with 'Old Pop In An Oak' (12) and 'Wild 'n Free' (55), which gives little indication of their popularity on the Continent. 'Wish You Were Here' and 'Spirit Of The Hawk' were number one in Germany, and 'Modern Talking' was number two for 19 weeks. Their albums, *Sex And Violins* and *Farm Out*! have been big sellers and they even have released a greatest hits, *The Best Of The West*.

Rednex with their charismatic girl singer, Scarlet, tours regularly and the changing line-up includes such personnel as Dagger, Bone Duster Crock and Ace Ratclaw. Yes, they sound like the contestants in a *Big Brother* house.

There is an even older song called 'Horkstow Grange' about another cotton-eye Joe, only this one was known as Steeleye Span.

716 Celine Dion
Think Twice

Label & Cat No.: **Epic 6606422**

Producers: **Chris Neil / Aldo Nova**

Writers: **Andy Hill / Pete Sinfield**

Date reached No.1: **25 March 1995**

Weeks at No.1: **7**

Celine Dion was born the youngest of 14 children in the French-speaking district of Charlemange, Quebec on March 30, 1968. A local music impresario, Rene Angelil, was knocked out by the child's voice and personality and her career started triumphantly when she won The Yahama Song Festival in Tokyo in 1982. This was followed by a best-selling album in France and Canada, *D'Amour Ou D'Amite*.

In 1988 she successfully represented Switzerland in The Eurovision Song Contest with 'Ne Partez Pas Sans Moi', although the record was not a UK hit. She had to wait until 1992 when she made the UK charts with the Oscar and Grammy winning title song from the Walt Disney animated film, *Beauty And The Beast,* sung with Peabo Bryson. The following year she revived 'When I Fall In Love' with the British singer, Clive Griffin, for the soundtrack of the romantic comedy, *Sleepless In Seattle*, with Tom Hanks and Meg Ryan.

Celine Dion had her biggest UK hit to date when her passionate revival of Jennifer Rush's 'The Power Of Love' made number four early in 1994. Both 'When I Fall In Love' and 'The Power Of Love' (a US number one) were included on her album, *The Colour Of My Love*, and 'Think Twice' was tried as a single in October 1994. It took four months to reach number one, although it barely made the US Top 100, and during its time at the top, *The Colour Of My Love*, was the number one album. Romance was in the offing in real life too as she married Rene Angelil: she talked about retiring to look after him but he was only in his fifties.

'Think Twice' was written by Andy Hill and Pete Sinfield, who had often worked with Bucks Fizz and had written 'Heart Of Stone' together. It's a strong ballad with overtones of 'Angel Of The Morning' in places but couldn't they have found a better rhyme than 'serious' and 'you or us?' The track featured Aldo Nova and Tim Renwick on guitars and Steve Piggot on drums, bass and keyboards and was produced in the UK by Chris Neil, best known for his role in the TV documentary, *The Big Time*, which established Sheena Easton.

The song won an Ivor Novello Award as the Best Song of the year and spent 31 weeks on the chart. Celine continued her hits with 'Only One Road' (8), 'Tu T'Aimes Encore' (7) and 'Falling Into You' (10), which was the title track of another number one album. She worked with many big name songwriters and producers including Diane Warren and Jim Steinman, but her work-out with Phil Spector was abandoned at four o'clock one morning when they both realised it was going nowhere.

717 Cher, Chrissie Hynde & Neneh Cherry with Eric Clapton
Love Can Build A Bridge

Label & Cat No.: **London COCD 1**

Producer: **Peter Asher**

Writers: **Naomi Judd / John Jarvis / Paul Overstreet**

Date reached No.1: **25 March 1995**

Weeks at No.1: **1**

In the Eighties the mother and daughter duo The Judds were one of the hottest acts in country music. Naomi and Wynonna worked with some of the best songwriters in Nashville, 'Love Can Build A Bridge' being a good example. This US country hit from 1990 was written with two established writers and performers. Paul Overstreet wrote many of Randy Travis' hits ('On The Other Hand', 'Forever And Ever, Amen') and has had several successes of his own ('Seein' My Father In Me', 'I Won't Take Less Than Your Love'). John Barlow Jarvis played piano on many hit records, toured as part of Rod Stewart's band and wrote 'I Still Believe In You' (Vince Gill). In 1996 his song 'The Flame' was sung by Trisha Yearwood at the closing ceremony for the Olympics. He has made several solo albums, the most recent being *View From A Southern Porch*. The lead guitar on The Judd's original of 'Love Can Build A Bridge' was played by Bonnie Raitt. Shortly after The Judds' single, Naomi became very ill with a liver disease and Wynonna blossomed as a solo star. They have, however, made occasional appearances together.

Despite several classy singles, The Judds never had any UK success and so, to all intents and purposes, 'Love Can Build A Bridge' was unknown when it was chosen as the Comic Relief song in 1995. Cher's producer, Peter Asher, assembled an impressive lineup – Cher herself, Chrissie Hynde from The Pretenders and Neneh Cherry. Neneh, the Swedish step-daughter of the jazz trumpeter Don Cherry, had had several hits including 'Buffalo Stance' (3, 1988), 'Manchild' (5, 1989) and '7 Seconds' (with Youssou N'Dour) (3,1994).

Cher's hit album in 1995 was *It's A Man's World* featuring songs associated with male performers. The title track was James Brown's 1966 hit, 'It's A Man's Man's Man's World' and the album led to the hit singles, 'Walking In Memphis' and 'One By One'. The James Brown song was also the foundation for Neneh Cherry's 1995 hit, 'Woman'.

In the Sixties, the walls were daubed "Eric Clapton is God" and over the years, the great blues guitarist has made some very commercial records including 'Layla' (as part of Derek & The Dominos with Duane Allman) (7, 1972), Bob Marley's 'I Shot The Sheriff' (9, 1974) and the reflective ballad about the loss of his son, 'Tears In Heaven' (5, 1992). 'Love Can Build A Bridge' is the only number one record to feature Eric Clapton. Presenting him with a Q award, Cher said of Eric Clapton, "He's the only man I know who's older than me."

Cher with Eric Clapton and Q award

718 Outhere Brothers
Don't Stop (Wiggle Wiggle)

Label & Cat No.: **Stip/WEA YZ 917CD**
Producer: **Outhere Brothers**
Writers: **Lemar Mahone / Ken Mayberry / Craig Simpkins / Aladino**
Date Reached No.1: **1 April 1995**
Weeks at No.1: **1**

In the past, songs about sex were almost guaranteed not to get airplay on the BBC unless the message was extremely well hidden. The Outhere Brothers made no attempt to hide it and, despite a number of complaints both in the UK and US, they topped the UK chart with a song about intercourse and had no problems getting airplay.

The Outhere Brothers were Hula (born Lemar Mahone), who first came to prominence as the producer of DJ Jazzy Jeff and The Fresh Prince's 1991 Top 10 hit 'Summertime', and Malik, who was born Ken Mayberry in Chicago, Illinois. Malik made his name as a member of the rap group Lidell Townsell & M.T.F (More Than Friends), who scored a US Top 30 hit with 'Nu Nu' in 1992. The following year he co-wrote DJ Jazzy Jeff & The Fresh Prince's number one hit 'Boom! Shake The Room'.

The pair, who met in 1987 through a friend of Jazzy Jeff's, originally formed The Outhere Brothers with two other pals. On their first trip to Europe, the two friends disappeared, leaving the group as a duo. Their first release, 'Pass The Toilet Paper' went largely unnoticed. Their next single, 'Don't Stop (Wiggle Wiggle)', was picked up by London's radio stations Kiss FM and Capital, but the BBC initially refused to play it. Further controversy raged after a parent from Bradford complained when her young daughter bought the debut album, *1 Polish, 2 Biscuits And A Fish Sandwich*, and found it contained lyrics like 'I'll lick your pussy'.

"The best songs are written from experience," proclaimed Malik. "We are very sexual in our songs. The sexual side of us is what everybody sees and what our music portrays. All of our songs reflect things that we, or friends close to us, have done and things that have been done to us." Hula revealed in an interview that he first had sex when he was five, with a girl who was seven. His brother, who was nine, had slept with her and told Hula that he'd be cool if he did it.

"Our music is very African-American as well as having that hard underground feel," insisted Malik. "It's also urban and very hip-hop. That's what is so fresh, the gay clubs support us for one sound and the pop culture supports us for another."

719 Take That
Back For Good

Label & Cat No.: **RCA 74321271462**
Producers: **Chris Porter / Gary Barlow**
Writer: **Gary Barlow**
Date reached No.1: **8 April 1995**
Weeks at No.1: **4**

Take That first sang 'Back For Good' at the 1995 Brits and this created a huge demand for the song. The radio stations were given copies, but it was not released for six weeks. As a result, the single sold 350,000 copies in the first week of release, making it the fastest-selling UK single in 10 years. It sold over a million copies in the UK, an indication that Take That had picked up MOR fans along with the adolescents.

Possibly because there were a number of similar bands in America, Take That couldn't repeat their US success, and 'Back For Good' was the group's only US Top 40 hit, making number seven.

The new album, *Nobody Else*, written entirely by Gary Barlow, entered at number one. Robbie Williams didn't take a lead vocal on the album and was missing from most of the recordings. It was taken as a sign that he was being marginalised within the group, but he hadn't bothered to learn the new songs and his voice was cracking up as a result of his partying.

His manager, Nigel Martin-Smith, wanted him in rehab, but he also knew that if it was made known such a move could be devastating for the clean-cut group.

In June 1995 Robbie Williams, now a bleached blond with a blacked-out tooth, went to Glastonbury with a crate of champagne and danced wildly on stage with Oasis. It heralded a year of partying in which he was voted the *NME* Ligger of the Year.

720 Oasis Some Might Say

Label & Cat No.:	**Creation CRESCD 204**
Producers:	**Owen Morris / Noel Gallagher**
Writer:	**Noel Gallagher**
Date reached No.1:	**6 May 1995**
Weeks at No.1:	**1**

NOEL GALLAGHER WAS BORN INTO A family of Irish Catholics in Burnage, south Manchester in 1967 and his brother Liam (actually William John Paul) followed in 1972. Their father, Tom, laid concrete floors but was also a country and western DJ, and their mother, Peggy, who worked in a biscuit factory, had to put up with his violence. They were divorced in 1984. Noel was a rebellious youngster, loving punk music and then The Smiths, and in 1980, he received six months probation for robbing a corner shop. He later remarked, "A lot of young people had accepted Conservative rule, dole culture, daytime telly and smoking spliffs for a living with the odd football match. Britain was dead in the Eighties."

In 1989 Noel went to see The Stone Roses and he asked someone who was taping the gig for a copy. It was Clint Boon from Inspiral Carpets and Noel became their roadie and guitar tech as they started to tour with their hit records: he would perform his own songs at soundchecks and he felt that his songs were better than Inspiral Carpets'.

Meanwhile, Liam had joined a local band, The Rain. He was the vocalist while Paul 'Bonehead' Arthurs played guitar, Paul McGuigan bass, and Tony McCarroll drums. Liam was shy and he sometimes sang with his back to the audiences, soon developing his famed stance of head thrust forward and hands clasped behind his back. At some stage, they became Oasis, taking their name from the clothing stores, which proved apt as Oasis was a key Manchester club during the British beat explosion of the Sixties.

In 1992 Noel told Oasis that he would join them if he could be lead guitarist and they would play his songs. This was some demand but when the band heard the songs especially 'Live Forever', they acquiesced. In May 1993 when a local girl group, Sister Lovers, said that they were going to support 18 Wheeler at King Tut's Wah Wah Hut in Glasgow, they invited Oasis along and said that they could play a few songs.

Back in 1984 Alan McGee, a tough-minded Glaswegian, had formed the record label, Creation, and had had success with Primal Scream, The Jesus And Mary Chain and My Bloody Valentine. He had hopes for The Boo Radleys, but the label was going through a bad patch, not helped by McGee's cocaine addiction. He went to King Tut's that night to see 18 Wheeler and get drunk but he was captivated by Oasis. Because of cash flow problems, he couldn't sign Oasis to Creation. Through his contacts, the band was signed to Sony worldwide, but their product was licensed to Creation in the UK. Oasis were given a £1,000 advance which was mostly spent by Noel on a guitar. Tony McCarroll, who needed a better drum-kit, was incensed and hardly spoke to Noel after that.

Johnny Marr from The Smiths recommended Marcus Russell as a manager and Owen Morris, who had been producing Electronic, came in as their producer. Owen said, "I go for the Shel Talmy technique and compress the hell out of everything." Oasis mostly recorded at the Rockfield Studios in Monmouth. The first Noel, the cynical 'Supersonic', reached the Top 40 but they were praised by the *NME* and *Melody Maker* as well as appearing on Channel 4's *The Word*. There was a buzz about Oasis and, despite being unknown, they made a huge impact at the Glastonbury Festival. To quote Liam: "There weren't any rock stars: they were dicks in tights. It was time for real lads to be up there and be in charge, and that is what we did."

Their second single, 'Shakermaker', made the Top 20 and then 'Live Forever', which Noel dedicated on stage to Alan McGee, made the Top 10. Oasis put a photo of John Lennon's Liverpool home on the CD sleeve and the video featured Tony McCarroll being buried. This statement of immortality is so well known that it is surprising that it wasn't a major hit. It coincided with the release of *Definitely Maybe*, and the cover picture included one of Noel's heroes, Burt Bacharach. It was targeted at lad's mags and football publications, thus giving some idea of the group's appeal. *Definitely Maybe* was a number one album which remained on the charts for over three years.

Oasis took 'Cigarettes And Alcohol' into the Top 10 and as if to emphasise their link to The Beatles, 'I Am The Walrus' was on the B-side. Their fifth single of 1994, the lushly orchestrated 'Whatever', reached number three, although they expected it to be their first number one.

When Oasis made their second album in 1995, a single, 'Some Might Say', was released first. It opened with a guitar solo rather reminiscent of Keith Richards, and the song captured the spirit of the day, that something was about to happen: "Some might say we will find a brighter day." Oasis plugged it on *Top Of The Pops* but Noel Gallagher and Tony McCarroll had an argument, which led to Tony being sacked. (Again shades of The Beatles with Pete Best.) He was replaced by the highly competent Alan White, the brother of Steve who played with Paul Weller. Noel said, "Right mate, you're in. You're not 30 stone, you look all right. Do you want the job?" Tony took Oasis to court and a settlement of £600,000 was agreed.

When 'Some Might Say' reached number one, Oasis hosted a spectacular party in Covent Garden. Kate Moss asked to be invited. Oasis are often associated with drugs, but Alan McGee realised that he had better get his head together as his act was becoming so big and he came off them. The ever-quotable Noel Gallagher reflected, "If I'd known we were making history, I would have gone to bed a little bit earlier and I would have tried to keep Liam off the sauce."

The Gallagher Brothers Liam (left) and Noel spent much of the Nineties at each others' throats, which guaranteed Oasis plenty of useful publicity

721 Livin' Joy
Dreamer

Label & Cat No.: **Undiscovered MCSTD 2056**

Producer: **Livin' Joy**

Writers: **Gianni Visnadi / Janice Robinson**

Date Reached No.1: **13 May 1995**

Weeks at No.1: **1**

IN 1994 ITALIAN BROTHERS PAOLO AND Gianni Visnadi made their mark on the chart as two thirds of the dance act Alex Party. The trio was completed by DJ Alex Natale. Their debut single, 'Alex Party (Saturday Night Party)' stiffed at number 49. It was re-issued four months later under the amended title 'Saturday Night Party (Read My Lips)' which reached number 29. They had one further attempt a couple of years later as a remix and called it 'Read My Lips', but that only went one place higher than before.

Next the brothers formed the techno dance act, Livin' Joy. They recruited New Jersey-born and Paris-based singer Janice Robinson, whom they saw singing with The Joe T. Vannelli Project. They went back to Italy and recorded 'Dreamer' at their studios in Venice. On release it only went to number 18 in the UK, yet topped the chart in 25 other countries. As Alex Party, the follow-up 'Don't Give Me Your Life' went to number two in February 1995. They felt that 'Dreamer' should have been a bigger hit, so they reissued it in May and it went to the top. Alex Party was abandoned.

After one single Janice left the group and returned to the US where she pursued a song-writing career and has since written songs for Wyclef Jean and Taylor Dayne. The Visnadi brothers returned to the UK where they stumbled on a soul singer Tameka Star performing at a club in Liverpool and asked her to join the group. Tameka's father had been in the army and so she'd had spent most of her child-hood on military bases across Europe. "It was a fantastic opportunity for me as I'd always wanted to be famous," said Tameka.

In 1996 the follow-up single, 'Don't Stop Movin'', the title track from the debut album, went into the Top 10, as did the next single 'Follow The Rules'. Two further singles, 'Where Can I Find Love' (12) and 'Deep In You' (17) were released in 1997. They took the following year off to record a new album *Just For The Sex Of It*, of which the title track, a song about practising safe sex, was released in 1999 and did well across Europe although it failed to chart in the UK.

722 Robson Green & Jerome Flynn
Unchained Melody / (There'll Be Bluebirds Over) The White Cliffs Of Dover

Label & Cat No.: **RCA 74321 284362**

Producers: **Mike Stock / Matt Aitken**

Writers: **Alex North / Hy Zaret : Walter Kent / Nat Burton**

Date reached No.1: **20 May 1995**

Weeks at No.1: **7**

JEROME FLYNN – SIX FOOT, BLONDE, broken nose – was born in Kent in 1963 and his injury came from playing rugby. He sang with local bands but his passion was acting and he studied at the Central School of Speech and Drama. He was in the original one-off production of ITV's *London's Burning*, but he turned down the series, preferring to play in *As You Like It* at the Royal Shakespeare Company.

Robson Green was born a year later and his father and uncle owned racehorses. He established himself as a hospital porter in *Casualty* and he and Jerome only met when they were cast in the ITV series, *Soldier, Soldier*, in 1991. The contemporary drama told of life in the King's Own Fusiliers, and Jerome played Lance Corporal Paddy Garvey and Robson Fusilier Dave Tucker. The first programme attracted nine million viewers: the public warmed to the friendship between Tucker and Garvey and the viewing figures increased to 16 million. As a result of its popularity, the second series was filmed in Hong Kong, the third in Germany and New Zealand, the fourth in Cyprus and the fifth in Australia.

In *Band Of Gold*, the ninth episode in the fourth series in 1994, the two friends were asked at the last minute to provide the cabaret at a

Robson and Jerome

wedding reception. They sang 'Unchained Melody', a song of undying devotion from someone away from his love.

Simon Cowell, then an executive at RCA, offered them a record deal and guaranteed them the Christmas number one. Both deeclined, and Jerome (usually called Rome) went to a retreat. Simon Cowell wooed Robson with a joint advance of £50,000 and he disturbed Jerome to tell him that the situation had changed. They agreed and the single became one of the fastest selling records of the Nineties, shifting a million copies in three weeks and finishing at 1.4m. They passed £18,000 of their royalties to Greenpeace, which they supported.

Robson and Jerome's was the eighth version of 'Unchained Melody' to make the UK charts, and their arrangement was inspired by The Righteous Brothers. Although most people believe that '(There'll Be Bluebirds Over) The White Cliffs Of Dover' was written for Vera Lynn, this wasn't so. It was an American song of hope, written in the wake of Judy Garland's 'Over The Rainbow (1939). The American songwriters lifted the idea of the bluebirds, having no idea whether bluebirds were seen in England or not. The song became a dance band favourite and naturally, its emotions were ideal for Vera Lynn, then the Forces' sweetheart. In 1966 the song was a Top 30 hit for The Righteous Brothers, so this single was more a homage to The Righteous Brothers than anything else.

723 Outhere Brothers Boom Boom Boom

Label & Cat No.: **Eternal YZ 938CD**

Producer: **Outhere Brothers**

Writers: **Lemar Mahone / Ken Mayberry**

Date Reached No.1: **8 July 1995**

Weeks at No.1: **4**

FOLLOWING FURTHER COMPLAINTS about the offensive language on their debut album *1 Polish, 2 Biscuits And A Fish Sandwich*, later copies were issued with a sticker advising parents that the Outhere Brothers' album contained lyrics of an offending nature, but it didn't seem to make much difference, the damage had been done and the album peaked at a lowly number 56.

Outhere Brothers

After 'Don't Stop (Wiggle Wiggle)', the next single was 'Boom Boom Boom'. It had more of a party feel with its opening line, 'I say boom boom boom let me hear you say way-oh' prompting any party crowd to repeat, 'Way-oh'. But it was the lyrics, 'slip my peter inside your folder, make you sweat get you wetter, pump it faster to make it better', in the second verse that caused the government to step in and attempt to get the album banned. Malik hit back, "It's sad that such ignorance exists worldwide. They even called us gangsta rappers."

It was at this point that a promoter at WEA Records had the idea to re-issue the album without the offensive material, so the album was re-recorded and given the new title *Party Album*. It fared slightly better but still missed the Top 40. In the US however, The Outhere Brothers failed to make both the singles and album charts.

"Sex is nothing negative," insisted Hula. "It's all about education. The kids in Europe are taught to use condoms as their society wants to make them more aware, whilst here in America they try and shut kids out."

They had two further Top 10 hits, with 'La La La Hey Hey' and 'If You Wanna Party'. Their second album, *The Other Side*, went nowhere and the pair stopped performing as a duo in 1998. Hula continued writing and had one further hit as co-writer and producer of Indo's 1998 Top 40 hit, 'R U Sleeping'. In 2003 a best of collection, accurately entitled *The Fuckin' Hits*, (and proving no lessons were learnt), was released...

724 Take That Never Forget

Label & Cat No.: **RCA 74321299572**

Producers: **Jim Steinman / Brothers In Rhythm / David James**

Writer: **Gary Barlow**

Date reached No.1: **5 August 1995**

Weeks at No.1: **3**

IN JULY 1995 ROBBIE WILLIAMS announced that he was quitting Take That after the obligatory six months' notice and he would embark on a solo career. Their manager, Nigel Martin-Smith, had had enough of him but he realised that the forthcoming tour was in jeopardy if Robbie behaved badly. As Robbie said, "I don't want to be one of Gary Barlow's backing dancers. I'll come to rehearsals and I'll be there but I'll do it my way," this seemed very likely.

Martin-Smith sacked him immediately, which led to legal action between the parties. The US release of their album, *Nobody Else*, was issued with a different cover, deleting Robbie and featuring the four remaining members, and with slightly amended contents. Import copies arrived in the UK and such was Take That's popularity that it even made the Top 30 albums.

The news of Williams' departure was discussed by *The Times*, where Martin Talbot, the editor of *Music Week*, was quoted as saying, "I don't rate his prospects of a solo career. He's a bit of a dancer, who can sing a few lines, and he can't play an instrument." Rather reminiscent of the assessment of Fred Astaire's screen test: "Can't act. Can't sing. Slightly bald. Can dance a little."

Thanks to Meat Loaf's producer, Jim Steinman, 'Never Forget' was as much an event as a single. The grandiose opening sets the tone and is followed by a children's choir before we get to Take That. The song was a swan song for the band as it featured a variety of lead vocalists and had an accompanying video containing childhood photographs and concert footage over the years. 'Never Forget' was a charity single in aid of Nordoff Robbins Music Therapy and it quickly became an anthem for the fans.

The comedian and DJ, Phill Jupitus, said in 2004, "It's not fashionable but I like 'Never Forget' by Take That. It has all the elements of a classic love song."

725 Blur
Country House

Label & Cat No.: **Food CDFOODS 63**

Producer: **Stephen Street**

Writers: **Damon Albarn / Graham Coxon / Alex James / Dave Rowntree**

Date reached No.1: **26 August 1995**

Weeks at No.1: **2**

DAMON ALBARN, BORN IN LONDON in 1968, came from a show business family: his father was the tour manager for Soft Machine and his mother a stage designer who had worked for the dissident director Joan Littlewood. The family moved to Colchester and Graham Coxon was impressed when the 12-year-old Damon sang 'Gee, Officer Krupke!' at a school assembly. It was an impressive performance and Damon was to prove himself a lively front man, pogoing and even diving into the audience, always a risky venture as it assumes the audience will catch you: see *School Of Rock*.

Damon studied for a fine arts degree at Goldsmith's College in London, and in 1989 he formed a band called Seymour with Graham (a proficient guitarist), Alex James (bass) and Dave Rowntree (drums). Damon's grandfather gave them cash to make demos and they were signed by Andy Ross and Dave Balfe to Food Records. They changed their name to Blur at the suggestion of Dave Balfe.

Blur's first album, *Leisure* (1991), sold well and they had their first chart entries with 'She's So High', 'There's No Other Way', 'Bang' and the sardonic 'Popscene', which became a concert favourite. They courted controversy (though not of Oasis proportions) with binge drinking, disputes with their manager and Damon's well reported relationship with Elastica's Justine Frischmann, former girlfriend of Brett Anderson of Suede, Blur's arch-rivals.

Blur's album, *Modern Life Is Rubbish* (1992), led to comparisons with The Kinks and then in 1994 they had their first Top 10 single with 'Girls And Boys', a song about sex-filled package holidays. It reached number five, their biggest single until 'Country House'.

Parklife (1994) was a number one album and sold a million copies. The title track (Madness + Kinks) featured a chirpy, spoken vocal from the actor Phil Daniels (*Quadrophenia*) and commented on both East End life and unemployment. Much of the album and 'Magic America', in particular, was the result of an unpleasant tour of America and Damon railed against obesity, junk food and shopping malls. Blur played Glastonbury and Damon performed 'Waterloo Sunset' with Ray Davies on Channel 4's *The White Room*.

By 1995 Blur were a top draw but had never had a number one single, and their last attempt, 'End Of A Century', only reached number 19. Encouraged by Steve Sutherland at the *NME*, they moved the release of 'Country House' to the same day as Oasis' 'Roll With It'. Oasis vs. Blur was a north vs. south war, "working-class heroes vs. middle-class wankers" (to quote Noel Gallagher), educated lads vs. lager louts ('Country House' referred to the nineteenth century French author, Honoré de Balzac), even smirking vs. sneering. Liam Gallagher upped the ante with some rude remarks about Justine.

'Country House' was a strong single, made with The Smiths' producer, Stephen Street. Opening with a nod to the *Batman* theme, the song had a similar storyline to The Kinks' 'Sunny Afternoon'. Such lines as "Everything going Jackanory" even sound like Ray Davies. The video with their four revolving bodies was influenced by Queen's 'Bohemian Rhapsody'. It also featured the model Joanne Guest polishing Graham Coxon's chest.

The country house in question was not owned by Blur. The picture shown on the single is Castle Neushwanstein in Bavaria, which was King Ludwig II's retreat in the 1860s. "It was a bit of an odd cover for me," explained Damon in *Record Collector*. "I don't really know what the point was behind it. We knew what the song was about, we had the lyrics and knew they were reportedly about Dave Balfe – but they could refer to any other streetwise person who moves out into the country when they get successful. We just took it to absurd limits."

Oasis distanced themselves from the showdown, Noel Gallagher describing it as Blur's "last chance to drag themselves up on the coat-tails of my band." Damon said, "The only thing we've got in common is that we are both doing shit in America."

It was a foregone conclusion that either Blur or Oasis would top the charts. Nobody said that Take That might hang around for another week or that Madonna's 'Human Nature' would defeat both of them. Blur won by selling 276,000 copies of 'Country House' against 'Roll With It''s 218,000.

Blur followed their success with a bittersweet album, *The Great Escape*, which had grunge leanings. The album featured Labour MP, Ken Livingstone, on 'Ernold Same', who had previously recorded with The Flying Pickets. This being the era when Ken was a rebel MP, he surmised it was better to be seen with Blur than Blair. In May 2000 Ken was elected Mayor of London, and re-elected in 2004.

Blur beat Oasis to number one in the Battle Of The Bands, but ultimately Oasis had greater success, left to right: Graham Coxon, Dave Rowntree, Alex James and Damon Albarn

726 Michael Jackson
You Are Not Alone

Label & Cat No.: **Epic 662 310 2**

Producer: **R.Kelly**

Writer: **R.Kelly**

Date Reached No.1: **9 September 1995**

Weeks at No.1: **2**

On August 24, 1993 Los Angeles Police Department were called in to investigate child abuse allegations made against Michael. They were made by the father of a 13-year old boy called Jordan Chandler, but Michael was never charged and made an out of court settlement for an alleged $20m (£14m). Michael suffered another blow when Pepsi pulled out of an advertising campaign worth $10m.

On a more positive if unlikely note, in May 1994, Michael married Elvis Presley's daughter Lisa Marie in a ceremony in the Dominican Republic. In her press statement, Lisa Marie said, "I am very much in love with Michael and I dedicate my life to being his wife" – well, 19 months of it anyway.

In June 1995 Epic Records released Michael's latest album, *HIStory: Past, Present and Future Book 1*. His record company were urging Michael to release a greatest hits package, but Michael wanted to record new material. They compromised and *HIStory: Past, Present and Future Book 1* became a double CD with one disc of hits and the other new material.

In 1994 Michael heard R.Kelly's US number one 'Bump And Grind' and liked it. On the strength of that, he called R.Kelly's manager and asked him if R.Kelly would write a song for him. After R.Kelly was assured by his management that it was a genuine request he went straight in the studio and came up with 'You Are Not Alone'. Jacko then joined R.Kelly in Chicago to lay down the track and asked Kelly to provide backing vocals. Kelly said, "I actually imitated Michael when I sent him the first copy. He was laughing at me because I was imitating him."

In America, Michael set a new record when the song became the first ever to enter the *Billboard* chart at number one. It gave Michael his 13th US number one, putting him in third place behind Elvis Presley (17) and The Beatles (20).

727 Shaggy
Boombastic

Label & Cat No.: **Virgin VSCDT 1536**

Producers: **Stonebridge / Nick Nice**

Writers: **Orville Burrell / Robert Livingston**

Date Reached No.1: **23 September 1995**

Weeks at No.1: **1**

Shaggy followed 'Oh Carolina', with his debut album *Pure Pleasure*, which made little impact. "I'm the only person who does songs that's leftfield," claimed Shaggy at the time. "When I did 'Oh Carolina', there was nothing around that sounded like it. When I had 'Boombastic' out, again there was nothing like it and all the DJs went mad for it."

Shaggy was offered a lucrative recording contract with Virgin Records and landed a Top five hit with 'In The Summertime'. "I loved this song as a kid and it's a great song to sample," he remembered.

He followed it with 'Boombastic', the title track from his second album. Not only was it a UK number one, it went on to top the US R&B and rap charts. It set a record when it spent a whole year at the top of the US reggae chart. Again it used a sample, this time from King Floyd's 1971 single,'Baby Let Me Kiss You'. It was the next in a long line of songs being used to advertise Levi's jeans.

Shaggy has a distinctive bass voice which he uses to create various sounds and this is combined with a repeated bass note on the piano. The lyric 'She call me Mr. Boombastic say me fantastic' led to Shaggy becoming known as Mr Boombastic. He also has the nickname Mr. Loverman because of his regular use of the line 'Mr. Lover-Lover'. And how did that come about? "I don't know, people just grabbed on to it. To me, I've said it and it's become a character. At the end of the day, I'll always do songs for the ladies, because I know there is a following for it and girls love it."

Boombastic, a play on the word bombastic, as well as a slang term for marijuana, first appeared on The Dream Warriors 1990 hit 'My Definition Of A Boombastic Jazz Style'.

The following year he teamed up with Grand Puba for 'Why You Treat Me So Bad' (11), followed by the double A-side 'Something Different' / 'The Train Is Coming' (15), the latter of which featured in the film *Money Train*. In 1997 he returned to the Top 10 with a ragga cover of Erma Franklin's 'Piece Of My Heart', using samples of the original. It was his last hit for Virgin who dropped him in favour of new talent.

728 Simply Red
Fairground

Label & Cat No.: **East West EW001**

Producers: **Mick Hucknall / Stewart Levine**

Writer: **Mick Hucknall**

Date Reached No.1: **30 September 1995**

Weeks at No.1: **4**

The darlings of MOR radio stations across the world, Simply Red evolved out of punk outfit The Frantic Elevators in 1984. They had released five singles on various independent labels between 1979 and 1982, the last being 'Holding Back The Years' in a sleeve that showed Mick Hucknall with a gun in his mouth. The track would later be re-recorded by Simply Red.

Taking the name from his flame-haired locks, Manchester-born singer Mick Hucknall assembled Simply Red with Fritz McIntyre (guitar), Tony Powers (bass), Tim Kellett (keyboards and trumpet) and Chris Joyce (drums). They opened their chart account in 1985 with a cover of The Valentine Brothers' 'Money's Too Tight (To Mention)' (13), a song many have associated with Thatcher's economic policies. Mick loved 'Holding

In order to promote his HIStory compilation album, Michael Jackson arranged for a giant statue of him to be floated down the Thames

Back The Years' and the new version was issued in late 1985. But the public didn't take to it and it peaked at number 51. With a new publicity campaign the song was re-issued the following May and it went to number two behind Dr & The Medics' 'Spirit In The Sky'.

Their first two albums *Picture Book* and *Men And Women*, both peaked at number two. In 1987 a note-for-note cover of Ella Fitzgerald's 'Ev'ry Time We Say Goodbye' reached number 11. In 1989 they finally landed a number one when the album *A New Flame* reached the top. But a number one single still eluded them when a cover of Harold Melvin & The Bluenotes' 'If You Don't Know Me By Now' reached number two. The extensive *New Flame* tour took up most of the year, but Mick was growing tired of the same routine with the same members of the band. "I want to keep Simply Red a rolling thing where different musicians come and go," he said, as he fired Bowers and Joyce.

Mick made 1990 a sabbatical year. He wanted to travel at leisure and often woke up thinking, 'which country shall I visit today?' Whilst in Milan he joined Barry White on stage for a duet

of 'Let The Music Play'. He was also spotted with Miles Davis at the Montreux Jazz Festival. In 1991 he released the album *Stars*, which sold 2.5 million copies in the UK alone and became the biggest selling British album of 1991 and 1992, earning Mick an Ivor Novello award for 'Songwriter Of The Year'.

He returned to the jazz festival two years later where he recorded four songs, 'Love For Sale', 'Drowning In My Own Tears', 'Granma's Hands' and 'Lady Godiva's Room' which collectively made up the *Montreux* EP and reached number 11. In 1993 Simply Red won Best Group at the Brit Awards and Mick was voted Best Male Singer. At that point Mick announced that he was taking some time off and would return when he had enough songs of 'appropriate quality'.

He proved that in September 1995 when he returned, essentially as a soloist, with his new single, the Latin-flavoured 'Fairground', which debuted at number one. It had all Mick's trademark soul qualities, but included a sample of 'Give It Up', a Top five hit for Dutch duo The Goodmen. Mick even acknowledged them in the lyric 'Let's make amends like all goodmen should'. It propelled the parent album, *Life* to number one, too. Further hits followed with 'Angel' (1996), 'Say You Love Me' (1998), and 'The Air That I Breathe' (1998) all making the Top 10.

Mick was growing tired of East West Records' policy. "The reason *Stars* didn't sell in the US was because they had a budget and they chose to promote En Vogue instead. We didn't get much support after they'd made that decision and I never really forgave them for it," Mick explained in an interview with Ron Slomowicz. "From then on, our relationship just went from bad to worse and by the time 1998 came around, I said to my management 'let's get out there and find another deal because I don't want to do it this way anymore. As far as I'm concerned I own that work that you might have on your table right now, a greatest hits or whatever, I own that work, I paid for it. They are currently custodians of my work, they think they own it but they don't neither morally nor financially and the only way that I can really get back at them if the law won't enable me to have what I own, is to create my own record company and create my own catalogue that would be in direct competition with that. Until they see the day that that work belongs to the artist.'"

In 2003 Mick set up his own simplyred.com label. The first single 'Sunrise', which sampled Hall & Oates' 'I Can't Go For That (No Can Do)', went to number seven. "It was my friend Andy Wright who came up with the sample, the same guy I first worked with on the Goodmen sample on 'Fairground'," remembered Mick. The album *Home*, didn't quite make it home to the number one slot. It stopped at number two behind *Meteora* by Linkin Park, but it proved that simplyred.com had the capability to compete with the major companies.

Subsequently in 2004 a poll compiled by the Radio Academy was released listing the Top 10 artists with the most plays on British radio in the last 20 years, Mick Hucknall/Simply Red came in at number nine. Just for the record the list was topped by George Michael.

729 Coolio featuring L.V. Gangsta's Paradise

Label & Cat No.: **Tommy Boy MCSTD 2104**

Producer: **Doug Rasheed**

Writers: **Artis Ivey Jr / Larry Sanders / Doug Rasheed / Stevie Wonder**

Date Reached No.1: **28 October 1995**

Weeks at No.1: **2**

COOLIO WAS A BRIGHT CHILD. "I WAS an A student," he admitted. As a young teenager his parents split and he was brought up by his mother. It was then that Coolio went off the rails. He left home and turned to drugs and thieving and ended up in prison for petty theft.

Born Artis Ivey Jr in Los Angeles in 1963, Coolio began rapping at 15. He trained as a firefighter as well as spending time in libraries trying to educate himself on subjects like the history of black people in America. He recorded his first

album in 1994. "I wrote the lyric 'It doesn't matter if you're black or white,' but I didn't really believe it, except in music," he remembered. "Now that I've travelled the world I know it's true. I've been to places where colour doesn't matter. But America isn't one of them, nor is England."

After a stint as a member of the rap act WC & The Maad Circle, Coolio released his first single 'Fantastic Voyage'. It went to number three in the US but fell one place short of the Top 40 in the UK.

It was whilst visiting his manager's office that he heard Stevie Wonder's 1976 album *Songs In The Key Of Life*. "That's where I met Larry Sanders, who is better known as L.V, which stood for Large Variety. He was working on a song using a sample of 'Pastime Paradise' from the album. I asked him if I could work with him on it," The song opens with the line, 'As I walk through the valley of the shadow of death' borrowed in part from Psalm 23. "The next line 'I take a look at my life' came straight in my head and I sat down and wrote the whole song on the spot. I remember trying to get people to understand the song at the time. People were calling it gothic rap because it was dark. That's true, but it was dark in a positive way, not a negative way. In the end I think they understood that it was a spiritual rap."

Kathy Nelson, music supervisor for the movie, *Dangerous Minds*, starring Michelle Pfeiffer, said, "The producers, Don Simpson and Jerry Bruckheimer, originally wanted more alternative music, but it didn't really work. I had recently heard this song 'Fantastic Voyage' and liked it, so I suggested an urban soundtrack." She invited Coolio to a preview and asked him if he could provide a song as the film's theme. Coolio agreed as he thought the inner-city classroom drama portrayed a positive message. In 1995 Coolio and Stevie Wonder performed a duet of the song at the Billboard Music Awards.

In December that same year, L.V released his debut solo single 'Throw Your Hands Up', which had his own re-recorded version of 'Gangsta's Paradise' on the other side. It peaked at number 24.

Coolio had two further Top 10 hits, a cover of Kool & The Gang's 'Too Hot' which reached number nine and 'C U When U Get There' (3), which sampled Pachelbel's 'Canon in D Major' and was featured in the film *Nothing To Lose*.

In 2000 he appeared as himself in the film *Lei Ting Zhan Jing*, the story of a young Chinese security officer who fights against the smuggling of drugs and corruption. In 2003 he had a small part in the film *Daredevil*, however "my scenes got edited out," said Coolio. "But you'll see me in the DVD version."

730 Robson & Jerome

I Believe / Up On The Roof

Label & Cat No.: **RCA 74321 326882**

Producers: **Mike Stock / Matt Aitken**

Writers: **Erwin Drake / Irvin Graham / Jimmy Shirl / Al Stillman : Gerry Goffin / Carole King**

Date reached No.1: **11 November 1995**

Weeks at No.1: **4**

ROBSON AND JEROME MADE VERY few performances as singers, among them The Royal Variety Performance in November 1995. This was the perfect opportunity to launch their latest single, 'I Believe' and so reach number one with their first two singles. The song had often been revived (including by R&J's favourites, The Righteous Brothers) but it hadn't been at number one since Frankie Laine in 1953.

The misconception that popular music was in decline immediately before The Beatles belies lovely pop songs like 'Up On The Roof'. Written by New Yorkers Carole King and Gerry Goffin and first recorded by Little Eva, it evokes the high-rise apartments in American cities where it's possible to escape the stresses of daily living by climbing up on the roof. The song is packed with Goffin's skilful imagery – "At night the stars put on a show for free" is a beautiful line.

The Drifters with Rudy Lewis on lead vocals recorded the song in June 1962 and it went to number five in the US. The Drifters never reached number one in the UK, their biggest hit being 'Save The Last Dance For Me', with Ben E. King on lead vocal, which reached number two in 1960. In the UK, 'Up On The Roof' was a hit for local singers, Kenny Lynch (10) and Julie Grant (33), but there were relatively few high-rise apartments in the early Sixties.

The single sold 900,000 copies and their album, *Robson & Jerome*, topped the charts – the ideal Christmas present, or maybe not – and sold 1.4m. *So Far So Good* topped the video charts and sold 400,000 copies. On the CD sleeve, Robson & Jerome thanked "all the writers for their lyrics": what about the music, chaps?

Coolio

731 Michael Jackson Earth Song

Label & Cat No.:	**Epic 662 695 2**
Producers:	**Michael Jackson / David Foster / Bill Bottrell**
Writer:	**Michael Jackson**
Date Reached No.1:	**9 December 1995**
Weeks at No.1:	**6**

DECEMBER 1995 WAS NOT A GOOD time for Michael. At the beginning of the month he was rehearsing for his *One Night Only* show in New York when he collapsed. Doctors diagnosed a gastrointestinal ailment and an electrolyte imbalance had caused his liver and kidneys to malfunction and his stomach became inflamed. Then more bad news came. The day after 'Earth Song' debuted at number one, his wife, Lisa Marie Presley, told him their marriage was over.

Jackson recovered within a couple of weeks and left hospital. In February the following year, Michael attended The Brits ceremony at London's Earls Court. While performing 'Earth Song', Pulp singer Jarvis Cocker invaded the stage and caused some disruption of Jacko's performance. Cocker was arrested on suspicion of assaulting three children on stage but was later cleared of all charges, maintaining he was protesting against Jacko's 'Christ-like' pose, a claim largely supported in the press.

'Earth Song' is Michael's biggest selling UK hit. It's the only one to sell over a million copies. To increase sales, a massive advertising campaign was launched, which included a 50ft statue of Michael being floated down the River Thames.

Compared to *Thriller* (50m), *Bad* (30m) and *Dangerous* (26m), *HIStory: Past, Present and Future Book 1*'s 14 million sales seems relatively low. As Tony Parsons in the *Daily Telegraph* wrote, "*HIStory* is the most personal record that any major artist has released since Bob Dylan's *Blood On The Tracks*. This is the King Of Pop seemingly on the verge of a nervous breakdown."

732 George Michael Jesus To A Child

Label & Cat No.:	**Virgin VSCDG 1571**
Producer:	**George Michael**
Writer:	**George Michael**
Date reached No.1:	**20 January 1996**
Weeks at No.1:	**1**

GEORGE MICHAEL'S *FAITH* (1987) ALBUM sold 15 million copies worldwide but *Listen Without Prejudice, Volume 1* (1990) could only manage five. Sony had bought his label, CBS, in 1988 and George associated the drop in sales with their "lack of creative and marketing talent" and not his own ability. He said, "Sony sees artists as little more than software" and sued them, demanding his release from the label. The evidence in the High Court case in 1993 lasted 74 days and must have been highly embarrassing for him. His fortune was laid bare and we learnt that he earned £16m in 1988.

To make matters worse, he lost the case, having to pay both sides' legal expenses and still being tied to the label. His answerphone message was "I'm never going to sing again, bastards, bastards" to the melody of 'Careless Whisper'. "He would have got more joy if he'd sued his hairdresser," joked Billy Bragg about the GM crop. In 1995 George Michael came to an agreement with Sony and he moved to the new DreamWorks label in the US, and Virgin elsewhere.

When George Michael was in Rio in 1991, he befriended dress designer Anselmo Feleppa, and he was to say, "For the first time I got together with someone who loved me, and I actually felt I loved him." Anselmo died from AIDS in 1993 and George wrote a lament, 'Jesus To A Child', in a couple of hours. "It's a special song," he said, "one of those songs that felt like it was handed to me."

In 1994 George performed 'Jesus To A Child', the first new song in five years, at the MTV awards in Berlin. When he had completed the single, he raised £50,000 for charity by presenting its first airing on London's Capital Radio. It was intended for release at Christmas, but the paperwork prevented it from being released before January. (Was this an example of Virgin also lacking creative and marketing talent?) By January, everybody had heard it on the radio and the single, despite being as bleak as anything by Nick Cave, shot to number one.

The album, *Older*, with his new look goatee beard, was a big seller and it maintained its link to Brazil as it was dedicated to the bossa nova maestro, Antonio Carlos Jobin, "who changed the way I listened to music".

733 Babylon Zoo Spaceman

Label & Cat No.:	**EMI CDEM 416**
Producers:	**Jas Mann / Steve Power**
Writer:	**Jas Mann**
Date Reached No.1:	**27 January 1996**
Weeks at No.1:	**5**

BABYLON ZOO'S JAS MANN MUST HAVE wondered if his career was ever going to get off the ground. The urban spaceman and former midfield player for Punjabi Rovers had three label changes before he landed himself the fastest-selling debut single in UK chart history.

Jaswinder, a Dudley-born Sikh had sowed his musical seeds as the lead singer with indie rock band The Sandkings. They had a deal with London Records and recorded the song, 'All's Well With The World'. They supported The Stone Roses and The Happy Mondays, but Jas wasn't happy. "It was wrong really. I'd left school and I should have chilled out and bummed around for a while, but suddenly I was in a group and it took me two years to find out that being in a group was not for me," he admitted. "I knew it was impossible for me to work with anybody as I need total control. I lived with my parents but had no friends, just my clothes, my guitar and a drum machine. I sold loads of my clothes to get some money to buy studio time. When I did, I recorded three songs in a day."

Jas worked better on his own. "I could never listen to a piece of music without pretending I could see things," he revealed. "I conceived the name Babylon Zoo in 1993 as a focus for films, gallery displays and kinetic art. I began writing more songs and using an Apple Mac. I wrote nine songs and sent them to the head of A&R at EMI, Clive Black."

Black was impressed after seeing a rehearsal in Wolverhampton in 1993 and a week later signed him. But six months later Black left EMI for a job at Warner Brothers as A&R director. Black was able to take Babylon Zoo with him even though an album had been started. Once at Warners, sleeves were immediately printed up for the first single 'Spaceman' and early copies were sent to radio stations. The single was all ready for release when Black was offered the Managing Director's job back at EMI, which he accepted and again took Babylon Zoo with him. It was a blessing in disguise that some radio stations had begun playing the track because that's how it came to the attention of Levi's. "The director tracked us down and said 'We love your tune: it's apt for the futuristic feel'," explained Jas. By August 1995 a deal had been secured with Levi's to use 'Spaceman' in their next advertising campaign. Three months later Levi's began using 'Spaceman' in cinemas all over the UK as well as on television and soon there was a big demand for the track. It would have been easy to get the single out in time for Christmas, but Black was looking for a more long-term thing. He said, "We spent two months working different stores with videos and album samplers to prove that Babylon Zoo was a real act, not just an advert."

When 'Spaceman' finally came out in January 1996, it sold 418,000 copies in the first week, far more than the parent album, *The Boy With The X-Ray Eyes*, which, despite reaching number six, dropped off the chart after only five weeks.

Although Babylon Zoo is generally classed as a one-hit wonder, he did chart three more singles. The follow-up, 'Animal Army' peaked at number 17 and the next single, the album's title track, faltered at number 32. In the Middle East, they were known as B. Zoo as 'Babylon' implies decadence in that part of the world.

Jas disappeared from the pop world for three years but he returned in 1999 with 'All The Money's Gone', but when it only reached number 46, not only had the money gone, so had Jas.

"'Spaceman' was too successful, too soon," Jas reflected in 2000. "When it stayed at the top for five weeks, I knew I was in trouble and that everything I did after was going to be compared with it. When EMI sent me round the world promoting the single, I became ill with exhaustion and went to India with my family to rest. After that I went to Italy but had a relapse and ended up in hospital for four months."

Jas now lives in Los Angeles with his wife and is still recording material, which he claimed in 2001, was for a solo album. "I'm constantly being approached to do another 'Spaceman', but there really is no point."

734 Oasis
Don't Look Back In Anger

Label & Cat No.: **Creation CRESCD 221**

Producers: **Owen Morris / Noel Gallagher**

Writer: **Noel Gallagher**

Date reached No.1: **2 March 1996**

Weeks at No.1: **1**

THE TERM BRITPOP WAS COINED BY the media to cover young British bands who took much of their inspiration from the Sixties. They included Blur, Pulp and Oasis, although Oasis had reservations about being marketed in this way.

After 'Some Might Say', Britpop was in full swing and although Oasis was not keen on the idea, their 'Roll With It' was released on the same day as Blur's 'Country House'. "Damon Albarn was on *News At Ten*. What the fuck was that about?" mused Noel Gallagher.

Blur won the chart race, but there were problems with the barcode on some Oasis singles and the difference between the sales figures (274,000 to 218,000 in that first week) might have been closer. Though Oasis lost in the short term, they were soon to eclipse Blur. Noel

Babylon Zoo

Gallagher, never at a loss for words when it came to hurling insults, went over the top when after Blur taunted Oasis for sounding like Status Quo. He retaliated, "I hope they catch AIDS and die because I fucking hate them."

Their second album, *(What's The Story) Morning Glory?*, was released in October 1995 and, despite mixed reviews, immediately topped the album charts. It included their next single, 'Wonderwall', which Noel had written for his wife, Meg Matthews: "You're gonna to be the one to save me". *Wonderwall* was the title of an instrumental soundtrack by George Harrison, and The Beatles' 'Till There Was You' was played at Noel and Meg's wedding.

Unlike The Beatles, Oasis songs have not been widely covered. The exception is 'Wonderwall', which was turned into an easy listening hit by Mike Flowers, a cabaret singer from a Liverpool seminary. With far less subtlety, the song was revived by The Wurzels in 2002. The first cover without an element of parody came from Ryan Adams in 2004. Much to Noel and Liam's delight (see – they can agree on something!), 'Wonderwall' was taken up at Maine Road by Manchester City supporters.

While Oasis were recording at Rockfield, Liam was drinking heavily. When he wandered off, Noel decided to record 'Don't Look Back In Anger' in his absence with Bonehead on piano. When Liam returned, they tried to keep him out of the studio. Liam attempted to smash Noel's guitar and Noel whacked him with a cricket bat. Noel said that he would leave and go solo, but he changed his mind within a week.

'Don't Look Back In Anger' was released as a single in March 1996 and gave Oasis their second number one. It was a big scale ballad very much in the late Sixties mould and Oasis/Beatle trainspotters can identify a shopping list of influences: after the piano opening reminiscent of John Lennon's 'Imagine' you can hear traces of The Casuals' 'Jesamine', Honeybus' 'I Can't Let Maggie Go', Pink Floyd's 'See Emily Play' and Lennon's 'Watching The Wheels'. The profusion of Sixties references suggests that Noel Gallagher was doing this deliberately to wind up the critics. The 'Sally' in the song didn't exist – "It was just words," he said.

'Wonderwall' was a hit single in America and Oasis were selling around the world. They turned down dates in Australia: Noel said, "We don't fucking want to fly to the other fucking end of the world and play like shit." They did in the end. When Oasis went to America, there was plenty of fighting within the group, and the tabloids loved their loutish behaviour.

Noel turned down an Ivor Novello songwriting award when he learnt he would have to share it with Damon Albarn and when Oasis won Best Video (for 'Wonderwall'), Best Group and Best Album at the Brits, they dismissed it by referring to the record industry as 'corporate pigs'.

Oasis put strong melodies and guitar bands back in fashion. Noel Gallagher said, "If we take anyone's first two albums against my first two albums, I'm there. I'm with The Beatles." (Note the 'my' rather than 'our'.)

735 Take That
How Deep Is Your Love?

Label & Cat No.: **RCA 74321355592**

Producers: **Chris Porter / Take That**

Writers: **Robin Gibb / Barry Gibb / Maurice Gibb**

Date reached No.1: **9 March 1996**

Weeks at No.1: **3**

IN FEBRUARY 1996 ROBBIE WILLIAMS reached an out-of-court settlement with BMG, enabling him to pursue a solo career. At the same time, the four remaining Take That members announced that they would be splitting after their current commitments. Both Childline and the Samaritans were deluged with calls from distraught fans.

For their final single, Take That revived The Bee Gees' 'How Deep Is Your Love?' and Gary Barlow said, rather curiously, "We wanted to prove that we could still do a cover version this far on in our career and do it very well." Even odder was the video with Take That tied to chairs with ropes. What were they saying?

Take That had sold around 10 million singles and so a *Greatest Hits* was bound to do well. Robbie Williams started legal proceedings to prevent its release, though it was hard to see why, and he soon dropped his action. *Greatest Hits* topped the album charts for four weeks.

How would Take That fare in their solo careers? The sensible money was on Gary Barlow, though Robbie might strike lucky with a one-off hit. We will meet both of them later in the book, but Mark Owen almost made the top with two Top Three hits, 'Child' (1996) and 'Clementine' (1997), and he did win *Celebrity Big Brother* in 2002.

736 Prodigy
Firestarter

Label & Cat No.: **XL Recordings XLS 70CD**

Producer: **Liam Howlett**

Writers: **Liam Howlett / Kim Deal / Anne Dudley / Jonathan J. Jeczalik / Gary Langan / Paul Morley / Trevor Horn**

Date Reached No.1: **30 March 1996**

Weeks at No.1: **3**

IN 1986 SOME LADS FROM ESSEX WERE out 'decorating' the local railway arches in graffiti. One of them signed his tag, Fame, and stood back to admire his work. Fame, known to his friends as Liam Howlett, went on to create music equally admirable.

Liam was into hip-hop and soon took up DJing under the name DJ Fame and became a member of a band Cut To Kill who put out one album in 1988. Soon after, Liam grew tired of the hip-hop scene and left. It was at a rave in 1989 that he met Keith Flint and Leeroy Thornhill. The following year they joined forces, recruited a rapper, Maxim Reality (born Keith Palmer) and called themselves The Prodigy, a name chosen by Liam in honour of his Moog Prodigy keyboard.

Their first single was a four-track 12-inch EP containing the tracks 'What Evil Lurks', 'We Gonna Rock', 'Android' and 'Everybody In The

Place', but it attracted few buyers. The next single, 'Charly', a slang name for cocaine, raced up to number three in the chart. It contained a sample from a Seventies public information film called *Say No To Strangers*, which was voiced by Kenny Everett. Over the next five years they registered Top 10 hits with 'Everybody In The Place', 'Out Of Space' / 'Ruff In The Jungle Bizness', 'One Love' and 'No Good (Start The Dance)'. In 1992 their debut album, *Experience*, reached number 12 and the follow-up, *Music For The Jilted Generation*, went all the way.

The original 'Firestarter' video was directed by the same team who worked on the Diesel jeans television ad that Keith and Liam loved, but as Liam said, "It just didn't represent us as people and it had to go." The new version was shot in a tube tunnel at the disused Aldwych station and showed Keith dressed in an American flag T-shirt with a mohican, looking very menacing. "It may be in black and white and shot in a cheap location but it ended up being the most expensive video we ever did," revealed Liam.

The week it aired on *Top Of The Pops*, the tabloids reared their heads in an attempt to ban the record, claiming it frightened young children and encouraged arsonists.

'Firestarter', which was inspired by The Foo Fighters' 'Weenie Beenie', a track on their debut album, *Foo Fighters*, lifted the guitar riff from The Breeders' album track, 'S.O.S.' and borrowed the 'hey, hey, hey' refrain from The Art Of Noise's 'Close (To The Edit)'. Both samples cost them dearly. The band were pleased with the finished article which brought together a darting break-beat, a whining guitar riff, and a keyboard sound resembling a siren. All this added to Keith's 'I'm a firestarter, twisted firestarter' growls gave the song a haunting, yet memorable sound.

737 Mark Morrison
Return Of The Mack

Label & Cat No.: **Creation CRESCD 221**

Producers: **Phil Chill / Mark Morrison**

Writer: **Mark Morrison**

Date reached No.1: **20 April 1996**

Weeks at No.1: **2**

Born in Hanover in 1973, Mark Morrison was raised partly in Florida and partly in Leicester where he was imprisoned between March and May 1994 after a fracas in a club. He turned to singing and 'Where Is Our Love?' was released on his own Joe'Mel label with backing from The Prince's Trust and Leicester Afro-Caribbean Arts Association. The single was played in clubs and as a result he was signed by Warners. Although he gave his influences as Bob Marley and Michael Jackson, the key inspiration was surely Marvin Gaye. Said Mark, "Nobody sings the way I do because it's a blend of singing, street talking and rapping all in one."

The first single, 'Crazy', was a club hit and made the UK Top 20, and was followed by 'Let's Get Down'. Mark Morrison was a disturbed man and perhaps in the light of this, it was unwise to market *Return Of The Mack* in the way they did. Holding a pair of handcuffs on the album cover, the slogan was "The Mack is back."

'Return Of The Mack' was a love song, but Mark added another dimension: "When I wrote that song, it was all about my moving from the negative to the positive. And that's how it turned out. Within the space of a year, I went from the lowest point in my life to return as The Mack and move forward to what's become the highest point in my life." 'Return Of The Mack' sampled the funky instrumental, 'N.T' by Kool & the Gang, and the single, and indeed the album, was produced by Phil Chill, who had worked with Neneh Cherry. The album's credits give thanks to God ("for continuing to answer my prayers and forgive my sins") and he adds as an aside to the Leicestershire police force – "Next time, better luck." Indeed.

The single was followed by four more hits from the album – a remixed 'Crazy' (6), 'Trippin'' (8), 'Horny' (5) and 'Moan And Groan' (7). 'Moan And Groan', especially, paid homage to Marvin Gaye and Mark laughs as he tells his girl to "Open my drawers." The 'Return Of The Mack' single was a huge European hit and climbed to number two in the US. The album sold nearly three million copies worldwide.

Although his career was going well, Morrison was constantly in trouble with the law,

culminating in him trying to take a stun-gun on a plane. He hired someone to complete a community service order on his behalf, hardly a wise move when he was very visibly on tour at the time. The paparazzi snapped the hapless worker and his deceit was all over the papers. Morrison was arrested again and, early in 1997, he was sentenced to a year in jail. At the same time, he was nominated for four Brits, though he did not win any.

Since then, Mark Morrison has had hits with 'Who's The Mack!' (13) and, with Connor Reeves, 'Best Friend' (23). There were reports that he converted to Islam and changed his name to Abdul Rahman, but he has since denied these reports. In 2004 he signed with the label, 2 Wikid, owned by the Everton striker Kevin Campbell but his new single, 'Just A Man' / 'Backstabbers' only reached number 50.

738 George Michael
Fastlove

Label & Cat No.: **Virgin VSCDG 1579**
Producer: **George Michael**
Writer: **George Michael**
Date reached No.1: **4 May 1996**
Weeks at No.1: **3**

WHILE GEORGE MICHAEL WAS IN limbo, refusing to record for Sony, he worked on an official biography with Tony Parsons. One of the chapters was tellingly entitled *A Very Early Masturbator*, but they called the book, *Bare*, instead of *Zip Me Up Before You Go-Go*.

'Fastlove', another track from George Michael's comeback album, *Older*, made the top and it includes a sample from Patrice Rushen's 1982 soul hit, 'Forget Me Nots'. According to the song, "Fastlove is all that I've got on my mind". The singer is not looking for a lasting relationship and simply wants to make love in his BMW. At the time, this was just a song rather than an indication of George's lifestyle, but there is a telling line with the dual interpretation of "Stupid Cupid keeps on calling me and I see lovin' in his eyes."

In 1998 George Michael was arrested for lewd behaviour after exposing himself to a policeman in the Will Rogers Memorial Park in Beverly Hills. Three days later, he admitted his sexuality on TV, gained a good deal of sympathy as many felt he had been hounded by the police.

A short while later, he wrote 'Outside' about his experience, possibly the most unlikely subject ever for a hit single but it went to number two. In the video, he parodied the policeman who had arrested him.

739 Gina G
Ooh Aah... Just A Little Bit

Label & Cat No.: **Eternal WEA 041CD**
Producer: **Steve Rodway**
Writers: **Simon Tauber / Stephen Rodway**
Date Reached No.1: **25 May 1996**
Weeks at No.1: **1**

GINA GARDENER, BORN IN BRISBANE on August 3, 1970, moved to Melbourne in 1987 and began DJing in the local nightclubs, which in turn led to her joining a dance act called Bass Culture. In 1992 they released their debut single 'Love The Life', written by Gina. In 1994 she decided to emigrate to the UK where she met Simon Tauber at the Warner Brothers' offices. He and former Motiv 8 producer and keyboard player Steve Rodway had written a song together which they had just submitted to Warners. Rodway had previously charted as the co-writer of Russ Abbott's 1984 Top 10 hit 'Atmosphere'. Gina heard the new track and asked to record it.

'Ooh Aah... Just A Little Bit' had an energetic Euro intro that was instantly recognisable and immediately got toes tapping and heads nodding. Once it was recorded, a copy found its way into the hands of Jonathan King, who at the time had taken over the organisation of A Song For Europe. He renamed it The Great British Song Contest and usually having a good eye (and ear) for spotting talent, it was his suggestion that 'Ooh Aah... Just A Little Bit' be put forward for the contest. It was performed and recorded at the BBC Television Centre and previewed on *Top Of The Pops*, followed by the *Live And Kicking* show the following Saturday morning. It was the public who voted and Gina won with 113,000 votes, nearly 72,000 ahead of Code Red's 'I Gave You Everything', who came second. When Code Red released that single later that year it faltered at number 50.

The contest was held at The Spektrum in Oslo in May and Gina only came seventh, but the song made the Top 10 across Europe. It also made the Top 20 in the US.

Gina had further UK hits with 'I Belong To You' (6), 'Fresh!' (6), 'Ti Amo' (11), 'Gimme Some Love' (25) and 'Every Time I Fall' (52). In 1998 Gina and the song's co-writer, Simon Tauber, claimed that they had earned no money from the hit and began a legal battle for their share of the royalties. The high court judge agreed that Tauber was entitled to £350,000 in unpaid royalties. But FX Music, the production company who held the royalties, went into liquidation. In 1998 Jonathan King invited Gina to be one of the judges for the preliminary stage of the contest to choose the final eight.

In 1999 Gina moved to America and signed with Warner Brothers there. Two singles and an album were issued within a year, but none of them troubled the UK or US charts. In 2001 the public were reminded of the song when Burger King started using it in their latest ad campaign.

Two years later Gina was invited to appear on a British reality TV show called *Reborn In The USA*. The programme also featured a parade of former chart stars: Sonia, Tony Hadley, Elkie Brooks, Go West's Peter Cox, Michelle Gayle, Imagination's Leee John, Dollar and Ultimate Kaos' Hayden Eshun. They toured the US and were voted off one by one by the British public. The show's reviews weren't favourable and Gina's voice seemed to have no range. The eventual winner was Tony Hadley.

In 2004 Gina returned to Australia and signed a deal with Dinky Records. Her first single in seven years was 'Heaven', a dance tune credited to Elemental featuring Gina G.

George Michael's indiscretion in a public toilet in Los Angeles didn't really harm his career

740 Baddiel & Skinner & The Lightning Seeds Three Lions

Label & Cat No.: **Epic 6632732**

Producers: **David Bascombe / Ian Broudie / Simon Rogers**

Writers: **David Baddiel / Frank Skinner / Ian Broudie**

Date reached No.1: **1 June 1996**

Weeks at No.1: **2 (2 runs)**

PAGES OF MISHEARD LYRICS ARE RIFE ON the internet, but many examples look too contrived to have evolved naturally. In 1985 Prince had a hit single with 'Raspberry Beret' and one of the lines was "Thunder drowns out what the lightning sees": the Liverpool musician Ian Broudie heard it as "Thunder drowns out what the lighting seeds".

The Lightning Seeds was the most successful Merseyside band of the Nineties. This was largely due to Ian's melodic songwriting and strong lead vocals, but the contributions at different times of Paul Hemmings (guitar), Martyn Campbell (bass) and Angie Pollock (keyboards, vocals) should not be overlooked. Chris Sharrock was the group's first drummer and for a time they also had Ringo Starr's son, Zak Starkey, in the band.

They had hit singles with 'Pure' (16, 1989), 'Change' (13, 1995), Perfect' (18, 1995) and 'Lucky You'(15, 1995), but the big hits eluded them. Asked to make a record for Euro 1996, Ian Broudie was in two minds. "I would never have bought a football single myself and I certainly didn't want to do one of those cheerleader records," he said. "Being a fan is being about losing and, if we did it, I wanted to write it from a fan's point of view." He asked the football-obsessed comedians, Frank Skinner and David Baddiel, to sing on the record and help with the words.

Ian recalls, "I remember when we played the single to Terry Venables and the team. They were training and we had this horrible ghetto-blaster. I was suddenly conscious of the words, 'Everyone knows the score, We've seen it all before' in other words, 'We're rubbish' and we did get some funny looks. But the song is from a fan's point of view and England fans are pretty long-suffering."

'Three Lions' was the first football single which suggested that the team might not win and was therefore more realistic. It turned out to be correct as England lost to Germany in a penalty shoot-out in the semi-final. The Lightning Seeds' 'The Life Of Riley', which Ian had written about the birth of his son, had been used for *Goal Of The Day* and a revamped 'Three Lions' hit the top in 1998. "The song has passed into folklore," says Broudie, "Everytime there's a big match, you can guarantee that some newspaper will be quoting from the song in their headlines."

741 Fugees Killing Me Softly

Label & Cat No.: **Columbia 663 343 2**

Producers: **Wyclef Jean / Lauryn Hill / Jerry Duplessis**

Writers: **Norman Gimbel / Charles Fox**

Date Reached No.1: **8 June 1996**

Weeks at No.1: **5 (2 runs)**

WITH THE CHART FULL OF TECHNO, trance and house tunes, The Fugees were a welcome breath of fresh air. Their music was R&B combined with light rap and traces of reggae, folk and rock and appealed to pop, easy listening and dance fans alike.

Lauryn Hill, who grew up in South Orange, New Jersey listening to the music of Stevie Wonder, Aretha Franklin and Curtis Mayfield, attended the same high school as keyboard player Pras Michel (born Prakazrel Michel). They, along with a female friend, began rapping in different languages and were combining them into one song, so decided to call themselves The Tranzlator Crew. One day in the studio, Pras' cousin, Wyclef Jean, who also played keyboards, came by and began contributing a few ideas. Before long he had replaced the other female as the new full-time member of the group.

Lauryn had acted in a number of soaps before being taking on the role of Rita Watson in the film *Sister Act II – Back In The Habit* alongside Whoopi Goldberg. The group renamed themselves The Fugees – short for Refugees which their parents had been from Haiti – and built their own basement studio and began auditioning for various record executives. They were signed by Ruffhouse Records' owner Chris Schwartz, who had also discovered Cypress Hill, and released their first album, *Blunted On Reality*. The album didn't sell and the one single from it, 'Nappy Heads' only reached number 49 Stateside and missed the charts completely in the UK. They then signed with Columbia, having walked in unannounced and doing an audition on the MD's desk. It worked. He signed them and their next album, *The Score*, was well received as was the next single, 'Fu-Gee-La', which sampled Teena Marie's 'Ooh La La La'. Next came 'Killing Me Softly', a beautifully sung cover, which vocally stayed true to the Robert Flack version of 1973. It added a heavy percussion bass-line and just a touch of rapping.

Starting life as 'Killing Me Softly With His Blues', the feeling which Don McLean engendered in singer Lori Leiberman when she caught him singing at the Troubadour club in L.A. in 1971, Lori took her proto-type lyrics to songwriters Norman Gimbel and Charles Fox who refined the song and changed the title for her to record. It appeared on her eponymous 1972 album, where she is also uncredited as a writer.

On a TWA flight from Los Angeles to New York, soul singer Roberta Flack was listening to the in-flight sound system when she first heard the song. In an interview with *NME* she said, "I was flicking through the in-flight magazine to see if they had done an article on me. After realising they hadn't, I saw this picture of a little girl called Lori Lieberman. I'd never heard of her before so I read it with interest to see what she had that I didn't." Roberta felt that the song wasn't complete, so on her arrival in New York she went into the studio to record it using a number of ideas, one being to change the end from a minor key to a major. After three months of fine-tuning the song was finally released and she was rewarded with a US number one in 1973.

Ian Broudie, David Baddiel and Frank Skinner lark around promoting their football anthem 'Three Lions'

NEW YORK

The Fugees took the song to number two in the US where it went on to win a Grammy for Best R&B Performance By A Vocal Group. In the UK it went one better by topping the chart for four weeks and then retuning to the top for a further week after relinquishing the position for one week to Baddiel & Skinner's football anthem, 'Three Lions'. It went on to sell 1.2 million copies and became the eighth biggest selling single of the Nineties.

742 Gary Barlow
Forever Love

Label & Cat No.: **RCA 74321397922**

Producers: **Chris Porter / Gary Barlow**

Writer: **Gary Barlow**

Date reached No.1: **20 July 1996**

Weeks at No.1: **1**

THE INDIVIDUAL MEMBERS OF TAKE That with most potential were Gary Barlow and Robbie Williams. When he left, Robbie was handicapped by a court action which cost him £1 million and it was agreed that Gary Barlow should have the first non-Take That single. If Gary's side thought that was a victory, they were in for a surprise because as soon as 'Forever Love' was released, Robbie was calling Gary "selfish, greedy, arrogant, thick and a clueless wanker." Apart from that, he's a great bloke. Even that was mild compared to Robbie's put-down of Jason Orange – "he's going to make a brilliant painter and decorator", and indeed, the future hasn't been Orange.

A ballad about an undying romance, 'Forever Love', was intended to be the first single on Gary's *Open Road* album, although that was delayed. The single was very much designed to appeal to Take That fans, but it had a limited life. Despite entering at number one, it was out of the Top 10 three weeks later. Still, it notched up UK sales of 270,000.

Unlike Liam Gallagher who was to rise to Robbie's taunts, Gary pretended not to notice and preferred playing tennis. He and Robbie even performed 'Let It Be' together at a charity concert in December 1997.

743 The Spice Girls
Wannabe

Label & Cat No.: **Virgin VSCDX 1588**

Producers: **Richard Stannard / Matt Rowe**

Writers: **Victoria Adams / Melanie Brown / Emma Bunton / Melanie Chisholm / Geri Halliwell / Richard Stannard / Matt Rowe**

Date reached No.1: **27 July 1996**

Weeks at No.1: **7**

IN MARCH 1994 AN ADVERT APPEARED IN *The Stage*: "R.U. 18-23 with the ability to sing/dance? R.U. streetwise, outgoing, ambitious and dedicated?" It was inserted by father and son Bob and Chris Herbert of Heart Management from Lightwater, Surrey. They conceived the idea of a girl group who would appeal to male and female adolescents alike. They decided on a quintet to avoid them dividing into pairs, and Bob told his 23-year-old son to go and find them.

Some 400 girls turned up at the Dance Works Studios off Oxford Street. Some of the auditions were filmed and later screened in a TV documentary, thus showing that the Herberts had invented the *Popstars* concept without realising it.

The five girls selected were 22-year-old Geraldine 'Geri' Halliwell from Watford, who had been a nude model and a host on the Turkish version of *The Price Is Right*; Victoria Adams (19), a sophisticated dancer and singer from Goff's Oak, Herts, who came from a privileged background; Melanie Chisholm (20), a soccer fanatic from Cheshire, who had the best singing voice but wanted to be a dancer – her mother, Joan, performed in Merseyside clubs as Tina Turner; the fiery Melanie Brown (18) from Leeds who loved hip-hop and had appeared on *Coronation Street*; and Michelle Stephenson (19) from Abington, Herts, who was a good singer but a poor dancer. All five could sing but only Mel B could play an instrument (drums), and although Geri had a stunning, forthright personality, her dancing lacked coordination.

The Herberts called them Touch as in "you can look but you can't touch", but Michelle didn't fit and became Pete Best Spice. Their singing teacher recommended an 18-year-old, blue-eyed blonde Emma Bunton. Emma had been to theatre school, been The Milky Bar Kid's accomplice in a TV campaign, appeared in *The Bill* and had reached the short list for a regular role in *EastEnders*. The girls bonded in a three-bedroom house in Maidenhead and discovered they could write together, their first song being 'It's Just One Of Those Days'.

They developed an unusual presentation insofar as none of the girls would take lead vocals or all five of them would, depending on how you view it. On the first records, the lines were shared throughout the songs, the only significant precedent for this approach being The Temptations around 1970. Their songs would also be written in this hit and miss fashion. Wisely, they decided that everything would be shared and so all five girls are listed as composers irrespective of their contribution – Victoria was missing the day 'Wannabe' was written.

Touch became The Spice Girls – as in "sugar and spice and all things nice" – and in March 1995 they audaciously dumped the Herberts and went to Simon Fuller, who managed Annie Lennox and Cathy Dennis. Fuller secured a deal with Virgin Records, which at the time was hungry to sign a major contemporary pop act.

The five girls recorded their first album, *Spice*, the producers including Richard Stannard and Matt Rowe (Matt & Biff), who had had success with East 17 and Ant and Dec and owned the Strong Room studio in East London. At first, they spent two days working on a sensual ballad, 'Feel Your Love', but this was discarded. Matt Rowe set up a loop with a strutting quality on his drum machine. It brought to mind 'You're The One That I Want' from *Grease* and within minutes the seven songwriters were composing 'Wannabe'.

Geri Halliwell recalled in her autobiography, *If Only*, "'Wannabe' took only about twenty

As pop careers go, few were more hectic than that of the Spice Girls, but in this shot Geri, Mel C, Emma, Mel B and Victoria look unusually relaxed

minutes to write. We started off simply mucking about with chords and raps. Right from that moment, we all realised that this was something special. It happened so naturally that the song seemed to symbolise what we were about."

The Girls coined the slogan 'girl power', as defined in 'Wannabe' with its partying video, shot next door to St. Pancras station, which was banned in Asia because of Mel B's erect nipples. The song was about doing what you want to do and not being compromised. If your boyfriend can't get along with your friends, dump him. If everyone criticises you, that's their problem. The phrase, "What you really, really want", is heard every day and is in *The Oxford Dictionary Of Twentieth Century Quotations*. If it was a feminist statement, then feminism could be fun.

The single and the album topped the UK and US charts and 'Wannabe' was number one in 31 countries. It sold 1.2 million copies in the UK alone and became the biggest selling single by a female group. The wannabes were, but what does 'zig-a-zig-ah' mean?

744 Peter Andre
Flava

Label & Cat No.: **Mushroom D 2003**

Producer: **Andy Whitmore**

Writers: **Peter Andre / Andy Whitmore / Wayne Hector / Cee Lo**

Date reached No.1: **14 September 1996**

Weeks at No.1: **1**

PETER JAY ANDREA HAS A COSMOPOLITAN background: a Greek Cypriot, the youngest of six children, born in Harrow, Middlesex on February 27, 1973. He moved with his family to the Gold Coast of Australia when he was 10. The teenage Peter Andre had two interests – building his body and building his reputation. He came second in a Michael Jackson lookalike contest and he performed in concert for an audience of 10,000 when he was only 16. The following year he won the Australian version of *New Faces* by performing Bobby Brown's 'Don't Be Cruel' with Michael Jackson-inspired dance steps.

His first single, 'Drive Me Crazy', made the Australian Top 40 in 1992. He had a great colour (not unusual in Australia!), combined with pin-up looks and an excellent physique honed during daily two-hour gym sessions. However, his subsequent singles, 'Gimme Little Sign', 'Funky Junky', 'Do You Wanna Dance?' and 'Let's Get It On' were only moderate hits.

He came to the UK in 1994, hoping for national stardom and knowing that it had worked for Kylie and Jason. He had minor success with 'Turn It Up', 'Mysterious Girl' and 'Only One' but then a reissue of 'Mysterious Girl' went to number two.

The next record was the hip hop disco sound of 'Flava', which included a rap by Cee Lo. It told of a wild party in Room 211 and gave no indication of what the occupants of Rooms 210 and 212 thought. The lyric included references to Bobby Brown and Mark Morrison – "The Mac's back wid da flava of the year." The record was produced by dance producer, Andy Whitmore, who had had success with 'Jump To The Beat' for Dannii Minogue (1991).

Peter Andre

745 Fugees
Ready Or Not

Label & Cat No.: **Columbia 663 721 2**

Producers: **Wyclef Jean / Lauryn Hill / Jerry Duplessis / Pras Michel**

Writers: **Wyclef Jean / Pras Michel / Lauryn Hill / William Hart / Thom Bell / Nicholas Ryan / Roma Ryan / Enya**

Date Reached No.1: **21 September 1996**

Weeks at No.1: **2**

'KILLING ME SOFTLY' DEBUTED AT number one after selling 160,000 copies. The third single from the million-selling album, *The Score*, 'Ready Or Not' sold 72,200 the week it went to number one, just 500 more than Peter Andre's 'Flava'.

The Fugees decided to cover the The Delfonics' last UK hit 'Ready Or Not Here I Come (Can't Hide The Love)' and borrowed a vocal refrain from 'Bodecia', a track on Enya's 1987 album *The Celts*. "The purpose of covering this song was because they gave us all inspiration when we were younger," admitted Lauryn Hill.

They followed 'Ready Or Not' with another cover, 'No Woman No Cry' which was The Fugees' tribute to their hero, Bob Marley. The song also featured Bob's son Steve on backing vocals. It might have given The Fugees their third consecutive number one had it not been for The Prodigy's 'Breathe'. They had one further Top 10 hit with 'Rumble In The Jungle', which sampled Abba's 'The Name Of The Game' and featured in the film *When We Were Kings*.

Their second album, *The Bootleg Versions*, which contained mixes of songs from their debut album, was released at the end of 1996. It made little impact and the group split up with all three members pursuing solo careers.

Pras Michel's first solo single, 'Ghetto Supastar (That Is What We Are)' (2, 1998) was featured in the film, *Bulworth*, and the follow-up, 'Blue Angels' (6), featured Lenny Kravitz on guitar. Wyclef, who had the solo hits 'Gone Till November' (3, 1998), 'Perfect Gentlemen' (4, 2001) and an R&B cover of Pink Floyd's 'Wish You Were

Here' (28, 2001), has also charted in collaboration with Destiny's Child, Bono and Mary J. Blige. He has also produced hit singles for Whitney Houston, Tom Jones, Santana and Simply Red. Lauryn Hill had solo hits with 'The Sweetest Thing' (18, 1997) from the film *Love Jones*, 'Doo-Wop (That Thing)' (3, 1998), 'Ex-Factor' (4, 1999), 'Everything Is Everything' (19) and a 'duet' with Bob Marley, 'Turn The Lights Down Low' (15) which appeared in the movie *The Best Man*.

Lauryn is married to Rohan Marley, one of Bob Marley's many sons, a professional US-style football player in Miami. Although the marriage has had its ups and downs, they have had three children. Lauryn had a remarkable year at the Grammys in 1999, winning Best New Artist, Best Female R&B Vocal Performance and Best R&B Song for 'Doo-Wop (That Thing)'. Her debut album, *The Miseducation Of Lauryn Hill*, won Best R&B Album and Album Of The Year. It also spent nearly 18 months on the UK chart.

746 Deep Blue Something
Breakfast At Tiffany's

Label & Cat No.: **Interscope IND 80032**

Producer: **David Castell**

Writers: **Todd Pipes / Deep Blue Something**

Date Reached No.1: **5 October 1996**

Weeks at No.1: **1**

"TONIGHT MATTHEW, I'M GOING TO BE Todd Pipes..." "Who?" asked 99% of the television audience of that night's popular and long-running ITV show, *Stars In Their Eyes*.

Todd (vocals, bass) along with his younger brother Toby (guitar, backing vocals) joined forces with fellow graduates from the University of North Texas, Clay Bergus (guitar, bass) and John Kirtland (drums). Originally called Leper Messiah (inspired by a line from David Bowie's 'Ziggy Stardust'), they changed their name to Deep Blue Something, after an instrumental they'd written. Clay left the band and was replaced by Kirk Tatam. Their first album, *11th Song*, which they sold at their gigs, featured the original version of 'Breakfast At Tiffany's'. The record had been financed by a wealthy youngster, Louis Bickel Jr. He had had no interest in the music world until one night when he chanced upon a performance of theirs. With promises of fame and fortune, according to the *Dallas Observer,* he paid a little over $2,000 for the band's studio time.

Todd Pipes was still working as an English teacher in a private Christian school in America's southwest, when an early version of 'Breakfast At Tiffany's' began receiving airplay on the local Texas radio station. Many parents complained that their children were 'being taught by a rock and roller' and the future popstar was asked to leave.

Initially inspired by the grunge sound that was popular at the time, they broke away and began to write and perform melody-filled, well-crafted pop tunes. "There are song writers who write everything in couplets and it's obvious what the next line is going to be because of the rhyme scheme. They have never heard of a blank verse or feminine endings. We have. That's one reason our songs are sound so different than what you hear every day," said Todd.

Their second album, *Home,* was released in June 1995 and contained a revamped version of 'Breakfast At Tiffany's', complete with a new layered guitar sound and tight harmonies. The song told of the breakdown of a couple from the male's point of view: 'You say that we've got nothing in common...' "I said what about Breakfast at Tiffany's'? She said, 'I think I remember the film. And as I recall, I think, we both kinda liked it.' And I said, 'Well, that's the one thing we've got.' Truman Capote's *Breakfast At Tiffany's* film version was released in 1961, and starred Audrey Hepburn in the lead role of Holly Golightly.

Deep Blue Something's 'Breakfast At Tiffany's' became an international hit. Life was looking good for the Texan boys. Then Louis

Fugees

Bickel reappeared, insisting on his percentage and a lengthy lawsuit ensued. Because of this the band were prevented from recording or releasing any new material, so they decided to take a break from the music world.

By 2001 when all their legal problems had been sorted out, they reformed with the original line-up and released their self-titled album.

747 The Chemical Brothers Setting Sun

Label & Cat No.: **Virgin CHEMSD 4**
Producers: **Tom Rowlands / Ed Simons**
Writers: **Tom Rowlands / Ed Simons / Noel Gallagher**
Date Reached No.1: **12 October 1996**
Weeks at No.1: **1**

"ED AND I HAVE ALWAYS BEEN ACID house fans. We called ourselves the Dust Brothers first because we really liked the US hip hoppers with that name but then we settled for Chemical Brothers. We only made records of our own because we couldn't find enough that sounded like the one we wanted to play," described Tom. "We used to hunt high and low to find records with huge, hard-hitting beats on them."

Tom Rowlands, born in Kingston, Surrey in 1971 and Ed Simons, born in Oxford in 1970 are both DJs who met in 1989 at the University Of Manchester where they were both studying history (they both studied to be teachers). Realising they preferred making music they began working together and released the singles 'Sea Of Beats', 'Rollercoaster' and 'Song To The Siren', all of which are now highly collectable 12-inch singles. In 1993 they began production work as the Dust Brothers but were forced to change their name after a US group with the same name objected. Their first hit, 'Leave Home', reached number 17 in 1995 and this led to them remixing tracks for The Prodigy, Primal Scream and The Charlatans. In return, The Charlatans' lead singer, Tim Burgess, sang (uncredited) lead vocals on their next hit 'Life Is Sweet'. The debut album, *Exit Planet Dust*, went to number nine and stayed on the chart for almost a year.

Ed and Tom share the same all-time favourite song, 'Tomorrow Never Knows' by The Beatles, which they regularly sampled in their DJ sets. For the next single, 'Setting Sun', they teamed up with Oasis' Noel Gallagher who co-wrote the lyrics. "He got wind that we wanted to do a track with him," remembered Ed. "He phoned us up and said, 'I'll come down now and do it'. I told him I would send him a tape of the track that we thought might appeal to him as it had a Beatlesque feel to it. The whole track took us a day in the studio with him, then us mixing for a while and it was in the can." Its original working title was 'Tomorrow Never Noels'.

Sony were sceptical about releasing it, but it was Noel who persuaded them in the end. It didn't receive much radio play and on the first week of release sold 99,000 copies. As Tom remembered, "I think it had the lowest number of radio plays ever for a number one hit. It was cool, circumventing all the conservatism, and still getting to number one with a banging record. It was our aim to make a record that stuck out. We wanted to make records that people just couldn't help but remember."

748 Boyzone Words

Label & Cat No.: **Polydor 5755372**
Producers: **Phil Harding / Ian Curnow**
Writers: **Barry Gibb / Maurice Gibb / Robin Gibb**
Date reached No.1: **19 October 1996**
Weeks at No.1: **1**

IRISH IMPRESARIO LOUIS WALSH, WHO had managed the Eurovision winners Johnny Logan and Linda Martin, was down on his luck but had no interest in signing Irish rock bands in the wake of Hothouse Flowers. He was unimpressed when he saw East 17 miming on stage but he knew what to do when he saw Take That at The Point arena in Dublin. He announced that he would form an Irish all singing, all dancing equivalent, who would be called Boyzone.

The 300 hopefuls had to sing, reveal their personality and dance to Right Said Fred's 'I'm Too Sexy'. His final choices were Shane Lynch, Keith Duffy, Stephen Gately, Ronan Keating (then only 15), Richard Rock (son of showband star Dickie Rock) and Mark Walton. Because of the publicity, they appeared the following day on Gay Byrne's *The Late Late Show*. Disaster. They had not rehearsed any songs – indeed, they hardly knew each other – and they danced to a record. Unfortunately, they had not rehearsed any routines and the cringe-making, uncoordinated performance has haunted Boyzone and Ronan Keating ever since. TV debuts don't come any worse than Shane Lynch's crotch-grabbing dance. Gay Byrne wished them well, presuming he would never hear from them again.

Richard and Mark came out of the group and Mikey Graham, who had been on the short list, joined the other four. Stephen and Shane, who were good dancers, helped with the choreography and when John Reynolds, a night-club owner and nephew of the Irish PM, Albert Reynolds, added finance, he became a joint manager. Louis Walsh had loved The Detroit Spinners' version of 'Working My Way Back To You' and with £10,000 from John Reynolds, they cut a track with Ian Levine in London. Ian thought that Ronan was not a strong enough vocalist and the lead vocals were taken by Stephen and Mikey instead. The B-side, made for £600, was the song that Ronan had performed at the audition, Cat Stevens' 'Father And Son'.

They gigged around Ireland for little money, singing live vocals over backing tracks at discos, often ducking bottles thrown by jealous males. The single made number three on the Irish charts and they performed in front of 80,000 football fans at the World Cup celebrations in Dublin.

Another of Louis' suggestions, their revival of The Osmonds' 'Love Me For A Reason' topped the Irish charts, but their managers could not secure a UK record deal. As special guests on a *Smash Hits* arena tour of the UK they did so well

The Irish Boyzone were quick to step into Take That's shoes; clockwise, from left: Ronan Keating, Steven Gately, Mikey Graham, Keith Duffy and Shane Lynch

that 'Love Me For A Reason' was released in the UK and reached number two. This was followed by 'Key To My Life' (3), 'So Good' (3), a new version of 'Father And Son' (2) and 'Coming Home Now' (4). A strong performance at the Royal Albert Hall in 1995 established them as a major act.

Take That bowed out at the start of 1996 with The Bee Gees' 'How Deep Is Your Love?'. Their successors, Boyzone, had their first UK number one with a heavily orchestrated version of The Bee Gees' 'Words', another suggestion from Louis Walsh whose record collection was proving invaluable.

In 1968 both Barry and Robin Gibb had been having arguments with friends, and they were in bad moods when they met. Robin said arguments were just words and from that, the song was formed. The Bee Gees' hit single was a solo showcase for Barry and featured a compressed, keyboard sound from Maurice, which sounded like several pianos combined. With Take That and Boyzone, there was a new acceptance of The Bee Gees, and Boyzone contributed 'Words '98' to the charity album, *Gotta Get A Message To You*. Maurice Gibb had called Boyzone's 'Words' the best cover of a Bees Gees song and they and Celine Dion were the guest acts on *An Audience With The Bee Gees*.

749 The Spice Girls
Say You'll Be There

Label & Cat No.: **Virgin VSCDT 1601**

Producers: **Absolute (Andy Watkins and Paul Wilson)**

Writers: **Victoria Adams / Melanie Brown / Emma Bunton / Melanie Chisholm / Geri Halliwell / Eliot Kennedy**

Date reached No.1: **26 October 1996**

Weeks at No.1: **2**

An interview with Peter Lorraine for the BBC's teen magazine, *Top Of The Pops*, was illustrated with a picture of The Spice Girls as a spice rack and gave them their aliases, Posh (the sultry Victoria in designer dresses), Baby (the blonde pixie Emma in pigtails or bunches), Ginger (Geri, the red-haired leader in Union Jack dress and wedge boots), Scary (Mel B, who, by her own admission was "loud, forthright and brash") and Sporty (the tattooed Mel C in her Adidas track suits). Lorraine should have been on the payroll as it proved crucial in creating the required image.

Perhaps for the first time since Abba, everybody knew the individual members of a group. A commonly asked question was, 'Who is your favourite Spice Girl?' – was it the black one (Mel B was actually mixed race), the blonde one, the ginger one, the posh one or the tomboy? Tony Blair knew the names of more Spice Girls than the current Prime Minister, John Major, something which may have contributed to Major's downfall. However, the *Daily Star* did run a front page headline that "Spice Girls Back Toriez." Mel C, much quieter than Geri and Mel B, acquiesced although her conscience opposed it.

'Wannabe' was a radical choice for a first single, but the second choice was more conventional. At first it was going to be 'Love Thing', but it was changed to the romantic R&B feel of 'Say You'll Be There'. Both tracks had been recorded at Eliot Kennedy's studio in Sheffield. Absolute (Andy Watkins and Paul Wilson) played the instruments, except the harmonica, which was played by Judd Lander, a Sixties beat musician from The Hideaways, who had also played on 'Karma Chameleon'.

Andy Watkins and Paul Wilson had met up at Bristol Polytechnic and they both have degrees in Food Science and Biology. They began their own studio in Bristol with a government grant and then Simon Fuller encouraged them to stop remixing and write their own material. They moved to Chertsey and their first big successes were with The Spice Girls.

Because The Spice Girls shared the vocals, they could make lively, energetic videos. 'Say You'll Be There' was among the best. It was shot in the Mojave desert and was a homage to the Russ Meyer film from 1965, *Faster, Pussycat! Kill Kill*. The Spice Girls were now such a phenomenon that they switched on the Christmas lights in Oxford Street.

750 Robson & Jerome
What Becomes Of The Broken Hearted? / Saturday Night At The Movies / You'll Never Walk Alone

Label & Cat No.: **RCA 74321 424732**

Producers: **Mike Stock / Matt Aitken**

Writers: **James Dean / Paul Riser / William Weatherspoon : Barry Mann / Cynthia Weil : Richard Rodgers / Oscar Hammerstein II**

Date reached No.1: **9 November 1996**

Weeks at No.1: **2**

Robson Green and Jerome Flynn left *Soldier, Soldier* in 1995 and the hit series soldiered on for a couple of years before finishing in 1997. Jerome was dissatisfied with the trappings of fame and found comfort in the book, *Embracing Heaven And Earth*, by the spiritual teacher, Andrew Cohen. Cohen contended that we were ruled by greed and lies and that we should live for the sake of others and not ourselves. Jerome lived up to the words himself, often carrying out charitable work and visiting Bosnia with the Red Cross. He also undertook a tour of Waterstone's bookshops reading Cohen's words.

Although their service in *Soldier, Soldier* had ended, Robson & Jerome were persuaded to record a further album, *Take Two*, for the Christmas market. Wise move as it sold 1.1 million. They also sold 300,000 copies of *Joking Apart*, a video recorded in front of a small audience of fans in Newcastle. The single made them the first act to enter at number one with their first three releases. It was also their final record together and the interest had so waned by Christmas 1997 that *The Best Of Robson & Jerome* stayed in the racks.

'What Becomes Of The Broken Hearted?' was a Motown song that was originally given to The Detroit Spinners, but, as so often happened with Motown, they tried it with a different act, Jimmy Ruffin, and released that instead. Jimmy, the brother of David Ruffin of The Temptations, said, "Motown wanted me to join The Contours but I wanted to remain a solo artist. I told the writer William Weatherspoon that I could do that song better than The Spinners and he was impressed by what I did. Motown didn't promote it at all as they felt the spiel at the start of the record was too monotonous. Two disc-jockeys in Chicago broke that record and then it became a big hit." Jimmy Ruffin's 'What Becomes Of The Broken Hearted?' became a UK Top Ten hit in 1966 and then again on reissue in 1974. Colin Blunstone, guesting with Dave Stewart, restored the song to the charts in 1981.

In 1964 Rudy Lewis of The Drifters collapsed and died following a drugs overdose. Johnny Moore became the lead singer and his light, wide-ranging voice was ideal for 'Saturday Night At The Movies'. Although a US hit, it was not a UK success until it was combined with another location song, 'At The Club', in 1972.

The third song on the single was 'You'll Never Walk Alone', a UK number one for Gerry & The Pacemakers in 1963 and then Gerry & The Crowd in 1985. Once again, this was a song that had been recorded by The Righteous Brothers.

Jerome Flynn starred in *Badger,* a series about a policeman with an interest in wildlife. He also played Bobby Charlton in *Best* about the life of George Best. In 2003 he played Tommy Cooper in *Jus' Like That!*, a West End success directed by Simon Callow. It was a brilliant recreation – he captured Cooper's 'huh huh huh' laugh and his inane grin when tricks didn't work, but most of all, he showed himself to be an excellent magician. The play went on a UK tour in 2004 and he plans to record his own songs about his spiritual beliefs.

Robson Green has been in several TV series including *Reckless* in which he played a surgeon involved in a steamy affair with Francesca Annis and *Grafters*, another series about Geordie builders with Stephen Tomkinson. He bought the rights to Val McDermid's novels about a clinical psychologist who works with serial killers and the series, *Wire In The Blood*, did very well. He has his own racehorse Magic Hour and he released a solo album, *Moment In Time* (2002), which spent less than that in the chart.

751 Prodigy
Breathe

Label & Cat No.: **XL Recordings XLS 80CD**

Producer: **Liam Howlett**

Writers: **Liam Howlett / Keith Flint / Maxim Reality / Dennis Coles / Gary Grice / Lamont Hawkins / Jason Hunter / Russell Jones / Prince Rakeem / Clifford Smith / Corey Woods**

Date Reached No.1: **23 November 1996**

Weeks at No.1: **2**

CHUFFED WITH THE SUCCESS OF 'Firestarter' the record company decided to re-issue all The Prodigy's previous singles. A promotional offer allowed fans to buy any three tracks for a tenner and so with the exception of 'One Love' all of them re-entered the Top 75. But the fans were waiting for something new.

Rumours had begun that the next single, 'Minefields', a track from their latest album *The Fat Of The Land*, was being limited to 10,000 copies. In actual fact, there were 100 promotional cassettes and 10 test vinyl pressings made before it was decided to withdraw the track, thus making them collectors items. "The only reason I kept the single back was because I decided the follow-on from 'Firestarter' had to be stronger," explained Liam Howlett. "'Minefields' is a good track, but it's a slow-building track that isn't direct. I decided that I wanted the next single to have a kick like 'Firestarter' without being 'Firestarter Part 2.'"

'Breathe' had more of a gothic sound than 'Firestarter'. The whiplashing sword sounds that lay across the heavy breakbeat is a sample of 'Da Mystery Of Chessboxin', a track on The Wu-Tang Clan's album *36 Chambers*. This time it was Keith and Maxim who shared the vocals in a verbal interplay. 'Breathe' entered the chart at number one by selling a whopping 195,000 in the first week. This fact was made all the more surprising as most radio stations only programmed the song into their evening shows and television coverage was restricted almost entirely to MTV. Still, no such problems abroad where there were no restrictions and the song topped the charts in Finland, Poland, Sweden, Denmark, Hungary, Iceland, Norway, Spain and The Czech Republic.

The accompanying video, set in two run-down adjacent apartment blocks, showed Maxim and Keith seemingly antagonising each other through a hole in the wall. In the 'Firestarter' video Keith had dyed his hair green. For 'Breathe' it was half green and half purple with an absurd number of body piercings, one of which included a bolt through his septum. Maxim was painted head to foot in black tiger-like stripes and had silver teeth. He also carried a walking stick.

One year on The Prodigy released their next single, the controversial 'Smack My Bitch Up' which fans had known for 18 months as it was a regular feature in their live sets. Needless to say it received little radio play and the video, which showed a naked couple romping on a bed having sexual intercourse, was restricted to a limited number of late-night viewings. The original artwork for the sleeve showed a VW Beetle wrapped round a lamppost, but Liam, as a compassionate gesture had it changed, along with the release date following the death of Princess Diana. Liam commented in *NME*, "It was the right sleeve at the wrong time." Instead a picture of Joel Botschinsky de Andrade at the 1996 Breakdancing Championship was shown.

Leeroy left the band in 2000 and The Prodigy continued as a three-piece having one further Top five hit in 2002, with 'Baby's Got A Temper'. Liam broke up with his long-term girlfriend, Angie, and in June 2002 married the former All Saint, Natalie Appleton. Liam had the idea of working with John Lydon. "I would still like to do the ultimate electronic punk track and I just thought it would be interesting to have Lydon on it, but I scrapped the idea because I can't get along with his attitude," admitted Liam.

The fire had seemingly gone out, but was re-started in August 2004 when The Prodigy, well Liam, returned with the first new album in seven years. *Always Outnumbered But Never Outgunned* saw them return to their old school roots by ditching the electronic punk sound. It also featured guest vocals from Twista and Liam Gallagher.

752 Peter Andre
I Feel You

Label & Cat No.: **Mushroom D 1521**

Producers: **Cutfather & Joe**

Writers: **Peter Andre / Glen Goldsmith / Terry Jones, Oliver Jacobs**

Date reached No.1: **7 December 1996**

Weeks at No.1: **1**

PETER ANDRE FOLLOWED HIS NUMBER one, 'Flava', with another one, 'I Feel You' and by now, his torso was as famous as he was. He was grateful for the success saying that otherwise he would be stuck in Australia with his "house and picket fence, beer and barbeque". He was the top-selling male artist of the year with three major singles and a number one album *Natural*. He toured with success and appeared triumphantly at Wembley.

'I Feel You' was written with Glen Goldsmith, who had made the Top 20 with 'Dreaming' in 1988 and had a hit album with *What You See Is What You Get*. The record was produced by the Danish team, Cutfather and Joe, who have worked with Ace of Base, Aqua, Atomic Kitten and Five. It was an explicit love song with the lyrics including "I'm thinking of the bedroom, baby."

However, the press can knock you down as well as set you up. His celebrity girlfriends were front page news but his reputation wasn't helped when a girl, Sharleen, described what he was like in bed. Switching to a high energy diet of bananas, he made himself ill and acquired the nickname of Monkey Boy.

In 1997 he had a Top 10 hit with 'Natural' and then 'All About Us' and 'Lonely', but he was about to be cast into the wilderness. The *Smash Hits* award of 1997 was his nadir as he was named as the Least Fanciable Male, The Loser of The Year and, horror of horrors, the recipient of the Worst Haircut. Surely his barber could have sorted that one out.

Although a Peter Andre calendar was manufactured for 1998, it was doubtful that his career would last the year. As it happened, he had further hits with 'All Right All Right' and 'Kiss The Girl', which was from the Walt Disney film, *The Little Mermaid*. He claimed, "I'm maturing. I don't want to record bubblegum songs just to sell records because that's not coming from within."

No one was listening. His second album, *Time*, only made the Top 30 and that, we thought, was that. How wrong we were.

753 Boyzone
A Different Beat

Label & Cat No.: **Polydor 5732052**

Producers: **Ray Hedges**

Writers: **Martin Brannigan / Keith Duffy / Stephen Gately / Ray Hedges / Ronan Keating / Shane Lynch**

Date reached No.1: **14 December 1996**

Weeks at No.1: **1**

BOYZONE'S 1995 ALBUM, *SAID AND Done*, was a well-crafted boy band affair, good performances from a group that might not last long. As Ronan Keating admitted, "We were no U2. We didn't try to be Take That or anyone else. We flaunted our Irish identities and we were five young men from the north side of Dublin just out for a good time." Certainly the record-buying public didn't see them as another U2, but the comparison with Take That was obvious to everyone (except, it seems, Ronan).

Their 1996 album, *A Different Beat*, displayed more maturity and included both strong originals and skilfully chosen covers. The first single, 'Words', went to number one and two months later, the title track was issued for Christmas, giving them another chart-topper and an anthem for their concert audiences.

Louis Walsh had been using Take That's producer, Ray Hedges, from time to time and had made 'Love Me For A Reason' and 'Daydream Believer' with him. Ray had been encouraging Boyzone to write, tossing out lines and asking them to complete them. Ronan Keating and Stephen Gately were becoming strong writers, and the best example of the group's songwriting is 'A Different Beat'.

'A Different Beat' has the most striking start of any boy band single. It begins with an African chant and moves into a plea for unity, although we all sing to different beats. Not for nothing was it followed on the album by Blue Mink's 'Melting Pot'. The song had come about as a result of their world tours, but, on the other hand, they might have been to see *The Lion King*.

A few weeks later, Boyzone were shooting a video for 'Isn't It A Wonder?', another track from *A Different Beat*, in the Australian outback. An engine on their 'plane failed and they had to make a crash landing. One of the headlines was "BOYZ ALIVE AFTER FLIGHT OF TERROR".

754 Dunblane
Knockin' On Heaven's Door / Throw These Guns Away

Label & Cat No.: **RCA 74321442182**

Producer: **Peter Cobbin**

Writers: **Bob Dylan : Ted Christopher**

Date Reached No.1: **21 December 1996**

Weeks at No.1: **1**

DUNBLANE WAS A SLEEPY SCOTTISH village a few miles north of Stirling with a population of less than 10,000. On Wednesday March 13, 1996 loner Thomas Hamilton walked into a school gymnasium and opened fire, killing 16 five and six-year-old children and their teacher, before turning the gun on himself. Within hours the world's media had descended on it and Dunblane became a name that people in all parts of the globe associated with mindless slaughter.

Local music shop owner and amateur musician Ted Christopher was inspired to re-record the Bob Dylan classic 'Knockin' On Heaven's Door' after singing it to himself shortly after the massacre. "I was singing the last verse where it says 'put all these guns in the ground, we can't shoot them any more.' With a few changes, it just became exactly what we wanted to say." With Bob Dylan's permission, Ted wrote an extra verse: 'Lord, these guns have caused too much pain, this town will never be the same. So for the bairns of Dunblane, we ask, please never again.'

Bob Dylan wrote the song for the film, *Pat Garrett And Billy The Kid,* the Sam Peckinpah-directed Western, starring James Coburn (Pat Garrett) and Kris Kristofferson (Billy The Kid). Dylan, who not only provided the soundtrack, also appears as 'Alias'. His version reached number 14 in the UK in 1973.

'Knockin' On Heaven's Door' has been covered by a multitude of artists, as varied as The Byrds, Eric Clapton, Elvis Costello, Randy Crawford, Avril Lavigne, Sisters Of Mercy, Roger Waters and Warren Zevon. Guns N'Roses narrowly missed out on getting their first chart topper, when their rendition – a live recording from the Freddie Mercury Tribute Concert – stalled at number two in 1992.

Ted asked Mark Knopfler if he would play guitar on the single and he readily agreed. Mark, who was born in Glasgow on August 12, 1949, moved with his family to Newcastle-Upon-Tyne when he was seven. Becoming interested in the guitar in his early teens, thanks largely to Hank Marvin and Django Reinhardt, he both joined and formed several bands. At the age of 16, he appeared on local television as one half of a duo with friend Sue Hercombe.

Before he was even asked, the manager of Abbey Road studios, Martin Benge had decided, "this was something with which Abbey Road had to be involved. The tragedy and the aim of the record are so important you couldn't be too busy to be involved." The single, which included 14 school children from Dunblane, some of who lost brothers and sisters in the tragedy, was recorded and mixed free of charge at the famed north London studios.

The sleeve featured a poignant picture of a clown drawn by Emma Crozier, one of the slain children. Proceeds went to three charities: Save The Children, Childline and Children's Hospice Association Of Scotland. After a long campaign by The Snowdrop Petition, made up of family and friends of the victims, the Firearms (amendment) Act of February 1997 was introduced, making it illegal to own, buy or sell any handgun .22-caliber and above in the UK.

755 The Spice Girls
2 Become 1

Label & Cat No.: **Virgin VSCDT 1607**

Producers: **Richard Stannard / Matt Rowe**

Writers: **Victoria Adams / Melanie Brown / Emma Bunton / Melanie Chisholm / Geri Halliwell / Richard Stannard / Matt Rowe**

Date reached No.1: **28 December 1996**

Weeks at No.1: **3**

THE FIRST CHRISTMAS SINGLE FROM The Spice Girls, '2 Become 1', was also the third release from their album, *Spice*. Unlike their first two singles, The Spice Girls had an orchestral backing and its warm sentiments were perfect for Christmas, but you might think that all the potential buyers would have it on the album. Apparently not as the single sold over a million copies in the UK.

Richard Stannard and Matt Rowe were the main songwriting and production team associated with The Spice Girls. Richard had been part of a boy band, 2wo Third3, and he acquired the nickname, Biff, after a fictitious fourth member of the group. When he met Matt Rowe, who had sung in Chester Cathedral, they decided to write together. They wrote 'Around The World' and 'Hold My Body Tight' for and with East 17 and then they started working with The Spice Girls.

'2 Become 1' was mostly written by Geri with the group's producers, Richard Stannard and Matt Rowe, and possibly it revealed the depth of feeling between Geri and Matt, although this has never been confirmed (or, for that matter, denied).

Although '2 Become 1' was intended as a romantic love song ("Tonight is the night when 2 become 1"), it could also be taken as a song promoting safe sex ("Free your mind of doubt and danger"), an ideal message for Christmas. It became the Christmas number one and the seasonal aspect was emphasised with special packaging and their version of 'Sleigh Ride' as a bonus track.

Although The Spice Girls had not envisaged their album to have a teenybop quality, they had now become the darlings of 10-year-old girls. Their posters went up on bedroom walls and what Christmas party didn't have some tot impersonating her favourite Spice Girl. All the more alarming when *The People* ran the story of 'Spice Girl's Cocaine Shame', but it transpired that Mel C had been at a party where people were taking drugs (it being highly unusual for pop stars ever to attend parties where people might take drugs). Kiss and sell stories were also everywhere: at least 13 former lovers told of their exploits with various Spice Girls, though not all in the same feature.

They also attracted a feminist following. Charlotte Raven wrote in *The Guardian*, "The boys want to fuck them, the girls want to be them and feminists want to hail them as the feisty new exponents of that post-oppression jive."

Germaine Greer was more circumspect: "The Spice Girls danced energetically if not well and they had a reasonable ratio of flesh on their bones – and they had achieved an educational level not aimed at by the dead-eyed emaciated models who are featured in *More*."

756 Tori Amos
Professional Widow (It's Got To Be Big)

Label & Cat No.: **Creation CRESCD 221**

Producers: **Armand van Helden / Tori Amos**

Writer: **Tori Amos**

Date reached No.1: **18 January 1997**

Weeks at No.1: **1**

THE DAUGHTER OF A MINISTER, MYRA Ellen Amos was born in 1963 in Newton, North Carolina. She was playing piano and learning songs from an early age. "I was always interested in songs and how they were constructed," she says. "Why did this song have a bridge and this one didn't. I loved a lot of the old songs and it doesn't get any better than 'I Can't Get Started'. I realised too that people often misunderstood them. I can remember the girls at school who were really short going 'I hate Randy Newman' and I was thinking, 'You're missing the whole point of the song, it's not about you.'"

Myra Ellen became Tori Amos for three reasons when she was 17: she was no-tori-ous for wearing red leather pants whilst teaching Sunday school, a boyfriend told her that she looked more like a Tori than an Ellen, and the Torrey is the rarest of all pine trees.

The young Tori started playing bars in Washington DC and Baltimore and relocated to Los Angeles in 1985. Within a few weeks, she was raped at gunpoint by a man who had driven her back to her apartment and she put the trauma into a compelling song, 'Me And A Gun'.

Tori Amos first recorded as a session singer, notably appearing on Al Stewart's *The Last Days Of The Century*, but after being signed to East West, she decided to launch her career in England. Her album, *Little Earthquakes* (1992), was produced by her boyfriend, Eric Rosse, and although it was hardly a commercial record, she promoted it on middle-of-the-road programmes like *Wogan*. She says, "People compared me to Kate Bush or Joni Mitchell but that was because I was a woman. You wouldn't know from my voice whether Led Zeppelin or John Lennon were influences. It's like I studied guitar players to get my piano style and I am more likely to seek visual artists rather than other songwriters for inspiration."

In 1994 Tori Amos had a hit album with *Under The Pink*, this time made in America, and a Top 10 single, 'Cornflake Girl', written about a friend of hers. She moved to Ireland for her next record, *Boys From Pele* (1996) and by now she had broken up with Eric Rosse. One of the songs, 'Professional Widow', was about someone giving head and relating it to her family life. It was released as a double-A side with an offbeat love song, 'Hey Jupiter', and made number 20.

Then came the remix. Tori says, "I was called by a friend who was the head of dance at Atlantic America and he had the feeling that Armand van Helden could do something with the album. *Boys For Pele* was a very extreme record and very acoustic and Armand said he understood the character of the girl in 'Professional Widow'. He did a great job on it but it's not really a song anymore – it is a vibe with a groove. After that I wanted to write a story that would work alongside a rhythm track and 'Cruel' and 'Raspberry Swirl' are like that."

Armand van Helden tells a slightly different story and it's likely that the record company was playing the two sides off to achieve a hit single. Armand discloses, "A man called Johnny D who worked as A&R and Street promotions manager at Atlantic had dinner with Tori Amos and he suggested that I remix 'Professional Widow'. Tori only made one suggestion and that was to make it different. I was free to experiment and having just returned from Ibiza, I was feeling extra creative."

The final product used only snippets of Tori Amos' original record but it created a new interest in her work. If you go and see her, be careful if you think the songs are about her. "I think it's hard to tell what is personal in my songs and what is not. I might be the guy in the song who is breaking the girl's heart. You write in that way in order to come to terms with parts of yourself that you can't stand."

757 White Town
Your Woman

Label & Cat No.:	**Chrysalis CDCHS 5052**
Producer:	**Jyoti Mishra**
Writer:	**Jyoti Mishra**
Date Reached No.1:	**25 January 1997**
Weeks at No.1:	**1**

WHITE TOWN IS ESSENTIALLY JYOTI Mishra who was born in Rourkela, India in 1966 but raised in Derby. He began playing the keyboard when he was 12 and learned to play guitar soon after. He and a group of friends formed White Town in 1989 but one by one his friends moved on and Jyoti was left as a one-man band. "The name White Town was taken from my childhood experiences of being raised in mostly white populated cities."

Jyoti spent a lot of time experimenting with music in his bedroom using a sequencer and various samples. "'Your Woman' was inspired by a 1932 song called 'My Woman' by Al Bowlly and played by Lew Stone and the Monseigneur Band. I heard it on the *Pennies From Heaven* soundtrack."

Bowlly, born in Mozambique in 1899, became Britain's most popular dance band singer in the Thirties. Such was his extravagance that he once sent his clothes to a pawnshop to raise money for his hotel bill. He was stuck in his room with no clothes and no money and had a recording session to attend some three miles away. He realised that the only way to get there was to pretend to be an athlete and run through the streets in his vest and underpants. He recorded the songs, collected his session fee then ran to the pawnshop to redeem his clothes.

Jyoti recorded the track using the organ sample from Al Bowlly and played it to his girlfriend who suggested he do something with it. With little money, he could only afford to press up five copies. "I used the internet a lot and met Anthony Chapman from the band Collapsed Lung via a music group. We started e-mailing each other and I sent him a copy and he offered to do a remix of it. A copy was also sent to Simon Mayo at Radio One who started playing it and it became the most requested record that week. I also sent a copy to a bloke in America who I met through net conversations. He owned the Parasol label but only wanted to press up 500 copies. I said 'we need much more than that like 20,000' but he disagreed."

Suddenly, Jyoti landed a deal with EMI in December 1996 and the following month 'Your Woman' was released as a single. It sold 165,000 copies in one week and shot to number one. Jyoti had no real aspirations to be a pop star. "Not many are interested in an Asian bloke who makes records in his bedroom". There was no video and he refused to appear on *Top Of The Pops*. "I knew then I would be a one-hit wonder," he said.

The week he was number one, the tabloid

press printed some very unflattering pictures one carrying the headline 'The Nerd from Nowhere', alongside jibes about his sexuality. This may have resulted from him singing the song from a woman's perspective, hence making it the first chart topper with a gender reversal. It didn't harm Joan Baez when she tried it in 1971, assuming the role of Virgil Cain in a cover of The Band's 'The Night They Drove Old Dixie Down'.

"I think my success annoyed the music industry because they don't like people having hits without their permission. Their tactic is to recruit pretty faces and combine them with million-pound studios, so when there's this fat Indian bloke having a hit with a song they rejected, it doesn't make them look good," said Jyoti Mishra in 2003.

758 Blur
Beetlebum

Label & Cat No.: **Food CDFOODS 89**
Producer: **Stephen Street**
Writers: **Damon Albarn / Graham Coxon / Alex James / Dave Rowntree**
Date reached No.1: **1 February 1997**
Weeks at No.1: **1**

After beating Oasis to the top with 'Country House' in 1995, Blur failed in successive bids to reach the top. There was 'The Universal' (5), 'Stereotypes' (7) and 'Charmless Man' (about being disillusioned on meeting Tony Blair, (5)). Both Blur and Damon Albarn, with a solo track, contributed to the soundtrack of *Trainspotting* in 1996.

Whereas Oasis' records were often more of the same, Blur experimented with their sound but only those who had heard some of their B-sides could have expected 'Beetlebum'. The song had a much fiercer sound but with Beatle overtones. Note the echo-laden Lennon vocal on "And when she lets me slip away": those who weren't impressed thought it was bum Beatle.

At the time the band neither confirmed nor denied that the song was about drugs, but Damon now admits, "It's about drugs basically. I'm not sure what a Beetlebum is. It's just a word I sang when I played the song to myself. I asked the others if I should change it, but they said no. If it felt right, we decided that we wouldn't tidy it up like we'd done in the past." The sleeve designer, Chris Thomas, followed this through with a mystifying cover shot on Richmond Common with his girlfriend playing dead.

'Beetlebum' was the first number one recorded in Iceland as Bjork had never quite made it. The single was followed by the joyous 'Song 2' with its insidious and oft-repeated 'whoo-hoo' phrase, which just missed the top.

By now there was considerable ill feeling within the band, although they did not break up, and Damon split with Justine Frischmann. On Blur's next album, *13*, 'No Distance Left To Run' was dedicated to her and included the line, "When you're coming down, think of me here." The languorous 'Tender', performed with The London Community Gospel Choir reached number two, but Blur had no more Top 10 hits until they moved (without Graham Coxon) to Parlophone Records in 2003. Then *Think Tank* topped the albums charts and 'Out Of Time' made number five. Graham Coxon has released his own album, *Happiness In Magazines*.

759 LL Cool J
Ain't Nobody

Label & Cat No.: **Geffen GFSTD 22195**
Producer: **James Todd Smith**
Writer: **David Wolinski**
Date Reached No.1: **8 February 1997**
Weeks at No.1: **1**

One of the original rap pack, LL Cool J, pretentiously abbreviated down from 'Ladies Love Cool James' after a young lady once questioned his sex appeal, burst on to the music scene in 1987 with his debut single 'I'm Bad'. In the charts he joined the likes of Public Enemy, Run-D.M.C. and The Beastie Boys who let us know that rap was here to stay.

LL was born James Todd Smith in St. Albans, Queens, New York on August 16, 1968. He grew up listening to his grandfather's jazz albums and became a regular viewer of the TV dance show, *Soul Train*. By nine he had learned to rap. Two years later his grandfather bought him a couple of turntables and a mixer so he could make his own music. In 1981 he put together some demo tapes and sent them to a variety of record labels. The only one to reply was Rick Rubin, owner of Def Jam, a fledgling dance label, who were looking for new talent. They signed him and within six months LL and Def Jam released their debut single, 'I Need A Beat'. Although it didn't chart on either side of the Atlantic, it received heavy rotation on the black radio stations. He was 17 when he did his first tour opening for Run-D.M.C. on their *Raising Hell* tour.

His second single, the rap ballad, 'I Need Love', made the UK Top 10 in the autumn of 1987 and also topped the US R&B chart. He seemed to have fallen out of favour in the UK when his next five singles, over nine years, all failed to make the Top 40. In 1996 'Hey Lover', which sampled Michael Jackson's 'Lady In My Life' and featured Boyz II Men on backing vocals, brought him back to the Top 20. The follow-up, 'Doin' It' using Grace Jones' 'My Jamaican Guy' as its base went to number 15. LL Cool J had found a new audience as proved when his next song, 'Loungin', went into the Top 10.

LL's album career had never taken off in the UK. *Radio* (1986), *Bigger And Deffer* (1987), *Walking With A Panther* (1989), *Mama Said Knock You Out* (1990) and *14 Shots To The Dome* (1993) all failed to make the Top 40.

Following in Will Smith's footsteps, LL made appearances in various films, including a rapper in *Wildcats* (1986), a detective in *The Hard Way* (1991) and as Captain Patrick Zevo in *Toys* (1992) alongside Robin Williams. On the small screen he spent four years playing Marion Hill in the US sitcom *In The House*. In 1995 he landed a part in the film *Out Of Sync*. "I had real high

hopes for that film as it was my first real starring role, but it bombed at the box office," admitted LL. "They spent $9 million making it – and it only made $9,000. It was in and out of the theatres so fast it should have gone straight to video."

In 1996 LL Cool J recorded 'Ain't Nobody', a song written by Rufus' keyboard player David Wolinski and first recorded by them with Chaka Khan as the lead singer in 1982. It appeared on their album *Stompin' At The Savoy*, but Warners were reluctant to release it as a single. David knew it had potential so gave them the ultimatum, 'release it or I'll give it to Quincy Jones for Michael Jackson and retire'. The song was released and although it only went to number 22 in the States, it made the Top 10 in Britain in 1984 and again in a remixed form five years later. LL's version was included in the movie *Beavis And Butthead Do America* and gave him his only UK number one, something he didn't achieve in America until 2002 when he duetted with Jennifer Lopez on 'All I Have'.

760 U2
Discothèque

Label & Cat No.: **Island CID 649**

Producer: **Flood**

Writers: **Bono / Paul Hewson / The Edge / Larry Mullen Jr. / Adam Clayton**

Date Reached No.1: **15 February 1997**

Weeks at No.1: **1**

In the mid-Nineties U2 ventured into movie soundtracks. 'Hold Me, Thrill Me, Kiss Me, Kill Me' was featured in the 1995 film *Batman Forever*, and the same year they wrote the theme for the new Bond movie, *Goldeneye*, which was recorded by Tina Turner. The following year Larry Mullen Jr. and Adam Clayton provided the soundtrack to *Mission Impossible*, which also made the Top 10. They also embarked on a project involving Brian Eno, Glaswegian DJ and remixer Howie B and Italian tenor Pavarotti, called 'Passengers'. They released the album, *Original Soundtracks Vol. 1* and one single, 'Miss Sarajevo', which was inspired by the TV documentary that reported on a beauty pageant in the besieged Bosnian capital.

During 1996 work began on their next album, *Pop*. One evening at the end of a long day's recording, Howie programmed some beats into his deck and began to play them. The Edge picked up a bass and joined in, Bono walked in and jammed along with some improvised vocals. That jam formed the template for 'Discothèque', which was earmarked as the first release from the album and eventually went to number one in 13 countries. To help get the right feel for the recording, the band decorated the studio in mirror balls and disco lighting.

A quick glance at the lyric to 'Discothèque' and they might seem meaningless, but according to Niall Strokes' book, *U2 Into The Heart*, he suggests that ''Discothèque' is an earnest little riddle about love disguised as trash'. U2 had further Top 10 hits with 'Staring At The Sun' and 'Last Night On Earth'.

In 1998 U2 made an appearance on *The Simpsons*. The episode, *Trash Of The Titans*, saw the group help Homer campaign for the position of Springfield Sanitation Director. It was a subject Bono had a great deal of experience with – campaigning. After Live Aid, he took to assisting the African nations manage their debt and help them to concentrate more on education and health issues.

761 No Doubt
Don't Speak

Label & Cat No.: **Interscope IND 95515**

Producer: **Matthew Wilder**

Writer: **Gwen Stefani**

Date Reached No.1: **22 February 1997**

Weeks at No.1: **3**

The British ska explosion made few commercial waves in America but in Anaheim, California in 1986 it inspired the formation of No Doubt. Keyboard player Eric Stefani bought a Madness record which he played to his school friend and singer John Spence, at which point they agreed to start a band. John's catchphrase was 'no doubt' so that was the name sorted, now they needed some musicians. Eric asked his sister Gwen to join as a co-lead singer and a few weeks later they brought in bassist Tony Kanal, who was born in north London to Indian parents.

Exactly one year after they formed, Spence took his own life in Anaheim Park. "It was a huge shock," said Gwen. "We were going to stop the band, but we thought that John would have wanted us to keep going, so we did." They recruited guitarist Tom Dumont and the following year, a 19-year-old Adrian Young lied his way into the band. "I told them I had been playing drums for eight years when it was actually one," he said.

They toured relentlessly and Gwen and Tony began a seven-year romance. In 1991 they landed a deal with Interscope Records. The following year they released their debut self-titled album, which sold 30,000 copies in the US, and reviewers weren't too complimentary about it either. One radio station owner in California who obviously wasn't keen commented, "It would take an act of God to get this group on the radio."

They soldiered on, but 1994 was not a good year. The record company kept insisting they write more and more songs, which took its toll on the band. Gwen and Tony split up and Eric left to pursue a career as an animator on *The Simpsons*. They continued as a four-piece and got working on their next album, *Tragic Kingdom*. The first single, the female-powered anthem, 'Just A Girl' was only a moderate hit in the States even though the album spent nine weeks at the top of the US chart.

By 1996 America had severely cut down on issuing CD singles, so if a radio station began playing a track, the consumer was forced to buy the album. Although they began taking more airplay tracks into account when compiling the *Billboard* singles chart, they also introduced an airplay-only chart of which No Doubt's next single, 'Don't Speak', a rock ballad became their first to head the listing and did so for 16 weeks.

'Don't Speak', written by Gwen about her

It took No Doubt six year from signing their record contract to registering a UK number one; left to right: Tony Kanal, Tom Dumont, Gwen Stefani and Adrian Young

break up with Tony, was produced by Matthew Wilder, who is best remembered for his 1984 Top five hit 'Break My Stride'. By the time it had made number one in the UK, *Tragic Kingdom* had sold over two million copies in the States, but would eventually sell over 10 million. It was on their 1996 US tour whilst supporting Bush that Gwen Stefani began dating Bush's lead singer Gavin Rossdale. The pair married in 2002.

'Just A Girl' had the potential to be a big hit and when it was re-issued as the follow-up, it went to number three. 'Spiderwebs', 'Sunday Morning' and 'Ex-Girlfriend' were all UK hits, but a pairing with Jamaican reggae singer, Bounty Killer, on 'Hey Baby' almost made it to number one in 2002. That was followed by 'Hella Good (12), the lilting ballad 'Underneath It All' (18) and a cover of Talk Talk's 'It's My Life' (20).

Christmas 2003 saw the release of *The Singles 1992-2003* and is a good reminder of their ever-changing musical style. Within a few years it'll be time for the next greatest hits package. No doubt!

762 The Spice Girls Mama / Who Do You Think You Are?

Label & Cat No.: **Virgin VSCDT 1623**

Producers: **Richard Stannard / Matt Rowe : Paul Wilson / Andy Watkins**

Writers: **Melanie B / Melanie C / Emma Bunton / Geri Halliwell / Victoria Adams / Richard Stannard / Matt Rowe : Melanie B / Melanie C / Emma Bunton / Geri Halliwell / Victoria Adams / Andy Watkins / Paul Wilson**

Date reached No.1: **15 March 1997**

Weeks at No.1: **3**

The success of the *Spice* album continued as The Spice Girls released their fourth consecutive number one from the record. The sentiments of a girl coming to appreciate her mother, 'Mama', would have suited any period of popular music and to pump up the emotion, The Spice Girls were supplemented by a choir. The song was Mel B's idea. Though cooler than Clive Dunn's 'Grandad', it mined the same seam.

The single was a charity record for Comic Relief, which no doubt helped sales. On the night itself, there was a parody from The Sugar Lumps with Dawn French as Posh and Jennifer Saunders as Ginger. The offical video showed the girls' mothers and was timed not only for Comic Relief but also for Mothering Sunday.

The Spice Girls had gone to Absolute's studio near Chertsey with the intention of writing a disco song with the studio's owners, Andy Watkins and Paul Wilsonand the joint A-side, 'Who Do You Think You Are' was the result. "When they wrote they were also writing the dance routine," said Paul Wilson, "constructing the video, at the same time as writing the song. They say that the mother of invention is copying somebody and getting it wrong. Their sound was actually not getting R&B quite right."

The final credit had seven writers, but possibly an eighth name should have been added – John Lennon. The line "Who do you think you are? Some kind of superstar?" paraphrases his 1970 hit, 'Instant Karma'.

The Spice Girls performed 'Who Do You Think You Are?' at the Brit Awards when Geri wore her Union Jack minidress, the perfect motif for British pop. The Spice Girls were now involved in numerous endorsement deals – Pepsi, British Telecom, Sony, Benetton, Asda, Walker's Crisps and Elizabeth David cakes. They recorded a new song based around Manfred Mann's '5-4-3-2-1' for the opening of Channel 5.

In May 1997 they flirted with Prince Charles at a charity concert in Manchester for the Prince's Trust. Geri planted a lipstick mark on his cheek and patted his bottom. They showed similar irreverence when they met Nelson Mandela in Pretoria in November, 1977, when Prince Charles was again present. A photo of this historic occasion made front pages around the world, perhaps the greatest PR coup of their short but illustrious career. When Geri left The Spice Girls in 1998, Prince Charles sent her his good wishes, recalling "your wonderfully friendly greeting". Beats a curtsey any day.

763 The Chemical Brothers Block Rockin' Beats

Label & Cat No.: **Virgin CHEMSD 5**

Producers: **Tom Rowlands / Ed Simons**

Writers: **Tom Rowlands / Ed Simons / Jesse B.Weaver**

Date Reached No.1: **5 April 1997**

Weeks at No.1: **1**

The Chemical Brothers had spent the majority of 1997 recording their third album *Dig Your Own Hole*, a title they took from some graffiti they had seen on a wall near their south London studios. 'Setting Sun' had already been a number one hit and 'Block Rockin' Beats' looked set to follow suit.

The album, which featured Noel Gallagher, Mercury Rev's Jonathan Donahue and Beth Orton, crashed into the chart at number one. 'Block Rockin' Beat' featured a sample of 'Gucci Again', a track sung by their old school mate Schoolly D. The track was laden with pitch-bending synthesizer stabs, but was less distorted than 'Setting Sun'. It went on to win a Grammy Award for Best Rock Instrumental, despite not being a US hit, not containing any guitars and not technically being an instrumental.

The duo spent the rest of 1997 on tour and the following year recovering from the hectic schedule. They returned in 1999 with the hit singles 'Hey Boy, Hey Girl' (3) and 'Let Forever Be' (9), this time featuring an uncredited Noel Gallagher as the lead singer. The accompanying album, *Surrender*, like *Dig Your Own Hole*, debuted at number one. In 1998 they appeared at Glastonbury.

In 2000 they were named Best UK Dance Act at the Brit Awards. The following year they were back in the Top 10 with 'It Began In Afrika', (which sampled 'Drumbeat' by Jim Ingram), and 'Star Guitar'. The next album, *Come With Us*, again flew to the top of the chart and endorsed the fact that they were still one of Britain's top dance acts.

In 2003 they teamed up with indie rockers,

Chemical Brothers Tom Rowlands (left) and Ed Simons met while studying history at Manchester Poly in 1989

The Flaming Lips for the Top 20 hit single 'The Golden Path'. The same year saw the release of their *Singles 93-03*, collection which made it into the Top 10.

764 R.Kelly
I Believe I Can Fly

Label & Cat No.: **Jive JIVECD 415**
Producer: **R.Kelly**
Writer: **R.Kelly**
Date Reached No.1: **12 April 1997**
Weeks at No.1: **3**

HAVING GROWN UP IN A ROUGH AREA on the south side of Chicago, Robert Kelly managed to stay away from gangs and drugs and turn his attention to basketball. He got a taste for performing one day in 1990 when one of his friends threw a hat onto the floor and passers-by began throwing money in as he sang Stevie Wonder songs. His next move was to front a quartet called MGM. They entered and won a televised talent show called *Big Break* and then split.

The following year he was singing at a barbeque at a friend's house where a fellow guest, an employee at Jive Records, heard him and signed him to the label. Robert was writing his own songs as well as playing a number of instruments. He formed a band of backing singers and dancers that he called Public Announcement.

His first single, 'She's Got That Vibe' was a club favourite all over the world although it didn't make much impact on the pop charts. His debut album in 1992, *Born Into The 90s*, sold well in the US and went platinum the following year.

In the UK his second single, 'Sex Me' went by almost unnoticed but a re-issue of 'She's Got That Vibe' in 1994 went to number three, followed by the sex-driven 'Bump N' Grind'. By now he had dispensed with Public Announcement to make his name as a solo artist. R wrote all his own songs and in 1995 received a call from his manager saying that Michael Jackson loved 'Bump N' Grind' and wanted R to write a song for him. The result was 'You Are Not Alone' which became the first song to enter the US chart at number one.

R. Kelly

In 1994 he met Gladys Knight's niece, Aaliyah, a teenage R&B singer, who was also his manager's niece. He wrote and produced her early hits which included 'Back & Forth', 'Down With The Clique' 'The Thing I Like' and 'Age Ain't Nothing But A Number'. He proved that point when he married her in the summer that year. It was a disaster and was soon annulled after it was discovered that Aaliyah had lied about her age.

With his love of basketball, he was delighted when Michael Jordan, star of the film *Space Jam*, asked him to contribute a song to the soundtrack. *Space Jam* was an animated film which also starred Bugs Bunny. "I've always wanted to write a song for kids, to let them know they can do anything they want to," he said. "There's no way I could've written this song without believing I could fly. My inspiration was George Benson's 'The Greatest Love Of All', a song I loved as a kid. I always wanted to write a song like that."

Although he lost out on Song Of The Year to Shawn Colvin's 'Sunny Came Home', 'I Believe I Can Fly' won Grammy Awards for Best Male R&B Performance, Best R&B Song and Best Song Written For A Motion Picture.

765 Michael Jackson
Blood On The Dance Floor

Label & Cat No.: **Epic 6644625**
Producer: **Teddy Riley**
Writers: **Michael Jackson / Teddy Riley**
Date Reached No.1: **3 May 1997**
Weeks at No.1: **1**

ONCE *THRILLER* HAD MADE MICHAEL Jackson a megastar, the press began calling him the King Of Pop. He sang ballads with great passion ('Ben' and 'She's Out Of My Life'), his dance tracks were always catchy and distinctive ('Billie Jean' and The Way You Make Me Feel') and his straightforward pop songs just brilliant ('Rock With You' and 'Leave Me Alone'). But from 1996, although his songs were still lyrically acceptable, the tunes became a bit nondescript.

Both, 'They Don't Care About Us' and 'Stranger In Moscow' entered and peaked at number four. The former spent three weeks in the Top 10, the latter just a week. When 'Blood On The Dance Floor' debuted at number one, it did so by selling just over 85,000 copies. The following week it plunged to number eight.

The album, *Blood On The Dance Floor – History In The Mix* also debuted at the top of the chart and contained only five new tracks plus a hoard of remixes from *HIStory: Past, Present and Future Book 1*. It received poor reviews with the press commenting that Jacko was now sounding 'predictable' and 'tired'. One website review noted that Michael Jackson could 'no longer craft a good melody'.

Michael needed a long rest away from the media spotlight and that's exactly what he tried to do. Every time Michael went out in public he would dress up in ridiculous outfits in an attempt to avoid the press, but in reality wound up courting even more publicity. He returned in 2001 with the number two hit 'You Rock My World'. As for the parent album, *Invincible*, Epic Records releasing it in a variety of different coloured sleeves in the hope that die-hard fans would buy one of each colour. However, the fans got wise and after six months, it had sold only five million copies… although still sufficient for him to afford another new nose.

766 Gary Barlow
Love Won't Wait

Label & Cat No.:	**RCA 74321470802**
Producer:	**Stephen Lipson**
Writers:	**Shep Pettibone / Madonna**
Date reached No.1:	**10 May 1997**
Weeks at No.1:	**1**

GARY BARLOW'S *OPEN ROAD* ALBUM should have been issued at the same time as his first single, 'Forever Love', but it was delayed because he wanted to re-record some of the tracks in the US. Both the album and the second single, 'Love Won't Wait', went in at number one, but soon dropped away. 'Love Won't Wait' spent only three weeks in the Top 20. Not that Robbie Williams helped the situation: he bought a copy of *Open Road* and took it back, saying, "This is crap. I want my money back."

For all that, 'Love Won't Wait' has an intriguing history. Madonna had a best-selling album with *Erotica* in 1992 and she and her producer, Shep Pettibone, planned more of the same, writing further songs including 'Love Won't Wait'. Madonna abandoned the project and instead made an album, *Bedtime Stories*, with different producers. As Madonna had songs she didn't want, her demos were passed around and Gary shortened 'Love Won't Wait' and took it somewhat faster. There are alternative mixes available by Junior Vasquez, CUCA and Monster Makers.

Robbie Williams' criticisms hit home and Gary Barlow's career nose-dived: his Take That fans had moved on and he hadn't found new ones. His next two singles failed to hit the top, and his 1999 album, *Twelve Months, Eleven Days*, only had one Top 20 single, 'Stronger'. Not to worry as Gary has developed a secondary career writing and producing for Blue ('Guilty'), Delta Goodrem ('Not Me, Not I) and Donny Osmond ('Breeze On By').

767 Olive
You're Not Alone

Label & Cat No.:	**RCA 74321473232**
Producers:	**Tim Kellett / Robin Taylor-Firth**
Writers:	**Tim Kellett / Robin Taylor-Firth**
Date Reached No.1:	**17 May 1997**
Weeks at No.1:	**2**

HAVING LEFT SIMPLY RED IN 1995, keyboard player Tim Kellett teamed up with dance programmer and ex-Nightmares On Wax member Robin Taylor-Firth to form a new group Olive.

Robin and Tim recorded demos in Tim's basement studio, one of which included 'You're Not Alone'. Before Simply Red, Tim had been a member of Durutti Column and had worked on sampling other people's vocals and making tape loops. He joined his old friends Durutti Column at a couple of gigs in Portugal and began messing around with a sample he found by Ruth-Ann Boyle. "I loved her voice and forgotten I had that sample," said Tim. "We tracked her down in a student union bar and asked her to join the group."

"We were keen to get some really strong backing track together using drum'n'bass, dub reggae and jungle," explained Tim. "But what's most important to us is to stick a good pop song on top. Through my experiences with Simply Red, I learned that people like a good song with a strong message, and I think Olive have both. I tend to write songs from a female perspective. Maybe it's because I grew up with three sisters and I was the only boy in the family. Once we brought Ruth-Ann in, I began writing about their experiences."

In 1996 they released their debut single, 'Miracle' which went completely unnoticed. The next release, 'You're Not Alone', limped to number 42. "We were very disappointed," remembered Tim. "The subject matter is something anyone can relate to and, unlike many bands we've been compared to, we don't shy away from writing songs with a beginning, a middle and an end. Every song on our album tells a story."

The debut album, *Extra Virgin*, was released in May 1997 and went to number 15 in Britain. It tackled a number of disturbing subjects including Ruth-Ann's memories of her father's death when she was three in 'Safer Hands', adultery in 'Curious' and domestic violence in 'Blood Red Tears'.

The next single was the re-issued 'Miracle', but it only bettered 'You're Not Alone' by one place. However, they were convinced the latter was capable of better, so 'You're Not Alone' was re-issued in May 1997 with additional new mixes by Paul Oakenfold, Roni Size and Nightmares On Wax and it finally made it to the top.

One further single, 'Outlaw' was issued and it reached number 14. In 1999 their contract with RCA ended and they were temporarily without a contract. Ruth-Ann contributed some vocals to two tracks on Enigma's 1999 album *Gravity Of Love*. The following year they signed with Madonna's Maverick record label and recorded a cover of 10cc's 'I'm Not In Love' which was included on the soundtrack to *The Next Best Thing*. The same year they released their second album, *Trickle*, but it attracted few buyers.

In 2003 Ruth-Ann rejoined Enigma and contributed vocals to a number of songs on their latest album, *Voyageur*.

768 Eternal with Bebe Winans
I Wanna Be The Only One

Label & Cat No.:	**EMI CDEM 472**
Producers:	**Nigel Lowis / BeBe Winans**
Writers:	**BeBe Winans / Rhett Lawrence**
Date Reached No.1:	**31 May 1997**
Weeks at No.1:	**1**

HAVING MET AT THE PRESTIGIOUS Italia Conti Stage School, Louise Nurding (born November 4, 1974) and Kelle Bryan (born March 12, 1975) became friends and shared an ambition to be in a pop group. Denis Ingoldsby, a record producer and manager who ran his own

First Avenue Management company, spotted Louise dancing in a nightclub. He approached her and asked if she could sing. Kelle was then introduced to Denis who teamed them up with two sisters Easther (born December 11, 1972) and Vernie (born May 17, 1971) Bennett, whom he'd already signed, and named them Eternal.

Their debut single, 'Stay' went to number four and was followed by the Top 10 hits 'Save Our Love' (8), 'Just A Step From Heaven' (8), 'Oh Baby I…' (4), 'Power Of A Woman' (5) and 'I Am Blessed' (7). In the summer of 1995 Louise announced that she was leaving and immediately signed a new solo contract with First Avenue. Eternal continued as a trio and had Top 10 hits with 'Good Thing' (8), 'Someday' (4), 'Secrets' (9) and 'Don't You Love Me' (3).

The Winans are 10 gospel-singing siblings from Detroit. Brothers Marvin, Ronald and Carvin, as The Winans, had one minor hit in 1985 with 'Let My People Go'. Another brother, Benjamin, known as BeBe and his sister, Priscilla, known as CeCe formed a duo in the early Nineties and had a US hit with a cover of the Staple Singers' 'I'll Take You There' which also featured Mavis Staples. CeCe teamed up with Whitney Houston for the 1996 hit 'Count On Me', from the film *Waiting To Exhale*, which made the Top 10 on both sides of the Atlantic.

In addition to singing, BeBe writes, produces and arranges and was part of the 1993 Grammy Award-winning team of producers who worked on *The Bodyguard* soundtrack. He then went on to write songs for Stephanie Mills, Bobby Brown, Brandy and Nancy Wilson. In 1996 he and Stephanie Mills appeared in the sold-out Broadway show *Your Arms Are Too Short To Box With God*.

Rhett Lawrence, who had written songs with Paula Abdul, teamed up with BeBe to write the upbeat 'I Wanna Be The Only One', on which BeBe joined the girls. A religious song, it was written to suggest that God is speaking to his children, saying 'I wanna be the only one you turn to, and if you do, I'll look after you.'

Eternal had one further Top 10 hit with 'Angel Of Mine' followed by the *Greatest Hits* collection which went to number two. The following year Louise, who had enjoyed half a dozen solo hits, married the footballer Jamie Redknapp aboard a yacht in Bermuda. Later the same year Easther married Boyzone member Shane Lynch but they split in 2000.

In 1999 Kelle admitted in an interview in *Smash Hits* that she learned from the newspapers that she was no longer a member of Eternal. After a six-month rest, she embarked on a solo career and had one hit with 'Higher Than Heaven'. She was replaced by TJ and Eternal had one further hit, 'Whatcha Gonna Do', written by the sisters. They split with their management company and were then dropped by EMI after it became their lowest charting hit. Eternal didn't live up to their name. The sisters then ousted TJ and decided to continue as a duo but haven't yet been seen on the chart.

769 Hanson
MMMBop

Label & Cat No.: **Mercury 5744992**

Producers: **Dust Brothers / Steve Lironi**

Writers: **Isaac Hanson / Taylor Hanson / Zach Hanson**

Date Reached No.1: **7 June 1997**

Weeks at No.1: **3**

UNFAIRLY DISMISSED AS JUST ANOTHER boy band, Hanson are a talented trio from Tulsa, Oklahoma who not only play their own instruments, but also write their own material.

The oldest of seven children raised on rock, R&B and gospel, Zak (born October 22, 1985), Taylor (born March 14, 1983) and Isaac (born November 17, 1980) started singing together acappella-style five years previous to their first chart topper before learning to play their instruments. By the time of their debut hit, they already were veterans of more than 300 performances. Once in their hometown – due to being underage – they had to do their gig *outside* the licensed Blue Rose Café.

Blessed with teenybopper looks and angelic voices, complete with infectious pop melodies and harmonising the way that only siblings can, it was only going to be a matter of time before one of the major labels snapped them up, which finally happened at the South by Southwest Music Conference in 1994. This annual event takes place in Austin, Texas, drawing thousands of hopeful musicians, all with the same goal; to get a record deal. Befriending a young entertainment lawyer, Christopher Sabec, at one of the convention's barbecues, the three lads offered to sing for him there and then. Impressed, Sabec became their manager and swiftly secured them a recording contract.

'MMMBop' was the first debut single to simultaneously top the UK and US charts and went to number one in an impressive 25 countries, including a nine-week stay in Australia. It was produced by the respected Dust Brothers (a.k.a. Mike Simpson and John King) better known for their work with Beck and the Beastie Boys.

As much as the song was adored, it was despised, mainly for being one of those tunes that you find impossible to get out of your head after hearing it a few times. When asked exactly what 'MMMBop' meant, Taylor replied, "It's really about friendships. The first verse said 'You have so many relationships in this life/Only one or two will last/You go through all the pain and strife/And you turn your back and they're gone so fast.' And that's what it's really about. It's deeper than it sounds."

Added Isaac, "It was originally written as a background part for a song. We liked the way the chorus sounded. A year later we finished the song. I don't know why we called it 'MMMBop'. It just worked."

The parent album, *Middle Of Nowhere*, eventually went on to sell over 10 million worldwide. Hanson had two further Top 10 hits with 'Where's The Love' (4) and 'I Will Come To You' (5), a song co-written with famed songwriting partnership Barry Mann and Cynthia Weil ('We've Got To Get Out Of This Place', 'You've Lost That Lovin' Feeling'. Things went quiet after that: Hanson released two further albums, *3 Car Garage- Indie Recordings 95-96* and *This Time Around*, which barely scraped into the Top 40 and spent a mere one week apiece on the UK chart. They spent the next couple of years working recording and writing songs for an eventual release, collaborating with artists such as Matthew Sweet, Ed Robertson (Barenaked Ladies), Gregg Alexander (New Radicals) and Carole King.

In 2004 they released the single 'Penny And Me', which went into the US Top 40 and an album, *Underneath*, which was released on their own label, 3CG.

770 Puff Daddy & Faith Evans (featuring 112) I'll Be Missing You

Label & Cat No.: **Puff Daddy 74321 499102**

Producers: **Puff Daddy / Stevie J**

Writers: **Sting / Todd Gaiter / Faith Evans**

Date reached No.1: **28 June 1997**

Weeks at No.1: **6 (2 runs)**

CAN YOU BE A GANGSTA RAPPER AND not be a gangster? Apparently not, if this entry is anything to go by.

The Bedford Stuyvesant (Bed Sty) area of New York was originally populated by former slaves and it became a poor, black, working-class district. In the Sixties it was considered one of the most dangerous ghetto localities in the US and several large-scale riots occurred there during the Seventies. Chris Wallace was born there in 1972 and grew up surrounded by pimps, prostitutes and drug dealers. He was soon dealing himself and by the time he was 15, he was earning $700 a day. He did some rapping and was signed by Sean Combs, aka Puff Daddy, to his Bad Boy record label.

Calling himself The Notorious B.I.G (and sometimes Biggie Smalls), Chris Wallace put his life into rhyme and the album, *Ready To Die* (1994), was a catalogue of misogyny, homophobia, drug dealing, a love of gangster films and gun lore. In 'One More Chance', Biggie admitted, "I'm a big black motherfucker." Indeed he was and at 6 foot 3 and weighing 22 stone, he was an easy target for even a short-sighted gunman. The album, *Ready To Die*, sold well and he had his first US Top 10 hit with 'Big Poppa', which sampled The Isley Brothers' 'Between The Sheets'.

The Notorious B.I.G was fined $25,000 when he beat up a promoter who had underpaid him. A few months later he beat up some autograph hunters with a baseball bat and was sentenced to community service. A succession of charges for drug and gun possession followed and he was fortunate to stay out of jail. Or not.

An east coast / west coast rap feud developed with Suge Knight who owned the Death Row label in Los Angeles. His main artist was Tupac Shakur and in one of his singles, 'Hit 'Em Up', he denounced the Bad Boy artists. Commenting on B.I.G's wife, Faith Evans, he said, "I fucked her, Biggie."

In July 1996 the Death Row gang attended the Mike Tyson vs. Bruce Seldon fight in Las Vegas. Tyson knocked out his opponent but the main bout was in the car park afterwards. Knight and Shakur got into a fight. They fled but not before Knight severely injured one opponent by stomping on his head. Hours later, Knight's car was riddled with bullets and Tupac Shakur was killed. Biggie declined to go to Shakur's memorial service. Knight meanwhile was arrested and was given a nine-year sentence.

Whether Notorious B.I.G or Puff Daddy were involved isn't known, but the two labels were at war and brought guns to an awards ceremony. Notorious B.I.G's new album was *Life After Death* and one of the tracks was 'You're Nobody ('Til Somebody Kills You)'. In March 1997, Biggie was murdered in LA..

Overcome by sentiment, Puff Daddy and Faith Evans reworked The Police's number one, 'Every Breath You Take', as 'I'll Be Missing You'. The packaging said *Tribute To The Notorious B.I.G.* and the royalties were for Biggie and Faith's daughter. They were backed by 112, an Atlanta group who were often used by Bad Boy. After 'I'll Be Missing You', they had a hit with Allure on 'All Cried Out'. Following the single, 'Mo Money Mo Problems' by Notorious B.I.G featuring Mase was a US number one and a Top 10 hit in the UK. It was number one the day that Princess Diana died.

When Puff Daddy picked up an award for the best R&B video for 'I'll Be Missing You', he commented on the death of Princess Diana, "Princess Diana made everybody feel good. You could tell her spirit and her vibe were so right. She's all right now." 'I'll Be Missing You' was included on the official tribute album to Diana, so like 'Candle In The Wind' the song had been used for two very different personalities.

In 1998 Puff Daddy sampled Jimmy Page's guitar riff from Led Zeppelin's 'Kashmir' and had a million-seller with 'Come With Me', which was on the soundtrack of *Godzilla*. Another single with Faith Evans, 'All Night Long', also did well. In 2000 Whitney Houston, supported by Faith Evans and Kelly Price, made the charts with the third hit song called 'Heartbreak Hotel'.

Despite all the violence in rap records, the Bed Sty district has become a 'neighbourhood in transition'. Rather like Notting Hill, some affluent people who work in the city have been moving to the area and fixing up houses and apartments. The poor blacks have been moving out to make room for those who can afford the property prices and rents.

The murders of both Tupac Shakur and The Notorious B.I.G remain unsolved.

Puff Daddy

771 Oasis D'You Know What I Mean?

Label & Cat No.: **Creation CRESCD 256**

Producers: **Owen Morris / Noel Gallagher**

Writer: **Noel Gallagher**

Date reached No.1: **19 July 1997**

Weeks at No.1: **1**

'D'YOU KNOW WHAT I MEAN?' WAS typical Oasis – insouciant, insolent and arrogant and with a gargantuan wall of sound. It may not have been one of Noel Gallagher's best tunes but it had a superb vocal from Liam

Gallagher, and the performance carried it. It also was the forerunner to Oasis' CD, *Be Here Now*, which was released in August 1997 and was their third number one album.

Noel Gallagher said of *Be Here Now*,"You write your first album when you're young and you're broke and you're hungry and you write your third album when you're a big fat drunken rock star. *Be Here Now* does nothing for me. We lost it down the drug dealers."

Commenting specifically on 'D'You Know What I Mean?', he said, "A good single is all down to the melody. 'D'You Know What I Mean?' has the same chords as 'Wonderwall' but it's got a different tune."

The album's title comes from one of John Lennon's final interviews. John was asked if rock-'n'roll had a message to the world and he said,"Be here now."The Beatles influence was still strong and by now everyone thought Noel nicked everything from 30 year old hits. Noel admitted writing songs around other's chord sequences, although it was never enough to be plagiarism. Like 'Wonderwall', 'Stand By Me' was written for Meg Matthews and made number two.

Alistair Campbell, Tony Blair's press secretary, said in October 1996, "Something has shifted, there's a new feeling on the streets. There's a desire for change. Britain is exporting pop music again. Now all we need is a new government." And in 1997 we had it – New Labour, New Brit-pop – and what could be more fitting than those working-class heroes, Oasis?

The Labour Party won the 1997 election and Tony Blair, depicted as a new Kennedy, became Prime Minster. The new government inherited huge problems with education, transport and the health service and they were determined to show that they would transform the UK. To win over the young, the concept of *Cool Britannia* came about where Britpop, art, film and fashion were encouraged by the Labour Party. 'Cool Britan-nia' was the opening track of *Gorilla,* the 1967 LP by The Bonzo Dog Doo-Dah Band, which was mocking the fashions of the time.

Tony Blair was photographed with a Fender guitar and his past with a rock band was raked up. In 1998 Blair held a now notorious party at Downing Street to which all the movers and shakers were invited. Liam Gallagher and Damon Albarn turned it down, but Noel Gallagher was seen chatting to the Prime Minister and shaking hands. *NME* was sceptical:"Tony Blair has always been more Cliff Richard than Keith Richards." D'you know what I mean?

772 Will Smith
Men In Black

Label & Cat No.: **Columbia 6648682**

Producers: **Poke & Tone (Jean Claude Olivier & Samuel Barnes)**

Writers: **Will Smith / Patrice Rushen / Gene McFadden / Freddie Washington**

Date Reached No.1: **16 August 1997**

Weeks at No.1: **4**

THERE'S A CERTAIN POIGNANCY THAT 'Men In Black' should be number one on a day when millions of people around the world might have been wearing black to mourn the death of Diana, Princess Of Wales.

At the end of 1996 Will had dropped his rap moniker, quit *The Fresh Prince Of Bel-Air* after six years and became a Hollywood movie star. He loved recording and the following year released his first album *Big Willie Style*, under his own name. He had finished filming his seventh movie, *Men In Black*, the title song of which appeared on the album. The story focused on two NYPD agents J (Will Smith) and K (Tommy Lee Jones) who alongside a pathologist, Laura Weaver, are asked to track down and wipe out an alien called Edgar who is out to assassinate two ambassadors. It was the executive producer, Steven Spielberg who brought in Will. He said, "He's funny and he's serious, all rolled into one. And he's a totally honest actor." Tommy Lee said of Will, "He is double cool. I just hoped I could keep up with him in the cool department."

'Men In Black' became the second number one in just over a year – after George Michael's 'Fastlove' – to sample Patrice Rushen's 1982 hit 'Forget Me Nots'. Will became a king of sam-pling. Over the next five years he had Top three hits with: 'Getting' Jiggy Wit It' (sampling Sister Sledge's 'He's The Greatest Dancer'), 'Miami' (using The Whispers' 'And The Beat Goes On'), 'Wild Wild West' from the film of the same name (using Stevie Wonder's 'I Wish) and 'Will 2K' (sampling The Clash's 'Rock The Casbah'). On New Years Eve 1997 Will married the actress Jada Pinkett.

His other films include: *Enemy Of The State* (1998), *The Legend Of Bagger Vance* (2000) and the sequel to *Men In Black*, *Men In Black II* (2002). His last hit, 'Black Suit's Comin' (Nod Ya Head)' was lifted from the *Men In Black II* soundtrack and reached number three.

Poke & Tone first came to prominence as writers and producers for a Long Island R&B act, Soul For Real in 1995. They have since pro-duced hits for Blackstreet, Jay-Z, LL Cool J, R.Kelly and Jennifer Lopez.

773 The Verve
The Drugs Don't Work

Label & Cat No.: **Hut HUTDG 88**

Producers: **Youth / The Verve / Chris Potter**

Writer: **Richard Ashcroft**

Date reached No.1: **13 September 1997**

Weeks at No.1: **1**

COMICS REGARD WIGAN AS A JOKE, ALL flat caps, whippets and working men's clubs, but George Orwell wrote a novel about the town and Buddy Holly played there. Novel-ty songs about the place abound and audiences, even Wigan ones, love The Houghton Weavers singing 'The Martians Have Landed In Wigan'. Limahl from Kajagoogoo was their first rock star but his success was eclipsed in the Nineties by The Verve who by 1997 had been playing around Lancashire towns for some time, often support-ing The Tansads. Although The Tansads released several albums and singles, they couldn't find commercial success. The strapline on their website reads, "The finest band ever to come from Wigan (and miles better than The Verve)."

'The Drugs Don't Work' was written about Verve singer Richard Ashcroft's father's illness; left to right: Nick McCabe, Pete Salisbury, Richard Ashcroft, Simon Tong and Simon Jones

The Verve were heading for national success – in the early Nineties they had a succession of minor hits ('History', based on William Blake's poem 'London', reached the Top 30 in 1995) and made two acclaimed albums, *A Storm In Heaven* (1993) and A *Northern Soul* (1995). However, their lead vocalist and songwriter, Richard Ashcroft, fell out with two of the members: lead guitarist Nick McCabe, who disliked touring, and drummer Peter Salisbury, who was punched on stage. The Verve disbanded.

Richard Ashcroft worked on a solo album, but he knew that Nick McCabe's creativity would strengthen his work. All differences were resolved and the proposed solo album became The Verve's third album, *Urban Hymns*. It contained 'Bitter Sweet Symphony' and 'The Drugs Don't Work' and sold seven million copies worldwide.

Richard Ashcroft's best idea was also his worst. Sampling Andrew Loog Oldham's very middle-of-the-road arrangement of The Rolling Stones' 'The Last Time' at the start of 'Bitter Sweet Symphony' resulted in Ashcroft having to share songwriting credits with the two Stones and settle with Oldham and Allen Klein, thereby losing £1 million in royalties. 'Bitter Sweet Symphony' made number two.

The Verve's follow-up, the downbeat but melodic anthem, 'The Drugs Don't Work', gave them a number one. Though most commentators assumed it was yet another song about recreational drugs, Ashcroft wrote the song after his father failed to respond to drugs prescribed to combat cancer. *Urban Hymns* can be viewed as a companion to Oasis' work, and Noel Gallagher wrote 'Cast No Shadow' about Richard's sensitivity as a songwriter and how his work has been tainted by success. Richard had a similar rock swagger to Liam Gallagher and he wrote 'A Northern Soul' about the Gallaghers' feuding on a US tour.

The Verve followed 'The Drugs Don't Work' with a third Top 10 single, 'Lucky Man', but they soon disbanded, saying goodbye in front of 30,000 people at Haigh Hall, just north of Wigan. Richard Ashcroft's solo career took off with 'A Song For The Lovers' and a number one album, *Alone With Everybody*, but he couldn't understand the critical mauling the album received. His second album, *Human Conditions* (2002), contained two more Top 20 singles, 'Check The Meaning' and 'Silence Of Silence', but why did the public all but ignore 'Buy It In Bottles' (26), which was every bit as strong as his major hits.

No longer in Wigan, Richard Ashcroft enjoys a family life in the Midlands with Kate Radley, who played keyboards for Spiritualised. He said, "There's a tradition of the lead singer leaving a group and his career petering out after three solo albums and the band reforming to play at Glastonbury. I'm going to break that mould."

774 Elton John
Something About The Way You Look Tonight / Candle In The Wind 1997

Label & Cat No.:	**Rocket PTCD 1**
Producers:	**Chris Thomas : George Martin**
Writers:	**Elton John / Bernie Taupin**
Date reached No.1:	**20 September 1997**
Weeks at No.1:	**5**

Marilyn Monroe was raised in foster homes, possibly raped as a child, endured loveless marriages and attempted suicide. She became a leading sex symbol/Hollywood actress via her giggle, her wiggle, her pout and her platinum blonde hair. She liked it hot and died in mysterious circumstances in 1962. The role the Kennedys played in her life – and possibly her demise – has been debated for years.

Bernie Taupin, who collected Monroe artefacts, felt compelled to write about her. "I wanted to say that it wasn't just a sex thing, that she was someone everybody could fall in love with. I could never come up with the right approach." Then Bernie read Ralph J. Gleason's obituary of the hard-drinking, hard-living Janis Joplin in *Rolling Stone*. It was entitled *Another Candle Blown Out* and Gleason, in turn, quoted a poem by the Pulitzer prize-winner, Edna St. Vincent Millay: "My candle burns at both ends, It will not last the night, But, ah, my foes and, oh, my friends, It gives a lovely light."

In 1973 Bernie passed his lyric to Elton, who also adored her and was discovering the two-edged nature of fame for himself. "When I think of Marilyn, I think of pain," he said. "I can't ever imagine her being happy." Bernie Taupin said, "'Candle In The Wind' is the best song we've ever written. The sentiment is how I feel, and the melody really suits the mood of it. It may come across as another schmaltzy song but people can listen to it and realise what the writers feel for her."

'Candle In The Wind' was the third single from the *Goodbye Yellow Brick Road* album and it reached number 11. In the US, it was the B-side of the funk inspired 'Bennie And The Jets', which became a US number one, and Elton was so fond of the song that he gave Bernie a dress and white satin stilettos that had been worn by the film star. In 1988 Elton made the Top five with an orchestral 'Candle In The Wind', recorded in concert in Australia.

Cut to 1997 – Elton's album, *The Big Picture*, is being released on September 22, and a single from it, 'Something About The Way You Look Tonight', is scheduled for September 8.

Elton was very friendly with Princess Diana, but he disagreed with her over a charity commitment and they both wrote letters they regretted. In January 1997 Elton John was depicted as the new Gianni Versace supermodel in a hilarious photospread in *The Sunday Times Magazine*. He was heartbroken when the designer was assassinated and Princess Diana comforted him at the funeral, thus renewing their friendship.

The People's Princess died on August 31 and many show-business names were invited to the funeral in Westminster Abbey. Pavarotti was too griefstricken to sing, but Elton John accepted. Diana loved 'Candle In The Wind', probably because she identified with the lyric – "They made you change your name", "Never knowing who to cling to when the rain set in" and "Even when you died, the press still hounded you". Such lyrics would never have been allowed at the

Elton John's moving tribute at Princess Diana's funeral was seen by 2.5 billion people around the world, far and away the biggest ever audience for a pop performance

Abbey, even though they would have complemented Earl Spencer's speech.

So Elton took a song that been written for someone else and rewrote it for Diana, or rather Bernie Taupin did. He called Bernie in California and within an hour, Bernie had faxed him new words. Emma Forrest in *The Guardian* called it 'drive-thru grief'. "'Her footsteps on England's greenest hills...' in Versace stilettos? Diana was always in London. She hated the countryside. What are you talking about, Elton?" The journalist had missed the point. The line has a resonance to William Blake's 'Jerusalem'.

Criticism of the opening phrase, 'Goodbye England's rose', might be more pointed. How did the people of Scotland and Wales view that, and she was, after all, the Princess of Wales? Nevertheless, she was born in Sandringham, Norfolk, so the farewell made sense. Bernie Taupin had removed the irony and anger from the original lyric, but one line was stunning, up there with his best work – "You were the grace that placed itself where lives were torn apart."

On September 6 Elton John performed in front of the biggest audience in his life, the biggest audience in anyone's life. The Prime Minister, Tony Blair, read the lesson and Elton moved to the piano. He sang with such warmth that everyone everywhere applauded. Even in the Abbey, the applause from the crowds watching on giant screens filtered through the walls.

The service had a UK audience of 31.5 million – ten million more than Charles and Diana's wedding. The broadcast was conveyed to 200 countries and the total viewing figure exceeded 2.5 billion. The funeral not only united the nation – it united the world. When the procession reached the Princess's resting place, the BBC ended its coverage by repeating 'Candle In The Wind'.

By then, Elton John had gone to a recording studio where George Martin was waiting. The 71-year-old had assembled woodwind and a string quartet for his final recording. A lesser producer would have overloaded the song, but George Martin gave it a quiet, sensitive arrangement – not unlike 'Yesterday' for Paul McCartney. Elton was technically perfect, but he couldn't match the emotion of that live performance before billions.

'Candle In The Wind 1997' was placed in-between two new songs: 'Something About The Way You Look Tonight' and 'You Can Make History (Young Again)'. Presumably this was so 'Something About The Way You Look Tonight' and 'Candle In The Wind 1997' could be listed as a double-header. 'Something About The Way You Look Tonight' wasn't inappropriate, but it was derivative of Berlin's 'Take My Breath Away'. Elton is hoarse in the chorus so he sounds at times like Rod Stewart.

The intention was to get 1.5 million singles pressed for the following Saturday. At midnight there was a queue at Tower Records in London and they sold 1,500 copies that night and their entire 5,000 stock by midday. Another million copies were pressed over the weekend. Shops had to limit purchasers to three copies, especially after con-men bought handfuls and offered them at higher prices on the streets.

Even those who thought Elton John totally naff bought the single and some, in true record collecting spirit, put them aside as mementos for their grandchildren. Paul Gambaccini has suggested that people transferred their grieving from giving flowers to buying CDs, which accounts for some people buying 40 or 50 copies. Millions were raised for the Memorial Fund and even the Chancellor, Gordon Brown, waived the VAT, which wasn't done for Band Aid.

The worldwide sales were colossal. If you grew sick of hearing the single, spare a thought for like-minded Canadians as 'Candle In The Wind 1997' topped their charts for 45 weeks. The single sold over five million copies in the UK and 11 million in the US. The total world sales were 33 million, making it the biggest-selling single of all-time.

Like Marilyn Monroe, Diana refuses to die. The fiasco of the her memorial in Hyde Park and the controversial lawsuit involving the Franklin Mint are mere distractions compared to more personal disclosures from former employees and romantic partners. Indeed, she continues to haunt the Royal Family, not only by these embarrassing revelations finding their way into books and magazines, but also – and more evocatively – in the handsome face of her son Prince William, the heir to the British throne.

775 The Spice Girls
Spice Up Your Life

Label & Cat No.: **Virgin VSCDT 1660**

Producers: **Richard Stannard / Matt Rowe**

Writers: **Victoria Adams / Melanie Brown / Emma Bunton / Melanie Chisholm / Geri Halliwell / Richard Stannard / Matt Rowe**

Date reached No.1: **25 October 1997**

Weeks at No.1: **1**

THE FILM, *SPICE WORLD*, IS *A HARD Day's Night* for the Nineties with The Monkees' *Head* thrown in for good measure. The Spice Girls, travelling in their Spicebus, are pursued by the media as they prepare for a concert at the Royal Albert Hall. And, er, that's it, but to be fair, there was scarcely any more plot in *A Hard Day's Night*. During the film, they fall out with their manager, Clifford, played by Richard E. Grant, and sack him. *Spice World* is "based on an idea by The Spice Girls" and was written by Simon Fuller's brother, Kim.

Shortly after the film opened, The Spice Girls sacked their manager, Simon Fuller, and, in an example of Girl Power, determined to manage themselves. The most likely reason for Simon Fuller's dismissal is that they were being worked too hard and wanted control of their destiny. Shortly afterwards Geri said, "The greatest irony about sacking Simon was that it had been triggered by my not being given a week off. Since then, we have worked twice as hard to prove that we didn't need him."

Spiceworld was also the title of the new album and the opening track, the bubbling, Latin-flavoured 'Spice Up Your Life', was the first single. By now The Spice Girls were so busy that quality was taking a back seat. One of the producers, Matt Rowe, recalls, "It had been booked in, that they were coming in to record their next single, and write it, with us. It was at Whitfield Street studios and there was going to be an MTV crew filming them as they did this. Well, how on earth can you possibly do this? You can't write and record a song in half-an-hour with a film crew watching. People in offices all round Whitfield Street were bombarding them – throwing things through the window, getting into the building, phoning up all the time. There were big crowds in the street outside. Eventually we got rid of the film crew and the song was done in one afternoon. All the writing and the recording of their vocals as well. But we did a lot of work on it afterwards."

Geri wrote in her diary, "Tomorrow our new single is released – 'Spice Up Your Life'. I think it will go to number one." The single did go to number one, but their success meant that rival female groups were everywhere – All Saints and N-Tyce, to begin with, followed by B*witched and Atomic Kitten. These groups were new and fresh and too much hype was having an effect on The Spice Girls. They were spreading themselves too thin and they would soon be as unfashionable as Old Spice.

The movie would never win them Oscars, and it was nominated for seven Razzies, the awards for the worst film performances of the year. When Phil Spector accepted a special award from Q, he added to his acceptance speech, "Are the Spice Girls the Antichrist? There's a big controversy in America about them being tantamount to a porno act. I disagree with that because there's a big difference between a Spice Girls video and a porno film. Some porno films have pretty good music."

The Spice Girls were also accused of exploiting their young fans. The CD booklet pushes the Official Merchandise – to have one of everything would cost £220.

776 Aqua
Barbie Girl

Label & Cat No.: **Universal UMD 80413**

Producers: **Johnny Jam / Felipe Delgado / Soren Rasted / Claus Norreen**

Writers: **Soren Rasted / Claus Norreen / René Dif / Lene Nystrøm**

Date Reached No.1: **1 November 1997**

Weeks at No.1: **4**

"I AM REALLY SORRY THAT WE MADE A record that millions of people like, and that we didn't wear boring clothes and play guitars and sing about what boring lives we have," said Soren Rasted, Aqua's songwriter and keyboard player in an *NME* headline.

Aqua assembled in 1989 when Danish-born musicians Claus Norreen and Soren Rasted, who had met whilst working in a filling station, began writing music together. They invited an ex-DJ, René Dif, and the Norwegian-born former television presenter Lene Nystrøm, who they had spotted singing Randy Crawford's 'Almaz', to join them as singers. Their first single, 'Itzy Bitzy' was released under the name Joyspeed, but went virtually unnoticed. Soon after they became Aqua, a name taken from a poster advertising the Danish National Aquarium. "We chose that because it's something you've got to jump into and enjoy," Soren explained.

Universal's marketing manager, Karl Badger, brought Aqua to the UK after attending a marketing meeting in Copenhagen. "Instantly I thought there was a bit of everything here: No Doubt and even Madonna," he recalled.

When he returned he sent out 800 copies of Aqua's next single, 'Roses Are Red' to club DJs. The reaction was disastrous and the record company didn't bother with 'My Oh My', their European follow-up. They also decided to hold back the release of their third single, 'Barbie Girl', until Aqua were available for UK promotion.

"It was René who came up with the original lyric 'Come on Barbie, let's go party' and we just wanted to put the voices to the dolls and try and imagine what they would say to each other," recalled Lene. "We can't understand why 'Barbie' exploded like it did. We knew it would be big but we wanted to promote it one country at a time. We didn't get the chance."

As soon as 'Barbie' was released in Europe, it ran into problems. Mattel, the Barbie doll manufacturers attempted to sue Aqua not only over the use of name, when it first appeared on the album *Aquarium*, but because they objected to the sexual innuendo in the lyrics which included 'Kiss me here, touch me there' and 'Hanky-panky'. They said it confused customers into thinking that Mattel backed it and tried to have all copies of the album recalled. MCA Records successfully negotiated with Mattel and agreed that future pressings would carry the sticker 'This product was not created or approved by the maker of the Barbie doll'. In the process, sales of *Aquarium* soared and eventually topped worldwide sales of 14 million. A month later MCA unsuccessfully counter-sued Mattel claiming that they had made MCA a subject of ridicule and

Aqua

had suffered a loss of reputation.

The accompanying video was done in comic style and was ultra cheesy. But it helped 'Barbie Girl' become Britain's 15th biggest selling single of all-time. It also failed to harm Mattel's profits of $1.5 billion a year in Barbie sales alone.

In 1998 a survey at London's HMV store in Oxford Street voted Aqua's 'Barbie Doll' the worst song of all-time, beating Black Lace's 'Agadoo' into second place. It prompted Colin Gibb of Black Lace to comment, "It's very disappointing not to be number one. I don't think it should be number two, 'Agadoo' is far more irritating than anything else."

777 Various Artists Perfect Day

Label & Cat No.: **Chrysalis CDNEED 01**

Producer: **Simon Hanhart**

Writer: **Lou Reed**

Date reached No.1: **29 November 1997**

Weeks at No.1: **2**

In 1966 Andy Warhol took time off from painting Campbell's soup cans, Brillo pads and other household goods to discover The Velvet Underground and their vocalist, Nico. With his patronage, they secured a record deal and he produced (at least, in name) their influential first LP with his banana on the cover. The Velvets weren't interested in hit singles; their songs, mostly written by Lou Reed, described life on the New York streets and included 'Heroin', 'I'm Waiting For The Man' (that is, the drug dealer), 'All Tomorrow's Parties' and 'Sister Ray'.

The Velvet Underground disbanded in 1970 and Lou Reed's first solo album, *Lou Reed*, had a critical mauling. Hard to believe but for a short time he retreated from the music business and worked for his father's accountancy practice. By 1972 David Bowie was a rising star and was developing his *Ziggy Stardust & The Spiders From Mars* album and stage show. He befriended first Iggy Pop and then Lou Reed. In August 1972 he brought Lou Reed to London and produced an album for him, assisted by The Spiders' lead guitarist, Mick Ronson. The result, *Transformer*, lived up to its name and brought Lou Reed into the mainstream. The distinctive cover photograph of Lou, captured by Mick Rock, with his white face, black lips and leather jacket was suggested by David's wife, Angie. It made him look tougher than most glam stars, something akin to an Eddy Izzard look.

The hit single from the album, 'Walk On The Wild Side', described life with Holly, Candy and Little Joe (the actor Joe Dallesandro) in Andy Warhol's Factory studio, a haven for avant garde artistic endeavours. The song, about addiction and prostitution, was the first hit single to explicitly refer to fellatio, which somehow bypassed the censors at the BBC. The B-side was another album track, the languid 'Perfect Day' in which Reed describes an idyllic day with his girlfriend, drinking Sangria in the park and going to the zoo, but more likely the song is about the effects of heroin.

In 1997 the song was revived for a campaign for the BBC's Children In Need. More intriguing than the Band Aid or USA For Africa singles, it featured many artists who wouldn't have a chart-topping single in a hundred years. By and large, the production team alighted on whoever happened to be in London and as a result, we have the gratifying result of Robert Cray, Emmylou Harris and Dr. John appearing on a number one record. In most cases, the artists were filmed performing the whole song and so the bonus tracks on the single could be separate male and female versions of 'Perfect Day'.

The order of play on the hit single is Lou Reed, Bono, Skye Edwards from the Bristol chill-out band Morcheeba, David Bowie, Suzanne Vega ('Tom's Diner' narrowly missed number one), Elton John, Boyzone, opera singer Lesley Garrett and reggae heroes Burning Spear on the first verse. Bono and opera star Thomas Allen, who was knighted in 1999, sing "You keep me hanging on" followed by an instrumental passage from The Brodsky Quartet.

For the second verse, there is Heather Small (whose record 'Proud' was used for the BBC's Olympics coverage in 2000), Emmylou Harris, Tammy Wynette and Shane McGowan with Sheona White from the Yorkshire Building Society Brass Band. Dr. John kicks in with "Just a perfect day", followed by David Bowie, Robert Cray, Huey from The Fun Lovin' Criminals, Ian Broudie (of The Lightning Seeds), Gabrielle and Dr. John again. This time "You keep me hanging on" is from Evan Dando of The Lemonheads and Emmylou Harris with an instrumental from jazz saxophonist Courtney Pine and The BBC Symphony Orchestra.

The closing coda, "You're going to reap just what you sow" comes from Brett Anderson of Suede, The Visual Ministry Choir (the British gospel equivalent of a super group), Joan Armatrading, Laurie Anderson, Heather Small, Tom Jones and concluding as it began with Lou Reed himself.

778 Teletubbies Teletubbies Say "Eh-Oh!"

Label & Cat No.: **BBC Worldwide Music WMXS 00092**

Producers: **Andrew McCrorie-Shand / Steve James**

Writers: **Andrew McCrorie-Shand / Andrew Davenport**

Date Reached No.1: **13 December 1997**

Weeks at No.1: **2**

The Teletubbies made their BBC TV debut on Monday, March 31, 1997. The furry, roly-poly creatures are Tinky-Winky (purple), Dipsy (green), Laa-Laa (yellow) and Po (red). All have an aerial sticking out of their heads, a beige face, big eyes, a twitchy nose and speak in a gurgling baby voice. They live in Tellytubbyland and can transmit television pictures on their tummies. The programme always starts with a rather sinister-looking loudspeaker rising up from a flowerbed to announce, "Time for Teletubbies". The sun, which shows a baby's face, giggles and also talks, with a voice provided by Toyah.

The half-hour programmes feature the cuddly foursome running around, singing songs and waving a lot. It gripped the nation's

After the success of the Teletubbies on children's TV, it was inevitable that (left to right) Po, Dipsy, Laa-Laa and Tinky-Winky would make a record

toddlers in a similar way that Andy Pandy did in the Fifties.

The Worldwide Music branch of the BBC label was launched in April 1997 with its first two releases being a two-CD set of some Led Zeppelin radio sessions and Radio Two archive material. They reached an agreement with the Teletubbies' independent production company, Ragdoll Productions' Anne Wood and Andrew Davenport, to release the theme as a single for the Christmas market

Before they decided to record a song the BBC were inundated with offers but turned them all down. The show's musical director, Andrew McCrorie-Shand, said, "The programme is the most important thing and by extension the young children who watch it, so to do anything else would be to betray the reason why it works. It would be so wrong to put a dance beat behind it and that's why we did it my way, by employing catchphrases from the show alongside the sort of music and instrumentation included in it." The BBC's legal department had threatened a number of parties who attempted to cash-in on the show's success. One musician had already recorded a song called 'Tubby Anthem'.

The Teletubbies was the latest in a long line of spin-off songs from children's television shows. The Chipmunks, The Wombles, The Smurfs, and The Simpsons all had chart success although Pinky & Perky must surely hold the record with over 30 singles released, yet their only chart hit was with 'Reet Petite' in 1993.

The single went on to sell over a million copies in Britain. It was followed by *The Album* and the inevitable plethora of official Teletubby merchandise which included dolls, videos, DVDs, cups, books, games and puzzles, crockery, cutlery and a Tubby-Go-Round.

The programme was aired in America in 1998 and the following year media controversy broke out when Christian leader Jerry Falwell wrote in the *National Liberty Journal* that Tinky-Winky was gay. His reasons were that purple was the gay pride colour, he had a triangle-shaped aerial (the gay pride symbol), and he carried a handbag. Even though the production company emphatically denied this, a new actor was brought in to play Tinky-Winky and the handbag disappeared.

The show has since been screened in over 85 countries and translated into 35 languages.

779 The Spice Girls
Too Much

Label & Cat No.: **Virgin VSCDR 1669**

Producers: **Absolute**

Writers: **Victoria Adams / Melanie Brown / Emma Bunton / Melanie Chisholm / Geri Halliwell / Andy Watkins / Paul Wilson**

Date reached No.1: **27 December 1997**

Weeks at No.1: **2**

OH, THE INDIGNITY OF IT ALL. THE Spice Girls, who had had five consecutive number ones, were competing with The Teletubbies for the Christmas number one. The Teletubbies had two weeks on top but The Spice Girls came straight in at number one for Christmas itself.

'Too Much' came from their film, *Spiceworld*, and had been written while they were filming. Geri told Andy Watkins and Paul Wilson that she had a good idea. She sang, "'Too much of something, Da-da-da-da-da'. Right. OK. You got that?" She scribbled some lines about love being blind and how words that appear deep may be meaningless. The others completed the song, the final bit coming after Geri saw someone wearing a T-shirt which read, "What part of no don't you understand?"

As usual, the song had to be structured for five people, and Andy and Paul used doo-wop records as the template. The format was for Emma to sing the high part, with Mel B, Victoria and Geri contributing in the middle, and Mel C adding ad-libs. They did all this while the film studio was besieged by fans. Listen to this subdued recording and bear in mind that it was recorded in a caravan in the middle of mayhem.

Another track on the album, 'Spice Invaders', features the girls talking over a backing track. It was getting harder and harder to find the time to make proper records.

780 All Saints
Never Ever

Label & Cat No.: **London LONCD 407**

Producers: **Cameron McVey / Magnus Fiennes**

Writers: **Sean Mather / Shaznay Lewis / Robert Jazayeri**

Date reached No.1: **17 January 1998**

Weeks at No.1: **1**

LOOKALIKE SISTERS NATALIE AND Nicole Appleton were born in Canada in 1973 and 1974 respectively and had unsettled childhoods. Their parents separated, reunited, separated and reunited and so on, and their four children were split up, sometimes living in North America, sometimes in England. Both Nat and Nic attended The Sylvia Young Theatre School in London, where Emma Bunton, Samantha Janus and Denise van Outen were fellow pupils. They built up their experience with bit parts: Nat in *Grange Hill* and Nic was in the films, *Brazil* and *Santa Claus: The Movie*.

Nic's best friend at the stage school was Melanie Blatt (born London, 1975), whose politically-minded parents had taken her on demos when she was young. Mel met Shaznay Lewis (born London, 1975) while doing session work at the ZTT studios in All Saints Road. They formed All Saints with Simone Rainford, and they released a single, 'If You Wanna Party' / 'Let's Get Started'. Simone would soon leave to be replaced by Mel but then Shaz left as she felt the group wasn't making any progress.

Meanwhile, Nat's marriage to a male stripper was breaking up, leaving her as a single parent in London. She joined Mel and Nic and they rehearsed Shaznay's songs, 'I Know Where It's At' and 'Never Ever'. When they passed an audition for London Records, Shaznay returned. Wearing combat jackets, they were presented as streetwise girls into contemporary R&B and rap, effectively The Rolling Stones to The Spice Girls' Beatles. The Saints came marching in when their first single, 'I Know Where It's At', made number four and for two months, they appeared on a *Smash Hits* tour with Ricky Martin and ★NSYNC.

From the start, All Saints were associated with celebrity boyfriends – Mel with Stuart Zender from Jamiroquai, Nat with *Top Of The Pops* presenter Jamie Theakston, and Nic with Robbie Williams. As if that were not enough, the spin-doctors concocted romances for Nic with Brad Pitt (they had never met) and Johnny Depp.

Their first album, *All Saints*, was mostly recorded in the UK and they described their producer, Karl Gordon as the fifth member of the group. Another producer, Cameron McVey had worked with Massive Attack and his wife, Neneh Cherry. Shaz had written 'Never Ever' with the hip-hop writers and producers, Rickidy Raw, otherwise Sean Mather and Robert 'Esmail' Jazayeri. When the album was released, they claimed that they had not been credited on 'Let's Get Started' and an agreement had to be reached with the record company. *All Saints* made number two and was on the charts for over a year.

'Never Ever' was recorded in Washington. Shaznay had written the song after splitting up with a boyfriend – "When you gonna take me out of this black hole?" – but the music conveyed the impression that all would be well. The melody, an off-shoot from 'Amazing Grace', was excellent but the song took two minutes to reach the chorus. The spoken intro, a nod to The Shangri-Las, was recited by Mel, and Shaz sang the lead vocal with the others adding harmonies. Towards the end of the session, Nat offered some ad-libs to complete the record but she was devastated when they were removed and replaced by Shaznay's.

The single entered the charts at number six, but the record had already sold 770,000 and had been on the charts for two months (even going down to number nine) before it reached the top. The Spice Girls may have beaten them to the Christmas number one, but those five girls must have been looking over the shoulders. Its total sales were 1.25m.

'Never Ever' won a Brit as Best Single and the ensuing video, showing a room exploding around them, also won Best Video. Nicole Appleton wrote in her joint autobiography with Nat, *Together* (2002): "So many times in my life, people dismissed and patronised me. Going to number one felt like a monumental 'fuck you' to them all. It was intensely satisfying."

781 Oasis
All Around The World

Label & Cat No.: **Creation CRESCD 282**

Producers: **Owen Morris / Noel Gallagher**

Writer: **Noel Gallagher**

Date reached No.1: **24 January 1998**

Weeks at No.1: **1**

OASIS WERE ON THE VERGE OF SPLITting up at the time of *Be Here Now*, but the strength of Noel's songs convinced them to stay. One was 'All Around The World', a huge anthemic song even by Oasis' standards. The optimistic lyric went, "All Around the world, You gotta spread the word, Tell 'em what you heard, We're gonna make a better day." The album track ran for nine minutes 38 seconds and it was not edited for single release. As a result, it became the longest single to make number one.

Noel Gallagher, eternally arrogant, denounced the opposition and issued statements like "We are bigger than God" but he often sounded more like The Rutles than Muhammad Ali. He later reflected, "You stop doing what comes naturally and you start to act like you're the biggest band in the world. You start wearing fur coat and sunglasses for breakfast and all that shite."

Liam was drinking heavily and his marriage to Patsy Kensit was in trouble, though she did bear him a son called Lennon in 1999. Similarly, Noel's marriage to Meg Matthews was on the rocks. This track is a reminder of happier times as both Patsy and Meg sing backing vocals. In 1999 Oasis released no new product, a sign that things had gone awry. The makeshift album *The Masterplan* was a collection of B-sides and rarities.

Oasis are often accused of nicking tunes so it's worth pointing out that Hear'Say's 2001 number one, 'Pure And Simple', appeared to owe a debt to Oasis' 'All Around The World'.

782 Usher
You Make Me Wanna...

Label & Cat No.: **LaFace 74321550502**

Producer: **Jermaine Dupri**

Writers: **Jermaine Dupri / Seal / Usher Raymond**

Date Reached No.1: **31 January 1998**

Weeks at No.1: **1**

USHER RAYMOND IV WAS BORN IN Chattanooga, Tennessee, on October 14, 1978. At the age of 12 he was briefly a member of the quartet NuBeginning before the family relocated to Atlanta, Georgia. "My mother introduced me to singing through church and I grew up listening to LL Cool J at home and when I went to my grandmother's house I'd listen to Donny Hathaway, Hall & Oates, Marvin Gaye, Fats Domino and Stevie Wonder so I got to know about the music of the Fifties and Sixties, which helped me to mature."

Once in Georgia, he entered a monthly talent show. "Everyone took part in it no matter what age you were." Usher won it for four consecutive months which led to him being invited on to the national television talent show, *Star Search* where he performed a cover of Boyz II Men's 'End of The Road', and won. It was through the talent contest he met the head of LaFace Records, L.A.Reid who asked him if he wanted to be a star.

His first US hit 'Can U Get Wit It' came in 1994, followed by 'Think Of You' and 'The Many Ways', all of which were medium hits. 'Think Of You' was his first UK hit but only spent one week at number 70. It was his next single, 'You Make Me Wanna...' that put Usher on the R&B map. In the US it made number two and sat there for seven weeks, unable to dislodge Elton's 'Candle In The Wind 1997'.

The British music press were comparing Usher to Bobby Brown and LL Cool J, but

Usher

Usher knew what he wanted. "My real ultimate is Michael Jackson. I really would like to be compared to him one day because he is the greatest."

Jermaine Dupri spent a couple of weeks hanging out with Usher before they worked together. "Jermaine paid a lot of attention to how I was and my everyday lifestyle and basically we wrote about that," Usher remembered. 'You Make Me Wanna' was about a man having problems with his girlfriend and turning to another female for comfort. Before long he found he was falling in love with this other girl. It was one of the last songs that we cut. As soon as we heard it, we knew that it should be the first one to release from the album."

His debut album, *Usher*, made little impact in the US but for the follow-up he was teamed with top R&B producer Jermaine Dupri who had worked with Kriss Kross, Mariah Carey and Snoop Doggy Dogg. The result was *My Way*, which went to number four in the US and number 16 here and was all about Usher's maturity from boy to man.

783 Aqua
Doctor Jones

Label & Cat No.: **Universal UMD 80457**

Producers: **Johnny Jam / Felipe Delgado / Soren Rasted / Claus Norreen**

Writers: **Anders Oland / Soren Rashed / Claus Norreen / René Dif**

Date Reached No.1: **7 February 1998**

Weeks at No.1: **2**

After 'Barbie Girl' had topped the chart in 35 countries and the video had been seen by millions, Aqua had to choose the next single from *Aquarium*. "People couldn't decide if we were a serious act or doing it with irony," offered Lene Nystrøm. "Grown-ups started to get the idea and we were surprised how many kids became fans. But we realised it was the cartoon image that was the appeal."

"Our songs don't have a specific message," added René. "It's not like we sing about politics. We try to do the opposite to what a lot of other bands do. We make fun of ourselves and of the record business without offending anyone. Well, we do, but they just don't know we're offending them!"

"'Doctor Jones' is about a boy and girl who fall in love on holiday but then separate, so she goes to the doctor to cure her love! It's very silly, but also funny," explained Lene. It incorporated a yodel from Lene and another nutty rap from René. Nonetheless, it was another catchy tune performed at a Hi-NRG speed. The accompanying video showed René dancing around at the back of a tent. He was wearing only underpants and a mask, but all you could see on the finished article was the shadows on the tent. "I felt a little bit stupid, to be honest, but I thought the final cut was ok." The style of the captions that flashed up on the screen was a homage to the Indiana Jones films.

They were just too late to be included in the nominations for the 1998 Brit awards, but they did have some consolation when asked to perform at the after show party, although instead of performing 'Doctor Jones', the audience had to settle for yet another helping of 'Barbie Girl'.

With the exception of Aqua, the first eight number ones of 1998 had all spent only one week at the top, which showed how much the singles-buying public enjoyed the light-heartedness of Scandinavian pop.

784 Celine Dion
My Heart Will Go On

Label & Cat No.: **Epic 6655472**

Producers: **Walter Afanasieff / James Horner**

Writers: **James Horner / Will Jennings**

Date reached No.1: **21 February 1998**

Weeks at No.1: **2 (in 2 runs)**

By 1996 Celine Dion had become a world superstar. Her dramatic vocal range put her alongside Whitney Houston and Mariah Carey, but because she was particularly partial to powerhouse ballads, Celine was most often compared to Barbra Streisand. It was appropriate that they should record a duet, 'Tell Me', which made number three.

The sinking of the luxury liner Titanic on its maiden voyage in 1912 has fascinated the public for years and there have been endless books, documentaries and exhibitions about the tragedy. There had been two films, the commendable *A Night To Remember* (1958) with Kenneth More and Honor Blackman and *Raise The Titanic!* (1980) with Jason Robards and Alec Guinness, which was a titanic disaster, as was a Broadway musical.

A new blockbuster about the Titanic had been discussed for years and James Cameron's film was the most expensive movie ever made – and, with box office takings of over $600 million, the most successful. If the film had done badly, the major Paramount studio might have gone under. The script was thin but the graphics and the sets were outstanding but what really ensured the film's success was heart-throb Leonardo DiCaprio.

The music for the film was written by James Horner, whose very varied CV included *Star Trek 2: The Wrath Of Khan* (1982), *The Name Of The Rose* (1986), *Honey, I Shrunk The Kids* (1989), *Patriot Games* (1992) and *Braveheart* (1995). The lyric for the theme song, 'My Heart Will Go On', came from the country music writer, Will Jennings. Quite by chance, he had met a survivor from the Titanic and when he was told that the story of a survivor would form the basis of the film, he decided that the lyric should echo her thoughts. 'My Heart Will Go On' was the first single by a female to debut at number one on both the US and UK charts.

On stage, Celine Dion lent on the railing at the prow of the Titanic and sang the ballad while a machine generated a strong wind for her hair. It became one of the most successful records of all time and is now much used at funerals.

Celine Dion followed it with a song from the West End production of *Saturday Night Fever*. The Bee Gees wrote one new song, 'Immortality', and Celine's version with them, although tipped as a number one and well publicised, only reached number five.

Celine Dion with the writers of 'My Heart Will Go On' James Horner (left) and Will Jennings

abc

2000-2005 1990-1999 1980-1989 1970-1979 1960-1969 1952-1959

785 Cornershop
Brimful Of Asha

Label & Cat No.: **Wiiija WIJ 81CD**

Producer: **Tjinder Singh**

Writer: **Tjinder Singh**

Date Reached No.1: **28 February 1998**

Weeks at No.1: **1**

SINGER AND GUITARIST TJINDER SINGH was born to Indian parents and grew up in Preston, Lancashire. In 1992 while studying at Preston University he formed Cornershop with guitarist and keyboard player Ben Ayres, another keyboardist Anthony Saffrey, percussionist Peter Bengry and drummer Nick Simms. Tjinder never told his father what he did. "An Asian on stage was unusual especially when I was playing guitar. It would have upset my father, so I told him I worked for a record company. My brother eventually told him."

By 1997 they had slimmed down to a duo consisting of Tjinder and Ben. Tjinder wrote the song as a tribute to Bollywood actress Asha Bhosle. On its initial release in August 1997, it faltered at number 60 on the chart.

Soon after, Fatboy Slim who liked the track, sped it up and began dropping it into his DJ set. It was well received by the crowd so Fatboy worked out a definitive remix and offered it to Cornershop's label, Wiiija, free of charge. They accepted it and issued it as a strictly limited white label 12" single. A couple of copies found their way into the hands of Radio 1 DJs Mary Anne Hobbs and Anne Nightingale who began playing it on every show. Then Steve Lamacq began playing it and within a week there was an on-air campaign to have it officially released. Part of the song was a celebration of the 45rpm single. Fatboy said, "All I did was speed it up, put a drum beat, a heavy breakbeat and a bassline on it and left the rest of the song as it was. It was brilliant."

The single was re-issued on seven inch and CD single, but Norman's remix was confined to the B-side or track two on the CD. The A-side was a straight re-issue and effectively everyone bought it for the A-side. However, hardly any radio station played the A-side so everyone thinks it was the Norman Cook remix that topped the chart.

Tjinder wasn't happy with the single's success. After releasing songs for over six years without success he was upset that his glory had been stolen by a remix and that the follow-up 'Sleep On The Left Side', which only reached number 23, was unfavourably compared with the remix. The second album, *Handcream For A Generation*, performed so badly that they were dropped from the label.

Norman said, "I thought I should apologise to Tjinder for fucking up the band's career. Tjinder said he wasn't bothered, but it doesn't feel good, making people sound jolly when it wasn't them."

Cornershop were out of the limelight for four years, but began recording again in 2002 on their own Meccico record label and returned to the chart in 2004 with 'Topknot'.

786 Madonna
Frozen

Label & Cat No.: **Maverick W0433CD**

Producers: **Madonna / William Orbit / Patrick Leonard**

Writers: **Madonna / Patrick Leonard**

Date Reached No.1: **7 March 1998**

Weeks at No.1: **1**

AMONG MADONNA'S MORE MEMORABLE gestures in the Nineties was the release of her notorious book, *Sex*, containing erotic pictures including one of her hitchhiking down a Florida highway stark naked. As fans flooded the bookshops for a copy, feminists united to condemn it. Madonna, never one to shirk from a controversy, argued, "I think I'm treated that way because people find it hard to believe that an ordinary little lady can become rich and powerful and stay sexy and disrespectful."

In the eight years that had passed since Madonna's last number one, she had launched her own Maverick record label, portrayed Eva Peron in the film version of *Evita* and, in October 1996, given birth to her first daughter, Lourdes Maria Ciccone Leon, (known as Lola). The father was fitness trainer Carlos Leon, whom she met whilst jogging in New York's Central Park.

The first single from *Evita*, was 'You Must Love Me'. When Madonna first saw the lyrics she felt they were not considerate enough towards either Evita's character or to her romance to Juan Peron. She rewrote them and duly faxed her version to Tim Rice who immediately sent a fax back informing Madonna that she had changed the song into a 'sloppy sentimental love song with abysmal and banal lyrics'. Uncharacteristically, Madonna gave in and recorded the song the way Rice had intended. It paid off: Tim received his third Academy Award for Best Original Song. Other singles released from the film were, 'Don't Cry for Me Argentina' (3) and 'Another Suitcase In Another Hall' (7).

Madonna teamed up with London-born producer William Orbit and renewed her acquaintance with lyricist Patrick Leonard for her new album *Ray Of Light*. The album had more of an electronic feel and a change of direction for which Madonna credits Rabbi Yardeni for his 'creative and spiritual guidance'. It also changed Madonna's persona. She had a calmer image and more mature outlook to motherhood.

The first single lifted from it was 'Frozen'. Both Madonna and William Orbit decided they would add a new synthesiser sound to Patrick's original arrangement to give the song a new techno feel. It tells a story of broken love which would seemingly be dedicated to Carlos Leon, with whom Madonna had split 10 months previously.

787 Run-D.M.C. Vs Jason Nevins It's Like That

Label & Cat No.: **SM:)E Communications SM 90652**

Producers: **Christian Smith / Joseph Simmons**

Writers: **Christian Smith / Joseph Simmons / Daryl McDaniels**

Date Reached No.1: **21 March 1998**

Weeks at No.1: **6**

Their trademark all-black Adidas clothing, thick gold chains and trilby hats made Run-D.M.C. one of the most recognisable hip-hop acts to come out of America.

New Yorkers Joseph Simmons, Daryl McDaniels and DJ Jam Master Jay (born Jason Mizell) all met at St Pascal's Catholic School and became lifelong friends. Once Joseph graduated in 1981, they decided that having grown up listening to the Sugarhill Gang they wanted to form a rap group and called themselves Orange Crush. The following year they changed their name, taking Joseph's nickname, Run, and Daryl's initials to became Run-D.M.C. A few years later, Run, who had overcome alcoholism, became an ordained minister and was known as Reverend Run.

They recorded a batch of demo tapes to circulate round American record companies, eventually landing a deal with Profile in 1983. Their first single, 'It's Like That' became a club favourite. The B-side, 'Sucker MC's' also created a stir and made MC one of rap's most common terms.

Their first UK hit, 'My Adidas' / 'Peter Piper' in 1986 made little impact peaking at number 62, but just a couple of months later they scored their first international Top 10 hit when they teamed up with Aerosmith's Steve Tyler and Joe Perry to create a rock/rap cover of Aerosmith's 1975 original 'Walk This Way'. When it was shown on MTV, they became the first rap act to have a video screened on that station. In addition they were the first rap act to be nominated for a Grammy and the first to appear on the cover of *Rolling Stone*.

They had further UK hits with 'You Be Illin" (1987), 'It's Tricky' (1987), 'Run's House' (1989), a rap cover of 'Ghostbusters' (1989), 'What's It All About' (1990) and 'Down With The King' (1993). Their biggest success came in 1998 when an unknown re-mixer, Jason Nevins, put his magic touch to their debut single.

"I grew up listening to hip-hop, especially Run-D.M.C. and I remember first hearing 'It's Like That' in the early Eighties," recalled Jason. "I remember when I took the record to the label, I said to them 'I don't think it'll sell a million copies, but I'm sure it'll do something.'"

The Reverend recalled the first time he heard the remix. "I was in the Profile Records office talking to a few people when the boss called me over. He said 'This guy has mixed "It's Like That" and has put a house beat behind it'. I liked it and thought it might sell 10,000 worldwide, maybe."

Jason was paid the $5,000 re-mixer's flat-rate by Profile Records. "Financially it wasn't a good deal for me," Jason remembered. "It was a good choice and a bad choice. Bad because I could have earned a lot more and good because without it, nobody would know who I was. Everyone has their own definition of what I did with that record. I personally think that I put their record over mine, but other people will think I put a beat over their record."

The accompanying video was a cheap effort, showing Run-D.M.C. and a bunch of kids break dancing in a multi-storey car park.

Dance radio stations began playing the track six weeks upfront and the song first entered the UK chart as a German import, spending three weeks on the chart and then a further week as an American import before its UK release, both copies being sold for upwards of £5.99. It crashed in at number one when officially released in the UK at less than £4 and in the process held off the Spice Girls' 'Stop' which became their only UK hit not to make the top.

Hoping to emulate 'It's Like That's' success, Jason Nevins had a go at remixing their 1987 hit, 'It's Tricky'. It only charted as a German import, spending one week at number 74. However, another remix of the same track, this time by Jacknife Lee, charted in 2003 and made number 20. Jason Nevins was back in the Top 10 in 2003 with 'I'm In Heaven' featuring Holly James.

On Wednesday October 30, 2002 two men were let into the second floor studio of a New York building where Jam Master Jay was recording. One of the men shot Jam in the head and he died instantly. It was the latest in a long line of pointless murders following the deaths of Tupac Shakur in 1996 and Notorious B.I.G. in 1997.

788 Boyzone
All That I Need

Label & Cat No.: **Polydor 5698732**
Producers: **Carl Sturken / Evan Rogers**
Writers: **Carl Sturken / Evan Rogers**
Date reached No.1: **2 May 1998**
Weeks at No.1: **1**

BOYZONE WENT THROUGH 1997 without a number one, albeit narrowly missing the top with three singles. The video for 'Isn't It A Wonder?' was shot in the Australian outback, while 'Picture Of You' came from the film *Mr. Bean* and had a comical video with Rowan Atkinson. Tracy Chapman's 'Baby Can I Hold You' was one side of their Christmas single, the other being a Stephen Gately solo, 'Shooting Star', from the cartoon film, *Hercules*.

Carl Sturken and Evan Rogers are a songwriting and production team from Connecticut who re-established Donny Osmond's career with the US number two, 'Soldier Of Love' in 1988. They had their own US number two as Rhythm Syndicate with 'P.A.S.S.I.O.N' in 1991. Since then they have worked with a multitude of performers including *NSYNC and Christina Aguilera and also worked on the *Love Actually* soundtrack and the US TV series, *American Idol* (2004). In 1998 they wrote, produced and largely played on 'All That I Need' for Boyzone. It was a strong ballad, very much in the Bee Gees tradition.

Around the time of its release, Ronan Keating's mother died from cancer, and he hated the media intrusion into a private matter. The day before Boyzone was to appear on *Top Of The Pops*, they held a press conference and, fed up with the questioning, Ronan walked out. He told the band he was taking a break and returned to Ireland. He took a holiday and the papers reported, erroneously, that he had suffered a breakdown. He returned to Boyzone a few days later and everything continued as before. But not for long.

789 All Saints
Under The Bridge / Lady Marmalade

Label & Cat No.: **London LONCD408**
Producers: **Nellee Hooper / Karl Gordon : Johnny Douglas / John Benson**
Writers: **Anthony Kiedis / Michael Balzary / John Frusciante / Chad Smith : Bob Crewe / Kenny Nolan**
Date reached No.1: **9 May 1998**
Weeks at No.1: **2 (in 2 runs)**

CONSIDERING THEIR VAST POPULARITY, it is surprising that the US rock band The Red Hot Chili Peppers are not featured in this book. In 1988 they achieved notoriety with their nude parody (except for the willy warmers) of The Beatles' *Abbey Road* sleeve. Four years later their single 'Under The Bridge', which they wrote themselves for their album *Blood Sugar Sex Magik*, made number 26, after being number two in the US. Their greatest commercial success in the UK was with 'By The Way', a number two in 2002, and their album of the same name was a number one. In 2004 they starred in a vast concert in Hyde Park.

Although the Chili Peppers are known for their hard rock/rap crossovers, 'Under The Bridge' is a mainstream classic which All Saints had no intention of covering until Karl Gordon suggested it. Their version included a sample of the Chili's record as well as 'Wild For Da Night' by Rampage.

Their cover of Labelle's 'Lady Marmalade' was deliberate, however. Patti LaBelle started recording in 1962 and nine years later formed an R&B group with space age outfits, Labelle, with Nona Hendryx and Sarah Dash. They recorded 'Lady Marmalade', a US number one and UK Top 20 entry, in 1974. The phrase, "Voulez-vous coucher avec moi ce soir (Do you want to sleep with me tonight?)", passed into the language, though Labelle had to change it to "Voulez-vous danser avec moi ce soir?" for US TV. No such trouble for All Saints, of course, and the revival was apt as Mel is part-French. The song, written in section by The Four Seasons' producer, Bob Crewe, and Kenny Nolan, was first recorded by Kenny's studio group, The Eleventh Hour.

Shaznay Lewis was never keen on All Saints recording cover versions and had to be persuaded to participate in the glorious, all-star celebration of Burt Bacharach's work, *One Amazing Night*, at the Hammerstein Ballroom in New York City. Nat took the lead on a spirited workout of '(There's) Always Something There To Remind Me', a third cover that surely would have been very successful as a single.

790 Aqua
Turn Back Time

Label & Cat No.: **Universal UMD 80490**
Producers: **Johnny Jam / Felipe Delgado / Soren Rasted / Claus Norreen**
Writers: **Soren Rashed / Claus Norreen**
Date Reached No.1: **16 May 1998**
Weeks at No.1: **1**

AQUA RETURNED FROM A SHORT TOUR of Australia in the summer of 1998 just in time to promote the third single from *Aquarium*, 'Turn Back Time', a ballad that highlighted the quality of Lene's voice.

Due for release in April, it was held back a month to coincide with the release of the film *Sliding Doors*, in which it was included. The film, starring Gwyneth Paltrow (with a convincing London accent), had an unusual story line about how random events can change lives.

Now that the British public were used to Aqua, Universal decided their next single would be the one they passed on in 1996, 'My Oh My'. They'll never know what would have happened if they had released it before 'Barbie Girl' but this time they were rewarded with a number six hit. 'Good Morning Sunshine' followed at the end of 1998 and Aqua spent the following year recording their next album *Aquarius*. When released in 2000 it only reached number 24, but the debut

All Saints offered a cool alternative to the frothy pop of The Spice Girls, left to right: Melanie Blatt, Nicole Appleton, Shaznay Lewis and Natalie Appleton

single, 'Cartoon Heroes' went to number seven. They took one further single from it, 'Around The World' which would become their final UK hit.

In late 2000 cracks were beginning to show and the band were on the verge of breaking up. They had maintained throughout that they had a special friendship but as Rene explained, "We had been together so much, I got the feeling we were almost too good friends. You should always keep a little distance from each other otherwise it becomes like a marriage." The following year, in their homeland, they performed a medley of their hits during the vote counting at the Eurovision Song Contest. Later the same year Lene and Soren, who had been dating secretly for months, married in Las Vegas.

791 The Tamperer featuring Maya
Feel It

Label & Cat No.: **Pepper 0530032**

Producers: **Falox (Giuliano Saglia)**

Writers: **Michael Jackson / Jackie Jackson / Steve Gittelman / Jim Dyke**

Date Reached No.1: **30 May 1998**

Weeks at No.1: **1**

When the Jackson 5 left Motown in 1976 and joined Epic Records as The Jacksons, only Jermaine remained with their original label and he had to wait four years for his first solo success in the UK when 'Let's Get Serious' made the Top 10 in 1980. Kenny Gamble and Leon Huff wrote the first five Jacksons' hits and after that Michael became the main songwriter. Jackie joined him on co-writing the Top 10 hit 'Shake Your Body (Down To The Ground)' and the follow-up 'Lovely One'. The next brother to have a go was Randy who co-wrote the back-to-back Top 10 hits 'Can You Feel It' and 'Walk Right Now'. So he would have been more than happy when an Italian dance act sampled the chimes and took it to number one.

Maya Dates had been a makeup artist in a strip club in her home state, Massachusetts, but when she was offered money to actually strip, she refused and left. Realising she wanted to be a performer she moved to Los Angeles and attended an open casting call for the Broadway show *Rent*. The Tamperer, who were Italian producers and keyboard players Alex Farolfi and Mario Fargetta, saw Maya in the show and asked her to join them as lead vocalist. Fargetta had already had some chart experience when he and The 49ers' lead singer, Anne-Marie Smith, took a dance version of John Miles' 'Music' into the Top 40 in 1993. They learned that Maya had already recorded a version of 'Feel It' but nothing happened with it. But they liked her more acappella version and knew they could do something with it.

'Feel It' was about infidelity and encouraged scorned women to confront their cheating partners and ask them what 'that hussy' would look like with a chimney on her. The Tamperer not only borrowed the tune from the Jacksons, they nicked half their title as well. As for the lyrics... no, they weren't original either. The hook line, "What will she look like with a chimney on her" was taken from 'Wanna Drop A House (On That Bitch)' by American dance act Urban Discharge featuring She. 'She' was actually a singer called Laura. They also forgot to credit Urban Discharge's composers, Steve Gittelman and Jim Dyke. Gittelman later became Maya's manager.

The Tamperer followed up their number one with the encouraging-titled 'If You Buy This Record Your Life Will Be Better', which made number three. Madonna's life was certainly better for it as they had sampled 'Material Girl' thus making her even more money. It was also the first time Madonna had allowed one of her tracks to be sampled.

Their third and final hit came in 2000 with 'Hammer To The Heart', reaching number six. At the same time, Maya was offered the part of Mary Magdelene in the Broadway revival of Andrew Lloyd Webber and Tim Rice's *Jesus Christ Superstar*, a role which in 1971 had made a star out of Hawaiian singer Yvonne Elliman.

792 B*Witched
C'est La Vie

Label & Cat No.: **Epic 6660532**

Producer: **Ray Hedges**

Writers: **Edele Lynch / Keale Lynch / Lindsay Armaou / Sinead O'Carroll / Ray Hedges / Tracy Ackerman / Martin Brannigan**

Date Reached No.1: **6 June 1998**

Weeks at No.1: **2**

Twins Edele and Keavy Lynch (born December 15, 1978), Lindsay Armouu (born in Athens, December 18, 1980) and Sinead O'Carroll (born May 14, 1973) were brought together when Sinead walked into a Dublin garage and befriended Keavy, who was a part-time mechanic there. Keavy then met Lindsay at a kick-boxing class and B★Witched, the youngest girl group to have a UK number one single, were born.

Lindsay and Sinead both learned piano from the age of seven. Edele and Keavy were inspired to write songs by their brother, Shane, a member of Boyzone. "All the stuff we write is based on our own experience," said Edele. "We believe in enjoying life to the max!"

Describing their sound as 'Irish hip-hop pop', the denim-clad B★Witched got their name from their producer Ray Hedges, best known for his work with Boyzone and Take That. Ray hadn't wanted to work with them initially as he thought there were too many girl bands around, but admitted that they would be 'bewitched' without him. "The asterisk was just to be pretty", explained Keavy.

Although they played several instruments between them, they made a conscious decision to let a backing band perform the music on record and during their concerts, preferring to put their energy into their dancing. As Keavy admitted, "We feel it would be a shame to put ourselves behind the instruments because we have so much energy. Besides, the best instrument anyone could ever have, and you can't exactly learn it, is a vocal cord. Anyone could learn to play an instrument." They felt it would take too long to play their own instruments on their recordings. "It takes a long, long time to write songs from scratch and then record the lead vocals and the backing vocals and instruments. We're not willing to take a year out just to record an album." Her twin Adele added, "Playing instruments is just a hobby. What we want to do is just sing and dance onstage."

The girls were received warmly Stateside and with tours of US shopping malls and supporting ★NSYNC, they were rewarded with a hit in the *Billboard* Top 100, where 'C'est La Vie' reached number nine.

At the time B★Witched were one of just a handful of artists who have entered the UK chart at number one with their debut single.

793 Baddiel, Skinner and Lightning Seeds
Three Lions '98

Label & Cat No.: **Epic 6660982**

Producers: **David Bascombe / Ian Broudie / Simon Rogers**

Writers: **David Baddiel / Frank Skinner / Ian Broudie**

Date reached No.1: **20 June 1998**

Weeks at No.1: **3**

After their number one with 'Three Lions', Lightning Seeds had further hits with 'Sugar Coated Iceberg' and 'You Showed Me' and then were asked to update 'Three Lions' for the 1998 World Cup. Again, England did not come through and the home team, France, won.

"We're like Spinal Tap," Broudie continues, "we've had hundreds of drummers, they keep appearing and disappearing." When they met up with Ringo Starr's son, Zak, he was playing with The Who who were not on the road at the time, so he joined them, playing drums on the remake of 'Three Lions'. Zak Starkey now divides his time between The Who and Oasis. According to Pete Townshend, "Keith [Moon] used to be a kind of musical godfather to him. He gave him his first drum kit, which I think is rather strange. It had nude women on it."

Lightning Seeds disbanded in 2000, and although a reunion tour has been mooted, it grows less likely as Ian Broudie has been producing hit singles and albums by The Coral and The Zutons.

794 Billie
Because We Want To

Label & Cat No.: **Innocent SINCD 2**

Producers: **Jim Marr / Wendy Page**

Writers: **Dion Rambo / Jacques Richmond / Wendy Page / Jim Marr**

Date reached No.1: **11 July 1998**

Weeks at No.1: **1**

The eldest of four children, Leanne Piper was born in Swindon on September 22, 1982, but her parents changed their minds about her name and she became Billie three weeks later. From the age of five, she wanted to be a singer and on holidays she would appear in talent contests. When she was seven, she became part of the Sixth Sense drama group in Swindon.

At the age of 12, Billie was awarded a half-scholarship at the Sylvia Young Theatre School in London. It was hard going "as you go from being the only person with ambition to a place where everyone is like that." Emma Bunton of The Spice Girls and Denise van Outen attended the school, and in Billie's year were Mattie Jay from Busted and Lee Ryan from Blue.

In 1996 Billie Piper had a small uncredited role in the film *Evita* and the following year she was chosen as the face of 1997 by the teenage magazine, *Smash Hits*. Hugh Goldsmith, the head of Virgin's Innocent label, liked the bubble-gum blowing youth and was also impressed by her singing talent. A team of stylists, songwriters and record producers was assembled to launch her. The cost was reported to be £1m, although Virgin would not confirm this figure.

The Los Angeles duo Dion Rambo and Jacques Richmond wrote a song of teenage rebellion, 'Because We Want To', which was produced in the UK by bassist Jim Marr and singer Wendy Page. The team go back to the Eighties with the band, Skin Games, which played important gigs but, largely because of their political content. The 1988 album, *Brilliant Shining*, was highly acclaimed. Wendy had a solo career but by the late Nineties, they were concentrating on writing and production. Wendy got a vocal credit on Tin Tin Out's hit single, 'Eleven To Fly'. On 'Because We Want To', Wendy arranged the backing vocals, singing some of them herself, and Jim played keyboards and bass and did the programming.

Many teenagers identified with the lyric of 'Because We Want To', and it can be compared to 'Don't Treat Me Like A Child', Helen Shapiro's first single, when she was 14. Helen, however, wants to be treated like an adult ("Don't think that I dream childish dreams"), while Billie wants to play loud music, dance all night and hold parties. The children in Helen's song were now the parents' in Billie's. 'Because We Want To' can also be seen as the junior version of The Spice Girls' declaration of girl power, 'Wannabe' (1996).

Neither sex nor drugs are mentioned in 'Because We Want To', but Billie went for the Lolita look in the video: a tousled-hair blonde with a bare midriff. Billie did a succession of live appearances before the single was released and also undertook a promotion tour around schools. (Times had certainly changed: in the early Sixties any teacher who even suggested Helen Shapiro might appear at their school would probably have been sacked!)

'Because We Want To' sold 80,000 in the first week and went straight in at number one. The paparazzi caught Billie drinking champagne to celebrate and the *Daily Mail* ran a full page feature entitled *Top Of The Poppets*. Comparing Billie with Helen Shapiro, it concluded, "A glance at the differing backgrounds of these two teenage starlets tells you a lot about how Britain has changed – little of it, many people will think, for the better." Billie had had a boyfriend for eight months and the feature commented without any evidence on their sex life. The comparison was unfair: Swindon's biggest star, Diana Dors, had been on the wild side of life since she was 13. Billie was annoyed by the feature and commented, "I don't think I am an immature 15-year-old. I know what I want out of life and I know what's stupid and what's sensible."

In 2004 Channel 4 presented a programme of the 100 Worst Pop Records and 'Because We Want To' was voted number seven, a harsh judgement for it doesn't belong with 'Agadoo', 'Mr. Blobby' and 'Orville's Song'. It was probably because the 13-year-olds who bought the record had grown up and didn't want to be reminded of their adolescence.

795 Another Level
Freak Me

Label & Cat No.: **Northwestside 74321582362**

Producer: **Fitzgerald Scott**

Writers: **Roy Murray / Keith Sweat**

Date Reached No.1: **18 July 1998**

Weeks at No.1: **1**

NEW YORK-BORN R&B SINGER/ songwriter Keith Sweat first arrived on the music scene in 1988 with his US Top five single 'I Want Her'. Despite airplay on UK dance shows it only reached number 26 here and would be the biggest of his eight UK hits. In 1991 Louise Ferguson, the wife of Keith's road manager Lonnie, saw a Georgia-based R&B group called Silk singing and invited them to her house to audition for her husband. The day they arrived there was a barbecue in progress and Keith was a guest. He heard them sing and was so impressed with their smooth harmonies that he wrote 'Freak Me' for them and the result was a US number one single. He also asked them to support him on his next tour.

Another Level were discovered by the American rapper Jay-Z. Jay-Z had been signed to Roc-A-Fella's UK subsidiary label, Northwestside Records, in 1997 by Nick Raphael and was delighted when he heard Another Level's demos. Another Level were Dane Bowers (born 1979), Wayne Williams (born 1977), Mark Baron (born 1974) and Bobak Kianoush (born 1978) and are all from London. "We are not a boy band," insisted Wayne. "There's been a huge gap in British pop as far as R&B is concerned but it's on the rise now. R&B is part of all cultures and we want to blow it up."

Their first single, the soulful and upbeat 'Be Alone No More' crashed into the chart at number six and featured a rap by Jay-Z. For the follow-up Jay-Z suggested a cover of a 1993 US hit 'Freak Me', with the lyric "I wanna be your nasty man, I wanna make your body scream." It was a sexually suggestive song which struck a chord with the young CD-buying public and won them Best Newcomer award at the 1998 MOBO Awards.

The third single, 'Guess I Was A Fool' went to number five and coincided with the release of their debut album *Another Level*. One further single, 'I Want You For Myself', featuring The Wu-Tang Clan's Ghostface Killah, was lifted and it went to number two.

In 1999 they were asked by London's Capital Radio to record a song for their annual charity, Help A London Child. They decided on a cover of Simply Red's 'Holding Back The Years', which was issued as a double A-side with a remixed version of 'Be Alone No More', but it only reached number 11. By now, Wayne had had enough and quit the band, leaving them as a trio. They had three further Top 10 hits with 'From The Heart' from *Notting Hill*, 'Summertime' and 'Bomb Diggy, which was used as the theme for the Channel 4 show *North Hollywood High*.

Dane Bowers embarked on a solo career and when he left the group broke up. Dane returned in 2000 with Truesteppers on the track 'Buggin', which reached number six. Later the same year came the second hit 'Out Of Your Mind' which got to number two and featured Dane's friend, Victoria Beckham.

In 2003 Wayne released two singles 'He Can't Love You' and 'All About The Sex' both of which missed the chart completely. Bobak and Mark have yet to start their solo career, so it looks like, at the moment, they are on another level.

796 Jamiroquai
Deeper Underground

Label & Cat No.: **Sony S2 6662182**

Producers: **Jay Kay / Toby Smith**

Writers: **Jay Kay / Toby Smith**

Date Reached No.1: **25 July 1998**

Weeks at No.1: **1**

GENERALLY CONSIDERED UNLUCKY, number 13 proved otherwise for Jamiroquai. Like Eternal a year earlier, both acts scored their first UK chart topper with their 13th hit single. With the chart becoming more volatile, and with songs peaking the week they enter and going into freefall theafter, registering their first number one so far into their career was unusual.

Named after a Native American Indian tribe, Jamiroquai were the permanently hat-wearing lead singer Jason Kay, often known as Jay Kay and whose mother, Karen, was a nightclub jazz singer, Toby Smith (keyboards), Stuart Zender (bass), Glenn Nightingale (guitar) Wallis Buchanan (didgeridoo) and Nick Van Gelder (drums). They formed in 1991 in London and with a chill out jazz sound and Jason's vocals reminiscent of Stevie Wonder, they landed a deal with the Acid Jazz label after Jay took a demo of what was to become their first single, 'When You Gonna Learn', to Kiss FM in London who played it a few times. They also employed an extensive horn and brass section.

'When You Gonna Learn?' became a favourite on the jazz and dance stations and dented the chart in October 1992. With London-based acts like Brand New Heavies and The James Taylor Quartet also making a name, Jamiroquai were snapped up by Sony and took the London acid jazz scene to a global audience.

Their next single, 'Too Young To Die' made the Top 10 and the debut album, *Emergency On Planet Earth* topped the chart. The next album in 1994, *The Return Of The Space Cowboy* saw the next three hit singles 'Stillness In Time', Half The Man' and 'Space Cowboy' all reach the Top 20. The same year Derrick McKenzie replaced Van

Jamiroquai, alias Jason Kay, is as well known for his hats, cars and partying as he is for his music

Gelder and Simon Katz replaced Nightingale.

In 1996 they released what was to be their most successful album *Travelling Without Moving*. It crashed into the chart at number two and the first three singles, 'Virtual Insanity', 'Cosmic Girl' and 'Alright' all made the Top 10.

Work had begun on the next album, *Synkronized* but half way through, Zender announced he was leaving the band and Jay scrapped all the tracks that he had co-written to start afresh. Zender began dating All Saint Melanie Blatt and Jay started seeing TV presenter Denise van Outen. Nick Fyffe was his replacement and before they began again, they were offered the chance to record a track for the forthcoming remake of *Godzilla*, starring Matthew Broderick.

In 1999 Jamiroquai released *Synkronized* which went straight to number one. The first single from it, 'Canned Heat', peaked at number four. In 2000 Katz left and was replaced by Rob Harris. With a few changes, which included Jay dropping the wind section and letting Buchanan go, work began on their new album, *A Funk Odyssey*. The following year they teamed up with Jools Holland for the hit single 'I'm In The Mood For Love'. *A Funk Odyssey* was released and went to number one with the first single, 'Little L' peaking at number four.

Toby Smith left the line-up in 2002 and began working with a new UK artist, Jamie Scott. His replacement was Matt Johnson. In 2004, after a two-year hiatus, Jamiroquai were ready to release their next album, *Dynamite*.

797 The Spice Girls
Viva Forever

Label & Cat No.: **Virgin VSCDT 1692**

Producers: **Richard Stannard / Matt Rowe**

Writers: **Victoria Adams / Melanie Brown / Emma Bunton / Melanie Chisholm / Geri Halliwell / Richard Stannard / Matt Rowe**

Date reached No.1: **1 August 1998**

Weeks at No.1: **2**

IN 1998 THE CRACKS WERE APPEARING in The Spice Girls. Sacking manager Simon Fuller created discord within the group with Geri and Mel B squabbling, usually over leadership, and Geri missing appearances. Although the others did their best to disguise the fact, Geri was the weakest stage performer, and while she was great at interviews, she was exposed when the group performed live.

Tarnished by overexposure on the merchandising front, the aptly named, Motown-sounding 'Stop', ended their run of number one hits, peaking at number two – a relative flop after six consecutive number ones. The worldwide sales of their first album, *Spice*, were 18 million, but *Spiceworld* managed only 12 million.

At the end of May 1998, Geri failed to appear with The Spice Girls on *The Lottery Show* and subsequent European dates. She left the group due to 'personal differences' and The Spice Girls would continued as a foursome.

The next single, 'Viva Forever', from the *Spiceworld* album, a slow ballad with several twists and turns, had already been scheduled. Their equivalent of Madonna's 'La Isla Bonita', a cartoon promotional video with Geri had already been made, so it was allowed to stand. Geri 's departure made little difference to ticket sales and the tour concluded with two huge shows at Wembley Stadium with a combined audience of 120,000.

798 Boyzone
No Matter What

Label & Cat No.: **Polydor 5675672**

Producers: **Jim Steinman / Andrew Lloyd Webber / Nigel Wright**

Writers: **Andrew Lloyd Webber / Jim Steinman**

Date reached No.1: **15 August 1998**

Weeks at No.1: **3**

"WHO ARE YOU?" ASKS HAYLEY MILLS, stumbling upon the escaped murderer. "Jesus Christ!" exclaims Alan Bates, thus setting in motion the touching, amusing and largely unsentimental story of mistaken identity in the 1961 film, *Whistle Down The Wind*. The film was based on a novel by Mary Hayley Bell, the wife of actor John Mills. Andrew Lloyd Webber loved the film and thought it would make a good stage musical, transferring it to the American 'Bible belt' with lyrics from Jim Steinman, who had been associated with Meat Loaf and Bonnie Tyler.

As usual, Lord Lloyd-Webber of Sydmonton planned an all-star album before the production was staged. Coincidentally, Boyzone had asked for a song when they met and they were surprised when he offered them 'No Matter What'. The uplifting song is performed by the children in the musical to assuage the pressures they're under, but the same lyrics work in a different setting as a love song.

'No Matter What' was not only Boyzone's biggest single, but also the biggest-selling record by an Irish act in the UK. The other hit from the musical was the title song, performed by Tina Arena. The musical became a long-running West End hit and has since toured the UK.

After four months, the Boyzone single ended its chart run in dramatic fashion. The band wanted to release 'I Love The Way You Love Me' for the Christmas market and Polydor felt that its chances would be improved if 'No Matter What' was no longer around. As the chart only recorded sales of singles over £1.79, the price was dropped to £1.78. Lloyd Webber and his former partner Tim Rice sent an indignant letter to *The Times*, which stated, "The company has made a highly popular record almost invisible in the hope that frustrated record buyers will unthinkingly hand over their cash for the next recording." No matter what they tell us, no matter what they say, 'I Love The Way You Love Me' made number two.

In 2001 Sir John and Lady Mills renewed their marriage vows in a church ceremony they had promised themselves since their registry office wedding during wartime in 1941. Their grandchild and Hayley's son, Crispin, enjoyed several hit records with his group, Kula Shaker, and as Lady Mills had a percentage of the musical, Sir John quipped, "I'm never going to get divorced now.

799 Manic Street Preachers
If You Tolerate This Your Children Will Be Next

Label & Cat No.: **Epic 6663452**

Producer: **Dave Eringa**

Writers: **Nick Jones / James Dean Bradfield / Sean Moore**

Date Reached No.1: **5 September 1998**

Weeks at No.1: **1**

IT TOOK THE MANIC STREET PREACHERS almost 20 single releases to reach the top. They came close with a cover of 'Theme From M.A.S.H. (Suicide Is Painless)' (7, 1992) and the anthemic 'A Design For Life' (2, 1996). All hailing from the South Wales mining town of Blackwood, they formed in 1988.

The Manics (as they are known) were originally named Betty Blue and comprised friends James Dean Bradfield (vocals/guitar), Nicky Wire (born Nick Jones, bass) and James' cousin, Sean Moore (drums). Richey James (born Edwards) – originally their driver – joined later on rhythm guitar.

Their first single, 'Suicide Alley', was funded with their dole money. Richey's involvement was designing the sleeve, as he was still driving them to gigs and not yet a fully-fledged member of the band. (These days, 'Suicide Alley' exchanges hands for up to £800.)

After Richey joined he become notorious for two incidents. The first followed a gig in Norwich in 1991 when Radio 1 DJ (then an *NME* journalist) Steve Lamacq, interviewed the group, commenting that they were 'just a re-hash of The Clash' and said "some people might regard you as just not for real." The self-mutilating, self-loathing guitarist then took a razor blade and carved '4 REAL' into his left arm. The wound required 17 stitches. The second occurred on February 1, 1995, two weeks before the band was due to begin a US promotional tour, when a troubled Richey checked out of a London hotel. This was to be his final incisive sighting; shortly afterwards, his car was found abandoned near a popular suicide spot, the Aust Services close to the Severn Bridge. His credit cards, anti-depressant pills and passport were found in his Cardiff flat.

It took a great deal of courage for the remaining members to play on as a trio, but they were given the blessing by Richey's family, and in 1996 they came back with their biggest-selling album up to that point, *Everything Must Go*. It won a multitude of awards, including two Brits for Best Album and Best Band.

This Is My Truth Tell Me Yours was released two years later. It was the first of their albums to sell a million, and topped the UK chart for three weeks. Apart from this chart topper, it also contained a further three hit singles, 'The Everlasting' (11), 'You Stole The Sun From My Heart' (5) and 'Tsunami' (11).

'If You Tolerate This Your Children Will Be Next' was inspired by a poster made famous by volunteers of the International Brigade who fought the fascists during the Spanish Civil War of the Thirties. The lyric was "inspired by Orwell's *Homage To Catalonia* and The Clash singing 'Spanish Bombs'," explained Nicky Wire. "It is meant to be a warning – a need for awareness in the modern world – of knowing your history, i.e. the International Brigade's bravery and courage."

The Manic Street Preachers have always been a popular touring band and have performed concerts all over the world. In February 2001 they became the first Western rock group to play in Cuba. Fidel Castro was in the audience.

Sightings of Richey are featured in the tabloids from time to time, from being seen drinking in a Canary Islands bar to shopping at an outdoor market in Goa. In March 2002 two fishermen in Gwent made the grim discovery of a pair of feet, still in training shoes, that had been washed up in the Severn Estuary. "We were in the studio and on the first day, the headline of the paper said 'Rock Star's feet found in River Severn'. They'd found this pair of trainers with bones in. Bizarrely, I knew by the make of trainers that Richey would never wear something so bad," declared Nicky. Richey James Edwards is missing, presumed dead, although his file is still open due to the insistence of his family. The rest of the band has a trust fund for him containing his 25% share of all royalties.

800 All Saints
Bootie Call

Label & Cat No.: **London LONCD 415**

Producer: **Karl Gordon**

Writers: **Shaznay Lewis / Karl Gordon**

Date reached No.1: **12 September 1998**

Weeks at No.1: **1**

ALL SAINTS BEGAN AS THE COOL alternative to The Spice Girls but, like the Spices, they found themselves losing their musical credibility as their love life and sometimes ladette behaviour was sensationalised by the tabloids. The most publicised romance was between Nicole Appleton and Robbie Williams and Nicole, much to her regret, was persuaded to have an abortion for the sake of her career. Robbie Williams himself was against this and even recorded 'Grace', a song for his unborn baby whom he had already named.

Natalie Appleton's romance with Jamie Theakston, on the other hand, was over when she was alleged to have beaten him up. In her autobiography *Together*, she denies this although she admits she did throw a tub of moisturiser at him. Jamie had allegedly dropped his trousers for Mariah Carey, but Nat wasn't entirely innocent as she had had a fling with Kevin Spacey.

There was a war of nerves within the group. According to the Appletons, Shaznay Lewis saw herself as the leader and was supported by Mel Blatt with Nic and Nat relegated, for the most part, to backing vocals. At one stage, Nic left the band and as Mel had taken leave to have her baby, Nat and Shaznay, never the best of friends, had to tour the US with two members of Chaka Khan's backing group. For all their rivalry, the Appletons never dissed Shaznay's songwriting and 'Bootie Call' was written with their regular producer, Karl Gordon. This dance track was recorded at Universal Studios in Hollywood and included the line, "You can bring it on with the rough stuff."

All Saints tried for their fourth number one in a year with the bitter-sweet 'War Of Nerves', but it only managed number seven and the Christmas number one went to The Spice Girls.

801 Robbie Williams
Millennium

Label & Cat No.: **Chrysalis CDCHS 5099**

Producers: **Guy Chambers / Steve Power**

Writers: **Robbie Williams / Guy Chambers / Leslie Bricusse / John Barry**

Date reached No.1: **19 September 1998**

Weeks at No.1: **1**

Was it Gary Barlow or was it Robbie Williams who most wanted to be George Michael? Robbie said as much by recording 'Freedom' as his first solo single: he appreciated George's musicianship and also the way he confronted Sony. Robbie's first album, *Life Thru A Lens*, offered his reflections on the excesses of fame as well as containing a venomous, hidden track directed at his careers master. 'Old Before I Die' and 'Lazy Days' were hit singles, but the album's sales did not go into the stratosphere until 'Angels' was issued as a single.

'Angels', an Elton-styled ballad, spent 13 weeks in the Top 10, reaching number four and selling 800,000 copies. Although the album did nothing at the Brits in February 1998, Robbie gave an electrifying performance of *Full Monty* material with Tom Jones. The following year his Brits and Ivors started coming.

The 1998 album, *I've Been Expecting You*, was about his relationship with Nicole Appleton of All Saints. Robbie invited Neil Tennant to sing backing vocals on 'No Regrets' and announced he had written a song in the style of The Pet Shop Boys, 'Millennium'. The song sampled John Barry's theme for *You Only Live Twice*, and at the time Robbie was named as a potential James Bond.

'Millennium' may have a Sean Connery feel but the lyric is about the pointlessness of life and his own, uninhibited lifestyle: "We all enjoy the madness 'cause we know we're going to fade away." 'Millennium' was released 15 months before the celebrations and was played incessantly at the turn of the century. Despite the hit records, 'Millennium' is the only number one with a James Bond connection.

In his autobiography, *Feel*, Robbie tells of being with a hooker in Santa Monica and telling her that he played for Liverpool FC. His cover was blown when the video for 'Millennium' was shown on TV.

802 Mel B featuring Missy 'Misdemeanor' Elliott
I Want You Back

Label & Cat No.: **Virgin VSCDT 1716**

Producers: **Missy Elliott / Gerard Thomas / Donald Holmes**

Writers: **Missy Elliott / Gerard Thomas / Donald Holmes**

Date reached No.1: **26 September 1998**

Weeks at No.1: **1**

Frankie Lymon's story is fraught with drama but *Why Do Fools Fall In Love* took place after his death and was about various women fighting for his assets. Instead of being packed with doo-wop classics, it had a contemporary soundtrack, organised by the female rapper, Missy 'Misdemeanor' Elliott. She was collaborating with Destiny's Child, Mace, Next, Timbaland and Usher, and she recognised Mel B's talent in The Spice Girls. It was the first time that one of them would be working independently of the others and they approved her move.

Mel B had one afternoon in New York to record 'I Want You Back' for the soundtrack, but she was unhappy with the lyric: "I didn't like the fact that this woman was a complete wreck and the only way she could express herself was by swearing." There and then, Missy rewrote the words and asked Mel to ad-lib an ending, which she did in her Leeds accent.

'I Want You Back' had a memorable video with Mel B looking like a tiger with black stripes down her legs. Her partner, Jimmy Gulzar, whom she had seen dancing in a cage in a gay club in Amsterdam, was also featured. They were married the week the single was number one and she started calling herself Mel G. Their daughter, Phoenix Chi, was born in February 1999, but the marriage lasted only 15 months. Mel poured her feelings into another song, 'Tell Me', a Top 10 hit in October 2000.

Why Do Fools Fall In Love? was no *La Bamba* and Frankie Lymon's story went straight to video. The record did give Missy 'Misdemeanor' Elliott her first UK Top 10 entry. Mel's second solo single, 'Word Up', also came from a film, *Austin Powers – The Spy Who Shagged Me*, but by stalling at number 14, it became the first record associated with a Spice Girl not to make the Top 10.

803 B*Witched
Rollercoaster

Label & Cat No.: **Epic 6664752**

Producer: **Ray Hedges**

Writers: **Edele Lynch / Keale Lynch / Lindsay Armaou Sinead O'Carroll / Ray Hedges / Tracy Ackerman / Martin Brannigan**

Date Reached No.1: **3 October 1998**

Weeks at No.1: **2**

Within a few short months, B*witched were bona fide popstars and their second release, 'Rollercoaster' reached the top spot like its predecessor.

"We're more interested in bringing joy to people's lives than becoming incredibly famous," claimed the girls. "We want B*Witched to be

At the time he left the group, few punters would have put their money on Robbie Williams becoming the most successful refugee from Take That

nothing less than a celebration of being alive."

They co-wrote nine of the dozen songs on their debut, self-titled album. When released in the UK it reached number three. Stateside it got to a respectable number 12.

B*Witched's brand of pop, which included an occasional tin whistle or fiddle, was appealing to the masses. Coming hot on the heels of The Spice Girls, the girl group admitted, "They opened the door for other girl groups. They basically showed the world that girls could do it too."

However, it was not so much 'girl power' as 'tomboy power'. Sinead explained, "They've kind of named us the first tomboy band. It's just the fact that Keavy was training as a mechanic and I did kickboxing and we all dress real casual. To wear a pair of high heels and a short skirt would be inappropriate."

Lindsay added, "We always, always, always wear denim. Denim's quite tomboyish. It's casual and it's uniformity between us and it looks good as a band."

804 Billie
Girlfriend

Label & Cat No.: **Innocent SIN CD3**

Producers: **Jim Marr / Wendy Page**

Writers: **Dion Rambo / Jacques Richmond**

Date reached No.1: **17 October 1998**

Weeks at No.1: **1**

The late Nineties was a fruitful era for young stars. Hanson hit the top with 'MMMBop' and a trio of girls from Manchester, Cleopatra, had a run of hits – 'Cleopatra's Theme', 'Life Ain't Easy' and 'I Want You Back', all in 1998. Billie the Kid, now 16, became the first female artist to go to number one with her first two singles. The dance song, 'Girlfriend', was by the same team as the first but it was more conventional and simply had Billie longing to be somebody's partner.

Billie was growing up away from her parents as they had to look after the rest of the family in Swindon. She went on the road with a chaperon and a private tutor. She split with her boyfriend and then had an on-off relationship with Ritchie Neville from 5ive.

Naturally, Billie wanted to be seen as more adult and possibly this affected her record sales. Her singles, 'Then She Wants' and 'Honey To The Bee', both stuck at number three and the album, called *Honey To The B,* stuck at number 14. She was featured on a Top 10 charity single, 'Thank ABBA For The Music', with B*Witched, Cleopatra, Tina Cousins and Steps. She had her own TV special, *Billie Wants You!*, and, in a sign that she was growing up, posed for the lad's mags, *FHM* and *Loaded*. But her main problem was the advent of Britney Spears in 1999: right from the start, Britney seemed much cooler than Billie.

805 Spacedust
Gym And Tonic

Label & Cat No.: **East West EW 188CD**

Producers: **Paul Glancey / Duncan Glasson**

Writer: **Thomas Bangalter**

Date Reached No.1: **24 October 1998**

Weeks at No.1: **1**

In January 1983 American actress Jane Fonda released the double album *Jane Fonda's Workout Record*, which consisted of exercise routines to the music of The Jacksons, REO Speedwagon, Linda Clifford and Billy Ocean. Disc one was for beginners and disc two was for the advanced fitness fanatic. It reached number seven and spent almost a year on the chart. The follow-up, *Jane Fonda's Workout Record: New and Improved*, arrived 18 months later.

In 1997 a Parisian nightclub DJ Christophe Le Friant, known as Chris The French Kiss, decided to record an album of house music. Chris, who was 23, ran his own Yellow Productions label and oversaw the sessions himself. He recorded the album *Paradise* and released it under the name Bob Sinclar, a variant on Bob St. Clair, a character played by Jean-Paul Belmondo in the James Bond spoof, *Le Magnifique* (1974). He borrowed, without permission, some samples from the Jane Fonda album for a track called 'Gym Tonic' and asked Daft Punk's keyboard player, Thomas Bangalter, who had written the song, to remix it. Bangalter's father had also had chart success in the Eighties as the writer of Ottowan's 1981 hit 'D.I.S.C.O.'. The track started receiving club play across Europe, especially in Ibiza and Chris was advised to have the track issued as a single, but Bangalter wouldn't allow his mix to be released. One reason may have been that he was already in the chart with his own track 'Music Sounds Better With You' under the name Stardust. It was a blessing in disguise as Jane Fonda had sought legal action for a breach of copyright.

When bootleg versions started appearing, two English producers, Paul Glancey and Duncan Glasson, who had first met in 1980 whilst filling freezers at Bejam, decided to do a cover. The pair had been working together since 1992 and had recorded under various guises including Dual, V Point, Aquarius and The Swimmer. As Paul recalled, "There was no real reason for another change of name, but we picked Spacedust after old sweets that used to explode in your mouth."

"We recorded a demo remix of 'Gym Tonic' as a possible remix to the original Bob Sinclar version," Paul remembered. "We had been remixing lots of pop projects at the time and thought that this one would be a good one to get a remix name on. We submitted it to Stuart Dashwood, the A&R man at East West Records and when he heard that Thomas Bangalter had blocked Bob Sinclar's version, he suggested that it would be a good idea to release ours. All I can remember about the girl on the recording is her name was Laurel and she was a Californian," remembered Duncan. "Paul picked her from an agency via East West after listening to four or five Jane Fonda soundalikes over the phone. She came in, read the lines and was paid £500 and off she went."

Paul and Duncan re-recorded it and slightly amended the title to 'Gym And Tonic' and it entered the chart at number one after selling 66,000 copies. "We were erroneously credited as the writers on the CD," admitted Paul. "Thomas wrote it and we just covered it." At the time they wished to remain anonymous, which Paul later explained, "I got a lot of grief from the dance press because our cover incensed a lot of the 'purist' dance journalists." The song spent eight weeks on the chart and the follow-up, 'Let's Get Down', which sampled Chic's 'I Want Your Love' reached number 20.

Four different girls were used for the promotion of the single. "The girl who mimed on *Top Of The Pops* is different from the girl who mimed in the video and different again from the girl we used at the club pa's. And all three were not the same girl who actually sang on the track. That always amused me," admitted Paul.

Paul still records under various names including Dirty Funker, Solaris, Grand Canyon and Red Kult. Duncan remixed many tracks for Paul Oakenfold and his Perfecto label under the pseudonyms Trailer Trash, Kowalski, Trash and Dash and Sabata.

806 Cher
Believe

Label & Cat No.: **WEA WEA 175CD**

Producers: **Mark Taylor / Brian Rawling**

Writers: **Brian Higgins / Paul Barry / Steve Torch / Matt Gray / Stuart McLennen / Timothy Powell**

Date reached No.1: **31 October 1998**

Weeks at No.1: **7**

ALTHOUGH CHER'S ADDICTION TO plastic surgery rivals that of Michael Jackson, she has never become the figure of fun that Jackson has, largely because she has a great sense of humour and can laugh at herself. In her fifties, she can appear scantily clad in the most tackily designed dresses and still look great. You can, if you wish, buy replicas of them on cher.com. Storage space for her wigs apparently takes up most of the third floor of Cher Castle in Malibu.

Cher combines the stadium sparkle of Tina Turner, the constant reinvention of Madonna and the kitsch of Dolly Parton with family dramas that put the Osbournes to shame. Her daughter, Chastity, is a lesbian activist, who wrote a savage book about her parents, Sonny and Cher, in *Family Outing*. Cher accepted the criticism and appeared on *Oprah* to help promote it. Her son with Gregg Allman, Elijah Blue, played in Deadsy, a band strongly influenced by the black magic practitioner, Aleister Crowley.

Cher was signed to the British arm of WEA and worked with UK musicians and producers. In 1998 she decided to pursue a similar Eurodisco feel to Madonna's 'Ray Of Light' and teamed up with the producers, Mark Taylor and Brian Rawling. Their electronic disco beat could be heard throughout her album, *Believe*, and there was a credit, "Vocal effects by Metrovision". Cher's voice had been put through a vocoder, very similar to what Neil Young had been using on his ground-breaking album, *Trans* (1980). Cher said of the single, 'Believe', "It was just a little fun thing, nothing deep, but my hopes for it were high."

'Believe' became the highest selling single by a female artist in the UK and won Cher her first Grammy. The accompanying album sold 10 million copies worldwide. The follow-up single, 'Strong Enough', written by Mark Taylor and Paul Barry, again featured the distorted vocal and disco thump and was another international hit. Since then she has made the UK Top 20 with a revival of 'All Or Nothing' and another Taylor / Rawling production, 'The Music's No Good Without You'.

At 52 Cher became the oldest solo female artist to top the UK charts but, of course, parts of her were much younger. In 2004 her farewell tour came to the UK with a series of massive stadium concerts. Her career, however, is bound to continue in other ways. It is, for example, a few years since Cher's last film, *Tea With Mussolini* (1999), in which she held her own against Judi Dench, Joan Plowright and Maggie Smith in a story about the director Franco Zeffirelli's wartime experiences.

In January 2005 this American Icon was still treading the boards on the ongoing Farewell Tour that visited the biggest US arenas.

807 B*Witched
To You I Belong

Label & Cat No.: **Epic 6667712**

Producer: **Ray Hedges**

Writers: **Edele Lynch / Keavy Lynch / Lindsay Armaou / Sinead O'Carroll / Ray Hedges / Martin Brannigan**

Date Reached No.1: **19 December 1998**

Weeks at No.1: **1**

B*WITCHED ENDED 1998 WITH THEIR third consecutive chart topper, 'To You I Belong', narrowly missing out on the Christmas number one to The Spice Girls.

'To You I Belong', a sensitive ballad, which was written for their close-knit families, showed how far their songwriting had progressed. "You can get inspiration any time of day," said Edele. "You could be sitting on a plane and maybe get inspiration for a melody or some lyric. Generally, what our music is about is just experiences that we have had or seen around us from other people. If we've got a message in our music, it's basically, 'live your life to the full.' That's essentially what we're about."

Dubbed by some members of the British press, 'The Nolans in Nike', B*Witched continued to perform as a foursome, touring the UK, the Far East and all 50 states to considerable success, although this single didn't chart in America, unlike their previous two, 'C'est La Vie' (9) and 'Rollercoaster' (67).

Reflecting on their achievements, Sinead said, "We just seemed to hit it off, both musically and socially. But we didn't want to hurry anything. We knew we had something good going, but we wanted to take our time with it. Between the four of us, we had all these different musical influences – everything from hip hop to pop, from soul to traditional Irish folk. And we wanted to take all our influences, absorb them, and create something that was entirely our own."

Added Keavy, "We don't really think about

limits, we're just busy enjoying the ride at the moment. We totally believe in the power of pop music to raise people's spirits. If our music can do that, then we're achieving our ambition."

And for most of the final 18 months of the last century, it appeared they had.

808 The Spice Girls
Goodbye

Label & Cat No.: **Virgin VSCDT 1721**

Producers: **Richard Stannard / Matt Rowe**

Writers: **Victoria Adams / Melanie Brown / Emma Bunton / Melanie Chisholm / Geri Halliwell / Richard Stannard / Matt Rowe**

Date reached No.1: **26 December 1998**

Weeks at No.1: **1**

THIS WAS THE FIRST SPICE GIRLS single not to come from a current album, but that was only because the four remaining girls – Emma, Victoria and the two Mels – were so tied up with their private lives that they hadn't got round to making a new one. Victoria was now married to the England striker, David Beckham, and they were living their lives as a soap opera.

Although The Spice Girls denied it at the time, 'Goodbye' is regarded as The Fad Four's farewell to Geri, and they were right. The song was written during sessions for the *Spiceworld* album while Geri was still in the group and recorded in Nashville while they were touring in America. Richard Stannard recalls: "They were absolutely knackered." It was one of the final sessions for the Stannard and Rowe partnership as Richard was moving to Dublin and opening his own studio there.

'Goodbye' was The Spice Girls' third consecutive Christmas number one: not bad for a song which had been left over. It was included on their third and final album, ironically called *Forever* in 2000. Mel B and Victoria were pregnant and so most of the promotion was undertaken by Mel C and Emma.

809 Chef
Chocolate Salty Balls (P.S. I Love You)

Label & Cat No.: **Columbia 6667982**

Producer: **Rick Rubin**

Writer: **Trey Parker**

Date reached No.1: **2 January 1999**

Weeks at No.1: **1**

FRITZ THE CAT (1972) IDENTIFIED THE market for adult cartoon features, mainly students, but it wasn't until the TV series, *South Park*, in the Nineties that the medium became really popular. *South Park* was created by Trey Parker and Matt Stone and recounted the exploits of the 10-year-olds Stan, Kyle, Cartman and Kenny. Going against all conventions, Kenny was killed in most of the episodes, only to reappear in the next. The script was packed with vulgarities, sexual humour and comic violence, never more so than in the film, *South Park: Bigger, Longer And Uncut*, in which the USA wages war on Canada. The film is noted for its grotesque parody of Disney musicals with Satan's 'Up There'.

Isaac Hayes played Jerome McElroy, otherwise known as Chef, in *South Park*. Hayes had had a career of great heights and lows. In the mid-Sixties, he was part of the house band at Stax Records in Memphis and he and his parter, David Porter, wrote and produced Sam & Dave's 'Hold On I'm Comin'' and 'Soul Man' and Carla Thomas' 'B-A-B-Y'. He also played organ on Otis Redding's staggering treatment of 'Try A Little Tenderness' (1967), which only made number 46 but is now regarded as one of the greatest records ever made.

Smashed at a party at Stax, Isaac Hayes went to the electric piano and talked his way through some standards. This led to some classic albums, notably *Hot Buttered Soul* (1969), in which he spent over 10 minutes on sensual interpretations of 'Walk On By' and 'By The Time I Get To Phoenix'. "It was like I was preaching a sermon," said Isaac, "and when I did them in a club, I found that some people were crying during the songs." Nicknamed Black Moses, Isaac in his gold chains and medallions became a major concert attraction.

Much to his annoyance, Hayes was turned down in favour of Richard Roundtree for the title role in the film, *Shaft*, but he wrote the score, including the trendsetting *Theme From Shaft*, thus becoming the first black musician to win an Oscar. Hayes was a star at the festival, *Wattstax*, and he turned to contemporary sounds with the hit single, 'Disco Connection', in 1976, but by then his musical approach had been copied very successfully by Barry White.

The following year Isaac Hayes was declared bankrupt. "I blame myself," he says now, "I was too preoccupied with producing, arranging and performing and I put blind trust in people I shouldn't have. By the time I realised what was happening, it was too late to reverse the process. I wasn't there the day they auctioned off all my stuff. I was in Atlanta working on a new LP. I knew I hadn't lost everything as I still had my talent."

In 1980 Isaac Hayes did well in a menacing role in the thriller, *Escape From New York*, and he re-established himself with albums, concerts and other, less memorable films. His earlier records were sampled by rap artists: "I take it as a great compliment and a validation of my work, but I will not give permission if the song promotes violence or insults women. I can't stand records that call girls 'bitches' or 'whores'."

Isaac Hayes had written music for the film, *Beavis And Butt-Head Do America* (1996), so landing the role of Chef in *South Park* was a natural progression. The lyric of the saucy 'Chocolate Salty Balls (P.S. I Love You)' was a recipe packed with innuendo: "Oooo, Suck on my chocolate salty balls, Put 'em in your mouth, and suck 'em, They're on fire, baby." The record was produced by Rick Rubin, who was noted for his work with The Beastie Boys and, in his later years, Johnny Cash. Its success led to *Chef Aid: The South Park Album* and a celebrity book edited by Isaac Hayes, *Cooking With Heart And Soul*. One of the participants, John Travolta, offers 'Royale with Cheese'.

Isaac Hayes had a cameo appearance in *Blues Brothers 2000*, but the film didn't rekindle the excitement of the original. He regularly appears in concert and does humanitarian work for The Isaac Hayes Foundation. In 2004 he did much to promote Memphis for the fiftieth anniversary of Elvis Presley recording 'That's All Right (Mama)' and although he still performs, he leads an active family life with 11 children and 16 grandchildren.

810 Steps
Heartbeat / Tragedy

Label & Cat No.: **Jive 0519142**

Producers: **Dan Frampton / Pete Waterman : Mark Topham / Karl Twigg / Pete Waterman**

Writers: **Jackie James : Barry Gibb / Maurice Gibb/ Robin Gibb**

Date Reached No.1: **9 January 1999**

Weeks at No.1: **1**

A FRIEND OF PETE WATERMAN'S, TIM Byrne, was managing a new band called Steps he had put together after placing an advert in *The Stage*. He arranged for Pete to attend an audition and when Pete asked what sort of music they made, his reply was: "They don't, they're line-dancers." Pete was sceptical because he'd never taken to country and western.

"I went along to the audition and what I saw blew me away," remembered Pete. "There was no image, they just looked like a bunch of ordinary dancers and they danced to this song called '5, 6, 7, 8', which sounded to me like a speeded up version of 'I Should Be So Lucky'. Their greatest strength was that they came across as lovely people who looked like they were enjoying themselves, and that fitted perfectly with my notion of them as Abba on speed."

Steps were Lisa Scott-Lee, Claire Richards, H (born Ian Watkins), Faye Tozer and Lee Latchford. The only one with previous experience in music was Claire who had been a member of TSD with former *Grange Hill* actress Bonnie Rachanski and ex-Baby D backing singer Costandia Costi. They charted two minor hits in 1996 including a cover of The Ronettes' 'Baby I Love You'.

They signed a record deal with Jive Records and '5, 6, 7, 8', co-written by Barry Upton, a brief member of Brotherhood Of Man, was issued as their first single. It spent 17 weeks on the chart despite only reaching number 14 and became the biggest-selling song of the Nineties not to reach the Top 10.

Next came the Pete Waterman composition 'Last Thing On My Mind', an Abba-esque cover of a song which hadn't really happened for Bananarama in 1993, but reached number six for Steps. This led to implications that they were merely Abba-soundalikes, but as Pete said, "I see it from a different perspective. I've been having hits for 30 years, and have written most of them, so I have built up this quality control and used it as a filter. Besides, my kids are six and eight and they don't see Steps as retro."

The 12-track debut album, *Step One*, which spent over a year on the chart, sold 41,000 on its first week and peaked at number two behind the Manic Street Preachers' *This Is My Truth Tell Me Yours*.

Claire took lead vocals on the next single 'One For Sorrow', which sounded even more like Abba. It connected with the record-buying public and went to number two. The fourth single lifted from the album was 'Heartbeat', a soulful ballad which was an obvious choice for the Christmas market and written by a former hairdresser Jackie James. Jackie was born in Edinburgh and always had an ambition to write songs. She was invited to a music industry party in London where she met her future manager, Billy Royle, who encouraged her to start writing. Jackie was a Motown and Atlantic soul fan and had studied the music of her idol, Burt Bacharach. She wrote 'Heartbeat' in 1994 and took it to Pete Waterman to ask his advice as to what she should do next, and to her delight, he offered her a publishing contract. But Pete held the song back until he had the right artist to record it. A worthwhile five year wait.

'Heartbeat' was issued as a double A-side with a new track not on the album, a cover of The Bee Gees' 1979 number one, 'Tragedy' which appeared on their next album *Steptacular*, and came with a wedding themed video and its own dance routine that every kid could copy. This received the most airplay and the song crashed in at number two after selling 66,000. At a time when records were beginning to regularly enter at the top, Steps took the more unusual route of 2-5-5-8-8-6-4-1. By the end of the year, Steps had sold a million singles in 1998.

Jive Records took the risk of releasing a fifth track from *Step One*, the disco stomping, 'Better Best Forgotten' which gave them a number two hit. Steps were ready to embark on a world tour as *Step One* had gone gold in Taiwan, Hong Kong and Australia and platinum in the Philippines. However, America was a different story. 'Tragedy' was their only US hit and that struggled to reach number 25.

811 Fatboy Slim
Praise You

Label & Cat No.: **Skint SKINT 42CD**

Producer: **Norman Cook**

Writers: **Norman Cook / Camille Yarborough**

Date Reached No.1: **16 January 1999**

Weeks at No.1: **1**

NORMAN, BORN QUENTIN COOK in Bromley, Kent in 1963 wasn't keen on his name. "Quentin Crisp was a famous homosexual and people at school seemed to think it was funny," he explained in Martin James' biography *Funk Soul Brother*. He acquired a variety of nicknames calling himself Q or Cookie. His siblings called him Julie, "Because I looked like Julie Andrews," he said. As a member of The Housemartins, Paul Heaton called him Quintox because he thought he looked like an ox! He then recorded under the names Freak Power, Pizzaman and Mighty Dub Katz. He eventually settled on

Norman Cook

Fatboy Slim, a name he chose because he said, "I like the way it sounded."

Fatboy decided to make Brighton his home and signed with a local label, Skint, in 1996. After a couple of minor hits, 'Going Out Of My Head' / 'Michael Jackson' and 'Everybody Needs A 303', he landed his first Top 10 hit with 'The Rockafella Skank', which used the sample line 'check it out now' from Lord Finesse's 'Vinyl Dogs Vibe' as well as the bassline from the northern soul classic 'Sliced Tomatoes' by the Just Brothers. It was followed by 'Gangster Trippin', which reached number three.

The album, *You've Come A Long Way, Baby*, went to number one and the third single from it, 'Praise You' followed suit. "Hopefully it's my anthem, my 'Sympathy For The Devil' or my 'Ferry 'Cross The Mersey'," proclaimed Norman.

Norman would always go out of his way to find the most obscure track to sample. For 'Praise You' he took a 1975 album track by the black soul singer Camille Yarborough called 'Take Yo Praise'. Norman said, "I used to go to shops in America and buy up lots of weird looking records for 49 cents each. Anyone pictured with long hair between 1968 and 1975 means they almost certainly took drugs, which means they probably made interesting music."

Camille wrote the track about African-American culture. She said, "It's about taking the time to give praise to someone you have loved and someone who has loved you. Coming out of the Civil Rights movement, so much drama was going on and so many of our people had really struggled to make things better that I really felt that I wanted to say 'we've come a long way together' to all of the brothers. I was so pleased that Fatboy Slim chose my song. I must say, I didn't like the way he once claimed that he takes something that has been discarded, that's no good, and makes it his own. 'Take Yo Praise' is still a good song and although I like his rhythms, it's the hook that makes it and that's mine."

The video, which showed seven adults seemingly aping around in a shopping precinct with an audience of passers-by, was directed by Spike Jonze, who is best remembered for making *Being John Malkovich*, and was named the number one video of all-time by *MTV* viewers.

Fatboy, who married Radio 1 DJ Zoë Ball in 1999 had further Top 10 hits with 'Right Here Right Now' (1999), 'Sunset (Bird Of Prey)' (2000) and 'Star 69 What The F★★k' (2001). The follow-up album, *Halfway Between The Gutter And The Stars* also made the Top 10.

812 911
A Little Bit More

Label & Cat No.: **Virgin**

Producers: **Trevor Steel / John Holliday**

Writer: **Bobby Gosh**

Date reached No.1: **23 January 1999**

Weeks at No.1: **1**

"IT'S WONDERFUL," SAID DENNIS Locorriere, the former lead singer of Dr. Hook, coming to the UK on tour in 1999, "'A Little Bit More' is on *Top Of The Pops* and everyone is thinking that we haven't aged at all. They're looking at 911 and saying, 'Isn't Dennis looking well?'"

Dennis recalled how Dr. Hook came to be singing 'A Little Bit More' in 1976. "We found 'A Little Bit More' on an album the songwriter Shel Silverstein had bought from a flea-market for 49 cents. The album was by Bobby Gosh and about eight years old. Shel thought the song would be right for us and of course it was. We didn't know Bobby and he didn't know that we had recorded his song. He'd given up trying to make it and he'd bought an antique shop and lived quietly with his wife, children and five goats on the side of a hill. The goats became big stars! No, actually, he sold them and he started writing again. I'm very glad about that record. It shows that a song doesn't have to surface tomorrow to be good. In fact, it doesn't have to surface at all."

That anecdote shows Dennis' skill as a raconteur but there is more to Bobby Gosh than that. Bobby had been the pianist for Kitty Kallen and he wrote songs with Sammy Cahn including 'The Need Of You' for Diahann Carroll. Sammy introduced him to Paul Anka and he toured the world as his pianist and conductor. He played piano on the demo of 'My Way', which was passed to Frank Sinatra. Bobby Gosh has made several solo albums and had his songs recorded by Engelbert Humperdinck and Roger Whittaker, although there have been no further hits. He has written several well-known advertising jingles in the US and his most recent album is *Love Stories* (2001).

The song's subject matter – the reality of a woman being able to enjoy multiple orgasms while a man might be worn out after one – was a first for a popular song. Dr. Hook's record reached number two in 1976.

Simon 'Spike' Dawbarn and Jimmy Constable were dancers on Pete Waterman's TV show, *The Hitman And Her*, and when they met Lee Brennan on one of the road shows, they decided to form a group. They were all good-looking, twenty-somethings and short: a Small Faces for the Nineties. The group was named after the US phone number for the emergency services, 911. In 1996 they won GMTV's *Search For The Next Big Thing* and acquired a record contract. By and large, they were a boy band with an awareness of disco favourites from the Sixties and Seventies.

Their first two releases, 'A Night To Remember' and 'Love Sensation' made the charts and then they reached the Top 10 with 'Don't Make Me Wait'. In 1997 they had four more Top 10 hits with 'The Day We Find Love' (4), 'Bodyshakin'' (3), 'The Journey' (3) and 'Party People – Friday Night' (5). Their album, *The Journey*, was also a big seller and if there had been a poster Top 10, 911 would have been on it.

In 1998 they had further Top 10 hits with 'All I Want Is You' (4), 'How Do You Want Me To Love You?' (10) and 'More Than A Woman' (2), which was also the opening track on The Bee Gees' tribute album, *Gotta Get A Message To You*. The second album, *Moving On*, made the Top 10.

In 1999 they got round to 'A Little Bit More' and the media ran stories on Jimmy's six-year-old son, whom he never saw. The follow-up, a revival of the soul classic 'Private Number', made number three but 'Wonderland', which many fans liked best, only reached number 13. Their third album was *There It Is*, but *The Greatest Hits And A Little Bit More* was not the anticipated

Dr Hook could only manage number two with 'A Little Bit More' in 1976, but 23 years later 911 – left to right, Spike, Lee and Jimmy – took it all the way

Christmas big seller. The group disbanded in February 2000. Had they continued, they would have had to change their name after 9/11 in 2001.

813 The Offspring Pretty Fly (For A White Guy)

Label & Cat No.: **Columbia 6668802**

Producer: **Dave Jerdan**

Writers: **Dexter Holland / Robert John 'Mutt' Lange / Joey Elliot / Steve Clarke**

Date Reached No.1: **30 January 1999**

Weeks at No.1: **1**

UNUSUAL FOR A PUNK ROCKER, THE Offspring's lead singer/guitarist Bryan Holland has a master's degree in molecular cell biology.

Earning his nickname 'Dexter' (due to being rather brainy – and his school's Valedictorian) whilst growing up in Orange County, California, on a diet of local punk bands and The Dead Kennedys, The Sex Pistols and The Ramones, he formed Manic Subsidal with schoolmate Greg Krisel (bass, born January 20, 1965) and the school janitor Kevin 'Noodles' Wasserman (guitar, born February 4, 1963). Aspiring 16-year-old drummer, Ron Welty (born February 1, 1971) begged Dexter to allow him to be in the band, after being introduced by his sister. Dexter (born December 29, 1966) was finally persuaded and in 1987 they became The Offspring.

After self-financing a single, they found they couldn't afford the extra 25 cents charge for each of the 1000 copies to stick both the front and back sleeves together, so they bought some beer and invited friends around to assist. Two-and-a-half years later, they finally sold the last copy.

In 1989 they released their eponymous album on a small label, which sold few copies. It was six years later that they came to the attention of the UK record-buying public, when 'Self-Esteem' reached the Top 40. This was followed by three further singles; 'Gotta Get Away', (43), 'All I Want', (31) and 'Gone Away', (42) over the next two years.

Their big break came in 1999 when they released the infectious 'Pretty Fly (For A White Guy)'. Fly is a slang term for 'cool' and it was a perfect blend of punk and pop, which sampled the intro to Def Leppard's 'Rock Of Ages'. Weird Al paid them a compliment by recorded an amusing version entitled 'Pretty Fly (For A Rabbi) for his *Running With Scissors* album.

The parent album, *Americana,* became their first album to reach the Top 10. An additional three singles were released from it: 'Why Don't You Get A Job?' (2), 'The Kids Aren't Alright' (11) and 'She's Got Issues' (41). However, for all their success in the UK, the lack of it in their homeland was a striking contrast. In America, their highest-charting single was 'Self-Esteem' (45). 'Pretty Fly' reached a paltry 53.

Not content with being a member of a successful band, Dexter runs his own record label, Nitro, which has included releases by his childhood heroes, T.S.O.L. and The Damned. He also has a pilot's license and eventually hopes to complete his Ph.D.

814 Armand Van Helden featuring Duane Harden You Don't Know Me

Label & Cat No.: **Ffrr FCD 357**

Producer: **Armand Van Helden**

Writers: **Armand Van Helden / Duane Harden**

Date Reached No.1: **6 February 1999**

Weeks at No.1: **1**

ARMAND VAN HELDEN'S FATHER WAS IN the armed forces, so having been born in New York, Armand spent time in Italy, Turkey and Holland before ending up in Boston. He hung around with the disco kids and early hip hoppers which gave him the incentive to become a DJ. He began recording under the guises Witch Doktor, New York Express and Pirates of the Caribbean.

In 1992 he became the promoter and DJ at the Loft club in New York and there he recorded his first single, 'Stay On My Mind' / 'The Anthem' for Nervous Records. "That's where I met Duane Harden because he used to sing at the top of his lungs over the records I was playing and he made the crowd go into a frenzy." Two years later he had his first UK success with 'Can U Feel It' under the name Deep Creed 94. Since then he has remixed countless songs yet has never had a hit in his own country. "It's not because of me, it's the dance scene in general in the States. I love the States for the artists that are pop here, I think they're great artists, and I would take them any day over those European pop artists," he revealed.

He concentrated on remixing and had his first success with 'Sugar Is Sweeter' by C.J.Bolland in 1996. "Johnny D, the A&R man at Atlantic records, suggested to Tori Amos that I should do a remix of 'Professional Widow', which I did and it resulted in a number one hit." Other hits like: 'Spin Spin Sugar' (Sneaker Pimps), 'Runaway' (Nuyorican Soul), 'Anybody Seen My Baby' (The Rolling Stones) and 'Been Around The World' and 'It's All About The Benjamins' (Puff Daddy) followed. This led to him becoming an in-demand remixer and he was once quoted that he charged £35,000 per remix. He also made the Top 40 in 1997 under his own name with the track 'The Funk Phenomena'. The following year he released the *2 Future 4 U* EP, which contained the track 'You Don't Know Me'. Despite airplay on the dance stations, it failed to cross over. Because of the length of the

Armand Van Helden

tracks, it was classed as a mini album but still fell short of the Top 75.

By experimenting with taking the deep basslines of jungle music and mixing them with house music, he came to invent a new genre known as speed garage. 'Ripgroove' by Double 99 and 'Never Gonna Let You Go' by Tina Moore are examples of this. "'You Don't Know Me' was a perfect example of putting two simple things together, the beats from Jaydee's 'Plastic Dreams' and a disco loop from Carrie Lucas. The vocalist will hear a few and pick a track and that's what happened with Duane," Armand explained.

Armand and Duane had both moved to New York City at different times and had lost touch. "But we reconnected somehow. A few years went by and I was starting to record a fully-fledged album, so I made a basic disco loop track and I liked how it grooved. Duane was around a lot, so it just happened to be that I told Duane he should bless that track. He had never recorded or written a song before and my only direction to him was that he could not write a song about love or an uplifting spirit or whatever all of the garage songs were singing about at the time. I think he wrote it overnight and came over to record it. I basically told him to sing the song 15 times or so and put him on record for one hour, meanwhile, I went to my bedroom for some afternoon loving. It's funny because I could hear him while I was making out, then he shouted to me through the door that he was leaving. The whole thing seemed very unforced and natural. Later, Duane told me that he wrote the song, thinking of how people used to judge me without even knowing me when we lived in Boston, which, by the way, was how he felt before he met me."

He followed-up his number one hit with 'Flowers' featuring Roland Clark and had one further Top 10 hit in 2000 with 'Koochy' which sampled Gary Numan's 'Cars'.

Armand spent four years out of the spotlight but returned in 2004 with a new CD *New York: A Mix Odyssey.* "It was a combo effort with the UK label, Southern Fried. They wanted to do a mixed CD that was a little different and that was exactly what I was trying to do," explained Armand. The CD contains mixes of 'Call Me' (Blondie), 'Black Betty' (Ram Jam), 'Tainted Love' (Soft Cell) and 'Don't Go' (Yazoo). The US copy contains the extra track 'Owner Of A Lonely Heart' by Yes.

815 Blondie
Maria

Label & Cat No.: **Beyond 74321645632**

Producer: **Craig Leon**

Writer: **Jimmy Destri**

Date Reached No.1: **13 February 1999**

Weeks at No.1: **1**

FOLLOWING BLONDIE'S SPLIT IN THE mid-Eighties, Deborah Harry launched a solo career and juggled it with nursing Chris Stein back to full health. He had been ill for some time and much speculation was made about his mystery illness, not least because he lost so much weight that he looked like a skeleton. Chris was eventually diagnosed with *pemphigus vulgaris*, which is an autoimmune blistering disorder of the skin that causes the person to suffer from burn-like lesions all over their body. Clem Burke played with Eurythmics, Jimmy Destri released an almost unnoticed solo album called *Heart On A Wall* and Nigel Harrison later joined Clem Burke in a new project called Chequered Past.

They reformed in 1999 as a foursome of Harry, Stein, Destri and Burke, releasing the album *No Exit,* which reached number three on the album chart, and set off on a UK tour. The press had their usual dig, that Debbie looked fat and worn. In fact she looked really good and had only put on a little weight. On stage musically though, it was as if they had never been away.

They signed a new contract to Beyond Records, an imprint of RCA. They also reunited with producer Craig Leon who had produced their eponymous debut album in 1976. The Florida born producer had relocated to the UK during the Eighties and had worked with The Ramones, Talking Heads, The Levellers, The Fall and Jesus Jones.

As for 'Maria', no such person existed. Jimmy Destri's exclusive revelation was that it was "Simply about pimply desire, sex drive without a license. Steering without a wheel and all that shit." Exactly!

816 Lenny Kravitz
Fly Away

Label & Cat No.: **Virgin VUSCD 141**

Producer: **Lenny Kravitz**

Writer: **Lenny Kravitz**

Date Reached No.1: **20 February 1999**

Weeks at No.1: **1**

LENNY KRAVITZ BURST ONTO THE music scene in the early Nineties, but if you listen to any of his songs, you'll realise he is a fan of Sixties and Seventies music although he's not always ready to admit it. In 1991 he said in an interview with *Q* magazine, "People are always hitting me with this retro thing. They are all missing the point. A lot of bands now are being psychedelic just to be cool, or puttin' on flared pants. That's not what I'm doing." Two years later, he revealed, "The people I gravitate to are the older ones – Mick Jagger and David Bowie, whoever. I was raised on good music and I haven't met a lot of musicians from this period that inspire me."

Leonard Albert Kravitz, who was born in New York on May 26, 1964 to a Russian father and a Bahamian mother, taught himself to play piano, bass, guitar and drums, as a child. At 13 his family relocated to Los Angeles and he attended the Beverly Hills High School with fellow classmates Maria McKee and Slash (from Guns N' Roses). His mother, Roxie, landed a TV role as Helen in *The Jeffersons* and Lenny followed in her footsteps and appeared in an episode of *The Cosby Show*.

Lenny began his career in music using the *nom de plume* Romeo Blue but soon reverted to Lenny Kravitz after landing a recording contract with Virgin. His debut album, *Let Love Rule*, had all the retro signs with hints of Seventies reggae mixed with Sixties soul. It peaked at number 56, but the first two singles from it, 'Mr. Cabdriver' and the title track failed to make an impact. He wrote his own material and really made his name when he co-penned Madonna's 1990 number two hit, 'Justify My Love'.

His second album, *Mama Said*, made the Top 10 and three singles were released from it; the Jimi Hendrix influenced 'Always On The Run', which he co-wrote with Slash, 'It Ain't Over 'Til It's Over', which was reminiscent of the Philly Sound and 'Stand By My Woman'. At this time, he was often seen in the tabloids with his girlfriend, the French singer Vanessa Paradis.

In 1993 Lenny released his third album *Are You Gonna Go My Way*, which shot to the top of the chart. The first single, the title track, made the Top 10. Later the same year he collaborated with David Bowie on the single 'Buddha Of Suburbia', which was the theme to the BBC television series of the same name.

In 1995 he just missed the Top 20 with 'Rock And Roll Is Dead', a title some people didn't take kindly to. "That song was completely misunderstood," insisted Lenny. "A lot of people just listened to the title and the chorus and did not take it that one layer deeper. I can't believe they thought I was serious, I was just clowning around." However, the parent album, *Circus*, made number five.

Thanks to two advertising campaigns, Lenny landed the biggest hit of his career. 'Fly Away', which was released in the US at the end of 1998, was used in the Nissan car commercials and made number 12. In the UK it was featured in another car commercial, this time for the Peugeot 206, but missed the chart completely. The following year an instrumental version was used by Sky Sports for their Scottish football coverage which prompted Virgin to re-issue it and it went all the way. It was the first track released from his fifth album, *5*.

Some copies of *5* don't include the track. Lenny explained, "'Fly Away' wasn't even going to be on the album. I had finished recording *5* and was in the studio trying out this guitar and amp, just jamming and I started to play chords. I suddenly started playing this riff because the guitar sounded chunky. As far as I was concerned it was a throwaway track because it happened too easily. It was only when a friend of mine heard it and said it was a hit, that I had the pressings stopped and the track added." A wise decision as it went on to win him a Grammy Award for Best Male Rock Vocal Performance.

Lenny was away from the spotlight for three years. Meanwhile a *Greatest Hits* was released and reached number 12. In 2004 he began recording a new album *Baptism* and the first single, 'California' deserved a far better chart placing than number 62. He was also making plans for a new film called *Barbecues and Barmitzvahs*. "It's a semi-autobiographical piece which deals with cultures, grace, love and family issues. It's like a real-life piece."

817 Britney Spears ...Baby One More Time

Label & Cat No.: **Jive 0522752**

Producers: **Max Martin / Rami Yacoub**

Writer: **Max Martin**

Date Reached No.1: **27 February 1999**

Weeks at No.1: **2**

The Mickey Mouse Club, which began in the Fifties, was a long-running television series produced and broadcast in America by Walt Disney Productions. Hosted by Jimmy Dodd and Roy Williams, a.k.a. Moose, it featured 30-odd children wearing Mickey Mouse T-shirts and Mickey Mouse ears. It ran for 360 episodes over four years with Annette Funicello emerging as its biggest star. Briefly revived in 1977 as *The New Mickey Mouse Club* with pretty much the same format, it was then reincarnated again in 1989. This was to be its longest run and introduced Justin Timberlake, Christina Aguilera and Britney Spears to America.

Britney, born in Kentwood, Louisiana on December 2, 1981, was enrolled at the Renee Donewar School Of Dance at the age of two by her mother, Lynne. In 1990 her mum spotted an advert announcing auditions for *The New Mickey Mouse Club*, but at the age of eight she was too young. Realising she had talent, they advised her to return when she was 11. Her mother thought Britney would have a better start in the Big Apple, so the family travelled by train to New York. It paid off – at the age of nine she was selected as the understudy in the off-Broadway production of *Ruthless*, a play loosely based on the 1956 film *The Bad Seed*.

Britney loved singing and was offered a part in the all-girl group Innosense, who were managed by Justin Timberlake's mum. In 1995 her father contacted an agent, Larry Rudolph who initially thought she was too young for the pop world, but when he saw acts like Hanson and the Backstreet Boys, he suspected there was a gap in the market for someone like Britney.

Britney's family didn't really have enough money to cut a proper demo tape, so Larry arranged for Britney to meet the vice president of Jive Records, Jeff Fenster. "I turned up with a backing track of Whitney Houston's 'I Have Nothing', which I sang followed by an acappella version of 'The Star Spangled Banner'," Britney admitted. Jeff was so impressed he signed the teenager on the spot and made a phone call to Swedish producer and songwriter Max Martin, who happened to be on holiday in Florida at the time. Jeff asked Max to visit him in New York with a view to working with her.

After the meeting, Max returned to Sweden to complete a song he'd begun writing with TLC in mind. "I recorded it on a dictaphone and played it to my new producer, Rami Yacoub who is much more into the urban sound than me, and it's thanks to him, the song sounds like it does. I originally wanted the song to be called 'Hit Me Baby One More Time' but changed the 'Hit Me' for an ellipsis because to me it was obvious it meant 'so let's do it again'". Rami had been working with Denniz Pop who had produced hits for Ace Of Base, *NSYNC and Five. Denniz passed away in 1998 and Rami was keen to impress Max with his production skills. He submitted it to Jive who in turn thought it was better suited to Five. Britney recalled, "When I first heard that song, I knew it was a hit and I wanted to record it."

Britney arrived at the Cherion studios in Stockholm for the recording. "We tried a couple

Britney Spears trod a fine line between images. On the one hand she was purity personified, on the other a sexual time-bomb

of different styles," recalled Max. "I could hear Britney's tummy rumbling and asked her if she wanted a break, but she was determined to get it finished, so we continued. It took over eight hours in the end."

Once it was completed, Britney returned to New York where Jive adopted a marketing strategy used by Debbie Gibson and Tiffany in the Eighties, a shopping mall tour. Britney was supported by two dancers and this led to her supporting *NSYNC on their concert tour the following year.

Jive Records decided that '...Baby One More Time' was to be her first single and suggested an animated Power Rangers-type video. Britney was horrified. "I couldn't believe they were really going to do it. They thought it was a good idea. I said 'no way', and told them my idea."

Her idea, which she'd had while travelling back to the States, was to appeal to girls her age by recording a video dressed in a school uniform. All the personnel at Jive thought it was a great concept and enlisted the help of Nigel Dick, the director who worked on The Backstreet Boys' 'As Long As You Love Me', who shot it at Rydell High School in Venice, California, the same setting used for *Grease* in 1978. Britney asked her cousin, Chad, to appear in the video as her love interest and an old family friend, Fe, appeared as the bespectacled teacher.

'...Baby One More Time' topped both the US and UK chart and spawned a number of unusual cover versions by the likes of Weezer, Type-O-Negative, Barenaked Ladies, Fountains Of Wayne and Ahmet & Dweezil Zappa. Britney's debut album, *...Baby One More Time*, was released four weeks after the single and entered at number eight. It took almost a year to reach its peak of number two behind Travis' *The Man Who*. Coincidentally, one of the hits from *The Man Who*, 'Turn' featured a cover of '...Baby One More Time' on the second CD single.

In Britain Britney sold 464,000 copies in the first week, the highest tally ever for a debut act. Before she had even left the chart, the press were speculating as to whether Britney was going to be a one-hit wonder, or could the babe do it one more time?

818 Boyzone
When The Going Gets Tough

Label & Cat No.: **Polydor 5699132**

Producer: **Steve Mac**

Writers: **Wayne Braithwaite / Barry Eastmond / Robert John 'Mutt' Lange / Billy Ocean**

Date reached No.1: **13 March 1999**

Weeks at No.1: **2**

After the mammoth success of 'No Matter What', Boyzone's next single was an anti-climax, although well chosen. It was a US country hit from John Michael Montgomery, 'I Love The Way You Love Me' (1993), a genre that was to prove very fruitful in Ronan Keating's solo career. The single went to number two and then Boyzone was back on top with their single for Comic Relief, 'When The Going Gets Tough'. Boyzone's version was a Xerox of the original, which had been a number one for Billy Ocean in 1986.

The Comic Relief single included Alison Moyet's lavish 'What A Wonderful World' and a documentary about the work of Comic Relief with Billy Connolly, Victoria Wood and Richard Wilson talking over the backing track of another number one single, 'Love Can Build A Bridge'.

Like the pop stars of the rock'n'rollin' Fifties, the boy bands had to appear single and therefore eligible to their fans. After some glamorous relationships, Ronan Keating married an Irish model, Yvonne Connolly, while Shane Lynch was married to Easther Bennett of Eternal. Keith Duffy had a celebrity marriage in Las Vegas, but it was revealed that both Keith and Mikey Graham had fathered children outside of marriage. Coming from a Catholic country compounded the problem, and Keith commented, "Having kids before marriage did not go down well at home. The whole Irish community was up in arms because they thought we were a bad influence on their kids."

Furthermore, Stephen Gately admitted he was gay and in love with a Dutch dancer, Eloy de Jong: "Eloy and I can relax without worrying who sees us. We're like any normal married couple."

But the biggest threat to Boyzone's stability was to come from within the band. Ronan Keating was managing Westlife, who had just made their first single.

819 B*Witched
Blame It On The Weatherman

Label & Cat No.: **Epic 6670335**

Producer: **Ray Hedges**

Writers: **Ray Hedges / Martin Brannigan / Tracy Ackerman / Andy Caine**

Date Reached No.1: **27 March 1999**

Weeks at No.1: **1**

With 'Don't Blame It On The Weatherman, B*Witched became the first act to enter the chart at number one with their first four releases (although they were soon to pass this mantle onto fellow countrymen, Westlife), and secured their place in music history.

Teaming up with Steps, Tina Cousins, Cleopatra and Billie for 'Thank Abba For The Music' a charity single comprising a medley of hits from the Swedish superstars, for the BRIT Trust, they achieved a number four record in April.

Their second album, *Awake And Breathe* was released in October and went to number five. Further hits followed: 'Jesse Hold On' (4) and 'I Shall Be There' (featuring Ladysmith Black Mambazo, 13). B*Witched parted company with their manager, Kim Glover, after returning from the States and feeling the need to change their image.

The Lynch mob continued when Keavy and Edele's younger sister, Naomi, and friend Olive Tucker, known as Buffalo G, reached the Top 20 in June 2000 with a cover of the Bananarama / Fun Boy Three (originally recorded by The Velvelettes) hit, 'We're Really Saying Something'.

In 2000 B*Witched's cover of Toni

Basil's 'Mickey' was included on the soundtrack to *Bring It On*, a rather dire American teen movie, starring Kirsten Dunst. However, it was only released as a single in the US, where it failed to chart.

Despite selling over 10 million records worldwide, in 2002 the girls were dropped by their record label, Epic. "A lot of people thought we'd be a one-hit wonder. People within the industry were saying we were a shame to pop music," claimed Sinead.

"We'll always be B★Witched, even when we're in our forties. We've experienced something together that no one can take away from us," confirmed Lindsay. "We were four best mates and we genuinely did get on brilliantly, and we had this fabulous job that we could all do together. We were so lucky. We're all still very close and see each other a lot, which is lovely. We're all very supportive of each other."

Edele co-wrote the track, 'Some Kind Of Miracle' for the debut Girls Aloud album, *Sound Of The Underground*. Sinead also still has her feet in the music world, managing new Irish girl band, MINX. "They're kind of like a punk rock Busted, but with girls," she explained. Lindsay is planning a solo career and the band is also attempting one more shot at the charts, currently working with producer Richard Stannard, who has worked with U2, Kylie Minogue and The Spice Girls.

820 Mr. Oizo Flat Beat

Label & Cat No.: **F Communications F104 CDUK**

Producer: **Quentin Dupieux**

Writer: **Quentin Dupieux**

Date Reached No.1: **3 April 1999**

Weeks at No.1: **2**

THE UNKNOWN MR. OIZO WOULD HAVE stayed that way had it not been for a last minute decision by Levi's to step in and use his tune for their latest ad campaign.

Mr. Oizo is the brainchild of French music and video director Quentin Dupieux. He explained the name, "Oiseau means 'bird' in French. A long time ago I was with a bunch of friends, we were all high and one of my friends saw me as a bird, so it became my nickname." As a teenager, Quentin directed short films for French television and between 1994 and 1998, produced eight of them. In 1997 he signed to the French F Communications label and made some short films with French DJ and the label's owner Laurent Garnier. In 1998 he turned his hand to music production and came up with the mid-tempo, heavily distorted, predominantly instrumental 'Flat Beat'.

More memorable than the tune was the yellow puppet, Flat Eric, in the accompanying video. "A representative from Levi's saw a music video called 'Kirk', that I wrote and directed in 1998 which contained the first version of Flat Eric. They loved the whole thing and asked me if they could adapt it for an advertisement with a new song," explained Quentin. "I did the design for Flat Eric and it was slightly reworked by the Muppets' designer, Jim Henson. I called him Flat Eric simply because he's got a flat head!"

The video showed Eric sitting behind a round green desk acting like the high-flying businessman. He then turns to a turntable, puts the needle on the record and proceeds to dial a friend and play them the tune down the phone whilst nodding his head furiously in time to the music. In the commercial, Eric was perched on the dashboard on the passenger's side of a car, driven by someone wearing Levi's and concentrating on the road.

There was an accompanying album, *Analog Worms Attack*, which failed to attract the record buyers and in turn – the chart. Mr. Oizo followed-up 'Flat Beat' the next year with 'Last Night A DJ Killed My Dog', which went nowhere and hence he remains a one-hit wonder. He also recorded a song on a similar theme called 'Last Night Herbert Murdered My Poodle'.

He spent the next couple of years working with Air (French Band), but returned to recording in 2004 with a new single, 'Stunt' and an album due in 2005.

821 Martine McCutcheon Perfect Moment

Label & Cat No.: **Innocent SIN CD7**

Producer: **Tony Moran**

Writers: **Wendy Page / Jim Marr**

Date Reached No.1: **17 April 1999**

Weeks at No.1: **2**

BRITAIN'S MOST POPULAR SOAP, *Eastenders*, has spawned its fair share of hit singles, but only Nick Berry, in 1987, had made it to the top after appearing in the show. Some 12 years later, Martine McCutcheon became the second.

Martine Ponting was born on May 14, 1976 in London's East End. When she was nine, her mother divorced Martine's natural father and married John McCutcheon and Martine eventually took his surname. She first got the taste for show business from watching Fifties and Sixties movies. "I was fascinated and intrigued by them," she recalled. "I was beginning to dream about following my heroines – such as Barbra Streisand and Marilyn Monroe – on to the big screen."

She won a place at Italia Conti, the Academy Of Theatre Arts, where among other things, she learned to speak eloquently. "I spoke really beautifully when I left there, it was only when I got into *Eastenders* that I went back to my old habits."

In 1989, just a few months after joining Italia Conti, Martine landed her first television job in a children's series called *Bluebird*, which starred Barbara Windsor and Lance Percival. "It only ran for six weeks but I learned so much about acting from Barbara, little did I know that years later she would end up as my mother-in-law – well, in the soap, anyway." At this time, her mum, Jenny, became her manager.

Still keen on singing, she auditioned successfully for the all-girl group Milan. They signed with Polydor and she, Claudia and

Dionne seemed ready to take on the world. As Martine noted, "At the time, all-girl groups were quite a rarity. Bananarama had had their day and The Spice Girls were years away." The only girl group making it big were Eternal. "We all loved Kylie and our image was vaguely Kylie-esque, with the emphasis on 'vaguely'." They recorded a cover of Rose Royce's 1979 hit 'Is It Love You're After', but it missed the chart completely. After a couple of years, things weren't going well. Their management preferred Claudia to do lead vocals and Martine was reduced to a backing vocalist. They received little airplay and had to resort to performing in the dingiest clubs. On one tour they supported East 17, but that ended in disaster. "The East 17 fans thought we were getting off with the boys backstage and used to throw mints at us on stage," recalled Martine. "As for their manager, Tom Watkins, he hated us too because he thought we were a distraction to his boys. It was time to quit."

To make ends meet, Martine took a job at Knickerbox when, just before Christmas 1994, her agent called informing her of an impending audition for the part of Tiffany Raymond in *Eastenders*. She got the part and made her first appearance a month later.

In the autumn of 1995 the dance act Uno Clio asked her if she would sing on their song 'Are You Man Enough?'. She agreed and it became a minor hit that November. Three years later Martine met Simon Cowell and Hugh Goldsmith and they got on well, but as she said, "Simon knew how to make money quickly for his artists, but a quick buck wasn't the issue. I wanted to have a long-term career in music." It was Hugh's friend, Cheryl Robson, an A&R expert who first played Martine a version of 'Perfect Moment'. "This is your song," she said. Written by Wendy Page and Jim Marr, who had written and produced hits for Billie, it was first recorded in 1997 by the Polish singer Edyta Górniak. Martine was growing tired of the *Eastenders*' storylines. "I was also getting fed up being strangled by my on-screen husband, Ross Kemp, every other episode. I made a fair amount of money from the soap, but the money Hugh was talking about convinced me of a career in music." She was put in touch with Tony Moran, who had previously worked with Celine Dion and Gloria Estefan, and he got it "spot on".

Having secured a deal with Virgin's Innocent label, Martine crashed in at number one and spent nearly four months on the chart. The follow-up, 'I've Got You' went to number six as did the next single, the double A-sided 'Talking In Your Sleep' (first recorded by Marmalade) / 'Love Me' with all proceeds being donated to the BBC's Children In Need Appeal. Her debut album, *You, Me & Us* reached number two.

In 2000 she returned to acting appearing as Mia in the movie *Kiss Kiss (Bang Bang)*. She also had two further hits, 'I'm Over You' (2, 2000) and an excellent cover of Donna Summer's 'On The Radio' (7, 2001). Martine landed the part of Eliza Doolittle in the West production of Lerner and Loewe's *My Fair Lady*. She won rave reviews but was dogged throughout with health problems and forced to quit after eight months. Even though the understudy had given more performances, Martine won an Olivier Award for her role. Having taken a long rest she returned the following year and recorded one further album, *Musicality*, a set of songs from the movies including 'The Lady Is A Tramp', 'Diamonds Are A Girl's Best Friend' and 'Can You Feel The Love Tonight'.

In 2003 she starred alongside Hugh Grant, Emma Thompson, Bill Nighy and Liam Neeson in the world-wide smash hit, *Love Actually*. In the film she gets her man, the Prime Minister (Hugh Grant), so that must have been her perfect moment.

822 Westlife
Swear It Again

Label & Cat No.: **RCA 74321 662062**
Producer: **Steve Mac**
Writers: **Steve Mac / Wayne Hector**
Date reached No.1: **1 May 1999**
Weeks at No.1: **2**

THE MANAGER OF BOYZONE, LOUIS Walsh, wanted a new challenge, another boy band from Ireland that he could build up from scratch. In 1998 while watching a TV programme from a hospital, he saw IOYOU and thought they might be right. The six lads came from Sligo and included Kian Egan, Mark Feehily and Shane Filan. Kian had worked as a singing kissogram so, in his own words he had experienced writing lyrics, making money and coping with screaming girls. IOYOU had made a single, 'Together Girl Forever', which had sold 2,000 copies. He asked them to support the American boy band, Backstreet Boys, when they came to Dublin.

Walsh decided that changes were needed and in a series of manoeuvres, Kian, Mark and Shane were joined by Bryan McFadden from the Dublin band, Cartel, and Nicky Byrne, who had been performing Boyzone songs in karaoke around Dublin. Graham Keighron stayed on in his new role as tour manager. Simon Cowell from RCA wanted to sign the band but thought Shane wasn't talented enough. The next time he saw them, Shane had changed his hair and Simon didn't realise it was the same boy. At first they were called Westside and they made their London debut at the Café De Paris in 1998. It was only a couple of days after Nicky's cousin, Kenneth Sherlock, had been killed in a car crash, which is why the first album is dedicated to him.

Westlife, as they became, were jointly managed by Louis Walsh and Ronan Keating and they were assigned to the hit producer, Steve Mac (Steve MacCutcheon). In 1991, when only 17, Steve had written his first hit song, '(I Wanna Give You) Devotion' for Nomad. He was impressed with Westlife, saying, "Some bands who come into the studio look great but can't sing very well, so Wayne Hector and I have to write simple songs for them. Westlife could sing anything we gave them."

Pete Waterman agreed, "Simon Cowell played me 'Swear It Again'. People tend to underestimate the power of the human voice, and to find five very unique and different voices is outstanding. For me, it was like finding three Rick Astleys in the same band."

Their debut single, 'Swear It Again', was released in Ireland in April and went straight to number one. It then did the same in the UK. This was no doubt helped by Ronan Keating mentioning Westlife at every opportunity.

Westlife were joined by Mohammed al-Fayed when they performed 'Swear It Again' at the opening of Harrod's sale. Among the band's detractors were Irish rock band, Ash, who called them a disgrace to the nation. They purchased 200 copies of Westlife's records and burnt them in a car park in Leeds. As they would have had to buy the records in the first place, they contributed towards their success.

823 Backstreet Boys I Want It That Way

Label & Cat No.: **Jive 0523392**

Producers: **Max Martin / Kristian Lundin**

Writers: **Max Martin / Andreas Carlsson**

Date Reached No.1: **15 May 1999**

Weeks at No.1: **1**

EXACTLY WHICH WAY THIS BAND OF five young men wanted it is not quite clear. Whatever, A.J. (known as Alexander James to his mother) McLean, Nick Carter, Kevin Richardson, Brian 'B-Rok' Littrell and Howard 'Howie' Dorough were sending the female population's hearts aflutter with their teen idol looks and close harmonies, and could have it any way they so desired.

The Backstreet Boys came together in Orlando, Florida in 1993. Local boys A.J. and Howie met New Yorker Nick at various auditions for television commercials, and after becoming firm friends, they began harmonising together. Kentuckian Kevin moved to Orlando and got a job as a tour guide at Disney World, at night the keyboard player concentrated on becoming a professional musician. After meeting the other three through a workmate, they decided to form a band and named themselves after a flea market, Backstreet, a local landmark. Kevin's cousin, Brian, was invited to join and flew in the next day from Kentucky.

A few days later they performed a concert at Sea World in front of 3,000 teenage girls, who went wild for the quintet. They continued touring around the States and eventually came to the attention of Jive Records who released their first single, 'We've Got It Going On', in 1995 to a disinterested public. It reached number 54 in the UK. Their second release, 'I'll Never Break Your Heart', fared a little better reaching number 42. However, a re-release of 'We've Got It Going On' nine months later saw them in the Top three for the first time, thanks largely to the rising popularity of boy groups.

Further singles followed over the next two and a half years; 'Quit Playing Games (With My Heart)' (2), 'Anywhere For You' (4), 'Everybody (Backstreet's Back)' and 'As Long As You Love Me' both reaching number three, and 'All I have To Give' just missing out on the top spot.

This success was being repeated the world over and there were scenes reminiscent of Beatlemania in their homeland. Their eponymous debut album became 1998's biggest seller Stateside (two years after its original release), with over eight million copies sold, and earned them a Grammy nomination for Best New Artist. The Backstreet Boys' next album, *Millennium* (from which 'I Want It That Way' was the first single released) came out in 1999 and went to number two in the UK. In the US it debuted at number one and broke the record for first week's sales. The album has since sold over 13 million worldwide.

Swedish songwriting and producing sensations Andreas Carlsson and Max Martin (born Martin Sandberg) have provided hits for Britney Spears ('Baby One More Time'), *NSYNC ('Tearin' Up My Heart'/'I Want You Back'), Westlife ('Obvious') and Celine Dion ('That's The Way It Is'). In 1999 Max received an award for ASCAP's Songwriter Of The Year. He won it again the following year.

The Backstreet Boys won many awards, from *MTV* Europe (Best Group) to *Billboard* (Album Of The Year, Artist Of The Year, Album Artist Duo/Group Of The Year and Album Artist Of The Year) to an American Music Award for Favourite Band/Duo/Group.

Black And Blue was released towards the end of 2000. Promotion was unique: the band travelled to Sweden, Japan, Australia, South Africa, Brazil and the USA in 100 hours, of which 55 were spent flying. It worked; the album sold five million in its first week.

Since the band's heyday, Nick Carter has released a solo album, *Now Or Never*, Kevin and Brian married their respective girlfriends and A.J. checked into rehab for alcohol abuse and depression.

In 2003 they released a statement: "As a group, we have decided not to record our next album at this time. We are not breaking up, but individually we are currently at different places in our lives, and our hearts and minds are focused in other areas. All of us are getting along great and are supporting each other in our individual endeavours."

824 Boyzone You Needed Me

Label & Cat No.: **Polydor 5639332**

Producer: **Steve Mac**

Writer: **Randy Goodrum**

Date reached No.1: **22 May 1999**

Weeks at No.1: **1**

ASTONISHING FACT: DESPITE BEING one of the biggest stars in North America, Anne Murray has never had a Top 20 hit in the UK. Even her US chart-topper, 'You Needed Me' only reached number 22. In 1978 Anne Murray was trying to balance her private and public lives: she had a husband and a son and she wanted to spend more time at home. She found the very song which expressed her emotions, 'You Needed Me': "I cried a tear, you wiped it dry. / I was confused, You cleared my mind."

Anne Murray found the song in a box of tapes. Unfortunately, only the writer's name, Randy Goodrum, was on the cassette. Her producer, Jim Ed Norman, found his name in the phone book. 'You Needed Me' became the central track on her album, *Let's Keep It That Way*, which has a dedication, "This album is for Bill – Love, Anne." To this day, it remains her favourite of her own recordings.

Boyzone might have shared the same thoughts as Anne Murray as the band was disintegrating, and perhaps that is why their manager, Louis Walsh, suggested the song. Mind you, he was part of the problem as he and Ronan Keating had put together a new and younger version of Boyzone in Westlife.

'You Needed Me' was Boyzone's 15th consecutive Top five single, but they would only have one more, 'Every Day I Love You'. The group would finish with a triumphant nine days at the Point in Dublin.

825 Shanks & Bigfoot
Sweet Like Chocolate

Label & Cat No.:	**Pepper 0530352**
Producers:	**Stephen Meade / Daniel Langsman**
Writers:	**Stephen Meade / Daniel Langsman**
Date Reached No.1:	**29 May 1999**
Weeks at No.1:	**2**

When the little-known Chocolate Boy label issued 'Sweet Like Chocolate' as a strictly limited edition, DJ-only, chocolate coloured 12-inch in December 1998 little did they know the reaction it would get. There was even one report of fisticuffs in the car park outside a club in Manchester when the DJ refused to hand over the scarce piece of vinyl.

Stephen Meade and Daniel Langsman, two London garage writers/producer/DJs, got together in 1997 when a friend of theirs, Simon Omer, took the opportunity to start a record label putting out good dance music. The label's first release, in August 1998, was a dance version of the *Starsky & Hutch* TV theme by Hoax. Next came Stephen and Daniel under the guise Doolally. The word comes from a town in India called Deolali, where British soldiers awaited transportation home after completing their tour of duty. The mixture of the heat and boredom drove them mad and the term doolally was coined.

Doolally's first single 'Straight From The Heart' featured the vocals of Sharon Woolf, who was introduced to Daniel by a friend when he suggested he was looking for a female singer. The track, which featured mixes by Tuff Jam and Bump & Flex, received strong backing from Kiss FM's Steve Jackson and reached number 20. It became a club favourite in Ibiza and was re-issued the following summer on XL Recordings' subsidiary label, Locked On, where it went to number nine. The duo then changed their name to Shanks & Bigfoot. Explaining his name, Stephen said, "I chose Shanks because I have long legs and a short torso, so I look shorter than short people sitting down." Daniel added, "I wanted a pseudonym to hide behind because I was a bit shy. I'm 5' 7" and have size nine shoes and someone commented that my feet looked big for my height."

The first release was a four-track EP, imaginatively titled *The E-P* and described in one music magazine as having 'freestyle grooves and obese basslines'. They signed with the Zomba Group's subsidiary dance label, Pepper and 'Sweet Like Chocolate' came out soon after. It was a double tribute to Omer, firstly as a thank you for getting them started, and secondly, as the duo had agreed to only make one track for his label and then move on, it was a farewell too. Once again, like 'Straight From The Heart', it featured Sharon Woolf on vocals. When it entered the chart at number one it was a huge surprise to both of them. Shanks commented, "I don't think you ever think 'this is a big record' when you make one. I think that would probably be complacent and very brave actually." Bigfoot added, "Somehow it's captured people's imaginations. To us it seems like a rather old record, but we're working on an album which will have some surprises on it." The album may have had some surprises, but it didn't sell enough to make the chart, so few would have found out. On its second week at the top, 'Sweet Like Chocolate' also topped the R&B, indie, and dance charts and became the first single to do so.

Shanks & Bigfoot were then commissioned by the Ministry Of Sound Label to remix a compilation called *Ayia Napa – The Album*, which went to number five. It took over a year for the follow-up single 'Sing-A-Long' to be issued when it went to number 12. In an interview with Radio 1, Bigfoot said, "Generally we're songwriters and producers and not DJs," so the plan was to move away from recording. Daniel is still writing and producing songs in the UK, whilst Stephen now lives in New York and is working on a multimedia project. "It may seem like a strange career path for a songwriter, but I was a prolific journalist and used to write for *Time Out*, *Arena*, *Big Issue* and *DJ Mixmag*. I was also a barrister before the hits started rolling in, but I have recently started writing songs again for the first time in three years."

826 Baz Luhrmann
Everybody's Free (To Wear Sunscreen) The Sunscreen Song (Class Of '99)

Label & Cat No.:	**EMI CDBAZ 001**
Producer:	**Nellee Hooper**
Writers:	**Tim Cox / Nigel Swanston / Mary Schmich**
Date Reached No.1:	**12 June 1999**
Weeks at No.1:	**1**

In the mid-forties the Swiss-based Piz Buin company invented the sun protection factor rating, which indicated how long one can safely stay in the sun before getting burnt. Now that advice has been immortalised on record (or CD to be precise) and credited to the Australian film director Baz Luhrmann, although he is not actually on the recording.

The song is a combination of a joke speech written by *Chicago Tribune* columnist Mary Schmich, although many thought it was a student graduation address made by the novelist Kurt Vonnegut. It's combined with 'Everybody's Free (To Feel Good)' as performed by Quindon Tarver on the soundtrack to the 1996 film *Romeo + Juliet*, which was directed by Baz Lurhmann and starred Leonardo DiCaprio and Claire Danes in the title roles.

"I was working with my assistant, Anton

Monsted and Josh Abrahams on a remix of 'Everybody's Free (To Feel Good)' when Ant showed me an e-mail of these words that appeared to be Kurt's graduation speech," remembered Baz. "His simple observations and ideas seemed to provide a profoundly useful guide for getting through life. We wanted to record it but only had two days and didn't know how to get hold of Kurt. Ant went onto the internet and discovered that a student had taken Mary's speech and linked it to Kurt's name in the style of a chain letter. To us it didn't matter who wrote it, it made sense and struck a chord with those who had read it, that we decided to record it."

The song made people feel good about themselves with the words: "You are not as fat as you imagine", "Remember compliments you receive. Forget the insults" and "Don't feel guilty if you don't know what you want to do with your life". It also dispensed advice like: "Don't be reckless with other people's hearts and don't put up with people who are reckless with yours", "Enjoy your body, use it every way you can. Don't be afraid of it or of what other people think of it". There was advice for children: "Get to know your parents. You never know when they'll be gone for good" and "Be nice to your siblings. They're your best link to your past and the people most likely to stick with you in the future".

Baz wanted Australian voice-over artist Lee Perry to record the song, so asked him over to his house. "I went in and met Baz at his house in Sydney," recalled Lee. "He described to me what he had in mind for the song." Lee adopted an American accent to sound more authoritative and the voice-over was done in about three hours on a DAT machine in Baz's house.

The original seven-minute track received plenty of airplay in Australia and even inspired a parody version, 'Not The Sunscreen Song'. Then interest died down and nothing happened for two years until it was released in America as an edited radio-friendly five-minute version. It reached number 45 and had the slightly amended title 'Everybody's Free (To Wear Sunscreen) The Speech Song'.

Baz produced and directed the 2001 film *Moulin Rouge* which starred Ewan McGregor and Nicole Kidman and spawned the duet 'Come What May' which charted at number 27.

827 S Club 7
Bring It All Back

Label & Cat No.: **Polydor 5610852**

Producers: **Eliot Kennedy / Mike Percy / Tim Lever**

Writers: **Eliot Kennedy / Mike Percy / Tim Lever**

Date Reached No.1: **19 June 1999**

Weeks at No.1: **1**

"BASICALLY THE S DOESN'T STAND FOR anything. It can stand for anything you want it to stand for," explained Jo O'Meara, about the origins of the name of one of the most successful girl/boy groups this country has seen. Jo, along with Tina Barrett, Hannah Spearritt, Rachel Stevens, Paul Cattermole, Jon Lee and Bradley McIntosh were the lucky ones chosen from 10,000 hopefuls who auditioned for a place in pop guru Simon Fuller's latest venture, S Club 7.

They went straight into a studio and began recording their debut album, *S Club* (2, 1999), then began filming *Miami 7*, a television series about seven youngsters trying to hit the big time in Florida. It proved enormously popular and was syndicated to over 100 countries, attracting four million viewers when it aired on the BBC. This surely helped 'Bring It All Back' sell 300,000 copies in a fortnight, of which 190,000 were within the first six days of release.

All the members of S Club 7 had previous backgrounds in performing. Paul had been a member of the National Music Theatre, Jon Lee worked on *EastEnders* (playing the role of Josh Saunders in 1997) and as a 12-year-old had starred in a West End production of *Oliver!*, Bradley and Tina were dancers, Jo was briefly in Solid Harmonie, but had left by the time they scored three Top 20 hits in 1998, and Rachel was a former model who had also done a bit of acting. Bradley's parents had found fame with the Cool Notes, who had half a dozen hits in the mid-Eighties.

S Club 7

Sheffield-based songwriting and producing team Eliot Kennedy, Mike Percy and Tim Lever have written a multitude of hits for artists including The Spice Girls, Take That, 5ive, Billie and Hear'Say.

'Bring It All Back' charted all over the world: Australia, Canada, Denmark, Germany, Ireland, Japan and New Zealand, where it reached the top spot. S Club 7 also received a Brit for 2000's Best Newcomer and several US awards, including Disney Channel Kids for Best Group Of The Year.

Their *Miami 7* series, was soon followed by *S Club 7 In L.A.*, about seven youngsters trying to hit the big time in Los Angeles. A second album, 7, was released in June 2000 and went to the top of the chart. Further hits followed: a hat trick of number twos, 'S Club Party', the double A-sided 'Two In A Million'/ 'You're My Number One' and 'Reach'. Their fifth release, 'Natural', got to number three in September 2000.

828 The Vengaboys
Boom Boom Boom Boom!!

Label & Cat No.: **Positiva CDTIVS 114**

Producers: **Danski / DJ Delmundo**

Writers: **Danski / DJ Delmundo**

Date Reached No.1: **26 June 1999**

Weeks at No.1: **1**

ORIGINALLY THE VENGABOYS WAS THE name for two Dutch DJs, Danski and Delmundo, who in 1992 toured around Spain in a schoolbus performing in various clubs and at beach parties. This continued until 1996 when they decided to ditch the bus and the name and record serious dance music under the new moniker Nakatomi. They scored a massive European hit with 'Children Of The Night', but in the UK it fell short of the Top 75. It was re-issued in 1998 when it made number 47.

In 1996 during one of their Spanish beach parties, they met and recruited four dancers; Kim Sasabone, Denice van Rijswijk, Roy den Burger and Robin Pors. Kim was born in Salvador, Brazil, Denice in Budapest, Robin in Barcelona and Roy in Port of Spain, Trinidad. They had all met on holiday in Spain, formed a dance troupe and like The Spice Girls, they had distinctive characters. Kim was a combat girl, Denice the glittery girl, Robin the sailor and Roy a cowboy.

In 1997 they performed a 'Cash Chaos Concert' in Barcelona. The idea was, at the end of the show, the four would throw $10,000 in the audience, but as Kim remembered, "We got overexcited and threw the money out at the beginning. It was total chaos." Although it delighted the fans, the concert only lasted eight minutes and Danski and Delmundo were arrested. Shortly after, they moved to Scandinavia and built their own recording studio.

The following year Danski and Delmundo decided to take a back seat from performing once they realised all their dancers could sing, so they re-introduced their old name and The Vengaboys became a four-piece.

So what does Venga mean? Roy explained, "It's pronounced Benga which means 'party', so it's like 'good time party music that's catchy and makes you feel good." Kim also confirmed that her and Denice didn't mind being in a group called 'Venga-boys'. "We liked the name in the first place and there are no feminist hassles at all."

Their debut hit, 'Up And Down', a fast trance track with very few lyrics, reached number four in the UK and was followed by the number three hit 'We Like To Party (The Vengabus)'. The debut album, *The Party Album*, went to number six and spent almost a year on the chart.

The next track released from the album, 'Boom Boom Boom Boom!!', entered the chart at number one after selling 134,000 copies. Roy commented at the time, "Being in the Vengaboys is still just a hobby for us and we never thought it was going to be this successful. It works really well now. Danski and Delmundo make all the decisions about the songs and we make all the decision about the shows. We know how to give people a good time."

829 ATB
9PM (Till I Come)

Label & Cat No.: **Sound Of Ministry MOSCDS 132**
Producer: **Andre Tenneberger**
Writer: **Andre Tenneberger**
Date Reached No.1: **3 July 1999**
Weeks at No.1: **2**

ATB IS THE ALIAS OF PRODUCER AND songwriter Andre Tanneberger who was born in Freilberg, Germany in 1973. He began making a name for himself in 1994 as a member of Sequential One with vocalist Morpha and Dutch DJ, Woody.

They released four singles, 'I Wanna Make U', 'Dreams', 'Imagination' and 'Angels, and an album, *Energy*, all of which were well received on the European club circuit. Both Woody and Andre were becoming increasingly busy with other projects and Sequential One was abandoned, although they continued working together.

Andre was DJing in various clubs and ended up with a residency at the legendary *Riu Palace* club in Mallorca in 1996. He began remixing for other acts including Miss Jane ('It's A Fine Day') and Future Breeze ('Why Don't You Dance with Me') both of which were UK hits. He set up two other projects, Love And Fate and ATB.

"One day Andre went into his studio to show a girl he'd just met how to make music," Woody described. "First you take a bass drum, then some percussion, then a guitar and so on and so on. He showed her how to pitch bend on the guitar and she was impressed. At nine o'clock he wanted to save the instrumental track he'd recorded in the computer and thought, 'Hey! It's 9pm' so he saved it under that name. A few days later, when he was finishing the track off, Andre used some whispering vocals from a Spanish girl he knew where she says 'Till I come' and so that's what the title became."

His debut album, *Movin' Melodies*, reached number 32 in 2000. The follow-up single, 'Don't Stop' reached number three, after spending two weeks on the chart on import. He had further hits with a cover of Adamski's 'Killer' (4, 2000), 'The Fields Of Love' (16, 2001) and 'Let U Go' (34, 2001). He continued to release albums in Europe and is a chart regular across the continent except, for some reason, in Holland and the UK. Andre has just completed his fifth album, *No Silence*, in 2004.

830 Ricky Martin
Livin' La Vida Loca

Label & Cat No.: **Columbia 667402**
Producer: **Desmond Child**
Writers: **Robi Rosa / Desmond Child**
Date reached No.1: **17 July 1999**
Weeks at No.1: **3**

RICKY MARTIN BECAME THE FIRST Puerto Rican to have a UK number one, although when he and other Latin performers such as Jennifer Lopez and Enrique Iglesias established themselves, they tended to merge contemporary American sounds with their native music.

Enrique Martin Morales was born in San Juan on Christmas Eve, 1971. He had singing lessons as a child and also appeared in TV commercials. In 1984 he joined a Puerto Rican boy band, Menudo, for five years then went solo. He had little luck in New York but when he moved to Mexico in 1990, he became a regular in the TV soap, *Alcanzar Una Estrella II*.

The Spanish language albums, *Ricky Martin* (1992) and *Me Amaras* (1993), did well and he transferred his allegiance to the US soap, *General Hospital*. Moving to Broadway, Ricky played the idealist student leader, Marius, in *Les Misérables* and his role included the key song, 'Empty Chairs At Empty Tables'. Whilst in New York, he befriended the songwriter and producer, Robi 'Draco' Rosa and they co-produced his next album, *A Medio Vivir* (1995), which merged Latin music with rock. In 1997 he had his first UK hit with '(Un, Dos, Tres) Maria' reaching number six.

Robi Rosa often wrote with Desmond Child, who had success writing with and for Kiss ('I Was Made For Lovin' You', 'Heaven's On Fire') and Jon Bon Jovi ('You Give Love A Bad Name', 'Livin' On A Prayer', 'Keep The Faith'). Other hits included 'Just Like Jesse James' for Cher, 'Poison' for Alice Cooper, 'How Can We Be Lovers?' for Michael Bolton and 'Old Before I Die' for Robbie Williams. In the mid-Nineties, Desmond Child moved to Miami and set up a studio in his garage. He was to produce, record and mix 'Livin' La Vida Loca' using his Pro Tools computer program.

Ricky Martin's fourth Spanish language album, *Vuelve* (1998) included 'La Copa De La Vida (The Cup Of Life)', which became the theme song for the World Cup in Paris and was written by Robi Rosa and Desmond Child. His album was a big Latin seller but after he sang with Madonna at the 1999 Grammys, he crossed over and became a major star.

His first English language CD, *Ricky Martin*, included 'Livin' La Vida Loca', with lyrics about a girl who will bewitch similar to Cliff Richard's 'Devil Woman'. With an energetic and sexy video, Ricky Martin was marketed as a Latin Tom Jones: unquestionably, this was *the* summer hit and led to other Latin-based number ones, 'Mi Chico Latino' and 'Mambo No. 5 (A Little Bit Of...)'. 'Livin' La Vida Loca' was on the charts for four months, while *Ricky Martin* was on the album charts for almost a year. Another hit, Sisqo's 'Thong Song' (2, 2000) mentions Ricky's record in its lyric.

Since then, Ricky Martin has had Top 20 hits with 'Shake Your Bon-Bon' (19), 'Private Emotion' (featuring Meja, 9), 'She Bangs' (another Desmond Child and Robi Rosa song, 3), 'Nobody Wants To Be Lonely' (with Christina Aguilera, 4) and 'Loaded' (19). He returned to his roots with another Spanish album, Almas Del Silencio, in 2003 and has given royalties to helping educate disabled children in Puerto Rico.

George W. Bush joined him on stage for 'The Cup Of Life' at his inauguration concert. In *Fahrenheit 9/11*, when Michael Moore comments on planes being grounded, he mentions that even Ricky Martin wasn't able to fly.

831 Ronan Keating
When You Say Nothing At All

Label & Cat No.: **Polydor 5612902**

Producers: **Stephen Lipson**

Writers: **Paul Overstreet / Don Schlitz**

Date reached No.1: **7 August 1999**

Weeks at No.1: **2**

KEITH WHITLEY HAD THE POTENTIAL TO be a major country star. He had played bluegrass in Ralph Stanley's Clinch Mountain Boys and, starting in 1988, had five consecutive US country number ones with 'Don't Close Your Eyes', 'When You Say Nothing At All', 'I'm No Stranger To The Rain', 'I Wonder Do You Think of Me' and, posthumously, 'It Ain't Nothin''.

'When You Say Nothing At All' was written by two leading country songwriters. Paul Overstreet wrote 'Love Can Build A Bridge' for The Judds and 'Forever And Ever, Amen' for Randy Travis, while Don Schlitz wrote about knowing when to hold and knowing when to fold for Kenny Rogers in 'The Gambler'. Paul and Don had met up for a writing session and when they came up with nothing at all, they realised that they had a good title. They were not over-impressed with the final song but Keith Whitley told them that they had written a classic.

Unfortunately, Keith Whitley did not have as much confidence in himself and he died from alcohol abuse in 1989 at the age of 33. 'When You Say Nothing At All' was a country hit for the second time when it was revived by the award-winning Alison Krauss & Union Station in 1995, but neither version had made the UK charts.

Ronan Keating

Screenwriter Richard Curtis is always keen to find the right songs to include in his films. Wet Wet Wet's revival of 'Love Is All Around' was integral to *Four Weddings And A Funeral*, and for the new Hugh Grant and Julia Roberts film, *Notting Hill*, he wanted a key song to be 'When You Say Nothing At All'. He suggested it to Ronan Keating from Boyzone, who said, "As soon as he mentioned the title, I was hooked." The record went further than being a hit single as it is now used at christenings, marriages and funerals.

Although Boyzone was still operative, the solo hit further distanced Ronan Keating from the group. Within a few months, he had topped the charts with Boyzone and as a solo act, while his protégés, Westlife, also had a number one. In addition, he was a popular TV presenter, having hosted *Eurovision*, *Miss World* and the MTV Awards. Much to the chagrin of the rest of Boyzone, when their greatest hits package, *By Request*, was released, Ronan's solo hit, 'When You Say Nothing At All', was included. The track is also included on his first solo album, *Ronan*, and on the soundtrack album, alongside Elvis Costello's poignant version of Charles Aznavour's 'She', which made the Top 20.

832 Westlife
If I Let You Go

Label & Cat No.: **RCA 74321 692352**

Producers: **Per Magnusson / David Kruger**

Writers: **Jörgen Elofsson / Per Magnusson / David Kreuger**

Date reached No.1: **21 August 1999**

Weeks at No.1: **1**

DESPITE ITS SIZE, IRELAND WAS becoming increasingly important for popular music. Several UK stars, including Elvis Costello, had moved there for tax reasons, but, more importantly, they had several home-grown hitmakers – U2, Boyzone, Samantha Mumba, B★Witched, and Westlife. Between March and August 1999, six UK number ones were by Irish acts and, ironically, Westlife dethroned their manager, Ronan Keating, with 'If I Let You Go'.

Following 'Swear It Again', Westlife were becoming big around the world and even had success in America. Their second single, 'If I Let You Go', was recorded with a different writing and production team, Per Magnusson and David Kruger, at the Cheiron Studios in Stockholm. Soon they would be recording hits with Will Young and Gareth Gates from *Pop Idol*. 'If I Let You Go' was a romantic ballad in the same style as 'Swear It Again'.

Not everyone was impressed with Westlife, particularly Boyzone. Keith Duffy, commenting after Boyzone had broken up, said, "Westlife copied everything we did. Kian Egan thinks he's a superstar. He's a big headed shit." Shane Lynch was also critical: "Westlife has nothing on us because we don't just mope around on stage. They stand around singing soppy ballads."

Shane Filan let the comments wash over him as he wanted to invest his money in his family's stables. His parents owned stables in Sligo and Shane had the abilty to be a top rider. He said, "I love unwinding by riding horses, but I never ride during concert tours because I don't think anyone would be amused if I fell off and broke my leg." However, the rest of Westlife visited his stables to sit on horses for a photo shoot.

833 Geri Halliwell
Mi Chico Latino

Label & Cat No.: **EMI CDEM 548**

Producers: **Absolute (Paul Wilson / Andy Watkins)**

Writers: **Geri Halliwell / Paul Wilson / Andy Watkins**

Date reached No.1: **28 August 1999**

Weeks at No.1: **1**

When Geri Halliwell walked out of The Spice Girls, many wondered if her 15 minutes of fame were up. She discussed her problems in much-publicised friendships with Chris Evans, George Michael and Robbie Williams. Commenting on her relationship with Robbie, she said, "We're friends who shag occasionally." In October 1998 she accepted a position as a United Nations 'goodwill' ambassador on reproductive health and later led a campaign concerning breast cancer. Geri was still a celebrity, and for a time it looked more likely that she would become a TV host than return to music.

The Absolute duo of Paul Wilson and Andy Watkins had worked on several tracks for The Spice Girls and Geri Halliwell asked them to produce her first solo album, *Schizophonic*. The remaining Girls gave them an ultimatum: if they worked with Geri, they couldn't work with them again. Irritated by this provocation, they sided with Geri. "Writing *Schizophonic* was almost like going back to writing the first Spice Girls album," said Paul Wilson. "It was that kind of energy and that's why we were glad we made the decision."

Geri and Absolute wrote the album together, but it was issued to weak reviews and the first single, 'Look At Me', only made number two. Mel C commented, "She's not a talented musician and she's not a very good singer", and Mel B thought she was only known for "her lips and her boobs". Emma Bunton said that she couldn't watch the video because "She tried to break up a great group."

Geri sacked her manager, Lisa Anderson, because the record failed to reach the top, and a Channel 4 documentary, *Geri*, directed by Molly Dineen, showed that a confused Geri was reading self-help books and battling with low self-esteem. For a time, her boyfriend was the super confident DJ and TV presenter Chris Evans.

At the time of the second single, *Schizophonic* was no longer a best-selling album, but Geri was lucky. Ricky Martin was on top with 'Livin' La Vida Loca' and the single chosen, 'Mi Chico Latino', had the same enthusiastic Latin-American feel and included a verse in Spanish. She didn't pull it off as convincingly as Ricky but it was an infectious record that was ideal for the summer. The video featured her on a yacht in a bikini with sexy boy dancers, demonstrating that her main audience was gays and young teenage girls.

834 Lou Bega
Mambo No. 5 (A Little Bit Of...)

Label & Cat No.: **RCA 74321 658012**

Producers: **Frank Lio / D. Fact / Zippy (Christian Pietschacher) / Lou Bega**

Writers: **Perez Prado / David LuBega / Zippy**

Date reached No.1: **4 September 1999**

Weeks at No.1: **2**

In the Fifties Cuba was run by the corrupt General Batista, who kept most of his citizens in poverty. It was liberated by Fidel Castro in 1959 when he and his bearded guerillas took control – they were actually known as 'Los barbudos' ('The bearded ones'). After US President Jack Kennedy failed to recognise Castro, he declared the country a socialist republic and aligned himself with Russia. If the Russians had not backed down in 1962, there could have been another world war.

The CIA had many, almost comic plans for removing Castro including presents of exploding cigars. He has survived assassination attempts and is still in control 45 years later. His compadre, his Ministry for Industry, Che Guevara, was less lucky: he left Cuba in 1965 and continued guerilla warfare in Bolivia. He was killed in 1967 but he lives on as a poster and t-shirt icon.

Although Castro appreciated the importance of song (his guerillas had guitars as well as rifles), the new order affected the lifestyle of the main Cuban musicians and they either emigrated to America (until that loophole was closed in 1964) or were reduced to poverty, The beautiful music continued, however, and the mambo and the cha-cha retained their native popularity. Because of the détente between America and Cuba, few Americans knew of the music.

Thirty years later, with the growing interest

in world music, fans realised they were missing out on some of the sweetest and most elegant music known to man. Ry Cooder must take credit for breaking down barriers with his work with The Buena Vista Social Club. In 1996 the 89-year-old Compay Segundo became a star and the film, *The Buena Vista Social Club*, directed by Wim Wenders, is a superb documentary.

Cuban bandleader Pérez Prado toyed with the concept of the mambo in the early Forties, adding American swing, especially the saxophone, to Afro-Cuban rhythms to create something more exciting than the rhumba. He said, "I am a collector of cries and noises, elemental ones like seagulls on the shore, winds through the trees and men at work in a foundry. Mambo is a movement back to nature by means of rhythms based on such cries and noises and on simple joys."

Pérez Prado recorded numerous mambos, giving his original compositions names like 'Olé Mambo', 'Manhattan Mambo' and 'Mambo-Jambo'. When he ran out of inspiration, he would simply number them and 'Mambo No. 5' in 1950 was one of a series of eight. When mambo became passé it was replaced by salsa.

Lou Bega was born in Germany in 1975, the son of two students, one from Uganda and one from Italy, and they both loved Pérez Prado's music. He made his first album as a rapper, *Bega*, in Munich in 1990, and became popular as a singer, rapper and trumpet player. In his lyrics to 'Mambo No. 5', he pays playful tribute to Monicas, Ericas and Ritas. His record was a hit in Germany and when import copies started to sell in the UK, RCA released it here and it went to the top. He looked elegant in his Thirties hat, white suit, pocket handkerchief and spats and he said, "Never lose your *joie de vivre*; there is more beauty around us than we can possibly imagine."

Several girls are listed in the song and it was reported that Angela, Pamela, Sandra, Rita, Monica, Erica, Tina, Mary and Jessica were Lou's old flames, something he never chose to deny. Statistically, it is unlikely that he dated eight girls whose names happen to end in 'a'. If this is true, the song becomes the musical equivalent of Tracey Emin's tent.

The follow-up, 'I Got A Girl', also dealt with his love for the dancing of a Cuban girl. "There is nothing better than to go out and dance the mambo," he claims, "with the right partner at your side, the fire is alight!"

When Channel 4 acquired the rights to Test cricket in 1999, they replaced the BBC's theme music (Booker T & The MG's 'Soul Limbo') with Lou Bega's 'Mambo No.5'.

835 The Vengaboys
We're Going To Ibiza

Label & Cat No.: **Positiva CDTIV 119**

Producers: **Danski / DJ Delmundo**

Writers: **Jeff Calvert / Max West**

Date Reached No.1: **18 September 1999**

Weeks at No.1: **1**

WHILST 'BOOM BOOM BOOM BOOM!!' was still on the UK chart, The Vengaboys' next single, 'We're Going To Ibiza', which was based around Typically Tropical's 1975 number one, 'Barbados', was filling dance-floors across Europe.

It was the cheesiest of all their songs, due mainly to the dreadful pronunciation of Ibiza, which came out as 'I-bits-a'. Import copies began to flood into the UK and were on sale at the same price as a British release at £3.99 and it entered the chart on import at number 69.

Chart rules state that when a UK version is released, the import copy gets eliminated from the chart, so when the UK version did come out the following week, it was eligible to enter at the top. That week saw, for the first time, a continental Top three with Holland's DJ Jean at three with 'The Launch' and Germany's Lou Bega with 'Mambo No.5 (A Little Bit Of...)' at number two.

In the summer of 1999 Robin announced he was leaving the group and was quickly replaced by Dutch-born Yorick Bakker who was formally a member of Velvet. His character was a seaman based on his life having been a dolphin trainer.

To promote their next single, 'Kiss (When The Sun Don't Shine)', they ran a kissing competition at the Daja Beach club. The winning couple's mouths finally separated after 34 hours, seven minutes and 41 seconds. Surely a record if only a Guinness World Records representative had been there to verify it. The single just missed out on the Christmas number one in 1999 to Westlife's 'I Have A Dream' / 'Seasons In The Sun' but they had two further Top 10 hits in 2000 with 'Shalala Lala' which was originally recorded by The Walkers in the Seventies and 'Uncle John

Lou Bega

From Jamaica'. Their second album, *The Platinum Album*, reached number nine and spent six months on the chart. By the end of 2000, their novelty, tongue-in-cheek, cheesy dance music was wearing a bit thin as proved when their next hit, 'Cheekah Bow-Bow (That Computer Song)' only reached number 19. The following February the video for their last single 'Forever As One', included footage of The Vengaboys with Westlife, but they were ordered by Westlife's management to edit out their appearance as they hadn't sought permission to use it.

The Vengaboys are still performing in parts of Europe and have announced that they have two ambitions to fulfil before they disappear. One is to record a duet with The Bloodhound Gang, the other is to record a Milli Vanilli tribute album.

836 Eiffel 65
Blue (Da Be Dee)

Label & Cat No.: **Eternal WEA 226CD1**

Producers: **Massimo Gabutti / Luciano Zucchet**

Writers: **Massimo Gabutti / Maurizio Lobina / Gianfranco Randone**

Date Reached No.1: **25 September 1999**

Weeks at No.1: **3**

EIFFEL 65 ARE THREE TECHNOLOGICAL Italian whiz kids, Maurizio Lobina (keyboards), Jeffrey Jey (born Gianfranco Randone, vocals) and Gabry Ponte (DJ/remixer) who all met in 1991 at the Bliss Corporation, the home of numerous successful dance acts run by its founder Massimo Gabutti.

For the first few years they worked individually on various dance tracks that became successful all over Europe. In 1999 they decided to form a group of their own and let a computer programme come up with a name. It randomly chose Eiffel. After a break, they returned to the studio to find that someone had written a phone number down on a piece of paper and where it ran off the edge of the paper, the last two digits ended up next to Eiffel. They kept it in feeling that it might be a lucky sign and they couldn't have been more right.

Maurizio, who had learned classical piano, was born in Turin while Jeffrey, although born in Sicily, spent many years growing up in Brooklyn, New York before returning to Italy at the age of 20. "Although we all share a passion for dance and electronic music, we want people to get a positive message from us," insisted Jeffrey. "We're more like an old fashioned Depeche Mode, a solid structure, but more futuristic."

In the studio Maurizio started playing a piano riff while Jeffrey was writing lyrics. He said, "I started thinking about this character I invented called Zoroti and the lifestyle he led, from the way he would buy his house, pick his girlfriend, his job or the neighbourhood he would live in. Then I came up with a colour, a colour that I thought described the way he saw things."

Like a number of dance tracks in 1999, it was first heard in Ibiza and so charted as an import spending five weeks on the chart prior to the UK release and reached number 39. It helped that the import price, which would normally be over £6 was the same as the UK release at £3.99.

Eiffel 65's follow-up 'Move Your Body' went to number three in February 2000, but the parent album, *Europop*, only spent four weeks on the chart despite reaching number 12. They released two further albums, *Contact* (2001) and *Eiffel 65* (2003), which both sold well in Europe, but failed to attract any buyers in the UK.

837 Christina Aguilera
Genie In A Bottle

Label & Cat No.: **RCA 74321705482**

Producers: **Steve Kipner / David Frank**

Writers: **Steve Kipner / David Frank / Pam Sheyne**

Date Reached No.1: **16 October 1999**

Weeks at No.1: **2**

"I WAS 17 YEARS OLD AND GLAD TO HAVE A record deal and fans, my dream had come true. But it wasn't who I wanted to be and the press saw it as manufactured," said a young, but mature Christina Aguilera.

Three of the biggest teen idols of the last five years; Britney Spears, Justin Timberlake and Christina Aguilera, all began their career in the same place. Christina was just 12 when she got the job on *The New Mickey Mouse Club* TV show in America. But it was her performance of 'Reflection' on the soundtrack to the Disney movie *Mulan* that convinced RCA to give her a record contract.

'Genie In A Bottle' was Christina's debut hit and it topped the chart on both sides of the Atlantic. The lyric 'I'm a genie in a bottle/You gotta rub me the right way', is a bit near the mark, but Christina explains the story, "It is a bit suggestive, but in a positive way. It's all about a girl who's a little sassy and likes to play hard to get, but equally wants sincerity in a relationship." Listen further to the lyric 'My body's saying let's go, but my heart is saying no' and you'll see what she means.

Even at 17, she was firm in her opinions. RCA weren't happy with her name because they thought it would be hard to pronounce and wanted to shorten it to Christina Agui, which surely would have been more confusing. They suggested names like Christina Maria and Christina Atee. "Then they were going to do one name, Christina, but I said no, I want to use my full name."

Co-writer Pam Sheyne is a New Zealander by birth but lives in London. A former backing singer for The Pet Shop boys and Celine Dion, she began writing songs in the mid-Nineties and has had songs recorded by Sheena Easton ('All I Ask Of You'), MN8 ('Baby It's You'), Kim Wilde ('This I Swear'), Kavana ('MFEO') and Billie ('She Wants You'). Steve Kipner has written hits for Olivia Newton-John ('Physical'), Chicago ('Hard Habit To Break') and George Benson ('20/20') whilst David Frank has worked on songs for Robert Palmer ('You Are In My System') and Ronan Keating ('Lost For Words'). For all three, this is their first UK chart topper.

Five weeks before 'Genie In A Bottle' topped the chart, the single spent five weeks below the Top 40 on import, which was a good indication that Christina was here to stay, at least for a while.

Like her rivals Britney Spears and Justin Timberlake, Christina Aguilera began her show-biz career on The Mickey Mouse Club TV show

838 Westlife
Flying Without Wings

Label & Cat No.: **RCA 74321 709162**

Producer: **Steve Mac**

Writer: **Steve Mac / Wayne Hector**

Date reached No.1: **30 October 1999**

Weeks at No.1: **1**

GETTING A NOVEL IDEA FOR A SONG IS half the battle, and Steve Mac and Wayne Hector had a winner by likening happiness to flying without wings. It is effectively a list song but Cole Porter would have shown more originality than simply choosing children, friendship and a lover's eyes. In the final verse, the singer finds satisfaction in his girlfriend, a factor he has already listed. Steve Mac states proudly that they wrote it in three hours but perhaps they should have spent more time in checking the scansion and rhymes and tightening the imagery. Still, it is a modern day standard and the key song in Westlife's stage act.

'Flying Without Wings' demonstrated the depth of Westlife's harmonies, and a New York gospel choir was added for the powerful finale. 'Flying Without Wings' was voted the Record of the Year, narrowly beating their manager's number one, 'When You Say Nothing At All'. Nicky Byrne had the award in his hand and when he hugged Wayne Hector, he broke it.

The group's first album, *Westlife,* was released at the same time. It made number two and although it couldn't dislodge Steps or Celine Dion, it was listed for over a year. *Westlife* contained three number ones, two future ones and 12 other tracks.

Although Westlife did not have any US hits, 'Flying Without Wings' became a US number two for the winner of *American Idol 2,* Ruben Studdard, in 2003.

By 2004 thousands of computer users were obtaining their music from PCs and a chart covering downloads was inevitable. Several contemporary bands wanted to secure the top position on the first chart. Westlife chose to make a live version of 'Flying Without Wings' available and it topped the chart in September 2004.

839 Five
Keep On Movin'

Label & Cat No.: **RCA 74321709862**

Producers: **Richard Stannard / Julian Gallagher**

Writers: **Richard Stannard / Julian Gallagher / Jason Brown / Abs Breen / Sean Conlon**

Date Reached No.1: **6 November 1999**

Weeks at No.1: **1**

"WE'RE NOT A BOY BAND, WE'RE A lad's band," insisted Ritchie Neville from one of pop's newest groups. Determined to avoid the boy band tag, Jason added, "Of course people will say we're manufactured because we met at an audition. The difference with us is that we're doing everything ourselves and we have a say in everything."

Five, or 5 as they were originally called , were put together by Richard Stannard and Julian Gallagher, who were involved with The Spice Girls three years earlier and as a result were initially referred to as The Spice Boys. The name was chosen by the group after a number of coincidences involving the number five. "One night whilst away in Denmark, we were sitting eating a Chinese when this brand new Mercedes parked outside and the number plate was '5'. Also that night, our manager, Chris' hotel room number was 555, so we decided to adopt that as our name," Ritchie recalled.

Five were Richard Abidin 'Abs' Breen (born 1979), Scott Robinson (born 1979), J (born Jason Brown 1976), Ritchie Neville (born Richard Dobson 1979) and Sean Conlon (born 1981). Their first single, 'Slam Dunk (Da Funk)', which sampled 'Clap Your Hands' by Herbie, and was reminiscent of The Spice Girls' 'Wannabe', slammed into the chart at number 10. It was followed by 'When The Lights Go Out' (4), 'Got The Feelin'' (3) and three number twos, 'Everybody Get Up', which sampled Joan Jett & The Blackhearts' 'I Love Rock And Roll', 'Until The Time Is Through' and 'If Ya Getting Down' which borrowed the bass line from Indeep's 'Last Night A DJ Saved My Life'. They finally got to number one with their seventh release, 'Keep On Movin''.

Their debut album, *Five*, was released in July 1998 and went straight to number one. The second album, *Invincible*, only went to number four, but spent longer on the chart.

Their energetic dance moves and clever rapping put them a cut above most of the other boy bands that flooded the charts around this time. In America they had three hits, two more than Take That and three more than Boyzone and Westlife, neither of whom got a look in.

'Keep On Movin'' was used as the backing theme for the 2002 World Cup.

840 Geri Halliwell
Lift Me Up

Label & Cat No.: **EMI CDEM 554**

Producers: **Absolute (Paul Wilson / Andy Watkins)**

Writers: **Geri Halliwell / Paul Wilson / Andy Watkins / Tracey Ackerman**

Date reached No.1: **13 November 1999**

Weeks at No.1: **1**

FOLLOWING HER NUMBER ONE WITH 'Mi Chico Latino', Geri Halliwell was doing something newsworthy almost every day. Quite how she found time to write her 400-page autobiography, *If Only*, is hard to say, but Geri was on the singles, albums and book charts at the same time. "Being a pop star isn't a long-term career," she noted. "It's something you do when you're young." Try telling that to Rod, Paul, Mick and Keith, but it presumably meant that Geri, rather like Cilla, would soon decide that enough was enough and, perhaps, become a TV presenter.

Her album, *Schizophonic*, was better than her critics would have you believe. She did not have a great voice, but the producers, the Absolute duo from Bristol, managed to extract some Karen Carpenter qualities from her for the fine ballad, 'Lift Me Up'. Geri commented, "It was in your face and full of attitude and that seemed to be the right message to send." It also sent a message to Emma Bunton whose single 'What I Am' with Tin Tin Out was released on the same day and lost the race for the top.

Geri's video looked at the various masks she wore, depicting her as a virgin bride, a vamp and a bitch as well as disposing of her previous image with a coffin and a floral display to 'Ginger'. Did Geri see herself as a Marilyn Monroe figure? For Prince Charles' 50th birthday, she replicated Marilyn's homage to President Kennedy by singing 'Happy Birthday To You'. As she sang on 'Heaven And Hell', "It's heaven, it's hell, being Geri Halliwell," adding "The only difference between you and I, is you get deadlines and I get headlines."

And as for 'Life Me Up' Geri has said, "If a song still sounds good 10 years after it came out, then you know it's a great record." We'll know in 2009.

841 Robbie Williams
It's Only Us / She's The One

Label & Cat No.: **Chrysalis CDCHS 5112**

Producers: **Guy Chambers / Steve Power**

Writers: **Guy Chambers / Steve Power: Karl Wallinger**

Date reached No.1: **20 November 1999**

Weeks at No.1: **1**

As a lyricist, Robbie Williams has collaborated with several songwriters, none more successfully than Guy Chambers, although they were to fall out spectacularly. His contribution to Robbie's 1998 *I've Been Expecting You* was invaluable and he was responsible for both the songs that were taken from the album and included on this single. Guy Chambers worked with Steve Power as a production team and one of their compositions was 'It's Only Us'.

Guy, a Liverpudlian, had played with World Party and then had minor successes with his group, The Lemon Trees, in 1992/3. One of the tracks on *I've Been Expecting You* was a revival of the World Party ballad, 'She's The One', with a restrained, almost whispered vocal from Robbie. The CD included the video, shot at an ice rink for which Robbie had tuition from Olympic gold medalist, Robin Cousins. When Robbie's friend and fellow entertainer, Jonathan Wilkes, was performing 'She's The One' in Brighton, Robbie walked on from the wings with the words, "Do you want a hand, mate?" He and Jonathan subsequently recorded 'Me And My Shadow' for the album, *Swing When You're Winning*.

Kurt Wallinger slagged off Robbie's version of 'She's The One' and, in annoyance, Robbie dropped it from stage performances. "Ungrateful bastard," said Robbie, "I bet he was fucking happy when the royalty cheque came in. It will go on the *Greatest Hits* and earn that bastard even more money."

One track on *I've Been Expecting You* was 'Jesus In A Camper Van' and Robbie and Guy were accused of plagiarising Loudon Wainwright's 'I Am The Way (New York Town)'. The judge awarded Wainwright 25% of the royalties and ordered that the song be removed from future pressings of the album. 'It's Only Us' was not initially on *I've Been Expecting You*, but has now replaced 'Jesus In A Camper Van'.

842 Wamdue Project
King Of My Castle

Label & Cat No.: **AM:PM CDAMPM 127**

Producer: **Chris Brann**

Writer: **Chris Brann**

Date Reached No.1: **27 November 1999**

Weeks at No.1: **1**

Feral, Santal, The Ananda Project and Wambonix, are all aliases of Georgia-native, Chris Brann. In 1994 he discovered house music and wanted to make his own. Later the same year he built himself a studio at home and began working with local DJs Chris Clarke and Chris Udoh under the guise Wamdue Kidz. This led to the release of 'Higher' on the Acacia label in the US. He signed to Strictly Rhythm Records in 1996 and released 'Resource Toolbook Volume 1', which was big on the underground scene but failed to cross over. The Wamdue Project is the moniker that would eventually bring him international success. But when 'King Of The Castle' was first issued in June 1998, so few people wanted to know that it only sold 350 copies.

Chris, who was born in Atlanta in 1974, met an Argentinean singer Victoria Frigerio singing in a club in the US and asked her to do some vocals for him. It was originally released on the now defunct Eruption record label and failed to connect. Chris then met English DJ and remixer Roy Malone in Italy who agreed to transform 'King Of My Castle' into a radio and club-friendly track. Chris knew it had potential and after some radical remixing, it was picked up by Sweden's Orange record label and became a major hit in most European countries. "It's been a kind of long slow build up," remembered Chris. "I was a bit put off artistically, but it's also a good thing because it brings the bulk of my art into mainstream awareness."

A&M, who were just about to be absorbed into Universal, launched their latest dance subsidiary label, AM:PM and where their previous dance off-shoots, Breakout and Funk A&Merica had failed, AM:PM landed a number one hit.

One thing that puzzled everyone was the song's lyrics. The verse, the chorus, in fact, the whole track, comprised of, "Must be the reason why I'm king of my castle, Must be the reason why it's free in my trapped soul, Must be the reason why I'm king of my castle, Must be the reason why I'm making examples to you."

Chris is a firm believer in the music he creates. "I think that music is first and foremost a language, second a technique. I'd like to be recognised less for my production and more for simply the musical content," he insists. "My intentions are being able to let music reveal itself, let the music breathe, don't force the music. That's my school of production: Let it exist, let it create itself a world. You don't, as a producer, have to force it or tell it to be a certain way."

Chris followed up his number one with 'You're The Reason', which only reached number 39 and within a few months the Wamdue Project was laid to rest. In 2000 he changed musical direction and began experimenting with jazz and Latin rhythms. He also uses a variety of vocalists and still releases tracks in Europe under his latest moniker P'Taah.

843 Cliff Richard
The Millennium Prayer

Label & Cat No.: **Papillon PROMISECD 01**

Producer: **Nigel Wright**

Writers: **Traditional (!) arranged by Paul Field / Stephen Deal / Cliff Richard / Nigel Wright**

Date reached No.1: **4 December 1999**

Weeks at No.1: **3**

ON THE DAY OF PRINCESS DIANA'S funeral in 1997, the songwriter Paul Field found himself on an unusually quiet motorway. Pulling into a service station, he was with the crowds watching the funeral on a large screen and as 'The Lord's Prayer' was recited, many joined in. Paul realised that although this was a secular age with falling church attendances, everyone knew 'The Lord's Prayer'. He set it to 'Auld Lang Syne' for a revue, *Hopes And Dreams*, for the Methodist church and a CD was recorded, using Cliff Richard, whom Paul knew. No one saw it as a potential single. Except Cliff.

Cliff realised it was a perfect single as 'The Lord's Prayer' celebrated Christmas and 'Auld Lang Syne' the turn of the year. It would be a charity release for Children's Promise and he asked EMI, his record company for 40 years, to release it. They refused, and in so doing created one of the great moments in pop history. Cliff took it to an independent label, Papillon. The record was turned down by Radios 1 and 2, and Andy Kershaw called it "sanctimonious old shite". Everyone said Cliff hadn't a prayer.

Then the publicity kicked in and it became a real Cliffhanger as to how the single would fare. Over 60,000 brave souls risked ridicule by buying it during the first week and it entered at number two without any airplay. When Cliff sang it on the *Royal Variety Performance* and *An Audience With Cliff Richard*, it went to number one, thus becoming the first number one in blank verse to make the top. It raised £1m for Children's Promise and Sir Cliff passed over the cheque at the Millennium Dome in March 2000.

Cliff's next album, *Wanted*, was on Papillon but he returned to EMI in 2003 for *Cliff At Christmas*. In 2004 Cliff signed with Decca, the label that had turned him down in 1958. He retains an enormous fan base and although he is more likely to be heard talking to David Hamilton on Saga Radio than on Radio 1 these days, his *Live And Kicking!* tour was a big success in 2004.

844 Westlife
I Have A Dream / Seasons In The Sun

Label & Cat No.: **RCA 74321 726012**

Producers: **Dan Frampton / Pete Waterman : Karl Twigg / Mark Topham**

Writers: **Benny Andersson / Björn Ulvaeus : Jacques Brel / Rod McKuen**

Date reached No.1: **25 December 1999**

Weeks at No.1: **4**

ON THE DAY THEY WOULD MAKE THEIR chart debut, Westlife were recording with Pete Waterman. Halfway through the day, they broke off to await the call, and Waterman opened the champagne when they found they had entered at number one with 'Swear It Again'. How did they record Abba's 'I Have A Dream' in the midst of such euphoria? It was considered the perfect contender for the Christmas number one and also for the turn of the century.

Because Westlife were so busy, only one day could be set aside for the videos. Two sets were assembled in the same building, and the members of the group rushed back and forth for the appropriate shots. Not for nothing does the video for 'I Have A Dream' end with Bryan McFadden asleep in the back of a car.

Abba had been foiled in their bid for a Christmas number one with 'I Have A Dream' in 1979 by Pink Floyd. The anthemic ballad came from their album, *Voulez-Vous*, and Abba often performed this song of hope on stage with choirs from local schools. Westlife used The Bodywork Theatre School Choir and, incidentally, the song was held back from their first album. The French chanson, 'Seasons In The Sun', had been a UK number one for Terry Jacks in 1974.

The main contenders for the Christmas number one were Cliff Richard's 'The Millennium Prayer', a reissue of John Lennon's 'Imagine' and the Spice Girls with a 'Perfect Day' workout of 'It's Only Rock'n'Roll'. Rockin' around the Christmas trees were the yodelling, dancing hamsters as well as 'Mr. Hanky The Christmas Poo', who was full of shit.

The serious money was on Cliff or Westlife, trying for their fourth number one with their fourth single. Fortunately for them, Cliff peaked early and their well-chosen version of Abba's simple, optimistic song soared to the top. Cliff didn't mind as, unbelievably, he was outselling both Boyzone and Liverpool footballer Michael Owen in the calendar stakes.

Pete Waterman was confident that 'I Have A Dream' would be the Christmas number one, and, even though it was May, he placed £1,000 on the outcome at 15 to 1. He said, "I wasn't even worried when Cliff Richard took the number one spot in December. I was sure Westlife would do it." Westlife became the first act since Elvis Presley in 1962 to have four number one records in the same year and what's more, all Westlife's records had all entered at the top.

So, at number one we had "I believe in angels", at number two "Our father, who art in heaven", and at number three, "Imagine there's no heaven": something for everyone.

2000-2005

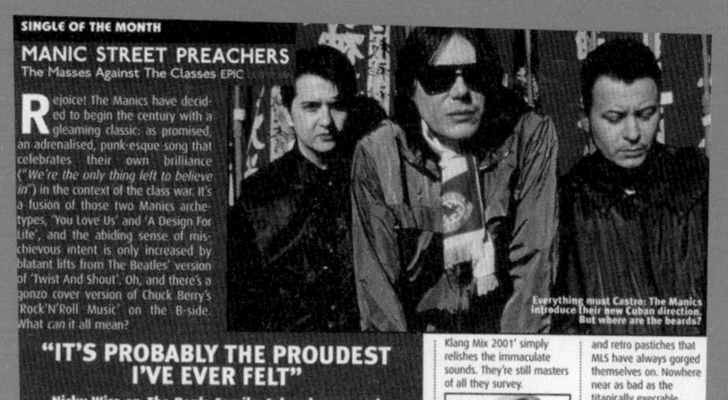
SINGLE OF THE MONTH

MANIC STREET PREACHERS
The Masses Against The Classes EPIC

Rejoice! The Manics have decided to begin the century with a gleaming classic: as promised, an adrenalised, punk-esque song that celebrates their own brilliance ("*We're the only thing left to believe in*") in the context of the class war. It's a fusion of those two Manics archetypes, 'You Love Us' and 'A Design For Life', and the abiding sense of mischievous intent is only increased by blatant lifts from The Beatles' version of 'Twist And Shout'. Oh, and there's a gonzo cover version of Chuck Berry's 'Rock'N'Roll Music' on the B-side. What *can* it all mean?

Everything must Castro: The Manics introduce their new Cuban direction. But where are the beards?

"IT'S PROBABLY THE PROUDEST I'VE EVER FELT"

Nicky Wire on *The Royle Family*, Cuban boxers and reclaiming The Beatles

Klang Mix 2001' simply relishes the immaculate sounds. They're still masters of all they survey.

and retro pastiches that MLS have always gorged themselves on. Nowhere near as bad as the titanically execrable 'Golden Mile' album and, therefore, a strange kind of let-down.

THE INTERNET IS STILL KILLING MUSIC

I'd just like to vent some anger about people like Dominic Tunon (*News*, May 17) who seem to think that downloading music for free off the internet is a God-given right. They don't seem to appreciate that the people who make the music they're stealing have to make a living just like everyone else. When you download (or fileshare) material like this, not only are you infringing copyright, ie breaking the law, you're also denying the musicians valuable income from record sales. Look at it this way: if you were struggling to make a living in a band and couldn't afford to eat because loads of tossers got your songs for free instead of paying for it, how would you feel? Mighty

right idea. Just think about what you're doing.
Jez Wright, West Sussex

It's funny: unless they're utter Luddites, you don't usually hear fledgling bands who are in desperate need of any kind of promotion complaining about people downloading their music for free. You'd think they'd be grateful for the attention.

JANUARY 2002 · £3.30

MOJO
The Music Magazine

George Harrison

Fatboy: 'Beach party is off'

'MP3? HOW GREAT IS THAT?'

Is MP3 the start of a new musical democracy? Or is it just a clunky, time-wasting way to hear some crappy unsigned bands? We ask industry insiders Alan McGee and Jonathan King – is it the bollocks or just bollocks...

FOR EVERYONE

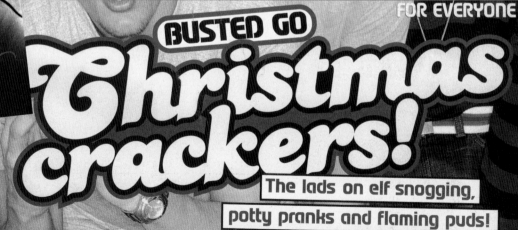

BUSTED GO Christmas crackers!

The lads on elf snogging, potty pranks and flaming puds!

"Eminem is one of the most charismatic and charming people I have ever met."

gibberish.

"This is the end of Robbie Williams, singer-cum-cabaret artist."

Two words, Robbie: Gary Barlow.

"I don't want to step onstage with someone wearing a fucking coronet and ermine."

Keith Richards. Not at all jealous of Mick's knighthood, then.

JOHN LENNON'S 'IPOD' FOUND!

Portable jukebox reveals what was on the legendary Beatle's playlist

Three fab facts about Natasha

- Natasha has had the same best friends since she was tiny and spends hours on the phone to them.
- The singer describes herself as fun, loving, crazy, happy and passionate.
- She quit her Psychology degree to be a pop star, but hopes to go back to uni and finish it one day.

This Week	Last Week	Weeks in Ch	ARTIST TI (Producer) Publisher (Writer)	
1	NEW		**BAND AID 20** DO THEY KNOW IT'S CHRISTMAS? (Godrich) Warner-Chappell (Geldof/Ure)	
2	NEW		**ICE CUBE FEAT. MACK 10 & MS TOI** YOU CAN DO IT (One Eye) Universal/Warner-Chappell/CC (Bambaataa/Jackson/Robie/Miller/Williams/Baker)	
3	2	5	**DESTINY'S CHILD** LOSE MY BREATH (Jerkins/Knowles) Sony ATV/EMI/Windswept (Jerkins/Garrett/Knowles/Rowland/Williams/Jerkins)	All Around The Work
4	1	3	**GIRLS ALOUD** I'LL STAND BY YOU (Higgins/Xenomania) EMI (Hynde/Kelley/Steinberg)	
5	NEW		**GREEN DAY** BOULEVARD OF BROKEN DREAMS (Cavallo/Green Day) Warner-Chappell (Green Day)	
6	NEW		**NATASHA BEDINGFIELD** UNWRITTEN (Rodrigues/Brisebois) EMI/CC (Bedingfield/Rodrigues/Brisebois)	
7	3	3	**LEMAR** IF THERE'S ANY JUSTICE (Rawling/Meehan) EMI/CC (Leeson/Vale)	Phonoge
8	NEW		**BABYSHAMBLES** KILLAMANGIRO (Epworth) EMI (Doherty)	So
9	5	2	**NELLY & CHRISTINA AGUILERA** TILT YA HEAD BACK (Doe) Warner-Chappell/Burning Bush (Nelly/Moore/Nexton/Mayfield)	Rough
10	NEW		**SNOOP DOGG FEAT. PHARRELL** DROP IT LIKE IT'S HOT (The Neptunes) EMI/BMG (Broadus/Hugo/Williams)	Un
11	8	3	**GWEN STEFANI** WHAT YOU WAITING FOR (Hooper) Barajuku Lover/Stuck In The Throat/Famous (Stefani/Perry)	
12	7	5	**EMINEM** JUST LOSE IT (Dr Dre/Elizondo) Windswept/EMI (Mathers/Young/Elizondo/Batson/Pope)	
13	6	2	**BRIAN MCFADDEN** IRISH SON (Chambers/Stacey) EMI (McFadden/Chambers)	
14	9	3	**JOJO FEAT. BOW WOW** BABY IT'S YOU (The Underdogs) First Avenue/BMG/EMI/Universal (Mason Jr/Thomas/Dawkins/Dixon)	Modest/So
15	4	2	**GERI** RIDE IT (Masterson) EMI/Windswept Music London (Quiz/Larossi/Kotecha/Halliwell)	
16	12	2	**UNITING NATIONS** OUT OF TOUCH (Keenan/Sampson) Warner-Chappell (Hall/Oates)	
17	15	5	**CHRISTINA AGUILERA & MISSY ELLIOTT** CAR WASH (Elliott/Herzberg/Styles/Bang Out/Silence/Urkill) Universal (Whitfield/Elliott)	
18	14	2	**JAY-Z/LINKIN PARK** NUMB/ENCORE (Shinoda) EMI/Zomba/Sony ATV (West/Linkin Park/Carter)	De
19	11	5	**USHER** CONFESSIONS PART II/MY BOO (Dupri/Cox:Dupri) EMI/BMG/EMI/Shaniah Cymone/Babyboy's Little Pub co/WC (Dupri/Cox/Raymond:Dupri/Seal/Shropshire/Keys)	L
20	NEW		**RAZORLIGHT** RIP IT UP (Cornfield/Razorlight) Sony ATV (Borrell/Razorlight)	
21	17	12	**ERIC PRYDZ** CALL ON ME (Prydz) EMI/Warner-Chappell/Rondor/Universal (Prydz/Winwood/Jennings)	
22	13	4	**U2** VERTIGO (Lillywhite) Blue Mountain/Fairwood (U2/Bono/The Edge)	
23	19	5	**JAMELIA** DJ/STOP (Soulshock & Karlin:Hogarth) Full Of Soul/EMI/Various/Universal (Soulshock/Karlin/White/Cantrall/Longott:Brown/Var.)	
24	[illegible]	[illegible]	**SHANIA TWAIN FEAT. MARK MCGRATH** PARTY FOR TW	

BBC1 pulls plug on Top Of The Pops

U2

Vertigo Island

'Vertigo' is from what Westwood calls the jump-off, absolutely brilliant and heavier than the Pope's nads to boot. Like four blokes in a small room making a killer racket. ***RF***

JOHN PEEL 1939-2004

HERO. LEGEND. GOOD BLOKE

ambrel

845 Manic Street Preachers The Masses Against The Classes

Label & Cat No.: **Epic 6685306**

Producer: **Dave Eringa**

Writers: **Nick Jones / James Dean Bradfield / Sean Moore**

Date Reached No.1: **22 January 2000**

Weeks at No.1: **1**

"ALL THE WORLD OVER, I WILL BACK THE masses against the classes." So said William Ewart Gladstone, the British Prime Minister between 1868-1874.

Fresh from their triumphant New Year's Eve 1999 gig at Cardiff's Millennium Stadium, the Manic Street Preachers now had something else to celebrate. Released on January 10, the Manics' new single was a limited edition, which was deleted on the day of issue. It was testament to the band's popularity that the song went straight in at number one. Disgusted by a chart full of pretty boy bands, bassist Nicky Wire begged the 50,000-strong crowd at the concert to go out and purchase their single in order to usurp Westlife from the top spot. Said Nicky, "It is a separate entity, a complete one-off and has nothing to do with the next album."

'The Masses Against The Classes', which also featured a raucous cover of Chuck Berry's 'Rock And Roll Music', sold almost 35,000 on its day of release, at a time when sales are traditionally slow due to a post-Christmas slump. By the end of the week it had sold 76,000 copies.

The opening sample, "This country was founded on the principle that the primary role of government is to protect property from the majority", is by respected linguist and socialist Noam Chomsky. Vocalist James Dean Bradfield quotes a line from the French novelist and playwright Albert Camus' 1951 tome, *The Rebel*, "The slave begins by demanding justice and ends by wanting to wear a crown," at the end of the song.

Since then, the Manics have released one further studio album, *Know Your Enemy* (2001), a greatest hits effort, *Forever Delayed* (2002) and a collection of B-sides and rarities, *Lipstick Traces* (2003). *Lipstick Traces* also contained some unlikely covers, including 'Last Christmas', 'Bright Eyes', 'Raindrops Keep Falling On My Head' and 'Out Of Time'.

They had two further Top 10 singles, both released on the same day, 'So Why So Sad' (8) and 'Found That Soul' (9).

In February 2004 the people of Wales voted for their '100 Welsh Heroes'. At number 17 was James Dean Bradfield, 10 places below Dylan Thomas but 27 higher than Anthony Hopkins. Richey Edwards was at number 23, still surpassing T.E. Lawrence (52), Neil Kinnock (58) and King Arthur (70). (And just in case you're wondering, Tom Jones was in third place, pipped to the post by founder of the NHS Aneurin Bevan, and Owain Glyndür, the 14th century rebel leader, who came in first and second respectively.)

846 Britney Spears Born To Make You Happy

Label & Cat No.: **Jive 9250022**

Producer: **Kristian Lundin**

Writers: **Kristian Lundin / Andreas Carlsson**

Date Reached No.1: **29 January 2000**

Weeks at No.1: **1**

THE FOLLOW-UP TO '...BABY ONE More Time', 'Sometimes' entered at number three and spent 16 weeks on the chart. During the filming of that video, Britney tore a cartilage in her knee while attempting a high kick and returned to her home town of Kentwood to recover.

After a couple of months she continued making the video, but soon found herself in the gossip columns, astute observers noticing that her breasts were larger than before the accident. She pointed out that at her age, a girl's breasts are naturally expected to balloon in size. Once the tabloids lost interest in her boobs, they started talking about her sex life and the fact that she was still a virgin. Again, she put up with none of it. She retorted, "Just because I look sexy on the cover of *Rolling Stone* doesn't mean I'm a naughty girl. I'd do it again."

Her next single, '(You Drive Me) Crazy' reached number five in the UK and was featured in the film Drive Me Crazy. She also made a cameo appearance in the TV show *Sabrina The Teen Witch* and became good friends with its star, Melissa Joan Hart. In September 1999 she appeared at the MTV Awards. She was also nominated for three awards for Best Female Artist, Best Pop Video and Best Choreography. She lost out on all three to Lauryn Hill, Fatboy Slim and Ricky Martin respectively and was desperately disappointed.

In the US, 'From The Bottom Of My Broken Heart' became the next single from ...*Baby One More Time*, but it only reached number 14. Jive's decision to release 'Born To Make You Happy' as the next single here paid off when it went to number one. The accompanying video showed Britney romping provocatively about on a bed, but filming was delayed when she suffered minor injuries after falling off it.

Britney returned to Stockholm to begin work on her next album, *Oops!... I Did It Again*, and because of the success of ...*Baby One More Time*, Britney was keen to continue working with Max Martin and Rami and so the title may have been a suggestion as to what we might expect.

To give it a different dimension she also enlisted the production skills of Robert 'Mutt' Lange who had worked with AC/DC, Bryan Adams and Def Leppard as well as Rodney Jerkins, who's CV includes Michael Jackson's Bad, as well as hit singles for Destiny's Child, Whitney Houston, Shola Ama, Brandy and Jennifer Lopez.

The album also contained 'Dear Diary', a beautiful ballad that gave Britney her first co-writing credit as well as a funky version of '(I Can't Get No) Satisfaction', albeit with slightly detoxified lyrics.

Manic Street Preachers built a career with songs that proclaimed their socialist ideals; left to right: James Dean Bradfield, Nicky Wire and Sean Moore

847 Gabrielle
Rise

Label & Cat No.: **Go. Beat GODCD 99**
Producer: **Johnny Dollar**
Writers: **Bob Dylan / Gabrielle / Ferdy Unger-Hamilton / Ollie Dagois**
Date Reached No.1: **5 February 2000**
Weeks at No.1: **2**

Gabrielle took a year's sabbatical following the birth of her son, Jordan, in 1995. She returned in 1996 with the Top five single, 'Give Me A Little More Time'. Later the same year she collaborated with East 17 on the number two hit 'If You Ever' followed by a true-to-the-original cover of Dionne Warwick's 'Walk On By'.

She spent the whole of 1998 recording her new album, *Rise*, which went straight to number one and spent over 18 months on the chart. The lead-off single, 'Sunshine', reached the Top 10, but it was the title track that took Gabrielle back to the top.

"'Rise' is very much a real song and people out there seem to relate to it. At the same time, it's an optimistic song," mused Gabrielle. Borrowing a sample from Bob Dylan's 'Knockin' On Heaven's Door', it was the first time Bob Dylan had allowed one of his songs to be sampled, rather than covered. She told Dotmusic, "I got really scared when they sent the demo to Bob Dylan but I got a note back saying he liked it and I could use the sample. It was really wonderful. Bob also agreed to waive half of his royalty rate saying 50% was the music and 50% was the lyrics."

Around this time, Gabrielle decided to have corrective eye surgery and got rid of the patch and her floppy wedge.

Gabrielle had further Top 10 hits with the upbeat 'When A Woman' and 'Out Of Reach' which featured in the film *Bridget Jones's Diary*. In 2001 her greatest hits album, *Dreams Can Come True*, reached number two and spent six months on the chart. Her last album, *Play To Win* was released in 2004 and reached the Top 10. The first single from it, 'Stay The Same', made number 20.

848 Oasis
Go Let It Out!

Label & Cat No.: **Big Brother REIDSD 001**
Producers: **Noel Gallagher / Mark Stent**
Writer: **Noel Gallagher**
Date reached No.1: **19 February 2000**
Weeks at No.1: **1**

By 2000 many wondered if Oasis had had their day. The group had released nothing during 1999, although Liam and Steve Cradock from Ocean Colour Scene had a Top 10 single with The Jam's 'Carnation'. The Gallaghers' personal lives still filled the tabloids, and each tour provoked traumas with one or the other of the brothers threatening to quit. Having split with Patsy Kensit Liam evidently approached Rod Stewart's ex, Rachel Hunter, with the chat-up line, "Do you think I'm sexy?" His new partner was Nicole Appleton from All Saints.

Would Oasis come up with anything worthwhile again? Their UK record label, Creation, was in disarray but their songs were still being published by Alan McGee. They formed their own label, called appropriately enough, Big Brother. The single, 'Go Let It Out!', was released at the start of the new millennium and Noel commented, "With 'Go Let It Out!', I know I can combine rock'n'roll with a contemporary feel and that gives me the confidence to go on."

The arrangement incorporated the Mellotron and lashings of psychedelic guitar. 'Go Let It Out' took a sample from Johnny Jenkins' 'Walk On Gilded Splinters' and the melody line shared some similarities with Abba's 'S.O.S'.

The title of their next album, *Standing On The Shoulder Of Giants*, released in March 2000, was taken with a slight adjustment from the wording around the rim of a two pound coin: Sir Isaac Newton has said, "If I have seen farther, it is by standing on the shoulders of giants." It was true of Oasis as they owe so much to The Beatles. Robbie Williams' comment on the album was, "Noel's run out of other people's ideas."

This was the last CD to feature Bonehead and indeed, Noel Gallagher did most of the bass playing. Liam, Noel and the drummer Alan White worked with two new members. Bonehead's replacement was Colin 'Gem' Archer, an excellent singer and guitarist who had been with The Contenders, Whirlpool and the Creation band, Heavy Stereo, and was working in a guitar shop at the time. New bassist Andy Bell was also with the Creation label, playing for Ride and Hurricane #1.

The second single from the album, the psychedelic 'Who Feels Love?', reached number four, a poor showing for Oasis, and the third, 'Sunday Morning Call', fared no better. Their next CD was *Familiar To Millions*, a live album from Wembley Stadium. If you couldn't catch them at an arena gig, you could see one of the tribute bands like No Way Sis, Wonderwall and Champagne Supernova. "I reckon we're busier than Oasis," said the lead singer of Wonderwall.

849 All Saints
Pure Shores

Label & Cat No.: **London LONCD 444**
Producer: **William Orbit**
Writers: **Shaznay Lewis / William Orbit / Suzanne Melvoin**
Date reached No.1: **26 February 2000**
Weeks at No.1: **1**

Dave Stewart wanted to direct a pop film, *Honest*, which was scripted by himself with Dick Clement and Ian LaFrenais, and it was a likely ladettes story set in 1969. He invited Nicole and Natalie Appleton and Melanie Blatt from All Saints to play the three East End Chase sisters. They agreed and insisted on doing their own stunts. From the start the film appeared to look disaster in the face: how could you publicise a film with only three of All Saints featured? The end result was no *Spice World*, and didn't it give the impression that the fourth All Saint, Shaznay Lewis, thought it naff? And it was.

There was only one song featuring any of the

band, namely, 'You're All I Need To Get By' by Nat with Bootsy Collins, but as all else was likely to fail, the film was sold on its shock value: see All Saints in the nude. Nobody paid much attention to that either. The film cost £4m and took £500 on its first weekend.

While the three girls were making *Honest*, Shaz went to the States to work with William Orbit, noted for his work with Madonna, on the songs and backing tracks for their second album. She hated the way that their celebrity boyfriends were tabloid fodder as she wanted All Saints to be taken seriously. Shaz maintained a long-standing relationship with the dancer Christian Storm and commented, "I remember a gig where someone held up a banner that read 'Pure Whores'. I knew for sure that they weren't talking about me."

Compared to *Honest*, *The Beach* was assured of a reasonable audience because it starred Leonardo DiCaprio and shared the same writer, director and producer as *Trainspotting*. It boasted a strong soundtrack with several original recordings. Melanie Blatt took the lead vocal on 'Pure Shores'. *The Beach* is a drugs story set in Thailand and the lyric of this slow dancer captures the main character's state of mind. The film disposed of Robert Carlyle in the first 10 minutes. Saints preserve us: you've got to be a Hitchcock to make something like that work.

850 Madonna
American Pie

Label & Cat No.: **Maverick W 519CD1**

Producers: **Madonna / William Orbit**

Writer: **Don McLean**

Date Reached No.1: **11 March 2000**

Weeks at No.1: **1**

MADONNA WAS STILL KEEN TO BE involved in the movie world and in 1999 her number two hit, 'Beautiful Stranger' – which bore more than just a passing resemblance to 'She Comes In Colors' by Love – was written for the Mike Myers film *Austin Powers II: The Spy Who Shagged Me*.

A year later Madonna landed the part of Abbie Reynolds in the comedy-drama, *The Next Best Thing*. In the movie a friend dies of an AIDS related disease. His last wishes were, that as a tribute, his nearest and dearest sing hand picked lines from 'American Pie' at his funeral. Madonna's co-star was Rupert Everett and it was he who convinced Madonna to sing the song in the movie. Madonna agreed on the proviso that Rupert was to be a part of it and he agreed to do backing vocals.

Don McLean was only 13 when his idol Buddy was killed in a plane crash and that childhood memory inspired the song he'll always be most remembered for, 'American Pie'. Don wrote the song in 1971 and it topped the US chart for four weeks. In the UK it reached number two. Over the years, he has often been questioned about the meaning of the lyrics but he remains enigmatic. In one interview he replied, "It means I don't have to work if I don't want to," although he did once concede, and revealed that he never intended the song to be about the death of music. He said, "The music never dies, and I was saying that people lack the basic trust to believe that music will happen again."

Don McLean's original version clocked in at just over eight and a half minutes. His single version had part one as the A-side and part two on the flip. Madonna wanted to record the full version, but was told she had to cut it down to about four and a half minutes. So she carefully chose the verses that she could identify with, using four from the first part and two from the second.

Many Don McLean fans were less than happy with Madonna's cover, but Don himself didn't mind it. He said, "Madonna is a myth in the music industry. She is a historic figure, as well as an excellent singer, composer and producer."

Don McLean's hits are fondly remembered and have been repackaged many times over the years, and each time they find a new audience, not least because he continues to tour and perform them. In June 2004 Don was elected into the National Academy of Popular Music Songwriters' Hall of Fame. "This is wonderful," he said, "an unexpected validation for an old lone wolf like me. I am deeply moved."

851 Chicane featuring Bryan Adams
Don't Give Up

Label & Cat No.: **Xtravaganza XTRAV 9CDS**

Producers: **Chicane / Ray Hedges**

Writers: **Nick Bracegirdle / Bryan Adams / Ray Hedges**

Date Reached No.1: **18 March 2000**

Weeks at No.1: **1**

"I AM FED UP WITH BAD DANCE RECORDS and pop records with no substance just being churned out one after the other," said Chicane a.k.a. Nick Bracegirdle. So he decided to market his own brand.

Nick, born in Amersham, Bucks in November 1979, is a classically trained pianist and guitarist who in 1995 was about to study graphic design at Oxford when he and fellow student Leo Elston decided to form a duo under the name Disco Citizens. "An old college friend, Alex Gold, owned Xtravaganza Records so he signed me up. I wasn't into the major record company stupidity, trying to sign me on stupid deals. With Alex, it was just like dealing with a mate." The first single, 'Right Here Right Now' which was licensed to the Deconstruction label, reached number 40.

The following year, Nick decided to record solo under the moniker Chicane. "The name had no deep meaning," he recalled. "I worked for quite a long time as a visual art designer and wanted to have an unusual name." The first single came in 1996 with 'Offshore', which reached number 14. The next single, 'Footprint' was released as Disco Citizens. From here on, Chicane would be his recording guise and Disco Citizens his remixing name.

Although Balearic conjures up thoughts of sun, sand and sea, Nick calls his music 'balearic style'. "I always try to produce summer music. Many people call my style 'balearic housy trance' and I quite like that."

A remix of 'Offshore '97' reached number 17 followed by 'Lost You Somewhere' and 'Strong In

Love' featuring Mason. Next, he teamed up with Maire Brennan from Clannad for the song 'Saltwater', which was effectively Chicane's 'Saltwater' with Maire singing lyrics to Clannad's song 'Harry's Game'. The debut album, *Far From The Maddening Crowd*, with its assortment of trance and house tunes failed to attract the record buying clubbers and it spent one week at number 49.

Nick had met Bryan Adams a couple of years earlier and remixed the Canadian rocker's Top 10 hit 'Cloud #9', so in return he asked Bryan if he would provide vocals for his new single 'Don't Give Up'. Bryan agreed, contributed some lyrics to the track and the song entered the chart at number one. Bryan and Nick have become good friends. "He's a great photographer," enthuses Nick. "He's even done some shots for my album *Inside Cover*."

Nick remixes in different styles under both names and has worked on hits for Everything But The Girl, Jose Padilla, Billie Ray Martin and B*Witched. But due to heavy work commitments he turned down the chance to remix tracks for both Minogue sisters.

His second album, *Behind The Sun*, which also contained the follow-ups, 'No Ordinary Morning' / 'Halcyon' and 'Autumn Tactics', reached number 10 and spent two months on the chart.

In 2003 'Saltwater' was re-issued after it was used as the theme for a TV commercial, Tourism Ireland, but few people went out and bought it again and it stiffed at number 43. A month later he teamed up with D:Ream's Peter Cunnah for the number 33 hit 'Love On The Run'.

In February 2004 Xtravaganza re-issued 'Don't Give Up', this time as a remix by the label's owner, Alex Gold. It failed to attract any new buyers, and like the re-issue of 'Saltwater', it only managed a number 43.

852 Geri Halliwell
Bag It Up

Label & Cat No.: **EMI CDEM 560**

Producers: **Absolute (Paul Wilson / Andy Watkins)**

Writers: **Geri Halliwell / Paul Wilson / Andy Watkins**

Date reached No.1: **25 March 2000**

Weeks at No.1: **1**

AGAINST THE ODDS, *SCHIZOPHONIC*, WAS a hugely successful album, producing several hit singles. 'Look At Me' was Geri's 'Wannabe', revealing that she craved media attention more than anything, and it reached number two. Then followed three number ones – 'Mi Chico Latino', 'Lift Me Up' and 'Bag It Up'.

To a driving disco beat and forceful backing vocals from Pepsi and Shirlie, 'Bag It Up' was a song about contrasts: Geri liked "chocolates and controversy" and he liked "Fridays and bad company" and so on, but it lacked the wit of the first song on that subject – Fred and another Ginger's 'Let's Call The Whole Thing Off' from *Shall We Dance?* (1937). In her song, Geri plays with the title of the best-selling book about gender, *Men Are From Mars, Women Are From Venus* by John Gray (1993), so it becomes "Men are from Venus and girls are from Mars".

The *Girl Powder* CD package was rounded off with Geri's covers of Nancy Sinatra's 'These Boots Are Made For Walkin'' and the Latin 'Perhaps, Perhaps, Perhaps', which is mostly associated with Doris Day, as well as the frenzied but very entertaining video for 'Bag It Up' showing Geri exerting her power over a host of hunks. Geri introduced the song at the Brits ceremony, appearing from between two enormous legs, presumably to symbolise her rebirth. She looked great, but was cavorting on a lap-dancing pole the right way to go about it?

853 Melanie C featuring Lisa 'Left-Eye' Lopes
Never Be The Same Again

Label & Cat No.: **Virgin VSCDT 1762**

Producer: **Rhett Lawrence**

Writers: **Melanie Chisholm / Rhett Lawrence / Paul F. Cruz / Lisa Lopes / Lorenzo Martin**

Date reached No.1: **1 April 2000**

Weeks at No.1: **1**

HAVING BEEN THE MEDIA SENSATION of the late Nineties, the individual Spice Girls went on to match The Beatles for celebrity status. Because Mel B (Scary Spice) and Mel C (Sporty Spice) had the best singing voices, it was assumed that they would fare better as solo artists.

After a hit single with Bryan Adams, 'When You're Gone' (3, 1998), Mel C released her first album, *Northern Star*, which covered many different styles and was produced by several top-name producers, including Rick Rubin and William Orbit. While she was in America, she befriended Steve Jones from The Sex Pistols whom she met in Hollywood. As a result, she appeared with him at the V99 festival in Staffordshire but the audience failed to appreciate a Spice Girl singing 'Anarchy In The UK'. They threw oranges, bread and bottles and she thanked the audience for "their presents".

With commendable pluck, Mel C booked a tour and despite the early setback, her shows of new songs and covers was well accepted. *Northern Star* made the Top 10 and was to remain on the chart for over a year. The singles 'Goin' Down' and 'Northern Star' went Top 10, but the third single, 'Never Be The Same Again', which included a rap from Lisa 'Left Eye' Lopes, went all the way. Much to Mel C's delight, it replaced

Geri Halliwell at number one.

Having Lopes on the single was a very cool move as it gave Mel C some much needed street cred. Lopes had had several hits as part of TLC including 'Waterfalls' (4, 1995) and 'No Scrubs' (3, 1999), but this was her first appearance on a number one.

854 Westlife
Fool Again

Label & Cat No.: **RCA 74321 751562**

Producers: **Per Magnusson / David Kreuger**

Writers: **Jorgen Elofsson / Per Magnusson / David Kreuger**

Date reached No.1: **8 April 2000**

Weeks at No.1: **1**

WESTLIFE HAD ONLY BEEN RECORDING for a year but they were breaking records as fast as they were making them. Endeavouring to become the first band ever to have their first five singles enter at number one, they went to Mexico to make a stunning video, which incorporated many local people. On the week of release, they were undertaking signings in record stores and making multiple TV appearances. It seems odd that they should pin so much hope on 'Fool Again', the fifth track from their album, *Westlife*. Surely most fans would have the song already, but perhaps they were tempted by the new up-tempo track, 'Tunnel Of Love', in the package.

'Fool Again' was a lovesick ballad with heavenly harmonies, written and produced by the same team who made 'If I Let You Go' with the group. The Swedish team had begun their international success with Britney Spears and they would soon be dominating the charts with songs for *Pop Idol* winners. Westlife were flying to New York when they heard via a mobile phone that they were back at number one. A party atmosphere developed on the plane as they yelled, "We're in *The Guinness Book Of Records*."

On July 1, 2000 Westlife were given the freedom of Sligo and Nicky Byrne impressed everyone with his 'thank you' speech in Irish.

855 Craig David
Fill Me In

Label & Cat No.: **Wildstar CCWILD 25**

Producer: **Mark Hill**

Writers: **Craig David / Mark Hill**

Date Reached No.1: **15 April 2000**

Weeks at No.1: **1**

BORN TO A GRENADIAN FATHER AND an English mother of Jewish faith, in Southampton in 1981, Craig David is a cut above your average R&B artist. He doesn't smoke, hardly drinks and rarely swears, and writes all his own songs. His father, George, played bass in an early Eighties band called Ebony Rockers, but they disbanded before Craig got a chance to see them. The music interested Craig and he was writing songs by the age of 12. Three years later he was MCing in a club of which his father was the chairman.

Artful Dodger were a Southampton-based two-step garage act made up of Mark Hill and Pete Devereux. Craig met Mark who was DJing at the Juice club and the two began writing songs together including 'What Ya Gonna Do', 'It Ain't Enough' and 'Re-rewind The Crowd Say Bo Selecta'. 'Re-rewind', with Craig David as uncredited vocalist, was issued on a white label in 1999 and became massive on the club scene, partly due to its infectious 'boink' sound after the 'Craig David all over your....' lyric. The north London label, La Bello Blanco, picked it up and started distributing it. Once the radio stations picked up on it, Relentless Records offered to sign them and the song went to number two, spending almost five months on the chart.

Artful Dodger continued without Craig who wanted to pursue a solo career as an R&B singer. They had four more Top 10 hits, of which he guested on a couple, namely 'Woman Trouble' (number six, 2000) and one of the earlier co-writes 'It Ain't Enough' (number 20, 2001).

Craig signed a deal with Wildstar Records through the Telstar group. London's Capital Radio had a vested interest in the label and began championing all the artists on it, which also included Lutricia McNeil and Connor Reeves.

He spent the early part of 2000 recording his debut album *Born To Do It*. When 'Fill Me In', the debut single, entered the chart at number one the tabloids claimed he was the youngest British male singer to top the chart. They had overlooked Craig Douglas, who was 10 months younger when he topped the chart in 1959.

'Fill Me In' did well in the US. It reached number 15 but as Craig commented, "It was interpreted there as a leftfield R&B track because it kicks into the two-step thing on the chorus and the people there don't know what two-step is." When asked what two-step is, Craig explained. "Two-step is a country dance. It's a hybrid of dance music, house music and R&B, quite hard to define really."

When *Born To Do It* was released in August 2000, it too entered the chart at number one and spent one year on the chart. He wasn't the youngest British solo male to have a number one album either. That honour went to Neil Reid, the *Opportunity Knocks* winner, who was 12 when his self-titled album topped the chart in 1972.

856 Fragma
Toca's Miracle

Label & Cat No.: **Positiva CDTIV 128**

Producer: **Ramon Zenker**

Writers: **Ramon Zenker / Dirk Duderstadt / Marco Duderstadt / Victor Imbres / Rob Davies**

Date Reached No.1: **22 April 2000**

Weeks at No.1: **2**

CLUB DJS MIXING TWO SONGS together has been going on for over 25 years. The art of playing the acappella vocals of one song over the backing track to another has been going on almost as long. Chicane's Nick Bracegirdle was one of the first acts to have a hit single using that method by mixing the instrumental 'Saltwater' with the vocals of Clannad's 'Harry's Game' in 1999. Fragma were the first to take one to the top.

Ramon Zenker, who hails from Dusseldorf in Germany, first found success in 1989 when he produced the Honesty 69's cover version of 'French Kiss', which was released before Lil' Louis' version and made number seven in the German chart. Three years later he teamed up with another keyboard player, Oliver Bondzio, to form the duo Hardfloor and released the *Hardtrance Acperience EP* on his own newly formed Harthouse label. He had one further UK hit with 'Trancescript'.

Throughout the Nineties Ramon has had European success under the guises Perplexer, Interactive and Calvin Rotane. As a writer he scored with the Top 10 hit 'Samba De Janeiro' as recorded by Bellini.

In 1999 he began working with two producer and songwriting brothers, Dirk and Marco Duderstadt and called himself Fragma. "It's a nonsense name, it doesn't mean anything at all, I just liked the sound of it," recalled Ramon. "One day Dirk and Marco gave me a rough demo with this magic plugged-guitar line which I thought was really good." It was on a visit to Ibiza, they met a singer called Eva Martinez and Ramon invited her to lend some vocals to the track. "I called it 'Toca Me'. Toca in Spanish means touch, so it became known as touch me."

It was DJ Vimto, in Britain, who had the idea to take the vocals of 'I Need A Miracle' by a British female singer known as Coco (born Sue Bryce), which was a minor UK hit in 1997 also on Positiva, and mix it with the almost instrumental 'Toca Me'. It worked perfectly and by amalgamating the titles, it became 'Toca's Miracle'. Coco had been the lead singer with the group Sub Love who later evolved into the dance act Way Out West.

The album, *Toca*, followed and reached number 19. Two further Top 10 singles were released, 'Everytime You Need Me' featuring Maria Rubia and 'You Are Alive' in 2001.

Ramon is still writing and recording dance material. His last hit was as the writer of 'Be Cool', a Top 10 hit for Germany four-piece Paffendorf in 2002.

857 Oxide And Neutrino
Bound 4 Da Reload (Casualty)

Label & Cat No.: **East West OXIDE 01CD1**
Producers: **DJ Oxide / MC Neutrino**
Writer: **Ken Freeman**
Date Reached No.1: **6 May 2000**
Weeks at No.1: **1**

BY 2000 TWO-STEP GARAGE WAS AT ITS peak with commercial acts like Bomfunk MC's and Artful Dodger being regular fixtures in the clubs and on the dance stations. DJ Ed Case had turned The Gorillaz hit 'Clint Eastwood' into an ear-friendly two-step tune and the production team, Sunship, worked wonders for Misteeq's hits' One Night Stand' and 'All I Want'. But it was two members of the south London 'Massif', The So Solid Crew, DJ Oxide and MC Neutrino who became leaders in this genre.

DJ Oxide (born Alex Rivers) and MC Neutrino (born Mark Oseitutu) in Battersea, south London in 1983 and 1982 respectively, chose their names before they had met. "I wanted to be different as there were a lot of MCs out there. I was good at science at school so that's why I chose Neutrino." Oxide added, "I chose mine just to be original."

The So Solid Crew were a hard-edged rap act who were yet to have chart success and although they didn't leave the fold, Oxide and Neutrino, who met at the Supreme FM pirate radio station in Brixton, made the decision to embrace mainstream.

In 1999 they began working on their debut album *Execute*. "Some tracks can take a day and other can take a week to put together," recalled Neutrino. "But the first track we worked on was 'Bound 4 Da Reload (Casualty)'." The album eventually reached number 11 and spent nearly five months on the chart.

'Bound 4 Da Reload (Casualty)' was built round a sample of the theme to the TV hospital drama *Casualty* and is interwoven with the line: "Ah! I've been shot. I don't believe this, can everyone stop getting shot" which was from dialogue spoken by actor and DJ Tony McMahon in the film *Lock, Stock And Two Smoking Barrels*, as well as some furious rapping by Neutrino. Radio 1 gave it limited airplay: however, through club play it entered the chart at number one after selling 70,000 copies.

The follow-up 'No Good 4 Me', which sampled the Prodigy's 'No Good (Start The Dance)' and featured three members of the So Solid Crew; Megaman, Romeo and Lisa Maffia, reached number six. The next single, 'Up Middle Finger' went to number seven. "I felt I had to express myself over the lack of support for the 'Casualty' track," said Neutrino of the song. "It wasn't directed at anyone specifically, it was just how I felt at the time."

Their final single 'Dem Girlz (I Don't Know Why)' reached number 10 in 2002. It was catchier than most of their previous hits and subsequently received more airplay. It coincided with the release of the album *2 Stepz Ahead*, which only spent two weeks on the chart.

In 2004 the pair were working on a new album. "Our early stuff was just a beat and a couple of fast lyrics that didn't make much sense. We've moved on from that. This is more grown up and lyrically we're on a different level now," said Neutrino.

858 Britney Spears
Oops!... I Did It Again

Label & Cat No.: **Jive 9250542**
Producer: **Max Martin**
Writers: **Max Martin / Rami**
Date Reached No.1: **13 May 2000**
Weeks at No.1: **1**

"I THINK GOD HAS A PLAN FOR EVERYONE and I think this is what he wanted me to do."

When Britney's second album, *Oops!...I Did It Again*, entered the chart at number two and the title track came in at number one, Britney had no need to be sorry for doing it again. Unfortunately her album came up against Whitney Houston's *Greatest Hits* and was unable to dislodge it. The album was more mature than her debut, but then Britney was growing up. In January 2000 Britney headed a long list of performers at the American Music Awards. Her revealing silver catsuit prompted further gossip about the size of her boobs.

'Oops!... I Did It Again', with its suggestive lyric, told the story of a girl flirting with a boy she didn't really care for, although he was smitten with her. It only reached number nine in the US, but became American radio's most requested track in history.

Two further singles were lifted from *Oops!... I Did It Again*, 'Lucky' reached number five and 'Stronger' got to number seven. Her third album, *Britney*, went to number three in the UK and spawned further Top 10 hits with 'I'm A Slave 4 U' (4) and 'Overprotected' (4) as well as 'I'm Not A Girl, Not Yet A Woman' (2) and 'I Love Rock 'N' Roll' (13) both from the film *Crossroads*, in which Britney made her acting debut. It was followed by 'Boys' from *Austin Powers In Goldmember*, in which she, alongside a string of famous names, made a cameo appearance.

In 2003 Britney teamed up with Madonna for the hit single 'Me Against The Music', which went to number three. At the Video Music Awards on MTV, they kissed one another, shocking some viewers. Asked if it was the first time she'd ever kissed a woman, Britney replied, "Yes! Oh my gosh." Was it planned? "In rehearsal, Madonna would play around a little bit. She said when we actually do it, let's just feel it out here because there was no choreography in that part. So we just felt it out. But it was just a kiss," she exclaimed. "There were no tongues."

Madison Avenue dancers with Cheyne Coates (centre)

859 Madison Avenue
Don't Call Me Baby

Label & Cat No.: **VC Recordings VCRD 64**

Producers: **Cheyne Coates / Andy Van Dorsselaer / Duane Morrison**

Writers: **Cheyne Coates / Andy Van Dorsselaer/ Duane Morrison**

Date Reached No.1: **20 May 2000**

Weeks at No.1: **1**

DANCER, CHOREOGRAPHER AND producer, Cheyne Coates met DJ Andy Van Dorsselaer in a Melbourne nightclub in 1998. Sharing a mutual love of Everything But The Girl, Moloko, C&C Music Factory and Soul II Soul, the pair became friends and made plans to record an album featuring an assemblage of vocalists singing songs written by Cheyne.

By chance, Cheyne provided the guide vocal for 'Don't Call Me Baby'. Andy preferred it to the singers they had hired, so they left it as it was. 'Don't Call Me Baby' was based around a large sample from an obscure Italian song from 1980, 'Ma Quale Idea', by Pino D'Angio.

When first released in the UK in November 1999, 'Don't Call Me Baby' reached number 30. Following a promotional tour in 2000, a re-issue made it all the way to the top. Said Andy, "We were in the UK for five weeks to promote it. We visited every radio and TV station, and had interviews with every magazine in the country. Each week we were getting updates that it was going to debut in the Top 20, then the Top five, etc. However we were up against artists like Britney Spears, but we just crossed our fingers that it would make number one. It was great when it happened, but it certainly wasn't the be all and end all."

Madison Avenue became the first Australian dance act to top the UK chart, and also the first Australian-produced number one single in the UK since Men At Work 17 years earlier. The success of the song led to the pair writing a number for fellow Melbournian, Kylie Minogue. However, this never came to fruition.

After further hits with 'Who the Hell Are You' (10), 'Everything You Need' (33), and a debut album, *The Polyester Embassy* (74), tension between the two flared and work on their next release was halted.

Madison Avenue split in 2003, with Cheyne embarking on a solo career. She released two Australian-only singles produced by Brian Canham, of Eighties band, Pseudo Echo. Andy remains a popular DJ and is working on another dance project, as well as running his label, Vicious Vinyl.

860 Billie Piper
Day & Night

Label & Cat No.: **Innocent SINCD 11**

Producers: **Eliot Kennedy / Tim Lever / Mike Percy**

Writers: **Eliot Kennedy / Tim Lever / Billie Piper / Mark Cawley**

Date reached No.1: **27 May 2000**

Weeks at No.1: **1**

By 1999 Billie Piper was exhausted. A three-month worldwide tour was followed by a period in hospital to cure a bladder infection. She was missing her youth, saying, "You've got to be on time, make sense, be logical, take care of yourself and make sure you get enough sleep. As a teenager you're not supposed to do those things."

Taking time off from the road, Billie worked on songs for her next album. Many were written by Billie with Eliot Kennedy and his partners at his Sheffield studios and they included the love song, 'Day & Night', the first single from her second album, *Walk Of Life*. It gave Billie, now billed as Billie Piper, her third number one and she was at a concert in Copenhagen when she got the news. However, the next single, 'Something Deep Inside', only reached number four and the title track only number 25.

At the end of 2000, Billie Piper was a guest on the Channel 4 show, *TFI Friday*. The programme was the brainchild of the 'ginger whinger' Chris Evans, the 35-year-old, quick-witted know-all. He had been a maverick DJ on Radio 1 and was now on Virgin Radio. *TFI Friday*, the work of his own production company, was making him extremely rich.

Evans, divorced and leading a playboy lifestyle, asked Billie for a date and gave her a Ferrari strewn with roses. She was only half-impressed as she swapped it for a Clio. To her record company, Chris Evans must have seemed the partner from hell. They went on binges together and newspapers carried picture of them stumbling from pubs. Billie was in tears when he went to watch lapdancing at Stringfellows.

Against the odds, Evans and Billie were married at the Little Church of the West, Las Vegas in May 2001 with Chris' friend, DJ Danny Baker, as the best man. Shortly afterwards, Chris was sacked as a breakfast presenter on Virgin Radio. He sued for wrongful dismissal but the judge called him 'a petulant prima donna'. Billie also fell out with her record label – Innocent was part of Virgin, as it happens – and her contract was terminated.

Billie Piper

Chris Evans' attempts at returning to big-time TV have not yet been successful, but Billie Piper is becoming a much-praised actress. She starred opposite Dennis Waterman and James Nesbitt in the BBC's update of *The Canterbury Tales,* and she played both a rebellious teenager and her sullen older self in a BBC play about care homes, *Bella And The Boys*. In 2004 her comedy with Orlando Bloom about boxing, *The Calcium Kid*, was not a critical success but is likely to do well on video. In 2005 she will be starring in the horror movie, *Spirit Trap*, and appearing as Dr. Who's assistant in a new BBC series.

861 Sonique
It Feels So Good

Label & Cat No.: **Universal MCSTD 40245**

Producers: **Sserious / Graeme Pleeth**

Writers: **Sonique / Sserious / Graeme Pleeth / Linus Burdick**

Date Reached No.1: **3 June 2000**

Weeks at No.1: **3**

"Music is something you're born with and I've always had this thing in me. Every Sunday was the day for loud music in our house," recalled Sonique fondly about the time she was growing up listening to Marvin Gaye, Roberta Flack, Otis Redding and Gladys Knight.

Born in north London's Crouch End on June 21, 1968, Sonia Clark, who was brought up by her Trinidadian mother had early ambitions to be an athlete. Her motto was 'Be the best or don't bother' and at the age of 15, after coming second in a race, she felt she wasn't good enough and decided to concentrate on her other love, music.

At the age of 17 she joined a reggae band called Fari but the guys in the band had expected her to bring some of her own music whereas she was yet to write her first song. She landed a recording contract with Cooltempo Records and her first release 'Let Me Hold You', became a club favourite and made its mark on the dance chart. She began writing songs and a chance meeting with Tim Simenon from Bomb The Bass led to them recording together. Tim's friend, Mark Moore, from S'Express spotted her and requested she work with him. "Mark needed a singer and a songwriter," she remembered. "So I was asked to collaborate on the 1990 album *Intercourse*. I tried to create my own style and identity, which I did, and it was all thanks to Mark." She co-wrote and sang on the hit 'Nothing To Lose' and sang on the follow-up, 'Find 'Em, Fool 'Em, Forget 'Em'.

Sonia became a DJ, specialising in improvised singing over the tracks she was playing. She had residencies at the Cream club in Liverpool, the Gatecrasher in Sheffield and spent two years at the Manumission in Ibiza.

In 1998 she signed to Serious Records and released the song 'I Put A Spell On You' (not the Nina Simone track) which reached number 36. The follow-up, 'It Feels So Good' reached number 24.

In the summer of 1999 a club DJ in Tampa, Florida began playing the track on an import 12-inch from the UK. It became a much requested song and suddenly it was a radio favourite too, so Sonique was quickly signed to Republic Records in the States. As she hadn't saved the original backing track, there was a problem when it came to live appearances. "As far as I was concerned that was it. I certainly didn't expect anything big to happen with the record. So when they asked me over to do some P.A's, I had to go back into the studio and re-record the backing." The song went to number eight on the US chart and the success helped her complete her debut album *Hear My Cry*.

Sonique re-recorded the vocals over the new backing track and it was re-released in the UK. This time it sold 195,000 copies in the first week and entered the chart at number one.

The next single lifted from the album was 'Sky' which reached number two, only held from the top by 'Lady (Hear Me Tonight)' by the French dance act Modjo. A re-issue of 'I Put A Spell On You' went to number eight before Sonique took a three year break. She returned in 2003 with the album *Born To Be Free*. The first single from it, 'Can't Make Up My Mind' reached number 17, but the follow-up, 'Alive', died at number 70.

862 Black Legend
You See The Trouble With Me

Label & Cat No.:	**Eternal WEA 262CD**
Producers:	**J-Reverse / Enrico Ferrari**
Writers:	**Barry White / Ray Parker Jr**
Date Reached No.1:	**24 June 2000**
Weeks at No.1:	**1**

Barry White registered his only UK number one in 1974 with 'You're The First, The Last, My Everything' which spent two weeks at the top. Some 18 months later he claimed his second biggest hit with 'You See The Trouble With Me' which stalled at number two behind Brotherhood Of Man's 'Save Your Kisses For Me'. In 2000 courtesy of two Italian producers/DJs he made it to the top again.

As a producer, Ciro uses the moniker J-Reverse. He met Enrico in the mid-Nineties and they occasionally worked together. Ciro created a house loop and decided that instead of using the 'static sounding' single version to sample Barry White's vocals, he would give the song a more exciting vibe by using a 1990 live concert appearance in Belgium that Enrico owned on videotape.

The track became a must-have for club DJs across Europe and made it into the Italian Top 10. When Barry White heard the version, he didn't take too kindly to the sample and ordered it to be withdrawn. At this point Enrico quit the project due to lack of technical skills, leaving Ciro to work as Black Legend by himself. Because the track was so popular, Ciro decided he would have the vocals recreated and after trying out many singers with no luck, he contacted a soul/house singer and voice coach, his friend Lisa Millett, to ask if she knew any Barry White soundalikes. At the time she was coaching a British singer called Elroy Powell. Elroy, also known as Spoonface, demonstrated his White impression to Lisa and the following week he was sent to Italy to record new vocals. Lisa has had a few UK hits as a featured artist with A.T.F.C., Goodfellaz and Sheer Bronze.

Import copies of 'You See The Trouble With Me', which still had the real Barry White on it, spent five weeks on the UK chart and climbed as high as number 52. When the British version was released, it entered at number one and spent 15 weeks on the chart.

Black Legend were almost classed as one hit wonders, but the follow-up, 'Somebody', reached number 37.

Ciro continues DJing around the world and producing/remixing quality dance music. He recently established his own record label called Reverse Records. Elroy, who now sports a Barry White-style beard, works as a writer and performance artist at Camden Town's Learning Education Arts Project (LEAP) in London..

863 Kylie Minogue
Spinning Around

Label & Cat No.:	**Parlophone CDRS 6542**
Producer:	**Mike Spencer**
Writers:	**Ira Shickman / Osborne Bingham / Kara Dio Guardi / Paula Abdul**
Date Reached No.1:	**1 July 2000**
Weeks at No.1:	**1**

Following 'Tears On My Pillow', Kylie continued with the Stock, Aitken & Waterman jingly pop songs, 'Better The Devil You Know' (2), 'Step Back In Time' (4), 'What Do I Have To Do' (6) and 'Shocked' (6). A smooth ballad with soul singer Keith Washington, 'If You Were With Me Now' and a cover of Chairmen Of The Board's 'Give Me Just A Little More Time' both made the Top five. Then things started to change. Was Kylie's appeal fading? 'Finer Feelings', 'What Kind Of Fool (Heard It All Before)' and a weak cover of Kool & The Gang's 'Celebration' all failed to make the Top 10.

In 1992 her *Greatest Hits* album went to number one and was her final collaboration with Stock Aitken and Waterman.

Throughout the Nineties Kylie went through a myriad image changes. She signed with the dance label deConstruction and her first album for them, *Kylie Minogue*, reached number four. The lead-off single, the haunting 'Confide In Me', reached number two. The follow-ups, 'Put Yourself In My Place' and 'Where Is The Feeling' failed to make the Top 10. However, the label change brought Kylie some street cred. Music magazines like *NME* and *Q*, who had more or less ignored her, were now keen to interview her. Nick Cave invited Kylie to record two duets for his album, *The Murder Ballads*. 'Where The Wild Roses Grow' was issued as a single and reached number 11.

In 1994 she appeared as Cammy, a kick boxing army lieutenant, in *Street Fighter* opposite Jean-Claude Van Damme. It received lukewarm reviews. The following year, her third film, the Hollywood comedy, *Bio Dome* went by almost unnoticed. In Australia it bypassed a cinema release and went straight to video. Around the same time, she published a 600-only limited edition copy of her *Art* book which showed her in various states of undress, prompting comparisons with Madonna's *Sex* book of three years earlier. The book was sent out to high flyers in the fashion, art and music worlds to promote the launch of her album.

The release of her next album, *Impossible Princess,* clashed with the death of Princess Diana in 1997 and was delayed for five months and confusingly given the same title as her previous album. It reached number 10 and the three singles released from it, 'Some Kind Of Bliss', 'Did It Again' and 'Breathe' all failed to make the Top 10, signalling the end of her relationship with deConstruction.

After initial negotiations with Mushroom Records, Matt Leonard, A&R at Parlophone, intervened and signed her. He said, "I think a lot of people thought that Kylie's career was over and were surprised when I signed her. Generally there's an idea that artists like Kylie are allowed one mistake and that's it."

Kylie spent time with her A&R man, Jamie Nelson. She told him, "I don't mind if I don't write the songs, let's just get the best songs." 'Spinning Around' was co-written by Paula Abdul about her divorce from her second husband, Brad Beckerman. Kylie recalled, "Jamie went to New York and arrived back with this demo, waving his arms saying, 'I've got this great song here and I think it'd be perfect for you.' We all listened to it and loved it straightaway, even in its demo form, it had something."

It was the first single from the album, *Light Years*. Both the album and single topped the UK chart. "I've never met those other people who wrote the song," said Kylie, "but I'm sure they're very pleased."

Kylie played to her biggest ever audience when she performed 'Dancing Queen' and her latest single, 'On A Night Like This', to four billion viewers at the closing ceremony of the Sydney 2000 Olympic Games.

864 Eminem
The Real Slim Shady

Label & Cat No.: **Interscope 4973792**

Producers: **Dr Dre / Mel-Man**

Writers: **Marshall Mathers III / Andre Young / Mike Bradford**

Date Reached No.1: **8 July 2000**

Weeks at No.1: **1**

NOT LONG AFTER MARSHALL BRUCE Mathers III was born, on October 17, 1972 in Missouri, his father walked out on his mother. Debbie Briggs-Mathers moved with her young son to Detroit.

"My father? I never knew him. Never even seen a picture of him. I don't like to give the sob story: growing up in a single-parent home, my mother never worked. We kept getting kicked out of every house we were in. There were times when my friends had to buy me fuckin' shoes!"

His childhood was not easy. His mother was on benefit and the two moved house many times. The longest time spent at any one school was not much more than three months. He was often bullied and was a poor student.

He discovered rap in his early teens, and would lip-synch to his favourite hip-hop tunes. In a friend's basement, the pair chose their 'rap' names, Manix and M&M (after his initials). Later, he would spell it in a different way to the famous chocolate. Being white was a disadvantage when it came to rap, but Eminem was determined to succeed. He performed at many improvisation nights in clubs, and also entered freestyle battles (basically a war of words. A winner is declared by the amount of abuse – in rhyming form – aimed at his opponent) on pirate radio stations.

In 1996 his independently released debut album *Infinite*, received unfavourable reviews and sold less than 1,000 copies.

The following year, a broke Eminem, now the proud father of a little girl, Hailie, went to Los Angeles to participate in the 1997 Rap Olympics. The first prize of $1,500 cash was well within his grasp as he got into the grand final but he finished as the runner-up. A member of staff at Interscope Records saw Eminem's performance and was impressed enough to pass a tape to his boss, Jimmy Iovine, who in turn sent it to rap legend Dr Dre. Together they produced *The Slim Shady LP* (1999), which went Top 10 in the UK and topped the *Billboard* R&B album chart in the US. It included Eminem's breakthrough single, 'My Name Is' (2), which sampled Labi Siffre's 'I Got The'. It also featured 'Guilty Conscience' (5), which sampled the track, 'Pigs Go Home', from the movie *Getting Straight*.

"I had this whole Slim Shady concept of being two different people, having two different sides of me. Slim Shady is just the evil thoughts in my head. Things I shouldn't be thinking about. People should be able to determine when I'm serious and when I'm fuckin' around. I got a warped sense of humour, I guess," said Eminem of his alter ego.

The Marshall Mathers LP was released in 2000. In the US it sold almost 1.8 million copies in its first week and won three Grammys. It also became the first ever rap album to be nominated for 'Album Of The Year', but lost out to Steely Dan's *Two Against Nature*.

'The Real Slim Shady' was taking a long time to write. His record company was getting

Eminem took his name from his initials but spelt it differently to avoid a confrontation with the manufacturers of M&M chocolate

RONNIE RIP

impatient. Finally Eminem was inspired by *MTV*, firstly after hearing a speech made by Will Smith, at the MTV Music Awards, where he stated he didn't need to swear to sell his records and then by Christina Aguilera, who, during an appearance with interviewer Carson Daly and Limp Bizkit frontman Fred Durst, mentioned she thought the controversial rapper was 'cute' but went on to caution female viewers to 'not let your man disrespect you', which Eminem took as a personal attack.

Still, it helped him finish the song, which included the lyrics, 'Will Smith don't gotta cuss in his raps to sell his records. Well I do, so fuck him and fuck you too!' and, 'I can sit next to Carson Daly and Fred Durst and hear 'em argue over who she gave head to first'. Continuing his rant against Christina, he raged, 'You little bitch, put me on blast on MTV.' 'Yeah, he's cute, but I think he's married to Kim, hee hee.' 'I should download her audio on MP3 and show the world how you gave Eminem VD.' We've come a long way from 'My Old Man's A Dustman'...

865 The Corrs
Breathless

Label & Cat No.:	**Atlantic AT0084CD**
Producer:	**Robert John 'Mutt' Lange**
Writers:	**Robert John 'Mutt' Lange / Sharon Corr / Andrea Corr / Caroline Corr / Jim Corr**
Date Reached No.1:	**15 July 2000**
Weeks at No.1:	**1**

The Corrs were the first Irish family since The Nolans to appear on the UK charts. The good-looking siblings were born and raised in Dundalk, County Louth, 50 miles north of Dublin, and all share vocal duties. Jim (born July 31, 1964, guitar and piano), Sharon (March 24, 1970, violin), Caroline (March 17, 1973, drums) and Andrea (May 17, 1974, lead vocals/tin whistle). Jim had once played in a band called Hughes Vision run by the film director John Hughes and that connection led to the formation of The Corrs in 1990, specifically to audition for the Alan Parker-directed film *The Commitments*, of which John was the musical director. Although they all appeared in the film, it was Andrea who made the greatest impression playing the character Sharon Rabbitte. The audition went well and John offered to become their manager. A few weeks later, the US Ambassador to Ireland, Jean Kennedy Smith, saw them play at Whelan's club in Dublin and invited them to Boston to play as part of the celebrations for the 1994 Soccer world cup held in Boston, MA in which Ireland were playing.

In 1994 they signed to 143 Records, a label owned by the American producer David Foster and recorded their debut album *Forgiven, Not Forgotten*. Two years later it was released internationally and received well in most countries except America. It went to number two in the UK, spending over two years on the chart and went nine times platinum in Ireland. But the first two singles from it, 'Runaway' and 'Love To Love You', only sold enough to reach numbers 49 and 62 respectively.

The second album, *Talk On Corners*, was a rockier album released in 1997. It topped the UK chart and spent nearly three years on it. "We thought we might have left it a bit too long between the first and second albums," Jim recalled. "The main reason for this long gap was due to the success of *Forgiven Not Forgotten*, which kept taking off in various places all over the world." From *Talk On Corners*, the first three singles; 'Only When I Sleep', 'I Never Loved You Anyway' and 'What Can I Do' all fell short of the Top 40 and proved that like Pink Floyd, Barbra Streisand and Eva Cassidy, they were an albums act. But that changed with the release of the fourth single 'Dreams', a song that fan Mick Fleetwood asked them to record for inclusion on a Fleetwood Mac tribute album. It was released on two CD singles, the second of which contained various mixes and a live version, and it went to number six. A new audience had just discovered The Corrs.

They were invited to appear at the Pavarotti And Friends War Child Concert For Liberia held in Modena, Italy. Another fan, Celine Dion, who was there, asked Andrea to play her Irish tin whistle on her live version of 'My Heart Will Go On'.

Next came a re-issue of 'What Can I Do', this time remixed by Tin Tin Out which went to number three. It was followed by 'So Young' (6) and another oldie, 'Runaway', again remixed by Tin Tin Out.

In 1999 they linked up with one of Ireland's premier bands, The Chieftans for the single, 'I Know My Love' and released their *Unplugged* album, which had been recorded for *MTV*, but part of the promotional tour was cancelled following the sudden death of their mother. Later the same year they won Best International Group at the Brit Awards and appeared at Glastonbury. In June they performed at Party In The Park in London, where they first met Robert 'Mutt' Lange.

The Corrs spent the first half of 2000 working on their new album, *In Blue*, which was released in July. It entered the chart at number one, as did its debut single, 'Breathless'.

"It was a bizarre situation, going to meet someone for the first time and trying to write a song with them, but it worked well", explained Andrea, of her work with Mutt. "We went to Switzerland where we wrote three songs; 'Breathless', 'Irresistible' and 'All The Love In The World'. 'Breathless' was all about tempting someone to make the first move – like come on and leave me breathless. It's that scenario when the daylight is fading and nothing else matters apart from the two people who are there." The accompanying video was shot in the Mahari Desert in California, near The Joshua Tree.

They had two further singles from *In Blue*; 'Irresistible' (20) and 'Give Me A Reason' (27). In November 2001 *The Best Of The Corrs* was released and 'Would You Be Happier?' was released to help promote it.

The Corrs then took three years off, but returned in 2004 with the new album *Borrowed Heaven*, which entered at number two. They also toured to promote the first single, 'Summer Sunshine', which reached number six and had a chorus resembling both 'Video Killed The Radio Star' and 'Ruby Tuesday'.

The Corrs gained their first exposure in the movie The Commitments; *left to right: Sharon, Caroline, Jim and Andrea*

866 Ronan Keating
Life Is A Rollercoaster

Label & Cat No.:	**Polydor 5619362**
Producers:	**Gregg Alexander / Rick Nowels**
Writers:	**Gregg Alexander / Rick Nowels**
Date reached No.1:	**22 July 2000**
Weeks at No.1:	**1**

THE AMERICAN GROUP, THE NEW Radicals, had a UK top five hit with 'You Get What You Give', in 1999, but Gregg Alexander didn't enjoy being in the spotlight. He preferred to write songs and so when he wrote the very commercial 'Life Is A Rollercoaster', he passed it to Ronan Keating. Ronan was delighted as he felt that the up-tempo song was far removed from Boyzone and would place him in the rock mainstream. Ronan felt it marked a significant turn in his career and he called his 2000 autobiography, *Life Is A Rollercoaster*. The same team also wrote and produced Ronan's 2002 hit, 'I Love It When We Do'. Gregg has also produced music for the film soundtracks, *A Walk To Remember* (2002) and *Scooby Doo 2* (2004).

And what of the other members of Boyzone? Stephen Gately sang 'Bright Eyes' on the soundtrack of *Watership Down* and, combined with 'New Beginnings', the single went to number three. The follow-up, 'I Believe', stalled at number 11. Mikey Graham's 'You're My Angel' fared poorly, reaching number 13, but the publicity surrounding his comments on cannabis being 'relatively harmless' may have gone against him. Shane Lynch and Keith Duffy took a pop at boy bands on the Christmas single, 'Girl You Know It's True', which didn't even crack the Top 40. Shane became a successful rally car driver for Ford.

The career of Keith Duffy, whose full name is Keith Peter Thomas Francis John Duffy, has taken some unusual twists and turns. At first he was Robbie Williams' drinking partner and in what was probably light relief after that, he became a very popular part of *Celebrity Big Brother* for Comic Relief. The public speculated as to whether there was a romance between him and housemate Claire Sweeney (there wasn't), and the winner was the downcast comedian Jack Dee. Since 2002, Keith has been a regular part of *Coronation Street*, playing a happy-go-lucky Irish barman who is planning to open his own restaurant.

867 Five + Queen
We Will Rock You

Label & Cat No.:	**RCA 74321774022**
Producers:	**Richard Stannard / Julian Gallagher**
Writers:	**Brian May / Jay Brown / Abs Breen**
Date Reached No.1:	**29 July 2000**
Weeks at No.1:	**1**

'WE WILL ROCK YOU' IS PROBABLY Queen's best-loved anthem. Yet it was only issued as the B-side of the 1977 number two hit, 'We Are The Champions'.

To try and prove they were the toughest boy band on the block, Five bravely attempted the huge stadium anthem. And to enforce its authenticity, they enlisted the talents of both Brian May (who played bass as well as lead guitar) and Roger Taylor. As Ritchie commented, "It's amazing working with Roger and Brian. They are both really cool guys and Brian has agreed to work on a couple of songs on our next album."

The performance was first aired to the British public at the 2000 Brit awards ceremony in March, where Five picked up the award for Best Pop Act.

Ronan Keating's 'Life Is A Rollercoaster' would have spent a second week at the top had Polydor not breached chart rules. By doing so, 'We Will Rock You' reached number one. An eagle-eyed official at C.I.N (Chart Information Network) noticed that CD1 of Ronan Keating's 'Life Is A Rollercoaster' contained a CD-Rom interview with Ronan about a unique track and not the main song, subsequently the sales of CD1 were deleted from the sales chart.

In April 2002 *We Will Rock You – The Musical* opened in London to popular acclaim. Written by comedian Ben Elton, it features over 30 Queen songs. It's not a biographical show, but one that's a celebration of their music and has made a star out of the lead character, Tony Vincent. In September 2003 the show opened in Australia and was attended by Brian and Roger. As soon as it opened down under, Ben revealed that there were plans for *We Will Rock You 2*.

868 Craig David
7 Days

Label & Cat No.:	**Wildstar WILD 30**
Producer:	**Mark Hill**
Writers:	**Craig David / Mark Hill / Darren Hill**
Date Reached No.1:	**5 August 2000**
Weeks at No.1:	**1**

CRAIG FOLLOWED-UP 'FILL ME IN' WITH the Spanish guitar-based '7 Days', which told the story of Craig meeting a beautiful woman on Monday then mapping out the week by explaining how he took her for a drink on Tuesday and then spent Wednesday, Thursday, Friday and Saturday making love to her and recovering on Sunday.

The accompanying video, with a nod to the film *Groundhog Day*, shows Craig continually waking up on the same Monday and attempting to make a date with this woman.

'7 Days' was less of the two-step and more of the smooth, slick R&B patter that we would come to see from Craig. The US took to it well as the single peaked at number 10 in 2001.

In October 2000 Craig attended the MOBO (Music Of Black Origin) Awards ceremony in London where he won three of the six categories he was nominated for. He won Best Single for 'Fill Me In', Best Newcomer and Best R&B Act. Craig set a record the following year when he was nominated for six Brits. Unfortunately for him, he didn't win any of them.

Craig released two further singles from *Born To Do It*; 'Walking Away' (3) and 'Rendezvous' (8). 2002 was spent working on his second album

Brought up in Southampton, Craig David was exposed to music early. "My father played bass in a reggae band and was always taking me to rehearsals," he says

English, so communication between him and Madonna for the first couple of weeks of recording was rather challenging. He began his career playing guitar in a French band called Taxi Girl. After he'd left the band, he moved into production. He loved the electronic disco scene and compiled an album called *Disco Science*. With an accompanying video, Mirwais sent some tracks to Maverick Records, which is where Madonna discovered him and liked what she heard.

Three weeks prior to the single's release, Madonna gave birth to her second child, a son called Rocco. The father was film director Guy Richie, whom she was planning to marry in the coming months.

A friend had sent her a video of Ali G's Christmas Special. She watched it, loved it and became a fan. She even told one newspaper that he was, "The Peter Sellers of our generation." Madonna contacted Ali G (the alter-ego of comedian Sacha Baron-Cohen) and asked him to appear in the video for 'Music'. He agreed and did so wearing his trademark yellow tracksuit and wraparound sunglasses.

873 A1

Take On Me

Label & Cat No.: **Columbia 6695902**

Producer: **Metro**

Writers: **Pal Waaktaar / Mags Furuholmen / Morten Harket**

Date Reached No.1: **9 September 2000**

Weeks at No.1: **1**

WITH THEIR GOOD LOOKS AND SLICK pop productions, you could be forgiven for thinking A1 were just another manufactured boy band. Although Ben Adams (born November 22, 1981), Christian Ingebrigtsen (born January 25, 1977), Mark Read (born November 7, 1978) and Paul Marazzi (born January 24, 1975) all won their role in the group through a management company searching for a classic boy band, the four young lads had individually spent their teen years honing their craft. Between them, they can play the piano, oboe, violin, drums and guitar.

Ben began singing at three and eventually became the head chorister at St Margaret's Church (between Westminster Abbey and the Houses Of Parliament), singing for the Queen. "I recorded two albums. I even sang for the Pope, so I'm sure he's a big fan of A1 already…"

Christian's father, Stein, had been a successful pop star in Norway in the Seventies, selling over one million records across Scandinavia. Christian took violin lessons when he was six, before going on to guitar and piano. At 16 he went to Kentucky for a year to study, and in 1997 Christian was among a handful of Norwegians invited to study at LIPA (Liverpool Institute for Performing Arts), Paul McCartney's acclaimed 'Fame' Academy.

Mark came from a musical family who performed on cruise ships. At 14 he was the youngest performer the ship ever had. His mother played drums in a band whilst pregnant with him. "I must have had the rhythm beaten into me!" he insisted.

Paul was the karaoke king. "I was discovered singing in my dad's bar in Spain. A producer who was in told me about the auditions for the band." Their name came to them when driving up the A1 one day. Thankfully they weren't travelling along the B1197, as it didn't have quite the same ring to it.

Although A1 are proud of being one of those rare teen bands who write their own songs, it was with a cover of A-Ha!'s number two hit from 1985 'Take On Me', that A1 received their first chart topper. Christian said, "We had the idea to revive an old classic. It was about the time Madonna did 'American Pie'. A lot of songs came up. It just stood out. I'm Norwegian, A-ha! were Norwegian, so it seemed a really cool thing to do." He added, "I was a big fan. They showed me as a young kid in Norway that it is possible to make it around the world."

Ben commented, "'Take On Me' was a complete surprise because we knocked Madonna off number one, which was great."

The second track on the CD was a Beatles Medley (as seen on LWT's *Stars Sing The Beatles*), a homage to the original fab four.

874 Modjo

Lady (Hear Me Tonight)

Label & Cat No.: **Sound Of Barclay 5877582**

Producers: **Yann Destagnol / Romain Tranchart**

Writers: **Yann Destagnol / Romain Tranchart / Bernard Edwards / Nile Rodgers**

Date Reached No.1: **16 September 2000**

Weeks at No.1: **2**

CONSIDERING OUR PROXIMITY TO France, a casual observer might have expected more than four French acts to top the UK charts. The language barrier is a factor, but it is probably that the cultural divide is too great.

Modjo are the Paris-born production duo Romain Tranchart and Yann Destagnol. Romain was brought up listening to classical music and after leaving school, took a job with the French Foreign Office. In 1996 he formed his first band, Seven Track, with Paul de Homem-Christo who later became one half of Daft Punk. Yann has been a rock music fan from an early age. He learned to play the flute, guitar, piano, clarinet and drums when he was young and by the time he was a teenager he had turned his hand to writing songs.

In 1998 Romain released his first single, 'What You're Gonna Do Baby' under the name Funk Legacy. Later that year he met Yann at the American School Of Modern Music in Paris and decided to team up, calling themselves Modjo. They signed to one of France's longest surviving labels, Sound Of Barclay, the same label the first French artist to top the chart, Charles Aznavour, signed to in 1973.

For their debut single, 'Lady (Hear Me Tonight)' they took the bassline from a little-known Chic song called 'Soup For One' and built it into a light, house groove. "We are young and we don't have the experience of songwriting," explained Yann. "We don't expect a lot of things from our lyrics, a bit like The Beatles used to in the beginning. 'Lady' is just a love story about a guy who falls for a girl in a disco."

Modjo released their debut album, *Modjo*, but it failed to attract the British record-buying

Unusually for a boy band, A1 write their own songs, though 'Take On Me' was a cover; clockwise, from top left: Ben Adams, Mark Read, Paul Marazzi and Christian Ingebrigtsen

public and missed the chart completely. They followed 'Lady (Hear Me Tonight)' with 'Chillin', which reached number 12, whilst their third single, 'What I Mean' stiffed at number 59.

In 2004 Romain said he would be releasing some new personal songs in addition to producing some up and coming French acts. Yann released his debut solo album *The Great Blue Scar* but you won't be seeing it in the UK chart, as it was released in France only.

875 Mariah Carey featuring Westlife
Against All Odds (Take A Look At Me Now)

Label & Cat No.: **Columbia 6698872**
Producers: **Mariah Carey / Steve Mac**
Writer: **Phil Collins**
Date reached No.1: **30 September 2000**
Weeks at No.1: **2**

GEOFFREY HOMES WROTE A DETECTIVE novel, *Build My Gallows High*, which became the *film noir*, *Out Of The Past* (1947), that made Robert Mitchum a star. The film was remade ("*film noir* in colour?") in 1984 as *Against All Odds* with Jeff Bridges, James Woods and Rachel Ward. The music was by Michel Colombier and Larry Carlton and the soundtrack was to be on Atlantic. The director, Taylor Hackford, was given a list of Atlantic artists and told to pick someone for the title song (this is true). He picked Phil Collins, a Virgin artist whose records were released by Atlantic in the US.

Taylor Hackford went to see Phil Collins in Chicago and showed him a rough cut of the film. He agreed to write a song, which would reflect the theme of the film. Although the phrase "against all odds" appears in the lyric, the most prominent line is "Take A Look At Me Now". The film did moderately well, helped by the hit single which topped the US charts and went to number two in the UK. The song was nominated for an Oscar and was performed at the ceremony by Ann Reinking (*All That Jazz, Annie*) because the Oscars' producer, Gregory Peck, hadn't heard of Phil Collins. Phil watched from the audience and Stevie Wonder won the Oscar itself with 'I Just Called To Say I Love You'.

Fast forward 15 years to the MTV Europe Awards. Mariah Carey was among the star performers and newcomers Westlife were on the bill. Mark Feehily wanted an autograph, but his request came out garbled because he was starstruck. She knew who Westlife were and she said, "I would like to work with you sometime." A couple of months later, the managements were talking, and Mark and Mariah were duetting on 'Against All Odds'. Shane Filan takes the opening lines but then Mark takes the solos. The record was made on the Isle of Capri, which presumably was absolutely necessary. The record was co-produced by Mariah Carey, and Shane commented, "We just did what she asked us to do, but she turned out to be very funny and liked having a laugh."

The video is infamous for the way Bryan McFadden stares at Mariah Carey's boobs, and who can blame him? "I only glanced at them," says Bryan, "but they edited the video to make it look like I was. When we did the video for 'Uptown Girl' with Claudia Schiffer, I made sure I was better behaved."

876 All Saints
Black Coffee

Label & Cat No.: **London LONCD 454**
Producer: **William Orbit**
Writers: **Tom Nichols / Alexander Von Soos / Kirsty Elizabeth**
Date reached No.1: **14 October 2000**
Weeks at No.1: **1**

ALL SAINTS SMILE OUT AT YOU AND look happy together in the CD booklet for *Saints And Sinners*, but it was an illusion. The band was having one internal squabble after another. Shaznay Lewis vetoed Nicole Appleton's song, 'Love Is Where I'm From', because it was written with Robbie Williams, and, according to her, his name wouldn't look right on an All Saints album.

'Black Coffee' was not one of the band's own songs. It had been written for a new singer, Kirsty Roper, but when it was played to Tracy Bennett, an executive at London Records, she wanted the song for All Saints. "William Orbit produced it," said Tom Nichols, "and it came out sounding fantastic. It was completely different from the demo."

All Saints' follow-up, Shaznay's 'All Hooked Up' stalled at number seven. There was an argument as to whether a jacket should be worn by Shaz or Nat and a further source of friction occurred when Mel mimed to Nat's voice on the video for 'All Hooked Up'. *Saints And Sinners* was a number one album, but All Saints had decided for the umpteenth time to split up – only this time it was final.

Melanie Blatt was the first All Saint to establish herself as a solo artist. She was featured with Artful Dodger on the Top 10 single, 'Twenty-fourseven', in 2001. The following year she was back in the charts with Rah Digga on Outsidaz's single, 'I'm Leavin". Then in 2003 Mel had her second Top 20 single with 'Do Me Wrong'.

Nic and Nat settled with their new partners, the two Liams – Liam Gallagher of Oasis with Nic and Liam Howlett of Prodigy with Nat. In 2002 they returned as The Appletons and had a number two single with 'Fantasy'. In 2003 they released a big-selling album, *Everything's Eventual*, and had another Top 10 single with 'Don't Worry'.

As the main songwriter, Shaznay Lewis did better than the other members of All Saints and is said to have a fortune of £7m. She had a small role in *Bend It Like Beckham*, took her time to return to the competitive market, but in 2004 she released her first solo album, the critically acclaimed *Open*. She had a hand in writing all the tracks and the first hit single was 'Never Felt Like This Before'.

What are the chances of All Saints reforming? Never ever.

'Against All Odds' was a number two hit for its writer Phil Collins but Mariah Carey and Westlife took it to number one

877 U2
Beautiful Day

Label & Cat No.: **Island CID 766**

Producer: **Daniel Lanois**

Writers: **Bono / The Edge / Adam Clayton / Larry Mullen Jr**

Date Reached No.1: **21 October 2000**

Weeks at No.1: **1**

BONO HAD AN IDEA FOR A MOVIE FOR some time and in 1999, as well as working on a new studio album, managed to find time to sit down and write it. *The Million Dollar Hotel* or, as it was known in the States, *The Billion Dollar Hotel*, received some awful reviews, and one video store owner in New York claimed it was 'the most refunded movie in the world'. Bono's story might have been based on The Clarence Hotel in Dublin, which he and The Edge purchased and restored in 1992.

The film's thin plot, which some critics tagged *The Million Dollar Flop*, starred Mel Gibson playing a cop sent to investigate the death of the son of a billionaire after falling off the roof of a hotel. The hotel's residents are all oddball characters. One even thinks he is a member of The Beatles.

For their new album, *All That You Can't Leave Behind*, they decided to drop the dance influence and return to regular songs, wisely bringing back the team of Daniel Lanois and Brian Eno who had worked on *The Joshua Tree*. 'Beautiful Day' was a long time in the making, with Eno eventually coming up with a beat reminiscent of Bo Diddley. Once Edge had found a lick to go with it, Eno recorded it about 10 times, seeking out the best bits from each.

The title came in a moment of spontaneity. Bono was feeling good and yelled out 'It's a beautiful dayeeeee', just like he had done a few years earlier on a song called 'I'm Not Your Baby', which appeared on the CD single of 'Please'.

Although it only reached number 21 on the US chart, 'Beautiful Day' won the 2000 Grammy Record Of The Year, which Daniel Lanois accepted on the band's behalf.

Three further singles were released from the album: 'Stuck In A Moment You Can't Get Out Of' (2), 'Elevation' (3) and 'Walk On' (5), which, as part of his world ambassador campaign, he dedicated to Aung San Suu Kyi, the elected leader of Burma who has been under house arrest since 1989.

878 Steps
Stomp

Label & Cat No.: **Jive 9201212**

Producers: **Mark Topham / Karl Twigg / Pete Waterman**

Writers: **Mark Topham / Karl Twigg / Pete Waterman / Rita Campbell / Bernard Edwards / Nile Rodgers**

Date Reached No.1: **28 October 2000**

Weeks at No.1: **1**

"STEPS SHOULD BE VERY PROUD OF WHAT they've achieved," announced Pete Waterman in 1999. "There's a lot of competition out there, but they do what they do so much better than anyone else." Rumours were flying around that Steps weren't making much money and that Pete Waterman only paid them a weekly wage, but the truth was that Steps were very astute. They had set up their own company and paid themselves a salary from it.

In 1999 they teamed up with B*Witched, Billie, Cleopatra and Tina Cousins for an Abba medley called 'Thank Abba For The Music', a charity record that reached number four with proceeds going to the Brits Trust. It was cleverly timed to tie in with the London West End production of *Mamma Mia!*, which opened the same week. They began work on their next album *Steptacular*, which was released at the end of the year. 'Tragedy', which was now included, had already been a number one and the next single 'Love's Got A Hold On My Heart', which reached number two, was followed by 'After The Love Has Gone' (5) and the double A-side 'Say You'll Be Mine' / 'Better The Devil You Know' which gave them a number four during Christmas week 1999.

In 2000 'Deeper Shade Of Blue', a song originally recorded by Tina Cousins, reached number four followed by another double A-side 'When I Said Goodbye' / 'Summer Of Love' (5).

'Stomp', a disco record based on Chic's 1977 hit 'Everybody Dance', was released in October 2000. The song, which the sleeve stated was a tribute to Bernard Edwards and Nile Rodgers, crashed in at number one after selling 48,000 copies. It was followed two weeks later by their third album, *Buzz*, which reached number four and spent only six months on the chart whereas the previous two had both spent over a year. Was their audience growing up?

They had a good start to 2001 with the next single from *Buzz*, 'The Way You Make Me Feel', reaching number two. It was listed as a double A-side with a non-album track, a cover of Marvin Gaye's 'Too Busy Thinking About My Baby'. Three further double A-sides followed that year: 'Here And Now' / 'You'll Be Sorry' (4), 'Chain Reaction' with a remix of 'One For Sorrow' (2) and their final single, 'Words Are Not Enough' / 'I Know Him So Well'. By now they'd had 15 hits which led to the inevitable compilation, *Gold – Greatest Hits*, which went straight to number one.

Rumours that Steps were about to split were denied so strenuously that it had to be true, and on Boxing Day 2001 television news programmes announced the group was breaking up. They issued the statement, "After five incredible years, we have decided it's time to move on to new challenges. We have always said that when the time came, we would leave as good friends and go out while we were on top, and although we are very sad, that's what we have done." As well as upsetting fans, it annoyed them because of the group's continued denial, so much so that they wanted nothing more to do with them. This was reiterated when Jive Records put together a two-CD set called *The Last Dance* comprising foreign-issued B-sides, previously unreleased remixes and 'Baby Don't Dance', a shelved track from the *Gold* album. It was issued in December 2002 and spent only one week on the chart at number 57.

Steps didn't care, H and Claire continued as a duo and charted three Top 10 hits in 2002, 'DJ',

'Half A Heart' and 'All Out Of Love', and Lisa Scott-Lee released two singles in 2003 'Lately' (3) and 'Too Far Gone' (11). As for Lee and Faye's careers, we are still waiting.

879 The Spice Girls
Holler / Let Love Lead The Way

Label & Cat No.: **Virgin VSCDT 1788**

Producers: **Rodney Jerkins : Rodney Jerkins / Harvey Mason Jr.**

Writers: **Mel B / Mel C / Emma Bunton / Victoria Adams / Rodney Jerkins / LeShawn Daniels / Fred Jerkins III : Mel B / Mel C / Emma Bunton / Victoria Adams / Rodney Jerkins / LeShawn Daniels / Fred Jerkins III / Harvey Mason Jr.**

Date reached No.1: **4 November 2000**

Weeks at No.1: **1**

A REVIVAL OF 'IT'S ONLY ROCK AND Roll' for the Children's Promise charity (which related to the final hour of the century) only made number 19. It featured The Spice Girls, and although it should have been better publicised, it was a fall from grace.

The Spice Girls released their *Forever* album in 2000 and 'Holler' / 'Let Love Lead The Way' was their first single for two years. The album made number two and the single topped the charts, but The Spice Girls were yesterday's news, not only with the public but also with the remaining four members, who, just like Geri, were pursuing individual careers. The third album was mostly made with one of America's top R&B producers, Rodney Jerkins, who had worked with Michael Jackson and Whitney Houston.

You know it's over when the record company doesn't even follow up a number one hit, when a top producer can't stop the rot, when your CD is remaindered within weeks, and when children stick their fingers down their throats at the mention of your name. The jokes were everywhere: What do you say to a Spice Girl in a year's time? Big Mac and fries, please.

Given a few years, The Spice Girls will be reassessed, no doubt leading to reunion appearances. Mel B wrote about the end of the group in her autobiography, *Catch A Fire*: "Feeling slightly detached and bewildered, I drove home and put on a video of The Spice Girls at Wembley. And it was then that it truly hit me how amazing our achievements were. When you're in it and you're working like a nutter, you don't actually realise what you've achieved, for yourself, for music, for your fans and for each other. That comes later. Still, I'm convinced that we will make music, perform together and entertain again as a group." Don't feel too sorry for them – they had amassed fortunes of around £20million each for their time in The Spice Girls.

880 Westlife
My Love

Label & Cat No.: **RCA 74321 802792**

Producers: **Per Magnusson / David Kreuger**

Writers: **Jorgen Elofsson / Pelle Nylen / David Kreuger / Per Magnusson**

Date reached No.1: **11 November 2000**

Weeks at No.1: **1**

WESTLIFE'S FIRST ALBUM, SIMPLY called *Westlife*, contained five number one singles. It went quadruple platinum in the UK and 12 times platinum in Ireland, which sounds impressive even if no one outside the industry is sure what it means. It represents 1.2m in the UK and 120,000 in Ireland. More to the point, *Westlife* sold five million copies worldwide.

They followed the CD with another value for money package, this time the 19-track *Coast To Coast*. The album topped the charts and included three number one singles ('I Have A Dream', 'Against All Odds (Take A Look At Me Now)', 'My Love') as well as a number two ('What Makes A Man'). 'What Makes A Man' was Westlife's eighth hit single and the first one not to make number one: Bob The Builder had built a wall to keep them out.

The album version of 'My Love' includes a spoken introduction in which Westlife are stuck in an airport. 'My Love' was a very commercial song featuring solo vocals from Shane Filan, Bryan McFadden and Mark Feehily, and included an intricate finale with counter-harmonies.

881 A1
Same Old Brand New You

Label & Cat No.: **Columbia 6705202**

Producer: **Eric Foster White**

Writers: **Eric Foster White / Ben Adams / Christian Ingebrigtsen / Mark Read**

Date Reached No.1: **18 November 2000**

Weeks at No.1: **1**

A1 HAD ALREADY ACHIEVED SUCCESS and a huge (mainly female) following by the time of their second – and final – chart topper.

Their first release, 'Be The First To Believe', back in 1999 had reached a respectable number six. They followed it two months later with 'Summertime Of Our Lives' (5). Two further singles, the double A-sided 'Everytime'/'Ready Or Not', and 'Like A Rose' went to numbers three and six respectively. *Here We Come*, the band's debut album released at the end of 1999 went Top 20. The follow-up, *The A List*, brought out a year later, peaked at number 14.

'Same Old Brand New You' was their sixth single release and co-written by Ben Adams, Christian Ingebrigtsen , Mark Read and Eric Foster White. Eric, an established writer, musician and performer has worked with Whitney Houston, Backstreet Boys, Britney Spears and Madonna. February 2001 saw A1 win the Best British Newcomer award at The Brits, while Ben was the recipient of the highly coveted Most Fanciable Male at the *Smash Hits* Awards.

A few weeks later tragedy struck on a promotional tour of Asia when four teenage girls were crushed to death during a record signing appearance at an Indonesian shopping centre. Organisers had expected a crowd of 1,000, but underestimated the band's popularity as several thousand more turned up. Eerily, the band had cancelled an in-store appearance in Glasgow three weeks earlier amid concerns over crowd safety. Christian confessed, "We're still haunted every day by what happened. The pain will never go away. I thought, 'Is it all worth it when four young lives can be lost like that?' We thought about giving it all up."

They admitted it was only the support of their fans that persuaded them to carry on as a band. Their latest single 'No More' got to number six that same month. It was followed almost a year later by 'Caught In The Middle' which entered the chart at number two. In May 2002 'Make It Good' reached number 11, hot on the heels of their third album of the same name.

In October 2002 A1 became a trio when Paul Marazzi, the first member to join became the first member to quit. His statement read: "After a lot of thought and deliberation I have made the difficult choice to leave the band due to personal reasons." His former bandmates said: "We are all heartbroken that Paul is leaving A1 but we understand his reasons and wish him all the very best. There is no way that we could ever replace him – he isn't just a band mate but a great friend. We will however be carrying on with our plans for the future and are very excited about our new single and album early next year."

Shortly after, the remaining members announced they were leaving their record company, Sony, and were going to concentrate on solo careers. A1 insisted they have not split up. Christian released his first solo album, *Take Back Yesterday* in 2003 and achieved two number one singles in his native country, Norway. Ben signed to Phonogenic in 2004 and released a solo album. Mark has submitted some of his songs for new releases by the Backstreet Boys, Charlotte Church and Tina Turner.

In May 2004 Ben and Mark joined Christian onstage at a Norwegian National Day celebration in Rotherhithe, London, for a version of 'Caught In The Middle' and revealed they have been writing together again.

882 LeAnn Rimes
Can't Fight The Moonlight

Label & Cat No.: **Curb CUBC 58**

Producer: **Trevor Horn**

Writer: **Diane Warren**

Date reached No.1: **24 November 2000**

Weeks at No.1: **1**

LEANN RIMES WAS BORN IN JACKSON, Mississippi in 1982 but she was an old hand and a polished performer by the time of her number one in 2000. Her father, Wesley, was a country musician who encouraged his daughter from the age of five. When the family moved to Texas, she was singing at rodeos and by the time she was seven, albums were being sold at gigs. When she was 11, she recorded 'Blue' at Norman Petty's studio in Clovis, New Mexico. The song had been written by Bill Mack for Patsy Cline, who had died before she could record it. Her performance of 'Blue' impressed Mike Curb of Curb Records, who signed her to his nationally distributed label. A new version of 'Blue' (as LeAnn was now 13) topped the US country chart and was also on the pop chart. She won three Grammys in 1997 and then set about recording more adult material and moving away from country.

In 1998 LeAnn recorded a new ballad by Diane Warren, 'How Do I Live', and although it was only number seven, it was on the charts for eight months and became almost as well known as the power ballad of the year, 'My Heart Will Go On'. Her flight from country music was particularly marked when she recorded the ballad, 'Written In The Stars', with Elton John and from his musical, *Aida*.

The Walt Disney film, *Coyote Ugly*, described how Violet Sanford, played by Piper Perabo, moved to New York to fulfil her dreams of being a songwriter. Her life then centres on the boisterous Coyote Ugly bar, where she works. LeAnn Rimes played herself and ends up performing Piper's hit composition, a strong disco number with a Latin feel, 'Can't Fight The Moonlight', with her. Despite being a dance number, it topped the US country charts because of LeAnn's background. In reality, the song was written by Diane Warren, effectively the Carole King of the Nineties.

Another song from the film, 'But I Do Love You', was tucked away as the second track on LeAnn Rimes' CD and was strong enough to have been a single in its own right. Although 'Can't Fight The Moonlight' was a huge hit, the film was not seen in the UK until 2000 and primarily will have its life on TV.

883 Destiny's Child
Independent Women (Part 1)

Label & Cat No.: **Columbia 6705932**

Producers: **Poke & Tone (Jean Claude Olivier & Samuel J. Barnes)**

Writers: **Samuel J. Barnes / Jean Claude Olivier / Cory Rooney / Beyoncé Knowles**

Date Reached No.1: **2 December 2000**

Weeks at No.1: **1**

A CAPPELLA FOUR-PART HARMONY ACTS were popular in the early part of the 20th century and were known as barber shop quartets. They were generally male, dressed in similar clothing and wore straw hats. Before Destiny's Child became famous, they could probably have qualified as one of the original female barber shop quartets. Beyoncé Knowles, Kelly Rowland, LeToya Luckett and LaTavia Robertson, who were all born in 1981 and grew up in Houston, Texas, began singing together at the age of 10 in Beyoncé's mother's hairdressing salon, Headliners.

Beyoncé's father, Mathew, had faith in his daughter's group, and gave up his job to become their manager. They were still performing under the name Girls' Tyme when they appeared in the

US TV show *Star Search*. They didn't win but soon afterwards they changed their name to Destiny's Child, a name taken from the *Book of Isaiah*, and were signed to Columbia Records.

Their first single, 'No No No', went to number three Stateside and number five here. Their next Top 10 hit was 'Bills Bills Bills' and gave them their first of four US number ones. 'Say My Name' (UK 3, US 1) and 'Jumpin' Jumpin'' (UK 3, US 3) followed and all had been lifted from their debut album *The Writing's On The Wall*.

One day in early 2000 Beyoncé had an argument with her boyfriend. She recalled, "I was like, I don't need a man, I'm independent," and with that went into a studio on her own and wrote the song. The only two people who heard it were her father and someone from the record label. Columbia were looking for some tracks for the new *Charlie's Angels* film which starred Drew Barrymore, Lucy Liu and Cameron Diaz, and as soon as they heard it, they knew it had to be included. Around the same time, Robertson and Luckett announced they were leaving and were quickly replaced by Farrah Franklin and Michelle Williams. Farrah didn't stick around and left after a few weeks, so the girls decided to continue as a trio.

The production duo Jean Claude Olivier and Samuel J. Barnes, who had began working together in the late-Eighties, and had produced hits for Notorious B.I.G., Nas, Mary J. Blige, Foxy Brown, Will Smith and Jay-Z, were called in to produce 'Independent Women'. Destiny's Child returned to the studio and altered some of the lyrics to suit the film and the track ended up on their next album *Survivor*.

"The initial idea was just to remix it," remembered Poke, "but we ended up remaking the record completely." This then became the single and because it was released before the one that appeared on *Survivor*, part one was added in brackets and the original album version became part two. It was part one that was used in the film.

The girls figured that since *Charlies Angels* were a trio, and they were now a trio it would be a great opportunity to focus on their own image and 'Independent Women' topped the US chart for 11 weeks.

884 S Club 7
Never Had A Dream Come True

Label & Cat No.: **Polydor 5879032**

Producer: **Cathy Dennis**

Writers: **Cathy Dennis / Simon Ellis**

Date Reached No.1: **9 December 2000**

Weeks at No.1: **1**

In 1999 S Club 7 were involved with their first charity record, as part of Various Artists For Children's Promise. The cover of the Rolling Stones' 'It's Only Rock 'N' Roll' featured the song's writers, Keith Richards and Mick Jagger and included Mary J. Blige, Jon Bon Jovi, Ozzy Osbourne, James Brown, The Spice Girls and Status Quo. It did rather poorly for an all-star charity single, and just scraped into the Top 20, proving that big names don't necessarily equate into big sales. The charity asked everyone to give the value of their last hour's pay of the millennium to 'create a better future for the children of the next millennium'.

'Never Had A Dream Come True' was chosen as the official single for the BBC's Children In Need appeal, with all proceeds going to the charity. Children In Need began in 1980 and has since raised more than £325 million to help disadvantaged and chronically ill British children lead a better life. The song raised over £200,000.

The single was also released in the US where it debuted at number 10. "We can't believe it," said the girl voted for the last three years running by *FHM* readers as Britain's sexiest, Rachel Stevens. "You always dream of cracking the States. Robbie and Westlife haven't yet managed it."

Cathy Dennis was born in Norwich in 1969. In her teens she was discovered by impresario Simon Fuller. Having achieved reasonable success in the late Eighties and Nineties, recording with D-Mob, where she reached the Top 20 with 'C'mon And Get My Love', and on her own, Cathy became disenchanted with performing and turned her talents to songwriting. The Spice Girls, Britney Spears, Janet Jackson, Kylie Minogue and many others have recorded her songs. Cathy wrote the theme to *Pop Idol* and *American Idol*, and also the debut singles for the winners and runners-up of the programmes.

885 Eminem
Stan

Label & Cat No.: **Interscope IND 97470**

Producer: **Mark the 45 King**

Writers: **Marshall Matthers III / Dido Armstrong / Paulie Herman**

Date Reached No.1: **16 December 2000**

Weeks at No.1: **1**

Eminem had been busy since his first chart topper five months earlier. Following an incident in June, where he was arrested for pistol-whipping a man whom he caught kissing Kim (now his wife) outside the Hot Rocks Café in Warren, Michigan where he grew up, Eminem was sent to court to be tried on charges of carrying a concealed weapon and assault with a dangerous weapon. Although the offence carried a five-year jail sentence, Judge Antonio Viviano sentenced him to two years probation and fined him $2,500.

Eminem's tempestuous and volatile marriage came to a head after a botched-up suicide attempt by Kim. Having had enough, he filed for divorce after less than 18 months of nuptials.

'Stan', is Eminem's greatest achievement to date. Beginning with a sample of 'Thank You' by Dido, followed by a menacing thunderclap, Eminem tells the sinister tale of an obsessed fan. 'Thank You' was originally featured in the romantic British film, *Sliding Doors* (1998), starring Gwyneth Paltrow and John Hannah.

"A hip-hop producer named DJ Mark 'The 45' King sampled the first part of 'Thank You' from the TV- and he put it on a beat tape, as they do, and sent it to Eminem and he used it. It's that simple," said Florian Cloud De Bounevialle Armstrong, better known as Dido, one of the biggest-selling female artists in the world today.

However, just a few short years ago, she was virtually unheard of. "I got this letter out of the blue one day," she told MTV. "It said, 'We like your album, we've used this track. Hope you don't mind and hope you like it.' When they sent it to me and I played it, I was like, 'Wow! This track's amazing.'"

Born on Christmas Day, 1971 to an Irish father and a French mother, her upper-middle-class upbringing couldn't have been more of a contrast to Eminem's. She earned her nickname for being interested in books (her unconventional parents didn't own a television) after *Dido, Queen Of Carthage.* the play by 16th century poet and playwright, Christopher Marlowe. Dido was a precocious and gifted child. At five years of age she began piano and violin lessons and attended the Guildhall School Of Music in London.

Her older brother Rollo, was the founding member of the band Faithless, and Dido would often hang out with him in the studio. One day when his scheduled vocalist failed to appear, he asked his sister to step in. She jumped at the chance. Soon she was singing with the group full-time. In 1999 she released *No Angel*, which after a slow start (and largely thanks to its inclusion of this song) became the biggest selling debut album by a female artist in the UK ever.

Among her many awards, she has received the Best British Solo Female and Best British Album awards at the Brits in 2002 and Best British Single (for 'White Flag', number two, 2003) and Best British Solo Female in 2004. 'White Flag' also earned Dido an Ivor Novello Award for International Hit Of The Year. She has also had Top 10 hits with 'Here With Me', 'Thank You' and 'Life For Rent'.

The video featured actor Devon Sawa (*Final Destination*) as Eminem lookalike Stan and Dido as his doomed pregnant girlfriend. It shows the rapper reading letters from Stan. They get darker and more deranged, climaxing with the weirdo telling his hero (via a suitably-placed recording device) that he has tied up his pregnant girlfriend and put her in the trunk, drunk a load of vodka and is about to drive his car off a bridge. Not realising he is too late, Eminem finally replies to Stan, his number one fan, apologising for his tardiness.

Partly to dispel the constant accusations of his hatred against homosexuals, Eminem duetted with Elton John on 'Stan' at the 2001 Grammy Awards. Sky News reports from June 2004 suggested that there has been a falling out between Dido and Eminem over royalties. It is said she has 'begun a legal battle to claim £1 million.'

886 Bob The Builder
Can We Fix It?

Label & Cat No.: **BBC Music WMSS 60372**

Producer: **Grant Mitchell**

Writer: **Paul K. Joyce**

Date Reached No.1: **23 December 2000**

Weeks at No.1: **3**

NOT FOR BOB THE USUAL BUILDERS' pessimism coupled with predictable forecasts that the job is far more difficult than it looks, will cost far more than you think, and take far longer too. Bob, with his team, could fix just about anything in no time at all.

Neil Morrissey was born in Stafford in 1962, the second youngest of four sons. His parents were psychiatric nurses, but the family was poor and Neil regularly played truant from school. In the evenings, Neil would often break into buildings and was once prosecuted for burglary. But something changed and he was placed with foster parents so he could concentrate on studying. It paid off and he won a scholarship to the Guildhall School of Music and Drama.

He graduated in 1983 and won his first role in *The Bounty* starring alongside Mel Gibson, Anthony Hopkins, Liam Neeson, Laurence Olivier, Edward Fox and Daniel Day-Lewis.

In 1986 he started a five-year residency as Rocky Cassidy in *Boon*, before taking over the role of Tony Smart from Harry Enfield in the award-winning comedy *Men Behaving Badly*, which ran from 1992-1998. He also appeared in a number of TV films, *Stuck On You* (1993), *Staggered* (1994), *The Vanishing Man* (1996) and *Jack And The Beanstalk* (1998).

Bob The Builder and all the other characters were devised by Keith Chapman and developed by HOT Animation. Neil had already worked with Jackie Cockle, the producer at HOT, so in 1999 it was suggested that Neil be brought in to provide voices for a number of characters in the show. Bob wears a yellow hard hat, checked shirt and blue dungarees with various tools hanging from his belt. As Neil explained, "Bob stands about nine inches high, he is made of strong plastic and has a full titanium skeleton inside."

The show's main characters are Bob and his partner, Wendy. However, other 'people' include JJ the mechanic, Molly who is JJ's daughter and hires out the skips, and Pilchard the cat. Bob's team comprised Muck the digger-dumper, Scoop the big digger, Lofty the crane, Trix the forklift, Dizzy the cement mixer, Roley the steamroller, and Skip the skip lorry. Another regular character is Farmer Pickles who owns Spud the scarecrow, Scruffty the dog and Travis the tractor. The voices for all the characters are provided by just three people; Neil voices Bob, Roley, Farmer Pickles, and Scruffty. Rob Rackstraw does Scoop, Muck, Travis and Spud, whilst Kate Harbour provides the voices of Wendy, Dizzy and Molly.

The composer Paul Kevin Joyce learned piano at an early age, which eventually led him to write his own songs. In 1983 he formed his own band, Sense, who supported Depeche Mode and Kim Wilde on tour. They had one hit single in France called 'Jamie'. In 1989 he turned his attention to writing and performing music for television and has worked on programmes for the BBC, ITV, Channel 4 and The Disney Channel. "I wrote the song quite quickly as I was well-briefed about what the producers were looking for. The phrase 'Can we fix it' was already established in the script so the challenge was to use it in the song in a way that would be both strong and appeal to kids and adults alike."

'Can We Fix It?', the programme's theme tune, won the BBC and the programme an Ivor Novello award. Neil explains: "We had the biggest selling single of the year 2000, which is a nice thing to get, and we were up against all kinds of people. We knocked Eminem off the number one spot and stopped Westlife matching a Beatles record of eight straight number ones. I remember sitting between Stevie Wonder and Annie Lennox at the awards ceremony and the place was rammed with every musical luminary you could think of. They announced 'Bob The Builder' as the winner and played the tune whilst I walked to the stage to a smattering of applause. I realised that we'd come in from the offside on this one, but it was great."

The single debuted at number one after selling more than 188,000 copies in one week. "Who would have realised that seven inches of plastic could give so many people so much pleasure," remarked Neil.

887 Rui Da Silva featuring Cassandra
Touch Me

Label & Cat No.: **Arista 74321823992**

Producer: **Rui Da Silva**

Writers: **Rui Da Silva / Cassandra Fox**

Date Reached No.1: **13 January 2001**

Weeks at No.1: **1**

ALTHOUGH BRITISH HOLIDAYMAKERS often make for Portugal, Rui Da Silva is the only charting Portuguese performer. 'Touch Me' was his only hit but he also recorded as part of The Obeah Men, Nylux, The Underground Sound Of Lisbon and Coco Da Silva as well as using the pseudonyms, Doctor J, Sound Projectors, Saffron, Teimoso, Mata Hari and The Four Elements.

Rui, born in 1968, began DJing and producing dance music in the early Nineties. "I was into things like Japan, David Sylvian, Brian Eno and Sonic Youth and the first record I did was the result of some experimental jamming sessions with some friends. I had a bass and an amplifier and I sold them and bought a drum machine and sampler," he recalled. After pressing a few tracks on 12-inch white labels, Rui went to London to gain a reaction. He then returned to Portugal and teamed up with DJ Vibe to form Underground Sound Of Lisbon and soon began releasing house tracks on his newly formed Kaos label, which were well received in Europe and America.

The Portuguese music scene was not the thriving industry seen by the likes of London and Ibiza, so Rui decided to move to London where he said, "This is the place where things are happening and where more people can be exposed to my music." He quickly built up a following and worked with big-name DJs, Danny Tenaglia, Sasha and John Digweed. He then formed the Kismet label in 2000, a name he chose because Kismet is the Turkish word for 'destiny'.

For his latest track, 'Touch Me', he wanted a female vocalist and brought in London-born singer Cassandra Fox. "I was coming out of the Denim bar in London and I asked these buskers if I could sing with them," recalled Cassandra. "Rui Da Silva came up to me and gave me a card and told me to call him. I did and we went into the studio. He gave me a backing track to take home and listen to and the next day I got the melody as I was walking to the station. By the time I got to my destination it was finished." The original version sampled the brass from Spandau Ballet's 1981 hit 'Chant No.1 (I Don't Need This Pressure On)' but he was sued by BMG for failing to seek permission to use it, so he was forced to re-record the track without the sample. "I wasn't impressed," he said, "but unfortunately if you incorporate someone else's song into your song it's still considered a crime. In music it is considered a crime but in painting it's not. Look at Andy Warhol. He used to do that with Campbell's soup and Marilyn Monroe images and he never got sued."

The follow-up single, 'Feel The Love' failed to make the Top 75, so he teamed up with DJ Hyper and called themselves Hyper DaSilva and released a couple of tracks that also failed to cross over to the pop chart.

In 2003 Rui's remixing skills were in demand and as well as mixing tracks for Jennifer Lopez, he was asked to rework Yoko Ono's minor 1981 hit 'Walking On Thin Ice', which was the last track she and John worked on together and the cassette John was carrying when he was shot.

"I have now developed my own website at www.kismetrecords.com where people can log on and download my music for a Euro each. It has become my main focus because everybody uses the internet now, so it's the best place to go and get music."

888 Jennifer Lopez
Love Don't Cost A Thing

Label & Cat No.: **Epic 6707282**

Producer: **Ric Wake**

Writers: **Damon Reinagle / Greg Lawson / Georgette Franklin / Jeremy Monroe / Amille Harris**

Date Reached No.1: **20 January 2001**

Weeks at No.1: **1**

JENNIFER LOPEZ WAS BORN TO PUERTO Rican parents in the Bronx on July 24, 1970. She studied singing and dancing from the age of five and continued her dancing lessons long after she graduated. She landed her first job, at the age of 20, as a fly girl – a dancer – in the American TV comedy series *In Living Colour*. She had to be slick, beautiful and have her own unique style. In 1993 she appeared in the video to Janet Jackson's hit 'That's The Way Love Goes'.

Jennifer was extremely ambitious and open to any challenge. Her other TV credits include *Nurses On The Line : The Crash Of Flight 7* (1993), *South Central* (1994) and *Hotel Malibu* (1994). Her movie debut was *My Little Girl* (1986) followed by *My Family, Mi Familia* (1995), *Jack* (with Robin Williams, 1996), *Selena* (1997) and opposite George Clooney in *Out Of Sight* (1998). In 1997 she was voted 16th in the *People* magazine's 50 Most Beautiful People. The same year at the launch party of *Selena*, her boyfriend, Ojani Noa, proposed in front of all the guests. The couple were married in February and by September they had separated. They were divorced the following March.

Sony Music's chairman, Tommy Mottola, was impressed with her performance as a Mexican-style singer in *Selena*, and arranged a meeting with her and a number of top producers. As she was keen to get her singing career going, they went straight into the studio and began recording a number of songs that would appear on her debut album, *On The 6*. At this time she began dating the R&B pioneer Sean 'Puff Daddy' Combs.

The album went to number eight in the States and number 14 here. The debut single, 'If You Had My Love' topped the US chart and reached number four in Britain. The next single, 'Waiting For Tonight', originally recorded by 3rd Party in 1997, went Top 10 in both the UK and the US.

She had doubts about her voice but was assured by her producer, Rodney Jerkins, that she had nothing to worry about. In 2001 her relationship with Puff Daddy was fizzling out following his arrest for gun possession and bribery charges. Whilst a third single was lifted from *On The 6*, Jennifer went back into the studio with Cory Rooney and Troy Oliver, who would become her permanent producers, to record her next album, *J-Lo*, the title of which came from Puff Daddy's pet name for her.

The first single from it, 'Love Don't Cost A Thing', topped the chart on both sides of the Atlantic. During the recording of the video, she met a new man, Cris Judd, who became her latest beau. Cris and Jennifer married in September 2001 but they split a year later. The week *J-Lo* went in at number one, her latest film, *The Wedding Planner*, was released and Jennifer became the first female to have the number one album and the number one film simultaneously in the US.

Most of Jennifer's UK releases went into the Top 10; 'Play' (3), 'Ain't It Funny' (3), 'I'm Real' (4), a remix of 'Ain't It Funny' with rapping from Ja Rule reached number four, 'I'm Gonna Be Alright' (3), 'Jenny From The Block' (3) and a duet with LL Cool J on 'All I Have' went to number two. In March 2002 an album, *J To Tha L-O! – The Remixes* climbed to number four.

Jennifer continued to notch up husbands as well as hits. In November 2002 she announced her engagement to Ben Affleck with whom she co-starred in *Gigli* (2003) and *Jersey Girl* (2004). *Gigli* received disastrous reviews. Everyone was accused of over-acting and the plot was non-existent. One reviewer said 'Tooth extraction without Novocain would have been less painful'. Soon after, Jennifer broke off the engagement to Ben and five months later she married the actor Marc Anthony, just four days after his divorce was finalised.

Jennifer Lopez

Jennifer has the most talked about buttocks in Hollywood. Her curvaceous rear-end, which she claims is insured for $1 billion, is now so famous that it could have been nominated in a Best Supporting role. The question is, on what grounds would an insurance company pay out? The bottom line is that it will always be there!

889 Limp Bizkit
Rollin'

Label & Cat No.: **Flip / Interscope IND97474**

Producer: **Terry Date**

Writers: **Wes Borland / Sam Rivers / John Otto / Fred Durst**

Date Reached No.1: **27 January 2001**

Weeks at No.1: **2**

"LIMP BIZKIT ARE DEFINITELY A DUMB rock band as far as the fact that our songs are written in a pop format," explained Wes Borland, Limp Bizkit's guitarist in an interview with *Rolling Stone*.

It all started in 1994 in Jacksonville, Florida when lead singer Fred Durst (born William Durst) called his long-time friend and bass player Sam Rivers and suggested they form a band. Sam brought his cousin John Otto in on drums and they recruited the guitarist Wes Borland. Fred and a friend were talking one day and his friend wasn't making much sense. When Fred pointed that out, he remarked, "Sorry, but my brain is like a limp biscuit." Fred thought that was a great name for the band and when the rest agreed, they adopted it and then they adapted it.

They began rehearsing and then recording, but were not making much headway so Fred began moonlighting as a tattoo artist from his home. One night Fred went to a Jacksonville concert by the rock band Korn. After the show they met and he invited the lead singer, Head, and bass player, Fieldy, to have some tattoos done. The next time they visited Fred, he handed them a demo tape, which Head passed to their producer, Ross Robinson. Ross loved their sound and Limp Bizkit were offered a recording contract. Their first professional gig was supporting House Of Pain. Fred invited DJ Lethal (born Leor DiMant) from the group to join as Limp Bizkit's fifth member.

They became known as a nu-metal group, a genre known for heavily distorted guitar with hip-hop influenced vocals. Their US hits made the chart only as album cuts and were not commercially available as singles, a situation that came about in December 1998 when *Billboard* decided that, due to an increasing number of tracks receiving airplay which were not commercially available, they were incorporated into the singles chart, but shown as album cuts.

In the UK their debut single, 'Take A Look Around', the theme from *Mission Impossible 2*, reached number three and went on to win them Best Rock Video award at the 2000 MTV Video Awards. Their first album, *Three Dollar Bill Y'All$*, went by completely unnoticed, but their second, *Significant Other*, went to number 10 and sold eight million worldwide.

In October 2000 they released their third album, the curiously titled *Chocolate St★rfish And The Hot Dog Flavored Water*. "People are always calling me an asshole, so I thought I'd make it the title of the album," Fred admitted. Although in another interview he claimed, "The title's kind of inspired by *Sgt. Pepper's Lonely Heart Club Band*," explained Fred. "But it's funny because the music is completely opposite of what Pepper is..."

'My Generation' (not The Who song) was the first single and it reached number 15. The follow-up, 'Rollin', will be best remembered for the $3 million video which showed Fred cruisin' in his Rolls-Royce cabriolet while other scenes featured shots of a helicopter swooping around the skyline of New York, weaving around the Statue Of Liberty and the roof of a building where the band are playing surrounded by scores of women with their breasts on display. Fred said, "We wanted it to be like Guns N' Roses."

Limp Bizkit had further Top 10 hits with 'My Way' (2001) and 'Eat You Alive' (2003). Later in 2003, Britney Spears became Fred's 'significant other'... for a short while anyway. Many fans wrote to Fred via his website telling him he was crazy for dating Britney, and that he needed his head tested. But he retorted with, "I really liked that girl, and it's not what you think. Trust me, she's cool. I mean, I hate her music, but I *really* like her as a person."

890 Atomic Kitten Whole Again

Label & Cat No.: **Innocent SINCD 24**

Producers: **Engine (Andy McCluskey / Stuart Kershaw)**

Writers: **Andy McCluskey / Stuart Kershaw / Bill Padley/ Jeremy Godfrey**

Date reached No.1: **10 February 2001**

Weeks at No.1: **4**

Eighties hitmakers, Orchestral Manoeuvres In The Dark (OMD) are one of the great acts never to make number one, although their near misses ('Enola Gay', 'Souvenir', 'Joan Of Arc', 'Sailing On The Seven Seas') are as well known as many of the chart-toppers. After a break from the business, their lead vocalist and songwriter, Andy McCluskey, looked for new Merseyside talent which he could produce. He worked with his songwriting partner Stuart Kershaw at their Engine Studios and their first attempt was a girl band called Honeyhead. They gave them 'Right Now' and 'Whole Again', but the band fell apart in 1998. Undeterred, they assembled a group of good-looking girls (Natasha Hamilton, Liz McClarnon, Kerry Katona) and called them Atomic Kitten. When they bought some clothes from a company called Automatic Kitten, Kerry misread the bill and Andy thought the name was perfect.

Atomic Kitten were signed to Innocent, a subsidiary of Virgin Records, and Andy and Stuart wrote and produced the first album, *Right Now*. The first three singles, 'Right Now', 'See Ya' and 'I Want Your Love', were Top 10 hits and then 'Follow Me' reached number 20. The killer single came at the start of 2001 with 'Whole Again'. "I loved The Shirelles," said Andy, "and in many ways that is the sort of song The Shirelles would have been doing now." The original intention was for 'Whole Again' to have a spoken introduction but that was dropped after All Saints hit the top with 'Never Ever'. At the suggestion of Virgin, Andy and Stuart gave 'Whole Again' to another songwriting team, Billy Padley and Jeremy Godfrey, to sharpen it up as it had the makings of an international hit.

The single was shunned by Radio 1, but Atomic Kitten promoted it on TV shows, appeared in the tabloids and did personal appearances, so it didn't matter. By the time, it made Radio 1's playlist, it was at number one.

Kerry Katona had had a traumatic upbringing with care homes and foster parents and although she didn't have the best voice in Atomic Kitten, she was the one who most wanted success. At the time of The Shirelles, a career would have been ruined by the revelations of earlier nude photographs, but the public shrugged off Kerry's nude photos. "We knew it was coming," said Andy, "Kerry showed me the pictures the first time I met her."

Atomic Kitten

891 Shaggy featuring Ricardo 'Rikrok' Ducent It Wasn't Me

Label & Cat No.: **MCA 1558022**

Producer: **Shaun Pizzonia**

Writers: **Orville Burrell / Ricardo Ducent / Shaun Pizzonia / Brian Thompson**

Date Reached No.1: **10 March 2001**

Weeks at No.1: **1**

Having spent four years without a recording contract, Shaggy moved to Long Island and built a studio in his basement. He began writing songs for films, contributing tracks to Kevin Costner's film *For The Love Of The Game*, *Speed II* and *Jungle To Jungle* before teaming up with noted writer/producers Jimmy Jam and Terry Lewis for 'Luv Me Luv Me', a duet between Shaggy and Janet Jackson, which was featured in the movie *How Stella Got Her Groove Back*. All this led to him being signed by MCA. "I don't hold any grudges against Virgin," maintained Shaggy. "I tell you, nothing clears up animosity like a hit record. I bet they are scratching their heads thinking, 'Damn! We should have kept him'."

He recorded the album *Hot Shot*, which initially failed to make any impact. It was only when a DJ in Honolulu, Pablo Sato, downloaded an MP3 of 'It Wasn't Me', a track from the album and began playing it to death on his KIKI-FM radio show that the public began to take notice.

The bulk of 'It Wasn't Me' features Ricardo 'Rikrok' Ducent, whom Shaggy met through one of his backing singers. Shaggy said, "He had a good personality, a good vibe and was a very humble kid. I let him demo the track with a view to getting someone else to sing on the final version, but when my producer Shaun Pizzonia heard his vocals, he convinced me to leave him on the track. Shaggy got the concept from a line in Eddie Murphy's film *Raw*. "Shaun came up with the beat, Brian came up with some words, Shaggy came up with the verses and I came up with the melody," recalled Rikrok.

The song tells of a guy who gets caught red-handed by his girlfriend, cheating with the girl next door. He then tries to deny all allegations despite her catching him on camera. "Everybody cheats at some time or another in their lives," Shaggy claimed. "I just wanted to put a funny twist on it. I think a lot of people saw themselves in it. Bill Clinton was a cheater, Jesse Jackson did it too."

Hot Shot shot to number one in both the UK and US. "The album is exceptional. I knew I had to come back with an album that was incredible and getting dropped by Virgin was fuel to my fire," insisted Shaggy.

'It Wasn't Me' initially spent three weeks on the chart as an import where it reached number 31. Once it was released in the UK it crashed into the chart at number one. A few weeks later, a bootleg parody surfaced about a mother who catches her son masturbating. It was called 'Caught Me One Handed' by The Parodies and was just a little too rude for radio.

892 Westlife
Uptown Girl

Label & Cat No.: **RCA 74321 842522**

Producer: **Steve Mac**

Writer: **Billy Joel**

Date reached No.1: **17 March 2001**

Weeks at No.1: **1**

WESTLIFE SEIZED THE OPPORTUNITY to get away from ballads with a perfunctory revival of Billy Joel's 'Uptown Girl' for Comic Relief. As it was more or less a straight copy, the critics said pants to the single, but many of the new fans wouldn't know the original.

One of the organisers of Comic Relief, scriptwriter Richard Curtis, knew supermodel Claudia Schiffer's agent and obtained her cooperation for the video, which would ape Billy Joel's original that featured his model wife Christie Brinkley. The video featured a chorus of city lads with the actors Tim McInnery, James Wilby, Ioan Gruffudd, Robin Bathurst and Crispin Bonham Carter as well as Westlife themselves.

Nicky Byrne from Westlife remarked, "Claudia had the most beautiful eyes and was really, really stunning. She was the perfect uptown girl for the video, but when we all stood beside her, the only one who was near her height was Bryan. We were looking up to her."

893 Hear'Say
Pure And Simple

Label & Cat No.: **Polydor 5870062**

Producers: **Pete Kirtley / Tim Hawes**

Writers: **Pete Kirtley / Tim Hawes / Alison Clarkson**

Date reached No.1: **24 March 2001**

Weeks at No.1: **3**

IN THE SEVENTIES, NIGEL LYTHGOE WAS a dancer with the TV troupe, *The Young Generation*. He became a television executive and while at London Weekend, he presided over *Blind Date*, *Gladiators* and *An Audience With*… In 2001 he adapted an Australian show, *Popstars*, for the UK market. Thousands of wannabes applied to take part, and the selection process with Nigel and his panel criticising the would-be Robbies and Kylies was filmed. His comments were so biting that the tabloids named him Nasty Nigel. As the series was pre-recorded, the five possible winners (three girls, two boys) shared a house in Mill Hill until the results, chosen by the judges and not the public, were announced. The outcome attracted 11 million viewers and the group, to avoid confusion with other versions of *Popstars*, was named Hear'Say. Nigel had wanted a one-word name but Resolution, Persona, Frenzy and Life were rejected.

As might be expected, the members of Hear'Say were quite experienced. Fashion-conscious Myleene Klass, who played several instruments, had studied at the Royal Academy of Music and was about to tour as a backing vocalist for Robbie Williams. Suzanne Shaw sang with the Abba tribute band The Right Stuff and had acted in *Holby City*. Mother of two, Kym Marsh made her first record when she was 13. Puppeteer Noel Sullivan sang with a Welsh male voice choir, and the ever-smiling club singer Danny Foster had been in Michael Barrymore's *My Kind Of Music*. Hear'Say were managed by Chris Herbert, who had formed The Spice Girls from auditions before they walked out on him and became managed by Simon Fuller.

Mel C felt sorry for them. "It's such an exploitation of those poor kids and I think the ones that haven't got through are the lucky ones. A lot of it is just a very public ritual humilation, but I'm sure that if I hadn't been in The Spice Girls, I would have been up there going for it myself."

One of Simon Cowell's less successful projects was Girl Thing. They had hits in 2000 with 'Last One Standing' and 'Girls On Top' and they had recorded 'Pure And Simple'. Simon reflected, "I knew it would be a hit but then Hear'Say released the same song and Girl Thing was doomed."

Hear'Say were allowed to perform 'Pure And Simple' on *The Brits*. They ignored the boos of rival record companies and 'Pure And Simple' became the fastest-selling debut single of all-time, going straight in at number one with sales of half a million and it sold 1.2 million in all. Some 8,000 fans went to Woolworth's in Milton Keynes for a signing session and counsellors had to deal with those who were overcome by meeting the group.

The album, *Popstars*, was equally successful, selling a million copies in the UK, but the question being asked by the public was, would it last? The question being asked by Hear'Say was, how much we will get out of this? *The Sunday Times* revealed the group would only be making 4p from the sale of each single. If true, the

Westlife secured the services of model Claudia Schiffer for their 'Uptown Girl' video; left to right: Mark Feehily, Bryan McFadden, Kian Egan, Nicky Byrne and Shane Filan

individual members would be making just £10,000 from their million seller.

894 Emma Bunton
What Took You So Long?

Label & Cat No.: **Virgin CDV 2935**
Producers: **Richard Stannard / Julian Gallagher**
Writers: **Emma Bunton / Julian Gallagher / Martin Harrington / Richard Stannard / John Themis**
Date reached No.1: **14 April 2001**
Weeks at No.1: **2**

DESPITE HER *POLLYANNA* LOOKS, EMMA might have been the contributory factor in the break-up of The Spice Girls as Geri objected to her friendship with their manager Simon Fuller. She denied that there anything in it, and her celebrity boyfriends have included Jade Jones of Damage and Justin Timberlake.

In November 1999 Emma recorded 'What I Am' with the instrumental and production team of Lindsay Edwards and Darren Stokes, known collectively as Tin Tin Out. It was a revival of a 1989 chart entry from Edie Brickell & The New Bohemians, and the new version went to number two.

With The Spice Girls' album, *Forever*, and her solo career, she ditched her Baby Spice image for a more adult look. Gone went the pigtails and her album, *A Girl Like Me*, was in line with her new sensuality. 'What Took You So Long?' is about a girl who is crowing over regaining her lover – "What took you forever to see I'm right?" The singalong melody had a Motown feel.

With 'What Took You So Long?' Emma became the fourth Spice Girl to have a solo number one. A few weeks earlier, Victoria Beckham lost a much-publicised race to the top with 'Not Such An Innocent Girl' only managing number six.

Even securing a number one and having a hit album wasn't enough to keep Virgin Records happy and Emma was dropped from the label. In 2003 she made a guest appearance in *Absolutely Fabulous* and was strongly featured in Marks & Spencer's campaign for Christmas. Of all The Spice Girls, Emma seems the one least changed by fame.

895 Destiny's Child
Survivor

Label & Cat No.: **Columbia 6711732**
Producer: **Anthony Dent**
Writers: **Anthony Dent / Beyoncé Knowles / Mathew Knowles**
Date Reached No.1: **28 April 2001**
Weeks at No.1: **1**

FOLLOWING THE SUCCESS OF 'Independent Women' in *Charlie's Angels*, Destiny's Child released the title track of their new album *Survivor* as a single. In it they sang, "Ain't no one come between us three", but things were changing. Beyoncé was shining through as the most talented of the trio and was considering a solo career.

'Survivor' topped the UK chart and spent seven weeks at number two in America, but it brought its share of problems. Soon after LaToya Luckett and LaTavia Robertson left in 2000, they tried to sue the remaining members claiming that 'Survivor' included derisive comments about them, but the suit was soon settled. Then came a $200 million lawsuit from a Miami-based producer, Terrence Robinson, who claimed that Beyoncé and her father had stolen the music from his 2000 song 'Glorious' after he had sent Mathew a copy. He also said in court that the song had not been copyrighted at the time, but he had secured one later. The matter was settled out of court. The song went on to win a Grammy for Best R&B Performance.

They followed 'Survivor' with 'Bootylicious' and a cover of Samantha Sang's 'Emotion', which was their final single. At the end of 2001 Destiny's Child split up. Beyoncé said at the time it was a temporary split, whilst Kelly likened the break to The Beatles. With thanks to technology, The Beatles did reunite, ('Free As A Bird' and 'Real love), but it seemed that Beyoncé was right and Destiny's Child did reform and in September 2004 Mathew said of their new album, *Destiny Fulfilled*, "It's the next stage and we hope it's going to be a hit. It's certainly a change of direction, they're older now and each lady performs their own track."

Beyoncé was the first to chart a solo single with 'Work It Out'. Kelly followed three months later with a collaboration with Texan-born rapper, Nelly.

896 S Club 7
Don't Stop Movin'

Label & Cat No.: **Polydor 5870832**
Producer: **Simon Ellis**
Writers: **Simon Ellis / Sheppard Solomon / Jon Lee / Rachel Stevens / Jo O'Meara / Paul Cattermole / Bradley McIntosh / Hanah Spearritt / Tina Barrett**
Date Reached No.1: **5 May 2001**
Weeks at No.1: **4 (2 runs)**

S CLUB 7'S SQUEAKY-CLEAN IMAGE WAS temporarily tarnished when the three male members, Jon Lee, Bradley McIntosh and Paul Cattermole, were arrested in London's Covent Garden for being in possession of marijuana. "We have been very stupid, we know we've made a mistake and we're very sorry," they claimed in a statement, after receiving a caution from police.

For a band with so many impressionable fans, it could have been the end of their career. However it didn't appear to hinder them at all, as proven when 'Don't Stop Movin'' debuted at the top spot a few weeks later. It stayed there for a fortnight, when it was usurped by Geri Halliwell's 'It's Raining Men', only to regain its position two weeks later for its second chart-topping run.

'Don't Stop Movin'' won ITV's *Record Of The Year*, as voted for by viewers, leaving Blue with 'All Rise' and Kylie's 'Can't Get You Out Of My Head' in respective second and third places.

The band also received the award for Best Single at The Brits in 2002.

It was Bradley's turn to perform lead vocals on this catchy, disco-flavoured number, taking over from the group's usual lead singer, Jo.

Later that month, they embarked on their first UK tour. It contained no less than four set changes, including a backdrop of the Hollywood sign, and a plethora of painstakingly choreographed dance routines.

Although their young fans lapped it up, they came under criticism for not singing live. Hannah admitted, "I'm not that good a singer, really. We mimed. We did sing the songs in the studio, but the amount of singing that we did in the band wasn't that much. We hardly did any singing."

897 Geri Halliwell

It's Raining Men

Label & Cat No.: **CDEMS 584**

Producer: **Stephen Lipson**

Writers: **Paul Jabara / Paul Schaffer**

Date reached No.1: **12 May 2001**

Weeks at No.1: **2**

BRIDGET JONES'S DIARY BEGAN AS A comic column in *The Independent*: Helen Fielding's creation worked for a London publisher and despaired about her weight and lack of boyfriends. When Fielding expanded the story to a novel, it became a publishing sensation. Using the same title, *Bridget Jones's Diary* was brought to the screen in 2001 with Renée Zellweger as Bridget, and Colin Firth and Hugh Grant as her quarries.

'It's Raining Men' was written in 1982 by Paul Schaffer, the music director for *Letterman*, and Paul Jabara, who had written for the soundtracks of *The Main Event* and *Thank God It's Friday*. It was given to the former gospel singers, Martha Wash and Izora Redman, who were backing the disco star, Sylvester. Taking a lead from the song, they called themselves The Weather Girls, and recorded it for the aptly named Fantasy label. The Weather Girls had powerful voices and, when it was promoted in 1984, the single made number two in the UK.

The key song on the soundtrack of *Bridget Jones's Diary* was a new recording of 'It's Raining Men', marking the return of the Geri. The musicians included Dave Stewart from Eurythmics on keyboards and Beverley Skeete from Bill Wyman's Rhythm Kings on backing vocals. The video for 'It's Raining Men' was a homage to the Eighties dance films, *Fame*, *Flashdance* and *Footloose*. Geri, now slimmed and glamorous, dances well, another example of how hard she was working.

Geri's publicist was Matthew Freud, the brother of Emma Freud, whose partner, Richard Curtis, wrote the screenplay of *Bridget Jones's Diary*. When they met at a London restaurant to discuss the film, Geri was worried that she might be pursued by fans. Richard Curtis said, "Don't worry, I'll go first. They'll run after me and you can disappear."

The single soon became a camp disco classic, and was included on Geri's new album, *Scream If You Wanna Go Faster*. The cover, showing Geri on roller skates clinging on the back of a car, was criticised by safety experts. Geri had had doubts about 'It's Raining Men', asking Emma Freud, "If I release a cover version, what about my artistic integrity?" When the subsequent singles, both originals, 'Scream If You Wanna Go Faster' and 'Calling', only made the Top Ten, it appeared that Geri's chart career was losing its impetus.

898 DJ Pied Piper & The Master Of Ceremonies

Do You Really Like It?

Label & Cat No.: **Relentless RELMOS 1CDS**

Producers: **DJ Pied Piper / Unknown MC**

Writers: **Eugene Nwohia / Steve Wickham / Paul Newman / Ashley Livingstone**

Date Reached No.1: **2 June 2001**

Weeks at No.1: **1**

IN 1990 THE BROTHERS EUGENE AND Ronald Nwohia from south London began recording together under the name DJ Supreme. American rapper Ice T was impressed enough to sign them to his Rhyme Syndicate label. Changing their name to Hijack, they made the lower end of the charts with 'The Badman Is Robbin'' (56).

The brothers joined up with MC Creed, Valerie M and PSG to form Da Click who had two hits in 1999 with 'Good Rhymes' (14), based around Chic's 'Good Times' and 'We Are Da Click' (38) sampling Tom Browne's 'Funkin' For Jamaica'.

By 2000 DJ Pied Piper (Eugene) and Unknown MC (Ronald) were playing the same clubs with MCs, Melody (born Ashley Livingstone), DT (born Paul Newman) and Sharkie P (born Steve Wickham). They all had catchphrases and they decided to put them into one song. "We put this gong on the front because it just sounded good and then DT came out with, 'Enter The Dragon' so we kept that in," recalled Piper, "Next was Sharkie P who came in with 'Do you really like it', followed by DT who sang 'We're lovin' it, lovin' it, lovin' it'. Melody started singing 'Uh, I'lla up, I'lla muh', which everyone thought sounded like Ayia Napa."

The brothers put the track out on their own Soul Food Records. "We sold them on the streets and at the gigs," Piper recalled, 'and then we got a call from Channel 4 who had heard 'Do You Really Like It?' and asked if we could provide music for a trailer to promote an Ali G series. Ronnie suggested that they use the same backing track with new lyrics rapped by Ronnie. Then the phone didn't stop ringing." They signed to Relentless Records and in the week of release, the single sold 148,000 copies and entered at number one.

DJ Pied Piper & The Master Of Ceremonies recorded a follow up, 'We Are Here', but it was never released. The MCs thought is was too commercial and were more interested in pursuing their own projects. The guys have since gone their separate ways. Piper still works in production and Melody owns the L4 management and production company with Simon Webbe from Blue.

899 Shaggy featuring Rayvon
Angel

Label & Cat No.: **MCA MCSTD 40257**

Producer: **Shaun Pizzonia**

Writers: **Orville Burrell / Ricardo Ducent / Nigel Staff / Shaun Pizzonia / Dave Kelly / Steve Miller / Eddie Curtis / Chip Taylor**

Date Reached No.1: **9 June 2001**

Weeks at No.1: **3**

WITH HIS *HOTSHOT* ALBUM GAINING platinum status and 'It Wasn't Me' becoming the biggest selling UK single of 2001, Shaggy had become an international star. "I got into this business to tour, that's actually why I became an artist and why I make records," he said. "I'm just at home on stage."

The next single was 'Angel'. "Shaun came to me with this beat, which was the Steve Miller bassline from 'The Joker'. I don't know what Steve was thinking, but it's actually reggae. I did a world music kind of vibe on it," Shaggy told *Billboard's* Fred Bronson. Neither Shaggy nor Shaun liked the way it was turning out so it was shelved. One day, one of *Hot Shot*'s co-producers, Dave Kelly, found the track and thought it was worth having another attempt at. He invited Rikrok, who had guested on 'It Wasn't Me', into the studio and started playing the track to them. All of a sudden, Rikrok began singing 'You're my angel in the morning, angel' and Shaggy knew that was it.

For the finished article they not only sampled 'The Joker', but also the chorus from Merrillee Rush's US hit version of 'Angel Of The Morning', which was written by the actor Jon Voight's brother, Chip Taylor, who had also written 'Wild Thing', an international hit for The Troggs. Shaggy said, "Because it's such a lively song, I thought it needed a voice with a different edge," so he brought in Barbados-born singer Rayvon (born Bruce Brewster), a singer he'd first met at a studio in New York where they collaborated on a cover of Air Supply's 'All Out Of Love' which was never released. "We gave the song to him and he came in and nailed it," said Shaggy.

Once it was recorded, Shaggy sent a copy to Chip Taylor for approval. "I thought that his version was really cool," said Chip. "We agreed that we'd call it another title because he used some other elements in it as well. We also worked out a deal and I own half of that copyright."

In 2002 Shaggy formed his own Big Yard record label with his long-term manager, Robert Livingston. The same year he won a multitude of awards including: Best International Male at the Brits, Best Selling Male Artist in the US, Best Selling American Artist at the World Music Awards and Best Selling Album at the Juno Awards in Canada. In addition, he won a *Billboard* award for Male Artist Of The Year.

Shaggy's singing voice is a put-on-gravely-Jamaican-patois. He said, "No one is interested in my normal speaking voice, it's an act I put on and everybody loves it." It certainly gave impressionist John Culshaw material for his act. I'm tellin' ya, you'd be hard pushed to spot the difference.

Shaggy

900 Christina Aguilera, Lil Kim, Mya And Pink
Lady Marmalade

Label & Cat No.: **Interscope 4975612**

Producers: **Ron Fair / Missy Elliott**

Writers: **Bob Crewe / Kenny Nolan**

Date Reached No.1: **30 June 2001**

Weeks at No.1: **1**

IN JUNE 2001 BAZ LUHRMANN'S written and directed movie *Moulin Rouge* was unleashed on the world and in the first 10 days, it netted $28 million. Why?

The hype, the stars and the humour played a big part, but it was the terrific music that paid homage to the 20th century's songbook, and frenzied energy that keeps the film moving. It features some unusual covers of classic songs including; 'Diamond Dogs' (Beck), 'Nature Boy' (John Leguizamo), 'Children Of The Revolution' (Marius Devries), 'The Sound Of Music' (Ewan McGregor), 'One Day I'll Fly Away' (Nicole Kidman) and 'Your Song' (Ewan McGregor with Placido Domingo). The highlight is the teaming up of R&B/hip-hop stars Christina Aguilera, Lil Kim (born Kimberley Jones), Mya (born Mya Harrison) and Pink (born Alecia Moore).

The story tells of Christian (Ewan McGregor), a Scottish lad who moves to Paris at the tail end of the 19th century. He's thrown into an untimely and tragic love affair with Satine, the highest paid singer at Paris' *Moulin Rouge* nightclub. The club's business is good but the owner spends more money than he is making on a new invention – the electric light. So with money tight, he needs a backer. Enter a rich English Duke who, in return for putting up the money, wants exclusive access to Satine. The film rests on a battle between love and money.

The US chart was now being compiled by a combination of sales and airplay. 'Lady Marmalade' was not released as a single, but received sufficient radio exposure to top the chart for five weeks as an airplay hit, and in the process became the first airplay-only single to spend more than one week on top.

The song was written in 1974 and first recorded by The Eleventh Hour, a group of studio musicians fronted by the co-writer Kenny Nolan. As Kenny remembered, "The song was written in bits, I had a section here and a section there, but still needed something to link it. Bob (Crewe) and I came up with the idea of 'Voulez-Vous Coucher Avec Moi Ce Soir?' and that seemed to be the missing bit of the puzzle." Labelle had a Top 20 hit with it in 1975 and group member Patti Labelle noted in her biography, that the song was written about Creole prostitutes.

901 Hear'Say
The Way To Your Love

Label & Cat No.: **Polydor 5871482**

Producers: **Stargate (Mikkel Eriksen / Hallgeir Rustan / Tor Erik Hermansen)**

Writers: **Mikkel Eriksen / Hallgeir Rustan / Tor Erik Hermansen**

Date reached No.1: **7 July 2001**

Weeks at No.1: **1**

ALTHOUGH HEAR'SAY WERE A NEW group created by the ITV show, *Popstars*, they were thrown in the thick of it. They performed 'Pure And Simple' at the Rugby League Cup Final at Twickenham, and they performed in arenas rather than theatres. They were given their own series, *Hear'Say: It's Saturday*, and David Cassidy, himself once a member of a manufactured band, was a guest.

Some of Hear'Say's recordings were made at the StarGate studios in Norway. All the group thought that 'The Way To Your Love' was a hit song and to quote Danny Foster, "It might sound a bit pants to say it, but 'The Way To Your Love' was one of those songs we did in the beginning that really bonded us vocally. When we heard it back, it was like, 'This is the one'." 'The Way To Your Love' featured strong harmonies and showed that all five members of the group could sing.

The manner in which Hear'Say came together was always going to be derided, but several factors led to their downfall. They were humiliated by Liberty X, a group formed from the losers on *Popstars*, who had much more street cred. When Kym Marsh left, they had a very public audition to choose a new member, but, when it became known that new boy Johnny Shentall was a friend of theirs, it looked like a publicity stunt gone wrong. Their singles, 'Everybody' and 'Lovin' Is Easy', reached the Top 10 and the group split up in October 2002.

Suzanne Shaw toured the UK opposite Darren Day in the very successful stage show, *Summer Holiday – The Musical*, and her romance with Darren helped ticket sales. In August 2004 Johnny Shentall married Lisa Scott-Lee from Steps. Noel Sullivan has been in a touring version of *Fame* and a solo album from Danny Foster is expected. Myleene Klass' career might go in a completely different direction following her classical album, *Moving On*, in 2003.

Hear'Say

902 Roger Sanchez
Another Chance

Label & Cat No.: **Defected DFECT 35CDS**

Producer: **Roger Sanchez**

Writers: **Roger Sanchez / Steve Lukather**

Date Reached No.1: **14 July 2001**

Weeks at No.1: **1**

AFTER 20 YEARS IN THE BUSINESS, one of the world's most sought-after producers and remixers, Roger Sanchez, has a reputation for getting what he wants.

Roger was born in New York in 1967 to Dominican parents and grew up in the disco era where his love of music prompted him to start DJing when he was just 13. That led on to his uncredited dance-on parts in the films *Breakdance* (1984) and *Krush Groove* (1985). DJing was a hobby, but his mixing abilities were proving popular and apart from now running the Ego Trip nightclub in Manhattan, he made mix tapes to sell. After a brief period studying architecture at the Manhattan School of Art and Design, he left in 1987 at his dad's suggestion that he should concentrate on DJing professionally.

He recorded his first single, 'Luv Dancin'', in 1990 under the pseudonym Underground Solution. He tried his hand at remixing which proved successful and was called in to work on tracks by Diana Ross, Janet Jackson, Michael Jackson, Chic, M People and Soul II Soul. Roger also recorded and remixed under the names Tribal Confusion, The S-Man and Transatlantic Soul. "I love production," he said. "I'm very much a person who knows what I want in terms of sound and production and that becomes an extension of myself."

His UK chart success came in 1993 as one half of Sound Of One with 'As I Am' (65), then in 1996 as El Mariachi with 'Cuba (38). Under his own name in 1997, Roger reached number 43 with 'Release Yo Self' and the following year he remixed Malcolm McLaren's 1982 hit 'Buffalo Gals', but it stalled at number 65. In 1998, under the guise Funk Junkeez, he charted with 'Got Funk'. This was followed by his first Top 40 hit 'I Want Your Love'. Every one of them was on different labels.

In 2001 he released his debut album, *First Contact*. The first single, 'I Never Knew' went to number 24, but using a sample from Toto's US Top 10 hit, 'I Won't Hold You Back' for his next single, 'Another Chance' saw him enter the chart at number one.

It was totally by accident that Toto's 'I Won't Hold You Back' was used. "The record happened to be sitting on the floor of my studio when I was working on my album and I just was listening to different tracks to get inspiration to do something and I came across that record and it had a line in it that basically I could relate to and that spoke to me."

The follow-up, 'You Can't Change Me', which featured Armand Van Helden, only reached number 25. Since then, Roger has written and produced album tracks for Dannii Minogue. He said, "The original idea was to do something so underground that no-one would know it was her until it was out, but then she got an album deal and it had to be more commercial."

Roger is still DJing and has a residency at the Pacha in Ibiza. He continues to release compilation mix albums under the titles *Release Yourself* and said of his most recent one, *Release Yourself 3*, "I think it has a solid track selection and is pretty party orientated."

903 Robbie Williams
Eternity / The Road To Mandalay

Label & Cat No.: **Chrysalis CDCHS 5126**
Producers: **Guy Chambers / Steve Power**
Writers: **Robbie Williams / Guy Chambers**
Date reached No.1: **21 July 2001**
Weeks at No.1: **2**

SING WHEN YOU'RE WINNING WAS Robbie Williams' third number one album – the title was a dig at Gary Barlow – and it contained a succession of hit singles – 'Rock DJ' (1), 'Kids' (a duet with Kylie Minogue, 2), 'Supreme' (4), 'Let Love Be Your Energy' (10) and 'The Road To Mandalay' (1).

'The Road To Mandalay' was not a revival of Rudyard Kipling's stirring song but a new, folksy ballad that worked very well. It was coupled with a new track, 'Eternity'. Both songs indicated that Robbie was not as happy with life as his media profile suggested. Indeed, he has separated Rob from 'Robbie' in many interviews. To keep the paparazzi at bay, he took to wearing the mask from the 'Eternity' video when he left and entered his house.

Robbie never cared for 'Eternity', saying in 2004, "I don't have to sing 'Eternity' ever again unless it's to save someone I love from death or some sheik offers me a million quid." He was incensed by a report in the *Daily Mail* that Guy Chambers' melodies were 'instantly hummable': "They've got me as Bernie Taupin and Guy as Elton John. I would find it hugely disrespectful if anybody in my record company thought that a huge lion's share of the songs weren't done by me."

Surprisingly, the most commercial song on *Sing When You're Winning* was not issued as a single. Robbie had written a song called 'Where's Your Saviour Now?', which he knew was substandard. He shouted, "John Lennon if you're there, send us a song", and an hour later, he had 'Better Man', a ballad which made a fine companion to 'Angels' and revealed that Robbie was realising his own limitations. Quite a change from "I'm a man machine, drinking gasoline".

904 Atomic Kitten
Eternal Flame

Label & Cat No.: **Innocent SINCD 27**
Producer: **Andy Wright**
Writers: **Susanna Hoffs / Billy Steinberg / Tom Kelly**
Date reached No.1: **4 August 2001**
Weeks at No.1: **2**

IN JANUARY 2001 KERRY KATONA announced she was expecting a child with her fiancé, Bryan McFadden from Westlife, and a few months later, she left the Kittens. Although Kerry had been an integral member of the Kittens, she knew that she did not have as strong a voice as the others and was happy with simply being a media personality.

Her replacement was another girl from the north-west, Jenny Frost, born of Liverpool parents but raised in Prestwich. She had been with the Eurovision group, Precious ('Say It Again', 6, 1999). Jenny had a stronger voice than Kerry which enhanced the group's harmonies.

Around the same time, Andy McCluskey fell out with their management and stopped working with them. Their revival of The Bangles' number one, 'Eternal Flame', was produced by the Londoner, Andy Wright. It stuck closely to the original. Jenny said, "Even though 'Eternal Flame' was a cover, it was a wicked version and I'm really proud of it." To Tash, 'Eternal Flame' was a new song: "I was a bit too young to remember it really, but I really loved performing it because there's a great little routine we did it to."

Liz added, "I was a massive fan of the original 'Eternal Flame' when I was younger and The Bangles thought our version was amazing." In 2003, Susanna Hoffs gave Atomic Kitten a new song, 'Love Don't Have To Hurt', which reached number four.

The Liverpool girls were becoming fashion icons. They performed on a concert to honour Nelson Mandela and sang 'Dancing In The Street' in a Motown medley at the Party In The Park at Buckingham Palace. Jenny said, "What on earth possessed me to grab the future King, pin an Atomic Kitten t-shirt to his chest, spin him round to the camera and then pull a really stupid face?" Publicity, probably.

905 So Solid Crew
21 Seconds

Label & Cat No.: **Relentless RELENT 16CD**
Producer: **Synth**
Writers: **Dwayne Vincent / Ashley Walters / Jermaine Williams / Shane Neil / Lisa Maffia / Michael Harvey / Marvin Dawkins / Jason Moore / Aminu Mahtari / Jason Philips / Les Weir**
Date Reached No.1: **18 August 2001**
Weeks at No.1: **1**

OFTEN REFERRED TO AS THE UK'S answer to the Wu-Tang Clan, So Solid Crew, most of whom had known each other since school, are made up of MCs Romeo, Megaman, Asher D, Face Skat D, Kowdean, Neutrino, Squami, JD, Harvey, Akira, Mac and Trigger. Then there are the DJs: Oxide, Dan Da Man, Sniper, TW7, Swiss, Timeless, PDs and Statix, vocalists Lisa Maffia, Kaish, Money, Tiger S and Thug Angel and finally producers G-Man, Mr. Shabz, AC Burrell, Synth, and Morgan. However, not all of them perform on this single.

Although various members quote varying

So Solid Crew

figures as to how many are actually part of the group at any one time, the ever-expanding Battersea-based rap crew were formed in 1998 when they all decided to meet up at the Killer Watt Carnival Soundsystem. "We were called SOS at first but there was a DJ called that on another station. He thought of the name So Solid Crew and everyone agreed that it was alright," explained Romeo. They released their first single 'Oh No, Sentimental Things' in December 2000, which only featured Lisa Maffia, Megaman and Romeo. It failed to make the chart.

"For our next single we tried to find a way to get the whole massive on one track to prove we were all equally part of the group," recalled Asher D. "We were thinking that there's about 20 guys and how long it would take to get every one of us out there. So we just sped up the process and divided the time equally which left us 21 seconds each."

The lyrics came in for criticism. '21 Seconds' opens with Megaman rapping, "21 seconds oh shit, I ain't got no time to smoke this" and "Say niggas wanna see nigga, get rich But niggas don't really want nigga to be rich," with Mac adding, "Shot Benz in a rave while I'm clubbin' Ladies come around an' they buggin'." The Culture minister, Kim Howells, launched an attack on So Solid Crew, alleging they helped to "Create a culture where killing is almost a fashion accessory." David Blunkett, the Home Secretary, supported him by agreeing that "The lyrics of some of these rap stars are appalling."

Their debut album, *They Don't Know*, was released just before Christmas 2001 and reached number six. The title track became their next hit single and got to number three. They had two further Top 10 hits 'Haters' (2002) and 'Broken Silence' (2003). Their second album, *2nd Verse*, sold few copies and spent one week on the chart at number 70.

Three members of the crew have had their share of trouble. G-Man and Kaish were arrested on gun and drug charges but later cleared. Asher D was arrested for possessing a gun and sent to a young offenders institution for 18 months.

Various members have pursued solo careers with Romeo being the most successful having had two Top 10 hits 'It's All Gravy' with Christina Milian (9) and 'Romeo Dunn' (3).

906 Five
Let's Dance

Label & Cat No.: **RCA 74321875962**

Producers: **Richard Stannard / Julian Gallagher**

Writers: **Richard Stannard / Julian Gallagher / Ash Howes / Martin Harrington / Jay Brown / Sean Conlon**

Date Reached No.1: **25 August 2001**

Weeks at No.1: **2**

AFTER THEIR COLLABORATION WITH Queen on 'We Will Rock You', Five were away from the chart for almost a year, but were constantly appearing in the tabloid gossip columns. If it wasn't Ritchie's romance with fellow pop star Billie Piper, it was Sean's health problems. One article claimed that J was engaged to TV presenter Dani Behr. Another said that Sean had quit the band because he couldn't handle the pressure. "Utter crap," retorted Ritchie. "I can't believe people read that crap. The truth is that Sean has glandular fever and is resting." That's the reason you'll notice a life-size cardboard cut-out of him in the 'Let's Dance' video.

Songwriters/producers Richard 'Biff' Stannard and Julian Gallagher were working at the Windmill Studios in Dublin. They liked the place so much they eventually bought it and renamed it Biffco Studios. Biff, a name he took from a character in *Back To The Future*, recruited the engineer and songwriter Ash Howes and more recently brought in an Irish songwriter Martin Harrington. As a team they have written hits for Atomic Kitten, Hear'Say and Kylie Minogue.

'Let's Dance' entered the chart at number one, but the cracks were beginning to show. Their songwriting commitments were about to split them up. "Abs, J and I write songs in Ireland with Jules and Biff, whilst Scott and Ritchie are working with Mikkel S.E, Hallgeir Rustan and Tor Erik Hermansen in Norway," revealed Sean. They all got together to complete what was to be their final studio album, *Kingsize*, which, when released, entered at number three.

They followed 'Let's Dance' with 'Closer To Me' which was to become their last hit and with the rush release of the *Greatest Hits* album less than three months after *Kingsize*, Five were about to say goodbye.

So far, only Abs has managed a successful solo career with three Top 10 singles, 'What You Got' (2002), 'Stop Sign' (2003), and 'Miss Perfect' with Nodesha (2003) and the Top 30 album *Abstract Theory*.

907 Blue
Too Close

Label & Cat No.: **Innocent SINCD 30**

Producer: **Ray Ruffin**

Writers: **Kier Gist / Darren Lighty / Robert Huggar / Raphael Brown / Robert Ford / Denzil Miller / James Moore / Kurtis Walker / Larry Smith**

Date Reached No.1: **8 September 2001**

Weeks at No.1: **1**

WITH FIVE HAVING JUST ANNOUNCED their split, Blue, hand-picked from 3,000 hopefuls at an audition set up by the same team who assembled The Spice Girls, were ready to step in to keep the boy band flag flying.

Blue are four London-based boys, Antony Costa, Simon Webbe, Lee Ryan and Duncan James. Duncan wanted to form a band and so he called Anthony, whom he had known for three years, and Lee, whom he had met at auditions. "I thought Lee had an amazing voice," Duncan recalled. "He then introduced us to his flatmate, Simon who became the fourth member and that was it." Antony added, "We don't take ourselves too seriously, we are just doing music for fun."

"Simon came up with the name. Basically it's just a colour and doesn't mean anything really, but I suppose Blue also has a bit of a naughty side to it," Duncan admitted. They formed in the winter of 1999 and with the help of their manager they signed a contract with Innocent Records.

Blue needed a song and they decided on the club classic, 'Too Close'. Kier Gist, or Kay Gee, as he likes to be known, was a former member of hip-hop group Naughty By Nature. Robert

Huggar, of the American R&B group Next, and cousin of Earth Wind & Fire's Philip Bailey, approached Gist in a shopping mall and told him he had a group. Gist asked them to drop off a demo and once he heard it, he signed them. Next's second single 'Too Close' spent five weeks at the top of the US chart and was also the biggest selling US hit of 1998. It sampled Kurtis Blow's 1979 hit 'Christmas' Rappin' and only made number 24 in the UK.

"'Too Close' is a club classic and still gets played everywhere. It's always been one of our favourite records as a group, so we couldn't resist doing our own version," said Simon.

The parent album, *All Rise*, contained 'something for everyone', explained Simon. "The first single and title track 'All Rise' was the R&B track, 'Too Close' was the soul track and the next single 'If You Come Back' will be the Motown-influenced track."

908 Bob The Builder
Mambo No.5

Label & Cat No.: **BBC Music WMS 560442**
Producer: **Grant Mitchell**
Writer: **Pérez Prado**
Date Reached No.1: **15 September 2001**
Weeks at No.1: **1**

With Bob The Builder now very much a fixture on children's TV, it seemed only right for him and his gang to release a follow-up to 'Can We Fix It?'. Coming exactly two years after Lou Bega took Pérez Prado's 1950 track to number one, Bob's version used the same backing as Lou's but had specially adapted lyrics with a chorus that went: "A little bit of timber and a saw, A little bit of fixing that's for sure, A little bit of digging up the roads, A little bit of moving heavy loads, A little bit of tiling on the roof, A little bit of making waterproof, A little bit of concrete mixed with sand, A little bit of Bob, the builder man."

Apart from the overabundance of Bob The Builder merchandise that included mugs, shoes, videos, bedding, Lego, games, sunglasses and a crockery set, there was the obligatory album. It was called *The Album* and reached number four in the chart. Apart from the two number one hits, it included cover versions of 'Painter Man' (Creation/Boney M), 'Dizzy' (Tommy Roe) and a duet with Elton John of 'Crocodile Rock'.

In 2000 Neil Morrissey and his *Men Behaving Badly* co-star, Leslie Ash, were asked to appear in the Homebase TV adverts. Neil's character had spent most of the programme's life trying to date Leslie's and eventually they did get it together. The storyline spilled over into real life with the media often making assumptions about their relationship. The ads just became a continuation of that storyline.

In 2002 Neil and Billy Bragg bought the four-room Hurst House Hotel in Laugharne, Carmarthenshire, South Wales, which is where Dylan Thomas wrote *Under Milk Wood*. Some work was carried out at the hotel, but Neil left the professional builders to do the job as he admitted, "Despite advertising DIY adverts, my own DIY skills leave a lot to be desired."

The Archies, Spitting Image, The Simpsons, Mr Blobby and The Teletubbies all did it once, but Bob The Builder is the only fictional character to have reached number one twice.

909 DJ Ötzi
Hey Baby (Uhh, Ahh)

Label & Cat No.: **EMI 8892462**
Producers: **Klaus Biedermann / Claus Marcus / Christian Seitz**
Writers: **Bruce Channel / Ed Cobb**
Date Reached No.1: **22 September 2001**
Weeks at No.1: **1**

Delbert McClinton played the harmonica on Bruce Channel's version of 'Hey Baby'. When Bruce and Delbert toured the UK in early 1962, one of the dates took in Liverpool where The Beatles were lower down in the bill and an impressed John Lennon asked Delbert to show him how to play it. A few months later that inspired sound could be heard on the intro to 'Love Me Do'.

Bruce's version of 'Hey Baby' topped the US chart and reached number two in the UK and has become a party sing-a-long favourite for over 40 years.

DJ Ötzi was born Gerry Friedle in Tyrol, Austria, the result of a one-night stand. His mother put him up for adoption and he spent two years with foster parents. Then his grandmother discovered his existence and brought him back to her hometown of Seelen-Dorf on Ötz, the place from which he would later take his name.

At 19 he left his grandmother's home and ended up living rough on the streets for a few months. When a passer-by call him a tramp, he decided enough was enough and became motivated to do something with his life. He sang karaoke in local bars, then became a DJ, taking the name DJ Ötzi and moving to Mallorca where he was well received. In 1998 he discovered he had testicular cancer, but after a short spell of chemotherapy, he made a full recovery.

One night during his DJ set, the tall, bleached-blond Ötzi was winding the crowd up into a frenzy by playing Bruce's 'Hey Baby' and adding his own 'Uuh Aahs' which the crowd were copying. So he recorded it and it was released by EMI's subsidiary label, Liberty, across Europe. It went to number one in Austria and Ireland, number two in Germany, Holland, Italy, Poland and Switzerland and number three in Belgium and Denmark. On import it reached number 45 in the UK, but such was its popularity that import copies ran short and EMI were forced to bring its UK release date forward. It was released the following week and sold over 90,000 copies. The song rocketed from 45 to number one but because the UK release carried the same catalogue number as the import, its leap to the top was not considered a new entry. It now holds the record for the biggest climb to number one in chart history. "I know I am no Mozart," Ötzi said. "I am the guy who can make any party rock. I'm successful because I am who I am and not a manufactured personality," he insisted.

During its seven-month residency on the

When his rewritten version of 'Mambo No 5' hit the top spot, Bob The Builder became the first kids' TV character to reach number one twice

chart, Ötzi's follow-up, a similar-styled cover of 'Do Wah Diddy Diddy' reached number nine and his Christmas offering 'X-Mas Time' attracted few buyers. In June 2002 the track was remixed by Humperfunk and Ötzi added some new lyrics. It became the unofficial World Cup anthem and was back in the chart at number 10.

DJ Ötzi's album, *Never Stop*, which included all his hits, was released in 2002 and was a 12-track non-stop party, but despite its success in Europe, the British people probably had enough uuh aah's for one year and it missed the chart completely.

"I loved DJ Ötzi's version very much," said Bruce Channel in 2004. "It went platinum, so not only did it make me a whole heap of money, it brought the song to a whole audience and I'm very grateful to him for that. It also shows how it has stood the test of time."

910 Kylie
Can't Get You Out Of My Head

Label & Cat No.: **Parlophone CDRS 6562**

Producer: **Cathy Dennis**

Writers: **Cathy Dennis / Rob Davis**

Date Reached No.1: **29 September 2001**

Weeks at No.1: **4**

KYLIE SLIPPED OUT OF FASHION DURING the mid-Nineties, but thanks to her flair for re-inventing herself by the turn of the century she was heralded as an iconic pop queen, a serious rival to Madonna. When she duetted with Robbie Williams on 'Kids', the press went into overdrive with speculation of a relationship. Although no romance materialised, the publicity did her no harm.

In 1989 dance-act D Mob's first two hits introduced us to the talents of Norwich-born singer Cathy Dennis. Two years later Cathy's first and biggest solo hit – a cover of Fonda Rae's 'Touch Me (All Night Long)' – got to number five in the UK and number two Stateside. She ran up a dozen UK hits, 11 of which she wrote herself. By 1998 she had decided to concentrate solely on songwriting.

Cathy's first success came in 1999 when S Club 7's 'Two In A Million' reached number two. She also co-wrote their party favourite, 'Reach'. Former Mud guitarist Rob Davis got into writing dance tunes in the late Eighties. "I met DJ Paul Oakenfold in 1988 and he said to me, 'I know exactly where music is going to go, the house thing is going to be big'. He started playing me all these tunes and I quite liked it, but it needed more melody," remembered Rob. "Then I saw an opening, to write top lines and add melody lines to it and get more vocals into the club tunes."

Simon Fuller, the man behind The Spice Girls and S Club 7, suggested that Cathy, whom he also managed, and Rob work together. "We did two songs in one day," continued Rob. "We'd done a really poppy thing for S Club and then, as an afterthought, we came up with 'Can't Get You Out Of My Head'." That afterthought has probably secured them financially for life.

Cathy voiced the demo of 'Can't Get you Out Of My Head', but was not convinced of its hit potential. Nonetheless, she took it to Parlophone where Kylie, on first hearing, leaped around yelling, 'When can I do it?'

'Can't Get You Out Of My Head' was the first track released from Kylie's new album, *Fever*, which went platinum in the UK within a week and four times platinum in Australia in a fortnight. The song sold over 300,000 copies in the first week, shot to number one in 15 countries and soon became affectionately known as the 'La-la-la song'. Such was her status now that she joined artists like Diana Ross, Tina Turner and Janet Jackson who felt it unnecessary to use their surname.

Kylie had an award-winning year in 2002. 'Can't Get You Out Of My Head' won Cathy Dennis three Ivor Novello awards for Best International Single, Best Dance Record and Most Played Record Of The Year. It contributed to Kylie's hat trick of MTV awards for Best Pop Act, Best Dance Act and Best Choreography In A Music Video. At the World Music Awards in Monaco, she was honoured as Best Selling Australian Artist Of The Year.

911 Afroman
Because I Got High

Label & Cat No.: **Universal MCSTD 40266**

Producers: **Afroman / Headfridge**

Writer: **Joseph Foreman**

Date Reached No.1: **27 October 2001**

Weeks at No.1: **3**

IN 1983 THE PROGRAMMING STAFF at Radio 1 refused to play Grandmaster Flash's 'White Lines (Don't Don't Do It)' because they were under the impression it promoted drugs. When it was pointed out that it was an anti-drug song, it was suddenly all over the airwaves and subsequently reached number seven and spent 43 weeks on the chart. 'Because I Got High' had more blatant drug references and, although it may be tongue-in-cheek, radio stations realised it was an anti-drug song describing the hazards of pot rather than its pleasures and had no reservations about playing it. It had a similar theme to the Dr Hook song 'I Got Stoned and I Missed It'.

Afroman was born Joseph Forman in Los Angeles in 1974. "I was gonna call myself all sorts of different names but for some reason this girl started calling me Afroman because I was broke, so I decided that would be my name," he explained. He learned drums and guitar as a child and started writing music in school. "My first song was about my eighth-grade teacher, Miss Dober, who had me kicked out of school for messing my pants, when I was about 13." I wrote this song about her and sold 400 copies to teachers and students, so even though I wasn't at school, I was really because my tapes were everywhere."

In the mid-Nineties he played drums in a church band as well as performing on the sidewalks. His parents bought him a tape recorder, mixer and microphone in the hope of keeping him out of mischief. He recorded and released his first album, *Sell Your Dope*, in November 1999, but soon became fed up with what he described as the 'L.A. vibe' and moved to Mississippi.

There he formed a band and signed with T-

Bone Records. He wrote the song 'Because I Got High' about his experiences with marijuana and all the things he couldn't do because he was high. "I wanted to take my negativity and generate something positive," he said. "I would wake up in the morning ready to take on the world and I was doing it, but then I got high and I messed around and lost the entire day doing nothing."

The song was included on his second album, *The Good Times*, which failed to chart in the UK, and also featured in the comedy film *Jay and Silent Bob Strike Back*, about two characters who sold drugs outside a convenience store for a living. After hearing of a movie being made inspired by their own life styles without permission, they set off on a journey from New Jersey to Hollywood to seek compensation.

'Because I Got High' initially charted in the UK on import 12-inch only sales and reached number 45. On its UK release it sold 130,000 copies. In his homeland it was released in August and climbed to number 13, but its progress was hindered by the events of 9/11. US radio and TV stations became very wary of the subject matter of many songs and, even though it seemed ludicrous in many instances, there was an instant ban of all songs with references to killing, drugs and violence.

912 Westlife
Queen Of My Heart

Label & Cat No.: **RCA 74321 899142**
Producer: **Steve Mac**
Writers: **Steve Mac / Wayne Hector / John McLaughlin / Steve Robson**
Date reached No.1: **17 November 2001**
Weeks at No.1: **1**

WITH COMMENDABLE SPEED, WESTLIFE followed their *Coast To Coast* album one year later with *World Of Our Own*. The 19-track, chart-topping album included the number one singles, 'Uptown Girl', 'Queen Of My Heart', 'World Of Our Own' as well as 'Bop Bop Baby' (number five and, unusually for a single, a song they had written themselves). The video for 'Bop Bop Baby' featured Westlife as five musketeers rescuing Ronnie Wood's daughter, Leah, from Vinnie Jones.

Following 'Swear It Again' and 'Flying Without Wings', the writer and producer, Steve Mac, repeated his success with another anthemic ballad, 'Queen Of My Heart'. Kian, Bryan, Shane and Mark had solo sections within the song.

913 Blue
If You Come Back

Label & Cat No.: **Innocent SINCD 32**
Producer: **Ray Ruffin**
Writers: **Ray Ruffin / Nicole Formescu / Ian Hope / Lee Brennan**
Date Reached No.1: **24 November 2001**
Weeks at No.1: **1**

"BASICALLY WE'D ALL BEEN DUMPED by our girlfriends and we were really upset," Duncan explained. He'd told their friend Lee Brennan, of 911, about the situation who, with Ray Ruffin, son of Motown legend, Jimmy, came up with 'If You Come Back'. He added, "I was in the car driving and feeling really gutted. Antony was in a café crying so we all got together and met up in this warehouse and just sung our hearts out."

The shoot for the accompanying video was underway in New York when the World Trade Center disaster struck, so filming continued in London.

The next single, 'Fly By II' which sampled Herb Alpert's 'Rise', went to number six and was followed by 'One Love', which reached number three.

In 2002 Blue ran into legal problems when the Seventies group with the same name sued them over its use. The original Blue weren't an active band, but were still issuing CDs. The judge, Mr Justice Laddie, decided there was no merit in the claim, as one band could not be mistaken for the other. The Seventies Blue faced a £100,000 bill for costs but the new Blue and EMI pledged it would not be enforced so long as the old band did not pursue their complaint by other means.

One person who wasn't blue was Elton John. He had signed the original Blue to his own Rocket label, played piano on their albums and produced their only UK hit, 'Gonna Capture Your Heart' in 1977. Now Elton was teaming up with the new Blue for a cover of his own song, 'Sorry Seemed To Be The Hardest Word' which went on to be number one.

914 S Club 7
Have You Ever

Label & Cat No.: **Polydor 5705002**
Producers: **Stephen Lipson**
Writers: **Cathy Dennis / Andrew Frampton / Chris Braide**
Date Reached No.1: **1 December 2001**
Weeks at No.1: **1**

'HAVE YOU EVER' WAS S CLUB 7'S fourth number one and their second for BBC's Children In Need appeal.

This pretty ballad, again penned by the busy Cathy Dennis and sung by Jo, debuted at the top spot. It was the third single released from their third album, *Sunshine*, which included their previous two chart-toppers and the future number two hit, 'You'.

Blue

Jon said 'Have You Ever' differed from their other singles, because it lacked a happy ending. "It's a very sad song really. It's aimed at anyone who has lost someone, especially young children who have lost a parent. The message is definitely awareness. It fits in well with Children In Need."

A specially recorded version of the song appeared on CD2 and the cassette copy, which put the band into the record books. It featured over 270,000 children chosen from more than 3,500 schools across the country.

In June 2002 following the band's performance at the Queen's Golden Jubilee 'Party In The Palace' celebration, Paul left the group. Paul, whose great-grandfather was once managing director of Abbey Road studios, said, "I've had some of the best times of my life over the past four years with S Club and I'd like to thank all my fans for that and also the other six guys. I love S Club to bits and I know they'll continue to be hugely successful. I'll be watching them every step of the way and wish them all the best. I'm going to rejoin my old school group." Speaking of the unsigned band, Skua (named after a bird that lives on the coast of Antarctica), he continued, "I was the lead singer for a number of years. I want to go back to my rock roots."

S Club 7 were determined to carry on as a six-piece, but dropped the digit. "Paul has left the band in a good way," commented Bradley. "There hasn't been a row, he just wants to do his kind of music."

Hannah, who was involved romantically with Paul, said she was looking forward to their being a normal couple after living in each other's pockets. "If you have some time apart, then you can have much more of a laugh because when you do get together and say, 'Hi, how was your day?' You don't already know the answer."

Obviously believing that the world was in desperate need of more S Clubbers, a team of nine children, all under the age of 15, were brought together by Simon Fuller after nationwide auditions. Originally called S Club Juniors, after four singles they changed their name to S Club 8 (one member had left before they hit the big time). They have so far achieved a 100% success rate with their half a dozen hits all reaching the Top 10.

Jo, regarded by many as the band's strongest singer, released a solo single. 'Every Kinda People', a cover of the hit by Robert Palmer which was featured on the *Guru* soundtrack. It failed to chart but Jo insisted she was not about to leave S Club.

Having completed their fourth successful TV series, *Viva S Club*, S Club were faced with a new challenge. Following in the steps of The Spice Girls, work began on their movie, *Seeing Double*. Paul had appeared in *Viva S Club*, documenting his farewell, but unexpectedly had a cameo in the flick when live footage of the original seven-piece was erroneously kept in.

Unsurprisingly, the movie was mauled by the press. *Seeing Double*, the tale of an evil scientist who manufactures clones of (manufactured) popstars, featured Gareth Gates in a brief role, and also Michael Jackson, Elton John and Madonna, although their parts were played by lookalikes. Two singles from the soundtrack were released. 'Alive' reached number five, whilst the double A-sided 'Say Goodbye'/'Love Ain't Gonna Wait For You' faltered at number two.

Both sets of S Club went out on tour together. The tour was called S Club United, and they played 12 dates across the UK. Before it was over, S Club, on stage at one of their London dates, announced they were splitting up at the end of May. The split coincided with their greatest hits package, which was held at number two by The Stereophonics' *You Gotta Go There To Come Back*.

Rachel was the first to receive a lucrative solo deal. She has had two number two singles, 'Sweet Dreams My L.A. Ex' and 'Some Girls', as well as a cover of Andrea True Connection's 'More More More', which reached number three. Meanwhile her debut album, *Funky Dory* reached number nine. Jo also signed up for a solo career, and is rumoured to be working with Richard Carpenter. Both girls are still on the payroll of Simon Fuller.

As for the other members, Tina has expressed a wish to get involved in writing music, Hannah has done some acting, Bradley is writing songs and Jon has gone into the world of theatre, playing the part of Marius in *Les Misérables*.

S Club 8, at time of press, are still going strong. One can only imagine the confusion if one of the members wishes to leave…

915 Daniel Bedingfield
Gotta Get Thru This

Label & Cat No.: **Relentless RELENT 27CD**

Producer: **Daniel Bedingfield**

Writer: **Daniel Bedingfield**

Date Reached No.1: **8 December 2001**

Weeks at No.1: **3 (2 runs)**

NEW ZEALAND-BORN, LONDON-raised Daniel Bedingfield wrote 'Gotta Get Thru This' while walking across Tower Bridge one day, to help him get over a broken heart.

"It's about this flaming redhead from New Jersey called Gina. I was passionately in love with her and I wanted to be with her, but didn't have the guts to. I really liked her. I was up in London and she was in the North of England. There was this tension about me wanting to be up there. So I wrote it, went home and put it on my computer. My friend said, 'Man, it's a great song.'" Daniel added, "It was all done in my bedroom. I made 'Gotta Get Thru This' with one computer and a mike – that's all I had."

When Daniel found that no major labels were interested in taking on his song, he decided to press up some of his own copies and sent them to various DJs. One garage DJ, EZ was impressed enough to put it on the compilation, *Pure Garage 4*, which soon saw him sign a lucrative deal with Polydor.

Proving to be possibly the best £1000 ever spent on the recording of a garage track, the single went on to top the UK chart twice, for a fortnight in December 2001 and a further week in mid-January 2002. It also went Top 10 in the US, making Daniel one of only a handful of British acts to achieve the feat in the last few years. He admitted, "I just can't believe what's been happening for me there. American radio stations are introducing it to something like a million new listeners every day." The song was also nominated for a Grammy for Best Dance Recording, but lost out to Dirty Vegas' 'Days Go By'.

To demonstrate 'Gotta Get Thru This' wasn't

Daniel Bedingfield wrote his number one hit 'Gotta Get Thru This' after a real-life romance went awry

a mere trendy garage hit and that he wasn't a one trick pony, Daniel was keen to perform an acoustic version of the song on many TV shows, including *Top Of The Pops*. It also appeared on his debut album, *Gotta Get Thru This* (2, 2002), which has so far sold in excess of two million copies in the UK alone.

And what does his ex-love Gina think of being the inspiration behind such a successful song? "She loves it. She's loving that song. It gets played everywhere."

916 Robbie Williams & Nicole Kidman Somethin' Stupid

Label & Cat No.: **Chrysalis CDCHS 5132**

Producers: **Guy Chambers / Steve Power / Montclare / Park**

Writer: **C. Carson Parks**

Date reached No.1: **22 December 2001**

Weeks at No.1: **3**

ROBBIE WILLIAMS WAS ASKED TO SING the standard, 'Have You Met Miss Jones?' for the soundtrack of *Bridget Jones's Diary*. He had always loved Frank Sinatra and Bobby Darin, and he kissed photos of the the Rat Pack and Muhammad Ali before going on stage – he also insisted on a prayer bonding addressed to Elvis. There is also a tattoo on his arm, "Elvis, grant me serenity". His enjoyment in recording 'Have You Met Miss Jones?' prompted him to record an album of his favourites, *Swing When You're Winning*.

As Robbie had been impressed with Nicole Kidman's performance in the film musical, *Moulin Rouge*, he met her in Los Angeles and suggested a duet. They decided on 'Somethin' Stupid', but they replaced the whimsical charm of the Sinatras with something more sensual, especially in the video. William Hill's was taking bids of 16/1 for them being married in 2002.

The CD was released in November 2001 and was promoted by a televised concert from the Royal Albert Hall in which Robbie in evening dress serenaded Nicole on a screen. In a similar way, he sang a duet of 'It Was A Very Good Year' with Sinatra. The single, released just before Christmas, included the video and the Royal Albert Hall performance of 'My Way'.

Robbie dedicated the album to his producer, Guy Chambers, "who is just as much Robbie as I am." Within a few months they had fallen out and recriminations went back and forth. The argument was over royalty rates and Rob's team argued that a new, highly lucrative deal with EMI would benefit Guy proportionately anyway.

The capricious Robbie signed an £80m deal with EMI, and the first album was *Escapology*. He took more interest in the production, saying that previously, "I've been pissed and haven't given a shit what the records sounded like." When Robbie was shown Stuart Maconie's derogatory review in Q, he said, "Wanker." The album sold three million copies and the Top 10 singles, 'Feel', 'Come Undone', 'Something Beautiful' and 'Sexed Up'.

917 Aaliyah More Than A Woman

Label & Cat No.: **Virgin VUSCD 230**

Producer: **Timbaland**

Writers: **Tim Mosely / Stephen Garrett**

Date Reached No.1: **19 January 2002**

Weeks at No.1: **1**

GLADYS KNIGHT'S NIECE, AALIYAH Dana Haughton, was born in Brooklyn, New York in January 1979 and raised in Detroit. Her name is a Swahili term for deity and she was discovered by R.Kelly who wrote her first hit 'Back & Forth' in 1994. They married later the same year, but the marriage was annulled soon after when it was discovered that she had lied about her age. Her next hit, '(At Your Best) You Are Love' was a cover of an Isley Brothers song and Kelly wrote and produced her next three hits, 'Age Ain't Nothing But A Number', 'Down With The Clique' and 'The Thing I Like'.

Aaliyah had aspirations to be an actress and her stunning looks certainly helped her achieve her goal. She made appearances in various movies as a singer and her songs can be heard in numerous films; 'Back & Forth' in *Never Ending Story III* (1994), 'The Thing I Like' in *A Low Down Dirty Shame* (1994), 'One In A Million' in *Sprung* (1997), 'Journey To The Past' in *Anastasia* (1997) and 'Are You That Somebody' in *Doctor Doolittle* (1998).

In 2000 she appeared in *Romeo Must Die* for which she also provided the songs 'Come Back In One Piece', 'I Don't Wanna' and 'Try Again', which gave her her only US chart topper.

Timbaland (Tim Mosely) and Stephen Garrett had become her regular songwriters having written 'Are You That Somebody' (1998), 'Try Again' (2000) and 'We Need A Resolution' (2001) which all made the Top 20.

In the summer of 2001 Aaliyah was in the Bahamas making a video for the song 'Rock The Boat', which would eventually be the follow-up to her only UK number one. On completion, she boarded a small privately-chartered Cessna plane, which crashed and exploded on take-off killing Aaliyah and the other eight people on board. The plane was overloaded, perhaps twice the maximum allowance and the pilot, Luis Morales, had been found guilty of possessing cocaine only a fortnight earlier. Both cocaine and alcohol were found in his bloodstream. The plane itself had not been regularly maintained and the pilot, even if he were clean, was unqualified for this trip.

Her album, *Aaliyah*, had been released just four weeks earlier and when the next single from it, 'More Than A Woman', went to number one, it made Aaliyah the only female to posthumously reach the top. "Beyond the music, she was a brilliant person, the most special person I ever met," commented her producer Timbaland. "'More Than A Woman' going to number one in Britain showed that she is still missed by music lovers and her fans." That, and as shown by departed artists such as Elvis Presley, John Lennon and Freddie Mercury before her, the public have an almost morbid fascination with celebrities who meet an untimely death.

After her tragic death in a plane accident, Aaliyah became the first woman to have a posthumous number one hit

918 George Harrison
My Sweet Lord

Label & Cat No.: **Parlophone CDR 6571**

Producers: **George Harrison / Phil Spector**

Writer: **George Harrison**

Date reached No.1: **26 January 2002**

Weeks at No.1: **1**

GEORGE HARRISON NEARLY DIED IN the same way as John Lennon when a deranged Liverpudlian, Michael Abrams, broke into his Henley home in 1999 and knifed him four times. Harrison chanted "Hare Krishna" as he struggled, then his wife, Olivia, attacked the intruder with a poker and the base of a lamp. The police arrested Abrams, who was detained in a psychiatric unit. George recovered from his wounds but his body was already ridden with cancer cells.

Shortly before his death on December 3, 2001 aged 58, George Harrison was looking at his past albums with a view of reissuing them on CD, digitally enhanced and with bonus tracks. The new version of his triple-album *All Things Must Pass* was very tastefully done, with 2CDs and an informative booklet in a smart box. Among the outtakes was the stunning 'I Live For You' that makes you wonder how George could have ignored it for 30 years.

To add to the 30th anniversary flavour, George created a new version, 'My Sweet Lord (2000)', replacing many of the original instruments and adding Sam Brown's vocals and his lookalike son Dhani on guitar. A CD single of the original version of 'My Sweet Lord' was issued with 'My Sweet Lord (2000)' as the second track and so one deceased singer followed another at the top of the charts.

The squabble over the copyright of 'My Sweet Lord' had been settled years earlier and George Harrison's estate now owned the copyright of the song he had plagiarised, 'He's So Fine'. This case, more than any other, had harmed George's reputation as a songwriter, but that was restored by plentiful testimonials after his death, the most lavish coming from Jim Capaldi of Traffic who likened his friend to Jesus Christ. The Labour MP Jane Griffiths was so overcome that she could not proceed with her Home Energy Conservation Bill, surely a topic close to George's heart: she told the Commons, "Some of us may be inclined to weep now that George's guitar gently weeps no more." An all-star tribute concert at the Royal Albert Hall featured the remaining Beatles, Eric Clapton and Ravi Shankar.

While The Beatles would be unthinkable without John Lennon or Paul McCartney, George Harrison was also an essential part of the group and quite probably their genius overshadowed his. He was a modest man who grew to hate publicity and he spent his later years tending the copious gardens at Friar Park, his Henley estate. The appreciation of his work is likely to increase as the years go by. However, George's CD booklet in *All Things Must Pass* hits a pessimistic note when he wonders if the planet Earth will even be here in another 30 years.

919 Enrique Iglesias
Hero

Label & Cat No.: **Interscope IND 97671**

Producer: **Mark Taylor**

Writers: **Enrique Iglesias / Paul Barry / Mark Taylor**

Date Reached No.1: **2 February 2002**

Weeks at No.1: **4**

"I LIKE BEING UNDERESTIMATED, BECAUSE that's what pushes me and drives me to make a great album. I keep having to prove myself," revealed Enrique Iglesias. When 'Hero' reached number one in the UK chart, Enrique and his dad, Julio, became the only father and son to do so individually.

Enrique was born in Madrid in 1975. His parents separated when he was three and at the age of eight, he went to live in Miami with his father. He first sang in a school production of *Hello Dolly* and decided to take singing lessons without telling his father. After a year doing business studies at the University of Miami he chose

to follow Julio into the business, but was determined to do it on his own. In 1995 he began promoting himself as Enrique Martinez from Central America and landed a recording contract with Fonovisa Records. It was at this point he told his father of his aspirations and moved to Toronto to record his first album.

Reverting to his real name, he released his Spanish-language debut album, *Enrique Iglesias*, which sold over a million copies in three months and won him a Grammy for Best Latin Performer. He continued the Latin sound with his next album *Vivir* (1997), for which he won *Billboard*'s Album Of The Year. Both albums contained songs he had written when he was a teenager. He signed a worldwide deal with Interscope Records and his next album, *Enrique*, not only showed him to possess a talent for songwriting, it was his first album sung in English.

His debut single, 'Bailamos', which is Spanish for 'we dance', featured in the Will Smith movie *Wild Wild West*, and went to number one in the US and number four in the UK. The follow-up, 'Rhythm Divine' attracted little interest, but the next single, 'Could I Have This Kiss Forever', a duet with Whitney Houston, flopped in the US, but reached the Top 10 here.

Enrique Iglesias

"'Hero' is a really simple song," claimed Enrique. "It's very difficult to write a simple song and still touch the heart. I wrote it in 20 minutes, I was in my house and I knew I had fallen in love with it. For me it's a career song, it's the song that I feel that I can sing 20 years from now and not feel like an idiot."

The song was released in the US in September 2001 and received extensive airplay across the country where it was used as a dedication to the emergency services personnel who were helping to save lives on 9/11.

Julio and Enrique don't speak to each other too often. "My father asked me to sing a duet with him, but the request came through the record company and I didn't think much of it. We spoke on the phone not long after that and he told me that he felt bad because I hadn't agreed to record with him. I said, 'Why didn't you call me direct?' All you needed to do was pick up the phone." No duet has yet materialised.

Enrique's parent album, *Escape*, went to number one and spent over a year on the chart. The title track became his next single and that went to number three. 'Love To See You Cry' and 'Maybe' both peaked at number 12 and a duet with Lionel Richie, 'To Love A Woman', reached number 19. Enrique did love a woman, the Russian tennis player, Anna Kournikova, whom he's been dating since December 2001, and playing games with the media over plans of a marriage.

920 Westlife
World Of Our Own

Label & Cat No.: **RCA 74321 919242**

Producer: **Steve Mac**

Writers: **Steve Mac / Wayne Hector**

Date reached No.1: **2 March 2002**

Weeks at No.1: **1**

WESTLIFE FANS WERE UNLIKELY TO read *Q Magazine* but the review of the *World Of Our Own* CD neatly summed up the feeling against them: "Unlike their predecessors Boyzone and Take That, Westlife are a thoroughly one-dimensional act who, while an accredited hit-making machine, appear completely devoid of character. With a record-breaking string of number one singles behind them, they have a singular quality: to sit on stools and croon as if in love with the whole darn world."

Clearly, Westlife had been releasing one sentimental ballad too many, and a change was needed – and *World Of Our Own* held the key. They released the upbeat and infectious title track and it went to the top, giving them their 10th number one. This was also a track for people who didn't like Westlife.

As well as the audio single, a video / DVD version was also available, containing the videos for 'World Of Our Own' and 'Angel' as well as documentary footage of the recording of 'World Of Our Own'.

921 Will Young
Anything Is Possible / Evergreen

Label & Cat No.: **RCA 74321 926142**

Producers: **Cathy Dennis : Per Magnusson / David Krueger**

Writers: **Cathy Dennis / Chris Braide : Jörgen Elofsson / Per Magnusson / David Krueger**

Date reached No.1: **9 March 2002**

Weeks at No.1: **3**

AFTER THE SUCCESS OF *POPSTARS*, THE same production team devised *Pop Idol*, where, instead of creating a group, they would find a solo performer. They received over 10,000 entrants and once the numbers had been pared down to 10, the public would vote for them. The hosts were Ant and Dec and the panel was Simon Cowell (chairman), Pete Waterman, Nicki Chapman (a *Popstars* judge) and Neil Fox (host of *The Pepsi Chart Show*).

Twenty-two-year-old Will Young from Hungerford had a degree in politics from Exeter University, but, in 1999, he had appeared on *This Morning* in a programme about forming a boy band. In his final year, he had played the lead in *Oklahoma!* and raised £20,000 for an AIDS charity. He wanted to be on stage professionally and, after graduating, enrolled at a drama college.

Pop Idol gripped the nation, especially when it reached the final 10. Then they were voted off one by one and finally, it was down to Will Young and Gareth Gates. Will had a warm, banana-like smile, but he was able to stand his ground, arguing with Simon Cowell when the criticisms were too personal. He quoted his father saying to his mother, "Get the shotgun, Annabel", when he saw Cowell, which became a catchphrase.

Before the play-off, they both recorded vocals for their potential single. 'Anything Is Possible' which was a middle-of-the-road ballad from the established writer, Cathy Dennis, and the newcomer, Chris Braide. The song was to win them an Ivor Novello award and Chris was to have his own success in the US with 'This Is The Night', recorded by Clay Aiken from *American Idol*. The more dramatic 'Evergreen' was taken from the recent Westlife album, *World Of Our Own*. Will wrote in his diary, which was printed as *Anything Is Possible* (Contender, 2002): "On first impression I wasn't over-struck on either of them. It felt like they had been chosen especially for Gareth – they were both great pop music but written in a style more suited to his voice."

In the days before the finale, the country was gripped by "Vote Will" / "Vote Gareth" fever. The TV contest was an unprecedented success, leading to the biggest telephone vote in the UK. 8.7 million people voted – 4.6 million for Will.

Straight after the show, Will went to Cuba to film the videos, which was unnecessary as the record was a surefire number one. It sold 330,000 on the first day of release and had passed 1.1 million by the end of the week. In that week, the single outsold the rest of the Top 75 combined. The total UK sales were 1.8 million.

This book shows that both Will Young and Gareth Gates have stickability, but spare a thought for another Pop Idol finalist, Rik Waller. He had a Top 10 hit with 'I Will Always Love You' but in 2004, a concert in Torquay was cancelled after only two people bought tickets.

922 Gareth Gates
Unchained Melody

Label & Cat No.:	**RCA 74321 930882**
Producer:	**Steve Mac**
Writers:	**Alex North / Hy Zaret**
Date reached No.1:	**30 March 2002**
Weeks at No.1:	**4**

In the early, pre-Beatle Sixties, the fashion was to have smartly suited, good-looking, flat-stomached youngsters like Eden Kane, Adam Faith, Danny Williams and Jimmy Justice singing beat ballads and wanting to be all-round entertainers. They smiled a lot and behaved impeccably – no swearing, no fighting, no controversial views and no lewd mannerisms on stage. Their managers treated them like puppets. What goes round comes around as the *Pop Idol* winners were precisely the same. They were chosen by pop managers and groomed as family entertainers and nothing illustrates this more than the number one CD, *Pop Idol – The Big Band Album*. Why were these youngsters working as lounge singers? Gareth Gates was swinging 'Mack The Knife' and Darius Danesh crooning 'Let There Be Love'. Their arena tour closed with Will Young singing 'My Way'. All good performances but the one thing they surely weren't doing was doing it their way.

Gareth Gates, an unfortunate name for a stammerer, was born in Bradford on July 12, 1984. His talent was quickly recognised as he sang in the school choir and had been part of their production of *Joseph And The Amazing Technicolor Dreamcoat*. He was also in the choir at Bradford Cathedral, singing in Mendelssohn's *Elijah* and performing 'Pie Jesu' on Michael Barrymore's *My Kind Of Music* in 1995. Two years later, he sang a solo in front of The Queen at a Maundy Thursday service.

He easily passed through the initial rounds of *Pop Idol* and became familiar for his spiky hairstyle. His mother's favourite song was 'Unchained Melody', which he knew from The Righteous Brothers' version in *Ghost*. It was the first song that Gareth had learnt to play on guitar. He knew it would be a great song to perform on *Pop Idol*: "It's a song you can sing very badly," he said, "lots of people mess up the 'I need your love' bit, but I knew I could do it okay."

After Will Young had been on top of the charts for three weeks, Gareth's 'Unchained Melody' was released. The CD single included Gareth's versions of 'Anything Is Possible' and 'Evergreen', which would have been the A-sides if he had won *Pop Idol*. The single sold 300,000 copies on its first day and 1.3 million copies overall.

Only 17, Gareth Gates became the youngest male solo artist to enter the chart at number one. This achievement pales into insignificance when you contrast the UK charts with the French one. In 1993 four-year-old Jordy was number one in France with 'Dur Dur D'Etre Bébé (It's Hard To Be A Baby)'.

923 Oasis
Thehindutimes

Label & Cat No.:	**Big Brother RKIDSCD 23**
Producer:	**The Band**
Writer:	**Noel Gallagher**
Date reached No.1:	**27 April 2002**
Weeks at No.1:	**1**

Interviews with Oasis, almost always punctuated by colourful language, are spirited affairs. The Gallagher brothers have different views as to why they are popular: Liam puts it down to their rebellious stance while Noel believes it's their great songs. In reality, it's a combination of the two.

However, in 2002, Oasis felt they were slipping and Noel was even contrasting the band with the little-known but influential Beta Band. He said, "If some people feel cheated when they listen to 'Thehindutimes' because it's not like the Beta Band, then that's not my problem." The record sounded like business as usual: even before Liam starts singing, this could only be an Oasis record. It featured drum loops and was modern psychedlia.

Like many of Noel Gallagher's songs, this started life as an instrumental track, somewhat similar to 'Cigarettes And Alcohol', and Noel had simply labelled it 'The Hindu Times' after seeing that on a T-shirt. The original lyric was "The ghost in your soul, it leaves me cold, babe" but it was changed to the more positive, "God gave me a soul in your rock'n'roll, babe." If Marc Bolan was still alive and making records in 2002, they might have sounded like 'Thehindutimes'.

The single was followed by the number one album, *Heathenchemistry,* the title again coming from a T-shirt. This is the last of six Oasis number ones as the subsequent singles haven't made it – 'Stopcryingyourheartout' (2), 'Little By Little' / 'She Is Love' (2) and 'Songbird' (3), which was written by Liam. The drummer Alan White left in 2004 and was replaced by Ringo Starr's son, Zak, who also plays with The Who, or Who Two as Pete Townshend now refers to his band.

Oasis are a huge concert attraction, but they have never reached the level of U2. They are to be congratulated for restoring good songwriting to the charts, but the comparison to The Beatles is not valid. They took a certain style from The Beatles, as they readily admit, but only a part of The Beatles' repertoire ,although they have been very original within those parameters. However, there is nothing like 'For No One' or 'Eleanor Rigby' in the Oasis catalogue, but who knows what Noel will do once he goes solo.

924 The Sugababes
Freak Like Me

Label & Cat No.:	**Island CID 798**
Producer:	**Richard X**
Writers:	**Eugene Hanes / Marc Valentine / Loren Hill / William Collins / George Clinton / Gary Numan**
Date Reached No.1:	**4 May 2002**
Weeks at No.1:	**1**

By the turn of the century there was not only a plethora of boy bands and

Sassy girl bands became all the rage after the success of Destiny's Child. The Sugababes are, left to right: Mutya Buena, Heidi Range and Keisha Buchanan

girl bands in the UK, but an increasing amount of R&B acts, especially females, following in the footsteps of America's TLC and Destiny's Child. The only serious British contenders were Mis-Teeq and The Sugababes.

The Sugababes were formed in 1998 and are London-born Keisha Buchanan, Mutya Buena and Siobhan Donaghy. Keisha and Mutya had known each other since school and they met Siobhan at a party in 1997. A friend of Siobhan's put them in touch with the manager Ron Tom. "It was Ron who gave us our name when we first got together. He used to call us his sugar babies," explained Keisha. When they signed to London Records, it was suggested that the babies should become babes, as it would have a sexier appeal as they matured. Their first three singles, 'Overload', 'New Year' and 'Run For Cover' all made the Top 20, but the debut album, *One Touch*, only made number 26 and spent just under four months on the chart. After their fourth single, 'Soul Sound', Siobhan left to pursue a solo career and was quickly replaced with the Liverpool-born Heidi Range who was once in a band with Liz and Kerry from Atomic Kitten.

Producer Richard X put together a bootleg mix of Adina Howard's 1995 hit 'Freak Like Me', which sampled George Clinton's 'I'd Rather Be With You', and Tubeway Army's 'Are Friends Electric' and gave it the title 'We Don't Give A Damn About Our Friends'. He pressed up a limited number of 12-inch white labels, credited it to Girls On Top and circulated them around the clubs. When Adina heard it she wasn't happy and refused to let her vocals be sampled. Heidi remembered, "Somebody had the bootleg and our A&R guy played it to us and we loved it and tried it out. It worked so we recorded it properly. It was getting really good feedback and everyone was liking it so we went with it." It won them a Brit Award for Best Dance Act.

Richard X has since collaborated with Liberty X, Kelis and Rachel Stevens. Because 'Soul Sound' only reached number 30, The Sugababes were dropped by London, although they retained Siobhan as a solo act. They were quickly picked up by Island Records and began working on their second album. They also began working with Trevor Horn and their next single is to be a remake of their debut hit, 'Overload 2004'.

925 Holly Valance
Kiss Kiss

Label & Cat No.: **London LONCD 464**

Producer: **Darran Bennett**

Writers: **Aksu Sezen / Juliette James / Steve Welton-Jaimes**

Date Reached No.1: **11 May 2002**

Weeks at No.1: **1**

BEFORE HER DEBUT SINGLE, 'KISS KISS' was released, Holly Valance was already a familiar name and face in Britain, thanks to her role as schoolgirl Felicity 'Flick' Scully on the Australian soap opera, *Neighbours*.

She was born Holly Vukadinovic (taking her stage name from the bed-sheet) in Melbourne on May 11, 1983, to a Serbo-Croatian father and English mother. Discovered at the age of 12 by a modelling agency, Holly was soon earning good money posing for teenage lingerie and supermarket catalogues. Although she harboured no childhood aspirations of becoming an actress, at 17 Holly starred in a steamy shower scene for a video by Australian boy band, Human Nature, which whetted her appetite. This led to her auditioning for and winning the role that would give her her big break, becoming a fantasy figure to many boys, from Melbourne to Manchester.

'Kiss Kiss' is based on a song by German-born Turkish popstar, Tarkan. It was called 'Simarik' (meaning 'Spoilt') and was a huge hit all over Europe, topping the Belgian chart. "I love the original," Holly commented. "I love Arabic, Turkish and all middle-eastern music, so when the record company asked if I would like to do this song and put it in English, I was all for it."

On not writing her own songs, Holly said, "That's nothing to be ashamed of really. It's all about interpretation. Look at Kylie's 'Can't Get You Out Of My Head.' She didn't write that, and yet it's her song completely. Can you imagine Alanis Morisette having the same success with it? I think not."

The promotional video that accompanied the single received much press coverage for giving the impression that Holly was dancing naked. The critics need not have got so worked up: Holly was actually wearing a flesh bikini. "I was cool with it. The post production was where they put in the strobes and special effects, so you can't slow it down and find anything." She added, "In a way, I was hoping it would cause a fuss rather than be just another boring video passing by."

Maybe there's a genetic link as Holly is a cousin, albeit several times removed, to one of the UK's cheekiest comedians, Benny Hill.

Holly's next release, 'Down Boy', stopped short of the top spot, reaching number two and her debut album, *Footprints*, went Top 10. The follow-up single, 'Naughty Girl' got to number 16 and 'State Of Mind', number eight.

By the time Holly's second album, *State Of Mind,* was released in November 2003, it appeared that her popularity had waned, as it reached a disappointing number 60, spending just one week on the chart.

926 Ronan Keating
If Tomorrow Never Comes

Label & Cat No.: **Polydor RONAN 9**

Producer: **Steve Mac**

Writers: **Garth Brooks / Kent Blazy**

Date reached No.1: **18 May 2002**

Weeks at No.1: **1**

IN 1989 THE ALBUM, *GARTH BROOKS*, radically transformed country music. "I looked at everything I could when I did that album," says Garth, "and went through 1,600 songs. I figured that the more I looked the better my odds of finding hits. I was too familiar with my own songs and I wanted other people to talk me out of doing them. Fortunately, everybody liked 'If Tomorrow Never Comes'."

"There are a lot of great writers in Nashville," continues Garth, "and Kent Blazy and his wife Sharon, who are wonderful people, had been trying to make a living from Kent's song-

Holly Valance had already tasted success as a model and actress before she decided on a career as a singer

writing. Kent had had some stuff recorded by Gary Morris but he hadn't had a number one. I thought we had something when we completed the song but I didn't really know it would be a hit until I heard it by chance on the radio in my truck and I knew we had got something. There was something in it that moved me and I could feel the tears come to my eyes."

The single topped the US country charts and with his albums and his arena shows he was to outsell and outgross every country music star before him. He was also the first country star to swing across the stage on ropes! Despite the fact that Garth Brooks recorded commercial songs and was on a major label, Capitol, his records meant little in the UK. His only UK Top 20 single was with 'The Red Strokes' (1994). It was a different story in Ireland where it was calculated that one person in two owned a Garth Brooks record. And Ronan Keating was amongst them.

Ronan Keating's solo career had had an impressive start with two international hit singles and an album, *Ronan*, that sold 1.4 million in the UK and four million worldwide. He looked set to repeat his success with his second album, *Destination*. 'If Tomorrow Never Comes' was Ronan's third solo number one and by giving the song a more middle of the road treatment, many of the purchasers would not realise that they were buying country music.

927 Liberty X
Just A Little

Label & Cat No.: **V2 VR 5018963**

Producer: **Big Pockets**

Writers: **Michelle Escoffery / George Hammond Hagan / John Hammond Hagan**

Date reached No.1: **25 May 2002**

Weeks at No.1: **1**

THE ITV SERIES *POPSTARS* LED TO THE hit group Hear'Say, but five of the losers – Michelle Heaton, Tony Lundon, Kevin Simms, Jessica Taylor and Kelli Young – came together not as *Popstars – The Rejects* but as Liberty. Losing to *Popstars* might have damned them, but they spent six months working on their act and writing songs, including their debut single, 'Thinking It Over', which made number five. Unwelcome publicity occurred when another band called Liberty took them to court for the use of their name and so they became Liberty X.

In between court appearances, Liberty X recorded their number one, 'Just A Little', an R&B dance tune which was deliberately raunchier than Hear'Say's offerings. 'Just A Little' won a Brit as the Best British Single and the songwriters won Ivor Novello awards, but the main prize was being chosen as the music for a Halifax Building Society campaign. Their album, *Thinking It Over*, entered at number three and stayed on the charts for a year, selling 600,000 copies. The next singles were 'Got To Have Your Love' (2) and 'Holding On For You' (5). Hear'Say split up in October 2002, shortly before Liberty X appeared in the Royal Variety Performance.

928 Eminem
Without Me

Label & Cat No.: **Interscope 4977282**

Producer: **Eminem**

Writers: **Marshall Mathers III / Jeff Bass**

Date Reached No.1: **1 June 2002**

Weeks at No.1: **1**

EMINEM COULDN'T HELP BUT COURT controversy. His mother sued him for $10 million for defamation in response to a *Rolling Stone* interview, and his estranged wife for a similar amount regarding his song, 'Kim' from his *Marshall Mathers LP*. 'Without Me' opens to the tune of Malcolm McLaren's 'Buffalo Gals', with Eminem going on to offend Moby, Limp Bizkit, N*SYNC, Prince, *MTV* and his mother (again).

Taken from his latest release, *The Eminem Show* (1), it also included the hit single, 'Cleaning Out My Closet' (4), a number where the chorus leads the listener to believe he is wishing to bury the hatchet with his mother. On closer listening, it's a hostile and hate-filled rant.

Eminem and Kim reconciled briefly, for the sake of their young daughter, Hailie. It wasn't to work, and this time Kim filed for divorce.

The video for 'Without Me', which featured Eminem dressed as Osama bin Laden, as well as Moby (who had accused Eminem of homophobia) being attacked by a man in a rabbit suit, won four MTV Video Music Awards, including Video Of The Year and Best Rap Video.

Love him or loathe him, there can be no denying the impact he has made on music the world over in the last few years. Perhaps Eminem, who boasted, 'Now this looks like a job for me. So everybody just follow me. 'Cause we need a little controversy, 'cause it feels so empty without me,' wasn't far wrong.

929 Will Young
Light My Fire

Label & Cat No.: **RCA 74321 943002**

Producers: **Absolute (Paul Wilson / Andy Watkins)**

Writers: **Jim Morrison / John Densmore / Ray Manzarek / Robby Krieger**

Date reached No.1: **8 June 2002**

Weeks at No.1: **2**

RAY MANZAREK, THE DOORS' ORGANist, came up with the riff for 'Light My Fire' and the lyrics were written by the vocalist, Jim Morrison, and guitarist, Robby Krieger. A seven minute version with a lengthy instrumental passage was included on their first album, *The Doors*, and an edited version was released as a single in both the UK and the US. The sensual song was controversial at the time – it ended on an orgasmic scream, but by the Eighties, it was a staple of cabaret singers everywhere.

Although The Doors are among the more iconic acts of the Sixties, they made little impression on the UK charts. In 1967 'Light My Fire', a US number one, only crept into the Top 50, but a re-issue around the time of Oliver Stone's bio-pic in 1991 did give them a Top 10 hit. A wonderfully intense version from José Feliciano made the Top 10 in 1968 and Amii Stewart's disco workout was a Top 10 hit in both 1979 and 1985. The song was also revived by UB40 as a Christmas single in 2000, but their fire didn't ignite the yule-logs.

Will Young knew he was playing to his strength by including 'Light My Fire' during the *Pop Idol* auditions. Young's version was modelled on Feliciano's, and although lacking his intensity, it was a fine, middle-of-the-road treatment. Simon Cowell was unimpressed, "I had a vision of Sunday lunch and after Sunday lunch you say to your family, 'I'm now going to sing a song for you.' Distinctly average, I'm afraid." Pete Waterman, on the other hand, described Will as the most impressive singer he had heard in 20 years. Waterman saw him as another Bobby Darin and the CD single included his big band treatment of Darin's 'Beyond The Sea'.

The competition for the top slot included a single from Ant and Dec, who had hosted *Pop Idol*. Their 'We're On The Ball – The Official England World Cup Song 2002' came in at number three.

930 Elvis vs JXL
A Little Less Conversation

Label & Cat No.: **RCA 74321 94357-2**
Producers: **Billy Strange / JXL**
Writers: **Billy Strange / Mac Davis**
Date reached No.1: **15 June 2002**
Weeks at No.1: **4**

'A LITTLE LESS CONVERSATION' WAS ONE of the four songs from Elvis Presley's 1968 film, *Live A Little, Love A Little*. The movie did little business and the single didn't even make the UK charts. That, in normal circumstances, would have been that, but it's a strange world.

In 2001 an alternate take of the song was used on the soundtrack of the George Clooney film, *Ocean's 11*. Altered by the film, Nike wanted to use it on their TV ads to coincide with the World Cup. The 34-year-old Dutch DJ Tom Holkenborg (Junkie XL) was asked to remix it, edit it and add additional sounds where he thought necessary.

The Elvis Presley Estate thought it was inappropriate for the King to be sharing the bill with someone called Junkie XL (though it's hard to see why!) and the name was shortened to JXL. The reaction to the advert, which also featured Eric Cantona, and then the single was overwhelmingly positive and it was predicted that it would go straight into the charts at number one. Which it did. It only lasted four weeks because BMG, who own RCA, wanted to pave the way for a new single by Gareth Gates and deleted it.

For years it seemed a perfect equilibrium that Elvis and The Beatles should both have 17 number one records, but with this Elvis edged ahead. Only a fool would predict for either of them that their time at the top was over.

931 Gareth Gates
Anyone Of Us (Stupid Mistake)

Label & Cat No.: **RCA 74321 946962**
Producers: **Per Magnusson / David Kreuger**
Writers: **Jorgen Elofsson / Per Magnusson / David Kreuger**
Date reached No.1: **20 July 2002**
Weeks at No.1: **3**

THE WRITING AND PRODUCTION TEAM of Will Young's number one, 'Evergreen', wrote Gareth Gates' second number one, the slow romantic ballad, 'Anyone Of Us (Stupid Mistake)', which was written and produced by the team known as A Side Productions. Gareth was uncomfortable performing the song as he disliked pronouncing the word 'stupid' with the American pronunciation of 'stoopid' but he accepted that it sounded better. The video was shot during a carnival in Venice. Gareth is searching for his girlfriend amongst masked figures.

Although 'Anyone Of Us (Stupid Mistake)' was number one for three weeks, total sales of 400,000 were disappointing after 1.3 million for 'Unchained Melody'. To balance that, it was Gareth's first European release and it went to number one in Holland and did well in Germany.

Will Young, Gareth Gates and the eight other finalists undertook a very successful *Pop Idol* tour of UK arenas: the show was split into halves and ended with a big band salute. Will performed at the *Party At The Palace* and sang 'We Are The Champions' with Queen, and both Will and Gareth were included in the Royal Variety Performance.

Gareth overcame his stammer and despite his youth, he was living the rock lifestyle, with the model Jordan as a girlfriend – that is growing up fast. Gareth's sister, Nicola, was featured in the 2003 series of *Pop Idol*, and made the Top 50. The panel disparaged her for sounding like a female Gareth, but she was allowed through to the next round because of her brother.

932 Darius
Colourblind

Label & Cat No.: **Mercury 0639652**
Producers: **Pete Glenister / Denny Lew**
Writers: **Pete Glenister / Denny Lew / Darius Danesh**
Date reached No.1: **10 August 2002**
Weeks at No.1: **2**

LIKE SO MANY OF THE *POPSTARS* AND *Pop Idol* finalists, Darius Danesh had a musical background. As an adolescent, Darius, whose father is from Persia, had performed in *Carmen* with the Scottish Opera, but his ambitions lay with pop music. When he was 16 he sang with a band in Glasgow called Jade and then read English Literature at Edinburgh University.

A friend persuaded him to enter *Popstars* and he arrived at the audition with his guitar, only to be told no instruments were allowed. Many thought he would win after a sweat-drenched performance of Tom Jones' *It's Not Unusual*. He didn't make the final but he was offered a recording contract. However, his tutors told him that he would have to leave university if he did not apply himself to his studies.

After graduating, he tried for *Pop Idol* and most viewers commended him for his persistence. He almost made the final 10 and was allowed in when Rik Waller dropped out with a throat infection. The massively overweight Waller was the choice of spoilers, those who wanted to ruin the programme, but he was to secure his own recording contract, having hits with covers of 'I Will Always Love You' (6) and '(Something Inside) So Strong' (25). Now he is more likely to be seen as part of a TV slimming campaign.

Darius came third in *Pop Idol*, but he fared even better on the charts. He had a number one with his own song, the lightweight and very catchy 'Colourblind', and since then there has been 'Rushes' (5), 'Incredible (What I Mean To Say)' (9) and 'Girl In The Moon' (21) as well as an album, *Dive In*. Although only 22, he wrote his autobiography, *Sink Or Swim*.

933 The Sugababes
Round Round

Label & Cat No.: **Island CID 804**

Producers: **Kevin Bacon / Jonathan Quarmby / Jeremy Wheatley**

Writers: **Brian Higgins / Miranda Cooper / Lisa Cowling / Tim Powell / Nik Coler / Keisha Buchanan / Mutya Buena / Heidi Range / Florian Pflüger / Felix Stecher / Robin Hofmann**

Date Reached No.1: **24 August 2002**

Weeks at No.1: **1**

THE SUGABABES HAD MOVED ON FROM producer Richard X and began working with Kevin Bacon (not the Hollywood actor) and Jonathan Quarmby, the London production duo who had worked with The Lighthouse Family, Audioweb, The Longpigs and Finley Quaye. They teamed up with Jeremy Wheatley who has produced hits for Space and Girls Aloud. The result was the number two album *Angels With Dirty Faces*, with all the tracks co-written by the girls, which spent 40 weeks on the chart.

The second single after 'Freak Like Me' was 'Round Round' which sampled Duplex Inc's 'Tangoforte'. It was also chosen to appear on the soundtrack for the 2002 film *The Guru*.

Two further tracks were released from *Angels With Dirty Faces*. The title track was coupled with 'Stronger' and made number seven whilst 'Shape', which sampled Sting's 'Shape Of My Heart', reached number 11.

The Sugababes spent the first half of 2003 working on their third album *Three*. There had been some promotion to break them in America, but the US market was flooded with R&B groups and, as yet, The Sugababes haven't found a place. However, they did write some songs with America's premier female songwriter, Diane Warren and former 4 Non Blondes singer, Linda Perry. On their return to England, they made a well-received appearance at Glastonbury.

934 Blazin' Squad
Crossroads

Label & Cat No.: **East West SQUAD 01 CD1**

Producers: **TNT Xplosive / Cutfather & Joe**

Writers: **Blazin' Squad / Bone Thugs-N-Harmony**

Date Reached No.1: **31 August 2002**

Weeks at No.1: **1**

IN 1999 10 KIDS, ALL FROM THE SAME school in Highams Park, east London, formed two separate groups of five; The Incredible Crew and the The Blazin' Squad, and all with a love of pirate radio, hip hop and garage. The following year they merged, ditched The Incredible Crew moniker and became known as The Blazin' Squad.

The Squad comprised nine MC's: Krazy (born Lee Bailey), Spike-e (born Sam Foulkes), Reepa (born Stuart Baker), Kenzie (born James Mackenzie), Flava (born James Murray), Melo-d (born Chris McKeckney), Strider (born Mustafa Omer), Freek (born Oliver Georgiou), Rocky B (born Marcel Sommerville), and one DJ, Tommy B (born Thomas Beasley). All were approximately 16 at the time.

"One of our mates from school suggested we should go into a studio and make a demo," recalled Flava. "We went into the studio and it cost £200 to make a demo with a producer. It was called 'Standard Flow' and Radio 1's Dreem Team started playing it, which is when East West Records picked it up."

'Crossroads' was originally recorded by the Cleveland rap act Bone Thugs-N-Harmony in 1996. "I heard the track on MTV," recalled Tommy B, "and thought it would be good to cover. It's one of the Top 10 biggest rap tracks of all-time in America, it spent eight weeks at number one there, but didn't reach those heights over here, so I thought we could give it a UK vibe."

The Bone Thugs-N-Harmony version, which was titled 'Tha Crossroads', sampled The Isley Brothers' 'Make Me Say It Again' hence its 13 writing credits. It was originally written as an elegy to a friend who was gunned down in Cleveland, but it ended up as a tribute to all their friends and family who had died including the rapper, Eazy-E (born Eric Wright), who got them together in the first place and had died of AIDS in 1995.

The release date of Blazin' Squad's version, coincided with the publication of nine of the members' GCSE results. It was a good result on both counts. The single went in at number one and the whole crew ended up with a total of 66 GCSE's between them.

Their debut album, *In The Beginning*, attracted few buyers. It only reached number 33 and spent six weeks on the chart. Proving they were more of a singles act, their next five hits all reached the Top 10, 'Love On The Line' (6), 'Reminisce' / 'Where The Story Ends' (8), 'We Just Be Dreamin' (3)', 'Flip Reverse (2) and 'Here 4 One' (6). Their second album, the 15-track *Now Or Never*, fared worse than *In The Beginning*, spending only two weeks on the chart and climbing no higher than number 37.

In April 2004 they were still proving a big live attraction by selling out a headline tour of the UK. "We're mixing every style of music now," enthused Krazy. "Some of our songs are about us, others are just proper love songs. We're rapping about everything from super heroes to bank robbers – basically stuff our mates can relate to."

On September 1, 2004 a new download Top 20 chart was introduced and the Blazin' Squad came in at number two with their new single, 'Blazin' Day'. That chart was headed by Westlife with a previously unavailable live version of 'Flying Without Wings'.

935 Atomic Kitten

The Tide Is High (Get The Feeling)

Label & Cat No.: **Innocent SINDX 38**

Producers: **Bill Padley / Jeremy Godfrey**

Writers: **John Holt / Bill Padley / Jeremy Godfrey / Howard Barrett / Tyrone Evans**

Date reached No.1: **7 September 2002**

Weeks at No.1: **3**

NOTHING WRONG WITH 'THE TIDE IS High', nothing wrong with Atomic Kitten, but their revival of Blondie's number one song appeared too calculated and too perfunctory. It was a number one record but the girls would have been better served with strong, original material. Not that their version of John Holt's famous song is without interest – they add a new section, effectively part of another song, 'Get The Feeling', which was written by their producers.

Atomic Kitten nearly had a further number one with the double-header, 'The Last Goodbye' / 'Be With You', the latter sampling some of ELO's 'Last Train To London'. Then came 'Love Don't Have To Hurt' (4), 'If You Come To Me' (3) and 'Ladies Night' with Kool & The Gang (8). *Ladies Night* was also the title of their third album, which reached a respectable number five, although their previous albums, *Right Now* and *Feels So Good*, had made the top.

In 2004 Atomic Kitten split up, temporarily at least, as Natasha Hamilton wanted to spend more time with her son. Liz McClarnon has appeared solo and made an album, and Jenny Frost is expected to do the same.

936 Pink

Just Like A Pill

Label & Cat No.: **Arista 74321959653**

Producer: **Dallas Austin**

Writers: **Pink / Dallas Austin**

Date Reached No.1: **29 September 2002**

Weeks at No.1: **1**

ALECIA MOORE WAS BORN NEAR Philadelphia on September 8, 1979 into a musical family. She earned her nickname as a child because her cheeks would turn pink when she was embarrassed. Later she would dye her blonde hair to match it.

Her Vietnam veteran father played guitar and introduced his young daughter to the music of Bob Dylan, The Mamas And The Papas, Janis Joplin and Billy Joel. "I'd watch him play and we'd sing together and that made me want to make music."

A rebellious teenager, Pink joined her first band at 13, doing backing vocals for a friend's group, Schools Of Thought. She began writing songs at 14 and frequented Philadelphia nightspot, Club Fever, where one night she was discovered by an executive from MCA Records. Following a successful audition, Pink joined an all-girl R&B quartet, Basic Instinct. However, they disbanded shortly after. Later she became a member of a trio, Choice and they signed to L.A. Reid and Babyface's label, LaFace. Although that band didn't last long either, Pink impressed L.A. Reid with her songwriting talent and was rewarded with a solo deal.

She first charted in the UK with 'There You Go' (6) in June 2000, followed by the Top 10 hits, 'Most Girls' (5) and 'You Make Me Sick' (9),

which were taken from her debut album, *Can't Take Me Home* (13). Pink's follow-up album, *Missundaztood*, which included this chart topper, also featured the number two hit, 'Get The Party Started' (written by ex-4 Non Blondes vocalist Linda Perry), 'Don't Let Me Get Me' (6) and 'Family Portrait' (11). *Missundaztood* has so far sold over 12 million sales worldwide.

'Just Like A Pill' is about an addictive and unhealthy relationship. The catchy number gave Pink a new image, making the move from R&B diva to rock chick.

"If I wasn't making music, I don't know if I'd be here at all. That's how much it means to me. It's been my escape for a long, long time," Pink professed. She added, "I decided at 15 that I didn't want to be one of those artists that gets up and sings love songs they don't mean. I decided that I was going to be me to the fullest extent, that my songs were going to reflect relationships I've had, things I've been through, and even the stuff I'm embarrassed about."

In 2003 Pink won a Brit award for Best International Female Artist, and was nominated for Best Female Pop Vocal Performance ('Get The Party Started') and Best Pop Vocal Album (*Missundaztood*) at the Grammys. She lost out on both counts to Norah Jones who swept the board.

Further singles followed: 'Feel Good Time' (3) and 'Trouble', which reached number seven, and for which Pink received a Grammy for Best Female Pop Vocal Performance in 2004. Her third album, *Try This* got to number three.

Pink is due to appear on the big screen in the title role in 2005 in *The Gospel According To Janis*, a biopic on Janis Joplin.

937 Will Young & Gareth Gates The Long And Winding Road / Gareth Gates Suspicious Minds

Label & Cat No.: **RCA 74321 965972**

Producers: **Steve Lipson : Steve Mac**

Writers: **John Lennon / Paul McCartney : Mark James**

Date reached No.1: **5 October 2002**

Weeks at No.1: **2**

ALISTAIR TAYLOR, THE GENERAL manager at Apple Records, saw Paul McCartney sitting at a piano at three in the morning in the Abbey Road studios: "He was picking out a melody and I said, 'I like that, it's a fabulous melody', and he said, 'It's just an idea'. He told the engineer to switch on the tape and he recorded 'The Long And Winding Road' then and there: it was full of la-la's as he'd only written a few lines, but it was quite fantastic."

The Beatles recorded 'The Long And Winding Road' during their filming of *Let It Be*, but rather than release a rough album, the tapes were given to Phil Spector. He added an orchestral backing incorporating The Mike Sammes Singers, but he did not, as many people assume, 'Spectorise' it. Paul McCartney did not discover this until it was too late, but he described the arrangement as 'tasteless' and would not let the song be issued as a single. He could not prevent its release in the US where it topped the charts for two weeks and became their biggest-selling single, topping six million copies.

During the later stages of *Pop Idol*, Will Young and Gareth Gates sang 'The Long And Winding Road' together, and the reception meant that it was always likely to be a single. The chart also listed Gareth Gates' version of Elvis Presley's 1969 hit, 'Suspicious Minds', which had been originally recorded a year earlier by its composer, Mark James. The third track, Will Young's version of Jackie Wilson's 'I Get The Sweetest Feeling' was not listed on the chart, although it was one of his strongest performances on *Pop Idol*.

The album coincided with the release of Will's album, *From Now On*, which topped the UK album charts and, amongst other things, included a new composition 'What's In Goodbye' by Burt Bacharach and Cathy Dennis. It was surprising that Bacharach should be writing for someone who was unknown a year earlier, but he enjoyed the *Pop Idol* concept and participated in the US version, *American Idols*.

938 Las Ketchup The Ketchup Song (Asereje)

Label & Cat No.: **Columbia 6731932**

Producer: **Manny Benito**

Writers: **Manuel Ruiz / Manny Benito**

Date Reached No.1: **19 October 2002**

Weeks at No.1: **1**

IN 1979 THE SUGARHILL GANG'S 'Rapper's Delight' became the first commercial rap/hip hop song to make the UK chart. They are still considered the pioneers of hip-hop and their music has influenced a multitude of rap acts. In 2002 the Spanish novelty trio, Las Ketchup, used the tune of the opening line, "I said a hip hop the hippie the hippie to the hip hip hop" for the chorus, but with their own tongue-twisting lyric "Asereje ja de jè de jebe tu de jebere seibiunouva, majavi an de bugui an de buididipi."

Las Ketchup are three attractive sisters, Pilar, Lola and Lucia Munoz who were born in Cordoba, southern Spain, an area known for its Flamenco dancing and bullfighting. They formed a group in honour of their father, Tomate, a renowned Flamenco guitarist and named their debut album *Hijas del Tomate* (*Daughters Of Tomate*). None of the girls had sung in public nor had any aspirations to be singers, although Lucia had once trained as a Flamenco dancer. Via their father, a Flamenco artist and producer, Manuel Ruiz, saw them and was impressed to the point that he signed them to a record deal.

Their debut single, 'The Ketchup Song (Asereje)' is a catchy summer song, telling the story of Diego, a Rastafarian gypsy, who likes 'Rapper's Delight' but as he doesn't know the words, he pronounces them as gibberish. The song is sung in Spanglish, a combination of English and Spanish, and has its own Macarena-style dance routine.

There has been confusion about what Asereje actually means. Pilar said, "The meaning of Asereje is an imitation of part of 'Rappers Delight'" For the UK and US market, it became known as 'The Ketchup Song', because, as Pilar added, "The band was called Las Ketchup and we thought it was easy and simple."

A massive hit throughout Europe, it topped the charts in Austria, Germany, France, Belgium, Finland, Italy, Sweden, Holland, Switzerland and Denmark. In the US it had a lukewarm reception and limped to number 54.

Their second release, 'Kusha Las Payas' in 2003, a more Latin-tinged song, failed to make the same impact and missed the UK and US chart completely, although it was nominated for a *Billboard* Latin Music Award.

939 Nelly featuring Kelly Rowland Dilemma

Label & Cat No.: **Universal MCSTD 40299**

Producers: **Bam (Antoine Macon) / Ryan Bowser**

Writers: **Kenny Gamble / Bunny Sigler / Nelly / Antoine Macon / Ryan Bowser**

Date Reached No.1: **26 October 2002**

Weeks at No.1: **2**

"I ALWAYS KNEW I HAD IT, BUT I NEVER knew things would happen so fast," admitted Nelly soon after his debut single '(Hot S+++) Country Grammar', peaked at number seven in both the US and UK. He also became only the

Classic songs by The Beatles and Elvis recorded by Pop Idol stars Will Young (left) and Gareth Gates could hardly fail to reach number one

third R&B artist to replace himself at the top of the US chart, after Puff Daddy and Ja Rule.

Nelly was born Cornell Haynes Jr in Travis, Texas in 1974. His father was in the Air Force and so he spent his first few years in Spain with his mother before moving back to St. Louis, Missouri. He was often in trouble at school and only excelled at baseball, so a career in sport looked inevitable, that was until he decided to form the rap group, St. Lunatics, with some friends.

In 1996 they had a local hit with 'Gimme What Ya Got'. "St. Louis didn't have a hip-hop scene and I wanted to do my bit," Nelly said. "I'm like a pioneer for the mid-West, give me a couple of years and I'll put St. Louis on the map."

He made his debut film appearance in *Snipes* in 2001 and charted four hits the same year; 'E.I' (11), 'Ride Wit Me' (3), 'Batter Up' (28) and a collaboration with another R&B group, Jagged Edge, 'Where The Party At?' (25). The following year he teamed up with *NSYNC for the hit 'Girlfriend' which just missed the top spot. His next single, 'Hot In Herre', peaked at number four in the UK, but gave him his first US chart-topper. His debut album, *Country Grammar*, reached number 14.

By the summer of 2002 Nelly had almost completed his second album, *Nellyville*, when he heard a tune written by his old friend Bam, and wanted to include it on the album. "We sat down at the keyboard," said Bam, "and just messed around. Then we added some drums and Nelly just began to write some words." It was almost finished when Bam put on the Patti LaBelle album *I'm In Love Again*. He started humming one of the tracks, 'Love, Need And Want You', which Nelly overheard and asked what it was. When Bam told him, he insisted they use the 'I love you' hook. When Nelly heard the finished track, he said, "I wanted to do something that nobody would think of, and that's why I brought in Kelly Rowland. I thought she would be better on her own as opposed to Destiny's Child." Kelly was nervous because, as she said, "When you cover a legend's song you have to do it correctly." But rather than Kelly hearing it from the album, she heard it directly from Patti herself, whom Nelly had invited to appear as Kelly's mother in the video.

'Dilemma' sold over 200,000 copies in the first week and entered at number one. In the US, it spent 10 weeks at the top in two runs. It paused for a couple of weeks to let US Pop Idol contestant, Kelly Clarkson, enjoy the limelight with 'A Moment Like This'.

For his next single he teamed up with Justin Timberlake for 'Work It', which reached number seven and the follow-up, 'Shake Ya Tailfeather' reached number 10 and was featured in the movie *Bad Boys II*.

940 DJ Sammy And Yanou featuring Do
Heaven

Label & Cat No.: **Data DATA 45CDS**

Producers: **DJ Sammy / Yanou**

Writers: **Bryan Adams / Jim Vallance**

Date Reached No.1: **9 November 2002**

Weeks at No.1: **1**

DJ SAMMY IS PROBABLY SPAIN'S MOST famous club DJ and certainly the most energetic. When asked, in 2003, if he was the maddest man in pop, he replied, "Yayayaya-hoolalalaaaa!, I'm certainly a little loopy. I just like to have good times, all the time."

Bryan Adams first hit the UK chart in 1985 with 'Run To You', which reached number 11. Later the same year, 'Heaven' reached number 38 and the follow-up, the anthemic 'Summer of '69' stiffed at number 42. It wasn't until 1991 when Bryan's first Top 10 hit, '(Everything I Do) I Do It For You', went to number one that he became a household name. However, 'Run To You' made number three in 1992 when raved up by the dance act Rage. Sammy did likewise with 'Heaven' and it hit the top. 'Summer of '69', in the meantime, has become a rock classic.

DJ Sammy, who was born Samuel Bouriah in Majorca in 1969, came from a musical family. His father was a guitarist and his sister was a piano teacher who taught Sammy how to play.

In 1984 he began DJing in various clubs and the same year he completed his training as a sound engineer at the music college in Palma. He joined a local radio station and built up a following playing techno.

DJ Sammy

In 1991 he met a Dutch singer/dancer Carisma (born Marie Jose van der Kolk), they recorded together and released the singles, 'Life Is Just A Game' (1995), 'You're My Angel' (1996), 'Prince Of Love' (1997), 'Golden Child' (1997) and 'Magic Moment' (1998).

After a spell DJing round the world, Sammy returned to Palma where he met Spanish producer Yanou (born Yann Pfeifer) and Dutch vocalist Do (born Dominique van Hulst). The pair had already decided to cover some Eighties rock songs in a dance style when Sammy joined them. Do was an in-demand singer for radio commercials and one particular one was produced by Yanou. "The reason I chose 'Heaven' is because I love it and it has a very special memory from my youth," recalled Yanou. "I asked Do to sing on the trance track which she agreed to, but she also insisted on recording a slower version true to the original." It must have disappointed Do that she didn't get any more credit because she added, "Everywhere I went people asked me if I was DJ Sammy, which was a bit annoying."

'Heaven' sold 120,000 copies in its first week and entered the chart at number one. It also reached number eight Stateside. The album, *Heaven*, was released in March 2003, and included Do's slow version of 'Heaven' with only piano accompaniment. This was known as the candlelight mix and it received airplay on late night radio, which boosted sales helping the album reach number 14. In July 2004 she released her debut solo album called *Do*, which also included the candlelight mix of 'Heaven'.

The next single, another firm favourite from Sammy's youth, 'The Boys Of Summer', this time featuring Loona on guest vocals, went to number two. One further single, 'Sunlight', was lifted from the album and it reached number eight.

941 Westlife
Unbreakable

Label & Cat No.: **RCA 74321 975182**

Producer: **Steve Mac**

Writers: **Jorgen Eloffson/John Reid**

Date reached No.1: **16 November 2002**

Weeks at No.1: **1**

IN JUST THREE YEARS WESTLIFE HAD 10 number ones, two Top 10 singles and three huge albums, so a greatest hits collection was compiled for the Christmas market, *Unbreakable, Volume 1: The Greatest Hits*. As was becoming standard practice, the greatest hits collection included new material, and 'Unbreakable' returned them to the top after the embarrassment of 'Bop Bop Baby' stalling at number five. A second single from the six new performances combined 'Tonight' with a remake of Cliff Richard's 'Miss You Nights' and made number three.

Although the package celebrated Westlife's success, it also highlighted their weakness. All too often they relied on sentimental ballads. Nothing wrong with that per se – the pop world is full of them – but could they be doing it too often? When Westlife moved away from this for a swinging Rat Pack homage in 2004, it seemed a little late for both their career and a tribute to Sinatra. Robbie Williams had, after all, swung when he was winning.

Still, in 2002, Westlife seemed 'Unbreakable'. The hit song featured lead vocals from Shane, Bryan and Mark with strong harmonies from all five for the chorus. Kian Egan remarked, "We have always said the most important thing is the song and we have worked really, really hard at it. We have kept trying to get the next song as good as the last one and luckily, it has worked."

Despite all their UK, Irish and international success, Westlife could not break through in America: 'Swear It Again' reached the US Top 20 but not even the duet with Mariah Carey was a hit there.

942 Christina Aguilera featuring Redman
Dirrty

Label & Cat No.: **RCA 74321962722**

Producers: **Rockwilder / Christina Aguilera**

Writers: **Christina Aguilera / Jasper Cameron / Batewa Muhammed / Dana Stinson**

Date Reached No.1: **23 November 2002**

Weeks at No.1: **2**

THROUGHOUT THE SEVENTIES, SLADE were the kings of misspelt titles, by the Noughties, it was becoming commonplace for R&B and rap acts to use a 'Z' instead of an 'S' and adding an extra 'R' into certain words. US rapper, Nelly started the trend earlier in 2003, when his hit 'Hot In Herre' got to number four.

Christina was born in Staten Island, New York on December 18, 1980. She likes to be known as Xtina, as she explains, "It's a joke nickname like Christmas is shortened to Xmas." She has said she is fed up with society being quick to judge females by saying, "If we want to be open or sexual then we are labelled a slut or whatever, so that's what 'Dirrty' is all about. It did exactly what it needed to do, it says I'm here, this is me and whether you like it or not, it's got your attention."

New Jersey born rapper, Reggie Noble, or Redman to his friends, was making a name for himself as a featured rapper on hits by artists like Beverley Knight, De La Soul and Dru Hill. In 2002, in collaboration with DJ Kool, he released the single 'Let's Get Dirty (I Can't Get In Da Club)' which failed to chart in Britain and only just crept into the US chart, but it made an impact on Christina who asked Redman to appear on her single. She said, "I loved 'Let's Get Dirty', so I asked the producer, Rockwilder, to put something together kind of like that for me. What I got was a little too close, but then I figured, Why not? The track is like an answer song to the original, only from a female point of view."

943 Daniel Bedingfield
If You're Not The One

Label & Cat No.: **Polydor 0658632**

Producer: **Mark Taylor**

Writer: **Daniel Bedingfield**

Date Reached No.1: **7 December 2002**

Weeks at No.1: **1**

ALTHOUGH THE CRITICS WERE circling when Daniel Bedingfield's second single, 'James Dean (I Wanna Know)' 'only' reached number four, they were sharply silenced when this stark ballad shot to the top spot.

Stateside, 'If You're Not The One' went Top 40, and the song appeared on the soundtrack to *Maid In Manhattan*, starring Jennifer Lopez in a modern-day Cinderella story. Couples everywhere declared it 'our song', apart from the Aussies, that is, who found the ballad version too slow for airplay. However, radio DJs chose to play a dance mix of the track, and it went into the Top 30.

"I did 'If You're Not The One' because it's so different to 'Gotta Get Through This'. I hope people can take the journey that I took on the album around these different styles. I'm not a dance artist, I'm not a ballad artist, I'm all of that, and I really want people to get that," he revealed to VH1.

Daniel remains tight-lipped about revealing which lucky lady was the inspiration behind this heartfelt number, pausing only to say she was 'an ex-girlfriend'.

In March 2003 Daniel embarked on a successful UK tour. Many fans, however, were surprised when during one number, the stage lights were dimmed and Daniel asked for quiet from the audience. Explaining how his faith got him where is he is today, he launched into 'Honest Questions', a song about his commitment to Christianity. "I'm a spiritual person, that's the foundation of who I am," Daniel admitted.

Of his achievements he added, "It really seems the world is my oyster at the moment. I feel tremendously blessed. It's been my dream since childhood and now that I've finally got here, everything's just as good as I always hoped. Standing in front of a crowd at Wembley Arena with everybody going nuts for you is fantastic. I just love it."

944 Eminem
Lose Yourself

Label & Cat No.: **Interscope 4978282**

Producer: **Eminem**

Writers: **Marshall Mathers III / Jeff Bass / Luis Resto**

Date Reached No.1: **14 December 2002**

Weeks at No.1: **1**

8 MILE OPENED IN CINEMAS ALL OVER the world in late 2002 to great critical and public acclaim, taking over $50 million in receipts on its opening weekend in the US.

Filming began in Eminem's hometown of Detroit to placard-waving demonstrators with the slogan, 'SLIM SHADY GO HOME!' Councillor Earl O Wheeler Jr said, "What Eminem stands for is the antithesis of what I stand for." Infuriated by accusations of giving Warren, the suburb he had grown up in, a bad name, Eminem fumed, "A bad name? The fucking white trash capital of the world? Shut the fuck up!"

Directed by Curtis Hanson (*Wonder Boys*, *L.A. Confidential*), *8 Mile* is a semi-biographical film set in 1995 starring Eminem as Jimmy 'Bunny Rabbit' Smith Jr, and Kim Basinger as his mother. Eminem, in particular, came in for some favourable reviews for his acting debut in a lead role.

After splitting up with his girlfriend, Rabbit has begrudgingly moved back to live with his mother in a trailer park, along with his young sister. A talented rapper, he dreams of securing a recording contract and getting out of 8 Mile (which refers to the road that separates the city of Detroit from its suburbs).

Rabbit enters freestyle contests in the local hip-hop clubs, where he who raps the wittiest and rhymes with the cruellest of 'dissing' is the victor. The soundtrack, which also contained songs by Jay-Z and Macy Gray, included Eminem's swear-filled number, 'Adrenaline Rush', featuring probably the only mention ever of a popular British TV chef in a rap song, 'I cook up the hot shit like Ainsley Harriott.'

The Mathers household wasn't short of doorstops in 2003. He won two Brits for Best International Male and Best International Album and a pair of Grammys for Best Male Rap Solo Performance and Best Rap Song for 'Lose Yourself', and received a further three nominations, including one for Song Of The Year, which was the first time a rap song had been nominated in the category. 'Lose Yourself' also earned him the Oscar for Best Original Song.

Eminem played a big part in the notorious rapper 50 Cent's (born Curtis Jackson) meteoric rise, when he signed the Queens, New York native to his own Shady Records label, part of a joint deal with his mentor, Dr Dre's label, Aftermath. They also co-produced his album, *Get Rich Or Die Tryin'*, which was only kept off the top spot by Justin Timberlake's *Justified*, and went on to be *Billboard's* biggest-seller of 2003 with 6.5 million Stateside sales alone. 50 went on to chart several songs, his best known being 'In Da Club', which reached number three the same year.

Eminem's follow-up singles 'Sing For the Moment' (which sampled the chorus of Aerosmith's 'Dream On' and featured vocals by Steven Tyler), and 'Business', both reached number six in 2003.

In July 2004, Eminem's ex-wife, Kim, was sentenced to a year in jail for 'leaving a court-ordered drug treatment programme without permission.'

945 Blue featuring Elton John
Sorry Seems To Be The Hardest Word

Label & Cat No.: **Innocent SINCD 43**

Producer: **StarGate (aka Mikkel S.E. / Hallgeir Rustan / Tor Erik Hermansen)**

Writers: **Elton John / Bernie Taupin**

Date Reached No.1: **21 December 2002**

Weeks at No.1: **1**

ELTON JOHN MUST ENJOY REMAKING his own songs. Following 'Don't Let The Sun Go Down On Me' with George Michael, 'Don't Go Breaking My Heart' with Rupaul, and the Princess Diana tribute, 'Candle In The Wind 1997', was 'Your Song' with Italian tenor Alessandro Safina. So, to keep him feeling youthful he was joined by boy band, Blue.

'Sorry Seems To Be The Hardest Word' was Lee Ryan's all time favourite song and it was his idea to cover the track. Their management company approached Elton's manager to ascertain his interest and Blue were delighted when Elton agreed to do a duet.

The original 1976 version reached number 11 and was the only single released from the parent album *Blue Moves*. The title seems to suggest a change of direction from the previous album *Rock Of The Westies* – it was more mellow and moody and focused on lost love. It is also Elton's own favourite album.

Elton began writing the song in 1975 in Los Angeles. Normally Elton would write the tune and Bernie, the lyrics, but as Elton explained, "I was sitting there and out it came, 'What have I got to do to make you love me'." Elton, being a blues fan, may have subconsciously taken the later line, 'What do I do when lightning strikes me, and I wake to find that you're not there', from the Ray Charles' song, 'Born To Lose' in which Ray sings, 'Born to lose / oh, it seems so hard to bear / when I awake and find that you're not there'. Elton also recorded a version of 'Born To Lose' with Leonard Cohen. For Elton, stopping seems to be the hardest word!

Blue had three further hits in 2003 with 'U Make Me Wanna' (4), 'Guilty' (2) and 'Signed, Sealed, Delivered I'm Yours', with guest artists Angie Stone and Stevie Wonder, (11). Their third album, *Guilty*, gave them their third consecutive chart topper and 'Bubblin', 'Breathe Easy' and 'Curtain Falls' gave them three more Top 10 hits in 2004.

946 Girls Aloud
Sound Of The Underground

Label & Cat No.: **Polydor 658272**

Producers: **Jeremy Wheatley**

Writers: **Miranda Cooper / Niara Scarlett / Brian Higgins / Xenomania**

Date reached No.1: **28 December 2002**

Weeks at No.1: **4**

THE FIRST SERIES OF *POPSTARS* produced the number one group, Hear'Say, and, in a surprising move, a group of also-rans, Liberty X, also had success. *Pop Idol* was even more popular than *Popstars*, largely because the public could vote, and so telephone voting was introduced for the second series, *Popstars: The Rivals*. The presenter was Davina McCall, more used to evicting contestants from the *Big Brother* house, and the judges were Geri Halliwell, Louis Walsh and Pete Waterman. The public interest was enormous as the members were selected for the girl band, Girls Aloud (to be managed by Walsh), and the boy band, One True Voice (to be managed by Waterman).

The winning members of Girls Aloud were Nadine Coyle (the 17-year-old lead vocalist from Derry), Sarah Harding, Nicola Roberts, Cheryl Tweedy and Kimberley Walsh. The surprise at Javine Hylton being voted out led to bets that she would have her own hits before the end of 2003 and, indeed, she found herself in the Top 20 with 'Real Things' and 'Surrender (Your Love)'. The members of One True Voice were Anton Gordon, Matt Johnson, Daniel Pearce, Keith Semple and Jamie Shaw.

Very skilfully, the groups hijacked the race for the Christmas number one. Pete Waterman had recorded 'Sound Of The Underground' earlier in 2002 with a new act, Orchid, but he decided not to release it and passed it to Girls Aloud. They put it out with their cover of East 17's 'Stay Another Day'. One True Voice went for a little-known Bee Gees' song, 'Sacred Trust', and Pete Waterman's 'Long After You've Gone'. With 213,000 sales, Girls Aloud sold 46,000 more than One True Voice and went to number one. They remained at the top while The Cheeky Girls' 'Cheeky Girls (Touch My Bum)' moved to number two. A UK tour featuring the two groups was cancelled due to poor ticket sales, and after a Top 10 hit with 'Shakespeare's Way With Words', One True Voice split up in August 2003.

Girls Aloud's second single, 'No Good Advice', went to number two, but couldn't dislodge R. Kelly. Their CD, *Sound Of The Underground*, was well received, combining elements of The Spice Girls, All Saints and Sugababes.

The group made unexpected headlines. Their road manager, John McMahon, was killed when their van crashed on Christmas Day with McMahon well over the limit. Also, Cheryl Tweedy was found guilty of assaulting a toilet attendant at The Drink Club in Guildford. She was fined £3,000 and sentenced to community service. Despite apologising to the group and to fans, she neglected to apologise to the victim.

947 David Sneddon
Stop Living The Lie

Label & Cat No.: **Mercury 0637292**

Producer: **Paul Meehan**

Writer: **David Sneddon**

Date reached No.1: **25 January 2003**

Weeks at No.1: **2**

FOLLOWING ITV'S SUCCESS WITH *Popstars* and *Pop Idol*, the BBC devised *Fame Academy*. This had a more serious intent as 12 singers would compete for a £1m contract with Mercury Records. They lived under constant scrutiny in the Fame Academy until they were asked to leave so the series added a *Big Brother* component. At first, the show had a critical mauling with complaints that it was wasting licence fees, but after a few weeks, the public was gripped. The weaker talents had gone and some talented youngsters remained (Sinead Quinn, Lemar Obika, Naomi Roper), who were encouraged to perform their own songs. Naomi couldn't make the final playoff because of illness and David Sneddon took her place.

With nearly seven million telephone votes, David Sneddon was the winner (as well as the BBC with a income from over 10 million calls). He was a 24 year old busker from Glasgow and as well as the recording contract, he was to have the lifestyle of a star for a year – a luxury flat in London, limousines, jets and even a personal trainer.

When he was 17, David had seen a lonely old man drinking coffee in a café for two hours and no one asked him if he was all right. He went home and wrote 'Stop Living The Lie', a compassionate song like 'Streets Of London'. The single, however, was very much in the boy band mould, and the record could have come out of *Popstars* or *Pop Idol*.

David Sneddon had further hits with 'Don't Let Go' (3), 'Best Of Order' (19) and 'Baby Get Higher' (which didn't, sticking at 38). His album, *Seven Years – Ten Weeks*, a reference to the *Fame Academy* experience, reached the Top Five.

In October 2003 David Sneddon announced that the fame game was not for him.

He would make occasional appearances but he would concentrate on songwriting. A few months later he had formed a rock band in Glasgow called The Sham and their first single, 'Goodbye Baby', was released in October 2004.

948 t.A.T.u
All The Things She Said

Label & Cat No.: **Interscope 0196972**

Producer: **Trevor Horn**

Writers: **Sergey Galoyan / Trevor Horn / Martin Kierszenbaum / Elina Kiper / Voitinskiy Polienko**

Date Reached No.1: **8 February 2003**

Weeks at No.1: **4**

ALTHOUGH ITS INFLUENCE ON MUSIC has been immense, Russia has not charted many acts outside her own country, save for one third of Dee-Lite and Ivan Rebroff. Indeed, until the arrival of these two teenagers, its contribution to the British chart had been minimal.

Lena Sergeyevna Katina (born October 4, 1984, Moscow) and Yulia Olegovna Volkova (born February 20, 1985, Moscow) first became friends in 1997 when they were both members of Neposedi, a pop group made up of youngsters. Discovered by psychologist, scriptwriter and director, Ivan Shapovalov, during auditions for a new girl duo, he became their manager.

Their name is an abbreviation of the Russian phrase, 'ta dyevushka lubit tu', meaning 'this girl loves that one', although it has been anglicised to 'Teens Against Tobacco Usage'. No sooner had t.A.T.u arrived on the music scene, rumours about their sexuality came flying from all directions. It was alleged that the pair were romantically involved, a clever marketing ploy that guaranteed them maximum promotion in the press. Lena offered that "t.A.T.u represented a new kind of teenager who is open to experience. It is not one type of sex, not one kind of experience, it is just to be who you are."

Their debut album, *200 KM/H In The Wrong Lane* sold over one million copies in Russia, and an estimated further four million bootlegs. 'All The Things She Said' was originally released in Russia in 2001, titled 'Ya Soshla S Uma' ('I've Lost My Mind'). It was rewritten in English with help from Trevor Horn as 'All The Things She Said' and contained the suggestive lyrics which only helped perpetuate the myth. And sell more records. It went to number 20 Stateside and hit the top in Australia, Austria, Denmark, Ireland, Italy, Mexico, New Zealand, Spain, Switzerland and Taiwan.

"It's a song about love between two girls," explained Yulia. Lena added, "Our songs are not silly. t.A.T.u is more sincere, more honest about ourselves and others. We don't shape ourselves for the audience. In Russia, life is not polite. If we don't like something, we say we don't like it. If we don't agree, we say 'fuck you.'"

The controversial video caused much hullabaloo and outrage in Britain, and indeed the rest of the world. It was banned in their home country, yet still managed to win MTV Russia's People's Choice Award. A censored version was shown for pre-watershed, although the uncut clip showed them as two schoolgirls behind iron bars, being stared at by curious onlookers. With an obligatory downpour, their skirts become soaked, clinging to them. In defiance of their disapproving audience, they turn to each other and begin kissing and caressing, and eventually walk off hand in hand into the distance. It became one of the most requested videos on MTV for the next few months.

In May 2003 they came third (behind Turkey and Belgium) in Eurovision, after much boasting that they would 'clobber all the competition'. The following year it seemed that all their lesbian antics were just a big gimmick, Julia Volkova fell pregnant and Lena recently got engaged to her long-term boyfriend.

Morrissey, on being asked his opinion of the girls' version of 'How Soon Is Now?',(which although was not given a single release in the UK, was a moderate hit in Europe), replied, "It was magnificent, although I don't know much about them." When told they were Russian lesbians, his response was, "Well, aren't we all?"

949 Christina Aguilera
Beautiful

Label & Cat No.: **RCA 82876502462**

Producer: **Linda Perry**

Writer: **Linda Perry**

Date Reached No.1: **8 March 2003**

Weeks at No.1: **2**

"ON MY OWN I'M TERRIBLE, I CAN barely write a song," said Linda Perry, who wrote this beautiful chart-topping ballad.

Linda made her mark on the world as lead singer and songwriter with Nineties US grunge/pop band 4 Non Blondes, whose hit 'What's Up?' reached number two in 1993. After a couple of years, she had become disillusioned with the industry and decided to break away for a solo career. Her record label at the time weren't keen on the idea, yet reluctantly agreed to let her record a solo album. It sold only 18,000 copies, which, after the six million selling Blondes album *Bigger, Better, Faster, More?*, was a major disappointment.

Her songwriting career happened by accident when Pink, who was a 4 Non Blondes fan, called her and threatened to stalk her if she didn't write a song for her. The result was 'Get The Party Started' which reached number two in 2002. As a result, she put her solo career on hold and started working with other female singers like Courtney Love and Christina Aguilera.

One day while feeling very depressed, Linda wrote 'Beautiful' with the intention of having it as her comeback single but hadn't recorded it. "I played it to Christina who immediately fell in love with it, so I gave her the chance to demo it. Her first vocal take, reading the lyrics from a piece of paper in my living room, were so fulfilling that we used that version on the single. It had a very raw feeling, which I liked, but Christina wanted it re-done to technical perfection, I said no and it took me seven months of arguments until she finally agreed."

Seeing the result of that hit, Linda decided it was time to give up the idea of a solo career and concentrate on writing for women she feels comfortable with.

The album, *Stripped*, which spent over a year on the chart, contained the Top 10 hits 'Fighter', which featured former Red Hot Chili Pepper Dave Navarro on guitar, 'Can't Hold Us Down', a duet with Lil' Kim and 'The Voice Within'.

950 Gareth Gates featuring Special Guests The Kumars
Spirit In The Sky

Label & Cat No.: **S 82876511192**

Producer: **Steve Mac**

Writer: **Norman Greenbaum**

Date Reached No.1: **22 March 2003**

Weeks at No.1: **2**

AFTER A LULL, TV COMEDY RETURNED with a vengeance with *The Office, Phoenix Nights* and *The Kumars At No. 42*. In 2001 The Kumars took the spoof chat show format of Mrs. Merton and Alan Partridge a stage further by having Ashwin and Madhuri Kumar (Vincent Ebrahim and Indira Joshi) build their son, Sanjeev (Sanjeev Bhaskar), a TV studio in the garden of their house in Wembley.

Sanjeev hosts a chat show with an audience but his attempts at asking sensible questions are foiled by the off-beat and crude contributions of Granny Sushila, played by Meera Syal. The guests have included Michael Parkinson, Mel B, Ronan Keating and Charlotte Church, and the result combines a chat show with comedy, and improvisation with scripted material. One of the 2003 episodes featured Gareth Gates, Pete Waterman and Samantha Mumba, who break into 'Spirit In The Sky'.

Gareth's album, *What My Heart Wants To Say*, had sold 600,000 copies, but his recent singles had not fared so well – 'Sunshine' (3) and 'What My Hearts Wants To Say' (5). Furthermore, Will Young's single for Children In Need, 'Don't Let Me Down', had entered at number two but fallen to number nine the next week. Still, a Pop Idol was teamed with The Kumars in a revival of 'Spirit In The Sky' for the annual Comic Relief appeal. All turned out well: the single sold 273,000 in its first week and had total sales of nearly 600,000.

It was the third time that 'Spirit In The Sky' made the top and each time – Norman Greenbaum (1970), Doctor & The Medics (1986) – it has sounded different. The CD single included a Gareth-only version of 'Spirit In The Sky'.

In 2003/4, chart positions became increasingly capricious, but the pricing structure adopted by record companies was a contributory factor. CD singles were on sale for £3.99, but in the first week, it could be £1.99 or £2.99, according to marketing policies. In September 2003 EMI released two-track CD singles for £1.99. A few companies followed suit and the week Gareth Gates' next single, 'Sunshine' entered the charts, it was the only one of 14 newcomers to be priced at £3.99. Maybe that's why Gareth stalled at number three.

951 Room 5 featuring Oliver Cheatham
Make Luv

Label & Cat No.: **Positiva CDTIV 187**

Producer: **Vito Lucente**

Writers: **Oliver Cheatham / Kevin McCord**

Date Reached No.1: **5 April 2003**

Weeks at No.1: **4**

BELGIAN-BASED ITALIAN DJ AND producer Vito Lucente, born in 1972, has been releasing tracks under various guises since 1996. His first track, 'Only House Muzik', under the name Mr Jack, made the club chart, but was blocked for commercial release because it contained an uncleared sample of Tom Wilson's minor 1995 hit 'Technocat'.

His next release, 'Wiggly World', was licensed in the UK by Xtravaganza Records and reached number 32 in 1997. Making his name as a big house producer, Vito launched his own Noisetraxx label and released tracks under different names including 'Shine On' as Hugh K and 'Can You See It' as Kafé. He also hired DJs Roger Sanchez, Erick 'More' Morillo, Mousse T and Robbie Rivera for their remixing skills.

In 1999 Vito began using the moniker Junior Jack and his tracks were licensed to Defected Records in the UK. His first release, 'My Feeling', which only reached number 31 in the UK, was a massive hit in Ibiza. His follow-up, 'Thrill Me', which sampled Vicki D's 'This Beat Is Mine' made number 29.

For his next project he went under the guise Room 5. This straightforward house track originally sampled Oliver Cheatham's 1983 hit 'Get Down Saturday Night', but Vito had the idea to contact Oliver to see if he would like to re-record his vocals for the track. Oliver was born in 1948 and was a former backing singer for Leo Sayer and Melissa Manchester. He agreed and the song became a bit hit in Europe. With a similar feel to Spiller's 'Groovejet' and Phats And Small's 'Turn Around' it was surprising that it went unnoticed in the UK. That changed over a year later thanks to Lynx, who employed the track for their latest deodorant commercial. The ad showed a man at a bar having a quiet drink, but when the track came on he moved to the middle of the pub floor and began dancing like a nerd, to the mockery of the entire pub.

Vito had no plans to continue with the Room 5 alias, because as he said, "That track was over a year old and it came as a surprise when it became popular in the UK, so I then had to do a Room 5 album very quickly. It was a little hard because to put on deep, underground, tribal tracks made no sense and I didn't want to disappoint the listeners who maybe wanted to hear similar stuff to 'Make Luv'." A follow-up, 'Music & You' was released but petered out at number 38.

Vito returned to his Junior Jack moniker and teamed up with The Cure's Robert Smith for the 2004 hit 'Da Hype', which reached number 25. The follow-up, 'Stupidisco' made number 26.

952 Busted
You Said No

Label & Cat No.: **Universal MCSTD 40318**

Producer: **Steve Robson**

Writers: **James Bourne / Matthew Jay / Charlie Simpson / Steve Robson / John McLaughlin**

Date Reached No.1: **3 May 2003**

Weeks at No.1: **1**

WHEN BUSTED ARRIVED ON THE music scene, they were quickly dismissed by cynics as yet another fly-by-night boy band. But the difference was that these three energetic lads not only wrote their own songs, they played their own instruments too.

Busted are James Bourne, Matthew Jay and Charlie Simpson. James was born in Southend on September 13, 1983 and as a teenager had passed an audition for one of Fagin's boys in a West End production of *Oliver!* After two years he was offered the title role. He learned guitar and admitted, "It was very frustrating and I nearly considered giving it up, but the first time I managed to play Michael Jackson's 'Earth Song', I knew it was all worth it."

Matthew was born in Tooting, south London on May 8, 1983 and grew up in Molesey, Surrey. His break came at a school karaoke competition. He sang Oasis' 'Don't Look Back In Anger' and was approached by a songwriter who had been in the audience. He said he was submitting a song for a Vivian Ellis Award – an annual prize for songwriters – and thought he would be perfect to sing his song. Although nothing came of the song, this songwriter heard of a place available at Sylvia Young's Theatre School and suggested Matt went along. Charlie was born in Ipswich on June 7, 1985 and at the age of 10 he also learned guitar.

Matt and James met in 2001 at an *NSYNC gig and decided to form their own band Buster. They auditioned numerous drummers, but none were satisfactory, so they placed an ad in the *NME* for a third member and Charlie got the gig and changed their name to Busted. They went to Universal Records to see the MD Paul Adam. He said, "I remember when they came into my office, we'd just moved offices and I had no chairs, so we all sat on the floor and they performed 'What I Go To School For', 'Year 3000' and 'Crash And Burn', the working title for 'You Said No'. They were such bloody good songwriters that they just blew me away."

'What I Go To School For' became their first single and entered the chart at number three. Their debut album, *Busted*, was released a fortnight later, going to number two and spending over a year on the chart. The next single, 'Year 3000', also went to number two and spent four months on the chart.

For the third single, they chose 'Crash And Burn'. "I remember we sat down for a writing session," said James, "and Charlie was talking about being blown out by a girl. He said 'I crashed and burned' which was something I had never heard before. Then we tied it in with a song we already had about a girl who was so fit and she knew it and we renamed it 'You Said No'."

953 Tomcraft
Loneliness

Label & Cat No.: **Data DATA 52CDS**

Producers: **Eniac (Robert Borrmann) / Tomcraft**

Writers: Andrea Martin / Ivan Mathias / Edmund Clement / Eniac (Robert Borrmann)

Date Reached No.1: **10 May 2003**

Weeks at No.1: **1**

IN A WEEK WHEN THE SALES OF SINGLES weren't particularly high, 36,000 was enough to give the Munich-based producer and DJ, Tomcraft, a surprise number one.

Tomcraft, born Thomas Brückner in 1975, started DJing in the mid-Nineties and wrote 'Loneliness' as an instrumental in 2001. "I'd been working on some ideas for tracks with my studio partner Eniac, but there was something missing," explained Thomas. "One day I was in my local charity shop, where I always buy my second-hand records, especially the Fifties and Sixties stuff, and I came across this amazing track, 'Share The Love' by Andrea Martin on an old Seventies album which I knew was exactly what I needed. I knew this British singer called Vivian and asked her to come in and update the sound, sped it up and it worked out brilliantly."

Tomcraft first played the track from a CD-R to a packed club in Zarbruken, Germany. "The reaction was unbelievable," he said proudly. "People were screaming and acting really crazy." With a reaction like that, he decided to press up a limited run of 50 white label 12-inch singles and passed them around to a number of top club DJs at Berlin's annual Love Parade festival. One copy found its way into the hands of Radio 1 DJ Judge Jules, who gave the track extensive airplay.

The lyrics seem a tad confusing as the word happiness appears as often as loneliness. Thomas said: "The lyrics say that happiness seems to be loneliness and loneliness killed my world. It doesn't really make much sense to me either, but I prefer it because of that. I like the idea that it is a bit crazy, it's just that kind of record."

954 R.Kelly
Ignition Remix

Label & Cat No.: **Jive 9254972**

Producer: **R.Kelly**

Writer: **R.Kelly**

Date Reached No.1: **17 May 2003**

Weeks at No.1: **4**

BEFORE 'I BELIEVE I CAN FLY' LEFT THE charts, R. Kelly's next hit, 'Gotham City' was all over the screen of another movie, *Batman And Robin*.

R idolised Marvin Gaye and saw himself as a modern-day version. Robert was at his best singing ballads as proved by his biggest UK hits 'Be Careful' (1998), 'I'm Your Angel' (with Celine Dion, 1998), 'If I Could Turn Back The Hands Of Time' (1999) and 'The World's Greatest' (2002) from the film *Ali*.

By playing their own instruments, Busted raised the ante for boy bands in the new millennium; left to right: Charlie Simpson, James Bourne and Matt Jay

erCard
CCCP

Following his catastrophic 1994 marriage to Aaliyah, who was only 15 at the time, suspicion was aroused about R. Kelly's involvement with young women. On June 5, 2002 Robert was arrested on 21 counts of child pornography. He was visibly shaken, his entire appearance changed. The trademark goatee was untrimmed, his hair was dishevelled, his eyes looked vacant and the tabloids photographed him in orange prison clothes. An earlier story broke that he had had sex with underage girls, but had settled out of court.

Whilst on bail in 2003 he worked on an album with the Isley Brothers as well as two new albums of his own. The first one, *Loveland*, was scrapped after he discovered it had been bootlegged. The other was *Chocolate Factory*, a set containing a bunch of songs about love, passion and sexual innuendos. Kelly wrote, produced and arranged the whole album that went to number one in the US and number 10 in the UK.

The first single lifted was 'Ignition Remix', (the album also contained a different song called 'Ignition') an R&B song full of sexual metaphors like 'Girl, please let me stick my key in your ignition', 'See, I'll be doin' about 80 on your freeway', 'Girl, back that thing up so I can wax it' and 'So tell me have you ever driven a stick, babe, You'll be screamin' every time we shiftin' gears'. "I've always got a few issues that I'm dealing with. In my music, I cry. It's a cry," he admitted. "People that listen to me know that. They know my heart is honest about the fact that I'm no angel here."

Two further singles were issued from *Chocolate Factory*, 'Snake' (10) and 'Step In The Name Of Love' / 'Thoia Thong' (14). As a writer he has had hits with 'Bump Bump Bump' (B2K & P.Diddy), 'Hell Yeah' (Ginuwine), 'One More Chance' (Michael Jackson), 'Clubbin' (Marques Houston), 'Ride Wit U' (Joe) and 'Calling All Girls' (ATL). In March 2004 he teamed up with Jennifer Lopez for the number three hit 'Baby I Love U' and two months later he joined a new young rapper, Cassidy, on another number three hit, 'Hotel'.

Kelly married Andrea Lee in 1996 and has three children with her. She has yet to comment on the allegations surrounding her husband.

955 Evanescence
Bring Me To Life

Label & Cat No.: **Epic 6739762**

Producer: **Dave Fortman**

Writers: **David Hodges / Amy Lee / Ben Moody**

Date Reached No.1: **14 June 2003**

Weeks at No.1: **4**

"WE'RE VERY SINCERE ABOUT WHAT we do. There's so much pre-packaged teen angst these days in music. That's not us. We're not trying to sell an angle, we're just here writing from our heart," states multi-instrumentalist Ben Moody, guitarist with Little Rock, Arkansas band Evanescence.

It was at youth camp in the mid-Nineties, that Ben heard Amy Lee perform Meat Loaf's 'I'd Do Anything For Love (But I Won't Do That)', and he was suitably impressed. "I went over to meet her and she started singing for me. I was pretty much blown away, so I suckered her into joining a band with me."

The two became friends and realising they shared many musical interests, began writing songs together. In December 1998 they recorded their first EP and put it out as a very limited edition on CD-R, selling it at their show at a popular pub, Vino's, in their hometown. Although Evanescence were essentially a duo, they recruited several local musicians to fill out the sound at their live gigs. Later, John LeCompt joined on guitar and Rocky Gray on drums.

While Evanescence were working on their first full-length CD, *Origin*, they came to the attention of producer Pete Matthews, who referred them to the predominantly Christian label, Wind-Up Records, to which they signed.

'Bring Me To Life' and the ballad, 'My Immortal' (7) which had appeared on their debut release, were featured in the action movie, *Daredevil*, starring Ben Affleck and Colin Farrell. It initially charted in the UK on import in May and reached number 60. When it was released locally two weeks later it went straight to the top.

After starting life as a ballad, 'Bring Me To Life' became a gothic rock classic, with help from producer Dave Fortman.

"'Bring Me To Life' is about discovering something or someone that awakens a feeling inside them that they've never had before. You discover there is a world that is bigger than just your safe bubble," explained Ben.

Whilst Amy and Ben are Christians, their displeasure at being wrongly labelled a 'Christian band' caused all their CDs to be taken off the shelves from Christian record stores in the US. It didn't seem to hinder the group's sales – the parent album, *Fallen*, which spent a week at number one in the UK, went on to sell over five million copies worldwide. "There are people hell-bent on the idea that we're a Christian band in disguise, that we have some secret message," claimed Amy. "We have no spiritual affiliation with this music. It's simply about life experiences."

The song helped earn them two Grammy awards in 2004, for Best Hard Rock Performance and Best New Artist. They were also nominated for another three awards; Best Rock Album, Album Of The Year and Best Rock Song, which were won by Foo Fighters, OutKast and The White Stripes respectively.

Ben Moody walked out of the band whilst on their 2003 European tour. He was replaced by Terry Balsamo, formerly of post-alternative metal band, Cold.

956 Beyoncé featuring Jay-Z
Crazy In Love

Label & Cat No.: **Columbia 6740672**

Producer: **Rich Harrison**

Writers: **Beyoncé Knowles / Rich Harrison / Shawn Carter / Eugene Record**

Date reached No.1: **12 July 2003**

Weeks at No.1: **3**

DESTINY'S CHILD ARE ONE OF THE best selling all-girl groups of recent times with albums sales of over 10 million, so when they split it was likely that there would be some solo success. Michelle moved into gospel music, Kelly followed the pop route and Beyoncé, with her looks and charm, launched a successful R&B career.

At school she hated her surname and after being constantly teased by other girls who would call her, among others things, 'knowlesitall', she decided to drop it. She landed a role in the Mike Myers film *Austin Powers In Goldmember* and contributed the track, 'Work It Out', which reached number seven. It was written and produced by the massively successful production duo, Chad Hugo and Pharrell Williams alias The Neptunes. Her next hit, a cover of Toni Braxton's 'Me & My Boyfriend' which was retitled '03 Bonnie & Clyde', was a duet with her rapper boyfriend, Jay-Z.

In early 2003 she began work on her debut album, *Dangerously In Love*, which contained a duet with Luther Vandross, 'The Closer I Get To You', and won a Grammy award for Best Performance By A Duo. "The album is a good balance of really beautiful ballads, great mid-tempos and some up-tempo club songs," said Beyoncé. She took home another Grammy for Best R&B Album.

The first single from it, 'Crazy In Love', sampled a Chi-Lites album track, 'You Are My Woman'. Beyoncé described it as "Very different from anything I've done and very different from most R&B songs. The beat is so hard it hurts your heart when you listen to it. The song is about a person who is in a relationship and they are at the point where they are so in love they are looking kind of crazy and doing things they don't normally do."

'Crazy In Love' topped the US chart for eight straight weeks and gave her a Grammy for Best R&B Song. She followed it with 'Baby Boy', a duet with dancehall reggae artist Sean Paul. It reached number two in the UK and went to number one in the US for 10 weeks. She had further UK hits with, 'Me, Myself And I' (11) and 'Naughty Girl' (10).

In September 2004 Destiny's Child reformed and an album was released in November. All three members will continue their solo projects. According to Mathew Knowles, "Destiny's Child will begin a world tour in April 2005, and Beyoncé will be making films in 2005 and 2006." Beyonce added, "The group will take a break in 2007 before releasing another Destiny's Child album in 2008."

957 Daniel Bedingfield
Never Gonna Leave Your Side

Label & Cat No.: **Polydor 9809362**
Producer: **Mark Taylor**
Writer: **Daniel Bedingfield**
Date Reached No.1: **2 August 2003**
Weeks at No.1: **1**

Daniel Bedingfield's debut album had so far generated four singles, which included two chart toppers, and two Top 10 hits (the fourth, 'I Can't Read You' reached number six).

Gotta Get Thru This was a record full of range: from R&B to pop to garage to soul to disco to ballads. "The album is so diverse, it's scary," claimed Daniel. "I wasn't even trying to make it so, but the music I love is so broad, everything from old musicals to house music, that I couldn't make it any other way." He added, "It's melody-based, it's beat-driven, there's lots of harmonies, lots of funk. I like to describe the record as what it would sound like if Sting and Michael Jackson and Stevie Wonder were in a basement, jamming together."

The fifth single, 'Never Gonna Leave Your Side', was a sentimental ballad, which Daniel had written when he was in America, trying to break into the lucrative US market. Performing the song on his UK tour received such a warm response that a re-issue of the album was released with its inclusion.

One final single was taken from *Gotta Get Thru This*. 'Friday' was his lowest-charting yet and stalled at number 28 in November.

In January 2004 on his annual visit to New Zealand, Daniel suffered serious injury, fracturing vertebrae in his neck, when his jeep overturned on a dirt road. Firemen had to cut him free from the wreckage. Daniel insisted he had been wearing a seatbelt, wasn't speeding and had not been drinking at the time of the crash. "Right now I feel OK and very grateful to be alive. I don't remember much about what happened, but I've seen pictures of the car and feel blessed to have got out of there at all."

On his release from hospital 10 days later, Daniel moved in with friends for the following two months to recover.

He had been nominated for three Brits, Best British Male Solo Artist, Best British Album and Best Pop Act, (of which he received an award for Best British Male Solo Artist, beating David Bowie and Will Young), although the accident meant he had to wear a head brace, which was screwed into his skull, leaving him unable to fly back to the UK to attend them. He joked in a phone interview with Radio 1 DJ, Chris Moyles, that he could have won an award for "best-looking male in a head brace", and that the device was "the biggest chick magnet I've ever had in my life!"

958 Blu Cantrell featuring Sean Paul
Breathe

Label & Cat No.: **Arista 82876545722**
Producer: **Mark Pitts**
Writers: **Andrea Martin / Ivan Matias / Richard Bembery / Melvin Bradford / Stephon Cunningham / Alvin Joiner / Marshall Mathers III / Charles Aznavourian**
Date reached No.1: **9 August 2003**
Weeks at No.1: **4**

Gentlemen, if you saw Blu Cantrell's first appearance on *Top Of The Pops*, and thought you'd seen her somewhere before, it just might have been in a top shelf magazine. Blu is not ashamed of her explicit nude photos and said she would happily do it again.

Blu, who chose the name after her favourite colour, was born Tiffany Cobb on December 13, 1976 in Providence, Rhode Island, and was brought up by her mum, a jazz singer whom she often watched perform whilst she was growing up.

The family moved to Atlanta and in 1994 Blu posed for *Playboy*, but opted to follow in her mother's footsteps and decided she wanted a career in music. One day her sister had an accident, fell into a coma and was rushed to hospital. Blu's offer to look after her whilst her mother carried on working, gave Blu her break. "I was standing in the hotel lobby next door," she explained, "and this guy, Tricky Stewart of Red Zone Entertainment, stopped me to tell me I looked like a singer. I thought he just wanted to get into my pants, but I realised he was serious and he introduced me to the president of Arista Records, Antonio 'LA' Reid." Initially she provided backing vocals for Puff Daddy and Faith Evans, but she was set for bigger things. Reid said, "The first time I heard her sing, I knew she was special, so I signed her."

Her debut album, *So Blu,* sold well in America but attracted few buyers in the UK. However, her first single, 'Hit 'Em Up Style (Oops!)', reached number 12 in the UK and number two in the US.

Just prior to recording her second album, Blu went through a particularly difficult break-up with a boyfriend. It left her devastated and suffering from depression. "That's why I called the album *Bittersweet*," she confessed. "I'm still bitter about a past relationship, but I've also experienced the sweetness of love." The album, of which Blu co-wrote four tracks, has a mixture of R&B flavours fused with her mother's jazz influences and it went to number two in the US and number 20 here.

For her next single, 'Breathe', which sampled Dr. Dre's 'What's The Difference', she teamed up with the Jamaican-born dancehall reggae star, Sean Paul. "That song is also a snapshot of that relationship. Sometimes you have to step back and give each other space," she admitted.

One further single was lifted from the album, the Caribbean-tinged 'Make Me Wanna Scream', which saw her duet with Ian Lewis of the reggae group Inner Circle.

Blu has established herself as a R&B singer alongside the likes of Beyoncé, Alicia Keys and Brandy, but if things don't work out, keep an eye out on that the top shelf.

959 Elton John
Are You Ready For Love?

Label & Cat No.: **Southern Fried ECB 50CDS**

Producer: **Thom Bell**

Writer: **Linda Bell / Thom Bell / Casey James**

Date Reached No.1: **6 September 2003**

Weeks at No.1: **1**

IT WORKED FOR ELVIS PRESLEY, WHEN JXL found an obscure track, added a heavier dance beat, remixed it and took it to number one, so why shouldn't it work for a long forgotten Elton John hit?

The original track was recorded with producer, Thom Bell, at Sigma Sounds Studios in Philadelphia. Thom had invited the Detroit Spinners to record backing vocals and two versions of the song were cut. One had all of The Spinners, the other with only lead singer Phillipe Wynne on backing vocals. It was the latter that was released as a single some two years after the recording. The other version is only available on the 1990s box set *The Complete Thom Bell Sessions*. The track wasn't released until 1979 because Elton wasn't entirely happy with the original mixes. He thought they were too cluttered, so asked sound engineer and producer Clive Franks to remix the track and make it less so. Clive remembered, "We mixed all the tracks in just two or three days, but I hate to admit, I've got no idea which mix was actually issued as a single – that was left up to Elton and (his manager) John Reid to decide."

In 1979 it was eventually released as a single but only reached number 42 in the UK. The same year The Spinners, as they were known in the States, recorded their own version of the song and it appeared on their album *From Here To Eternally*. Later in 1979 Elton embarked on his first tour for three years, which included a performance in Israel, where only one westerner, Leonard Cohen, had performed before.

In the summer of 2003 Ashley Beedle from the dance act X-Press 2 remixed the track. Although little was done to the original sound, it became a nightclub smash. Its profile was boosted when Sky TV used it as backing music for their soccer coverage. When DJ Fatboy Slim heard it, he wanted it issued on his own Southern Fried record label. Initially, a strictly limited edition of 6000 pink vinyl 12" copies were released, which sold enough to enter the chart at number 66. Two months later, the track got a full CD release following its use by the Sky Sports channel to advertise the new season of football coverage. But the bizarre thing is that the remixed version does not appear on the CD single or the cassette single, it only appeared on the B-side of the 12" copy. So how many fans bought the CD, only to discover they already had it in their collection.

960 Black Eyed Peas
Where Is The Love?

Label & Cat No.: **A&M 9810996**

Producers: **Will I. Am / Ron Fair**

Writers: **Will Adams / Allan Pineda / Jamie Gomez / Justin Timberlake / Michael Fratantuno / George Pajon Jr / Priese Board**

Date reached No.1: **13 September 2003**

Weeks at No.1: **6**

AFTER 9/11 MILLIONS OF PEOPLE found it hard to convey their feelings of shock, horror and most of all, anger. Songwriters expressed their emotions in song. The country star Alan Jackson reflected their feelings best with 'Where Were You (When The World Stopped Turning?)', Paul McCartney organised and appeared on the same bill as Elton John, Billy Joel, Bon Jovi, The Who, James Taylor, Destiny's Child and many other acts, at the Madison Square Garden tribute concert, and performed his specially written tribute 'Freedom'. The

Black Eyed Peas' number one 'Where Is The Love?' was written as a reaction to the 9/11 World Trade Center atrocity; left to right: Apl.de.Ap, Will I.Am, Fergie and Taboo

Black Eyed Peas summed up their feelings with their R&B response 'Where Is The Love?' especially with the poignant opening line, "What's wrong with the world, mama."

Black Eyed Peas were formed in 1992 when friends Will I. Am (born William Adams) and Apl.de.Ap (born Allan Pineda) met Taboo (born Jamie Gomez) at a break dancing club in Los Angeles and signed to the rapper, Eazy-E's Ruthless label. After Eazy-E died of AIDS in 1995, they recruited Kim Hill as lead singer and signed an international deal with Interscope Records.

Their debut album, *Behind The Front*, sold few copies and failed to chart, but the first single, 'Joints And Jam' became a minor UK hit (53). They looked set to be one hit wonders as there was no follow-up for three years. In 2001 they returned with 'Request + Line', a collaboration with R&B singer Macy Gray, which made the UK Top 40, but the accompanying album, *Bridging The Gap*, went unnoticed in the UK. The following year Kim was replaced by Fergie (born Stacy Ferguson), a former singer and dancer in the US TV series *Kids Incorporated*.

The Peas supported Justin Timberlake on his 2002 tour, and he agreed to sing, uncredited, on their next track, 'Where Is the Love?'. "The song itself relates to the tension of the world today with personal struggles the members of the different groups have gone through," said Will. "The last couple of years haven't been easy. Is it guilt? Or is it stress? But there is uncertainty over what's gonna happen in the next five years." The track was included on their third album *Elephunk*, which features Sergio Mendes on piano and incorporates different musical styles. "We like to take risks," continued Will. "We like to utilise different instruments, whether it's a tuba or a kazoo. We went to Australia and saw this dude playing some bagpipes and we asked him to come on tour and he did five shows with us there." When 'Where Is The Love?', which features a 40-piece orchestra, spent six weeks at the summit, it became the longest any single had stayed at the top since Cher's 'Believe' five years earlier. It was also the best-selling single of 2003.

The follow-up single, 'Shut Up' made number two and was held off by Will Young's 'Leave Right Now'. They had two further singles from the album, 'Hey Mama' (6, 2004) and 'Let's Get It Started' (11, 2004).

They have also recorded the title track to the 2004 film *Dirty Dancing : Havana Nights*.

961 The Sugababes
Hole In The Head

Label & Cat No.: **Island CID 836**

Producers: **Brian Higgins / Xenomania / Jeremy Wheatley**

Writers: **Brian Higgins / Miranda Cooper / Tim Powell Nick Coler / Mutya Buena / Heidi Range / Keisha Buchanan / Niara Scarlett**

Date Reached No.1: **25 October 2003**

Weeks at No.1: **1**

For their third album, *Three*, the Sugababes began working with established songwriters Jony Rockstar, Stuart Crichton, Brian Higgins and Guy Sigsworth. They all gathered together at Linford Manor studios in Milton Keynes and began writing songs.

"It was a really good way of doing an album," said Keisha. "I would be with one songwriter in one room and the girls would be with another with someone else and we would all swap rooms during the day."

The first single from it, 'Hole In The Head', is a mixture of house, ska and R&B with a hint of reggae. "The song is basically about a guy that's broken up with you and at first you sulk and are upset," explained Keisha. "Then after a few hours you say, 'You know what...I'm going to get my hair done and get myself ready to go out, because I'd rather sell my ass than think of you again!" The accompanying video shows the girls pushing their dumped boyfriends off the stage.

The follow-up, 'Too Lost In You' was featured in *Love Actually*, starring Hugh Grant, Bill Nighy and Liam Neeson.

Their third album, *Three*, spent nine months on the chart and one further single, the ballad, 'Caught In A Moment', reached number eight.

962 Fatman Scoop featuring The Crooklyn Clan
Be Faithful

Label & Cat No.: **Def Jam UK 9812716**

Producer: **Crooklyn Clan**

Writers: **Fatman Scoop / Edmund Bini / Joe Rizzo / Andres Titus / William McLean / Allen Jones / Johnny Hammond / Ben Cauly / James Alexander / Bernard Edwards / Nile Rodgers / Schon Crawford / Ronald Lawrence**

Date Reached No.1: **1 November 2003**

Weeks at No.1: **2**

Harlem-born Fatman, Isaac Freeman III, grew up listening to hip-hop and knew he wanted to be a part of the scene. In the early Nineties he was offered a job with the small hip-hop label Chemistry Records, but in 1993 they folded and Scoop joined the successful independent label, Tommy Boy. He was soon promoting acts like Naughty By Nature, Coolio and De La Soul.

He posed for *The Source*, a magazine of hip-hop music and culture, which, in turn, led to him appearing in the videos for De La Soul's 'Itsoweezee', Puff Daddy's 'We'll Always Love Big Poppa' and The Fugees' 'Killing Me Softly'. In 1995 he was offered the overnight slot on New York's Hot 97FM station and in addition to playing the latest hip-hop and rap tunes, he was inundated with voiceover requests for commercials to promote Coolio, LL Cool J, Foxy Brown and Notorious B.I.G. In 1998 he was offered the breakfast show, but after a few months returned to his night-time show.

In addition he was offered a syndicated radio show, which broadcast to various cities in Missouri, Texas, Tennessee and Arizona. He linked up with two Brooklyn-born DJ's, Riz and Sizzahandz alias Joe Rizzo and Edmund Bini, who, for production purposes called themselves The Crooklyn Clan. They signed to AV8 Records in New York in 1996 and recorded three songs, 'Hands Up', 'Where U @' and 'Be Faithful', which sampled Faith Evans' 'Love Like This', The

Black Sheeps' 'The Choice Is Yours' and Chic's 'Chic Cheer'.

'Be Faithful' was released on 12-inch only and became a nightclub favourite in the US. It was picked up by Def Jam UK in 2003 who edited it down to just under three minutes for radio purposes. The Fatman, who also records under the moniker Big Colorado, scooped the number one slot by selling 62,000 copies.

963 Kylie Minogue
Slow

Label & Cat No.: **Parlophone CDR 6625**

Producers: **Dan Carey / Emiliana Torrini**

Writers: **Kylie Minogue / Dan Carey / Emiliana Torrini**

Date Reached No.1: **15 November 2003**

Weeks at No.1: **1**

AT THE BEGINNING OF 2003 'CAN'T Get You Out Of My Head' was still ruling the dance floors and TV stations. Kylie had concluded her European and Australian Fever tour and on its completion, she began work on her next album, Body Language, which was recorded in London, Ireland and Spain. It was the year that Kylie was awarded a Centenary Medal by the Governor General of Australia for Outstanding Contribution To The Music Industry. In addition, VH1 viewers voted her Sexiest Pop Pin-Up in the world.

Body Language was similar to *Fever*, albeit perhaps slightly more mature, with the added touch of Eighties synth pop. Like her two previous albums, the debut single went straight to the top. It was also Kylie's first number one as a writer, although she shared the accolade with Dan Carey and Emiliana Torrini, an Italian singer/songwriter whose 2000 album, *Love In The Time Of Science* received critical acclaim.

The accompanying video was rated PG. Kylie's outfits were getting skimpier but she knew where to draw the line. "I've always been on the right side of the line. Before we did the video for 'Slow', I hadn't seen any videos for a while, so I watched some and said 'I'm not doing that,'" Where Madonna and Christina Aguilera attempt to shock, *Body Language* shows that Kylie has quietly matured and retained some dignity, because in the early days, the Stock, Aitken & Waterman team was too authoritative leaving her little control, but she was now more important than the records, earning herself a reputation for making creditable music. And becoming a gay icon.

In 2003 Kylie launched her own lingerie range, *Love Kylie*, in London's Selfridges. The sales were incredible, and it caused massive media frenzy.

The next two singles, 'Red Blooded Woman' and 'Chocolate' were co-written by Brian Poole's daughter and former Alisha's Attic member Karen, and reached number five and six respectively.

964 Busted
Crashed The Wedding

Label & Cat No.: **Universal MCSTD 40245**

Producer: **Steve Power**

Writers: **James Bourne / Tom Fletcher**

Date Reached No.1: **22 November 2003**

Weeks at No.1: **1**

IN THE SUMMER OF 2003, BUSTED SET out on a sell-out arena tour. To help promote it Universal Records released a fourth single from *Busted*. 'Sleeping With The Light On' was the first song Matt and James ever wrote. Matt said, "It's all about coming home drunk. Put the lights on, keep one hand touching the floor, and it stops the room spinning."

They spent the latter half of 2003 recording their second album *A Present For Everyone*, which was another energetic release that kept their trademark melodies. It entered the chart at number two, only 575 copies shy of beating Michael Jackson's *Number Ones* album to the top.

The album's debut single 'Crashed The Wedding', crashed into pole position. The opening line, 'I'm so rushed off my feet, Looking for Gordon Street' is a line from *Wayne's World II*. "There's a bit where Wayne tries to stop a wedding, and asks Charlton Heston where Gordon Street is. When Wayne eventually crashes the wedding it's done in a parody of *The Graduate*," James explained.

In a world of manufactured bands, Busted stand out as an original force. "To call us a boy band is seriously underrating us," James insisted. "We're not a serious rock band – we're a pop band, but we're not a boy band."

965 Westlife
Mandy

Label & Cat No.: **RCA 82876 570732**

Producer: **Steve Mac**

Writers: **Scott English / Richard Kerr**

Date reached No.1: **23 November 2003**

Weeks at No.1: **1**

RICHARD KERR RECORDED FOR Deram but his first hit was as writer of 'Blue Eyes' for the one-man band, Don Partridge (1968). In 1971 he wrote a couple of small hits for the reggae band, Greyhound. He befriended Scott English, an American singer living in London, and they started writing together. "I went round to his house and as there was something going on, we wrote at his neighbours on a very rickety, upright piano, and it happened to be a creative day for me. I wrote the music first and then Scott wrote the lyric, 'Brandy'. I thought it would be a hit but Scott knew it would be a hit." Scott English recorded the song himself and it made the Top 20 in October 1971.

Four years later Richard Kerr was in Los Angeles: "My publishers wanted me to team up with some American writers and I went to the publishers' office in Los Angeles. I heard a really nice track coming through the walls and it took me two minutes to realise that it was my song, but the singer was singing 'Mandy'

instead of 'Brandy'. No one had asked us and they had made the change because there was a hit record in America called 'Brandy, You're A Fine Girl' by Looking Glass. I was furious at first but when it started zooming up the charts, I was very happy indeed."

Barry Manilow's 'Mandy' topped the US charts and made number 11 here and was covered by many middle of the road stars such as Andy Williams and Johnny Mathis. As a result, Richard wrote further songs for Barry Manilow, notably 'Somewhere In The Night'.

In 2003 the first single from Westlife's forthcoming *Turnaround* album, 'Hey Whatever' made number four but the group returned to the top with a remake of Barry Manilow's 'Mandy'.

966 Will Young
Leave Right Now

Label & Cat No.: **S 82876578562**

Producer: **Stephen Lipson**

Writer: **Francis Eg White**

Date reached No.1: **6 December 2003**

Weeks at No.1: **2**

WITH ALL THE PUBLICITY SURROUNDING *Pop Idol,* Will Young's first single, 'Anything Is Possible' / 'Evergreen', was expected to top the charts. His manager, Simon Fuller, strengthened the probability by making the single a double A-side. Will's revivals of 'Light My Fire' and 'The Long And Winding Road' were also chart-toppers and then a single for the BBC's *Children In Need*, 'Don't Let Me Down' / 'You And I', in November 2002 made number two.

After all this activity, it was a strange logic which determined that Will wouldn't have a new single until December 2003. He spent the time working on a second album and he said, "The great thing about taking time out is that it has enabled me to explore my creativity." He was writing songs himself and he was developing a light, soulful voice for material similar to Mick Hucknall's.

The single, 'Leave Right Now' was a gentle, well sung ballad with guitars played by the songwriter Eg White (!) and keyboards from Anne Dudley of The Art Of Noise. Will was lost at a party in the engaging video. The single was produced by Stephen Lipson, whose credits include Simple Minds, Sting, Annie Lennox and Geri Halliwell. It was by no means certain that Will would make number one, but the single beat Shane Richie from *EastEnders* with his colourful cover of Wham!'s 'I'm Your Man'.

'Leave Right Now' was a strong performance, but certainly the record's pricing was a factor in its success. Will's single was £1.99 for its first week while Shane Richie's was the standard £3.99. If you are a 10 year old with £5 pocket money and you are torn between the two artists, wouldn't you buy Will because you will still have £3 to spend on sweets?

The single was featured on Will's second album, *Friday's Child*. Although many people sneered at *Pop Idol*, the CD achieved rave reviews. It topped the UK album charts and sold as many copies in the first two weeks as *From Now On* had sold in the first two months.

967 Ozzy & Kelly Osbourne
Changes

Label & Cat No.: **Sanctuary SANXD 234**

Producer: **Mark Hudson**

Writers: **Ozzy Osbourne / Geezer Butler / Tommy Iommi / Bill Ward / Kelly Osbourne**

Date Reached No.1: **21 December 2003**

Weeks at No.1: **1**

JOHN MICHAEL 'OZZY' OSBOURNE, born December 3, 1948, Birmingham, is famous for many things: singing with Black Sabbath, biting the head off a bat, urinating on the Alamo and, since 2002, starring with his madcap family and menagerie for three fly-on-the-wall television series. *The Osbournes*, made by MTV and shown on Channel 4 in the UK, shot Ozzy, his wife Sharon and two of his three children, Kelly and Jack into stardom. Oldest daughter Aimee declined to appear.

The original version of 'Changes' appeared on the album, *Black Sabbath Vol. 4* which reached number eight in 1972. Black Sabbath, formed in Birmingham in the late Sixties, were pioneers of heavy metal, and comprised Tony Iommi (guitar), Terry 'Geezer' Butler (bass), Bill Ward (drums) and Ozzy on vocals. Very influential in HM circles, they have left their mark on Iron Maiden, Metallica, and Marilyn Manson, among others.

In 1979 Ozzy left to embark on a solo career. Black Sabbath carried on with a multitude of replacement musicians and lead singers. The original line-up reunited for Live Aid in 1985, but Butler quit shortly after. It wasn't until 1998 with the live double CD release, *Reunion*, which was recorded in December 1997 at the N.E.C. in Birmingham, that all four original members appeared together on record again. It just missed the Top 40, spending one week in the chart. In the US however, it got to number 11 and achieved platinum status.

Kelly Lee Osbourne (born October 27, 1984, in London) released her first single in 2002. The cover of Madonna's 'Papa Don't Preach' initially charted on import and reached number 65. When it came out locally it was a number three hit. Her second single, 'Shut Up' reached number 12. Kelly's debut album, *Shut Up* (31), was shrewdly re-titled *Changes* and reissued with the song's inclusion in a calculated attempt to cash in on its success. They needn't have bothered. It struggled to reach the Top 30.

"We always thought it would be a cliché to cover one of my father's songs," claimed Kelly. "Then I sat with the song for a day and rewrote the lyrics. And we recorded the song in three hours."

Whereas the former was a lament of a lost love, the new version is about a child who has grown up and about to leave the family home. Instead of, "She was my woman," Ozzy now sings, "She was my baby", and "My heart was blinded/ Love went astray" was amended to, "My baby's grown now/ She's found her way."

Family friend Elton John convinced Ozzy and Kelly to use a choir on 'Changes'. Kelly recalled,

Ozzy Osbourne first hit the charts with Black Sabbath in 1970, then waited 33 years to reach the top, duetting with daughter Kelly on another Sabbath song

"It was weird because we both fought so much. Ozzy wanted the choir on there and I didn't. We were out at Elton's house this summer, and his was the final decision on whether to put the choir on there."

She added, "It really is a sweet song. It's really hard to sing in front of your dad but I think he was actually more embarrassed than I was."

Just days before this became Ozzy's first chart-topper, he was involved in a serious accident at his Buckinghamshire home, breaking his collarbone, several ribs and a vertebra when his quadbike flipped over and landed on top of him. After spending a fortnight in intensive care, Ozzy was moved to a private clinic. He has since made a full recovery… well, by Ozzy's standards anyway.

968 Michael Andrews featuring Gary Jules
Mad World

Label & Cat No.:	**Adventures In Music/Sanctuary SANXD 250**
Producer:	**Michael Andrews**
Writer:	**Roland Orzabel**
Date reached No.1:	**27 December 2003**
Weeks at No.1:	**3**

"JOHN LENNON IS MY MAIN INSPIRATION," says Roland Orzabel of the duo, Tears For Fears. "He was a brilliant writer, but he was in primal therapy for six months and I studied it for six years." Like John Lennon, Roland and his musical partner, Curt Smith, were intrigued by the theories of Dr. Arthur Janov. They took the name of their group, Tears For Fears, from Janov's belief that crying is a good way to allay your worries.

Tears For Fears' first album, *The Hurting*, was inspired by Janov's teaching and the moody 'Mad World' was an introspective song about alienation. It contains the line, "The dreams in which I'm dying are the best I've ever had." 'Mad World' was their first hit single, reaching number three in 1982. Although the duo did not have a UK number one, they topped the US charts with 'Everyone Wants To Rule The World' and 'Shout' and they sold nine million copies of their album, *Songs From The Big Chair.*

Gary Jules

Gary Jules is a Los Angeles singer, guitarist and songwriter who made an album, *Greetings From The Side*, that was produced by his childhood friend, Michael Andrews, for A&M in 1997. When the label was involved in a merger, his work was overlooked and the album was released without any fanfare.

In 2001 Michael Andrews was writing the music for the science fiction film, *Donnie Darko*, which was being directed by 26-year-old Richard Kelly and produced by Drew Barrymore. Jake Gyllenhaal plays the title role, an adolescent who may or may not be schizophrenic but is alienated from his family and talks to a giant rabbit who tells him to prepare for the end of the world. Richard Kelly was keen to have contemporary music from the Eighties on the soundtrack including 'The Killing Moon' (Echo & The Bunnymen) and 'Notorious' (Duran Duran).

Michael Andrews knew that Gary Jules had 'Mad World' in his repertoire and he thought it would be ideal for the title credits. The rather eerie recording was made in an hour. For a key scene towards the end of the film, Richard Kelly wanted U2's 'MLK', but this proved too costly. As a result, 'Mad World' was promoted to this section and it was a perfect fit.

Donnie Darko was not immediately successful, but it was a film that students would discuss. By 2003, with its release on DVD, it had a cult following and viewers could watch it over and over. The soundtrack album did well and 'Mad World' was also included on Gary's second album, *Snakeoil For Wolftickets* (2001), although this was not given a UK release until 2004. 'Mad World' was issued as a single and curiously it became a contender for the Christmas number one.

The Christmas number one is normally uplifting, whether it be a Christmas song or not, and this ghostly record was a surprising victor. The Darkness with 'Christmas Time (Don't Let The Bells End)' had to make do with second place, although in a sense, it was the darkness that had won.

969 Michelle
All This Time

Label & Cat No.:	**S 82876590652**
Producer:	**Steve Mac**
Writers:	**Steve Mac / Wayne Hector / Neil Tennant**
Date reached No.1:	**17 January 2004**
Weeks at No.1:	**3**

TWENTY THOUSAND HOPEFULS HOPED to become ITV's latest Pop Idol and the winner who beat off all the skinny wannabes was 23-year-old Michelle McManus, a hotel events organiser from Baillieston, near Glasgow. The judges had been harsh, thinking her size went against her and that her voice, clearly modelled on Celine Dion, was too nasal. Meat Loaf, on the other hand, wished her luck in the final and sent her flowers. The show isn't over till the fat lady sings and the majority of the telephone votes went to Michelle.

Judges Pete Waterman and Neil Fox were surprised at the outcome. Simon Cowell said that she had 'broken the norm' of pop stars, although Mama Cass and Alison Moyet were big girls with even bigger voices. There are also, in different decades and genres, Big Mama Thornton, Barry White, Pavarotti and the XXL Elvis, not to mention all the fat rappers, although this has sometimes made them particularly easy targets for assassins.

Was it the sympathy vote? Even if she thought so, Michelle wasn't admitting it and with commendable self-esteem, she commented, "I am part of the British public myself and we won't vote for people because we feel sorry for them. We vote for them because they are talented."

Fifteen million people had watched the final and as 10 million of them had voted, this series was certainly profitable. The Lord Provost of Glasgow said that the result showed "It is not just skinny people who are pop stars."

The Scottish First Minister Jack McConnell said, "Michelle brought sparkle to the contest and real hope and pride to Scotland. This is a big signal to young Scots. If you have the ambition and go for it, you can win." He was ignoring all the Scots who had entered and lost. However, *Pop Idol* and similar shows contained a very serious message for politicians: how can there be such poor turnouts at elections and such interest in a manufactured TV talent contest? *Pop Idol* is, in time, certain to have an effect on the means for electing politicians.

Although the viewers of *Pop Idol 2* admired her voice, it was her physique that attracted attention. Professor Phil Hanlon, a health expert from Glasgow University, said, "I'm delighted for her success, although I think that Scotland has an obesity issue that it must confront." He saw Michelle as a role model but added, rather curiously, "I don't think we're saying that from now on the body shape everyone in Scotland aspires to is an overweight one." Precisely – you're a health expert, mate.

During the series, Michelle had stunned audiences with 'I Say A Little Prayer' and 'Without You', but she showed her quieter side with the carol, 'O Holy Night'. A big ballad, 'All This Time', was chosen for the first single and it was created by the team who had worked on the first *Pop Idol*. Michelle also led the *Pop Idol* choir on a remake of John and Yoko's 'Happy Xmas (War Is Over)'. It came in at number five and disappeared

quickly once Christmas was over. Michelle's album, *The Meaning Of Love*, featured one ballad after another and a more wide-ranging CD would have been better. You could listen to the CD while reading Simon Cowell's best-selling autobiography, *I Don't Mean To Be Rude But…*

In the world we live in, not looking svelte may count against Michelle having a sustained career. Still, if she does decide to slim, there is bound to be a Celebrity Fit Club that will welcome her as a contestant.

970 LMC vs U2
Take Me To The Clouds Above

Label & Cat No.: **All Around The World CDGLOBE 313**

Producer: **Lee Monteverde**

Writers: **Bono / Larry Mullen / David Evans / Adam Clayton / George Merrill / Shannon Rubicam / Narada Michael Walden**

Date Reached No.1: **7 February 2004**

Weeks at No.1: **2**

Like ABBA, M/A/R/R/S and KWS, LMC took the initials of its members to obtain their name. LMC are All Around The World label's in-house producer Lee Monteverde, general manager Matt Cadman and MD Cris Nuttall. Cris' mother, Marie, had a connection with a number one artist in 1964. She used to manage Reidys record shop in Penny Street, Blackburn. She knew The Four Pennies (named after the street) and the producer Johnny Franz and had arranged an audition for them. Lee, Matt and Cris are involved with remixing and have worked on tracks for Lasgo and Erasure.

All Around The World is the Lancashire-based independent dance label, formed in 1991. The label had registered 27 Top 20 hits including three number twos, 'Stayin' Alive' and 'Set You Free' both by N-Trance (1995) and 'Pretty Green Eyes' by Ultrabeat (2003), but LMC gave them their first chart topper.

The song was an amalgamation of two songs, using the bass riff from U2's 1987 hit 'With Or Without You' and a vocal copied from Whitney Houston's 1986 hit 'How Will I Know', the second line of which lent the song its title.

"We chose to credit ourselves as LMC vs U2 instead of LMC vs Whitney because we think it had more kudos," said Matt. "Also it was easier to clear a music sample than a vocal one. We decided to bring in former Loveland lead singer Rachel McFarlane to reproduce the Whitney lyric. She's got a great voice and certainly did it justice." Loveland had four Top 40 hits in the mid-Nineties, the biggest being 'Let The Music (Lift You Up)'.

On its first week in the shops it sold 69,000 copies, enough for it to enter the chart at number one. But the song was far more successful in the north of the country. Sales figures showed that London was the poorest selling area for the track.

"There are no immediate plans for a follow-up," Matt said. "We did it as a mash-up and it worked well, so we decided to release it under our own names, although I wouldn't rule out the possibility of us doing it again."

For their next hit, Lee, Matt and Cris teamed up with the production duo Flip & Fill, alias Graham Turner and Mark Hall, for a cover version of 'Hungry Eyes' under the moniker Eyeopener. The track, which reached number 16 was originally recorded by Eric Carmen and his version, although not a UK hit, is best remember for it's appearance in the film *Dirty Dancing*.

Michelle

971 Sam & Mark
With A Little Help From My Friends / Measure Of A Man

Label & Cat No.: **19 19RECS 9**

Producer: **David Eriksen**

Writers: **John Lennon / Paul McCartney : Cathy Dennis / Steve Morales / David Siegel**

Date reached No.1: **21 February 2004**

Weeks at No.1: **1**

THE JUDGES AND MANY MILLIONS OF viewers thought that 17-year-old Sam Nixon from Barnsley stood a good chance of winning ITV's *Pop Idol 2*. The cheeky, tousle-haired lad was this year's Gareth Gates and he performed a fine version of Rod Stewart's 'Maggie May' in the semi-final but it was not enough. He was eliminated, although many callers complained that their calls had been diverted to other contestants. They cried, 'Fix!', though why anyone should want to fix it is unknown.

Others eliminated along the way included Gareth Gates' sister, Nicola, and Andy Scott Lee from the boy band, 3SL, and brother of Steps' star, Lisa. One finalist, Susanne Manning, had the misfortune of having her father's affairs reported in *News Of The World*, which illustrated one of the drawbacks of celebrity.

The final, gladatorial contest was between Mark Rhodes and Michelle McManus. Mark Rhodes, the 22-year-old Yummie Brummie, had nearly been eliminated in an earlier round and his presence in the final irritated Pete Waterman, one of the judges. He remarked, "Mark is far out of his depth and this show is not about talent or singing any more."

Michelle won but, not leaving any stone unturned, the runners-up, Sam Nixon and Mark Rhodes, were hastily put into a recording studio for a single, which was released as a double A-side. Sam had sung 'With A Little Help From My Friends' on the Beatles Night edition of *Pop Idol 2* and now it worked so well as a duet with Mark Rhodes that it is surprising that it hadn't been done this way before by, say, Sam and Dave. The other side, 'Measure Of A Man', had been sung by Mark on the final and was again changed to a duet. It was co-written by Cathy Dennis in her new career of writing for *Pop Idol* contestants. Further chart success didn't really go their way. The follow-up, 'The Sun Has Come Your Way', reached number 19 but had completely disappeared three weeks later.

Mark always went on stage in his lucky stud muffin underpants. Sometimes you can be given too much information.

972 Busted
Who's David?

Label & Cat No.: **Universal MCSTD 40355**

Producer: **Steve Power**

Writers: **James Bourne / Tom Fletcher**

Date Reached No.1: **28 February 2004**

Weeks at No.1: **1**

THE SECOND TRACK FROM THE NOW million-selling album, *A Present For Everyone*, was a quality three-track CD single which contained a cover of The Undertones' debut hit, 'Teenage Kicks' and a video with a fly-on-the-wall style documentary of the boys getting ready to take the stage at one of their concerts.

At the beginning of 2004 Busted were nominated for three Brit Awards for which they won two; Best British Breakthrough Artist and Best Pop Act.

'Who's David?' was written by James and future McFly member Tom Fletcher during their 2003 tour. "James and Tom were in a room at the Lowry Hotel in Manchester," recalled Charlie. "All my mates were at the gig that night so I was downstairs in the bar having a drink and every so often I'd run upstairs and see how James and Tom were getting on. They finished the song at eight o'clock the next morning." The song tells the story of a jealous and paranoid boyfriend who goes through his girlfriend's mobile phone only to find a stack of texts from someone called David.

If you're wondering who David is, James explains, "It isn't about anyone at all. I just chose that name because it rhymed with 'invaded'."

973 Peter Andre
Mysterious Girl

Label & Cat No.: **A&E PA 001CDX**

Producer: **Ollie J**

Writers: **Peter Andre / Oliver Jacobs / Phillip Jacobs / Glen Goldsmith / Bubbler Ranx**

Date reached No.1: **6 March 2004**

Weeks at No.1: **1**

AT FIRST PETER ANDRE CALLED HIS song, 'Mysterious Man', but his record company said that he might be considered gay so he changed it to 'Mysterious Girl'. He told his Australian girlfriend, Katharine Maddock, that she was his mysterious girl as he couldn't be seen with a permanent companion. He shot a video in Thailand and he was to lose Katharine when he had a relationship with the girl in the film, Jan Pen. Not to mention an actress from *Home And Away*, a female wrestler, Mel B, Caprice and Melanie from All Saints etc etc etc. An impressive collection of conquests but not up to Eddie Fisher standards.

In 1995 Peter Andre had recorded 'Mysterious Girl' with a rap from Bubbler Ranx. On its first outing, it only reached number 53, but it was reissued in 1996 and went to number two with Bubbler receiving a label credit. It sold two million copies worldwide but Bubbler was a mysterious man as nobody knew much about him.

By 1999 Peter Andre's career was belly up and his records were in bargain bins. He had had his moment in *The Sun* and in 2000, he returned to Australia to work at his parent's Koolamara Beach Resort on the Gold Coast. When they sold the business in 2002, he moved to Cyprus to work at his brother's gym. The only news was a fling with Tania from *Big Brother*: maybe he realised that a reality show might be the way back.

Early in 2004 he joined the other contestants on *I'm A Celebrity... Get Me Out Of Here!* and was at an advantage as he lived in Australia. It was not the spiders and cockroaches that made his blood pressure rise but the pneumatic model, Jordan, and soon the public was wondering – did they or didn't they? When he leftthe camp, he fell ill having being bitten by a spider on one of his tasks. The winner was Kerry Katona, a founder member of Atomic Kitten.

Chris Moyles on Radio1 mounted a campaign to return 'Mysterious Girl' to the charts. The single gave him his third number one and he has been able to tour again and make new records for East West. While in the rainforest, he claimed to have written 'Insania' (3), while dreaming, the word being a mixture of insane and mania. However, he was peddling a song he had demoed in 1999. Was Peter Andre suffering from amnesia as well as insania?

974 Britney Spears
Toxic

Label & Cat No.: **Jive 8286602092**

Producers: **Bloodshy / Avant (Christian Karlsson / Pontus Winnberg)**

Writers: **Cathy Dennis / Christian Karlsson / Pontus Winnberg / Henrik Jonback**

Date Reached No.1: **13 March 2004**

Weeks at No.1: **1**

BRITNEY'S PRIVATE LIFE WAS ANYTHING but. Her ongoing romance with Justin Timberlake continued to fill the gossip columns but by the end of 2002 they were no longer together, although they admitted they still had feelings for each other. At the beginning of 2003 rumours were flying that Britney was now dating Limp Bizkit's lead singer, Fred Durst. On Saturday January 3, 2004 in a spur-of-the-minute decision, Britney married her childhood sweetheart, Jason Allen Alexander. The marriage lasted just 55 hours before a judge granted them an annulment. Her lawyer said, "Britney Spears lacked understanding of her actions to the extent that she was incapable of agreeing to the marriage." James, who agreed, commented, "It was just crazy, man!"

In 2003 Britney released her fourth album, *In The Zone*, which reached number 13. With this, and her public kiss with Madonna, Britney was ready to show the world she'd grown up.

'Toxic' was produced by the Swedish production duo Bloodshy and Avant, alias Christian Karlsson and Pontus Winnberg. The pair had already produced hit singles for Christina Milian, Samantha Mumba and Ms Dynamite. The CD single also came with a remix from Armand Van Helden.

The accompanying video was similar to that of her former lover Justin Timberlake's hit 'Cry Me A River'. Whereas Justin just follows his cheating ex, Britney's detective-style production sees her chase her cheating partner (played by actor Martin Henderson) through various European locations, with the intention of killing him by way of a poisonous potion. Was this the effect Justin really had on her we wonder?

975 DJ Casper
Cha Cha Slide

Label & Cat No.: **All Around The World CDGLOBE 329**

Producer: **Hardino**

Writer: **Marvel Thompson**

Date Reached No.1: **20 March 2004**

Weeks at No.1: **2**

DJ CASPER, WHO IS ALSO KNOWN AS 'Mr C The Slide Man', was born William Perry in Chicago, Illinois in 1965. "I got the name Casper from when I was young and roller-skated a lot. I would always wear white whatever I did stage-wise."

The opening line to 'Cha Cha Slide' states, "This is something new". Well it's not. "I wrote 'Cha Cha Slide' in 1996 as an aerobics workout programme for a gym trainer friend of mine, David Wilson, and I recorded and released my own version in 1998," remembered Casper. It made little impact. In 2003 it surfaced in clubs across Europe and All Around The World Records picked it up for a UK release.

Although Casper wrote the song, it is credited to Marvel Thompson, a Chicago entrepreneur involved with M.O.B. Records, to which Casper was originally signed.

The infectious 2-step novelty song entered the chart at number two, having received virtually no airplay on mainstream radio. In an ever-sliding singles market, the song made the rare one step climb to number one, the first time a song had climbed to the top since DJ Ötzi in the spring of 2001.

In the Fifties it was common for numerous versions of the same song to appear in the chart simultaneously. These days it's almost unheard of. One exception was 'Macarena' by the similarly titled Los Del Rio and Los Del Mar. Customers who went into a shop and didn't specify which version they wanted could have ended up with either. Los Del Mar's version stiffed at number 43, whereas Los Del Rio's version peaked at number two in the UK and spent 14 weeks at number one in the US.

It's a similar story with 'Cha Cha Slide'. DJ Casper's version may have lost out on a few sales to a cover version by the mysterious MC Jig, but Casper reached number one whilst the cover only reached number 33. "I didn't appreciate his version," said Casper, "because he was trying to make people think he was the creator but he used my music and my words."

The dance moves to 'Cha Cha Slide' involve Casper getting the audience to slide to the left and then to the right as well as asking them to clap, hop and stomp their feet. The follow-up single was another party favourite. Adopting the same instructing method, Casper, using a sample from the Gap Band original, rowed up the chart with a remake of 'Oops Upside Your Head'.

976 Usher featuring Lil' Jon And Ludacris Yeah!

Label & Cat No.: **Arista 82876606002**

Producers: **Jonathan Smith**

Writers: **Jonathan Smith / Sean Garrett / Patrick Smith / Christopher Bridges**

Date Reached No.1: **27 March 2004**

Weeks at No.1: **2**

In 1998 Usher was offered his first movie part as Gabe Santora in *The Faculty*, a story of school children who discover that their teachers are from another planet. The following year he played Lester Dewitt in *Light It Up*, another school story about a bunch of kids who are trying to improve the conditions of their run-down high school. Later the same year he appeared as a DJ in yet another school movie, *She's All That*, in which two school-mates have a bet that one of them can transform the school geek into a prom queen.

'Nice & Slow' was the follow-up to his first number one, 'You Make Me Wanna...' and although it only reached number 24 in the UK, it gave Usher his first US number one. Following the movies he returned to music and spent most of 2000 recording his new album *8701*, taken from the date it was released in America. It was the album that introduced Usher to a new audience with his laid back, mellow, yet catchy choruses. The first single, 'Pop Ya Collar' made number two here followed by 'U Remind Me' (3) and 'U Got It Bad' (5) which both topped the US chart.

Usher then began a highly publicised relationship with Rozonda 'Chilli' Thomas from TLC. Their equally highly publicised break up over a year later would take Usher's music to new heights as his next album, *Confessions*, was mostly written about the split. Similarly when Justin Timberlake and Britney Spears broke up a couple of years earlier, the media's assistance in keeping their names in the spotlight worked wonders for their music, especially for Justin's *Justified* album.

The first single, 'Yeah', which spent 12 weeks at the top of the US singles chart, saw Usher team up with the Atlanta-born producer and R&B singers Lil' Jon (born Jonathan Smith) and Ludacris (born Christopher Bridges). 'Yeah' has also been described in America as the first 'crunk' record. Lil' Jon's explanation of crunk is, "A state of high energy." Usher added, "Me and Lil' Jon worked together a long time ago, before crunk took off. I brought Jon in because I love to be right in the middle of what's hot and no-one had really done a crunk record before."

977 McFly 5 Colours In Her Hair

Label & Cat No.: **Universal MCSTD 40357**

Producer: **Craig Hardy**

Writer: **Tom Fletcher / Danny Jones / James Bourne**

Date Reached No.1: **10 April 2004**

Weeks at No.1: **2**

McFly got off to a McFlying start as protégés of Busted. Like Busted, they write their own songs and play their own instruments. "I just think it's good to introduce a bit of musicianship into the pop world, I think people are bored of boy bands," said McFly's guitarist and co-vocalist Danny Jones, a member of one himself.

McFly are Danny Jones (born Bolton, Lancs, March 12, 1986), vocalist/guitarist Tom Fletcher (born Harrow, Middx, July 17, 1985), bass player Dougie Poyner (born Orsett, Essex, November 30, 1987) and drummer Harry Judd (born Chelmsford, Essex, December 23, 1985).

Tom and Danny met in 2002 in a pub where Danny used to play songs by The Verve. They both auditioned for Busted but neither got the gig even though Tom was short listed but lost out to Charlie. However, Busted's manager signed Tom as a songwriter and he wrote four of their hits including three number ones. But Tom wanted his own band, so the following year he got together with Danny and they placed an ad in the *NME* for two more members.

Taking their name from Michael J. Fox's character, Marty McFly, in the 1985 film *Back To The Future* was Tom's idea. "I was with Busted when they were doing a soundcheck for 'Year 3000' and the name sprung into my head. Danny wasn't sure at first, but we watched the film again and when he saw the bit where Biff crashes into the side of a manure truck which had the name D. Jones on the side, that clinched it."

McFly had already had a taste of being at number one before they had released any of their own material. They collaborated with Busted on a revival of 'Build Me Up Buttercup', which appeared on the B-side of Busted's 'Crashed The Wedding'.

'5 Colours In Her Hair', which was co-written by James from Busted, was inspired by a Channel 4 soap called *As If*. "It's about this gorgeous actress with dreadlocks and piercings called Emily Corrie who plays Sooz," explained Tom. "Basically Danny and I both fancied her because she's got this 'no bullshit' attitude which we also found attractive." The song was coupled with Busted and McFly duetting on a cover of 'Lola'.

Danny's mum was also pleased with their success. "She's a hairdresser," explained Danny, "and she kept getting all these girls coming in and asking to have five colours put in their hair."

McFly took their name from a character in the film Back To The Future; *left to right: Tom Fletcher, Danny Jones and Dougie Poyner*

978 Eamon
F**k It (I Don't Want You Back)

Label & Cat No.: **Jive 828766 08520**

Producers: **Mark Passey / Milk Lee**

Writers: **Eamon Doyle / Kirk Robinson / Mark Passey**

Date reached No.1: **24 April 2004**

Weeks at No.1: **4**

THE FIRST KNOWN USE OF THE WORD 'fuck' was in 1503 in the poetry of William Dunbar and so Eamon's single could have been paraded as the 500th anniversary edition. The expletive 'fuck' has been used as a crude description of sexual intercourse and the phrase, 'fuck it!' meaning to 'to hell with it' for half as long. 'Fuck' was banned from polite conversation and from broadcasting for many years and the first person to say 'fuck' on the BBC was the theatre critic, Ken Tynan, in an arts programme in 1965. The generally held view is that John Lennon was the first person to include 'fuck' in a song on a commercial record with 'Working Class Hero' (1970) but surprisingly and probably much to his chagrin, Al Stewart, had beaten him to it with 'Love Chronicles' (1969). How extraordinary that a gentle folkie should have the edge on John Lennon, Frank Zappa, The Fugs and The Rolling Stones.

Eamon

The floodgates opened and Dory Previn, Jimmy Webb, Joni Mitchell, Nilsson, Buffy Sainte-Marie, Commander Cody & His Lost Planet Airmen, and Monty Python's Flying Circus were soon incorporating the word into their songs. In 1971 Isaac Hayes was jokingly prevented from saying 'motherfucker' in 'Theme From Shaft' and in 1973 the Rolling Stones recorded a song about groupies, 'Starfucker', although they were made to call it 'Star Star' on the track listing. During the punk era, Wayne County & The Electric Chairs topped the indie charts with 'Fuck Off' and The Dead Kennedys, made the Top 40 with 'Too Drunk To Fuck' but their name was thought more objectionable than the song.

From the mid-Eighties, Britain and America have been in a moral panic as the expletives have encroached into standard conversation, and both rap and heavy metal are very heavy with four letter (and 12 letter) words. In 1993 Rage Against The Machine's Top 30 single, 'Killing In The Name', contained 20 fucks and Bruno Brookes was reprimanded after playing it on Radio 1.

It was inevitable that there would be a chart-topper with 'fuck' in its title and it is only surprising that it took so long. Eminem was the most likely suspect, but it turned out to be someone with a similar name, Eamon, another white rapper but with a softer sound. The Staten Islander had been singing for over 10 years, part of the time with his father's doo-wop group where he developed a love of Frankie Lymon.

Eamon wrote a regretful song after discovering that his girlfriend was cheating on him. It was a soul ballad that combined Smokey Robinson with rap and he called it 'F★★k It (I Don't Want You Back)'. The 20 instances of 'fuck' were bleeped for airplay by taking the word and reversing it whenever it occurred, giving the record a curious splicing sound. The six instances of 'shit' were bleeped and also the reference to head, although that had been permitted in Lou Reed's 'Walk On The Wild Side' (1974). The recent black US term for a prostitute 'ho' was permitted, and Eamon has called his music, Ho-Wop.

There were seven versions of the song on the hit single – the dirty version, the clean version and various other mixes and remixes. Eamon's single also did very well in America and the album, *I Don't Want You Back*, included the titles 'Get Off My Dick' and 'I'd Rather Fuck With You'. The follow-up, 'Love Them', which sampled The Flamingos' 'I Only Have Eyes For You', had no swear words and missed the Top 20 completely. Eamon promoted the album on stadium dates, opening for Britney Spears. "I come from a nice home," he said, "I'm not talking about gang-banging or guns or stuff like that because that's not what I'm about."

979 Frankee
F.U.R.B. (F U Right Back)

Label & Cat No.: **All Around The World CDGLOBE 355**

Producers: **Ty Real / Jessi Jordan**

Writers: **Eamon Doyle / Mark Passy / Kirk Robinson / Jennifer Graziano / Frankee**

Date reached No.1: **22 May 2004**

Weeks at No.1: **3**

WAS IT A MASSIVE PUBLICITY HYPE OR the real thing? Eamon's single of 'F★★k It (I Don't Want You Back)' recounted the problems with his girlfriend, and instead of suing him, the stunning-looking Frankee, also from Staten Island, thought she wouldn't get mad, but get even. She retaliated with 'F U Right Back', which, amongst other things, said that she was faking orgasms and accused him of having pubic lice (another first for a number one record): "You thought you could really make me moan / I had better sex alone" and "I'm glad I didn't catch your crabs", respectively.

Eamon was said to be surprised by her outburst, but, and it's a big BUT, how come Frankee was allowed to use the same backing tape and simply write new words to Eamon's song? As it stands, Eamon's name is on a song which portrays him as a lousy lover. So let's just say, in a manner of speaking, they are in bed with each other.

Frankee began singing at age of six and she was taking both singing and dancing lessons as a teenager. She went to the University of Tampa but left after a year to continue singing in New York. Her instincts were correct and her demo tapes led to offers from several record labels.

What's more, she had been recording long before her single or even Eamon's. She had been working with several well-known songwriters and producers for her debut album, which was about her and her friends' relationships, *The Good, The Bad And The Ugly*. She commented, "The most important thing is that the material had to be great and that the songs had an authenticity, a believability about them. I'm a 20-year-old living in New York so I'm bound to have seen and been through some stuff because New Yorkers generally are exposed to a lot."

980 Mario Winans featuring Enya and P.Diddy I Don't Wanna Know

Label & Cat No.: **Bad Boy MCSTD 40369**

Producer: **Mario Winans**

Writer: **Mario Winans / Enya / Nicholas Ryan / Roma Ryan / Michael Jones / Chauncey Hawkins / Erick Sermon / Parish Smith**

Date Reached No.1: **12 June 2004**

Weeks at No.1: **2**

THE WINANS ARE A 10-STRONG GOSPEL singing family from Detroit, Michigan. They are no relation to The Winans who had a hit with 'Let My People Go' in 1985. Cece and Bebe had already had some UK chart success, duetting with Whitney Houston on 'Count On Me' and featuring on Eternal's number one 'I Wanna Be The Only One', respectively. But Mario looks set to become a chart regular.

Mario, born on August 29, 1974, showed an early interest in learning the piano but it was drums and percussion that excited him the most. "I was always banging on pots and pans with wire coat hangers," he remembered. His gospel-singing mother, Vickie, has a recording studio at home and Mario taught himself to operate the equipment that would later give him an interest in production. After he graduated he produced an album for a local gospel group which led to a chance meeting with top producer Dallas Austin. He was signed as an in-house producer for the label and worked with R. Kelly, Mary J. Blige, Lil' Kim and Jennifer Lopez.

He enjoyed production work, and never seriously considered a career as a solo recording artist, but in 1997 he signed to Motown and released his debut album *Story Of My Heart*. It made little impact and the only single released from it, 'Don't Know', only scraped into the lower end of the US R&B chart. A mutual friend then introduced him to Puff Daddy who signed him to his Bad Boy label. In 1998 he played drums on Puff and Jimmy Page's number two hit 'Come With Me', which featured in the film *Godzilla*. Two years later he was a guest vocalist on Puff Daddy's US hit single and ode to God, 'Best Friend'.

Mario started recording his debut solo album, *Hurt No More*, in 2002. "It's all about relationships," he said. "We all have a heart and sometimes you have to look deeper into what we're saying and doing to the people we care about."

The debut single, 'I Don't Wanna Know', a song about a man who has to deal with his girlfriend's infidelity, features a rap from Puff, now known as P.Diddy and a sample from Enya's 1986 recording 'Boadecia', which the Fugees also sampled in 'Ready Or Not'. "'Boadecia' is one of my favourite songs by Enya," said Mario. "I discovered it on the soundtrack to the film *Sleepwalkers* in 1992. It's a very moving song which really touches me." The album reached number three, but the single sold 61,000 copies and entered the chart at number one.

The second single, 'Never Really Was' failed to make the same impact and missed the Top 40 completely. However, keeping the story going, an answer version by The Pirates featuring Enya, Shola Ama, Naila Boss & Ishani called 'You Should Really Know' entered the chart the same week and reached number eight.

981 Britney Spears Everytime

Label & Cat No.: **Jive 82876626202**

Producer: **Guy Sigsworth**

Writers: **Britney Spears / Annette Stamatelatos**

Date Reached No.1: **26 June 2004**

Weeks at No.1: **1**

WITH SINGLES SALES AT MORE OR LESS an all-time low, Britney's third single from *Into The Zone*, 'Everyday' sold a mere 54,000 copies to reach number one.

The same month 'Everytime' topped the chart, Britney announced her engagement to dancer Kevin Federline who has two daughters from a previous relationship. She said, "I've kissed a bunch of frogs and finally found my prince." She spent the summer recovering from yet another knee injury, which forced the cancellation of her latest tour. Britney put the time towards compiling her forthcoming album due for release in November, *Greatest Hits: My Prerogative*.

In September Britney was due to make a cameo appearance in the film *Pauly Shore Is Dead* alongside Eminem, Whoopi Goldberg, Sean Penn, Fred Durst, Pamela Anderson and Snoop Dogg. It tells the story of a Hollywood actor/comedian who loses everything in the world and is forced to move back to live with his mum. One day he climbs into the attic and the ghost of a famous dead comedian appears to advise Pauly to kill himself as he would be better received as the comic genius who died before his time. Instead, Pauly fakes his own death, the media goes wild and the world is suddenly talking about Pauly Shore – which is all he wanted in the first place. For the finale, Pauly tried to persuade Britney to marry Kevin Federline at which point she pulled out of the movie because she claimed movie fans would laugh at her and not with her.

In September 2004 Britney recorded her new single, a cover of Bobby Brown's 'My Prerogative' and the accompanying video showed her getting married to Kevin. Three days later she did it for real.

982 McFly
Obviously

Label & Cat No.: **Universal MCSTD 40364**

Producer: **Hugh Padgham**

Writer: **Tom Fletcher / Danny Jones / James Bourne**

Date Reached No.1: **3 July 2004**

Weeks at No.1: **1**

ALTHOUGH ALL FOUR MEMBERS OF McFly share a three-storey house in north London (Tom, the key songwriter has the whole of the third floor to himself), it was actually a hotel room that Tom and Danny once shared that became the inspiration for the title of their 13-track debut album, *Room On The 3rd Floor*.

Two weeks before it hit the shops, McFly released 'Obviously' as the second single. It was a less energetic track than '5 Colours In Her Hair', with harmonies that reflected the music that Tom in particular had grown up with. He enjoyed The Beatles and The Beach Boys and said, "I've always loved the fact that there's a really unique quality to Sixties music."

The album sold 61,000 copies, enough to enter the album chart at the top, something their mentors, Busted, had yet to achieve.

A big selling point for McFly was the fact that their B-sides, often cover versions, weren't on the album. 'Obviously' was coupled with the Undertones' 'Get Over You', which was on the album, but was a hidden track and can only be accessed by holding the reverse button at the beginning of track one. If you play it through a computer, you have no chance. The third single, 'That Girl', which reached number two, featured a close cover of The Beatles' 'She Loves You'.

At the end of November 2004, the album's title track became the fourth single. It peaked at number five and, again, came with a cover version, this time doing justice to Queen's 1979 hit 'Crazy Little Thing Called Love'

At this year's Record Of The Year show, McFly attained second place for '5 Colours In Her Hair', only beaten by Busted's 'Thunderbirds'.

983 Usher
Burn

Label & Cat No.: **LaFace 82876633212**

Producers: **Jermaine Dupri**

Writers: **Jermaine Dupri / Bryan Michael Cox / Usher Raymond**

Date Reached No.1: **10 July 2004**

Weeks at No.1: **2**

CONFESSIONS SOLD 1.1 MILLION COPIES in America in the first week – the biggest first week sale for an R&B act. Chilli claimed during a radio interview that they split because Usher had cheated on her. Whether it's true or not is unknown, but much of Usher's album tells the story.

'Burn' was the second single lifted from the album. Was it a track written about his former lover, TLC's Chilli? Usher offers, "I wrote 'Burn' in 2003, so it's not written about Chilli, but it does apply in a way." Usher confessed in an interview with VH1 of the first single released from his latest album. "It's a product of growing up. No one can really explain that gut-wrenching feeling you get when you're going through it."

As 'Burn' hit the UK chart, Usher embarked on his latest UK tour, which he called the *Truth Tour*. 'Burn' also replaced 'Yeah' at the top of the US chart and he repeated that feat a few weeks later when his next single, 'Confessions Part II', replaced 'Burn'. *Confessions* was the biggest-selling album in America in 2004 having sold over five millions copies in the US alone.

There was talk of MTV making a film version of *Confessions*, but it came to nothing. There were also plans for Usher to appear as Jackie Wilson in Ray, a Ray Charles biopic, but his part never materialised although the film did. 'Confessions Part II' was his next single and it was coupled with 'My Boo', a duet with Alicia Keys, which stopped at number five in the UK, but at the time of going to press, was still at the top of the US chart having already spent four weeks there.

984 Shapeshifters
Lola's Theme

Label & Cat No.: **Positiva CDTIVS 207**

Producers: **Simon Marlin / Max Reich**

Writers: **Simon Marlin / Max Reich / Karen Poole / Gianni Bini / Fulvio Permiola / Patrick Moten**

Date Reached No.1: **24 July 2004**

Weeks at No.1: **1**

THROUGHOUT THE 21ST CENTURY THE music press have speculated that house music is dying and the clubbing days are over, then every once in a while a tune comes along that proves them wrong. It happened with Spiller, Modjo and Room 5, among many others that didn't reach the top. The Shapeshifters' song became the summer anthem of 2004.

The Shapeshifters are English-born Simon Marlin and Swedish-born Max Reich. Simon is a DJ and in 1995 was an A&R manager for a small independent label. "I met Max when I was DJing in Sweden," he recalled. "Max played me his stuff and I signed him to the label straight away. Max had been DJing since he was 14 and had played alongside Carl Cox and Laurent Garnier. We've been working together ever since and in 2003, with Simon's wife, Lola, we set up the house label, Nocturnal Groove." He also runs the London nightclub of the same name. "That's where we decided to form the Shapeshifters," a name they took from a race of people known as changelings in the *Star Trek* spin-off series, *Deep Space Nine*. A Shapeshifter is someone who can change themselves into anything they want.

Later in 2003 Lola became the inspiration for an instrumental track they had written. "'Lola's Theme' was a working title due to the original string sample being taken from one of Lola's favourite records. It just stuck and gave us the inspiration to add a vocal about her," Simon explained. The string sample was taken from 'What About My Love' by Johnnie Taylor, a track from his 1982 album *Just Ain't Good Enough*.

Promotional copies first appeared in November 2003 and around the same time they attended the annual Miami Winter Music Conference where it was showcased and well received, but Simon felt that it needed some lyrics. "If house music is to survive it needs to be represented by daytime radio and a vocal track is usually better than an instrumental," he remarked. The vocal sample was pinched from 'Rock Me Tonight' by F.O.S. (Fathers Of Soul), "But we changed around the order of the lyrics to make our own line. 'I'm a different person, turn my world around' was not in the original," Simon added. They also brought in female singer, Cookie, a former member of the London Community Gospel Choir who had previously sung with Kylie Minogue, Depeche Mode and Ms Dynamite.

'Lola's Theme' sold 52,000 in its first week in the shops and entered the chart at number one. The chart rules state that up to 40 minutes of music is allowed if the CD single contains only one song, so the Shapeshifters utilised that time with various mixes including one by Victor Caldrone and one by Eric Prydz who just two months later registered his first chart topper.

Simon continues to DJ at Nocturnal and the pair do P.A.s as the Shapeshifters. It's difficult to follow-up such a huge anthem and indeed, Spiller, Modjo and Room 5 all struggled, but as Simon said, "We're really busy DJing at the moment and we're working on a mix compilation, but we will get round to the album soon and then we'll look to release a single from it."

985 The Streets
Dry Your Eyes

Label & Cat No.: **Locked On/679 679L077CD1**

Producer: **Mike Skinner**

Writer: **Mike Skinner**

Date Reached No.1: **31 July 2004**

Weeks at No.1: **1**

In 1997, at the age of 19, Birmingham-born street poet Mike Skinner, armed with his sampler, followed his girlfriend to Australia. They soon split up, but Mike stayed on without her, and spent the best part of a year in Sydney, working in bars.

On his return to the UK he gave himself the moniker The Streets. ("It's such a good name, because it's just what you see wherever you go. It's just working-class England," was his reasoning) and attempted to start up his own record label. When that failed, he began working on his debut album, *Original Pirate Material* (2002), which was picked up by the UK's premier 2-step/garage/hip-hop label, Locked On. Most of it was recorded in his old bedroom at his mother's house. If you listen carefully, you can hear her asking her son to 'turn the music down, it's dinner time' on the track 'Turn The Page'.

Original Pirate Material won Mike rave reviews and it was nominated for a Mercury Music Prize, although it was awarded to Ms Dynamite's *A Little Deeper*. Stateside, *Rolling Stone* called it 'The number one debut album of the year'. Being a white rapper has had critics naming him the British Eminem, something Mike disagrees with. "The most predictable thing I could do would be to come out and say I don't really like Eminem because I keep getting compared to him, but I quite like him, you know. He's a really good rapper." Although Mike's influences were De La Soul and The Beastie Boys, The Streets has a distinctive English feel to it. He is a storyteller, an Ian Dury for the new millennium.

Several singles were released from his debut, although none charted. It was not until 2004 that The Streets finally achieved commercial success with his second album, *A Grand Don't Come For Free*. Also nominated for a Mercury Music Prize (this time losing out to Franz Ferdinand's self-titled debut), its first single, 'Fit But You Know It' received extensive airplay and reached number four.

Carefully selecting this weepy ballad as the second single was a sharp move. It brought The Streets a whole new audience and gave both his albums a new lease of life. *Original Pirate Material* achieved its highest position (10) and *A Grand Don't Come For Free* went all the way to the top.

Coldplay's Chris Martin performed on the original version, but as he explained, "There was this version of it in which I sang the chorus, but I didn't think it was as good as the version where Mike sang the chorus. Then he didn't think that was as good as the version where some other dude sang the chorus, so neither him nor me sings on the chorus."

With Mike's new-found fame came an accusation from songwriter Michael Gagliano who claimed it was his orchestral arrangement on 'Dry Your Eyes', taken from one of his own compositions, 'Yesterday And Today Part 1'. Mike denied it and claimed to have never heard the track. A statement by his record company read, "The strings in The Streets single 'Dry Your Eyes' were taken from a sample CD which provides royalty-free samples for artists. This is standard practice nowadays."

986 Busted
Thunderbirds / 3AM

Label & Cat No.: **Universal MCSTD 40375**

Producers: **Steve Power : The Matrix (Lauren Christy Scott Spock / Graham Edwards)**

Writers: **James Bourne / Matthew Willis / Charlie Simpson / Tom Fletcher / Barry Gray : Lauren Christy / Scott Spock / Graham Edwards / Charlie Simpson / Matthew Willis / James Bourne**

Date Reached No.1: **7 August 2004**

Weeks at No.1: **2**

'Air Hostess' was the third single from *A Present For Everyone* and reached number two behind Eamon, but the lads were happy with that as their album had now gone triple platinum.

Universal chose to pick a fourth track for single release. Had '3AM' been released as a single A-side, it's unlikely that it would have made number one. But because it was coupled with the previously unavailable 'Thunderbirds', the theme to the new adventure movie, it became their highest first week sale with 70,000 copies going over the counter.

'3AM' was co-written and produced by the musicians Lauren Christy (piano), Scott Spock (trumpet) and Graham Edwards (guitar), the

Scottish team collectively known as The Matrix. Lauren and Graham (who was a former touring bass player in the Eighties and has worked with Adam & The Ants, Mick Jagger and Go West) are married. In the early Nineties he moved to Los Angeles and turned his hand to songwriting as well as joining the band Dollshead, which is where he met Scott. The trio's first writing project was for Christina Aguilera's *My Kind Of Christmas* album (2000). Their manager put them in touch with a then unknown Canadian singer called Avril Lavigne and they wrote a number of tracks for her *Let's Go* album, including the hit single 'Complicated'. "We came up with The Matrix because it was easier than keep describing ourselves every time and it's a name for the womb which everything comes from," explained Christy. "It's not inspired by the film, that came later."

Tom Fletcher, who narrowly missed out to Charlie for a place in the band, still wanted to be a member of a band, so in 2004 he became the lead singer and guitarist with McFly. James returned the songwriting compliment by co-penning their first three hit singles.

987 3 Of A Kind
Baby Cakes

Label & Cat No.: **Relentless RELDX 6**

Producers: **3 Of A Kind**

Writers: **Liana Caruana / Nicholas Gallante / Marc Portelli**

Date Reached No.1: **21August 2004**

Weeks at No.1: **1**

3 OF A KIND WERE SO NAMED BECAUSE, although all three members were quite different in character and looks, when they came together musically, they were very similar.

The 2-step garage trio from east London are Miz Tipzta (born Liana Caruana), Devine (born Nicholas Gallente) and Marky P (born Marc Portelli).

Tipzta, a former NHS hospital worker, wrote the lyrics in 1998 after watching the film *Baby Cakes* starring Ricki Lake. Tipzta said, "The words are written about someone I knew, but generally it's based on the film's love story. Basically, the girl knows the man is 'the one' but he doesn't realise it." She had put it aside and forgotten about it. She rediscovered it in 2002 and sang them to her friend, Devine, whom she had met at the hospital, but was now a DJ on a London pirate radio station, Supreme FM. Devine's friend, Marky P was a DJ and producer and he played Devine an instrumental track he had written. At that point, Devine had the idea to match Tipzta's song to Marky P's tune.

The trio all met up for the first time on the day they recorded the track in March 2003. A copy found its way to Jiggy B, a DJ on an east London pirate station, Rinse FM, who began playing the short version on the radio and the Angel Farringdon mix in the clubs. DJs from other local pirate stations got copies and began championing it too. Marky P recalled, "I remember that I saw the whole club I was in singing the chorus. I knew we had to release it and it would be a big hit."

3 Of A Kind went into the studio to record their debut album and are planning to release the follow-up single in February 2005.

988 Natasha Bedingfield
These Words

Label & Cat No.: **Photogenic 82876639182**

Producers: **Steve Kipner / Andrew Frampton / Wayne Wilkins**

Writers: **Steve Kipner / Andrew Frampton / Wayne Wilkins / Natasha Bedingfield**

Date Reached No.1: **28 August 2004**

Weeks at No.1: **2**

"I DIDN'T WIN THE LOTTERY, YOU KNOW – I worked hard for this," says Natasha Bedingfield of her success. As Daniel's younger sister, the accusations from the media of 'cashing in' are inevitable, although Natasha insists, "We agreed early on that Dan would not help me to write or produce anything. That way I couldn't be accused of using him and his connections."

Natasha, Daniel and their youngest sister, Nikola, formed their first band, DNA Algorhythm, when they were all in their teens. Their influences were mainly contemporary R&B and dance artists. The trio performed at some of their social worker parents' counselling seminars.

Her first solo release, 'Single', a song she co-wrote embracing the advantages of being unattached, reached number three in May 2004. 'These Words' is a love song explaining the problems with writing a love song. It describes the struggle in finding inspiration: "Read some Byron, Shelley and Keats, recited it over a hip-hop beat, I'm having trouble saying what I mean, with dead poets and drum machines." Natasha explained, "It's about trying to express love in a clever way, but at the end of the day the only way to really say it is 'I love you'. Even though it's cheesy and it's clichéd, it's the only way to say it."

The number one status for 'These Words' means that Natasha and Daniel are the first sister and brother to individually hit the top spot, a feat not even managed by The Jacksons or The Osmonds. However, Eden Kane ('Well I Ask You', 1961) and Peter Sarsdedt ('Where Do You Go To (My Lovely)', 1969) were the first ever brothers to achieve number one singles (and almost made it a hat trick, but brother Robin's 'My Resistance Is Low' stalled at number three in 1976).

Unwritten was released in September 2004 and entered the chart in pole position, making Natasha only the third female artist, along with Annie Lennox and Bonnie Tyler, to have her debut album enter at number one. It features a collaboration with smitten rapper, Bizarre, from D12, who claims to have never even heard of Natasha's famous sibling when he made the offer to work with her.

These words aren't entirely Natasha's own. Although she had a hand in the lyrics, it was co-written by the songwriting team made up of Steve Kipner, Andrew Frampton and Wayne Wilkins.

Steve was born in Cincinatti, Ohio and

Natasha Bedingford and her brother Daniel are the first siblings to reach number one individually

moved to Australia when he was one, with his mother and his US Air Force father, who was stationed in Brisbane. Steve received an early musical education. In the Sixties, his father Nat, signed the Bee Gees to his newly launched Spin Records label, whetting Steve's interest with the industry. Nat had written 'Too Much, Too Little, Too Late' for Johnny Mathis and Deniece Williams. Steve followed in his footsteps, and went on to co-write America's biggest selling hit single of the Eighties, Olivia Newton-John's 'Physical', and 'Hard Habit To Break' (8 UK, 3 US) for Chicago. Andrew has co-written hits for Steps, S Club 7 and Victoria Beckham.

989 Nelly featuring Jaheim
My Place / Flap Your Wings

Label & Cat No.: **Universal MCSTD 40379**

Producers: **Neptunes**

Writers: **Randy Edelman / Nelly / Dorian Moore / Eldra DeBarge / William DeBarge / Etterlene Jordan / Kenny Gamble / Leon Huff : Nelly / Pharrell Williams / Chad Hugo**

Date Reached No.1: **11 September 2004**

Weeks at No.1: **1**

NELLY HAD A VERY SUCCESSFUL 2003. His hit single 'IZ U' was featured in the Disney film *Haunted Mansion* and his recently launched clothing range, Vokal, was raking in large profits.

He spent the early part of 2004 recording not one, but two albums. Following Guns N' Roses in 1991 (*Use your Illusion I* and *Use your Illusion II*) and Bruce Springsteen in 1992 (*Human Touch* and *Lucky Town*), Nelly released *Sweat* and *Suit* on the same day.

"I started out recording one album," Nelly said, "but I had so much material that I did two. *Sweat* will feature club anthems and more hardcore material, whilst *Suit* is all about being grown up and sexy and offers more melodic tracks." The album also features contributions from Ronald Isley, Christina Aguilera and US country star, Tim McGraw.

The debut single, the double A-sided 'My Place' / 'Flap Your Wings' entered the UK chart at number one. The laidback 'My Place', which features Jaheim, samples 'Isn't It A Shame' by Patti LaBelle, 'Come Go With Me' by Teddy Pendergrass and a track he'd already sampled on his 2001 hit, 'Ride Wit Me', 'I Like It' by DeBarge. "I knew I had to get Jaheim on the track," Nelly said. "He is like the Teddy Pendergrass of our day. He is a crooner and sings with real emotion." The upbeat 'Flap Your Wings' is from *Sweat* and as Nelly commented, "I have always had great success in the clubs and I like to party, so when I heard the song, I liked it immediately, and I wanted to do it because I knew it would work."

In the summer of 2004 he extended his clothing range with the new line Apple Bottoms and his own energy drink, Pimp Juice. He is also getting back into films and, at time of going to press, was about to start filming a remake of Burt Reynolds' 1974 film *The Longest Yard* alongside Adam Sandler and Burt himself.

990 Brian McFadden
Real To Me

Label & Cat No.: **Sony 6753032**

Producer: **Guy Chambers**

Writer: **Guy Chambers / Brian McFadden**

Date Reached No.1: **18 September 2004**

Weeks at No.1: **1**

LEAVING THE UK'S MOST SUCCESSFUL ever boy band, with 12 number one singles and four chart-topping albums under their belt, was a brave move. But Brian, (who reverted to the original spelling of his name – he used Bryan as a stage name, as he thought it would make him stand out more, and he claimed the 'y' made it easier to sign autographs!) like Robbie Williams in Take That, never seemed to fit in with his former bandmates. More comfortable singing rockier songs, he revealed, "I have always been into guitar stuff, from Bryan Adams to Nirvana. I was drinking heavily towards the end of my days with the band and I wasn't happy. All I wanted to do was quit and get my life back."

Even on the first listen of 'Real To Me', Brian's disenchantment with Westlife is patently obvious. The album version contains the line, 'Bullshit dinners and the free champagne, Men in suits who think they know it all, No one knows me but they know my name, That's not real to me.'

"It's everything I hated about being in Westlife, from the hectic schedule, showbiz parties and non-stop travelling all over the place, and boring record company meetings. It's about feeling trapped everywhere I went, from the cars to the hotel rooms." He added, "It's only now I have kids that I realise what the important things in life are."

On hearing the news that his debut single had reached the top, 24-year-old football fan Brian remarked, "I feel like Coventry City have won the FA Cup."

The main reason Brian claimed to have left Westlife was to spend more time with his wife, former Atomic Kitten and Queen Of The Jungle in 2004's *I'm A Celebrity, Get Me Out Of Here!*, Kerry Katona and their two children. However, mere days after 'Real To Me' hit the top spot, the couple broke up, blaming the split on the fact they never saw each other due to work commitments.

As well as writing songs for Girls Aloud, Phixx and Ireland's entry for the 2004 Eurovision contest (it came an embarrassing 23rd out of 24), Brian is managing a young South African rock band, Franklin, a group he discovered performing at Sun City during his honeymoon.

Future ambitions for Brian include becoming the President of Ireland. "When the time comes, I'll run for president. I think I'd be very good but I'm too young at the

Brian McFadden

moment. Look at it this way, you get a huge house, a private jet and about 15 security guards."

991 Eric Prydz
Call On Me

Label & Cat No.: **Data DATA 68CDS**

Producer: **Eric Prydz**

Writers: **Eric Prydz / Steve Winwood / Will Jennings**

Date Reached No.1: **25 September 2004**

Weeks at No.1: **5 (2 runs)**

IN 1966 STEVE WINWOOD REGISTERED two number ones as guitarist, keyboard player and singer with the Spencer Davis Group. There followed a brief spell with Blind Faith and a seven-year stint with Traffic, before embarking on a solo career in 1975. After a seven-year wait he returned to the chart with the stunning 'While You See A Chance'. The follow-up, 'Valerie', missed the Top 50 until a remix of it made number 19 in 1987. Since then, apart from a couple of albums in the Nineties, *Refugees Of The Heart* and *Junction Seven*, Steve been out of the public eye. Thanks to Eric Prydz, he got back to number one.

Born in 1977 in Stockholm, aviophobe Eric Prydz (rhymes with quids) has rarely ventured out of his home country. In 2002 he was in the studio when he had the idea of using Steve Winwood's 'Valerie' as the basis for a dance tune to play as an end-of-the-night anthem at his resident club, Grodal. He tried it out, put it on to a CD-R and gave a copy to his friend DJ Falcon, asking him to put it in his set in the UK. The track found its way onto the internet which is how Steve Winwood first heard it. Although he liked the song, he wasn't happy that no permission had been sought, so he advised his lawyers to find and deal with the culprit. After it was discovered that Eric was behind it, Steve agreed to go back into the studio and re-record his vocals.

In 2004 Eric contributed a mix to the Shapeshifters' number one, 'Lola's Theme', and collaborated with Swedish producer, Steve Angello. Their single, 'Woz Not Woz' reached number 55. Later the same year, Eric signed to Data Records, a subsidiary of Ministry Of Sound.

Eric spent three weeks at the top before Robbie knocked him off for a week. When he returned to the top a week later, the tabloids made big news of the fact it was the lowest selling week ever for singles. They were happy to report that Eric climbed back to the top after only 23,000 copies were sold in the shops, but failed to mention that the track was available to download as well as appearing on numerous compilation albums.

992 Robbie Williams
Radio

Label & Cat No.: **Chrysalis CDCHSS 5156**

Producers: **Robbie Williams / Stephen Duffy / Andy Strange**

Writers: **Robbie Williams / Stephen Duffy**

Date Reached No.1: **16 October 2004**

Weeks at No.1: **1**

EMI'S DIRECTORS MUST HAVE BEEN worried when Robbie Williams fell out with his songwriting partner Guy Chambers, especially as the recriminations on both sides implied they would be unlikely to work together again for some years.

His new partner was Stephen 'Tin Tin' Duffy, a founder member of Duran Duran who had hits as Tin Tin and more recently had been part of The Lilac Time. Their first session was cancelled when Robbie realised that England was playing, but they were soon writing songs in Stephen's attic studio. In late 2003 and early 2004, over 40 songs were started and some completed. True to form, Robbie then lost interest and spent his time on the golf course. His Knebworth performance became the UK's biggest-selling music DVD to date and he recorded Dougal's voice for an animated film of *The Magic Roundabout*.

Robbie was amused when George Michael criticised his £80m deal with EMI, calling it "a huge betrayal of any sense of community." He commented, "I must have been a huge thorn in George's side for a long time. I'll bring it up at the next community meeting." Taking George Michael's *Patience* CD, he crossed out the title and renamed it *Lonely At The Top*.

EMI were issuing a *Greatest Hits* for Christmas 2004 and wanted to include at least two new tracks which could be singles. There were many contenders, including 'Boom Boom' and 'Misunderstood' and Robbie regarded 'Ghosts' as a potential 'Vienna'. However, he was very keen that the first single should sound different. The second single would be 'Misunderstood', which was for the soundtrack of *Bridget Jones: The Edge Of Reason*. In the end Robbie said, "I've always seen 'Radio' as an album track that's weird and great, but I like it for a single. You could play that song to anyone and they wouldn't say 'Robbie Williams'."

'Radio' is an eccentric and unusual song about an entertainer suffering madness. The first verse was complete but Robbie couldn't be bothered to write the second. Stephen did it for him, continuing with the random images, and Robbie liked it. The reason for 'effervescent' in the first verse is because Robbie thought this was the name of the group Evanescence. The lyric could be an ad for his *Greatest Hits* with the line, "Listen to the radio and you will hear the songs you know." The arrangement owed something to electro-pop of David Bowie and Human League with the campness of *Cabaret* thrown in.

Video thrills the 'Radio' star and the lavish but occasionally distasteful film shows Robbie intoning "I am the god of romance", surrounded by gymnastic cheerleaders wearing Lone Ranger masks. Something stirs in Robbie's leg and he sprouts a devil's tail. Ouch.

The single went straight in at number one. On the same week, Duran Duran entered at number five with '(Reach Up For The) Sunrise'. Robbie's single included a B-side, '1974', the year that he was born. He told of his unrequited love for Lisa Parkes, a girl a year above him at school. The package included a DVD on the making of the video. Someone remarks, "There's no you in tomorrow. "That's good," says Robbie, "That's the next line I need for the song I'm writing."

993 Ja Rule featuring R. Kelly & Ashanti Wonderful

Label & Cat No.: **Def Jam 9864606**

Producer: **Jimi Kendrix**

Writers: **Jeffrey Atkins / Kendred Smith / Irving Lorenzo / R. Kelly**

Date Reached No.1: **6 November 2004**

Weeks at No.1: **1**

If you thought LL Cool J was being conceited when he stated that his name stood for Ladies Love Cool James, then it's quite likely you'll think the same for Ja Rule. Ja, who was born in New York on February 29, 1976, says that his name is an acronym for Jeffrey Atkins Represents Unconditional Love's Existence.

Musically, the rapper grew up listening to Sam Cooke and Otis Redding, but there were other influences too. "In my home town I used to watch Run D.M.C. riding around in a black Cadillac. I loved the glamour of it all and the fact they didn't do drugs showed me that I could have that glamour too. It really opened my eyes."

He started rapping when he was 16 and began working with Jay-Z and the rap producer Irv Gotti. His debut album, *Venni Vetti Vecci* in 1999 showcased his rapping and reached number three in the US. The follow-up, *Rule 3:36*, in 2000 went to number one. After the rappers Tupac and Notorious B.I.G. were murdered he decided to concentrate more on singing than rapping. In the UK his first success came in 2001. The singles, 'Between Me And You', a duet with Christina Milian, reached number 26 and the follow-up, 'Livin' It Up', which sampled Stevie Wonder's 'Do I Do', peaked one place lower. However, it was his third single, 'Always On Time', a collaboration with female R&B singer Ashanti, that put him in the Top 10. The co-writer of that song, 7 Aurelius, said of Ja, "The amazing thing about him is that he never writes anything down during recording. He does it all from memory. Sometimes I'll have this song and he'll just walk in and start vibing to it in a deep, rich melodic way."

After a re-issue of 'Livin' It Up' went to number five in 2002, Ja then collaborated with Mary J. Blige on 'Rainy Dayz' and joined Jennifer Lopez on 'Ain't It Funny'. 'Wonderful' is a love song in which Ja Rule asks 'If I didn't have all the things I have, would you still love me?' It was the first single taken from his sixth album *R.U.L.E.*

Ashanti Douglas is a New York R&B singer who has had five UK Top 10 hits including three collaborations with Ja Rule. R. Kelly was touring with Jay-Z in 2004 when the two fell out. Kelly claimed at a show in Madison Square Garden that he saw two men brandishing guns and walked off stage. He later stated that members of Jay-Z's entourage had attacked him with pepper spray.

Like Will Smith, Ja has a taste for appearing in films and can be seen in *The Fast And The Furious* (2001), *Half Past Dead* (2003), *The Cookout* and *Back In The Day* (both 2004).

So is Ja Rule, who is married with two children, going to be around for years? He said in 2004, "I think I'm gonna retire after two more albums. I'm gonna be the first rapper to really retire. I don't want to stop making music because I love to make music. But I want to retire from the actual job of being an artist. I want to be able to star in movies and do soundtracks just because I love to do it."

994 Eminem Just Lose It

Label & Cat No.: **Interscope 2103183**

Producers: **Dr Dre / Mike Elizondo**

Writers: **Marshall Mathers III / Andre Young / Mike Elizondo / Mark Batson / Christopher Pope**

Date Reached No.1: **13 November 2004**

Weeks at No.1: **1**

Eminem's fourth album, *Encore*, was leaked onto the internet several weeks before its intended release. The record company, nervous of the potential millions in profit it could be losing, brought forward the release date. Nevertheless, the first single lifted from it, 'Just Lose It', went straight to number one here, Australia and Switzerland, and Top 10 in Hong Kong, Ireland, Japan, Lebanon, Lithuania, Turkey, United States and Venezuela, proving that this foul-mouthed rapper is one of the most popular artists in the world today.

This time it's a tirade against Michael Jackson, both lyrically and visually. In the second verse, Eminem raps, "Come here little kiddies, On my lap, Guess who's back with a brand new rap? And I don't mean rap as in a new case of child investigation accusation." The highly amusing, yet undeniably cruel accompanying video depicts Eminem as Michael. It begins with a scene similar to 'Billie Jean' and includes a re-enactment of the 1984 Pepsi incident in which Michael received serious burns due to a mishap. Further on, Eminem, dresses in complete Jackson garb, is on a dance floor, searching for his nose that has fallen off, mocking the former King Of Pop's excessive plastic surgery. The video ends with Eminem (as Michael) sitting on a bed with young boys jumping up and down on it, a derisive response to the singer's current legal position.

Naturally, Michael Jackson was not pleased, and attempted to get the clip banned. During a phone call to L.A. DJ, Steve Harvey, he stated, "I feel that it is outrageous and disrespectful. It is one thing to spoof, but it is another to be demeaning and insensitive. I've never had a problem with Eminem. I've admired him as an artist, and was shocked by this. The video was inappropriate and disrespectful to me, my children, my family and the community at large."

Asked by *Rolling Stone* if he was picking on Michael, Eminem replied, "I didn't do anything in the video that he hasn't done himself. With the little boys jumping on the bed and all that – they're just jumping on the bed. People can take what they wanna take, decipher it how they wanna decipher it. But it's not actually Michael Jackson, it's me playing Michael Jackson, studying the moves and doing the impressions. I don't have an opinion really against Michael Jackson. When *Thriller* came out, you couldn't tell me nothin' about Michael: Dude was the ultimate, dude is a legend."

Eminem is trying to show the world he is a devoted father to his nine-year-old daughter Hailie. "Last year I went and read to the class. It was reading month or something." He also has custody of his niece, Alaina and his half-brother, Nate.

995 U2
Vertigo

Label & Cat No.: **Island CIDX 878**

Producer: **Steve Lillywhite**

Writers: **Bono / The Edge / Larry Mullen Jr / Adam Clayton**

Date Reached No.1: **20 November 2004**

Weeks at No.1: **1**

At the beginning of 2003, U2 began work on their 11th studio album, *How To Dismantle An Atomic Bomb*. "It's such a personal record that it may just be our best," Bono said. "The atomic bomb in the title refers to me. I was at my father's bedside when he died in 2001 and a bomb went off inside my head and I had no idea how to deal with it."

They began recording it with producer Chris Thomas, but scrapped over a year's work because, as The Edge commented, "We didn't gel for whatever reason." So they returned to working with their original producer, Steve Lillywhite.

The album's first single, 'Vertigo', was available for download four weeks prior to the physical single. The physical single entered at the top after selling just under 52,000 copies, but then dropped to number seven the following week, while remaining at number one on the download chart. "It was originally called 'Native Son' and had a very different feel," explained Adam Clayton. "Bono and Edge rewrote it when we started working with Steve (Lillywhite). The bass and drums have a little bit of Echo & The Bunnymen in there, a nice wink to where we came from."

So where is 'Vertigo'? Bono explained, "It's a dizzy feeling, a sick feeling, when you get up to the top of something and there's only one way to go. That's not a dictionary definition, that's mine and in my head I created a club called Vertigo, with all these people in it and the music is not the music you want to hear and the people are not the people you want to be with. Then you see somebody and she's got a cross around her neck and you focus on it, because you can't focus on anything else. You find a little tiny fragment of salvation in there."

U2, keeping up with trends, went into partnership with Apple to produce a customised iPod. It carried the new album as well as a number of songs from U2's back catalogue. They also recorded a TV ad for the iPod, which shows the band in silhouette and has an instrumental version of 'Vertigo' as the backing. *How To Dismantle An Atomic Bomb* was released two weeks after 'Vertigo' and sold just over 200,000 copies in the first week.

996 Girls Aloud
I'll Stand By You

Label & Cat No.: **Polydor 9869130**

Producer: **Brian Higgins**

Writers: **Chrissie Hynde / Tom Kelly / Billy Steinberg**

Date Reached No.1: **27 November 2004**

Weeks at No.1: **2**

Girls Aloud from *Popstars : The Rivals* had demonstrated their staying power when they followed up their debut single, the chart-topping 'Sound Of The Underground', with 'No Good Advice' (2), 'Life Got Cold' (3), 'Jump' (which was used in the film *Love Actually*, 2), 'The Show' (2) and 'Love Machine' (2), but a second number one had eluded them.

In 1994 The Pretenders recorded the emotive ballad 'I'll Stand By You', with Chrissie Hynde employing minimal piano accompaniment by the song's co-writer, Tom Kelly. In 2004 Girls Aloud's version of 'I'll Stand By You' was chosen to represent one of Britain's biggest annual charity events, Children In Need – the year it celebrated its 25th anniversary.

Nadine Coyle said, "We've all grown up with Children In Need and it's great that we can now be so involved with this year's anniversary appeal." Sarah Harding said of the song, "When we recorded it for our album, *What Will The Neighbours Say?*, we were drawn to the lyrics straight away, we've all been in situations where we have needed someone or been there for someone."

Billy Steinberg remembered, "'I'll Stand By You', like the other hits that Tom and I wrote, started out as a lyric that I had in a notebook. I had the title and the chorus lyric. Chrissie is a very, very strong songwriter in her own right. She would cross out any lines I had written that she didn't like, and usually the lines that she didn't like would be ones that were too tender or too poetic. She would toughen up stuff I'd written."

"I remember when we wrote it I felt two things," said Billy. "I felt we had written a hit song and I felt a little sheepish that we had written something a little soft, a little generic for The Pretenders. I know that Chrissie felt that way too to some extent. I don't think she really entirely embraced it to begin with, but she certainly does now because when she plays it live, it's one of the songs that gets the strongest response. It's done really well for her and for us."

997 Band Aid 20
Do They Know It's Christmas?

Label & Cat No.: **Mercury 9869413**

Producer: **Nigel Godrich**

Writers: **Bob Geldof / Midge Ure**

Date Reached No.1: **11 December 2004**

Weeks at No.1: **4**

By 2004 Band Aid's 'Do They Know It's Christmas?' had become a standard, securing a regular income for The Band Aid Trust by being included on seasonal compilations. The trust had distributed £75m, notably in Ethiopia, and Comic Relief was continuing its cause. *The Sun* journalist, Dominic Mohan, suggested that Bob Geldof and Midge Ure should organise a new version for the 20th anniversary and, unlike the first time where some performers had to be cajoled into appearing, Midge Ure commented, "The phones are ringing off the hook."

After recording a backing track, the single was completed one Sunday at George Martin's recording studio in Hampstead. The performers were Natasha Bedingfield, Turin Brakes, Dido, Jamelia, Beverley Knight, Paul McCartney (playing bass), Katie Melua, Ms Dynamite, Est'Elle, Lemar, Shaznay Lewis, Moloko, Rachel Stevens, Joss Stone, Robbie Williams and Will Young, alongside members of Ash, Busted, Coldplay, The Darkness, The Divine Comedy, Feeder, Keane, Morcheeba, Oasis, Radiohead, Snow Patrol, The Sugababes, Supergrass, The Thrills, Travis and U2. For reasons best known to himself, Damon Albarn was there but only serving tea.

Three actions stand out from the day: Bono's quieter retake of "Tonight, thank God, it's them instead of you" chosen over Justin Hawkins' more frenzied approach; Dizzee Rascal's memorable rap line "Help the helpless"; and young soul singer Joss Stone's ad-libs at the end. Introduced to Bob Geldof, she said, "You're that Bob Godorf or is it Gandalf?"

Twenty years earlier The Cars had made a video for Live Aid showing the poverty in Ethiopia. After Bob Geldof, or is it Gandolf, showed it to today's stars a girl featured in the video was brought into the studio – she is being trained in cultivating the barren land.

The single sold at £3.99 and, depending on the retailer, at least £2.43 went to charity. It sold 72,000 on its first day and topped quarter of a million within a week. It was available on downloads and ringtones, thus creating a Lord of the Ringtones. Geldof also authorised a Live Aid DVD set with only Led Zeppelin and Carlos Santana refusing permission for their contributions to be included.

The funds received a huge boost when millionaire businessman Tom Hunter was so moved by a documentary on Ethiopa that he doubled the amount raised from sales of the single.

998 Steve Brookstein
Against All Odds

Label & Cat No.: **Sony 82876672732**
Producer: **Steve Mac**
Writer: **Phil Collins**
Date Reached No.1: **8 January 2005**
Weeks at No.1: **1**

THE *POP IDOL* JUDGE AND MUSIC mogul Simon Cowell established his own TV production company, Syco, and launched *The X Factor* on ITV1. The concept was similar to *Pop Idol* in that nationwide auditions were filmed, but this time the entry was open to anyone over 16. As with *Pop Idol*, the bickering between the judges (here, Cowell, Louis Walsh and Sharon Osbourne) became the main attraction and the best moments were when they were confronted with abominable acts such as Jurasso and his song about bonfire night.

Steve Brookstein (pronounced 'Brookstine') was a 35-year-old pub singer from Mitcham, Surrey who had previously appeared on Jonathan Ross' *Big Big Talent Show* and opened for Dionne Warwick. His disarming smile and laidback attitude engaged viewers: he didn't appear to care whether he won or not. Louis Walsh said that Steve reminded him of a serial killer: "He just stands there and smiles like Fred West." He was sponsored by Simon Cowell while his rivals in the final, G4, were an operatic quartet under Louis Walsh's guidance. To compound the rivalry, Cowell had just launched a similar group, Il Divo.

The bitterness intensified with Sharon Osbourne dismissing Steve as a fake and saying he was "full of crap". Cowell looked aghast at Osbourne's outburst and she was shouted down by the TV audience: their pent-up emotions probably secured Steve's victory.

The final was on the same Saturday as the final of BBC's *Strictly Come Dancing*, and between them they had 15m phone-in votes. The winner of *Strictly Come Dancing* was Jill Halfpenny of *EastEnders* and her teacher, Darren Bennet, but the real winner was BT.

Reality TV became reality when Steve released 'Against All Odds', a chart-topper for Mariah Carey featuring Westlife in 2000. The single, released on December 20, entered at number two, but climbed to the top after Simon Cowell announced all proceeds would go to the Tsunami disaster appeal. In a telling remark, Simon Cowell added that the single should make several hundred thousand pounds for charity, adding, "The cost to Steve will be a few thousand but he didn't even think about it. He said, 'I want to do it.'"

As Ronan Keating/Yusuf's revival of 'Father And Son' was also for Band Aid, three of the top four singles were for charity.

Steve Brookstein

999 Elvis Presley
Jailhouse Rock

Label & Cat No.: **RCA 82876667152**
Producer: **Steve Sholes**
Writers: **Jerry Leiber / Mike Stoller**
Date Reached No.1: **15 January 2005**
Weeks at No.1: **1**

TO CELEBRATE THE 70TH ANNIVERSARY of Elvis Presley's birth, RCA/BMG reissued each of Elvis' UK number ones in chronological order on a weekly basis. The first two number ones, 'All Shook Up' (1957) and 'Jailhouse Rock' (1958), were issued in the first week. Because 'All Shook Up' came with a cardboard storage case to hold all the other number one discs, it was ineligible for the charts. In the event, 'All Shook Up' sold over 17,000 copies that week, which would have placed it at number two behind 'Jailhouse Rock' with 21,000.

Creatively, the CD singles were disappointing. In their regular, mail order *Follow That Dream* CD series for fans, RCA issued outtakes from Elvis' recording sessions. The new CD singles contained an occasional bonus track ('Heartbreak Hotel', a number two, was added to the 'All Shook Up' single and the film version of 'Treat Me Nice' to 'Jailhouse Rock'), but most are simply the original A- and B-side. A neat touch though was to issue them with original US covers, previously unseen in the UK. They were also issued on 10-inch vinyl playing at 45rpm with sleeves that replicated the RCA paper bags of the period with the original serial number (RCA 1028).

Most critics welcomed these releases but there was an extraordinary outburst from Tim Luckhurst in *The Times*, who was dismayed by the attention on Elvis. He wrote, "American giants such as Bob Dylan and Frank Zappa merit our affection. If he had started singing after John Lennon, Presley would not even merit a place on *I'm A Celebrity... Get Me Out Of Here!*"

We can only speculate on John Lennon's reaction to such risible remarks, but in all probability, he would have written an open letter to *The Times* stating that he wouldn't have found his own voice without Elvis leading the way. Indeed, Elvis' rasping vocal on 'Jailhouse Rock' could have inspired John's performance on 'Twist And Shout'.

RCA has reissued 'Jailhouse Rock' several times as a single but come 2009, when the record will be over 50 years old, anybody will be able to release it as it will fall into the public domain. There are currently moves to change the law, but with strong arguments on both sides, the industry's attempts may not be successful.

1000 Elvis Presley
One Night

Label & Cat No.: **RCA 82876666682**

Producer: **Steve Sholes**

Writers: **Dave Bartholomew / Pearl King**

Date Reached No.1: **22 January 2005**

Weeks at No.1: **1**

In 1958 'Jailhouse Rock' was the first record to enter the chart at number one and in 2005 it became the first record to enter the chart for the second time at number one. This time, however, its stay at the top was limited as it was replaced by 'One Night', previously a chart topper in 1959. Elvis beat off new material from Manic Street Preachers and The Killers and a reissue from Iron Maiden, despite some poor distribution as many potential buyers found the Elvis singles weren't in stock. He became only the third act to replace themselves at number one, following The Beatles (1963) and John Lennon (1981).

Although Elvis was at his peak in the Fifties, his records did not automatically go to number one. His follow-up to 'Jailhouse Rock', 'Don't' was a number two and 'Hard Headed Woman' and 'King Creole', also failed to reach the top. He secured his third number one with the double header, 'One Night' / 'I Got Stung' in 1959.

The new CD single was enhanced by Elvis' original recording of Smiley Lewis' 'One Night Of Sin', cut in January 1957 while he was making the *Loving You* soundtrack. This was too raunchy for a supposedly clean-living teen idol to release and Elvis must have known that at the time. Both Colonel Parker and RCA told Elvis it was unacceptable but Elvis liked the song so much that they agreed to negotiate a revised lyric with the publisher.

A month later he returned to the studio with an amended lyric and this version, with Scotty Moore (guitar), Bill Black (bass), Dudley Brooks (piano) and D.J. Fontana (drums), is the one that made the top – twice. However, because Elvis had been recording a treasure-trove of riches, its release was held back until he went in the army.

The majority of those who bought 'Jailhouse Rock' probably already had it in their collection and were buying this reissue to support Elvis. 'One Night' is less iconic and so hopefully some fans were hearing it (and enjoying it) for the first time.

So Elvis' 20th chart-topper became the 1,000th number one and few will dispute the merit of this achievement. It rekindled interest in the singles chart and there was speculation as to whether Elvis could continue hitting the top with his former number ones ('Wooden Heart' anyone?) or if normality would return to the charts.

As we go to press, a slew of charity songs are being recorded for the Tsunami appeal and all could potentially be the first of the second thousand of number ones. There is an all-star cover of Eric Clapton's 'Tears In Heaven' put together by Simon Cowell and Sharon Osbourne, featuring the likes of Elton John, Rod Stewart, Ozzy Osbourne and Gwen Stefani. The former Radio 1 DJ, Mike Read, who was moved to tears after seeing orphaned children wandering around aimlessly in search of their parents, decided to get involved by using a song he had already written called 'Grief Never Grows Old'. He called the project One World, and among the celebrities invited were Boy George, Cliff Richard, Russell Watson, Brian Wilson, Steve Winwood and, performing together for the first time since the death of their brother Maurice, Barry and Robin Gibb.

To appeal to all markets, Bluey from the soul group Incognito, brought together a collection of urban stars including Chaka Khan, Lemar and Omar to record the song 'Give & Let Live' under the name The Hope Collection. Also, two British Asian acts, Sahara and RDB have collaborated on a single called 'Saathi'. Whatever their chart performances, all the money raised will go to The Disaster Emergency Committee.

In the spring of 2005, there are plans to incorporate the download chart into the main singles chart. When this takes place, we will see a substantial rise in recorded sales figures and in all probability, more stability returning to the chart.

It's taken 52 years to reach 1000 chart-toppers, but at the current rate we will reach 2,000 in another 25.

Next page: Elvis, once and forever the King of Rock'n'Roll, at Fox Studios in Los Angeles, September, 1956. Nothing was ever the same again

THERE'S A LEAK IN THIS OLD BUILDING
MENS VOICES
Gibson